HIPPOCRENE STANDARD DICTIONARY

POLISH-ENGLISH
ENGLISH-POLISH

Iwo Cyprian Pogonowski

with
Complete Phonetics
Menu Terms
Business Terms

HIPPOCRENE BOOKS
New York

Library of Congress Cataloging-in-Publication Data
Pogonowski, Iwo Cyprian, 1921-
      Dictionary, Polish-English, English-Polish
      1. Polish language-Dictionaries-English.
      2. English language-Dictionaries-Polish.
      1. Title.
      PG6640.P54   491.8'5321   82-9211
                    AACR2
ISBN 0-7818-0282-2

Printed in the United States of America.

Contents

a.	– attribute	– przydawka
adj.	– adjective	– przymiotnik
adj. f.	– adjective feminine	– przymiotnik żeński
adj. m.	– adjective masculine	– przymiotnik męski
adj. n.	– adjective neuter	– przymiotnik nijaki
adv.	– adverb	– przysłówek
am.	– American	– amerykański
chem.	– chemistry	– chemia
conj.	– conjunction	– spójnik
constr.	– construction	– budowa
etc.	– and so on	– i tak dalej
excl.	– exclamation	– wykrzyknik
expr.	– expression	– wyrażenie
f.	– substantive feminine	– rzeczownik żeński
gram.	– grammar	– gramatyka
hist.	– history	– historia
hyp.	– hyphen	– łącznik
indecl.	– indeclinable	– nieodmienny
inf.	– infinitive	– bezokolicznik
m.	– substantive musculine	– rzeczownik męski
m.in.	– among others	– między innymi
n.	– substantive neuter	– rzeczownik nijaki
num.	– numeral	– liczebnik
part.	– particle	– partykuła
pl.	– substantive plural	– rzeczownik liczba mnoga
poet.	– poetry	– poezja
polit.	– politics	– polityka
p.p.	– past participle	– imiesłów czasu przeszłego
prep.	– preposition	– przyimek
pron.	– pronoun	– zaimek
s.	– substantive	– rzeczownik
sb.	– somebody	– ktoś
slang	– slang	– gwara, żargon
v.	– verb	– czasownik
vulg.	– vulgarity	– ordynarność
wg	– according to	– według
W.W. II	– World War II	– druga wojna światowa
zob.	– see	– zobacz

POLISH-ENGLISH

A

a [a][as"a" in car] conj. and; or; but; then; at that time

a jakże! [a-yak-zhe] excl.: oh yes... ; yes indeed!

a to [a to] conj. and so

abażur [a-ba-zhoor] m. lamp shade; a device to screen light

abdykować [ab-di-ko-vaćh] v. abdicate, abdicate the throne

abecadło [a-be-tsa-dwo] n. A.B.C., alphabet; rudiment

abonament [a-bo-na-ment] m. subscription, season ticket

abonent [a-bo-nent] m. subscriber, holder of a season ticket; contract passenger

abonować [a-bo-no-vaćh] v. subscribe to a periodical etc.

absencja [ab-sen-tsya] f. absence, non-attendance

abstrakcja [ab-strak-tsya] f. abstraction; abstract

absurd [ab-soord] m. absurdity

aby [a-bi] conj. to; in order to, in order that, only to; that

ach! [akh] excl.: oh! ah!

aczkolwiek [ach-kol-vyek] conj. though; although, albeit

adapter [a-dap-ter] m. record player, adapter; pick-up

administracja [ad-mee-ńees-trats -ya] f. administration; (management); authorities

admirał [ad-mee-raw] m. admiral

adres [ad-res] m. address

adwokat [ad-vo-kat] m. lawyer

afera [a-fe-ra] f. swindle

aferzysta [a-fe-zhis-ta] m. swindler; confidence man

afisz [a-feesh] m. poster

afiszować [a-fee-sho-vaćh] v. advertise; flaunt; parade

agrafka [a-graf-ka] f. safety pin; hist.: buckle; brooch

agrest [ag-rest] m. gooseberry

aha! [akh-a!] excl.: oh yes...

akacja [a-kats-ya] f. acacia; locust tree; locust shrub

akcja [a-ktsya] f. action; share; plot; campaign; operation

AK [a-ka] f. Polish Home Army (W.W.II) (Armia Krajowa)

akowiec [a-kov-yets] m. soldier of the Polish Home Army (World War II)

aksamit [ak-sa-meet] m. velvet

akt kupna [akt koop-na] f. purchase deed; deed

akta [ak-ta] pl. documents; deeds; dossier; files; records

aktualny [ak-too-al-ni] m. timely; current; up to date; topical

akumulator [a-koo-moo-la-tor] m. battery; storage battery

akuszerka [a-koo-sher-ka] f. midwife; accoucheuse

akwarela [ak-va-re-la] f. a watercolor; painting in (with) watercolors; the watercolors

albo [a-lbo] conj. or; else

albowiem [al-bo-vyem] conj. for; as; since; because; on account of

ale [a-le] conj. however; but; still; yet; not at all; n. defect

aleja [a-le-ya] f. avenue; alley

ależ [a-lesh] conj. why (yes)

alfa [al-fa] f. alpha

alfabet [al-fa-bet] m. alphabet

alfons [al-fons] m. pimp; cadet

alimenty [a-lee-men-ti] pl. alimony for separated wife

alkohol [al-ko-khol] m. alcohol

alpejski [al-pey-skee] adj. m. Alpine; of the Alps

aluzja [a-looz-ya] f. hint; allusion; insinuation; dig

ałun [a-woon] m. alum

amant [a-mant] m. lover; beau

ambasada [am-ba-sa-da] f. embassy; ambassador and his staff; the embassy building

ambicja [am-beets-ya] f. ambition; aspiration; self esteem

ambona [am-bo-na] f. pulpit

Amerykanin [A-me-ri-ka-ńeen] m. American; man native of America

Amerykanka [A-me-ri-kan-ka] f. American; American woman
amerykański [a-me-ri-kań-skee] adj. m. American; of America
amnestia [am-nest-ya] f. amnesty; act of pardon
amortyzacja [a-mor-ti-zats-ya] f. depreciation; amortization
amory [a-mo-ri] pl. flirtation; courting; love affairs
amperomierz [am-pe-ro-myesh] m. ammeter; meter of amperes; amperometer
amputować [am-poo-to-vaćh] v. amputate; to cut off
amunicja [a-moo-ńee-tsya] f. ammunition; munitions
analfabeta [a-nal-fa-be-ta] m. illiterate; an ignorant
analiza [a-na-lee-za] f. analysis; parsing; analysis of a sentence
analogia [a-na-log-ya] f. analogy; parallelism; parallel; parity
ananas [a-na-nas] m. pineapple; rascal; rogue; blighter
andrus [an-droos] m. rough kid
andrut [an-droot] m. wafer
anegdota [a-neg-do-ta] f. anecdote; story; theme
aneksja [a-neks-ya] f. annexation; rape of a country
anemia [a-ne-mya] f. anemia
angażować [an-ga-zho-vaćh] v. engage; undertake; hire; bind
angielski [an-gyel-skee] adj. m. English; English language
ani [a-ńee] conj. neither; nor; not; not even; not as much; or
anielski [a-ńel-skee] adj. m. angelic; cherubic; angelical
animusz [a-ńee-moosh] m. courage; verve; vigor; zest
anioł [a-ńow] m. angel
aniżeli [a-ńee-zhe-lee] part. rather; then; rather then
ankieta [an-ke-ta] f. poll; inquiry; questionnaire; survey form
anons [a-nons] m. advertisement (in a newspaper); ad
antybiotyki [an-ti-bee-yo-ti-kee] pl. antibiotics
antyk [an-tik] m. antique
aparat [a-pa-rat] m. apparatus; appliance; camera; gadget; device; mechanism; machinery
apartament [a-par-ta-ment] m. residence; suite of rooms
apel [a-pel] m. appeal; muster; roll-call; roll; parade
apetyt [a-pe-tit] m. appetite
apostolski [a-pos-tol-skee] adj. m. apostolic; missionary
aprobować [a-pro-bo-vaćh] v. approve; endorse; sanction
aprowizacja [a-pro-vee-zats-ya] f. food supply; provisions
apteczka [ap-tech-ka] f. first aid kit; medicine chest
apteka [ap-te-ka] f. pharmacy
arbuz [ar-boos] m. watermelon
architekt [ar-khee-tekt] m. architect
arcydzieło [ar-tsi-dźhe-wo] n. masterpiece
arena [a-re-na] f. arena; stage
areszt [a-resht] m. arrest; jail
argument [ar-goo-ment] m. argument; reason; contention
arkusz [ar-koosh] m. sheet
armata [ar-ma-ta] f. cannon
armator [ar-ma-tor] m. ship owner; skipper; charterer
armia [ar-mya] f. army; array
arogancja [a-ro-gan-tsya] f. arrogance; insolence; conceit
arteria [ar-ter-ya] f. artery
artretyzm [ar-tre-tizm] m. arthritis; gout
artykuł [ar-ti-koow] m. article
artyleria [ar-ti-ler-ya] f. artillery; gunnery; ordnance
artysta [ar-ti-sta] m. artist
arytmetyka [a-rit-me-ti-ka] f. arithmetic
as [as] m. ace; A flat
asceta [as-stse-ta] m. ascetic
asekuracja [a-se-koo-ra-tsya] f. insurance; assurance
aspiryna [as-pee-ri-na] f. aspirin
astma [ast-ma] f. asthma
asygnata [a-sig-na-ta] f. order (of payment, early check
asymilować [a-si-mee-lo-vaćh] v. assimilate; absorb; liken
asystować [a-sis-to-vaćh] v. accompany; attend; court;

assist; escort; wait upon

atak [a-tak] m. attack; charge (fit); spasm; offensive

atlas [at-las] m. atlas

atleta [at-le-ta] m. athlete

atłas [at-was] m. satin

atmosfera [at-mos-fe-ra] f. atmosphere; air; climate; tone

atol [a-tol] m. atoll

atom [a-tom] m. atom

atomowy [a-to-mo-vi] adj. m. atomic; nuclear

atrakcja [a-trak-tsya] f. attraction; high light

atrament [a-tra-ment] m. ink

atut [a-toot] m. trump

audycja [aw-dits-ya] f. broadcast; program; pop

aukcja [awk-tsya] f. auction

autentyczny [aw-ten-tich-ni] adj. m. authentic; genuine

auto [aw-to] n. motor car

autor [aw-tor] m. author

autostrada [aw-to-stra-da] f. superhighway; freeway

awans [a-vans] m. promotion; advancement; preferment

awantura [a-van-too-ra] f. brawl; fuss; row; scandal

azot [a-zot] m. nitrogen

aż [ash] part. as much; up to; till; until; as far as; down to

ażeby [a-zhe-bi] conj. that; in order that; so that; to

ażurowy [a-zhoo-ro-vi] adj. m. lace-like; transparent

B

ba [ba] excl.: hey?; nay; indeed...; and even; what more; or rather; of course

baba [ba-ba] f. woman (old, simple); grandmother; ram

babiarz [bab-yash] m. lady chaser; ladies' man

babie lato [ba-bye la-to] n. Indian Summer

babka [bab-ka] f. grandmother; lass; chick; cake; flat hammer

babrać [bab-rach] v. smear; stain; dabble; soil; fumble

bachor [ba-khor] m. kid; brat

baczność [bach-noshch] f. attention; watchfulness; care

bać się [bach shan] v. fear

badacz [ba-dach] m. researcher

badać [ba-dach] v. investigate; examine; research; explore

badyl [ba-dil] m. steam; weed

badylarz [ba-di-lash] m. marketing gardener (slang)

bagatela [ba-ga-te-la] f. trifle; easy matter; a mere trifle

bagaż [ba-gash] m. luggage

bagażowy [ba-ga-zho-vi] m. porter; adj. m. baggage-; luggage-

bagnet [bag-net] m. bayonet

bagno [bag-no] m. swamp; fen; morass; marsh; bog; quagmire

bajka [bay-ka] f. fairy-tale; gossip; scandal; story; fable

bajoro [ba-yo-ro] n. muddy pool

bak [bak] m. gasoline tank; can; pl. side-whiskers; sideburns

bakterie [bak-ter-ye] pl. bacteria; germs; microbes

bal [bal] m. ball; bale; log

balet [ba-let] m. ballet

balia [bal-ya] f. wash tub

balkon [bal-kon] m. balcony

balustrada [ba-loos-tra-da] f. railing; hand rail; guard rail

bałagan [ba-wa-gan] m. mess; disorder; disarray; confusion

bałamucić [ba-wa-moo-cheech] v. lead astray; loiter; flirt; coax; seek to seduce

bałwan [baw-van] m. snowman; ass; breaking wave crest; blockhead; fool; nitwit; fetish; idol; lump; block; snow-mass

banał [ba-naw] m. stoke phrase; tag; banality; truism; triviality

banan [ba-nan] m. banana

banda [ban-da] f. band; gang

bandaż [ban-dash] m. bandage

bandera [ban-de-ra] f. flag

bandyta [ban-di-ta] m. bandit

bank [bank] m. bank; pool

bankiet [ban-ket] m. banquet
banknot [bank-not] m. banknote
bankrut [bank-root] m. bankrupt
baptysta [bap-tis-ta] m. baptist
bar [bar] m. bar; barium
barak [ba-rak] m. barrack
baran [ba-ran] m. ram; tup; idiot
baraszkować [ba-rash-ko-vaćh]
v.frolic; gambol; romp; caper
barbarzyńca [bar-ba-zhiń-tsa]
m. barbarian; savage; vandal
barczysty [bar-chis-ti] m. broad
-shouldered; square built
bardziej [bar-dźhey] adv. more;
(emphatic "bardzo"); worse
bardzo [bar-dzo] adv. very
bariera [bar-ye-ra] f. rail; barrier;
hand rail; obstacle; dike; dyke
barki [bar-kee] pl. shoulders
barłóg [bar-woog] m. litter bed
barman [bar-man] m. barman
barszcz [barshch] m. beet soup
barwa [bar-va] f. color; hue
bary [ba-ri] pl. large shoulders;
broad shoulders; parallel bars
barykada [ba-ri-ka-da] f.
barricade; barrier; obstacle
baryłka [ba-riw-ka] f. barrel
basen [ba-sen] m. pool; tank
bastard [bas-tard] m. bastard
baśń [baśhń] f. fable; myth
bat [bat] m. whip; lash
bateria [ba-ter-ya] f. battery
bawełna [ba-vew-na] f. cotton
bawialnia [ba-vyal-ńa] f. sitting
room; parlor; drawing room
bawić [ba-veećh] v. amuse;
entertain; recreate; stay
bawidamek [ba-vee-da-mek] m.
ladies' man; gallant
bawół [ba-voow] m. buffalo
baza [ba-za] f. base; basis
bazgrać [baz-graćh] v. scribble;
scrawl; scratch; daub; splotch
bażant [ba-zhant] m. pheasant
bąbel [bown-bel] m. blister
bądź [bownćh] v. be this; conj.
either-or; anyhow at any rate
bąk [bownk] m. horse fly;
blunder; vulg. fart
bąkać [bown-kaćh] v. mumble;
hint; mutter; hum; allude
bebechy [be-be-khi] pl. guts

beczka [bech-ka] f. barrel
bednarz [bed-nash] m. cooper
befsztyk [bef-shtik] m. beefsteak (broiled or fried)
beksa [bek-sa] f. cry baby
beletrystyka [be-le-tris-ti-ka] f.
fiction; belles-lettres
belka [bel-ka] f. beam; bar
bełkot [bew-kot] m. mumbling
benzyna [ben-zi-na] f. gasoline
berbeć [ber-bećh] m. small kid;
toddler; brat; dot
berek [be-rek] m. tag play
beret [be-ret] m. beret; cap
bestia [bes-tya] f. beast
besztać [besh-taćh] v. scold;
rebuke; chide; rebuke: trounce
beton [be-ton] m. concrete
bety [be-ti] pl. bedding
bez [bes] prep. without
bez [bes] m. lilac
bez- [bes] prefix = suffix less
beza [be-za] f. meringue
bezbarwny [bez-barw-ni] adj. m.
colorless; plain; drab; dull
bezbłędny [bez-bwand-ni] adj. m.
faultless; correct; perfect
bezbolesny [bez-bo-les-ni] m.
painless; without pain
bezbronny [bez-bron-ni] adj. m.
defenseless; helpless; unarmed
bezcelowy [bez-tse-lo-vi] adj. m.
aimless; pointless; useless
bezcenny [bez-tsen-ni] adj. m.
priceless; invaluable; inestimable; beyond price
bezchmurny [bez-khmoo-rni] adj.
m. cloudless; serene; clear
bezdomny [bez-dom-ni] adj. m.
homeless; houseless; m.
homeless person; outcast
bezdzietny [bez-dźhet-ni] adj. m.
childless; without offspring
bezdźwięczny [bez-dźhvanch-
-ni] adj. m. soundless; voiceless; sounded with the breath
bezecny [be-zets-ni] adj. m.
wicked; infamous; ignominious
bezgotówkowy [bez-go-toov-ko-
-vi] adj. m. without cash
bezgrzeszny [bez-gzhesh-ni] adj.
m. sinless; innocent; chaste
bezkonkurencyjny [bez-kon-koo-

-ren-tsiy-ni] adj. m. unrivaled
bezkrwawy [bez-**krva**-vi] adj. m.
bloodless; free of bloodshed
bezkształtny [bez-**kshtawt**-ni]
adj.m. shapeless; formless
bezład [bez-**wat**] m. disorder
bezmiar [bez-myar] m.
immensity; boundlessness; no
end of; vastness; host; swarm
bezmyślność [bez-**miśhl**-
-**nośhćh**] f. thoughtlessness;
wantonness; inconsideration
beznadziejny [bez-na-**dźhey**-ni]
adj. m. hopeless; desperate
bez ogródek [bez o-**groo**-dek]
adv. bluntly; unequivocally
bezokolicznik [bez-o-ko-**leech**-
-**ńeek**] m. infinitive (mood)
bezowocny [bez-o-**vots**-ni] m.
fruitless; vain; unsuccessful
bezpieczeństwo [bez-pye-**cheń**-
-stvo] m. security; safety
bezpłatnie [bez-**pwat**-ńe] adv.
free of charge; gratuitously
bezpłciowy [bez-**pwćho**-vi] adj.
m. sexless; neutral; insipid
bezpodstawny [bez-pod-**stav**-ni]
adj. m. groundless; baseless
bezpośrednio [bez-po-**śhred**-
-ńo] adv. directly; personally
bezprawny [bez-**prav**-ni] adj. m.
lawless; illegal; illicit
bezprzedmiotowy [bez-**pshed**-
-myo-to-vi] adj. m. aimless
bezprzykładny [bez-pshi-**kwad**-ni]
adj. m. unprecedented
bezradny [bez-**rad**-ni] adj. m.
helpless; baffled; at a loss
bezręki [bez-**ran**-kee] adj. m.
armless; handless (cripple)
bezrobotny [bez-ro-**bo**-tni] adj. m.
unemployed; out of work
bezrolny [bez-**rol**-ni] adj. m.
landless; with no land
bezsenny [bez-**sen**-ni] adj. m.
sleepless; restless; wakeful
bezsens [bez-sens] m. nonsense
bezsilny [bez-**śheel**-ni] adj. m.
powerless; weak; helpless
bezskuteczny [bez-skoo-**tech**-ni]
adj. m. to no avail; futile;
ineffective; nugatory
bezsporny [bez-**spor**-ni] adj. m.

incontestable; undebatable
bezsprzeczny [bez-**spshech**-ni]
adj. m. indisputable; evident
bezstronność [bez-**stron**-
-nośhćh] f. impartiality;
fairness; open-mindedness
beztroski [bez-**tros**-kee] adj. m.
carefree; careless; jaunty
bezustanny [bez-oos-tan-ni] adj.
m. ceaseless; endless
bezużyteczny [bez-oo-zhi-**tech**-ni]
adj. m. useless; idle
bezwartościowy [bez-var-to**śh**-
-ćho-vi] adj. m. worthless
bezwarunkowy [bez-va-roon-**ko**-
-vi] adj. m. unconditional; utter
bezwładność [bez-**vwad**-
-nośhćh] f. inertia; torpor;
decline; palsy; inertness
bezwstydny [bez-**vstid**-ni] adj. m.
shameless; lewd; flagrant
bezwyznaniowy [bez-viz-na-**ńo**-
-vi] adj. m. nonsectarian
bezwzględny [bez-**vzgland**-ni]
adj. m. ruthless; despotic
bezzębny [bez-**zanb**-ni] adj. m.
toothless; edentate
bezzwłoczny [bez-**zvwoch**-ni] adj.
m. immediate; prompt
bezzwrotny [bez-**zvrot**-ni] adj. m.
not to be refunded
beż [besh] m. beige
bęben [**ban**-ben] m. drum; kid;
brat; barrel; cylinder; tumbler
bęcwał [**bants**-vaw] m.
nincompoop; dullard; chickle-
head; jolt-head; dolt
bękart [**ban**-kart] m. bastard
biadać [**bya**-daćh] v. moan
białaczka [bya-**wach**-ka] f.
leukemia; leukaemia
białko [**byaw**-ko] n. egg white;
protein; white of the eye
biały [**bya**-wi] adj. m. white
biba [**bee**-ba] f. drinking spree
biblia [**beeb**-lya] f. Bible
biblioteka [beeb-lyo-**te**-ka] f.
library; bookcase; book series
bibuła [bee-**boo**-wa] f. blotting
paper; illegal political
publication; literary trash
bicz [beech] m. whip; whiplash
bić [beećh] v. beat; defeat

biec [byets] v. run; trot; flow

bieda [bye-da] f. poverty; want; trouble; distress; evil days

biedny [byed-ni] adj. m. poor

bieg [byek] m. run; race; course

biegle [bye-gle] adv. fluently

biegun [bye-goon] m. pole; rocker; spindle; trunnion

biegunka [bye-goon-ka] f. diarrhea; dysentery

biel [byel] f. whiteness; white

bielizna [bye-leez-na] f. linen

bielmo [byel-mo] n. cataract

bierny [byer-ni] adj. m. passive

bieżący [bye-zhown-tsi] adj. m. current; flowing; running

bieżnia [byezh-ńa] f. runway; track; racecourse; tire tread

bigos [bee-gos] m. hashed meat and cabbage dish (traditional Polish food)

bijatyka [bee-ya-ti-ka] f. fight; brawl; tussle; scrimmage

bila [bee-la] f. billiard ball

bilans [bee-lans] m. balance sheet; balance; rest; outcome; result

bilet [bee-let] m. note; ticket

biodro [byod-ro] n. hip; huckle

biszkopt [beesh-kopt] m. biscuit; sponge cake; cracker

bitny [beet-ni] adj. m. valiant

bitwa [beet-va] f. battle; fight

biuro [byoo-ro] n. office

biust [byoost] m. bust; breast

biustonosz [byoos-to-nosh] m. brassiere; bra; bust-bodice

biżuteria [bee-zhoo-ter-ya] f. jewelry; jewels

blacha [bla-kha] f. sheet metal; cook top; the range; tinware

blady [bla-di] adj. m. pale

blaga [bla-ga] f. lie; bluff

blankiet [blan-ket] m. blank form; printed form; blank

blask [blask] m. flush; luster

bliski [blees-kee] adj. m. near; imminent; near by; close

blizna [bleez-na] f. scar

bliźni [bleezh-ńee] m. fellow man; fellow creature; twin; identical; neighbor

blokować [blo-ko-vaćh] v.

block; blockade; obstruct; stall; take up space; interlock

blondynka [blon-din-ka] f. blonde (girl); fair haired girl

bluzka [blooz-ka] f. blouse

bluźnić [blooźh-ńeećh] v. curse; blaspheme; talk nonsense; revile; profane

błahość [bwa-khośhćh] f. triviality; futility

błagać [bwa-gaćh] v. beseech

błazen [bwa-zen] m. clown; buffoon; fool; low comedian

błąd [bwownt] m. error; mistake; lapse; slip-up; fallacy; fault

błąkać się [bwown-kaćh śhan] v. wander; stray; roam; rove

błękit [bwan-kit] m. blue (color); azure; blue pigment; sky

błocić [bwo-ćheećh] v. get muddy; soil with mud; spatter

błogi [bwo-gee] adj. m. blissful; delightful; sweet; rapturous

błogosławić [bwo-go-swa-veećh] v. bless; praise; exalt; thank; commend; glorify

błona [bwo-na] f. membrane; coat; film; tunic; velum; web

błonie [bwo-ńe] n. meadow; plain; public grassy land

błotnik [bwot-ńeek] m. (car) fender; mudguard; (front end fender) splash-board

błoto [bwo-to] n. mud; muck

błysk [bwisk] m. flash; flare

bo [bo] conj. because; for; or; as;since; or else; but then

bochenek [bo-khe-nek] m. loaf

bocian [bo-ćhan] m. stork

boczny [boch-ni] adj. m. lateral; side; collateral (line)

boczyć się [bo-chyćh śhan] v. sulk; be angry; look askance

bodaj [bo-day] part. may be; should be...; would be...

bodziec [bo-dźhets] m. stimulus

bogactwo [bo-gats-tvo] n. riches; wealth; means; fortune; plenty

bogaty [bo-ga-ti] adj. m. rich

bogobojny [bo-go-boy-ni] adj. m. pious; devout; church going

bohater [bo-kha-ter] m. hero

boisko [bo-ees-ko] n. stadium;

field; threshing floor; gridiron
bojaźń [bo-yaźhń] f. fear;
  fright; anxiety; terror
boja [bo-ya] f. buoy; beacon
bojkot [boy-kot] m. boycott
bojownik [bo-yov-ńeek] m.
  fighter; militant; champion
bok [bok] m. side; flank
boks [boks] m. boxing; stall
boleć [bo-lećh] v. pain; ache
bolesny [bo-les-ni] adj. m.
  sore; painful; sad; woeful;
  acute; dismal; agonizing
bomba [bom-ba] f. bomb; bomb
  shell; a sensation; beer-mug
bombowiec [bom-bo-vyets] m.
  bomber; bombing plane
borykać się [bo-ri-kaćh **śhan**]
  v. cope; struggle; wrestle
bosak [bo-sak] m. boat hook
boso [bo-so] adv. barefoot
bosy [bo-si] adj. m. barefoot
bowiem [bo-vyem] conj. for;
  because; since; as; hence
boży [bo-zhi] adj. m. God's
Bóg [book] m. God
bój [booy] m. fight; battle
ból [bool] m. pain; ache; sore
bór [boor] m. forest; wood
bóść [boośhćh] v. gore; sting
bóżnica [boozh-ńee-tsa] f.
  synagogue; house of prayer
bractwo [brats-tvo] n. fraternity;
  brotherhood; guild; sodality
brać [braćh] v. take; hold
brak [brak] m. lack; need; want;
  scarcity; shortage; absence;
  fault; privation; poverty
brama [bra-ma] f. gate; gateway;
  front door; wicket; port
bransoletka [bran-so-let-ka] f.
  bracelet; wristlet; bangle
brat [brat] m. brother; mate
bratać [bra-taćh] v. unite;
  fraternize; chum up
bratanek [bra-ta-nek] m. nephew
bratanica [bra-ta-ńee-tsa] f.
  niece (brother's daughter)
brednie [bred-ńe] n. nonsense
brew [brev] f. eyebrow
brewerie [bre-ver-ye] n. brawl
brezent [bre-zent] m. tarpaulin;
  (waterproof) canvas

brnąć [brnownćh] v. wade
broczyć [bro-chićh] v. bleed
broda [bro-da] f. beard; chin
brodzić [bro-dźheećh] v. wade
broić [bro-eećh] v. make
  mischief; frolic; romp; gambol
brom [brom] m. bromine
brona [bro-na] f. harrow
bronić [bro-ńeećh] v. defend;
  protect; shield; interdict
bronz [brons] m. bronze
broń [broń] f. weapon; arms
broszka [brosh-ka] f. brooch
broszura [bro-shoo-ra] f.
  pamphlet; folder; booklet
browar [bro-var] m. brewery
bród [brood] m. ford
brud [brood] m. dirt; filth
bruk [brook] m. pavement
brukiew [broo-kyev] f. turnip
brulion [brool-yon] m. rough
  draft copy; notebook; exercise
  book; preliminary draft
brunatny [broo-na-tni] adj. m.
  brown; tawny; tan colored
brunetka [broo-net-ka] f.
  brunette; dark-haired woman
brutal [broo-tal] m. brute
bruzda [brooz-da] f. furrow;
  groove; deep wrinkle; streak
brwi [brvee] pl. eye brows
brykać [bri-kaćh] v. prance
bryła [bri-wa] f. lump; mass
bryzg [brizk] m. splash
bryzgać [briz-gaćh] v. splash
brzeg [bzhek] m. shore; margin
brzemię [bzhe-myan] n. burden
brzęk [bzhank] m. clink; chink;
  rattle; ping; buzz; hum; drone
brzuch [bzhookh] m. belly;
  abdomen; stomach; tummy;
  guts; abdomen (of an insect)
brzydki [bzhid-kee] adj. m. ugly;
  unsightly; hideous; foul
brzydzić się [bzhi-dźheećh
  śhan] v. feel disgust; loathe;
  abhor; detest; hold in disgust
brzytwa [bzhit-va] f. razor
buchać [boo-khaćh] v. squirt
bucik [boo-ćheek] m. shoe; boot
buda [boo-da] f. shed (stall)
budowa [boo-do-va] f.
  construction; erection;

framework; structure
budowla [boo-**dov**-la] f. building
(large); edifice; house
budzić [boo-dźheećh] v. wake
up; awaken; rouse; stir; arise
budzik [boo-dźheek] m. alarm
clock; alarm
budżet [boo-jet] m. budget
bujać [boo-yaćh] v. rock; lie
bufor [boo-for] m. buffer
bułka [boow-ka] f. roll
(breakfast); bread roll; loaf
bunt [boont] m. mutiny
bura [boo-ra] f. reprimand
burak [boo-rak] m. beet
burda [boor-da] f. scuffle; row;
brawl; disturbance; wrangle;
rough neck; hoodlum
burmistrz [boor-meestsh] m.
mayor
bursztyn [boor-shtin] m. amber
burta [boor-ta] f. ship's side
bury [boo-ri] adj. m. dark gray
burza [boo-zha] f. tempest;
storm; wind storm; rain storm
burżuazja [boor-zhoo-az-ya] f.
bourgeoisie; middle class
busola [boo-so-la] f. compass
but [boot] m. boot; shoe; sabot
buta [boo-ta] f. arrogance
butelka [boo-tel-ka] f. bottle
butny [boot-ni] adj. m. arrogant;
insolent; overbearing
buzia [boo-źha] f. face; mouth
by [bi] conj. in order that;
(conditional) as if; at least
byczy [bi-chi] adj. m. 1. bull's;
2. very good; glorious
być [bićh] v. be; exist; live
bydlę [bid-lan] n. beast; brute
byle [bi-le] conj. in order to; so
as to; pron. any; slap-dash
były [bi-wi] adj. m. former
bynajmniej [bi-nay-mńey] adv.
by no means; not at all
bystrość [bis-troshćh] f.
swiftness; shrewdness
byt [bit] m. existence
bytność [bit-noshćh] f. stay
bywać [bi-vaćh] v. frequent
bywalec [bi-va-lets] m. patron
frequenter; man of the world
bzdura [bzdoo-ra] f. nonsense

bzik [bźheek] adj. m. crank;
loony; crazy; m. fad; craze
bzykać [bzi-kaćh] v. buzz

C

cackać się [tsats-kaćh śhan]
v. fondle; pamper; humor;
coddle; handle delicately
cacko [tsats-ko] n. jewel; trinket;
plaything; toy; beauty
cal [tsal] m. inch
całka [tsaw-ka] f. integral
całkiem [tsaw-kem] adv. quite;
entirely; completely; totally
całkowity [tsaw-ko-vee-ti]
adj. m. total; complete
cało [tsa-wo] adv. (in one piece)
safely; safe and sound
całować [tsa-wo-vaćh] v. kiss;
embrace; give a kiss
całus [tsa-woos] m. kiss
cap [tsap] m. billy goat
cąber [tsown-ber] m. rump; fillet
cążki [tsownzh-kee] pl. small
tongs; pliers; pincers
ceber [tse-ber] m. bucket
cebula [tse-boo-la] f. onion
cech [tsekh] m. trade; guild
cecha [tse-kha] f. feature; mark;
characterize; calibrate
cedr [tsedr] m. cedar
cedzić [tse-dźheećh] v. strain;
filter; percolate; sip; trickle
cegielnia [tse-gel-ńa] f.
brickyard; brick factory
cegła [tseg-wa] f. brick
cel [tsel] m. purpose; aim
cela [tse-la] f. cell
celnik [tsel-ńeek] m. customs
inspector; customs officer
celować [tse-lo-vaćh] v. aim;
excel; exceed; be very good
celuloza [tse-loo-lo-za] f.
cellulose
cembrować [tsem-bro-vaćh] v.
case(well); timber (a shaft)
cement [tse-ment] m. cement

cena [tse-na] f. price; value
cenić [tse-ńeećh] v. value;
rate; esteem; prize; evaluate
cennik [tsen-ńeek] m. price list;
price catalogue; price-current
centnar [tsent-nar] m.
hundredweight
centrala [tsen-tra-la] f. head
office; main office; exchange
centrum [tsent-room] n. center
centryfuga [tsen-tri-foo-ga] f.
centrifuge; separator
centymetr [tsen-ti-metr] m.
centimeter
cep [tsep] m. flail; blockhead
cera [tse-ra] f. complexion; skin;
mend; darn; darned place
ceramiczny [tse-ra-meech-ni] adj.
m. ceramic; earthenware
cerata [tse-ra-ta] f. oilcloth
ceregiele [tse-re-ge-le] n. fuss;
petty formalities; ceremony
certować się [tser-to-vaćh
śhan] v. pretend; stand on
ceremony; fuss; be ceremonious; pretend to decline
cewka [tsev-ka] f. spool
cęgi [tsan-gee] pl. tongs; pliers;
nippers; pincers; pipe-wrench
cętka [tsant-ka] f. dot
chałat [kha-wat] m. lab. coat
chałastra [kha-was-tra] f. mob
chałupa [kha-woo-pa] f. hut
cham [kham] m. roughneck; boor
charakter [kha-rak-ter] m.
disposition; character; quality
charczeć [khar-chećh] v.
wheeze; snort; be hoarse
chata [kha-ta] f. hut; cabin
chcieć [khćhećh] v. want
chciwiec [khćhee-vyets] m.
greedy man; grasping man
chełpić się [khew-peećh śhan]
v. boast; brag; bluster; vaunt;
swagger; glory; pride
chemia [khe-mya] f. chemistry
chemiczny [khe-meech-ni]
adj. m. chemical
cherlak [kher-lak] m. weakling
chęć [khanćh] f. wish; desire
chędogi [khan-do-gee] adj. m.
neat; clean; tidy; orderly
chichot [khee-khot] m. giggle;

laughter; chuckle; titter
chimera [khee-me-ra] f. whim
chinina [khee-ńee-na] f. quinine
chiński [kheeń-skee] adj. m.
Chinese; of China
chirurg [khee-roorg] m. surgeon;
sawbones (slang)
chlapać [khla-paćh] v. splash
chleb [khleb] m. bread
chlew [khlev] m. pigsty; pigpen
chlor [khlor] m. chlorine
chluba [khloo-ba] f. glory; pride
chlubić się [khloo-beećh śhan]
v. boast; flatter oneself
chlusnąć [khloos-nownćh] v.
splash; fling; spout; spurt
chłeptać [khwep-taćh] v. lap
up; lap down; swill
chłodzić [khwo-dźeećh] v.
cool; refresh; refrigerate
chłonąć [khwo-nownćh] v.
absorb; devour; drink in;
inhale; imbibe; take in
chłop [khwop] m. peasant; man
chłosta [khwos-ta] f. lashing
chłód [khwoot] m. cold;
freshness; coolness; iciness;
shiver; chilly atmosphere
chłystek [khwis-tek] m. squirt
chmara [khma-ra] f. swarm
chmiel [khmyel] m. hop; hops
chmura [khmoo-ra] f. cloud
chociaż [kho-ćhash] conj. albeit;
even if; though, tho'; while
chociaż = choćby = chociażby
choć [khoćh] conj. at least
chodnik [khod-ńeek] m.
sidewalk; pathway; stair
carpet; foot-path; pavement
chodzić [kho-dźheećh] v. go;
walk; move; creep; pace;
attend; come; thread; stalk
choinka [kho-een-ka] f. fir
cholera [kho-le-ra] f. cholera;
excl.: damn! hell! the devil!
cholewa [kho-le-va] f. boot
chorągiew [kho-rown-gev] f.
flag; standard; ensign
choroba [kho-ro-ba] f. sickness
chory [kho-ri] adj. m. sick; ill;
ailing; infirm; unwell
chować [kho-vaćh] v. hide
chód [khoot] m. gait; walk

chór [khoor] m. choir
chów [khoof] m. breeding
chrabąszcz [khra-b<u>own</u>shch] m.
  beetle; May-bug
chrapać [khra-paćh] v. snore
chroniczny [khro-ńeech-ni] adj.
  m. chronic; habitual
chronić [khro-ńeećh] v.
  shelter; protect; guard; shield;
  fence; give refuge; prevent
chropowaty [khro-po-va-ti] adj.
  m. rough; callous; coarse;
  harsh; uneven; rugged; harsh
chrust [khroost] m. kindling
chrupać [khroo-paćh] v. crunch
chrypka [khrip-ka] f. hoarseness;
  sore throat
Chrystus [khris-toos] m. Christ
chrzan [khzhan] m. horseradish
chrząstka [khzh<u>own</u>st-ka] f.
  cartilage; gristle; copula
chrząszcz [khsh<u>own</u>shch] m.
  May bug; beetle; cockchafer
chrzcić [khzhćheećh] v.
  baptize; christen; initiate
chrześcijanin [khshe-śhćhee-
  -ya-ńeen] m. Christian
chrząst [khzh<u>an</u>st] m. clatter
chrzęścić [khzh<u>an</u>-śhćheećh]
  v. clank; jangle; grate; crunch
chuchać [khoo-khaćh] v. puff
chuchro [khookh-ro] m. weakling
chuć [khoochoćh] f. lust
chudnąć [khood-n<u>own</u>ćh] v.
  lose weight; grow thin; lose
  flesh; become thin; thin
chuligan [khoo-lee-gan] m.
  hoodlum; ruffian; roughneck
chustka [khoost-ka] f.
  handkerchief; kerchief; scarf
chwacki [khvats-kee] adj. m.
  brave; plucky; gallant; rakish
chwalić [khva-leećh] v. praise
chwała [kva-wa] f. praise; glory;
  splendor; pride of; a credit to
chwast [khvast] m. weed
chwiać [khvyaćh] v. waver
chwila [khvee-la] f. moment
chwycić [khvi-ćheećh] v.
  grasp; seize; get hold; grip
chwyt [khvit] m. grasp; grip
chyba [khi-ba] part. maybe
chybotać [khi-bo-taćh] v. rock

chybić [khi-beećh] v. miss
chylić [khi-leećh] v. bow
chyłkiem [khiw-<u>k</u>em] adv.
  stealthily; on the sly
chytry [khit-ri] adj. m. sly
chyży [khi-zhi] adj. m. swift
ci [ćhee] pron. these; they;
  part.: for you; well, well!
ciało [ćha-wo] n. body; substance; frame; anatomy; staff;
  aggregate; corpse; carcass
ciarki [ćhar-kee] pl. shudder
ciasnota [ćhas-no-ta] f.
  tightness; narrow-mindedness
ciastko [ćhast-ko] n. cake; pie
ciasto [ćhas-to] n. dough
ciąć [ćh<u>own</u>ćh] v. cut; clip
ciągnąć [ćh<u>own</u>g-n<u>own</u>ćh] v.
  pull; draw; tag; lug; drag;
  haul; have in tow; trail;.
  obtain; pump; deduce; infer;
  suck; inhale; attract; stretch;
  expand; extend; continue;
  proceed; blow; sweep; run;
  tend; lean; dilate; wear on
ciągnik [ćh<u>own</u>g-ńeek] m.
  tractor; agrimotor; crawler
ciąża [ćh<u>own</u>-zha] f. pregnancy
ciążenie [ćh<u>own</u>-zhe-ńe] v.
  gravitation; tendency
cichaczem [ćhee-kha-chem] adv.
  stealthily; on the quiet
cichnąć [ćheekh-n<u>own</u>ćh] v.
  quiet down; subside; abate
cicho [ćhee-kho] adv. silently;
  noiselessly; softly; privately
cichy [ćhee-khi] adj. m. quiet;
  still; low; gentie; calm; serene
ciec [ćhets] v. leak; flow
ciecz [ćhech] f. liquid
ciekawy [ćhe-ka-vi] adj. m.
  cute; curious; interesting;
  prying; inquiring; inquisitive
cielak [ćhe-lak] m. calf
cielesny [ćhe-les-ni] adj. m.
  carnal; bodily; sexual
ciemię [ćhe-my<u>an</u>] n. crown of
  the head; septum of the skull
ciemiężenie [ćhe-my<u>an</u>-zhe-ńe]
  n. oppression; subjugation
ciemnia [ćhem-ńa] f. darkroom
ciemno [ćhem-no] adv. darkly
ciemny [ćhem-ni] adj. m. dark

cieniować [ćhe-ńo-vaćh] v.
    shade; modulate; grade
cienisty [ćhe-ńees-ti] adj. m.
    shady; shade giving
cienki [ćhen-kee] adj. m. thin
cień [ćheń] m. shade; shadow
cieplarnia [ćhep-lar-ńa] f.
    greenhouse; hothouse; stove
ciepło [ćhep-wo] adv. warm
ciepławy [ćhep-wa-vi] adj. m.
    lukewarm; tepid; not enthused
ciepły [ćhep-wi] adj. m. warm
cierń [ćherń] m. thorn; prickle
cierpiący [ćher-pyown-tsi]
    adj. m. suffering; ailing; ill
cierpieć [ćher-pyećh] v. suffer;
    anguish; be troubled; endure
cierpki [ćherp-kee] adj. m. tart;
    acid; surly; acrid; sour; harsh
cierpliwość [ćher-plee-
    -vośhćh] f. patience; endu-
    rance; forbearance
cierpliwy [ćher-plee-vi] adj. m.
    enduring; patient; forbearing
cierpnąć [ćherp-nownćh] v.
    grow numb; creep; go to sleep
ciesielstwo [ćhe-śhel-stvo] n.
    carpentry (in construction]
cieszyć [ćhe-shićh] v. cheer
cieśla [ćheś-la] m. carpenter;
    wood worker; shipwright;
    wood construction worker
cietrzew [ćhe-tshev] m.
    black-cock (male); black
    grouse; grey hen (female)
cieśnina [ćheśh-ńee-na] f.
    straits; narrows; sound; ravine
cięcie [ćhan-ćhe] n. cut; gash
cięciwa [ćhan-ćhee-va] f.
    chord (in geometry); bow
    string; string; subtense
cięgi [ćhan-gee] pl. lashing
cięty [ćhan-ti] adj. m. sharp-
    tongued; biting; dogged; inci-
    sive; keen-witted; ready; tipsy
ciężar [ćhan-zhar] m. weight;
    burden; gravity; onus; duty;
    charge; task; encumbrance
ciężeć [ćhan-zhećh] v. grow
    heavy; become heavy; be-
    come a burden; encumber
ciężki [ćhanzh-kee] adj. m.
    heavy; weighty; bulky;

oppressive; clumsy; dull; inapt
ciężko [ćhanzh-ko] adv. heavily
ciocia [ćho-ćha] f. auntie; aunt
cios [ćhos] m. blow; stroke; hit;
    shock; ashlar; block; joint
cioteczny brat [ćho-tech-ni brat]
    m. cousin
ciotka [ćhot-ka] f. aunt
ciosać [ćho-saćh] v. hew;
    chop out; dress building stone
cis [ćhees] m. yew
cisawy [ćhee-sa-vi] adj. m.
    chestnut (horse)
ciskać [ćhees-kaćh] v. fling;
    cast; throw; hurl; sling; plunk;
    let fly; fret; fume; storm; rage
cisnąć [ćhees-nownćh] v.
    press; squeeze; bear; urge;
    hurt; pinch; crowd; tighten
cisza [ćhee-sha] f. calm; silence
ciśnienie [ćheeśh-ńe-ńe] n.
    pressure; blood pressure;
    thrust; stress
ciuch [ćhookh] m. used clothing
ciułać [ćhoo-waćh] v. hoard
ciurkiem [ćhoor-kyem] adv. in a
    trickle; with big drops
ciupa [ćhoo-pa] f. jail; clink
ciupasem [ćhoo-pa-sem] adv.
    under convoy; (transport)
    under an armed convoy
ciżba [ćheezh-ba] f. crowd
ckliwy [tsklee-vi] adj. m. qualmy;
    sickly; faint; sloppy
clić [tsleećh] v. collect custom
    duty; lay a custom duty
cło [tswo] n. customs
cmentarz [tsmen-tash] m.
    cemetery; burial ground
cmokać [tsmo-kaćh] v. smack
cnota [tsno-ta] f. virtue
co [tso] pron. part. what; which
codzień [tso-dźheń] adv. daily
cofać się [tso-faćh śhan] v.
    back up; retreat; regress;
    retire; remove; withdraw
cokolwiek [tso-kol-vyek] pron.
    anything; whatever; somewhat
comber [tsom-ber] m. saddle (of
    mutton); rump; loin; haunch
coraz [tso-raz] adv. ever
coś [tsośh] pron. something
córka [tsoor-ka] f. daughter

cóż [tsoosh] pron. what then
cuchnąć [tsookh-no̱wnćh] v.
　stink foul; smell foul
cucić [tsoo-ćheećh] v. revive
cud [tsoot] m. wonder; miracle
cudzołożyć [tsoo-dzo-wo-zhićh]
　v. commit adultery
codzoziemiec [tsoo-dzo-żhe-
　-myets] m. alien; foreigner
cudzy [tsoo-dzi] adj. m. someone
　else's; alien; foreign
cudzysłów [tsoo-dzi-swoof] m.
　quotation marks
cukier [tsoo-ker] m. sugar
cuma [tsoo-ma] f. mooring
cwał [tsvaw] m. full gallop
cwaniak [tsva-ńak] m. city
　slicker; sly dog; crafty guy
cwany [tsva-ni] adj. m. sly;
　cunning; crafty; artful
cyc [tsits] m. nipple (vulg.)
cyfra [tsif-ra] f. number
cygan [tsi-gan] m. gipsy; cheat;
　Gipsy; swindler; liar
cykl [tsikl] m. cycle
cylinder [tsi-leen-der] m. cylinder;
　barrel; (men's) top hat
cyna [tsi-na] f. tin
cynamon [tsi-na-mon] m.
　cinnamon; spice of laurel bark
cynober [tsi-no-ber] m. vermilion
cyngiel [tsin-gyel] m. trigger
cynik [tsi-ńeek] m. cynic
cynk [tsink] m. zinc; tutenag
cypel [tsi-pel] m. cape; tip
cyprys [tsi-pris] m. cypress
cyrk [tsirk] m. circus
cyrkiel [tsir-kel] m. compass
cysterna [tsis-ter-na] f. cistern;
　tank car; vat; storage tank
cytadela [tsi-ta-de-la] f. citadel;
　fortress; stronghold
cytata [tsi-ta-ta] f. quotation
cytryna [tsi-tri-na] f. lemon
cywil [tsi-veel] m. civilian
cyzelować [tsi-ze-lo-vaćh] v.
　engrave; carve; elaborate
czad [chat] m. carbon monoxide
czaić się [cha-eećh śhan] v.
lie in wait; lurk; stalk; crouch
czajnik [chay-ńeek] m. tea-pot
czajka [chay-ka] f. gull
czako [cha-ko] f. shako

czapka [chap-ka] f. cap; pileus
czapla [chap-la] f. heron
czaprak [chap-rak] m. horse
　blanket; caparison; trappings
czar [char] m. spell; charm
czarno [char-no] adv. blackly
czart [chart] m. devil; deuce
czas [chas] m. time; duration
czaszka [chash-ka] f. skull
czaty [cha-ti] pl. watch; lookout;
　wait; ambush; outpost
cząstka [cho̱wnst-ka] f. particle
czcić [chćheećh] v. adore;
　worship; idolize; venerate
czcigodny [chćhee-god-ni]
　adj. m. honorable; revered;
　venerable
czcionka [chćhon-ka] f. type;
　character; letter in print
czczo [chcho] adv. empty
　(stomach); emptily; vainly; idly
czego [che-go] conj. why? what?
czek [chek] m. check (in
　banking); cheque
czekać [che-kaćh] v. wait;
　await; stand by; expect;
　waste time; be in store for
czekanie [che-ka-ńe] n. wait
czekan [che-kan] m. pickhammer
czekolada [che-ko-la-da] f.
　chocolate; slab of chocolate
czeladnik [che-lad-ńeek] m.
　apprentice; journeyman
czelność [chel-nośhćh] f.
　impudence; effrontery; nerve
czeluść [che-loośhćh] f.
　abyss; gulf; precipice; depths
czemu [che-moo] part. why? to
　what? what to? what for?
czepek [che-pek] m. bonnet;
　hood; night cap; caul; calyptra
czepiać się [chep-yaćh śha̱n]
　v. cling; hang on; peck at
czereda [che-re-da] f. gang;
　throng; crowd; swarm; pack
czerep [che-rep] m. shell; skull;
　fragment; splinter; shard
czereśnia [che-reśh-ńa] f.
　cherry; cherry tree; gean
czernić [cher-ńeećh] v.
　blacken; black; paint black
czerń [cherń] f. black color
czerpać [cher-paćh] v. scoop;

draw; ladle; derive (benefit)
czerstwy [chers-tvi] adj. m.
stale; robust (man); firm
czerw [cherv] m. worm; grub
czerwienić się [cher-vye-ńeećh
śhan] v. blush (redden)
czerwony [cher-vo-ni] adj. m.
red; scarlet; crimson; ruddy
czesać [che-saćh] v. comb;
brush; dress hair; do hair
czeski [ches-kee] adj. m. Czech
czesne [ches-ne] n. tuition
cześć [cheśhćh] f. honor;
cult; worship; respect;
adoration; reverence; good
name; greeting: hullo! cheerio!
często [chans-to] adv. often
częstokroć [chan-sto-kroćh]
adv. often; repeatedly
częstość [chans-tośhćh] f.
frequency; recurrence
częstotliwość [chan-sto-tlee-
-vośhćh] f. frequency; recurrence; rapid occurrence
częstować [chan-sto-vaćh] v.
treat to something; regale
częsty [chans-ti] adj. m.
frequent; repeated often
częściowy [chan-śhćho-vi]
adj. m. partial; fragmentary
część [chanśhćh] f. part;
share; section; piece; quota
czkawka [chkav-ka] f. hiccups
człon [chwon] m. element;
segment; link; member; clause
członek [chwo-nek] m. limb;
member; man's sex organ
człowiek [chwo-vyek] m. man;
individual; chap; somebody
czmychnąć [chmikh-nownćh]
v. bolt; steal out; whisk away
czochrać [chokh-raćh] v.tousle;
ripple; hackle; scratch
czołg [chowg] m. tank (military);
reptile; crawler
czołgać [chow-gaćh] v. crawl
czoło [cho-wo] n. forehead
czop [chop] m. peg; plug; pin
czosnek [chos-nek] m. garlic
czterdzieści [chter-dźheśh-
-ćhee] num. forty
czternaście [chter-naśh-ćhe]
num. fourteen, 14

czteropiętrowy [chte-ro-pyan-tro
-vi] adj. m. four stories high;
four storied (building)
cztery [chte-ri] num. four
czub [choop] m. tuft; crest
czucie [choo-ćhe] n. feeling;
smelling; sense perception
czuć [chooćh] v. feel; smell
czujka [chooy-ka] f. sentry
czułość [choo-wośhćh] f.
tenderness; affection; caress
czuły [choo-wi] adj. m. tender;
affectionate; sensitive; keen
czupurny [choo-poor-ni] adj. m.
pugnacious; boastful; defiant
czuwać [choo-vaćh] v. watch;
nurse; look-out; stay up; tend
czwartek [chvar-tek] m.
Thursday
czwarty [chvar-ti] num. fourth
czworobok [chvo-ro-bok] m.
quadrilateral; square; tetragon
czworokąt [chvo-ro-kownt] m.
quadrangle; quad; tetragon
czwórka [chvoor-ka] f. foursome;
crew of four; good mark
czy [chi] conj. if; whether
czychać [chi-khaćh] v. lurk
czyj [chiy] pron. whose
czyjś [chiyśh] pron.
somebody's; anybody's;
someone else's
czyli [chi-lee] conj. or; otherwise;
that is to say; in other words
czym...tym... [chim...tim] adv.
the sooner... the; the more
the...; the less... the...
czyn [chin] m. act; deed
czynsz [chinsh] m. rent
czynić [chi-ńeećh] v. do;
render; act; amount; cause
czyrak [chi-rak] m. boil; furuncle;
abscess; anbury; rising
czynnik [chin-ńeek] m. factor
czysto [chi-sto] adv. clean
czysty [chis-ti] adj. m. clean
czyszczenie [chish-che-ńe] n.
cleaning; brushing; diarrhoea
czyścić [chiśh-ćheećh] v.
clean; scour; brush; rub; purge
czyściec [chiśh-ćhets] m.
purgatory; woundwort
czytać [chi-taćh] v. read

czytelnia [chi-tel-ńa] f. reading room; lending library

czytelnik [chi-tel-ńeek] m. reader; reading individual

czytelny [chi-tel-ni] adj. m. legible; readable

czyż [chish] part. if; whether

ćma [ćhma] f. obscurity; swarm; night butterfly; night moth; darkness; dark night

ćmić [ćhmeećh] v. obscure; dim; darken; eclipse; smoke; sicken; blind; dazzle; glimmer

ćwiartka [ćhvyart-ka] f. one quarter; one fourth of a liter

ćwierć [ćhvyerćh] f. one fourth (of a liter etc.)

ćwiczenie [ćhvee-che-ńe] n. exercise; instruction; drill

ćwiek [ćhvyek] m. nail; stud

ćwikła [ćhveek-wa] f. red beet with horseradish (salad)

D

dach [dakh] m. roof; shelter

dać [daćh] v. give; pay; result

daktyl [dak-till] m. date

dal [dal] f. distance; remoteness; far away; aloof; distant

dalece [da-le-tse] adv. further; by far; so far; (so) much so

dalej [da-ley] moreover; further off; so on; later; further back

dalmierz [dal-myesh] m. range finder; telemeter

dalszy [dal-shi] adj. m. further; later; outlying; another

dama [da-ma] f. lady; partner

dana [da-na] adj. f. given (data)

danie [da-ńe] m. serving (of food); dish; course

danser [dan-ser] m. dancer

dane [da-ne] pl. data

dar [dar] m. gift; present

daremnie [da-rem-ńe] adv. in vain; without success

daremny [da-rem-ni] adj. m. futile; vain; idle; ineffective

darmo [dar-mo] adv. free; gratuitously; to no avail

darować [da-ro-vaćh] v. give; forgive; overlook; spare

data [da-ta] f. date

datek [da-tek] n. small gift

dawać [da-vaćh] v. give (often)

dawno [dav-no] adv. long ago

dąb [downp] m. oak tree (wood)

dąć [downćh] v. blow; resound

dąsać się [down-saćh śhan] v. sulk; be in the pouts; mump

dążyć [down-zhićh] v. aspire; tend; aim; be bound; trend

dbać [dbaćh] v. care; set store

dach [dakh] m. breath; gust

decydować [de-tsi-do-vaćh] v. decide; resolve; determine

decyzja [de-tsis-ya] f. decision; ruling; resolve; resolution

defekt [de-fekt] m. defect; flaw;

delikatność [de-lee-kat-nośhćh] f. delicacy; gentleness; softness; subtleness; daintiness; tact; consideration; thoughtfulness; sensitiveness; frailness; nicety; fragility

defekt [de-fekt] m. defect; flaw; fault; damage; injury; reject

demaskować [de-mas-ko-vaćh] v. unmask; uncover; denounce

demokracja [de-mo-krats-ya] f. democracy; rule by the people

denerwować [de-ner-vo-vaćh] v. bother; make nervous; vex; irritate; upset; exasperate

dentysta [den-tis-ta] m. dentist

depesza [de-pe-sha] f. wire; telegram; cable; dispatch

deponować [de-po-no-vaćh] v. deposit; put in safe keeping

depozyt [de-po-zit] m. deposit

deptać [dep-taćh] v. trample (the soil); tread; pace up and down; stain; soil; muddy

derka [der-ka] f. rug; blanket

deseń [de-seń] m. pattern; design; decorative design

deska [des-ka] f. plank; board

desperacja [des-pe-rats-ya] f. desperation; despair

deszcz [deshch] m. rain

detal [de-tal] m. detail; trifling matter; retail trade

determinacja [de-ter-mee-nats-ya] f. determination; resoluteness

dewiza [de-vee-za] f. foreign money; motto; slogan; device

dąbina [dan-bee-na] f. oak wood; oak bark; oak stand

dętka [dant-ka] f. pneumatic tire; tube; air chamber

diabeł [dya-bew] m. devil

dieta [dye-ta] f. diet; regimen

dla [dla] prep. for; to; towards

dlaczego [dla-che-go] prep. why; what for; why are you ...?

dlatego [dla-te-go] prep. because; this is why; and so

dławić [dwa-veech] v. choke; squash; throttle; strangle

dłoń [dwoń] f. palm of the hand; hand; metacarpus; quart

dłubać [dwoo-bach] v. groove; poke; pick one's teeth

dług [dwook] m. debt; obligation

długi [dwoo-gee] adj. m. long

długo [dwoo-go] adv. a long time; a long way; long before

dłuto [dwoo-to] n. chisel

dłutować [dwoo-to-vach] v. chisel; cut with chisel

dłużnik [dwoozh-ńeek] m. debtor; borrower; mortgager

dmuchać [dmoo-khach] v. blow

dniówka [dńoov-ka] f. day's work; work by day; time work

dno [dno] n. bottom; utterness

do [do] prep. to; into; up; till

doba [do-ba] f. 24 hours

dobić [do-beech] v. deal a death blow; drive home (a point, etc.); reach (a shore)

dobierać [do-bye-rach] v. match; take more; select

dobitny [do-beet-ni] adj. m. expressive; emphatic; distinct

doborowy [do-bo-ro-vi] adj. m. choice; select; picked

dobosz [do-bosh] m. drummer

dobór [do-boor] m. selection; assortment; choice

dobra [dob-ra] n. riches

dobranoc [do-bra-nots] (indecl.) good-night

dobrany [do-bra-ni] adj. m. matching; becoming; well-chosen; accordant

dobre [dob-re] adj. n. good

dobro [dob-ro] n. good; right

dobrobyt [do-bro-bit] m. well being; prosperity; welfare

dobroczynność [do-bro-chin-nośhćh] f. charity; works of mercy; philanthropy

dobroć [dob-roćh] f. kindness

dobroduszny [do-bro-doosh-ni] adj m. kindhearted; kindly

dobrodziej [do-bro-dźhey] m. benefactor; his reverence

dobrotliwy [do-bro-tlee-vi] adj. m. kind; good natured

dobrowolny [do-bro-vol-ni] adj. m. voluntary; gratuitous

dobry [dob-ri] adj. m. good; kind; right; hearty; retentive

dobrze [dob-zhe] adv. well; OK; rightly; properly; okay

dobudówka [do-boo-doov-ka] f. building extension

dobyć [do-bićh] v. pullout

dobytek [do-bi-tek] m. belongings; effects; livestock

doceniać [do-tse-ńach] v. duly appreciate; value; esteem

docent [do-tsent] m. associate professor; lecturer

dochodzenie [do-kho-dze-ńe] n. investigation; inquiry

dochodzić [do-kho-dźeećh] v. draw near; investigate; reach

dochód [do-khoot] m. income; revenue; profit; returns

dociąg [do-ćhownćh] c. sting; taunt; fit by cutting off

dociec [do-ćhets] v. find out

dociekać [do-ćhe-kaćh] v. search; investigate; find out

docierać [do-ćhye-raćh] v. draw near; reach; reduce friction; rub up; get at

docinek [do-ćhee-nek] m. taunt

doczekać [do-che-kaćh] v. wait; live to see; wait 'til

doczepiać [do-che-pyaćh] v. fix append; attach; hitch; link

doczesny [do-ches-ni] adj. m. temporal; worldly; mundane

dodać [do-daćh] v. add; sum up; join; affix; impart

dodatek [do-da-tek] m. supplement; addition; fixture; extra; appendage; bonus

dodatni [do-dat-ńee] adj. m. positive; advantageous; active

dodawanie [do-da-va-ńe] n. addition

dogadać się [do-ga-daćh śhan] v. scoff; jibe; gibe; flout; bicker; remark; come to terms; communicate well

dogadzać [do-ga-dzaćh] v. please; accommodate; satisfy

doglądać [do-glown-daćh] v. supervise; tend; oversee

dogmat [dog-mat] m. dogma

dogodny [do-god-ni] adj. m. convenient; suitable; handy

dogonić [do-go-ńeećh] v catch up; overtake; be in hot pursuit; be hot on the track

dogryzać [do-gri-zaćh] v. vex; tease; finish munching; disturb

doić [do-eećh] v. milk; fleece

dojarka [do-yar-ka] f. milk maid; milking machine

dojazd [do-yazt] m. access; drive; approach; means of transport; journey

dojechać [do-ye-khaćh] v. reach; arrive; approach; bang; hit; give a blow; jeer; peck

dojeżdżać [do-yezh-dzhaćh] v. commute; be coming; pull in

dojmujący [doy-moo-yown-tsi] adj. m. acute; piercing; sharp; keen; tormenting; stinging

dojrzały [doy-zha-wi] adj. m. ripe; mellow; mature; adult

dojrzeć [doy-zhećh] v. glimpse; notice; ripen; be ripen; mellow

dojście [doy-śhćhe] n. access; (avenue of) approach

dok [dok] m. dock

dokarmić [do-kar-meećh] v. nourish additionally

dokazać [do-ka-zaćh] v. prove; achieve; accomplish; do the trick; get by effort

dokazywać [do-ka-zi-vaćh] v. frolic; gambol; romp and play

dokąd [do-kownt] adv. where; till when? whither; where to? how far? till when? how long?

dokładać [do-kwa-daćh] v. add; throw in; say more; give more

dokładny [dok-wad-ni] adj. m. accurate; exact; precise

dokoła [do-ko-wa] adv. round; round about; all round

dokonać [do-ko-naćh] v. achieve; accomplish; carry out; fulfil; do; execute

dokończenie [do-koń-che-ńe] n. conclusion; completion; end

doktor [dok-tor] m. doctor

dokręcać [do-kran-tsaćh] v. tighten; screw tight; turn off

dokuczać [do-koo-chaćh] v. vex; annoy; nag; bully; sting; trouble; spite; worry; torment

dola [do-la] f. fortune; lot

dolar [do-lar] m. dollar

doliczyć [do-lee-chićh] v. count up; add; charge more; reckon

dolina [do-lee-na] f. valley; dale; glen; coomb; (slang) pocket

dolny [dol-ni] adj. m. lower

dołączyć [do-wown-chićh] v. add; join; enclose; affix; tack on; annex; accede; crop up

dołek [do-wek] m. dimple; pit

dom [dom] m. house; home

domagać się [do-ma-gaćh śhan] v. demand; claim; insist

domiar [do-myar] m. additional assessment; surtax; adv.: on top of it all; in addition

domniemany [do-mńe-ma-ni] adj. m. supposed; assumed; alleged; presumed

domostwo [do-mos-tvo] n. household; homestead; farmstead; family's home

domownik [do-mov-ńeek] m. inmate; household member

domowy [do-mo-vi] adj. m. domestic; homemade; private

domysł [do-misw] m. guess

doniesienie [do-ńe-śhe-ńe] m. denunciation; report; news

doniosły [do-ńo-swi] adj. m. significant; far reaching

donosiciel [do-no-śhee-ćhel] m.

denunciator; informer
donośny [do-**nośh**-ni] adj. m.
resounding; ringing; loud
dookoła [do-o-**ko**-wa] adv. round;
round about; all around; all
around; right round
dopaść [do-**paśhćh**] v. run
up; overtake; reach at a run;
catch up; hunt down; seize
dopalać [do-pa-**laćh**] v.
after burn; finish burning; burn
out; finish smoking
dopasować [do-pa-**so**-vaćh] v.
fit; adapt; adjust; match; tone
dopatrywać [do-pa-**tri**-vaćh] v.
see to it; find out; keep an
eye; perceive; detect; watch
dopełnić [do-**pew**-ńeećh] v.
fulfil; fill up; complete; make
up; complement; supplement
dopędzić [do-**pan**-dźheećh] v.
catch up with; overtake; gain
on; drive (cattle to...)
dopiąć [do-py**ownćh**] v. attain;
buckle up; button up; obtain
dopiero [do-**pye**-ro] adv. only;
just; hardly; barely; not till
dopilnować [do-peel-no-vaćh]
v. see something done; make
sure; supervise; take care
dopisek [do-**pee**-sek] m.
postscript; foot note
dopłata [do-**pwa**-ta] f. extra
payment; surcharge; extra fare
dopływ [do-**pwif**] m. tributary
dopomagać [do-po-ma-**gaćh**] v.
help; be of assistance
dopominać się [do-po-**mee**-
-naćh **śhan**] v. put in a
claim; demand; call for
dopóki [do-**poo**-kee] conj. as
long; as far; while; until; till
dopóty [do-**poo**-ti] conj. till; until;
so far; up to here; as long as
dopraszać się [do-pra-**shaćh**
śhan] v. solicit; beg; insist
doprawdy [do-**prav**-di] adv. truly;
indeed; really; is that so?
doprawiać [do-pra-**vyaćh**] v.
add (to taste); replace
doprowadzić [do-pro-**va**-
-dźheećh] v. lead to; cause;
provoke; reduce; achieve;

convey; result; bring
dopust Boży [do-**poost bo**-zhi]
m. calamity; scourge; act of
God; decree of Providence
dopuszczać [do-**poosh**-chaćh]
v. admit; allow; permit; be
open; give access; be patient
dopytać się [do-pi-taćh **śhan**]
v. find out; inquire; question
dorabiać [do-ra-**byaćh**] v. make
additionally; replace; finish
doradca [do-**rad**-tsa] m. adviser;
counselor; guide; consultant
dorastać [do-**ras**-taćh] v.
mature; grow; grow up; reach
doraźnie [do-**raźh**-ńe] adv.
(immediately) on the spot
doręczyć [do-**ran**-chićh] v.
hand in; deliver; transmit
dorobek [do-**ro**-bek] m.
acquisition; rise to affluence
dorobkiewicz [do-rob-**ke**-veech]
m. upstart; parvenu; new rich
doroczny [do-**roch**-ni] adj. m.
yearly; annual; recurring yearly
dorodny [do-**rod**-ni] adj. m.
handsome; fine-looking;
shapely; good-looking
dorosły [do-**ros**-wi] adj. m. adult;
grown up; mature; grown
dorożka [do-**rosh**-ka] f. cab
dorównywać [do-roov-ni-vaćh]
v. match; equal; catch up with
dorsz [dorsh] m. cod (fish)
dorywczy [do-**riv**-chi] adj. m.
occasional; improvised; fitful;
off-and-on; hit-and-run
dorzecze [do-**zhe**-che] n. river
basin; drainage area
dorzeczny [do-**zhech**-ni] adj. m.
reasonable; sensible; efficient;
adequate; acceptable; logical
dorzucać [do-**zhoo**-tsaćh] v.
throw in; add; throw as far as
dosadny [do-**sad**-ni] adj. m.
forceful; expressive; crisp
dosiadać [do-**śha**-daćh] v.
mount (horse); bestride
dosięgać [do-**śhan**-gaćh] v.
reach; attain; catch up with
doskonalić [do-sko-na-leećh] v.
perfect; improve; cultivate
doskwierać [do-**skvye**-raćh] v.

pinch; gripe; trouble; worry
dosłowny [do-**swov**-ni] adj. m.
literal; verbal; textual
dosłyszeć [do-**swi**-shećh] v.
hear well; catch a sound
dostać [dos-**tać**h] v. obtain;
reach; take out
dostarczyć [do-**star**-chićh] v.
provide; supply; deliver
dostateczny [do-sta-**tech**-ni] adj.
m. sufficient; adequate
dostatek [do-**sta**-tek] m.
abundance; wealth; affluence
dostawca [do-**stav**-tsa] m.
supplier; provider
dostawa [do-**sta**-va] f. delivery
dostawać [do-**sta**-vaćh] v.
reach; receive; be attended to
dostęp [dos-<u>tanp</u>] m. access
dostojnik [do-**stoy**-ńeek] m.
dignitary; notable of high rank
dostosować [do-sto-so-vaćh] v.
accommodate; subordinate; fit
dostroić [do-**stro**-eećh] v. tune
up; conform; adapt
dostrzec [dos-tshets] v. notice;
behold; perceive; spot; spy;
see
dostudzić [do-**stoo**-dźheećh] v.
cool off
dosyć [do-sićh] adv. enough;
plenty; sufficient
dosztukawać [do-shtoo-**ko**-
-vaćh] v. piece on; eke out;
sew on; add on; patch with
dość [doshćh] adv. enough
dośrodkowy [do-śhrod-**ko**-vi]
adj. m. centripetal; concentric
doświadczyć [do-śhvyad-
-chićh] v. experience; sustain;
feel; undergo; suffer; scourge
dotarcie [do-**tar**-ćhe] n.
reaching; overcoming friction
dotąd [do-<u>townt</u>] adv. up till
now; here to fore; hitherto;
thus far; so far; yet; by then;
till then; still; not...as yet
dotkliwy [do-**tklee**-vi] adj. m.
painful; keen; intense; severe
dotknąć [dot-kn<u>own</u>ćh] v.
touch; finger; offend; hurt
dotknięcie [dot-kń<u>an</u>-ćhe] n.
touch; contact; feeling; stroke

dotrzeć [do-tshećh] v. reach;
overcome friction; rub up
dotrzymać [do-**tshi**-maćh] v.
keep; stick to one's
commitment; adhere; redeem
dotychczas [do-tikh-chas] adv.
up to now; hitherto; to date
dotyczyć [do-ti-chićh] v.
concern; relate; regard; affect
dotyk [do-tik] m. touch; feel
dowcip [dov-ćheep] m. wit;
joke; jest; gag; quip; sally
dowiedzieć się [do-**vye**-dźhećh
śhan] v. get to know; learn
do widzenia [do vee-**dze**-ńa]
good bye; see you later
dowierzać [do-**vye**-zhaćh] v.
trust; have confidence in
dowieść [do-vyeśhćh] v.
prove; bring; vindicate
dowieźć [do-vyeźhćh] v. 1.
supply; 2. drive to
dowodzić [do-**vo**-dźheećh] v.
conduct; keep proving
dowolnie [do-**vol**-ńe] adv. at
will; optionally; freely
dowolny [do-**vol**-ni] adj. m.
optional; any; whichever
dowód [do-**voot**] m. proof;
evidence; record; token
dowódca [do-**vood**-tsa] m.
commander
dowóz [do-**voos**] m. supply;
delivery
doza [do-za] f. dose
dozbroić [do-zbro-eećh] v.
rearm; supplement weapons
dozgonny [do-**zgon**-ni] adj. m.
lifelong; lasting till death
doznać [doz-naćh] v. go
through; undergo; endure;
feel; suffer; experience
dozorca [do-**zor**-tsa] m.
caretaker; watchman; overseer
dozorować [do-zo-ro-vaćh] v.
oversee; supervise; attend
dozór [do-zoor] m. surveillance
dozwolić [do-zvo-leećh] v.
allow to happen; let happen
dożynki [do-**zhin**-kee] pl. harvest
festivities
dożywocie [do-zhee-**vo**-ćhe] n.
life estate; life pension

dół [doow] m. pit; bottom part
drab [drap] m. ruffian; scamp
drabina [dra-bee-na] f. ladder
dramat [dra-mat] m. drama
drań [drań] m. scoundrel;
  crumb; rotter; cad
drapacz [dra-pach] m. scraper
drapać [dra-pać] v. scratch
drapieżnik [dra-pyezh-ńeek] m.
  beast of prey; plunderer
drastyczny [dra-stich-ni] adj. m.
  drastic; rough; violent
dratwa [drat-va] f. pitched tread;
  shoemaker's twine
drażliwy [dra-zhlee-vi] adj. m.
  touchy; irritable; ticklish
drażnić [drazh-ńeećh] v. vex;
  tease; irritate; whet; annoy;
  jar; provoke; stimulate; gall
drąg [drownk] m. pole; bar
drążyć[drown-zhićh] v. hollow
  out; bore; torment; fret; gnaw
drelich [dre-leekh] m. denim
dren [dren] m. drain (pipe)
dreptać [drep-tać] v. triptrot;
  toddle; totter; patter
dreszcz [dreshch] m. chill;
  shudder; thrill; flutter; shiver
dreszczowiec [dresh-cho-vyets]
  m. thriller (novel or movie)
drewno [drev-no] n. piece of
  wood; timber; log; xylem
dręczyć [dran-chićh] v. torment
drętwieć [drant-vyećh] v. grow
  numb; grow stiff; stiffen
drgać [drgać] v. tremble;
  vibrate; quiver; throb; wobble
drobiazg [dro-byazk] m. trifle;
  detail; trinket; small fry
drobina [dro-bee-na] f. particle
drobne [drob-ne] pl. small
  change; petty cash; small coin
drobnica [drob-ńee-tsa] f. small
  goods; small size packages
drobnostka [drob-nost-ka] f.
  trifle; small mater; trinket
drobny [drob-ni] adj. m. small;
  tiny; trivial; petty; slight
droga [dro-ga] f. 1. road; 2.
  journey; 3. adj. f. dear
drogeria [dro-ger-ya] f. drugstore;
  drysaltery
drogi [dro-gee] adj. m. dear;

expensive; costly; beloved
drogowskaz [dro-gov-skas] m.
  road sign; signpost
drozd [drozt] m. thrush
drożdże [drozh-dzhe] pl. yeast
drożeć [dro-zhećh] v. grow
  dear; rise in price; appreciate
drożyzna [dro-zhiz-na] f. high
  cost of living; high prices
drób [droop] pl.paltry
dróżka [droozh-ka] f. path
druciany [droo-ćha-ni] adj. m. of
  wire; made out of wire
drugi [droo-gee] num. second ;
  other; the other one; latter
druh [drookh] m. buddy;
  companion; friend; boy scout
druk [drook] m. print; printing
drut [droot] m. wire
druzgotać [drooz-go-tać] v.
  smash; shatter; crush to
  pieces; pulverize; crush
drużba [droozh-ba] m. best man
drużyna [droo-zhi-na] f. team
drwal [drval] m. lumber jack
drwić [drveećh] v. mock; deride; sneer; scoff; jeer; jibe
drwiny [drvee-ni] pl. mockery
dryg [drik] m. knack; flair for
drzazga [dzhaz-ga] f. splinter
drzeć [dzhećh] v. tear; pull
drzemka [dzhem-ka] f. nap
drzewo [dzhe-vo] n. tree
drzeworyt [dzhe-vo-rit] m.
  woodcut; wood engraving
drzwi [dzhvee] n. door
drżeć [drzhećh] v. shiver;
  shake; tremble; quiver; quake
dubeltówka [doo-bel-toov-ka] f.
  double barrel gun; shotgun
duch [dookh] m. spirit; ghost;
  state of mind; intendment
duchowieństwo [doo-kho-vyeń-
  -stvo] pl. clergy; priesthood
dudek [doo-dek] m. 1. hoopoe;
  2. dupe; fool; dolt; booby
dudnić [dood-ńeećh] v.
  resound; rumble; roll; thump
dudy [doo-di] pl. bagpipe
dukat [doo-kat] m. ducat
dulka [dool-ka] f. oarlock
duma [doo-ma] f. pride; epic
dumać [doo-mać] v. meditate

dumny [doom-ni] adj. m. proud
dupa [doo-pa] f. ass (vulg.)
dur [door] m. typhoid fever
dureń [doo-reń] m. fool; ass
durzyć [doo-zhich] v. fool;
  infatuate; bewilder; dupe
dusić [doo-śheech] v. strangle
dusigrosz [doo-śhee-grosh] m.
  penny pincher; niggard;
  cheapskate; miser; skinflint
dusza [doo-sha] f. soul; psyche
dużo [doo-zho] adv. much; many
duży [doo-zhi] adj. m. big; large;
  great; fair-sized; pretty large
dwa [dva] num. two; 2
dwakroć [dva-kroch] num.
  twice; two times
dwanaście [dva-naśh-che]
  num. twelve; 12
dwieście [dvyeśh-che] num.
  two hundred; 200
dwoić [dvo-eech] v. double
dwojaczki [dvo-yach-kee] pl.
  twins; double pot
dwoje [dvo-ye] num. the two;
  two; in two; couple; two
  (fold); two (ways); 2
dworski [dvors-kee] adj. m.
  courtly; manorial; of court
dworzec [dvo-zhets] m. (rail)
  station; depot
dwókrotnie [dvoo-krot-ńe] adv.
  twice; twice over; two times
dwór [dvoor] m. country manor
dwunastka [dvoo-nast-ka] f.
  twelve; (team) of twelve
dwustronny [dvoo-stron-ni] adj.
  m. two-sided; bilateral
dyg [dik] m. curtsy; bob
dygnitarz [dig-ńee-tash] m.
  dignitary; high ranking man
dygotać [di-go-tach] v. tremble
dykta [dik-ta] f. plywood
dyktator [dik-ta-tor] m. dictator;
  absolute ruler; tyrant
dylemat [di-le-mat] m. dilemma;
  perplexity; fix
dym [dim] m. smoke; fumes
dymić [di-meech] v. smoke
dynamit [di-na-meet] m.
  dynamite; W.W.II German
  ersatz (artificial) bread
dyndać [din-dach] v. dangle

dynia [di-ńa] f. pumpkin
dyplom [di-plom] m. diploma
dyplomacja [di-plo-mats-ya] f.
  diplomacy; policy; tact
dyrekcja [di-rek-tsya] f.
  management; headquarters
dyrygent [di-ri-gent] m. orchestra
  conductor; orchestra leader
dyscyplina [di-sci-plee-na] f.
  discipline; branch; line
dysk [disk] m. disc; discus
dyskrecja [dis-kre-tsya] f.
  discretion; management
dyskusja [dis-koo-sya] f. discussion; debate; controversy
dysponować [dis-po-no-vach]
  v. dispose; control; order
dysputa [dis-poo-ta] f. dispute;
  debate; controversy
dystans [dis-tans] m. distance
dystyngowany [dis-tin-go-va-ni]
  adj. m. distinguished
dysza [di-sha] f. nozzle; blast
  pipe; snout; twyer
dyszeć [di-shech] v. gasp; pant
dywan [di-van] m. carpet; rug
dywidenda [di-vee-den-da] f.
  dividend; bonus
dywizja [di-veez-ya] f. division
dyżurny [di-zhoor-ni] adj. m. on
  call; on duty; orderly
dzban [dzban] m. jug; pitcher
dziać się [dźhach śhan] v.
  occur; happen; take place
dziadek [dźha-dek] m.
  grandfather
dział [dźhaw] m. section
działacz [dźha-wach] m. activist
  (in politics, religion etc.)
działać [dźha-waćh] v. act;
  work; be active; be effective
działka [dźhaw-ka] f. parcel
działo [dźha-wo] n. cannon
dziarski [dźhars-kee] adj. m.
  brisk; lively; swinging; rakish
dziąsło [dźhown-swo] n. gum
dzicz [dźheech] pl. savages
dzida [dźee-da] f. spear; pike
dzieci [dźhe-chee] pl. children
dzieciństwo [dźhe-cheeń-
  -stvo] n. childhood; boyhood;
  infancy; babyhood
dziecko [dźhets-ko] n. child;

baby; trot; brat; kiddie; kid

dziedziczyć [dźhe-dźhee--chićh] v. inherit (property, features); come into (money)

dziedzina [dźhe-dźhee-na] f. realm; area; sphere; domain

dziedziniec [dźhe-dźhee-ńets] m. yard; court; backyard

dziegieć [dźhe-gyećh] m. tar

dzieje [dźhe-ye] pl. history

dziejowy [dźhe-yo-vi] adj. m. historical; historic

dziekan [dźhe-kan] m. dean

dzielić [dźhe-leećh] v. divide; share; split; distribute

dzielnica [dźhel-ńee-tsa] f. province; quarter; section

dzielny [dźhel-ni] adj. m. brave; resourceful; efficient

dzieło [dźhe-wo] n. achievement; work; composition; cause; result; outcome; doing

dziennik [dźhen-ńeek] m. daily news; daily; journal; diary

dzienny [dźhen-ni] m daily; diurnal; day's (pay, work, etc.)

dzień [dźheń] m. day; daylight

dzień dobry [dźheń dob-ri] exp. good morning; good day

dzierżawa [dźer-zha-va] f. lease; rental; holding; household

dzierżyć [dźher-zhićh] v. wield (power); hold tight; grip

dziesiątka [dźhe-śhownt-ka] f. ten; (team of) ten; 10

dziesięć [dźhe-śhanćh] num. ten; 10

dziewczyna [dźhev-chi-na] f. girl; lass; wench; maid

dziewica [dźhe-vee-tsa] f. virgin; maiden

dziewięć [dźhe-vyanćh] num. nine; 9

dziewiętnaście [dźhe-vyant--naśh-ćhe] num. nineteen

dzięcioł [dźhan-ćhow] m. woodpecker

dziękczynienie [dźhank-chi-ńe--ńe] n. thanksgiving

dziękować [dźhan-ko-vaćh] v. thank; give thanks

dzik [dźheek] m. boar; tusker

dziobać [dźho-baćh] v. peck

dziób [dźhoop] m. beak; bill

dzisiejszy [dźhe-śhey-shi] adj. m. today's; modern

dziś [dźheeśh] adv. today

dziupla [dźhoop-la] f. (tree) hollow; (tree) cavity

dziura [dźhoo-ra] f. hole

dziurawy [dźhoo-ra-vi] adj. m. leaky; full of holes

dziw [dźheef] m. wonder

dziwactwo [dźhee-vats-tvo] n. crank; fad; craze; peculiarity

dziwić [dźhee-veećh] v. astonish; surprise; wonder

dziwny [dźheev-ni] m. strange; odd; queer; peculiar; singular

dzwon [dzvon] m. bell; chime

dźwięczeć [dźhvyan-chećh] v. ring; sound; jingle; clang

dźwięk [dźhvyank] m. sound

dźwig [dźhveek] n. crane

dźwigać [dźhvee-gaćh] v. lift; hoist; raise; heave; erect; carry; upheave; elevate; erect

dżdżysty [dzhdzhis-ti] adj. m. wet; rainy; drizzly (weather

dżem [dzhem] m. jam; fruit jam

dżet [dzhet] m. jet

dżinsy [dzheen-si] pl. blue jeans (pants); jeans

dżokej [dzho-key] m. jockey

dżudo [dzhoo-do] n. judo (sport)

dżuma [dzhoo-ma] f. plague

dżungla [dzhoon-gla] f. jungle

E

echo [ekho] n. echo; response

edukacja [e-doo-ka-tsya] f. education; formal schooling; instruction; teaching

efekt [e-fekt] m. effect

efektowny [e-fek-tov-ni] adj. m. showy; striking; attractive

efektywny [e-fek-tiv-ni] adj. m. efficient; effective; real

egida [e-gee-da] f. protection; auspices; protectorate

egoista [e-go-ees-ta] m. egotist
egoistyczny [e-go-ees-tich-ni]
adj. m. selfish; self seeking
egzamin [eg-za-meen] m.
examination; exam; standing a
test; a set of questions
egzekucja [eg-ze-kuts-ya] f.
execution; seizure; flogging
egzemplarz [eg-zem-plazh] m.
copy (sample); specimen
egzystencja [eg-żis-ten-tsya] f.
existence; livelihood
ekierka [e-ker-ka] f. set square;
draftsman's triangle
ekipa [e-kee-pa] f. team; crew
ekonomia [e-ko-no-mya] f.
economics; thrift; economy
ekran [ek-ran] m. screen; shield
ekspedient [eks-pe-dyent] m.
salesperson; clerk; salesman
ekspedycja [eks-pe-dits-ya] f.
dispatch; expedition; service
ekspert [eks-pert] m. expert
eksploatować [eks-plo-a-to-
-vaćh] v. exploit; sweat;
utilize (machines); operate
eksponat [eks-po-nat] m. exhibit
ekspozytura [eks-po-zi-too-ra] f.
agency; branch office; branch
ekwipować [ek-vee-po-vaćh]
v. equip; fit out; provide with
elaborat [e-la-bo-rat] m. study
elaborate essay; dissertation
elastyczność [e-las-tich-
-nośhćh] f. elasticity; resilience; flexibility; buoyancy
elegancja [e-le-gan-tsya] f.
elegance; fashion; style
elektrociepłownia [e-lek-tro-
-ćhep-wov-ńa] f. steam plant
elektryczność [e-lek-trich-
-nośhćh] f. electricity
element [e-le-ment] m. element
elementarny [e-le-men-tar-ni] adj.
m. fundamental; primary
elewator [e-le-va-tor] m.
(grain) elevator; hoist
emalia [e-ma-lya] f. enamel
emeryt [e-me-rit] m. retired
person; pensioner; pensionary
emigracja [e-mee-grats-ya] f.
emigration; exile; emigrants
emisja [e-mees-ya] f. emission

emocja [e-mots-ya] f. thrill
entuzjazm [en-tooz-yazm] m.
enthusiasm; rapture
energia [e-ner-gya] f. energy
energiczny [e-ner-geech-ni] adj.
m. energetic; vigorous
epoka [e-po-ka] f. epoch
epitet [e-pee-tet] m. epithet
era [e-ra] f. era; epoch
erotyczny [e-ro-tich-ni] adj. m.
erotic; sexual; amatory
eskadra [es-kad-ra] f. squadron;
aerial fleet
eskorta [es-kor-ta] f. escort
estetyczny [es-te-tich-ni] adj. m.
aesthetic; in good taste
etap [e-tap] m. stage (of
development); halting place
etatowy [e-ta-to-vi] adj. m.
permanent (job); full time
eter [e-ter] m. ether
etyczny [e-tich-ni] adj. m.
ethical; moral (standard)
etykieta [e-ti-ke-ta] f. label;
etiquette; formality; ceremonial; acceptable manners
ewakuacja [e-va-koo-ats-ya] f.
evacuation; removal; emptying
ewangelia [e-van-gel-ya] f.
gospel; gospel truth
ewangielik [e-van-ge-leek] m.
protestant; Lutheran
ewentualność [e-ven-too-al-
-nośhćh] f. possibility
ewentualnie [e-ven-too-al-ńe]
adv. possibly; if need be
ewidencja [e-vee-den-tsya] f.
records; lists; files; roll
ewolucja [e-vo-loo-tsya] f.
evolution; development
ex- see eks-

F

fabryczny [fab-rich-ni] adj. m.
manufactured; machine made
fabryka [fa-bri-ka] f. factory
fabuła [fa-boo-wa] f. fable; story

facet [fa-tset] m. guy
fachowiec [fa-kho-vyets] m.
  expert; specialist; connoisseur
fajdać [fay-daćh] v. shit (vulg.)
fajans [fa-yans] f. earthenware
fajerka [fa-yer-ka] f. cook-top
  unit; gas stove lid; burner
fajka [fay-ka] f. pipe (for
  smoking); wild boar's tusk
fajtłapa [fay-twa-pa] m. all
  thumbs guy (awkward, clumsy
  man); dangling hand; crock
fakt [fakt] m. fact; reality
faktor [fak-tor] m. broker; agent;
  factor (math.); intermediary
faktycznie [fak-tich-ńe] adv. in
  fact; actually; indeed; truly
fala [fa-la] f. wave; tide; surge
falisty [fa-lees-ti] adj. m. wavy;
  rolling; corrugated
falochron [fa-lokh-ron] m.
  breakwater; pier; jetty; mole
falsyfikat [fal-si-fee-kat] m.
  forgery; counterfeit; fake
fałd [fawt] m. fold (wrinkle)
fałsz [fawsh] m. falsehood
fałszować [faw-sho-vaćh] v.
  falsify; fake; forge; sing flat
fama [fa-ma] f. fame; rumor
fanaberie [fa-na-be-rye] pl.
  whims; fads; frills; ostentation
fanatyk [fa-na-tik] m. fanatic;
  enthusiast; bigot; maniac
fanfaron [fan-fa-ron] m. braggart;
  coxcomb; swaggerer
fantastyczny [fan-tas-tich-ni] adj.
  m. fantastic; wild; odd
fantazja [fan-taz-ya] f. dash;
  imagination; fiction; whim
fara [fa-ra] f. parish church
farba [far-ba] f. paint; dye color;
  dyeing; oil color; ink; blood
farbować [far-bo-vaćh] v. dye
farsa [far-sa] f. farce; mockery
farsz [farsh] m. stuffing
fartuch [far-tookh] m. apron
fasola [fa-so-la] f. bean
fasonować [fa-so-no-vaćh] v.
  fashion; shape; mold model
fastryga [fas-tri-ga] f. tack;
  basting; baste; tacks
faszyzm [fa-shizm] m. fascism
fatalny [fa-tal-ni] adj. m. fatal; ill

-fated; awful; nasty; fateful
fatyga [fa-ti-ga] f. trouble;
  fatigue; bother; pains
fatałaszki [fa-ta-wash-kee] pl.
  knick-knacks; frippery; trinkets
febra [feb-ra] f. fever; the shakes
faworyzować [fa-vo-ri-zo-vaćh]
  v. favor; play favorites
felczer [fel-cher] m. male nurse;
  medical assistant
federacja [fe-de-rats-ya] f.
  federation; union
feralny [fe-ral-ni] adj. m. unlucky;
  ill-fated; hapless; disastrous
ferie [fe-rye] pl. holidays
ferma [fer-ma] f. farm; ranch
ferment [fer-ment] m. ferment
festyn [fes-tin] m. festival
fetor [fe-tor] m. stench; reek
figa [fee-ga] f. fig; nix
figiel [fee-gel] m. practical joke;
  prank; trick; ill turn
figura [fee-goo-ra] f. figure;
  shape; form; image; big wig
fikcja [feek-tsya] f. fiction
filar [fee-lar] m. pillar
filatelista [fee-la-te-lees-ta] m.
  stamp-collector; philatelist
filc [feelts] m. felt
filia [fee-lya] f. branch (store);
  branch-office; branch
filiżanka [fee-lee-zhan-ka] f. cup;
  cupful; coffee-cup
film [feelm] m. film; picture
filolog [fee-lo-log] m. philologist;
  linguist; linguistics teacher
filozof [fee-lo-zof] m. philosopher
filtr [feeltr] m. filter; strainer
filut [fee-loot] m. jester; rogue;
  joker; fox; sly boots
finanse [fee-nan-se] pl. finances;
  funds; money resources
finisz [fee-ńeesh] m. end (of a
  run); the finish; finis; the end
fiołek [fyo-wek] m. violet
fiołkowy [fyow-ko-vi] adj. m.
  purple; violet; of the violet
firanka [fee-ran-ka] f. curtain;
  drapery; pl. hangings
firma [feer-ma] f. business; firm;
  name of a firm; establishment
fisharmonia [fees-har-moń-ya] f.
  philharmonic orchestra

fizjognomia [fees-yo-gnom-ya] f. face; external aspect

fizjonomia [fees-yo-nom-ya] f. face; physiognomy

fizjolog [feez-yo-log] m. physiologist

fizyczny [fee-zich-ni] adj. m. physical; bodily; manual

fizyk [fee-zik] m. physicist

flaczki [flach-kee] pl. tripe

flaga [fla-ga] f. banner; flag; ensign; standard; signal

flaki [fla-kee] pl. bowels

flakon [fla-kon] m. vase

flanela [fla-ne-la] f. flannel

flaszka [flash-ka] f. bottle

flama [fla-ma] f. lady-love

flądra [flown-dra] f. flounder

flegma [fleg-ma] f. phlegm

flejtuch [fley-tookh] m. slut

flet [flet] m. flute

flirt [fleert] m. flirt

flisak [flee-sak] m. raft-man

flora [flo-ra] f. flora

floret [flo-ret] m. foil

flota [flo-ta] f. navy; fleet

fluksja [flooks-ya] f. tooth -infection; swelling

fluid [floo-eet] m. fluid

fochy [fo-khi] pl. blues; whims; sulks; pouts; sudden fancy

foka [fo-ka] f. seal

folgować [fol-go-vaćh] v. slacken; relax; indulge; abate

folklor [fol-klor] m. folklore

folusz [fo-loosh] m. fulling mill

folwark [fol-vark] m. farm

fonetyczny [fo-ne-tich-ni] adj. phonetic; of speech sounds

fontanna [fon-tan-na] f. fountain; spurt of water; waterworks

foremny [fo-rem-ni] adj. m. shapely; handsome; regular; symmetrical; well-proportioned

forma [for-ma] f. shape; mold

format [for-mat] m. size

formularz [for-moo-lazh] m. (application) form; blank

formuła [for-moo-wa] f. formula

fornir [for-ńeer] m. veneer

forsa [for-sa] f. dough; chink; bread; tin; a pot of money

forsować [for-so-vaćh] v.

force; strain; urge; exhort; advocate; overcome; exert

fort [fort] m. fort; stronghold

forteca [for-te-tsa] f. fortress; citadel; stronghold

fortel [for-tel] m. stratagem; ruse; subterfuge; trick; device

fortepian [for-te-pyan] m. grand piano; stringed keyboard

fortuna [for-too-na] f. fortune

fosa [fo-sa] f. moat; broad ditch

fosfat [fos-fat] m. phosphate

fosfor [fos-for] m. phosphorus

fotel [fo-tel] m. armchair

fotograf [fo-to-graf] m. photographer

fotografia [fo-to-gra-fya] f photograph; snap shot; picture

fracht [frakht] m. freight

fragment [frag-ment] m. fragment; episode; excerpt; scrap

frak [frak] m. evening formal

framuga [fra-moo-ga] f. recess (structure); bay; embrasure

frant [frant] m. sly dog; knave

frasunek [fra-soo-nek] m. worry; grief; sorrow; care; trouble

fraszka [frash-ka] f. trifle

frazes [fra-zes] m. platitude

frekwencja [frek-ven-tsya] f. attendance; turnout; frequency

frędzla [frandz-la] f. fringe

fresk [fresk] m. fresco

front [front] m. front; face, etc.

froterować [fro-te-ro-vaćh] v. rub; polish; wax (floors)

frunąć [froo-nownćh] v. fly away; fly about; flee

frymarczyć [fri-mar-chićh] v. barter; trade; traffic

fryzjer [fri-zyer] m. barber; hairdresser; beautician

fujara [foo-ya-ra] m. & f. all thumbs; nincompoop; pan-pipe; oaf; ninny; (muz.) pipe

fukać [foo-kaćh] v. scold; puff

fundacja [foon-da-tsya] f. foundation; endowment

fundament [foon-da-ment] m. foundation; substructure

fundusz [foon-doosh] m. fund

funkcja [foon-ktsya] f. function; functions; office; duties

funt [foont] m. pound (weight)
fura [foo-ra] f. cart; wagon
furgon [foor-gon] m. truck; van
furia [foo-rya] f. fury; rage
furiat [foo-ryat] m. madman
furman [foor-man] m. carter
furora [foo-ro-ra] f. sensation
furtka [foort-ka] f. gate; door
fusy [foo-si] pl. lees; dregs
fuszer [foo-sher] m. bungler
futerał [foo-te-raw] m. (gun)
    case; holster; sheath; box
futro [foot-ro] n. fur (skin, coat)
futryna [foo-tri-na] f. door-frame;
    window-frame; opening-frame
futrzarz [foot-shash] m. furrier
fuzja [fooz-ya] f. fusion; merger;
    amalgamation; shotgun; rifle

G

gabardyna [ga-bar-di-na] f.
    gabardine; twilled cloth
gabinet [ga-bee-net] m. study;
    (ruling) cabinet; office
gablotka [gab-lot-ka] f. showcase
gad [gat] m. reptile; mean guy
gadać [ga-daćh] v. talk; yak;
    prattle; talk nonsense; chat
gaduła [ga-doo-wa] m. clapper
gaj [gay] m. grove
gala [ga-la] f. gala; festivity
galanteria [ga-lan-te-rya] f.
    gallantry; haberdashery
galareta [ga-la-re-ta] f. jelly
galeria [ga-le-rya] f. gallery
galimatias [ga-lee-ma-tyas] m.
    gibberish; hotchpotch; mess
galon [ga-lon] m. gallon
galop [ga-lop] m. gallop; run
galwaniczny [gal-va-ńeech-ni]
    adj. m. galvanic; volcanic
gałąź [ga-wownźh] f. branch
gałgan [gaw-gan] m. rag; rascal;
    good-for-nothing; scamp
gałganiarz [gaw-ga-ńazh] m.
    ragtagman; rag-picker; ragman
gałka [gaw-ka] f. knob; ball

gama [ga-ma] f. scale
gamoń [ga-moń] m. lout; oaf
ganek [ga-nek] m. balcony
gangrena [gan-gre-na] f.
    gangrene; depravity; cor-
    ruption; decay of tissue
ganić [ga-ńeećh] v. blame;
    criticize; rebuke; upbraid
gapa [ga-pa] f. oaf; stowaway
gapić się [ga-peećh śhan] v.
    gape; star-gaze; moon; stare
gapie [ga-pye] pl. gapers
garaż [ga-razh] m. garage
garb [garp] m. hunch; hump
garbarnia [gar-bar-ńa] f. tannery;
    tan-yard; tanning hides place
garbować [gar-bo-vaćh] v. tan
garbaty [gar-ba-ti] adj. m. hunch
    -backed; humpy; uneven; hilly
garbus [gar-boos] m. = garbaty
garbić [gar-beećh] v. stoop
garderoba [gar-de-ro-ba] f.
    wardrobe; dressing-room
gardło [gard-wo] n. throat
garłować [gard-wo-vaćh] v.
    talk big; clamor; cry for
gardłowy [gard-wo-vi] adj. m.
    guttural; punishable by death
gardzić [gar-dźheećh] v. de-
    spise; scorn; have in con-
    tempt; hold in contempt
gardziel [gar-dźhel] f. throat;
    fauces; choke; gorge; jaws
garnąć [gar-nownćh] v. gather
garncarz [garn-tsazh] m. potter
garnek [gar-nek] m. pot; potful
garnirować [gar-ńee-ro-vaćh]
    v. garnish; trim (a dres etc.)
garnitur [gar-ńee-toor] m. set;
    suite (clothes); assortment
garnizon [gar-ńee-zon] m.
    garrison; stationed troops
garnuszek [gar-noo-shek] m. cup
garstka [garst-ka] f. handful
garść [garśhćh] f. handful
gasić [ga-śheećh] v. expire;
    go out; die down; extinguish;
    quench; put out; eclipse
gasnąć [gas-nownćh] v.
    die down; go out; wane; fade
gaśnica [gaśh-ńee-tsa] f. fire
    -extinguisher
gastronomiczny [gas-tro-no

-meech-ni] adj. m. gastro-
nomic; of good cooking
gastryczny [gas-trich-ni] adj. m.
gastric; in or near the stomach
gatunek [ga-too-nek] m. kind;
quality; sort; class; species
gawęda [ga-van-da] f. chat
gawiedź [ga-vyedźh] f. mob;
rabble; populace; gaping
crowd; the common people
gawron [gav-ron] m. rook
gaz [gaz] m. gas; open throttle
gaza [ga-za] f. gauze
gazeciarz [ga-ze-ćhash] m. pa-
perboy; newsstand (kiosk)
gazeta [ga-ze-ta] f. newspaper
gazolina [ga-zo-lee-na] f.
gasoline; gasolene; petrol
gazomierz [ga-zo-myezh] m. gas
meter; gas gauge
gazownia [ga-zov-ńa] f.
gas plant; gas works
gaźnik [gaźh-ńeek] m. carbu-
rettor (for air-gasoline mixing)
gaża [ga-zha] f. wage; salary
gąbczasty [gownb-cha-sti] adj.
m. spongy; squashy; mushy
gąbka [gownb-ka] f. sponge
gąsienica [gown-śhe-ńee-tsa] f.
caterpillar; band; track
gąsior [gown-śhor] m. gander;
jar; demijohn; ridge tile
gąszcz [gownshch] m. thicket
gbur [gboor] m. rude; boor
gburowaty [gboo-ro-va-ti] adj. m.
boorish; rude; churlish; surly
gdakać [gda-kaćh] v. cackle;
yak; sound like a hen
gderać [gde-raćh] v. grumble
gdy [gdi] conj. when; as; that
gdyby [gdi-bi] conj. if
gdyż [gdizh] conj. for; because
gdzie [gdźhe] adv. conj. where
gdzie indziej [gdźhe een-dźhey]
elsewhere; somewhere else
gdziekolwiek [gdźhe-kol-vyek]
adv. anywhere; wherever
gdzieniegdzie [gdźhe-ńeg-
-dźhe] adv. here and there; in
places; at intervals
gdzieś [gdźheśh] adv. somewhere; (vulg. exp.: in my ass)
gejzer [gey-zer] m. geyser

gen [gen] m. gene
genealogia [ge-ne-a-lo-gya] f.
genealogy; origin; pedigree
generacja [ge-ne-rats-ya] f.
generation; production
generalny [ge-ne-ral-ni] adj. m.
general; widespread; full-scale
generał [ge-ne-raw] m. general
genetyczny [ge-ne-tich-ni] adj. m
genetic
geneza [ge-ne-za] f. origin;
genesis; birth; the beginning
genialny [ge-ńal-ni] adj. m.
ingenious; genial; great
geniusz [ge-ńyoosh] m. genius
geodezja [ge-o-dez-ya] f.
geodesy (grid of polygons)
geografia [ge-o-gra-fya] f.
geography; the physical traits
geologia [ge-o-lo-gya] f. geology
geometra [ge-o-met-ra] m.
surveyor; land surveyor
geometria [ge-o-met-rya] f.
geometry (of points, lines, etc)
georginia [ge-or-gee-ńa] f. dahlia
germański [ger-mań-skee]
adj. m. Germanic (languages)
gest [gest] m. gesture; motion
gestykulować [ges-ti-koo-lo-
-vaćh] v. gesticulate
getto [get-to] n. ghetto
gęba [gan-ba] f. mug; mouth;
puss; snout; muzzle; face; gob
gęgać [gan-gaćh] v. cackle
gęś [ganśh] f. goose
gęśl [ganśhl] f. lute
gęstość [gan-stośhćh] f. density; thickness; closeness
gęstwina [ganst-vee-na] f.
thicket; array; accumulation
giąć [gyownćh] v. bow; bend
gibki [geeb-kee] adj. m. pliant;
flexible; limber; supple
giełda [gew-da] f. stock
-exchange; money-market
giez [ges] m. gadfly; breeze
giątki [gant-kee] adj. m. flexible;
nimble; elastic; adaptable
gigant [gee-gant] m. giant
gilza [geel-za] f. (cartridge) case;
cartridge-shell; cigarette tube
gimnastyczny [geem-na-stich-ni]
adj. m. gymnastic; athletic

gimnazjum [geem-**naz**-yoom] n.
  high-school; middle-school
ginąć [gee-n<u>own</u>ćh] v. perish
ginekolog [gee-ne-**ko**-log] m.
  gynecologist
gips [geeps] m. gypsum; plaster
gitara [gee-**ta**-ra] f. guitar
glazura [gla-**zoo**-ra] f. glaze
gleba [**gle**-ba] f. soil
glejt [gleyt] m. safe-conduct
ględzić [<u>glan</u>-dźheećh] v. talk
  through one's hat; talk nonsense; twaddle; blather; prate
gliceryna [glee-tse-ri-na] f.
  glycerin (soap. etc)
glin [gleen] m. aluminum
glina [glee-na] f. clay; loam
glista [glees-ta] f. earth-worm;
  warm; ascaris; nema
glob [glop] m. globe; sphere
gładki [**gwad**-kee] adj. m. plain;
  smooth; sleek; even; level;
  glib; straight; lank; fluent
gładzić [gwa-**dźheećh**] v. level; smooth; sleek; (put to
  death); mangle; stroke; press
głaskać [**gwas**-kaćh] v. caress;
  fondle; stroke; pet; tickle
głaz [gwaz] m. boulder; rock
głąb [g<u>wownp</u>] f. depth; abyss
głąb [g<u>wownp</u>] f. stalk; fool
głębia [g<u>wan</u>-bya] f. depth;
  deep; interior; intensity
głęboki [gw<u>an</u>-bo-kee] adj. m.
  deep; distant; remote; intense
głębokość [gw<u>an</u>-**bo**-kośhćh]
  f. depth; profundity; keenness
głodny [**gwod**-ni] adj. m. hungry
głodować [gwo-**do**-vaćh] v.
  starve; hunger; lay off food
głodzić [gwo-**dźheećh**] v. deprive, stint (of food); starve
  (someone); underfeed
głos [gwos] m. voice; sound;
  tone; toot; vote; opinion
głosować [gwo-**so**-vaćh] v.
  vote; cast one's vote
głośnik [**gwośh**-ńeek] m.
  loudspeaker; public-address
  system; speaking trumpet
głośno [**gwośh**-no] adv. loud
głośny [**gwośh**-ni] adj. m. loud
głowa [**gwo**-va] f. head; chief

głowić się [gwo-veećh **śhan**]
  v. beat one's brains out;
  puzzle; rack one's brains
głód [gwoot] m. hunger; famine
głóg [gwook] m. hawthorn
główka [**gwoov**-ka] f. pinhead;
  knob; tip; top; boss; heading
głównodowodzący [gwoov-no
  -do-vo-d<u>zown</u>-tsi] m. commander-in-chief (of an army)
główny [**gwoov**-ni] adj. m. main;
  predominant; foremost; chief
głuchy [**gwoo**-khi] adj. m. deaf
głupi [**gwoo**-pee] adj. m. silly;
  stupid; foolish; asinine
głupiec [**gwoo**-pyets] m.
  addle-brain; fool; idiot; loony;
  goof; numskull; addle-brain
głupota [gwoo-**po**-ta] f. stupidity;
  imbecility; foolishness
głupstwo [**gwoop**-stvo] n. nonsense; trifle; blunder; mistake
głuszec [**gwoo**-shets] m. grouse
gmach [gmakh] m. large building
gmatwać [**gmat**-vaćh] v. mix
  up; tangle; embroil; complicate; muddle; jumble; confuse
gmerać [gme-raćh] v. pry; poke
gmin [gmeen] m. populace
gmina [**gmee**-na] f. county;
  parish; community; commune
gnat [gnat] m. bone (slang)
gnębić [gn<u>an</u>-beećh] v. oppress
gniady [**gńa**-di] adj. m. bay
  (horse); dark brown horse
gniazdo [**gńaz**-do] n. nest
gnić [gńeećh] v. rot; decay
gnida [**gńee**-da] f. nit
gnieść [gńeśhćh] v. squeeze
gniew [gńev] m. anger; wrath
gnieździć się [**gńeźh**-
  -dźheećh **śhan**] v. nestle;
  cluster; assemble; collect
gnilny [**gńeel**-ni] adj. m. putrid;
  of rot; septic; putrefactive
gnoić [gno-eećh] v. putrefy
gnojówka [gno-**yoov**-ka] f. liquid
  manure; manure pit; dunghill
gnój [gnooy] m. manure; dung;
  stinker (vulg.); lousy bum
gnuśny [**gnoośh**-ni] adj. m.
  sluggish; lazy; idle; listless
godło [**god**-wo] n. emblem

godność [god-noshćh] f. dignity; name; pride; self-esteem; self-respect; post; high rank

godny [god-ni] adj. m. worthy

gody [go-di] pl. nuptials; mating

godzić [go-dźheećh] v. reconcile; hire; square; engage; aim

godzien [go-dźhen] adj. m. deserving; worth; worthy

godzina [go-dźhee-na] f. hour

godziwy [go-dźhee-vi] adj. m. proper; suitable; just; fair

goić [go-eećh] v. heal; cure

goleń [go-leń] m. shin-bone

golić [go-leećh] v. shave

golonka [go-lon-ka] f. pig's feet dish; ham below the knee

gołąb [go-wownb] m. pigeon

gołoledź [go-wo-ledźh] f. glazed frost; frozen; dew

gołosłowny [go-wo-swov-ni] adj. m. unfounded; proofless; vain

goły [go-wi] adj. m. naked

gonić [go-ńeećh] v. chase; hunt; pursue; track; run after

goniec [go-ńets] m. messenger

gonitwa [go-ńeet-va] f. chase

gont [gont] m. shingle

gorąco [go-rown-tso] n. heat

gorący [go-rown-tsi] adj. m. hot; sultry; warm; hearty; lively

gorączka [go-rownch-ka] f. fever; shakes; excitement; heat; temperature; heat; passion

gorczyca [gor-chi-tsa] f. white mustard; charlock

gorętszy [go-rant-shi] adj. m. hotter; fervent; more intense

gorliwiec [gor-lee-vyets] m. zealot; ardent supporter

gorliwy [gor-lee-vi] adj. m. zealous; keen; eager; devout

gorset [gor-set] m. girdle

gorszy [gor-shi] adj. m. worse

gorszyć [gor-shićh] v. demoralize; scandalize; shock; deprave; make improper; corrupt

gorycz [go-rich] f. bitterness

goryl [go-ril] m. gorilla

gorzałka [go-zhaw-ka] f. brandy spirits; booze; spirit

gorzeć [go-zhećh] v. be ablaze

gorzej [go-zhey] adv. worse

gorzelnia [go-zhel-ńa] f. distillery; still; smell of booze

gorzki [gozh-kee] adj. m. bitter

gospoda [gos-po-da] f. inn

gospodarczy [gos-po-dar-chi] adj. m. economic; farm; charring

gospodarka [gos-po-dar-ka] f. economy; housekeeping; farming; husbandry; management

gospodarny [gos-po-dar-ni] adj. m. economical; thrifty

gospodarstwo [gos-po-dar-stvo] n. household; farm; property; possession; holding

gospodarz [gos-po-dash] m. landlord; landholder; host; farmer; manager; home-steward

gospodyni [gos-po-di-ńee] f. landlady; hostess; manageress

gosposia [gos-po-śha] f. housekeeper; maid; servant

gościć [gośh-ćheećh] v. receive; entertain; treat; stay at; to enjoy hospitality

gościna [gośh-ćhee-na] f. visit; stay at sb. house

gościnność [gośh-ćheen-nośhćh] f. hospitality

gość [gośhćh] m. guest; caller; visitor; customer

gościec [gośh-ćhets] m. gout; arthritis; rheumatism

gotować [go-to-vaćh] v. cook; boil; get ready; prepare

gotowość [go-to-vośhćh] f. readiness; willingness

gotowy [go-to-vi] adj. m. ready; done; complete; willing

gotówka [go-toov-ka] f. cash

gotyk [go-tik] m. Gothic

goździk [gośh-dźheek] m. carnation; clove; lily-flower

góra [goo-ra] f. mountain

góral [goo-ral] m. mountaineer

górnictwo [goor-ńeets-tvo] n. mining; mining industry

górnik [goor-ńeek] m. miner

górnolotny [goor-no-lot-ni] adj. m. lofty; soaring; gaudy

górny [goor-ni] adj. m. upper

górować [goo-ro-vaćh] v. prevail; excel; dominate; rise

górski [goor-skee] adj. m.

górzysty [goo-zhis-ti] adj. m.
  hilly; mountainous
gówniarz [goov-ńazh] m. (vulg.)
  shit-ass; whipster; squirt
gówno [goov-no] n. shit (vulg.)
gra [gra] f. game; sham; acting
grab [grab] m. hornbeam tree;
  hardbeam tree
grabarz [gra-bazh] m. grave
  -digger; sexton; burying beetle
grabić [gra-beećh] v. rake;
  plunder; rob; sack; rake up
grabie [gra-bye] n. rake
grabież [gra-byezh] f. plunder
graca [gra-tsa] f. rabbler; hoe
gracja [gra-tsya] f. grace
gracować [gra-tso-vaćh] v.
  scrape; rake; mix mortar; hoe
gracz [grach] m. player; gambler;
  crafty double-dealer; sly fox
grać [graćh] v. play; act;
  gamble; pretend; pulsate
grad [grad] m. hail; volley
grafika [gra-fee-ka] f. graphics;
  arts; art of writing; engraving
gram [gram] m. gram
gramatyka [gra-ma-ti-ka] f.
  grammar; grammar book
gramofon [gra-mo-fon] m. record
  player (turntable); phonograph
gramolić się [gra-mo-leećh
  śhan] v. clamber; climb
granat [gra-nat] m. grenade
granatnik [gra-nat-ńeek] m.
  mortar; howitzer
granatowy [gra-na-to-vi] adj. m.
  navy blue; of grenades
granda [gran-da] f. swindle
graniastosłup [gra-ńa-sto-swoop]
  m. prism (regular, right, etc.)
granica [gra-ńee-tsa] f. border; boundary; limit; frontier;
  range; reach; confines; bounds
granit [gra-ńeet] m. granite
granulować [gra-noo-lo-vaćh] v.
  granulate (form into grains)
grań [grań] f. mountain ridge;
  crest; edge; razor's edge
grasować [gra-so-vaćh] v. ravage; roam; about; prowl; maraud; stalk; overrun; rove
grat [grat] m. run down furniture

(or man); crock; trash
gratis [gra-tees] adv. free of
  charge; something given free
gratka [grat-ka] f. windfall
gratulacja [gra-too-lats-ya] f.
  congratulations; felicitation
grawer [gra-ver] m. engraver
grawitacja [gra-vee-tats-ya] f.
  gravitation (pull of gravity)
grdyka [grdi-ka] f. Adam's apple
grecki [grets-kee] adj. m. Greek
gremialnie [gre-myal-ńe] adv. in
  -a-mass; collectively; altogether; in a group; one and all
grobla [grob-la] f. dike; dam
grobowiec [gro-bo-vyets] m.
  tomb; sepulchre; family vault
grobowy [gro-bo-vi] adj. m.
  grave; deathly; gloomy; dismal
groch [grokh] m. pea; pea plant
grom [grom] m. thunderclap
gromada [gro-ma-da] f. crowd;
  throng; community; team
gromadzić [gro-ma-dźheećh] v.
  amass; hoard; gather; attract
gromić [gro-meećh] v. storm;
  rout; reprimand; defeat
grono [gro-no] n. bunch of
  grapes; cluster; group; body of
  people; company; circle
gronostaj [gro-no-stay] m. ermine
grosz [grosh] m. grosz; penny
groszek [gro-shek] m. green pea;
  spotted pattern; (sweet) pea
grot [grot] m. dart; spike
grota [gro-ta] f. grotto; cave
groza [gro-za] f. dread; horror
grozić [gro-źheećh] v. threaten
groźba [groźh-ba] f. threat
grób [groop] m. grave; tomb
gród [groot] m. (fortified) town
gródź [groodźh] m. f. bulkhead
grubiański [groo-byań-skee] adj.
  m. rude; coarse; obscene
grubość [groo-bośhćh] f.
  thickness; girth; size; grist
gruby [groo-bi] adj. m. thick; fat;
  big; stout; large; low-pitched
gruchotać [groo-kho-taćh] v.
  shatter; batter; rattle; crash
gruczoł [groo-chow] m. gland
gruda [groo-da] f. lump; clod
grudzień [groo-dźheń] m.

(the month of) December
grunt [groont] m. ground; soil
grupa [groo-pa] f. group; class
grusza [groo-sha] f. pear-tree
gruz [groos] m. rubble; ruins
gruzeł [groo-zew] m. clot
gruzy [groo-zi] pl. debris
gruźlica [grooźh-**lee**-tsa] f.
tuberculosis; consumption
gryka [gri-ka] f. buckwheat
grymas [gri-mas] m. grimace
grypa [gri-pa] f. flu; influenza
grysik [gri-śheek] m. grits
gryzoń [gri-zoń] m. rodent
gryźć [griźhćh] v. bite;
gnaw; chew; prick; torment
grzać [gzhaćh] v. warm; fire;
warm up; beat; shoot; thrash
grządka [gzhownd-ka] f. flower
bed; patch; (hen-) roost
grząść [gzhownśhćh] v.
wade; proceed with difficulty
grząski [gzhown-skee] adj. m.
quaggy; slimy; slushy; miry
grzbiet [gzhbyet] m. back; spine;
ridge; butt; edge; rib
grzebać [gzhe-baćh] v. bury;
rummage; dig; rake up; fumble
grzebień [gzhe-byeń] m. comb;
crest of a wave; teaser
grzech [gzhekh] m. sin; fault
grzechotka [gzhe-khot-ka] f.
rattle; flapper; clapper
grzechotnik [gzhe-khot-ńeek] m.
rattlesnake
grzeczność [gzhech-nośhćh]
f. politeness; favor; attentions
grzęznąć [gzhanz-nownćh] v.
get stuck; wade; flounder;
sink in (a quagmire, mud)
grzmiący [gzhmyown-tsi] adj. m.
thundering; thunderous; booming; fulminatory
grzmot [gzhmot] m. thunder; hag
grzyb [gzhip] m. mushroom;
fungus; snuff; dry-rot
grzywa [gzhi-va] f. mane
grzywna [gzhiv-na] f. fine
gubernator [goo-ber-na-tor] m.
governor (general)
gubić [goo-beećh] v. loose; ruin
gula [goo-la] f. knob; bump
gulasz [goo-lash] m. meat soup

gulgotać [gool-go-taćh] v.
gurgle; bubble; mumble
guma [goo-ma] f. rubber
gumno [goom-no] n. barn (yard)
gust [goost] m. taste; palate
guz [goos] m. bump; tumor
guzdrać się [gooz-draćh śhan]
v. dawdle; dally; waste time in
trifling; trifle; delay; lag
gwałcić [gvaw-ćheećh] v.
rape; violate; compel; coerce;
force; outrage; transgress
gwałt [gvawt] m. rape; outrage
gwałtowny [gvaw-tov-ni] adj. m.
outrageous; urgent; violent
gwar [gvar] m. hum; noise; buzz
gwara [gva-ra] f. dialect; slang;
jargon; lingo; cant; patter;
colloquial regional language
gwarancja [gva-ran-tsya] f.
warranty; guarantee; pledge
gwardia [gvar-dya] f. guard
gwarny [gvar-ni] adj. m. noisy
gwarzyć [gva-zhićh] v. chat
gwiazda [gvyaz-da] f. star
gwint [gveent] m. thread (mech.)
gwintować [gveen-to-vaćh] v.
cut thread; tap; rifle
gwizd [gveezt] m. whistle
gwoli [gvo-lee] conj. for the sake
of; because of; in order to
gwóźdź [gvooźhćh] m. nail
gzyms [gzims] m. molding;

H

habit [kha-beet] m. monk's
frock; habit; nun's frock
haczyk [kha-chik] m. small hook;
barb; snag; catch
hafciarka [khaf-ćhar-ka] f.
embroiderer
haft [khaft] m. embroidery
haftka [khaft-ka] f. clasp
hak [khak] m. hook; clamp;
clasp; grapnel; upper-cut (box)
hala [kha-la] f. (sports)hall
halka [khal-ka] f. petticoat

halny wiatr [khal-ni **vyatr**] m.
Tatra wind (foehn)
halucynacja [kha-loo-tsi-**nats**-ya]
f. hallucination
hałas [kha-was] m. noise; din
hałasować [kha-wa-**so**-vaćh] v.
make noise (racket); be noisy
hałastra [kha-**wast**-ra] f. mob;
rabble; riff-raff; ragtag mob
hałaśliwy [kha-wa-**śhlee**-vi] adj.
m. noisy; loud; rackety; rowdy
hamak [kha-mak] m. hammock
hamować [kha-mo-vaćh] v.
apply brakes; restrain; hamper;
curb; cramp; delay; retard
hamulec [kha-**moo**-lets] m. brake
hamulec ręczny [kha-**moo**-lets
ranch-ni] m. hand brake
handel [khan-del] m. commerce
handlarz [khand-lash] m.
merchant; shopkeeper; peddler
handlować [khand-lo-vaćh] v.
trade; deal; be in business
hangar [khan-gar] m. hangar
haniebny [kha-**ńeb**-ni] adj. m.
disgraceful; dirty; foul; vile
hańba [khań-ba] f. disgrace
hańbić [khań-beećh] v. disgrace; bring shame; dishonor
haracz [kha-rach] m. tribute
harcerstwo [khar-**tsers**-tvo] n.
scouting; Boy Scouts
harcerz [khar-tsezh] m. boy
scout
hardy [khar-di] adj. m. haughty
harfa [khar-fa] f. harp
harmider [khar-**mee**-der] m.
hullabaloo; clatter; din; row
harmonia [khar-mo-**ńa**] f.
harmony; accordion; harmo-
nics; concord; chord
harować [kha-**ro**-vaćh] v. toil
harpun [khar-poon] m. harpoon
hart [khart] m. fortitude;
hardness; sternness; temper;
endurance; inflexibility; grit
hartować [khar-**to**-vaćh] v.
temper; harden; anneal; season; inure; quench; toughen
hasać [kha-saćh] v. frisk; frolic;
romp; gambol; dance; caper
hasło [khas-wo] m. password
haubica [khaw-**bee**-tsa] f.

howitzer (a short cannon)
haust [khaust] m. gulp; swing
hazard [kha-zard] m. risk;
hazard; the gaming table
heban [khe-ban] m. ebony
hebel [khe-bel] m. plane (tool)
hebrajski [kheb-**rays**-kee] adj. m.
Hebrew (language); Hebraic
heca [khe-tsa] f. fun; fuss
hegemonia [khe-ge-mo-**ńa**] f.
hegemony; dominance
hej [khey] excl.: hey! ho!
hejnał [khey-naw] m. trum-
-pet call; bugle-call; reveille
hektar [khek-tar] m. hectare
hełm [khewm] m. helmet; dome
hemoroidy [khe-mo-**roy**-di] pl.
piles; hemorrhoids
hen [khen] adv. far; away
herb [kherp] m. coat-of-arms
herbaciarnia [kher-ba-**ćhar**-ńa]
f. tea-house; tea-room
herbata [kher-ba-ta] f. tea
herbatnik [kher-bat-**ńeek**] m.
biscuit; small dry cake
heretyk [khe-**re**-tik] m. heretic
herezja [khe-rez-ya] f. heresy
hermetyczny [kher-me-**tich**-ni]
adj. m. air-tight; hermetic
heroiczny [khe-ro-**eech**-ni] adj. m.
heroic; daring and risky
heroizm [khe-ro-**eezm**] m.
heroism (qualities and actions)
herszt [khersht] m. ringleader
het [khet] adv. far; away
hetman [khet-man] m. commander-in-chief; (chess) queen
hiacynt [khya-tsint] m. hyacinth
hiena [khee-**ye**-na] f. hyena
hierarchia [khye-**rar**-khya] f.
hierarchy; order of ranks
hieroglif [khye-**ro**-gleef] m.
hieroglyph; illegible writing
higiena [khee-**ge**-na] f. hygiene;
sanitation; hygienics
hinduski [kheen-**doos**-kee]
adj. m. Hindu
hiperbola [khee-per-**bo**-la] f.
hyperbola; hyperbole
hipnotyczny [kheep-no-**tich**-ni]
adj. m. hypnotic; mesmeric
hipochondryk [khee-po-**khon**-drik]
m. hypochondriac

hipokryta [khee-po-kri-ta] m.
hypocrite; one who pretends
or dissembles; dissembler
hipopotam [khee-po-po-tam] m.
hippopotamus; hippo
hipoteka [khee-po-te-ka] f. title;
mortgage; records office
hipoteza [khee-po-te-za] f.
hypothesis; assumption
histeria [khee-ster-ya] f. hysteria;
outbreak of a hysterical fit
historia [khee-stor-ya] f. story;
history; affair; show; fuss
hiszpański [khee-shpań-skee]
adj. m. Spanish; of Spain
hitlerowiec [khee-tle-ro-vyets] m.
hitlerite; German Nazi
hodować [kho-do-vaćh] v. rear;
breed; rise; keep; nurse
hodowca [kho-dov-tsa] m.
breeder; grower; farmer; riser;
grower; cultivator
hojny [khoy-ni] adj. m. generous;
lavish; liberal; profuse; ample
hokej [kho-key] m. hockey
holenderski [kho-len-ders-kee]
adj. m. Dutch; of Holland
holować [kho-lo-vaćh] v. tow;
haul; drag; tug; truck
hołd [khowd] m. tribute
hołota [kho-wo-ta] f. riff-raff
honor [kho-nor] m. honor
honorarium [kho-no-rar-yoom] n.
fee; honorarium; charge
horda [khor-da] f. horde; throng
horendalny [kho-ren-dal-ni] adj.
m. awful; horrible; exorbitant
hormon [khor-mon] m. hormone
horoskop [kho-ros-kop] m.
horoscope; prophesy; prospect
horyzont [kho-ri-zont] m. horizon;
vistas; prospect; possibilities
hotel [kho-tel] m. hotel
hoży [kho-zhi] adj. m. brisk;
handsome; comely; fresh
hrabia [khra-bya] m. count
hrabina [khra-bee-na] f. countess
hrabianka [khra-byan-ka] f.
countess (miss)
hrabstwo [khrab-stvo] n. county
hreczka [khrech-ka] f. buckwheat
hreczkosiej [khrech-ko-śhey] m.
country bumpkin; clod-breaker

hubka [khoob-ka] f. tinder
huczeć [khoo-chećh] v. roar
hufnal [khoof-nal] m. horseshoe
nail; horseshoe fastener
huk [khook] m. bang; roar
hulać [khoo-laćh] v. carouse;
riot; make merry; run wild
hulajnoga [khoo-lay-no-ga] f.
scooter (without motor)
hulaka [khoo-la-ka] m. carouser;
debaucher; rioter; rake
hulanka [khoo-lan-ka] f. riot;
debauch; junket; carouse
hultaj [khool-tay] m. libertine;
rascal; good-for-nothing
humanista [khoo-ma-ńees-ta] m.
humanist; classical scholar
humanitarny [khoo-ma-ńee-tar-
-ni] m. humane; humanitarian
humor [khoo-mor] m. humor
hura [khoo-ra] hurrah! cheers!
long live! hurray
huragan [khoo-ra-gan] m.
hurricane; cyclone; storm
hurmem [khoor-mem] adv. in
swarms; in a mass; altogether
hurt [khoort] m. wholesale
humus [khoo-moos] m. humus
husarz [khoo-sash] m. Polish
winged-armor cavalryman;
light cavalryman (hist.)
huśtać [khoo-śhtaćh] v.
swing; rock; dandle; toss up
and down; see-saw; sway
huśtawka [khoośh-tav-ka] f.
swing; seesaw; swing boat
huta [khoo-ta] f. metal or glass
mill; smelting works
hutnik [khoot-ńeek] m. metal or
glass (man) worker; iron
master; metallurgist
hycel [khi-tsel] m. dogcatcher;
rascal; good for nothing
hydrant [khid-rant] m. hydrant
hydraulika [khid-raw-lee-ka] f.
hydraulics; plumbing
hymn [khimn] m. anthem; hymn

I

i [ee] conj. and; also; too
ichtiologia [eekh-tyo-**log**-ya] f.
   ichthyology; zoology of fish
idea [ee-de-a] f. idea; aim
idealista [ee-de-a-**lees**-ta] m.
   idealist; dreamer; visionary
idealny [ee-de-**al**-ni] adj. m. ideal;
   perfect; visionary; sublime
identyczny [ee-den-**tich**-ni] adj.
   m. identical; similar
ideologia [ee-de-o-**log**-ya] f.
   ideology; doctrines; opinions
idiosynkrazja [ee-dyo-sin-**kraz**-ya]
   f. idiosyncrasy; mannerism
idiota [ee-dyo-ta] m. idiot
idiotka [ee-**dyot**-ka] f. idiot
iglaste drzewo [eeg-**las**-te **dzhe**-
   -vo] m. coniferous tree
iglica [eeg-**lee**-tsa] f. spire
igła [eeg-wa] f. needle
ignorancja [eeg-no-ran-tsya] f.
   ignorance; lack of knowledge
igrać [eeg-rach] v. play; trifle
igrzysko [eeg-**zhis**-ko] n.
   spectacle (games); contest
ikra [eek-ra] f. spawn; roe
ile [ee-le] adv. how much
ilekroć [ee-le-kroch] adv. every
   time; whenever; when
iloczas [ee-lo-chas] m. quantity
   (of a vowel or syllable)
iloczyn [ee-lo-chin] m.
   (multiplication) product
iloraz [ee-lo-raz] m. (division)
   quotient
ilościowy [ee-**losh-cho**-vi]
   adj. m. quantitative; numerical
ilość [ee-**loshch**] f. quantity
iluminacja [ee-loo-mee-**nats**-ya] f.
   illumination; floodlight
ilustracja [ee-loo-**strats**-ya] f.
   illustration; figure; picture
iluzja [ee-**looz**-ya] f. illusion
ił [eew] m. loam; rich soil
im [eem] conj. the more...

imać [ee-mach] v. size upon
imadło [ee-mad-wo] n. (shope)
   vice; chuck; holder; vise
imaginacja [ee-ma-gee-**nats**-ya] f.
   imagination; empty fancy
imbir [eem-beer] m. ginger
imbryk [eem-brik] m. teapot
imieniny [ee-mye-**nee**-ni] n.
   name-day; name-day party
imiennie [ee-myen-ńe] adv. by
   name; personally; individually
imiennik [ee-**myen**-ńeek] m.
   namesake
imiesłów [ee-**mye**-swoov] m.
   participle
imię [ee-myan] n. name (given)
imigracja [ee-mee-**grats**-ya] f.
   immigration; the immigrants
imigrant [ee-**meeg**-rant] m.
   immigrant; foreign settler
imigrować [ee-mee-**gro**-vach] v.
   immigrate; settle in a new
   land; come into a new land
imitacja [ee-mee-**tats**-ya] f.
   imitation; counterfeit; fake
imitować [ee-mee-to-vach] v.
   imitate; mimic; simulate
impas [eem-pas] m. deadlock
imperialista [eem-pe-rya-**lees**-ta]
   m. imperialist; empire builder
imperium [eem-pe-ryoom] n. empire; countries under one ruler
impertynent [eem-per-ti-nent] m.
   an arrogant; pert, impertinent,
   saucy, cheeky person
impet [eem-pet] m. impetus
imponować [eem-po-no-vach]
   v. impress; impose on sb; inspire respect; dazzle
import [eem-port] m. import
impregnować [eem-pre-**gno**-
   -vach] v. impregnate; make
   waterproof; saturate; soak
impreza [eem-pre-za] f.
   entertainment; spectacle;
   show; stunt; meet; venture
improwizować [eem-pro-vee-**zo**-
   -vach] v. improvise; extempo-
   rize; arrange on the spot
impuls [eem-pools] m. impulse
inaczej [ee-na-chey] adv.
   otherwise; differently; unlike
inauguracja [ee-naw-goo-**rats**-ya]

f. inauguration; opening
inaugurować [ee-naw-goo-ro-
-vaćh] v. inaugurate; initiate
in blanko [een blan-ko] adv. in
blank; blank check, document
incydent [een-tsi-dent]
m. incident; happening; event
indagacja [een-da-gats-ya] f.
investigation; questioning
indeks [een-deks] m. index
indemnizacja [een-dem-ńee-zats-
-ya] f. indemnity (for a loss)
indukcja [een-dook-tsya] f.
induction; reasoning leading to
a general conclusion
indyk [een-dik] m. turkey
indyczka [een-dich-ka] f. turkey
-hen; dish of turkey-hen
indywidualny [een-di-vee-doo-al-
-ni] adj. m. individual
inercja [ee-nerts-ya] f. inertia;
inaction; inertness
infekcja [een-fekts-ya] f.
infection; contamination
infiltracja [een-feel-trats-ya] f.
infiltration; penetration
inflacja [een-flats-ya] f. inflation
influenza [een-floo-en-za] f.
influenza; flu; grippe
informacja [een-for-mats-ya] f.
information; intelligence; news
informacyjny [een-for-ma-tsiy-ni]
adj. m. information (office)
informować [een-for-mo-vaćh]
v. inform; instruct; post up
ingerencja [een-ge-rents-ya] f.
interference; meddling
inhalacja [een-kha-lats-ya] f.
inhalation; breathing in
inicjał [ee-ńee-tsyaw] m. initial
(letter); ornate letter
inicjator [ee-ńee-tsya-tor] m.
originator; mover; founder
inicjatywa [ee-ńee-tsya-ti-va] f.
initiative; enterprise; lead
inkasować [een-ka-so-vaćh] v.
collect (money); get a blow
inklinacja [een-klee-nats-ya] f.
inclination; liking for; bias
inkwizycja [een-kvee-zits-ya] f.
inquisition; investigation
innowacja [een-no-vats-ya] f.
innovation; novelty

innowierca [een-no-vyer-tsa] m.
dissenter; heretic
inny [een-ni] adj. m. other;
different; another (one)
inscenizacja [een-stse-ńee-zats-
-ya] f. putting on stage
inspekcja [een-spek-tsya] f.
inspection; review; examination; parade; inspectorate
inspekty [een-spek-ti] n. hotbed;
glass covered frame
inspiracja [een-spee-rats-ya] f.
inspiration; breathing in
instalacja [een-sta-lats-ya] f.
installation; plumbing etc.
instalator [een-sta-la-tor] m.
plumber; fitter; electrician
instrukcja [een-struk-tsya] f.
instruction; order; training
instrument [een-stru-ment] m.
instrument; tool; deed; legal
instrument; appliance
instynkt [een-stinkt] m. instinct;
inborn aptitude; knack
instytucja [een-sti-too-tsya] f.
institution; establishment
insynuacja [een-si-noo-ats-ya] f.
insinuation; innuendo
integralny [een-te-gral-ni] adj. m.
integral; whole; entire
intelekt [een-te-lekt] m. intellect;
(high) intelligence; mind
intelektualista [een-te-lek-too-a-
-lees-ta] m. intellectual
inteligencja [een-te-lee-gents-ya]
f. intelligentsia; intelligence;
ability to learn, grasp, cope
inteligentny [een-te-lee-gent-ni]
adj. m. intelligent; clever; wise
intencja [een-ten-tsya] f.
intention; purpose; anything
intended; determination to act
intensywny [een-ten-siv-ni] adj.
m. intensive; strenuous
interes [een-te-res] m. interest;
business; store; matter
interesowny [een-te-re-sov-ni]
adj. m. selfish; greedy
interesujący [een-te-re-soo-<u>yown</u>-
-tsi] adj. m. interesting
internat [een-ter-nat] m. boarding
school (for boys or for girls)
interpretacja [een-ter-pre-tats-ya]

f. interpretation; explanation
interwencja [een-ter-**ven**-tsya] f.
  intervention; interference
intratny [een-**trat**-ni] adj. m.
  lucrative; profitable; paying
introligator [een-tro-lee-**ga**-tor] m.
  bookbinder; bookbinder's shop
intruz [een-troos] m. intruder
intryga [een-tri-ga] f. plot;
  intrigue; machination
intuicja [een-too-**eets**-ya] f.
  intuition; insight; feeling
intuicyjny [een-too-ee-**tsiy**-ni] m.
  adj. intuitive; subconscious
inwalida [een-va-lee-da] m.
  invalid; disabled (soldier)
inwazja [een-**vaz**-ya] f. invasion
inwencja [een-**ven**-tsya] f.
  inventiveness; invention
inwentarz [een-**ven**-tash] m.
  inventory; stock; list
inwestycja [een-ve-**stits**-ya] f.
  investment; capital outlay
inżynier [een-zhi-ńer] m.
  engineer; graduate engineer
inżynieria [een-zhi-ńer-ya] f.
  engineering (science)
ircha [eer-kha] f. suede-leather;
  chamois-leather; suede
irlandzki [eer-landz-kee] adj. Irish
irys [ee-ris] m. iris
ironia [ee-ro-ńya] f. irony
irygacja [ee-ri-**gats**-ya] f.
  irrigation; watering
irytacja [ee-ri-**tats**-ya] f. irritation;
  vexation; chafe; annoyance
iskać [ees-kać] v. seek lice;
  cleanse of vermin; delouse
iskra [ees-kra] f. spark; flash
istnieć [eest-ńech] v. exist
istnienie [eest-ńe-ńe] n.
  existence; being; entity
istny [eest-ni] adj. m. real;
  veritable; downright; sheer
istota [ees-to-ta] f. being;
  essence; gist; sum; entity
istotny [ees-tot-ni] adj. m. real;
  substantial; vital; radical
istotnie [ees-tot-ńe] adv. indeed;
  truly; really; in fact; in reality
iście [eeśh-ćhe] adv. indeed;
  truly; really; in truth
iść [eeśhćh] v. go; walk

izba [eez-ba] f. room; chamber
izba handlowa [eez-ba khan-**dlo**-
  -va] f. Chamber of Commerce
izolacja [ee-zo-**lats**-ya] f.
  isolation; insulation; seal
izolator [ee-zo-la-tor] m.
  insulator; non-conductor
izolacyjna taśma [ee-zo-la-**tsiy**-
  -na taśh-ma] f. insulating
  tape; electrician's tape
izoterma [ee-zo-ter-ma] f.
  isotherm; line plotted to show
  an equal temperature
izotop [ee-**zo**-top] m. isotope
izraelicki [eez-ra-e-**leets**-kee] adj.
  m. Israeli; of Israel
izraelita [eez-ra-e-lee-ta] m.
  Israelite; citizen of Israel
iż [eesh] conj. that (literary)
iżby [eezh-bi] conj. m. in order
  that; in order to; lest

J

ja [ya] pron. I; (indecl.) self
jabłecznik [yab-**wech**-ńeek] m.
  apple cider; apple pie
jabłko [yab-ko] n. apple
jabłoń [yab-woń] f. apple tree
jacht [yakht] m. yacht
jachtklub [yakht-kloob] m. yacht
  club (for cruises, racing, etc.)
jad [yat] m. venom; poison
jadalnia [ya-dal-ńa] f.
  dining-room; mess; mess-hall
jadalny [ya-dal-ni] adj. m. eat-
  -able; edible; dining (room)
jadło [yad-wo] n. food; edibles
jadłodajnia [ya-dwo-day-ńa] f.
  restaurant; eating house
jadłospis [yad-wo-spees] m.
  menu; bill of fare
jaglana kasza [ya-gla-na ka-sha]
  f. millet-groat (porridge)
jaglica [yag-lee-tsa] f. trachoma;
  viral eye infection
jagnię [yag-<u>ńan</u>] n. lamb
jagoda [ya-go-da] f. berry

jajecznica [ya-yech-ńee-tsa] f.
  scrambled eggs
jajko [yay-ko] n. egg (small)
jajko na twardo [yay-ko na tvar-
  -do] hard-boiled egg
jajko na miękko [yay-ko
  na myank-ko] soft-boiled egg
jajnik [yay-ńeek] m. ovary
jajo [ya-yo] n. egg; ovum
jak [yak] adv. how; as; if; than
jakby [yak-bi] adv. as if; if
jak gdyby [yak-gdi-bi] adv. as if;
  seemingly; sort of; so to say
jaka [ya-ka] pron. f. what; which
jaki [ya-kee] pron. m. what;
  which one? that; some; like
jakie [ya-ke] pron. n. what;
  which=jaki (fem. & neuter)
jakiś [ya-keeśh] pron. some
jakkolwiek [yak-kol-vyek] conj.
  though; pron. somehow; anyhow; whichever; adv. somehow; anyhow; however
jako [ya-ko] adv. as; by way of
jako tako [ya-ko ta-ko] adv. so
  -so; tolerably well
jakoś [ya-kośh] adv. somehow
jakość [ya-kośhćh] f. quality
jakościowo [ya-kośh-ćho-vo]
  adv. m. qualitatively
jakże [yak-zhe] pron. how; sure;
  yes indeed; how can this be?
jałmużna [yaw-moozh-na] f.
  alms; charity; (endowment)
jałowcówka [ya-wov-tsoov-ka] f.
  gin; juniper-flavored vodka
jałowiec [ya-wo-vyets] m. juniper
  tree (Juniperus)
jałowieć [ya-wo-vyećh] v. grow
  -sterile; grow unproductive
jałowy [ya-wo-vi] adj. m. barren;
  sterile; arid; aseptic
jałówka [ya-woov-ka] f. heifer
jama [ya-ma] f. pit; hole; den;
  cavity; cave; burrow; hollow
jamnik [yam-ńeek] m.
  dachshund
jankes [yan-kes] m. Yankee
Japończyk [ya-poń-chik] m.
  Japanese; of Japan
japoński [ya-pońs-kee] adj. m.
  Japanese; of Japan
jar [yar] m. canyon; ravine

jarmark [yar-mark] m. fair
jarosz [ya-rosh] m. vegetarian
jarski [yar-skee] adj. m.
  vegetarian; meatless
jary [ya-ri] adj. robust; vigorous;
  hale; spring (wheat, rye, etc.)
jarzębiak [ya-zhan-byak] m. sorb
  brandy; rowan-berry vodka
jarzębina [ya-zhan-bee-na] f. sorb
  tree; rowan; rowan berry
jarzmo [yazh-mo] n. yoke
jarzyć [ya-zhićh] v. sparkle;
  glitter; glow; shimmer
jarzyna [ya-zhi-na] vegetable;
  dish of vegetables
jasełka [ya-sew-ka] pl. crib;
  Nativity play; creche
jasiek [ya-śhek] m. little pillow;
  bean; beans; bean dish
jaskinia [yas-kee-ńa] f. cave
jaskiniowiec [ya-skee-ńo-vyets]
  m. cave dweller; cave man
jaskółka [yas-koow-ka] f.
  swallow; martin; harbinger
jaskrawy [yas-kra-vi] adj. m.
  glowing; showy; vivid; bright;
  striking; glaring; extreme
jasno [yas-no] adv. clearly;
  brightly; cheerfully; plainly
jasny [yas-ni] adj. m. clear;
  bright; light; shining; noble
jasnowidz [yas-no-veets] m.
  clairvoyant person; crystal
  gazer; seer (of future events)
jastrząb [yas-tzhownp] m.
  falcon; hawk; goshawk
jaszczyk [yash-chik] m. muni-
  -tions box; ammunition trailer
jaśmin [yaśh-meen] m. jasmine
jaśnieć [yaśh-ńećh] v. shine;
  sparkle; radiate; gleam; pale
jatka [yat-ka] f. shambles;
  butcher's shop; massacre
jatki [yat-kee] pl. shambles
jaw [yav] m. reality; v. expose
jawić [ya-vićh] v. appear; show
jawny [yav-ni] adj. m. evident;
  public; open; notorious; sheer
jawor [ya-vor] m. plane tree;
  maple tree; sycamore tree;
  sycamore wood (lumber)
jaz [yaz] m. weir; milldam
jazda [yaz-da] f. ride; driving

jaźń [yaźhń] f. ego; self; the
I; the inner man; psyche
jąć [yownćh] v. seize; begin
jądro [yown-dro] n. nucleus;
testicle; kernel; core
jąkać [yown-kaćh] v. stutter
jątrzyć [yown-tshićh] v. irritate;
fester; vex; embitter; inflame
jechać [ye-khaćh] v. ride; drive
jeden [ye-den] num. one; some
jedenaście [ye-de-naśh-ćhe]
num. eleven; 11
jedlina [yed-lee-na] f. fir grove;
fir and spruce branches
jednać [yed-naćh] v. conciliate
jednak [yed-nak] conj. however;
yet; still; but; after all; though
jednaki [yed-na-kee] adj. m.
identical; similar; equal; alike
jedno- [yed-no] one-; uni-; single-
jednocześnie [yed-no-cheśh-
-ńe] adv. simultaneously; also
jednoczyć [yed-no-chićh] v.
unify; merge; join; unite
jednogłośnie [yed-no-gwośh-
-ńe] adv. unanimously; in a
chorus; with one voice, assent
jednokrotnie [yed-no-krot-ńe]
adv. one time; once (only)
jednostka [yed-nost-ka] f. unit;
individual; entity; measure;
digit; specimen; denomination
jedność [yed-nośhćh] f. unity
jedwab [yed-vap] m. silk
jedynaczka [ye-di-nach-ka] f.
an only daughter; only child
jedynak [ye-di-nak] m. only son
jedynie [ye-di-ńe] adv. only;
merely; solely; nothing but
jadyny [ye-di-ni] adj. m. the only
one; the sole; unique; dearest
jedzenie [ye-dze-ńe] n. meat;
food; victuals; feed; eats
jemioła [ye-myo-wa] f. mistletoe
jeleń [ye-leń] m. stag; deer
jelito [ye-lee-to] n. intestine;
bowel; gut; pl. entrails
jełczeć [yew-chećh] v. grow
rancid; become rancid
jeniec [ye-ńets] m. captive
jerzyna [ye-zhi-na] f. black berry
jasień [ye-śheń] f. autumn;
fall; the fall of the leaf

jesienny [ye-śhen-ni] adj. m.
autumnal; of autumn
jesion [ye-śhon] m. ash tree
jasionka [ye-śhon-ka] f. fall
overcoat; light overcoat
jesiotr [ye-śhotr] m. sturgeon
jestestwo [yes-tes-tvo] n. being;
nature; creature; existence
jeszcze [yesh-che] adv. still;
besides; more; yet; way back
jeść [yeśhćh] v. eat; feed sb
jeśli [yeśh-lee] conj. if
jezdnia [yezd-ńa] f. roadway
jezuita [ye-zoo-ee-ta] m. Jesuit;
member of Jesuit Order
jeździec [yeźh-dźhets] m.
horseman; rider; equestrian
jeż [yesh] m. porcupine
jeżdżenie [yezh-dzhe-ńe] n.
riding; driving; tyrannizing
jeżeli [ye-zhe-lee] conj. if
jeżyć się [ye-zhićh śhan] v.
bristle up; stand on end
jeżyna [ye-zhi-na] f. blackberry;
blackberry bush; bramble
jęczeć [yan-chećh] v. moan;
groan; wail; whine; complain
jęczmień [yanch-myeń] m.
barley; a cereal grass
jędrny [yandr-ni] adj. m. firm;
robust; strong; terse; pithy
jędza [yan-dza] f. witch; shrew
jęk [yank] m. groan; moan; wail
jęknąć [yank-nownćh] v. complain; moan; groan; whine;
grumble; wail; bellyache
język [yan-zik] m. tongue
jod [yod] m. iodine
jodła [yod-wa] f. fir tree; spruce
jodyna [yo-di-na] f. tincture of
iodine (antiseptic); iodine
jon [yon] m. ion
jowialny [yo-vyal-ni] adj. m.
jovial; debonair; genial
jubiler [yoo-bee-ler] m. jeweler
(store or profession)
jubileusz [yoo-bee-le-oosh] m.
jubilee; anniversary
jucht [yookht] m. Russian
leather; water-proof leather
juczny koń [yooch-ni koń]
adj. m. pack-horse; beast of
burden; carrying saddle-bags

judzić [yoo-dźheećh] v. instigate; incire; provoke; set on
juki [yoo-kee] pl. packsaddle
junak [yoo-nak] m. brave.
swaggerer; dashing fellow
jurysdykcja [yoo-ris-dik-tsya]
f.jurisdiction; legal authority
juta [yoo-ta] f. jute; jute plant
jutro [yoot-ro] adv. tomorrow
jutrzejszy [yoo-tshey-shi] adj. m.
tomorrow's; future
jutrzenka [yoo-tshen-ka] f. day
-break; morning star; dawn
już [yoozh] conj. already; at any
moment; by now; no more
jużci [yoozh-ćhee] conj. of
course; certainly; sure thing!

K

kabalarka [ka-ba-lar-ka] f. fortune
teller (by looking at cards)
kabała [ka-ba-wa] f. cabala
kabaret [ka-ba-ret] m. cabaret
kabel [ka-bel] m. cable
kabestan [ka-bes-tan] m.
capstan; winch; windlass
kabina [ka-bee-na] f. cabin
kabłąk [kab-wownk] m. bow;
hoop; bail; trigger-guard
kabotyn [ka-bo-tin] m. poser;
buffoon; second-rate actor
kabriolet [ka-bryo-let] m.
convertible car; gig
kabza [kab-za] f. purse
kac [kats] m. hangover
kacerz [ka-tsesh] m. heretic
kacet [ka-tset] m. Nazi-Ger-
man concentration camp
kaczka [kach-ka] f. duck
kadłub [kad-woop] m. trunk;
hull; fuselage; framework
kadra [ka-dra] f. staff; cadre
kadzić [ka-dźheećh] v.
incense; flatter; fart (vulg.)
kadzidło [ka-dźhee-dwo] n.
incense (at an altar); frank-
incense; (fragrance)

kadź [kadźh] f. tub; tubful
kafar [ka-far] m. pile driver
kafel [ka-fel] m. tile (ceramic)
kaftan [kaf-tan] m. jacket
kaftan bezpieczeństwa [kaf-tan
bez-pye-cheń-stva] m.
straight jacket; "waistcoat"
kaftanik [kaf-ta-ńeek] m. bodice;
vest; (baby's) jacket; caftan
kaganiec [ka-ga-ńets] m.
muzzle; gag; oil lamp; cresset;
torch of learning
kajać się [ka-yaćh shan] v.
repent; confess with contrition
kajak [ka-yak] m. kayak; canoe
kajdany [kay-da-ni] pl. hand
-cuffs; shackles; chains; bonds
kajuta [ka-yoo-ta] f. ship-cabin
kajzerka [kay-zer-ka] f. fancy roll
of bread; kaiser roll
kakao [ka-ka-o] n. cocoa
kaktus [kak-toos] m. cactus
kalać [ka-laćh] v. pollute; foul
up; stain; sully; befoul
kalafior [ka-la-fyor] m.
cauliflower (a vegetable)
kalarepa [ka-la-re-pa] f. turnip
-cabbage; kohlrabi
kalectwo [ka-lets-tvo] n.
disability; lameness; inva-
lidism; cripplehood
kaleczyć [ka-le-chićh] v. cut;
wound; mutilate; hurt; injure;
lacerate; cripple; mangle
kalejdoskop [ka-ley-do-skop] m.
kaleidoscope; medley; miscellany; riot (of colors)
kaleka [ka-le-ka] m. f. cripple
kalendarz [ka-len-dash] m.
calendar; almanac
kalesony [ka-le-so-ni] pl.
underwear; drawers; shorts;
underpants; trunk drawers
kalina [ka-lee-na] f. guelder-rose;
cranberry shrub (tree)
kalka [kal-ka] f. carbon paper
kalkulacja [kal-koo-lats-ya] f.
calculation; computation
kalkulować [kal-koo-lo-vaćh] v.
calculate; compute; work out
kaloria [ka-lo-rya] f. calorie
kaloryfer [ka-lo-ri-fer] m. radiator;
steam heater; (water) heater

kalosz [ka-losh] m. rubber
overshoe; galosh; rubber boot
kalumnia [ka-loom-ńa] f.
calumny; slander; aspersion
kalwin [kal-veen] m. Calvinist
kał [kaw] m. excrement; stool
kałamarz [ka-wa-mash] m. ink
-stand; ink pot; ink-well
kaluża [ka-woo-zha] f. puddle
kamelia [ka-me-lya] f. camellia
kameralna muzyka [ka-me-ral-na
moo-zi-ka] chamber music
kamerdyner [ka-mer-di-ner] m.
butler; valet (de chambre)
kamerton [ka-mer-ton] m. tuning-
-fork ("U" shaped); pitch pipe
kamfora [kam-fo-ra] f. camphor
kamgarn [kam-garn] m. worsted
kamienica [ka-mye-ńee-tsa] f.
apartment house; tenants
kamienieć [ka-mye-ńéćh] v.
petrify; turn into stone
kamieniołom [ka-mye-ńo-wom]
f. quarry; stone pit
kamień [ka-myeń] m. stone
kamizelka [ka-mee-zel-ka] f.
waistcoat; vest; camisole
kampania [kam-pa-ńa] f.
campaign; drive (promotional)
kamrat [kam-rat] m. chum; pal
kamyk [ka-mik] m. pebble
kanadyjski [ka-na-diy-skee] adj.
m. Canadian; of Canada
kanalia [ka-na-lya] f. scoundrel
kanalizacja [ka-na-lee-zats-ya] f.
sewers; sanitation; drainage
kanał [ka-naw] m. channel; dike;
(storm) sewer; duct; ditch;
conduit; tube; gully; gutter
kanapa [ka-na-pa] f. sofa
kanapka [ka-nap-ka] f. sandwich;
small size sofa; love seat
kanarek [ka-na-rek] m. canary
kancelaria [kan-tse-la-rya] f.
office; chancellery; archives
kancerować [kan-tse-ro-vaćh]
v. damage; mangle; lacerate;
hack; tear jaggedly (roughly)
kanciarz [kan-ćhash] m.
swindler; trickster; con man
kanciasty [kan-ćha-sti] adj. m.
angular; awkward; stiff
kanclerz [kan-tslesh] m.

chancellor (chief of a government); church official
kandelabr [kan-de-labr] m.
chandelier; street lamp
kandydat [kan-di-dat] m.
candidate; applicant; aspirant
kangur [kan-goor] m. kangaroo
kanon [ka-non] m. canon (priest)
kanonierka [ka-no-ńer-ka] f.
gunboat; patrol boat
kanonik [ka-no-ńeek] m. canon
(priest); monsignor; prelate
kanonizować [ka-no-ńee-zo-
-vaćh] v. canonize; glorify
kant [kant] m. edge; crease;
swindle; trick; racket; chant
kantar [kan-tar] m. halter
kantor [kan-tor] m. exchange office; counter; cantor (singer)
kantyna [kan-ti-na] f. canteen
kanwa [kan-va] f. canvas
kapa [ka-pa] f. bedspread; cover
kapać [ka-paćh] v. dribble;
trickle; drip; fall drop by drop
kapela [ka-pe-la] f. band (of mu-
musicians); (church) choir
kapelan [ka-pe-lan] m. chaplain
(in armed forces, hospital)
kapelusz [ka-pe-loosh] m. hat
kapilarny [ka-pee-lar-ni] adj. m.
capillary; of capillary tube
kapiszon [ka-pee-shon] m. hood
kapitalista [ka-pee-ta-lees-ta] m.
capitalist; wealthy person
kapitalizm [ka-pee-ta-leezm] m.
capitalism (private or state)
kapitał [ka-pee-taw] m. capital
kapitan [ka-pee-tan] m. captain
kapitulacja [ka-pee-too-lats-ya] f.
surrender; capitulation; giving
up to an enemy
kapitulować [ka-pee-too-lo-
-vaćh] v. surrender; give up
kaplica [ka-plee-tsa] f. chapel
kapliczka [ka-pleech-ka] f. shrine
(in a church); wayside shrine
kapłan [ka-pwan] m.priest
kapłon [ka-pwon] m. capon
kapota [ka-po-ta] f. long coat
kapral [kap-ral] m. corporal
kaprys [kap-ris] m. caprice; fad;
whim; fancy; freak; vagary
kaptować [kap-to-vaćh] v. win

over; bring over; canvas

kaptur [kap-toor] m. hood

kapturowy sąd [kap-too-ro-vi **sownt**] kangaroo court

kapusta [ka-**poos**-ta] f. cabbage; a dish of cabbage

kapuś [ka-poośh] m. stool-pigeon; informer; police spy

kapuśniak [ka-poośh-ńak] m. cabbage soup; drizzle; mizzle

kara [ka-ra] f. penalty; fine; punishment; correction; chastisement; retribution; requital; a judgement; nuisance; pest

karabin [ka-ra-been] m. rifle

karać [ka-raćh] v. punish

karafka [ka-raf-ka] f. carafe; serving-bottle; (glass or metal) bottle; flagon; decanter

karakuły [ka-ra-koo-wi] pl. astrakhan sheep fur

karalny [ka-ral-ni] adj. m. punishable; deserving a fine

karaluch [ka-ra-lookh] m. cockroach; black beetle

karambol [ka-ram-bol] m. collision; cannon; carom

karaś [ka-raśh] m. crucian

karat [ka-rat] m. carat

karawaniarz [ka-ra-**va**-ńash] m. undertaker; coffin bearer

karb [karb] m. notch; score; crease; fold; nick; tally; curl

karbid [kar-beed] m. carbide

karbol [kar-bol] m. carbolic acid; phenol; (diluted) an antiseptic

karbować [kar-bo-vaćh] v. notch; curl; tally; crimp; fold

karbunkuł [kar-boon-koow] m. ulcer (under skin); carbuncle

karburator [kar-boo-ra-tor] m. carburetor (fuel mixing device)

karcer [kar-tser] m. prison; dark cell; detention (in a school)

karciarz [kar-ćhash] m. (cards) gambler; card player; gamester

karcić [kar-ćheećh] v. reproof; admonish; scold; castigate

karczemny [kar-chem-ni] adj. m. rude; vulgar; coarse

karczma [karch-ma] f. tavern

karczoch [kar-chokh] m. artichoke (thistle like plant)

karczować [kar-cho-vaćh] v. dig up (stumps); clear land

kardiografia [kar-dyo-gra-fya] f. (electro-) cardiography

kardynalny [kar-di-nal-ni] adj. m. fundamental; essential

kardynał [kar-di-naw] m. cardinal; prince (in the Catholic Church; elector of the pope)

karetka [ka-ret-ka] f. ambulance; (prison or mail) van; chaise

kariera [ka-**rye**-ra] f. career

kark [kark] m. neck; nape

karkołomny [kar-ko-**wom**-ni] adj. m. breakneck; neck-breaking

karłowaty [kar-wo-**va**-ti] adj. m. dwarfish; undersized

karamel [ka-ra-mel] m. caramel

karmić [kar-meećh] v. feed; nourish; nurse; suckle; nurture

karmin [kar-meen] m. carmine

karnawał [kar-na-vaw] m. carnival; period of feasting

karnie [kar-ńe] adv. penally; in perfect order (discipline)

karność [kar-nośhćh] f. discipline; orderly conduct

karny [kar-ni] adj. m. disciplined; penal (code, colony); punitive

karo [ka-ro] n. diamonds (in cards); square cut (bodice)

karoseria [ka-ro-**se**-rya] f. car (truck) body; enclosing frame

karp [karp] m. carp (fish)

karta [kar-ta] f. card; page; note; sheet; leaf; ticket; charter

kartel [kar-tel] m. (industrial) trust; cartel; combine; pool

kartofel [kar-to-fel] m. potato

kartoflanka [kar-to-flan-ka] f. m. potato soup; type of onion

kartograf [kar-to-graf] m. cartographer; map maker

karton [kar-ton] m. cardboard

kartoteka [kar-to-te-ka] f. card index; file

karuzela [ka-roo-**ze**-la] f. merry-go-round; carousel

kary koń [ka-ry koń] m. black horse

karygodny [ka-ri-god-ni] adj. m. unpardonable; guilty; gross

karykatura [ka-ri-ka-too-ra] f.

cartoon; caricature; parody
karykaturzysta [ka-ri-ka-too-**zhis**-
-ta] m. cartoonist
karzeł [ka-zhew] m. dwarf
kasa [ka-sa] f. cashier's desk;
cash register; ticket office
kasjer [kas-yer] m. cashier
kask [kask] m. helmet; tin hat
kaskada [kas-**ka**-da] f. cascade
kasować [ka-**so**-vaćh] v. cancel
kasta [kas-ta] f. caste
kastrować [kas-tro-vaćh] v.
castrate; geld; (sterilization)
kasyno [ka-**si**-no] n. casino; club;
mess-hall; mess-room
kasza [ka-sha] f. grits; groats;
cereals; gruel; porridge; mess
kaszel [ka-shel] m. cough
kaszkiet [kash-ket] m. cap
kasztan [kash-tan] m. chestnut
kat [kat] m. executioner
katafalk [ka-ta-falk] m. bier
kataklizm [ka-ta-kleezm] m.
cataclysm; disaster; calamity
katalizator [ka-ta-lee-**za**-tor] m.
catalyst; agent of catalysis
katalog [ka-ta-log] m. catalog
katar [ka-tar] m. head cold;
running nose; catarrh
katarakta [ka-ta-**rak**-ta] f.
cataract; opaque eye lens
kataryniarz [ka-ta-ri-**ńash**] m.
(street) organ grinder
katarynka [ka-ta-rin-ka] f. barrel
organ; street organ
katastrofa [ka-ta-**stro**-fa] f.
catastrophe; disaster; crash
katecheta [ka-te-**khe**-ta] m.
teacher of catechism
katedra [ka-te-dra] f. pulpit; univ.
dept. chair; cathedral
kategoria [ka-te-**go**-rya] f.
category; division; class
kategoryczny [ka-te-go-**rich**-ni]
adj. m. absolute; categorical
katoda [ka-**to**-da] f. cathode
katolicki [ka-to-**leets**-kee] adj. m.
Catholic; of the Cath. Church
katować [ka-to-vaćh] v.
torture; beat cruelly; hack
kaucja [kaw-tsya] f. bail; deposit;
security; recognizance
kauczuk [kaw-chook] m. India

natural rubber; caoutchouc
kaukaski [kaw-**kas**-kee] adj. m.
Caucasian; of Caucasus
kawa [ka-va] f. coffee
kawaler [ka-**va**-ler] m. bachelor;
suitor; beau; cavalier
kawaleria [ka-va-**le**-rya] f.
cavalry; young folks
kawalkada [ka-val-**ka**-da] f.
cavalcade (procession)
kawał [ka-vaw] m. piece; joke;
cheat; lump; funny business
kawałek [ka-**va**-wek] m. bit;
morsel; scrap; chunk
kawiarnia [ka-**vyar**-ńa] f. cafe
kawior [ka-vyor] m. caviar
kawka [kav-ka] f. jackdaw
kawon [ka-von] m. watermelon
kawowy [ka-**vo**-vi] adj. m. (of)
coffee; coffee-(plantation)
kazać [ka-zaćh] v. order; tell;
make sb. do sth; command
kazanie [ka-za-ńe] n. sermon
kazić [ka-**źheećh**] v. pollute;
corrupt; blemish; contaminate
kazirodztwo [ka-źhee-**rodz**-tvo]
n. incest
kaznodzieja [ka-zno-**dźhe**-ya] m.
preacher; evangelist
kaźń [kaźhń] f. execution
każdorazowy [kazh-do-ra-**zo**-vi]
adj. m. every time; each time;
every single (time)
każdy [kazh-di] pron. every;
each; respective; any; all
kącik [kown-ćheek] m. nook
kąkol [kown-kol] m. cockle;
corn cockle (in grainfield)
kąpać [kown-paćh] v. v. bathe;
bath; bask; soak; be steeped
kąpiel [kown-pyel] f. bath
kąpielisko [kown-pye-**lees**-ko] n.
resort; spa; public bath
kąsać [kown-saćh] v. bite
kąsek [kown-sek] m. bit; nip
kąt [kownt] m. corner; angle
kątomierz [kown-to-myesh] m.
protractor; dial-sight
kciuk [kćhook] m. thumb
kelner [kel-ner] m. waiter
kelnerka [kel-ner-ka] f. waitress;
bar maid; woman waiter
keson [ke-son] m. caisson

kędzierzawy [kan-dźhe-zha-vi]
adj. m. curly; curled; fuzzy
kędzior [kan-dźhor] m. curl;
lock (of hair); ringlet
kąpa [kan-pa] f. cluster; holm;
hurst; clump (of trees); tuft
kęs [kans] m. bit; mouthful
kibic [kee-beets] m. kibitzer
kibić [kee-beećh] f. figure of a
person; waist; middle
kichać [kee-khaćh] v. sneeze
kiecka [kets-ka] f. frock; skirt;
petticoat (inelegant)
kiedy [ke-di] conj. when; as;
ever; how soon?; while; since
kiedy indziej [ke-di een-dźhey]
some other time
kiedykolwiek [ke-di-kol-vyek]
adv. whenever; at any time
kiedyś [ke-diśh] adv. someday;
in the past; once; one day
kiedyż ? [ke-dish] adv. when
then?; when on earth ?
kielich [ke-leekh] m. goblet;
chalice; cup; cupful; glassful
kielnia [kel-ńa] f. trowel
kieł [kew] m. tusk; fang;
canine tooth; cutting bit
kiełbasa [kew-ba-sa] f. sausage
kiełek [ke-wek] m. sprout
kiełkować [kew-ko-vaćh] v.
sprout; germinate; spring up
kiełzać [kew-zaćh] v. bridle
kiep [kep] m. oaf; fool; gull
kiepski [kep-skee] adj. m. mean;
bad; poor; second-rate
kier [ker] m. (cards) hearts
kierat [ke-rat] m. thrasher
kiermasz [ker-mash] m. fair
kierować [ke-ro-vaćh] v. steer;
manage; run; show the way
kierownik [ke-rov-ńeek] m.
manager; director; supervisor
kierunek [ke-roo-nek] m.
direction; course; trend; line
kiesa [ke-sa] f. purse
kieszeń [ke-sheń] f. pocket
kij [keey] m. stick; cane; staff
kijanka [kee-yan-ka] f. tadpole
kikut [kee-koot] m. stump; stub
kilim [kee-leem] m. rug; carpet
kilka [keel-ka] num. a few; some
kilkakroć [keel-ka-kroćh] adv.

repeatedly; again and again
kilkakrotny [keel-ka-krot-ni] adj.
m. repeated; recurring
kilkudniowy [keel-koo-dńo-vi]
adj. m. of several days
kilkoro [keel-ko-ro] num. some;
several; one or two; a number
kilof [kee-lof] m. pick; hack
kilogram [kee-lo-gram] m.
kilogram = 2.2 pounds
kilometr [kee-lo-metr] m.
kilometer = 3,280.8 feet
kiła [kee-wa] f. syphilis
kinetyka [kee-ne-ti-ka] f. kine-
matics; science of motion
kino [kee-no] n. cinema; movies
kiosk [kyosk] m. kiosk; booth
kipieć [kee-pyećh] v. boil
kisić [kee-śheećh] v. ferment
kisnąć [kees-nownćh] v. turn
sour; ferment; pickle; fug
kisza [kee-sha] f. intestine
kiść [keeśhćh] f. bunch; wrist
kit [keet] m. putty; mastic
kiwać [kee-vaćh] v. v. rock;
nod; wag; dangle; fool; dodge;
jink; sway; swing; motion to
klacz [klach] f. mare
klajster [klay-ster] m. glue;
paste; water base glue
klakson [klak-son] m. car horn
klamka [klam-ka] f. door knob
klamra [klam-ra] f. buckle; clasp;
bracket; fastener; staple
klapa [kla-pa] f. lapel; valve
klapsy [klap-si] pl. spanking
klarować [kla-ro-vaćh] v.
clarify; filter; clear; purify
klarnet [klar-net] m. clarinet
klasa [kla-sa] f. class; classroom;
rank; order; division
klaskać [klas-kaćh] v. clap
klasowy [kla-so-vi] adj. m. class;
of classes; class- (distinction)
klasyczny [kla-sich-ni] adj. m.
classic; standard; conventional
klasyfikować [kla-si-fee-ko-
-vaćh] v. classify; sort; grade
klasztor [klash-tor] m.
monastery; convent; cloister
klatka [klat-ka] f. cage; crate
klatka schodowa [klat-ka skho-
-do-va] f. staircase; stairway

klatka piersiowa [klat-ka pyer-śho-va] f. rib cage; chest

klauzula [klaw-zoo-la] f. clause; proviso; reservation

klawisz [kla-veesh] m. (piano) key; stool pigeon; jailer

kląć [klownćh] v. curse; swear

klątwa [klown-tva] f. curse; ban; excommunication; anathema

klecić [kle-ćheećh] v. botch

kleić [kle-eećh] v. glue; stick together; fudge; shape; size

kleik [kle-eek] m. gruel

klej [kley] m. glue; cement

klejnot [kley-not] m. jewel

klekotać [kle-ko-taćh] v. clatter; rattle; chatter; prate

kleks [klex] m. blot; ink-spot

klepać [kle-paćh] v. hammer; flatten; prattle; pat; blab; clap

klepka [klep-ka] f. stave

klepsydra [klep-sid-ra] f. hour-glass; obituary notice

kleptomania [klep-to-ma-ńa] f. kleptomania; impulse to steal

kler [kler] m. clergy; priesthood

kleszcz [kleshch] m. tick

kleszcze [klesh-che] pl. pliers; tongs; claws; pincers; nippers

klękać [klan-kaćh] v. kneel down; bend the knee; kneel

klęska [klans-ka] f. defeat; disaster; calamity; repulse

klęsnąć [klans-nownćh] v. shrink; subside; go down

klient [klee-ent] m. customer

klika [klee-ka] f. clique

klimat [klee-mat] m. climate

klin [kleen] m. wedge; cotter

klinga [kleen-ga] f. (sword) blade; sabre-blade

kliniczny [klee-ńeech-ni] adj. m. clinical (diagnosis); clinic-

klinika [klee-ńee-ka] f. clinic

klisza [klee-sha] f. (photo) plate; printing plate; woodcut; cliche

klitka [kleet-ka] f. cubicle; cell

kloc [klots] m. log; block; chunk

klomb [klomp] m. flower bed

klon [klon] m. maple (tree)

klops [klops] m. meat loaf

klosz [klosh] m. glass cover; lamp shade; dish cover

klozet [klo-zet] m. toilet

klub [kloop] m. club; union

klucz [klooch] m. key; wrench

kluska [kloos-ka] f. boiled dough strip; dumpling; lump

kładka [kwad-ka] f. foot-bridge; gangway; gangplank; brow

kłaki [kwa-kee] pl. oakum; shaggy hair; matted hair

kłam [kwam] m. lie; falsehood

kłamać [kwa-maćh] v. lie

kłamca [kwam-tsa] m. liar

kłaniać się [kwa-ńaćh śhan] v. salute; bow; greet; worship

kłaść [kwaśhćh] v. lay; put down; place; set; deposit

kłąb [kwownp] m. clew; ball

kłąbek [kwown-bek] m. ball (of thread); hunk of yarn

kłębić się [kwan-beećh śhan] v. whirl; swirl; surge; billow

kłoda [kwo-da] f. log; clog

kłopot [kwo-pot] m. trouble

kłopotać [kwo-po-taćh] v. trouble; disturb; worry

kłopotliwy [kwo-pot-lee-vi] adj. m. troublesome; baffling

kłos [kwos] m. (corn) ear

kłócić [kwoo-ćheećh] v. stir; agitate; mix; disturb; quarrel

kłódka [kwood-ka] f. padlock

kłótliwy [kwoot-lee-vi] v. quarrelsome; cantankerous

kłótnia [kwoot-ńa] f. quarrel

kłuć [kwooćh] v. stab; prick

kłus [kwoos] m. trot; jog trot

kłusownik [kwoo-sov-ńeek] m. poacher; trespassing hunter

kmieć [kmyećh] m. peasant

kminek [kmee-nek] m. cumin

knajpa [knay-pa] f. tavern

knebel [kne-bel] m. gag

knocić [kno-ćheećh] v. bungle

knot [knot] m. (candle) wick; fuse; kid; bad mark; bungle

knuć [knooćh] v. plot; scheme

koalicja [ko-a-lits-ya] f. coalition; temporary union (alliance)

kobiałka [ko-byaw-ka] f. wicker-basket; chip basket; pottle

kobieciarz [ko-bye-ćhash] m. lady chaser; lady's man

kobiecość [ko-bye-tsośhćh] f.

womanhood; feminity
kobiecy [ko-bye-tsi] adj. m.
  female; womanish; feminine
kobierzec [ko-bye-zhets] m.
  carpet; anything like a carpet
kobieta [ko-bye-ta] f. woman
kobyła [ko-bi-wa] f. mare
kobza [kob-za] f. bagpipe
koc [kots] m. blanket; coverlet
kochać [ko-khaćh] v. love
kochanie [ko-kha-ńe] n. love;
  darling; sweetheart; affection
kochany [ko-kha-ni] adj. m.
  beloved; loving; affectionate
kochliwy [kokh-lee-vi] adj. m.
  easily in love; amorous
koci [ko-ćhee] adj. m. catlike
kociak [ko-ćhak] m. kitty-cat;
  lassie; lass; pinup girl
kocioł [ko-ćhow] m. kettle;
  boiler; pot; encirclement
kocur [ko-tsoor] m. tomcat
koczować [ko-cho-vaćh] v.
  lead nomadic life; wander
  about; be encamped; bivouac
koczownik [ko-chov-ńeek] m.
  nomad; wanderer; vagrant
kodeks [ko-dex] m. (legal) code
koedukacja [ko-e-doo-kats-ya] f.
  coeducation (of both sexes)
koegzystencja [ko-eg-zis-ten-
  -tsya] f. coexistence
kofeina [ko-fe-ee-na] f. caffeine;
  alkaloid in coffee
kogut [ko-goot] m. cock; rooster
koić [ko-eećh] v. soothe
kojarzenie [ko-ya-zhe-ńe] n.
  matching; association; union
kojarzyć [ko-ya-zhićh] v. unite;
  bind; join; link; connect
kojący [ko-yown-tsi] adj. m.
  soothing; comforting; balmy
kojec [ko-yets] m. coop; pen
kokaina [ko-ka-ee-na] f. cocaine;
  an alkaloid addicting drug
kokarda [ko-kar-da] f. rosette;
  bow; slip-knot; true-love knot
kokietka [ko-ket-ka] f. flirt
kokietować [ko-ke-to-vaćh] v.
  flirt; court; woo; coquet
koklusz [kok-loosh] m. whooping
  cough; hooping cough
kokos [ko-kos] m. coconut

kokos [ko-kos] m. good
  business; a grand thing
kokoszka [ko-kosh-ka] f.
  brood hen; laying hen
koks [kox] m. coke; gas coke
koksownia [kok-sov-ńa] f.
  coking plant; cokery
kolaboracja [ko-la-bo-rats-ya] f.
  collaboration; collaborators
kolacja [ko-lats-ya] f. supper
kolano [ko-la-no] n. knee; bend
kolarstwo [ko-lar-stvo] n.
  cycling; bicycle sport
kolarz [ko-lash] m. cyclist
kolący [ko-lown-tsi] adj. m.
  prickly; thorny; spiked
kolba [kol-ba] f. (riffle) butt
kolczasty [kol-chas-ti] adj. m.
  barbed; thorny; spiny
kolczyk [kol-chik] m. earring;
  earmark; ear tag; eardrop
kolebka [ko-leb-ka] f. cradle
kolec [ko-lets] m. thorn
kolega [ko-le-ga] m. buddy;
  colleague; fellow worker
koleina [ko-le-ee-na] f. truck rut;
  wheel groove; wheel trace
kolej [ko-ley] f. railroad
kolejaka [ko-ley-ka] f. (waiting)
  line; narrow-gage railroad; turn
kolejno [ko-ley-no] adv. by turns;
  one after the other; in turns
kolejny [ko-ley-ni] adj. m. next;
  successive; following
kolekcja [ko-lek-tsya] f.
  collection; things collected
kolektywizacja [ko-le-kti-vee-zats-
  -ya] f. collectivization
koleżeństwo [ko-le-zheń-stvo]
  n. fellowship; comradeship
kolęda [ko-lan-da] f. Christmas
  carol; song of joy or praise
kolędować [ko-lan-do-vaćh] v.
  sing carols; wait a long time
koliber [ko-lee-ber] m. hum-
  -ming-bird; Trochilidae
kolia [ko-lya] f. necklace
kolidować [ko-lee-do-vaćh] v.
  collide; interfere; clash
koligacja [ko-lee-gats-ya] f.
  (family) relationship
kolisty [ko-lees-ti] adj. m.
  circular; round

kolizja [ko-**leez**-ya] f. collision; clash; interference

kolka [**kol**-ka] f. colic

kolokwium [ko-lo-**kvyoom**] m. oral examination; test

kolonia [ko-lo-**ńa**] f. colony

kolonista [ko-lo-**ńees**-ta] m. settler; colonist; colonial

kolońska woda [ko-**loń**-ska vo--da] cologne water

kolor [**ko**-lor] m. color; tint; hue

koloryt [ko-**lo**-rit] m. coloring

kolosalny [ko-lo-**sal**-ni] adj. m. colossal; vast; tremendous

kolportaż [kol-**por**-tash] m. (paper) distribution

kolumna [ko-**loom**-na] f. column

kołatać [ko-**wa**-tać] v. knock; rattle; beg; throb; bang

kołczan [**kow**-chan] m. quiver

kołdra [**kow**-dra] f. quilter-cover; quilt; coverlet; eiderdown

kołek [**ko**-wek] m. peg; stake

kołnierz [**kow**-ńesh] m. collar

koło [**ko**-wo] n. wheel; circle

koło [**ko**-wo] prep. around; near; about; by; in vicinity; close to

kołodziej [ko-wo-**dźhey**] m. wheelwright; wheeler

kołowacizna [ko-wo-va-**ćheez**--na] f. dizziness; confusion

kołować [ko-wo-**vać**] v. stray; revolve; confuse; circle; whirl; be in a whirl; prevaricate

kołowrotek [ko-wo-**vro**-tek] m. spinning-wheel; reel; winch

kołowrót [ko-wo-**vroot**] m. gin; windlass; hoist; whip; turn-pike; turnstile; large reel

kołowy ruch [ko-**wo**-vi **rookh**] vehicular traffic; traffic

kołpak [**kow**-pak] m. pointed fur cap; calpack; calpac

kołtun [**kow**-toon] m. hair snarl; tangle; bigot; moron; Philistine

kołysać [ko-**wi**-sać] v. rock; sway; toss to and fro; roll

kołysanka [ko-wi-**san**-ka] f. lullaby; cradle song; berceuse

kołyska [ko-**wis**-ka] f. cradle

komar [**ko**-mar] m. mosquito

kombajn [**kom**-bayn] m. combine

kombinacja [kom-bee-**nats**-ya] f. combination; union; scheme; arrangement; (woman's) slip

kombinować [kom-bee-**no**-vać] v. combine; speculate; arrange; think; contrive

komedia [ko-**me**-dya] f. comedy

komenda [ko-**men**-da] f. word of command; command; head-quarters; an order

komentarz [ko-**men**-tash] m. commentary; glossary; remark

kometa [ko-**me**-ta] f. comet

komfort [**kom**-fort] m. comfort

komiczny [ko-**meech**-ni] adj. m. comic; amusing; funny; droll

komin [**ko**-meen] m. chimney

kominek [ko-**mee**-nek] m. fire-place; hearth; open fire

kominiarz [ko-**mee**-ńash] m. chimney-sweep

komis [**ko**-mees] m. (on) commission sale; commission shop; commission agent

komisariat [ko-mee-**sa**-ryat] m. police station; commissariat

komisja [ko-**mees**-ya] f. commission; board (of inquiry) (standing) committee

komitet [ko-**mee**-tet] m. committee; board

komitywa [ko-mee-**ti**-va] f. intimacy; good friendly terms

komiwojażer [ko-mee-vo-**ya**-zher] m. travelling salesman

komnata [kom-**na**-ta] f. chamber

komoda [ko-**mo**-da] f. chest of drawers; low-boy; commode

komora [ko-**mo**-ra] f. chamber

komora celna [ko-**mo**-ra **tsel**-na] f. customs office; custom house (where duties are paid)

komorne [ko-**mor**-ne] n. (apartment) rent; rental

komórka [ko-**moor**-ka] f. cell

kompan [**kom**-pan] m. chum; pal

kompania [kom-pa-**ńya**] f. company; (stock, military) company; society; pilgrimage

kompas [**kom**-pas] m. compass

kompensata [kom-pen-**sa**-ta] f. compensation; indemnity

kompetentny [kom-pe-**ten**-tni] adj. m. competent; qualified

kompleks [kom-plex] m.
complex (of buildings); group;
(inferiority) complex; whole
komplement [kom-ple-ment] m.
compliment; complement
komplet [kom-plet] m. complete
set; complete (full) group
kompozytor [kom-po-zi-tor] m.
composer (of music)
kompot [kom-pot] m. compote
kompres [kom-pres] m. compress
kompromis [kom-pro-mees] m.
compromise; accommodation
kompromitacja [kom-pro-mee-
-tats-ya] f. disgrace; loss of
face; shame; humiliation
komuna [ko-moo-na] f. commune
komunał [ko-moo-naw] m.
platitude; banality; trite
remark; commonplace
komunia [ko-moo-ńa] f. Communion (in Catholic church)
komunikacja [ko-moo-ńee-kats-
-ya] f. communication; contact
komunikat [ko-moo-ńee-kat] m.
bulletin; report; communique
komunikować [ko-moo-ńee-ko
-vać] v. inform; give news;
report; receive Communion
komunista [ko-moo-ńees-ta] m.
communist (party member)
konać [ko-nać] v. agonize;
expire; be dying; die (with
greed, with laughter)
konar [ko-nar] m. limb; branch
koncentryczny [kon-tsen-trich-ni]
adj. m. concentric; converging
koncept [kon-tsept] m. concept;
idea; joke; plan; brain wave
koncert [kon-tsert] m. concert
koncesja [kon-tses-ya] f.
concession; conceding; right
to sell; licence; licence to do...
koniec [ko-ńets] m. end; finish
konkurencja [kon-koo-ren-tsya] f.
competition; rivalry; contest
konkurs [kon-koors] m. contest
konnica [kon-ńee-tsa] f. cavalry
konno [kon-no] adv. on horse
-back; sit astraddle; mounted
konny [kon-ni] adj. m. mounted
konopie [ko-no-pye] pl. hemp
konował [ko-no-vaw] m. farrier;

quack doctor; sawbones
konserwa [kon-ser-va] f.
preserve; conservatists
konserwatorium [kon-ser-va-tor-
-yoom] n. conservatory
konsola [kon-so-la] f. console
konspirować [kon-spee-ro-vać]
v. plot; conspire; keep secret
konstatować [kon-sta-to-vać]
v. state; ascertain; find
konsternacja [kon-ster-nats-ya] f.
consternation; dismay; shock
konstrukcja [kon-strook-tsya] f.
construction; design; plan
konstruować [kon-stroo-o-vać]
v. construct; build; make
konstytucja [kon-sti-toots-ya] f.
constitution; physique
konsulat [kon-soo-lat] m. consulate (office of a consul)
konsumować [kon-soo-mo-
-vać] v. consume; eat up;
drink up; use up; waste (fuel)
konsylium [kon-sil-yoom] n.
consultation (usually medical)
konszachty [kon-shakh-ti] pl. collusion; (underhand) scheming
kontakt [kon-takt] m. contact
kontaktować się [kon-tak-to-
-vać śhan] v. be in contact;
be in touch; communicate
konto [kon-to] n. account
kontrabanda [kon-tra-ban-da] f.
smuggled goods; contraband
kontrakt [kon-trakt] m. contract
enforceable by law
kontraktować [kon-trak-to-
-vać] v. contract (to supply);
hire; engage (an employee)
kontrast [kon-trast] m. contrast
(pointing the differences)
kontrastować [kon-tras-to-
-vać] v. contrast (with);
stand in contrast; stand out
kontratak [kontr-a-tak] m. count-
er-attack (opposing an attack)
kontrola [kon-tro-la] f. control;
checking; check up; inspection
kontrolny [kon-trol-ni] adj. m. of
inspection; of supervision
kontrolować [kon-tro-lo-vać]
v. control; check; verify
kontrpropozycja [kontr-pro-po-

-zits-ya] f. counter-proposal
kontrrewolucja [kontr-re-vo--loots-ya] f. counterrevolution
kontrowersja [kon-tro-**ver**-sya] f. controversy; quarrel; dispute
kontuar [kon-**too**-ar] m. counter
kontur [kon-**toor**] m. outline
kontusz [kon-**toosh**] m. split-sleeve Polish overcoat (of old)
kontuzja [kon-**tooz**-ya] f. shock
kontynent [kon-ti-nent] m. continent; mainland; any main land area of the earth
konwalia [kon-**va**-lya] f. lily of the valley; convallaria
konwikt [kon-**veekt**] m. boarding school (for boys or girls)
konwój [kon-**vooy**] m. convoy
konwulsja [kon-**vool**-sya] f. convulsion; a fit; a spasm
koń [koń] m. horse; steed
koń mechaniczny [koń me-kha--ńeech-ni] m. mechanical horsepower; horsepower
końcowy [koń-**tso**-vi] adj. m. final; terminal; last; late
końcówka [koń-**tsoov**-ka] f. ending; remainder; tail-piece
kończyć [koń-**chich**] v. end; finish; quit; be dying; stop
kończyna [koń-**chi**-na] f. extremity; limb; member; leg
kooperacja [ko-o-pe-**rats**-ya] f. cooperation; acting together
koordynacja [ko-or-di-**nats**-ya] f. coordination (mental & phys.)
kopa [ko-pa] f. threescore (60); pile; dozens; stack
kopa siana [ko-pa **śha**-na] f. hay-stack; hayrick
kopać [ko-**pach**] v. kick; dig
kopalnia [ko-pal-ńa] f. mine
koparka [ko-**par**-ka] f. excavator; mechanical shovel; stripper
kopcić [kop-**ćheech**] v. soot; smoke; blacken with smoke
kopciuszek [kop-**ćhoo**-shek] m. Cinderella; drudge; slavey
kopeć [ko-**pech**] m. soot
koper [ko-per] m. dill; fennel
koperta [ko-per-ta] f. envelope; quilt-case; (watch-)case
kopiasty [ko-**pyas**-ti] adj. m.

heaped; piled up; heaped (plate); lying in a heap
kopiec [ko-**pyets**] m. mound; barrow; heap; knoll; clamp
kopiować [ko-**pyo**-vach] v. copy; reproduce; imitate
kopuła [ko-**poo**-wa] f. dome
kopyto [ko-pi-to] n. hoof
kora [ko-ra] f. bark; cortex
koral [ko-ral] m. coral (red)
korale [ko-**ra**-le] pl. bead necklace; coral beads; gills
korba [kor-ba] f. crank; winch
kordon [kor-don] m. cordon
korek [ko-rek] m. cork; fuse; stopper; traffic-jam; tie-up
korekta [ko-**rek**-ta] f. proof
korepetycja [ko-re-pe-**tits**-ya] f. tutoring; private lesson
korespondencja [ko-res-pon--**dents**-ya] f. correspondence; letters; mail; post
korespondent wojenny [ko-res--pon-dent vo-**yen**-ni] war correspondent; war reporter
korkociąg [kor-ko-**ćhowng**] m. corkscrew; tail-spin; twist
korniszon [kor-ńee-shon] m. pickled cucumber; gherkin
korny [kor-ni] adj. m. humble
korona [ko-ro-na] f. crown
koronacja [ko-ro-**nats**-ya] f. coronation; crowning
koronka [ko-**ron**-ka] f. lace
koronować [ko-ro-**no**-vach] v. crown; be crowned
korowód [ko-ro-vood] m. procession; pageant; train; pl. difficulties; exertions
korporacja [kor-po-**rats**-ya] f. corporation; association; guild
korpulentny [kor-poo-lent-ni] adj. m. fat; corpulent; obese; stout
korpus [kor-poos] m. body; staff; (army) corps; all army officers
korsarz [kor-sash] m. pirate
kort tenisowy [kort te-ńee-**so**-vi] tennis court
korupcja [ko-**roop**-tsya] f. corruption; venality; bribery
korygować [ko-ri-**go**-vach] v. correct; rectify; put right
korytarz [ko-ri-tash] m. corridor;

passage-way; lobby; tunnel
koryto [ko-ri-to] n. through; river
-bed; channel; chute; road-bed
korzec [ko-zhets] m. bushel
korzeń [ko-zheń] m. root; spice
korzyć [ko-zhich] v. humble;
humiliate; prostrate; mortify
korzystać [ko-zhis-tach] v.
profit; gain; enjoy a right
korzystny [ko-zhist-ni] adj. m.
profitable; favorable
korzyść [ko-zhiśhćh] f. profit
kos [kos] m. blackbird
kosa [ko-sa] f. scythe; tress
kosiarka [ko-śhar-ka] f. mower; mowing machine (time)
kosić [ko-śheećh] v. mow;
scythe; rake; sweep
kosmaty [kos-ma-ti] adj. m.
shaggy; hairy; fleecy
kosmetyczka [kos-me-tich-ka] f.
vanity bag; beautician
kosmetyk [kos-me-tik] m.
cosmetic; makeup (skin and
hair); cosmetic preparation
kosmiczny [kos-meech-ni] adj. m.
cosmic; outer space; vast
kosmopolita [kos-mo-po-lee-ta]
m. cosmopolite; cosmopolitan
kosmyk [kos-mik] m. wisp;
strand; tuft; flock (of hair)
kosodrzewina [ko-so-dzhe-vee-
-na] f. dwarf mountain pine
kosooki [ko-so-o-kee] adj. m.
with slanting eyes; with
scowling eyes; cross-eyed
kostium [kos-tyoom] m. suit;
dress; garb; tailor made suit
kostka [kost-ka] f. small bone;
ankle; knuckle; die; dice; lump
kostnica [kost-ńee-tsa] f.
morgue; mortuary; dead house
kostnieć [kost-ńećh] v. grow
stiff (numb); ossify; freeze
kosy [ko-si] adj. m. slanting
kosz [kosh] m. basket; grab-bag;
Tartar military camp
koszary [ko-sha-ri] pl. barracks
(military); caserns
koszenie [ko-she-ńe] n. mowing
koszerny [ko-sher-ni] adj. m.
kosher (clean or fit to eat)
koszmar [kosh-mar] m.

nightmare; frightening
experience (dream)
koszt [kosht] m. cost; price;
expense; charge; economic
costs; production cost etc.
kosztorys [ko-shto-ris] m.
estimate; cost calculation
kosztowny [kosh-tov-ni] adj. m.
expensive; costly; precious
koszula [ko-shoo-la] f. shirt
koszyk [ko-shik] f. small basket;
grab bag; hilt guard; basketful
koszykówka [ko-shi-koov-ka] f.
basketball
kościany [kośh-ćha-ni] adj. m.
bone (handle etc.); osseous
kościec [kośh-ćhets] m.
skeleton; framework; frame
kościelny [kośh-ćhel-ni] adj.
m. of church; ecclesiastical;
m. sexton; sacristan
kościotrup [kośh-ćho-troop]
m. skeleton; thin man (vulg.)
kościół [kośh-ćhoow] m.
church; church organization
kościsty [kośh-ćhees-ti]
adj. m. bony; angular; raw-
boned; teleostean (fish)
kość [kośhćh] f. bone; spine
koślawić [kośh-la-veećh] v.
deform; distort; crook
koślawy [kośh-la-vi] adj. m.
crooked; lame; lopsided
kot [kot] m. cat; pussy cat; puss
kotara [ko-ta-ra] f. curtain
kotek [ko-tek] m. kitten; puss
kotlet [kot-let] m. cutlet
kotlina [kot-lee-na] f. dale
kotłować [kot-wo-vaćh] v.
whirl; seethe; surge; drive
crazy; bother; worry
kotłownia [kot-wov-ńa] f. boiler
room; boiler house; fire room
kotwica [kot-vee-tsa] f. anchor
kotwiczyć [kot-vee-chićh] v.
anchor; lie at anchor
kowadło [ko-va-dwo] n. anvil
kowal [ko-val] m. blacksmith
kowalny [ko-val-ni] adj. m.
malleable; ductile; forgeable
koza [ko-za] f. goat; jail
kozioł [ko-źhow] m. buck;
somersault; trestle; stack

koźlę [koźh-lan] n. kid; goatling
kożuch [ko-zhookh] m.
　sheepskin (coat); fur coat;
　coating on hot milk; film; hide
kół [koow] m. stake; post
kółko [koow-ko] m. small wheel;
　small circle; (soc.) circle
kpiarz [kpyash] m. scoffer
kpić [kpeećh] v. jeer; sneer
kpiny [kpee-ni] n. mockery; this
　is preposterous! (exp.)
kra [kra] f. ice flow; ice float
krach [krakh] m. crash; slump
kraciasty [kra-ćhas-ti] adj. m.
　chequered; grated; checkered
kradzież [kra-dźhesh] f. theft
kradziony [kra-dźho-ni] adj. m.
　stolen (object); robbed
kraina [kra-ee-na] f. land; region;
　province; country
kraj [kray] m. country; verge;
　edge; hem of a garment; land
krajać [kra-yaćh] v. cut; slice;
　carve; operate; hack; saw
krajobraz [kra-yo-bras] m.
　landscape; scenery painting
krajowy [kra-yo-vi] adj. m.
　native; nationally made
krajoznawczy [kra-yo-znav-chi]
　adj. m. hiking; touring
krakać [kra-kaćh] v. croak
kram [kram] m. booth; mess;
　trouble; stall; odds and ends
kramarz [kra-mash] m. huckster
kran [kran] m. tap; faucet
kraniec [kra-ńets] m. border;
　edge; end; extremity; margin
krańcowy [krań-tso-vi] adj. m.
　extreme; marginal; excessive
krasa [kra-sa] f. grace; beauty;
　loveliness; splendor
krasić [kra-śheećh] v. decorate
krasomówca [kra-so-moov-tsa]
　m. orator (very eloquent)
kraść [kraśhćh] v. steal; rob
kraśnieć [kraśh-ńećh] v.
　blush; grow beautiful; redden
krata [kra-ta] f. grate; grill
krater [kra-ter] m. crater
krawat [kra-vat] m. neck (tie)
krawcowa [krav-tso-va] f.
　seamstress; tailor's wife
krawędź [kra-vandźh] f. edge

krawężnik [kra-vanzh-ńeek] m.
　curb (stone); roof-hip
krawiec [kra-vyets] m. tailor
krąg [krownk] m. ring; vertebra;
　disk; range; circle; sphere
krążek [krown-zhek] m. small
　disk; potter's wheel; pulley
krążyć [krown-zhićh] v. rove;
　circulate; rotate; wander; stray
kreacja [kre-ats-ya] f. (dress)
　creation (of a theater part)
kreda [kre-da] f. chalk
kredens [kre-dens] m. china
　cabinet; cupboard; buffet
kredka [kred-ka] f. crayon;
　lipstick; chalk for writing
kredowy [kre-do-vi] adj. m.
　cretaceous; chalky; made of
　chalk; white like chalk
kredyt [kre-dit] m. credit
krem [krem] m. cream; custard
krematorium [kre-ma-to-ryoom]
　n. crematorium; crematory
kremowy [kre-mo-vi] adj. m.
　cream-colored; cream yellow
kreować [kre-o-vaćh] v. create;
　act; set up; institute; appoint
krepa [kre-pa] f. crepe
kres [kres] m. end; limit; term
kreska [kres-ka] f. dash (line);
　stroke; hatch; scar; accent
kreślić [kreśh-leećh] v. draw;
　trace; sketch; cross out
kret [kret] m. mole; schemer
kretowisko [kre-to-vees-ko] n.
　molehill (made by burrowing)
krew [krev] f. blood; race
krewetka [kre-vet-ka] f. shrimp
krewki [krev-kee] adj. m. rash;
　quick-tempered; impetuous
krewny [krev-ni] m. relative
kręcić [kran-ćheećh] v. twist;
　turn; shoot film; fuss; boss
kręcony [kran-tso-ni] adj. m.
　twisted; curled; winding; spiral
kręgle [kran-gle] n. bowling;
　(ninepins) game of bowling
kręgosłup [kran-go-swoop] m.
　spine; vertebral column; spinal
　column; backbone; willpower
kręgowiec [kran-go-vyets] m.
　vertebrate; animal with spine
krępować [kran-po-vaćh] v.

bind; embarrass; hamper; hinder; tie up; shackle; impede; fetter; peg down; cramp

krępy [kran-pi] adj. m. stocky; thickset; sturdy; short; squat

krętactwo [kran-tats-tvo] n. cheat; foul dealing; shuffle

krętacz [kran-tach] m. double -dealer; dodger; quibbler; cheat; crooked (lawyer etc.)

kręty [kran-ti] adj. m. curved; curly; winding; spiral; devious

krnąbrny [krnownb-rni] adj. m. stubborn; unruly; restive; insubordinate; balky; fractious

krochmal [krokh-mal] m. starch

krochmalić [krokh-ma-leećh] v. starch; beat up; stiffen

krocie [kro-ćhe] pl. thousands

kroczyć [kro-chićh] v. stride

kroić [kro-eećh] v. cut; slice

krok [krok] m. step; pace; march

krokiew [kro-kev] f. rafter

krokodyl [kro-ko-dil] m. crocodile; split flap (aviation)

kromka [krom-ka] f. slice

kronika [kro-ńee-ka] f. chronicle

kropić [kro-peećh] v. sprinkle

kropka [krop-ka] f. dot; point

kropkować [krop-ko-vaćh] v. dot; speckle; spot

kropla [krop-la] f. drop

krosno [kros-no] n. loom

krosta [kros-ta] f. pimple

krotochwila [kro-to-khvee-la] f. joke; burlesque; farce

krowa [kro-va] cow; mine

krój [krooy] m. cut; fashion

król [krool] m. king; rabbit

królestwo [kroo-les-tvo] n. kingdom; the realms; sphere

królewicz [kroo-le-veech] m. crown prince; king's son

królewski [kroo-lev-skee] adj. m. royal; kingly; majestic; king's

królik [kroo-leek] m. rabbit

królikarnia [kroo-lee-kar-ńa] f. warren; rabbit warren

królowa [kroo-lo-va] f. queen

krótki [kroot-kee] adj. m. short; brief; terse; concise; curt

krótko [kroot-ko] adv. briefly; shortly; tersely; (hold) tightly

krtań [krtań] f. larynx

kruchy [kroo-khi] adj. m. brittle; frail; tender; crisp; crusty

krucjata [kroots-ya-ta] f. crusade; action for some cause

krucyfiks [kroo-tsi-feeks] m. crucifix; cross of Jesus

kruczek [kroo-chek] m. trick

kruczy [kroo-chi] adj. m. jet -black; raven's color

kruk [krook] m. raven

krupy [kroo-pi] pl. groats

kruszec [kroo-shets] m. (metal) ore; metal; gold; silver

kruszeć [kroo-shećh] v. crumble; grow brittle; repent

kruszyć [kroo-shićh] v. crush; crumb; destroy; shatter; disrupt; break into pieces

kruszyna [kroo-shi-na] f. crumb

krużganek [kroozh-ga-nek] m. portico; gallery; ambulatory

krwawica [krva-vee-tsa] f. hard won money; toil; labor

krwawić [krva-veećh] v. bleed

krwawy [krva-vi] adj. m. bloody; bloodthirsty; bloodstained

krwiobieg [krvyo-byeg] m. blood circulation; circulation

krwisty [krvees-ti] adj. m. sanguineous; blood-red

krwotok [krvo-tok] m. hemorrhage; heavy bleeding

kryć [krićh] v. hide; conceal; cover; roof over; shield; mask

kryjówka [kri-yoov-ka] f. hiding place; hide-out; cache

kryminalista [kri-mee-na-lees-ta] m.criminal; felon; criminologist

kryminał [kri-mee-naw] m. jail; prison; crime; felony; thriller

krynica [kri-ńee-tsa] f. spring

krystalizować [kris-ta-lee-zo-vaćh] v. crystallize; shape

kryształ [krish-taw] m. crystal

kryterium [kri-te-ryoom] n. criterion; touchstone; test

kryty [kri-ti] adj. m. covered

krytyczny [kri-tich-ni] adj. m. critical; decisive; crucial

krytyk [kri-tik] m. critic

krytyka [kri-ti-ka] f. criticism; review; censure; critique

kryzys [kri-zis] m. crisis
krzaczasty [kzha-chas-ti] adj. m.
  bushy; shaggy (thick); beetle
krzak [kzhak] m. bush
krzątać [kzhown-tać] v. bustle
krzątanina [kzhown-ta-ńee-na] f.
  bustle; comings and goings
krzem [kzhem] m. silicone
krzemień [kzhe-myeń] f. flint
krzepić [kzhe-peećh] v. brace
  up; refresh; invigorate; fortify
krzepki [kzhep-kee] adj. vigorous;
  lusty; robust; husky; sprightly
krzepnąć [kzhep-nownćh] v.
  coagulate; gather strength; set
krzesać [kzhe-saćh] v. strike
  fire (out of); strike sparks
krzesiwo [kzhe-śhee-vo] n.
  tinder-box; flint (and steel)
krzesło [kzhes-wo] n. chair
krzew [kzhev] m. shrub
krzewić [kzhe-veećh] v. spread;
  propagate; teach; graft
krzta [kzhta] f. whit; bit
krztusiec [kzhtoo-śhets] m.
  whooping-cough
krztusić się [kzhtoo-śheećh
  śhan] v. choke; stifle
krzyczeć [kzhi-chećh] v. shout;
  cry; scream; yell; clamor
krzyk [kzhik] m. cry; scream;
  shriek; yell; outcry; call
krzykacz [kzhi-kach] m. bawler;
  crier; shouter; agitator
krzykliwy [kzhik-lee-vi] adj. m.
  noisy; clamorous; loud; showy
krzywa [kzhi-va] f. curve
krzywda [kzhiv-da] f. harm; a
  sense of wrong; wrong; injury
krzywdzący [kzhiv-dzown-tsi]
  adj. m. harmful; injurious
krzywdzić [kzhiv-dźheećh] v.
  harm; wrong; damage; be unfair (unjust); be prejudicial
krzywica [kzhi-vee-tsa] f. rickets;
  rachitis; sweep (turning) saw
krzywić [kzhi-veećh] v. bend
krzywić się [kzhi-veećh śhan]
  v. make faces; bend; warp
krzywo [kzhi-vo] adv. crooked
krzywy [kzhi-vi] adj. m. crooked;
  skew; distorted; slanting
krzyż [kzhish] m. cross

krzyżować [kzhi-zho-vaćh] v.
  cross; thwart; crucify
krzyżówka [kzhi-zhoov-ka] f.
  crossword puzzle; hybrid
ksiądz [kśhownts] m. priest
książę [kśhown-zhan] m.
  prince; duke; ruler of a duchy
książka [kśhownzh-ka] f. book
księga [kśhan-ga] f. register;
  large book; volume; tome
księgarnia [kśhan-gar-ńa] f.
  bookstore; books; book shop
księgarz [kśhan-gash] m.
  bookseller; owner of a
  bookstore
księgować [kśhan-go-vaćh] v.
  keep books; enter in books
księgowy [kśhan-go-vi] m.
  bookkeeper; accountant
księgozbiór [kśhan-go-zbyoor]
  m. book collection; library
księstwo [kśhans-tvo] n. duchy
księżna [kśhan-zhna] f.
  princess; wife of a prince
księży [kśhan-zhi] adj. m.
  priestly; belonging to a priest
księżyc [kśhan-zhits] m. moon
kształcić [kshtaw-ćheećh] v.
  educate; train; form; school
kształt [kshtawt] m. form;
  shape; configuration; figure
kształtny [kshtawt-ni] adj. m.
  shapely; neat; nicely made
kształtować [kshtaw-to-vaćh]
  v. shape; form; mold; fashion
kto [kto] pron. who; all; those
kto bądź [kto bowndźh]
  anybody; no one; just anyone
kto inny [kto een-ni] somebody
  else; someone else
ktoś [ktośh] pron. somebody
którędy [ktoo-ran-di] adv. which
  way; how to get there?
który [ktoo-ri] pron. who; which;
  that; any; whichever; that
któż [ktoosh] pron. whichever
ku [koo] prep. towards; to
kubatura [koo-ba-too-ra] f.
  (building) volume; cubature
kubek [koo-bek] m. cup; mug
kubeł [koo-bew] m. pail; bucket
kucharka [koo-khar-ka] f. cook
kucharz [koo-khash] m. cook

kuchenka gazowa [koo-khen-ka ga-zo-va] f. (gas) hot plate
kuchnia [kookh-ña] f. kitchen; kitchen stove; cooking range
kucnąć [koots-nownćh] v. squat down; squat; crouch
kucyk [koo-tsik] m. small pony
kuć [kooćh] v. hammer; shoe a horse; forge; cram lessons; peck; pick; coin; whack
kudłaty [kood-wa-ti] adj. m. shaggy; hairy; hirsute
kudły [kood-wi] pl. shaggy hair
kufel [koo-fel] m. beer mug
kufer [koo-fer] m. trunk
kuglarz [koog-lash] m. juggler
kukiełkowy teatr [koo-kew-ko-vi te-atr] puppet-show
kukła [kook-wa] f. puppet
kukułka [koo-koow-ka] f. cuckoo bird; cuckoo clock
kukurydza [koo-koo-ri-dza] maize; corn; Indian corn
kula [koo-la] f. sphere; bullet crutch; ball; globe; shot
kulawy [koo-la-vi] adj. m. lame
kulbaczyć [kool-ba-chićh] v. saddle (a horse, a pony, etc.)
kuleć [koo-lećh] v. limp
kulić się [koo-leećh śhan] v. snuggle; crouch; cringe; nestle
kulinarny [koo-lee-nar-ni] adj. m. culinary; of cooking (cookery)
kulisy [koo-lee-si] pl. theater scenes; the inner facts; links
kulisty [koo-lees-ti] adj. m. spherical; ball-shaped; round
kulminacyjny [kool-mee-na-tsiy-ni] adj. m. culminating; final; climactic; of a turning point
kult [koolt] m. cult; worship
kultura [kool-too-ra] f. culture; good manners; cultivation
kuluar [koo-loo-ar] m. lobby
kułak [koo-wak] m. fist; punch
kum [koom] m. godfather; crony
kumoterstwo [koo-mo-ters-tvo] n. favoritism; log rolling
kumulacja [koo-moo-lats-ya] f. accumulation; merger; fusion
kuna [koo-na] f. marten
kundel [koon-del] m. mongrel
kunszt [koonsht] m. art; skill

kunsztowny [koon-shtov-ni] adj. m. artistic; artful; ingenious
kupa [koo-pa] f. heep; pile; lot; excrement; assemblage; set
kupczyć [koop-chićh] v. bargain; trade; influence peddling; traffic (in one's influence)
kupić [koo-peećh] v. buy
kupiec [koo-pyets] m. shopkeeper; merchant; dealer
kupno [koop-no] n. purchase
kupon [koo-pon] m. coupon
kur [koor] m. cock; cock crow
kura [koo-ra] f. hen; hen bird
kuracja [koo-rats-ya] f. cure
kuratorium [koo-ra-tor-yum] n. board of trustees (of schools)
kurcz [koorch] m. cramp; shrinking; twitching
kurczę [koor-chan] n. chicken
kurczyć [koor-chićh] v. shrink
kurek [koo-rek] m. tap; cock
kurier [koor-yer] m. courier
kurnik [koor-ñeek] m. chicken house; hen house; hen roost poultry house; hen cote
kuropatwa [koo-ro-pat-va] f. partridge (game bird)
kurować [koo-ro-vaćh] v. heal; cure; treat for an illness
kurs [koors] m. course; rate; fare
kursować [koor-so-vaćh] v. circulate; ferry; run; ply
kurtka [koor-tka] f. jacket
kurtyna [koor-ti-na] f. curtain
kurwa [koor-va] f. whore (vulg.)
kurz [koosh] m. dust
kurza ślepota [koo-zha śhle-po-ta] night blindness
kusić [koo-śheećh] v. tempt
kustosz [koos-tosh] m. curator; conservator
kusy [koo-si] adj. m. short; scanty; skimpy; meager
kusza [koo-sha] f. crossbow
kuśnierz [koośh-ñesh] m. furrier; fur dealer
kuter [koo-ter] m. cutter
kutwa [koot-va] f. miser
kuty [koo-ti] adj. m. forged; shod; cunning; sly; shrewd
kuzyn [koo-zin] m. cousin
kuźnia [kooźh-ña] f. forge

kwadra [kvad-ra] f. quarter moon
kwadrans [kvad-rans] f. quarter
of an hour; fifteen minutes
kwadrat [kvad-rat] m. square
kwakać [kva-kaćh] v. quack
kwalifikacja [kva-lee-fee-kats-ya]
f. qualification; evaluation
kwalifikować [kva-lee-fee-ko-
-vaćh] v. qualify; class; appraise; describe; evaluate
kwapić się [kva-peećh shan]
v. be eager; be in a hurry
kwarantanna [kva-ran-tan-na] f.
quarantine; period of isolation
kwarc [kvarts] m. quartz
kwarta [kvar-ta] f. quart
kwartalny [kvar-tal-ni] adj. m.
quarterly; occurring quarterly
kwas [kvas] m. acid; pl. discord
kwasić [kva-sheećh] v. sour;
ferment; embitter; be idle
kwaskowaty [kvas-ko-va-ti] adj.
m. acrid; sourish; acidulous
kwasy [kva-si] pl. fusses; bad
-blood; ill humor; dissent
kwaśny [kvaśh-ni] adj. m. sour
kwatera [kva-te-ra] f. quarters;
lodging; living accommodation
kwaterka [kva-ter-ka] f. quarter
of a liter; quarter liter bottle
kwesta [kves-ta] f. collection
(for); passing the hat around
kwestia [kves-tya] f. question
kwestionariusz [kves-tyo-na-
-ryoosh] m. questionnaire
kwękać [kvan-kaćh] v. be for
ever sickly (ailing); complain
kwiaciarka [kvya-ćhar-ka] f.
florist; flower girl
kwiaciarnia [kvya-ćhar-ńa] f.
flower shop; florist's
kwiat [kvyat] m. flower
kwiczeć [kvee-chećh] v. make
a shrill cry; squeak; squeal
kwiczoł [kvee-chow] m. field-fare
(Turdus pilavis)
kwiecień [kvye-ćheń] m. April
kwiecisty [kvye-ćhees-ti] adj. m.
flowery; colorful; ornate
kwietnik [kvyet-ńeek] m. flower
-bed; carpet bed
kwik [kveek] m. squeal; squeak
kwit [kveet] m. receipt

kwitnąć [kveet-nownćh] v.
blossom; grow moldy; look
healthy; thrive; prosper
kwitować [kvee-to-vaćh] v.
give receipt; relinquish; forgo
kwoka [kvo-ka] f. sitting hen
kwota [kvo-ta] f. amount;
amount (of money); allocation
kynologiczny związek [ki-no-lo-
-geech-ni zvyown-zek] kennel
club; kennel association

L

labirynt [la-bee-rynt] m.
labyrinth; maze
laborant [la-bo-rant] m. lab.
technician. assistant chemist
laboratorium [la-bo-ra-tor-yoom]
n. laboratory; lab
lać [laćh] v. pour; shed; (spill)
lada [la-da] part. any; whatever;
the least; paltry; s. counter
lada kto [la-da kto] anybody
ladacznica [la-dach-ńee-tsa] f.
harlot; prostitute; strumpet
laik [la-eek] m. layman
lak [lak] m. sealing wax
lakier [la-ker] m. varnish
lakmus [lak-moos] m. litmus
lakoniczny [la-ko-ńeech-ni] adj.
m. terse; brief; curt; laconic
stating much in few words
lakować [la-ko-vaćh] v. seal
lalka [lal-ka] f. doll; puppet
laktoza [lak-to-za] f. lactose
lament [la-ment] m. lament
lamować !la-mo-vaćh] v. trim;
edge; border (with lace etc.)
lamówka [la-moov-ka] f. trim;
border; edge; trimming; piping
lampa [lam-pa] f. lamp
lampart [lam-part] m. leopard
lampas [lam-pas] m. side stripe
(on pants); lampas; stripe
lampion [lam-pyon] m. lampion
lamus [la-moos] m. storeroom
lanca [lan-tsa] f. lance; spear

lancet [lan-tset] m. lancet; fleam
landara [lan-da-ra] f. jalopy; old
  crate; rumble-tumble; jumbo
lanie [la-ńe] n. pouring; casting;
  beating; trashing; licking
lanolina [la-no-lee-na] f. lanolin;
  wool-fat (in ointments)
lansady [lan-sa-di] pl. prancing
  gait; skips; leaps; bounds
lansować [lan-so-vaćh] v. promote; launch; initiate; start
lapidarny [la-pee-dar-ni] adj. m.
  terse; concise; curt; crisp
lapis [la-pees] m. silver nitrate;
  lunar caustic
lapsus [lap-soos] m. lapse (slip)
laryngologia [la-rin-go-lo-gya] f.
  laryngology
las [las] m. wood; forest; thicket
lasek [la-sek] m. grove; copse
laska [las-ka] f. cane; stick
laskowy orzech [las-ko-vi o-
  -zhekh] m. hazelnut
lasować [la-so-vaćh] v. slake
lata [la-ta] pl. years
latać [la-taćh] v. fly; be running
latarka [la-tar-ka] f. flashlight;
  (electric) torch; small lamp
latarnia [la-tar-ńa] f. streetlight;
  lantern; beacon; lamppost
latarnia morska [la-tar-ńa mors-
  -ka] lighthouse; beacon
latarnik [la-tar-ńeek] m.
  lighthouse keeper; lamplighter
latawiec [la-ta-vyets] m. kite
lato [la-to] n. summer
latorośl [la-to-roshl] f. shoot;
  offspring; scion; spring; sprout
laubzega [law-bze-ga] f. fretsaw;
  jigsaw; scroll saw
laufer [law-fer] m. runner (foot-
  man); (chess) bishop
laury [law-ri] pl. laurels
laureat [law-re-at] m. laureate;
  prize-winner; prizeman
lawa [la-va] f. volcanic lava
lawenda [la-ven-da] f. lavender;
  lavender water
laweta [la-ve-ta] f. gun carriage;
  heavy artillery gun base
lawina [la-vee-na] f. avalanche;
  shover (of words, rock, etc.)
lawirować [la-vee-ro-vaćh] v.

veer; tack; intrigue; shift
lazaret [la-za-ret] m. field
  hospital (for infections)
lazur [la-zoor] m. azure; sky blue;
  the blue; blue pigment
ląd [lownd] m. 1.land;
  2. mainland; 3. continent
lądować [lown-do-vaćh] v.
  land; disembark; go ashore;
  alight; save oneself
lecieć [le-ćhećh] v. fly; run;
  hurry; wing; drift; drop; fall
leciutko [le-ćhoot-ko] adv.
  barely touching; very lightly
leciwy [le-ćhee-vi] adj. m. up in
  years; advanced in years;
  aged; elderly
lecz [lech] conj. but; however
leczenie [le-che-ńe] n. healing;
  cure; treatment
lecznica [lech-ńee-tsa] f.
  hospital; clinic; nursing home
leczyć [le-chićh] v. heal; treat;
  nurse; practice medicine
ledwie [led-vye] adv. hardly; no
  sooner; scarcely; barely; almost; nearly; only just
ledwo że nie [led-vo zhe ńe]
  adv. almost; nearly; hardly
legacja [le-gats-ya] f. legation;
  legacy; bequest
legalizować [le-ga-lee-zo-vaćh]
  v. legalize; certify; attest
legalny [le-gal-ni] adj. m. legal;
  lawful; allowed by law
legat [le-gat] m. bequest; papal
  muncio; anything bequeathed
legawiec [le-ga-vyets] m. pointer;
  setter (a large hunting dog)
legenda [le-gen-da] f. legend
legendarny [le-gen-dar-ni] adj. m.
  legendary; fabulous; storied
legia [leg-ya] f.legion; multitude
legion [leg-yon] m. legion
legitymacja [le-gee-ti-mats-ya] f.
  i-d card; identification papers;
  membership card etc.; warrant
legitymować się [le-gee-ti-mo-
  -vaćh śhan] v. prove one's
  identity; identify oneself
legnąć [leg-nownćh] v. fall in
  battle; perish; lie down
legowisko [le-go-vees-ko] n.

berth; bedding; encampment;
den; pallet; lair; encampment
legumina [le-**goo-mee**-na] f.
dessert; sweet dish; legumin
lej [ley] m. crater; funnel
lejce [ley-tse] pl. reins
lejek [le-yek] m. small funnel
lek [lek] m. medicine; drug
lekarski [le-**kars**-kee] adj. m.
medical; medicinal; officinal
lekarz [le-kash] m. physician
lekceważący [lek-tse-va-**zhown**-
-tsi] adj. m. disrespectful
lekceważenie [lek-tse-va-zhe-ńe]
n. disdain; disrespect; scorn
lekceważyc [lek-tse-**va**-zhich] v.
slight; scorn; neglect; disdain
lekcja [lek-tsya] f. lesson; class
lekki [lek-kee] adj. m. light; light
-hearted; graceful; slight
lekko [lek-ko] adv. easily; lightly
lekkoatletyka [lek-ko-at-le-ti-ka] f.
field & track sports; athletics
lekkomyślny [lek-ko-**myśhl**-ni]
adj. m. careless; thoughtless;
reckless; rash; fickle; hasty
lektura [lek-**too**-ra] f. reading
matter; reading list; reading
lemiesz [le-myesh] m. plough-
share; (shear) blade; vomer
lemoniada [le-mo-**ńa**-da] f.
lemonade; lemon squash
len [len] m. flax; linen
lenić się [le-ńeech śhan] v.
be idle; be lazy; shed hair
lenieć [le-ńeć] v. shed hair;
slough (skin); moult(feathers)
leninizm [le-ńee-ńeezm] m.
Leninism; Lenin's system
lenistwo [le-**ńeest**-vo] n.
laziness; idleness; sloth;
sluggishness
leniwy [le-**ńee**-vi] adj. m. lazy
lennik [len-ńeek] m. vassal
pledging fealty to overlord
lenno [len-no] n. fief; feud
leń [leń] m. lazy-bones; idler;
lazy bum; sluggard
lep [lep] m. glue; flypaper
lepianka [le-**pyan**-ka] f. adobe;
mud hut; mud cabin
lepić [le-**peeć**] v. stick; glue
lepiej [le-pyey] adv. better;

rather; (feel) better
lepki [lep-kee] adj. m. sticky
lepszy [lep-shi] adj. m. better;
improved; superior; preferable
lesbijka [les-**beey**-ka] f. lesbian;
homosexual women
lesisty [le-**śhees**-ti] adj. m.
wooded; woody; forested
leszcz [leshch] m. bream
leszczyna [lesh-chi-na] f.
hazelnut tree; hazel grove
leśnictwo [leśh-**ńeets**-tvo] n.
forestry; forest-range
leśniczówka [leśh-ńee-**choov**-
ka] f. ranger's house
leśniczy [leśh-ńee-chi] m.
ranger; forest-ranger; forester
leśnik [leśh-ńeek] m. forester
leśny [leśh-ni] adj. m. of forest;
of forestry; forest-
letarg [le-tark] m. lethargy
letni [let-ńee] adj. m. lukewarm;
half-hearted; summer
letnik [let-ńeek] m. vacationer
letnisko [let-ńees-ko] n. summer
resort; summer vacation spot
lew [lev] m. lion; lady's man
lewa [le-va] f. left (side)
lewar [le-var] m. lever; jack
lewatywa [le-va-ti-va] f. enema
lewica [le-**vee**-tsa] f. the left
(polit.); left-hand side
lewo [le-vo] adv. to the left
lewy [le-vi] adj. m. left; false
leźć [leźhć] v. crawl; creep-
along; climb; shuffle; lob
leżak [le-zhak] m. folding
(canvas) chair; deck-chair
leżeć [le-zheć] v. lie; (fit)
lędźwie [landźh-vye] pl. loins
lęgnąć [lang-nownch] v. hatch
lęk [lank] m. fear; anxiety; dread
lękać się [lan-kaćh śhan] v.
be afraid; dread; stand in awe
lękliwy [lank-lee-vi] adj. m. timid;
faint-hearted; apprehensive
lgnąć [lgnownch] v. adhere;
sink; stick; be partial; feel
attracted; get stuck; cling
libacja [lee-**bats**-ya] f. drinking
party; drinking bout
liberalny [lee-be-**ral**-ni] adj. m.
liberal; broad-minded

liberał [lee-be-raw] m. liberal

libertyn [lee-ber-tin] m. libertine; free thinker; promiscuous man

lice [lee-tse] n. face; cheek; the right side; evidence (of guilt)

licencja [lee-tsen-tsya] f. license (permission to practice)

licho [lee-kho] adv. poorly; badly; indifferently; scantily

licho [lee-kho] n. evil; devil

lichota [lee-kho-ta] f. rubbish

lichtarz [leekh-tash] m. candlestick; candelabra

lichwa [leekh-va] f. usury

lichwiarz [leekh-vyash] m. usurer; loan shark; money lender (at high interest rate)

lichy [lee-khi] adj. m. shoddy; shabby; poor; mean; rotten; petty; miserable; inferior; paltry; flimsy; trivial; rotten

lico [lee-tso] n. face; cheek; surface; front; outer part

licować [lee-tso-vaćh] v. fit for...; comport; veneer; face

licytacja [lee-tsi-tats-ya] f. auction; bidding; the bid

licytować [lee-tsi-to-vaćh] v. auction; bid; offer; call

liczba [leech-ba] f. number; figure; integer; group; class

liczbowy [leech-bo-vi] adj. m. numerical; numeral

licznik [leech-ńeek] m. counter; numerator; gas meter; electric meter; etc.; taximeter; register

liczny [leech-ni] adj. m. numerous; large; abundant; plentiful; frequent

liczyć [lee-chićh] v. count; reckon; compute; calculate

liczydło [lee-chid-wo] n. abacus; counter; register

liga [lee-ga] f. league; alliance

lik [leek] m. lot; countless

lignia [leeg-ńa] f. lignin

likier [lee-ker] m. liquor

likwidacja [leek-vee-dats-ya] f. liquidation; closing down

likwidować [leek-vee-do-vaćh] v. liquidate; do away with

lila [lee-la] adj. m. (color) pale -violet; lily-; lilac (blue)

lilia [leel-ya] f. lily; nenuphar

liliowy [leel-yo-vi] adj. m. lilac (color); lily-; purple

liliput [lee-lee-poot] m. little dwarf; midget; pygmy

limfa [leem-fa] f. lymph

limit [lee-meet] m. limit

limuzyna [lee-moo-zi-na] f. limousine; pilot's enclosure

lin [leen] m. tench (fish)

lina [lee-na] f. line; rope

lincz [leench] m. lynch

linczować [leen-cho-vaćh] v. lynch; kill by mob action

lingwista [leen-gvees-ta] m. linguist (specialist)

linia [leeń-ya] f. line; lane

linijka [lee-ńeey-ka] f. ruler

liniować [lee-ńo-vaćh] v. rule; line (paper); rule paper

liniowy okręt [lee-ńyo-vi ok-rant] liner (ship); battleship

linoleum [lee-no-le-oom] n. linoleum (floor covering)

linoskoczek [lee-no-sko-chek] m. tightrope artist; rope walker

linotyp [lee-no-tip] m. linotype (typesetting machine)

linowa kolejka [lee-no-va ko-ley-ka] cable car

lipa [lee-pa] f. 1. linden tree; 2. fake; cheat; fraud; trash

lipiec [lee-pyets] m. July

lira [lee-ra] f. lyre

liryczny [lee-rich-ni] adj. m. lyric (poetry etc.); lyrical (poet etc.)

liryka [lee-ri-ka] f. lyric poetry

lis [lees] m. fox; sly man

list [leest] m. letter; note

lista [lees-ta] f. list; roll; register; (attendance, time) record

listonosz [lees-to-nosh] m. postman

listopad [lees-to-pad] m. November

listownie [lees-tov-ńe] adv. by letter; by mail

listwa [lees-tva] f. trim

liszaj [lee-shay] m. herpes

liszka [leesh-ka] f. caterpillar; vixen; sly fox

liściasty [leeśh-ćhas-ti] adj. m. leafed; leafy; foliaceous

liść [leeśhćh] m. leaf; frond
litania [lee-ta-ńya] f. litany
litera [lee-te-ra] f. letter
literacki [lee-te-rats-kee] adj. m.
 literary; of letters
literat [lee-te-rat] m. writer
literatura [lee-te-ra-too-ra] f.
 literature; writings
litewski [lee-tevs-kee] adj. m.
 Lithuanian; Lithuanian
 language
litograf [lee-to-graf] m.
 lithographer
litościwy [lee-tośh-ćhee-vi]
 adj. m. merciful; pitying;
 compassionate
litość [lee-tośhćh] f. pity;
 mercy; compassion
litowac sie [lee-to-vaćh śhan]
 v. have pity; feel pity
litr [leetr] m. liter
liturgia [lee-toor-gya] f. liturgy;
 religious ritual
lity [lee-ti] adj. m. massive; solid;
 cast; pure-; pure stand (trees)
lizać [lee-zaćh] v. lick; taste
lizol [lee-zol] m. lysol
lizus [lee-zoos] m. bootlicker
lniany [lńa-ni] adj. m. linen;
 flaxen (thread); linseed (oil)
loch [lokh] m. dungeon; cellar
lodołamacz [lo-do-wa-mach] m.
 icebreaker; ice shield
lodowaty [lo-do-va-ti] adj. m. icy;
 ice-cold; chilling; frigid
lodowiec [lo-do-vyets] m. glacier;
 mass of ice and snow
lodowisko [lo-do-vees-ko] n. ice
 field; skating-rink; ice rink
lodownia [lo-dov-ńa] f. ice
 -chamber; ice-cellar; icy cold
lodowy [lo-do-vi] adj. m. of ice
lodówka [lo-doov-ka] f. refrigerator; ice box; ice chest
lody [lo-di] pl. ice cream
logarytm [lo-ga-ritm] m. loga-
 rithm; exponential expression
logiczny [lo-geech-ni] adj. m.
 logical; consistent; sound
logik [lo-geek] m. logician; expert
 in logic (cause and effect)
logika [lo-gee-ka] f. logic
lojalność [lo-yal-nośhćh] f.

loyalty; straightforwardness
lojalny [lo-yal-ni] adj. m. loyal;
 staunch; low-abiding; true
lok [lok] m. curl; coil
lokaj [lo-kay] m. lackey
lokal [lo-kal] m. premises
lokalizować [lo-ka-lee-zo-vaćh]
 v.localize; locate; range
lokalny [lo-kal-ni] adj. m. local;
 regional; of a place
lokata [lo-ka-ta] f. investment
lokator [lo-ka-tor] m. tenant
lokomocja [lo-ko-mots-ya] f.
 locomotion; communication
lokomotywa [lo-ko-mo-ti-va] f.
 train engine; locomotive
lokować [lo-ko-vaćh] v. place
lombard [lom-bard] m. pawnshop
lont [lont] m. fuse; slow-match
lornetka [lor-net-ka] f. field
 glasses; opera glasses
los [los] m. lot; fate; chance;
 lottery ticket; destiny; hazard
losować [lo-so-vaćh] v. draw
 lots; raffle; draw cuts
lot [lot] m. flight; speed
loteria [lo-ter-ya] f. lottery
lotnia [lot-ńa] f. hang glider
lotnictwo [lot-ńeets-tvo] n.
 aviation; aeronautics; air force
lotnik [lot-ńeek] m. aviator
lotnisko [lot-ńees-ko] n. airport;
 airfield; aerodrome
lotniskowiec [lot-ńees-ko-vyets]
 m. aircraft carrier
lotny [lot-ni] adj. m. bright;
 quick; swift; sharp; subtle
lotos [lo-tos] m. lotus
loża masońska [lo-zha ma-soń-
 -ska] shriners' lodge
lód [loot] m. ice; pl. ice cream
lśniący [lśhńown-tsi] adj. m.
 shining; bright; glossy; sleek
lśnić [lśhńeećh] v. glitter;
 shine; gleam; glimmer; shimmer; glisten; sparkle
lub [loop] conj. or; or else
luba [loo-ba] f. sweetheart
lubić [loo-beećh] v. like; be
 fond; enjoy; be partial
lubieżny [loo-byezh-ni] adj. m.
 lustful; voluptuous; lewd
lubość [loo-bośhćh] f. delight

lubować się [loo-bo-vaćh śhan] v. take delight; find pleasure; relish; be fond (of)

lud [loot] m. people; nation

ludność [lood-nośhćh] f. population (of a given territory, city, country, etc.)

ludny [lood-ni] adj. m. populous; teeming; crowded

ludobójstwo [loo-do-booys-tvo] n. genocide; killing of a nation

ludowy [loo-do-vi] adj. m. populist; popular; country

ludożerca [loo-do-zher-tsa] m. cannibal; man-eater

ludzie [loo-dźhe] pl. people

ludzkość [loots-kośhćh] f. mankind; humaneness; humanity; human feelings; kindness

lufa [loo-fa] f. gunbarrel

luk [look] m. hatch; skylight

luka [loo-ka] f. gap; blank; break

lukier [loo-ker] m. sugar icing; frosting (on a cake)

lukratywny [loo-kra-tiv-ni] adj. m. lucrative; profitable

luksus [look-soos] m. luxury

lunatyk [loo-na-tik] m. 1. sleepwalker; 2. loony

lunąć [loo-nownćh] v. rain in torrents; slap; lash down in sheets; whack; fail; flunk

luneta [loo-ne-ta] field-glass; spy -glass; telescope; lunette

lupa [loo-pa] f.magnifying glass; jeweler's glass (loop); lens

lusterko [loos-ter-ko] n. hand glass; rear-view mirror (in a car); pocket looking-glass

lustro [loos-tro] n. mirror

lustrować [loo-stro-vaćh] v. inspect; review; check; audit

lut [loot] m. solder (brazing)

luteranin [loo-te-ra-ńeen] m. Lutheran (church member)

lutnia [loot-ńa] f. flute

lutować [loo-to-vaćh] v. solder

luty [loo-ti] m. February

luty [loo-ti] adj. m. bleak; grim; severe; m. February

luz [loos] m. clearance; play

luzak [loo-zak] m. loose; led horse; (replacement) horse

luzować [loo-zo-vaćh] v. replace; relieve; loosen; slacken; relay; ease off

luźny [looźh-ni] adj. m. loose

lwi [lvee] adj. m. lion's

lżej [lzhey] adv. lighter; easier; with less weight

lżenie [lzhe-ńe] n. abuse; insults; vituperation

lżyć [lzhićh] v. abuse; insult

Ł

łabędź [wa-bandźh] m. swan

łach [wakh] m. rang; clout

łacha [wa-kha] f. sandbank

łachman [wakh-man] m. rag

łachudra [wa-khood-ra] m. scoundrel; ragamuffin

łaciarz [wa-ćhash] m. patcher

łaciaty [wa-ćha-ti] adj. m. in patches; pinto (horse)

łacina [wa-ćhee-na] f. Latin

łaciński [wa-ćheeń-skee] adj. m. Latin; of Latin

ład [wad] m. order; orderliness

ładnie [wad-ńe] adv. nicely

ładnieć [wad-ńećh] v. grow pretty; grow (look) prettier

ładny [wad-ńi] adj. m. nice

ładować [wa-do-vaćh] v. load; charge(a battery); cram; fill

ładownica [wa-dov-ńee-tsa] f. cartridge pouch; charger

ładunek [wa-doo-nek] m. load; cargo; (electr.) charge; shipload; burden; freight; bulk

łagodność [wa-god-nośhćh] f. gentleness; kindliness; suavity

łagodny [wa-god-ni] adj. m. gentle; mild; soft; meek; easy

łagodzący [wa-go-dzown-tsi] adj. m. alleviating; extenuating

łagodzić [wa-go-dźheećh] v. soothe; relieve; alleviate; attenuate; mitigate; smooth

łajać [wa-yaćh] v. scold; chide

łajdactwo [way-dats-tvo] n.

łajdak

mean trick; scoundrels; rabble
łajdak [**way**-dak] m. scoundrel;
rascal; villain; rogue; wretch
łajno [**way**-no] n. dung; shit
łaknąć [**wak**-n<u>own</u>ćh] v. hunger for; thirst for; crave for
łakocie [wa-ko-ćhe] pl. deli-
-cacies; sweets; tidbits; candy
łakomić się [wa-**ko**-meećh
** śhan**] v. covet; lust; be temp-
ted (by); be greedy (of)
łakomy [wa-ko-mi] adj. m.
greedy; covetous; avid
łakomstwo [wa-**koms**-tvo] n.
greed; gluttony; greediness
łamać [**wa**-maćh] v. break;
crush; quarry; shatter; crack;
snap; smash; fracture (a bone)
łamigłówka [wa-mee-gwoov-ka]
f. riddle; puzzle; jigsaw puzzle
łamistrajk [wa-**mee**-strayk] m.
scab; strikebreaker
łamliwy [wam-lee-vi] adj. m.
fragile; frail; brittle; breakable
łan [wan] m. stand of wheat
łania [**wa**-ńa] f. hind; doe
łańcuch [**wań**-tsookh] m. chain;
range; series; train; succession
łańcuchowa reakcja [wań-tsoo-
-kho-va re-ak-tsya] chain
reaction (of nuclear fission)
łapa [wa-pa] f. paw; claw; arm
łapać [wa-paćh] v. catch; get
hold (of); snatch; grasp; seize
łapanka [wa-pan-ka] f. roundup
łapcie [wap-ćhe] pl. bast
sandals; moccasins
łapczywość [wap-chi-vośhćh]
f. greed; greediness; avidity
łapczywy [wap-chi-vi] adj. m.
greedy; money-grubbing; avid
łapka [wap-ka] f. (mouse) trap
łapówka [wa-poov-ka] f. bribe
łapserdak [wap-**ser**-dak] m.
rogue; ragamuffin; scoundrel
łasica [wa-**śhee**-tsa] f. weasel
łasić się [wa-śheećh **śhan**] v.
fawn; fawn on sb.; toady
łaska [**was**-ka] f. grace;
clemency; favor; generosity;
mercy; condescension; pity
łaskawy [was-ka-vi] adj. m.
gracious; kind; generous

łaskotać [wa-**sko**-taćh] v.
tickle; titillate; delight
łaskotliwy [wa-sko-**tlee**-vi]
adj. m. ticklish; titillating
łasy [**wa**-si] adj. m. greedy
łaszczyć się [**wash**-chićh
śhan] v. covet; lust
łata [**wa**-ta] f. patch
łatać [**wa**-taćh] v. patch up
łatanina [wa-ta-**ńee**-na] f. patch
work; mending; bungled work
łatwo [**wat**-vo] adv. easily
łatwopalny [wa-tvo-**pal**-ni]
adj. m. (easily) inflammable
łatwość [**wat**-vośhćh] n.
easy; facility; aptitude; fluency
łatwowierny [wa-tvo-**vyer**-ni] adj.
m. credulous; gullible
łatwy [**wat**-vi] adj. m. easy;
simple; effortless; light
ława [**wa**-va] f. bench; footing
ławica [wa-**vee**-tsa] f. (fish)
shoal; sandbank; shelf; layer
ławka [**wav**-ka] f. pew; bench
ławnik [**wav**-ńeek] m. juror;
alderman; assessor
łazić [**wa**-źheećh] v. crawl;
loiter; slouch about; creep
łazienka [wa-**źhen**-ka] f.
bathroom; toilet; bath
łazik [wa-źheek] m. tramp; jeep
łaźnia [**waźh**-ńa] f. bath
łażący [wa-zh<u>own</u>-tsi] adj. m.
dragging; crawling; scansorial
łączący [w<u>own</u>-ch<u>own</u>-tsi] adj.
m. uniting; joining; connecting
łącznica [w<u>own</u>-**chńee**-tsa] f.
junction; (phone) switchboard
łącznie [**wownch**-ńe] adv. together; including; inclusive of;
along with; jointly; conjointly
łącznik [**wownch**-ńeek] m.
hyphen; liaison man; link; tie;
bond; connecting rod; fastener
łączność [**wownch**-nośhćh] f.
contact; communication; unity; signal service; connection;
communion; liaison
łączny [**wownch**-ni] adj. m. joint;
combined; total; global
łączyć [**wown**-chićh] v. join;
unite; merge; link; bind; weld
łąka [**wown**-ka] f. meadow

łeb [wep] m. head; pate; top
łechtać [wekh-tać] v. tickle;
flatter; titillate; lure
łęk [wank] m. saddlebow;
syncline; arch; bow; pommel
łgać [wgać] v. lie; brag; boast
łgarstwo [wgar-stvo] n. lie
łgarz [wgash] liar; braggart
łkać [wkać] v. sob; weep
łobuz [wo-boos] m. rogue;
rascal; scamp; scoundrel
łodyga [wo-di-ga] f. stem
łoić [wo-eeć] v. tallow; beat
up; wallop; curry
łokieć [wo-kyeć] m. elbow
łom [wom] m. crowbar; scrap;
junk; rubble; block chocolate
łomot [wo-mot] m. crash; crack
łono [wo-no] n. lap; bosom;
womb; pubes
łopata [wo-pa-ta] f. spade
łopot [wo-pot] m. (sail) flutter
łoskot [wos-kot] m. clatter;
bang; din; rumble; racket;
boom; bluster (of a storm)
łosoś [wo-sośh] m. salmon
łoś [wośh] m. elk; moose
łotewski [wo-tev-skee] adj. m.
Latvian; Latvian language
łotr [wotr] m. scoundrel; knave;
rascal; rogue; thief
łowczy [wov-chi] adj. m.
hunting; huntsman's; hunter's
łowić [wo-veeć] v. trap; fish;
catch (sounds); hunt; chase
łowiectwo [wo-vyets-tvo] n.
hunting; game shooting
łowy [wo-vi] pl. hunt; chase
łozina [wo-żhee-na] f. wicker;
sallow; osier; osier-bed
łoże [wo-zhe] n. bed; cradle
łożyć [wo-zhić] v. spend
łożyska [wo-zhis-ko] n. (river)
bed; (ball) bearing
łódka [wood-ka] f. small boat
łódź [woodźh] f. boat; craft
łój [wooy] m. tallow; suet
łów [woov] m. hunt; chase
łóżeczko [woo-zhech-ko] n.
(child's) bed; small bed
łóżko [woozh-ko] n. bed; bunk
łubin [woo-been] m. lupin
łucznik [wooch-ńeek] m. archer

łuczywo [woo-chi-vo] n. resinous
kindling; resinous chips
łudzący [woo-dzown-tsi] adj. m.
delusive; deceptive; illusive
łudzić [woo-dźheeć] v. delude; deceive; give false hope;
dangle hopes before someone
ług [woog] m. lye
ługować [woo-go-vać] v.
leach; lixiviate
łuk [wook] m. bow; arch; bent;
curve; vault; flying buttress
łuna [woo-na] f. glow (of light)
łup [woop] m. booty; spoils;
plunder; loot; prey; quarry
łupać [woo-pać] v. cleave;
split; ache; give shooting pain
łupek [woo-pek] m. slate; shale
łupić [woo-peeć] v. plunder
łupież [woo-pyesh] m. dandruff
łupieżca [woo-pyezh-tsa] m.
plunderer; looter; pillager
łupina [woo-pee-na] f. husk;
shell; peel; skin; hull; rind
łuska [woos-ka] f. scale; husk;
shell; pod; flake; rind
łuskać [woos-kać] v. scale;
husk; peel; pod; hull (rice)
łuszczyć [woosh-chić] v. peel;
pare; flake off; shell off
łuza [woo-za] f. billiard pocket
łydka [wit-ka] f. calf (leg-shank)
łyk [wik] m. gulp; sip; draft
łykać [wi-kać] v. swallow;
gulp; sip; bolt; gorge; drink
łyko [wi-ko] n. bast; phloem
łykowaty [wi-ko-va-ti] adj. m.
wiry; tough; fibrous
łypać [wi-pać] v. blink; wink
łysek [wi-sek] m. (bold head)
bold; bold-faced animal
łysieć [wi-śheć] v. become
bold; grow bold; lose hair
łysina [wi-śhee-na] f. pate
łyskać [wis-kać] v. flash
łysy [wi-si] adj. m. bold
łyżeczka [wi-zhech-ka] f.
teaspoon; dessert spoon;
curette; small spoonful
łyżka [wizh-ka] f. spoon;
spoonful; tablespoonful
łyżwa [wizh-va] f. skate
łyżwiarz [wizh-vyash] m. skater

łyżwowy [wizh-vo-vi] adj. of
skates; of a sledge runner
łza [wza] f. tear
łzawy [wza-vi] adj. m. tearful
łzowy kanał [wzo-vi ka-naw] tear
canal; tear duct

M

maca [ma-tsa] f. matzos
macać [ma-tsaćh] v. feel; try;
grope; finger; probe; cuddle
machać [ma-khaćh] v. wave;
whisk; swing; swish; lash;
wag; run; flap; brandish
macher [ma-kher] m. trickster
machina [ma-khee-na] f. (large)
machine; bureaucratic machine
machinacja [ma-khee-na-tsya] f.
machination; dodge; intrigue
machlojka [ma-khloy-ka] f.
swindle; defraudation
macica [ma-ćhee-tsa] f. uterus;
womb; screw nut; tap root
macierz [ma-ćhesh] f. mother
country; matrix; mother
macierzanka [ma-ćhe-zhan-ka] f.
thyme; wild thyme; mint
macierzyński [ma-ćhe-zhiń-
-skee] adj. m. maternal; ma-
ther's; motherly; like a mother
macierzyństwo [ma-ćhe-zhiń-
-stvo] n. maternity; motherhood; parenthood
macierzysty [ma-ćhe-zhi-sti] adj.
m. maternal; (parental)
maciora [ma-ćho-ra] f. sow
macka [mats-ka] f. tentacle;
feeler; antenna; horn; palp
macocha [ma-tso-kha] f.
stepmother; not as good as
(treating worse than) mother
maczać [ma-chaćh] v. dip in a
liquid; dip; soak
maczuga [ma-choo-ga] f. bat;
club; bludgeon; cudgel
magazyn [ma-ga-zin] m. store;
warehouse; repository; store

magazynier [ma-ga-zi-ńer] m.
warehouseman; storekeeper
magia [ma-gya] f. sorcery
magiczny [ma-geech-ni] adj. m.
magic; conjuring tricks
magister [ma-gees-ter] m. master
(diploma); chemist; apothecary
magisterium [ma-gees-ter-yum]
n. (university) master's degree
magistrat [ma-gees-trat] m. city
hall; municipal authorities
maglować [ma-glo-vaćh] v.
mangle; calender; bother;
crush; tire with; harp on
magnat [mag-nat] m. magnate
magnes [mag-nes] m. magnet
magnetofon [mag-ne-to-fon] m.
tape-recorder
magnetyczny [mag-ne-tich-ni]
adj. m. magnetic
magnetyzm [mag-ne-tizm] m.
magnetism; personal charm
magnez [mag-nes] m. mag-
nesium (metallic element)
magnezja [mag-nez-ya] f.
magnesia; magnesium
magnolia [mag-no-lya] f.
magnolia (bot. Magnolia)
mahometanin [ma-kho-me-ta-
-ńeen] m. Mohammedan;
Moslem; follower of Islam
mahoń [ma-khoń] m. mahogany
maić [ma-eećh] v. decorate
with green leaves (verdure)
maj [may] m. May; verdure
majaczyć [ma-ya-chićh] v.
rave; loom; be delirious
majątek [ma-yown-tek] m.
fortune; estate; property;
wealth; one's possessions
majdan [may-dan] m. parade
ground; open space; clearing;
personal junk; traps; chattels
majeranek [ma-ye-ra-nek] m.
marjoram; fragrant plant of
mint family used for cooking
majestat [ma-ye-stat] m.
majesty; kingship; stateliness
majętność [ma-yant-noshćh]
f. wealth; fortune; property
majętny [ma-yant-ni] adj. m. well
to do; wealthy; affluent; rich
majonez [ma-yo-nes] m.

yonnaise; egg yoke dressing
major [ma-yor] m. major
majówka [ma-joov-ka] f.
  Mayouting; picnic; junket
majster [may-ster] m. qualified
  craftsman; boss; master (carpenter; baker, etc.); foreman
majstersztyk [may-ster-shtik] m.
  masterpiece; greatest work
majstrować [may-stro-vaćh] v.
  tinker; make (an object)
majtek [may-tek] m. deck hand
majtki [may-tkee] pl. panties
mak [mak] m. poppy seed
makaron [ma-ka-ron] m. macaroni; pasta in tubular form
makata [ma-ka-ta] f. tapestry
makler [mak-ler] m. broker
makolągwa [ma-ko-lowng-va] f.
  linnet; young lass; lassie
makrela [ma-kre-la] f. mackerel
maksyma [mak-si-ma] f. axiom;
  maxim; adage; rule of conduct
maksymalny [mak-si-mal-ni] adj.
  m. maximum; top-:peak-;most-
makulatura [ma-koo-la-too-ra] f.
  waste-paper; spoilage; rubbish
makuch [ma-kookh] m. oilcake
malaria [ma-lar-ya] f. malaria
malarstwo [ma-lar-stvo] n.
  painting (art); house painting
malarz [ma-lash] m. painter
malec [ma-lets] m. youngster
maleć [ma-lećh] v. shrink;
  dwindle; grow smaller; lessen
maleńki [ma-leń-kee] adj. m.
  very small; tiny; insignificant
maleństwo [ma-leń-stvo] n. tiny
  thing; little one; little mite
malina [ma-lee-na] f. raspberry
malować [ma-lo-vaćh] v. paint;
  stain; color; make up; depict
malowidło [ma-lo-vid-wo] n.
  painting; picture (painted)
malowniczy [ma-lov-ńee-chi]
  adj. m. picturesque; vivid
maltretować [mal-tre-to-vaćh]
  v. abuse; mistreat; ill treat
malwersacja [mal-ver-sats-ya] f.
  embezzlement; peculation
mało [ma-wo] adv. little; few;
  seldom; lack; not enough
małoduszny [ma-wo-doosh-ni]

adj. m. small-minded; narrow-
  minded; cheap; fainthearted
małoletni [ma-wo-let-ńee]
  adj. m. minor; under age;
  juvenile; immature; young
małomówny [ma-wo-moov-ni]
  adj. m. reticent; laconic;
  taciturn; uncommunicative
małostkowy [ma-wo-stko-vi] adj.
  m. fussy; mean; small-minded
małpa [maw-pa] f. ape; monkey
małpować [maw-po-vaćh] v.
  ape; imitate poorly; trifle
mały [ma-wi] adj. m. little; small
  size; low; modest; slight
małżeński [maw-zheń-skee]
  adj. m. matrimonial; conjugal
małżeństwo [maw-zheń-stvo]
  n. married couple; wedlock
małżonek [maw-zho-nek] m.
  husband; spouse; consort;
  mate; bedfellow; partner
małżonka [maw-zhon-ka] f. wife
mama [ma-ma] f. mamma; ma-
  ther; mum; mummy; mama
mamałyga [ma-ma-wi-ga] f.
  maize; gruel; hominy
mamić [ma-meećh] v. deceive;
  delude; beguile; lure; tempt
mamidło [ma-mee-dwo] n.
  illusion; delusion; lure; seduction; enticement; temptation
mamona [ma-mo-na] f. mammon
mamlać [mam-laćh] v. mumble
mamrotać [mam-ro-taćh] v.
  mutter; mumble; gibber
mamut [ma-moot] m. mammoth
manatki [ma-nat-kee] pl. personal
  belongings; traps; chattels
mandaryn [man-da-rin] m.
  mandarin; Chinese dignitary
mandat [man-dat] m. mandate;
  traffic ticket; fine
mandolina [man-do-lee-na] f.
  mandolin with 8 to 10 strings
manekin [ma-ne-keen] m. manne-
  quin; model of human body
manewr [ma-nevr] m. maneuver
manewrować [ma-ne-vro-vaćh]
  v. manoeuver; steer; handle;
  switch; shunt; plot; intrigue
maneż [ma-nesh] m. riding
  school; horse-driven thrasher

mangan [man-gan] m.
  manganese (used in alloys)
mania [ma-ńya] f. mania; fad
maniak [ma-ńyak] m. maniac;
  crank; widely insane person
manicure [ma-ńee-keer] m.
  manicure; trimming, polishing
  doing, etc. one's fingernails
manić [ma-ńeećh] v. deceive;
  tempt; delude; beguile; lure
maniera [ma-ńe-ra] f. manner
manierka [ma-ńer-ka] f. canteen
manifest [ma-ńee-fest] m.
  manifesto; a public declaration
manifestacja [ma-ńee-fes-ta-
  -tsya] f. manifestation; demonstration; ostentatious display
manifestować [ma-ńee-fes-to-
  -vaćh] v. demonstrate; stage
  a manifestation; display
manipulacja [ma-ńee-poo-lats-
  -ya] f. manipulation; handling
manipulować [ma-ńee-poo-lo-
  -vaćh] v. manipulate; handle;
  tinker; manage artfully
mankiet [man-ket] m. cuff; turn
  -up; wristband; ruffle
mankament [man-ka-ment] m.
  defect; shortcoming; fault
manko [man-ko] n. (acc.)
  shortage; allowance to cashier
  for errors; cash shortage
manna [man-na] f. cream of
  wheat; a godsend manna
manometr [ma-no-metr] m.
  pressure gauge; steam gauge
manowce [ma-nov-tse] pl. mis-
  guided direction; road less
  area; wrong way
manufaktura [ma-noo-fak-too-ra]
  f. fabric; manufacture; shop
manuskrypt [ma-noo-skript] m.
  manuscript; (hand or typewritten) document, book, etc.
mańkuctwo [mań-koots-tvo] n.
  left-handedness
mapa [ma-pa] f. map; chart
mara [ma-ra] f. ghost; apparition;
  nightmare; dream; vision
marazm [ma-razm] m. torpor;
  sluggishness; stagnation
marchew [mar-khev] f. carrot
marcepan [mar-tse-pan] m.

marzipan; marchpane
margaryna [mar-ga-ri-na] f.
  margarine; marge (slang)
margines [mar-gee-nes] m.
  margin; edge; border; minor
  incidental, secondary) thing
mariaż [mar-yash] m. marriage
marionetka [ma-ryo-net-ka] f.
  puppet; dummy; figurehead
marka [mar-ka] f. mark; brand;
  stamp; trade mark; reputation
markotno [mar-kot-no] adv. sad;
  in low spirits; in bad humor;
  gloomily; sullenly; moodily
markotny [mar-kot-ni] adj. m.
  peevish; moody; sullen; sad
marksistowski [mar-kśhee-
  -stovs-kee] adj. m. Marxist
  (socialist or communis)
marksizm [mar-kśheezm] m.
  Marxism; Marxist believes
marmolada [mar-mo-la-da] f.
  marmalade; jam; shambles
marmur [mar-moor] m. marble
marnieć [mar-ńećh] v. deteriorate; waste; decline; perish;
  languish; fade; droop; pine
marność [mar-nośhćh] f.
  futility; flimsiness; vanity
marnotrawny [mar-no-trav-ni]
  adj. m. wasteful; prodigal
marnować [mar-no-vaćh] v. run
  to waste; squander; spoil
marny [mar-ni] adj. m. poor;
  meager; sorry; of no value
marsz [marsh] m. march; walk
marsz! [marsh] excl.: (command)
  forward march! split! get out!
  off you go! out! double!
marszałek [mar-sha-wek] m.
  marshal; Polish Seym speaker
marszczyć [mar-shchićh] v.
  wrinkle; frown; crease; ripple
marszruta [mar-shroo-ta] f. route;
  itinerary; a record of a journey
martwica [mar-tvee-tsa] f.
  necrosis; sinter; travertine
martwić [mar-tveećh] v. distress; grieve; vex; worry; sadden; afflict; (cause) trouble
martwy [mar-tvi] adj. m. dead
martyr [mar-tir] m. martyr
maruder [ma-roo-der] m.

marauder; straggler; loiterer
marudzić [ma-roo-dźheećh] v.
loiter; grumble; lag behind
mary [ma-ri] pl. mar; bier
marynarka [ma-ri-nar-ka] f.
jacket; sports coat; navy
marynarz [ma-ri-nash] m.
mariner; sailor; seaman
marynata [ma-ry-na-ta] f. pickle
marynować [ma-ri-no-vaćh] v.
pickle; marinade; side-track
marzec [ma-zhets] m. March
marzenie [ma-zhe-ńe] n. dream;
reverie; day dream; pensiveness; daydreaming
marznąć [marz-nownćh] v. be
frozen; freeze; freeze to death
marzyciel [ma-zhi-ćhel] m.
dreamer; fantast; visionary
marzyć [ma-zhićh] v. dream
masa [ma-sa] f. bulk; mass
masa perłowa [ma-sa per-wo-va]
f. mother of pearl
masakra [ma-sak-ra] f. massacre;
carnage; wholesale butchery
masakrować [ma-sa-kro-vaćh]
v. massacre; slaughter; butcher; mangle (a text); hack
masarnia [ma-sar-ńa] f. pork
-meat (pork butcher's) shop
masarz [ma-sash] m.
pork-butcher; pork meat
worker;·pork sausage maker
masaż [ma-sash] m. massage
masażysta [ma-sa-zhis-ta] m.
masseur; rubber
maselniczka [ma-sel-ńeech-ka] f.
butter-dish; small churn
maska [mas-ka] f. mask; hood
maskować [mas-ko-vaćh] v.
disguise; mask; hide; screen
masło [mas-wo] n. butter
masoński [ma-soń-skee] adj. m.
masonic; freemason's
masować [ma-so-vaćh] v. give
a massage to; massage; rub
masowo [ma-so-vo] adv. wholesale; in a mass; in masses; in
great numbers (quantities)
masywność [ma-siv-nośhćh]
f. massiveness; solidity
masywny [ma-siv-ni] adj. m.
massive; solid; bulky; massy

maszerować [ma-she-ro-vaćh]
v. march; march on; keep
marching; advance steadily
maszkara [mash-ka-ra] f.
monster; scarecrow; eyesore
maszt [masht] m. mast; flagstaff
maszyna [ma-shi-na] f. machine
maszynka do golenia [ma-shin-
-ka do go-le-ńa] f. safety
razor; shaver
maszyneria [ma-shi-ner-ya] f.
machinery; mechanism
maszynista [ma-shi-ńees-ta] m.
railroad engineer; machinist
maszynistka [ma-shi-ńeest-ka] f.
typewriter typist; typist
maszynopis [ma-shi-no-pees] m.
typescript; typewritten copy
maść [maśhćh] f. ointment;
horse color; unguent; salve
maślanka [ma-śhlan-ka] f.
buttermilk; sour liquid; (a
product of churning butter)
mat [mat] m. flat color;
checkmate (one's opponent)
mata [ma-ta] f. mat; matting
matactwo [ma-tats-tvo] n. legal
trickery; fraudulence; deceit
matczyny [mat-chi-ni] adj. m.
maternal (love etc.); mother's
matematyczny [ma-te-ma-tich-ni]
adj. m. mathematical
matematyk [ma-te-ma-tik] m.
mathematician (also student)
matematyka [ma-te-ma-ti-ka] f.
mathematics; science of numbers, quantities, forms, etc.
materac [ma-te-rats] m. mattress
materia [ma-ter-ya] f. matter;
stuff; subject; point; puss;
cloth; any specified substance
materialista [ma-te-rya-lees-ta]
m. materialist; money grabber
materialistyczny [ma-te-rya-lee-
-stich-ni] adj. m. materialistic
(opposite to spiritual)
materiał [ma-te-ryaw] m.
material; substance; stuff;
cloth; fabric; assignment
matka [mat-ka] f. mother
matnia [mat-ńa] f. snare; trap
matowy [ma-to-vi] adj. m. flat
color; dull; lackluster

matrona [mat-ro-na] f. matron
matryca [mat-ri-tsa] f. matrix;
die; type; mold; stencil; swage
matrykuła [mat-ri-koo-wa] f.
register of university students
matrymonialny [ma-tri-mo-ńyal-
-ni] adj. m. matrimonial (a-
gency, office); marital
matura [ma-too-ra] f. final
high school examination
mauretański [maw-re-tań-skee]
adj. m. Moorish; of Moors
mazać [ma-zać] v. smear; defile; scribble; blot; stain; daub
mazgaj [maz-gay] m. crybaby
Mazur [ma-zoor] m. mazurka
rhythm; Mazurian
maź [maźh] f. grease; tallow
mącić [mown-ćheećh] v. blur;
ruffle; muddy; cloud; confuse
mączka [mownch-ka] f. fine
flour; powder; dust; starch
mądrość [mownd-rośhćh] f.
wisdom; intelligence; sagacity
mądry [mownd-ri] adj. m. sage
mąka [mown-ka] f. flour; meal
mąż [mownsh] m. husband; man
mąż stanu [mownsh sta-noo]
statesman; outstanding politician; outstanding diplomat
mdleć [mdlećh] v. faint; lose
consciousness; fail; weaken;
go off into a faint; droop; flag
mdlić [mdleećh] v. nauseate
mdłość [mdwośhćh] f. nau-
sea; fuzziness; indistinctness
mdło [mdwo] adv. dull;
nauseating; sickening; faintly
meble [meb-le] pl. furniture
macenas [me-tse-nas] m. lawyer
mech [mekh] m. moss; down
mechaniczny [me-kha-ńeech-ni]
adj. m. mechanical; automatic
mechanik [me-kha-ńeek] m.
mechanic; Jack of all trades
mechanika [me-kha-ńee-ka] f.
mechanics; (practical, political,
strategic etc.) mechanics
mechanizm [me-kha-ńeezm] m.
mechanism; gear; device
mecz [mech] m. sport match
meczet [me-chet] m. mosque
medal [me-dal] m. medal

mediacja [me-dya-tsya] f.
mediation; settling of differences between persons (nations)
meduza [me-doo-za] f. jellyfish
medycyna [me-di-tsi-na] f.
medicine; art of healing
medyczny [me-dich-ni] adj. m.
medical; medicinal
medyk [me-dik] m. medical
student; medic (physician)
medykament [me-di-ka-ment] m.
drug; medicine (hist. expr.)
medytacja [me-di-tats-ya] f.
meditation; thinking deeply
megafon [me-ga-fon] m.
loudspeaker; megaphone
megaloman [me-ga-lo-man] m.
megalomaniac; self appointed
boss; self-important person
melancholia [me-lan-kho-lya] f.
melancholy; the blues; dejection; despondency; low spirits
melasa [me-la-sa] f. molasses
meldować [mel-do-vaćh] v.
report; register; announce; inform; notify; give an account
meldunek [mel-doo-nek] m.
report; announcement; notification; registration
melioracja [me-lyo-rats-ya] f.
reclamation of land; drainage
melodia [me-lod-ya] f. melody
meloman [me-lo-man] m. music
lover; music enthusiast
melon [me-lon] m. melon
melonik [me-lo-ńeek] m. bowler
hat; derby; bowler; billycock
memoriał [me-mo-ryaw] m. memorial; minutes' journal;
written communication
menażeria [me-na-zher-ya] f.
menagerie; animal collection
menażka [me-nazh-ka] f. mess
kit; canteen; mess-tin; dixie
mennica [men-ńee-tsa] f. mint
menstruacja [men-stroo-ats-ya] f.
menstruation; menses; period
mentalność [men-tal-nośhćh]
f. mentality; way of thinking
menu [me-noo] m. menu; bill of
fare; list of foods served
mer [mer] m. mayor
merdać [mer-daćh] v. wag tail

merytoryczny [me-ri-to-**rich**-ni]
adj. m. of substance; essential
meszek [**me**-shek] m. down; nap
meta [**me**-ta] f. goal; hang-out
metafizyka [me-ta-**fee**-zi-ka] f.
metaphysics (speculative phil.)
metal [**me**-tal] m. metal
metalowy [me-ta-**lo**-vi] adj. m.
metallic (luster, sound etc.)
metalurgia [me-ta-**loor**-gya] f.
metallurgy; science of metals
metamorfoza [me-ta-mor-**fo**-za] f.
metamorphosis; a change
inform etc.; metamorphism
meteor [me-**te**-or] m. meteor
meteorologia [me-te-o-ro-**lo**-gya]
f. meteorology (weather etc.)
metoda [me-**to**-da] f. method;
system of doing or handling
metodyczny [me-to-**dich**-ni] adj.
m. methodical; systematic
metr [metr] m. meter; 39.97in.
metro [**met**-ro] n. subway
metropolia [me-tro-**pol**-ya] f.
metropolis; main large city
metryczny [met-**rich**-ni] adj. m.
metric; of metrical system
metryka [**met**-ri-ka] f. birth
-certificate; the public register
metys [**me**-tys] m. metis
mewa [**me**-va] f. sea-gull
mezalians [me-**za**-lyans] m.
misalliance; improper alliance
mezanin [me-**za**-ńeen] m. mez-
zanine (between two stories)
męczarnia [man-**char**-ńa] f.
torture; torment; anguish; agony; tribulation; anxiety
męczennik [man-**chen**-ńeek] m.
martyr; sufferer for faith etc.
męczyć [man-**chićh**] v. bother;
torment; oppress; tire; exhaust; trouble; torture; agonize
mędrek [man-drek] m. smart
aleck; know-it-all; wiseacre
mędrzec [mand-zhets] m. sage
męka [man-ka] f. fatigue; torment; pain; distress; nuisance;
suffering; anguish; vexation
męski [man-skee] adj. m. masculine; manly; man's; virile;
male; gentleman's; manlike
męskość [mans-kośhćh] f.

manhood; virility; manliness
męstwo [mans-tvo] n. bravery;
courage; prowess; fortitude
mętny [mant-ni] adj. m. turbid;
dull; dim; blurred; vague; fishy
męty [man-ti] pl. dregs; scum of
society; underworld; raffle
mężatka [man-zhat-ka] f. married woman; femme covert
mężczyzna [manzh-chiz-na] m.
man (on toilets: Gentleman)
mężnieć [manzh-ńećh] v.
grow manly; muster courage;
take heart; grow into a man
mężny [manzh-ni] adj. m. brave
mglisty [mglees-ti] adj. m. foggy;
misty; dim; nebulous; vague
mgła [mgwa] f. fog; mist; cloud
mgławica [mgwa-**vee**-tsa] f.
nebula; cloud; hazy idea; haze
mgnienie [mgńe-ńe] n. blink;
twinkle; wink; flash; jiffy; trice
miał [myaw] m. dust; powder
miałki [myaw-kee] adj. m. fine
(sugar; sand etc.); powdered
miano [mya-no] n. name; designation; appellation (label)
mianować [mya-no-vaćh] v.
appoint; promote; give a title
mianowicie [mya-no-**vee**-ćhe]
adv. namely; to wit; that is ...
mianownik [mya-**nov**-ńeek] m.
denominator; nominative
miara [mya-ra] f. measure;
gauge; yard-stick; foot-rule;
amount; measuring rod; limit
miarkować [myar-ko-vaćh] v.
guess; note; mitigate oneself
miarodajny [mya-ro-**day**-ni] adj.
m. authoritative; competent
miarowy [mya-**ro**-vi] adj. m.
rhythmic; steady; regular
miasteczko [mya-**stech**-ko] n.
borough; small country town
miasto [myas-to] n. town
miałczeć [myaw-chećh] v. mew
miazga [myaz-ga] f. pulp; squash
miażdżyć [myazh-dzhićh] v.
crush; squash; smash; grind;
lacerate; reduce to a pulp
miąć [myownćh] v. crumple;
wrinkle; crease; rumple; crush
miąższ [myownsh] m. pulp;

flesh of fruit; pomace; squash
miech [myekh] m. bellows
miecz [myech] m. sword
mieć [myećh] v. have; hold;
run; own; keep; have to do
miednica [myed-ńee-tsa] f. hand
washtub; pelvis; wash basin
miedza [mye-dza] f. farm
boundary strip; bounds; balk
miedź [myedźh] f. copper
miedziak [mye-dźhak] m. copper
penny; copper coin
miedziany [mye-dźha-ni] adj. m.
of copper; coppery; of brass
miedzioryt [mye-dźho-rit] m.
copperplate engraving
miejsce [myeys-tse] n. place;
location; spot; room; space;
seat; employment; berth; point; scene; occupation; job
miejscowość [myey-stso-
-vośhćh] f. locality; place;
town; village; spot
miejscowy [myey-stso-vi] adj. m.
local; native; indigenous
miejski [myey-skee] adj. m. of
town; of city; urban
mielizna [mye-leez-na] f. shoal;
shallow water; sandbank
mielenie [mye-le-ńe] n. grinding;
milling; mincing; jabber;
prattling incoherently
mielony [mye-lo-ni] adj. m.
ground; milled; minced; pul-
verized; chewed up
mieniać [mye-ńaćh] v. change;
swap; exchange; convert
mienić [mye-ńeećh] v. call;
glitter; shimmer; change color; show a play of colors
mienić się [mye-ńeećh śhan]
v. change one's color; glitter
mienie [mye-ńe] n. property;
belongings; estate; effects
miernictwo [myer-ńeets-tvo] m.
surveying; land measuring
mierniczy [myer-ńee-chi] m.
surveyor; adj. m. geodetic
mierność [myer-nośhćh] f.
mediocrity; average range
miernota [myer-no-ta] average
intelligence; mediocrity
mierny [myer-ni] adj. m.

mediocre; mean; of moderate
means; moderate; indifferent
mierzeja [mye-zhe-ya] f. sand-bar
mierzić [myer-źheećh] v. be
disgusting; sicken; make (render) unbearable; disgust
mierznąć [myerz-nownćh] v.
become disgusting; pall on sb.
mierzwa [myezh-va] f. litter
mierzwić [myezh-veećh] v. manure a field; tousle; ruffle; mat
mierzyć [mye-zhićh] v. measure; judge; try on; aim; tend
towards; estimate; evaluate
miesiąc [mye-śhownts] m.
month; moon; lunar month
miesić [mye-śheećh] v.
massage; knead (dough, clay)
miesięcznie [mye-śhanch-ńe]
adv. monthly; every month
miesięcznik [mye-śhanch-ńeek]
m. monthly paper; monthly
mieszać [mye-shaćh] v. mix;
mingle; shuffle; confuse
mieszać się [mye-shaćh śhan]
v. meddle; become confused
mieszanina [mye-sha-ńee-na] f.
mixture; compound; medley
mieszanka [mye-shan-ka] f.
blend; mix; mixture; miscellany; composition; compound
mieszczanin [myesh-cha-ńeen]
m.burgher; townsman; citizen
mieszczaństwo [myesh-chań-
-stvo] n. middle class; towns
people; narrow-mindedness
mieszek [mye-shek] m. small
bellows; bag; money-bag
mieszkać [myesh-kaćh] v.
dwell; live; stay; have a flat;
lodge; reside; inhabit; abide
mieszkalny [myesh-kal-ni] adj. m.
inhabitable; habitable
mieszkanie [myesh-ka-ńe] n.
apartment; rooms; lodgings
mieszkaniec [myesh-ka-ńets] m.
inhabitant; lodger; resident
mieść [myeśhćh] v. sweep;
fling; hurl; blow (leaves etc.)
mieścić [myeśh-ćheećh] v.
contain; fit; hold; store; place
mieścina [myeśh-ćhee-na] f.
small town; out-of-the-way

miewać [mye-vaćh] v. have
occasionally; feel sometimes
mięczak [myan-chak] m. mollusk
międlić [myand-leećh] v.
bruise; hackle; crush; swingle;
scutch; hold forth; twaddle
między [myan-dzi] prep.
between; among; in the midst
międzymorze [myan-dzi-mo-zhe]
n. isthmus; narrow strip of
land (with water on each side)
międzynarodowy [myan-dzi-na-
-ro-do-vi] adj. m. international
międzyplanetarny [myan-dzi-pla-
-ne-tar-ni] adj. m. inter-
planetary; of cosmic space
miękczyć [myank-chićh] v.
soften; move; touch; palatalize
miękisz [myan-keesh] m. pulp
miękki [myank-kee] adj. m. soft;
flabby; limp; supple
miękko [myank-ko] adv. softly;
gently; tenderly; limply; supply
miękkość [myank-kośhćh] f.
softness; irresolution; pliancy
mięknąć [myank-nownćh] v.
soften up; relax; relent
mięsień [myan-śheń] m.
muscle; muscular strength
mięsisty [myan-śhees-ti] adj. m.
fleshy; meaty; pulpous
mięsiwo [myan-śhee-vo] n.
meat dish; dish of meat
mięso [myan-so] n. flesh; meat
mięsożerny [myan-so-zher-ni]
adj. m. carnivorous; meat-eat-
ing; insect-eating (as plants)
mięta [myan-ta] f. mint; trifle
miętosić [myan-to-śheećh] v.
crumble; knead; crush up
mig [meek] m. split second;
twinkle; sign language
migać [mee-gaćh] v. twinkle
migawka [mee-gav-ka] f. camera
shutter; news in brief
migdał [meeg-daw] m. almond;
tonsil; good and tasty thing
migi [mee-gee] pl. sign language;
speaking by (hand made) signs
migotać [mee-go-taćh] v. waver; twinkle; flicker; whisk;
flit; glimmer; shimmer; glitter
migracja [mee-grats-ya] f.

migration; migrating (of groups
of people, birds, etc.)
migrena [mee-gre-na] f. migraine;
sick headache; hemicrania
mijać [mee-yaćh] v. go past;
pass by; pass away; go by
mijać się z prawdą [mee-yaćh
śhan z prav-down] v. swerve
from the truth; to be untrue
mika [mee-ka] f. mica (mineral)
mikrob [mee-krob] m. microbe
mikrofon [mee-kro-fon] m.
microphone; transmitter
mikroskop [mee-kros-kop] m.
microscope
mikroskopijny [mee-kros-ko-peey-
-ni] adj. m. microscopic
mikstura [meek-stoo-ra] f.
mixture; concoction; medicine
mila [mee-la] f. mile
(1609.35 m.; 5,280 ft.;)
mila morska [mee-la mor-ska] f.
nautical mile (1853.2 m.)
milczący [meel-chown-tsi]
adj. m. silent; reticent; mum;
tacit; implicit; unspoken
milczeć [meel-chećh] v. be
silent; quit talking; be quiet
milczenie [meel-che-ńe] n.
silence; keeping still; stillness
milczkiem [meelch-kem] adv.
secretly; stealthily; on the sly
mile [mee-le] adv. pleasantly;
kindly; warmly; courteously
miliard [mee-lyard] m. thousand
million; billion (in America)
milicja [mee-leets-ya] f. militia;
police; constabulary
milicjant [mee-leets-yant] m.
policeman; constable
miligram [mee-lee-gram] m.
milligram; 1/1000 of a gram
milion [mee-lyon] m. million
milioner [mee-lyo-ner] m.
millionaire; a person owning at
least a million dollars (pounds)
milionowe miasto [mee-lyo-no-ve
myas-to] city of million people
militarny [mee-lee-tar-ni] adj. m.
military; fit for war (army)
militaryzować [mee-lee-ta-ri-zo-
-vaćh] v. militarize
milknąć [meel-knownćh] v.

abate; cease talking; die a-
way; calm down; be hushed
miło [mee-wo] adv. nicely;
pleasantly; agreeably
miło poznać [mee-wo poz-
-nаćh] exp. glad to meet; de-
lighted to meet; nice to meet
miłosierdzie [mee-wo-śher-
-dźhe] m. charity; mercy;
compassion; mercy
miłosierny [mee-wo-śher-ni] adj.
m. merciful; charitable
miłosny list [mee-wos-ni leest]
love letter
miłostka [mee-wost-ka] f. little
love affair
miłość [mee-wośhćh] f. love
miłośnik [mee-wośh-ńeek] m.
fancier; amateur; fan
miłować [mee-wo-vaćh] v. love
miły [mee-wi] adj. m. pleasant;
beloved; likable; nice; enjoy-
able; prepossessing; attractive
mimiczny [mee-meech-ni] adj. m.
mimic; imitative; make-believe
mimo [mee-mo] prep. in spite of;
notwithstanding; (al)though
mimo [mee-mo] adv. past; by
mimo woli [mee-mo vo-lee]
involuntarily; unintentional
mimo wszystko [mee-mo
vshist-ko] after all; in spite of
all; for all you may say
mimichodem [mee-mo-kho-dem]
adv. by the way; incidentally
mimowolny [mee-mo-vol-ni] adj.
m. involuntary; unintentional
mina [mee-na] f. facial
expression; look; appearance
mina [mee-na] f. mine; air
minaret [mee-na-ret] m. minaret
minąć [mee-nownćh] v. pass
by; go past; elapse; cease
mineralny [mee-ne-ral-ni] adj. m.
mineral; containing minerals
mineralogia [mee-ne-ra-lo-gya] f.
mineralogy
minerał [mee-ne-raw] m. mineral
minia [mee-ńya] f. minium; red
lead base; red lead
miniatura [mee-ńa-too-ra] f.
miniature; miniature copy
minimalny [mee-ńee-mal-ni] adj.

m. minimal; the least possible
minimum [mee-ńee-moom] n.
minimum; adv. at the very
least; at the lowest point
miniony [mee-ńo-ni] adj. m. by-
-gone; of long ago; olden
minister [mee-ńees-ter] m.
minister; cabinet member
ministerialny [mee-ńees-te-ryal-
-ni] adj. m. ministerial
ministerstwo [mee-ńees-ter-
-stvo] n. ministry; department
under a government minister
minorowy [mee-no-ro-vi] adj. m.
in minor key; low-spirited
minuta [mee-noo-ta] f. minute
minutowy [mee-noo-to-vi] adj. m.
of one minute
miodownik [myo-dov-ńeek] m.
gingerbread; bastard balm
miodowy miesiąc [myo-do-vi
mye-śhownts] honeymoon
miodosytnia [myo-do-sit-ńa] f.
mead bar; mead brewery
miot [myot] m. throw; cast;
littler; brood; animal birth;
fling; shooting party
miotacz [myo-tach] m. thrower
miotacz ognia [myo-tach og-ńa]
m. flamethrower
miotać [myo-taćh] v. throw;
fling; toss; hurl; stir; rave;
storm; sputter (abuse, curses)
miotła [myot-wa] f. broom
miód [myoot] m. honey; mead
mir [meer] m. esteem; respect
miriady [mee-rya-di] pl. myriads;
large numbers of persons etc.
mirra [meer-ra] f. myrrh
mirt [meert] m. myrtle
misa [mee-sa] f. platter; bowl
misja [mees-ya] f. mission
misjonarz [mees-yo-nash] m.
(religious) missionary
miska [mees-ka] f. dish; pan
misterny [mees-ter-ni] adj. m.
fine; delicate; subtle; clever
mistrz [meestsh] m. master;
maestro; champion; expert
mistrzostwo [mees-tzhos-tvo] m.
championship; mastery
mistrzowski ruch [mees-tzhov-
-skee rookh] master stroke

mistycyzm [mees-ti-tsizm] m.
mysticism; intuitive knowledge
mistyczny [mees-tich-ni] adj. m.
mystic; mystical; occult
mistyfikacja [mees-ti-fee-kats-ya]
f. mystification; hoax; catch
mistyfikować [mees-ti-fee-ko-
-vaćh] v. mystify; hoax; deceive; puzzle; perplex
mistyk [mees-tik] m. mystic
misyjny [mee-siy-ni] adj. m.
missionary; mission-
miś [meeśh] m. Teddy bear;
nylon fur coat or jacket
mit [meet] m. myth; mythology
mitologia [mee-to-lo-gya] f.
mythology; study of myths
mitologiczny [mee-to-lo-geech-ni]
adj. m. mythologic
mitra [meet-ra] f. mitre (hat)
mitręga [mee-tran-ga] f. delay;
waste of time; dawdler
mitrężyć [mee-tran-zhićh] v.
loiter; waste time; delay; lag
mityczny [mee-tich-ni] adj. m.
mythical; mythic; fictitious
mitygować [mee-ti-go-vaćh] v.
quiet; appease; check; restrain
mityng [mee-ting] m. (mass)
meeting; a mass gathering of
people; a coming together
mizantrop [mee-zan-trop] m.
misanthrope; hater of people
mizdrzyć się [meez-dzhićh
śhan] v. ogle; wheedle;
make eyes; cajole; coquet
mizerak [mee-ze-rak] m. poor
soul; weakling; poor devil
mizeria [mee-ze-rya] f. cucumber
salad; shabby possessions
mizerny [mee-zer-ni] adj. m.
meager; ill-looking; wretched;
paltry; haggard; poor; gaunt
mknąć [mknownćh] v. fleet;
rush; dash; speed; scurry; spin
mlaskać [mlas-kaćh] v. lap;
smack; make smacking noises
mlecz [mlech] m. marrow; milt
mleczarnia [mle-char-ńa] f.
dairy; creamery; milk bar
mleczny [mlech-ni] adj. m. milk;
milky; dairy; lactic; milk-white
mleć [mlećh] v. grind; mill

mleko [mle-ko] n. milk
młocarnia [mwo-tsar-ńa] f.
thresher; threshing-machine
młocka [mwots-ka] f. threshing
młoda [mwo-da] adj. f. young
młode [mwo-de] adj. pl. young;
n. pl. the young; litter
młodociany [mwo-do-ćha-ni]
adj. m. juvenile; youthful
młodość [mwo-dośhćh] f.
youth; early stage
młody [mwo-di] adj. m. young
młodzian [mwo-dźhan] m.
young man; lad; youth
młodzieniaszek [mwo-dźhe-ńa-
-shek] m. sprig; stripling; lad
młodzieniec [mwo-dźhe-ńets]
m. young man; lad; youth
młodzieńczy [mwo-dźheń-chi]
adj. m. youthful; immature
młodzież [mwo-dźhesh] f.
youth; young generation
młodzik [mwo-dźheek] m.
youngster; teenager; youngling
młokos [mwo-kos] m. kid
młot [mwot] m. sledge; hammer
młotek [mwo-tek] m. hammer;
tack-hammer; clapper
młócić [mwoo-ćheećh] v.
thresh (out); pommel; pound
młyn [mwin] m. mill; grinder
młynarz [mwi-nash] m. miller
młynek [mwi-nek] m. hand-
grinder; winnow mill; flay
młyński [mwiń-skee] adj. m.
mill-; of a mill
mnich [mńeekh] m. monk; friar
mniej [mńey] adv. less; fewer
mniej więcej [mńey vyan-tsey]
more or less; about; round
mniejsza o to [mńey-sha o to]
never mind that (exp.)
mniejszość [mńey-shośhćh]
f. minority; the lesser part
mniejszy [mńey-shi] adj. m.
smaller; lesser; less; minor
mniemać [mńe-maćh] v. suppose; deem; imagine; think;
consider; be of opinion
mniemanie [mńe-ma-ńe] n.
opinion; notion; conviction
mniszka [mńeesh-ka] f. nun
mnoga [mno-ga] num. plural

mnogi [mno-gee] adj. m.
numerous; of the plural
mnogość [mno-goshćh] f.
abundance; plurality; multitude
mnożenie [mno-zhe-ńe] n.
multiplication; increase; pro-
liferation; breeding
mnożyć [mno-zhićh] v. multiply
mnóstwo [mnoos-tvo] n. very
many; multitude; swarm; loads
mobilizacja [mo-bee-lee-zats-ya]
f. mobilization; call-up
mobilizować [mo-bee-lee-zo-
-vaćh] v. mobilize; call up
moc [mots] f. power; might;
great-deal; vigor; strength
mocarstwo [mo-tsar-stvo] n.
strong country; (world) power
mocarz [mo-tsash] m. strong
man; potentate; powerful man
mocny [mots-ni] adj. m. strong
mocować się [mo-tso-vaćh
śhan] v. wrestle; exert oneself; fight against (disease)
mocz [moch] m. urine
moczar [mo-char] m. bog; marsh
moczopędny [mo-cho-pand-ni]
adj. m. diuretic
moczowy [mo-cho-vi] adj. m.
uric; urinary; of urine
moczyć [mo-chićh] v. wet;
drench; steep; soak; urinate
moda [mo-da] f. fashion; style
model [mo-del] m. model; type
modelować [mo-de-lo-vaćh] v.
model; shape; mold; fashion
modernizować [mo-der-ńee-zo-
-vaćh] v. modernize; bring up
to date; make modern
modlić się [mod-leećh śhan] v.
pray; say one's prayer
modlitewnik [mod-lee-tev-ńeek]
m. prayer-book
modlitwa [mod-leet-va] f. prayer;
grace (at meal time)
modła [mod-wa] f. mold;
standard; fashion; model;
pattern; distinctive character
modniarka [mod-ńar-ka] f.
milliner; modiste; hat maker
modny [mod-ni] adj. m.
fashionable; in fashion; in
vogue; stylish; up to date

modry [mod-ri] adj. m. azure
-blue; deep blue; cerulean blue
modrzew [mod-zhev] m. larch
modulacja [mo-doo-lats-ya] f.
modulation; inflection
modulować [mo-doo-lo-vaćh] v.
modulate; inflect; regulate
modyfikacja [mo-di-fee-kats-ya]
f. modification; alteration
modyfikować [mo-di-fee-ko-
-vaćh] v. modify; alter; qualify; change partially
modystka [mo-dist-ka] f.modiste;
milliner; hat maker
mogący [mo-gown-tsi] adj. m.
able; capable; competent
mogiła [mo-gee-wa] f. tomb
mojżeszowy [moy-zhe-sho-vi]
adj. m. Mosaic; of Moses
mokka [mok-ka] f. natural
coffee; mocha; Mocha coffee
moknąć [mok-nownćh] v. get
wet; get soaked; drenched; be
soaked; be out in the rain
mokradło [mo-krad-wo] n. bog
mokry [mok-ri] adj. m. wet;
moist; watery; rainy; sweaty
molekularny [mo-le-koo-lar-ni]
adj. m. molecular; of molecule
molekuła [mo-le-koo-wa] f.
molecule (smallest particle)
molestować [mo-les-to-vaćh] v.
molest; annoy; vex; trouble
molo [mo-lo] n. pier; mole; jetty;
breakwater; quay
moment [mo-ment] m. moment
momentalny [mo-men-tal-ni] adj.
m. instantaneous; immediate
monarcha [mo-nar-kha] f.
monarch; sovereign; king
monarchista [mo-nar-khees-ta]
m. monarchist; royalist
moneta [mo-ne-ta] f. coin; chink
moneta brzęcząca [mo-ne-ta
bzhan-chown-tsa] cash; coins
mongolski [mon-gol-skee] adj. m.
Mongol; of Mongolia
monitor [mo-ńee-tor] m. monitor
monitować [mo-ńee-to-vaćh]
v. admonish; monitor; check
on (a person or timing)
monogram [mo-no-gram] m.
monogram; initials in a design

monokl [mo-nokl] m. eye-glass
monolog [mo-no-log] m.
monologue; soliloquy of one
actor; skit for one actor only
monopol [mo-no-pol] m.
monopoly; exclusive control
monoteizm [mo-no-te-eezm] m.
monotheism; belief in one god
monotonia [mo-no-to-ńya] f.
monotony; tiresome same-
ness; lack of variety;
monotonny [mo-no-ton-ni]
adj. m. monotonous; drab; dull
monstrualny [mon-stroo-al-ni]
adj. m. monstrous; horrible
monstrum [mon-stroom] n.
monster; monstrosity
montaż [mon-tash] m. mounting;
assembling; installation; set-up
monter [mon-ter] m. mechanic
montować [mon-to-vaćh] v.
install; put together; put up
monumentalny [mo-noo-men-tal-
-ni] adj. m. monumental
mops [mops] m. pug-dog
moralizator [mo-ra-lee-za-tor] m.
moralizer; moralist
moralizować [mo-ra-lee-zo-
vaćh] v. moralize; discuss
moral questions (tediously)
moralność [mo-ral-nośhćh] f.
morals; morality; ethics
moralny [mo-ral-ni] adj. m.
moral; ethical; of good (sexual) conduct or character
morał [mo-raw] m. moral lesson
moratorium [mo-ra-to-ryoom] n.
moratorium; legalized delay
mord [mort] m. murder; unlawful killing; slaughter
morda [mor-da] f. snout; muzzle,
vulg.: mug; kisser; puss
morderca [mor-der-tsa] m.
murderer; assassin; cutthroat
morderczy [mor-der-chi] adj. m.
murderous; cutthroat; deadly
morderstwo [mor-der-stvo] n.
murder; assassination
mordęga [mor-dan-ga] f. toil;
drudge; moil; fag; strain
mordować [mor-do-vaćh] v.
kill; torment; harass; toil;
sweat; worry; assassinate

mordować się [mor-do-vaćh
śhan] v. kill oneself with
work; toil; sweat (over);
drudge; murder one another
morela [mo-re-la] f. apricot
morena [mo-re-na] f. moraine
morfina [mor-fee-na] f. morphine
(derivative of opium)
morfologia [mor-fo-lo-gya] f.
morphology; science of forms
morga [mor-ga] f. acre
morowy [mo-ro-vi] adj. m.
pestilential; clever; good
buddy; fine fellow; first-rate
mors [mors] m. walrus
morska choroba [mor-ska kho-ro-
-ba] seasickness; dizziness
morski [mor-skee] adj. m.
maritime; sea; nautical; naval
morwa [mor-va] f. mulberry
morze [mo-zhe] n. sea; ocean
morzyć [mo-zhićh] v. starve
mosiądz [mo-śhownts] m. brass
moskit [mos-keet] m. mosquito
most [most] m. bridge
mościć [mośh-ćheećh] v.
pad (a nest); make a bed of
straw; cushion (a seat etc.)
motać [mo-taćh] v. reel;
embroil; entangle; intrigue;
spool; involve in difficulty
motek [mo-tek] m. reel; ball
motłoch [mot-wokh] m. mob
motocykl [mo-to-tsikl] m.
motorcycle; motor bike
motor [mo-tor] m. motor; engine;
motive power; motor bike
motorówka [mo-to-roov-ka] f.
motorboat
motoryzacja [mo-to-ri-za-tsya] f.
motorization; mechanization
motoryzować [mo-to-ri-zo-vaćh]
v. motorize; mechanize
motyka [mo-ti-ka] f. hoe
motyl [mo-til] m. butterfly
motyw [mo-tiv] m. motif; motive
motywować [mo-ti-vo-vaćh] v.
give reasons; explain; justify
mowa [mo-va] f. speech; language; tongue; talk; address
mozaika [mo-zay-ka] f. mosaic
mozolić [mo-zo-leećh] v. toil;
take pains; exert oneself

mozolny [mo-zol-ni] adj. m.
toilsome; strenuous arduous
mozół [mo-zoow] m. exertion
moździerz [moźh-dźhesh] m.
mortar; mine thrower
może [mo-zhe] adv. perhaps;
maybe; very likely; how a-
bout? suppose...?
możliwość [mozh-lee-voshćh]
f. possibility; chance; con-
tigency; capabilities; power
możliwości [mozh-lee-vośh-
-ćhee] pl. scope; vistas;
capabilities; chances; power
możliwy [mozh-lee-vi] adj.
possible; fairly good; passable
można [mozh-na] v. imp. it is
possible; one may; one can
możność [mozh-noshćh] f.
power; freedom to; free
choice to; ability; opportunity
możny [mozh-ni] adj. m. potent;
powerful; mighty; convincing
móc [moots] v. be free to; to
be able; be capable of (doing)
mój [mooy] pron. my; mine
mól [mool] m. moth
mól książkowy [mool
kśhownzh-ko-vi] bookworm
mór [moor] m. pestilence;
epidemic; plague; pest
mórg [moorg] m. acre
mówca [moov-tsa] m. speaker
mówić [moo-veećh] v. speak;
talk; say; tell; say things
mównica [moov-ńee-tsa] f.
(pulpit); speaker's platform
mózg [moozg] m. brain; mind
mózgowy [mooz-go-vi] adj. m.
cerebral; of the brain
mroczny [mroch-ni] adj. m.
dusky; gloomy; obscure; dark
mrok [mrok] m. dusk; twilight
mrowić się [mro-veećh śhan]
v. swarm; teem; be alive (with
people, with insects etc.)
mrowie [mro-vye] n. swarm;
tingle; gooseflesh; creeps
mrowisko [mro-vees-ko] n.
anthill; ants' nest
mrozić [mro-źheećh] v. freeze;
congeal; refrigerate; chill
mroźny [mroźh-ni] adj. m.

frosty; icy; freezing
mrówka [mroov-ka] f. ant;
emmet; pismire
mróz [mroos] m. frost; the cold
mruczeć [mroo-chećh] v.
mumble; mutter; purr; murmur; grumble; growl; grunt
mrugać [mroo-gaćh] v. twinkle;
blink; wink; flicker; flinch
mruk [mrook] m. mumbler; man
of few words; growler
mrukliwy [mroo-klee-vi] adj. m.
mumbling; sulky; gruff; taciturn; speaking indistinctly
mrużyć [mroo-zhićh] v. blink;
wink; squint; half-shut (eyes)
mrzonka [mzhon-ka] f. illusion
msza [msha] f. mass (in church)
mszalny [mshal-ni] adj. m. for
mass; of mass (in the church)
mszał [mshaw] m. missal
mściciel [mśhćhee-ćhel] m.
avenger; retaliator
mścić [mśhćheećh] v. take
vengeance; avenge; retaliate
mściwy [mśhćhee-vi] adj. m.
vindictive; vengeful
mszczenie [mshche-ńe] n.
vengeance; retaliation
mszyca [mshi-tsa] f. mite
mszysty [mshis-ti] adj. m. mossy
mucha [moo-kha] f. fly; trifle
mufka [moof-ka] f. muff
mularz [moo-lash] m. mason
mulat [moo-lat] m. mulatto
mulisty [moo-lees-ti] adj. m.
muddy; oozy; slimy; sludgy
muł [moow] m. ooze; slime
muł [moow] m. mule
mumia [moo-mya] f. mummy
mundur [moon-door] m. uniform
municypalny [moo-ńee-tsi-**pal**-ni]
adj. m. municipal
munsztuk [moon-shtook] m.
(bridle) bit; mouthpiece
mur [moor] m. brick wall
murarz [moo-rash] m. bricklayer
murawa [moo-ra-va] f. lawn
murować [moo-ro-vaćh] v. lay
bricks; build in brick (in stone)
murowany [moo-ro-**va**-ni] adj. m.
of bricks; of stone; certain
murzyn [moo-zhin] m. negro

mus [moos] m. necessity;
compulsion; constraint
mus [moos] m. froth; mousse
musieć [moo-śheći] v. be ob-
liged to; have to; be forced;
must do; got to have it; want
muskać [moos-kaći] v. touch
lightly; skim; stroke
muskularny [moos-koo-lar-ni] adj.
m. muscular; strong; hefty;
sinewy; beefy; strong; brawny
muskuł [moos-koow] m. muscle
musować [moo-so-vaći] foam;
froth; bubble; fizz; sparkle
muszka [moosh-ka] f. fly;
gunbead; face skin-spot; bow-
tie; midge; dry-fly; patch (on
the face); spot; gun sight
muszkat [moosh-kat] m. nutmeg
muszkiet [moosh-ket] m.
musket; smooth bore firearm
muszla [moosh-la] f. shell; conch
musztarda [moosh-tar-da] f.
mustard seasoning
musztra [moosh-tra] f. training;
exercise; (military) drill
muślin [moośh-leen] m. muslin
mutacja [moo-ta-tsya] f.muta-
tion; (voice) change; variation
muterka [moo-ter-ka] f. (bolt)
nut; female screw
muza [moo-za] f. Muse
muzealny [moo-ze-al-ni] adj. m.
of a museum; of museums
muzeum [moo-ze-oom] n.
museum; exhibition building
muzułmanin [moo-zoow-ma-
-ńeen] m. Moslem; Muslim;
follower of Islam (Mussulman)
muzyczny [moo-zich-ni] adj. m.
musical; set to music
muzyk [moo-zik] m. musician
muzyka [moo-zi-ka] f. music
muzykalność [moo-zi-kal-
-nośhći] f. ear for music
muzykalny [moo-zi-kal-ni] adj. m.
having an ear for music
muzykant [moo-zi-kant] m. low
class musician; bandsman
my [mi] pron. we; us
myć [mići] v. wash
mycka [mits-ka] f. skull-cap
mydlarnia [mi-dlar-ńa] f.

soap store; soap works;
perfumery
mydlarstwo [mi-dlar-stvo] n.
soap-making; soap-boiling
mydlarz [mid-lash] m. soap-
-maker; soap boiler
mydlić [mid-leeći] v. soap;
froth; dress someone down
mydlić oczy [mid-leeći o-chi]
pull wool over eyes
mydliny [mid-lee-ni] pl. soap
-suds; lather
mydło [mid-wo] n. soap; soft
soap; cake of soap
mylić [mi-leeći] v. mislead;
misguide; confuse; deceive
mylny [mil-ni] adj. m. wrong
mysz [mish] f. mouse
myszkować [mish-ko-vaći] v.
covertly explore; trace scent
myśl [miśhl] f. thought; idea
myślący [mi-śhlown-tsi] adj. m.
thoughtful; reflective
myśleć [miśh-leći] v. think
myśliciel [miśh-lee-ćhel] m.
thinker; one who thinks a lot
myśliwiec [miśh-lee-vyets] m.
fighter plane; fighter pilot
myśliwy [miśh-lee-vi] m. hunter
myślnik [miśhl-ńeek] m. dash
(mark); hyphen
myślowy [miśh-lo-vi] adj. m.
mental; reflective; intellectual
myto [mi-to] n. toll; tollgate
mżyć [mzhići] v. drizzle

N

na [na] prep. on; upon; at; for;
by; in (NOTE : verbs with
prefix na NOT INCLUDED
HERE: CHECK WITHOUT THE
PREFIX na")
nabawić się [na-ba-veeći
śhan] v. bring upon oneself;
incur; contract; catch (cold)
nabawić strachu [na-ba-veeći
stra-khoo] v. frighten

nabiał [na-byaw] m. dairy
products including eggs
nabiegać się [na-bye-gaćh
śhan] v. have run a lot; exert
oneself; run about a great deal
nabić [na-beećh] v. load a
weapon; beat up (somebody);
whack; kill (a mass of); pack
nabiegły krwią [na-byeg-wi
krvy<u>own</u>] adj. m. bloodshot
nabierać [na-bye-raćh] v. take;
take in; tease; cheat; amass
nabijać [na-bee-yaćh] v. stud;
(repeatedly) load gun
nabijać się [na-bee-yaćh śhan]
v. make fun of (somebody)
nabożeństwo [na-bo-zheń-stvo]
n. church service
nabożny [na-bozh-ni] adj. m.
pious; religious; godly;
devoutly; devotional (hymn)
nabrać [nab-raćh] v. take; take
in; tease; cheat; gather; swell
nabój [na-booy] m. charge;
cartridge; round of ammunition
nabrzeże [na-bzhe-zhe] n. wharf;
embankment; landing pier
nabrzmiały [na-bzhmya-wi] adj.
m. swollen; distended
nabytek [na-bi-tek] m.
acquisition; purchase; new
recruit (new employee)
nabrzmiewać [na-bzhmye-vaćh]
v. swell; plump up; plump out
nabywać [na-bi-vaćh] v. buy;
acquire; obtain; gain; procure;
purchase; get; develop (habit)
nabywca [na-biv-tsa] m. buyer
nacechowany [na-tse-kho-va-ni]
adj. m. marked; characterized
nachodzić [na-kho-dźheećh] v.
intrude; (abstraction:) haunt
nachylać [na-khi-laćh] v. stoop;
bend; incline; lean; tilt; slant
nacięcie [na-ćhan-će] n. cut;
incision; notch; nick; score;
indentation; scarification
naciągać [na-ćh<u>own</u>-gaćh] v.
stretch; draw; strain; pull
one's leg; take sb. in; infuse
naciek [na-ćhek] m. infiltration;
leak; swelling; (fluid) gathering
nacierać [na-ćhe-raćh] v. rub;

attack; harass; demand
nacinać [na-ćhee-naćh] v. cut
a great deal; notch; score;
nick; scarify; hoax; dupe
nacisk [na-ćheesk] m. pressure;
stress; accent; thrust; push
naciskać [na-ćhees-kaćh] v.
press; urge; bear on; push
nacjonalista [na-tsyo-na-lees-ta]
m. nationalist
nacjonalizacja [na-tsyo-na-lee-
-zats-ya] f. nationalization
nacjonalizm [na-tsyo-na-leezm]
m. nationalism
nacjonalizować [na-tsyo-na-lee-
-zo-vaćh] v. nationalize
naczekać się [na-che-kaćh
śhan] v. wait too long; tire of
waiting; wait indefinitely
na czczo [na chcho] adv. on an
empty stomach; unfed; fasting
naczelnik [na-chel-ńeek] m.
manager; chief; head; master
naczelny [na-chel-ni] adj. m.
chief; head; paramount; primate; principal; main; front
naczerpać [na-cher-paćh] v. dip
up; draw (fluid); scoop up
naczynie [na-chi-ńe] n. vessel
nad [nad] prep. over; above; on;
upon; beyond; at; of; for
nadajnik [na-day-ńeek] m.
transmitter; feeder
nadal [na-dal] adv. still; in future;
continue (to do); as before
nadaremnie [na-da-rem-ńe] adv.
in vain; unsuccessfully; to no
purpose; without result
nadaremny [na-da-rem-ni] adj. m.
fruitless; vain; unsuccessful
nadarzać się [na-da-zhaćh
śhan] v. happen; occur; turn
up; present itself; offer (of)
nadawać [na-da-vaćh] v. confer
bestow; grant; endow; christen; invest; vest; offer; cause
nadawca [na-dav-tsa] m. sender
nadąć [na-d<u>own</u>ćh] v. puff up
nadąsany [na-d<u>own</u>-sa-ni]
adj. m. sulky; sullen; stuffy
nadążać [na-d<u>own</u>-zhaćh] v.
keep up with; cope with; keep
pace; lag behind; follow

nadbałtycki [nad-baw-tits-kee] adj. m. on the Baltic; Baltic

nadbiec [nad-byets] v. come running up; hasten up; run up

nadbrzeże [nad-bzhe-zhe] n. shore; coast; littoral

nadbrzeżny [nad-bzhezh-ni] adj. m. coastal; sea-shore

nadbudowa [nad-boo-do-va] f. superstructure; added floor

nadbudować [nad-boo-do-vaćh] v. build on; add an upper floor

nadchodzić [nad-kho-dźheećh] v. approach; arrive; come; be forthcoming; be imminent

nadciągać [nad-ćhown-gaćh] v. draw near; be nearing; be imminent; be setting in; come

nadciśnienie [nad-ćhee-śhńe-ńe] n. hypertension

nadczłowiek [nad-chwo-vyek] m. superman; superhuman man

nadejście [na-dey-śhćhe] n. coming; arrival; oncoming

nadepnąć [na-dep-nownćh] v. step on; tread on (crushing)

nader [na-der] adv. greatly; excessively; highly; most

nadesłać [na-de-swaćh] v. send in; forward; remit (a sum)

nade wszystko [na-de vshist-ko] adv. above all (else)

nadęty [na-dan-ti] adj. m. puffed up; inflated; superior

nadgraniczny [nad-gra-ńeech-ni] adj. m. near-border; frontier-

nadjechać [nad-ye-khaćh] v. drive up; come up; arrive

nadlecieć [nad-le-ćhećh] v. fly in; arrive (drive up) in a hurry

nadleśniczy [nad-leśh-ńee-chi] m. chief ranger; forest inspector; head (chief) of rangers

nadliczbowy [nad-lich-bo-vi] adj. m. overtime; additional

nadludzki [nad-loots-kee] adj. m. superhuman; divine; terrific

nadmiar [nad-myar] m. excess

nadłamać [nad-wa-maćh] v. break slightly; cause a slight break; break off; fracture

nadmienić [nad-mye-ńeećh] v. mention; allude; hint; add

nadmierny [nad-myer-ni] adj. m. excessive; extravagant; undue

nadmorski [nad-mors-kee] adj. m. seaside-(resort); maritime

nadmuchać [nad-moo-khaćh] v. inflate; blow up with air

nadobny [na-dob-ni] adj. m. handsome; comely; pretty

nadobowiązkowy [nad-o-bo-vyown-sko-vi] adj. m. optional; elective; voluntary

na dół [na doow] adv. down; downstairs; downwards

nadpić [nad-peećh] v. take a sip; start overfilled drink

nadpłynąć [nad-pwi-nownćh] v. sail in; swim in; arrive

nadprodukcja [nad-pro-doo-ktsya] f. excess production

nadprogramowy [nad-pro-gra-mo-vi] adj. m. extra; additional

nadprzyrodzony [nad-pzhi-ro-dzo-ni] adj. m. supernatural

nadpsuty [nad-psoo-ti] adj. m. partly spoiled; impaired

nadrabiać [nad-ra-byaćh] v. catch up with; make up; work ahead of schedule; compensate for (a deficiency); out do

nadruk [nad-rook] m. overprint

nadrzędny [nad-zhand-ni] adj. m. superior; primary; precedent

nadskakiwać [nad-ska-kee-vaćh] v. try to ingratiate oneself; curry favor (with)

nadsłuchiwać [nad-swoo-khee-vaćh] v. strain to listen

nadspodziewany [nad-spo-dźhe-va-ni] adj. m. unexpected

nadstawiać [nad-sta-vyaćh] v. expose; risk; hold out; cock

nadto [nad-to] adv. moreover; furthermore; nor; besides; too much; too many; amply

nadużycie [nad-oo-zhi-ćhe] n. abuse; excess; misuse

nadużywać [nad-oo-zhi-vaćh] v. abuse; take advantage; strain (relations); misuse

nadwaga [nad-va-ga] f. overweight; allowance of extra weight (in travel)

nadwartość [nad-var-tośhćh]

f. overvalue in economics
nadwątlić [nad-**vownt**-leećh] v.
weaken; impair; damage
nadwiślański [nad-vee-**śhłań**-
-skee] adj. m. on the Vistula
nadwodny [nad-**vod**-ni] adj. m.
near water; riverside; aquatic
nadwozie [nad-vo-**źhe**] n. car
-body; body of a car or truck
nadwyrężać [nad-vi-**ran**-zhaćh]
v. impair; strain; weaken
nadwyżka [nad-**vizh**-ka] f.
surplus; excess amount
nadymać [na-di-**maćh**] v. puff
up; inflate; swell out; fill out;
bulge; blow out; pump up; distend; bulge; put on airs
nadymić [na-di-**meećh**] v. fill
(a rooom) with smoke; make a
lot of smoke
nadzieja [na-**dźhe**-ya] f. hope
nadziemski [nad-**źhem**-skee]
adj. m. celestial; heavenly;
divine; super terrestrial
nadzienie [na-**dźhe**-ńe] n.
stuffing (of fowl, etc.) ; filling;
nadziewać [na-**dźhe**-vaćh] v.
stuff; pierce with; put on; fill
nadzorca [nad-**zor**-tsa] m.
overseer; superintendent;
supervisor (of work, workers)
nadzór [nad-**zoor**] m. supervision
nadzwyczaj [nad-**zvi**-chay] adv.
unusually; extremely; most
nadzwyczajny [nad-zvi-**chay**-ni]
adj. m. extraordinary; extreme
nafta [**naf**-ta] f. petroleum
naftalina [na-fta-**lee**-na] f.
naphthalene (moth repellent)
nagabywać [na-ga-bi-**vaćh**] v.
annoy; accost; trouble; molest
nagana [na-**ga**-na] f. blame
nagi [**na**-gee] adj. m. naked; in
buff; bare; nude; bald; empty
naginać [na-gee-**naćh**] v. bend
down; submit to; adapt; bow
nagle [**nag**-le] adv. suddenly
naglić [nag-**leećh**] v. urge
nagłość [nag-**wośhćh**] f.
urgency; suddenness; instancy
nagłówek [na-**gwoo**-vek] m.
heading; caption; title; headline; letter-head; headstall

nagły [**nag**-wi] adj. m. sudden;
urgent; instant; abrupt; pressing; unexpected; immediate
nagminny [nag-**meen**-ni] adj. m.
universal; usual; current;
general; epidemic; enzootic
nagniotek [nag-**ńo**-tek] m. (skin)
corn; callus (on the skin)
nagonka [na-**gon**-ka] f. campaign
against; hue and cry against
nagość [na-**gośhćh**] f. nudity
nagradzać [na-gra-**dzaćh**] v.
reward; give prize; recompense; indemnify; make up for
nagrobek [na-**gro**-bek] m. tomb
nagroda [na-**gro**-da] f. reward
nagrodzić [na-gro-**źeećh**] v.
reward; requite; recompense
nagromadzić [na-gro-ma-
-**źeećh**] v. accumulate; congregate; amass; heap up
nagrzewać [na-gzhe-**vaćh**] v.
warm up; heat up; preheat
naigrawać [na-ee-gra-**vaćh**] v.
mock; scoff; deride; ridicule
naiwny [na-**eev**-ni] adj. m. naive
najazd [na-**yazd**] m. invasion
najbardziej [nay-bar-**dźhey**] adv.
most (of all)
najechać [na-ye-**khaćh**] v.
overrun; invade; run into; ram;
crowd; run over; crush into
najedzony [na-ye-**dzo**-ni] adj. m.
full (of food); satiated
najem [na-**yem**] m. hire; renting
najemnik [na-**yem**-ńeek] m.
hireling; mercenary; free lance;
soldier of fortune; wage earner
najemny [na-**yem**-ni] adj. m.
venal; mercenary; hired labor
najeść się [na-ye**śhćh śhan**]
v. eat plenty of; eat a lot
najeźdźca [na-**yeźhdźh**-tsa]
m. invader; assailant; violator
najeżdżać [na-**yezh**-dzhaćh] v.
invade; run into; attack; ram
najeżony [na-ye-**zho**-ni] adj. m.
bristling; bristly; beset
najgorszy [nay-**gor**-shi] adj. m.
the worst; the worst of all
najgorzej [nay-**go**-zhey] adv.
worst of all; worst possible
najlepiej [nay-le-**pyey**] adv. best;

best of all
najlepszy [nay-lep-shi] adj. m.
best; best of all; best possible
najmniej [nay-mńey] adv. least
najmniejszy [nay-mńey-shi] adj.
m. least; smallest; least of all
najmować [nay-mo-vaćh] v.
rent; hire; engage; lease
najpierw [nay-pyerv] adv. first of
all; in the first place; at first
najście [nay-śhćhe] n. intrusion; inroad; invasion; incursion; irruption; encroachment
najść [nayśhćh] v. intrude; fill
najwięcej [nay-vyan-tsey] adv.
most of all (worst of all)
największy [nay-vyan-kshi] adj.
m. biggest; largest; extreme
najwyżej [nay-vi-zhey] adv.
highest; at the very most
najwyższy [nay-vizh-shi] adj. m.
highest; top; utmost; extreme
nakarmić [na-kar-meećh] v.
feed (population); give food
nakaz [na-kaz] m. order; writ
nakazywać [na-ka-zi-vaćh] v.
order; demand; command
nakleić [na-kle-eećh] v. stick
on; paste up; mount; post
nakład [na-kwad] m. outlay
nakładać [na-kwa-daćh] v. lay
on; put on; place; set; spread
nakładca [na-kwad-tsa] m.
publisher (of printed work)
nakłaniać [na-kwa-ńaćh] v.
persuade; induce; bring; get;
urge; incite; incline; prevail
na koniec [na ko-ńets] adv.
finally; at the (very) end
nakreślać [na-kre-śhlaćh] v.
delineate; sketch; draft; write
nakręcać [na-kran-tsaćh] v.
wind up; shoot (movie); turn;
direct; set on; cheat; swindle
nakrętka [na-krant-ka] f. (screw)
nut; female screw; jam nut
nakrycie [na-kri-ćhe] n. cover
nakrywać [na-kri-vaćh] v. cover
nakrywka [na-kriv-ka] f. lid
na kształt [na kshtawt] in form
of...; in shape of; a kind of...
nalać [na-laćh] v. pour in; pour
on (liquid only, no sand etc.)

nalegać [na-le-gaćh] v. insist
naleganie [na-le-ga-ńe] n.
insistence; urgent demand
nalepiać [na-le-pyaćh] v. stick
on; paste on; mount; glue on
nalepka [na-lep-ka] f. sticker
naleśnik [na-leśh-ńeek] m.
pancake wrap around stuffing
nalewać [na-le-vaćh] v. pour in
należeć [na-le-zhećh] v. belong
należność [na-lezh-nośhćh] f.
due; ration; charge; fee
należy [na-le-zhi] adj. m. due;
owing; rightful; proper
należycie [na-le-zhi-ćhe] adv.
properly; duly; suitably
należyty [na-le-zhi-ti] adj. m.
proper; right; appropriate
nalot [na-lot] m. air raid; (skin)
rush; coating; incursion; blitz
naładować [na-wa-do-vaćh] v.
load; charge; cram; freight
nałogowiac [na-wo-go-vyets] m.
addict; chain-smoker; drunkard
nałogowy [na-wo-go-vi] adj. m.
addicted; inveterate; habitual
nałogowy pijak [na-wo-go-vi pee-
-yak] alcoholic; drunkard
nałóg [na-woog] m. addiction
namacalny [na-ma-tsal-ni] adj.
m. tangible; substantial
namaszczać [na-mash-chaćh]
v. anoint; grease; smear
namaszczenie [na-mash-che-ńe]
n. solemnity; anointing
namawiać [na-ma-vyaćh] v.
persuade; prompt; urge; exhort; instigate; encourage
namazać [na-ma-zaćh] v. daub;
anoint; scrawl (scribble)
namiastka [na-myast-ka] f.
substitute; ersatz; stopgap
namiernik [na-myer-ńeek] m.
direction finder; pelorus
namiestnik [na-myest-ńeek] m.
regent; governor; viceroy
namiętność [na-myant-
-nośhćh] f. passion; infa-
tuation; fervor; keenness
namiętny [na-myant-ni] adj. m.
passionate; keen; ardent; lusty
namiot [na-myot] m. tent; booth
namoczyć [na-mo-chićh] v.

wet; soak; steep; drench
namoknąć [na-mok-<u>own</u>ćh] v.
get soaked; become saturated
namowa [na-mo-va] f. instigation; suggestion; persuasion
namulić [na-moo-leećh] v. slime up; silt up; mud up; ooze up
namydlić [na-mid-leećh] v. soap up; put soap lather on
namysł [na-misw] m. reflection
namyślać się [na-mi-śhlaćh śhan] v. ponder; reflect; think over; make up one's mind
nanosić [na-no-śheećh] v. bring; deposit; plot; track (mud); drift; mark (on a map)
na nowo [na no-vo] adv. anew
naocznie [na-och-ńe] adv. by eye; visually; clearly
naoczny świadek [na-och-ni śhvya-dek] eyewitness
na odwrót [na od-vroot] adv. inversely; the other way around; directly opposite
na ogół [na o-goow] adv. (in general) generally; on the whole; not specifically
na około [na o-ko-wo] adv. all around; about; right round
naokoło [na-o-ko-wo] prep. all around; about; on all sides
naonczs [na-on-chas] adv. at that time; then; in those days
naoliwić [na-o-lee-veećh] v. oil; lubricate; grease; make slippery or smooth; apply oil
na opak [na o-pak] adv. backward; perversely; the wrong way; upside-down
na ostatek [na o-sta-tek] adv. finally; in the end; at last
naostrzyć [na-ost-zhićh] v. sharpen up; become sharp
na oścież [na ośh-ćhesh] adv. wide open; opened all the way
na oślep [na ośh-lep] adv. blindly; full tilt; headlong
na ówczas [na oov-chas] adv. at that time; then; in those days
napad [na-pat] m. assault; fit; attempt; attack; outburst; invective; outbreak; onset
napadać [na-pa-daćh] v. assail

napar [na-par] m. infusion; brew; a beverage brewed
naparstek [na-par-stek] m. thimble; dram; thimble full
naparzyć [na-pa-zhićh] v. infuse; fight; beat up (badly)
napaskudzić [na-pas-koo-dźheećh] v. soil up; make a mess; dirty; foul; make trouble
napastliwy [na-past-lee-vi] adj. m. aggressive; malicious; bitter; quarrelsome
napastnik [na-past-ńeek] m. aggressor; assailant; forward, forward center (sport)
napastować [na-pas-to-vaćh] v. pester; attack; wax; molest; worry; assail; persecute
napaść [na-paśhćh] f. assault
napawać [na-pa-vaćh] v. fill up (with feelings, panic, wander)
napatrzyć się [na-pat-shićh śhan] v. see enough; have a good look; see a lot of
napełniać [na-pew-ńaćh] v. fill up; inspire; imbue; pervade
na pewno [na-pev-no] adv. surely; certainly; for sure; without fail; with assurance
napęd [na-p<u>and</u>] m. propulsion; drive; force; driving gear
napędowy [na-p<u>an</u>-do-vi] adj. m. motive; driving; impulsive
napędzać [na-p<u>an</u>-dzaćh] v. chase in; propel; round up; drift in; carry along; egg on
napić się [na-peećh śhan] v. have a drink; quench one's thirst; have to drink
napierać [na-pye-raćh] v. press forward; insist; advance
napięcie [na-p<u>yan</u>-ćhe] n. tension; strain; voltage; intensity; stress; stretch
napiętek [na-p<u>yan</u>-tek] m. heel
napiętnować [na-p<u>yan</u>t-no-vaćh] v. brand; stigmatize; censure; condemn as being very bad; stamp
napięty [na-p<u>yan</u>-ti] adj. m. tense; taut; strained; tight
napinać [na-pee-naćh] v. strain
napis [na-pees] m. inscription

napitek [na-**pee**-tek] m. drink
napiwek [na-**pee**-vek] m. tip
napluć [na-plooćh] v. spit on
napływ [na-pwiv] m. influx
napływać [na-pwi-vaćh] v.
inflow; flow in; flock; pour in
napływowy [na-pwi-**vo**-vi]
adj. m. alluvial; immigrant;
alien; extraneous; foreign
napoczynać [na-po-chi-naćh] v.
start up; open; broach
napominać [na-po-**mee**-naćh] v.
admonish; reprimand; rebuke
napomknąć [na-pom-kn**own**ćh]
v. mention; hint at; allude to
napomnienie [na-po-mńe-ńe] n.
admonition; reprimand; rebuke
na pomoc! [na po-mots] excl.:
help! give help! please, help!
napotny [na-**pot**-ni] adj. m.
perspiratory; diaphoretic
napotykać [na-po-ti-kaćh] v.
run in; come across; be faced
with; happen; be confronted
napowietrzny [na-po-**vyetsh**-ni]
adj. m. aerial; overhead-
na powrót [na po-vroot] adv.
return; again; on the way back
na pozór [na po-zoor] adv.
apparently; on the face of it
napój [na-pooy] m. drink
na pół [na poow] adv. in half
napór [na-poor] m. pressure
naprawa [na-pra-va] f. repair;
redress; renovation; reform
naprawdę [na-prav-d**an**] adv.
indeed; really; truly; positively
naprawiać [na-pra-vyaćh] v.
repair; fix; mend; rectify;
reform; mend; set (put) right
naprędce [na-pr**and**-tse] adv.
hastily; in a hurry; slapdash
naprężenie [na-pr**an**-zhe-ńe] n.
tension; strain; tautness
naprężyć [na-pr**an**-zhićh] v.
tighten; stretch; strain
naprowadzać [na-pro-**va**-
-dzaćh] v. lead in; direct to;
point out to; advise; suggest
na próżno [na proozh-no] adv. in
vain; uselessly; to no avail
naprzeciw [na-pzhe-ćheev] adv.
opposite; vis-a-vis

naprzeć [na-pzhećh] press;
urge; press hard; insist on
na przekór [na pzhe-koor] adv. in
despite; just to spite
na przełaj [na pzhe-way] adv.
shortcut (across obstacles)
na przemian [na pzhe-myan] adv.
alternately; by turns
naprzód [na-pzhood] adv. in
front; forwards; first; in the
first place; forward; onward
na przykład [na pzhi-kwad] adv.
for instance; for example
naprzykrzać się [na-pshik-
shaćh **shan**] v. bother; molest; pester; obtrude oneself
napuchnąć [na-poo-khn**own**ćh]
v. swell; become swollen
napuchły [na-poo-khwi] adj. m.
swollen; bulging; distended
napuścić [na-poo-**shćh**eećh]
v. set up; impregnate; let in
napuszony [na-poo-**sho**-ni] adj.
m. puffed up; bristling; ruffled
napychać [na-pi-khaćh] v.
stuff; cram; fill; pack; crowd;
stow; line one's purse; gorge
narada [na-ra-da] f. consultation;
council; conference; meeting
naradzać się [na-ra-dzaćh
shan] v. consult on; confer
with; deliberate; hold a council
naramiennik [na-ra-myen-ńeek]
m . epaulet; shoulder-strap
narastać [na-ra-staćh] v. grow
on; increase; accumulate; ac-
crete; accrue (interest); gather
naraz [na-raz] adv. suddenly
na razie [na ra-źhe] adv. for the
time being; for the present
narażać [na-ra-zhaćh] v. expose to danger; endanger
narciarstwo [nar-ćhars-tvo] n.
skiing (sport); gliding on skis
narciarz [nar-ćhazh] m. skier
narcyz [nar-tsiz] m. narcissus
nareszcie [na-resh-ćhe] adv. at
last; finally; at long last
naręcze [na-r**an**-che] n. armful
narkotyczny [nar-ko-tich-ni] adj.
m. narcitic; causing numbness
narkotyk [nar-ko-tik] m. narcotic;
drug for sleep and relief

narkoza [nar-ko-za] f. anesthesia; loss of sense of pain, touch
narobić [na-ro-beećh] v. mess up; cause nuisance; make a mess; cause a lot of (trouble)
narodowość [na-ro-do--vośhćh] f. nationality; national status (attachment)
narodowy [na-ro-do-vi] adj. m. national; of national character
narodzenie [na-ro-dzhe-ńe] n. birth; a being born; the beginning; Nativity; Christmas
narodzić się [na-ro-dźheećh śhan] v. be born; originate; a- rise; come into existence
narodziny [na-ro-dźhee-ni] pl. birth; origin; the beginning
narośl [na-rośhl] f. tumor; growth; excrescence; wart
narowisty [na-ro-vees-ti] adj. m. restive; vicious; skittish
narożnik [na-rozh-ńeek] m. corner; angle; cross-roads; gusset; quoin; corner brick
narożny [na-rozh-ni] adj. m. corner-; at the street corner
naród [na-root] m. nation; people; the nation; crowd
narów [na-roov] m. vice (restiveness); bad habit; fault
narta [nar-ta] f. ski; sleigh
naruszać [na-roo-shaćh] v. disturb; violate; injure; harm
naruszenie [na-roo-she-ńe] n. offense; disturbance; breach
narwany [nar-va-ni] adj. m. hot -headed; reckless; rash; fitful
narybek [na-ri-bek] m. small fry; coming generation
narząd [na-zhownt] m. organ
narzecze [na-zhe-che] n. (primitive) dialect
narzeczona [na-zhe-cho-na] f. fiancee; an engaged woman
narzeczony [na-zhe-cho-ni] m. fiance; an engaged man
narzekać [na-zhe-kaćh] v. complain; grumble; lament
narzekanie [na-zhe-ka-ńe] n. complaints; kick; bitching
narzędzie [na-zhan-dźhe] n. tool; utensil; implement

narzucać [na-zhoo-tsaćh] v. throw over; impose; shovel on
nasada [na-sa-da] f. base
nasenna pigułka [na-sen-na pee--goov-ka] f. sleeping pill
nasiadówka [na-sia-doov-ka] f. sitzbath; hip-bath
nasiąknąć [na-śhownk--nownćh] v. soak up; become saturated; imbibe; soak in
nasienie [na-śhe-ńe] n. seed; sperm; semen; posterity
nasilenie [na-śhee-le-ńe] n. intensification; intensity
naskórek [na-skoo-rek] m. outer skin; epidermis; cuticle
naskarżyć [na-skar-zhićh] v. denounce; lodge a complaint
nasłuchać się [na-swoo-khaćh śhan] v. hear plenty
nasłuchiwać [na-swoo-khee--vaćh] v. monitor (radio); listen; be on the watch for
nasmarować [na-sma-ro-vaćh] v. smear over; grease; oil; lubricate; rub with ointment
nastać [na-staćh] v. set in; enter; occur; come about
nastanie [na-sta-ńe] n. arrival; setting-in; advent; coming
nastarczyć [na-star-chićh] v. supply enough; keep pace with; cope with the demand
nastawać [na-sta-vaćh] v. in- sist; start service; be against
natawiać [na-sta-vyaćh] v. set up; set right; tune in; point
nastawienie [na-sta-vye-ńe] n. attitude; bias; disposition
następca [na-stanp-tsa] m. successor; heir (to the throne)
następnie [na-stanp-ńe] adv. next; then; subsequently
następny [na-stanp-ni] adj. m. next; the next; the following
następować [na-stan-po-vaćh] v. follow; tread; come after; ensue; step on; take place
następstwo [na-stanp-stvo] n. result; succession; upshot
następujący [na-stan-poo-yown--tsi] adj. m. the successive; the following; the next

nastraszyć [na-stra-shićh] v.
frighten; intimidate; scare
nastręczać [na-stran-chaćh] v.
afford; present; offer; procure
nastroić [na-stro-eećh] v.
attune; tune up; dispose to
nastroszyć [na-stro-shićh] v.
bristle up; perk up; heap up
nastrój [na-strooy] m. mood
nasturcja [na-stoor-tsya] f.
nasturtium; lark-heel
nasuwać [na-soo-vaćh] v.
shove up; draw over; afford;
overthrust; offer possibilities
nasycać [na-si-tsaćh] v.
satiate; satisfy; sate; saturate
nasycenie [na-si-tse-ńe] n.
satiation; saturation; satisfaction; gratification
nasycony [na-si-tso-ni] adj. m.
satiate; saturated; replete
nasyłać [na-si-waćh] v. send
on (to pester, badger; kill)
nasyp [na-sip] m. embankment
nasypać [na-si-paćh] v. pour in;
spread up (dry powder etc.)
nasz [nash] pron. our; ours
naszyć [na-shićh] v. sew on;
trim (with fur, ribbons, etc.)
naszkicować [na-shkee-tso-
vaćh] v. sketch; make a
sketch of; draw up; outline
naszyjnik [na-shiy-ńeek] m.
necklace; neck jewelry
naśladować [na-śhla-do-vaćh]
v. imitate; mimic; reproduce
naśladowanie [na-śhla-do-va-
-ńe] n. imitation; copy
naśladowca [na-śhla-dov-tsa]
m. imitator
naśmiewać się [na-śhmye-
-vaćh śhan] v. laugh at;
deride; laugh to the full
naświetlać [na-śhvyet-laćh] v.
explain; irradiate; expose
natarcie [na-tar-ćhe] n. 1.
rubbing; 2. onslaught; attack;
offensive; advance
natarczywość [na-tar-chi-
-vośhćh] f. insistence; obtrusiveness; urgency; pressure
natarczywy [na-tar-chi-vi] adj.
m. insistent; pressing; urgent

natchnąć [natkh-nownćh] v.
inspire; infuse; penetrate
natchnienie [nat-khńe-ńe] n. inspiration; brain wave; impulse;
afflation; happy thought
natenczas [na-ten-chas] adv.
then; at that time; as
natężać [na-tan-zhaćh] v.
strain; intensify; strengthen;
exert; heighten; enhance
natężenie [na-tan-zhe-ńe] n.
tension; strain; effort; pitch
natężony [na-tan-zho-ni] adj. m.
intense; strained; concentrated
natknąć [nat-knownćh] v.
come across; butt; stick; stud
natłoczony [na-two-cho-ni] adj.
m. crowded; packed; huddled
natłoczyć [na-two-chićh] v.
cram; pack; crowd; huddle
natłok [nat-wok] m. crowd;
throng; pressure accumulation
natomiast [na-to-myast] adv.
however; yet; on the contrary
natłuścić [na-twoo-
-śhćheećh] v. oil; grease;
lubricate; supply a lubricant
natrafić [na-tra-feećh] v.
encounter; come across
natręctwo [na-tran-tstvo] n. in-
trusiveness; obtrusiveness
natręt [na-trant] m. intruder
natrętny [na-tran-tni] adj. m.
intrusive; bothersome
natrysk [na-trisk] m. shower
-bath; shower; spraying
natrząsać się [na-tzhown-saćh
śhan] v. scoff at; sneer at;
poke fun; hold in derision
natrzeć [na-tzhećh] v. rub;
attack; harass; scold; rate
natura [na-too-ra] f. nature
naturalizacja [na-too-ra-lee-za
-tsya] f. naturalization
naturalizować [na-too-ra-lee-zo-
-vaćh] v. naturalize
naturalny [na-too-ral-ni] adj. m.
natural; true to life
natychmiast [na-tikh-myast] adv.
at once; instantly; right away
natychmiastowy [na-tikh-myas-
-to-vi] adj. m. instantaneous
nauczać [na-oo-chaćh] v.

teach; instruct; tutor; train
nauczanie [na-oo-**cha**-ńe] n.
teaching; instruction
nauczka [na-**ooch**-ka] f. (pointed)
lesson (unpleasant)
nauczyciel [na-oo-chi-ćhel] m.
teacher; instructor
nauczyć się [na-oo-chićh
śhan] v. learn; come to know
nauka [na-**oo**-ka] f. science; research work; learning; study;
teaching; knowledge; lesson
naukowiec [na-oo-ko-vyets] m.
scientist; scholar; researcher
naukowość [na-oo-ko-vośhćh]
f. erudition; scholarship; learning; scientific nature; erudition
naukowy [na-oo-ko-vi] adj. m.
scientific; scholarly; academic
naumyślnie [na-oo-miśhl-ńe]
adv. on purpose; of set purpose; deliberately; intentionally
nawa [na-va] f. nave; aisle
nawadniać [na-vad-ńaćh] v.
irrigate; saturate with water
nawalić [na-va-leećh] v. pile
up; fail; bungle; break down
nawał [na-vaw] m. no end of;
an overwhelming amount
nawała [na-va-wa] f.
overwhelming mass; swarms;
onslaught; enormous amount
nawałnica [na-vaw-ńee-tsa] f.
tempest; storm; hurricane
nawarstwienie [na-var-stvye-ńe]
n. stratification
nawarzyć [na-va-zhićh] v.
brew; cook; concoct; get in
trouble; cause trouble
nawet [na-vet] adv. even
nawet gdyby [na-vet gdi-bi] adv.
even if; even though; even
nawias [na-vyas] m. parenthesis
nawiasem [na-vya-sem] adv.
incidentally; by way of di-
gression; by the way
nawiasowy [na-vya-so-vi] adj. m.
parenthetical; incidental
nawiązać [na-vyown-zaćh] v.
tie to; refer to; enter in
nawiązanie [na-vyown-za-ńe] n.
connection; reference to
nawiedzać [na-vye-dzaćh] v.

visit; haunt; afflict; obsess
nawierzchnie [na-vyezh-khńa] f.
surface (finish); pavement
nawijać [na-vee-yaćh] v. wind
up; reel; roll up; spool; coil
nawlekać [na-vle-kaćh] v.
thread; string; slip on
nawodnienie [na-vod-ńe-ńe] n.
irrigation; saturation with
water; washing out (a cavity)
nawoływać [na-vo-wi-vaćh] v.
call; hail; exhort; urge; lure
nawozić [na-vo-źheećh] v.
fertilize; manure; truck; cart;
fill (a ditch); bring (gravel)
nawóz [na-vooz] m. manure;
dung; muck; fertilizer
na wpół [na vpoow] adv. half;
semi-; half-(finished, boiled)
nawracać [na-vra-tsaćh] v. turn
around; convert; turn back
nawrócenie [na-vroo-tse-ńe] n.
conversion; being converted
nawrót [na-vroot] m. return;
relapse; recurrence; set-back
na wskroś [na vskrośh] adv.
throughout; from end to end
nawyk [na-vik] m. habit; wont
nawykać [na-vi-kaćh] v.
accustom; fall into a habit
nawykły [na-vik-wi] adj. m.
accustomed; get used to...
na wylot [na vi-lot] adv. through
and through; right through
nawymyślać [na-vi-mi-śhlaćh]
v. revile; abuse; insult; invent
na wyrywki [na vi-riv-kee] adv.
at random; haphazardly
nawzajem [na-vza-yem] adv.
mutually; same to you
na wznak [na vznak] adv. on
one's back; supine
nazad [na-zat] adv. back (wards)
nazajutrz [na-za-yootsh] adv.
next morning; next day
nazbierać [naz-bye-raćh] v.
gather up; collect; assemble
nazbyt [naz-bit] adv. too much
na zewnątrz [na zev-nowntsh]
adv. out; outward; outside
naznaczyć [na-zna-chićh] v.
mark; fix; appoint; outline

nazwa [naz-va] f. designation; name; appellation; title

nazwisko [naz-**vees**-ko] n. family name; surname; reputation

nazywać [na-zi-vaćh] v. call; name; term; denominate; label; christen; give a name

nażarty [na-zhar-ti] adj. m. gorged; stuffed (greedily)

nażreć się [na-zhrećh śha͟n] v. gorge; stuff oneself (vulg.)

negacja [ne-gats-ya] f. negation; opposite of positive

negatyw [ne-ga-tiv] m. negative

negatywny [ne-ga-tiv-ni] adj. m. negative; saying "no"

negliż [ne-gleesh] m. undress; morning dress; dishabille

negocjacje [ne-go-tsya-tsye] pl. negotiations; settling a treaty

negować [ne-go-vaćh] v. deny

nekrolog [ne-kro-log] m. obituary notice; obituary

nektar [nek-tar] m. nectar

neofita [ne-o-fee-ta] m. convert; neophyte; proselyte

neologizm [ne-o-lo-geezm] m. neologism; new word; new meaning; new coined word

neon [ne-on] m. neon light

nepotyzm [ne-po-tizm] m. nepotism; favoritism shown to relatives in securing jobs, etc.

nerka [ner-ka] f. kidney

nerw [nerv] m. nerve; vigor; ardor; coolness in danger

nerwica [ner-vee-tsa] f. neurosis; nervous disturbance

nerwoból [ner-vo-bool] m. neuralgia; severe pain along a nerve; neuralgy

nerwowość [ner-vo-vośhćh] f. nervosity; irritability; fidgets

nerwowy [ner-vo-vi] adj. m. nervous (breakdown); made up of nerves; fearful; excitable

neseser [ne-se-ser] m. dressing case; make-up case

netto [net-to] adv. net (cost, price, profit, weight, result)

neutralizować [ne-oo-tra-lee-zo-vaćh] v. neutralize

nautralność [ne-oo-tral-

-nośhćh] f. neutrality; neutral status; impartiality

neutralny [ne-oo-tral-ni] adj. m. neutral; indifferent

neutron [ne-oo-tron] m. neutron

newralgia [ne-vral-gya] f. neuralgia; pain along a nerve

newroza [nev-ro-za] f. neurosis

nęcić [nan-ćheećh] v. entice; court; allure; tempt; be seductive; be inviting; tantalize

nędza [nan-dza] f. misery

nędzarz [nan-dzash] m. destitute wretch; beggar; pauper

nędznik [nan-dźneek] villain

nędzny [nandz-ni] adj. m. wretched; miserable; shabby; sorry; beggarly; abject; trashy

nękać [nan-kaćh] v. molest; hurry; torment; harass; annoy; worry; gnaw; press hard

ni to ni owo [ńee to ńee o-vo] adv. neither this nor that

ni stąd ni zowąd [ńee stownt ńee zo-vownt] without any reason; suddenly; for no reason whatever; unexpectedly

niania [ńa-ńa] f. (baby's) nurse; nanny; dry nurse

niańczyć [ńań-chićh] v. nurse

niańka [ńań-ka] f. nurse

niby [ńee-bi] adv. as if; pretending; as it were; like; a sort of; as though; supposedly

nic [ńeets] pron. nothing at all; not a bit; nothing whatever

nic a nic [ńeets ah ńeets] expr.: nothing at all; nothing whatever; not a bit

nic nie szkodzi [ńeets ńe shko-dźhee] expr.: does not matter; do not mention it!

nic z tego [ńeets z te-go] expr.: no use; to no purpose; to no avail; no use for it

nici [ńee-ćhee] f. pl. 1. threads 2. nothing; nothing of it

nici będą z tego [ńee-ćhee ban-down s te-go] it will come to nothing; it will do no good

nicość [ńee-tsośhćh] f. nothingness; oblivion; nihility; nonentity; a mere nothing

nicpoń [ńeets-poń] m. good-for
-nothing; "nogoodnik"; scamp
niczego [ńee-che-go] pron. not
bad; quite good; ont unsightly
niczyj [ńee-chiy] adj. m. nobody's; no one's; ownerless
nić [ńeećh] f. thread
nie [ńe] part; no; not (any)
nie jeszcze [ńe yesh-che] not
yet; not for a long time
nieagresja [ńe-a-gre-sya] f.
nonaggression (treaty or pact)
nieaktualny [ńe-ak-too-al-ni] adj.
m. out of date; off the map;
no longer considered; stale
nieaktywny [ńe-ak-tiv-ni] adj. m.
niebaczny [ńe-bach-ni] adj. m.
imprudent; rush; inconsiderate
niebawem [ńe-ba-vem] adv. by
and by; before long; soon
niebezpieczeństwo [ńe-bez-pye-
-cheń-stvo] n. danger; peril
niebezpieczny [ńe-bez-pyech-ni]
adj. m. dangerous; risky;
tricky; unsafe; hazardous
niebiański [ńe-byań-skee]
adj. m. heavenly; divine
niebieskawy [ńe-bye-ska-vi] adj.
m. bluish; off blue
niebieski [ńe-byes-kee] adj. m.
blue; heavenly; of the sky
niebieskooki [ńe-byes-ko-o-kee]
adj. m. blue-eyed
niebiosa [ńe-byo-sa] pl.
Heavens; the visible sky
niebo [ńe-bo] n. sky
nieborak [ńe-bo-rak] m. poor
soul; poor devil
nieboszczyk [ńe-bosh-chik] m.
deceased; dead person
niebosiężny [ńe-bo-śhanzh-ni]
adj. m. sky-high; towering
niebotyczny [ńe-bo-tich-ni] adj.
m. sky-high; sky reaching
nieboże [ńe-bo-zhe] n. poor
soul; poor thing; poor devil
nie byle jak [ńe bi-le yak]
expr.:not just any way; not
carelessly; unusually well
niebyły [ńe-bi-wi] adj. m. null
and void; non-existent
niebywale [ńe-bi-va-le] adv.
unusually; exceptionally

niebywały [ńe-bi-va-wi] adj. m.
unheard-of; unusual; uncommon; unparalleled; exceptional
niecały [ńe-tsa-wi] adj. m.
incomplete; defective; fragmentary; somewhat less than
niecenzuralny [ńe-tsen-zoo-ral-
-ni] adj. m. indecent; un-
printable; obscene; suggestive;
coarse; broad; ribald
niech [ńekh] part. let; suppose
niechcący [ńekh-tsown-tsi] adv.
unintentionally; unawares
niechęć [ńe-khanćh] f.
disinclination; aversion; ill-will
niechętny [ńe-khant-ni] adj. m.
unwilling; reluctant; averse
niechluj [ńe-khluy] m. grub;
sloppy; dirty; sloven; pig; slut
niechybny [ńe-khib-ni] adj. m.
without fail; certain; unerring
niechże [ńekh-zhe] part. let
niecić [ńe-ćheećh] v. kindle;
stir up; light (a fire)
nieciekawy [ńe-ćhe-ka-vi]
adj. m. blank; void of interest
niecierpliwić się [ńe-ćher-plee-
-veećh śhan] v. be impatient
niecierpliwy [ńe-ćher-plee-vi]
adj. m. impatient; restless
niecnota [ńets-no-ta] m. scamp;
rogue; rascal; roguery; infamy
niecny [ńets-ni] adj. m. vile
nieco [ńe-tso] adv. somewhat; a
little; a trifle; slightly
niecodzienny [ńe-tso-dźhen-ni]
adj. m. uncommon; unusual
nieczesany [ńe-che-sa-ni]
adj. m. unkempt; disorderly
nieczęsty [ńe-chan-sti] adj. m.
infrequent; not frequent
nieczuły [ńe-choo-wi] adj. m.
callous; heartless; insensible
nieczynny [ńe-chin-ni] adj. m.
inert; inactive; out of order
nieczysty [ńe-chis-ti] adj. m.
unclean; polluted; dirty; shady
nieczytelny [ńe-chi-tel-ni] adj. m.
illegible; cramped; crabbed
niedaleki [ńe-da-le-kee] adj. m.
near; not distant; at hand
niedaleko [ńe-da-le-ko] adv.
near; not far; a short way off

niedawno [ńe-dav-no] adv.
recently; not long ago; newly
niedbale [ńed-ba-le] adv. neg-
lectfully; carelessly; casually;
nonchalantly; heedlessly
niedbalstwo [ńed-bal-stvo] n.
negligence; laxity; care-
lessness; laxity; nonchalance
niedbały [ńed-ba-wi] adj. m.
negligent; untidy; lax; careless
niedługi [ńed-woo-gee] adj. m.
short; not long; brief; curt
niedługo [ńed-woo-go] adv.
soon; not long; before long;
by and by; a short time
niedobitki [ńe-do-beet-kee] pl.
survivors; routed soldiers
niedobór [ńe-do-boor] m. deficit;
shortage; scarcity; loss
niedobrany [ńe-do-bra-ni] adj. m.
ill-suited; ill-matched
niedobry [ńe-do-bri] adj. m. no
-good; bad; wicked; nasty
niedobrze [ńe-dob-zhe] adv. not
well; badly; wrong; improperly
nie doceniać [ńe do-tse-ńać]
v. underestimate; estimate too
low; set too low an estimate
niedociągnięcie [ńe-do-ćhown-
-gńan-ćhe] n. shortcoming
niedogodność [ńe-do-god-
-nośhćh] f. inconvenience;
drawback; lack of comfort
niedogodny [ńe-do-god-ni]
adj. m. inconvenient; undesirable; causing bother, etc.
niedogotowany [ńe-do-go-to-va-
-ni] adj. m. underdone; half-
cooked; half-raw
nie dojadać [ńe do-ya-dać] v.
under-nourish; not eat enough
niedojda [ńe-doy-da] m. nitwit;
bungler; fumbler; lout
niedojrzały [ńe-doy-zha-wi] adj.
m. unripe; immature; under
age; green; raw; half-grown
niedokładny [ńe-do-kwad-ni] adj.
m. inaccurate; inexact
niedokończony [ńe-do-koń-cho-
-ni] adj. m. unfinished;
incomplete; uncompleted
niedokrwisty [ńe-do-krvees-ti]
adj. m. anemic; anaemic

niedola [ńe-do-la] f. adversity
niedołęga [ńe-do-wan-ga] m.
blunderer; cripple; duffer
niedołęstwo [ńe-do-wans-tvo] n.
inefficiency; clumsiness
niedomagać [ńe-do-ma-gać]
v. be unwell; be ailing
nie domknięty [ńe dom-kńan-ti]
adj. m. ajar; slightly open
niedomówienie [ńe-do-moo-vye-
-ńe] n. vague hint; insinuation
niedomyślny [ńe-do-miśhl-ni]
adj. m. slow thinking
niedopałek [ńe-do-pa-wek] m.
(cigarette) butt; stub; ember
niedopatrzenie [ńe-do-pa-tshe-
-ńe] n. oversight; neglect
niedopuszczalny [ńe-do-poosh-
-chal-ni] adj. m. inadmissible
niedorozwinięty [ńe-do-roz-vee-
-ńan-ti] adj. m. under-
developed; mentally retarded
niedorzeczność [ńe-do-zhech-
-nośhćh] f. (pure) nonsense
niedorzeczny [ńe-do-zhech-ni]
adj. m. absurd; ridiculous;
nonsensical; ludicrous
niedoskonały [ńe-do-sko-na-wi]
adj. m. imperfect; deficient
niedosłyszalny [ńe-do-swi-shal-
-ni] adj. m. inaudible
niedosmażony [ńe-do-sma-zho-
-ni] adj. m. underdone
nie dospać [ńe dos-pać] v.
sleep too short time
niedostateczny [ńe-do-sta-tech-
-ni] adj. m. insufficient
niedostatek [ńe-do-sta-tek] m.
shortage; indigence; poverty
niedostępny [ńe-do-stan-pni]
adj. m. inaccessible; out of
reach; unattainable
niedostosowanie [ńe-do-sto-so-
-va-ńe] n. maladjustment
niedostrzegalny [ńe-do-stzhe-gal-
-ni] adj. m. imperceptible
niedościgły [ńe-do-śhćheeg-
-wi] adj. m. matchless; in-
imitable; peerless; unique
niedoświadczenie [ńe-do-
-śhvyad-che-ńe] n. inex-
perience; lack of experience
niedouczony [ńe-do-oo-cho-ni]

adj. m. half-educated
nie dowarzony [ńe do-va-zho-ni]
half-boiled; rough; immature
niedowiarek [ńe-do-vya-rek] m.
unbeliever; atheist; skeptic
niedowidzieć [ńe-do-vee--dźhećh] v. be short-sighted
nie dowierzać [ńe do-vye--zhaćh] v. distrust; disbelieve
niedowład [ńe-do-vwat] m.
paresis; partial paralysis
niedozwolony [ne-do-zvo-lo-ni]
adj. m. not allowed; illicit
niedrogi [ńe-dro-gee] adj. m.
cheap; inexpensive; low priced
nieduży [ńe-doo-zhi] adj. m.
small; little; not big; not tall
niedwuznaczny [ńe-dvoo-znach--ni] adj. m. unequivocal; clear
niedyskrecja [ńe-di-skrets-ya] f.
indiscretion; indelicacy
niedyspozycja [ńe-di-spo-zits-ya]
f. indisposition; ill-health
niedziela [ńe-dźhe-la] f. Sunday
niedźwiadek [ńe-dźhvya-dek]
m. bear cub; Teddy bear
niedźwiedzica [ńedźh-vye--dźhee-tsa] f. female bear
niedźwiedź [ńedźh-vyedźh]
m. bear; bearskin; clumsy man
nieelastyczny [ńe-e-la-stich-ni]
adj. m. inelastic
nieestetyczny [ńe-e-ste-tich-ni]
adj. m. unesthetic
nieetyczny [ńe-e-tich-ni] adj. m.
unethical; immoral
niefachowy [ńe-fa-kho-vi] adj.
m. incompetent; inexpert; unprofessional; amateurish
nieforemny [ńe-fo-rem-ni]
adj. m. shapeless; deformed
nieformalnie [ńe-for-mal-ńe]
adv. informally; illegally
niefortunny [ńe-for-toon-ni] adj.
m. unlucky; regrettable
niefrasobliwy [ńe-fra-so-blee-vi]
adj. m. care-free; jaunty
niegdyś [ńeg-diśh] adv.
formerly; once; at one time
niegodny [ńe-god-ni] adj. m.
unworthy; undignified; vile;
base; discreditable; shameful
niegodziwy [ńe-go-dźhee-vi]

adj. m. wicked; vile; base;
mean; foul; unscrupulous
niegościnny [ńe-go-śhćheen--ni] adj. m. inhospitable; desolate; forbidding; bleak
niegrzeczny [ne-gzhech-ni] adj.
m. rude; impolite; unkind; bad
niegustowny [ńe-goo-stov-ni]
adj. m. tasteless; in bad taste
niehigieniczny [ńe-khee-gye--ńeech-ni] adj. m. unsanitary
niehonorowy [ńe-kho-no-ro-vi]
adj. m. dishonorable; unfair
nieistotny [ńe-ee-stot-ni] adj. m.
inessential; immaterial
niejaki [ńe-ya-kee] adj. m. one;
certain; some; slight
niejasno [ńe-yas-no] adv. dimly;
vaguely; ambiguously; darkly;
obscurely; indistinctly
niejasny [ńe-yas-ni] adj. m. dim;
unclear; indistinct; vague; obscure; ambiguous; hazy; foggy
niejeden [ńe-ye-den] adj. m.
many a; quite a number
niejednokrotnie [ńe-yed-no-krot--ńe] adv. repeatedly; recurrently; more than once
nie karany [ńe ka-ra-ni] adj. m.
with a clean record; not
convicted before
niekiedy [ńe-ke-di] adv. now
and then; sometimes; at times
niekonsekwentny [ńe-kon-se--kvent-ni] adj. m. inconsistent
niekorzystny [ńe-ko-zhist-ni] adj.
m. disadvantageous
niekorzyść [ńe-ko-zhiśhćh] f.
disadvantage; detriment
niekształtny [ńe-kshtawt-ni] adj.
m. unshapely; formless
niektóry [ńe-ktoo-ri] adj. m.
some; one here and there
nieledwie [ńe-led-vye] adv. all
but; almost; practically
nielegalny [ńe-le-gal-ni] adj. m.
illegal; unlawful; illicit
nieletni [ńe-let-ńee] pl. under
age; juvenile; minor
nieliczny [ńe-leech-ni] adj. m.
not numerous; scarce; rare;
small; pl. some few; rare
nielitościwy [ńe-lee-to-

-śhćhee-vi] adj. m. unmerciful; pitiless; ruthless
nielogiczny [ne-lo-**geech**-ni] adj. m. illogical; nonsensical;
nieludzki [ńe-**loodz**-kee] adj. m. inhuman; atrocious; ruthless
nieład [ńe-wad] m. disorder; disarray; confusion; mess
nieładnie [ńe-**wad-**ńe] adv. not nicely; unattractively; wrongly
nielaska [ńe-**was**-ka] f. disgrace; disfavor; loss of respect
niemal [ńe-mal] adv. almost; nearly; pretty nearly; well-nigh
niemało [ńe-**ma**-wo] adv. not a few; pretty much; not a little
niemały [ńe-**ma**-wi] adj. m. pretty big; fair-sized; goodly; no mean; of considerable size
niemądry [ńe-**mown**-dri] adj. m. unwise; ill-judged; silly; stupid
niemczyć [ńem-**chićh**] v. Germanize (under pressure)
niemęski [ńe-**man**-skee] adj. m. unmanly (without nerve, etc.)
niemiecki [ńe-**myets**-kee] adj. m. German; German language
niemiły [ńe-**mee**-wi] adj. m. unpleasant; unsightly; harsh; surly; disagreeable; offensive
niemniej jednak [**ńem**-ńey **yed**-nak] nevertheless; all the same; none the less; however
niemoc [ńe-mots] f. impotence
niemodny [ńe-**mod**-ni] adj. m. outmoded; out of fashion
niemoralny [ńe-mo-**ral**-ni] adj. m. immoral; dishonest; depraved
niemowa [ńe-**mo**-va] m. & f. mute; dumb; speechless
niemowlę [ńe-mo-**vlan**] n. baby
niemożliwy [ńe-mo-**zhlee**-vi] adj. m. impossible; unfeasible
niemrawy [ńe-**mra**-vi] adj. m. sluggish; tardy; indolent
niemy [**ńe**-mi] adj. m. dumb
nienaganny [ńe-na-**gan**-ni] adj. m. blameless; faultless
ninaruszalny [ńe-na-roo-**shal**-ni] adj. m. inviolable; sacred
nienaruszony [ńe-na-roo-**sho**-ni] adj. m. intact; undisturbed
nienasycony [ńe-na-si-co-ni] adj.

m. insatiable; voracious; (chem. unsaturated)
nienaturalny [ńe-na-too-**ral**-ni] adj. m. unnatural; insincere
nienawistny [ńe-na-**veest**-ni] adj. m. hateful; full of hatred
nienawiść [ńe-na-**veeśhćh**] f. hate; abomination; detestation
nie nazwany [**ńe** na-zva-ni] adj. m. unnamed; not maned
nienormalny [ńe-nor-**mal**-ni] adj. m. abnormal; insane
nieobecność [ńe-o-**bets**-**nośhćh**] f. absence; non-attendance; truancy
nieobecny [ńe-o-**bets**-ni] adj. m. absent; not present; not in
nieobeznany [ńe-o-bez-**na**-ni] adj. m. uninformed; ignorant
nieobliczalny [ńe-o-blee-**chal**-ni] adj. m. unreliable; incalculable; irresponsible; unpredictable
nieobyczajny [ńe-o-bi-**chay**-ni] adj. m. immoral; ill-mannered
nieoceniony [ńe-o-tse-**ńo**-ni] adj. m. inestimable; priceless
nieoczekiwany [ńe-o-che-kee-**va**-ni] adj. m. unexpected
nieodłączny [ńe-o-**dwown**-chni] adj. m. inseparable; inherent
nieodmienny [ńe-od-**myen**-ni] adj. m. invariable; undeclinable
nieodparty [ńe-od-**par**-ti] adj. m. irrefutable; compelling; cogent
nieodpowiedni [ńe-od-po-**vyed**-ńee] adj. m. inadequate; inappropriate; improper; wrong
nieodpowiedzialny [ńe-od-po-vye-**dźhal**-ni] adj. m. irresponsible; unpredictable
nieodstępny [ńe-od-**stanp**-ni] adj. m. inseparable
nieodwołalny [ńe-od-vo-**wal**-ni] adj. m. irrevocable; final; irreversible; beyond recall
nieodzownie [ńe-od-**zov**-ńe] adv. inevitably; absolutely
nieodzowny [ńe-od-**zov**-ni] adj. m. indispensable; irrevocable
nieodżałowany [ńe-od-zha-wo-**va**-ni] adj. m. never enough regretted; much regretted
nieoględny [ńe-o-**gland**-ni]

adj. m. inconsiderate; reckless; rash; heedless; too hasty

nieograniczony [ńe-o-gra-ńee--cho-ni] adj. m. infinite; boundless; unrestricted; unstinted; unlimited; indefinite; absolute

nieokiełzany [ńe-o-kew-za-ni] adj. m. unbridled; rampant; reinless; uncontrollable

nieokreślony [ńe-o-kre-śhlo-ni] adj. m. indefinite; undetermined; nondescript; uncertain

nieokrzesany [ńe-o-kzhe-sa-ni] adj. m. rude; crude; ill-mannered; coarse; uncouth

nieomal [ńe-o-mal] adv. almost; pretty nearly; practically

nieomylny [ńe-o-mil-ni] adj. m. infallible; unerring; sure

nieopatrzny [ńe-o-patsh-ni] adj. m. unguarded; inconsiderate

nieopisany [ńe-o-pee-sa-ni] adj. m. indescribable; excessive; extreme; inexpressible

nieopłacalny [ńe-o-pwa-tsal-ni] adj. m. unprofitable

nieopłacony [ńe-o-pwa-tso-ni] adj. m. unpaid; not paid for

nieopodal [ne-o-po-dal] adv. near by; close at hand; next door

nieorganiczny [ńe-or-ga-ńeech--ni] adj. m. inorganic (compound); inanimate

nieosobowy [ńe-o-so-bo-vi] adj. m. inpersonal; not personal

nieostrożny [ńe-o-strozh-ni] adj. m. careless; imprudent

nieoswojony [ńe-o-svo-yo-ni] adj. m. untamed; unfamiliar

nieoświecony [ńe-o-śhvye-tso--ni] adj. m. dark; ignorant

nieoznaczony [ńe-oz-na-cho-ni] adj. m. indefinite; unmarked

niepalący [ńe-pa-lown-tsi] adj. m. not smoking; non smoking; m. non-smoker

niepalność [ńe-pal-nośhćh] f. incombustibility

niepalny [ńe-pal-ni] adj. m. incombustible; uninflammable

niepamięć [ńe-pa-myanćh] f. oblivion; forgetfulness; unconsciousness; negligence

niepamiętny [ne-pa-myant-ni] adj. m. forgetful; immemorial

nieparlamentarny [ńe-par-la-men--tar-ni] adj. m. rough (language); using vulgar words

nieparzysty [ńe-pa-zhis-ti] adj. m. odd; uneven; unpaired

niepełnoletni [ńe-pew-no-let--ńee] adj. m. minor; underage

niepewność [ńe-pev-nośhćh] f. uncertainty; incertitude

niepewny [ńe-pev-ni] adj. m. uncertain; insecure; unsafe

niepisany [ńe-pee-sa-ni] adj. m. unwritten; not in writing

niepiśmienny [ńe-peeśh-myen--ni] adj. m. illiterate; unlettered

niepłacący [ńe-pwa-tsown-tsi] adj. m. non-paying

niepłodny [ńe-pwod-ni] adj. m. sterile; barren; infertile

niepłonny [ńe-pwon-ni] adj. m. well-founded; motivated

niepochlebny [ńe-po-khleb-ni] adj. m. unfavorable

niepocieszony [ńe-po-ćhe-sho--ni] adj. m. desolate

niepoczciwy [ńe-po-chćhee-vi] adj. m. wicked; unkind

niepoczytalny [ńe-po-chi-tal-ni] adj. m. irresponsible; insane

niepodejrzany [ńe-po-dey-zha-ni] adj. m. unsuspected

niepodległość [ńe-po-dleg--wośhćh] f. independence; sovereignty (of state, ruler)

niepodległy [ńe-po-dleg-wi] adj. m. independent; sovereign

niepodobieństwo [ńe-po-do--byeń-stvo] n. impossibility

niepodobna [ńe-po-dob-na] adv. it's impossible; there is no way; one cannot possibly

niepodobny [ńe-po-dob-ni] adj. m. (altogether) unlike; unlikely; (quite) dissimilar

niepodzielny [ńe-po-dźhel-ni] adj. m. indivisible; undivided

niepogoda [ńe-po-go-da] f. bad weather; foul weather

niepogwałcony [ńe-po-gvaw-tso--ni] adj. m. inviolate

niepohamowany [ńe-po-kha-mo-

-va-ni] adj. m. unrestrained
niepojętny [ńe-po-yant-ni]
adj. m. dull (man); stupid
niepojęty [ńe-po-yan-ti] adj. m.
inconceivable; incomprehensible; unimaginable; beyond
understanding
niepokalany [ńe-po-ka-la-ni] adj.
m. immaculate; faultless
niepokaźny [ńe-po-kaźh-ni]
adj. m. inconspicuous; modest; plain; shabby; wretched
niepokoić [ńe-po-ko-eećh] v.
disturb; trouble; annoy; pester
niepokonany [ńe-po-ko-na-ni]
adj. m. invincible; irresistible
niepokój [ńe-po-kooy] m. anxiety; unrest; trouble; agitation; concern; worry; disquiet
niepolityczny [ńe-po-lee-tich-ni]
adj. m. impolitical; inexpedient; improper; impolitic; nonpolitical; injudicious
niepomierny [ńe-po-myer-ni] adj.
m. excessive; extreme
niepomny [ńe-pom-ni] adj. m.
forgetful; oblivious
niepomyślny [ńe-po-miśhl-ni]
adj. m. adverse; unlucky
niepopłatny [ńe-po-pwat-ni] adj.
m. unprofitable; unrewarding
niepoprawny [ńe-po-prav-ni] adj.
m. incorrigible; incorrect
niepopularny [ńe-po-poo-lar-ni]
adj. m. unpopular
nieporadny [ńe-po-rad-ni] adj. m.
awkward; helpless; unskillful
nieporęczny [ne-po-ranch-ni] adj.
m. cumbersome; unhandy
nieporozumienie [ńe-po-ro-zoo-
-mye-ńe] n. misunderstanding
nieporównany [ńe-po-roov-na-ni]
adj. m. incomparable
nieporuszony [ńe-po-roo-sho-ni]
adj. m. immovable; firm
nieporządek [ńe-po-zhown-dek]
adj. m. disorder; mess
nieporządny [ńe-po-zhownd-ni]
adj. m. disorderly; untidy;
messy; slipshod; chaotic
nieposłuszeństwo [ńe-po-swoo-
-sheń-stvo] n. disobedience
nieposłuszny [ńe-po-swoosh-ni]

adj. m. disobedient; unruly
niepospolity [ńe-pos-po-lee-ti]
adj. m. uncommon; rare
niepostrzeżenie [ńe-po-stshe-
-zhe-ńe] adv. imperceptibly;
without being noticed
niepotrzebny [ńe-po-tzheb-ni]
adj. m. unnecessary; useless
niepowetowany [ńe-po-ve-to-
va-ni] adj. m. irreparable
niepowodzenie [ńe-po-vo-dze-
-ńe] n. failure; adversity
niepowołany [ńe-po-vo-wa-ni]
adj. m. uncalled for; incompetent; unfit; undesirable; wrong
niepowrotny [ńe-pov-rot-ni] adj.
m. irrevocable; irrecoverable;
beyond recall; irretrievable
niepowsrzymany [ńe-pov-stzhi-
-ma-ni] adj. m. irresistible
niepowszedni [ńe-pov-shed-ńee]
adj. m. uncommon; unusually
good; exceptional
niepowściągliwy [ńe-pov-
-śhćhowng-lee-vi] adj. m.
intemperate; uncontrollable
niepozorny [ńe-po-zor-ni] adj. m.
inconspicuous; modest
niepożądany [ńe-po-zhown-da-
-ni] adj. m. undesirable; unwanted; objectionable
niepożyteczny [ńe-po-zhi-tech-
-ni] adj. m. useless; unprofitable; to no purpose
niepraktyczny [ńe-prak-tich-ni]
adj. m. impractical; unwieldy
niepraktykujący [ńe-prak-ti-koo-
-yown-tsi] adj. m. noncommunicant; retired (professional)
nieprawda [ńe-prav-da] f.
untruth; falsehood; lie; exp.:
impossible! isn't that so?
nieprawdopodobny [ńe-prav-do-
-po-dob-ni] adj. m. improbable
nieprawdziwy [ńe-prav-dźhee-
-vi] adj. m. untrue; false; bogus; faked; fictitious; unreal
nieprawidłowość [ńe-pra-vee-
-dwo-vośhćh] f. anomaly; irregularity; falsity; incorrectness; abnormality; faultiness
nieprawidłowy [ńe-pra-vee-
dwo-vi] adj. m. anomalous;

irregular; contrary to the rules
nieprawny [ńe-**prav**-ni] adj. m.
illegal; unlawful; invalid
nieprawomyślny [ńe-pra-vo-
-**miśhl**-ni] adj. m. unorthodox;
disloyal; unfaithful; not loyal
nieprawy [ńe-**pra**-vi] adj. m.
unrighteous; adulterous;
bastard; unlawful; illegitimate
nieproporcjonalny [ńe-pro-por-
-**tsyo-nal**-ni] adj. m. dispro-
portional; out of proportion
nieproszony [ńe-pro-**sho**-ni] adj.
m. uncalled for; self-invited;
unwelcome (guest)
nieprzebaczalny [ńe-pzhe-ba-
chal-ni] adj. m. unpardonable
nieprzebłagany [ńe-pzhe-bwa-
ga-ni] adj. m. implacable
nieprzebrany [ńe-pzhe-**bra**-ni]
adj. inexhaustible; countless
nieprzebyty [ńe-pzhe-**bi**-ti]
adj. m. impassable
nieprzejednany [ńe-pzhe-yed-**na**-
-ni] adj. m. irreconcilable; un-
compromising; implacable
nieprzejrzysty [ńe-pzhey-**zhis**-ti]
adj. m. not clear; opaque
nieprzekupny [ńe-pzhe-**koop**-ni]
adj. m. unbribable; incorrupt-
ible; refusing to take bribes
nieprzemakalny [ńe-pzhe-ma-**kal**-
-ni] adj. m. waterproof
nieprzeniknony [ńe-pzhe-ńeek-
-**ńo**-ni] adj. m. impenetrable;
impassable (area); inscrutable
nieprzepuszczalny [ńe-pzhe-
-**poosh**-chal-ni] adj. m.
impervious; impenetrable
nieprzerwany [ńe-pzher-**va**-ni]
adj. m. continuous; ceaseless
nieprześcigniony [ńe-pzheśh-
-**ćheeg**-ńo-ni] adj. m.
unsurpassable; unexcelled
nieprzewidziany [ńe-pzhe-vee-
-**dźha**-ni] adj. m. unforeseen
nieprzezorny [ńe-pzhe-**zor**-ni]
adj. m. improvident; unforsee-
ing; wanting of foresight
niprzeźroczysty [ńe-pzhe-źhro-
-**chis**-ti] adj. m. opaque
nieprzezwyciężony [ńe-pzhez-vi-
-ćh<u>an</u>-**zho**-ni] adj. m.

invincible; insurmountable
nieprzychylny [ńe-pzhi-**khil**-ni]
adj. m. unfriendly; prejudiced
nieprzydatny [ńe-pzhi-**dat**-ni] adj.
m. useless; unserviceable
nieprzygotowany [ńe-pzhi-go-to-
-**va**-ni] adj. m. unprepared
nieprzyjaciel [ńe-pzhi-ya-**ćhel**]
m. enemy; foe; ill-wisher
nieprzyjacielski [ńe-pzhi-ya-**ćhel**-
-skee] adj. m. enemy; hostile;
enemy's (tanks, guns, etc.)
nieprzyjazny [ńe-pzhi-**yaz**-ni] adj.
m. unfriendly; inimical
nieprzyjaźń [ńe-pzhi-**yaźhń**] f.
hostility; unfriendliness
nieprzyjemność [ńe-pzhi-**yem**-
-nośhćh] f. unpleasantness
nieprzyjemny [ńe-pzhi-**yem**-ni]
adj. m. unpleasant; disagee-
able; distasteful; annoying
nieprzystępny [ńe-pzhis-**tanp**-ni]
adj. m. inaccessible; grumpy
nieprzytomność [ńe-pzhi-**tom**-
-nośhćh] f. unconsciousness;
absentmindedness; senseless-
ness; foolishness
nieprzytomny [ńe-pzhi-**tom**-ni]
adj. m. unconscious; absent-
minded; frantic; mad; wild
nieprzyzwoitość [ńe-pzhi-zvo-
-ee-tośhćh] f. indecency
nieprzyzwoity [ńe-pzhi-zvo-**ee**-ti]
adj. m. indecent; obscene
nieprzyzwyczajony [ńe-pzhiz-vi-
-cha-**yo**-ni] adj. m. not
accustomed to; unaccustomed
niepunktualny [ńe-poon-ktoo-**al**-
-ni] adj. m. unpunctual; late
nierad [ńe-rad] adj. m. unwilling;
annoyed; adv. unwillingly
nieraz [**ńe**-raz] adv. often; again
and again; many a time
nierdzewny [ńe-**rdzev**-ni] adj. m.
rustproof; stainless; rustless
nierealny [ńe-re-**al**-ni] adj. m.
imaginary; unreal; unrealizable
nieregularność [ńe-re-goo-**lar**-
-nośhćh] f. irregularity
nieregularny [ńe-re-goo-**lar**-ni]
adj. m. irregular; erratic
niereligijny [ńe-re-lee-**geey**-ni]
adj. m. not religious; profane;

impious; irreligious
nierogacizna [ńe-ro-ga-**ćheez**-
-na] f. pl. swines; hogs
nierozdzielny [ńe-roz-**dźhel**-ni]
adj. m. inseparable
nierozerwalny [ńe-ro-zer-**val**-ni]
adj. m. indissoluble
nierozgarnięty [ńe-roz-gar-**ńan**-
-ti] adj. m. dull; (dim-witted)
nieskuteczny [ńe-skoo-**tech**-ni]
adj. m. ineffective; futile
niesłabnący [ńe-swab-**nown**-tsi]
adj. m. unabated; unflagging
niesława [ńe-**swa**-va] f. infamy
niesławny [ńe-**swav**-ni] adj. m.
infamous; inglorious; disgraceful; having a bad reputation
niesłowny [ńe-**swov**-ni] adj. m.
unreliable; undependable
niesłuszność [ńe-**swoosh**-
-nośhćh] f. injustice; unfair-
ness; groundlessness
nisłuszny [ńe-**swoosh**-ni] adj. m.
unjust; wrong; groundless
niesłychany [ńe-swi-**kha**-ni] adj.
m. unheard of; unprecedented
niesmaczny [ńe-**smach**-ni]
adj. m. tasteless; unsavory;
unseemly; unpalatable; coarse
niesmak [**ńes**-mak] m. bad
taste; disgust; repugnance;
nasty taste (in the mouth)
niesnaski [ńe-**snas**-kee] pl.
dissension; discord; quarrels
niespełna [ńe-**spew**-na] adv.
nearly; not all; not quite;
about; somewhat less than
niespodzianka [ńe-spo-**dźhan**-
-ka] f. surprise; surprise gift
niespodziewany [ńe-spo-**dźhe**-
-va-ni] adj. m. unexpected;
unlooked for; unforeseen
niespokojny [ńe-spo-**koy**-ni] adj.
m. restless; fussy; upset;
fretful; turbulent; ill at ease
niesporo [ńe-**spo**-ro] adv. slowly
nie sposób [ńe **spo**-soop] adv.
it's impossible; by no means
niespożyty [ńe-spo-**zhi**-ti]
adj. m. durable; indefatigable
niesprawiedliwość [ńe-spra-
-vye-dlee-vo**śhćh**] f. injustice
niesprawiedliwy [ńe-spra-vyed-

-lee-vi] adj. m. unjust; unfair
niesprawny [ńe-**sprav**-ni] adj. m.
ineffective; inefficient
nie sprzyjający [ńe spzhi-ya-
-**yown**-tsi] adj. m. adverse
niestały [ńe-**sta**-wi] adj. m.
unsteady; inconsistent; variable; fickle; unsteady; shifting
niestaranny [ńe-sta-ran-ni]
adj. m. careless; sloppy;
dowdy; neglectful; slapdash
niestateczny [ńe-sta-**tech**-ni] adj.
m. unstable; fickle; flighty
niestety [ńe-**ste**-ti] adv. alas;
unfortunately; exp.: I am sorry
niestosowny [ńe-sto-**sov**-ni] adj.
m. improper; unsuitable; unfit;
inappropriate; out of place
niestrawność [ńe-**strav**-
-nośhćh] f. indigestion; dys-
pepsia; difficulty in digesting
niestrawny [ńe-**strav**-ni] adj. m.
indigestible; stodgy; dull
niestrudzony [ńe-stroo-**dzo**-ni]
adj. m. indefatigable; untiring
niestworzony [ńe-stvo-**zho**-ni]
adj. m. unreal; nonsense
niesumienny [ńe-soo-**myen**-ni]
adj. m. unscrupulous; uncon-
scientious; unreliable; careless
nieswojo [ńe-**svo**-yo] adv.
uneasily; strangely; qualmishly
nieswój [ńe-**svooy**] adj. m. ill at
ease; uncomfortable; seedy;
strange; off color
niesymetryczny [ńe-si-met-**rich**-
-ni] adj. m. asymmetrical
niesympatyczny [ńe-sim-pa-**tich**-
-ni] adj. m. unpleasant
nieszczególny [ńe-shche-**gool**-ni]
adj. m. mediocre; so-so
nieszczelny [ńe-**shchel**-ni]
adj. m. leaky; not shut tight
nieszczery [ńe-**shche**-ri] adj. m.
insincere; double dealing
nieszczęsny [ńe-**shchans**-ni] adj.
m. miserable; ill-fated
nieszczęście [ńe-**shchan**-
-śhćhe] n. misfortune; disaster; adversity; bad luck
nieszczęśliwy [ńe-shchan-
-śhlee -vi] adj. m. unhappy;
ill-starred; luckless; wretched

nieszkodliwy [ńe-shko-dlee-vi]
adj. m. harmless; not grave;
inoffensive; innoxious

nieszlachcic [ńe-shlakh-ćheets]
m. commoner (not a noble)

nieszpetny [ńe-shpet-ni] adj. m.
fairly good-looking

nieszpory [ńe-shpo-ri] pl.
vespers; evening prayers

nieścisły [ńe-śhćhees-wi]
adj. m. inexact; inaccurate;
faulty; imprecise; incoherent

niéściśliwy [ńe-śhćheeśh-lee-
-vi] adj. m. incompressible

nieść [ńeśhćh] v. carry;
bring; bear; lay; afford; drive;
bear along; give as a sacrifice

nieślubny [ńe-śhloob-ni]
adj. m. illegitimate; born out
of wedlock; natural

nieśmiały [ńe-śhmya-wi]
adj. m. coy; shy; timid; faint-
hearted; bashful; sheepish

nieśmiertelny [ńe-śhmyer-tel-
-ni] adj. m. immortal; everlasting; undying; imperishable

nieświadomy [ńe-śhvya-do-mi]
adj. m. ignorant (of); unaware;
unknowing (of); involuntary

nietakt [ńe-takt] m. lack of tact;
slip; tactlessness; indelicacy

nietaktowny [ńe-tak-tov-ni] adj.
m. tactless; indelicate

nietknięty [ńe-tkńan-ti] adj. m.
intact; virgin; untouched

nietolerancja [ńe-to-le-ran-tsya]
f. intolerance

nietoperz [ńe-to-pesh] m. bat

nietowarzyski [ńe-to-va-zhis-kee]
adj. m. unsociable

nietrafny [ńe-traf-ni] adj. m.
wrong; missing the mark

nietrzeźwy [ńe-tzheźh-vi]
adj. m. drank; tipsy; unsound

nietutejszy [ńe-too-tey-shi]
adj. m. stranger; non-resident

nietykalny [ńe-ti-kal-ni] adj. m.
immune; inviolable

nie tyle [ńe ti-le] adv. not so
much; not exactly; but; rather

nie tylko [ńe til-ko] adv. not
only; anything but; not merely

nieubłagalny [ńe-oo-bwa-gal-ni]

adj. m. implacable; irrevocable

nieuchronny [ńe-oo-khron-ni]
adj. m. inevitable; inescapable

nieuchwytny [ńe-oo-khvit-ni]
adj. m. elusive; evasive; inaudible; imperceptible

nieuctwo [ńe-oots-tvo] n. lack
of education; ignorance

nieuczciwy [ńe-ooch-ćhee-vi]
adj. m. dishonest; foul; unfair

nieuczynny [ńe-oo-chin-ni] adj.
m. unobliging; disobliging

nieudolny [ńe-oo-dol-ni] adj. m.
awkward; clumsy; decrepit

nieufny [ńe-oof-ni] adj. m.
distrustful; suspicious

nieugaszony [ńe-oo-ga-sho-ni]
adj. m. unextinguished;
unquenchable; unsuppressible

nieugięty [ńe-oo-gyan-ti] adj. m.
inflexible; unyielding

nieuk [ńe-ook] m. know-nothing

nieukojony [ńe-oo-ko-yo-ni] adj.
m. inconsolable (grief, etc.)

nieuleczalny [ńe-oo-le-chal-ni]
adj. m. incurable

nieumiarkowany [ńe-oo-myar-ko-
-va-ni] adj. m. intemperate

nieumiejętny [ńe-oo-mye-yant-
-ni] adj. m. inexpert; unskilled

nieumyślny [ńe-oo-miśhl-ni]
adj. m. unintentional

nieunikniony [ńe-oo-ńeek-ńo-ni]
adj. m. unavoidable; inevitable

nieuprzedzony [ńe-oo-pzhe-dzo-
-ni] adj. m. unbiased; not
forewarned; not prejudiced

nieuprzejmy [ńe-oo-pzhey-mi]
adj. m. impolite; discourteous;
unkind; lacking compassion

nieurodzaj [ńe-oo-ro-dzay] m.
bad harvest; bad crops;
scarcity (of crops, etc.)

nieusprawiedliwiony [ńe-oo-
-spra-vye-dlee-vyo-ni] adj. m.
unexcused; unjustified

nieustanny [ńe-oos-tan-ni] adj.
m. constant; perpetual; unceasing; continual; incessant

nieustraszony [ńe-oos-tra-sho-ni]
adj. m. fearless; intrepid

nieusuwalny [ńe-oo-soo-val-ni]
adj. m. immovable (object);

irremovable (from office)
nie uszkodzony [ńe oosh-ko-**dzo**-
-ni] adj. m. unhurt; not hurt
undamaged; not damaged
nieuwaga [ńe-oo-**va**-ga] f.
inattention; absentmindedness
nieuważny [ńe-oo-**vazh**-ni]
adj. m. inattentive; careless
nieuzasadniony [ńe-oo-za-sad-
-ńo-ni] adj. m. unfounded;
unjustified; groundless
nieuzbrojony [ńe-ooz-bro-**yo**-ni]
adj. m. unarmed; disarmed
nieużyteczny [ńe-oo-zhi-**tech**-ni]
adj. m. useless; superfluous
nieużyty [ńe-oo-**zhi**-ti] adj. m.
unused; not worn; uncoope-
rative; disobliging
niewart [ńe-vart] adj. m. not
worth; unworthy (of reward,
praise, etc.); not deserving
nie warto [ńe **var**-to] adv. not
worth (talking about it); not
worthwhile (considering it)
niważny [ńe-**vazh**-ni] adj. m.
invalid; trivial; null and void
niewątpliwy [ńe-**vownt**-plee-vi]
adj. m. sure; doubtless
niewczesny [ńe-**vches**-ni]
adj. m. untimely; late; ill-
timed; inopportune; premature
niewdzięczny [ńe-**vdźhanch**-ni]
adj. m. ungrateful; thankless
niewesoły [ńe-ve-**so**-wi] adj. m.
sad; joyless; pretty bad
niewiadomy [ńe-vya-do-mi] adj.
m. unknown (direction, origin,
quantity, reason, etc.)
niewiara [ńe-**vya**-ra] f. disbelief
(in); mistrust (of); unbelief
niewiasta [ńe-**vyas**-ta] f. woman
niewidomy [ńe-vee-do-mi]
adj. m. blind; lacking insight
niewidzialny [ńe-vee-**dźhal**-ni]
adj. m. invisible; obscure
niewiedza [ńe-**vye**-dza] f.
ignorance (of); unawareness
niewiela [ńe-**vye**-le] adv. not
much; not many; little; few
niewielki [ńe-**vyel**-kee] adj. m.
small; little; unimportant
niewierny [ńe-**vyer**-ni] adj. m.
disloyal; infidel; unfaithful

niewieści [ńe-**vyeśh**-ćhee]
adj. m. womanly; feminine
niewinność [ńe-**veen**-
-nośhćh] f. innocence; purity; chastity; unsophistication
niewinny [ńe-**veen**-ni] adj. m.
not guilty; innocent; harmless
niewłaściwy [ńe-vwaśh-ćhee-
-vi] adj. m. improper; unsuitable; wrong; inappropriate
niewola [ńe-**vo**-la] f. captivity;
bondage; servitude; slavery
niewolić [ńe-**vo**-leećh] v.
enslave; compel; oppress
niewolnica [ńe-vol-**ńee**-tsa] f.
slave; serf; prisoner of war
niewolnik [ńe-**vol**-ńeek] m.
slave; serf; prisoner of war
nie wolno [ńe **vol**-no] v. not allowed; not permitted
niewód [ńe-voot] m. dragnet
niewprawny [ńe-**vprav**-ni]
adj. m. unversed; unskilled; inexpert; incompetent; clumsy;
awkward; inefficient
niewspółmierny [ńe-vspoow-
-**myer**-ni] adj. m. incommen-
surable; out of proportion
nie wtajemniczony [ńe vta-yem-
-ńee-cho-ni] adj. m. uninitiated; uninformed; not privy
niewyczerpany [ńe-vi-cher-**pa**-ni]
adj. m. inexhaustible
niewygoda [ńe-vi-**go**-da] f.
discomfort; trouble; hardship
niwygodny [ńe-vi-**god**-ni] adj. m.
uncomfortable; awkward
niewykonalny [ńe-vi-ko-**nal**-ni]
adj. m. unfeasible; unworkable
niewykształcony [ńe-vi-kshtaw-
-**tso**-ni] adj. m. uneducated
niewymierny [ńe-vi-**myer**-ni] adj.
m. irrational; surd
niewymowny [ńe-vi-**mov**-ni] adj.
m. unspeakable; inexpressible
niewymuszony [ńe-vi-moo-**sho**-
-ni] adj. m. unconstrained;
voluntary; natural; unaffected
niewymyślny [ńe-vi-**miśhl**-ni]
adj. m. unsophisticated; plain
niewypał [ńe-**vi**-paw] m. dud
niewypłacalny [ńe-vi-pwa-**tsal**-
-ni] adj. m. insolvent

niewypowiedziany [ńe-vi-po-vye-
-dźha-ni] adj. m. untold
niewyraźnie [ńe-vi-raźh-ńe]
adv. indistinctly; seedily
niewyraźny [ńe-vi-raźh-ni]
adj. m. queer; indistinct
niewyrobiony [ńe-vi-ro-byo-ni]
adj. m. raw; inexperienced
niewyrozumiały [ńe-vi-ro-zoo-
-mya-wi] adj. m. intolerant
niewysłowiony [ńe-vi-swo-vyo-
-ni] adj. m. ineffable
niewyspany [ńe-vis-pa-ni]
adj. m. sleepy (not enough
sleep); heavy with sleep
niewystarczający [ńe-vis-tar-
-cha-yown-tsi] adj. m.
insufficient; inadequate
niewystawny [ńe-vis-tav-ni] adj.
m. frugal; modest; simple
niewytłumaczony [ńe-vi-twoo-
-ma-cho-ni] adj. m. inexplicable; incomprehensible
niewytrwały [ńe-vi-trva-wi]
adj. m. not persistent
niewytrzymały [ńe-vi-tzhi-ma-wi]
adj. m. not enduring
niewzruszony [ńe-vzroo-sho-ni]
adj. m. unmoved; rigid
niezachwiany [ńe-za-khvya-ni]
adj. m. unshaken; undeterred
niezadowolenie [ńe-za-do-vo-le-
-ńe] n. discontent; displeasure
niezadowolony [ńe-za-do-vo-lo-
-ni] adj. m. dissatisfied; displeased (with); unsatisfied
niezakłócony [ńe-za-kwoo-tso-ni]
adj. m. undisturbed; unmarred
niezależnośhćh [ńe-za-lezh
-nośhćh] n. independence;
self-sufficiency; detachment
niezależny [ńe-za-lezh-ni]
adj. m. independent; self-
contained; self-sufficient
niezamężna [ńe-za-manzh-na]
adj. f. unmarried; single
niezamożny [ńe-za-mozh-ni] adj.
m.poor; indigent; unpropertied
niezapominajka [ńe-za-po-mee-
-nay-ka] f. forget-me-not
nizapomniany [ńe-za-pom-ńa-ni]
adj. m. not-to-be-forgotten;
unforgettable; memorable

niezaprzeczalny [ńe-za-pzhe-
chal-ni] adj. m. undeniable
niezaradny [ńe-za-rad-ni] adj. m.
helpless; shiftless
niezasłużony [ńe-za-swoo-zho-
-ni] adj. m. undeserved
niezawisły [ńe-za-vees-wi]
adj. m. independent; self-reliant; self-governing; free
niezawodnie [ńe-za-vod-ńe]
adv. surely; without fail;
infallibly; unfailingly
niezawodny [ńe-za-vod-ni]
adj. m. sure; never failing;
safe; unerring; steadfast
niezbadany [ńe-zba-da-ni]
adj. m. unexplorable; in-
scrutable; unfathomable
niezbędny [ńe-zband-ni] adj. m.
indispensable; essential
niezbity [ńe-zbee-ti] adj. m.
irrefutable; incontrovertible
niezbyt [ńe-zbit] adv. not very
(much); none too; not too
niezdarny [ńe-zdar-ni] adj. m.
clumsy; awkward; bungled
niezdatny [ńe-zdat-ni] adj. m.
unfit (for use); unqualified (for
doing); unserviceable
niezdecydowany [ńe-zde-tsi-do-
-va-ni] adj. m. undecided
niezdolność [ńe-zdol-nośhćh]
f. inability; unfitness
niezdolny [ńe-zdol-ni] adj. m.
incapable; unable; unfit; dull
niezdrowy [ńe-zdro-vi] adj. m.
unhealthy; unwell; ill; sickly
niezdyscyplinowany [ńe-zdis-tsi-
-plee-no-va-ni] adj. m.
undisciplined; unruly
niezgłębiony [ńe-zgwan-byo-ni]
adj. m. inscrutable; abyssal
niezgoda [ńe-zgo-da] f. discord;
disagreement; dissension
niezgodność [ńe-zgod-
-nośhćh] f. inconsistency; in-
compatibility; disagreement
niezgodny [ńe-zgod-ni] adj. m.
discordant; incompatible
niezgrabny [ńe-zgrab-ni] adj. m.
unhandy; clumsy; shapeless
nieziszczalny [ńe-zeesh-chal-ni]
adj. m. unattainable

niezliczony [ńe-zlee-cho-ni] adj.
m. uncountable; countless
niezłomny [ńe-zwom-ni] adj. m.
inflexible; firm; steadfast
niezmącony [ńe-zmown-tso-ni]
adj. m. unruffled; undisturbed
niezmienny [ńe-zmyen-ni]
adj. m. invariable; constant;
fixed; unchanging; permanent
niezmierny [ńe-zmyer-ni] adj. m.
immense; vast; boundless
niezmordowany [ńe-zmor-do-va-
-ni] adj. m. indefatigable;
tireless; untiring; unflagging
nieznaczny [ńe-znach-ni] adj. m.
trivial; insignificant
nieznajomość [ńe-zna-yo-
-mośhćh] f. ignorance; unawareness; unacquaintance
nieznajomy [ńe-zna-yo-mi]
adj. m. unknown (people);
strange; m. stranger
nieznany [ńe-zna-ni] adj. m.
unknown; unfamiliar; obscure
nieznośny [ńe-znośh-ni]
adj. m. unbearable; annoying;
nasty; pesky; intolerable
niezręczny [ńe-zranch-ni] adj. m.
awkward; clumsy; tactless
niezrozumiały [ńe-zro-zoo-mya-
-wi] adj. m. unintelligible
niezrównany [ńe-zroov-na-ni]
adj. m. matchless; incomparable; peerless; unique; grand;
beyond compare; unrivalled
niezwłoczny [ńe-zvwoch-ni] adj.
m. instant; prompt; immediate
niezwyciężony [ńe-zvi-ćhan-
-zho-ni] adj. m. invincible
niezwykły [ńe-zvik-wi] adj. m.
unusual; extreme; rare; odd
nieżonaty [ńe-zho-na-ti] adj. m.
unmarried; single; bachelor
nieżyczliwy [ńe-zhich-lee-vi] adj.
m. unfriendly; ill-disposed
nieżyt [ńe-zhit] m. inflammation;
catarrh; hay fever; colitis
nieżywy [ńe-zhi-vi] adj. m.
dead; lifeless; inanimate
nigdy [ńeeg-di] adv. never
nigdzie [ńeeg-dźhe] adv.
nowhere; anywhere (after
negation)

nijaki [ńee-ya-kee] adj. m. none;
neuter (gender); indistinct
nikczemnik [ńeek-chem-ńeek]
m. villain; scoundrel; wretch
nikczemny [ńeek-chem-ni] adj.
m. vile; abject; despicable;
base; shabby; mean; dirty
nikiel [ńee-kel] m. nickel
nikły [ńeek-wi] adj. m. scanty
niknąć [ńeek-nownćh] v. vanish; dwindle; waste away
nikotyna [ńee-ko-ti-na] f.
nicotine; poisonous tobacco
extract causing nicotinism
nikt [ńeekt] pron. nobody
nim [ńeem] conj. before; till
nimb [ńeemp] m. halo; aureole
niniejszy [ńee-ńey-shi] adj. m.
this; present; the present
niski [ńees-kee] adj. m. low
nisko [ńees-ko] adv. low
nisza [ńee-sha] f. niche; recess
niszczący [ńeesh-chown-tsi] adj.
m. destructive; disruptive
niszczeć [ńeesh-chećh] v.
waste away; deteriorate; get
wasted; decay; go to ruin
niszczyciel [ńeesh-chi-ćhel] m.
devastator; destroyer; waster
niszczyć [ńeesh-chićh] v.
destroy; spoil; ruin; wreck;
damage; demolish; lay waste
nit [ńeet] m. rivet
nitke [ńeet-ka] f. thread
nitować [ńee-to-vaćh] v. rivet
niwa [ńee-va] f. field; soil
niweczyć [ńee-ve-chićh] v.
destroy; annihilate; lay waste
niwelacja [ńee-ve-lats-ya] f.
leveling; survey; surveying
nivelować [ńee-ve-lo-vaćh] v.
make level; demolish; survey
nizina [ńee-żhee-na] f. lowland
niż [ńeezh] m. lowland; depression; atmospheric low; low
niż [ńeesh] conj. than
niżej [ńee-zhey] adv. lower;
below; down; further down
niższość [ńeesh-shośhćh] f.
inferiority (complex etc.)
niższy [ńeezh-shi] adj. m. lower;
inferior; shorter; subordinate
no [no] part. why; well; now;

then; just; there; there now!

noc [nots] f. night

nocleg [nots-leg] m. place to
sleep; night's lodging

nocny [nots-ni] adj. m.
nocturnal; night-

nocować [no-tso-vaćh] v.
spend night; stay (accommodation) overnight; sleep

noga [no-ga] f. leg; foot

nogawica [no-ga-vee-tsa] f.
legging; trouser leg

nomenklatura [no-men-kla-too-ra]
f. nomenclature; terminology

nominacja [no-mee-nats-ya] f.
appointment; nomination

nominalny [no-mee-nal-ni] adj. m.
nominal; (face) value

nonsens [non-sens] m. nonsense

nora [no-ra] f. burrow; den

norma [nor-ma] f. standard;
norm; rule; general principle

normalizacja [nor-ma-lee-zats-ya]
f. normalization; standard

normalizować [nor-ma-lee-zo-
-vaćh] v. normalize (metal);
standardize; make standard

normalny [nor-mal-ni] adj. m.
normal; standard; ordinary

normować [nor-mo-vaćh] v.
regulate; standardize; make
standard or uniform; normalize

nos [nos] m. nose; snout

nosić [no-śheećh] v. carry;
wear; bear; have about one

nosorożec [no-so-ro-zhets] m.
rhinoceros (with horn)

nostalgia [nos-tal-gya] f.
nostalgia; homesickness

nosze [no-she] pl. stretchers

nota [no-ta] f. note; grade

notariusz [no-tar-yoosh] m.
notary public

notatka [no-tat-ka] f. note

notatnik [no-tat-ńeek] m.
notebook; diary; notes

notes [no-tes] m. pocket
notebook; small notebook

notoryczny [no-to-rich-ni] adj. m.
notorious; flagrant; arrant

notować [no-to-vaćh] v. make
notes; take notes; write down

notowanie [no-to-va-ńe] n.

quotation; record (of facts)

nowela [no-ve-la] f. short story;
amendment (to a constitution)

nowelista [no-ve-lees-ta] m.
short story writer

nowicjat [no-vee-tsyat] m.
novitiate; novitiate

nowicjusz [no-veets-yoosh]
novice; beginner; freshman

nowina [no-vee-na] f. news

nowinka [no-veen-ka] f. fad

nowiutki [no-vyoot-kee] adj. m.
brand-new; spick-and-span

nowoczesny [no-vo-ches-ni] adj.
m. modern; up to date; present day; newest; progressive

noworoczny [no-vo-roch-ni] adj.
m. New Year's; of New Year

nowość [no-vośhćh] f. novelty; newness; strangeness;

nowotwór [no-vo-tvoor] m.
tumor; newly-coined word

nowożytny [no-vo-zhit-ni] adj. m.
(of) modern (period)

nowy [no-vi] adj. m. new

nozdrze [noz-dzhe] n. nostril

nożownik [no-zhov-ńeek] m.
knifer; cutthroat; gangster

nożyce [no-zhi-tse] pl. shears;
clippers; large shears

nożyczki [no-zhich-kee] pl.
scissors; small scissors

nożyk [no-zhik] m. pocketknife

nów [noov] m. new moon

nóż [noosh] m. knife; cutter

nucić [noo-ćheećh] v. hum

nuda [noo-da] f. boredom;

nudności [nood-nośh-ćhee] pl.
nausea; impulse to vomit

nudny [nood-ni] adj. m. boring;
nauseating; dull; sickening

nudysta [noo-dis-ta] m. nudist

nudziarz [noo-dźhash] m. bore

nudzić [noo-dźheećh] v. bore

numer [noo-mer] m. number

numerować [noo-me-ro-vaćh]
v. number; give a number to

numerowy [noo-me-ro-vi] m.
porter; bell-boy; hotel waiter

numizmatyka [noo-meez-ma-ti-
-ka] f. numismatics; study (or
collection) of coins, medals

nuncjusz [noon-tsyoosh] m.

nuncio; papal ambassador
nurek [noo-rek] m. diver
nurkować [noor-ko-vaćh] v.
dive; plunge; duck; nose-dive
nurt [noort] m. current (flowing);
stream; trend; wake
nurtować [noor-to-vaćh] v.
fret; penetrate; pervade; ferment in; rankle; pray on
nurzać [noo-zhaćh] v. dip;
welter in; plunge into; wallow
in; immerse in; steep into
nuta [noo-ta] f. (sound) note
nuty [noo-ti] pl. written music;
printed music; music score
nuż [noozh] adv. if; and if
nużący [noo-zh<u>own</u>-tsi] adj. m.
tiring; tiresome; wearisome
nużyć [noo-zhićh] v. tire;
weary; make tired; oppress
nygus [ni-goos] m. lazybones
nygusować [ni-goo-so-vaćh] v.
lounge about; loiter; loaf
nylon [ni-lon] m. nylon
nyża [ni-zha] f. niche; alcove

O

o [o] prep. of; for; at; by; about;
against; with; to; over; oh!
oaza [o-a-za] f. oasis
oba [o-ba] pron. both
obabrać [o-ba-braćh] v. besmear; smear over; make dirty
obaj [o-bay] pron. both
obalenie [o-ba-le-ńe] n.
overthrow; subversion; refutation; reversal; abolition
obalić [o-ba-leećh] v.
overthrow; knock down; fell;
refute; throw down; subvert
obarczyć [o-bar-chićh] v.
encumber; saddle; load; weigh
down; burden; saddle (with)
obarzanek [o-ba-zha-nek] m.
round cracknel (torus shaped)
obawa [o-ba-va] f. fear;
apprehension; phobia; anxiety

obawiać się [o-ba-vyaćh **śhan**]
v. be anxious; fear; dread
obcas [ob-tsas] m. heel
obcążki [ob-ts<u>ownzh</u>-kee] pl.
(small) tongs; pincers; pliers
obcesowo [ob-tse-**so**-vo] adv.
headlong; outright; abruptly
obcęgi [ob-**tsan**-gee] pl. tongs
obchodzić [ob-kho-dźheećh] v.
go around; evade; elude;
celebrate; inspect; by-pass
obchód [ob-khoot] m. (daily)
beat; celebration; circuit
obciągać [ob-ćh<u>own</u>-gaćh] v.
pull down; cover; pull tight
obciążać [ob-ćh<u>own</u>-zhaćh] v.
burden; charge (account)
obcierać [ob-ćhe-raćh] v. wipe
obcinać [ob-ćhee-naćh] v. cut
off; clip; crop; chop off
obcisły [ob-ćhees-wi] adj. m.
tight; close fitting; clinging
obcokrajowiec [ob-tso-kra-yo-
-vyets] m. foreigner; alien
obcokrajowy [ob-tso-kra-yo-vi]
adj. m. foreign; alien
obcować [ob-tso-vaćh] v. associate; mix with; have sex
obcowanie [ob-tso-va-ńe] n.
intercourse; association
obcy [ob-tsi] adj. m. strange;
foreign; unfamiliar; unrelated
obczyzna [ob-chiz-na] f. foreign
country; exile; foreign land
obdarować [ob-da-ro-vaćh] v.
bestow; lavish gifts on...
obdarty [ob-dar-ti] adj. m.
ragged; in rags; tattered
obdarzyć [ob-da-zhićh] v.
bestow; lavish gifts on...
obdzielić [ob-dźhe-leećh] v.
divide; distribute; deal; endow
obdzierać [ob-dźhe-raćh] v. rip
off; skin off; strip; fleece
obecnie [o-bets-ńe] adv. at
present; just now; to-day
obecność [o-bets-nośhćh] f.
presence (in); attendance (at)
obejmować [o-bey-mo-vaćh] v.
embrace; enfold; span; enfold;
include; take over; take in;
hug; grasp; clasp; encircle
obejrzeć [o-bey-zhećh] v.

inspect; glance at; see
obejście [o-bey-śhćhe] n. by
-pass; farmyard; manner
obejść [o-beyśhćh] v. go a-
round; by-pass; affect
obelga [o-bel-ga] f. (open) insult;
affront; invective; pl. abuse
obelżywy [o-bel-zhi-vi] adj. m.
insulting; abusive; opprobrious
oberwać [o-ber-vaćh] v. tear
off; cop it; pluck; get a nock
oberża [o-ber-zha] f. inn; tavern
oberżysta [o-ber-zhis-ta] m.
innkeeper; owner of an inn
oberżnąć [o-ber-zhnownćh] v.
cut off; trim; clip; edge; cheat
obeschnąć [o-bes-khnownćh]
v. dry up; get dry; dry
obetrzeć [o-bet-zhećh] v. wipe
out; dust; rub sore; skin
obezwładnić [o-bez-vwad-
-ńeećh] v. overpower; subdue; disable; make helpless
obeznany [o-bez-na-ni] adj. m.
familiar (with); acquainted
(with); conversant (with)
obfitość [ob-fee-tośhćh] f.
plenty; abundance; profusion
obfity [ob-fee-ti] adj. m.
abundant; ample; profuse; liberal; plentiful; abounding in
obgadywać [ob-ga-di-vaćh] v.
talk ill; talk over; crab
obgryzać [ob-gri-zaćh] v. nibble
bare; gnaw; pick a bone; bite
obiad [o-byat] m. dinner
obicie [o-bee-ćhe] n. upholstery;
(door) padding; chip; beating;
bruise; drubbing
obiecywać [o-bye-tsi-vaćh] v.
promise; look forward to
obieg [o-byek] m. circulation
obiegać [o-bye-gaćh] v. run
around; circulate; revolve;
skirt; make the round; orbit
obiekcja [o-byek-tsya] f.
objection; demur; hesitation
obiekt [o-byekt] m. object;
subject; building; target
obiektyw [o-byek-tiv] m. object
-lens; object-glass; objective
obiektywny [o-byek-tiv-ni]
adj. m. objective; impartial

obierać [o-bye-raćh] v. choose;
elect; peel; pick; strip; adopt
obierzyny [o-bye-zhi-ni] pl.
peelings; parings; offals
obieralny [o-bye-ral-ni] adj. m.
elective; eligible
obietnica [o-byet-ńee-tsa] f.
promise; engagement
obijać [o-bee-yaćh] v. chip;
hoop; loaf; hurt; injure
objadać się [ob-ya-daćh śhan]
v. gorge; overeat; cram; gnaw
objaśniać [ob-yaśh-ńaćh] v.
explain; make clear; gloss
objaw [ob-yav] m. symptom
objawić [ob-ya-veećh] v. reveal
objazd [ob-yazt] m. tour; circuit;
detour; diversion; bypass
objąć [ob-yownćh] v. embrace;
assume; grasp; encompass;
enfold; hug; span; take over
objeżdżać [ob-yezh-dzhaćh] v.
ride; around; break in a horse
objętość [ob-yan-tośhćh] f.
volume; bulk; capacity; size;
measurement; content
obkładać [ob-kwa-daćh] v. cover (up); wrap; line (a pipe);
impose; hit; buffet; deal blows
oblegać [ob-le-gaćh] v. besiege
oblać [ob-laćh] v. pour on
(water); spill; drench; fail
oblekać [ob-le-kaćh] v. clothe;
put on; cover; encase; don
oblepiać [ob-le-pyaćh] v. paste
over; stick; post; plaster over
oblewać [ob-le-vaćh] v. pour
on; drench; bathe; sprinkle;
wash; spill; celebrate; fail
oblężenie [ob-lan-zhe-ńe] m.
siege; state of siege
obliczać [ob-lee-chaćh] v.
count; reckon; figure out; calculate; estimate; design; mean
oblicze [ob-lee-che] n. face
obliczenie [ob-lee-che-ńe] n.
calculation; evaluation; count
obligacja [ob-lee-gats-ya] f.
obligation; bond; share
oblizać [ob-lee-zaćh] v. lick
obładować [ob-wa-do-vaćh] v.
load down; heap; burden
obława [ob-wa-va] f. roundup;

posse; man hunt; chase; raid
obłąkany [ob-w<u>own</u>-ka-ni]
adj. m. insane; loony; madman
obłęd [ob-w<u>ant</u>] m. insanity
obłędny [ob-w<u>and</u>-ni] adj. m.
mad; wild; insane; crazy
obłok [ob-wok] m. cloud
obłowić się [ob-**wo**-veećh
ś<u>han</u>] v. pick up a lot; make
a pile; fill (line) one's pockets
obłożnie [ob-**wozh**-ńe] adv. bed
-ridden; severely (ill)
obłożyć [ob-**wo**-zhićh] v. cover up; wrap; line; impose; hit;
buffet; seize; put dues on
obłuda [ob-**woo**-da] f. hypocrisy
obłudnik [ob-**wood**-ńeek] m.
hypocrite; snuffler; dissembler
obłudny [ob-**wood**-ni] adj. m.
hypocritical; false; canting
obłupać [ob-**woo**-paćh] v. shell;
peel; bark; flay; skin; fleece
obłuszczać [ob-**woosh**-chaćh]
v. scale; shell; husk; flay; skin
obły [ob-wi] adj. m. oval;
tapering; cylindrical
obmacać [ob-ma-tsaćh] v. feel
about; explore with fingers;
palpate; handle (a fabric etc.)
obmawiać [ob-ma-vyaćh] v.
slander; gossip; speak ill
obmierznąć [ob-myerz-n<u>own</u>ćh]
v. get sick of (something)
obmowa [ob-mo-va] f. slander;
detraction; backbiting
obmurować [ob-moo-ro-vaćh]
v. brick in; brick veneer
obmyślać [ob-miśh-laćh] v.
design; contrive; reflect
obmywać [ob-mi-vaćh] v. wash
-up; sponge down; give a
wash; wash the dirt off
obnażać [ob-na-zhaćh] v.
denude; bare; unclothe; strip
off clothes; uncover; lay bare
obniżać [ob-ńee-zhaćh] v.
lower; sink; drop; abate; level
down; draw down; reduce
obniżenie [ob-ńee-zhe-ńe] n.
decrease; reduction; lowering
obniżka [ob-ńeezh-ka] f.
reduction; depreciation; drop;
fall; diminution; decrease

obojczyk [o-boy-chik] m. collar
bone; clavicle; amice; gorget
obnosić [ob-no-śheećh] v.
take around; flaunt; parade
obojętnie [o-bo-y<u>ant</u>-ńe] adv.
indifferently; slang: no matter
obojętność [o-bo-y<u>ant</u>-
-nośhćh] f. indifference; in-
sensibility; neutrality
obojętny [o-bo-y<u>ant</u>-ni] adj. m.
indifferent; neutral
obok [o-bok] adv. prep. beside;
next; about; close by; by;
close; next door; alongside
obopólny [o-bo-pool-ni] adj. m.
common; mutual; reciprocal
obora [o-bo-ra] f. cow barn
obosieczny [o-bo-śhech-ni] adj.
m. two-edged; double edged
obowiązek [o-bo-vy<u>own</u>-zek] m.
duty; obligation; responsibility
obowiązkowy [o-bo-vy<u>own</u>z-ko-
-vi] adj. m. dutiful; compulsory
obowiązany [o-bo-vy<u>own</u>-za-ni]
adj. m. obligated; compelled
obowiązujący [o-bo-vy<u>own</u>-zoo-
-y<u>own</u>-tsi] adj. m. obligatory
obowiązywać [o-bo-vy<u>own</u>-zi-
-vaćh] v. be in force (law
etc.); bind; compel; oblige
obozować [o-bo-zo-vaćh] v.
camp; camp out; tent; tent it;
(lie) encamp(ed); bivouac
obój [o-booy] m. oboe; (horn)
obóz [o-boos] m. camp
obrabiać [o-bra-byaćh] v.
machine (metal, wood etc.);
work-over; fashion; shape; till;
hem; stitch; gosip; rifle; beat
obrabiarka [ob-ra-byar-ka] f.
machine tool; lathe
obrabować [ob-ra-bo-vaćh] v.
rob (a train); strip of money
obracać [ob-ra-tsaćh] v. turn
-over; turn into; rotate; crank
obrachować [ob-ra-kho-vaćh]
v. compute; figure out; calculate; count; reckon; estimate
obrachunek [ob-ra-khoo-nek] m.
settlement; bill; "day of
reckoning"; count; reckoning
obrada [ob-ra-da] f. conference
obradować [ob-ra-do-vaćh] v.

confer; deliberate; debate; sit

obradzać [ob-ra-dzać] v. bear crops; yield a crop; be plentiful; yield an abundant crop

obramować [ob-ra-mo-vać] v. frame; encircle; encase; hem; edge (a garment); border

obrastać [ob-ras-tać] v. over-grow; grow; grow all over

obraz [ob-raz] m. picture; image; painting; drawing; likeness

obraza [ob-ra-za] f. affront; offense; insult; outrage; feeling of offence; transgression

obrazek [ob-ra-zek] m. illustration; small picture

obrazić [ob-ra-źheećh] v. offend; affront; insult; sting

obrazowy [ob-ra-zo-vi] adj. m. pictorial; picturesque; vivid

obrażenie [ob-ra-zhe-ńe] n. offense (s); injury; insults

obraźliwy [ob-raźh-lee-vi] adj. m. offensive; touchy; resentful; abusive; insulting

obrażać [ob-ra-zhaćh] v. offend; (repeatedly) insult; affront; transgress (against)

obrąb [ob-rownb] m. cutoff

obrąbek [ob-rown-bek] m. hem

obrączka [ob-rownch-ka] f. ring

obręb [ob-ranb] m. compass; area; reach; extent; precincts

obrębiać [ob-ran-byaćh] v. hem

obręcz [ob-ranch] f. hoop; tire; rim; band; girdle; ring; circle

obrobić [ob-ro-beećh] v. machine; fashion; shape; till; hem

obrok [ob-rok] m. feed; fodder

obrona [o-bro-na] f. defense

obronność [ob-ron-nośhćh] f. defense capability; defenses

obronny [ob-ron-ni] adj. m. defensive; fortified; protective

obrońca [ob-roń-tsa] f. defender guard; barrister; advocate (of a cause); counsel for

obrośnięty [ob-rośh-ńan-ti] adj. m. overgrown; unshaven

obrotny [ob-rot-ni] adj. m. active; skillful; nimble; agile; shrewd

obrotowy [ob-ro-to-vi] adj. m. turnover (tax); rotary; rota-

tive; revolving; circulating

obroża [ob-ro-zha] f.(dog) collar; neck band; a circular band

obrócić [ob-roo-ćheećh] v. rotate; revolve; turn; go

obrót [ob-root] m. turn; turn-over; revolution; slew; sales

obrus [ob-roos] m .tablecloth

obruszać [ob-roo-shaćh] v. loosen up; irritate; bring down

obrywać [ob-ri-vaćh] v. tear off; tear away; pluck; wrench off; curtail; get (spanking)

obryzgiwać [ob-riz-gee-vaćh] v. splash; spatter (with mud)

obrzęd [ob-zhant] m. rite; ceremony; custom; dispensation

obrzęk [ob-zhank] m. swelling

obrzękły [ob-zhank-wi] adj. m. swollen; tumid; bulged

obrzmiały [obzh-mya-wi] adj. m. swollen; tumid; bulged

obrzucać [ob-zhoo-tsaćh] v. throw upon; hurl; pelt; fell

obrzydliwy [ob-zhid-lee-vi] adj. m. revolting; disgusting

obrzydzenie [ob-zhi-dze-ńe] n. aversion; nausea; disgust

obrzynać [ob-zhi-naćh] v. clip; cut; cut off; edge; trim; cheat

obsada [ob-sa-da] f. cast; crew; garrison; staff; mounting

obsadka [ob-sad-ka] f. penholder; small mounting

obsadzać [ob-sa-dzaćh] v. plant; staff; set; fix; occupy; stock; border; line; mount; fill

obserwacja [ob-ser-vats-ya] f. observation; remark

obserwator [ob-ser-va-tor] m. observer; look out man; witness; viewer (of something)

obserwatorium [ob-ser-va-tor-yoom] m. observatory

obserwować [ob-ser-vo-vaćh] v. watch; observe; take stock

obsługa [ob-swoo-ga] f. attendance; service; staff

obsługiwać [ob-swoo-gee-vaćh] v. wait-upon; service

obstalować [ob-sta-lo-vaćh] v. order (a suit of clothes etc.)

obstalunek [ob-sta-loo-nek] m.

order; a request to supply
obstawać [ob-**sta**-vaćh] v.
insist on; hold to; stand by;
persist in; abide by; stick to
obstąpić [ob-**stown**-peećh] v.
surround; form a circle; cluster
obstrzał [ob-stzhaw] m. gun-fire;
scope of fire; firing
obstrukcja [ob-**strook**-tsya] f.
obstruction; constipation
obsuwać [ob-**soo**-vaćh] v. slide
down; creep; lower; bring
down; push down; give way
obsuwisko [ob-soo-**vees**-ko] n.
landslide; mud slide
obsychać [ob-si-khaćh] v. dry
up; get parched; run dry; go
dry; get dry; become dry
obsyłać [ob-**si**-waćh] v. send
around (messengers etc.)
obsypywać [ob-si-pi-vaćh] v.
strew; sprinkle; shower; heap
obszar [ob-shar] m. area; range
obszarnik [ob-shar-ńeek] m.
landowner; large scale farmer
obszerny [ob-sher-ni] adj. m.
spacious; extensive; vast;
broad; wide; roomy; ample
obsztorcować [ob-shtor-**tso**-
-vaćh] v. snub; give hard time
obszukać [ob-shoo-kaćh] v.
search; ransack; make a thorough search; plunder; pillage
obszyć [ob-shićh] v. sew
around; hem; trim; mend
obuch [/o-bookh] m. back of an
axe; sledge; head of an axe
obudzić [o-boo-dźheećh] v.
wake up; awaken; excite; stir
up; rouse from sleep; arise
obumarły [o-boo-mar-wi] adj. m.
deadened; half dead; decaying
obumierać [o-boo-mye-raćh] v.
wither; atrophy; decay; shrink
oburącz [o-boo-**rownch**] adv.
with both hands (arms)
oburzać [o-boo-zhaćh] v.
revolt; shock; rouse (provoke)
indignation; be revolting; be
disgusting; be outrageous
oburzony [o-boo-zho-ni] adj. m.
indignant (at); resentful (of)
obustronny [o-boo-**stron**-ni] adj.

m. bilateral; mutual; reciprocal
obuwie [o-boo-vye] n. footwear
obwarowywać [ob-va-ro-**vi**-
-vaćh] v. fortify (a town); en-
trench (a position); secure
obwąchiwać [ob-**vown**-khee
-vaćh] v. sniff around; smell
around; sniff at; smell at
obwiązywać [ob-**vyown-zi**-
-vaćh] v. bind up; bandage;
tie around something
obwieszczać [ob-**vyesh**-chaćh]
v. announce; proclaim; notify
obwieszczenie [ob-vyesh-**che**-
-ńe] n. proclamation; notice
obwiniać [ob-vee-ńaćh] v.
accuse of; charge with
obwisać [ob-**vee**-saćh] v. sag;
droop; hang loosely; flag
obwodowy [ob-vo-do-vi] adj. m.
circumferential; district
obwoluta [ob-vo-**loo**-ta] f.
wrapper; book-jacket; file
(cardboard) cover; frame
obwołać [ob-**vo**-waćh] v.
acclaim; proclaim; call names
obwód [ob-voot] m. perimeter
oby [o-bi] part. may...; may you
obycie [o-bi-ćhe] n. good
manners; experience; good
breeding; familiarity (with)
obyczaj [o-bi-chay] m. custom
obyczajność [o-bi-**chay**-
-nośhćh] f. decency; good
conduct; morality; morals
obyczajny [o-bi-chay-ni] adj. m.
decent; of moral conduct
obydwaj [o-bi-dvay] num. both
obyty [o-bi-ti] adj. m. familiar;
easy mannered; polished
obywać się [o-bi-vaćh **śhan**]
v. do without; dispense with
obywatel [o-bi-va-tel] m. citizen;
squire; inhabitant; freeman
obywatelka [o-bi-va-**tel**-ka] f.
(female) citizen; inhabitant
obywatelstwo [o-bi-va-tel-stvo]
m. citizenship; nationality
obznajomić [ob-zna-**yo**-meećh]
v. familiarize; acquaint; inform
obżarstwo [ob-zhar-stvo] n.
gluttony; stuffing oneself
ocaleć [o-tsa-lećh] v. survive

(danger); rescue; save
ocalenie [o-tsa-le-ńe] n. rescue;
salvation; escape; rescuing
ocalić [o-tsa-leećh] v. rescue
ocean [o-tse-an] m. ocean
ocena [o-tse-na] f. grade; estimate; appraisal; criticism
ocet [o-tset] m. vinegar
och! [okh!] excl. oh!
ochędożyć [o-khan-do-zhićh] v.
clean; put in order; tidy up
ochlapać [o-khla-pać h] v.
splash; splatter (with mud)
ochładzać [o-khwa-dzaćh] v.
cool; chill; refresh
ochłap [o-khwap] m. offal; trash;
scrap of meat; offal; remnant
ochłonąć [o-khwo-nownćh] v.
calm down; get cooler; cool
ochoczo [o-kho-cho] adv. eager-
ly; cheerfully; gladly; gaily;
willingly; readily; with zest
ochota [o-kho-ta] f. eagerness;
forwardness; willingness
ochotnik [o-khot-ńeek] n.
volunteer; serving of free will
ochraniać [o-khra-ńaćh] v.
protect; preserve; shield
ochrona [o-khro-na] f. (shelter)
protection; conservation
ochronny [o-khron-ni] adj. m.
protective; preventive
ochrypły [o-khrip-wi] adj. m.
hoarse; husky; raucous
ochrypnąć [o-khrip-nownćh] v.
hoarsen; grow hoarse
ochrzcić [okh-zhćheećh] v.
baptize; christen; name; dub
ociągać się [o-ćhown-gaćh
śhan] v. linger; delay; put off
ociec [o-ćhets] v. drain; drip
ociekać [o-ćhe-kaćh] v. drain;
drip; stream; overflow; dry
ociemniały [o-ćhem-ńa-wi] adj.
m. blind; blind man
ocieniać [o-ćhe-ńaćh] v.
shade over; protect from the
sun; overshadow; shade
ocieplać [o-ćhe-plaćh] v. warm
up; make warmer; get warm
ocierać [o-ćhe-raćh] v. wipe
off; rub sore; gall; abrade
ociężały [o-ćhan-zha-wi] adj. m.

inert; (lazy) heavy; tardy; dull;
ponderous; languid; bovine
ociosać [o-ćho-saćh] v. hew
ocknąć się [ots-knownćh
śhan] v. wake up (from a
nap, meditation, etc,-.); awake
oclić [ots-leećh] v. assess
custom; collect duty; levy
duty (for); pay duty (for)
oczarować [o-cha-ro-vaćh] v.
charm; enchant; fascinate;
ravish; cast a spell; bewitch
oczekiwać [o-che-kee-vaćh] v.
wait for; await; expect; hope
oczekiwanie [o-che-kee-va-ńe]
n. expectation; prospect
oczerniać [o-cher-ńaćh] v.
slander; malign; defame; vilify
oczko [och-ko] n. (needle) eyelet;
little eye; mesh; stitch
oczny [och-ni] adj. m. optic
oczyszczać [o-chish-chaćh] v.
clean; purify; dust; clear
oczytany [o-chi-ta-ni] adj. m.
well-read; of wide reading
oczywisty [o-chi-vees-ti] adj. m.
obvious; self-evident; plain
oczywiście [o-chi-veeśh-ćhe]
adv. obviously; of course
od [od] prep. from; off; of; for;
since; out of; with; per; by
(the line); then (idiomatic)
odbarwić [od-bar-veećh] v.
bleach; decolonize
odbicie [od-bee-ćhe] n. reflection; bounce; ricochet; beating
back; deflection; repercussion;
reflex; reverberation; repulse
odbić [od-beećh] v. bounce
back; rescue; recover; reflect;
print; divert; deflect; detach
odbiegać [od-bye-gaćh] v.
desert; deviate; stray; digress
odbijać [od-bee-yaćh] v. reflect; print; put off; fend off;
stand out; leave a trace; kick
odbiorca [od-byor-tsa] m.
receiver; customer; addressee
odbiornik [od-byor-ńeek] m.
(radio) receiver; collector
odbiór [od-byoor] m. receipt;
reception; (money) collection
odbitka [od-beet-ka] f. copy;

reprint; impression; proof; slip

odblask [od-blask] m. reflection of light; gleam; irradiation

odbudowa [od-boo-do-va] f. reconstruction; restoration

odbudować [od-boo-do-vaćh] v. rebuild; restore; reconstruct

odbyt [od-bit] m. 1. sale, 2. anus; end of alimentary tract

odbywać [od-bi-vaćh] v. do; perform; be in progress

odcedzić [od-tse-dźheećh] v. strain; strain out; drain away

odchodzić [od-kho-dźheećh] v. go away; leave; walk off; split; sail; retire; withdraw

odchudzać [od-khoo-dzaćh] v. reduce (weight); slim; make slimmer; slenderize

odchylać [od-khi-laćh] v. deflect; slant; slope; bend back; deviate; half-open

odchylenie [od-khi-le-ńe] n. deviation; declination; deflection (of rays); variation

odciągać [od-ćhown-gaćh] v. draw aside; retract; divert; delay; pull back; withdraw

odciążać [od-ćhown-zhaćh] v. relieve; unburden; lighten; ease; take the strain off

odcień [od-ćheń] m. shade (of difference); tint; undertone; tinge; hue; cast; (semi) tone

odcierpieć [od-ćher-pyećh] v. suffer for; expiate; atone

odcinać [od-ćhee-naćh] v. cut off; sever; amputate; detach

odcinek [od-ćhee-nek] m. sector; segment; space; portion; period; fragment; passage

odcisk [od-ćheesk] m. imprint; skin-corn; stamp; trace; impression; squeeze; mark

odcyfrować [od-tsif-ro-vaćh] v. decipher; make out; decode

odczekać [od-che-kaćh] v. wait out; wait for the right moment

odczepić [od-che-peećh] v. detach; unhook; get rid; disconnect; unhitch; unfasten

odczuć [od-choućh] v. feel; notice; resent; smart from

odczyn [od-chin] m. (chem.) reaction; chemical change

odczynnik [od-chin-ńeek] m. reagent; reacting substance

odczyt [od-chit] m. lecture

odczytać [od-chi-taćh] v. read over; take the reading; call

oddać [od-daćh] v. give back; pay back; render; deliver

oddalać [od-da-laćh] v. remove; send away; drive away

oddalony [od-da-lo-ni] adj. m. distant; remote; far away

oddany [od-da-ni] adj. m. given up; devoted; loving; intent

oddawać [od-da-vaćh] v. give back; pay back; return; repay

od dawna [od dav-na] since a long time; long since

oddech [od-dekh] m. breath

oddychać [od-di-khaćh] v. breathe; take breath; respire

oddział [od-dźhaw] m. division; section; ward; branch; detail

oddziaływać [od-dźha-wi-vaćh] v. influence; affect

oddzielać [od-dźhe-laćh] v. separate; divorce; split

oddzielny [od-dźhel-ni] adj. m. separate; individual; discrete

oddzierać [od-dźhe-raćh] v. tear off; pull off; pull away

oddźwięk [od-dźhvyank] m. echo; resonance; repercussion

odebrać [o-de-braćh] v. take away from; receive; withdraw; take back; regain; deprive of

odechcieć się [o-dekh-ćhećh śhan] v. lose interest; cease liking; be sick of (it, etc.)

odegnać [o-deg-naćh] v. chase away; drive away; drive off

odegrać się [o-de-graćh śhan] v. win back; recover; take revenge; retrieve; recoup losses

odejmować [o-dey-mo-vaćh] v. subtract; deduct; take away; diminish; withdraw; deprive

odejście [o-dey-śhćhe] n. departure; withdrawal; divergence; deviation (from a line)

odejść [o-deyśhćh] v. depart; go away; leave; abandon

odemknąć [o-dem-knowńch] v. open; half open (a door, window, etc.); set ajar; unbolt

odepchnąć [o-dep-khnowńch] v. shove away; beat back; elbow aside; drive back; spurn

odeprzeć [o-dep-zheć́h] v. repel; repulse; fight off; retort

oderwać [o-der-vać́h] v. tear off; break off; detach; sever

odesłać [o-des-wać́h] v. send back; return; refer; direct

odetchnąć [o-det-khnowńch] v. breathe (freely); respire

odetkać [o-det-kać́h] v. unstop; uncork; unchoke; fall out

odezwa [o-dez-va] f. proclamation (to the nation); appeal; urgent request (to the people)

odgadywać [od-ga-di-vać́h] v. guess; surmise; solve a riddle

odgałęziać [od-ga-**wan**-źhać́h] v. branch away; fork off; ramify; branch out; branch off

odganiać [od-ga-ńać́h] v. chase away; drive off; dismiss

odgarniać [od-gar-ńać́h] v. shove away; rake aside; push aside; clear (the snow, etc.)

odginać [od-gee-nać́h] unbend; fold back; straighten curve

odgłos [od-gwos] m. echo; resonance; sound; noise; thud

odgniatać [od-gń́a-tać́h] v. bruise; wrinkle (the dress, etc.); crease (the skin, etc.)

odgradzać się [od-gra-dzać́h **śhan**] fence off; screen off; separate; shut oneself off

odgrażać się [od-gra-zhać́h **śhan**] v. talk big; threaten

odgrodzić [od-gro-dźhee¢́h] v. divide off; fence off; shut off

odgruzować [od-groo-**zo**-vać́h] v. clear off rubbish from a space; remove the rubble

odgrywać [od-**gri**-vać́h] v. play off; perform; act; make believe; pretend; sham; recover

odgryzać [od-gri-zać́h] v. bite off; snap off; gnaw off

odgrzebywać [od-gzhe-bi-vać́h] v. dig up; rake up; unearth; turn up; clear (the rubble)

odgrzewać [od-gzhe-vać́h] v. rewarm; rehash (an old story); warm up (food, soup, etc.)

odjazd [od-yazt] m. departure

odjeżdżać [od-**yezh**-dzhać́h] v. depart; be off; abandon; start

odjęcie [od-**yan**-ć́he] n. amputation; deduction; withdrawal; subtraction; weaning

odkazić [od-ka-źheeć́h] v. disinfect; sterilize

odkażać [od-ka-zhać́h] v. disinfect (repeatedly); sterilize

odkażenie [od-ka-zhe-ńe] n. disinfection; sterilization

odkąd [od-**kownt**] adv. since; since when?; ever since; from

odkleić [od-kle-eeć́h] v. unglue; unstick; detach; ungum

odkładać [od-**kwa**-dać́h] v. put aside; save; put back; put off

odkłonić się [od-**kwo**-ńeeć́h **śhan**] v. greet back

odkopać [od-ko-pać́h] v. dig up

odkorkować [od-kor-ko-vać́h] v. uncork; unjam (the traffic)

odkręcić [od-**kran**-ć́heeć́h] v. unscrew; turn around

odkroić [od-kro-eeć́h] v. cut off; carve off; slice off

odkryć [od-krić́h] v. discover; uncover; lay bare; expose; dig up; unearth; notice; reveal

odkrycie [od-kri-ć́he] n. discovery; exploration (of the unknown); exposure; (a) find

odkupić [od-koo-peeć́h] v. repurchase; redeem; buy back; replace; compensate; ransom

odkupienie [od-koo-pye-ńe] n. redemption; repurchase

odkurzacz [od-koo-zhach] m. vacuum cleaner; dust exhauster; carpet sweeper; sl. vac

odkuwać się [od-koo-vać́h **śhan**] v. recoup losses; make money (out of); make up (for)

odlać [od-lać́h] v. pour off

odlatywać [od-la-ti-vać́h] v. fly away; fly off; take off

odległość [od-**leg**-woś́hć́h] f. distance; remoteness; interval

odległy [od-leg-wi] adj. m.
distant; remote; far away;
long ago; far removed

odlepiać [od-le-pyaćh] v.
unglue; unstick; detach (a
stamp, etc.); ungum

odlew [od-lef] m. cast; pour

odlewać [od-le-vaćh] v. pour
off; cast; mould; pour out

odlewacz [od-le-vach] m. founder

odlewnia [od-lev-ńa] f. foundry

odliczać [od-lee-chaćh] v.
deduct; count off; reckon off;
allow (for sale's tax, etc.)

odliczenie [od-lee-che-ńe] n.
deduction; allowance

odlot [od-lot] m. departure (by
plane); take-off; start

odludek [od-loo-dek] m. recluse

odludny [od-lood-ni] adj. m.
solitary; lonely; secluded

odłam [od-wam] m. fraction

odłamać [od-wa-maćh] break
off; sever; snap off

odłamek [od-wa-mek] m. chip;
splinter; fragment; chip; stub

odłazić [od-wa-źheećh] v.
crawl away; get unstuck;
come off (the shoe, etc.)

odłączyć [od-wown-chićh] v.
sever; disconnect; separate

odłożyć [od-wo-zhićh] v. set
aside; put off; put back

odłóg [od-wook] m. fallow

odłupać [od-woo-paćh] v. split
off; chip off; break off

odma płucna [od-ma pwoots-na]
f. pneumothorax; pneumatosis

odmarznąć [od-marz-nownćh]
v. thaw (the snow, etc.); melt;
get warm; unfreeze

odmawiać [od-ma-vyaćh] v.
refuse; say prayers; decline
(an offer, etc.); recite

odmeldować [od-mel-do-vaćh]
v. take a formal leave

odmęt [od-mant] m. chaotic
whirlpool; confusion; depths

odmiana [od-mya-na] f. change;
alteration; modification

odmieniać [od-mye-ńaćh] v.
change; alter; decline; conjugate (a verb); modify

odmienny [od-myen-ni] adj. m.
mutable; different; unlike

odmierzać [od-mye-zhaćh] v.
measure off; mark off

odmłodzić [od-mwo-dźheećh]
v. rejuvenate; make (look)
younger; infuse new blood

odmowa [od-mo-va] f. refusal to
do; denial; saying "no"

odmówić [od-moo-veećh] v.
refuse; say prayers; say "no"

odmrozić [od-mro-źheećh] v.
get frostbite; get frozen; thaw

odmrożenie [od-mro-zhe-ńe] n.
frostbite; kibe; chilblain

odmruknąć [od-mrook-nownćh]
v. mutter back; grunt out

odnająć [od-na-yownćh] v.
sublet (rent) a room (from)

odnawiać [od-na-vyaćh] v.
renew; renovate; restore; recondition; reform; resume

odnajdywać [od-nay-di-vaćh] v.
recover; find; discover

od niechcenia [od ńe-khtse-ńa]
adv. carelessly; willy-nilly

odniemczać [od-ńem-chaćh] v.
remove German influence; de-
Germanize (language etc.)

odniesienie [od-ńe-śhe-ńe] n.
carrying back; reference (line)

odnieść [od-ńeśhćh] v. bring
back; take back; sustain

odnoga [od-no-ga] f. spur;
branch; offshoot; river pass

odnosić [od-no-śheećh] v.
take back; carry back; bring
back (repeatedly); refer (to)

odnośnie [od-nośh-ńe] prep.
concerning; in comparison

odnośnik [od-nośh-ńeek] m.
reference; footnote (in a text)

odnośny [od-nośh-ni] adj. m.
relative; respective; proper

odnotować [od-no-to-vaćh] v.
check off; note down; state

odnowa [od-no-va] f. renewal;
restoration; regeneration

odnowić [od-no-veećh] v.
renew; renovate; reform; revive; restore; condition; do up

odosobnić [o-do-sob-ńeećh] v.
isolate; confine; stand alone

odosobnienie [o-do-sob-**ńe**-ńe]
n. isolation; privacy; seclusion
odór [o-door] m. reek; smell
odpad [od-pad] m. refuse; drop
-out; waste; muck; scraps
odpadać [od-pa-daćh] v. drop
off; come off; fall off; peel off
odpadki [od-pad-kee] pl. waste
odparcie [od-par-ćhe] n.
repulsion; rejection; refutation
odparować [od-pa-ro-vaćh] v.
parry; repel; evaporate
odparzenie [od-pa-zhe-ńe] n.
gall; scald; chafe (skin)
odparzyć [od-pa-zhićh] v.
blister; chafe one's skin
odpędzać [od-p<u>an</u>-dzaćh] v.
chase away; repel; expel; keep
back (away, off); banish
odpiąć [od-py<u>own</u>ćh] v.
unfasten; unbuckle; unclasp
odpieczętować [od-pye-ch<u>an</u>-to-
-vaćh] v. unseal; open (a
letter); break the seal (of)
odpinać [od-pee-naćh] v. unbutton; disconnect; undo; detach; unclasp; unbuckle
odpierać [od-pye-raćh] v. repel;
refute; force back; disprove
odpiłować [od-pee-wo-vaćh] v.
saw off; file off; cut off
odpis [od-pees] m. copy
odpisać [od-pee-saćh] v. copy;
write back; answer; deduct
odpłacić [od-pwa-ćheećh] v.
repay; reciprocate; get back at
odpłata [od-pwa-ta] f. reim-
bursement; retribution; repayment; retaliation; recompense
odpłynąć [od-pwi-n<u>own</u>ćh] v.
float away; sail away; swim
away; put to sea; row away
odpływ [od-pwif] m. low tide;
ebb; outflow; drainage; spout
odpoczynek [od-po-chi-nek] m.
rest; repose; relax from work
odpoczywać [od-po-chi-vaćh]
v. rest; have a rest; take a
rest; repose (on a sofa, etc.)
odpokutować [od-po-koo-to-
-vaćh] v. expiate; atone; pay
dearly; suffer a penalty (for)
odporność [od-por-nośhćh] f.

immunity; (power of) resistance; hardiness (of plants)
odpowiadać [od-po-vya-daćh]
v. answer to; correspond to
odpowiedni [od-po-**vyed**-ńee]
adj. m. respective; adequate;
suitable; fit; right; due; opportune; competent (official)
odpowiedzialność [od-po-vye-
-dźhal-nośhćh] f. respon-
sibility; liability; civil liability;
accountability (personal, etc.)
odpowiedzialny [od-po-vye-
-dźhal-ni] adj. m. responsible;
liable; accountable; trustworthy; reliable; sl. spanking
odpór [od-poor] m. opposition;
resistance; making a stand
odprasować [od-pra-so-vaćh] v.
press; iron; press out; express
odprawa [od-pra-va] f. dispatch;
rebuff; briefing; debriefing
odprawiać [od-pra-vyaćh] v.
dispatch; dismiss; celebrate
(mass); order away; rebuff;
send away; pay off; discharge
odprężać [od-pr<u>an</u>-zhaćh] v.
relax; slacken; let down; recoil
odprężenie [od-pr<u>an</u>-zhe-ńe] m.
relaxation; easing of tension;
detente; slackening
odprowadzać [od-pro-va-dzaćh]
v. divert; drain off; escort
odpruwać [od-proo-vaćh] v. rip
off (buttons); rip away
odpust [od-poost] m. indulgence
odpuszczenie [od-poosh-che-ńe]
n. forgiveness; remission
odpychać [od-pi-khaćh] v. repel
odpychanie [od-pi-kha-ńe] n.
repulsion; repelling
odra [od-ra] f. measles; pl.
rubeola (high fever & skin
eruption, usually of children)
odrabiać [od-ra-byaćh] v. work
off; work out; get done; undo
odraczać [od-ra-chaćh] v. put
off; postpone; defer; delay
odradzać [od-ra-dzaćh] v.
advise against; regenerate;
revive; infuse new life (into)
odrapać [od-ra-paćh] v.
scratch; dilapidate; scrape off

odrastać [od-ras-taćh] v. grow back; sprout again; shoot again; grow again; sucker

odraza [od-ra-za] f. aversion

odrazu [od-ra-zoo] adv. at once

odrażający [od-ra-zha-yown-tsi] adj. m. repulsive; hideous

odrąbać [od-rown-baćh] v. chop off; hew away; cut off

odrębność [od-ranb-nośhćh] n. distinction; individuality

odrębny [od-ranb-ni] adj. m. distinct; individual; separate

odręczny [od-ranch-ni] adj. m. freehand; personal; longhand

odrętwiały [od-rant-vya-wi] adj. m. numbed; torpid; stiff

odrobić [od-ro-beećh] v. work off; work out; get done; do

odrobina [od-ro-bee-na] f. small bit; particle; shred; a dash

odroczenie [od-ro-che-ńe] n. adjournment; postponement

odroczyć [od-ro-chićh] v. put off; delay; defer; postpone

odrodzenie [od-ro-dze-ńe] m. rebirth; renaissance

odrodzić [od-ro-dźheećh] v. regenerate; renew; revive

odróżniać [od-roozh-ńaćh] v. distinguish; differentiate

odróżniać się [od-roozh-ńaćh śhan] v. differ; be different

odruch [od-rookh] m. reflex

odrywać [od-ri-vaćh] v. tear off; sever; separate; break off

odrzeć [od-zhećh] v. reply

odrzucać [od-zhoo-tsaćh] v. reject; repulse; cast away

odrzutowiec [od-zhoo-to-vyets] m. jet-propelled plane; jet

odrzwia [odzh-vya] pl. door -frame; mine prop set

odrzynać [od-zhi-naćh] v. cut off; cut away; detach; sever

odsądzać [od-sown-dzaćh] v. deny (talent); deprive of merit; refuse to acknowledge

odsetka [od-set-ka] f. interest point; percentage; proportion

odsiadywać [od-śha-di-vaćh] v. sit out; serve (sentence)

odsiecz [od-śhech] f. rescue (of besieged fortress, etc.)

odskoczyć [od-sko-chićh] v. jump off; spring back; dart away; make a leap aside

odsłonić [od-swo-ńeećh] v. unveil; expose; display; show

odsprzedać [od-spshe-daćh] v. resell; sale at second hand

odsprzedaż [od-spshe-dash] f. resale; sale at second hand

odstawać [od-sta-vaćh] v. hang loose; not fit; come off

odstawić [od-sta-veećh] v. put aside; deliver; play (dumb)

odstąpić [od-stown-peećh] v. step back; secede; cede

odstęp [od-stanp] m. margin; space; interval; lapse (of time)

odstępca [od-stanp-tsa] m. renegade; deserter; turncoat

odstępne [od-stanp-ne] n. payment for giving up a lease

odstraszyć [od-stra-shićh] v. deter; frighten away; scare

odstręczyć [od-stran-chićh] v. dissuade; turn away; repel; deter; be repulsive; frighten

odstrzał [od-stshaw] m. shooting off; firing (game, mine)

odsunąć [od-soo-nownćh] v. push away; shove away; put away; brush aside; remove

odsyłacz [od-si-wach] m. reference mark; footnote mark

odsyłać [od-si-waćh] v. send back; refer; return; direct

odsypać [od-si-paćh] v. pour off (not liquid); alluviate

odsypiać [od-si-pyaćh] v. catch up on sleep; sleep off

odszkodowanie [od-shko-do-va-ńe] n. indemnity; compensation; (war) damages; award

odszukać [od-shoo-kaćh] v. retrieve; run down; seek out; find; detect (a leak, etc.)

odśrodkowy [od-śhrod-ko-vi] adj. m. centrifugal

odświerzyć [od-śhvye-zhićh] v. refresh; recondition; restore

odświętny [od-śhvyant-ni] adj. m. festive; ceremonial; showy; one's Sunday best

odtąd   109   odzywać się

odtąd [od-<u>town</u>t] adv. hence
-forth; from now on; from
here; thereafter; since then
odtłuścić [od-twoośh-
-ćheeć] v. degrease; reduce
weight; extract the fat; scour
odtrącać [od-<u>trown</u>-tsać] v.
repel; jostle; knock off; deduct
(charges); thrust aside; spurn
odtrutka [od-troot-ka] f. antidote
against poison; counterpoison
odtwarzać [od-**tva**-zhać]
v. reproduce; reconstitute
odtwórca [od-**tvoor**-tsa] m. ren-
derer; reproducer; performer
oduczać [o-doo-chać] v. dis-
accustom; unteach; unlearn;
break (cure, correct) a habit
odurzać [o-doo-zhać] v. stun;
make dopey; stupefy; daze;
dizzy; intoxicate; fuddle
odurzenie [o-doo-zhe-ńe] n.
stupor; giddiness; intoxication
odwadniać [od-vad-ńać] v.
drain; dehydrate; desiccate
odwaga [od-va-ga] f. courage
odwalić [od-va-leeć] v. push
away; beat it; copy; get over
with; roll aside; remove; sham
odwar [od-var] m. decoction
odważnik [od-vazh-ńeek] m.
scale-weight; (pound) weight
odważny [od-vazh-ni] adj. m.
brave; courageous; bold
(man); daring; plucky; spunky
odważyć [od-va-zhić] v.
weigh; weigh out; consider
odważyć się [od-va-zhić
śh<u>an</u>] v. dare; have the
courage (the pluck); risk
odwdzięczyć się [od-vdźhan-
-chić śh<u>an</u>] v. repay (with
gratitude); return; requite
odwet [od-vet] m. retaliation;
retort; revenge; requital
odwiązać [od-vy<u>own</u>-zać] v.
untie; unfasten; unbuckle;
undo; unbend (a wire, etc.)
odwieczny [od-vyech-ni] adj. m.
eternal; immemorial; age long
odwiedzać [od-vye-dzać] v.
visit; call on; pay a visit; pay a
call; come and see; frequent

odwiedziny [od-vye-dźhee-ni] n.
visit; call; coming to see
odwijać [od-**vee**-yać] v.
unwrap; draw back one's fist
odwilż [od-veelzh] f. thaw
odwlekać [od-**vle**-kać] v. put
off; postpone; delay; drag
away; haul aside; defer
odwodnić [od-**vod**-ńeeć] v.
drain; desiccate; dehydrate
odwodzić [od-**vo**-dźheeć] v.
draw off; draw aside; dissuade; abduct; cock (a gun)
odwołać [od-**vo**-wać] v. take
back; appeal; refer; recall
odwołanie [od-vo-wa-ńe] n.
recall; appeal; repeal; cancellation; withdrawal; revo-
cation; annulment; removal
odwozić [od-**vo**-źheeć] v.
take back (by car); drive back
odwód [od-voot] m. reserve
odwracać [od-**vra**-tsać] v.
reverse; turn around; invert
odwrotny [od-**vrot**-ni] adj. m.
reverse; opposite; converse
odwrót [od-vroot] m. retreat;
reverse (side); withdrawal
odwykać [od-**vi**-kać] v. break
a habit; loose a habit
odwzajemniać [od-vza-**yem**-
-ńać] v. reciprocate (a
feeling, etc,); repay; return
odyniec [o-di-ńets] m. boar
odzew [od-zev] m. echo; reply
odziedziczyć [o-dźhe-dźhee-
-chić] v. inherit; succeed
odzienie [o-dźhe-ńe] n. clothing
odzież [o-dźhesh] f. clothes
odznaczać [od-zna-chać] v.
distinguish; decorate; mark off
odznaczenie [od-zna-che-ńe] n.
distinction; award; decoration
odznaka [od-zna-ka] f. badge
odzwierciedlać [od-zvyer-ćhe-
-dlać] v. reflect (something)
odzwyczajać [od-zvi-cha-yać]
v. break (cure, correct) a
habit; make loose a habit
odzyskać [od-zis-kać] v.
retrieve; regain; recover; win
back; resume possession
odzywać się [od-zi-vać śh<u>an</u>]

v. speak up; drop a line; respond; address; pass a word
odźwierny [o-dźhvyer-ni] m.
doorman; janitor; caretaker
odżyć [od-zhićh] v. come back to life; be reborn; reappear
odżywczy [od-zhiv-chi] adj. m. nutritious; nourishing; alimentary; nutritive; refreshing
odżywiać [od-zhi-vyaćh] v. nourish; feed; supply a person with (food) nourishment
odżywienie [od-zhi-vye-ńe] n. food; nourishment; diet
ofensywa [o-fen-si-va] f. offensive; push; attack
oferma [o-fer-ma] f. sad sack
oferta [o-fer-ta] f. offer
ofiara [o-fya-ra] f. victim; offering; sacrifice; dupe
oficer [o-fee-tser] m. (military) officer (in the army)
oficjalny [o-feets-yal-ni] adj. m. official; formal; reserved
oficyna [o-fee-tsi-na] f. back house; printing shop; annex; outbuilding
ofuknąć [o-fook-nownćh] v. rebuke (severely or formally); reprimand; trounce; rate
ogar [o-gar] m. bloodhound
ogarek [o-ga-rek] m. candle-end; stump; stub; cigarette end
ogarniać [o-gar-ńaćh] v. seize; comprehend; take in; grasp
ogień [o-gyeń] m. fire; flame
ogier [o-gyer] m. stallion
oglądać [o-glown-daćh] v. inspect; consider; see
oględny [o-gland-ni] adj. m. circumspect; moderate; cautious; gentle (words, etc.)
ogłada [o-gwa-da] f. good manners (delicacy and elegance); refinement; urbanity
ogłaszać [o-gwa-shaćh] v. advertise; declare; publish
ogłuchnąć [o-gwookh-nownćh] v. become deaf; be hushed
ogłupieć [o-gwoo-pyećh] v. become stupid; grow silly
ognie sztuczne [o-gńe shtooch-ne] pl. fireworks

ogniotrwały [o-gńo-trva-wi] adj. m. fireproof; incombustible
ognisko [og-ńees-ko] n. hearth; focus; camp fire; fire place
ognisty [og-ńees-ti] adj. m. fiery; flaming; passionate
ogniwo [o-gńee-vo] n. link
ogolić [o-go-leećh] v. shave
ogon [o-gon] m. tail; trail; scut
ogonek [o-go-nek] m. waiting line; queue; diacritical mark
ogorzały [o-go-zha-wi] adj. m. sunburnt; tanned; weather beaten (man, car, etc,); tawny
ogólnie [o-gool-ńe] adv. generally; as a rule; universally
ogólny [o-gool-ni] adj. m. general; prevailing; global; total; universal; common (room)
ogół [o-goow] m. people; public
ogółem [o-goo-wem] adv. on the whole; as a whole; altogether
ogórek [o-goo-rek] m. cucumber
ogórkowy sezon [o-goor-ko-vi se-zon] slack time (season)
ograbić [o-gra-beećh] v. rob
ograniczony [o-gra-ńee-cho-ni] adj. m. narrow-minded; limited
ogrodnik [o-grod-ńeek] m. gardener; horticulturist
ogrodzić [o-gro-dźheećh] v. fence in (one's farm, property, etc.); enclose; wall in; rail in;
ogromny [o-grom-ni] adj. m. huge; tremendous; colossal
ogród [o-groot] m. garden
ogryzać [o-gri-zaćh] v. gnaw away; nimble at; pick (a bone)
ogrzewać [o-gzhe-vaćh] v. heat
ohydny [o-khid-ni] adj. m. hideous; ghastly; abominable; vile; offensive; filthy; horrid
o ile [o ee-le] conj. as far as
ojciec [oy-ćhets] m. father
ojciec chrzestny [oy-ćhets khzhest-ni] godfather
ojczym [oy-chim] m. stepfather
ojczysty język [oy-chis-ti yan-zik] native tongue; mother tongue
ojczyzna [oy-chiz-na] f. native country (land, soil); motherland; homeland; fatherland
okaleczyć [o-ka-le-chićh] v.

maim; cripple; lame; mutilate
oka mgnienie [o-ka mgńe-ńe] n.
eye blink; split second
okap [o-kap] m. eaves; overlap
okaz [o-kas] m. specimen; type
okazać [o-ka-zać] v. show;
demonstrate; evidence; exhibit
okazały [o-ka-za-wi] adj. m.
magnificent; stately; grand
okaziciel [o-ka-źhee-ćhel] m.
bearer (of a check etc.)
okazja [o-ka-zya] f. opportunity
okazyjny [o-ka-ziy-ni] adj. m.
occasional; opportune (buy);
chance (acquaintance, etc.)
okazywać [o-ka-zi-vać] v.
demonstrate; show (one's
passport); manifest; display
oklaski [o-klas-kee] pl. applause;
clapping; acclamation
oklaskiwać [o-klas-kee-vać] v.
applaud; clap (one's hands)
okleić [o-kle-eeć] v. paste-
-over; stick over; smear over
oklepany [o-kle-pa-ni] adj. m.
commonplace; (well) worn
okład [o-kwat] m. compress;
hot pad; lining; wrapping
okładka [o-kwad-ka] f. (book)
cover; book binding
okłamać [o-kwa-mać] v.
deceive; tell a lie; delude
okno [o-kno] n. window
oko [o-ko] n. eye; eye sight
okolica [o-ko-lee-tsa] f. region;
surroundings; vicinity
okoliczność [o-ko-leech-
-nośhć] f. circumstance;
fact; occasion
około [o-ko-wo] prep. near;
about; more or less; on; or
okoń [o-koń] m. perch; bass
okop [o-kop] m. trench
okopcić [o-kop-ćheeć] v.
soot; blacken with smoke
okopcony [o-kop-tso-ni] adj. m.
sooty; blackened with soot
okostna [o-kost-na] f.
periosteum; (very sensitive)
lining of the bones
okólnik [o-kool-ńeek] m. circular
(letter); corral; poultry yard
okpić [o-kpeeć] v. pull wool

over eyes; deceive; cheat; gull
okradać [o-kra-dać] v. pick
-pocket; burglarize; rob
okrakiem [o-kra-kem] adv.
astraddle; with legs wide apart
okrasa [o-kra-sa] f. fat;
ornament; embellishment; flavoring; seasoning; gravy; lard
okrasić [o-kra-śheeć] v.
adorn; season; add a
condiment; embellish a dish
okratować [o-kra-to-vać] v.
grate; bar (a window)
okratowanie [o-kra-to-va-ńe] m.
grating; railings; bars
okrąg [o-krownk] m. district
okrągły [o-krown-gwi] adj. m.
round; spherical; full (month,
hour, etc.); well-mannered
okrążać [o-krown-zhać] v.
encircle; circle; revolve; detour
okres [o-kres] m. period; phase
określać [o-kreśh-lać] v.
define; qualify; fix; appoint
okręcać [o-kran-tsać] v. coil
around; wrap; turn around
okręt [o-krant] m. ship; boat
okrężny [o-kranzh-ni] adj. m.
roundabout; indirect; devious
(ways); circuitous; circular;
travelling-peddlar's (trader)
okropność [o-krop-nośhć] f.
horror; atrocity; outrage
okropny [o-krop-ni] adj. m.
horrible; fearful; awful; extreme; ghastly; atrocious
okruch [o-krookh] m. crumb
okrucieństwo [o-kroo-ćheń-
-stvo] n. cruelty; atrocities
okrutny [o-kroot-ni] adj. m. cruel;
savage; excessive; sore
okrycie [o-kri-ćhe] n. covering;
wrap; garment; overcoat
okrywać [o-kri-vać] v. cover
okrzyczany [o-kzhi-cha-ni]
adj. m. notorious; famous;
renowned; far-famed (person)
okrzyk [o-kzhik] m. outcry
okrzyknąć [o-kzhik-nownć] v.
proclaim; declare; brand
oktawa [o-kta-va] f. octave
okucie [o-koo-ćhe] n. hardware;
ferrule; fitting; fixtures

okuć [o-kooćh] v. shoe a
horse; hackle; fit a lock and
hinges; fix metal fittings
okularnik [o-koo-lar-ńeek] m.
cobra; poisonous snake of
Asia (Naja naja)
okulary [o-koo-la-ri] pl.
eyeglasses; eyepiece
okulista [o-koo-lees-ta] m. eye
doctor; eye surgeon; oculist
okultyzm [o-kool-tizm] m.
occultism; hidden knowledge
okup [o-koop] m. ransom
okupacja [o-koo-pats-ya] f.
occupation; occupancy
okupować [o-koo-po-vaćh] v.
occupy; invade a territory
okupywać [o-koo-pi-vaćh] v.
pay ransom; pay dearly; buy;
compensate; redeem; atone
olbrzym [ol-bzhim] m. giant
olbrzymi [ol-bzhi-mee] adj. m.
gigantic; huge; colossal; excessive; tremendous; untold
olcha [ol-kha] f. alder tree
oleander [o-le-an-der] m.
oleander (an evergreen shrub)
olej [o-ley] m. oil; oil paint
olej lniany [o-ley lńa-ni] m.
linseed-oil (from flaxseed)
oligarchia [o-lee-gar-khya] m.
oligarchy; the ruling persons
oliwa [o-lee-va] f. olive; oil
oliwić [o-lee-veećh] v. oil
oliwka [o-leev-ka] f. olive-tree
olszyna [ol-shi-na] f. alder-tree
stand (forest); alder wood
olśniewać [ol-śhńe-vaćh] v.
dazzle; ravish; enchant
ołów [o-woof] m. lead; lead shot
ołówek [o-woo-vek] m. lead
pencil; drawing in pencil
ołtarz [ow-tash] m. altar
omackiem [o-mats-kem] adv.
gropingly; blindfold
omal [o-mal] adv. nearly
omamić [o-ma-meećh] v.
deceive; beguile; delude
omaścić [o-maśh-ćheećh] v.
add fat; add butter (on bread
etc.); flavor (a dish)
omawiać [o-ma-vyaćh] v.
discuss (a subject, etc.)

omdlały [om-dla-wi] adj. m.
fainted; faint; languid
omdleć [om-dlećh] v. faint
omen [o-men] m. omen
omieszkać [o-myesh-kaćh] v.
fail; omit; neglect (to do)
omijać [o-mee-yaćh] v. pass
omlet [om-let] m. omelet
omłócić [om-woo-ćheećh] v.
thrash out; give a thrashing
omotać [o-mo-taćh] v. entangle
omówić [o-moo-veećh] v.
discuss (pending matters)
omylić [o-mi-leećh] v. mislead
omylny [o-mil-ni] adj. m. fallible;
misleading; deceitful
omyłka [o-miw-ka] f. error
on [on] pron. he; this (man)
ona [o-na] pron. she
ondulacja [on-doo-lats-ya]
f. (hair) wave; (permanent
hair) wave; wave in the hair
ondulacja trwała [on-doo-lats-ya
trva-wa] permanent (wave)
onegdaj [o-neg-day] adv. the
other day; two days ago
ongiś [on-geeśh] adv. (arch) at
one time; once upon a time
oni [o-ńee] pron. m. pl. they
oniemiały [o-ńe-mya-wi] adj. m.
mute; dumb; speechless
onieśmielać [o-ńe-śhmye-
-laćh] v. intimidate; browbeat;
cow; overawe; abash
ono [o-no] pron. it
opactwo [o-pats-tvo] n. abbey
opaczny [o-pach-ni] adj. m.
wrong; mistaken; improper
opad [o-pat] m. (rain) fall
opadać [o-pa-daćh] v. subside
(na) opak [na o-pak] adv. upside
down; reverse; wrong way
opakowanie [o-pa-ko-va-ńe] n.
wrapping; packing; wrappage
opal [o-pal] m. opal
opalać się [o-pa-laćh śhan] v.
suntan; tan; bronze; lie (bask)
in the sun; get sunburnt
opalanie [o-pa-la-ńe] n. heating
(house etc.); fire marking
opalenizna [o-pa-le-ńeez-na] f.
suntan; tan; scorched remains
opał [o-paw] m. fuel for heating

opamiętać [o-pa-**myan**-taćh] v.
  sober up; bring to reason
opanować [o-pa-no-vaćh] v.
  master; conquer; seize; learn
opanowany [o-pa-no-**va**-ni] adj.
  m. cool-headed (person); composed; calm; self-possessed
opary [o-**pa**-ri] pl. fumes
oparcie [o-**par**-ćhe] n. support
oparzyć [o-**pa**-zhićh] v. scald
opasać [o-**pa**-saćh] v. belt;
  girdle; grid; encircle; surround
opaska [o-**pas**-ka] f. band
opasły [o-**pas**-wi] adj. m. obese
opaść [o-**paśh**ćh] v. drop;
  sink; hang loose; settle; collapse; slump; fall away
opatentować [o-pa-ten-to-vaćh]
  v. patent; take out a patent
opatrunek [o-pa-**troo**-nek] m.
  dressing; bandage; field
  dressing (of a wound, etc,)
opatrywać [o-pa-tri-vaćh] v.
  fix; dress; provide; prepare
opera [o-**pe**-ra] f. opera; opera
  house; no end of a joke
operacja [o-pe-**rats**-ya] f. surgery;
  operation; action; process
operować [o-pe-ro-vaćh] v.
  operate (on a person); manipulate; act; handle; use; run
  carry on (financial operations)
opętanie [o-pan-ta-**ńe**] n.
  obsession (demonical, etc.)
opieczętować [o-pye-**chan**-to
  -vaćh] v. seal up; seal
opieka [o-**pye**-ka] f. care
opiekować [o-pye-ko-vaćh] v.
  take care of; care for; have
  charge of; nurse (a patient)
opiekun [o-**pye**-koon] m.
  guardian; curator; foster-
  parent; curator; warden
opierać się [o-pye-raćh **śhan**]
  v. lean; base; relay; rest; defy
opieszały [o-pye-**sha**-wi] adj. m.
  slow; tardy; lazy; inert
opinia [o-**pee**-ńya] f. opinion;
  view; reputation; sentiment
opis [o-**pees**] m. description
oplątać [o-**plown**-taćh] v.
  ensnare; entangle; entwine
opluwać [o-**ploo**-vaćh] v. spit

on; spit at; slander; defame
opłacać [o-**pwa**-tsaćh] v. pay;
  bribe; cover the cost; reward
opłakany [o-pwa-**ka**-ni] adj. m.
  deplorable; sad; pitiful
opłakiwać [o-pwa-**kee**-vaćh] v.
  lament; deplore; mourn
opłata [o-**pwa**-ta] f. fee
opłatek [o-**pwa**-tek] m. wafer
opłucna [o-**pwoots**-na] f. pleura;
  membrane around the lungs
opłukiwać [o-pwoo-**kee**-vaćh]
  v. rinse; wash with water
opływać [o-**pwi**-vaćh] v. sail
  around; abound; encircle; roll
opływowy [o-pwi-**vo**-vi] adj. m.
  streamlined; streamline
opodal [o-**po**-dal] adv. near by
opodatkować [o-po-dat-**ko**-
  -vaćh] v. tax; impose a tax
opona [o-**po**-na] f. tire
oponować [o-po-**no**-vaćh] v.
  oppose; take exception
opornie [o-**por**-ńe] adv. with
  difficulty; arduously
oporny [o-**por**-ni] adj. m. balky;
  recalcitrant; refractory
opowiadać [o-po-**vya**-daćh] v.
  tell-tale; relate; record
opozycja [o-po-**zits**-ya] f.
  opposition; resistance
opór [o-**poor**] m. resistance
opóźniać [o-**poozh**-ńaćh] v.
  delay; retard; slow down;
  defer; hold back; detain
opóźnienie [o-poo zh-ńe-ńe] n.
  delay; deferment; tardiness
opracować [o-pra-**tso**-vaćh] v.
  work up; elaborate; compile
oprawa [o-**pra**-va] f. frame;
  binding; framework; handle
oprawca [o-**prav**-tsa] m. skinner;
  executioner; torturer; assassin
opresja [o-**pres**-ya] f. oppression
oprocentowanie [o-pro-tsen-to-
  -va-ńe] n. interest (on money)
oprowadzać [o-pro-**va**-dzaćh] v.
  show around; act as a guide
oprócz [o-**prooch**] prep. except;
  besides; apart from; but; save
opróżniać [o-**proozh**-ńaćh] v.
  empty; clear; evacuate; unload
opryskliwy [o-**pris**-klee-vi] adj. m.

peevish; gruff; harsh
opryszek [o-pri-shek] m.
hoodlum; hooligan; rowdy
(man); rough-neck; gangster
oprzeć [o-pzhećh] v. lean on;
base; rest; prop up; resist;
become inflamed; inflame
oprzytomnieć [o-pzhi-tom-
-ńećh] v. recover; collect
oneself; regain consciousness
optyk [op-tik] m. optician
optymista [op-ti-mees-ta] m.
optimist; one of cheerful
views that good prevails
opublikować [o-poo-blee-ko-
-vaćh] v. publish; make public
opuchły [o-pookh-wi] adj. m.
swollen; dilated; distended
opuchlina [o-pookh-lee-na] f.
swelling; dilatation
opuszczać [o-poosh-chaćh] v.
leave; omit; abandon; lower;
let down; lower (a price)
opustoszały [o-poos-to-sha-wi]
adj. m. deserted; desolate;
empty; abandoned; vacant
opuszczenie [o-poosh-che-ńe] n.
omission; lowering; reduction
orać [o-raćh] v. till; plough
oranżeria [o-ran-zher-ya] f.
greenhouse; hothouse
oraz [o-ras] conj. as well as
orbita [or-bee-ta] f. orbit
order [or-der] m. decoration;
order (for service rendered)
ordynarny [or-di-nar-ni] adj. m.
gross; coarse; vulgar; trashy;
uncouth; unrefined; boorish
orędzie [o-ran-dźhe] n. (official)
message; proclamation
oręż [o-ransh] m. weapon
organiczny [or-ga-ńeech-ni] adj.
m. organic; constitutional
organista [or-ga-ńees-ta] m.
organist; organ player
organizacja [or-ga-ńee-zats-ya] f.
organization; organized group
organizm [or-ga-ńeezm] m.
organism; any living thing
orgia [or-gya] f. orgy
orka [or-ka] f. tillage
orkiestra [or-kes-tra] f.
orchestra; orchestra pit

orny [or-ni] adj. m. arable
orszak [or-shak] m. retinue
ortodoksja [or-to-doks-ya] f.
orthodoxy; conventionality
ortografia [or-to-gra-fya] f.
orthography; correct spelling
oryginalny [o-ri-gee-nal-ni]
adj. m. original; inventive; new
orzech [o-zhekh] m. nut; walnut
orzeczenie [o-zhe-che-ńe] m.
decision; sentence; ruling
orzeł [o-zhew] m. eagle; genius
orzeźwiać [o-zheźh-vyaćh] v.
refresh; brace up; invigorate
osa [o-sa] f. wasp; vixen; shrew
osad [o-sat] m. sediment; dregs
osada [o-sa-da] f. settlement
osadnik [o-sad-ńeek] m. settler
osadzać [o-sa-dzaćh] v. plant;
seat; settle; place; fix; steady
osamotnienie [o-sa-mot-ńe-ńe]
n. isolation; loneliness
osądzać [o-sown-dzaćh] v.
sentence; judge; prejudge
oschły [oskh-wi] adj. m. arid;
dry; cold; stiff; stand-offish
osełka [o-sew-ka] f. whetstone
oset [o-set] m. thistle; teasel
osiadać [o-śha-daćh] v. settle;
subside; make a settlement
osiągnąć [o-śhowng-nownćh]
v. attain; achieve; gain; reach
osiedlać [o-śhed-laćh] v.
settle; make a settlement
osiem [o-śhem] num. eight; 8
osiemdziesiąt [o-śhem-dźhe-
-śhownt] num. eighty; 80
osiemnaście [o-śhem-naśh-
-ćhe] num. eighteen; 18
osiemset [o-śhem-set] num.
eight hundred; 800
osierocić [o-śhe-ro-ćheećh] v.
orphaned (a child); desert
osika [o-śhee-ka] f. aspen
osikać [o-śhee-kaćh] v.
sprinkle; piss on (vulg.)
osiodłać [o-śhod-waćh] v.
saddle; reduce to subjugation
osioł [o-śhow] m. donkey; ass
oskarżać [os-kar-zhaćh] v.
accuse; charge with; indict
oskrzela [os-kshe-la] pl. n.
bronchia; two main branches

of the windpipe
oskrzydlać [os-**kshid**-laćh] v.
outflank; go beyond; cut off
oskubać [os-koo-baćh] v.
fleece; feather; pluck (a fowl,
etc.); skin; soak (somebody)
osłabiać [o-**swa**-byaćh] v. impair; weaken; reduce; lessen;
diminish; attenuate; abate
osłabienie [o-swa-**bye**-ńe] n.
weakness; diminution; debili-
tation; mitigation; abatement
osłona [o-**swo**-na] f. shield;
cover; protection; defense
osładzać [o-swa-dzaćh] v.
sweeten; put sugar; cheer up
osłupiały [o-swoo-**pya**-wi] adj. m.
amazed; aghast; astounded
osmarować [o-sma-**ro**-vaćh] v.
besmear; libel; run down; soil
osoba [o-**so**-ba] f. person
osobisty [o-so-**bees**-ti] adj. m.
personal; private; particular
osobiście [o-so-**beeśh**-ćhe]
adv. personally; in person
osobnik [o-sob-ńeek] m.
individual; specimen; person
osobny [o-sob-ni] adj. m.
separate; private; individual
osobowość [o-so-bo-**vośh**ćh]
f. personality; individuality
osowiały [o-so-**vya**-wi] adj. m.
depressed; dejected; glum;
mopish; chap-fallen (person)
ospa [os-pa] f. smallpox
ospały [os-**pa**-wi] adj. m.
drowsy; sleepy; sluggish; dull
ostatecznie [o-sta-**tech**-ńe] adv.
finally; after all; at last
ostateczny [os-ta-**tech**-ni]
adj. m. final; ultimate; decisive; eventual; extreme
ostatek [o-sta-tek] m. reminder;
rest; remains; scrap; leavings
ostatni [o-**stat**-ńee] adj. m. last;
late; end; closing; parting
ostatnio [o-sta-**tńo**] adv. of late;
lately; not long ago; recently
ostoja [o-**sto**-ya] f. mainstay
ostroga [o-**stro**-ga] f. spur
ostrokątny [o-stro-**kownt**-ni] adj.
m. sharp-angled (object)
ostrożność [o-strozh-**no**śhćh]

f. caution; prudence; care
ostrożny [o-**strozh**-ni] adj. m.
careful; prudent; cautious;
wary; circumspect; discreet
ostry [o-stri] adj. m. sharp
ostryga [o-**stri**-ga] f. oyster
ostrze [o-stshe] n. cutting edge;
spike; blade; point; prong
ostrzegać [o-stshe-gaćh] v.
warn of; warn against; admonish; put on guard; advise
ostrzeliwać [o-stshe-lee-vaćh]
v. shoot at; strafe; fire at;
accustom to gun fire
ostrzeżenie [o-stshe-zhe-ńe] n.
warning; danger sign; notice
ostrzyć [o-stshićh] v. sharpen;
whet; grind; put an edge
ostrzygać [o-stshi-gaćh] v. cut
(hair); shear sheep; trim
ostudzać [o-stoo-dzaćh] v. cool
ostygać [o-sti-gaćh] v. cool
down; chill; cool off; abate
osuszać [o-soo-shaćh] v. dry;
drain; dehumidify; wipe; mop
oswobodzić [o-svo-bo-
-dźheećh] v. free; liberate;
rescue; rid of; set free
oswoić [o-svo-eećh] v. tame;
familiarize; domesticate
oszacować [o-sha-tso-vaćh] v.
evaluate; estimate; appraise
oszczep [osh-chep] m. javelin
oszczerstwo [osh-cher-stvo] n.
calumny; libel; defamation
oszczędności [osh-**chand-nośh**
-ćhee] pl. savings (money)
oszklenie [osh-kle-ńe] n. glazing
(of windows); window panes
oszołomić [o-sho-**wo**-meećh] v.
stun, daze; stupefy; bewilder
oszpecić [o-shpe-ćheećh] v.
deface; disfigure; deform; mar
oszukać [o-shoo-kaćh] v. cheat
oszust [o-shoost] m. cheater
oś [ośh] f. axle (axis)
ościenny [ośh-ćhen-ni] adj. m.
bordering; adjoining; adjacent
ość [ośhćh] f. (fish) bone
oślepiać [o-śhle-pyaćh] v.
blind; dazzle; strike blind
ośmieszać [o-śhmye-shaćh]
v. ridicule; deride; make fun of

ośrodek [o-śhro-dek] m. center

oświadczenie [o-śhviad-che--ńe] n. declaration; assertion; pronouncement

oświadczyny [o-śhvyad-chi-ni] pl. marriage proposal

oświata [o-śhvia-ta] f. education; learning

oświecać [o-śhvye-tsaćh] v. light up; enlighten; educate

oświetlenie [o-śviet-le-ńe] n. lighting; light; illumination

otaczać [o-ta-chaćh] v. surround; enclose; turn on a lathe; embrace; encircle

otchłań [ot-khwań] f. abyss

otępienie [o-tan-pye-ńe] n. dullness; stupor; stupefaction

oto [o-to] part. here; there

otoczenie [o-to-che-ńe] n. environment; setting; neighborhood; (one's) associates

otoczyć [o-to-chićh] v. surround; enclose; turn on a lathe; embrace; encircle

otomana [o-to-ma-na] f. couch

otóż [o-toosh] conj. now

otruć [o-trooćh] v. poison

otrucie [o-troo-ćhe] n. poisoning

otrzaskać [o-tzhas-kaćh] v. acquaint with; accustom to

otrząsać [o-tzhown-saćh] v. shake loose; shudder; strew

otrzewna [o-tzhev-na] f. peritoneum; lining of abdomen

otrzeźwieć [o-tzheźh-vyećh] v. sober up; be disillusioned; brisk up; bring around (back)

otrzymać [o-tzhi-maćh] v. receive; get; be given; acquire

otulić [o-too-leećh] v. tuck in; wrap; wrap up; shroud; envelop; enfold with; lag with

otwarcie [o-tvar-ćhe] adv. 1. openly; frankly; in plain words; outright; 2. n. opening

otwarty [o-tvar-ti] adj. m. open; frank; overt; professed

otwierać [o-tvye-raćh] v. open

otwór [ot-voor] m. opening

otyły [o-ti-wi] adj. m. obese

owa [o-va] f. pron. that

owad [o-vad] m. insect

owal [o-val] m. oval

owca [ov-tsa] f. sheep

owczarek [ov-cha-rek] m. sheep-dog

owczarnia [ov-char-ńa] f. sheep-fold; fold

owdowiały [ov-do-vya-wi] adj. m. widowed; a man who lost wife and did not remarry

owe [o-ve] pl. f. pron. that

owacja [o-vats-ya] f. ovation

owies [o-vyes] m. oats

owi [o-vee] pl. m. pron. that

owiewać [o-vye-vaćh] v. blow upon; sweep over; encompass; inspire; enwrap

owijać [o-vee-yaćh] v. wrap up

owłosiony [o-vwo-śho-ni] adj. m. hairy; hirsute; pilose (man); shaggy (animal)

owo [o-vo] n. pron. that; that thing; the said (thing)

owoc [o-vots] m. fruit; fruitage

owrzodzenie [o-vzho-dze-ńe] n. ulceration; sore; sores

owsianka [ov-śhan-ka] f. oatmeal; kasha; porridge

owszem [ov-shem] part. yes; certainly; on the contrary

ozdabiać [oz-da-byaćh] v. decorate; adorn; trim; garnish

ozdoba [oz-do-ba] f. decoration

oziębiać [o-źhan-byaćh] v. cool off; chill; cool down; damp (spirits); refrigerate

oziębły [o-źhanb-wi] adj. m. frigid; cold; reserved; dry

oznaczać [o-zna-chaćh] v. mark; signify; indicate; fix; spell out; denote; determine

oznajmiać [o-znay-myaćh] v. announce; inform; notify; state (one's opinion, etc.)

oznaka [o-zna-ka] f. sign; symptom; badge; mark; token

ozór [o-zoor] m. (bull's) tongue; gossiping tongue; (ox) tongue

ożenić [o-zhe-ńeećh] v. marry

ożywiać [o-zhi-vyaćh] v. bring to life; animate; brisk up

ożywienie [o-zhi-vye-ńe] n. animation; liveliness; stir

ożywiony [o-zhi-vyo-ni] adj. m.

animated; lively; brisk

Ó

ósemka [oo-sem-ka] f. eight; 8
ósma godzina [oos-ma go-
-dźhee-na] eight o'clock
ósmak [oos-mak] m. eighth
grader; eighth grade pupil
ów [oof] m. pron. that
ówczesny [oov-ches-ni] adj. m.
the then; of those days
ówdzie [oov-dźhe] adv.
elsewhere; there

P

pa ! [pa] excl.: bye-bye !
pacha [pa-kha] f. armpit
pachnąć [pakh-nownćh] v.
smell (good); have a fragrance
pachołek [pa-kho-wek] m. boy;
page; servant; menial; flunky
pachwina [pakh-vee-na] f. groin
pacierz [pa-ćhesh] m. prayer
pacierzowy stos [pa-ćhe-zho-vi
stos] m. spinal column; spine
paciorki [pa-ćhor-kee] pl. string
of beads; short prayer
pacjent [pa-tsyent] m. patient
pacyfista [pa-tsi-fees-ta] m.
pacifist; believer in peace
pacyfizm [pa-tsi-feezm] m.
pacifism; ideology of peace
paczka [pach-ka] f. parcel
paczyć [pa-chićh] v. warp
padać [pa-daćh] v. fall down
padalec [pa-da-lets] m. blind
-worm; slow warm
padlina [pa-dlee-na] f. carrion
pagórek [pa-goo-rek] m. hill
pająk [pa-yownk] m. spider
pajęczyna [pa-yan-chi-na] f.
cobweb; spider's web;

gossamer
paka [pa-ka] f. crate; lock-up
pakować [pa-ko-vaćh] v. pack;
cram; wrap; pack off; pack up
pakunek [pa-koo-nek] m. baggage; package; parcel; bundle
pal [pal] m. pile; stake; picket
palący [pa-lown-tsi] m. smoker
palec [pa-lets] m. finger; toe
palenie [pa-le-ńe] n. smoking
palenisko [pa-le-ńees-ko] n.
hearth; fireplace; grate
paleta [pa-le-ta] f. palette
palić [pa-leećh] v. burn; smoke
cigarette; heat; scorch; shoot
paliwo [pa-lee-vo] n. fuel
palma [pal-ma] f. palm tree
palnik [pal-ńeek] m. burner
palto [pal-to] m. overcoat
pałac [pa-wats] m. palace
pałka [paw-ka] f. stick; club
pamflet [pam-flet] m. pamphlet
pamiątka [pa-myownt-ka] f.
souvenir; keepsake; token of
remembrance; reminder; relic
pamięć [pa-myanćh] f. memory
pamiętać [pa-myan-taćh] v.
remember; recall; be careful
pamiętnik [pa-myant-ńeek] m.
diary; memoirs; album
pan [pan] m. lord; master;
mister; you; gentleman; squire
pan młody [pan mwo-di] m.
bride groom; groom
pani [pa-ńee] f. lady; you;
madam; mistress (in school)
panika [pa-ńee-ka] f. panic;
scare; an unreasoning fear
panna [pan-na] f. miss; girl; lass
panna młoda [pan-na mwo-da] f.
bride (about to be married)
panoszyć się [pa-no-shićh
śhan] v. domineer; boss; run
the show; lord it; be rife
panować [pa-no-vaćh] v. rule
(a nation); reign (supreme); be
master of; command; control;
dominate (over a people); prevail; be rife; predominate
panteizm [pan-te-eezm] m.
pantheism; the doctrine that
the entire universe is God
pantera [pan-te-ra] f. panther

pantoflarz [pan-to-flash] m.
  henpecked (subdued) husband
pantofel [pan-to-fel] m. slipper;
  light shoe; light low shoe
pantomima [pan-to-mee-ma] f.
  pantomime; a drama of action
  and gestures -- no words
panujący [pa-noo-yown-tsi] adj.
  m. prevailing; ruling
pański [pańs-kee] adj. m.
  lord's; your's; lordly
państwo [państ-vo] n. state;
  nation; married couple
papa [pa-pa] f. felt paper
papier [pa-pyer] m. paper
papieros [pa-pye-ros] m.
  cigarette; a small cigar
papieski [pa-pyes-kee] adj. m.
  papal; of the Pope
papież [pa-pyesh] m. pope
papka [pap-ka] f. pulp; mash;
  pap; gruel; paste; slurry
paplać [pap-laćh] v. prattle
paproć [pa-proćh] f. fern
papryka [pa-pri-ka] f. red-pepper;
  paprica; paprika
papuga [pa-poo-ga] f. parrot
para [pa-ra] f. 1. couple; 2.
  steam; the power of steam
  under pressure; vigor; energy
parabola [pa-ra-bo-la] f. parabola
parada [pa-ra-da] f. parade
paradoks [pa-ra-doks] m.
  paradox; apparent self-con-
  tradictory statement
parafia [pa-ra-fya] f. parish
parafina [pa-ra-fee-na] f. paraffin
  (waxy petroleum in candles)
paragraf [pa-ra-graf] m.
  paragraph (a distinct section)
paraliż [pa-ra-leesh] m. paralysis;
  crippling of activities
parametr [pa-ra-metr] m.
  parameter; element of an orbit
parapet [pa-ra-pet] m. window
  -sill; stool; rail; breastwork
parasol [pa-ra-sol] m. umbrella
parawan [pa-ra-van] m. screen
parcelować [par-tse-lo-vaćh] v.
  parcel out (land); cut up
parcie [par-ćhe] n. thrust
park [park] m. park (wooded)
parkan [par-kan] m. fence; net;

  hoarding (hiding)
parlament [par-la-ment] m.
  parliament; national legislative body (council)
parny [par-ni] adj. m. sultry
parobek [pa-ro-bek] m. farm
  -hand; plough man; rustic
parodia [pa-ro-dya] f. parody
parokrotnie [pa-ro-krot-ńe] adv.
  repeatedly; a couple of times
parostatek [pa-ro-sta-tek] m.
  steamboat; steamer; steamship (driven by steam power)
parować [pa-ro-vaćh] v. 1.
  evaporate; vaporize; cook by
  steam; 2. parry (a blow)
parowiec [pa-ro-vyets] m.
  steamboat; steamer; steamship (driven by steam power)
parowóz [pa-ro-voos] m. steam
  locomotive; railroad engine
parów [pa-roov] m. ravine
parówki [pa-roov-kee] pl. hot
  dogs; sausages; frankfurters
parszywy [par-shi-vi] adj. m.
  mangy; scabby; lousy; horrid
partacki [par-tats-kee] adj. m.
  bungled up; botched; fudged
partacz [par-tach] m. bungler
parter [par-ter] m. ground floor;
  first floor; parterre
partia [par-tya] f. party; card
  game; political party; game
partner [part-ner] m. partner
partyjny [par-tiy-ni] adj. m. party
  -(member); party member
partykuła [par-ti-koo-wa] f.
  particle; tiny fragment
partyzantka [par-ti-zant-ka] f.
  guerrilla; partisan war
parytet [pa-ri-tet] m. parity
parzyć [pa-zhićh] v. scald;
  steam; burn; percolate; couple
parzysty numer [pa-zhis-ti noo-
  -mer] m. even number
pas [pas] m. belt; traffic lane
pasat [pa-sat] m. trade wind
pasażer [pa-sa-zher] m.
  passenger; chap; fellow; liner
pasek [pa-sek] m. belt; band
pasieka [pa-śhe-ka] f. apiary
pasierb [pa-śherb] m. stepson
pasierbica [pa-śher-bee-tsa] f.

stepdaughter
pasja [pas-ya] f. passion
paskarz [pas-kazh] m. profiteer
pasmo [pas-mo] n. streak; tract;
range; traffic lane
pasożyt [pa-so-zhit] m. parasite;
sponger (living as a parasite)
pasta [pas-ta] f. paste
pasterka [pas-ter-ka] f. midnight
mass; shepherdess
pasterz [pas-tesh] m. shepherd
pastwa [pas-tva] f. prey
pastwisko [pas-tvees-ko] n.
pasture; grass land; pasturage
pastylka [pas-tii-ka] f. tablet
pasywny [pa-siv-ni] adj. m.
passive; acted upon; inactive
pasza [pa-sha] f. fodder
paszcza [pash-cha] f. jaw
paszport [pash-port] m. passport;
certificate of identity
paść [paśhćh] v. fall down;
graze; tend cattle; feed
patelnia [pa-tel-ña] f. frying pan
patent [pa-tent] m. patent
patetyczny [pa-te-tich-ni] adj. m.
pathetic; pompous; turgid
patolog [pa-to-lok] m.
pathologist; specialist in
pathology (of abnormalities)
patriarcha [pa-tryar-kha] m.
patriarch; high ranking bishop
patriota [pa-tryo-ta] m. patriot
patron [pa-tron] m. sponsor;
stencil; pattern; protector
patronat [pa-tro-nat] m.
patronage; power to grant
favors, support, etc.
patroszyć [pa-tro-shićh] v.
disembowel; gut; draw fowl
patrzeć [pa-tshećh] v. look at;
look on; stare at; see in retrospect; glare at; watch
patyk [pa-tik] m. stick
patyna [pa-ti-na] f. patina
pauza [paw-za] f. pause
paw [pav] m. peacock
paznokieć [paz-no-kyećh] m.
(finger) nail; toe nail
pazur [pa-zoor] m. claw
paź [paźh] m. page
październik [paźh-dźher-ñeek]
m. October

pączek [pown-chek] m. bud
pąsowy [pown-so-vi] adj. m. red;
crimson; bright red; poppy red
pchać [pkhaćh] v. push; thrust;
shove; impel; propel; urge;
egg on; drive; cram; stuff; dispatch; send; rush
pchła [pkhwa] f. flea
pchnięcie [pkhñan-ćhe] n.
push; thrust; jostle; shove
pech [pekh] m. bad luck
pechowiec [pe-kho-vyets] m.
unlucky fellow; luckless chap
pedagog [pe-da-gok] m.
pedagogue; educator
pedał [pe-daw] m. 1. pedal; 2.
gay; homosexual; pansy boy
pedant [pe-dant] m. pedant
pejcz [peych] m. horsewhip
pejzaż [pey-zash] m. landscape
peleryna [pe-le-ri-na] f. cape
pelikan [pe-lee-kan] m. pelican
pełnia [pew-ña] f. fullness
pełnić [pew-ñeećh] v. fulfill
pełno [pew-no] adv. plenty
pełnoletni [pew-no-let-ñee] adj.
m. adult; of age; mature
pełnomocnictwo [pew-no-mo-
-tsñeets-tvo] n. power of
attorney; full powers (legal)
pełny [pew-ni] adj. m. full
pełzać [pew-zaćh] v. creep;
crawl; fawn; drag; cringe
penicylina [pe-ñee-tsi-lee-na] f.
penicillin (antibiotic)
pensja [pens-ya] f. salary;
pension; allowance; wages
pensjonat [pen-syo-nat] m.
boarding house; pension
perfidny [per-feed-ni] adj. m.
perfidious; double dealing
perfumy [per-foo-mi] pl. scent;
perfume; perfumes
pergamin [per-ga-meen] m.
parchment; sheep skin
period [pe-ryod] m. period
perkal [per-kal] m. calico
perła [per-wa] f. pearl
peron [pe-ron] m. train-platform
perski [pers-kee] adj. m. Persian;
Iranian; of Iran
personalny [per-so-nal-ni] adj. m.
personal; personnel officer

personel [per-so-nel] m. staff;
 personnel; employees
perpektywa [per-spe-kti-va] f.
 perspective; vista; sense of
 proportion; view; outlook
perswazja [per-sva-zya] f.
 persuasion; power of per-
 suading; arguments
pertraktacja [per-tra-kta-tsya] f.
 negotiation; parley
peruka [pe-roo-ka] f. wig
peruwiański [pe-roo-vyań-skee]
 adj. m. Peruvian; of Peru
peryskop [pe-ris-kop] m.
 periscope (optical instr.)
pestka [pest-ka] f. kernel; pip;
 drupe; stone; trifle
pesymista [pe-si-mees-ta] m.
 pessimist expecting the worst
petent [pe-tent] m. petitioner
pewien [pe-vyen] adj. m. certain;
 one; a; an; some; sure
pewnik [pev-ńeek] m. axiom
pewniak [pev-ńak] m. cinch;
 surefooted man; certainty
pewny [pev-ni] adj. m. sure;
 secure; dependable; safe
pęcak [pan-tsak] m. peeled
 barley; hulled barley
pęcherz [pan-khesh] m. bladder
pęcznieć [panch-ńéch] v.
 swell; heave; bulge; bilge
pęd [pand] m. rush; dash; run;
 speed; impetus; urge; shoot;
 sprout; onward rush; scud
pędzel [pan-dzel] m. (paint)
 brush; tuft of hair
pędzić [pan-dźheéch] v. drive;
 run; lead; distill; hurry
pęk [pank] m. bunch
pękać [pan-kaćh] v. burst;
 split; crack; go off; flaw;
 snap; cleave; rift; break
pępek [pan-pek] m. navel
pętać [pan-taćh] v. shackle;
 hobble; knock about; clog
pętak [pan-tak] m. squirt
pętelka [pan-tel-ka] f. loop;
 small noose; small knot
piać [pyaćh] v. crow; sing
piana [pya-na] f. foam
pianino [pya-ńee-no] n. piano
piasek [pya-sek] m. sand

piasta [pyas-ta] f. hub; nave
piastować [pya-sto-vaćh] v.
 nurse; tend; hold (an office)
piąć się [pyownćh śhan] v.
 climb up; rise; creep; aspire
piątek [pyown-tek] m. Friday
piątka [pyownt-ka] f. five; 5
piąty [pyown-ti] num. fifth; 5th
picie [pee-ćhe] n. drinking
pić [peećh] v. drink; booze
picuś [pee-tsoośh] m. dandy
piec [pyets] m. stove; oven;
 furnace; kitchen stove; kiln
piec [pyets] v. bake; roast; burn;
 scorch; sting; smart
piechota [pye-kho-ta] f. infantry;
 a variety of beans
piechotą [pye-kho-town] adv. on
 foot; (go) on foot
piecza [pye-cha] f. care; charge
pieczarka [pye-char-ka] f.
 meadow mushroom
pieczątka [pye-chownt-ka] f.
 seal; stamp; signet
pieczeń wołowa [pye-cheń vo-
 -wo-va] f. roast beef
pieczyste [pye-chi-ste] f. roast
 meat; meat course; joint; roast
pieczywo [pye-chi-vo] n. bakery
 -goods; bread; baking
pieg [pyek] m. freckle; ephelis
piegowaty [pye-go-va-ti] adj. m.
 freckled (with brownish spots)
piekarnia [pye-kar-ńa] f. bakery;
 baker's shop; baked goods
piekarz [pye-kash] m. baker
piekielny [pye-kel-ni] adj. m.
 infernal; of hell; hellish
piekło [pye-kwo] n. hell
pielęgniarka [pye-lan-gńar-ka] f.
 nurse; hospital nurse
pielęgnować [pye-lan-gno-vaćh]
 v. nurse; tend; care; cultivate
pielgrzym [pyel-gzhim] m.
 pilgrim; wanderer to a holy
 place (often in a group)
pielucha [pye-loo-kha] f. diaper;
 baby's napkin; napkin
pieniądz [pye-ńownts] m.
 money; coin; currency; funds
pienić [pye-ńeećh] v. foam;
 sparkle; cover with foam
pieniężny [pye-ńanzh-ni] adj. m.

monetary; pecuniary; moneyed
pień [pyeń] m. trunk; stem;
   stump; snag; stock; root
pieprz [pyepsh] m. pepper
pierdzieć [pyer-dźhećh] v. fart
   (vulg); stink up; shit
pierdzioch [pyer-dźhokh] m. old
   fart (vulg.); old stinker
piernat [pyer-nat] m. feather-bed
piernik [pyer-ńeek] m. 1. ginger
   bread; 2. an old fogey; duffer
pierś [pyerśh] f. breast; chest
pierścień [pyerśh-ćheń] m.
   ring; collar; circle; hoop
pierścionek [pyer-śhćho-nek]
   m. ring; engagement ring
pierwej [pyer-vey] adv. of first;
   sooner; before; first
pierwiastek [pyer-**vya**-stek] m.
   root; element; radical
pierworodny [pyer-vo-rod-ni] adj.
   m. firstborn (son or daughter)
pierwotny [pyer-**vot**-ni] adj. m.
   primitive; primary; original
pierwszeństwo [pyerv-sheń-
   -stvo] n. priority; precedence
pierwszy [pyerv-shi] num. first
pierzchać [pyezh-khaćh] v. run
   away; fly; flee; disperse;
   scatter; take flight; vanish
pierze [pye-zhe] n. feathers
pierzyna [pye-zhi-na] f.
   featherbed; eider down; quilt
pies [pyes] m. 1. dog; 2. cur
piesko [pyes-ko] adv. badly
pieszczota [pyesh-cho-ta] f.
   caress; endearment
pieszo [pye-sho] adv. on foot
pieścić [pyeśh-ćheećh] v.
   fondle; caress; pet; hug;
   babble; handle lovingly
pieśń [pyeśhń] f. song
pietruszka [pye-troosh-ka] f.
   parsley (used for garnishing)
pięciobój [pyan-ćho-booy] m.
   pentathlon (of five events)
pięcioletni [pyan-ćho-let-ńee]
   adj. m. five years old
pięć [pyanćh] num. five; 5
piędź [pyandźh] f. palm. span
pięćdziesiąt [pyanćh-dźhe-
   -śhownt] num. fifty; 50
pięćset [pyanćh-set] num.

five hundred; 500
piękność [pyank-nośhćh] f.
   beauty; good looks; loveliness
piękny [pyank-ni] adj. m.
   beautiful; lovely; fine; handsome; good-looking; pretty
pięściarz [pyanśh-ćhash] m.
   boxer; prize-fighter
pięść [pyanśhćh] f. fist
pięściarstwo [pyanśh-ćhar-
   -stvo] n. box; boxing; pugilism
pięta [pyan-ta] f. heel
piętnastoletni [pyan-tna-sto-let-
   -ńee] adj. m. fifteen years old
piętnasty [pyant-nas-ti] num.
   fifteenth; 15th
piętnaście [pyant-naśh-ćhe]
   num. fifteen; 15
piętno [pyant-no] n. mark;
   stigma; brand; stamp; impress
piętro [pyant-ro] n. story; floor;
piętrzyć [pyant-shićh] v. pile
   up; bank up; heap; accumulate; rise; tower; be heaped
   high (with crates, boxes, etc.)
pigułka [pee-**goow**-ka] f. pill
pijak [pee-yak] m. drunk
pijany [pee-ya-ni] adj. m. drunk;
   tipsy; intoxicated; elated
pijawka [pee-yav-ka] f. leech
pikantny [pee-kant-ni] adj. m.
   spicy; piquant; pungent; sharp
piknik [peek-ńeek] m. picnic
pilnik [peel-ńeek] m. file
pilność [peel-nośhćh] f.
   diligence; urgency; industry;
   care; assiduity; urgency
pilny [peel-ni] adj. m. diligent;
   urgent; industrious; careful
pilot [pee-lot] m. pilot
pilśń [peelśhń] f. felt
piła [pee-wa] f. saw; bore
piłka [peew-ka] f. ball; handsaw;
   football; socker; shot
piłować [pee-**wo**-vaćh] v. saw;
   bore (a person); rasp on...
pingwin [peen-gveen] m. penguin
piołunówka [pyo-woo-**noov**-ka] f.
   absinth flavored liqueur
pion [pyon] m. plumb (line)
pionek [pyo-nek] m. pawn
pionier [pyo-ńer] m. pioneer
pionowy [pyo-**no**-vi] adj. m.

vertical; upright; plumb
piorun [pyo-roon] m. thunderbolt;
lightning shaft; lightning
piorunochron [pyo-roo-no-khron]
m. lightning-rod (conductor)
piosenka [pyo-sen-ka] f. song
piórko [pyoor-ko] n. (small)
feather; pen; plume
pióro [pyoo-ro] n. feather; pen
piramida [pee-ra-mee-da] f.
pyramid (polygonal figure)
pirat [pee-rat] m. pirate
pirotechnika [pee-ro-tekh-ńee-ka]
f. pyrotechnics (display)
pisać [pee-saćh] v. write
pisarz [pee-sash] m. writer
pisemnie [pee-sem-ńe] adv. in
writing; in black and white
pisk [peesk] m. squeal; squeak
piskliwy [pees-klee-vi] adj. m.
shrill; squeaky; thin; strident;
piping; high-pitched
piskle [pees-kle] n. chicken;
nestling; squealer
piskorz [pees-kosh] m. (long) eel
pismo [pees-mo] n. writing;
letter; newspaper; scripture;
alphabet; type; print
pisownia [pee-sov-ńa] f.
spelling; orthography
pistolet [pee-sto-let] m. pistol;
handgun; gun; spray gun
pisuar [pee-soo-ar] m. urinal
piszczeć [peesh-chećh] v. 1.
creak; squeak; screech; make
high-pitched sounds; 2. claim
piszczel [peesh-chel] m.
shinbone; tibia; blow pipe
piśmiennictwo [peeśh-myen-
-ńeets-tvo] n. literature
piśmiennie [peeśh-myen-ńe]
adv. in writing; in black and
white (written on paper)
piwiarnia [pee-vyar-ńa] f. beer
hall; beer house; saloon
piwnica [peev-ńee-tsa] f. cellar;
basement; coal cellar
piwny [peev-ni] adj. m. brown
(color); hasel; beer-
piwo [pee-vo] n. beer
piwonia [pee-vo-nya] f. peony
piwowar [pee-vo-var] m. brewer
piżama [pee-zha-ma] f. pajamas

plac [plats] m. square; area;
ground; building site; field
plac boju [plats bo-yoo] m. battle
field; field of battle; the field
placek [pla-tsek] m. cake; pie
placówka [pla-tsoov-ka] f.
sentry; post; outpost; agency
plaga [pla-ga] f. plague
plagiator [pla-gya-tor] m.
plagiarist (male)
plakat [pla-kat] m. poster
plama [pla-ma] f. blot; stain
plamić [pla-meećh] v. blot;
stain; soil; tarnish; defile
plan [plan] m. plan; design; map
planeta [pla-ne-ta] f. planet
planować [pla-no-vaćh] v. plan
planowo [pla-no-vo] adv.
according to (a fixed) plan;
systematically; methodically
plantacja [plan-ta-tsya] f.
(sugar, etc.) plantation
plaster [plas-ter] m. plaster;
patch; tape; adhesive; slice
plastyczne sztuki [plas-tich-ne
shtoo-kee] fine arts
plastyczny [plas-tich-ni] adj. m.
plastic; artistic; vivid
plastyk [plas-tik] m. artist;
plastic (substance)
platerować [pla-te-ro-vaćh] v.
plate (with na other metal)
platforma [plat-for-ma] f.
platform; truck; lorry; shelf
platoniczny [pla-to-ńeech-ni] adj.
m. Platonic; unsubstantial
platyna [pla-ti-na] f. platinum
plazma [plaz-ma] f. plasma
plaża [pla-zha] f. beach
plażować [pla-zho-vaćh] v. sun
bathe; lie on the beach
plądrować [plown-dro-vaćh] v.
plunder; ransack; ravage; loot
pląsy [plown-si] pl. dance
plątać [plown-taćh] v. entangle
plebania [ple-ba-ńya] f. rectory
plebiscyt [ple-bees-tsit] m.
plebiscite; people's direct vote
plecak [ple-tsak] m. rucksack;
backpack; (soldier's) knapsack
plecionka [ple-ćhon-ka] f. plaid
braid; wattle; basket work
plecy [ple-tsi] pl. back; backing

pleć [plećh] v. weed (a garden)
plemienny [ple-myen-ni] adj. m.
tribal; of a tribe
plemię [ple-myan] n. tribe
plemnik [plem-ńeek] m. sperm
plenum [ple-noom] n. plenary
session; plenary assembly
pleść [pleśhćh] v. twist; blab;
weave; interlace; talk nonsense; blab; jabber; tangle
pleśnieć [pleśh-ńećh] v.
mold; go mouldy; mildew
pletwa [plet-va] f. fin; dovetail
plewić [ple-veećh] v. weed
plik [pleek] m. bundle; sheaf
plisa [plee-sa] f. pleat
plomba [plom-ba] f. lead seal;
tooth filling; stopping
plon [plon] m. crop; yield
plotka [plot-ka] f. gossip; rumor;
piece of gossip; pl. tales
pluć [plooćh] v. spit; abuse
plugawy [ploo-ga-vi] adj. m.
filthy; squalid; foul; obscene
plus [ploos] m. plus; asset
plusk [ploosk] m. splash
pluskać [ploos-kaćh] v. splash
pluskiewka [ploos-kev-ka] f.
thumbtack; drawing pin
pluskwa [ploos-kva] f. bedbug
plusz [ploosh] m. plush
plutokracja [ploo-to-kra-tsya] f.
plutocracy (of the wealthy)
pluton [ploo-ton] m. platoon
plwocina [plvo-ćhee-na] f.
spittle; expectoration; spit
płaca [pwa-tsa] f. wage; salary
płachta [pwakh-ta] f. sheet
płacić [pwa-ćheećh] v. pay
płacz [pwach] m. cry; weep
płakać [pwa-kaćh] v. cry; weep
płaski [pwas-kee] adj. m. flat
płaskorzeźba [pwa-sko-zheźh-
-ba] f. low relief; bas-relief
płaskowyż [pwa-sko-vish] m.
high plateau; high table land
płaszcz [pwashch] m. overcoat
płaszczyć [pwash-chićh] v.
flatten; become flat; fall flat
płaszczyzna [pwash-chiz-na] f.
plane; surface; area; sheet (of
water, etc.); plain; expanse
płat [pwat] m. slice; lobe

płatać [pwa-taćh] v. cut; play
(tricks); slice; split; fell
płatek [pwa-tek] m. flake
płatność [pwat-nośhćh] f.
payment; remittance; bill
pławić [pwa-veećh] v. float;
wallow; duck; drown; soak
płaz [pwas] m. 1. reptile
płaz [pwas] m. 2. flat of a sabre
płciowy [pwćho-vi] adj. m.
sexual; genital; sex-(urge etc.)
płeć [pwećh] f.sex; complexion
płetwa [pwet-va] f. (swim-) fin
płochliwy [pwo-khlee-vi] adj. m.
timid; shy; skittish; scared
płochy [pwo-khi] adj. m.
frivolous; shy; timid; fickle
płodny [pwod-ni] adj. m. fertile;
productive; prolific; fruitful
płodzić [pwo-dźheećh] v.
beget; procreate; sire; breed
płomień [pwo-myeń] m. flame
płonąć [pwo-nownćh] v. be on
fire; blaze; be inflamed; glow
płonny [pwon-ni] adj. m. sterile;
useless; vain; of no avail
płoszyć [pwo-shićh] v. frighten
płot [pwot] m. fence; hoarding
płowieć [pwo-vyećh] v. fade
płowy [pwo-vi] adj. m. flaxen;
fair; buff; fallow; fawn
płód [pwoot] m. fetus; fruit
płócienny [pwoo-ćhen-ni]
adj. m. linen (sheets, etc.);
canvas-(sail, shoes etc.)
płótno [pwoot-no] n. linen;
canvas; cloth; scrim; painting
płuco [pwoo-tso] n. lung
płucny [pwoots-ni] adj. m.
pulmonary; of the lungs
pług [pwook] m. plough; plow
płukać [pwoo-kaćh] v. rinse;
wash; gargle one's throat
płyn [pwin] m. liquid; fluid
płynąć [pwi-nownćh] v. flow;
swim; sail; drift; go by; come
płynny [pwin-ni] adj. m. liquid;
fluent; fluid; smooth; graceful
płyta [pwi-ta] f. plate; slab; disk;
sheet; board; (musical) record
płyta gramofonowa [pwi-ta gra-
-mo-fo-no-va] f. (musical)
record; (gramophone) disk

płytki [pwit-kee] adj. m. shallow; flat; trivial; pointless

pływać [pwi-vaćh] v. 1. swim; float; navigate; be afloat; sail 2. quibble; be evasive

pływak [pwi-vak] m. swimmer; float; quibbler; buoy

pniak [pńak] m. stump; trunk

po [po] prep. after; to; up to; till; upon; for; at; in; up; of; next; along; about; over; past; behind; as far as; how (much)

pobicie [po-bee-će] n. battery

pobić [po-beećh] v. beat up; defeat; beat in; thrash; spank

pobielać [po-bye-laćh] v. whiten; tin; make white; paint white; whitewash; grow white

pobierać [po-bye-raćh] v. take; collect; receive; get; draw (rations, etc.); charge; derive

pobliski [po-blees-kee] adj. m. nearby; neighboring (inn, etc.)

pobłażać [po-bwa-zhaćh] v. indulge; forbear; be tolerant

pobłażliwy [po-bwa-zhlee-vi] adj. m. lenient; forgiving; tolerant

poboczny [po-boch-ni] adj. m. lateral; secondary; accessory

poborca [po-bor-tsa] m. (tax) (tax) collector; tax gatherer

poborowy [po-bo-ro-vi] adj. m. recruit; recruiting (board)

pobory [po-bo-ri] pl. salary

pobrać [po-braćh] v. receive; collect; get; draw; gather

pobudka [po-boot-ka] f. incentive; motive; reveille

pobudliwy [po-boo-dlee-vi] adj. m. excitable; ebullient

pobyt [po-bit] m. stay; visit

pocałować [po-tsa-wo-vaćh] v. give a kiss; kiss (good-bye)

pocałunek [po-tsa-woo-nek] m. kiss; caress with the lips

pochlebiać [po-khle-byaćh] v. flatter; adulate; expect; fawn

pochlebny [po-khleb-ni] adj. m. flattering; complimentary

pochłaniać [po-khwa-ńaćh] v. absorb; swallow up; engulf

pochmurny [po-khmoor-ni] adj. m. gloomy; cloudy; overcast

pochodnia [po-khod-ńa] f. torch

pochodny [po-khod-ni] adj. m. derivative; derived

pochodzenie [po-kho-dze-ńe] n. origin; descant; source

pochopny [po-khop-ni] adj. m. hasty; eager; rush; ready

pochować [po-kho-vaćh] v. bury; hide; conceal; put away

pochód [po-khoot] m. march; procession; parade; progress

pochwa [pokh-va] f. vagina; sheath (of a sword); scabbard

pochwała [pokh-va-wa] f. praise; eulogy; approval; applause

pochylić [po-khi-leećh] v. incline; slope; slant; droop

pochyły [po-khi-wi] adj. m. inclined; stooped; sloping; out of the vertical; oblique

pociąć [po-ćhownćh] v. cut up into pieces; slash; sting; saw up; furrow; intersect

pociąg [po-ćhownk] m. train; affinity; inclination

pociągać [po-ćhown-gaćh] v. pull; draw; attract; tug; coat

pociągnięcie [po-ćhowng-ńan--ćhe] n. pull; move; stroke; pluck; a tug; a swig (at)

po cichu [po ćhee-khoo] adv. secretly; silently; softly

pocić [po-ćheećh] v. sweat

pociecha [po-ćhe-kha] f. comfort; joy; solace; satisfaction; consolation; offspring

po ciemku [po ćhem-koo] adv. in the dark; while in the dark

pocierać [po-ćhe-raćh] v. rub

pocieszać [po-ćhe-shaćh] v. console; comfort; cheer up; solace; bring consolation

pocieszenie [po-ćhe-she-ńe] n. consolation; comfort; solace

pocieszny [po-ćhesh-ni] adj. m. funny; amusing; droll; comic

pocisk [po-ćheesk] m. missile; (gun, etc.) bullet; projectile

po co ? [po tso] what for ?

począć [po-chownćh] v. begin; conceive; become pregnant

początek [po-chown-tek] m. beginning; start; outset; fore-

part; early stage; outset
początkujący [po-ch<u>ow</u>n-tkoo-
-y<u>ow</u>n-tsi] adj. m. beginner
poczciwy [poch-ćhee-vi] adj. m.
good-hearted; friendly; kindly
poczekać [po-che-kaćh] v. wait
poczekalnia [po-che-kal-ńa] f.
waiting room; waiting hall
poczęstować [po-chan-sto-
-vaćh] v. treat to; entertain;
serve (food); regale (with)
poczęstunek [po-chan-stoo-nek]
m. treat; drinks; entertainment
poczta [poch-ta] f. post; mail
pocztówka [poch-toov-ka] f.
postcard; picture postcard
poczucie [po-choo-ćhe] n.
feeling; sense; consciousness
poczwórny [po-chvoor-ni] adj. m.
fourfold; four times as large,
as tall; as long, as big
poczynać [po-chi-naćh] v.
begin (aggressively); conceive
poczytalny [po-chi-tal-ni] adj. m.
accountable; sane; responsible
poczytny [po-chit-ni] adj. m.
popular (book); widely read
pod [pod] prep. under; below;
towards; on in underneath
podać [po-daćh] v. give; hand;
pass; serve; shake (hand)
podanie [po-da-ńe] n.
application; request; legend
podarek [po-da-rek] m. gift
podarty [po-dar-ti] adj. m. torn
podatek [po-da-tek] m. tax; duty
podatnik [po-dat-ńeek] m. tax-
-payer; rate payer
podaż [po-dash] f. supply
podążać [po-d<u>ow</u>n-zhaćh] v.
make for; draw to; make
one's way (towards a place)
podbicie [pod-bee-ćhe] n.
conquest; instep; lining; ceiling
podbiec [pod-byets] v. run up
podbiegunowy [pod-bye-goo-no-
-vi] adj. m. polar; near pole
podbój [pod-booy] m. conquest
podbudowa [pod-boo-do-va] f.
substructure; base course
podbródek [pod-broo-dek] m.
chin; bib; feeder
podburzać [pod-boo-zhaćh] v.

stir up; incite to revolt
podchmielony [pod-khmye-lo-ni]
adj. m. tipsy; in drink
podchodzić [pod-kho-dźheećh]
v. approach; assume an attitude; walk up; step up; climb;
treat; seep; steel up; outwit
podchwycić [pod-khvi-ćheećh]
v. catch up; snatch up; spot
podchwytliwy [pod-khvi-tlee-vi]
adj. m. captious (question)
podciągać [pod-ćh<u>ow</u>n-gaćh]
v. draw up; pull up; improve;
raise; elevate; include; class
podczas [pod-chas] prep. during;
while; when; whereas
podczerwony [pod-cher-vo-ni]
adj. m. infrared
poddać [pod-daćh] v.
surrender; suggest; submit;
expose; subject; bare a hand
pod dostatkiem [pod do-stat-
-kem] adv. plenty; enough
podejmować [po-dey-mo-vaćh]
v. take up; entertain; pick up
podejrzany [po-dey-zha-ni] adj.
m. suspect; suspicious; shady
podejrzliwy [po-dey-zhlee-vi] adj.
m. suspicious; distrustful
podeptać [po-dep-taćh] v.
tramp (under foot); bustle
(about a purchase, etc.)
poderwać [po-der-vaćh] v. jerk
up; pick up; weaken; rouse
podeszwa [po-desh-fa] f. sole
podginać [pod-gee-naćh] v.
tuck up (one's shirt, etc.);
cock; turn up; bend (a knee)
podglądać [pod-gl<u>ow</u>n-daćh] v.
(play a) spy; peep; pry; snoop
podgórski [pod-goor-skee]
adj. m. foot-hill; piedmont
podjechać [pod-ye-khaćh] v.
drive up; ride up hill; come up
podgrzewać [pod-gzhe-vaćh] v.
warm up (some food); heat up
podjudzać [pod-yoo-dzaćh] v.
stir up; incite (to evil)
podkasać [pod-ka-saćh] v. tuck
up; turn up (sleeves); rise
podkład [pod-kwat] m. base;
railroad tie; undercurrent; bedding; groundwork; foundation

podkładać [pod-**kwa**-daćh] v.
lay under; put under; plant as
evidence; underlay; set (fire)
podkop [pod-kop] m. mine; sap
podkowa [pod-**ko**-va] f. horse
-shoe; semicircle
podkradać [pod-**kra**-daćh] v.
thieve; pilfer; creep up
podkreślać [pod-**kre**-śhlaćh]
v. stress; underline (an error);
emphasize; accentuate; insist
podkuwać [pod-**koo**-vaćh] v.
shoe (horse); hobnail a shoe;
cram (for an examination)
podlegać [pod-le-gaćh] v. be
subject; be liable; succumb;
undergo; be submitted to
podległość [pod-le-gwośhćh]
f. dependence; subjection;
subordination; submission
podlewać [pod-le-vaćh] v.
water (flowers); baste
podlizywać się [pod-lee-zi-vaćh
śh<u>an</u>] v. suck up to; make up
to somebody; toady somebody
podlotek [pod-**lo**-tek] m.
fledgling (girl); flapper (girl);
girl in her teens
podłoga [pod-**wo**-ga] f. floor
podłość [pod-**wo**śhćh] f. dirty trick; meanness; baseness
podług [pod-**wook**] prep.:
according to; in conformity
with; after (masters, etc.)
podłużny [pod-**woozh**-ni] adj. m.
oblong; longitudinal; elongated
podły [pod-**wi**] adj. m. mean
podmiejski [pod-**myeys**-kee] adj.
m. suburban; of the suburbs
podminować [pod-mee-no-
-vaćh] v. undermine; sap
podmiot [pod-**myot**] m. subject
podmuch [pod-mookh] m. gust;
blow; puff; waft; breath; blast
podmywać [pod-mi-vaćh] v.
wash under; sap; undermine;
wash away; wash up
podniebienie [pod-ńe-bye-ńe] n.
palate; roof of the mouth
podniecać [pod-ńe-tsaćh] v.
flurry excite; agitate; rouse;
egg on; fluster; rouse; stir up
podnieść [pod-ńeśhćh] v.

lift; hoist (a flag); rise; elevate;
rear; increase (wages, etc,)
podnieta [pod-**ńe**-ta] f. stimulus;
impulse; spur; stimulant
podniosły [pod-**ńo**-swi] adj. m.
sublime; elevated; lofty
podnosić [pod-no-śheećh] v.
hoist; raise (a question); lift;
take up; elevate; increase; rear
podnóżek [pod-**noo**-zhek]
footstool; ottoman; leg rest
podobać się [po-do-baćh
śh<u>an</u>] v. please; be attractive;
take sombody's fancy; enjoy
podobny [po-**dob**-ni] adj. m.
similar; like; congenial
podoficer [pod-o-**fee**-tser] m.
noncommissioned officer
podołać [po-do-waćh] v. be up
to; cope; manage; be equal to
podomka [po-**dom**-ka] f.
houserobe; dressing gown
podówczas [pod-**oof**-chas] adv.
at that time; at the time; then
podpadać [pod-pa-daćh] v. be
spotted; fall under a category
podpalenie [pod-pa-le-ńe] n.
arson; setting of fire
podpatrzyć [pod-pa-**tshi**ćh] v.
spy; peep; find out; pry
podpierać [pod-pye-raćh] v.
prop up; support; bolster
podpinać [pod-**pee**-naćh] v. pin;
buckle up; strap; fasten; gird
podpis [pod-pees] m. signature
podpływać [pod-**pwi**-vaćh] v.
swim up; sail up; row up
podpora [pod-**po**-ra] f. prop
podporucznik [pod-po-**rooch**-
-ńeek] m. second lieutenant
podporządkować [pod-po-
-z<u>ho</u>wnd-ko-vaćh] v. subordinate; submit; conform
podprowadzić [pod-pro-**va**-
-dźheećh] v. bring near
podpułkownik [pod-poow-**kov**-
-ńeek] m. lieutenant colonel
podrażnić [pod-**razh**-ńeećh] v.
displease; irritate; vex; gall
podręcznik [pod-**ranch**-ńeek] m.
handbook; textbook; manual
podrożeć [pod-ro-zheećh] v. go
up; grow dear; rise in price

podróż 127 podziewać

podróż [pod-roosh] f. travel;
voyage; journey; passage
podróżnik [pod-roozh-ńeek] m.
traveler; voyager; wayfarer
po drugie [po droo-ge] adv. in
the second place; second
podrzeć [pod-zheć] v. tear up
podrzędny [pod-zhand-ni] adj. m.
subordinate; secondary
podsądny [pod-sownd-ni] m.
defendant; the person sued
podskakiwać [pod-ska-kee-
-vać] v. leap; jump up; hop;
skip; frisk; bounce; soar; jolt
podsłuch [pod-swookh] m.
eavesdropping; wire tapping;
listening in (on the phone)
podstawa [pod-sta-va] f. base;
basis; footing; mount; rest;
foundation; principle
podstawić [pod-sta-veeć] v.
substitute; put under; bring
round; place under; push to
podstęp [pod-stanp] m. trick;
ruse; guile; piece of deceit;
stratagem; cunning devices
podstępny [pod-stanp-ni] adj. m.
deceitful; tricky; crafty;
insidious; scheming; guileful
podstrzygać [pod-stshi-gać] v.
trim the hair; shorten the hair
podsuwać [pod-soo-vać] v.
push near; plant; suggest; slip
under; move to; prompt with
(an answer); offer (an opinion)
podsycać [pod-si-tsać] v.
foment; feed; fan (a quarrel)
podsypywać [pod-si-pi-vać] v.
pour (sand etc.); strew;
sprinkle (with sugar, etc.)
podszept [pod-shept] m.
suggestion; prompting; insinuation; instigation
podszeptywać [pod-shep-ti-
-vać] v. prompt; suggest;
hint; insinuate; whisper into
somebody's ear; instigate
podszewka [pod-shev-ka] f.
lining; inside information
podświadomy [pod-śhvya-do-
-mi] adj. m. subconscious
podupadać [pod-oo-pa-dać] v.
decline; deteriorate; fall into

decay; fall into poverty
poduszka [po-doosh-ka] f. pillow;
pad; cushion; ball (of the
thumb); cushion pad; finger tip
podwajać [pod-va-yać] v.
double; duplicate; increase
twofold; reduplicate;
podważyć [pod-va-zhić] v.
lever up; pry up; shake (an
opinion); prize a lid open
podwiązka [pod-vyownz-ka] f.
garter; suspender; ligature
podwieczorek [pod-vye-cho-rek]
m. afternoon tea (snack)
podwieźć [pod-vye żhć] v.
give a ride; give a lift (in one's
car); bring to doorstep; provide with; supply (groceries)
podwładny [pod-vwad-ni] adj. m.
subordinate (to somebody);
inferior; m.subordinate
podwodna łódź [pod-vod-na
woodżh] f. submarine
podwoić [pod-vo-eeć] v.
double; increase twofold; duplicate; reduplicate
podwozie [pod-vo-żhe] n.
chassis; under-carriage
podwórko [pod-voor-ko] n.
backyard; farmyard; court;
courtyard; barnyard
podwyżka [pod-vish-ka] f. raise
podzelować [pod-ze-lo-vać] v.
resole (shoes; boots; foot)
podziać [po-dźhać] v. loose;
put somewhere; mislay
podział [po-dźhaw] m. division
podziałka [po-dźhaw-ka] f.
scale; graduation; division
podzielać [po-dźhe-lać] v.
share; participate; concur
podzielić [po-dźhe-leeć] v.
divide (into parts)
podzielny [po-dźhel-ni] adj. m.
divisible (easily)
podziemie [pod-żhe-mye] n.
basement; underworld
podziemny [pod-żhem-ni]
adj. m. underground; secret
podziękować [po-dźhan-ko-
-vać] v. thank; decline with
thanks (for something)
podziewać [po-dźhe-vać] v.

loose; mislay; leave
somewhere; put somewhere
podziw [po-dźheef] m. admiration; wander; an admiration
podzwrotnikowy [pod-zvrot-ńee-ko-vi] adj. m. tropical
podżegacz [pod-zhe-gach] m. instigator; warmonger; abettor
poemat [po-e-mat] m. poem
poeta [po-e-ta] m. poet
poetka [po-et-ka] f. poet
poezja [po-e-zya] f. poetry
pogadanka [po-ga-dan-ka] f. talk; chat; chatty (talk) lecture
poganiać [po-ga-ńać] v. drive; egg on; urge on; prod on; hustle; urge forwards
poganin [po-ga-ńeen] m. pagan
pogarda [po-gar-da] f. contempt
pogarszać [po-gar-shać] v. make worse; aggravate; worsen; deteriorate; grow worse
pogawędka [po-ga-vand-ka] f. chat; chit-chat; chatty talk
pogląd [po-glownd] m. opinion
pogłębiać [po-gwan-byać] v. deepen; dig deeper; dredge
pogłoska [po-gwos-ka] f. rumor
pogniewać się [po-gńe-vać śhan] v. get angry; be angry
pogoda [po-go-da] f. weather; cheerfulness; fine weather
pogodny [po-god-ni] adj. m. serene; cheerful; sunny
pogodzić [po-go-dźheeć] v. reconcile; square (things)
pogoń [po-goń] f. pursuit; chase; hunt; quest; pursuers
pogorszenie [po-gor-she-ńe] n. worsening; deterioration
pogorszyć [po-gor-shić] v. make worse; aggravate
pogorzelisko [po-go-zhe-lees-ko] n. after fire ruins
pogotowie [po-go-to-vye] n. ambulance service; readiness
pogranicze [po-gra-ńee-che] n. borderland; border line
pogrom [po-grom] m. rout; pogrom; crushing defeat
pogromca [po-grom-tsa] m. (animal) tamer; conqueror
pogróżka [po-groosh-ka] f.

threat; threatening expression
pogrzeb [po-gzhep] m. funeral
pogrzebacz [po-gzhe-bach] m. poker (for stirring a fire)
pogwałcić [po-gvaw-ćheeć] v. violate; outrage; transgress
poić [po-eeć] v. water; ply
pojawić się [po-ya-veeć śhan] v. appear; emerge; become visible; occur; arise
pojazd [po-yazt] m. car; vehicle
pojąć [po-yownć] v. grasp; marry; comprehend; understand; conceive; imagine
pojechać [po-ye-khać] v. go; leave; take (train; boat etc.)
pojednać [po-yed-nać] v. reconcile (two or more parties)
pojednawczy [po-yed-nav-chi] adj. m. conciliatory
pojedynczy [po-ye-din-chi] adj. m. single; individual; one-fold; single-entry (books)
pojedynek [po-ye-di-nek] m. duel; encounter; single combat
pojemnik [po-yem-ńeek] m. container; vessel; receptacle
pojemność [po-yem-nośhćh] f. capacity; cubic content
pojezierze [po-ye-źhe-zhe] n. lake land; lake district
pojęcie [po-yan-ćhe] n. notion; idea; concept; comprehension
pojętny [po-yant-ni] adj. m. intelligent; sharp; teachable
pojmować [poy-mo-vać] v. comprehend; conceive; grasp; imagine; understand
pojutrze [po-yoot-zhe] adv. the day after tomorrow
pokarm [po-karm] m. food; feed
pokaz [po-kas] m. display; shaw
pokazywać [po-ka-zi-vać] v. show; point; exhibit; let see
pokaźny [po-kaźh-ni] adj. m. respectable; appreciable
pokład [po-kwat] m. deck; layer
pokątny [po-kownt-ni] adj. m. underhanded; secret; illegal
pokłon [po-kwon] m. bow before (sb); homage; greeting
pokłócić się [po-kwoo-ćheeć śhan] v. fall out with; quarrel

pokochać [po-ko-khaćh] v. fall
in love; become fond of
pokoik [po-ko-eek] m. little room;
little cozy room
pokojówka [po-ko-yoof-ka] f.
housemaid; chamber maid
pokolenie [po-ko-le-ńe] n.
generation; about 30 years
pokonać [po-ko-naćh] v. defeat
(an army); conquer; subdue
pokorny [po-kor-ni] adj. m.
humble; meek; submissive
pokost [po-kost] m. varnish
pokrajać [po-kra-yaćh] v. cut
up; carve up; slice; slash
pokój [po-kooy] m. room; peace
pokrapiać [po-kra-pyaćh] v.
sprinkle; wash down (a meal)
pokrewieństwo [po-kre-vyeń-
-stvo] n. kinship; kindred;
relation; relationship; affinity
pokrewny [po-krev-ni] adj. m.
related; kindred; akin; cognate
pokrótce [po-kroot-tse] adv. in
short; in brief; concisely
pokrycie [po-kri-ćhe] n. cover
pokryć [po-krićh] v. cover
po kryjomu [po kri-yo-moo] adv.
secretly; on the sly; in secret
pokrywa [po-kri-va] f. lid
pokrywać [po-kri-vaćh] v.
cover; upholster; serve (mare)
pokrzepić [po-kzhe-peećh] v.
invigorate; refresh; fortify
pokrzywa [po-kzhee-va] f. nettle
pokrzyżować [po-kzhi-zho-
-vaćh] v. cross up; confound;
tangle; put crosswise; thwart
pokup [po-koop] m. demand
pokupny [po-koop-ni] adj. m. in
demand; sellable; salable
pokusa [po-koo-sa] f. temptation
pokuta [po-koo-ta] f. penance
pokwitować [po-kvee-to-vaćh]
v. receipt; acknowledge
receipt (of a sum, etc,)
pokwitowanie [po-kvee-to-va-ńe]
n. receipt; written receipt
polać [po-laćh] v. (liquid) pour;
pour over; flow; shed; gusher
Polak [po-lak] m. Polonian; Pole;
Polonius (as in Hamlet)
polana [po-la-na] f. glade

polano [po-la-no] n. billet; log
polarny [po-lar-ni] adj. m. polar;
of the polar (axis, direction)
pole [po-le] n. field; area
polec [po-lets] v. fall; be killed
(in battle); bite the dust; die
polecać [po-le-tsaćh] v. recommend; commend; instruct;
order; enjoin; tell (to do)
polegać [po-le-gaćh] v. rely
polemika [po-le-mee-ka] f.
polemics; controversy
polepszać [po-lep-shaćh] v.
improve; ameliorate; mend;
get better; grow better
polerować [po-le-ro-vaćh] v.
polish; furbish; burnish; refine
polewać [po-le-vaćh] v. water;
glaze; enamel; ice (cakes)
polewka [po-lev-ka] f. broth
polędwica [po-land-vee-tsa] f.
sirloin; loin; fillet (of beef)
policja [po-leets-ya] f. police
policzek [po-lee-chek] m. cheek
politechnika [po-lee-tekh-ńee-ka]
f. polytechnic institute; technical university or college
politowanie [po-lee-to-va-ńe] n.
pity; compassion; sympathy
polityk [po-lee-tik] m. politician
experienced in government
polka [pol-ka] f. polka (dance)
polka [pol-ka] f. Polish girl; Polish
women; Pole; Polish lady
polny [pol-ni] adj. m. field
polon [po-lon] m. polonium
polonez [po-lo-nez] m. polonaise
Polonia [po-lo-ńa] f. Polish
colony; Polish emigrants
Polonus [po-lo-noos] m. Pole of
old; typical Pole of the past
polot [po-lot] m. elan; ima-
ginativeness; loftiness
polować [po-lo-vaćh] v. hunt
polski [pol-skee] adj. m. Polish;
Polish language
polskość [pol-skośhćh] f. Polish character; traits, etc.
polszczyć [polsh-chićh] v.
Polonize; invest with Polish
traits, culture, language, etc.
polszczyzna [pol-shchiz-na] f.
Polish language; Polish traits

polubić [po-**loo**-beećh] v. get to like; become fond of; take a fancy to; take a liking to

polubownie [po-loo-**bov**-ńe] adv. amicably; by compromise

połamać [po-**wa**-maćh] v. break

połączenie [po-w<u>own</u>-che-ńe] n. connection; linkage; contact

połknąć [pow-kn<u>own</u>ćh] v. swallow; gulp down; drink down; gulp bach (tears, etc.)

połowa [po-**wo**-va] f. half

położenie [po-wo-**zhe**-ńe] n. position; situation; site

położna [po-**wozh**-na] f. midwife

położnica [po-**wozh**-ńee-tsa] f. woman lying-in (in childbed)

położyć [po-**wo**-zhićh] v. lay down; place; deposit; fell; ruin

połóg [po-**wook**] m. childbirth

połów ryb [po-**woov** rib] fish catch; fishing; fish haul

południe [po-**wood**-ńe] n. noon; south; midday; the South

południk [po-**wood**-ńeek] m. meridian; the line of longitude

południowo-wschodni [po-wood--ńo-vo vskhod-ńee] adj. m. south-east; of south-east

południowo-zachodni [po-wood--ńo-vo za-khod-ńee] adj. m. south-west; of south west

południowy [po-**wood**-ńo-vi] adj. m. south; midday; southerly

połykać [po-**wi**-kaćh] v. swallow; gulp down; bolt

połysk [po-**wisk**] m. glitter; gloss; luster; sheen; sparkle

pomadka [po-**mad**-ka] f. lipstick

pomagać [po-ma-**gać**h] v. help

pomaleńku [po-ma-**leń**-koo] adv. little by little; very slowly

pomału [po-ma-**woo**] adv. little by little; slowly; leisurely

pomarańcza [po-ma-**rań**-cha] f. orange; orange tree

pomarszczony [po-mar-**shcho**-ni] adj. m. wrinkled; creased

pomazać [po-ma-**zaćh**] v. smear-over; anoint; soil; scrawl; spread (butter, etc.)

pomawiać [po-ma-**vyać**h] v. accuse; impute; charge with

pomiar [po-**myar**] m. measurement; survey; surveying; mensuration; measurements

pomiatać [po-mya-**tać**h] v. push around; spurn; hold in contempt; ill-treat; sweep

pomidor [po-**mee**-dor] m. tomato

pomieszać [po-**mye**-shaćh] v. mix up; mingle; blend; stir; tangle; muddle up; embroil; mistake; jumble up; drive mad

pomieszanie zmysłów [po-mye--**sha**-ńe zmis-woov] insanity; madness; mental derangement

pomieszczać [po-**myesh**-chaćh] v.admit;contain; accommodate

pomiędzy [po-**my<u>an</u>**-dzi] prep. between; among; in the midst

pomijać [po-**mee**-yaćh] v. pass over; omit; overlook; leave out

pomimo [po-**mee**-mo] prep. in spite of; notwithstanding

pomnażać [po-**mna**-zhaćh] v. multiply; increase; intensify

pomniejszać [po-**mńey**-shaćh] v. diminish; lessen; reduce; dwarf; belittle; minimize

pomnik [pom-**ńeek**] m. monument (to a great man, etc,)

pomoc [po-**mots**] f. help; aid

pomocnik [po-mots-**ńeek**] m. helper; assistant; helpmate; (an) aid; one who assists

pomocny [po-**mots**-ni] adj. m. helpful in; instrumental in

pomorski [po-**mors**-kee] adj. m. Pomeranian; of Pomerania

pomost [po-**most**] m. platform

pomóc [po-**moots**] v. help; assist

pompa [pom-**pa**] f. pump; pomp

pompować [pom-po-**vać**h] v. pump; blow up (inflate a tire)

pomsta [pom-**sta**] f. vengeance

pomruk [pom-**rook**] m. murmur; grumble; growl; purr; rumble

pomstować [pom-sto-**vać**h] v. curse; swear; revile; vituperate

pomyje [po-**mi**-ye] pl. dishwater; hog-wash; swill; lap; slops

pomylić [po-mi-**leeć**h] v. confound; mistake (facts); be mistaken; mislead; misinform

pomyłka [po-**miw**-ka] f. error

pomysł [po-misw] m. idea
pomyślność [po-miśhl-
-nośhćh] f. prosperity; success; happiness; welfare
pomyślny [po-miśhl-ni] adj. m.
successful; favorable; good
pomywaczka [po-mi-vach-ka] f.
dishwasher; scullery maid
ponad [po-nat] prep. above;
over; beyond; upwards of;
super-; more than; over and
above; besides; apart from
ponadto [po-nad-to] prep.
moreover; besides; over and
above; furthermore; also
ponaglać [po-na-glaćh] v. rush;
urge; remind; press; urge on
ponaglenie [po-na-gle-ńe] n.
reminder; pressure; urging
ponawiać [po-na-vyaćh] v.
renew (efforts); reiterate
ponętny [po-nant-ni] adj. m.
seductive; attractive; alluring
poniechać [po-ńe-khaćh] v.
give up; relinquish; renounce;
forsake; desist; forbear; drop
poniedziałek [po-ńe-dźha-wek]
m. Monday (week's 2nd day)
poniekąd [po-ńe-kownt] adv.
partly; in a way; in a sense
ponieść [po-ńeśhćh] v. sustain; carry; bear; suffer; incur;
push; take; overcome; bolt
ponieważ [po-ńe-vash] conj.
because; as; since; for
poniewczasie [po-ńe-vcha-śhe]
adv. too late; after the event
poniewierać [po-ńe-vye-raćh]
v. kick around; slight; hold in
contempt; ill-treat; mishandle
poniżej [po-ńee-zhey] adv.
below; beneath; hereunder;
under; lower down; less than
poniżyć [po-ńee-zhićh] v.
degrade; humble; tread down
ponosić [po-no-śheećh] v.
bear; carry (away); suffer; incur; bolt (a rider); push; carry
ponowić [po-no-veećh] v. renew; reiterate (demands, etc.)
ponownie [po-nov-ńe] adv.
anew; again; afresh; a second
time; another time; re-(do)

ponowny [po-nov-ni] adj. m.
repeated; renewed; reiterated
ponton [pon-ton] m. pontoon
ponury [po-noo-ri] adj. m.
gloomy dismal; sullen; dreary
pończocha [poń-cho-kha] f.
stocking; piece of hosiery
popadać [po-pa-daćh] v. fall in
poparcie [po-par-ćhe] n.
support; backing; promotion;
push; advancement; advocacy
popaść [po-paśhćh] v. fall in
popatrzeć [po-pa-tshećh] v.
look awhile (at); glance; see
popchnąć [pop-khnownćh] v.
push; shove up (down, along);
hassle; jostle; steer; direct
popelina [po-pe-lee-na] f. poplin
popełniać [po-pew-ńaćh] v.
commit (an error, crime, etc.);
perpetrate (crime, murder)
popęd [po-pant] m. impulse
popędliwy [po-pan-dlee-vi] adj.
m. impetuous; rush; hot headed; irritable; impulsive
popędzać [po-pan-dzaćh] v.
drive on; urge; push on; prod;
spur; goad; hustle on; hurry
popielaty [po-pye-la-ti] adj. m.
charcoal-grey; ashen; gray
popielec [po-pye-lets] m. Ash
Wednesday (1st day of Lent)
popielniczka [po-pyel-ńeech-ka]
f. ash-tray; ash pan
popierać [po-pye-raćh] v.
support; back; promote; favor;
uphold; give one's backing to
popiersie [po-pyer-śhe] n. bust
popić [po-peećh] v. rinse down
popiół [po-pyoow] m. ashes;
ash; cinders; slag
popis [po-pees] m. show; parade
popisywać się [po-pee-si-vaćh
śhan] v. show off; flaunt; parade; make a show (of wit)
popleczmik [po-plech-ńeek] m.
backer; upholder; partisan
popłatny [po-pwat-ni] adj. m.
profitable ; lucrative
popłoch [po-pwokh] m. panic
popołudnie [po-po-wood-ńe] n.
afternoon; after 12 at noon
po południu [po po-wood-ńu] in

(during) the afternoon
poprawa [po-**pra**-va] f.
improvement; change for the better; (signs of) recovery
poprawka [po-**prav**-ka] f.
correction; amendment; alteration; (final) rectification
poprawny [po-**prav**-ni] adj. m.
correct; faultless; proper
po prostu [po **pros**-too] adv.
simply; openly; candidly; unceremoniously; in plain words
poprzeczka [po-**pshech**-ka] f.
crossbar; crossbeam; the bar
poprzedni [po-**pshed**-ńee]
adj. m. previous; preceding; former; foregoing; anterior
poprzedzać [po-pshe-**dzać**] v.
precede; prelude; go before
poprzestać [po-pshes-**tać**] v.
settle for; be satisfied
popularny [po-poo-**lar**-ni] adj. m.
popular; prevalent; in vogue
popychać [po-pi-**khać**] v.
push (along, up, down, aside); shove; ill treat; hustle; jostle;
popychadło [po-pi-**khad**-wo] n.
(a slow) drudge; scapegrace
popyt [**po**-pit] m. demand
pora [**po**-ra] f. time; season
porachunek [po-ra-**khoo**-nek] m.
reckoning; a bone to pick
porada [po-**ra**-da] f. advice
poradnia [po-**rad**-ńa] f.
information bureau; (also) dispensary, clinic etc.
poradnik [po-**rad**-ńeek] m. guide; handbook; reference book
poradzić [po-ra-**dźheeć**] v.
advise to do; cope with; help
poranek [po-**ra**-nek] m. morning
porastać [po-ras-**tać**] v.
overgrow; grow; become overgrown with; cover; sprout
poratować [po-ra-to-**vać**] v.
help in distress; recuperate
porażenie [po-ra-**zhe**-ńe] n.
stroke; shock; paralysis
porażka [po-**razh**-ka] f. defeat; set back; reverse; a beating
porcelana [por-tse-**la**-na] f. china; porcelain; crockery; dishes
porcja [**por**-tsya] f. portion

poręcz [po-**ranch**] f. banister
poręczenie [po-**ran**-che-ńe] n.
guarantee; bail; warranty; pledge to guarantee for
poręka [po-**ran**-ka] f. guaranty; pledge; sponsorship; surety
poronić [po-ro-**ńeeć**] v. abort; miscarry; have a miscarriage
porost [**po**-rost] m. growth
porowaty [po-ro-**va**-ti] adj. m.
porous; full of pores
porozdawać [po-roz-da-**vać**] v.
give away; pass around
porozumianie [po-ro-zoo-**mye**-ńe]
n. understanding; agreement
poród [**po**-root] m. child delivery; childbirth; parturition
porównać [po-roov-**nać**] v.
compare; draw a comparison; liken; parallel (two items)
porównanie [po-roov-**na**-ńe] n.
comparison; equalization
poróżnić [po-**roozh**-ńeeć] v.
disunite; divide; embroil
port [port] m. port; harbor
portfel [**port**-fel] m. wallet
portier [**por**-tyer] m. doorman
portki [**port**-kee] pl. pants (vulg.); breeches; (sloppy) trousers
portmonetka [port-mo-**net**-ka] f.
purse; billfold; wallet
porto [**por**-to] n. postage
portret [**por**-tret] m. portrait
portugalski [por-too-**gals**-kee] adj.
m. Portuguese; of Portugal
poruczać [po-roo-**chać**] v.
entrust; charge with
porucznik [po-**rooch**-ńeek] m.
Lieutenant; Flying Officer
poruszać [po-roo-**shać**] v.
move; touch; sway; set in motion; keep in motion; wag
poruszenie [po-roo-**she**-ńe] n.
agitation; movement; stir; disturbance; touch; commotion
poryw [**po**-riv] m. impulse; rapture; gust; onrush; elation
porywać [po-ri-**vać**] v. snatch; carry off; whisk away; grab; thrill; snap up; sweep away
porywacz [po-**ri**-vach] m.
kidnaper; abductor; ravisher
porywczy [po-**riv**-chi] adj. m.

rash; irritable; impetuous; hasty; impulsive; hot-tempered
porządek [po-zhown-dek] m.
order; tidiness; regularity; system; arrangement; sequence
porządny [po-zhownd-ni] adj. m.
neat; decent; accurate; reliable
porzucać [po-zhoo-tsać] v.
abandon; desert; forsake; jilt; leave; cast away; give up
porzucić [po-zhoo-ćheeć] v.
abandon; give up; cast away
posada [po-sa-da] f. employment
posadzka [po-sadz-ka] f. parquet floor; tile (marble) floor
posąg [po-sowng] m. statue
poselstwo [po-sels-tvo] n.
legation; deputation; envoys
poseł [po-sew] m. envoy; congressman; deputy; legate
posępny [po-sanp-ni] adj. m.
gloomy; dismal; dreary; dark
posiadacz [po-śha-dach] m.
bearer; holder; possessor; owner (of properties, etc.)
posiadać [po-śha-dać] v.
hold; own; possess; acquire; dominate; be in possession
posiadłość [po-śhad-wośhćh] f. estate; property; dominion
posiedzenie [po-śhe-dze-ńe] n.
session; conference; meeting
posilać [po-śhee-lać] v.
refresh; nourish; feed
posiłek [po-śhee-wek] m. meal; refreshment; reinforcement
posłać [po-swać] v. send; make a bed; dispatch somewhere; dispatch; forward
posłanie [po-swa-ńe] n. bed; bedding; message; dispatch
posłaniec [po-swa-ńets] m.
messenger; commissioner
posłuchać [po-swoo-khaćh] v.
listen; obey; take advice
posługa [po-swoo-ga] f. service
posługacz [po-swoo-gach] m.
servant; orderly (in a hospital); attendant; commissioner
posłuszny [po-swoosh-ni] adj. m.
obedient; submissive; docile
pospolity [pos-po-lee-ti] adj. m.
vulgar; common; ordinary;

commonplace; everyday
posrebrzać [po-sreb-zhaćh] v.
silver (plate); silver foil
post [post] m. fast; fast day
postać [po-staćh] v. form; human shape; personage
postanowić [po-sta-no-veećh] v. decide; enact; resolve; determine; make up one's mind
postanowienie [po-sta-no-vye-ńe] n. decision; resolve; provision (of the law); resolution
postarać się [po-sta-raćh śhan] v. procure; obtain; get; try (one's best); find; attempt
postawa [po-sta-va] f. attitude; posture; pose; bearing; stature; demeanor; mien; position
postawny [po-stav-ni] adj. m.
portly; handsome; well made
postawić [po-sta-veećh] v. set up; put up; put on; bet; raise; erect; build; stake
postąpić [po-stown-peećh] v.
proceed; act; deal; follow; advance; progress; treat; behave
posterunek [po-ste-roo-nek] m.
outpost; sentry; police station
postęp [po-stanp] m. progress; advance; march; headway
postępowanie [po-stan-po-va-ńe] n. behavior; advance; conduct; (legal) procedure
postojowe [po-sto-yo-ve] n.
demurrage; adj. n. parking
postój [pos-tooy] m. halt; stop; stand; parking; stopping place
postrach [po-strakh] m. terror; dread; scare; fright; bugaboo
postrzał [po-stshaw] m. gunshot; wound; (gun) shot; rifle shot; rifle shot wound; lumbago
postrzelony [po-stshe-lo-ni] adj. m. wounded; crazy; cracked
postulat [po-stoo-lat] m.
demand; claim; requirement
postument [po-stoo-ment] m.
pedestal (of a statue); socle
posucha [po-soo-kha] f. drought
posuw [po-soov] m. feed (of a drill); feed of a lathe
posuwać [po-soo-vaćh] v.
move; shove; push on; carry;

dash; speed; shift; advance
posyłać [po-**si**-waćh] v. send
over; send to; dispatch
posyłka [po-**siw**-ka] f. errand
posypywać [po-si-pi-vaćh] v.
dust; pour; sprinkle (dry)
poszanowanie [po-sha-no-**va**-ńe]
n. respect; observance (of a
law); esteem; good opinion
poszarpać [po-**shar**-paćh] v.
maul; tear up; jag up; mangle;
rend; rough up; pull about
poszczególny [po-shche-**gool**-ni]
adj. m. individual
poszerzać [po-**she**-zhaćh] v.
widen; broaden; extend; ream;
spread; open out; let out
poszewka [po-**shev**-ka] f. pillow
case; pillow slip
poszkodowany [po-shko-do-**va**-ni]
adj. m. victim; sufferer
poszlaka [po-**shla**-ka] f. trace;
circumstantial evidence; sign
poszukiwać [po-shoo-kee-vaćh]
v. search; look for; inquire;
seek; claim; be in want of
poszukiwanie [po-shoo-kee-**va**-
-ńe] n. search; quest; research; investigation; inquiry
pościć [pośh-ćheećh] v. fast
pościel [pośh-ćhel] f. bedclothes sheets and blankets
pościg [pośh-ćheeg] m. chase;
pursuit (of a criminal, etc.)
pośladek [po-śhla-dek] m.
buttock; rump; bum
poślizgnąć się [po-śhleez-
-**nown**ćh **śhan**] v. slip; make
a slip; lose footing, etc.
poślubić [po-śhloo-beećh] v.
marry; take in marriage
pośmiertny [po-śhmyert-ni] adj.
m. posthumous (child; works,
obituary notice, etc.)
pośmiewisko [pośh-mye-**vees**-
-ko] n. laughingstock; butt of
ridicule; object of ridicule
pośpiech [pośh-pyekh] m.
haste; hurry; dispatch
pośredni [po-śhred-ńee]
adj. m. intermediate; indirect
pośrednik [po-śhred-ńeek] m.
go-between; intermediary

pośredniczyć [po-śhred-**ńee**-
-ćhićh] v. mediate; be a go-
between; run a sales' agency
pośród [po-śhroot] prep. in
the midst of; among; amid(st)
poświadczać [po-**śhvyad**-
-chaćh] v. attest; certify; au-
thenticate; testify; witness
poświadczenie [po-śhvyad-
-**che**-ńe] n. certificate; attestation; certification of
poświęcać [po-śhvyan-tsaćh]
v. sacrifice; sanctify
poświęcenie [po-śhvyan-**tse**-
-ńe] n. devotion; sacrifice
pot [pot] m. sweat; perspiration
potajemny [po-ta-yem-ni] adj. m.
secret; clandestine; underhand
potakiwać [po-ta-kee-vaćh] v.
assent; agree; acquiesce
potas [po-tas] m. potassium
potaż [po-tash] m. potash
potąd [po-townt] adv. up to
here; up to this place
potem [po-tem] adv. after;
afterwards; then; later on
potencjalny [po-ten-tsyal-ni] adj.
m. potential; virtual
potęga [po-tan-ga] f. power;
might; force; impressiveness
potęgować [po-tan-go-vaćh] v.
intensify; raise to a power
potępiać [po-tan-pyaćh] v.
damn; run down; condemn
potępienie [po-tan-pye-ńe] n.
damnation; disapproval; blame
potężny [po-tanzh-ni] adj. m.
mighty; tremendous; powerful
potknąć się [pot-knownćh
śhan] v. slip on; trip over;
stumble against; make a slip
potknięcie [pot-kńan-ćhe] v.
slip; stumble; trip; a lapse
potoczny [po-toch-ni] adj. m.
current; common; everyday;
daily; of frequent occurrence
potok [po-tok] m. stream; brook
potomek [po-to-mek] m.
descendant; offspring; scion
potomność [po-tom-nośhćh]
f. posterity; future generations
potomstwo [po-tom-stvo] pl.
issue; progeny; offspring;

breed of animals; young
potop [po-top] m. deluge; flood
potrafić [po-tra-feećh] v. know
how to do; manage to do; be
able to do; be capable to do
potrawa [po-tra-va] f. dish
potrawka [po-traf-ka] f.
fricassee; ragout
potrącić [po-trown-ćheećh] v.
knock; deduct; poke; push;
jostle; nudge; touch upon
po trochu [po tro-khoo] little by
little; gradually; by driblets
potrójny [po-trooy-ni] adj. m.
triple; triplicate; treble
potrask [po-tshask] m. trap
potrząsać [po-tshown-saćh] v.
shake; brandish; agitate; strew
potrzeba [po-tzhe-ba] f. need;
want; call for; emergency; extremity; necessity; evacuation
potrzebny [po-tsheb-ni] adj. m.
necessary; needed; wanted
potulny [po-tool-ni] adj. m.
docile; submissive; humble;
meek; easy to discipline
poturbować [po-toor-bo-vaćh]
v. manhandle; rough up; beat;
maul; batter; knock about; ill-
treat; give a rough handling
potwarz [po-tvash] f. slander;
calumny; libel (against)
potwierdzać [po-tvyer-dzaćh] v.
confirm; attest; corroborate
potwór [po-tvoor] m. monster
potykać się [po-ti-kaćh śhan]
v. stumble; skirmish; joust
potylica [po-ti-lee-tsa] f. occiput;
back part of the skull
pouczać [po-oo-chaćh] v.
instruct; teach; give instructions; tutor; brief; admonish
pouczenie [po-oo-che-ńe] n.
instruction; giving instructions
poufalić się [po-oo-fa-leećh
śhan] v. take liberties; hob-
nob (with); be familiar (with)
poufały [po-oo-fa-wi] adj. m.
intimate; unceremonious; free
with; too familiar; mately;
hobnobbing with (somebody)
poufny [po-oof-ni] adj. m.
confidential; private; secret

powab [po-vap] m. charm; attraction; lure; seduction; loveliness; grace; attractiveness
powabny [po-vab-ni] adj. m.
attractive; charming; alluring
powaga [po-va-ga] f. gravity;
seriousness; dignity; prestige
powalać [po-va-laćh] v. soil;
dirty; overthrow; kill; slay
powalić [po-va-leećh] v. knock
down; floor (an adversary);
overthrow; kill; slay; fell
powała [po-va-wa] f. ceiling
poważać [po-va-zhaćh] v.
respect; esteem; have regard
poważny [po-vazh-ni] adj. m.
earnest; grave; dignified; serious; solemn; business-like
powątpiewać [po-vownt-pye-
-vaćh] v. doubt; have doubts
about; be dubious about
powetować [po-ve-to-vaćh] v.
make up for a loss; indemnify
oneself for; retrieve; repair
powiadać [po-vya-daćh] v. say;
tell; speak; (a legend, a rumor, etc.) has it that...
powiadomić [po-vya-do-meećh]
v. inform; notify; let know
powiastka [po-vyast-ka] f. tale
powiat [po-vyat] m. county;
district; district authorities
powicie [po-vee-ćhe] n.
swaddling (child) clothes
powidła [po-veed-wa] pl. jam;
marmalade; (plum) jam
powiedzieć [po-vye-dźhećh] v.
say to; tell; intend to say;
express; declare; make known
powieka [po-vye-ka] f. eyelid
powielacz [po-vye-lach] m.
mimeograph for making copies
powiernica [po-vyer-ńee-tsa] f.
confidante; trusted friend
powierzać [po-vye-zhaćh] v.
confide; charge with a task
powierzchnia [po-vyezh-khńa] f.
surface; plane; area; acreage
powiesić [po-vye-śheećh] v.
hang (a person, picture, etc.);
suspend; hung up; ring off
powieść [po-vyeśhćh] f.
novel; v. lead somebody

powieść się [po-vyeśhćh śhan] v. succeed; be successful; come off

powietrze [po-vyet-zhe] n. air

powiew [po-vyef] m. breeze

powiększać [po-vyank-shaćh] v. enlarge; augment; extend; add; magnify; aggrandize

powiększenie [po-vyank-she-ńe] n. enlargement; magnification

powijaki [po-vee-ya-kee] pl. swathing; initial stage

powikłać [po-vee-kwaćh] v. complicate; embroil; confuse

powinność [po-veen-nośhćh] f. duty; obligation

powinowaty [po-vee-no-va-ti] adj. m. related; akin

powitać [po-vee-taćh] v. welcome; salute; bid welcome

powlekać [po-vle-kaćh] v. cover; drag; coat; smear; spread; put on bed-linen

powłoczka [po-vwoch-ka] f. pillowcase; envelope; covering

powłoka [po-vwo-ka] f. (paint) coat; covering; envelope; shell

powłóczysty [po-vwoo-chis-ti] adj. m. trailing; enticing

powodować [po-vo-do-vaćh] v. cause; bring about; touch off; effect; induce; give occasion

powodzenie [po-vo-dze-ńe] n. success; well-being; prosperity

powodzić się [po-vo-dźheećh śhan] v. fare (well, ill); be well off; be prospering

powojenny [po-vo-yen-ni] adj. m. post-war; after-war

powoli [po-vo-lee] adv. slow

powolny [po-vol-ni] adj. m. slow; tardy; leisurely; gradual

powołanie [po-vo-wa-ńe] n. vocation; call; appointment; quotation; reference; plea of

powonienie [po-vo-ńe-ńe] n. sense of smell; smell

powód [po-voot] m. cause; reason; ground; motive; rise; provocation; the plaintiff

powódź [po-voodźh] f. flood

powój [po-vooy] m. bindweed

powóz [po-voos] m. carriage

powracać [po-vra-tsaćh] v. return; come back; resume; recover; ride back; drive back

powrotny [po-vrot-ni] adj. m. return; return (ticket)

powrót [po-vroot] m. return

powróz [po-vroos] m. rope

powstanie [po-vsta-ńe] n. rising (to honor); uprising; revolt; rebellion origin; rise; birth

powstaniec [po-vsta-ńets] m. insurgent; rebel (soldier)

powstawać [po-vsta-vaćh] v. rise up; stan up; revolt

powstrzymać [po-vstzhi-maćh] v. restrain; refrain; hold back

powszechny [po-vshekh-ni] adj. m. universal; general; public

powszedni [po-vshed-ńee] adj. m. everyday; commonplace; daily; ordinary; common

powściągliwość [pov-śhćhowng-lee-vośhćh] f. abstinence; temperance; moderation; restraint; reserve

powściągliwy [po-vśhćhown-glee-vi] adj. m. reserved; abstinent; moderate; reticent; temperate; self-restrained

powtarzać [po-vta-zhaćh] v. say again; go over; repeat; reproduce; reiterate; retell

po wtóre [po vtoo-re] adv. secondly; in the second place; in the second group; then

powtórnie [po-vtoor-ńe] adv. anew; again; a second time

powtórny [po-vtoor-ni] adj. m. repeated; renewed; second-

powyżej [po-vi-zhey] adv. above; here in before; higher up; over

powziąć [po-vźhownćh] v. take up; form; decide; conceive (a plan, suspicion, etc.)

poza [po-za] f. pose; attitude; posture; affection; sham

poza [po-za] prep. beyond; besides; except; apart; outside; apart from; past; extra-

pozagrobowy [po-za-gro-bo-vi] adj. m. of beyond the grave; from the hereafter; from beyond the grave; of the beyond

pozbawiać [po-zba-vyaćh] v.
deprive; dispossess of; take
away; divest; strip; remove
pozbyć się [poz-bićh śh<u>an</u>] v.
rid oneself; get rid; shake off
pozdrawiać [po-zdra-vyaćh] v.
greet; send one's greetings
pozew [po-zef] m. summons; order to came; writ; citation
poziom [po-źhom] m. level
poziomka [po-źhom-ka] f. wild
strawberry (fruit or plant)
poziomy [po-źho-mi] adj. m.
horizontal; level; uninspired
pozłota [po-zwo-ta] gilding
poznać [po-znaćh] v. get to
know; come to know; recognize; taste; acquaint; see
poznajomić [po-zna-yo-meećh]
v. acquaint; introduce
poznanie [po-zna-ńe] n.
cognition; acquaintance;
learning; study; knowledge
pozornie [po-zor-ńe] adv.
apparently; on the surface
pozostać [po-zos-taćh] v.
remain; stay behind; continue
pozostały [po-zo-sta-wi] adj. m.
remaining; residual; left
pozostawiać [po-zo-sta-vyaćh]
v. leave (behind); bequeath
pozór [po-zoor] m. appearance;
pretext; sham; look; mask;
cloak; face; show; semblance
pozwać [po-zvaćh] v. summon
pozwalać [po-zva-laćh] v. let;
allow; permit; tolerate; suffer
pozwany [po-zva-ni] m.
defendant; person sued or accused in a court of law, etc.
pozwolenie [po-zvo-le-ńe] n.
permission; consent; permit
pozycja [po-zits-ya] f. position;
item; status; posture; place
pozyskać [po-zis-kaćh] v. gain;
win over (to); gain good will
pozytywny [po-zi-tiv-ni] adj. m.
positive; affirmative; favorable
pozywać [po-zi-vaćh] v. sue;
cite; summon; cite (to court)
pożałować [po-zha-**wo**-vaćh] v.
repent; regret; take pity
pożar [po-zhar] m. fire (woods,

buildings); conflagration
pożądać [po-zh<u>own</u>-daćh] v.
desire; covet; lust after
pożądany [po-zh<u>own</u>-da-ni] adj.
m. desirable; welcome; desired
pożądliwy [po-zh<u>own</u>-dlee-vi]
adj. m. greedy; covetous; lascivious; lewd; lustful; leer
pożegnać [po-zheg-naćh] v. bid
goodbye; see off; dismiss
pożerać [po-zhe-raćh] v. devour; glut; gorge (one's food)
pożoga [po-zho-ga] f. fire;
conflagration; ravages (of war)
pożółknąć [po-zhoow-
-kn<u>own</u>ćh] v. grow yellow;
turn yellow; become yellow
pożycie [po-zhi-ćhe] n.
intercourse; conjugal life
pożyczka [po-zhich-ka] f. loan
pożyteczny [po-zhi-tech-ni] adj.
m. useful; profitable
pożytek [po-zhi-tek] m. use;
advantage; usefulness; benefit
pożywić [po-zhi-veećh] v. feed;
nourish; refresh; give food
pożywny [po-zhiv-ni] adj. m.
nutritious; nourishing
pójść [pooyśhćh] v. go; go
(home, school) away; go up...;
leave; fly; drift; pan out
póki [poo-kee] conj. till; until; as
long as; while; when; before
pół [poow] num. half; semi-;
demi; a one half; mid (way); in
mid course; half-way; hemi-
półbucik [poow-boo-ćheek] m.
half boot; low shoe
półgłosem [poow-gwo-sem] adv.
in a low voice; in an undertone; under one's breath
półgłówek [poow-gwoo-vek] m.
half-wit; fool; simpleton; dolt
półka [poow-ka] f. shelf; ledge
półkole [poow-ko-le] n. semi
-circle; half-circle; hemicycle
półksiężyc [poow-kśh<u>an</u>-zhits]
m. half-moon; crescent; the
Crescent of Islam; Islam
półkula [poow-koo-la] f. hemi-
-sphere; half of a sphere
półmisek [poow-**mee**-sek] m.
charger dish; (serving) dish

półnagi [poow-na-gee] adj. m.
    half naked; half dressed
północ [poow-nots] f. midnight;
    north; North; the North
północno-wschodni [poow-nots-
    -no vskhod-ńee] northeast
północno-zachodni [poow-nots-
    -no za-khod-ńee] northwest
północny [poow-nots-ni] adj. m.
    north; Northern; Northerly
półroczny [poow-roch-ni] adj. m.
    half-yearly; semi-annual
półświatek [poow-shvya-tek]
    m. love industry; demimonde
półtora [poow-to-ra] num. one
    and half; a (day etc.) and half
półurzędowy [poow-oo-zhan-do-
    -vi] adj. m. semi-official
półwysep [poow-vi-sep] m.
    peninsula; almost an island
póty [poo-ti] conj. as long
później [poozh-ńey] adv. later
    on; afterwards; at a later date
późno [poozh-no] adv. late;
    well on; tardily; late-
późny [poozh-ni] adj. m. late
prababka [pra-bab-ka] great
    grandmother; ancestor
praca [pra-tsa] f. work; job
pracodawca [pra-tso-dav-tsa] m.
    employer; adj. m. (man) em-
    ploying people for wages
pracowity [pra-tso-vee-ti] adj. m.
    industrious; hard-working
pracownik [pra-tsov-ńeek] m.
    worker;employee;clerk;official
praczka [prach-ka] f. wash-
    (washer)woman; laundress
prać [praćh] v. wash clothes;
    launder; thrash; strike; beat up
pradziad [pra-dźhat] m. great
    grandfather; ancestor
pragnąć [prag-nownćh] v. be
    thirsty; desire; wish; long for
pragnienie [prag-ńe-ńe] n. wish;
    thirst; desire; lust for
praktyczny [prak-tich-ni] adj. m.
    practical; sensible; expedient
praktyka [prak-ti-ka] f. practice;
    usage; apprenticeship
praktykować [prak-ti-ko-vaćh]
    v. practice; be in training
pralka [pral-ka] f. washing

machine; washer; wash board
pralnia [pral-ńa] f. laundry
pranie [pra-ńe] n. washing
praojciec [pra-oy-ćhets] m.
    forefather; ancestor
prasa [pra-sa] f. press; print
prasować [pra-so-vaćh] v. iron
    (linen etc.); press; print
prawda [prav-da] f. truth
prawdomówność [prav-do-
    -moov-noshćh] f. veracity;
    truthfulness; truth of words
prawdopodobny [prav-do-po-dob-
    -ni] adj. m. probable; likely
prawdziwie [prav-dźhee-vye]
    adv. truly; genuinely; indeed
prawdziwy [prav-dźhee-vi] adj.
    m. true; real; authentic
prawica [pra-vee-tsa] f. the
    Right; right hand; right wing
prawić [pra-veećh] v. talk; say
prawidło [pra-veed-wo] n. rule;
    boot tree; law; centering
prawidłowy [pra-vee-dwo-vi] adj.
    m. regular; correct; proper
prawie [pra-vye] adv. almost;
    nearly; practically; all but
prawnik [prav-ńeek] m. lawyer
prawnuczka [prav-nooch-ka] f.
    great granddaughter
prawnuk [prav-nook] m. great
    grandson (grandson's son)
prawny [prav-ni] adj. m. legal;
    lawful; legitimate; rightful
prawo [pra-vo] adv. right; law
prawo [pra-vo] n. law; (driving)
    license; statute; claim
prawodawca [pra-vo-dav-tsa] m.
    legislator; lawmaker; lawgiver
prawodawstwo [pra-vo-dav-stvo]
    n. legislation; legislature
prawomocny [pra-vo-mots-ni]
    adj. m. legal; valid
prawosławny [pra-vo-swav-ni]
    adj. m. (also m.) Orthodox
prawość [pra-voshćh] f.
    honesty; integrity; rectitude;
    righteousness; uprightness
prawować się [pra-vo-vaćh
    shan] v. litigate a cause; sue
    for; be engaged in a lawsuit;
    be at law with somebody
prawowity [pra-vo-vee-ti] adj. m.

legal (heir apparent, heir, etc.)
prawy [pra-vi] adj. m. honest;
right; right hand-; upright; lawful; right (wheel, hand, side)
prażyć [pra-zhićh] v. grill; roast
burn; keep heavy gunfire on
prąd [prownd] m. current; flow
stream; air flow; tendency;
trend; movement (air, water)
prądnica [prownd-ńee-tsa] f.
electric generator; dynamo
prąd stały [prownd sta-wi] m.
direct (electric) current
prąd zmienny [prownd zmyen-ni]
m. alternating (electric) current
prążek [prown-zhek] m. stripe
precyzja [pre-tsi-zya] f. precision;
accuracy; definiteness
precyzować [pre-tsi-zo-vaćh] v.
define; state precisely; define
precz! [prech] adv. go away; do
away with; down (off) with
prefabrykować [pre-fa-bri-ko-;
-vaćh] v. prefabricate
prefiks [pre-feeks] m. prefix
prelegent [pre-le-gent] m.
lecturer (presenting a lecture)
prelekcja [pre-lek-tsya] f. lecture
(informative talk); talk
preliminarz [pre-lee-mee-nash] m.
estimate of a budget, etc.
premedytacja [pre-me-di-tats-ya]
f. premeditation
premia [pre-mya] f. premium;
bonus; bounty; prize; gift
premier [pre-myer] m. prime
minister of a country; premier
premiera [pre-mye-ra] f. first
night show; first night
prenumerata [pre-noo-me-ra-ta] f.
subscription (to a paper etc.)
preparat [pre-pa-rat] m.
preparation; concoction; specimen (also for scientific use)
prerogatywa [pre-ro-ga-ti-va] f.
privilege; prerogative (power)
presja [pres-ya] f. pressure
prestiż [pres-teesh] m. prestige;
high esteem (influence power)
pretekst [pre-tekst] m. pretext;
excuse; false reason or motive
pretensja [pre-ten-sya] f. claim;
grudge; debt; pretentiousness

prezerwatywa [pre-zer-va-ti-va] f.
contraceptive sheath; condom
prezent [pre-zent] m. gift
prezes [pre-zes] m. chairman
prezydent [pre-zi-dent] m.
president; mayor; Lord Mayor
prącik [pran-ćheek] m. (small)
stick; stamen; rod; graphite
prądki [prand-kee] adj. m. swift;
quick; rapid; fast; prompt; immediate; hasty; instant; nimble
prędko [prand-ko] adv. quickly;
fast; soon; at once; rapidly
prędkość [prand-kośhćh] f.
speed; swiftness; velocity; impetuosity; impulsiveness
prędzej [pran-dzey] adv. quicker;
sooner; rather; with all haste
pręga [pran-ga] f. stripe; wale
pręgierz [pran-gesh] m. pillory
pręgowaty [pran-go-va-ti] adj. m.
striped; with stripes (wales)
pręt [prant] m. rod; bar; pole;
switch; stick; wand; twig;
perch; (gauging-) rod; stave
prężność [pranzh-nośhćh] f.
resilience; elasticity; energy
prężny [pranzh-ni] adj. m.
elastic; resilient; supple
prężyć [pran-zhićh] v. strain
probierczy kamień [pro-byer-chi
ka-myeń] m. touchstone
problem [pro-blem] m. problem
probostwo [pro-bos-tvo] n.
parsonage; parish; rectory
proboszcz [pro-boshch] m.
pastor; parish priest; parson
probówka [pro-boof-ka] f. test
-tube; (laboratory) test glass
proca [pro-tsa] f. sling; catapult
proceder [pro-tse-der] m. trade;
(shady) dealings; a plot
procedura [pro-tse-doo-ra] f.
procedure; legal practice
procent [pro-tsent] m.
percentage; interest on money
procentować się [pro-tsen-to-
-vaćh śhan] v. bring interest
proces [pro-tses] m. lawsuit
procesja [pro-tses-ya] f.
procession; (marching, proceeding) moving as in parade
procesować [pro-tse-so-vaćh]

proch [prokh] m. powder; dust

proch strzelniczy [prokh stzhel-
-ńee-chi] m. gunpowder

producent [pro-doo-tsent] m.
producer; manufacturer; maker

produkcja [pro-dook-tsya] f.
production; (factory, literary)
output; produce; performance

produkować [pro-doo-ko-vaćh]
v. produce; grow; generate;
manufacture; turn out; stage

produkt [pro-dookt] m. product

profanować [pro-fa-no-vaćh] v.
profane; desecrate; despoil

profesor [pro-fe-sor] m.
(university) professor; teacher

profil [pro-feel] m. profile

profilaktyczny [pro-fee-lak-tich-ni]
adj. m. prophylactic

prognoza [prog-no-za] f.
prognosis; forcast (of weather)

program [pro-gram] m. program;
plan; agenda (of a meeting)

progresja [pro-gres-ya] f.
progression; sequence

prohibicja [pro-khee-beets-ya] f.
prohibition; forbidden

projekcja [pro-yek-tsya] f.
projection (on a screen etc.)

projekt [pro-yekt] m. project

projektować [pro-yek-to-vaćh]
v. design; plan; lay out; draft

proklamować [pro-kla-mo-vaćh]
v. proclaim; announce official-
ly; announce to be

prokurator [pro-koo-ra-tor] m.
public prosecutor

proletariat [pro-le-ta-ryat]
proletariat; working class

prolog [pro-log] m. prologue

prolongować [pro-lon-go-vaćh]
v. prolong; extend; renew

prom [prom] m. ferry (boat)

promienieć [pro-mye-ńećh] v.
radiate; beam (with joy etc.)

promieniotwórczy [pro-mye-ńo-
-tvoor-chi] adj. m. radioactive
(matter; isotopes etc.)

promieniować [pro-mye-ńo-
-vaćh] v. radiate (heat, light);
beam; glow; brim over (with)

promienisty [pro-mye-ńees-ti]
adj. m. radial; radiant; radiate

promienny [pro-myen-ni] adj. m.
radiant; beaming; bright

promień [pro-myeń] adj. m. ray
beam; gleam; radius; fin ray

promocja [pro-mots-ya] f.
promotion; conferment of a
university (doctoral) degree

propaganda [pro-pa-gan-da] f.
propaganda; publicity; popula-
rization; information; boosting

propagować [pro-pa-go-vaćh]
v. propagate; publicize; boost

proponować [pro-po-no-vaćh]
v. propose; put forwards; suggest; submit (a plan); offer

proporcja [pro-por-tsya] f.
proportion; ratio; relation

proporcjonalny [pro-por-tsyo-nal-
-ni] adj. m. proportional

proporzec [pro-po-zhets] m.
pennon; banner; streamer;
pennant; (stem) jack

propozycja [pro-po-zits-ya] f.
proposal; offer; suggestion

proroctwo [pro-rots-tvo] n.
prophecy; prediction (future)

prorok [pro-rok] m. prophet

prosić [pro-śheećh] v. beg;
pray; ask; invite; request

prosię [pro-śhan] n. young pig

proso [pro-so] n. millet

prospekt [pro-spekt] m.
prospect; folder; view; pano-
rama; outlook; anticipation

prosperować [pro-spe-ro-vaćh]
v. prosper; be prosperous; be
doing well; thrive; succeed

prostacki [pro-stats-kee] adj. m.
boorish; rude; vulgar; coarse

prostak [pros-tak] m. boor; gull

prostata [pro-sta-ta] f. prostate
(gland at the male bladder)

prosto [pros-to] adv. straight;
right; upright; simply; candidly

prostoduszny [pro-sto-doosh-ni]
adj. m. simple-hearted; naive

prostokąt [pro-sto-kownt] m.
rectangle (four-sided plane
figure with four right angles)

prostolinijny [pro-sto-lee-ńeey-ni]
adj. m. straightforward

prostopadła [pro-sto-pad-wa] f.
perpendicular; normal; sheer
prostota [pro-sto-ta] f. simplicity;
neatness; boorishness
prostować [pro-sto-vaćh] v.
straighten; correct; revise
prosty [pros-ti] adj. m. straight;
direct simple; vulgar; plain
prostytucja [pro-sti-too-tsya] f.
prostitution; streetwalking
prostytutka [pro-sti-toot-ka] f.
prostitute; streetwalker
proszek [pro-shek] m. powder
(for baking etc.); wafer
proszę [pro-shan] please
prośba [prośh-ba] f. request;
demand; petition; application
proszkować [prosh-ko-vaćh] v.
pulverize; grind to powder
protegowany [pro-te-go-va-ni]
adj. m. protege (helped, etc.)
protekcja [pro-tek-tsya] f. pull;
patronage; backing; influence;
push; a person that protects
protest [pro-test] m. protest
protestant [pro-te-stant] m.
Protestant; evangelical
protestantyzm [pro-te-stan-tizm]
m. Protestantism
proteza [pro-te-za] f. artificial
limb, tooth, or denture, etc.
protokół [pro-to-koow] m.
record; protocol; minutes; official record; formal record
prototyp [pro-to-tip] m.
prototype; archetype; proto-
plast; proterotype; model
prowadzenie [pro-va-dze-ńe] n.
management; conduct; leadership; directing; prosecution
prowadzić [pro-va-dźheećh] v.
steer; lead; conduct; guide;
keep; live; carry on (a conversation); show the way; escort;
run; manage (an institution)
prowadzić auto [pro-va-
-dźheećh aw-to] **drive a car**
prowiant [pro-vyant] m.
provisions; eatables; rations
prowincjonalny [pro-veen-tsyo-
-nal-ni] adj. m. provincial
prowizja [pro-veez-ya] f.
commission; percentage; pro-

vision; brokerage
prowizoryczny [pro-vee-zo-rich-
-ni] adj. m. provisional
prowodyr [pro-vo-dir] m.
ringleader; gang leader
prowokacja [pro-vo-kats-ya] f.
provocation; stirring trouble
proza [pro-za] f. prose; dullness
próba [proo-ba] f. trial; test;
proof; ordeal; acid test; try; go
próbka [proob-ka] f. sample
próbny [proob-ni] adj. m. ex-
perimental; tentative; test-
próbować [proo-bo-vaćh] v.
try; test; taste; put to the
test; make an attempt; offer
próchnica [prookh-ńee-tsa] f.
molder; (tooth) decay; humus
próchno [prookh-no] n. rotten
wood; mould; rot; wood dust
prócz [prooch]prep.save; except;
besides; apart from; moreover
próg [proog] m. threshold
prószyć [proo-shićh] v. sift;
flake; make dust; sprinkle
(dust, snow); spray (powder)
próżnia [proozh-ńa] f. vacuum
próżniaczy [proozh-ńa-chi]
adj. m. lazy; idle; inactive;
leisure; work-shy; sluggish
próżniak [proozh-ńak] m. idler
próżno [proozh-no] adv. vainly;
empty-; in vain; to no avail
próżność [proozh-nośhćh] f.
vanity; false pride; futility
próżny [proozh-ni] adj. m. 1.
empty; void; 2. vain; futile
pruć [prooćh] v. rip; unsew
pruski [proos-kee] adj. m.
Prussian; of Prussia
prychać [pri-khaćh] v. snort
prycza [pri-cha] f. plank-bed
pryk stary [prik sta-ri] m. old
goat; old duffer; old codger
prym [prim] m. lead; first place;
superiority; the lead
prymas [pri-mas] m. primate
prymka [prim-ka] f. chewing
tobacco (a plug of)
pryskać [pris-kaćh] v. splash;
spray; splatter; sputter; fly;
clear out; bolt; scamper away;
burst; hop it; dissolve; vanish

pryszcz [prishch] m. pimple
prysznic [prish-ńeets] m. shower bath; shower (fixture)
prywatny [pri-vat-ni] adj. m. private; personal; confidential
pryzmat [priz-mat] m. prism
prządka [pshownd-ka] f. spinner
prząść [pshownśhćh] v. spin
przebaczać [pshe-ba-chaćh] v. forgive; pardon; condone
przebaczenie [pshe-ba-che-ńe] n. pardon; forgiveness; remittal (of sins); absolution
przebąkiwać [pshe-bown-kee-vaćh] v. mutter; hint (that); allude to something; mention
przebić [pshe-beećh] v. pierce; perforate; puncture; stab; dig; recoin; transfix; bore; punch
przebieg [pshe-byek] m. course; run; progress; process; milage
przebiegać [pshe-bye-gaćh] v. run cross; take place; proceed
przebiegły [pshe-byeg-wi] adj. m. cunning; sly; wily; crafty
przebierać [pshe-bye-raćh] v. choose; sort; change clothes; sift; disguise; manipulate
przebijać [pshe-bee-yaćh] v. pierce; puncture; stab; reveal; show through; make visible
przebłysk [pshe-bwisk] m. glimpse; ray; flash; sparkle; glimmer; stroke of (genius)
przebłyskiwać [pshe-bwi-skee-vaćh] v. gleam; shine; flash
przeboleć [pshe-bo-lećh] get over; put up with; get over it
przebój [pshe-booy] m. hit; success; breakthrough; clou
przebranie [pshe-bra-ńe] n. disguise; being disguised
przebrnąć [psheb-rnownćh] v. muddle through; wade through
przebrzmiały [psheb-zhmya-wi] adj. m. overblown; has-been
przebudowa [pshe-boo-do-va] f. remodeling; rebuilding
przebudzić [pshe-boo-dźheećh] v. wake up; awake; rouse; revive; awaken; make active
przebyć [pshe-bićh] v. be over through; surmount; ride out

storm; travel; cross; pass; dwell; cover distance (space)
przebywać [pshe-bi-vaćh] v. stay; reside; dwell; inhabit
przecedzać [pshe-tse-dzaćh] v. filter; strain through a sieve
przeceniać [pshe-tse-ńaćh] v. overrate; lower the price
przechadzka [pshe-khadz-ka] f. walk; stroll; tour; airing
przechadzać się [pshe-kha-dzaćh śhan] v. take a walk; stroll; go for a walk; saunter
przechodzić [pshe-kho-dźheećh] v. pass (through)
przechodzień [pshe-kho-dźheń] m. passerby; pedestrian
przechowanie [pshe-kho-va-ńe] n. safekeeping; storage
przechowywać [pshe-kho-vi-vaćh] v. store; preserve; harbore; keep; retain; shelter
przechrzcić [pshekh-shćheećh] v. convert; change name
przechwalać [pshe-khva-laćh] v. talk big; overpraise; extol; puff; give exaggerated praise
przechwycić [pshe-khvi-ćheećh] v. intercept; seize
przechylić [pshe-khi-leećh] v. tilt; lean; tip; incline
przechytrzyć [pshe-khit-zhićh] v. outwit; overreach; outsmart
przeciąć [pshe-ćhownćh] v. cut; cross; intersect; slice; cleave; cut across; bisect
przeciąg [pshe-ćhowng] m. draught; span; spell; time lapse; space (stretch) of time
przeciągać [pshe-ćhown-gaćh] v. draw; drag; delay; stretch
przeciążać [pshe-ćhown-zhaćh] v. overload; overburden; overwork; congest
przecie [pshe-ćhe] conj. yet; of course but; after all; still
przeciekać [pshe-ćhe-kaćh] v. leak; ooze; drain; percolate
przecierać [pshe-ćhe-raćh] v. rub; wipe clear; threadbare; fret; polish (shoes); clear up
przecierpieć [pshe-ćher-pyećh] v. endure; bear; suffer

przecież [pshe-ćhesh] conj. yet;
still; after all; now; though
przeciątny [pshe-ćhant-ni]
adj. m. average; ordinary; indifferent; mediocre; common
przecinać [pshe-ćhee-naćh] v.
cut; intersect; slice; cleave
przecinek [pshe-ćhee-nek] m.
comma (mark of punctuation)
przeciskać się [pshe-ćhees-
-kaćh śhan] v. squeeze
(press) through; push through;
elbow one's way through
przeciw [pshe-ćheev] prep.
against; versus; contrary to
przeciwko [pshe-ćheev-ko] prep.
against; contrary; versus
przeciwdziałać [pshe-ćheev-
-dźha-waćh] v. counteract
przeciwległy [pshe-ćheev-leg-wi]
adj. m. opposite; contrary
przciwlotniczy [pshe-ćheev-lot-
-ńee-chi] adj. m. antiaircraft
(artillery, defence etc.)
przeciwnie [pshe-ćheev-ńe]
adv. on the contrary; reverse
przeciwnik [pshe-ćheev-ńeek]
m. opponent; adversary; enemy; foe; antagonist
przeciwność [pshe-ćheev-
-nośhćh] f. adversity; set-
back; reverse (of fortune)
przeciwstawiać [pshe-ćheev-sta
-vyaćh] v. oppose; set a-
gainst; contrast; resist; defy
przeciwwaga [pshe-ćheev-va-ga]
f. counterweight; balance
weight; counterbalance
przecudny [pshe-tsood-ni] adj. m.
most wonderful; just simply
marvelous; most admirable
przeczący [pshe-chown-tsi] adj.
m. negative; contradictory
przeczenie [pshe-che-ńe] n.
negation; negative (answer);
denial; answer in the negative
przecznica [pshech-ńee-tsa] f.
side-street; cross street
przeczucie [pshe-choo-ćhe] n.
foreboding; presentiment
przeczulony [pshe-choo-lo-ni] adj.
m. high-strung; oversensitive;
touchy; easily irritated

przeczyć [pshe-chićh] v. deny;
belie; negate; contradict
przeczyszczać [pshe-chish-
-chaćh] v. purge; cleanse;
scour; wipe; purge; clean out
przeczytać [pshe-chi-taćh] v.
read through; peruse; read
over again; re-read
przeć [pshećh] v. insist on;
urge; press on; push; exert
pressure; impel; drive; insist;
bear down; urge; impel; strive
przed [pshet] prep. before; in
front of; ahead of; previous
to; from; since; ago; against
przedajny [pshe-day-ni] adj. m.
venal; open to bribery
przedawnienie [pshe-dav-ńe-ńe]
n. expiration of validity
przedawniony [pshe-dav-ńo-ni]
adj. m. of expired validity
przeddzień [pshed-dźheń] m.
on the eve; the day before
przede wszystkim [pshe-de
vshist-keem] adv. above all;
first and foremost; first of all;
in the first place; to start with
przedhistoryczny [pshed-khee-
-sto-rich-ni] adj. m. prehistoric;
before the recorded history
przedimek [pshed-ee-mek] m.
article (in grammar)
przedkładać [pshed-kwa-daćh]
v. submit; refer; propose;
present; give priority
przedłużać [pshe-dwoo-zhaćh]
v. lengthen; prolong; extend
przedmieście [pshed-myeśh-
-ćhe] n. suburb; a district on
the outskirts of a city
przedmiot [pshed-myot] m.
object; subject; subject matter
przedmiotowy [pshed-myo-to-vi]
adj. m. objective; at issue
przedmowa [pshed-mo-va] f.
preface; foreword; introduction (a preliminary section)
przedmówca [pshed-moov-tsa]
m. previous speaker
przedni [pshed-ńee] adj. m.
leading; front (seat, tooth);
forward; choice; fine; foremost; superior; high-quality

przedostać się [pshe-do-staćh
śhan] v. penetrate; get in;
(pass, work, force) through
przedostatni [pshe-do-**stat**-ńee]
adj. m. last but one
przedpłata [pshed-**pwa**-ta] f.
advance payment; subscription
przedpokój [pshed-**po**-kooy] m.
(waiting-room) lobby; ante-
chamber; anteroom; entry hall
przedpole [pshed-**po**-le] n.
foreground; foreland
przedpołudnie [pshed-po-**wood**-
-ńe] n. morning; forenoon
przdpotopowy [pshed-po-to-**po**-
-vi] adj. m. fossil; fossilized;
obsolete; antediluvian
przedramię [pshed-ra-myan] n.
forearm; antebrachium
przedrostek [pshed-**ros**-tek] m.
prefix (in grammar)
przedruk [pshe-drook] m. reprint;
reimpression; impression
przedrzeć [pshed-zhećh] v. tear
up; tear through; rend; break
through; penetrate; burst
przedrzeźniać [pshed-**zheźh**-
-ńaćh] v. ape; mimic; mock;
take off; imitate like an ape
przedsiębiorca [pshed-**śhan**-
-byor-tsa] m. contractor;
businessman; entrepreneur
przedsiębiorstwo [pshed-**śhan**-
-byor-stvo] n. business;
concern; enterprise; firm
przedsiębrać [pshed-**śhan**-
-braćh] v. undertake; embark
on (upon); enter upon (on)
przedsionek [pshed-**śho**-nek] m.
lobby; vestibule; porch; auricle
przedsmak [pshed-smak] m.
foretaste; earnest (of future
events, what is to come)
przedstawić [pshed-**sta**-veećh]
v. present; represent; introduce to; recommend; imagine
przedstawiciel [pshed-sta-**vee**-
-ćhel] m. representative
przedstawicielstwo [pshed-sta-
-vee-ćhel-stvo] n. agency
przedstawienie [pshed-sta-**vye**-
-ńe] n. performance; show;
version; play; introduction

przedszkole [pshed-**shko**-le] n.
kindergarten; nursery school
przedświt [pshed-**śhveet**] m.
predawn; daybreak; harbinger
przedtem [**pshed**-tem] adv.
before; beforehand; before
that; before then; formerly; in
advance; before now; earlier
przedterminowy [pshed-ter-mee-
-no-vi] adj. m. advance;
premature; done ahead of time
przedwczesny [pshed-**vches**-ni]
adj. m. premature; untimely
przedwczoraj [pshed-**vcho**-ray]
adv. the day before yesterday
przedwieczny [pshed-**vyech**-ni]
adj. m. eternal; primeval; ancient; secular; everlasting
przedwiośnie [pshed-**vyośh**-ńe]
n. early spring (springtime)
przedwojenny [pshed-vo-**yen**-ni]
adj. m. prewar; before the war
przedział [pshe-dźhaw] m.
partition; compartment; section; interstice; parting
przedzielić [pshe-dźhe-leećh]
v. divide; part; separate
przedzierać [pshe-dźhe-raćh]
v. tear down; tear up; rend
przedziurawić [pshe-dźhoo-ra-
-veećh] v. perforate; make a
puncture; riddle; pierce; make
a hole (holes); poke a hole
przedziwny [pshe-dźheev-ni]
adj. m. prodigious; admirable;
quite (very) odd; strange
przeforsować [pshe-for-**so**-
-vaćh] v. ram through; force
through; overstrain
przegapić [pshe-ga-peećh] v.
let slip; over look; miss
przeginać [pshe-gee-naćh] v.
bend (over); turn up; turn
down; incline; inflect; bow
przegląd [pshe-glownd] m.
review; inspection; survey
przegłosować [pshe-gwo-**so**-
-vaćh] v. outvote; take a vote
przegonić [pshe-go-ńeećh] v.
overtake; drive out; drive
through; drive away; rush past
przegotować [pshe-go-to-vaćh]
v. boil; overcook; over boil

przegrać [pshe-grać] v. lose (war, game, battle, lawsuit, fortune, etc.); gamble away
przegradzać [pshe-gra-dzać] v. partition; divide; separate
przegrana [pshe-gra-na] f. defeat; loss; beating; licking
przegryzać [pshe-gri-zać] v. bite through; bite in two
przegroda [pshe-gro-da] f. partition; division; stall; cell
przegub [pshe-goob] m. wrist; ball-and-socket joint
przeholować [pshe-kho-lo-vać] v. overshoot; rush into excess
przeistoczyć [pshe-ee-sto--chić] v. transform; remold; convert (turn) into; refashion
przejaśnienie [pshe-yaśh-ńe--ńe] n. clearing up; bright interval; break in the clouds
przejaw [pshe-yav] m. symptom; sign; indication; manifestation
przejawiać [pshe-ya-vyać] v. reveal; display; manifest; evidence; show (satisfaction etc.)
przejazd [pshe-yazt] m. crossing; passage; thoroughfare; journey
przejąć [pshe-yownć] v. take over; seize; adopt; master; succeed; perturb; make fret
przejechać [pshe-ye-khać] v. pass; ride; cross; run over
przejęty [pshe-yan-ti] adj. m. impressed; upset; deeply stirred; perturbed; wrapped up
przejmować [pshey-mo-vać] v. take over; seize; penetrate
przejrzeć [pshey-zheć] v. see through; recover sight; revise
przejrzysty [pshey-zhis-ti] adj. m. transparent; clear; sheer
przejście [pshey-śhćhe] n. pass; transition; conversion; roadway; alley; aisle; ordeal
przejściowo [pshey-śhćho-vo] adv. temporarily; provisionally
przejść [psheyśhćh] v. pass; cross; experience; go across
przekaz [pshe-kas] m. transfer; money order; remittance
przekazywać [pshe-ka-zi-vać] v. transfer; pass on; send on;

transmit; deliver; direct
przekaźnik [pshe-kaźh-ńeek] m. relay; repeater; transmitter
przekąsem [pshe-kown-sem] adv. ironically; mockingly; contemptuously; sneeringly
przekąska [pshe-kown-ska] f. snack; refreshment
przekątna [pshe-kownt-na] f. diagonal (line)
przekleństwo [pshe-kleń-stvo] n. curse; profanity; damnation
przekład [pshe-kwat] m. translation; rendering; rearrangement; transposition
przekładać [pshe-kwa-dać] v. shift; transfer; prefer; move; translate; reach; put between
przekładnia [pshe-kwad-ńa] f. gearbox; clutch; transposition
przekłuć [pshe-kwooćh] v. prick (a bubble); pierce; puncture (a tire); perforate
przekonać [pshe-ko-naćh] v. convince; persuade; bring round; reason with; urge; talk
przekonanie [pshe-ko-na-ńe] n. conviction; persuasion; opinion
przekop [pshe-kop] m. trench; ditch; tunnel; cutting; piercing
przekopać [pshe-ko-paćh] v. dig-through; turn over; excavate; cut (a passage, ditch)
przekora [pshe-ko-ra] f. spite
przekraczać [pshe-kra-chaćh] v. overstep; cross; surpass
przekradać się [pshe-kra-daćh śhan] v. steal through
przekreślić [pshe-kreśh-leećh] v. cross out; delete; annul
przekręcić [pshe-kran-ćheećh] v. twist; distort (a statement)
przekroczenie [pshe-kro-che-ńe] n. crossing; offence; transgression; sin (against)
przekroczyć [pshe-kro-chićh] v. cross; trespass; exceed; offend; violate; transgress (the law); step over; overstep
przekroić [pshe-kro-eećh] v. cut
przekrój [pshe-krooy] m. cross section; profile; review
przekrwienie [pshe-krvye-ńe] n.

hyperemia; congestion
przekształcić [pshe-kshtaw-
-ćheećh] v. transform
przekupić [pshe-koo-peećh] v.
bribe; buy over; corrupt
przekupka [pshe-koop-ka] f.
huckstress; vendor; wrangler
przekupny [pshe-koop-ni] adj. m.
venal; bribable; corruptible
przekupstwo [pshe-koop-stvo] n.
bribery; graft; corruption
przekwitać [pshe-kvee-taćh] v.
wither; fade; decay; shed
blossom; come out of bloom
przelatywać [pshe-la-ti-vaćh] v.
fly through; cross; run; pass
przelew [pshe-lef] m.
transfusion; transfer; overflow
przelewać [pshe-le-vaćh] v.
overfill; transfer; shed
przelękły [pshe-lank-wi] adj. m.
frightened; intimidated
przeleknąć [pshe-lank-nownćh]
v. frighten; scare; terrify
przelicytować [pshe-lee-tsi-to-
-vaćh] v. outbid (one another)
przeliczyć [pshe-lee-chićh] v.
miscalculate; count over
przelot [pshe-lot] m. overflight;
flight; passage; transit by air
przelotny [pshe-lot-ni] adj. m.
fleeting; passing; transient
przeludnienie [pshe-lood-ńe-ńe]
n. overpopulation; congestion
przeładować [pshe-wa-do-vaćh]
v. overload; transship; reload
przeładunek [pshe-wa-doo-nek]
m. load transfer; reloading
przełamać [pshe-wa-maćh] v.
break through; break in two
przełazić [pshe-wa-źheećh] v.
climb over; creep across
przełącznik [pshe-wownch-ńeek]
m. switch; shift; commutator
przełącz [pshe-wanch] f. pass;
saddle; mountain pass
przełknąć [pshew-knownćh] v.
swallow; swallow down
przełom [pshe-wom] m. break
-through; turning point; gorge
przełożony [pshe-wo-zho-ni] m.
principal; superior; chief
przełożyć [pshe-wo-zhićh] v.

transfer; prefer; shift; reach
przełyk [pshe-wik] m. gullet; eso-
phagus; oesophagus; throat
przemakać [pshe-ma-kaćh] v.
ooze; get wet; be permeable
przemarsz [pshe-marsh] m.
marching past; march of
troops; passage of troops
przemarznąć [pshe-mar-
-znownćh] v. be chilled to the
marrow; be (get) frozen stiff;
przemawiać [pshe-ma-vyaćh] v.
speak; harangue; address
przemądrzały [pshe-mownd-zha-
-wi] adj. m. too smart; wise
guy; smart; pert; too clever
przemęczać [pshe-man-chaćh]
v. overstrain; overwork; spend
przemęczenie [pshe-man-che-ńe]
n. strain; overwork; tiredness
przemiał [pshe-myaw] m.
grinding (of grain); milling (of
grain); meal; grist; shoal
przemiana [pshe-mya-na] f.
change; transformation; alteration; conversion; mutation
przemianować [pshe-mya-no-
-vaćh] v. rename; change
name; give an other name
przemienić [pshe-mye-ńeećh]
v. change; transform; alter;
turn; convert; transmute into
przemieścić [pshe-myeśh-
-ćheećh] v. displace; dislocate; shift; trans-locate
przemijać [pshe-mee-yaćh] v.
go by; be over; pass; cease
przemilczeć [pshe-meel-chećh]
v. keep secret; leave unsaid
przemoc [pshe-mots] f. force;
violence; constraint; compulsion; (act of force) violence
przemoczyć [pshe-mo-chićh] v.
soak; drench; wet; seep; sop
przemoknąć [pshe-mok-
-nownćh] v. be soaked; get
wet; soak through to the skin
przemowa [pshe-mo-va] f.
(long) speech; oration; for- mal
address; harangue; tirade
przemóc [pshe-moots] v.
overcome; conquer; defeat;
master; prevail; predominate

przemówić [pshe-moo-veech]
v. speak up; make a mistake
(speaking); recover speech
przemówienie [pshe-moo-vye-
-ńe] n. speech; oration
przemycać [pshe-mi-tsaćh] v.
smuggle (into a country, etc.)
przemyć [pshe-mićh] v. rinse;
scrub; wash off (the dirt); give
a wash; lavage; flush; rinse
przemysł [pshe-misw] m.
industry; trade; ingenuity
przemysłowy [pshe-mi-swo-vi]
adj. m. industrial; factory
(workers); manufacturing
przemyśliwać [pshe-mi-śhlee-
-vaćh] v. ponder; think over
przemyślny [pshe-miśhl-ni] adj.
m. ingenious; clever; cunning
przemyt [pshe-mit] m. smuggling
przemytnik [pshe-mit-ńeek] m.
smuggler; contrabandist
przemywać [pshe-mi-vaćh] v.
rinse; wash; scrub; lavage;
flush; give a wash (scrub etc.)
przenieść [pshe-ńeśhćh] v.
transfer; surpass; carry over;
remove; convey; move (to);
retrace; exceed; overshoot
przenigdy [pshe-ńeeg-di] adv.
nevermore; never again
przenikać [pshe-ńee-kaćh] v.
penetrate; pierce; permeate
przenikliwy [pshe-ńee-klee-vi]
adj. m. penetrating; acute;
sharp; piercing; keen; shrewd
przenocować [pshe-no-tso-
-vaćh] v. pass the night; put
up for the night; sleep
przenośnia [pshe-nośh-ńa] f.
metaphor; figure of speech
przenośny [pshe-nośh-ni]
adj. m. portable; mobile; transferable; metaphorical
przeobrażać [pshe-o-bra-zhaćh]
v. transform; modify; change
przeoczenie [pshe-o-che-ńe] n.
oversight; omission
przeoczyć [pshe-o-chićh] v.
overlook; leave out; omit
przepadać [pshe-pa-daćh] v. be
lost; be extremely fond; vanish; disappear; perish; fail

przepalić [pshe-pa-leećh] v.
burn through; overheat; fire in
a stove occasionally; scorch
przepasać [pshe-pa-saćh] v.
gird; belt; tie; overfeed
przepaska [pshe-pas-ka] f. band
przepaść [pshe-paśhćh] v.
abyss; precipice; chasm; gulf
przepchać [pshep-khaćh] v.
push through; pass through;
clean out; swab (a pipe)
przepełniać [pshe-pew-ńaćh]
v. overfill; cram; over cram
przepełnienie [pshe-pew-ńe-ńe]
n. overfill; crowd; excess
przepędzać [pshe-pan-dzaćh] v.
drive away; spend; distill; stay
przepić [pshe-peećh] v. spend
on drinking; drink away;
waste money on drinking
przepierać [pshe-pye-raćh] v.
launder; wash clothes
przepierzenie [pshe-pye-zhe-ńe]
n. partition (wall etc.)
przepiękny [pshe-pyank-ni] adj.
m. very beautiful; gorgeous
przepiłować [pshe-pee-wo-
-vaćh] v. saw through; file
through; saw off; file away
przepiórka [pshe-pyoor-ka] f.
quail (migratory game bird)
przepis [pshe-pees] m. regulation
przepis [pshe-pees] m. recipe
przepisać [pshe-pee-saćh] v.
prescribe; write over again
przepisać [pshe-pee-saćh] v.
copy; transfer (property)
przepłacać [pshe-pwa-tsaćh] v.
overpay; pay too much; bribe
przepłukać [pshe-pwoo-kaćh]
v. rinse; gargle; scour; wash
przepłynąć [pshe-pwi-nownćh]
v. swim across; row across
przepływać [pshe-pwi-vaćh] v.
flow; float across; swim
across; row across; sail across
przepocić [pshe-po-ćheećh] v.
sweat through; sweat (a shirt)
przepoić [pshe-po-eećh] v.
impregnate; saturate; fill
przepona [pshe-po-na] f.
diaphragm; midriff; stiffener
przepowiadać [pshe-po-vya-

-dać] v. predict; foretell;
prophesy; repeat one's lesson;
foretell future events; divine
przepracować się [pshe-pra-tso-
-vaćh śhan] v. overwork
(oneself); overtrain oneself
przepraszać [pshe-pra-shaćh] v.
apologize; excuse oneself
przeprawa [pshe-pra-va] f.
passage; crossing; journey
przeprawa [pshe-pra-va] f. fight;
incident; scene; row
przeprawiać [pshe-pra-vyaćh]
v. cross over; carry across
przeproszenie [pshe-pro-she-ńe]
n. apology; apologies
przeprowadzać [pshe-pro-va-
-dzaćh] v. convey; lead;
conduct; escort; see across
przeprowadzka [pshep-ro-vadz-
-ka] f. moving (from a house)
przepuklina [pshe-poo-klee-na] f.
hernia (protrusion); rupture
przepustka [pshe-poost-ka] f.
pass; permit; liberty; sluice
przepuszczać [pshe-poosh-
-chaćh] v. let pass; promote;
leak; miss; let slip; waste;
squander away; be pervious
przepuszczalność [pshe-poosh-
-chal-nośhćh] f. permeability
przepych [pshe-pikh] m. luxury;
pageantry; splendor; ostentation; magnificence; glamor
przepychać [pshe-pi-khaćh] v.
push through; force through
przepytywać [pshe-pi-ti-vaćh]
v. examine; inquire; question
przerabiać [pshe-ra-byaćh] v.
do over; revise; remodel; alter
przerachować [pshe-ra-kho-
-vaćh] v. miscalculate; count
over again; re-count; convert
przeradzać się [pshe-ra-dzaćh
śhan] v. change (into)
przerastać [pshe-ras-taćh] v.
outgrow; rise above; surpass
przerazić [pshe-ra-źheećh] v.
terrify; appall; consternation
przeraźliwy [pshe-raźh-lee-vi]
adj. m. appalling; terrifying
shrill; awesome; acute; sharp
przerażenie [pshe-ra-zhe-ńe] n.

terror; horror; dread; dismay
przerażony [pshe-ra-zho-ni] adj.
m. horror stricken; terrified
przeróbka [pshe-roob-ka] f.
revision; reshaping; alteration
przerwa [psher-va] f. pause;
break; recess; interval
przerys [pshe-ris] m. tracing
przerysować [pshe-ri-so-vaćh]
v. trace; copy; retrace
przerwać [psher-vaćh] v.
interrupt; pause; cut-off
przerzedzić [pshe-zhe-
-dźheećh] v. thin out;
decimate (a population)
przerzucić [pshe-zhoo-ćheećh]
v. throw over; shift; move;
flip; browse; transfer
przerzynać [pshe-zhi-naćh] v.
cut through; cut in two
przesada [pshe-sa-da] f.
exaggeration; overstatement
przesadzać [pshe-sa-dzaćh] v.
exaggerate; jump (leap) over
przesadzać [pshe-sa-dzaćh] v.
transplant; bed out seedlings
przesalać [pshe-sa-laćh] v.
oversalt; put too much salt
przesąd [pshe-sownt] m.
prejudice; superstition; fallacy
przesądny [pshe-sownd-ni] adj.
m. superstitious; prejudiced
przesiadać się [pshe-śha-daćh
śhan] v. change (places, bus,
train); move to another seat
przesiedlać [pshe-śhed-laćh] v.
displace; migrate; transplant
przesiewać [pshe-śhe-vaćh] v.
sift; sieve; screen out; riddle
przesilać się [pshe-śhee-laćh
śhan] v. subside; get over;
culminate; overcome; over-
strain; rich high point
przesilenie [pshe-śhee-le-ńe] n.
crisis; turning point
przeskoczyć [pshes-ko-chićh]
v. jump over; vault; outstrip;
skip; leap across (a ditch etc.)
przesłać [pshes-waćh] v. send
przesłać [pshes-waćh] v. make
a bed over; rearrange a bed
przesłaniać [pshe-swa-ńaćh] v.
screen off; veil; cover; hide;

shade; conceal; dim (lights)
przesłanka [pshe-**swan**-ka] f.
premise; prerequisite;(necessary) condition; reason; datum
przesłuchiwać [pshes-woo-khee-
-vаć] v. interrogate; hear;
examine; question (witnesses)
przesmyk [**pshes**-mik] m. strait
przesolony [pshe-so-lo-ni] adj. m.
oversalted; with excess salt
przespać [**pshes**-pаć] v. sleep
over; fail to wake up for
przestać [**pshes**-tаć] v. cease
przestanek [pshes-**ta**-nek] m.
pause; rest; stop; (bus) stop
przestankować [pshes-tan-ko-
-vаć] v. punctuate (written
matter; text; letter, etc.)
przestarzały [pshe-sta-zha-wi]
adj. m. obsolete; time worn
przestawać [pshe-sta-vаć] v.
stop; cut out; break off
przestawać [pshe-sta-vаć] v.
associate; hobnob; keep
company; stand (some time)
przestawiać [pshe-sta-vyаć] v.
displace; transpose; shift
przestąpić [pshe-**stown**-peеć]
v. step over; transgress; cross
przestępca [pshe-**stanp**-tsa] m.
criminal; felon; law breaker
przestępny [pshe-**stanp**-ni] adj.
m. leap (year); felonious
przestępstwo [pshe-**stanp**-stvo]
n. offense; crime; transgression; misdemeanor; felony
przestrach [pshe-strakh] m.
fright; alarm; fear; terror
przestraszyć [pshe-**stra**-shić]
v. scare; startle; alarm
przestroga [pshe-stro-ga] f.
warning; admonition; caution
przestronny [pshe-**stron**-ni] adj.
m. spacious; roomy; vast
przestrzegać [pshe-**stshe**-gаć]
v. observe (rules); caution
przestrzelić [pshe-stshe-leеć]
v. shoot through; shoot down
przestrzenny [pshe-**stshen**-ni]
adj. m. spatial; roomy; vast
przestrzeń [pshe-stsheń] f.
space; outer space; room
przestworze [pshe-**stvo**-zhe] n.

expanse; infinity; space
przesunięcie [pshe-soo-**ńan**-
-ćhe] n. shift; transfer;
displacement; reshuffle (of)
przesuwać [pshe-**soo**-vаć] v.
move; shift; shove; transfer
przesycać [pshe-**si**-tsаć] v.
saturate; glut; impregnate
przesyłać [pshe-**si**-wаć] v.
send; dispatch; forward
przesyłka [pshe-**siw**-ka] f.
shipment; mail; parcel
przesypiać [pshe-**si**-pyаć] v.
oversleep; sleep away
przesyt [pshe-sit] m. glut
przeszczep [pshe-shchep] m.
transplant; graft; grafting
przeszkadzać [pshe-shka-dzаć]
v. hinder; trouble; prevent
przeszkoda [pshe-shko-da] f.
obstacle; hitch; obstruction
przeszkolenie [pshe-shko-le-ńe]
n. training; instruction course
przeszło [pshesh-wo] adv. more
than; over (an amount); last
przeszłość [pshesh-**wość**]
f. past; record; antecedents
przeszukać [pshe-shoo-kаć] v.
search over; ransack; scour
przeszyć [pshe-shić] v. sew
-through; pierce; gore; quilt
prześcieradło [pshe-śhćhe-ra-
-dwo] n. bedsheet; sheet
prześcignąć [pshe-śhćheeg-
-**nown**ć] v. outdistance;
outdo; outstrip; overtake; excel; surpass; exceed; out-rival
prześladować [pshe-śhla-**do**-
-vаć] v. persecute; harass;
haunt; pester; molest; worry
prześladowanie [pshe-śhla-do-
-va-ńe] n. persecution; oppression; obsession; molesting
prześliczny [pshe-śhleech-ni]
adj. m. most beautiful; lovely
prześliznąć [pshe-śhleez-
-**nown**ć] v. slip through;
glide past; sneak through
przeświadczenie [pshe-śhvyad-
-che-ńe] n. conviction; persuasion; certitude; confidence
prześwietlać [pshe-**śhvyet**-
-laćh] v. shine through;

fluoroscope (through)
przetak [pshe-tak] m. riddle
przetaczać [pshe-ta-chać] v.
1. roll; wheel; pour; decant
przetaczać [pshe-ta-chać] v.
2. transfuse (blood)
przetapiać [pshe-ta-pyać] v.
recast; smelt (metals); melt
przetarg [pshe-tark] m. auction
przetarty [pshe-tar-ti] adj. m.
threadbare; rubbed through
przetłumaczyć [pshe-twoo-ma--chić] v. translate; explain
przeto [pshe-to] conj. therefore;
accordingly; consequently
przetrawić [pshe-tra-veeć] v.
digest; ruminate; etch; corrode
przetrwać [pshe-trvać] v.
survive; outlast; remain; keep
przetrwonić [pshe-trvo-ńeeć]
v. squander; waste away; fritter away (money, fortune etc.)
przetrząsnąć [pshe-tshowns--nownć] v. search (shake through); ransack; comb out
przetrzymać [pshe-tshi-mać]
v. endure; outdo; keep waiting
przetwarzać [pshe-tva-zhać]
v. remake; manufacture
przetwórnia [pshe-tvoor-ńa] f.
factory; processing plant
przewaga [pshe-va-ga] f.
predominance; overbalance; lead; superiority; majority
przeważać [pshe-va-zhać] v.
outweigh; prevail; overbalance; predominate
przeważający [pshe-va-zha--yown-tsi] adj. m. prevailing;
superior; predominant
przeważnie [pshe-vazh-ńe] adv.
mainly; mostly; chiefly; largely
przewiązać [pshe-vyown-zać]
v. bind up; change dressing
przewidywać [pshe-vee-di--vać] v. anticipate; foresee
przewiercić [pshe-vyer-ćheeć]
v. drill through (pierce)
przewiesić [pshe-vye-śheeć]
v. sling over; hang over; rehang (pictures, etc.)
przewietrzyć [pshe-vyet-shić]
v. ventilate; be aerated

przewiew [pshe-vyev] m. gust
of wind; draught; breeze; breath of (fresh) air; whiff
przewiezienie [pshe-vye-źhe-ńe]
n. transport; transportation; carriage; conveyance; move
przewijać [pshe-vee-yać] v.
wrap up; change dressing
przewinienie [pshe-vee-ńe-ńe]
n. offence; delinquency
przewlekły [pshe-vlek-wi] adj. m.
protracted; lingering; lasting
przewodni [pshe-vod-ńee]
adj. m. leading; guiding (light, principle, notion etc.)
przewodniczący [pshe-vod-ńee--chown-tsi] m. chairman
przewodnik [pshe-vod-ńeek] m.
guide; conductor; leader
przewodzić [pshe-vo-dźheeć]
v. head; command (a unit); lead (a group); conduct; carry
przewozić [pshe-vo-źheeć] v.
convey; transport; cart across
przewoźnik [pshe-voźh-ńeek]
m. ferryman; carter; carrier
przewód [pshe-voot] m. conduit;
channel; wire; procedure
przewóz [pshe-voos] m.
transport; freight; cartage
przewracać [pshe-vra-tsać] v.
overturn; turn over; upset; toss; topple; invert; reverse
przewrotność [pshe-vrot--nośhć] f. perversity; perfidy; deceit; perverseness
przewrót [pshe-vroot] m.
revolution; upheaval; coup
przewyższać [pshe-vizh-shać]
v. out do; exceed; surpass
przez [pshes] prep. across; over
(the fence); through; during; within; in; on the other side
przeziębić się [pshe-źhan--beeć śhan] v. catch cold; become cold; grow cold
przezimować [pshe-źhee-mo--vać] v. winter; hibernate
przeznaczać [pshez-na-chać]
v. intend; earmark; mean; destine; assign; allocate; design; appropriate (for)
przeznaczenie [pshez-na-che-ńe]

n. destiny; purpose; fate
przezorność [pshe-zor-
-nośhćh] f. caution; pru-
dence; foresight; cautiousness
przeźrocze [psheźh-ro-che] n.
transparency; slide; open work
przeźroczysty [pshe-źhro-chis-
-ti] adj. m. transparent
przezwisko [pshez-vees-ko] n.
1. nickname; surname
przezwisko [pshez-vees-ko] n.
2. abusive (bad) name
przezwyciężać [pshe-zvi-ćhan-
-zhaćh] v. overcome; conquer
przezywać [pshe-zi-vaćh] v.
revile; abuse; call names
przeżegnać się [pshe-zheg-
-naćh śhan] v. cross oneself
przeżuwać [pshe-zhoo-vaćh] v.
chew; masticate; ponder over
przeżycie [pshe-zhi-ćhe] n. (bad,
good) experience; survival
przeżyć [pshe-zhićh] v.
survive; live through; outlive
przeżytek [pshe-zhi-tek] m. relic
of the past; old timer
przędza [pshan-dza] f. yarn
przędzalnia [pshan-dzal-ńa] f.
spinning mill; spinning room
przęsło [pshans-wo] n. (bridge)
bay; (stair) flight; span
przodek [psho-dek] m. ancestor
przodek [psho-dek] m. front;
heading; end; top
przodować [psho-do-vaćh] v.
lead; excel; be the best
przodownictwo [psho-dov-ńeets-
-tvo] n. leadership; hegemony
przodownik [psho-dov-ńeek] m.
leader; foreman (head of a
group); police inspector
przód [pshoot] front; ahead; bow
przy [pshi] prep. by; at; nearby;
with; on; about; close; beside
przybić [pshi-beećh] v. nail
down; fasten; fix; dishearten
przybiec [pshi-byets] v. run up;
hasten; come up running
przybierać [pshi-bye-raćh] v.
dress up; put on; adopt; adorn
przybliżać [pshi-blee-zhaćh] v.
bring near; draw near; magnify
przybliżony [pshi-blee-zho-ni] adj.

m. approximate; very near
przyboczny [pshi-boch-ni] adj. m.
side (kick); personal (aide);
body (guard); adjutant (officer)
przybory [pshi-bo-ri] pl.
accessories; outfit; tools; fittings; tackle; (toilet) articles
przybór [pshi-boor] m. rise (of a
river); flood (rising waters)
przybrać [pshi-braćh] v. adorn;
put on; assume; adopt; rise;
grow; increase; swell (a river)
przybrzeżny [pshi-bzhezh-ni] adj.
m. coastal; riverside; inshore
przybudówka [pshi-boo-doov-ka]
f. annex; addition (to a building); penthouse; lean to
przybycie [pshi-bi-ćhe] n. arrival;
gain; growth; accession
przybysz [pshi-bish] m. newcomer; new arrival; stranger
przybytek [pshi-bi-tek] m.
increase; sanctuary; repository
przybywać [pshi-bi-vaćh] v.
arrive; come; reach; attain
przybywać [pshi-bi-vaćh] v.
increase; rise; attain; reach
przychodnia [pshi-khod-ńa] f.
outpatient clinic; ambulatory
przychodzić [pshi-kho-
-dźheećh] v. come over, a-
round, along, to, again; turn
up; arrive; be first at; follow
przychód [pshi-khoot] m.
income; profit; takings; proceeds; receipts; receipt (book)
przychylać [pshi-khi-laćh] v.
incline; comply; bend; stoop
przychylny [pshi-khil-ni] adj. m.
favorable; kind; friendly
przyciągać [pshi-ćhown-gaćh]
v. attract; draw near; appeal;
lure; entice; come; arrive
przyciąganie ziemskie [pshi-
-ćhown-ga-ńe źhem-ske]
gravitation; gravitational pull
przyciemniać [pshi-ćhem-
-ńaćh] v. dim; darken; shade;
black out; obscure; subdue
przycinać [pshi-ćhee-naćh] v.
1. cut off; shorten; clip; trim
przycinać [pshi-ćhee-naćh] v.
2. make fun of; sting; peck at

przycisk [pshi-ćheesk] m.
1. pressure; stress; squeeze
przycisk [pshi-ćheesk] m.
2. accent; emphasis; stress
przycisk [pshi-ćheesk] m.
3. weight; (paper-weight, etc.)
przyciskać [pshi-ćhees-kać]
v. press; keep down; squeeze
przycupnąć [pshi-tsoop-
-nownćh] v. squat down; lie
in wait; crouch; cower; lurk
przyczaić się [pshi-cha-eećh
śhan] v. lurk; sulk; ambush;
lie in ambush; hide; be hidden
przyczepić [pshi-che-peećh] v.
attach; fasten; link; fix; pin;
hook; charge with an offense
przyczepić się [pshi-che-peećh
śhan] v. cling; pick a quarrel;
find fault; hold tight; attach
przyczepka [pshi-chep-ka] f.
trailer; exp.: on top of it all
przyczółek [pshi-choo-wek] m.
abutment; bridgehead; beachhead; fronton; frontal; pedi-
ment (an ornamental gable)
przyczyna [pshi-chi-na] f. cause;
reason; ground; intersection
przyrzyczynek [pshi-chi-nek] m.
contribution (to science etc.)
przyczyniać [pshi-chi-ńach] v.
add; add to; contribute
przyczynowość [pshi-chi-no-
-vośhćh] f. causation; cau-
sality; a causing
przyćmiewać [pshi-ćhmye-
-vach] v. dim; tarnish; obscure; outshine; overshadow;
darken; eclipse; cloud over
przydać [pshi-dach] v. add;
append; lend; add weight
przydatny [pshi-dat-ni] adj. m.
useful; helpful; serviceable
przydawka [pshi-dav-ka] f.
attribute (gram.); qualifier
przydeptać [pshi-dep-tach] v.
thread upon; step on (upon)
przydługi [pshi-dwoo-gee] adj. m.
lengthy; somewhat too long
przydomek [pshi-do-mek] m. by
-name; surname; nickname
przydreptać [pshi-drep-tach] v.
trip along; come tripping

przydrożny [pshi-drozh-ni]
adj. m. roadside (shrine etc.)
przydusić [pshi-doo-śheećh] v.
throttle; smother; press down
przydybać [pshi-di-bach] v.
overtake; take unawares; nab
przydymać [pshi-di-mach] v.
foot it along; run up (slang)
przydymiony [pshi-di-myo-ni] adj.
m. smoky (food); tinted (glass)
przydział [pshi-dźhaw] m.
allotment; ration; allowance
przydzielać [pshi-dźhe-lach] v.
assign; allocate; allot
przyganiać [pshi-ga-ńach] v.
blame; find fault with;
criticize; rebuke; reprimand
przygarnąć [pshi-gar-nownćh]
v. take up; adopt; hug; grasp;
clasp; gather; press; shelter
przygasać [pshi-ga-sach] v.
dim; subside; abate; go out;
die down; diminish; subside
przyglądać się [pshi-glown-
-dach śhan] v. observe; look
on; scan; see; watch; survey
przygnać [pshi-gnach] v. drive
near; bring; run up; hasten
przygnębiać [pshi-gnan-byach]
v. depress; deject; dishearten
przygnębienie [pshi-gnan-bye-
-ńe] n. depression; low spirits
przygniatać [pshi-gńa-tach] v.
crush; overwhelm; oppress;
burden; press down; squeeze;
pinch; bow down; weigh on
przygoda [pshi-go-da] f.
adventure; accident; experience (pleasant, unpleasant)
przygodny [pshi-god-ni] adj. m.
occasional; casual; accidental
przygotować [pshi-go-to-vach]
v. prepare; get ready; worn;
fit; coach; train; make ready;
pack up; turn on (the bath)
przygotowanie [pshi-go-to-va-
-ńe] n. preparation; getting
ready; pl. arrangements, etc.
przygotowawczy [pshi-go-to-vav-
-chi] adj. m. preparatory; initial
przygrywać [pshi-gri-vach] v.
1. play the accompaniment
przygrywać [pshi-gri-vach] v.

2. play (music for pleasure)
przygrzewać [pshi-gzhe-vaćh]
v. warm up; heat up; swelter
przygwoździć [pshi-gvo-
-źhdźheećh] v. nail down;
pin down; fasten permanently
przyimek [pshi-ee-mek] m.
preposition (relation word)
przyjaciel [pshi-ya-ćhel] m.
friend; good friend; close
friend; intimate friend
przyjaciółka [pshi-ya-ćhoow-ka]
f. girl friend; close friend
przyjazd [pshi-yazt] m. arrival;
scheduled time of arrival
przyjazny [pshi-yaz-ni] adj. m.
friendly; amicable; kindly
przyjaźń [pshi-yaźhń] m.
friendship; friendly relations;
amity; kindest regards etc.
przyjaźnić się [pshi-yaźh-
-ńeećh śhan] v. be friends,
on friendly terms; pal; chum
przyjechać [pshi-ye-khaćh] v.
come (over); arrive; come
przyjemność [pshi-yem-
-nośhćh] f. pleasure; (keen)
enjoyment; gusto; zest;
przyjemny [pshi-yem-ni] adj. m.
pleasant; attractive; nice; cosy
przyjezdny [pshi-yezd-ni] m.
stranger; sightseer; visitor
przyjeżdżać [pshi-yezh-dzhaćh]
v. arrive (by transportation)
przyjęcie [pshi-yan-ćhe] n.
admission; adoption; reception
przyjęty [pshi-yan-ti] adj. m.
customary; acceptable
przyjmować [pshiy-mo-vaćh] v.
receive; accept; entertain
przyjście [pshiyśh-ćhe] n.
arrival; coming; advent
przyjść [pshiyśhćh] v. come
-over; come along; come in
(around); arrive; turn up
przykazać [pshi-ka-zaćh] v.
order; tell; enjoin to do
przykazanie [pshi-ka-za-ńe] n.
commandment; injunction
przyklasnąć [pshi-klas-nownćh]
v. applaud; commend; praise
przykleić [pshi-kle-eećh] v.
stick; glue; paste; stick on

(stamp, sticker, label, etc.)
przyklękać [pshi-klan-kaćh] v.
genuflect; bend the knee
przykład [pshi-kwat] m. example;
instance; pattern; sample
przykładać [pshi-kwa-daćh] v.
apply; affix; lend a hand
przykładać [pshi-kwa-daćh] v.
beat up with; apply a force
przykładny [pshi-kwad-ni] adj. m.
exemplary; well fitting
przykrajać [pshi-kra-yaćh] v.
cut off length; cut to fit; cut
out (a cloth, garments etc.)
przykrawać [pshi-kra-vaćh] v.
cut out (a cloth, garments,
etc.); cut off (the length)
przykręcać [pshi-kran-tsaćh] v.
1. screw on; screw down
przykręcać [pshi-kran-tsaćh] v.
2. turn (off, on) tight
przykrość [pshi-krośhćh] f.
annoyance; irritation; vexation
przykry [pshi-kri] adj. m.
disagreeable; painful; nasty;
bad; unpleasant; annoying
przykrywać [pshi-kri-vaćh] v.
cover; roof over; put on a cap
przykrywka [pshi-kriv-ka] f. lid;
(under the) cover (of love etc.)
przykrzyć się [pshi-kshićh
śhan] v. be bored; having nothing to do; pall on; be weary;
bore; yearn; become tedious
przykucnąć [pshi-koots-
-nownćh] v. squat down; sit
down (low); crouch; squat
przykuć [pshi-kooćh] v.
chain; grip; hammer on; rivet;
attach with chains, etc.
przykuć [pshi-kooćh] v. arrest
(attention); chain; grip; rivet;
fascinate; hold spellbound
przylatywać [pshi-la-ti-vaćh] v.
fly in; fly into (a room)
przylądek [pshi-lown-dek] m.
cape; tip of land; headland
przylecieć [pshi-le-ćhećh] v.
fly in; arrive; come running
przylegać [pshi-le-gaćh] v. fit;
cling; adhere; lie close
przylegać [pshi-le-gaćh] v.
adjoin; abut; be contiguous

przylegly [pshi-leg-wi] adj. m.
adjacent; adjoining; contiguous
przylepić [pshi-le-peećh] v.
stick; glue on; stick to; post
przylepiec [pshi-le-pyets] m.
adhesive tape; court plaster
przylgnąć [pshil-gnownćh] v.
stick; cling; adhere; nestle up
przylot [pshi-lot] m. plane arrival
przylutować [pshi-loo-to-vaćh]
v. solder on; sweat on
przyłączać [pshi-wown-chaćh]
v. annex (to); join (with); add;
connect; attach; incorporate
przyłączenie [pshi-wown-che-
-ńe] n. annexation; incorporation; connection; addition
przyłbica [pshiw-bee-tsa] f. visor;
beaver; welder's helmet
przymawiać [pshi-ma-vyaćh] v.
criticize; rebuke; pinprick;
nettle; nag; allude to; hint
przymawiać się [pshi-ma-vyaćh
śhan] v. hint around for
przymiarka [pshi-myar-ka] f.
fitting on; trying on clothes
przymierać [pshi-mye-raćh] v.
starve; be half dead; be dying
przymierzać [pshi-mye-zhaćh]
v. try on; set to; apply to
przymierze [pshi-mye-zhe] n.
alliance; covenant; Testament; (Ark of the) Covenant
przymierzyć [pshi-mye-zhićh] v.
try on; set on; apply to
przymieszka [pshi-myesh-ka] f.
admixture; addition; modicum;
dash (of salt, spirits, etc.)
przymiot [pshi-myot] m. (man's)
quality; trait; attribute
przymiotnik [pshi-myot-ńeek] m.
adjective (grammar)
przymknięty [pshim-kńan-ti] adj.
m. half-closed; shut up
przymocować [pshi-mo-tso-
-vaćh] v. fasten down; fix to;
secure to; attach; make fast
przymówka [pshi-moov-ka] f.
gibe; hint; allusion; scoff; jeer
przymrozek [pshi-mro-zek] m.
slight frost; ground frost
przymrużyć oczy [pshi-mroo-
-zhićh o-chi] blink; narrow

(half-close) one's eyes; wink
przymus [pshi-moos] m.
compulsion; constraint; pressure; coercion; duress
przymusić [pshi-moo-śheećh]
v. compel; force(into a decision, etc.); oblige; coerce
przymusowy [pshi-moo-so-vi]
adj. m. obligatory; coercive
(measures, etc.); forced
przynaglać [pshi-na-glaćh] v.
urge; haste; push on; hustle;
spur on; impel; hurry
przynajmniej [pshi-nay-mńey]
adv. at least; at any rate; anyway; in the smallest degree
przynależeć [pshi-na-le-zhećh]
v. belong; be a member (of a
party); be affiliated with
przynależność [pshi-na-lezh-
-nośhćh] v. (nationality)
membership; affiliation; (national) status; pl. pertinents
przynależny [pshi-na-lezh-ni] adj.
m. belonging; appurtenant
przynęta [pshi-nan-ta] f. bait;
lure; enticement; lure; decoy
przynosić [pshi-no-śheećh] v.
1. bring (up, down etc.); fetch
przynosić [pshi-no-śheećh] v.
2. bear; yield; bring (profit,
honor, ill luck, news); afford;
przyobiecać [pshi-o-bye-tsaćh]
v. promise; give a promise
przyobiecywać [pshi-o-bye-tsi-
-vaćh] v. promise; give a
promise (to do or not to do)
przypadać [pshi-pa-daćh] v. be
due; fall; come; happen; take
przypadek [pshi-pa-dek] m.
event; chance; case; incident
przypadkiem [pshi-pad-kem]
adv. by chance; accidentally
przypadkowo [pshi-pad-ko-vo]
adv. accidentally; by chance;
unintentionally; by accident
przypadłość [pshi-pad-
-wośhćh] f. affliction; indisposition; ailment; disease
przypalić [pshi-pa-leećh] v.
singe; burn(the food, milk)
smoke; scorch; sear; light up
przypasać [pshi-pa-saćh] v.

attach (to belt); grid on
przypatrywać się [pshi-pa-tri-
-vaćh **śhan**] v. observe; look
at (this or that); contemplate;
have a look at this (or that)
przypatrzyć się [pshi-pa-tshićh
śhan] v. observe; look at; see
(in detail); contemplate
przypędzać [pshi-**pan**-dzaćh] v.
1. come in haste; run up (to)
przypędzać [pshi-**pan**-dzaćh] v.
2. drive up; drive (cattle)
przypiąć [pshi-py**own**ćh] v. pin;
fasten; attach; buckle; pin on
przypieczętować [pshi-pye-
-**chan**-to-vaćh] v. seal up; set
one's seal to papers; confirm
przypisek [pshi-pee-sek] m. note;
postscript; added note
przypisywać [pshi-pee-si-vaćh]
v. ascribe; attribute; credit
przypłacać [pshi-pwa-tsaćh] v.
pay (with life, health, property, etc.); pay (very dearly)
przypłynąć [pshi-pwi-n**own**ćh]
v. arrive sailing or swimming;
come to shore; swim up; sail
up; row up; come; arrive
przypływ [pshi-pwif] m. high
tide; inflow; influx; high water
przypodobać się [pshi-po-do-
-baćh **śhan**] v. get into good
graces of; endear oneself to
przypominać [pshi-po-mee-
-naćh] v. remind; recollect;
resemble; recall(to mind)
przypomnienie [pshi-pom-ńe-ńe]
n. reminder; memento; souvenir; a cause to remember
przypowieść [pshi-po-
-vyeśhćh] f. tale; parable (a
simple moral lesson); allegory
przyprawa [pshi-pra-va] f.
seasonings; spice (relish, pe-
per, etc,); sauce; condiment
przyprawiać [pshi-pra-vyaćh] v.
1. season; flavor; spice
przyprawiać [pshi-pra-vyaćh] v.
2. cause a loss; fasten; put on
przyprowadzać [psi-pro-va-
-dzaćh] v. bring along; fetch
przypuszczać [pshi-poosh-
-chaćh] v. suppose; let ap-

proach; admit; let enter
przypuszczalnie [pshi-poosh-**chal**-
-ńe] adv. supposedly; likely
przypuszczalny [pshi-poosh-**chal**-
-ni] adj. m. supposed
przypuszczenie [pshi-poosh-**che**-
-ńe] n. guess; supposition
przyroda [pshi-ro-da] f. nature
przyrodni brat [pshi-rod-ńee
brat] half brother
przyrodnia siostra [pshi-**rod**-ńa
śhos-tra] half sister
przyrodnik [pshi-rod-ńeek] m.
naturalist; natural historian
przyrodzony [pshi-ro-dzo-ni] adj.
m. innate; natural; inborn
przyrost naturalny [pshi-rost na-
-too-ral-ni] birthrate
przyrostek [pshi-ros-tek] m.
suffix (grammatical term)
przyrząd [pshi-zh**ownt**] m.
instrument; tool; appliance;
device; gadget; contraption
przyrządzać [pshi-zh**own**-
-dzaćh] v. make ready; prepare; cook; get ready; dress
przyrzeczenie [pshi-zhe-che-ńe]
n. promise; plighted word
przyrzekać [pshi-zhe-kaćh] v.
promise to do (something)
przysadka [pshi-sad-ka] f.
pituitary gland; stipule
przysądzać [pshi-**sown**-dzaćh]
v. award; adjudge; allocate
przysiad [pshi-śhat] m. squat
przysiadać [pshi-śha-daćh] v.
sit down; crouch; sit up
przysięga [pshi-śhan-ga] f. oath;
sworn attestation (in a court)
przysięgać [pshi-śhan-gaćh] v.
swear to do; take an oath
przysięgły [pshi-śhang-wi]
adj. m. sworn (jury man)
przysłać [pshi-swaćh] v. send
in; send along; send up
przysłaniać [pshi-swa-ńaćh] v.
shade; vail; cover up; screen
przysłona [pshi-swo-na] f. veil;
shade; screen; diaphragm;
stop; curtain to conceal
przysłowie [pshi-**swo**-vye] n.
proverb; byword
przysłówek [pshi-**swoo**-vek] m.

adverb (grammatical term)
przysłuchiwać się [pshi-swoo-
-khee-vaćh **śhan**] v. listen to
przysługa [pshi-**swoo**-ga] f.
service; good turn; favor;
kindness; a good deed
przysługiwać [pshi-swoo-**gee**-
-vaćh] v. to have right to; be
vested in; be entitled to
przysłużyć się [pshi-**swoo**-
-zhićh **śhan**] v. render
service; do (be of) service to
przysmak [pshi-smak] m. tid-
-bit; delicacy; choice morsel
przysmażyć [pshi-**sma**-zhićh] v.
roast; fry a little; brown; devil
przysparzać [pshi-spa-zhaćh] v.
1. increase; add to; enlarge
przysparzać [pshi-spa-zhaćh] v.
2. cause (trouble); bring (add)
unpleasantness (misery, etc.)
przyśpieszać [pshi-**śhpye**-
-shaćh] v. accelerate; urge;
speed up; hasten; rush; hurry
przyśpieszenie [pshi-śhpye-she-
-ńe] n. acceleration (of gravity); speeding up; activation
przysposabiać [pshi-spo-**sa**-
-byaćh] v. prepare; adapt; a-
dopt; fit; qualify; train
przystać [**pshis**-taćh] v. join;
comply; cohere; fit together;
befit; be suitable; consent
przystanąć [pshi-sta-**nown**ćh]
v. stop; pause; halt
przystanek [pshi-**sta**-nek] m.
stop; station; bus stop etc.
przystań [pshi-stań] f. small
(boat) harbor (inland); port
przystawać [pshi-sta-vaćh] v.
fit; enlist; coincide; halt
przystawiać [pshi-sta-vyaćh] v.
place near; set against; put
przystawka [pshi-stav-ka] f. side
dish; hors-d'oeuvre
przystęp [pshi-stanp] m. access
przystępny [pshi-**stanp**-ni]
1. adj. m. accessible; easy to
approach; affable
przystępny [pshi-**stanp**-ni]
2. adj. m. intelligible; clear; lucid; plain; straightforward;
moderate (conditions, prices)

przystojny [pshi-**stoy**-ni] adj. m.
handsome; decent; suitable
przystosować [pshi-sto-**so**-
-vaćh] v. adjust; fit; accommodate; adapt; conform
przystrajać [pshi-**stra**-yaćh] v.
decorate; adorn; dress; trim
przysunąć [pshi-**soo**-nownćh]
v. move near; push nearer
przyswajać [pshi-**sva**-yaćh] v.
acquire (a knowledge); assimilate; adopt; familiarize with
przysyłać [pshi-**si**-waćh] v.
send; send along; send up
przysypać [pshi-**si**-paćh] v.
cover (with earth; snow, etc.)
przyszłość [pshish-**wośh**ćh] f.
the future; days to come
przyszyć [pshi-shićh] v. sew on
przyszykować [pshi-shi-**ko**-
-vaćh] v. prepare; make ready
przyśnić się [pshiśh-**ńeeć**h
śhan] v. appear in a dream
przyśrubować [pshi-śhroo-**bo**-
-vaćh] v. screw on; screw
down; fasten with a screw
przyświadczyć [pshi-**śhvyad**-
-chićh] v. agree with; attest
przytaczać [pshi-ta-**chaćh**] v.
quote; cite; wheel up; bring
up; roll up; mention; allege
przytakiwać [pshi-ta-kee-vaćh]
v. say yes; assent; acquiesce
przytępić [pshi-**tan**-peećh] v.
dull; blunt somewhat; dim;
befog (memory etc.); deaden
przytępienie [pshi-**tan**-pye-ńe] n.
dullness; bluntness; dimness
przytknąć [pshit-**known**ćh] v.
place touching; set to; apply
to; join; meet; abut; border
przytłaczać [pshi-**twa**-chaćh] v.
overwhelm; press to earth;
crush to earth; weigh down
przytłumić [pshi-**twoo**-meećh]
v. damp; deaden; stifle; subdue (a passion); dim; muffle
przytoczyć [pshi-to-chićh] v.
quote; cite; roll up; bring up
przytomnie [pshi-tom-ńe] adv.
with presence; of mind; lucidly
przytomność [pshi-tom-
-nośhćh] f. consciousness;

(one's) senses; lucid intervals
przytomny [pshi-**tom**-ni] adj. m.
conscious; quick-witted
przytrafiać się [pshi-**tra**-fyaćh
śhan] v. happen; occur; befall
przytrzymać [pshi-**tshi**-maćh] v.
hold; detain; keep in place; arrest; hold back; apprehend
przytulić [pshi-**too**-leećh] v.
snuggle; cuddle; hug; fold
przytułek [pshi-**too**-wek] m.
shelter; alms-house; poor
house; (place of) refuge
przytwierdzić [pshi-**tvyer**-
-**dźheećh**] v. fasten; fix; affix; attach to; acquiesce in
przytyk [pshi-tik] m. dig; allusion;
hint at; reference to; junction
przytykać [pshi-ti-kaćh] v. 1. a-
but; meet; join to; adjoin to
przytykać [pshi-ti-kaćh] v. 2.
set; be contiguous to; border
przy tym [pshi tim] adv. besides
przyuczać [pshi-oo-chaćh] v.
train; accustom an animal
przywabiać [pshi-**va**-byaćh] v.
decoy; lure (with a bait)
przywara [pshi-**va**-ra] f. vice;
fault; defect; shortcoming
przywiązać [pshi-**vyown**-zaćh]
v. bind; tie; attach; hitch;
lash; fasten; connect; endear
przywdziewać [pshi-**vdźhe**-
vaćh] v. put on (clothes)
przywidzenie [pshi-vee-dze-ńe]
n. illusion; delusion; phantasm
przywieźć [pshi-**vyeśhćh**] v.
import; bring; drive up; recall
przywilej [pshi-**vee**-ley] m.
privilege; prerogative; a special right or favor granted
przywitać [pshi-**vee**-taćh] v.
welcome; greet; bid (each
other) good morning
przywłaszczać [pshi-**vwash**-
-chaćh] v. usurp; appropriate
przywodzić [pshi-**vo**-dźheećh]
v. lead; bring about (back) the
(realization of); remind; recall
przywłaszczenie [pshi-**vwa**-
-shche-ńe] n. appropriation;
usurpation (of rights etc.)
przywołać [pshi-**vo**-waćh] v.

summon; call in; signal; sign
przywozić [pshi-**vo**-źheećh] v.
bring (by car); import; deliver
przywódca [pshi-**vood**-tsa] m.
leader; ringleader; chieftain
przywóz [pshi-voos] m. import;
delivery; transport; carriage
przywracać [pshi-**vra**-tsaćh] v.
restore; bring back; reappoint
przywrócenie [pshi-vroo-tse-ńe]
n. restoration; reinstatement
przywyknąć [pshi-vi-**known**ćh]
v. get accustomed; get used
przyznać [pshi-znaćh] v. ad-
mit; award; allow; grant; acknowledge; recognize; concede
przyzwalać [pshi-zva-laćh] v.
consent; approve; agree; concede; acquiesce in; assent to
przyzwoitość [pshi-zvo-ee-
-tośhćh] f. decency; propriety; decorum; ordinary decency
przyzwoity [pshi-zvo-ee-ti] adj.
m. decent; proper; seemly; becoming; suitable; appropriate
przyzwolenie [pshi-zvo-le-ńe] n.
consent; acquiescence; assent
przyzwyczajać [pshi-zvi-**cha**-
-yaćh] v. accustom; habituate
przyzwyczajenie [pshi-zvi-cha-**ye**-
-ńe] n. habit; custom
przyzywać [pshi-zi-vaćh] v.
call in; call sb.; beckon; sign
psalm [psalm] m. psalm
pseudonim [psew-do-ńeem] m.
pen name; fictitious name
psiarnia [**pśhar**-ńa] f. kennel
psie pieniądze [pśhe pye-**nown**-
-dze] dirt cheap; dog cheap
psikus [pśhee-koos] m. prank
psota [pso-ta] f. prank; mischief;
practical joke; (nasty) trick
psotnik [psot-ńeek] m. prank-
ster; practical joker; jester;
scamp; roguish kid; tomboy
pstrąg [pstrowng] m. trout; kelt
pstry [pstri] adj. m. mottled;
speckled; spotted; colorful
pstry [pstri] adj. m. gaudy;
showy in bad taste; freaked
psuć [psooćh] v. spoil; decay;
waste; corrupt; deprave; damage; put out of order; mess

up; throw out of gear; injure
psychiatra [psi-**khyat**-ra] m.
psychiatrist; shrink; alienist
psychiczny [psi-**kheech**-ni] adj.
m. mental (state, disease)
psycholog [psi-**kho**-lok] m.
psychologist; behaviorist dealing with mental processes
pszczelarstwo [pshche-lar-stvo]
n. beekeeping; apiculture
pszczelarz [**pshche**-lash] m.
beekeeper; apiarist
pszczoła [**pshcho**-wa] f. bee
pszenica [pshe-**ńee**-tsa] f. wheat
ptactwo [**ptats**-tvo] pl. fowl;
birds; the species of birds
ptak [ptak] m. bird; fowl
ptaszek [pta-shek] m. little bird;
small bird; confidence man
publicysta [poo-blee-**tsis**-ta] m.
columnist; journalist
publiczność [poo-**bleech**-
-nośhćh] pl. public; com-
munity; audience; the house
publikacja [poo-blee-**kats**-ya] f.
publication; something publish-
ed (as a periodical, book, etc.)
puch [pookh] m. down; fluff
puchacz [poo-khach] m. eagle
owl (night bird of prey)
puchar [poo-khar] m. cup; bowl
puchlina wodna [pookh-lee-na
vod-na] f. dropsy; hydropsy
puchnąć [pookh-<u>nown</u>ćh] v.
swell; (sport) flag
puchowy [poo-**kho**-vi] adj. m.
downy; fluffy; eiderdown
pucołowaty [poo-tso-wo-**va**-ti]
adj. m. chubby (-cheeked)
pucz [pooch] m. Putsch
pudełko [poo-**dew**-ko] n. (small)
box; tin; can; hand box
puder [poo-der] m. powder
puderniczka [poo-der-**ńeech**-ka]
f. powder box; compact; puff
box; a small cosmetic case
pukać [poo-**kać**h] v. knock; rap
pugilares [poo-gee-la-res] m.
billfold; pocket book; wallet
pukiel [poo-kyel] m. curl; lock
pula [poo-la] f. pool; kitty
pularda [poo-lar-da] f. poularde;
fattened boiler (chicken)

pulchny [**pool**-khni] adj. m.
plump; mellow; loose; spongy
pulower [poo-lo-ver] m. pull-over
pulpit [**pool**-peet] m. desk;
lectern; shelf; book rest
puls [pools] m. pulse; vibration
pulsować [pool-**so**-vaćh] v.
pulsate; palpitate; throb;
vibrate; beat rhythmically
pułap [poo-wap] m. ceiling
pułapka [poo-**wap**-ka] f. trap
pułk [poowk] m. regiment; group
pułkownik [poow-**kov**-ńeek] m.
colonel; group captain
pumeks [poo-meks] m. pumice
punkt [poonkt] m. point; mark
punktualny [poon-ktoo-**al**-ni] adj.
m. punctual; exact; prompt
pupa [poo-pa] f. behind;
buttocks; bottom; an ass
pupil [poo-peel] m. ward; pupil;
favorite; pet (like a pet)
purchawka [poor-**khav**-ka] f. puff
-ball (lycoperdon)
purchawka [poor-**khav**-ka] f.
grumpy fellow
purpura [poor-**poo**-ra] f. purple
purytanin [poo-ri-ta-**ńeen**] m.
Puritan; man of strict religion
pustelnia [poos-tel-**ńa**] f.
hermitage; solitary secluded
place; secluded retreat
pustelnik [poos-**stel**-ńeek] m.
hermit; (secluded) recluse
pustka [**poost**-ka] f. solitude;
empty (place); emptiness; void
pustkowie [poost-**ko**-vye] n.
deserted place; desert; solitude; barren desolation
pustoszyć [poos-to-**shić**h] v.
devastate; ravage; lay waste;
overrun; override; ruin
pusty [**poos**-ti] adj. m. empty
pustynia [poos-ti-**ńa**] f. desert
puszcza [**poosh**-cha] f. primeval
forest; wilderness
puszczać [poosh-**chać**h] v. let
go; let fall; set afloat; free;
fade; drop; let out; emit; start;
release; relinquish (a hold)
puszczać się [**poosh**-chaćh
ś<u>han</u>] v. draw apart; dart after; let go; be a permissive

girl; go to bed with; set out
puszek [poo-shek] m. down
puszka blaszana [poosh-ka bla-
-sha-na] tin can; tin box
puszysty [poo-shis-ti] adj. m.
downy; fluffy (snow); flossy;
flaky (snow); nappy (carpet)
puścić [poosh-ćheeć] v. let
go; let free; release; let fall
puzon [poo-zon] m. trombone
(one octave below trumpet)
pycha [pi-kha] f. 1. pride;
conceit; haughtiness
pycha [pi-kha] f. 2. excellent tid-
-bit; fine stuff
pykać [pi-kać] v. puff; pop
pylić [pi-leeć] v. dust; be
dusty; rise dust; pollen
pył [piw] m. dust; powder
pyskować [pis-ko-vać] v. be
saucy; bark; bawl
pysk [pisk] m. muffle; snout;
mug; muzzle; phiz; rowdyism
pyskaty [pis-ka-ti] adj. m.
foulmouthed; saucy; pert;
bawling (quarrelsome)
pyszałek [pi-sha-wek] m.
boaster; braggart; coxcomb
pysznić się [pish-ńeeć śhan]
v. swagger; prance; swank;
strut; put on airs; flaunt
pysznie [pish-ńe] adv. proudly;
admirably; in grand fashion
pytać [pi-tać] v. ask; inquire;
question; interrogate
pytanie [pi-ta-ńe] n. question;
inquiry; query; interrogation
pytel [pi-tel] m. bolter
pytlować [pit-lo-vać] v. sift;
bolt (flour); be a chatterbox
pyton [pi-ton] m. python
pyza [pi-za] f. dumpling
pyzaty [pi-za-ti] adj. m. chubby;
full-cheeked; full-moon face

R

rab [rab] m. slave; servant

rabarbar [ra-bar-bar] m. rhubarb
rabat [ra-bat] m. discount;
rebate; reduction (in price)
rabin [ra-been] m. rabbi
rabować [ra-bo-vać] v. rob;
maraud; plunder; pirate; take
by force; steal; pirate
rabunek [ra-boo-nek] m. robbery;
plunder; holdup; depredation
rabuś [ra-boośh] m. robber;
plunderer; pillager; holdup man
rachityczny [ra-khee-tich-ni] adj.
m. rickety; rachitic
rachmistrz [rakh-meestsh] m.
(public) accountant; calculator
rachować [ra-kho-vać] v.
calculate; count; reckon; compute; rely; estimate; suppose
rachunek [ra-khoo-nek] m. bill to
be paid or settled; account;
calculation; sum; addition
rachunkowość [ra-khoon-ko-
-vośhćh] f. book-keeping
racica [ra-ćhee-tsa] f. cloven
hoof; cow hoof; split hoof
racja [ra-tsya] f. reason; right;
ration; propriety; correctness
racjonalizować [ra-tsyo-na-lee-
-zo-vać] v. rationalize (food,
etc.); improve (a process)
racjonalny [ra-tsyo-nal-ni] adj. m.
rational; reasonable; sensible
raczej [ra-chey] adv. rather;
sooner (than); rather than
raczkować [rach-ko-vać] v. go
on all fours; crawl on all four
raczyć [ra-chić] v. treat
to; condescend; deign; stoop
to do; treat; be pleased to do
rad [rad] adj. m. pleased; glad
rad [rad] m. radium
rada [ra-da] f. advice; counsel
radar [ra-dar] m. radar
radca [rad-tsa] m. advisor;
counselor; legal advisor
radcostwo [rad-tsos-tvo]
n. councillorship; post of a
(legal) advisor (councillor)
radio [ra-dyo] n. radio; wireless;
broadcasting (system)
radiofonia [ra-dyo-fo-ńya] f.
broadcasting; radiotelephony
radioaktywny [ra-dyo-ak-tiv-ni]

adj. m. radioactive
radiostacja [ra-dyo-**stats**-ya] f.
radio station
radiodepesza [ra-dyo-de-pe-sha]
f. radio telegram
radioterapia [ra-dyo-te-ra-pya] f.
radiotherapy; X-ray teraphy
radny [rad-ni] m. alderman
radosny [ra-dos-ni] adj. m. gay;
glad; festive (day etc.)
radość [ra-dośhćh] f. joy;
gladness; delight; merriment;
glee; feeling of happiness
radykalny [ra-di-kal-ni] adj. m.
radical; man of radical views
radykał [ra-di-kaw] m. radical
radzić [ra-dźheećh] v.
deliberate; suggest; give an
advice; (give, hold) counsel
radziecki [ra-dźhets-kee] adj. m.
Soviet; of Soviet Union
(should use "**sowiecki**")
rafa [ra-fa] f. reef; rim; ripple
rafineria [ra-fee-ne-rya] f.
refinery; refining works
rafinować [ra-fee-no-vaćh] v.
refine; purify; distill
raid [rayd]m. sport rally (race)
raj [ray] m. paradise; heaven
rak [rak] m. crayfish; cancer
rakieta [ra-kye-ta] f. rocket; flare
rakieta [ra-kye-ta] f. (tennis)
racket; a light bat for tennis
rama [ra-ma] f. frame; scheme;
case; stretcher (for oil canvas)
ramie [ra-myan] n. shoulder
ramowy [ra-mo-vi] adj. m. frame
rampa [ram-pa] f. ramp; loading
platform; bar; barrier; float
rana [ra-na] f. wound; injury;
sore; hurt (to man, plant etc.)
randka [rand-ka] f. date
ranek [ra-nek] m. morning; day
-break; break of day
ranga [ran-ga] f. rank; standing
ranić [ra-ńeećh] v. wound;
hurt; inflict a wound; maul
ranny [ran-ni] adj. m. 1. wound-
-ed, injured person; casualty
ranny [ran-ni] adj. m. morning;
early morning (hours, time)
rano [ra-no] adv. early
rano [ra-no] adv. morning;

forenoon; too early
rapier [ra-pyer] m. rapier
raport [ra-port] m. report;
account; statement; log
raptem [rap-tem] adv. suddenly;
abruptly; no more than; all in
all; all of a sudden
raptowny [rap-tov-ni] adj. m.
abrupt; sudden; impulsive; unexpected; heady; impetuous
rasa [ra-sa] f. race; stock; breed;
(plant) variety; blood
rasizm [ra-śheezm] m. racism
rasowy [ra-so-vi] adj. m. racial;
thoroughbred; purebred; racy
raszpla [rash-pla] f. rasp
rata [ra-ta] f. instalment
(payment); part payment (plan)
ratować [ra-to-vaćh] v. rescue
(from drowning); save; deliver
(from danger, predicament)
ratownictwo [ra-tov-ńeets-tvo]
n. life saving (system)
ratownik [ra-tov-ńeek] m. life
-guard; rescuer; life saver
ratunek [ra-too-nek] m. rescue;
salvation; help; assistance; the
last resort; deliverance
ratunkowy pas [ra-toon-ko-vi
pas] m. life belt; life jacket
ratusz [ra-toosh] m. city hall
ratyfikacja [ra-ti-fee-kats-ya] f.
ratification; validation
raut [rawt] m. evening party
raz [ras] m. 1. one time
raz [ras] m. 2. blow; stroke
raz [ras] adv. 3. once; at one
time; at last; time being
razem [ra-zem] adv. together
razić [ra-źheećh] v. 1. strike
razić [ra-źheećh] v. 2. offend
razić [ra-źheećh] v. 3. dazzle;
shock; hit
razowy [ra-zo-vi] adj. m. brown
(bread); whole meal (bread)
razowiec [ra-zo-vyets] m. brown
bread; whole meal bread
rażący [ra-zhown-tsi] adj. m.
1. glaring; gaudy; blinding
rażący [ra-zhown-tsi] adj. m.
2. flagrant; rank; gross
raźnie [ra-źhńe] adv.
cheerfully; briskly; at a lively

pace; safely; securely
rąb [rownb] m. rim; pane;
clearing of a forest
rąbać [rown-baćh] v. chop;
hew; fell (trees); hack out ice
rąbać [rown-baćh] v. say truth
to somebody's face; slash
rączka [rownch-ka] f. handle;
small hand; handgrip; holder
rączy [rown-chi] adj. m. swift
rdza [rdza] f. rust; mildew; blight
rdzenny [rdzen-ni] adj. m.
essential; original; specific
rdzeń [rdzeń] m. core; pith;
marrow; gist; essence; log
rdzoodporny [rdzo-od-por-ni] adj.
m. rust-proof; stainless
rdzewieć [rdze-vyećh] v.
corrode; rust; get rusty; gather rust; get the color of rust
reagować [re-a-go-vaćh] v.
react; respond; be susceptible
reakcja [re-ak-tsya] f. reaction
reakcjonista [re-ak-tsyo-ńees-ta]
m. reactionary
reakcyjny [re-ak-tsiy-ni] adj. m.
reactionary; retrograde
reaktywować [re-ak-ti-vo-vaćh]
v. start (make active) again
reaktywować [re-ak-ti-vo-vaćh]
v. reactivate; bring back to life
(military duty); recall
realia [re-al-ya] pl. realia; realities
realista [re-a-lees-ta] m. realist;
advocate of realism
realizm [re-a-leezm] m. realism
facing facts; being practical
realizować [re-a-lee-zo-vaćh] v.
actualize; realize; cash (assets)
realność [re-al-nośhćh] f. real
estate; land including buildings
realność [re-al-nośhćh] f.
reality; the real (fact)
realny [re-al-ni] adj. m. real;
concrete; actual; genuine; true
rebelia [re-be-lya] f. rebellion;
uprising against government
recenzent [re-tsen-zent] m. critic;
reviewer (of books, plays)
recenzja [re-tsen-zya] f. review
(of books, plays, etc.)
recepcja [re-tsep-tsya] f.
reception (desk, office); formal

social function
recepis [re-tse-pees] m. receipt;
recipe; written receipt
recepta [re-tsep-ta] f.
prescription; doctor's order
rechot [re-khot] m. shrieking;
laughter; croak (of frogs)
recydywista [re-tsi-di-vees-ta] m.
recidivist; old offender
recytować [re-tsi-to-vaćh] v.
recite; give a recitation
redagować [re-da-go-vaćh] v.
edit; draw up; formulate; draft
redakcja [re-dak-tsya] f. editing
redakcja [re-dak-tsya] f. editor's
office; editorial stuff
redaktor [re-dak-tor] m. editor
redukcja [re-dook-tsya] f.
reduction (in size, price, etc.)
redukować [re-doo-ko-vaćh] v.
reduce; lay off; cut down
referat [re-fe-rat] m. report
referencja [re-fe-ren-tsya] f.
reference; testimonial
referent [re-fe-rent] m. clerk
refleks [re-fleks] m. reflex
refleksja [re-fleks-ya] f.
reflection; thought; cogitation
reflektor [re-flek-tor] m. reflector;
searchlight; headlight
reflektować [re-flek-to-vaćh] v.
1. apply for; want; make a bid
reflektować [re-flek-to-vaćh] v.
2. reflect; bring (listen) to
reason; moderate; restrain
reforma [re-for-ma] f. reform
reformacja [re-for-mats-ya] f.
reformation; Reformation
reformować [re-for-mo-vaćh] v.
reform; reorganize
regaty [re-ga-ti] pl. boat race
regencja [re-gen-tsya] f. regency;
regency style (in furniture)
regionalny [re-gyo-nal-ni] adj. m.
regional; local
regulacja [re-goo-lats-ya] f.
regulation; control; regulator
regularny [re-goo-lar-ni] adj. m.
regular; even; systematic
regulować [re-goo-lo-vaćh] v.
1. regulate; control; set (time)
regulować [re-goo-lo-vaćh] v.
2. settle; adjust; regularize

reguła [re-goo-wa] f. rule; law
rehabilitować [re-kha-bee-lee-to-
-vaćh] v. rehabilitate
reja [re-ya] f. yardarm
rejent [re-yent] m. notary public;
notary's office; regent
rejestr [re-yestr] m. register; file;
index; roll; register mark
rejestracja [re-yes-trats-ya] f.
registration; licensing
rejestrować [re-yes-tro-vaćh] v.
register; enroll; record
rejon [re-yon] m. region
rejwach [rey-vakh] m. uproar;
hullabaloo; row; hurly-burly
rekin [re-keen] m. shark
reklama [re-kla-ma] f.
advertising; publicity (commercial, political, etc.)
reklamacja [re-kla-mats-ya] f.
complaint; demand for compensation, damages, etc.
reklamować [re-kla-mo-vaćh] v.
complain; make formal charge
reklamować [re-kla-mo-vaćh] v.
advertise; make publicity
rekolekcje [re-ko-lek-tsye] pl.
retreat; period of contemplation (in a quiet place)
rekomendacja [re-ko-men-dats-
-ya] f. recommendation;
(personal, etc.) reference
rekompensata [re-kom-pen-sa-ta]
f. compensation; recompense
rekonwalescent [re-kon-va-les-
-tsent] m. convalescent
rekord [re-kord] m. (sports)
record; (world) record
rekordzista [re-kor-dźhees-ta] m.
record holder; champion
rekreacja [re-kre-ats-ya] f.
recreation; amusement
rekrut [re-kroot] m. recruit;
conscript; recently enlisted
man; sl. rookie; rooky
rekrutować [re-kroo-to-vaćh] v.
recruit; enlist (new people)
rektor [rek-tor] m. university
president; university head
rektyfikować [re-kti-fee-ko-
-vaćh] v. rectify; correct; put
right; purify; convert current
rekwizycja [re-kvee-zits-ya] f.

requisition; seizure
relacja [re-lats-ya] f. report
relacja [re-lats-ya] f. rate; relation
relatywizm [re-la-ti-veezm] m.
relativity; relativism
relegacja [re-le-gats-ya] f.
expulsion; relegation; exile
religia [re-lee-gya] f. religion
religijny [re-lee-geey-ni] adj. m.
religious; godly; sacred
relikwia [re-leek-vya] f. relic
remanent [re-ma-nent] m.
remainder; inventory; stock
remis [re-mees] m. (sport) draw
remiza [re-mee-za] f. engine
-shed; engine-house; depot;
barn; coach-house; fire-station
remont [re-mont] m. 1. repair(s)
remont [re-mont] m. 2. (horse)
remount; replacement horse
remontować [re-mon-to-vaćh]
v. repair; recondition; overhaul
renumeracja [re-noo-me-rats-ya]
f. re-enumeration; recount
ren [ren] m. reindeer; caribou
renegat [re-ne-gat] m. renegade
renifer [re-ńee-fer] m. reindeer;
(domesticated) arctic deer
renoma [re-no-ma] f. renown
renta [ren-ta] f. rent; fixed
income; annuity; pension
rentowność [ren-tov-nośhćh]
f. profitability; earning capacity; financial feasibility
rentgenolog [rent-ge-no-lok] m.
radiologist; roentgenologist
rentowny [ren-tov-ni] adj. m.
profitable; remunerative
reorganizacja [re-or-ga-ńee-zats-
-ya] f. reorganization
reperacja [re-pe-rats-ya] f. repair
reperacja [re-pe-rats-ya] f.
reparation; war reparation
repatriacja [re-pat-ryats-ya] f.
repatriation (home, etc.)
reperować [re-pe-ro-vaćh] v.
mend; repair; fix; set right
repertuar [re-per-too-ar] m.
repertory; repertoire
repetycja [re-pe-tits-ya] f.
repetition (of a lesson etc.)
replika [re-plee-ka] 1. f. replica;
2. f. rebuttal; 3. f. (theatre)

cue; retort; rejoinder
replikować [re-plee-ko-vaćh] v.
  answer back; rejoin; retort
reportaż [re-por-tash] m. account
reportaż [re-por-tash] m. report-
  ing; commentary; coverage (of
  an event, news report, etc.)
represja [re-pre-sya] f. reprisal;
  repressive measures, etc.
reprezentacja [re-pre-zen-tats-ya]
  f. representation; dignity
reprezentant [re-pre-zen-tant] m.
  representative (typical)
reprezentować [re-pre-zen-to-
  -vaćh] v. represent; display
reprodukcja [re-pro-dook-tsya] f.
  reproduction; copy; replica
republika [re-poo-blee-ka] f.
  republic (based on elections)
republikański [re-poo-blee-kań-
  -skee] adj. m. republican
reputacja [re-poo-tats-ya] f.
  reputation; (character)
resor [re-sor] m. (car) spring
resort [re-sort] m. 1. agency
resort [re-sort] m. 2. competence; scope; province
respekt [res-pekt] m. respect
restauracja [res-taw-rats-ya] f.
  1. restaurant; diner
restauracja [res-taw-rats-ya] f.
  2. restoration (of objects of
  art, historic buildings, etc.)
restrykcja [res-trik-tsya] f.
  restriction; reservation
restytucja [res-ti-toots-ya] f.
  restitution; restoration
reszta [resh-ta] f. rest; reminder;
  change; residue; the rest
retoryka [re-to-ri-ka] f. rhetoric;
  manual (text) of rhetorics
retusz [re-toosh] m. retouch
retuszować [re-too-sho-vaćh] v.
  touch up; retouch
reumatyczny [rew-ma-tich-ni]
  adj. m. rheumatic
reumatyzm [rew-ma-tizm] m.
  rheumatism (pain in the joints)
rewanż [re-vansh] m. 1. rematch
rewanż [re-vansh] m. 2. re-
  -venge; recompense, etc.
rewelacja [re-ve-lats-ya] f.
  revelation; striking disclosure

rewers [re-vers] m. 1. receipt
rewers [re-vers] m. 2. reverse
  (side of a coin, etc.)
rewia [re-vya] f. parade
rewia [re-vya] f. (theatre) revue
rewidować [re-vee-do-vaćh] v.
  revise; reconsider; review
rewidować [re-vee-do-vaćh] v.
  house-search; make a search
rewidować [re-vee-do-vaćh] v.
  audit (accounts); inspect
rewizja [re-veez-ya] f. revision;
  search; audit; inspection; re-
  trial; (customs) examination
rewizjonizm [re-veez-yo-ńeezm]
  m. revisionism (change)
rewizyta [re-vee-zi-ta] f. return
  (somebody's) visit
rewolucja [re-vo-loots-ya] f.
  revolution; complete change
rewolucyjny [re-vo-loo-tsiy-ni]
  adj. m. revolutionary
rewolwer [re-vol-ver] m.
  revolver; hand gun (with revolving cylinder)
rezerwa [re-zer-va] f. reserve
rezerwat [re-zer-vat] m.
  reservation; game preserve
rezerwować [re-zer-vo-vaćh] v.
  reserve; set aside; book
rezerwuar [re-zer-voo-ar] m.
  reservoir; (storage) tank
rezolutny [re-zo-loot-ni] adj. m.
  resolute; determined; game
rezonans [re-zo-nans] m.
  resonance (intensifying vibrations, often destructive)
rezultat [re-zool-tat] m. result;
  effect; numerical answer
rezydencja [re-zi-den-tsya] f.
  residence; dwelling place
rezydent [re-zi-dent] m. resident
  (permanent, not a transient)
rezygnacja [re-zig-nats-ya] f. f.
  resignation; patient submission
reżim [re-zheem] m. regime
reżyser [re-zhi-ser] m. stage
  manager; (film) director
ręcznie [ranch-ńe] adv. by hand
ręcznik [ranch-ńeek] m. towel
ręczny [ranch-ni] adj. m. manual;
  hand made; wrist (watch)
ręczyć [ran-chićh] v. guarantee

ręka [ran-ka] f. hand; arm; touch
rękaw [ran-kav] m. sleeve
rękawica [ran-ka-vee-tsa] f.
  mitten; gauntlet; mitt; glove
rękawiczka [ran-ka-veech-ka] f.
  glove (fur lined, velvet, etc.)
rękodzielnik [ran-ko-dźhel-ńeek]
  m. craftsman; handicraftsman
rękojeść [ran-ko-yeśhćh] f.
  hilt; handle; handgrip; helve
rękojmia [ran-koy-mya] f.
  guarantee; pledge (to replace);
  gage (security); warranty
rękopis [ran-ko-pees] m.
  manuscript; script; MS
robactwo [ro-bats-tvo] n. vermin
robak [ro-bak] m. worm; beetle;
  grub; maggot; anxiety; worry
rober [ro-ber] m. (bridge) rubber
  (in a card game of bridge)
robić [ro-beećh] v. make; do;
  act; work; become; get; feel;
  turn; knit; raise (an alarm)
robociarz [ro-bo-ćhash] m.
  common laborer (slang);
  mechanic; working man
robocizna [ro-bo-ćheez-na] f.
  wages; cost of labor; labor
roboczogodzina [ro-bo-cho-go-
  -dźhee-na] f. man-hour
robot [ro-bot] m. robot
robota [ro-bo-ta] f. work; job
robotnica [ro-bot-ńee-tsa] f.
  workwoman; operative; factory girl; female farmhand
robotnik [ro-bot-ńeek] m.
  worker; operative; mechanic
robótki [ro-boot-kee] pl.
  needlework; fancy work
rocznica [roch-ńee-tsa] f.
  anniversary
rocznie [roch-ńe] adv. yearly
rocznik [roch-ńeek] m. annual;
  yearbook; annual set (volume,
  edition, etc.); age group
roczny [roch-ni] adj. m. annual;
  one year's (duration etc.)
rodak [ro-dak] m. compatriot
rodowity [ro-do-vee-ti] adj. m.
  native; by birth; true-born
rodowód [ro-do-voot] m.
  genealogy; origin; pedigree;
  descent; lineage; filiation

rodzaj [ro-dzay] m. kind; sort;
  gender; type; race; manner; a-
  spect; nature; type; genre
rodzajnik [ro-dzay-ńeek] m.
  article (definite od indefinite)
rodzeństwo [ro-dzeń-stvo] n.
  siblings; brothers and sisters
rodzice [ro-dźhee-tse] pl.
  parents; father and mother
rodzić [ro-dźheećh] v. bear;
  procreate breed; yield (crops)
rodzina [ro-dźhee-na] f. family
rodzinny [ro-dźheen-ni] adj. m.
  family; native; home (life etc.)
rodzynek [ro-dzi-nek] m. raisin;
  currant; plum (for cakes)
rogacz [ro-gach] m. stag
rogacz [ro-gach] m. cuckold;
  deer; stag; deceived husband
rogatka [ro-gat-ka] f. toll-gate;
  toll-bar; toll-booth; turnpike
rogaty [ro-ga-ti] adj. m. horned;
  haughty; deceived (husband)
rogatywka [ro-ga-tiv-ka] f. four
  -corned cap (Polish style)
rogowacieć [ro-go-va-ćhećh]
  v. grow horny; become horny;
  grow (become) corneous
rogowaty [ro-go-va-ti] adj. m.
  corneous; horny; keratose
rogówka [ro-goov-ka] f. cornea
rogóżka [ro-goozh-ka] f. (door)
  mat (flat, woven of straw)
roić [ro-yeećh] v. 1. dream;
  imagine or fancy (all sorts of
  things, very many things)
roić [ro-yeećh] v. swarm; teem;
  run; be alive with; crawl
rojalista [ro-ya-lees-ta] m.
  royalist; supporter of the king
rojny [roy-ni] adj. m. teeming;
  swarming (crowds etc.)
rojowisko [ro-yo-vees-ko] n. hive;
  swarm; gathering place
rok [rok] m. year; a twelvemonth
rok przestępny [rok pzhe-stanp-
  -ni] leap year (bissextile)
rokować [ro-ko-vaćh] v. 1. negotiate; augur (ill, well)
rokować [ro-ko-vaćh] v. 2. expect; promise oneself; hope
rokowania [ro-ko-va-ńa] 1. pl.
  negotiations 2. pl. prognosis

rola [ro-la] 1. f. arable land
2. f. (theatre) part; scroll;
weight; (political, etc.) role
rolka [rol-ka] f. roll; spool; reel;
runner; pulley; castor; trolley
rolnictwo [rol-ńeets-tvo] n.
agriculture; farming; animal
husbandry; land cultivation
rolnik [rol-ńeek] m. farmer
romans [ro-mans] 1. m. novel
of love, adventure, etc.
2. love affair; liaison
romantyczny [ro-man-tich-ni] adj.
m. romantic; full of romance
romantyk [ro-man-tik] m. romantic; not practical; visionary;
suited for (full of) romance
romantyzm [ro-man-tizm] m.
romanticism (literary style)
romański [ro-mań-skee] adj. m.
Romance; Romanesque
romb [romb] m. rhomb; diamond
rondel [ron-del] m. stew-pan
rondo [ron-do] n. brim; circular
plaza; traffic circle; circus
ronić [ro-ńeećh] v. 1. shed
ronić [ro-ńeećh] v. 2. miscarry; drop; cast; emit; moult
ropa [ro-pa] f. 1. puss
ropa [ro-pa] f. 2. crude oil; rock
oil; naphtha; petroleum
ropieć [ro-pyećh] v. fester;
have oozing sore; suppurate
ropień [ro-pyeń] m. abscess
ropny [rop-ni] adj. m. purulent;
oil fired; oil- (derrick etc.)
ropucha [ro-poo-kha] f. toad
rosa [ro-sa] f. dew
rosły [ros-wi] adj. m. tall; big
frame; stalwart; strong; sturdy
rosnąć [ros-nownćh] v. grow
rosół [ro-soow] m. broth;
bouillon; clear soup; pickle
rostbef [rost-bef] m. roast-beef;
baked beef; (beef or ox) rump
rosyjski [ro-siy-skee] adj. m.
Russian; of Russia
roszczenie [rosh-che-ńe] n.
claim; pretension; pretence
rościć [rośh-ćheećh] v. claim
roślina [rośh-lee-na] f. plant;
vegetable; living plant
roślinność [rośh-leen-

-nośhćh] f. flora; vegetation
rowek [ro-vek] m. (small)
channel; groove; (small) gutter; rut; furrow
rower [ro-ver] n. bike; cycle
rowerzysta [ro-ve-zhis-ta] m.
cyclist; a cycle rider
rozbawiony [roz-ba-vyo-ni] adj.
m. merry; amused; in high
spirits; in festive mood
rozbestwić [roz-best-veećh] v.
enrage; turn into a wild beast
rozbicie [roz-bee-ćhe] n. break;
wreck; jumble; defeat; rout;
hurt; smash; breakage; failure
rozbić [roz-beećh] v. smash;
defeat; wreck; shatter; disrupt
rozbiegać się [roz-bye-gaćh
śhan] v. scatter; run in all directions; swarm; take off; bolt
rozbierać [roz-bye-raćh] v.
undress (somebody); strip; dismount; seize; analyze; divide
rozbieżny [roz-byezh-ni] adj. m.
divergent; different; discordant
rozbijać [roz-bee-yaćh] v. break
up; rout; crush; bluster; storm
rozbiór [roz-byoor] m. analysis
rozbiór [roz-byoor] m.
dismemberment; partition
rozbiórka [roz-byoor-ka] f.
demolition; taking to pieces
rozbitek [roz-bee-tek] m. ship
-wrecked person; castaway;
wreck; down-and-out; waif
rozbój [roz-booy] m. robbery;
piracy; banditry; high-jacking
rozbójnik [roz-booy-ńeek] m.
bandit; robber; cutthroat; hi-
jacker; brigand; highwayman
rozbrajać [roz-bra-yaćh] v.
disarm (a person, a country, a
mine, etc.); dismantle (a ship);
appease; pacify
rozbrat [roz-brat] m. split;
dis-union; gap between two
things; break with somebody
rozbrojenie [roz-bro-ye-ńe] n.
disarmament; reduction of
arms; discharge (a battery)
rozbrojeniowy [roz-bro-ye-ńo-vi]
adj. m. disarmament
rozbrzmiewać [roz-bzhmye-

-vać] v. resound; ring out; re
(echo); sound with (applause)
rozbudowa [roz-boo-do-va] f.
build up; extension; expansion
rozbudować [roz-boo-do-vać]
v. extend; enlarge; expand;
develop; increase in size etc.
rozbudzić [roz-boo-dźheeć] v.
rouse up; wake up; excite; stir
rozchmurzyć [roz-khmoo-zhić]
v. clear up; brighten up
rozchodzić [roz-kho-dźheeć]
v. 1. stretch, wear (shoes)
rozchodzić [roz-kho-dźheeć]
v. 2. spread come apart
rozchodzić [roz-kho-dźheeć]
v. 3. get into the swing of
walking, marching, etc.
rozchód [roz-khoot] m.
expenditure; expenses etc.
rozchwytać [roz-khvi-tać] v.
snatch up; scramble for;
sweep off; snatch away
rozchylać [roz-khi-lać] v.
open; force apart; spread
rozciągać [roz-ćhown-gać] v.
stretch; extend; widen; expand; distend; dilate; spread
rozcieńczyć [roz-ćheń-chić]
v. thin (down); dilute; rarefy;
attenuate; weaken with water
rozcierać [roz-ćhe-rać] v. rub;
grind; crush; spread (ointment)
rozcinać [roz-ćhee-nać] v. cut
up (open); dissect; rip open
rozczarować [roz-cha-ro-vać]
v. disappoint disenchant
rozczesać [roz-che-sać] v.
comb down; brush out (hair)
rozczłonkować [roz-chwon-ko-
-vać] v. dismember; divide
up; break up; partition
rozczulić [roz-choo-leeć] v.
move; touch; affect; stir
(feelings, the heart, soul etc.)
rozczyn [roz-chin] m. solution
(chem.); leaven (yeast)
rozdać [roz-dać] v. distribute;
give away; deal out; dispense
rozdarcie [roz-dar-ćhe] n. tear
rozdarcie [roz-dar-ćhe] n.
disruption; (internal) split
rozdeptać [roz-dep-tać]

v. trample (crush, grind) under
foot; tread on (out of shape)
rozdęcie [roz-dan-ćhe] n.
swelling; inflation; expansion
rozdmuchać [roz-dmoo-khać]
v. fan; inflate; blow about;
amplify; scatter; dishevel hair
rozdrapać [roz-dra-pać] v.
1. scratch (a pimple, etc.)
rozdrapać [roz-dra-pać] v.
2. snatch up; scramble for
rozdrażnić [roz-drazh-ńeeć] v.
irritate; exasperate; vex
rozdrobnić [roz-drob-ńeeć] v.
split up; divide; crumble; morsel; fritter down; granulate
rozdroże [roz-dro-zhe] n.
crossroads; parting of the
ways; condition of doubt etc.
rozdwoić [roz-dvo-eeć] v.
split; cleave; divide in two
rozdymać [roz-di-mać] v.
inflate; swell; expand; puff out
rozdział [roz-dźhaw] m.
distribution; disunion; parting
(hair); dispensation; chapter
rozdzielać [roz-dźhe-lać] v.
divide; distribute; set at odds
rozdzierać [roz-dźhe-rać] v.
tear up; tear asunder; rend;
pierce; rip open; break (heart)
rozdźwięk [roz-dźhvyank] m.
discord; dissonance; clash
rozebrać [ro-zeb-rać] v.
undress; analyze; take apart
rozedma [ro-zed-ma] f.
emphysema (distended lungs
deprived of elasticity)
rozejm [ro-zeym] m. truce
rozejrzeć się [ro-zey-zheć
śhan] v. look around
rozejść się [ro-zeyśhćh
śhan] v. split; part; separate
rozerwać się [ro-zer-vać
śhan] v. divert oneself; get
torn; burst; come apart; snap
rozgałęzić [roz-ga-wan-
-źheeć] v. branch out; fork
off (out); branch off; ramify
rozgałęzienie [roz-ga-wan-żhe-
-ńe] n. branching; ramification
rozgardiasz [roz-gard-yash] m.
bustle; chaos; confusion

rozgarnąć [roz-**gar**-no**wn**ćh] v.
rake aside; part; brush apart
rozgarnięty [roz-gar-**ńan**-ti] adj.
m. bright; clever; sharp
rozglądać się [roz-**glown**-daćh
śhan] v. look around; look for
rozgłaszać [roz-**gwa**-shaćh] v.
make known ; broadcast
rozgłos [roz-gwos] m. publicity;
fame; renown; repute; notorie-
ty; publication; promulgation
rozgłośnia [roz-**gwośh**-ńa] f.
broadcasting station
rozgmatwać [roz-**gmat**-vaćh] v.
disentangle; extricate
rozgnieść [roz-gńeśhćh] v.
flatten; squash (once)
rozgniatać [roz-**gńa**-taćh] v.
squash; flatten (often)
rozgniewać [roz-**gńe**-vaćh] v.
anger; vex; irritate
rozgoryczenie [roz-go-ri-che-ńe]
n. bitterness; exasperation
rozgoryczyć [roz-go-ri-chićh] v.
embitter; exacerbate; disgust
rozgotować [roz-go-to-vaćh] v.
cook to a pulp; cook to rags
rozgraniczyć [roz-gra-**ńee**-
-chićh] v. delimit; mark the
boundaries; demarcate; divide
rozgromić [roz-**gro**-meećh] v.
rout (the enemy); crush (an
army); put to the flight
rozgrywać [roz-**gri**-vaćh] v. play
one's game; put through a policy etc.; fight (a battle)
rozgryźć [roz-gri**źh**ćh] v. bite
through; bite in two; crack
(nuts, etc.); crush (a pill)
rozgrzać [roz-gzhaćh] v. warm
up; heat up; get hot; rouse
rozgrzebać [roz-**gzhe**-baćh] v.
dig up; rake up; scatter
rozgrzeszyć [roz-**gzhe**-shićh] v.
absolve (of sins); forgive
rozgrzewać [roz-**gzhe**-vaćh] v.
warm up; rouse; stimulate
rozhukany [roz-khoo-ka-ni] adj.
m. wild; unruly; riotous
rozhuśtać [roz-**khoośh**-taćh]
v. set swinging; set rocking
roziskrzyć [roz-**ees**-kzhićh] v.
start sparkle; make sparkle

rozjaśnić [roz-**yaśh**-ńeećh] v.
brighten; clear up; clarify
rozjątrzyć [roz-**yownt**-zhićh] v.
exasperate; irritate; chafe
rozjemca [roz-**yem**-tsa] m.
referee; arbiter; umpire
rozjeżdżać się [roz-**yezh**-
-dzhaćh **śhan**] v. disperse;
part; be for ever travelling
rozjuszyć [roz-**yoo**-shićh] v.
enrage; infuriate; exasperate
rozkapryszony [roz-ka-pri-**sho**-ni]
adj. m. whimsical; fitful
rozkaz [roz-kas] m. order
rozkiełznąć [roz-**kew**-
-zno**wn**ćh] v. unbridle; unchain; let (make) loose
rozkleić [roz-**kle**-eećh] v. 1.
unglue; unstick; weaken, etc.
rozkleić [roz-**kle**-eećh] v. 2.
post up (posters, notices, etc.)
rozkład [roz-kwat] m. dissolution;
decay; disposition; timetable;
train schedule; breakdown
rozkładać [roz-**kwa**-daćh] v.
decompose; spread; display;
stagger (hours); lay out; distribute; arrange; dispose
rozkołysać [roz-ko-**wi**-saćh] v.
set rocking; set swinging;
agitate; swing with great force
rozkopywać [roz-ko-pi-vaćh] v.
dig up; rip up; kick apart;
tumble; make excavations
rozkosz [roz-kosh] f. delight
rozkrajać [roz-**kra**-yaćh] v. cut
up; carve; slice; divide
rozkręcić [roz-**kran**-ćheećh] v.
unscrew; un-reel; take to
pieces; loosen a screw; uncurl
rozkruszyć [roz-**kroo**-shićh] v.
crush up; grind; disintegrate
rozkrzewić [roz-kzhe-veećh] v.
propagate; increase; diffuse
rozkuć [roz-koóćh] v.
unshackle; unshod (a horse);
unchain, un-fetter (a convict,
etc.); hammer out (a metal);
rozkulbaczyć [roz-kool-**ba**-
-chićh] v. unsaddle (a horse)
rozkupić [roz-**koo**-peećh] v. buy
up; buy everything; buy all
rozkwit [roz-kveet] m. bloom

rozkwitać [roz-**kvee**-tać] v.
burst into flower; bloom; o-
pen; blossom; beam; light up
rozlatywać się [roz-la-ti-vać
śhan] v. fly away; break up;
scatter; disperse; run away;
scamper away; burst asunder
rozlazły [roz-laz-wi] adj. m. slack;
loose; spread out; sloppy
rozległy [roz-leg-wi] adj. m.
spacious; vast; wide; far-
flung; extensive (knowledge)
rozleniwiać [roz-le-**ńee**-vyać]
v. make lazy; induce to laziness; induce to sloth
rozlepić [roz-le-peećh] v. post;
put up; paste up; stick; unstick (sheets of paper, etc.)
rozlew [roz-lev] m. flood
rozlew krwi [roz-lev **krvee**] m.
bloodshed; killing; slaughter
rozlewać [roz-le-vać] v. spill;
slop; splash; shed; diffuse;
pour (out); ladle out (soup)
rozliczenie [roz-lee-**che**-ńe] n.
settling; reckoning; settlement
rozliczny [roz-**leech**-ni] adj. m.
manifold; diverse; numerous
rozliczyć [roz-lee-chićh] v.
settle up (accounts); calculate
rozlokować [roz-lo-ko-vać] v.
put up; make at home; quarter
rozlosować [roz-lo-**so**-vać] v.
allot; distribute by lot
rozluźnić [roz-looźh-ńeećh]
v. slacken; relax; unfasten
rozluźnienie [roz-looźh-ńe-ńe]
n. loosening; laxity; slackness
rozładować [roz-wa-do-vać] v.
unload; discharge (a battery)
rozłam [roz-wam] m. breach;
split; break; division; dissent
rozłamać [roz-**wa**-mać] v.
break (in two); split
rozłazić się [roz-wa-źheećh
śhan] v. fall apart; disperse
rozłączenie [roz-**wown**-che-ńe]
n. separation; dis-junction
rozłączyć [roz-**wown**-chićh] v.
disconnect; sever; uncouple
rozłąka [roz-**wown**-ka] f.
separation (of people)
rozłożyć [roz-**wo**-zhićh] v.

spread; lay out; disassemble
rozłupać [roz-**woo**-pać] v.
split; cleave; rift; slit (logs);
crack (nuts, heads, etc.); rive
rozmach [roz-makh] m. impetus;
dash; verve; grand style; momentum; force; swing; vigor;
spirit; kick; (swinging) blow
rozmaitości [roz-ma-ee-**tośh**-
-ćhee] pl. miscellany; vaude-
ville theater; variety theater
rozmaity [roz-ma-**ee**-ti] adj. m.
varied; miscellaneous; diverse
rozmaryn [roz-ma-rin] m.
rosemary (Rosmarinus)
rozmarzenie [roz-ma-zhe-ńe] n.
daydream; dreaminess; reverie
rozmawiać [roz-ma-vyać] v.
converse; talk; speak with
rozmazać [roz-ma-zać] v. blur;
smear; daub; let out (a secret)
rozmiar [roz-myar] m. dimension;
size; proportion; scale
rozmienić [roz-mye-ńeećh] v.
change (money, bank-note,
etc.); get the change
rozmieszczać [roz-**myesh**-
-chać] v. arrange; dispose;
place; put; assign places
rozmieszczenie [roz-myesh-che-
-ńe] n. distribution; layout
rozmiękczyć [roz-**myank**-chićh]
v. soften (clay, a man, etc.);
soak; steep; make soft
rozmięknąć [roz-**myank**-
-nownćh] v. become soft; get
soaked; get drenched; sop
rozmijać się [roz-mee-yać
śhan] v. miss; swerve from;
pass; fail to (meet, notice)
rozmiłować się [roz-mee-**wo**-
-vać **śhan**] v. take a liking
to; develop a love for
rozminąć się [roz-mee-nownćh
śhan] v. miss (on road); pass
each other; fail to meet
rozmnażać [roz-mna-zhać] v.
breed; multiply; propagate;
increase in numbers; augment
rozmoczyć [roz-mo-chićh] v.
soak; steep; wet thoroughly;
sodden; make (very) soggy
rozmoknąć [roz-mo-knownćh]

v. become soaked; get soggy
rozmowa [roz-**mo**-va] f.
conversation; talk; discourse
rozmowny [roz-**mov**-ni] adj. m.
communicative; talkative
rozmówca [roz-**moov**-tsa] m.
interlocutor (in conversation)
rozmówić się [roz-**moo**-veećh
śhan] v. talk over; make oneself understood; speak with
rozmysł [**roz**-misw] m. intent;
premeditation; consideration;
intention; purpose; design
rozmyślać [roz-**miśh**-laćh] v.
meditate; ponder how to do
rozmyślanie [roz-miśh-la-**ńe**] n.
meditation; contemplation
rozmyślić się [roz-**miśh**-leećh
śhan] v. change one's mind
rozmyślny [roz-**miśhl**-ni] adj. m.
deliberate; intentional; wilful
roznamiętnić [roz-na-**myant**-
-**ńeećh**] v. impassion; excite
rozniecić [roz-**ńe**-ćheećh] v.
inflame; enkindle a fire; inspire
roznosić [roz-no-**śheećh**] v.
carry (take) around; serve; deliver; rout; distribute; smash
rozochocić [roz-o-kho-**ćheećh**]
v. make merry; animate
rozogniać się [roz-**og**-ńaćh
śhan] v. inflame; become excited; flare up; flush
rozpacz [**roz**-pach] f. despair;
distress; (utter) desperation
rozpad [**roz**-pat] m. decay; break
up; collapse; disintegration
rozpakować [roz-pa-**ko**-vaćh] v.
unpack (one's luggage); un-
wrap (a parcel, a package)
rozpalić [roz-pa-**leećh**] v. fire
up; ignite; start a fire; set
ablaze; light (a cigarette)
rozpamiętywać [roz-pa-**myan**-ti-
-**vaćh**] v. contemplate; reflect
upon; ponder over; recollect
rozpaplać [roz-pa-**plaćh**] v. blab
out; divulge; babble out
rozpasany [roz-pa-**sa**-ni] adj. m.
unbridled; dissolute; licentious
rozpatrywać [roz-pa-**tri**-vaćh] v.
consider; act upon; examine
rozpęd [**roz**-pant] m. impetus;

dash; momentum; taking a run
rozpędzać [roz-**pan**-dzaćh] v.
pick up speed; scatter; disperse; dispel; dissipate; give
an impetus; accelerate
rozpętać [roz-**pan**-taćh] v.
unshackle; unleash; let loose
rozpiąć [roz-**pyown**ćh] v.
unbuckle; undo; stretch (sail)
rozpieczętować [roz-pye-**chan**-
-to-vaćh] v. unseal; open
rozpierać [roz-**pye**-raćh] v.
expand; extend; push aside
rozpierzchnąć się [roz-**pyezh**-
-khno**wn**ćh **śhan**] v. scatter
rozpieszczać [roz-**pyesh**-chaćh]
v. pamper; spoil; coddle up
rozpiętość [roz-**pyan**-to**śh**ćh]
f. span; spread; range; stretch
rozpinać [roz-**pee**-naćh] v.
unbutton; unbuckle; stretch;
spread (sails, nets, etc.)
rozplątać [roz-**plown**-taćh] v.
untangle; untie (a knot); unravel (a plot); disentangle
rozpleść [**roz**-pleśhćh] v.
unbraid; un-twine (a cord); un-
plait (hair); unravel; unclasp
rozpłakać się [roz-**pwa**-kaćh
śhan] v. burst into tears;
start weeping; become tearful
rozpłaszczyć [roz-**pwash**-chićh]
v. flatten out; flat (metal)
rozpłatać [roz-**pwa**-taćh] v. slit;
split; split into two
rozpłodowy [roz-pwo-**do**-vi] adj.
m. (for) breeding; breeding-
rozpłodzić [roz-pwo-**dźheećh**]
v. propagate; cause reproduction (of a specie, clan, etc.)
rozpłód [**roz**-pwoot] m.
propagation; reproduction
rozpływać się [roz-**pwi**-vaćh
śhan] v. melt away; outbreak; dissolve; flow; spread
rozpoczęcie [roz-po-**chan**-ćhe] n.
start; outbreak; beginning;
commencement; lead-off
rozpoczynać [roz-po-**chi**-naćh]
v. begin; start going; open;
initiate; launch; embark upon
rozpogodzić się [roz-po-go-
-**dźheećh śhan**] v. clear up;

brighten up; cheer up
rozporek [roz-po-rek] m. fly; slit
rozporządzać [roz-po-zh<u>own</u>-
-dzaćh] v. dispose; decree;
order; control; command
rozpościerać [roz-posh-ćhe-
-raćh] v. unfurl; spread out;
expand; stretch; fling out
rozpowiadać [roz-po-**vya**-daćh]
v. tell tales (left and right);
divulge; talk (at length) about
rozpowszechniać [roz-pov-
-shekh-ńaćh] v. widespread;
diffuse; disseminate; propagate; spread (around, all over)
rozpowszechnienie [roz-pov-
-shekh-ńe-ńe] n. propagation;
spread; diffusion; prevalence
rozpoznać [roz-**poz**-naćh] v.
recognize; spot; diagnose
rozpoznanie [roz-poz-na-ńe] n.
diagnosis; identification;
reconnaissance; recognition
rozpoznawczy [roz-poz-**nav**-chi]
adj. m. diagnostic; distinctive
rozpraszać [roz-**pra**-shaćh] v.
scatter; dispel; distract; disperse; dissipate; make vanish
rozprawa [roz-**pra**-va] f. trial;
showdown; dissertation; de-
bate; court trial (hearing)
rozprawiać [roz-**pra**-vyaćh] v.
debate; argue; dispute; reason; talk at length; discuss
rozprawić się [roz-pra-veećh
shan] v. settle matters; fight
out; dispose of; floor
rozprężyć [roz-**pran**-zhićh] v.
distend; expand; dilate; resile;
deprive of elasticity; relax
rozprostować [roz-pros-**to**-vaćh]
v. straighten; unbend; stretch
(legs, etc.); smooth out
rozproszyć [roz-**pro**-shićh] v.
disperse; scatter; dispel; distract; diffuse (light); spread
rozprowadzić [roz-pro-**va**-
-dźheećh] v. spread; retail;
distribute; dilute; convey; thin
down; attenuate; smear
rozpruć [roz-proo ćh] v. rip up;
open; un-sew; unravel; rip
open; unstitch; unpick; slit

rozprzedać [roz-pzhe-daćh] v.
sell out; sell (successively)
rozprzedaż [roz-pzhe-dash] f.
sale; complete sale; retailing
rozprzestrzenić [roz-pzhe-**stshe**-
-ńeećh] v. spread; propagate
rozprzęgać [roz-**pzhan**-gaćh] v.
1. unhitch; unharness (horses)
rozprzęgać [roz-pzh<u>an</u>-gaćh] v.
2. disorganize; dislocate
rozprzężenie [roz-pzhan-zhe-ńe]
n. anarchy; demoralization
rozpusta [roz-**poos**-ta] f.
debauch; riot; licentiousness
rozpustnica [roz-poost-**ńee**-tsa]
f. rake; rip; libertine;
debauchee; profligate
rozpustnik [roz-**poost**-ńeek] m.
rake; rip; libertine; debauchee;
profligate; reprobate
rozpuszczać [roz-**poosh**-chaćh]
v. dissolve; dismiss; let go;
disband; dilute; thaw; melt;
defrost; unfreeze; extend
rozpuszczalnik [roz-poosh-**chal**-
-ńeek] m. solvent; dis-solvent
rozpuszczalny [roz-poosh-**chal**-ni]
adj. m. soluble; dissolvable
rozpychać się [roz-pi-khaćh
shan] v. shove aside; jostle
one's way; elbow one's way;
push one's way though
rozpylacz [roz-pi-lach] m.
sprayer; nozzle; atomizer
rozpylać [roz-pi-laćh] v. spray;
pulverize; atomize
rozpytywać [roz-pi-ti-vaćh] v.
ask for; inquire around; ask all
sorts of questions
rozrachować [roz-ra-kho-vaćh]
v. settle accounts; calculate
rozrachunek [roz-ra-khoo-nek] m.
squaring up accounts
rozradzać się [roz-ra-dzaćh
shan] v. breed; propagate
rozrastać się [roz-ras-taćh
shan] v. grow larger (stronger); increase; develop; expand
rozrąbać [roz-r<u>own</u>-baćh] v. cut
asunder; hew apart; chop up
rozrobić [roz-**ro**-beećh] v. stir
up; dilute; scheme; intrigue;
make trouble; kick up a row

rozrodczość [roz-rod-
-chośhćh] f. reproduction;
reproductiveness; generation
rozróżniać [roz-roozh-ńaćh] v.
distinguish; tell apart; discern
rozruchy [roz-roo-khi] pl. riots;
disturbances; violent disorders
rozruszać [roz-roo-shaćh] v.
start up; stir up; put in motion; set in motion; animate
rozrywać [roz-ri-vaćh] v. burst;
disrupt; tear open; entertain
rozrywka [roz-riv-ka] f.
amusement; recreation; entertainment; pastime; diversion
rozrządnica [roz-zhownd-ńee-
-tsa] f. control panel
rozrzedzić [roz-zhe-dźheećh] v.
dilute; rarefy; thin down
(paint, a soup, etc.); weaken
rozrzewnić [roz-zhev-ńeećh] v.
move; touch (pathetically); affect; stir (the soul, the heart)
rozrzucać [roz-zhoo-tsaćh] v.
scatter; squander; distribute
rozrzutność [roz-zhoot-
-nośhćh] f. extravagance;
wastefulness; lavishness
rozrzutny [roz-zhoot-ni] adj. m.
wasteful; extravagant; thriftless; squandering; prodigal;
spendthrift; lavish
rozsada [roz-sa-da] f. seedling;
seedlings (grown from seeds)
rozsadzać [roz-sa-dzaćh] v.
space-out; place; seat separately; blow up; explode; split
rozsądek [roz-sown-dek] m.
good sense; discretion; intellect; reason; judgement; sense
rozsądny [roz-sownd-ni] adj. m.
sensible; reasonable;
advisable; sound; judicious
rozsiadać się [roz-śha-daćh
śhan] v. sit stretched; sprawl
round; settle comfortably
rozsiekać [roz-śhe-kaćh] v. cut
up; slash asunder; hack up
rozsiewać [roz-śhe-vaćh] v.
saw; disseminate; spread; diffuse; shed; propagate (gossip)
rozsiodłać [roz-śhod-waćh] v.
unsaddle; take the saddle off

rozsławiać [roz-swa-vyaćh] v.
glorify; make famous; extol
rozstać się [roz-staćh śhan] v.
part; give up; part with
rozstanie [roz-sta-ńe] n. parting
1. separation; 2. leave-taking
rozstawać się [roz-sta-vaćh
śhan] v. part with; give up
rozstawiać [roz-sta-vyaćh] v.
disperse; place apart; space;
spread; put at intervals
rozstąpić się [roz-stown-peećh
śhan] v. step aside; come
apart; draw aside (apart); split
rozstęp [roz-stanp] m. gap;
space; slit; interval; heave
rozstroić [roz-stro-eećh] v. put
out of tune; upset; disarray;
derange; disorder; un-tune
rozstrój [roz-strooy] m. upset;
disorder; confusion; derangement; (nervous) breakdown
rozstrzelać [roz-stzhe-laćh] v.
1. scatter; distract (attention)
rozstrzelać [roz-stzhe-laćh] v.
2. execute by shooting; put
before a firing squad
rozstrzygać [roz-stzhi-gaćh] v.
try out; decide; fight out; determine; judge; arbitrate; settle
rozstrzygnięcie [roz-stzhig-ńan-
-ćhe] f. decision; settlement
rozsuwać [roz-soo-vaćh] v.
part; draw aside; separate; expand; spread; part; extend
rozsyłać [roz-si-waćh] v.
distribute; circulate; send out
rozsypać [roz-si-paćh] v.
disperse (a granular sub-
stance); spill; scatter; spread
rozszarpać [roz-shar-paćh] v.
tear up; claw; disjoin; mangle
rozszczepiać [roz-shche-pyaćh]
v. split; cleave; fissure
rozszczepienie [roz-shche-pye-
-ńe] n. split; diffraction
rozszerzać [roz-she-zhaćh] v.
widen; broaden; enlarge; expand; spread out; extend; dilate; open; propagate; spread
rozszerzenie [roz-she-zhe-ńe] n.
enlargement; dilation
rozsznurować [roz-shnoo-ro-

-vać] v. unlace; loosen the
lace; come (become) unlaced
rozszyfrować [roz-shif-ro-vać]
v. decode; break the code
rozścielać [roz-śhćhe-lać] v.
spread (out); make the bed
rozśmieszać [roz-śhmye-
-shać] v. amuse; make
laugh; be amusing; be funny
rozświecić [roz-śhvye-
-ćheećh] v. light up; throw
light on; shine on; brighten up
roztaczać [roz-ta-chać] v. roll
out; spread; unfold; display;
bore; take under (protection)
roztajać [roz-ta-yać] v. thaw
roztapiać [roz-ta-pyać] v.
melt; smelt (metal); thaw (ice)
roztargać [roz-tar-gać] v. tear
to pieces; ruffle; dishevel
roztargniony [roz-tar-gńo-ni] adj.
m. absentminded; distracted;
scatterbrained; far-away
rozterka [roz-ter-ka] f. tearing
between; dissension; suspense
roztkliwiać [roz-tklee-vyać] v.
feel for; touch; move; stir
roztłuc [roz-twoots] v. smash up
roztopy [roz-to-pi] pl. thaw
roztratować [roz-tra-to-vać] v.
run over; trample; tread under
foot; trample to death
roztrąbić [roz-trown-beećh] v.
broadcast; blaze abroad
roztrącić [roz-trown-ćheećh] v.
push aside; elbow; part; jostle
rozstropność [roz-strop-
-nośhćh] f. prudence; cir-
cumspection; thoughtfulness
rozstropny [roz-strop-ni] adj. m.
wise; cautious; circumspect;
politic; sensible; cautious;
well-advised; discriminating
roztrwonić [roz-trvo-ńeećh] v.
squander (a fortune, money)
roztrzaskać [roz-tzhas-kać] v.
smash; shatter; crash; dash;
break (to pieces with a noise)
roztrzepanie [roz-tzhe-pa-ńe] n.
scatterbrain; fickleness
roztrzepany [roz-tzhe-pa-ni] adj.
m. scatterbrain; giddy
roztwór [roz-tvoor] m. (chem.)

solution (colloidal, molal, etc.)
roztyć się [roz-tićh śhan] v.
grow (very) fat; become fat
rozum [ro-zoom] m. mind;
reason; intellect; under-
standing; wit; senses; judgment; brains; intelligence;
senses; judiciousness; wits
rozumieć [ro-zoo-myećh] v.
understand; get; perceive
rozumny [ro-zoom-ni] adj. m.
rational; reasonable; wise
rozumować [ro-zoo-mo-vać] v.
reason (out); argue (about)
rozwaga [roz-va-ga] f. deli-
beration; thoughtfulness; prudence; reflection; caution
rozwalać [roz-va-lać] v.
shatter; demolish; smash; pull
down (building, etc.); sprawl
rozwarty kąt [roz-var-ti kownt]
m. obtuse angle
rozważać [roz-va-zhać] v.
1. weigh out (quantities of...)
rozważać [roz-va-zhać] v.
2. consider; ponder; meditate
rozweselić [roz-ve-se-leećh] v.
cheer up; put in good humor
rozwiać [roz-vyać] v. blow
away; scatter; disperse; dispel
rozwiązać [roz-vyown-zać] v.
untie; solve; undo; dissolve;
loosen; unbind; unravel; undo
rozwiązanie [roz-vyown-za-ńe]
n. solution; way out; (child)
delivery; realization; execution
rozwiązły [roz-vyownz-wi]
adj. m. fast; dissolute; de-
bauched; licentious; profligate
rozwidniać [roz-veed-ńać] v.
dawn; be lit up; become lit up
rozwiedziona [roz-vye-dźho-na]
adj. f. divorcee (a woman)
rozwiedziony [roz-vye-dźho-ni]
adj. m. divorced (a man)
rozwierać [roz-vye-rać] v.
open wide; fling (wide) open
rozwieszać [roz-vye-shać] v.
hang about; stretch; spread
out; hung up (here and there)
rozwieść się [roz-vyeśhćh
śhan] v. divorce; dwell upon
rozwijać [roz-vee-yać] v.

rozwikłać [roz-**veek**-waćh] v.
disentangle; unravel; clear up
rozwikłanie [roz-veek-**wa**-ńe] n.
unraveling; disentanglement
rozwlekać [roz-**vle**-kaćh] v.
drag out; protract; spread
rozwlekły [roz-**vlek**-wi] adj. m.
verbose; lengthy; long-spun
rozwodnić [roz-**vod**-ńeećh] v.
dilute; water down; weaken
rozwodnik [roz-**vod**-ńeek] m.
divorced man; divorcee
rozwodowy [roz-vo-**do**-vi] adj. m.
divorce (proceedings etc.)
rozwodzić [roz-**vo**-dźheećh] v.
divorce (a married couple)
rozwojowy [roz-vo-**yo**-vi] adj. m.
evolutional; developmental
rozwolnienie [roz-vol-**ńe**-ńe] n.
diarrhea; lax bowels; open
bowels; too frequent bowels
rozwozić [roz-**vo**-źheećh] v.
transport; deliver (mail etc.)
rozwód [roz-vood] m. divorce
rozwódka [roz-**vood**-ka] f.
divorcee; divorced woman
rozwój [roz-vooy] m.
development; evolution; extension; progress; (up)growth
rozwścieczony [roz-**vśhćhe**-
-cho-ni] adj. m. enraged;
furious; mad with rage; rabid
rozwydrzony [roz-vid-zho-ni] adj.
m. rampant; wild; lawless
rozzłościć [roz-**zwośh**-
-ćheećh] v. irritate; provoke;
make angry; vex; anger
rozżalenie [roz-zha-le-ńe] n.
grudge; resentment; bitterness
rozżarzyć [roz-zha-zhićh] v.
inflame; set on fire; fire
rożek [ro-zhek] m. small horn;
croissant; small corner
rożen [ro-zhen] m. roasting spit
ród [rood] m. clan; breed; family;
stock; race; origin; line
róg [roog] m. horn; corner; ant-
ler; bugle; corner kick (sport);
pl. woman's marital infidelity
rój [rooy] m. swarm; hive; bevy;
cluster; colony; galaxy

róść [roośhćh] v. grow; age;
go up; shoot up; spring up
rów [roov] vm. ditch; trench;
trough; drainage ditch
rówieśnik [roo-**vyeśh**-ńeek] m.
peer of the same age; contemporary (man); equal (age)
równać [roov-naćh] v. equalize;
level; make even; smooth out
równanie [roov-na-ńe] n.
equation; equalization; comparison; making equal
równia [roov-ńa] f. plane; level
równie [roov-ńe] adv. equally
również [roov-ńesh] conj. also;
too; likewise; as well
równik [roov-ńeek] m. equator
równina [roov-ńee-na] f. plain;
flat country; level landscape
równo [roov-no] adv. even;
flat; level; straight; equi-
równoboczny [roov-no-**boch**-ni]
adj. m. equilateral
równoczesny [roov-no-**ches**-ni]
adj. m. simultaneous
równoległobok [roov-no-leg-**wo**-
-bok] m. parallelogram
równoległy [roov-no-**leg**-vi] adj.
m. parallel to; collateral
równoleżnik [roov-no-**lezh**-ńeek]
m. parallel (of latitude)
równomierny [roov-no-**myer**-ni]
adj. m. even; uniform; steady
równoramienny [roov-no-ra-
-**myen**-ni] adj. m. isosceles
(triangle); of equal sides
równorzędny [roov-no-**zhand**-ni]
adj. m. equal rank; equivalent
równość [roov-**nośhćh**] f.
equality; parity; identity
równouprawnienie [roov-no-oo-
-prav-ńe-ńe] n. equality of
rights (of women, men, etc.)
równowaga [roov-no-**va**-ga] f.
equilibrium; balance; poise
równowartościowy [roov-no-
-var-tośh-ćho-vi] adj. m.
equivalent; equipollent
równoważny [roov-no-**vazh**-ni]
adj. m. equivalent; equipollent; equiponderant
równoważyć [roov-no-va-zhićh]
v. balance; equalize; even up

równoznaczny [roov-no-znach-ni] adj. m. synonymous; tantamount; amounting to (a denial)

rózga [rooz-ga] f. switch; cane

róż [roozh] m. rouge; pink

róża [roo-zha] f. rose

różaniec [roo-zha-ńets] m. (praying with a) rosary; beads

różdżka [roozhdzh-ka] f. dowsing rod; twig; diving rod; magic wand; fairy's wand

różnica [roozh-ńee-tsa] f. difference; disparity; dissimilarity; result of subtraction

różniczka [roozh-ńeech-ka] f. differential; small difference

różnić się [roozh-ńeeć śhan] v. differ; be at variance

różnobarwny [roozh-no-barv-ni] adj. m. many colored; motley

różnojęzyczny [roozh-no-yan-zich-ni] adj. m. many-tongued

różnolity [roozh-no-lee-ti] adj. m. diverse; varied; heterogenous

różnorodny [roozh-no-rod-ni] adj. m. heterogenous; various

różnoznaczny [roozh-no-znach-ni] adj. m. ambiguous; vague

różny [roozh-ni] adj. m. different; miscellaneous; sundry; varied

różowy [roo-zho-vi] adj. m. pink; rosy; ruddy; rose color

rtęciowy [rtan-ćho-vi] adj. m. mercuric (compounds etc.)

rtęć [rtanć] f. mercury

rubaszny [roo-bash-ni] adj. m. coarse; ill-mannered; gruff

rubin [roo-been] m. ruby (red)

rubryka [roo-bri-ka] f. space; column; blank space; rubric

ruch [rookh] m. move; movement; traffic; motion; gesture; circulation; agitation; rush

ruchawka [roo-khaw-ka] f. riot

ruchliwy [rookh-lee-vi] adj. m. busy; mobile; agile; active

ruchomości [roo-kho-mośh-ćhee] pl. movables (personal property); belongings; chattels personal effects; one's things

ruchomy [roo-kho-mi] adj. m. mobile; moving; shifting; flexible; floating; dis-placeable

ruczaj [roo-chay] m. brook

ruda [roo-da] f. ore (metallic)

rudera [roo-de-ra] f. run-down house; shanty; ruin; hovel

rudy [roo-di] adj. m. red (haired); russet; ginger; foxy; ruddy

rufa [roo-fa] f. stern; poop

rugować [roo-go-vaćh] v. eject; oust; evict; eliminate; displace

ruina [roo-ee-na] f. ruin; wreck

ruja [roo-ya] f. heat; rut

rujnować [rooy-no-vaćh] v. ruin; undo; destroy; wreck

ruleta [roo-le-ta] f. roulette

rulon [roo-lon] m. roll; rouleau

rum [room] m. rum (drink)

rumak [roo-mak] m. charger; steed; palfrey; courser

rumianek [roo-mya-nek] m. camomile; chamomile (tea)

rumiany [roo-mya-ni] adj. m. rosy; ruddy; browned; florid

rumienić [roo-mye-ńeećh] v. blush; brown; redden; color

rumieniec [roo-mye-ńets] m. blush; ruddiness; floridity

rumor [roo-mor] m. racket; uproar; rumble; clatter; din

rumowisko [roo-mo-vees-ko] n. debris; rubble; brash

rumuński [roo-mooń-skee] adj. m. Rumanian; of Rumania

runąć [roo-nownćh] v. fall down; collapse; crash; swoop; come down; topple; resound

runda [roon-da] f. bout; round; lap; fall (in wrestling)

runo [roo-no] n. fleece; nap

rupiecie [roo-pye-ćhe] pl. rubbish; rash; junk; stuff; oddments; odds and ends

ruptura [roop-too-ra] f. hernia

rura [roo-ra] f. tube; pipe

rurka [roor-ka] f. small pipe

rurociąg [roo-ro-ćhowng] m. pipeline; run of pipes; piping

rusałka [roo-saw-ka] f. undine; naiad; water nymph; vanessa

ruszać [roo-shaćh] v. move; stir; start; take away; withdraw; touch; tamper; remove

rusznikarz [roosh-ńee-kash] m. gunsmith (man or shop)

rusztowanie [roosh-to-va-ńe] n.
scaffold; cradle (hanging)
rutyna [roo-ti-na] f. routine
rutynowany [roo-ti-no-va-ni] adj.
m. experienced; competent
rwać [rvaćh] v. pluck; tear; pull
out; pull up; rush; burst
rwący [rvown-tsi] adj. m. rapid;
racking (pain); swift flowing
rwetes [rve-tes] m. bustle; ado;
racket; turmoil; agitation; stir
ryba [ri-ba] f. fish; the Fish
rybak [ri-bak] m. fisherman
rybny staw [rib-ni stav] fish pond
(artificially made pond)
rybołóstwo [ri-bo-woos-tvo] n.
fishery; fishing industry
rycerski [ri-tser-skee] adj. m.
chivalrous; courteous; gallant
rycerz [ri-tsesh] m. knight
rychło [rikh-wo] adv. soon;
quickly; early; soon after
rychły [rikh-wi] adj. m. speedy;
early; prompt; approaching
rycina [ri-ćhee-na] f. engraving;
illustration; cartoon; drawing;
plate; figure; picture
rycynus [ri-tsi-noos] m. castor
oil; castor oil plant
ryczałt [ri-chawt] m. lump sum;
global sum; the lump
ryczeć [ri-chećh] v. roar; moo;
bellow; low; growl; bray; (elephant) trumpet; hoot; yell
ryć [rićh] v. dig; root; engrave;
carve; excavate; burrow; incise; plough; tunnel; inscribe
rydel [ri-del] m. spade; spud
rydwan [rid-van] m. chariot
rygiel [ri-gel] m. bolt; bar; lock
rygor [ri-gor] m. rigor; severity;
discipline; penalty; strictness
ryj [riy] m. snout; phiz; mug
ryk [rik] m. roar; moo; low; yell
rylec [ri-lets] m. burin; graver;
chisel; etching needle; dry
point; (cyclostyle) pen
rym [rim] m. 1. rhyme; 2. bang!
rymarz [ri-mash] m. saddler
rymować [ri-mo-vaćh] v. rhyme
rynek [ri-nek] m. market (square)
rynna [rin-na] f. gutter; chute
rynsztok [rin-shtok] m. sewer

rynsztunek [rin-shtoo-nek] m.
armor; armature; outfit; kit
rys [ris] m. feature; trait
rysa [ri-sa] f. crack; flow;
fissure; scratch; rift; crevice;
chink; cranny; a partial break
rysopis [ri-so-pees] m.
description (of a person for a
passport, military service, etc.)
rysować [ri-so-vaćh] v. draw;
design; sketch; draft; trace;
pencil; describe; delineate; line
rysownica [ri-sov-ńee-tsa] f.
drawing board; drafting table
rysownik [ri-sov-ńeek] m.
draftsman; illustrator; designer
rysunek [ri-soo-nek] m. sketch;
drawing; draft; outline; deline-
ation; draftsmanship; cartoon
rysunkowy [ri-soon-ko-vi] adj. m.
tracing; drawing (board, block,
etc.); cartoon (film); drawn
ryś [riśh] m. lynx
rytm [ritm] m. rhythm; cadence
rytmiczny [rit-meech-ni] adj. m.
rhythmic; regular; measured
rytownictwo [rit-ov-ńeets-tvo] n.
engraving (trade); dye sinking
rytownik [ri-tov-ńeek] m.
engraver; master dye sinker
rytuał [ri-too-aw] m. ritual
rywal [ri-val] m. rival; contestant
rywalizacja [ri-va-lee-zats-ya] f.
rivalry; competition; emulation
ryza [ri-za] f. ream; restraint
ryzyko [ri-zi-ko] n. risk; venture
ryzykować [ri-zi-ko-vaćh] v.
risk; venture; gamble; hazard
ryzykowny [ri-zi-kov-ni] adj. m.
risky; hazardous; venturesome
ryż [rizh] m. rice; rice paddy
ryży [ri-zhi] adj. m. red (haired);
russet; ginger; foxy (person);
red-brown; ginger-haired
rzadki [zhad-kee] adj. m. rare;
thin; watery; weak; loose
rzadko [zhad-ko] adv. seldom;
thinly; rarely; far apart; exceptionally; sparsely
rzadkość [zhad-kośhćh] f. rarity; sparseness; curiosity; curio; rareness; thinness
rząd [zhownt] m. row; rank; file;

line up; government; rule
rządca [zh<u>own</u>-tsa] m.
　administrator; land steward
rządowy [zh<u>own</u>-do-vi] adj. m.
　governmental; government-;
　state-(schools, administration)
rządzić [zh<u>own</u>-dźheećh] v.
　rule over; govern; control; di-
　rect; be in power; run; boss
rzec [zhets] v. say; utter
rzecz [zhech] m. thing; matter;
　act; stuff; deal; work; subject;
　theme; object; business; con-
　cern; point; purpose; question
rzeczka [zhech-ka] f. small river;
　river; brook; (small) stream
rzecznik [zhech-ńeek] m.
　spokesman; attorney; patent
　agent; intercessor; advocate
rzeczownik [zhe-chov-ńeek] m.
　noun; substantive (grammar)
rzeczowo [zhe-cho-vo] adv.
　factually; terse; business like;
　to the point; objectively
rzeczoznawca [zhe-cho-znav-tsa]
　m. expert; specialist (authority
　in a special field)
rzeczpospolita [zhech-pos-po-lee-
　-ta] f. republic; commonwealth
rzeczywistość [zhe-chi-vees-
　-tośhćh] f. reality; actuality
rzeczywisty [zhe-chi-vees-ti] adj.
　m. real; actual; virtual
rzednieć [zhed-ńećh] v. grow
　thin; become rare; scatter;
　thin; become scarce; disperse
rzeka [zhe-ka] f. river; stream
rzekomo [zhe-ko-mo] adv. would
　be; allegedly; supposedly; by
　all accounts; pretendedly
rzekomy [zhe-ko-mi] adj. m.
　make believe; reputed; sup-
　posed; sham; alleged; imagi-
　nary; so called; would be
rzemień [zhe-myeń] m. leather
　strap; leather bond; leather
　belt; thong; shoulder strap
rzemieślniczy [zhe-myeśhl-ńee-
　-chi] adj. m. trade; craft-
rzemieślnik [zhe-myeśhl-ńeek]
　m. artisan; craftsman; me-
　chanic; tradesman
rzemiosło [zhe-myos-wo] n.

(handi) craft; craft; trade; job;
　business; craftsmanship
rzemyk [zhe-mik] m. thong;
　leather strap; chin strap
rzepa [zhe-pa] f. turnip
rzepak [zhe-pak] m. rape-seed
rzesza [zhe-sha] f. crowd; Reich
　throng; multitude; mass(es)
rzeszoto [zhe-sho-to] n. sieve
rześki [zheśh-kee] adj. m.
　lively; brisk; spry; fresh
rześkość [zheśh-kośhćh] f.
　vigor; sprightliness; briskness
rzetelny [zhe-tel-ni] adj. m.
　honest; upright; fair; real;
　straightforward; just; reliable
rzewny [zhev-ni] adj. m. wistful
　moving; touching; mournful
rzezać [zhe-zaćh] v. slaughter;
　castrate; circumcise (ritually)
rzezimieszek [zhe-źhee-mye-
　-shek] m. cutpurse; thief; pick-
　pocket; cutthroat; criminal
rzeź [zheźh] f. carnage; mas-
　sacre; slaughter; shambles;
　carnage; butchering (people)
rzeźba [zheźh-ba] f. sculpture
rzeźbiarstwo [zheźh-byar-stvo]
　n. sculpture; sculpturing
rzeźbiarz [zheźh-byash] m.
　sculptor (a creating artist)
rzeźbić [zheźh-beećh] v.
　carve; cut; sculpture; weather
　(the earth, mountains, etc.)
rzeźnia [zheźh-ńa] f. slaughter
　-house; knackery (for horses)
rzeźnik [zheźh-ńeek] m.
　butcher; brutal killer
rzeźwić [zheźh-veećh] v. re-
　fresh; cool; invigorate; sober
rzeźwość [zheźh-vośhćh] f.
　agility; briskness; sprightliness
rzeźwy [zheźh-vi] adj. m. agile;
　brisk; smart; spry; lively; re-
　freshing; bracing; crisp (air)
rzeżączka [zhe-zh<u>ow</u>nch-ka] f.
　gonorrhea (a venereal disease)
rzędem [zh<u>an</u>-dem] adv. in a row
rzędna [zh<u>an</u>d-na] f. ordinate
rzępolić [zh<u>an</u>-po-leećh] v.
　scrape (on fiddle); rasp (on the
　fiddle, violin, etc.); fiddle
rzęsa [zh<u>an</u>-sa] f. eyelash

rzęsisty [zhan-**shees**-ti] adj. m.
profuse; heavy; abundant; copious; perky; warm (applause)
rzęzić [zhan-źheech] v. death
rattle; ruckle (in sickness)
rznąć [zhnownch] v. cut;
carve; butcher; saw; slaughter; vulg.: screw; have sex
rzodkiew [zhod-kyev] f. radish
rzodkiewka [zhod-kyev-ka] f.
radish (the pungent root)
rzucać [zhoo-tsach] v. throw;
fling; pitch; dash; hurl; toss;
chuck at; lay down; leave
rzucić [zhoo-cheech] v. throw;
cast; plunge; dash; pitch; fling
rzut [zhoot] m. throw; cast;
projection; view; sketch
rzutki [zhoot-kee] adj. m. brisk;
lively; enterprising; active
rzutkość [zhoot-koshch] f.
briskness; initiative
rzyć [zhich] v. f. (vulg.) ass
rzygać [zhi-gach] v. vomit;
belch out; spew; eject; emit
rzymski [zhim-skee] adj. m.
Roman; of Rome (church, rite)
rżeć [rzhech] v. whinny; neigh
rżnąć [rzhnownch] v. cut;
saw; engrave; carve; butcher;
bang; play cards; do with
zest; (vulg.) screw; have sex;
rżnięcie [rzhńan-che] n. colic;
bellyache; (slang) beating
rżysko [rzhis-ko] n. stubble-field;
rye field; short, bristly growth

S

sabat [sa-bat] m. Sabbath
sabotaż [sa-bo-tash] m.
sabotage; act of sabotage
sacharyna [sa-kha-ri-na] f.
saccharin (a sugar substitute)
sad [sad] m. orchard
sadło [sad-wo] n. lard; suet
sadowić [sa-do-veech] v. place;
show to a seat; seat
sadownik [sa-dov-ńeek] m. fruit
-grower; fruit farmer; orchard-
ist; orchard-man (owner)
sadyba [sa-di-ba] f. dwelling-
house; human habitation;
home; abode; hamlet; village
sadysta [sa-dis-ta] m. sadist
sadza [sa-dza] f. soot; black
sadzać [sa-dzach] v. show to a
seat; seat; make sit down
sadzawka [sa-dzav-ka] f. pool
sadzić [sa-dźheech] v. plant
(seedlings, etc.); set; run;
grow; speed; stud (decorate)
sadzonka [sa-dzon-ka] f.
seedling; quick-set; cutling
sadzone jajka [sa-dzo-ne yay-ka]
s. fried eggs sunny side up
safanduła [sa-fan-doo-wa] f.
bungler; yes-man; oaf; muff;
duffer; clumsy spoiler
safian [sa-fyan] m. morocco
(leather); saffian (leather)
sagan [sa-gan] m. kettle; pot
sak [sak] m. dip-net; sack
sakrament [sa-kra-ment] m.
sacrament (of matrimony etc.)
sakwa [sak-fa] f. wallet; purse
money-bag; travelling bag;
feed bag; (horse's) nose bag
sala [sa-la] f. hall; room
sala [sa-la] f. audience (in a hall)
salaterka [sa-la-ter-ka] f. salad
bowl; vegetable dish
salceson [sal-tse-son] m. head
-cheese; (mock) brawn
saletra [sa-let-ra] f. niter;
saltpeter; potassium nitrate
salina [sa-lee-na] f. salt-works;
saline; salt mine
salmiak [sal-myak] m. ammonium
chloride; sal-ammoniac
salon [sa-lon] m. drawing-room
salonka [sa-lon-ka] f. club car
(railroad); parlor car
salutować [sa-loo-to-vach] v.
salute; dip the flag
salwa [sal-va] f. volley; salvo
sałata [sa-wa-ta] f. lettuce; salad
sam [sam] adj. m. alone; oneself; myself; yourself; nothing
but; very; right; mere

samica [sa-mee-tsa] f. female
samiec [sa-myets] m. male
samobójca [sa-mo-booy-tsa]
m.suicide; suicidal man
samobójczy [sa-mo-booy-chi] adj.
m. suicidal; leading to suicide
samobójstwo [sa-mo-booy-stvo]
n. suicide; act of killing
oneself, committing suicide
samochód [sa-mo-khood] m.
mobile; car; motor car
samochwał [sa-mo-khvaw] m.
braggart; boaster; blow hard
samodział [sa-mo-dźhaw] m.
homespun (cloth)
samodzielność [sa-mo-dźhel-
-nośhćh] f. independence
samodzielny [sa-mo-dźhel-ni]
adj. m. self-reliant; independent; self-contained
samogłoska [sa-mo-gwos-ka] f.
vowel; vocal (speech sound)
samogon [sa-mo-gon] m.
moonshine (unlawfully made)
samoistny [sa-mo-eest-ni] adj. m.
independent; autonomous
samokrytyka [sa-mo-kri-ti-ka] f.
self-criticism; self-accusation
samokształcenie [sa-mo-kshtaw-
-tse-ńe] n. self-education
samclot [sa-mo-lot] m. airplane
samolub [sa-mo-loob] m. egoist
samolubstwo [sa-mo-loob-stvo]
n. selfishness; egoism
samolubny [sa-mo-loob-ni] adj.
m. selfish; self-seeking;
egoistic; conceited
samoobrona [sa-mo-o-bro-na] f.
self-defense
samopas [sa-mo-pas] adv. alone;
by oneself; loosely; unheeded
samopoczucie [sa-mo-po-choo-
-će] n. frame of mind; self-
consciousness; feeling (good)
samopomoc [sa-mo-po-mots] f.
self-help; mutual aid (society)
samorodek [sa-mo-ro-dek] m.
(gold) nugget of native gold
samorodny [sa-mo-rod-ni] adj. m.
autogenous; natural; virgin
samorząd [sa-mo-zhownt] m.
autonomy; self-government
samotnik [sa-mot-ńeek] m.

recluse; hermit; solitary; rogue
samostanowienie [sa-mo-sta-no-
-vye-ńe] n. self-determination
samotność [sa-mot-nośhćh] f.
solitude; loneliness; retirement
samouctwo [sa-mo-oots-tvo] n.
self-education; self instruction
samouczek [sa-mo-oo-chek] m.
handbook (for self-instruction)
samouk [sa-mo-ook] m. self
-taught (man, person, etc.)
samowładczy [sa-mo-vwad-chi]
adj. m. autocratic; arbitrary
samowola [sa-mo-vo-la] f.
license (arbitrariness); law-
lessness (abuse of freedom)
samowystarczalny [sa-mo-vis-tar-
-chal-ni] adj. m. self-sufficient;
self contained; unsubsidized
samozachowawczy instynkt [sa-
-mo-za-kho-vav-chi een-stinkt]
m. self-preservation instinct
samozapalenie się [sa-mo-za-pa-
-le-ńe śhan] n. spontaneous
combustion; self ignition
samozwaniec [sa-mo-zva-ńets]
m. usurper; pretender
sanatorium [sa-na-tor-yoom] m.
sanitorium; sanatorium
sandacz [san-dach] m. perch-
-pike (a fresh water fish)
sandał [san-daw] m. sandal
sanie [sa-ńe] pl. sleigh; sledge
sanitariuszka [sa-ńee-tar-yoosh-
-ka] f. nurse (military, etc.)
sanitarny [sa-ńee-tar-ni] adj. m.
sanitary; of sanitation; health-
sankcja [sank-tsya] f. sanction
(international, etc.); approval
sankcjonować [sank-tsyo-no-
-vaćh] v. sanction; authorize
sanki [san-kee] pl. sled; sleigh
sanskryt [san-skrit] m. Sanskrit;
Sanscrit; old Aryan language
sapać [sa-paćh] v. gasp; pant;
heave; snort; puff and blow;
chug; breathe heavily; wheeze
saper [sa-per] m. combat engineer; sapper; army engineer
sardynka [sar-din-ka] f. sardine
sarkać [sar-kaćh] v. grumble
at (against); complain about
(at); snort out (an order etc.)

sarkastyczny [sar-kas-tich-ni] adj.
m. sarcastic (smile etc.)
sarna [sar-na] f. roe deer
sarnia skóra [sar-ña skoo-ra] f.
buckskin; roe deer's hide
satelita [sa-te-lee-ta] f. satellite;
attendant; planet pinion
satyna [sa-ti-na] f. satin
satyra [sa-ti-ra] f. satire
satysfakcja [sa-tis-fak-tsya] f.
satisfaction; compensation
sączyć się [sown-chićh śhan]
v. drip; trickle; distill; sift;
ooze out; seep; percolate
sąd [sownd] m. judgment; court
sądownictwo [sown-dov-ñeets-
-tvo] n. judicature; jurisdiction
sądowy [sown-do-vi] adj. m.
judicial; of court; judiciary
sądzić [sown-dźheećh] v. try;
judge; think; believe; expect;
guess; pass judgement; doom
sąg [sowng] m. cord (of wood)
sąsiad [sown-śhad] m. neighbor
sąsiadka [sown-śhad-ka] f.
neighbor; lady next door
sąsiedni [sown-śhed-ñee]
adj. m. adjacent; neighboring
sąsiedztwo [sown-śhedz-tvo] n.
neighborhood; nearness; proxi-
mity; vicinity; environs
sążeń [sown-zheń] m. fathom;
cord; approximately six feet
scalić [stsa-leećh] v. integrate
scedzić [stse-dźheećh] v.
strain off; decant (a liquid);
pour off (a liquid)
scena [stse-na] f. scene; stage
scenariusz [stse-nar-yoosh] m.
scenario; script; screenplay
sceneria [stse-ner-ya] f. scenery;
stage decorations; backdrops
sceptyczny [stsep-tich-ni] adj. m.
skeptic; skeptical (smile etc.)
sceptyk [stsep-tik] m. skeptic
schab [skhab] m. pork chop
schadzka [skhadz-ka] f. date
scheda [skhe-da] f. inheritance;
inheritance; heirloom
schemat [skhe-mat] m. scheme;
plan; draft; outline; diagram
schematyczny [skhe-ma-tich-ni]
adj. m. schematic (drafting...)

schizma [skheez-ma] f. schism
schlebiać [skhle-byaćh] v.
flatter; wheedle; adulate; gratify somebody's whims, fancies
schludny [skhlood-ni] adj. m.
neat; clean; trim; slick; tidy
schnąć [skhnownćh] v. dry;
dry up; wane; waste; parch;
wither; become dry; go dry
schodki [skhod-kee] pl. steps
(small); small stairs
schodowa klatka [skho-do-va
klat-ka] staircase
schody [skho-di] pl. stairs
schodzić [skho-dźheećh] v.
get down; go down stairs;
step down; come (walk) down
scholastyka [skho-las-ti-ka] f.
scholasticism; Scholasticism
schorowany [skho-ro-va-ni] adj.
m. invalid; ailing; ill; sick
schować [skho-vaćh] v. hide;
pocket; conceal; put away;
tuck away; save (for future)
schowek [skho-vek] m. closet;
safe; hiding place; recess
schód [skhood] m. stair; step
schron [skhron] m. shelter;
pillbox; air raid shelter etc.
schronić się [skhro-ñeećh
śhan] v. take refuge; take
cover; find shelter (from the
cold, the rain, etc.);
schronisko [skhro-ñees-ko] n.
shelter; hiding place; refuge
schudnięcie [skhood-ñan-ćhe]
n. loss of fat; loss of weight;
slimming down; slimming
schwycić [skhvi-ćheećh] v.
seize; catch hold of; grasp
schylać [skhi-laćh] v. bend;
bow; incline; stoop down
schyłek [skhi-wek] m. decline
scyzoryk [stsi-zo-rik] m. pocket
knife; clasp knife; pen knife
seans [se-ans] m. seance; sitting; showing; performance
secesja [se-tses-ya] f. secession;
Secession style (architecture)
sedes [se-des] m. toilet seat
sedno [sed-no] n. crux; core;
gist; essence (of the matter)
sejm [seym] m. Polish parliament

(bicameral since 1493)
sekcja [**sek**-tsya] f. dissection;
section; cross-section; division
sekret [**se**-kret] m. secret
sekretarz [se-**kre**-tash] m.
secretary; reporter; minuter
seksualny [se-ksoo-al-ni] adj. m.
sexual; sex- (appeal, urge)
sekta [**sek**-ta] f. sect
sektor [**sek**-tor] m. sector
sekunda [se-**koon**-da] f. second
sekundnik [se-**koond**-ńeek] m.
second-hand (of a watch)
sekutnica [se-koot-**ńee**-tsa] f.
shrew; scold; vixen
seledynowy [se-le-di-**no**-vi] adj.
m. aquamarine; willow green
selekcja [se-**lek**-tsya] f. selection
(by elimination, natural, etc.)
seler [**se**-ler] m. celery
semafor [se-**ma**-for] m. se-
maphore (signaling system)
semicki [se-**meets**-kee] adj. m.
Semitic (character etc.)
seminarium [se-mee-**nar**-yoom] n.
seminar; seminary; training
school (doing research)
sen [sen] m. sleep; slumber;
dormancy; torpidity; dream
senat [**se**-nat] m. senate (in
Poland evolved from royal
council in XV c.); Upper
House of the parliament
senator [se-**na**-tor] m. senator
senior [**se**-ńyor] m. senior
senny [**sen**-ni] adj. m. sleepy
sens [sens] m. sense;
significance; meaning; point
sensacja [sen-**sats**-ya] f.
sensation; a hit; making a hit
sensacyjny [sen-sa-**tsiy**-ni] adj.
m. sensational; exciting
sentencja [sen-**tents**-ya] f.
maxim; dictum; pronounce-
ment; concise rule of conduct
sentyment [sen-ti-ment] m. sentiment; partiality; fondness; o-
pinions and feelings combined
separacja [se-pa-**rats**-ya] f.
separation (from bed and
board); isolation (in general)
separatka [se-pa-**rat**-ka] f.
private-room; solitary cell

separować [se-pa-ro-**vać**] v.
separate (a couple); isolate
seplenić [se-ple-**ńeeć**] v. lisp;
have a lisp; speak with lisp
ser [ser] m. (cottage etc.) cheese
serce [**ser**-tse] n. heart; kindness
sercowy [ser-**tso**-vi] adj. m.
cardiac; love- (affair, secret,
etc.); heart (attack, disease)
serdak [**ser**-dak] m. sleeveless
(furred traditional) waistcoat
serdeczność [ser-**dech**-
-nośhć] f. cordiality; hearti-
ness; caresses; warmth; love
serdeczny [ser-**dech**-ni] adj. m.
hearty; cordial; sincere
serdelek [ser-**de**-lek] m. small
sausage (specially smoked)
serenada [se-re-**na**-da] f.
serenade (music and song at
night under lady's window)
seria [**ser**-ya] f. series; chain;
set; train (of events etc.)
serio [**ser**-yo] adv. seriously
sernik [**ser**-ńeek] m. cheese-
cake; (biology) casein
serwatka [ser-**vat**-ka] f. whey
serweta [ser-**ve**-ta] f. (small)
table cloth; doily; serviette
serwetka [ser-**vet**-ka] f. napkin
serwilizm [ser-**vee**-leezm] m.
servility; humbly submission
serwis [**ser**-vees] m. dinner set;
service (tennis); turn of serving; set; tea-service etc.
serwować [ser-vo-**vać**] v.
serve; do services; aid; help
seryjny [se-**riy**-ni] adj. m. serial;
consecutive; repetitive (work)
sesja [**ses**-ya] f. session; sitting
setka [**set**-ka] f. hundred, 100
setny [**set**-ni] adj. m. hundredth
sezon [**se**-zon] m. season
sędzia [**san**-dźha] m. judge;
referee; magistrate; umpire
sędziwy [san-**dźhee**-vi] adj. m.
aged; old; grey headed; hoary;
ancient; of great antiquity
sęk [sank] m. knot; knag; knar
sękaty [san-ka-ti] adj. m. knotty;
knaggy; gnarly; nodose; rug-
ged; obstinate; self-willed
sęp [sanp] m. vulture

sfera [sfe-ra] f. sphere; zone
   atmosphere; area; domain; orb
sferyczny [sfe-rich-ni] adj. m.
   spherical (geometry, triangle)
sfinks [sfeenks] m. sphinx
sfora [sfo-ra] f. pack of dogs
siać [śhaćh] v. sow (corn);
   sift; loose; drop; spread; pour
siadać [śha-daćh] v. sit down;
   take a seat; get stranded; go
   flat; squat down; go aground
siano [śha-no] n. hay
sianokosy [śha-no-ko-si] pl.
   hay-making; hay cutting
siarczan [śhar-chan] m. sulfate
siarka [śhar-ka] f. sulfur
siarkowy [śhar-ko-vi] adj. m.
   sulfuric (acid etc.)
siatka [śhat-ka] f. net; screen
siatkówka [śhat-koov-ka] f. re-
   tina (anatomy); volley-ball
siąść [śhownśhćh] v. sit
   down; take a seat (a chair)
sidło [śheed-wo] n. snare; trap
siebie [śhe-bye] pron. (for) self;
   oneself; one; each other
siec [śhets] v. cut; mow; whip
sieczka [śhech-ka] f. chop
   straw; chaff; (empty) head
sieczna [śhech-na] f. secant
sieczna broń [śhech-na broń]
   f. cutting weapons
sieć [śhećh] f. net; network;
   grid; fishing net; trap; snare;
   web; ramification (of a plot);
   system; network; grid; mains
siedem [śhe-dem] num. seven
siedemdziesiąt [śhe-dem-dźhe-
   -śhownt] num. seventy; 70
siedemdziesiąty [śhe-dem-
   -dźhe-śhown-ti] num.
   seventieth; 70th
siedemnasty [śhe-dem-nas-ti]
   num. seventeenth; 17th
siedemnaście [śhe-dem-naśh-
   -ćhe] num. seventeen; 17
siedemset [śhe-dem-set] num.
   seven hundred; 700
siedlisko [śhed-lees-ko] n. seat;
   abode; habitation; hotbed (of
   sedition, etc.); nest; habitat
siedmiokrotny [śhed-myo-krot-
   -ni] adj. m. seven-fold

siedmioletni [śhed-myo-let-ńee]
   adj. m. seven year (old, etc.)
siedzący [śhe-dzown-tsi] adj. m.
   sitting (posture); sedentary
siedzenie [śhe-dze-ńe] n. seat;
   (person's) bottom; behind
siedziba [śhe-dźhee-ba] f. seat;
   abode; habitat (of an animal);
   seat (of government, etc.)
siedzieć [śhe-dźhećh] v. sit
   (stay); be perched; be settled
siejba [śhey-ba] f. sowing;
   sowing time; sowing season
siekacz [śhe-kach] m. incisor;
   chopping knife; chopper
siekanina [śhe-ka-ńee-na] f.
   hash; chopping up; cutting up
siekiera [śhe-kye-ra] f. hatchet;
   small axe; small hatchet
sielanka [śhe-lan-ka] f. idyll
sielankowy [śhe-lan-ko-vi]
   adj. m. idyllic; pastoral; rural;
   bucolic; of a pastoral life
sielski [śhel-skee] adj. m. rural;
   idyllic; pastoral; rural
siemię [śhe-myan] n. bird seed
siennik [śhen-ńeek] m. straw
   -mattress; pallet; paillasse
sień [śheń] f. hallway;
   corridor; vestibule; entrance
   hall (of a manorial residence)
siepacz [śhe-pach] m. (rough)
   henchman; hired assassin
sierota [śhe-ro-ta] f. m. orphan;
   lonesome person; poor fellow
sierp [śherp] m. sickle
sierpień [śher-pyeń] m. August
sierść [śherśhćh] f. hair
   (coat); fur; game beasts
sierżant [śher-zhant] m.
   sergeant (military rank)
siew [śhev] m. sowing; seeds
siewca [śhev-tsa] m. sower
siewnik [śhev-ńeek] m. seeder;
   sowing-machine (for wheat)
się [śhan] pron. self (oneself,
   myself, etc.; of itself, by
   itself, one, you); each other
sięgać [śhan-gaćh] v. reach
sikać [śhee-kaćh] v. squirt;
   spout; gush; piss (vulg.)
sikawka [śhee-kav-ka] f. fire
   hose; squirt; fire engine

sikora [śhee-**ko**-ra] f. titmouse
siksa [**śheek**-sa] f. hussy of low
   morals; small girl piddler
silnik [**śheel**-ńeek] m. motor
silnik spalinowy [**śheel**-ńeek
   spa-lee-**no**-vi] combustion
   engine (oil or gas fuel)
silny [**śheel**-ni] adj. m. strong;
   powerful; mighty; hefty; lusty;
   sturdy; stiff; robust; nasty
silos [**see**-los] m. silo; (store) pit
siła [**śhee**-wa] f. force; might;
   strength; power; energy; vigor
siła [**śhee**-wa] f. many; much
siłacz [**śhee**-wach] m. strong-
   man; athlete; weight lifter
siłownia [śhee-**wov**-ńa] f.
   power plant; power station;
   power house; electricity works
sinawy [śhee-**na**-vi] adj. m.
   bluish; somewhat blue
siniak [**śhee**-ńak] m. bruise
sinus [**see**-noos] m. sine of an
   angle (trigonometric function)
siny [**śhee**-ni] adj. m. livid; blue;
   purple; blue in the face
siodełko [śho-**dew**-ko] n. bicycle
   seat; small (pony) saddle
siodlarz [**śhod**-lash] m. saddler
siodłać [**śhod**-waćh] v. saddle
siodło [**śhod**-wo] n. saddle
sioło [**śho**-wo] n. hamlet; village
siostra [**śhos**-tra] f. sister
siostrzenica [śhos-tshe-**ńee**-tsa]
   f. niece
siostrzeniec [śhos-tshe-**ńets**] m.
   nephew
siostrzyczka [śhos-**tshich**-ka] f.
   little sister
siódemka [śhoo-**dem**-ka] f.
   seven; 7
siódmy [**śhood**-mi] num.
   seventh; 7th
sito [**śhee**-to] n. sieve; strainer
sitowie [śhee-**to**-vye] n. bulrush
siusiać [**śhoo**-śhaćh] v. tinkle;
   urinate; piss; pee; piddle
siwek [**śhee**-vek] m. gray horse
siwieć [**śhee**-vyećh] v. grow
   gray; become gray-haired
siwucha [śhee-**voo**-kha] f. low
   grade vodka; rot gut
siwy [**śhee**-vi] adj. m. gray;

blue; grizzly; gray-haired;
   hoary; darkish; dreary
skafander [ska-fan-der] m. diving
   suit; pressure suit; wind jacket
skakać [ska-kaćh] v. jump;
   spring; bounce; leap; pop;
   skip; dive; gambol; plunge
skakanka [ska-**kan**-ka] f. jumping
   rope; skipping rope
skala [ska-la] f. scale; extent
skaleczenie [ska-le-**che**-ńe] n.
   cut; injury; hurt; wound
skaleczyć [ska-le-chićh] v. hurt;
   injure; cut; prick; wound
skalisty [ska-**lees**-ti] adj. m.
   rocky (mountain, etc.)
skalp [skalp] m. scalp
skała [ska-wa] f. rock; stone
skamieniały [ska-mye-**ńa**-wi] adj.
   m. petrified; fossil-; stone-
skamienieć [ska-**mye**-ńećh] v.
   become petrified; turn into
   stone; turn into rock
skandal [skan-dal] m. scandal
skarb [skarb] m. treasure;
   treasury; riches; beloved
   person; darling; love; hoard
skarbiec [**skar**-byets] m.
   treasury; strong room; safe
   deposit box; treasure-house
skarbnik [**skarb**-ńeek] m.
   treasurer; cashier; paymaster
skarbonka [skar-**bon**-ka] f. piggy
   bank; money box; poor box
skarcić [skar-**ćheećh**] v.
   admonish; rebuke; reprimand;
   scold; un-braid; rate
skarga [skar-ga] f. complaint;
   suit; claim; charge; grievance
skarłowaciały [skar-wo-va-**ćha**-
   -wi] adj. m. stunted; dwarfish
skarpa [skar-pa] f. scarp;
   buttress; slope; escarpment
skarpetka [skar-**pet**-ka] f. sock; a
   short stocking
skarżyć [skar-zhićh] v. sue;
   denounce; complain; tell tales
skarżypyta [skar-zhi-pi-ta] m.
   squealer; informer; telltale
skaza [ska-za] f. tarnish; brab;
   blot; flaw; spot; speck
skazać [ska-zaćh] v. condemn;
   sentence; pass judgement;

pass sentence; doom (to)

skazaniec [ska-za-ńets] m.
condemned man (to death)

skazić [ska-źheećh] v. spoil;
corrupt; adulterate; pollute

skąd [skownd] adv. from where;
since when; where from?

skądinąd [skownd-ee-nownt]
adv. otherwise; on the other
hand; from somewhere else

skąpić [skown-peećh] v.
skimp; stint; begrudge (food,
money, hospitality, etc.)

skąpiec [skown-pyets] m. miser

skąpstwo [skownp-stvo] n.
parsimony; avarice; stinginess

skąpy [skown-pi] adj. m. stingy;
scanty; meager; avaricious;
niggardly; miserly; mean

skiba [skee-ba] f. clod

skinąć [skee-nownćh] v. signal;
motion; nod; bow (one's head)

skinienie [skee-ńe-ńe] n. nod;
bow; sign; gesture; motion

sklejać [skle-yaćh] v. glue
together; stick; paste; patch

sklejka [skley-ka] f. plywood

sklep [sklep] m. store; shop

sklepienie [skle-pye-ńe] n. vault;
vaulting; dome; canopy

sklepikarz [skle-pee-kash] m.
shopkeeper; tradesman

sklepowa [skle-po-va] f.
saleslady; saleswoman

skleroza [skle-ro-za] f. sclerosis;
hardening of body tissues

skład [skwat] m. composition;
warehouse; store; framework

składać [skwa-daćh] v. make
up; compose; piece; fold; set
together; assemble; deposit

składacz [skwa-dach] m. type
-setter; compositor

składany [skwa-da-ni] adj. m.
compound; folding; collapsible;
miscellaneous; plicate (leaf)

składka [skwad-ka] f.
contribution; membership fee

składnia [skwad-ńa] f. syntax

składnica [skwad-ńee-tsa] f.
depository; warehouse; depot

składnik [skwad-ńeek] m.
ingredient; component; con-

stituent; element

składowe [skwa-do-ve] n. warehouse fee; storage charges

skłamać [skwa-maćh] v. tell a
lie; tell an untruth; lie

skłaniać [skwa-ńaćh] v. bend;
lean; incline; induce; impel;
dispose; prompt; determine to
do; bow down; defer to; rest

skłon [skwon] m. slope; bow

skłonność [skwon-nośhćh] f.
inclination to do; tendency to
do; disposition; proneness to

skłonny [skwon-ni] adj. m.
disposed; inclined; prone; apt

skłócić [skwoo-ćheećh] v. stir
up; agitate; cause to disagree

sknera [skne-ra] m. f. miser

skobel [sko-bel] m. staple

skoczek [sko-chek] m. jumper

skocznia [skoch-ńa] f. ski-jump
(rump); take off ramp

skoczny [skoch-ni] adj. m. brisk;
lively; vivacious; saltatory

skoczyć [sko-chićh] v. leap;
jump; make a dash; hurry

skojarzenie [sko-ya-zhe-ńe] n.
association; union; conjunction

skok [skok] m. jump; leap; hop

skok tłoka [skok two-ka] m.
piston stroke (the length of)

skołatany [sko-wa-ta-ni] adj. m.
worn; battered; shattered

skołować [sko-wo-vaćh] v.
confound; muddle; exhaust

skomleć [skom-lećh] v. whine

skomplikowany [skom-plee-ko-
-va-ni] adj. m. complex; intricate; full of details

skonać [sko-naćh] v. expire;
die; pass away; stop living

skończyć [skoń-chićh] v.
finish; end; stop; have done

skoro [sko-ro] conj. after; at;
since; as; soon; if; once; as
soon as; now that; seeing that

skoro [sko-ro] adv. very soon; by
and by; quickly; as soon as

skoroszyt [sko-ro-shit] m. folder;
letter file; folder with letters

skorowidz [sko-ro-veetz] m.
index; indexed note book

skorpion [skor-pyon] m.

scorpion with poisonous sting

skorupa [sko-**roo**-pa] f. crust;
shell; incrustation; carapace

skory [**sko**-ri] adj. m. quick;
eager; prompt (to act); swift

skostniały [skost-**ńa**-wi] adj. m.
ossified; numb; stiff; fossilized

skośny [**skoś**-ni] adj. m.
slanting; oblique; inclined

skotłować [skot-**wo**-vaćh] v.
whirl; bewilder; agitate; swirl;
seethe; bother; drive crazy

skowronek [sko-**vro**-nek] m. lark;
skylark (old-world songbird)

skowyczeć [sko-vi-**chećh**] v.
yelp; whine; squeal; whimper;
whine with high-pitched sound

skowyt [**sko**-vit] m. yelp; squeal

skóra [**skoo**-ra] f. skin; hide;
leather; coat; pelt; fell

skórka [**skoor**-ka] f. skin; peel;
crust; cuticle; agnail; pelt; fur

skórny [**skoor**-ni] adj. m.
cutaneous; dermal; skin-
(disease department, etc.)

skórzany [skoo-**zha**-ni] adj. m.
leather made; leathery;
leather-(gloves, shoes, etc.)

skra [skra] f. spark (poetic)

skracać [skra-**tsaćh**] v. shorten;
cut down; lessen; abridge

skradać się [skra-daćh **śhan**]
v. steal up; creep up; advance
stealthily; slink; sneak up

skraj [skray] m. border; edge;
brink; margin; fringe; rand;
outskirts; border; periphery

skrajać [skra-**yaćh**] v. cut off;
cut (cloth); cut up (to pieces)

skrajność [**skray**-nośhćh] f.
extremism; (the) extreme

skrajny [**skray**-ni] adj. m.
extreme; intense; utmost; ul-
tra; utter; radical; abject; dire

skrapiać [skra-**pyaćh**] v. damp;
sprinkle; moisten; water

skraplać [**skrap**-laćh] v. liquefy;
condense; precipitate

skrawek [skra-**vek**] m. shred;
snip; strip; patch; chip; fragment; patch; pl. parings

skreślić [**skreśh**-leećh] v.
sketch; cancel; jot down;

delete; erase; depict; note

skręcać [skran-**tsaćh**] v. twist;
turn off; break (neck); strand

skrępować [skran-**po**-vaćh] v.
tie up; restrict; embarrass; impede; cramp; hinder; cumber

skręt [**skrant**] m. twist; twisting;
turn; torsion; veer; winding

skrobaczka [skro-**bach**-ka] f.
rasp; scrapper; foot scrapper

skrobać [skro-**baćh**] v. scrape;
rasp; scratch; scale (fish);
tread on; stab; spear; scribble

skromny [**skrom**-ni] adj. m. coy;
modest; simple; lowly; chaste;
unassuming; scant; frugal

skroń [skroń] f. temple

skropić [skro-**peećh**] v. liquefy;
sprinkle; water; moisten; damp

skrócić [skroo-**ćheećh**] v. abbreviate; shorten; cut down;
curtail; lessen; abridge

skrót [skroot] m. abbreviation

skrucha [**skroo**-kha] f. contrition;
repentance; compunction

skrupulatny [skroo-poo-**lat**-ni]
adj. m. scrupulous; precise;
exact; conscientious

skrupuł [**skroo**-poow] m. scruple

skruszyć [skroo-**shićh**] v.
crumble; crush; bring to repentance; break down

skrycie [skri-**ćhe**] adv. secretly

skryć [skrićh] v. hide; obscure

skrypt [skript] m. script;
mimeographed lecture; I.O.U.

skrytka pocztowa [skrit-ka poch-
-**to**-va] post office box

skrytość [skri-**tośhćh**] f.
secrecy; secretiveness

skryty [**skri**-ti] adj. m.
underhanded; secret; reticent

skrzek [**skshek**] m. scream;
croak; frog-spawn; screeching

skrzep [**skshep**] m. clot;
coagulation (of blood); grume

skrzepnąć [skshep-**nownćh**] v.
clot; coagulate; set; freeze;
solidify; congeal; stiffen;
acquire new vigor; harden

skrzętnie [skshant-**ńe**] adv.
sedulously; diligently; busily

skrzętny [skshant-ni] adj. m.

industrious; busy; diligent
skrzydlaty [skshi-**dla**-ti] adj. m.
winged; wing shaped
skrzydło [**skshid**-wo] n. wing of
(bird, plane, insect); leaf; brim;
(fan) arm; extension; flank
skrzynia [**skshi**-ńa] f. chest; bin;
box; hutch; case; crate; coffer
skrzynka [**skshin**-ka] f. box;
chest; (gear) case; coffer
skrzynka biegów [**skshin**-ka **bye**-
-goov] f. gearbox; gear case
skrzypce [**skship**-tse] n. violin;
fiddle; person playing fiddle
skrzypek [**skshi**-pek] m. violinist;
violin player; fiddler
skrzypieć [**skshi**-pyećh] v.
crunch; creak; screech; grind;
squeak; gride; scratch; gride
skrzywiać [**skshi**-vyaćh] v.
bend; distort (facts); twist;
contort; put awry; make faces
skrzyżowanie dróg [skshi-zho-**va**-
-ńe droog] pl. f. cross-roads;
crossing; intersection
skrzyżowany [skshi-zho-**va**-ni]
adj. m. crossbred
skubać [skoo-**baćh**] v. nibble;
pluck; pick; fleece; graze;
tease; pinch; nibble; browse
skuć [skooćh] v. shackle; chain
skulić [skoo-**leećh**] v. curl up;
cuddle up; squat; lie low;
crouch; bend one's shoulders
skup [skoop] m. purchasing
center (of farm products, etc.)
skupiać [skoo-**pyaćh**] v. concentrate; bring together; gather; collect; rally; cluster
skupienie [skoo-**pye**-ńe] n.
concentration; focussing; compression; conglomeration
skupiony [skoo-**pyo**-ni] adj. m.
collected; concentrated; dense
skupować [skoo-po-**vaćh**] v.
buy; buy up; keep buying; buy
out; purchase (a lot)
skurcz [skoorch] m. cramp;
shrinking; spasm; twitch;
systole; contraction
skurczyć [skoor-**chićh**] v. draw
in; shrink; contract; lessen;
diminish; retract; reduce

skuteczność [skoo-**tech**-
-nośhćh] f. efficiency; efficacy; good result, results
skutecznie [skoo-**tech**-ńe] adv.
with good result; effectively
skuteczny [skoo-**tech**-ni] adj. m.
effective; efficient; operative
skutek [**skoo**-tek] m. effect;
result; outcome; consequence
skuter [**skoo**-ter] m. motor-
-scooter; scooter
skutkować [skoot-ko-**vaćh**] v.
have effect; work; operate
skwapliwy [skvap-**lee**-vi] adj. m.
eager; willing; ready
skwar [skvar] m. scorching heat
skwarek [**skva**-rek] m. crackling
skwaśniały [skvaśh-**ńa**-wi] adj.
m. sour; turned sour; glum
skwer [skver] m. square
słabiutki [swa-**byoot**-kee] adj. m.
very weak (in diminutive)
słabnąć [swab-**nownćh**] v.
weaken; grow feeble; decline;
diminish; grow weaker; abate
słabość [swa-**bośhćh**] f. infirmity; weakness; illness; debility; fragility; impotence
słabowity [swa-bo-**vee**-ti] adj. m.
weakly; feeble; fragile; puny
słaby [**swa**-bi] adj. m. weak;
frail; feeble; infirm; faint;
flimsy; poor; lacking character
słać [swaćh] v. send; make
bed; spread (a table cloth etc.)
słaniać się [swa-**ńaćh** **śhan**]
v. totter; stagger; lurch; reel
sława [**swa**-va] f. glory; renown;
fame; celebrity; reputation; repute; good (ill) name; celebrity
sławetny [swa-**vet**-ni] adj. m.
notorious; famous; ill famous
sławić [**swa**-veećh] v. praise;
celebrate; glorify; laud; blazon
sławny [**swav**-ni] adj. m. famous; glorious; celebrated; illustrious; well-known; of note
słodkawy [swod-**ka**-vi] adj. m.
sweetish; slightly sweet
słodki [**swod**-kee] adj. m. sweet
słodycze [swo-**di**-che] pl. sweets
słodzić [swo-**dźheećh**] v. sugar; sweeten; put some sugar

słoik [swo-eek] m. jar; gallipot;
glass; pot; little jar
słojowaty [swo-yo-va-ti] adj. m.
grained; veined; showing grain
słoma [swo-ma] f. straw
słomianka [swo-myan-ka] f.
straw mat; doormat of straw;
basket of plaited straw
słomiany wdowiec [swo-mya-ni
vdo-vyets] m. grass widower
słomka [swom-ka] f. small straw
słonecznik [swo-nech-ńeek] m.
sunflower (daisy-like flower)
słoneczny [swo-nech-ni] adj. m.
sunny; solar (system, year,
etc.); sun-(bath, rays, spots)
słonina [swo-ńee-na] f. lard
słoniowa kość [swo-ńo-va
kośhćh] f. ivory (tusk)
słonka [swon-ka] f. wood-cock
słony [swo-ni] adj. m. salty
słoń [swoń] m. elephant
słońce [swoń-tse] n. sun;
sunlight (self-luminous)
słota [swo-ta] f. foul weather
słotny dzień [swot-ni dźheń]
m. rainy day; bad weather day
słowacki [swo-vats-kee] adj. m.
Slovak; Slovakian: of Slovakia
słowianin [swo-vya-ńeen] m.
Slav (of the Slavic group)
słowiański [swo-vyań-skee] adj.
m. Slav; Slavonic; of Slavdom
słowik [swo-veek] m.
nightingale; good singer
słownictwo [swov-ńeets-tvo] n.
vocabulary; list of words
słownik [swov-ńeek] m.
dictionary; vocabulary; language (word listing book)
słowny [swov-ni] adj. m. verbal;
reliable; dependable (man)
słowo [swo-vo] n. word
słoworód [swo-vo-rood] m.
etymology; origin of words
słowotwórstwo [swo-vo-tvoor-
-stvo] n. word formation
słód [swood] m. malt; grist
słój [swooy] m. jar; (annual
tree) ring; pot; vain; grain
słówko [swoov-ko] n. (little or
sweet) word; nice word
słuch [swookh] m. hearing

słuchacz [swoo-khach] m.
listener; (university) student;
hearer; auditor; pl. audience
słuchać [swoo-khaćh] v. hear;
obey; listen; obey orders
słuchawka [swoo-khav-ka] f.
(tel.) receiver; earphone
słuchowisko [swoo-kho-vees-ko]
n. radio-(drama, play, comedy,
etc.); broadcast drama
słuchy [swoo-khi] pl. rumors;
(animal) ears; uncertain news
sługa [swoo-ga] f. servant
słup [swoop] m. pillar; column;
post; pole; pylon; landmark
słupek [swoo-pek] m. pillaret;
small post; stake; stud; rail
słuszność [swoosh-nośhćh] f.
rightness; equity; rightfulness;
legitimacy; aptness; justice
słuszny [swoosh-ni] adj. m. just;
fair; right; pertinent; apt
służalczy [swoo-zhal-chi] adj. m.
servile; cringing; subservient
służąca [swoo-zhown-tsa] f.
maid; servant; cleaning woman; domestic woman servant
służący [swoo-zhown-tsi] m.
servant; manservant; domestic
służba [swoozh-ba] pl. service
służbowy [swoozh-bo-vi] adj. m.
official; business (trip etc.)
służyć [swoo-zhićh] v. serve
słychać [swi-khaćh] v. people
say; one hears; be heard
słynąć [swi-nownćh] v. be
famed (renowned, celebrated)
słynny [swin-ni] adj. m. famous
słyszalny [swi-shal-ni] adj. m.
audible; within hearing range
słyszeć [swi-shećh] v. hear
smacznego! [smach-ne-go] exp.
(have a) good apatite!
smaczny [smach-ni] adj. m. tasty
smagać [sma-gaćh] v. lash;
whip; flog; swish; slash
smagły [smag-wi] adj. m.
swarthy; dark-complexioned
smak [smak] m. taste; relish;
savor; palate; liking; appetite
smakołyk [sma-ko-wik] m. tidbit;
delicacy; dainty; choice morsel
smakować [sma-ko-vaćh] v.

taste; relish; delight (in)
smakowity [sma-ko-**vee**-ti] adj.
   m. savory; appetizing; tasty
smalec [sma-lets] m. lard; fat
smar [smar] m. grease; lubricant
smarkać [smar-kaćh] v. blow
   one's nose; wipe one's nose
smarkacz [smar-kach] m. squirt;
   snot; whippersnapper; raw lad
smarkaty [smar-ka-ti] adj. m.
   snotty; callow; raw; nasty
smarować [sma-ro-vaćh] v.
   smear; oil; lubricate; grease
smarowidło [sma-ro-**veed**-wo] n.
   grease; lubricant; ointment
smażyć [sma-zhićh] v. fry;
   scorch; bake in the sun
smętny [sman-tni] adj. m.
   melancholy; blue; doleful
smoczek [smo-chek] m. nipple;
   pacifier; dummy; comforter
smok [smok] m. dragon; cowl
smoking [smo-king] m. dinner
   jacket; tuxedo; formal jacket
smolny [smol-ni] adj. m.
   resinous; pitchy; tarry
smoła [smo-wa] f. pitch; tar
smrodliwy [smrod-lee-vi] adj. m.
   rank; stinky; smelly; foul
smród [smroot] m. stench; fetor
smucić [smoo-ćheećh] v. sadden; grieve; afflict; distress
smukły [smook-wi] adj. m.
   slender; slim; willowy; gracile
smutek [smoo-tek] m. sorrow;
   sadness; grief; mournfulness
smutny [smoot-ni] adj. m. sad
smycz [smich] f. leash; dog lead
smyczek [smi-chek] m. (violin)
   bow; fiddle stick; pl. strings
smyk [smik] m. whippersnapper;
   brat; kid; small (lively) boy
snop [snop] m. sheaf; bunch
snop światła [snop śhvyat-wa]
   light beam; light shaft
snuć [snooćh] v. spin; reel off
snycerz [sni-tsesh] m. sculptor
sobek [so-bek] m. egoist
sobota [so-bo-ta] f. Saturday
sobowtór [so-**bov**-toor] m.
   double; second (other) self
soból [so-bool] m. sable (fur)
sobór [so-boor] m. synod

socjalista [so-tsya-**lees**-ta] m.
   socialist (a believer)
socjalizacja [so-tsya-lee-**zats**-ya]
   f. socialization (nationalization)
socjalizm [so-**tsya**-leezm] m.
   socialism (state control etc.)
socjologia [so-tsyo-lo-gya] f.
   sociolog; social science
soczewica [so-che-**vee**-tsa] f.
   lentil; lentils (pottage)
soczewka [so-**chev**-ka] f. lens
soczysty [so-**chis**-ti] adj. m.
   juicy; sappy; mellow; coarse
soda [so-da] f. soda
sodowa woda [so-**do**-va **vo**-da] f.
   soda water (with sodium)
sofa [so-fa] f. lounge; sofa
sofistyczny [so-fees-**tich**-ni] adj.
   m. sophistical; captious
sojusz [so-yoosh] m. alliance
sojusznik [so-**yoosh**-ńeek] m.
   ally; associate joined for a
   common and specific purpose
sok [sok] m. sap; juice
sokół [so-koow] m. falcon
solanka [so-lan-ka] f. salt spring;
   salted bread roll; brine
solić [so-leećh] v. salt; add salt
solidarność [so-lee-**dar**-
   -nośhćh] f. solidarity
Solidarność [so-lee-**dar**-
   -nośhćh] s. Solidarity Labor
   Union formed in Poland (1980)
solidarny [so-lee-dar-ni] adj. m.
   solidary; sympathetic
solidny [so-leed-ni] adj. m. solid;
   firm; sound; reliable; safe
solista [so-**lees**-ta] f. soloist
soliter [so-lee-ter] m. tapeworm
   (parasite in the intestines); solitary tree; solitaire (gem)
solniczka [sol-ńeech-ka] f.
   salt-shaker; saltcellar
solo [so-lo] adv. solo
solny [sol-ni] adj. m. saline
solony [so-lo-ni] adj. m. salted;
   corned (beef); salt cured
sołtys [sow-tis] m. village head
   (officer below wójt)
sonata [so-na-ta] f. sonata
sonda [son-da] f. probe; feeler;
   sonde; searcher; explorer; plummet; lead; sounding balloon

sonet [so-net] m. sonnet
sopel [so-pel] m. icicle
sopran [sop-ran] m. soprano
sortować [sor-to-vaćh] v. sort
sos [sos] m. gravy; sauce
sosna [sos-na] f. pine (tree)
sośnina [sośh-ńee-na] f. pine
-wood; pine tree; pine branches; pine (boards) lumber
sowa [so-va] f. owl (bird)
sowiecki [so-vyets-kee] adj. m.
of Soviet Union; of the USSR
sowity [so-vee-ti] adj. m. lavish;
ample; abundant; plentiful
sód [sood] m. sodium (element)
sól [sool] f. salt (mineral)
spacerować [spa-tse-ro-vaćh]
v. walk; stroll; walk about
spacja [spats-ya] f. (print) space
spaczać [spa-chaćh] v. warp;
pervert; twist; distort
spaczenie [spa-che-ńe] n.
distortion; perversion; warp
spać [spaćh] v. sleep; slumber
spad [spat] m. slope; drop
spadać [spa-daćh] v. fall; drop
spadek [spa-dek] v. fall;
inheritance; downfall; slope;
dip; drop; decline; down grade
spadkobierca [spad-ko-byer-tsa]
f. heir; inheritor; successor
spadochron [spa-do-khron] m.
parachute (statichute, etc.)
spadzisty [spa-dźhees-ti] adj. m.
steep; sloping; precipitous
spajać [spa-yaćh] v. weld;
solder; link; joint; unite; bond
spalenizna [spa-le-ńeez-na] f.
(smell of) burning (smoke)
spalić [spa-leećh] v. burn out
spalony [spa-lo-ni] adj. m. parched; (sport) offside; burned up
sparzyć [spa-zhićh] v. burn;
sting; scald; blister; scorch
spasły [spas-wi] adj. m. fat
spaść [spaśhćh] v. fall; fatten
spawacz [spa-vach] m. welder
spawać [spa-vaćh] v. weld;
solder (pipes etc.); weld metal
spawanie [spa-va-ńe] n. welding
(of metals, structures, etc.)
spazm [spazm] m. spasm; convulsion; convulsive sobbing

spec [spets] m. specialist;
expert; craftsman; dab hand;
dab; sharp-(shooter, etc.))
specjalizacja [spe-tsya-lee-zats-
-ya] f. specialization; major
specjalność [spe-tsyal-
-nośhćh] f. specialty; peculiarity; specialty; special-
specjalny [spe-tsyal-ni] adj. m.
special; express; particular
specyficzny [spe-tsi-feech-ni] adj.
m. specific; peculiar; concrete
spedytor [spe-di-tor] m. shipping
agent; forwarding agent
spekulacja [spe-koo-lats-ya] f.
speculation; (business) venture
spekulant [spe-koo-lant] m.
profiteer; speculator; gambler
spekulować [spe-koo-lo-vaćh]
v. speculate; profiteer; gamble
spelunka [spe-loon-ka] f. joint
spełniać [spew-ńaćh] v. perform; fulfill; comply with; accomplish; answer; satisfy; do
spędzać [span-dzaćh] v. round
up (cattle); spend (time); a-
bort; drive away; gather; pass
(time); gather; bring together
spichlerz [speekh-lesh] m.
granary (storage of grain)
spiczasty [spee-chas-ti] adj. m.
pointed (sharply); peaked; acu-
minate; tapering; sharp
spiec [spyets] v. burn; scorch;
sun-blister; blush; parch; singe
spieniężyć [spye-ńan-zhićh] v.
cash (checks); sell (property)
spieniony [spye-ńo-ni] adj. m.
foamy; foaming; (horse, etc.)
covered with foam
spierać się [spye-raćh śhan] v.
argue; contend; quarrel; dispute; come off in the wash
spieszny [spyesh-ni] adj. m.
hasty; quick; hurried
spieszyć się [spye-shićh śhan]
v. hurry; dismount; be eager
spięcie [spyan-ćhe] n. buckle;
short circuit; collision; clash
spiętrzyć [spyan-tshićh] v. pile
up; heap up; bank up; dam up
spiker [spee-ker] m. (radio)
announcer; speaker

spinacz [spee-nach] m. fastener
spinać [spee-naćh] v. fasten;
pin up; clasp; spur (horse)
spinka [speen-ka] f. clasp
spirala [spee-ra-la] f. spiral; coil;
volute; helix; spiral glide
spiralny [spee-ral-ni] adj. m.
spiral; helical; involuted
spirytus [spee-ri-toos] m. spirits;
alcohol; rectified (proof) spirit
spis [spees] m. list; register;
inventory; record; roll; census
spis rzeczy [spees zhe-chi] table
(list, etc.) of contents
spisać [spee-saćh] v. record;
write down; make a list (of);
acquit oneself (well...)
spisek [spee-sek] f. plot
conspiracy; hatching a plot
spiskowiec [spees-ko-vyets] m.
conspirator; (secret) plotter
spiż [speezh] m. brass; bronze
spiżarnia [spee-zhar-ńa] f.
pantry; buttery; cupboard
spiżowy [spee-zho-vi] adj. m.
brass; bronze; booming (voice)
splatać [spla-taćh] v. braid;
interlace; interlock; plait
splątać [splown-taćh] v. snarl
up; mat; ravel; confuse; in-
terweave; interlace; muddle up
spleśniały [spleśh-ńa-wi]
adj. m. moldy; musty; mouldy;
mildewy; covered with fungus
splot [splot] m. twine; twist;
coil; tangle; plait coincidence
splunąć [sploo-nownćh] v. spit
spluwaczka [sploo-vach-ka] f.
spittoon; cuspidor
spłacić [spwa-ćheećh] v. pay
off; repay (a debt, a creditor)
spłaszczyć [spwash-chićh] v.
flatten out; humble (another)
spłata [spwa-ta] f. refund;
instalment payment; amortization; repayment; part payment
spłatać figla [spwa-taćh feeg-
-la] v. play a trick; play a joke
spław [spwav] m. rafting; river (flotilla) trade; floating
spławiać [spwa-vyaćh] v. float;
get rid; shunt; raft (timber);
participate in the river trade

spławik [spwa-veek] m. (fishing)
float (dipping when fish bites)
spławny [spwav-ni] adj. m. navigable (river, waterway, etc.)
spłodzić [spwo-dźheećh] v.
beget; generate; put out; produce; be delivered; cause
spłonąć [spwo-nownćh] v.
burn down; go up in flames;
be consumed by fire; redden
spłonka [spwon-ka] f. percussion
cap; primer; detonator
spłoszyć [spwo-shićh] v. scare
away; frighten; startle; flush
spłowiały [spwo-vya-wi] adj. m.
faded (appearance); discolored
spłukać [spwoo-kaćh] v. rinse;
flush; swill out; wash away
spływać [spwi-vaćh] v. flow
(down); drift (with the current,
down-stream); float (with the
current); be streaming (with)
spochmurnieć [spo-khmoor-
-ńećh] v. grow cloudy, gloomy; cloud over; grow sullen
spocić się [spo-ćheećh śhan]
v. sweat; become sweaty; be
in perspiration; perspire
spoczynek [spo-chi-nek] m. rest
spoczywać [spo-chi-vaćh] v.
sit; rest; lie down; be at rest;
rest on; sit down; lie; be at
spod [spod] prep. from under
spodek [spo-dek] m. saucer
spodenki [spo-den-kee] pl. knee
-pants; shorts; knickers
spodlić [spod-leećh] v. debase;
degrade; disgrace; demean
spodnie [spod-ńe] pl. trousers;
pants; slacks; breeches
spodobać się [spo-do-baćh
śhan] v. take a liking; take a
fancy; feel inclined (like)
spodziewać się [spo-dźhe-
-vaćh śhan] v. expect; hope
for; think that it will happen
spoglądać [spo-glown-daćh] v.
look out; look at; contemplate
spoić [spo-eećh] v. make
drunk; weld; ply with liquor
spoistość [spo-ees-tośhćh] f.
cohesion; compactness; density; tenacity; closeness; unity

spoisty [spo-**ees**-ti] adj. m.
compact; cohesive; dense; tenacious; closely packed; terse

spojenie [spo-**ye**-ńe] n. weld;
joint; public symphysis

spojówka [spo-**yoov**-ka] f.
conjunctiva (eyelid membrane)

spojrzeć [spoy-**zheć**] v. look;
glance at; gaze at; view

spojrzenie [spoy-**zhe**-ńe] n.
glance; look; gaze; peep

spokojny [spo-**koy**-ni] adj. m.
quiet; calm; peaceful; still

spokój [spo-**kooy**] m. peace;
calm; quiet; serenity; placidity

spokrewniony [spo-krev-**ńo**-ni]
adj. m. related to; related

spoliczkować [spo-leech-**ko**-vać] v. slap in the face

społeczeństwo [spo-we-**cheń**-stvo] n. society; public;
community; the public; people

społeczny [spo-**wech**-ni] adj. m.
social (evil, psychology, etc.);
public; welfare; collective

społem [spo-**wem**] adv. together
in common; jointly; unitedly

spomiędzy [spo-**myan**-dzi] prep.
from among; from the midst

sponad [spo-**nat**] prep. from
above; from over (the top)

sponiewierać [spo-ńe-**vye**-rać]
v. abuse; ill-treat; maltreat;
revile; batter; put in distress

spontaniczny [spon-ta-**ńeech**-ni]
adj. m. spontaneous; voluntary

sporadyczny [spo-ra-**dich**-ni] adj.
m. sporadic; occasional; stray

sporny [**spor**-ni] adj. m.
controversial; debatable; questionable; contestable; litigious

sporo [**spo**-ro] adv. good deal; a
lot of; briskly; quite a few

sport [sport] m. sport; athletics

sportowiec [spor-**to**-vyets] m.
sportsman; athlete; sporting
man (acting sportsmanlike)

spory [**spo**-ri] adj. m. pretty big;
fast; useful; considerable; fair

sporządzać [spo-**zhown**-dzać]
v. make up; draw up; make
out; prepare; write out

sposobić [spo-**so**-beeć] v.

prepare; make ready (colloquial exp.); make up for

sposobność [spo-**sob**-nośhćh]
f. opportunity to do; occasion
(much scope); chance for

sposobny [spo-**sob**-ni] adj. m.
convenient; capable; able

sposób [**spo**-soop] m. means;
way; manner; fashion; method

spostrzegać [spos-**tshe**-gać] v.
notice; perceive; observe; spot

spostrzegawczy [spos-tshe-**gav**-chi] adj. m. quick to notice;
keen; observant; perceptive

spostrzeżenie [spos-tshe-**zhe**-ńe]
n. observation; awareness; realization; remark; perception

spośród [spo-**śh**-rood] prep.
from among; from the midst

spotęgować [spo-**tan**-**go**-vać]
v. intensify; increase; intensify; strengthen; enhance

spotkać [spot-**kać**] v. come
across; meet; run across; befall; come across; happen; find

spotkanie [spot-**ka**-ńe] n.
meeting; date; encounter

spotwarzać [spo-**tva**-zhać] v.
calumniate; defame; slander

spoufalać się [spo-oo-fa-**lać**
śhan] v. become intimate

spowiadać [spo-**vya**-dać] v.
confess; listen to confession

spowiednik [spo-**vyed**-ńeek] m.
confessor; father confessor

spowiedź [spo-**vyedźh**] f.
confession; confided secrets

spowijać [spo-**vee**-yać] v.
swathe; wrap; shroud; cover

spowodować [spo-vo-**do**-vać]
v. cause; induce; set off

spoza [**spo**-za] prep. from
behind; from beyond; from
outside; from across

spozierać [spo-**źhe**-rać] v.
glance at; look; gaze at

spożycie [spo-**zhi**-ćhe] n.
consumption; intake (food, calories, fluids, etc.)

spożywać [spo-**zhi**-vać] v.
consume; eat; drink; have a
meal; take (partake of) a meal

spożywca [spo-**zhiv**-tsa] m.

consumer (of food, etc.)
spożywcze artykuły [spo-zhiv-
-che ar-ti-**koo**-wi] pl. n.
groceries; food products
spód [spoot] m. bottom; foot
spódnica [spood-**ńee**-tsa] f.
skirt; petticoat; apron strings
spójnia [**spooy**-ńa] f. bond; link;
union; tie; glue; junction
spójnik [**spooy**-ńeek] m.
conjunction (grammar)
spółdzielczość [spoow-**dźhel**-
-chośhćh] f. cooperation
spółdzielnia [spoow-**dźhel**-ńa] f.
coop; cooperative (society)
spółgłoska [spoow-**gwos**-ka] f.
consonant (grammar)
spółka [**spoow**-ka] f. partnership;
(joint stock) company; society
spór [spoor] m. strife; dispute
spóźniać się [spooźh-**ńaćh
śhan**] v. be late; be slow; be
behind time; be delayed; lose
spóźnienie [spooźh-**ńe**-ńe] n.
delay; late coming; late arrival
spóźniony [spooźh-**ńo**-ni]
adj. m. late; delayed; belated;
tardy (excuses etc.); backward
spracować się [spra-**tso**-vaćh
śhan] v. be tired; be exhausted; have worked hard
spracowany [spra-tso-**va**-ni] adj.
m. overworked; exhausted;
tired out (by too much work)
spragniony [sprag-**ńo**-ni] adj. m.
thirsty; thirsting for
sprawa [**spra**-va] f. affair;
matter; cause; case; question;
job; business; deal; action
sprawca [**sprav**-tsa] f. doer;
author; culprit; originator
sprawdzić [sprav-**dźheećh**] v.
verify; examine; test; check
sprawdzian [sprav-**dźhan**] m.
test; gauge; criterion; template
sprawiać [spra-**vyaćh**] v.
cause; bring to pass; occasion; afford; bring about; give
sprawiedliwość [spra-vyed-lee-
-**vośhćh**] f. justice; equity
sprawiedliwy [spra-vyed-lee-vi]
adj. m. just; righteous; fair
sprawka [**sprav**-ka] f. doing;

trick; small offense; prank
sprawność [sprav-**nośhćh**] f.
efficiency; dispatch; skill
sprawny [**sprav**-ni] adj. m. able;
efficient; deft; dexterous
sprawować [spra-**vo**-vaćh] v.
perform; discharge; hold;
exercise; fulfil (duties etc.)
sprawowanie [spra-vo-**va**-ńe] n.
conduct; behavior; perform-
ance; discharge (of duties)
sprawozdanie [spra-voz-da-ńe]
n. report; account; statement
sprawozdawca [spra-voz-**dav**-tsa]
m. reviewer; reporter
sprawunek [spra-**voo**-nek] m.
purchase (made while shopping); pl. shopping
sprężać [spr<u>an</u>-zhaćh] v.
compress; tense; pre-stress
sprężarka [spr<u>an</u>-**zhar**-ka] f.
compressor; air compressor
sprężenie [spr<u>an</u>-**zhe**-ńe] n.
compression; prestress; pretension (of concrete, etc.)
sprężyna [spr<u>an</u>-**zhi**-na] f. spring;
mainspring; impulse; incentive
sprężystość [spr<u>an</u>-**zhis**-
-**tośhćh**] f. elasticity; energy;
resilience; buoyancy; firmness
sprężysty [spr<u>an</u>-**zhis**-ti] adj. m.
elastic; springy; energetic
sprostować [spros-**to**-vaćh] v.
rectify; correct; right
sprostowanie [spros-to-**va**-ńe] n.
rectification; correction
sproszkować [sprosh-**ko**-vaćh]
v. pulverize; levigate; triturate
sprośny [**sprośh**-ni] adj. m.
obscene; lewd; foul (language)
sprowadzać [spro-**va**-dzaćh] v.
bring; import; fetch; call in
spróchniały [sprookh-**ńa**-wi] adj.
m. rotten; decayed; moulded
spróchnieć [sprookh-**ńećh**] v.
rot (wood, etc.); decay
(teeth); moulder; grow carious
spryciarz [spri-**ćhash**] m.
dodger; trickster; sly-boots
spryskać [spris-**kaćh**] v. splash
spryt [sprit] m. shrewdness;
cunning; gumption; knack
sprytny [**sprit**-ni] adj. m. tricky;

clever; cunning; cute
sprzączka [spshownch-ka] f.
buckle; clasp; fastening
sprzątaczka [spshown-tach-ka] f.
cleaning woman; charwoman
sprzątać [spshown-tać] v.
tidy up; clean up (the mess,
etc.); clear up; pitch up; take
away; snatch away; remove
sprzątanie [spshown-ta-ńe] n.
clearing; tidying up; housework; house (office) cleaning
sprzeciw [spshe-ćheev] m.
objection; opposition; resistance; objection; demur
sprzeciwiać się [spshe-ćhee-
-vyać śhan] v. object;
oppose; stand against; resist
sprzeczać się [spshe-chać
śhan] v. fight; argue; dispute
(about); squabble; quarrel (a-
bout parking, etc.); contend
sprzeczka [spshech-ka] f.
quarrel; squabble; altercation;
tiff; flare-up; dispute
sprzeczność [spshech-
-nośhćh] f. contradiction;
discrepancy; inconsistency
sprzeczny [spshech-ni] adj. m.
contradictory; incompatible
sprzedać [spshe-dać] v.
dispose of; sell; trade away
sprzedajny [spshe-day-ni] adj. m.
venal; corrupt; corruptible
sprzedawca [spshe-dav-tsa] m.
salesman; shopkeeper; dealer
sprzedawczyni [spshe-dav-chi-
-ńee] f. saleslady; saleswoman; vendor; seller
sprzedaż [spshe-dash] f. sale
sprzedaż detaliczna [spshe-dash
de-ta-leech-na] f. retail; sale at
retail prices (in retail stores)
sprzedaż hurtowa [spshe-dash
khoor-to-va] f. wholesale
sprzeniewierzenie [spshe-ńe-vye-
-zhe-ńe] n. embezzlement
sprzęgać [spshan-gać] v.
couple; tie; link; team up
(horses); connect (wagons)
sprzęgło [spshan-gwo] n. clutch;
coupling; coupler; attachment
sprzęt [spshant] m. implement;

furniture; accessories; utensils; tackle; outfit; chattels
sprzyjać [spshi-yać] v. favor;
be friendly; promote; further
sprzykrzyć [spshik-shićh] v. get
sick of; get fed up with
sprzymierzeniec [spshi-mye-zhe-
-ńets] m. ally; confederate
sprzymierzony [spshi-mye-zho-ni]
adj. m. allied; confederated
sprzysiągać się [spshi-śhan-
-gać śhan] v. conspire; plot
sprzysiążenie [spshi-śhan-zhe-
-ńe] n. plot; conspiracy
spuchnąć [spookh-nownćh] v.
swell; bulge; curve out
spulchniać [spoolkh-ńać] v.
fluff up; loosen; cultivate (soil)
spust [spoost] m. release; catch;
slip; trigger; appetite; drain
spustoszenie [spoos-to-she-ńe]
n. devastation; ravage; ruin
spustoszyć [spoos-to-shićh] v.
devastate; ravage; make havoc (of a country); lay waste
spuszczać [spoosh-chać] v.
let down; drop; droop; lower;
drain; let fall; throw down; roll
down; put down; let loose
spuścizna [spoośh-ćheez-na] f.
inheritance; legacy; heritage
spychacz [spi-khach] m.
bulldozer; stripper
spychać [spi-khać] v. push
down; relegate; drive away
spytać się [spi-tać śhan] v.
ask; ask a question
srać [srać] v. shit (vulg.)
srebrnik [srebr-ńeek] m. silver
-coin; silversmith
srebrny [srebr-ni] adj. m. silver
srebro [sreb-ro] n. silver
srebrzyć [sreb-zhićh] v. sil-
verplate; wash with silver
srebrzysty [sreb-zhis-ti] adj. m.
silvery (glow, color, etc.)
srogi [sro-gee] adj. m. fierce;
cruel; severe; strict; grim
sroka [sro-ka] f. magpie
srokaty [sro-ka-ti] adj. m. piebald
(horse); with patches
srom [srom] m. disgrace; vulva
sromota [sro-mo-ta] f. shame;

ignominy; disgrace
sromotny [sro-mot-ni] adj. m.
shameful; disgraceful; infamous; disreputable (act, deed)
srożyć [sro-zhićh] v. rage;
torment; storm; oppress; be
(look) severe; harass; be rife
ssać [ssaćh] v. suck; exploit
ssak [ssak] m. mammal;
mammalian (milk sucking)
ssawka [ssav-ka] f. sucker
ssąca pompa [ss<u>own</u>-tsa pom-pa] f. suction pump
stabilizować [sta-bee-lee-zo-vaćh] v. stabilize; fix
stacja [stats-ya] f. station
stacja benzynowa [stats-ya ben-zi-no-va] f. filling or service
station; gas station
stacjonować [sta-tsyo-no-vaćh]
v. be stationed; be in garrison
staczać [sta-chaćh] v. roll
down; fight (a battle, etc.)
staczać się [sta-chaćh <u>śhan</u>]
v. roll down; go from bad to
worse; be on the down grade
stać [staćh] v. stand; be
stopped; farewell; ill-afford;
rise; be at a station; stagnate
stać się [staćh <u>śhan</u>] v.
become; grow; occur; happen
stadion [sta-dyon] m. stadium
stadło [sta-dwo] n. couple
stadnina [stad-ńee-na] f. stud
stado [sta-do] n. flock; herd
stagnacja [stag-nats-ya] f.
stagnation; recession; stagnancy; depression; at low ebb
stajnia [stay-ńa] f. stable
stal [stal] f. steel
stale [sta-le] adv. constantly;
always; for ever; incessantly
stalownia [sta-lov-ńa] f. steel
-mill; steel plant; steel works
stalowy [sta-lo-vi] adj. m. steel;
steely; steel gray
stała [sta-wa] f. constant
stałość [sta-wośhćh] f.
stability; firmness; steadiness
stały [sta-wi] adj. m. stable;
permanent; solid; fixed; firm
stamtąd [stam-t<u>ownt</u>] prep.
from there; from over there;

out of it;
stan [stan] m. state; status;
condition; order; estate; class
stanąć [sta-n<u>own</u>ćh] v. stand
up; stop at; put up; rise; set
foot; get on one's feet, etc.
standaryzować [stan-da-ri-zo-vaćh] v. standardize
stanik [sta-ńeek] m. bodice; bra;
brassiere; waste; corsage
staniol [sta-ńol] m. tin foil
stanowczość [sta-nov-chośhćh] f. determination;
finality; assertiveness; fixity
stanowczy [sta-nov-chi] adj. m.
final; positive; decided; firm
stanowić [sta-no-veećh] v.
establish; determine; constitute; decide; proclaim
stanowisko [sta-no-vees-ko] n.
position; post; status; stand;
rank; appointment; attitude
starać się [sta-raćh śhan] v.
take care; try one's best
staranie [sta-ra-ńe] n. care;
endeavor; exertion; pains
staranny [sta-ran-ni] adj. m.
careful; accurate; nice; exact
starcie [star-će] n. clash;
collision; friction; squabble
starczy [star-chi] adj. m. senile;
starczy [star-chi] v. it is enough
starczyć [star-chićh] v. suffice
starodawny [sta-ro-dav-ni] adj.
m. old time; ancient; antique
staromodny [sta-ro-mod-ni] adj.
m. old fashioned; outmoded
starosta [sta-ros-ta] m. country
-head; wedding host; foreman
starość [sta-rośhćh] f. old
age; very old age; antiquity
staroświecki [sta-ro-śhvyets-kee] adj. m. old fashioned
starożytność [sta-ro-zhit-nośhćh] f. antiquity; ancient times (period, epoch)
starożytny [sta-ro-zhit-ni] adj. m.
ancient; antique; old world
starszeństwo [star-sheń-stvo]
n. seniority; superiority
starszy [star-shi] adj. m. older;
elder; superior (officer)
starszyzna [star-shiz-na] f. the

elders; the seniors; the chiefs
start [start] m. take-off; start
startować [star-to-vaćh] v.
start; take off; make a start
staruszek [sta-roo-shek] m. old
fellow; old man, gentleman
stary [sta-ri] adj. m. old; old-
-looking; former; stale
starzec [sta-zhets] m. old man
starzeć się [sta-zhećh śhan] v.
grow old; age; grow stale; go
bad; be sensecent (food)
stateczny [sta-tech-ni] adj. m.
stable; buoyant; staid
statek [sta-tek] m. ship; craft;
vessel; boat; steamship
statki [stat-kee] pl. kitchen pots
and pans; kitchen utensils
statua [sta-too-a] f. statue
statut [sta-toot] m. statute
statyka [sta-ti-ka] f. statics
statysta [sta-tis-ta] m.
supernumerary (actor with a
nonspeaking part); dummy
statystyczny [sta-tis-tich-ni] adj.
m. statistical; statistic
statystyka [sta-tis-ti-ka] f.
statistics; returns
statyw [sta-tiv] m. stand;
(camera) support; tripod
staw [stav] m. pond; joint
stawać się [sta-vaćh śhan] v.
become; grow (scarce, big)
stawiać [sta-vyaćh] v. place;
erect; put; stand; offer; lay
down; post; station; put upright; give (grades); defy; rise;
set (sail); move (a resolution)
stawka [stav-ka] f. stake
stąd [stownt] prep. from here;
away; therefore; that is why
stągiew [stown-gev] f. vat
stąpać [stown-paćh] v. pace;
tramp; tread (softly); plod
along; lumber along; strut
stchórzyć [stkhoo-zhićh] v.
show fear; shrink with fright
stearyna [ste-a-ri-na] f. stearin
stek [stek] m. 1.steak; 2. pile of
(lies, insults, etc.); pack of
(insults); shower of abuse
stelmach [stel-makh] m.
cart-wright; wheelwright

stempel [stem-pel] m. stamp;
prop; ramrod; punch; die
stemplowany [stem-plo-va-ni]
adj. m. cancelled; used
stenograf [ste-no-graf] m.
stenographer; shorthand writer
stenografia [ste-no-gra-fya] f.
shorthand; stenography
stenotypistka [ste-no-ti-peest-ka]
f. stenotypist; steno
step [step] m. steppe
ster [ster] m. helm; rudder
sterczeć [ster-chećh] v. stand
out; stick out; tower; bulge
stereoskop [ste-re-os-kop] m.
stereoscope (two eyepieces)
stereotypowy [ste-re-o-ti-po-vi]
adj. m. stereotyped (notion)
sternik [ster-ńeek] m. pilot
sterować [ste-ro-vaćh] v. steer
sterta [ster-ta] f. stack; rick
stebnować [steb-no-vaćh] v.
stitch; quilt; backstitch
stęchlizna [stan-khleez-na] f.
fusty smell; musty smell
stęchły [stankh-wi] adj. m.
musty; stale; foul; fusty; no
longer fresh
stękać [stan-kaćh] v. moan;
groan; utter a groan; complain
stępić [stan-peećh] v. blunt;
dull; take the edge off
stępienie [stan-pye-ńe] n.
dullness (of knife, mind, etc.)
stęskniony [stan-skńo-ni]
adj. m. sick for; yearning for;
hankering for; nostalgic
stężały [stan-zha-wi] adj. m.
hardened; stiff; concentrated;
solidified; coagulated
stężeć [stan-zhećh] v. harden;
stiffen; coagulate; concentrate
stężenie [stan-zhe-ńe] n.
concentration; strength (of a
solution, etc.); rigor (mortis)
stłoczyć [stwo-chićh] v. cram;
compress; jam; squeeze; pack;
pile up; crowd things together
stłuc [stwoots] v. smash; break;
bruise; shatter; injure; beat up
stłuczenie [stwoo-che-ńe] n.
bruise; break; contusion; injury
stłumiać [stwoo-myaćh] v.

dampen; muffle; deaden; dull;
suppress; stifle; restrain
sto [sto] num. hundred; 100
stocznia [stoch-ña] f. shipyard
stodoła [sto-do-wa] f. barn
stoik [sto-eek] m. Stoic
stoisko [sto-ees-ko] n. stand
stojak [sto-yak] m. stand
stojący [sto-**yown**-tsi] adj. m.
standing; stagnant; erect;
upright; stan-up (collar, etc.)
stok [stok] m. slope; hillside
stokroć [sto-kroćh] adv.
hundred times; hundredfold
stokrotka [sto-**krot**-ka] f. daisy
stokrotny [sto-**krot**-ni] adj. m.
hundredfold repeated
stolarnia [sto-lar-ña] f. joiner's
shop; carpenter's shop
stolarz [sto-lash] m. cabinet
maker; joiner; carpenter
stolec [sto-lets] m. stool; faeces;
excrement; bowel movement
stolica [sto-lee-tsa] f. capital (of
a country, state, island, etc.)
stolik [sto-leek] m. small table;
nice little (card, etc.) table
stolnica [stol-ñee-tsa] f. molding
board; paste board (kitchen)
stołeczny [sto-**wech**-ni] adj. m.
metropolitan (taxes, etc.);
capital (city); of capital (city)
stołek [sto-wek] m. small stool
stołować [sto-**wo**-vaćh] v.
board; serve meals to lodgers
stołownik [sto-**wov**-ñeek] m.
boarder (provided with meals)
stołówka [sto-**woov**-ka] f. mess
(dining) hall; mess; canteen
stonka [ston-ka] f. potato beetle;
potato bug; Colorado beetle
stonoga [sto-no-ga] f. centipede;
(warm-like) wood louse
stop [stop] m. (metal) alloy;
melt; traffic sign; stop; halt
stopa [sto-pa] f. foot; standard
stopa procentowa [sto-pa pro-
-tsen-to-va] f. interest rate
stopa życiowa [sto-pa zhi-ćho-
-va] f. living standard
stoper [sto-per] m. stopwatch
stopić [sto-peećh] v. melt
stopień [sto-pyeń] m. (stair)

step; degree; grade; extent
stopniały [stop-**ña**-wi] adj. m.
molten away; dwindled; soft-
ened; shrunk; unfrozen
stopnieć [stop-ñećh] v. melt
down; melt away; shrink; soft-
en; dwindle; become smaller
stopniowo [stop-ño-vo] adv.
gradually; little by little
stopniowy [stop-ño-vi] adj. m.
gradual; progressive
stora [sto-ra] f. shade; blind
storczyk [stor-chik] m. orchid
stos [stos] m. (wood) pile
stos atomowy [stos a-to-mo-vi]
m. atomic pile; atomic reactor
stosować [sto-**so**-vaćh] v. use
stosownie [sto-sov-ñe] adv.
accordingly; in compliance
stosowny [sto-sov-ni] adj. m.
proper; convenient; opportune
stosunek [sto-**soo**-nek] m. rate;
relation; proportion; attitude
stosunek płciowy [sto-**soo**-nek
pwćho-vi] m. sexual relations;
sexual intercourse; sex
stosunki handlowe [sto-**soon**-kee
khand-lo-ve] pl. trade
relations; commercial relations
stosunkowy [sto-soon-**ko**-vi] adj.
m. relative; proportional
stowarzyszenie [sto-va-zhi-she-
-ñe] n. association; club
stożek [sto-zhek] m. cone
stożkowaty [stozh-ko-**va**-ti] adj.
m. conical; cone shaped
stóg [stook] m. stack (rick)
stół [stoow] m. table; fare
stracenie [stra-tse-ñe] n.
execution; loss; doom
straceniec [stra-tse-ñets] m.
desperado; madcap (man)
strach [strakh] m. fear; fright
stracić [stra-ćheećh] v. lose;
execute (a man); shed (teeth
etc.); sustain a loss
stragan [stra-gan] m. booth;
stand; (market) stall
straganiarz [stra-ga-ñash] m.
stand owner; stall holder
strajkować [stray-ko-vaćh] v.
go on strike; strike; be out
strapić [stra-peećh] v. sadden;

pain; distress; afflict; grieve;
worry; inflict pain, distress
strapienie [stra-**pye**-ńe] n.
worry; distress; heartbreak
strapiony [stra-**pyo**-ni] adj. m.
worried; dejected; distressed
straszak [stra-shak] m. noisy toy
pistol; scarecrow; bugbear
straszliwy [strash-**lee**-vi] adj. m.
horrible; fearsome; awful
straszny [strash-ni] adj. m.
awful; terrible; awesome; ee-
rie; gruesome; dreadful; frightful; terrific; horrible
straszyć [stra-shich] v.
frighten; haunt; threaten; bluff
straszydło [stra-**shid**-wo] n.
scarecrow; (unsightly) fright
strata [stra-ta] f. loss
strateg [stra-teg] m. strategist
strategia [stra-**teg**-ya] f. strategy
strategiczny [stra-te-**geech**-ni]
adj. m. strategic; of strategy
strategik [stra-**te**-geek] m.
strategist (using stratagems)
stratny [strat-ni] adj. m. one that
lost something; being the loser
stratować [stra-to-vaćh] v.
trample; tread under foot
strawa [stra-va] f. food; meal
strawić [stra-veećh] v. digest;
consume; bear; stomach; sap;
stand; ruin; destroy; etch
strawna [strav-na] adj. f.
digestible; palatable (food)
strawne [strav-ne] n. food ration
(in the army etc.); adj. n.
digestible; palatable (food)
strawny [strav-ni] adj. m.
digestible; palatable (food)
straż [strash] f. guard; watch;
safe custody; strict guard;
escort; convoy; (van-) guard
straż pożarna [strash po-zhar-na]
f. fire brigade; fire department
straż przednia [strash pshed-ńa]
f. vanguard; advance guard
straż tylna [strash til-na] f.
rear-guard; rear guard
strażak [stra-zhak] m. fireman
strażnica [strazh-ńee-tsa] f.
guardhouse; watchtower
strażnik [strazh-ńeek] m. guard;

watchman; sentry
strącić [**strown**-ćheećh] v.
knock off (apples); throw, hurl
down; down; deduct
strączek [**strown**-chek] m.
(small) pod; hull; husk; legume
strąk [**strownk**] m. pod; hull;
husk; legume pod or seed
strefa [stre-fa] f. zone; area
stres [stres] m. stress
streszczać [stresh-chaćh] v.
sum up; summarize; boil
down; condense; abbreviate
streszczenie [stresh-**che**-ńe] n.
resume; summary; digest
stręczyciel [stran-**chi**-ćhel] m.
pimp; procurer; broker
stręczyć [**stran**-chićh] v.
procure (women); recommend
stroczyć [stro-chićh] v. strap
strofa [stro-fa] f. strophe
strofować [stro-**fo**-vaćh] v.
reprimand; admonish; scold;
chide; sermonize; reprimand
stroić [stro-eećh] v. dress up;
tune up; make fun; trim; add
beauty; adorn; arrange; mock
strojnie [stroy-ńe] adv.
beautifully (richly) dressed
strojny [stroy-ni] adj. m. dressed
up; elegant; smart; spruce
stromo [stro-mo] adv. steeply;
abruptly; precipitously; sheer
stromy [stro-mi] adj. m. steep
strona [stro-na] f. page; side;
region; aspect; part; party
stronić [stro-ńeećh] v. avoid;
shun; keep oneself away
stronnictwo [stron-ńeets-tvo] n.
party (political)
stronniczy [stron-ńee-chi]
adj. m. partial; biased; unfair
stronnik [stron-ńeek] m.
partisan; supporter; follower;
henchman; backer; adherent
strop [strop] m. (room) ceiling;
(house) roof; (sailing) sling
stropić [stro-peećh] v.
discourage; confound; abash;
put out of countenance
stroskany [stros-ka-ni] adj. m.
worried; sorrowful; dejected
strój [strooy] m. attire; dress

stróż [stroosh] m. watchman
stróżka [stroozh-ka] f. (woman)
caretaker; wife of a caretaker
struchlały [strookh-la-wi] v.
terrified; paralysed with fear
strucie [stroo-che] n. food
poisoning; dejection (feeling)
struć [strooch] v. poison;
depress; deject; dishearten;
embitter (another person)
strudzony [stroo-dzo-ni] adj. m.
weary; tired; exhausted
strug [strook] m. plane (wood
working tool used to smooth)
struga [stroo-ga] f. stream;
creek; trickle; flow in streams
strugać [stroo-gach] v. whittle;
scrape; carve; cut out
struktura [strook-too-ra] f.
structure; texture; framework
strumień [stroo-myeń] m.
stream; flow; flux; jet; torrents
strumyk [stroo-mik] m. brook;
creek; streamlet
struna [stroo-na] f. string; chord;
note; wire; (metal) wire; cord
struna głosowa [stroo-na gwo-
-so-va] f. vocal cord
strup [stroop] m. scab; crust
strupieć [stroo-pyech] v. to be
a dead body; form a scab
strupieszały [stroo-pye-sha-wi]
adj. m. decrepit; worn out
strupieszeć [stroo-pye-shech]
v. grow decrepit; become
obsolete; become antiquated
strupowaty [stroo-po-va-ti] adj.
m. scabby; having many scabs
struty [stroo-ti] adj. m. dejected;
crestfallen; poisoned
struś [strooś] m. ostrich
strwonić [strvo-ńeech] v.
squander away (a fortune etc.)
strych [strikh] m. attic
strychnina [strikh-ńee-na] f.
strychnine (poisonous alkaloid)
stryczek [stri-chek] m. (hanging)
rope; noose; the halter
stryj [striy] m. uncle
stryjeczny brat [stri-yech-ni brat]
m. cousin; uncle's son
strzał [stshaw] m. shot
strzała [stsha-wa] f. arrow

strzaskać [stshas-kach] v.
smash to pieces; shatter
strząsać [stshown-sach] v.
shake off; shake down; flick
off (ash); brush away; shake
strzec [stshets] v. guard; watch;
keep an eye on; protect; keep
strzelać [stshe-lach] v. shoot;
fire; slap; score; blunder
strzelanie [stshe-la-ńe] n.
shooting (practice); gunfire
strzelanina [stshe-la-ńee-na] f.
gunfire; shots; gunplay
strzelba [stshel-ba] f. shotgun
strzelec [stshe-lets] m. shooter;
rifleman; sniper; gunner;
scorer; fusilier; marksman
strzelnica [stshel-ńee-tsa] f.
shooting range; rifle range
strzelniczy proch [stshel-ńee-chi
prokh] m. gunpowder
strzemienne [stshe-myen-ne] n.
parting drink; stirrup cup
strzemię [stshe-myan] n. stirrup
strzepać [stshe-pach] v. brush
off; flick off; shake off (away)
strząp [stshanp] m. shred; tatter
strzępek [stshan-pek] m. shred;
(small) fragment; (small) scrap
strzępić [stshan-peech] v.
shred; reduce to shreds; fray
strzępić się [strzan-peech
śhan] v. be reduced to shreds
strzępić język [stshan-peech
yan-zik] v. wag one's tongue;
waste breath; talk nonsense
strzyc [stshits] v. cut; clip;
shear; mow; trim; graze
strzyc uszami [stshits oo-sha-
-mee] v. prick up ears
strzykać [stshi-kach] v. squirt;
spray; inject; ache
strzykawka [stshi-kav-ka] f.
syringe; hypodermic syringe
strzyżenie [stshi-zhe-ńe] n.
(hair) cut; sheep shearing
strzyżony [stshi-zho-ni] adj. m.
cropped; cut; clipped
student [stoo-dent] m. student
studenteria [stoo-den-ter-ya] pl.
students; student folks
studia [stoo-dya] pl. university
studies; university research

studio [stoo-dyo] n. atelier;
(film, artist's, etc.) studio
studiować [stoo-dyo-vaćh] v.
study; investigate; peer
studium [stoo-dyoom] n. investigation; university studies
studnia [stood-ńa] f. well
studzić [stoo-dźheećh] v. cool
down (one's tea, coffee, etc.)
studzienny [stoo-dźhen-ni] adj.
m. well- (shaft, water, etc.)
stuk [stook] m. knock; clutter
stukać [stoo-kaćh] v. knock;
tap; hit; rap; patter; rattle;
drum; clatter; clink (glasses)
stulecie [stoo-le-ćhe] n. century;
an age; hundred years
stuletni [stoo-let-ńee] adj. m.
hundred years old; age old
stulić [stoo-leećh] v. press
tight; close up; coil up
stuszować [stoo-sho-vaćh] v.
touch up (photo); tone down
stutonowy [stoo-to-no-vi] adj.
weighing one hundred ton
stwardnieć [stvard-ńećh] v.
harden; stiffen; grow callous
stwardniały [stvard-ńa-wi]
adj. m. hardened; hard-set;
grown hard; hard; sclerotic
stwardnienie [stvard-ńe-ńe] n.
hardening; callosity (of skin)
stwierdzać [stvyer-dzaćh] v.
state; find out; confirm
stwierdzenie [stvyer-dze-ńe] n.
statement; ascertainment
stworzenie [stvo-zhe-ńe] n.
creature; formation; creation
stworzyciel [stvo-zhi-ćhel] m.
creator; maker (of the world)
stworzyć [stvo-zhić] v. create;
produce; set up; compose
stwór [stvoor] m. monster
Stwórca [stvoor-tsa] f. Creator
(of the universe, etc.) Maker
styczeń [sti-cheń] m. January
styczna [stich-na] f. tangent; adj.
f. adjacent (wall, side, etc.)
styczność [stich-nośhćh] f.
contact; tangency; adjacency
styczny [stich-ni] adj. m.
adjacent; contiguous
stygmat [stig-mat] m. stigma

stygnąć [stig-nownćh] v. cool
down; cool off; be cooling off
styk [stik] m. contact; butt
stykać się [sti-kaćh śhan] v.
contact; touch; adjoint; meet
stykowy [sti-ko-vi] adj. m.
contact (effect, print, etc.)
styl [stil] m. style; fashion; order
stylisko [sti-lees-ko] n. helve;
shaft; handle (of a spade etc.)
stylista [sti-lees-ta] m. stylist
stylistyka [sti-lees-ti-ka] f. art of
composition; syntax; stylistics
stylizacja [sti-lee-zats-ya] f.
stylization (in art, etc.); mode
of expression (in writing, etc.)
stylizować [sti-lee-zo-vaćh] v.
adapt to a certain style; conform to a style (mode); stylize
stylowy [sti-lo-vi] adj. m. stylish;
(forms) of style; in a style
stypa [sti-pa] f. wake; funny
confusion; funeral banquet
stypendium [sti-pend-yoom] n.
scholarship; stipend; grant
subiekcja [soob-yek-tsya] f.
inconvenience (of a delay)
subiektywny [soo-byek-tiv-ni]
adj. m. subjective
sublokator [soob-lo-ka-tor] m.
lodger; subtenant
subordynacja [soo-bor-di-nats-ya]
f. subordination
subskrypcja [soob-skrip-tsya] f.
subscription; a subscribing
substancja [soob-stan-tsya] f.
substance; (physical) matter
subsydiować [soob-sid-yo-
-vaćh] v. subsidize
subtelność [soob-tel-nośhćh]
f. subtlety; niceness; delicacy
subtelny [soob-tel-ni] adj. m.
subtle; nice; fine; refined
subwencja [soob-ven-tsya] f.
subsidy; grant in aid
suchar [soo-khar] m. dry-bread
ration; cracker; biscuit
sucharek [soo-kha-rek] m.
cracker; (a dry) biscuit
sucho [soo-kho] adv. dryly;
uninterestingly; dry weather
suchość [soo-khośhćh] f.
dryness; abruptness

suchotnik [soo-**khot**-ńeek] m.
consumptive (patient)
suchoty [soo-**kho**-ti] pl.
consumption; phthisis
suchy [soo-khi] adj. m. dry;
withered; lean; uninteresting
sudecki [soo-**dets**-kee] adj. m. of
Sudeten, Sudetic Mountains
sufit [soo-feet] m. ceiling
suflować [soof-lo-vaćh] v.
prompt (an actor on stage)
sugerować [soo-ge-ro-vaćh] v.
suggest; allude; hint
sugestia [soo-**ges**-tya] f.
suggestion; motion; proposal
sugestywny [soo-ges-**tiv**-ni] adj.
m. suggestive (speech etc.)
suka [**soo**-ka] f. bitch
sukces [**sook**-tses] m. success
sukcesja [sook-**tses**-ya] f.
succession; inheritance; devo-
lution; the act of succeeding
sukcesor [sook-**tse**-sor] m. heir
sukcesorka [sook-tse-**sor**-ka] f.
heiress (of an inheritance)
sukienka [soo-**kyen**-ka] f. dress
sukiennice [soo-kyen-**ńee**-tse] n.
weaver's or draper's market
hall; clothier's hall
sukiennik [soo-**kyen**-ńeek] m.
draper; clothier (dealer)
suknia [**sook**-ńa] f. gown; dress
sukno [**sook**-no] n. woolen cloth
sułtan [**soow**-tan] m. sultan
sum [soom] m. catfish
suma [**soo**-ma] f. sum; total;
high mass; entirety; whole
sumaryczny [soo-ma-**rich**-ni] adj.
m. summary; total; global
sumienie [soo-**mye**-ńe] n.
conscience (clear, guilty etc.)
sumienny [soo-**myen**-ni] adj. m.
conscientious; scrupulous
sumować [soo-**mo**-vaćh] v.
sum up; add up; reckon
sunąć [**soo**-nownćh] v. glide;
push; move; skim along
supeł [**soo**-pew] m. knot
supernowoczesny [soo-per-no-
-vo-ches-ni] adj. m. ul-
tramodern; the most modern
supersam [soo-per-sam] m.
supermarket (of groceries)

surdut [**soor**-doot] m. frock;
coat; overcoat; long jacket
surogat [soo-ro-gat] m.
surrogate; substitute for
surowica [soo-ro-**vee**-tsa] f.
serum (any animal fluid)
surowiec [soo-ro-vyets] m. raw
material; staple; rawhide
surowo [soo-ro-vo] adv.
severely; strictly; sternly;
harshly; austerely; in the raw
surowość [soo-ro-**vośhćh**] f.
severity; crudeness; rigor
surowy [soo-ro-vi] adj. m.
severe; raw; coarse; harsh
surówka [soo-**roov**-ka] f. pig
iron; fruit salad; raw hide
susza [**soo**-sha] f. drought;
dryness; (very) dry weather
suszarka [soo-**shar**-ka] f. (hair,
clothes) dryer; desiccator
suszarnia [soo-**shar**-ńa] f. drying
shed; drying plant; kiln
suszka [**soosh**-ka] f. blotter
suszyć [**soo**-shićh] v. dry
sutanna [soo-**tan**-na] f. cassock
sutener [soo-te-ner] m. cadet;
soutener; bully; ponce
suterena [soo-te-re-na] f.
basement (below the ground)
sutka [**soot**-ka] f. nipple
suty [**soo**-ti] adj. m. copious;
abundant; lavish; plentiful; rich
suwać [**soo**-vaćh] v. shove
suwak [**soo**-vak] m. slide rule
swada [**sva**-da] f. eloquence
swar [svar] m. squabble; quarrel;
rife; dissension; contention
swarliwy [svar-**lee**-vi] adj. m.
quarrelsome; cantankerous
swastyka [svas-**ti**-ka] f.
swastica; swastika (emblem)
swat [svat] m. matchmaker
swatać [sva-taćh] v. match-
make; want to match (with)
swaty [sva-ti] n. matchmaking
swawola [sva-vo-la] f. anarchy
swawolny [sva-**vol**-ni] adj. m.
unruly; playful; frolicsome;
wilful; immoral; dissolute
swąd [svownt] m. reek; stench
sweter [**sve**-ter] m. sweater
swędzenie [svan-dze-ńe] n. itch;

an itch; tingle (int he skin)
swędzić [svan-dźheećh] v.
itch; itch to do something
swoboda [svo-bo-da] f. freedom;
ease; latitude; liberty
**swoboda działania [svo-bo-da
dźha-wa-ńa]** f. freedom to
act; discretion; be free to do
swobodny [svo-bod-ni] adj. m.
free; easy; at liberty; loose;
lax; unconstrained; at large
swoisty [svo-ees-ti] adj. m.
specific; characteristic
swojski [svoy-skee] adj. m.
homely; familiar; friendly;
tame; (well) domesticated
sworzeń [svo-zheń] m. carriage
bolt; lug bolt; cotter; pin
swój [svooy] pron. his; hers; my;
its; our; your; their; one's own
**swój człowiek [svooy chwo-
-vyek]** m. trustworthy man
sybaryta [si-ba-ri-ta] m. Sybarite;
sybarite; voluptuary
syberyjski [si-be-riy-skee] adj. m.
Siberian; of Siberia
sycić [si-ćheećh] v. satiate
syczeć [si-chećh] v. hiss
syfon [si-fon] m. siphon
**sygnalizować [sig-na-lee-zo-
-vaćh]** v. signalize; signal
sygnał [sig-naw] m. signal
sygnatura [sig-na-too-ra] f.
(official) signature
sygnet [sig-net] m. signet; seal
ring; imprint; colophon
syk [sik] m. hiss; sizzle; fizzle
sylaba [si-la-ba] f. syllable
sylogizm [si-lo-geezm] m.
syllogism (form of reasoning)
sylweta [sil-ve-ta] f. silhouette;
outline; profile; figure
symbioza [sim-byo-za] f.
symbiosis; living together
symbol [sim-bol] m. symbol
symboliczny [sim-bo-leech-ni]
adj. m. symbolic; symbolical
**symbolizować [sim-bo-lee-zo-
-vaćh]** v. symbolize; stand for
symetria [si-metr-ya] f. symmetry
symetryczny [si-me-trich-ni] adj.
m. symmetrical
symfonia [sim-foń-ya] f.

symphony (of sounds, colors)
symfoniczny [sim-fo-ńeech-ni]
adj. m. symphonic (orchestra)
sympatia [sim-pat-ya] f. liking
sympatyczny [sim-pa-tich-ni] adj.
m. congenial; attractive
sympatyk [sim-pa-tik] m. well
-wisher; sympathizer
**sympatyzować [sim-pa-ti-zo-
-vaćh]** v. like; go along; feel
with; share the feelings, ideas
symptom [simp-tom] m. symptom (of a particular disease)
symulacja [si-moo-lats-ya] f.
simulation; make believe;
sham; false appearance
symulować [si-moo-lo-vaćh] v.
simulate; feign; pretend; affect
syn [sin] m. son; (a descendant)
synagoga [si-na-go-ga] f. synagogue (Jews' worship place)
syndykat [sin-di-kat] m.
syndicate; syndicate; labor
union; (criminal) organization
synek [si-nek] m. sonny (boy)
synekura [si-ne-koo-ra] .f
sinecure; cosy job; fat job
synod [si-nod] m. synod; council
synonim [si-no-ńeem] m. synonym (word of same meaning)
synowa [si-no-va] f. daughter-in-
-law (the wife of a son)
synowiec [si-no-vyets] m.
nephew (son of a relative)
syntetyczny [sin-te-tich-ni] adj.
m. synthetic; artificial
synteza [sin-te-za] f. synthesis
sypać [si-paćh] v. strew; pour;
scatter (dry matter); shower
(blows, etc.); betray secrets
sypialnia [si-pyal-ńa] f. bedroom;
bedroom furniture suite
sypki [sip-kee] adj. m. loose
(rocks); granular (substance);
friable; dry (goods, etc.)
sypki towar [sip-kee to-var] m.
granular goods; dry goods
syrena [si-re-na] f. siren;
mermaid; hooter; the emblem
of Warsaw, capital of Poland
syrop [si-rop] m. syrup
syryjski [si-riy-skee] adj. m.
Syrian; of Syria

system [sis-tem] m. system
systematyczny [sis-te-ma-tich-ni]
adj. m. systematic; neat
syt [sit] m. satiate; full
sytny [sit-ni] adj. m. filling up;
nourishing; satiating
sytuacja [si-too-ats-ya] f.
situation; circumstances; position; things; state of affairs
sytuować [si-too-o-vaćh] v.
situate; locate; position
sytuowany [si-too-o-va-ni]
adj. m. situated; placed; located; conditioned; (well) off
syty [si-ti] adj. m. satiate; dilled
up; well-fed; nourishing
szabla [shab-la] f. sabre
szablon [shab-lon] m. stencil;
pattern; model; stereotype
szablonowy [sha-blo-no-vi] adj.
m. routine; stereotype
szach-mat [shakh-mat] m. check
-mate (in the chess game)
szachista [sha-khees-ta] m.
chess player (man)
szachować [sha-kho-vaćh] v.
check (in the chess game)
szachownica [sha-khov-ńee-tsa]
f. chessboard; checker board
szachraj [shakh-ray] m. cheat
szachrować [shakh-ro-vaćh] v.
cheat; swindle; jockey
szachy [sha-khi] pl. chess
szacować [sha-tso-vaćh] v.
evaluate; estimate; size up
szacunek [sha-tsoo-nek] m.
1. valuation; assessment
szacunek [sha-tsoo-nek] m.
2. respect; esteem; deference
szafa [sha-fa] f. chest; wardrobe;
bookcase; cupboard
szafir [sha-feer] m. sapphire
szafka nocna [shaf-ka nots-na] f.
night table; bedside table
szafot [sha-fot] m. (execution)
scaffold; execution block
szafować [sha-fo-vaćh] v.
lavish; squander; be liberal
szafran [shaf-ran] m. saffron
ka [shay-ka] f. gang
szakal [sha-kal] m. jackal
szal [shal] m. shawl; scarf
szala [sha-la] f. scale

szalbierstwo [shal-byer-stvo] n.
swindle; fraud; imposition
szalbierz [shal-byesh] m. fraud;
swindler; quack; impostor
szaleć [sha-lećh] v. rage; rave
szalenie [sha-le-ńe] adv. madly;
terribly; awfully; like mad
szaleniec [sha-le-ńets] m.
madman; daredevil; desperado
szaleńczy [sha-leń-chi] adj. m.
frantic; mad; insane; reckless
szaleństwo [sha-leń-stvo] n.
fury; madness; craze; frenzy
szalik [sha-leek] m. scarf
szalony [sha-lo-ni] adj. m. mad
szał [shaw] m. rage; fury; frenzy
szałas [sha-was] m. tent; shanty;
shed; shelter; chalet; hut
szamotać się [sha-mo-taćh
śhan] v. scuffle; struggle;
tussle; jerk; pull about
szampan [sham-pan] m. champagne (of Champagne, France)
szaniec [sha-ńets] m. bastion
szanować [sha-no-vaćh] v.
respect (person, tradition)
honor; have regard; esteem
szanowny [sha-nov-ni] adj. m.
honorable; worthy; dear (sir)
szansa [shan-sa] f. chance
szantaż [shan-tash] m.
blackmail; extortion
szantażować [shan-ta-zho-
-vaćh] v. blackmail; make
squeal; extort (money, etc.)
szantażysta [shan-ta-zhis-ta] m.
blackmailer; extortioner
szarak [sha-rak] m. hare; average
man of the street; yeoman
szarańcza [sha-rań-cha] f.
locust; swarm of locust;
swarm of any flying insects
szarfa [shar-fa] f. scarf; sash
szargać [shar-gaćh] v.
besmear; foul up; slander;
tarnish; slur (a reputation)
szarlatan [shar-la-tan] m.
confidence man; charlatan
szarotka [sha-rot-ka] f. edelweiss
szarość [sha-rośhćh] f.
greyness; drabness; dullness;
duskiness; gray tint (color)
szarpać [shar-paćh] v. jerk;

pull; tear; tousle; knock about;
assail; prey; impair; slander
szaruga [sha-roo-ga] f. gray, foul
(bad) weather; gray skies
szary [sha-ri] adj. m. gray; drab
szarzeć [sha-zheéh] v. loom;
gray; grow dusky; show gray
szarzyzna [sha-zhiz-na] f.
grayness; drabness; duskiness
szarża [shar-zha] f. (cavalry)
charge; (military) rank; officer
szarżować [shar-zho-vaćh] v.
charge (recklessly); overact
szastać [shas-taćh] v. squander
szata [sha-ta] f. garment; gown
szatan [sha-tan] m. satan; devil;
a very strong coffee drink
szatański [sha-tań-skee] adj. m.
devilish; infernal; satanic
szatkować [shat-ko-vaćh] v.
cut; chop; shred; slice
szatnia [shat-ńa] f. locker room;
coat-room; a large coat closet
szatynka [sha-tin-ka] f. dark
-blond girl; auburn haired
(woman, girl, lady, etc.)
szczać [shchaćh] v. piss (vulg.)
szczapa [shcha-pa] f. split log;
splint; chip; sliver; thin man
szczaw [shchav] m. sorrel
szczątek [shchown-tek] m.
remnant; vestige; fragment
szczebel [shche-bel] m. (ladder)
rung; spoke; grade; round
szczebiot [shche-byot] m.
chatter; chirp (of birds); lisp;
prattle; chirrup; warble; babble
szczebiotać [shche-byo-taćh] v.
chirrup; chirp; chatter; bable
szczebiotanie [shche-byo-ta-ńe]
n. chatter; prattle; chirp; lisp
(of children); warble; chirrup
szczecina [shche-ćhee-na] f.
bristle (of hogs); stubble beard
szczególnie [shche-gool-ńe] adv.
particularly; in particular;
especially; principally; chiefly;
above all; peculiarly; singularly
szczególność [shche-gool-
-nośćh] f. peculiarity; singularity; specific character
szczególny [shche-gool-ni] adj.
m. peculiar; special; specific

szczegół [shche-goow] m. detail
szczgółowo [shche-goo-wo-vo]
adv. in detail; in full; with full
particulars; closely; narrowly
szczegółowość [shche-goo-wo-
-vośćh] f. minuteness of
detail; full particulars; in full
szczegółowy [shche-goo-wo-vi]
adj. m. detailed; minute;
thorough; lengthy (document)
szczekać [shche-kaćh] v. bark
szczekanie [shche-ka-ńe] n. bark
szczekotanie [shche-ko-ta-ńe] n.
rattle; sharp short sounds
szczelina [shche-lee-na] f. slot;
crevice; cleft; slit; rift; crack
szczelny [shchel-ni] adj. m.
(water, air, etc.) tight
szczeniak [shche-ńak] m. puppy;
kid; pup; young dog; bad boy
szczep [shchep] m. graft; tribe;
seedling (grown from a seed)
szczepić [shche-peećh] v.
graft; vaccinate; inoculate
szczepienie [shche-pye-ńe] n.
grafting; vaccination
szczepionka [shche-pyon-ka] f.
vaccine (for a specific disease)
szczerba [shcher-ba] f. jag;
notch; gap; nick; chip; dent
szczerbaty [shcher-ba-ti] adj. m.
gap-toothed; jagged; notched
szczerbić [shcher-beećh] v. jag
szczerość [shche-rośćh] f.
sincerity; open-heartedness
szczerozłoty [shche-ro-zwo-ti]
adj. m. of pure gold; golden
szczery [shche-ri] adj. m.
sincere; frank; candid
szczędzić [shchan-dźheećh] v.
spare; economize; grudge; be
sparing (in giving, using); stint
szczęk [shchank] m. clink; clash;
clang; rattle; ringing sound
szczęka [shchan-ka] f. jaw;
mandible; clamp; denture plate
szczękać [shchan-kaćh] v.
clink; clang; jangle; rattle
szczęścić się [shchanśh-
-ćheećh śhan] v. be thriving; have a good luck
szczęście [shchanśh-ćhe] n.
happiness; good luck; success

szczęśliwy [shch<u>an</u>-śhlee-vi]
adj. m. happy; lucky; successful; thriving; prosperous; joyful
szczodrość [shchod-rośhćh]
f. generosity; open-handed-
ness; munificence
szczodry [shchod-ri] adj. m.
generous; abundant; ample
szczoteczka [shcho-tech-ka] f.
small brush; toothbrush
szczotka [shchot-ka] f. brush
szczotkarski [shchot-kar-skee]
adj. m. brush; brush maker's
szczotkować [shchot-ko-vaćh]
v. brush down; brush (a coat,
etc.); polish (floors, etc.)
szczuć [shchooćh] v. hiss; bait;
embitter against; set dogs on
szczudło [shchood-wo] n. stilt;
crutch; pole with a footrest
szczupak [shchoo-pak] m. pike
szczupleć [shchoo-plećh] v.
slim down; reduce; diminish
szczupłość [shchoop-wośhćh]
f. slimness; scantiness
szczupły [shchoop-wi] adj. m.
slim; slender; thin; lean
szczur [shchoor] m. rat
szczwany [shchva-ni] adj. m. sly;
cunning; crafty; slyly deceitful
szczycić się [shchi-ćheećh
śh<u>an</u>] v. boast; take pride; be
(very) proud of; take glory in
szczypać [shchi-paćh] v. pinch;
tweak; squeeze; nip; sting
szczypce [shchip-tse] pl. tongs;
pliers; pincers; clippers
szczypczyki [shchip-chi-kee] pl.
tweezers; forceps; small tongs
szczypiorek [shchi-pyo-rek] m.
chive (used for flavoring)
szczypta [shchip-ta] f. pinch
szczyt [shchit] m. top; summit;
peak; apex; climax; vortex
szczytnie [shchit-ńe] adv.
laudably; commendably; loftily
szczytny [shchit-ni] adj. m. lofty;
sublime; commendable; proud
szczytowy [shchi-to-vi] adj. m.
peak; culminant; uppermost;
top; climactic; supreme; gable-
szef [shef] m. boss; chief
szefostwo [she-fost-vo] n.

management (of a business);
leadership; post of a chief
szejk [sheyk] m. sheik
szelest [she-lest] m. rustle
szeleścić [she-leśh-ćheećh]
v. rustle; whisper (in the wind)
szelka [shel-ka] f. strap; belt
szelki [shel-kee] pl. suspenders;
(pair of) straps; belts; braces
szelma [shel-ma] f. rogue;
scoundrel; wretch; knave
szelmostwo [shel-mos-tvo] n.
piece of roguery; rascally trick
szemrać [shem-raćh] v.
murmur; grumble; prattle;
whisper; ripple; mutter; repine
szept [shept] m. whisper
szeptać [shep-taćh] v. whisper
szepnąć [shep-n<u>own</u>ćh] v.
whisper; murmur; conspire;
scheme; prompt a thought to
szereg [she-rek] m. row; file;
series; range; chain (of events)
szeregować [she-re-go-vaćh] v.
rank; classify; arrange
szeregowy [she-re-go-vi] adj. m.
1. series (mathematical)
szeregowy [she-re-go-vi] m.
2. soldier in the ranks
szermierka [sher-myer-ka] f.
fencing; swordsmanship; fight
szermierz [sher-myesh] m. fencer
szeroki [she-ro-kee] adj. m. wide
range; broad; ample; extensive
szeroko [she-ro-ko] adv. widely;
broadly; wide; far and wide
szerokość [she-ro-kośhćh] f.
width; latitude; breath
szerokotorowa kolej [she-ro-ko-
-to-ro-va ko-ley] f. wide gauge
railroad (mainly Russian)
szerszeń [sher-sheń] m. hornet;
large yellow and black wasp
szerzenie [she-zhe-ńe] n. spread;
propagation; dissemination
szerzyć [she-zhićh] v. spread;
propagate; promulgate; disseminate; pervade; radiate
szesnastka [shes-nast-ka] f. the
figure sixteen; 16
szesnastoletni [shes-nas-to-let-
-ńee] adj. m. sixteen-year-old
szesnastowieczny [shes-nas-to-

-vyech-ni] adj. m. sixteenth-
century; of the 16th century
szesnasty [shes-nas-ti] num.
sixteenth; 16th
szesnaście [shes-naśh-ćhe]
num. sixteen; 16
sześcian [sheśh-ćhan] m.
cube (number's third power)
sześcienny [sheśh-ćhen-ni]
adj. m. cubic (third power)
sześciobok [sheśh-ćho-bok] m.
hexagon; hexahedron
sześciokrotny [sheśh-ćho-krot-
-ni] adj. m. six-fold
sześciolatek [sheśh-ćho-la-tek]
m. boy of six; six year old
sześcioro [śheśh-ćho-ro]
num. six (children)
sześć [śheśhćh] num. six; 6
sześćdziesiąt [sheśhćh-dźhe-
-śhownt] num. sixty; 60
sześćdziesiąty [sheśhćh-dźhe-
-śhown-ti] adj. m. sixtieth
sześćdziesięcioletni [sheśh-
-dźhe-śhan-ćho-let-ńee] adj.
m. sixty years old; of sixty
(60) years' duration
sześćset [sheśhćh-set] num.
six hundred; 600
szew [shev] m. seam; stitch;
juncture; raphe; suture
szewc [shevts] m. shoemaker;
boot-maker; (mending) cobbler
szewstwo [shev-stvo] n. shoe
-making; shoe-making trade
szkalować [shka-lo-vaćh] v.
slander; defame; calumniate
szkapa [shka-pa] f. screw; jade,
a worthless horse; crock
szkarada [shka-ra-da] f. eyesore;
an abomination; fright
szkaradny [shka-rad-ni] adj. m.
hideous; ugly; abominable;
nasty; repulsive; revolting
szkarlatyna [shkar-la-ti-na] f.
scarlet fever; scarlatina
szkarłat [shkar-wat] m. scarlet
szkarłatny [shkar-wat-ni] adj. m.
scarlet; crimson; purple
szkatuła [shka-too-wa] f. box;
casket; financial means; funds
szkic [shkeets] m. outline;
sketch; essay; study; tracing

szkicować [shkee-tso-vaćh] v.
sketch; outline; draw up; design; trace; pencil; chalk out
szkicownik [shkee-tsov-ńeek] m.
sketch pad; sketchbook
szkielet [shke-let] m. skeleton;
framework; shell; carcass
szkiełko [shkew-ko] n. small
glass; pane; slide; crystal
szkiełko od zegarka [shkew-ko
od ze-gar-ka] n. watch-glass
szklanka [shklan-ka] f. (drinking)
glass; glassful (of water etc.)
szklany [shkla-ni] adj. m. glass;
glassy (eye, etc.); vitreous
szklarz [shklash] m. glazier
szklić [shkleećh] v. glaze; brag
szkisty [shklees-ti] adj. m.
glassy; glazy; vitreous; hyaline
szkliwo [shklee-vo] n. enamel;
glaze; (desert) varnish
szkło [shkwo] n. glass; pane
szkocki [shkots-kee] adj. m.
Scottish; of Scotland
szkoda [shko-da] f. damage;
harm; detriment; mischief; injury; hurt; exp.: that's too
bad! what a pity! what a
shame! how annoying!
szkodliwy [shkod-lee-vi] adj. m.
harmful; detrimental; damag-
ing; destructive; pernicious
szkodnik [shkod-ńeek] m. wrong
-doer; pest; nuisance
szkodzić [shko-dźheećh] v.
do harm; injure; be harmful;
cause damage; disagree with
szkolenie [shko-le-ńe] n.
training; instruction; schooling
szkolić [shko-leećh] v. school;
train; give instruction; instruct
szkolnictwo [shkol-ńeets-tvo] n.
school system; education
szkolny [shkol-ni] adj. m. school;
scholastic; of school; school-
szkoła [shko-wa] f. school
szkop [shkop] m. Kraut; Hun
(vulg.); (an invading) German
szkopuł [shko-poow] m. obstacle
szkorbut [shkor-boot] m. scurvy
szkuner [shkoo-ner] m. schooner
szkwał [shkvaw] m. squall; flaw
szlaban [shla-ban] m. tollgate;

barrier; train crossing barrier
szlachcic [shlakh-ćheets] m.
squire; nobleman; gentleman
szlachecki [shla-khets-kee] adj.
m. noble; gentle; gentleman's
szlachetny [shla-khet-ni] adj. m.
noble; noble-minded; elegant
szlachta [shlakh-ta] f. gentry
szlachtować [shlakh-to-vaćh] v.
slaughter; brutal killing
szlafrok [shlaf-rok] m.
house-robe; woman's wrapper
(at home); dressing gown
szlak [shlak] m. trail; track;
border; (trade) route; band;
selvage; (animal) scent
szlam [shlam] m. slime; ooze; slit
szlem [shlem] m. big slam
(in bridge, a card game)
szlemik [shle-meek] m. little slam
(in bridge, a card game)
szlifa [shlee-fa] f. epaulettes
szlifierka [shlee-fyer-ka] f.
grinding machine; grinder
szlifierz [shlee-fyesh] m. polisher;
(diamond, etc.) cutter; grinder
szlifować [shlee-fo-vaćh] v.
polish; burnish; cut (diamonds)
szlify [shlee-fi] pl. epaulets
szlochać [shlo-khaćh] v. sob
szmaciany [shma-ćha-ni] adj. m.
rag (doll); made out of rags
szmaragd [shma-ragd] m.
emerald; emerald green color
szmat [shmat] m. large piece;
long way; a good bit; expanse
szmata [shma-ta] f. clout; rag
szmatławiec [shma-twa-vyets]
m. shabby newspaper; smear
sheet; rag; cheep tabloid
szmelc [shmelts] m. scrap; junk;
rubbish; scrap-heap (of metal)
szmer [shmer] m. murmur; rustle
szmerać [shme-raćh] v.
murmur; whisper (of trees)
szmergiel [shmer-gel] m. emery
szminka [shmeen-ka] f. lipstick;
paint; rouge; make up
szmira [shmee-ra] f. literary
garbage; trash; muck
szmirowaty [shmee-ro-va-ti] adj.
m. trashy (literature, paper)
szmonces [shmon-tses] m.

Jewish quip or joke; nonsense
(slang); sarcastic remark
szmugiel [shmoo-gel] m.
smuggle; smuggling; contraband; smuggled goods
szmuglować [shmoo-glo-vaćh]
v. smuggle (goods, etc.)
szmuklerstwo [shmook-ler-stvo]
n. haberdashery (ties, shirts)
szmuklerz [shmook-lesh] m.
haberdasher (men's apparel)
sznur [shnoor] m. rope; cord;
line; twine; twist; raft
sznurek [shnoo-rek] m. string
sznurować [shnoo-ro-vaćh] v.
lace up; lace; tie; purse
sznurowadło [shnoo-ro-**vad**-wo]
n. shoe lace; lace; shoe string
sznurowany [shnoo-ro-**va**-ni] adj.
m. laced (shoes, etc.)
sznycel po wiedeńsku [shni-tsel
po vye-deń-skoo] m. Wiener
cutlet; veal cutlet (minced)
szofer [sho-fer] m. chauffeur;
driver; (bus) driver; (truck)
driver; (lorry) driver
szopa [sho-pa] f. shed; lark; fun;
thatch (hairdo) (slang)
szopka [shop-ka] f. puppet
show; little shed; lark; fun;
farce; home-made Christ's crib
szorować [sho-ro-vaćh] v. rub;
scour; scrub; wash; grate; run
szorstki [shorst-kee] adj. m.
coarse; rough; crude; harsh
szorstko [shorst-ko] adv.
roughly; coarsely; bluntly;
crudely; curtly; rudely
szorstkość [shorst-kośhćh] f.
roughness; harshness; bluntness; rudeness; crudeness
szosa [sho-sa] f. highway; road
szowinizm [sho-vee-ńeezm] m.
chauvinism; jingoism
szóstka [shoost-ka] f. the figure
six; 6
szósty [shoos-ti] adj. m. num.
sixth; 6th
szpachelka [shpa-khel-ka] f.
small spatula; small putty-
knife; stopping knife
szpachla [shpakh-la] f. spatula;
putty-knife; palette knife

szpachlówka [shpakh-loov-ka] f.
filler; putty; caulking
compound; painter's putty
szpada [shpa-da] f. sword; epee
(fencing sword like a foil)
szpadel [shpa-del] m. spade
szpagat [shpa-gat] m. string;
(ballet) split; cord; twine; twist
szpaler [shpa-ler] m. double
(tree) row; double lane of
people; hedge; two rows of
people (one on each side)
szpalta [shpal-ta] f. (newspaper,
magazine, etc.) column; (printer's) slip; (tanner's) split
szpara [shpa-ra] f. gap; slot; rift;
chink; crack; slit; crevice;
cranny; interstice
szparag [shpa-rak] m. asparagus
szpareczka [shpa-rech-ka] f.
narrow chink; small crack
szpargał [shpar-gaw] m. scrap
paper; scrap of paper
szpatułka [shpa-toow-ka] f.
spatula; tongue-depressor
szpecić [shpe-ćheećh] v.
disfigure; make ugly; mar
beauty; blemish; impair
szperacz [shpe-rach] m. ferreter;
(military) scout; sniper; rum-
mager; searcher (in archives)
szperać [shpe-raćh] v. forage;
burrow; poke about; search (in
books; archives, etc.)
szpetnie [shpet-ńe] adv. in an
ugly fashion; uglily; badly;
shabbily; basely; odiously
szpetny [shpet-ni] adj. m. ugly;
unsightly; shabby; base; vile
szpetota [shpe-to-ta] f. ugliness;
unsightliness; shabbiness
szpic [shpeets] m. spike; peak;
(sharp) point; Pomeranian dog
(Scandinavian Samoyed)
szpica [shpee-tsa] f. picket; head
of an advance military guard
szpicel [shpee-tsel] m. stool
pigeon; informer; sl. nark;
plain-clothes man; spy
szpiczasty [shpee-chas-ti] adj. m.
pointed; tapering (sharply)
szpieg [shpyeg] m. spy; sleuth
szpiegostwo [shpye-gos-tvo] n.
espionage; spying; intelligence
szpiegować [shpye-go-vaćh] v.
spy upon; shadow somebody;
watch somebody; eavesdrop
szpik [shpeek] m. marrow;
medulla; (fatty) bone marrow
szpikować [shpee-ko-vaćh] v.
stuff (with information); lard
(meat etc.); run through
szpilka [shpeel-ka] f. pin (small)
szpilkowy [shpeel-ko-vi] adj. m.
conifer (tree); pegged (soles)
szpikulec [shpee-koo-lets] m.
sharp pin; larding pin; skewer;
spit; (ice) pick
szpila [shpee-la] f. bodkin
szpilka [shpeel-ka] f. pin
szpilkowaty [shpeel-ko-va-ti] adj.
m. needle-like; sharply pointed
szpinak [shpee-nak] m. spinach
szpital [shpee-tal] m. hospital
szpon [shpon] m. claw; talon
pl. (evil, etc.) clutches
szponder [shpon-der] m. flank
(meat); sirloin
szprotka [shprot-ka] f. sprat
szpryca [shpri-tsa] f. syringe
szprycha [shpri-kha] f. spoke
szprycować [shpri-tso-vaćh] v.
sprinkle; syringe
szpula [shpoo-la] f. spool; reel
(for wire, film, etc.); coil
szpulka [shpool-ka] f. bobbin
szpunt [shpoont] m. plug;
stopper; bung; peg; (cabinet
maker's) tongue; feather
szpuntować [shpoon-to-vaćh]
v. bung (barrel); plug; peg
szrama [shra-ma] f. scar; slash
szranki [shran-kee] pl. lists;
bounds; reins; tilt (tournament) yard; barriers; leash
szreń [shreń] f. neve; frost
szron [shron] m. hoar frost; rime;
coat of rime; very light frost
sztab [shtab] m. staff;
headquarters; (General) Staff
sztaba [shta-ba] f. bar; (gold)
ingot; ingot (of silver)
sztabowy [shta-bo-vi] adj. m.
staff (officer, plan, etc.)
sztachety [shta-khe-ti] pl.
(picket) fence; railing

sztafeta [shta-fe-ta] f. relay (race); (military, etc.) courier

sztaluga [shta-loo-ga] f. easel

sztama [shta-ma] f. good understanding (sl.); stay friends

sztanca [shtan-tsa] f. die; stamp; punch (used with a die)

sztandar [shtan-dar] m. banner; (national) flag; infantry colors

sztanga [shtan-ga] f. iron bar; bar-bells; weight-lifting bar

sztangista [shtan-gees-ta] m. weight-lifter (sportsman)

sztokfisz [shtok-feesh] m. stock-fish; cod; codfish

sztolnia [shtol-ńa] f. gallery

sztora [shto-ra] f. blind

sztorm [shtorm] m. gale; storm

sztos [shtos] m. blow; stroke; sexual connection (vulg.)

sztuba [shtoo-ba] f. sl. school

sztubak [shtoo-bak] m. school kid; grade school pupil

sztucer [shtoo-tser] m. rifle (gun); sporting rifle

sztuciec [shtoo-ćhets] m. fork

sztuczka [shtooch-ka] f. trick; small piece; dodge; manoeuvre

sztuczne tworzywo [shtoo-chne tvo-zhi-vo] n. plastic

sztuczny [shtooch-ni] adj. m. artificial; sham; false; immitation

sztućce [shtooćh-tse] pl. (table) silver; knife, fork, and spoons

sztuka [shtoo-ka] f. art; piece; head of cattle; (stage) play; stunt; craft; art (of war); unit

sztukateria [shtoo-ka-ter-ya] f. stucco work; stucco

sztukować [shtoo-ko-vaćh] v. piece; patch up; eke out (a living); lengthen (dress, etc.)

szturchać [shtoor-khaćh] v. poke; dig; prod; jab; push; jostle; knuckle; knock about

szturm [shtoorm] m. attack; storm; assault; onslaught

szturmować [shtoor-mo-vaćh] v. storm; attack; assault; harass; molest; beset

sztych [shtikh] m. stab; engraving; etching; woodcut; spade thrust (in fencing, etc.)

sztyft [shtift] m. tag; pin; peg; prong; fang; needle

sztylet [shti-let] m. stiletto; dagger; poniard; bodkin; spike

sztywnieć [shtiv-ńećh] v. stiffen; grow stiff; become stiff; grow (become) rigid

sztywno [shtiv-no] adv. stiffly

sztywny [shtiv-ni] adj. m. stiff; rigid; inflexible; unbending; fixed; stark; puffed up; offish

szubienica [shoo-bye-ńee-tsa] f. gallows (for hanging men)

szubrawiec [shoo-bra-vyets] m. scoundrel; rascal; rogue

szubrawstwo [shoob-rav-stvo] n. villainy; rascally trick; rabble

szufelka [shoo-fel-ka] f. scoop; small shovel; small scoop

szufla [shoof-la] f. shovel

szuflada [shoo-fla-da] f. drawer; shunting; shelving

szuja [shoo-ya] f. scoundrel; rascal; rogue; confidence man

szukać [shoo-kaćh] v. look for; seek; search; cast about for; be bent on; be out for

szukanie [shoo-ka-ńe] n. search; quest; a probing; a seeking

szuler [shoo-ler] m. gambler; card-cheat; cheat; sharp

szulernia [shoo-ler-ńa] f. gambling den; gambling house

szum [shoom] m. (wind) noise; hum; roar; uproar; murmur; scum; spatter; frost

szumieć [shoo-myećh] v. buzz; roar; froth; hum; rustle; fizz; sparkle; revel; carouse

szumnie [shoom-ńe] adv. noisily; boisterously; uproariously; with pump

szumny [shoom-ni] adj. m. roaring; noisy; boisterous; humming; buzzing; frothy; high sounding; bombastic; pompous; uproarious; sonorous

szumowiny [shoo-mo-vee-ni] pl. scum; scum, dregs, lees of society; scum of society

szurać [shoo-raćh] v. scrape; shuffle; rasp; kick up a row;

bluster

szurgać [shoor-gaćh] v. shuffle noisily; scrape one's foot on the floor; pick up a trouble

szus [shoos] m. freak; **ski run** straight down

szuter [shoo-ter] m. gravel; broken stone

szuwary [shoo-va-ri] pl. rushes in wet lands

szwab [shvab] m. roach; cockroach; Hun; detested German invader

szwabić [shva-beećh] v. cheat; swindle

szwaczka [shvach-ka] f. seamstress; needle woman

szwadron [shvad-ron] m. squadron; (cavalry) squadron; troop

szwagier [shva-ger] m. brother-in -law

szwagierka [shva-ger-ka] f. sister -in-law

szwagrostwo [shvag-rost-vo] pl. brother-in-law and wife

szwagrowa [shvag-ro-va] f. wife of brother-in-law

szwajcar [shvay-tsar] m. doorman

Szwajcar [shvay-tsar] m. Swiss

szwajcarski [shvay-tsar-skee] adj. m. Swiss; of Switzerland

szwajcować [shvay-tso-vaćh] v. weld

szwalnia [shval-ńa] f. underwear factory; tailoring shop

szwank [shvank] m. injury, loss

szwankować [shvan-ko-vaćh] v. be faulty; be deficient; be defective; be out of order

szwarc [shvarts] m. smuggling; contraband (slang)

szwarcować [shvar-tso-vaćh] v. smuggle in; smuggle out; steal in; steal out; dodge the customs officials; gate-crush

szwargot [shvar-got] m. gibberish; jabber; lingo

szwargotać [shvar-go-taćh] v. gibber; jabber

szwedzki [shvedz-kee] adj. m. Swedish; of Sweden

szwejsować = szwajcować (to weld)

szwendać się [shven-daćh śhan] v. loiter; hang about; lop about; gad about

szwindel [shveen-del] m. swindle; trickery; hanky-panky; shenanigan

szwindlarz [shveend-lash] m. swindler; crook; trickster

szwoleżer [shvo-le-zher] m. light -cavalryman

szyb [shib] m. shaft; (oil) well; pit; coal shaft; groove; stack

szyba [shi-ba] f. (glass) pane; wind-shield; sheet of water

szybciej [shib-ćhey] adv. hurry up! jump to it!

szybka [shib-ka] f. small glass panel; piece of glass

szybki [shib-kee] adj. m. quick; fast; prompt; rapid; sharp (walk); smart (pace)

szybko [shib-ko] adv. quickly; fast; promptly; swiftly; rapidly; speedily; apace; hurry up!

szybkodziałający [shib-ko-dźha -wa-yown-tsi] adj. quick-acting

szybkostrzelny [shib-ko-stshel-ni] adj. rapid-firing

szybkość [shib-kośhćh] f. speed; rate; velocity; rapidity; fastness; quickness

szybować [shi-bo-vaćh] v. glide; soar; tower; sail; plane

szybowiec [shi-bo-vyets] m. glider (motor-less)

sztychta nocna [shtikh-ta nots- -na] f. night shift

szycie [shi-ćhe] n. sewing

szyć [shićh] v. sew; sew up

szydełko [shi-dew-ko] n. crochet -needle; crochet hook

szydełkować [shi-dew-ko-vaćh] v. make by crochet; crochet

szyderca [shi-der-tsa] m. scoffer; giber; railer

szderczo [shi-der-cho] adv. scoffingly; sneeringly; jeeringly

szyderczy [shi-der-chi] adj. m. scoffing; sarcastic; derisive; sneering; jeering; railing

szyderstwo [shi-der-stvo] n.

scoff; jeer; sneer; gibe;
derision; flout; raillery
szydło [shid-wo] n. awl; pricker
szydzić [shi-dźheećh] v. scoff
at; sneer at; jeer at; gibe at;
flout at; rail at; deride
szyfr [shifr] m. code; cipher
szyfrant [shif-rant] m.
cryptographer; coder
szyja [shi-ya] f. neck; bottleneck;
gullet; throat
szyk [shik] m. order; elegance;
(battle) array; formation
szykana [shi-ka-na] f. chicanery;
vexation; difficulties; petty
annoyances; (great) style
szykanować [shi-ka-no-vaćh] v.
vex; chicane; annoy; nag; pick
at; worry; persecute
szykować [shi-ko-vaćh] v.
make ready; prepare; get
ready; array; marshal
szykować się [shi-ko-vaćh
śhan] v. get ready; be in
prospect; prepare
szykownie [shi-kov-ńe] adv. in
style; smartly; elegantly;
fashionably; with elegance
szykowność [shi-kov-nośhćh]
f. elegance; smartness; style;
chic; recent fashion
szykowny [shi-kov-ni] adj. m.
smart; elegant; fashionable;
classy; dressy; chic
szyld [shild] m. sign-board; shop
sign; facia
szyldwach [shild-vakh] m.
sentry; military guard
szyling [shi-leeng] m. shilling
szympans [shim-pans] m.
chimpanzee
szympansica [shim-pan-śhee-
-tsa] f. female chimpanzee
szyna [shi-na] f. rail; slide-bar;
splint; pl. track, see: szyny
szynel [shi-nel] m. military
overcoat; greatcoat
szynk [shink] m. bar; saloon; pub
szynka [shin-ka] f. ham
szynkarka [shin-kar-ka] f.
barmaid
szynkarz [shin-kash] m. barman
szyny [shi-ni] pl. (railroad) track

szyper [shi-per] m. skipper
szypuła [shi-poo-wa] f. stalk;
stem; peduncle
szypułka [shi-poow-ka] f. small
stalk; stem; shank
szyszak [shi-shak] m. helmet
szyszka [shish-ka] f. (tree) cone;
strobile; bigwig; top-dog
szyzma [shiz-ma] f. schism

Ś

ściana [śhćha-na] f. wall
ścianka [śhćhan-ka] f.
partition; bulkhead; small wall
ściągać [śhćhown-gaćh] v.
draw down or together; cheat
in class; assemble; collect
(taxes, debts, etc.)
ściągaczka [śhćhown-gach-ka]
f. cheat note; crib
ścieg [śhćhek] m. stitch
ściec [śhćhets] v. drain off;
run off; trickle down; drip
ściek [śhćhek] m. sewer;
gutter; sink; sewage; drain;
gully; sullage
ściekać [śhćhe-kaćh] v.
drain off; flow down; trickle
down; drip; gutter
ściemniać [śhćhem-ńaćh] v.
darken; dim; obscure; dim the
lights; turn down the lights
ścienny [śhćhen-ni] adj. m.
mural (painting); wall (map
clock, calendar etc.)
ścierać [śhćhe-raćh] v. rub
off; grind down; wear off
ścierka [śhćher-ka] f. duster;
rug; kitchen towel; clout
ściernisko [śhćher-ńees-ko] n.
stubble field; stubble
ścierń [śhćherń] m. stubble
ścierpły [śhćherp-wi] adj. m.
numb; gone to sleep
ścierwo [śhćher-vo] n. carrion
ścieśniać [śhćheśh-ńaćh]
v. cramp; tighten; narrow;

restrict; close; confine

ścieżka [śhćhezh-ka] f. trail;
pass; (foot) pass; alley

ścięcie [śhćhan-ćhe] n.
beheading; cutting off;
truncation; coagulation

ścięgno [śhćhang-no] n.
tendon; sinew

ścięty [śhćhan-ti] adj.
m. truncated; cut off;
beheaded; coagulated

ścigacz [śhćhee-gach] m.
torpedo boat; motor gun boat

ścigać [śhćhee-gaćh] v.
chase; pursue; run after; hunt
for; prosecute

ścinać [śhćhee-naćh] v. cut
off; cut down; fell (tree); clip;
clot; shear; remove; behead

ścinać się [śhćhee-naćh
śhan] v. coagulate; congeal;
fix; clot; fail (an examination)

ściółka [śhćhoow-ka] f. litter
bed; litter bedding; barn litter

ścisk [śhćheesk] m. throng;
press; crowd; squeeze; crush;
clamp; cleat; hand-screw

ściskać [śhćhees-kaćh] v.
compress; shake (hand); hug;
squeeze; press; clench; pack

ścisłość [śhćhees-wośhćh]
f. exactness; accuracy; compactness; density; reliability;
cohesion; strictness; fidelity

ścisły [śhćhees-wi] adj. m.
exact; precise; compact;
accurate; dense; close-knit

ściśle [śhćheeśh-le] adv.
exactly; tightly; compactly

ślad [śhlat] m. trace; track;
(foot) print; footstep

ślamazara [śhla-ma-za-ra] f.
sluggard; slow headed person

ślamazarny [śhla-ma-zar-ni] adj.
m. sluggish; listless

śląski [śhlown-skee] adj. m.
Silesian; of Silesia

śledczy [śhled-chi] adj. m.
inquisitional; of inquiry

śledzić [śhle-dźheećh] v.
spy; watch; investigate;
observe; shadow; follow

śledziona [śhle-dźho-na] f.

spleen; milt

śledziowy [śhle-dźho-vi]
adj. m. herring (oil, salad, etc.)

śledztwo [śhledz-tvo] n.
investigation; inquest; inquiry

śledź [śhledźh] m. herring

ślepie [śhle-pye] n. (animal's)
eye; eye; lights

ślepnąć [śhlep-nownćh] v. go
blind; loose one's eyesight

ślepa ulica [śhle-pa oo-lee-tsa]
s. dead-end street

ślepota [śhle-po-ta] f.
blindness; cecity; lack of
foresight

ślepy [śhle-pi] adj. m. blind

ślęczeć [śhlan-chećh] v. drag
study or reading; drudge; pore
(over a book); plod; slog
away; boggle; grind

śliczny [śhleech-ni] adj. m.
pretty; lovely; dandy

ślimacznica [śhlee-mach-ńee-
-tsa] f. road access ramp;
helix; warm-wheel; scroll

ślimak [śhlee-mak] m. snail

ślina [śhlee-na] f. saliva

śliniak [śhlee-ńak] m. bib

śliski [śhlees-kee] adj. m.
slippery; slimy; scabrous

śliwa [śhlee-va] f. plum tree

śliwka [śhleev-ka] m. plum

śliwowica [śhlee-vo-vee-tsa] f.
plum brandy; plum vodka

ślizgacz [śhleez-gach] m. speed
-boat; gliding boat

ślizgać się [śhleez-gaćh
śhan] v. slide; glide; slip;
skid; skate (on ice)

ślizgawka [śhleez-gav-ka] f.
skating rink; kid's slide

ślizgowiec [śhleez-go-vyets] m.
hydrofoil; gliding boat; speed
boat

ślub [śhloop] m. wedding; vow

ślubna obrączka [śhloob-na o-
-brownch-ka] f. wedding ring

ślubny [śhloob-ni] adj. m.
nuptial; wedding-(ring);
legitimate (son)

ślubować [śhloo-bo-vaćh] v.
vow; take an oath; pledge

ślusarz [śhloo-sash] m. lock

-smith; ironworker; metal
worker

śluz [śhloos] m. slime; phlegm

śluza [śhloo-za] f. sluice

śmiać się [śhmyaćh śhan] v.
laugh; laugh at; chuckle; scoff
at; make sport of

śmiałek [śhmya-wek] m.
daredevil; mad cap

śmiałość [śhmya-wośhćh]
f. boldness; courage; bravery;
daring; guts; pluck; audacity

śmiały [śhmya-wi] adj. m. bold

śmiech [śhmyekh] m. laughter

śmieci [śhmye-ćhee] pl.
rubbish; garbage; rag; shred;
scrap of paper; refuse

śmiecić [śhmye-ćheećh] v.
litter; throw litter about

śmiecie [śhmye-ćhe] pl.
rubbish; garbage; rag; shred;
scrap; refuse; sweepings

śmieć [śhmyećh] m. litter;
rag; scrap; shred

śmiercionośny [śhmyer-ćho-
-nośh-ni] adj. m. lethal;
deadly; murderous

śmierć [śhmyerćh] f. death

śmierdzieć [śhmyer-dźhećh]
v. stink; smell; reek (of vodka,
nicotine, carrion)

śmiertelnik [śhmyer-tel-ńeek]
m. mortal man; mortal

śmiertelność [śhmyer-tel-
-nośhćh] f. mortality;
deadliness; death rate

śmiertelny [śhmyer-tel-ni]
adj. m. mortal; deadly; death-
(throes, blow, rattle); fatal

śmieszność [śhmyesh-
-nośhćh] f. comic trait; the
ridiculous; drollery

śmieszny [śhmyesh-ni] adj. m.
funny; ridiculous; comic;
absurd; amusing; droll

śmieszyć [śhmye-shićh] v.
make (people) laugh; cause
laughter; amuse

śmietana [śhmye-ta-na] f. sour
cream; clotted cream

śmietanka [śhmye-tan-ka] f.
cream; flower (of society etc.)

śmietnik [śhmyet-ńeek] m.

garbage can; garbage dump

śmiga [śhmee-ga] f. (windmill)
sail

śmigło [śhmeeg-wo] n. propeller; adv. swiftly; nimbly

śmigłowiec [śhmee-gwo-vyets]
m. helicopter

śniadanie [śhńa-da-ńe] n.
breakfast; luncheon

śniady [śhńa-di] adj. m.
swarthy; sun-tanned; dusky;
tawny; dark-skinned

śnić [śhńeećh] v. dream
(about something); have a
dream; dream that

śniedź [śhńedźh] f. verdigris

śnieg [śhńek] m. snow;
snow-scape

śniegowce [śhńe-gov-tse] pl.
snow boots; overshoes;
galoshes

śnieg pada [śhńek pa-da] exp.
it snows

śnieżka [śhńezh-ka] f.
snowball; Snow White

śnieżnobiały [śhńezh-no-bya-
-wi] adj. m. snow-white

śnieżny [śhńezh-ni] adj. m.
snowy; snow white; snow-

śnieżyca [śhńe-zhi-tsa] f.
snow -storm; blizzard

śpiący [śhpyown-tsi] adj. m.
sleepy; drowsy; slumberous

śpiączka [śhpyownch-ka] f.
sleeping sickness

śpieszyć się [śhpye-shićh
śhan] v. hurry; hasten; be in
a hurry; make haste; be fast

śpiew [śhpyev] m. song;
singing; singing lesson

śpiewaczka [śhpye-vach-ka] f.
singer (girl or woman)

śpiewać [śhpye-vaćh] v. sing

śpiewak [śhpye-vak] m. singer

śpiewnik [śhpyev-ńeek] m.
songbook; hymn-book

śpiewny [śhpyev-ni] adj. m.
melodious; singsong- (accent)

śpioch [śhpyokh] m. sleepy
head; lie-abed; slug-abed

śpiwór [śhpee-voor] m.
sleeping bag

średni [śhred-ńee] adj. m.

average; medium; mean; intermediary; middle; mediocre
średnica [śhred-ńee-tsa] f.
diameter; bore; middle register
średnik [śhred-ńeek] m.
semicolon
średnio [śhred-ńo] adv.
average; medium-; fairly well
średniowiecze [śhred-ńo-vye-
-che] n. Middle Ages
średniowieczny [śhred-ńo-
-vyech-ni] adj. m. medieval
środa [śhro-da] f. Wednesday
środek [śhro-dek] m. center;
middle; measures; means;
remedy; interior; midst; inside;
agent; medium; device
środkowy [śhrod-ko-vi] adj. m.
central; center- (line); middle
środowisko [śhro-do-vees-ko]
n. surroundings; environment;
habitat; range; (chem.)
medium
śródmieście [śhrood-myeśh-
-će] n. city center; center of
town; down town area
Śródziemne Morze [śhrood-
-źhem-ne mo-zhe] n.
Mediterranean sea;
Mediterranean
śruba [śhroo-ba] f. screw
śrubokręt [śhroo-bo-krant] m.
screwdriver; turn-screw
śrut [śhroot] m. (lead) shot
świadczenie [śhvyad-che-ńe]
n. benefit; charge; testimony
świadczyć [śhvyad-chićh] v.
witness; attest; bear witness
świadectwo [śhvya-dets-tvo] n.
certificate; bill of health
świadek naoczny [śhvya-dek
na-och-ni] m. exp.: an
eyewitness
świadomość [śhvya-do-
-mośhćh] f. consciousness;
awareness; notice (of sth)
świadomy [śhvya-do-mi]
adj. m. conscious; aware;
wilful; cognizant; voluntary
świat [śhvyat] m. world
światło [śhvyat-wo] n. light
światłomierz [śhvya-two-
-myesh] m. light meter

photometer
światopogląd [śhvya-to-po-
-glownt] m. ideology; outlook
on life; philosophy of life
światowy [śhvya-to-vi] adj. m.
world; worldly; global; society-
świąteczny [śhvyown-tech-ni]
adj. m. festive; holiday
(mood); solemn
świątynia [śhvyown-ti-ńa] f.
temple; place of worship
świder [śhvee-der] m. drill;
auger; bore; borer; perforator
świdrować [śhvee-dro-vaćh]
v. drill; bore; perforate; pierce
świeca [śhvye-tsa] f. candle
świecić [śhvye-ćheećh] v.
light up; shine; glitter; sparkle
świecki [śhvyets-kee] adj. m.
secular; mundane; laic; lay
świecki ksiądz [śhvyets-kee
kśhownts] m. secular priest
świeczka [śhvyech-ka] f.
(small) candle
świecznik [śhvyech-ńeek] m.
chandelier; candlestick
świergot [śhvyer-got] m.
twitter; chirp; warble; chirrup;
tweet; short and shrill tone
świergotać [śhvyer-go-taćh]
v. chirp; chirrup; warble;
tweet; sound like a bird
świerk [śhvyerk] m. fir tree
świerkowy [śhvyer-ko-vi]
adj. m. fir; spruce; of spruce
świerszcz [śhvyershch] m.
cricket; grasshopper
świerzb [śhvyezhb] m. scabies
świerzbieć [śhvyezh-byećh]
v. itch; be itching
świetlica [śhvyet-lee-tsa] f.
reading hall; community center
świetlik [śhvyet-leek] m.
firebug; glow worm; skylight;
firefly; glowing beetle
świetlny [śhvyetl-ni] adj. m.
lighting (gas etc.)
świetność [śhvyet-nośhćh]
f. splendor; magnificence;
glamor; luster
świetny [śhvyet-ni] adj. m.
splendid; excellent; first rate
świeżo [śhvye-zho] adv. fresh

świeży [śhvye-zhi] adj. m.
  fresh; new; recent; fresh; raw;
  ruddy; brisk; crisp; breezy

święcenie [śhvyan-tse-ńe] n.
  celebration; blessing;
  observance; consecration

święcić [śhvyan-ćheećh] v.
  celebrate; keep a holiday;
  bless; observe; ordain

święcone [śhvyan-tso-ne] n.
  Easter blessed food (Polish
  style traditionally displayed)

święta [śhvyan-ta] pl. holiday

święto [śhvyan-to] n. holiday

świętokradztwo [śhvyan-to-
  -krads-tvo] n. sacrilege

świętoszek [śhvyan-to-shek]
  m. bigot; sanctimonious
  hypocrite

świętość [śhvyan-tośhćh] f.
  sanctity; holiness; sainthood

święty [śhvyan-ti] adj. m.
  saint; holy; saintly; pious;
  sacred; sacrosanct; inviolate

świnia [śhvee-ńa] f. swine;
  hog; pig; exp.: dirty pig

świnić [śhvee-ńeećh] v.
  make a mess; litter up; play
  dirty or shabby tricks

świnka morska [śhveen-ka
  mors-ka] f. guinea pig; cavy

świństwo [śhveeńs-tvo] n.
  dirty deed; meanness; nasty
  stuff; dross

świsnąć [śhvees-nownćh] v.
  whistle; pilfer; bolt

świst [śhveest] m. whistle
  sound; bullet sound

świstak [śhvees-tak] m.
  ground hog; woodchuck

świstawka [śhvees-tav-ka] f.
  whistle

świstek [śhvees-tek] m. scrap
  of paper; slip of paper

świt [śhveet] m. daybreak;
  dawn; sunrise; break of day

świtać [śhvee-taćh] v. dawn
  (upon); rise (of sun or moon)

świtezianka [śhvee-te-źhan-ka]
  f. water-nymph

T

tabaka [ta-ba-ka] f. snuff

tabakierka [ta-ba-ker-ka] f.
  snuff box

tabela [ta-be-la] f. table; index;
  list; tabulated figures

tabletka [tab-let-ka] f.
  tablet; pill (aspirin etc.)

tablica [tab-lee-tsa] f.
  blackboard; switchboard; slab;
  signboard; bulletin-board

tablica rozdzielcza [tab-lee-tsa
  roz-dźhel-cha] f. switchboard

tabliczka mnożenia [tab-leech-ka
  mno-zhe-ńa] f. multiplication
  table

tabor kolejowy [ta-bor ko-le-yo-
  -vi] m. rolling stock (r.r.)

taboret [ta-bo-ret] m. taboret

tabu [ta-boo] n. taboo

tabun [ta-boon] m. horse herd

taca [ta-tsa] f. tray; salver

taczki [tach-kee] pl. wheelbarrow

tafla [taf-la] f. plate; slab

taić [ta-eećh] v. hide; conceal

tajać [ta-yaćh] v. thaw; melt

tajemnica [ta-yem-ńee-tsa] f.
  secret; mystery; secrecy

tajemniczy [ts-yem-ńee-chi] adj.
  m. mysterious; inscrutable;
  weird; uncanny; secret

tajny [tay-ni] adj. m. secret

tak [tak] part. yes; adv. thus; as;
  indecl.: like this; so

tak czy tak [tak chi tak] exp.
  anyhow; either way; in any
  case; one way or the other

taki [ta-kee] adj. m. such

taki sam [ta-kee sam] adj. m.
  identical; similar

takielunek [ta-ke-loo-nek] m.
  rig; rigging; tackle

taksa [tak-sa] f. tariff; rate

taksacja [tak-sa-tsya] f. tax
  -appraisal

taksować [tak-so-vaćh] v.

estimate; rate; appraise; value
taksówka [tak-**soov**-ka] f. taxi
takt [takt] m. tact; stroke
taktowny [tak-tov-ni] adj. m.
tactful; considerate
taktyczny [tak-tich-ni] adj. m.
tactical; political
taktyka [tak-ti-ka] f. tactics
także [tak-zhe] adv. also; too; as
well; likewise; alike
talent [ta-lent] m. talent
talerz [ta-lesh] m. (food) plate;
plateful; disk; planting scalp
talerzyk [ta-le-zhik] m. small
plate; ski-stick disk; scale
talia [ta-lya] f. waist; card deck;
pack of cards; tackle; middle
talk [talk] m. talcum; talc
talon [ta-lon] m. coupon
tam [tam] adv. there; yonder
tama [ta-ma] f. dam; dike
tamować [ta-mo-vaćh] v. dam
up; block; check; stem; clog
tamtejszy [tam-tey-shi] adj. m.
from there; living there
tamten [tam-ten] pron. that
tamtędy [tam-tan-di] adv. that
way; the other way
tamże [tam-zhe] adv. there in; in
the same place; at which
place; (by the same author)
tancerka [tan-tser-ka] f. dancer;
ballet-dancer; partner
tancerz [tan-tsesh] m. dancer
tandeta [tan-de-ta] f. trashy
products; shoddy goods
taneczny [ta-nech-ni] adj. m.
dancing-(school, master, hall);
dance-(step; music etc.)
tangens [tan-gens] m. tangent
tani [ta-ńee] adj. m. cheap
taniec [ta-ńets] m. dance
tanieć [ta-ńećh] v. get
cheaper; cheapen; grow
cheaper; fall in price
taniość [ta-ńośhćh] f.
cheapness; low prices
tańczyć [tań-chićh] v. dance
tankowiec [tan-ko-vyets] m.
tanker (ship)
tapczan [tap-chan] m. couch;
convertible bed
tapeta [ta-pe-ta] f. wallpaper

tapicer [ta-pee-tser] m.
upholsterer; upholsterer's shop
taran [ta-ran] m. battering ram
tarapaty [ta-ra-pa-ti] pl. trouble;
predicament; sad fix
taras [ta-ras] m. terrace
tarasować [ta-ra-so-vaćh] v.
block; stand in the way
tarcica [tar-ćhee-tsa] f. plank;
deal; sawn board
tarcie [tar-ćhe] n. friction;
frictional resistance
tarcza [tar-cha] f. shield; disk
tarczowa piła [tar-cho-va pee-
-wa] f. circular saw
tarczyca [tar-chi-tsa] f. thyroid
gland
targ [tark] m. country market
targować [tar-go-vaćh] v. sell;
bargain; trade; haggle; deal
tarka [tar-ka] f. rasp; grater
tartak [tar-tak] m. sawmill
taryfa [ta-ri-fa] f. tariff
tarzać się [ta-zhaćh śhan] v.
wallow; welter; roll (in mud)
tasak [ta-sak] m. chopper;
broad blade cleaver
tasiemiec [ta-śhe-myets] m.
tapeworm; cestoid; taenia
tasiemka [ta-śhem-ka] f. ribbon;
tape; narrow strip
tasować [ta-so-vaćh] v. shuffle
taśma [taśh-ma] f. band; tape
taśma ruchoma [taśh-ma roo-
-kho-ma] f. belt conveyor
tatarka [ta-tar-ka] f. buckwheat
taternik [ta-ter-ńeek] m.
mountain climber; alpinist
tatuować [ta-too-o-vaćh] v.
tattoo; make a tattoo mark
tatuś [ta-toośh] m. daddy; dad
tchawica [tkha-**vee**-tsa] f.
trachea; windpipe
tchnąć [tkhnownćh] v. inspire
tchnienie [tkhńe-ńe] n. breath
tchórz [tkhoosh] m. skunk;
coward; craven; poltroon; funk
tchórzliwy [tkhoo-**zhle**-vi] adj.
m. cowardly; chicken-hearted
tchórzostwo [tkhoo-**zhost**-vo] n.
cowardice; lack of courage
teatr [te-atr] m. theatre; the
stage

teatralny [te-a-**tral**-ni] adj. m.
theatrical; scenic; stage-
techniczny [tekh-**ńeech**-ni] adj.
m. technical (terms, school,
staff); technological (progress)
technik [tekh-**ńeek**] m.
technician; engineer; mechanic
technika [tekh-**ńee**-ka] f.
technique; engineering;
technology
technologia [tekh-no-**lo**-gya] f.
technology; production
engineering; technique
teczka [**tech**-ka] f. briefcase;
folder; portfolio; jacket; binder
tegoroczny [te-go-**roch**-ni]
adj. m. this year's
teka [**te**-ka] f. (large) briefcase;
portfolio; file; folder; case
tekst [tekst] m. text; wording
tekstylny [tek-**stil**-ni] adj. m.
textile; textile-; draper;
clothier-
tektura [tek-**too**-ra] f. cardboard;
pasteboard (corrugated)
telefon [te-le-**fon**] m. telephone;
phone; phone receiver
telefonistka [te-le-fo-**ńeest**-ka] f.
telephone operator
telefonować [te-le-fo-**no**-vaćh]
v. ring up; telephone; call up
telegraf [te-le-**graf**] m. telegraph;
telegraph office
telegraficzny [te-le-gra-**feech**-ni]
adj. m. telegraphic
telegrafować [te-le-gra-fo-**vaćh**]
v. cable; wire; telegraph
telegram [te-le-**gram**] m.
telegram; cable; wire;
cablegram
telepatia [te-le-**pa**-tya] f.
telepathy; tough transference
teleskop [te-le-**skop**] m.
telescope; telescopic spring
teleskopowy [te-le-sko-**po**-vi] adj.
m. telescopic
telewizja [te-le-**veez**-ya] f.
television; TV
telewizor [te-le-**vee**-zor] m.
television set; TV set
temat [**te**-mat] m. subject
temblak [**tem**-blak] m. sling
temperament [tem-pe-ra-**ment**]

m. temper; nature; mettle
temperatura [tem-pe-ra-**too**-ra] f.
temperature; fever
temperować [tem-pe-**ro**-vaćh]
v. temper; sharpen; mitigate
tamperówka [tem-pe-**roov**-ka] f.
pencil sharpener
tempo [**tem**-po] n. rate; tempo
temu [**te**-moo] adv. ago
ten; ta; to [ten, ta, to] m.f.n.
pron. this; this one
ten sam [ten sam] pron. the
same (man, pencil, etc.)
tendencja [ten-**den**-tsya] f.
tendency; inclination; drift;
trend; bias; proclivity
tendencyjny [ten-den-**tsiy**-ni] adj.
m. biased; tendentious
tenis [te-**ńees**] m. tennis
tenor [te-**nor**] m. tenor (voice)
tenuta [te-**noo**-ta] f. land holding;
rent; tenure; lease
tenże [ten-zhe] m. pron. the
same (individual etc.)
teolog [te-o-**lok**] m. theologian
teologia [te-o-**lo**-gya] f. theology;
Faculty of Theology
teoretyczny [te-o-re-**tich**-ni] adj.
m. theoretical; speculative
teoretyk [te-o-re-**tyk**] m.
theoretician; theorist
teoria [te-o-**rya**] f. theory
terapia [te-ra-**pya**] f.
therapeutics; therapy
teraz [te-**ras**] adv. now;
nowadays; at present
teraźniejszość [te-raźh-**ńey**-
-shośhćh] f. present (time)
teraźniejszy kurs [te-raźh-**ńey**-
-shi **koors**] m. present rate
teren [te-**ren**] m. terrain
terenowy samochód [te-re-**no**-vi
sa-mo-khood] m. cross-
country car (four wheel drive)
terkotać [ter-ko-**taćh**] v. rattle;
clatter; chatter (away)
termin [ter-**meen**] m. term;
expression; apprenticeship;
time limit; fixed date
termin ostateczny [ter-meen o-
-sta-**tech**-ni] m. deadline
terminator [ter-mee-**na**-tor] m.
apprentice; terminator

terminarz [ter-mee-nash] m.
appointment calendar; agenda
terminologia [ter-mee-no-lo-gya]
f. terminology; nomenclature
terminowo [ter-mee-no-vo] adv.
on time; in due time;
punctually; promptly
termit [ter-meet] m. termite
termometr [ter-mo-metr] m.
thermometer
termos [ter-mos] m. thermos
-bottle; vacuum bottle (flask)
terpentyna [ter-pen-ti-na] f.
turpentine (oil)
terror [ter-ror] m. terror
terroryzować [ter-ro-ri-zo-vaćh]
v. terrorize; bully
terytorialny [te-ry-tor-yal-ni] adj.
m. territorial
terytorium [te-ri-tor-yoom] n.
territory
testament [te-sta-ment] m.
testament; (last) will
teściowa [teśh-ćho-va] f.
mother-in-law
teść [teśhćh] m. father-in-law
teza [te-za] f. thesis; argument
też [tesh] adv. also; too;
likewise; as well
tęchnąć [tankh-nownćh] v. get
musty; grow mouldy; reduce
swelling; become reduced
tęcza [tan-cha] f. rainbow
tęczówka [tan-choov-ka] f. iris
tędy [tan-di] adv. this way
tęgi [tan-gee] adj. m. stout;
strong; solid; fat; big; portly
tego [tan-go] adv. stoutly; ably;
amply; mightily; powerfully
tępak [tan-pak] m. dullard
tępić [tan-peećh] v. dull; blunt;
destroy; combat; exterminate;
oppose; fight; persecute
tępota [tan-po-ta] f. dullness;
stupidity; obtuseness; stolidity
tępy [tan-pi] adj. m. dull; point
less; slow-witted; stolid
tęsknić [tansk-ńeećh] v. long
(for); yearn; be nostalgic
tęsknota [tans-kno-ta] f. longing;
hankering; nostalgia
tęskny [tansk-ni] adj. m.
melancholy; wistful; longing;

yearning; lingering;sad
tętent [tan-tent] m. hoof beat
tętnica [tan-tńee-tsa] f. artery
tętnić [tant-ńeećh] v. pulsate
tętno [tant-no] n. pulse rate;
heartbeats; vibrations
tężec [tan-zhets] m. tetanus
tężeć [tan-zhećh] v. stiffen;
solidify; set; clot; curdle;
coagulate; grow stronger;
acquire strength and vigor
tężyzna [tan-zhiz-na] f. vigor
tkacki [tkats-kee] adj. m. textile;
weaver's; of textiles
tkactwo [tkats-tvo] n. weaving
tkacz [tkach] m. weaver (man)
tkać [tkaćh] v. weave; poke
tkanina [tka-ńee-na] f. fabric
tkanka [tkan-ka] f. tissue
tkliwość [tklee-vośhćh] f.
tenderness; love; affection
tkliwy [tklee-vi] adj. m. tender;
loving; affectionate; sensitive
tknąć [tknownćh] v. touch;
strike; size; affect
tkwić [tkveećh] v. stick; stay
tleć [tlećh] v. smoulder
tlen [tlen] m. oxygen
tlenek [tle-nek] m. oxide
tlić się [tleećh śhan] v.
smoulder; glow; burn lightly
tło [two] n. background
tłocznia [twoch-ńa] f. press
tłoczyć [two-chićh] v. press;
crowd; print; stamp; crush
tłok [twok] m. piston; crowd
tłuc [twoots] v. pound; hammer;
batter; smash; shatter
tłuczek [twoo-chek] m. pestle
tłuczeń [twoo-cheń] m.
macadam; broken stone; road
gravel; break-stone
tłum [twoom] m. crowd; mob;
host; throng; multitude
tłumacz [twoo-mach] m.
interpreter; translator
tłumaczenie [twoo-ma-che-ńe]
n. translation; explanation;
interpretation; excuse
tłumaczyć [twoo-ma-chićh] v.
translate; interpret; justify
tłumić [twoo-meećh] v. muffle;
put down; dampen; suppress;

stifle; stamp out; deaden
tłumik [twoo-meek] m. muffler
tłumny [twoom-ni] adj. m.
  crowded; numerous; populous
tłumok [twoo-mok] m. bundle
tłusty [twoos-ti] adj. m. obese;
  fat (meat; pig etc.); rich; oily;
  greasy; corpulent; fatty
tłuszcz [twooshch] m. fat;
  grease
tłuszcza [twoosh-cha] f. mob
tłuścić [twoośh-ćheećh]
  grease; smear with grease
to [to] pron it; this; that; so
toaleta [to-a-le-ta] f. toilet;
  dress; dressing table
toaletowe przybory [to-a-le-to-ve
  pzhi-bo-ri] pl. toilet-articles;
  cosmetics
toast [to-ast] m. toast
tobół [to-boow] m. pack; bundle
toczony [to-cho-ni] adj. m.
  turned; shaped; rounded
toczyć [to-chićh] v. roll;
  machine; wage (war); wheel;
  carry on; shape; fester
toga [to-ga] f. gown; Roman
  toga
tok [tak] m. course; progress
tokarka [to-kar-ka] f. lathe
tokarnia [to-kar-ńa] f. lathe
tokarz [to-kash] m. machinist;
  turner; lathe operator
tokować [to-ko-vaćh] v. toot
tolerancja [to-le-rants-ya] f.
  tolerance; broad-mindedness
tolerować [to-le-ro-vaćh] v.
  tolerate; suffer; stand for
tom [tom] m. volume
ton [ton] m. sound; tone; note
tona [to-na] f. ton (metric etc.)
tonacja [to-na-tsya] f. pitch; key;
  mode; tone; tonal character
tonaż [to-nash] m. tonnage
tonąć [to-nownćh] v. drown
toń [toń] f. deep (water); flood;
  deep sea; depth of water
topaz [to-pas] m. topaz
topić [to-peećh] v. drown;
  thaw; melt down; smelt
  (metals); sink; flux
topiel [to-pyel] f. abyss; gulf
topliwy [to-plee-vi] adj. m.

meltable; fusible; liquescent
topnieć [top-ńećh] v. melt
topografia [to-po-gra-fya] f.
  topography; lay of the land
topola [to-po-la] f. poplar
toporek [to-po-rek] m. hatchet
topór [to-poor] m. (big) hatchet;
  axe; battle axe
tor [tor] m. track; lane; path
tor kolejowy [tor ko-le-yo-vi] m.
  rail-track; railroad track
torba [tor-ba] f. bag; bagful
torcik [tor-ćheek] m. small layer
  cake
torebka [to-reb-ka] f. (hand) bag;
  purse; small bag (or pouch)
torf [torf] m. peat
torfowisko [tor-fo-vees-ko] n.
  peat bog; turbary
torować [to-ro-vaćh] v. clear;
  pave; clear a path; show the
  way; pave the way for
torpeda [tor-pe-da] f. torpedo;
  motor driven rail car
torpedować [tor-pe-do-vaćh] v.
  torpedo; scuttle; obstruct
torpedowiec [tor-pe-do-vyets] m.
  torpedo boat
tors [tors] m. torso
tort [tort] m. tort (multi-layer)
  fancy cake
tortura [tor-too-ra] f. torture
torturować [tor-too-ro-vaćh] v.
  torture; torment; put to torture
totalny [to-tal-ni] adj. m.
  totalitarian; total; entire
towar [to-var] m. merchandise
towarowy dom [to-va-ro-vi dom]
  m. department store
towarzyski [to-va-zhis-kee] adj.
  m. sociable; social
towarzystwo [to-va-zhist-vo] n.
  company; society; companionship; entourage
towarzysz [to-va-zhish] m.
  companion; pal; associate;
  comrade; chum; mate
towarzyszka [to-va-zhish-ka] f.
  companion (female); associate
towarzyszyć [to-va-zhi-shićh] v.
  accompany; escort; keep company; attend; go together
tożsamość [tozh-sa-mośhćh]

f. identity; sameness
tracić [tra-ćheećh] v. lose;
waste; shed (leaves); execute
tradycja [tra-di-tsya] f.
tradition; handing down orally
customs, beliefs, etc.
tradycyjny [tra-di-tsiy-ni] adj. m.
traditional
traf [traf] m. happenstance;
chance; luck; coincidence
trafem [tra-fem] adv. by chance
trafiać [tra-fyaćh] v. hit
(target); guess right; home
trafność [traf-nośhćh] f.
accuracy (of aim); rightness;
soundness; relevancy; fitness
trafny [traf-ni] adj. m. exact;
correct; right; fit; apt
tragarz [tra-gash] m. porter
tragedia [tra-ge-dya] f. tragedy;
very sad or tragic event
tragiczny [tra-geech-ni] adj. m.
tragic; disastrous; very sad
tragikomedia [tra-gee-ko-me-dya]
f. tragicomedy
trajkotać [tray-ko-taćh]
v. chatter; jabber; rattle;
gabble
trak [trak] m. square saw;
frame sawing machine
trakcja [tra-ktsya] f. traction
trakt [trakt] m. highway; course
traktat [tra-ktat] m. treaty
traktor [trak-tor] m. tractor
traktować [trak-to-vaćh] v.
deal; treat; negotiate; discuss
trampolina [tram-po-lee-na] f.
spring board; diving board
tramwaj [tram-vay] m. tramway
tramwajarz [tram-va-yash] m.
tramway worker
tran [tran] m. (cod or whale) oil;
cod liver oil; whale oil
trans [trans] m. trance; ecstasy
transakcja [trans-akts-ya] f.
transaction; deal
transatlantycki [trans-at-lan-tits-
-kee] adj. m. transatlantic
transformator [trans-for-ma-tor]
m. transformer; converter
transfuzja [trans-fooz-ya] f.
transfusion (of blood etc.)
transmisja [trans-mees-ya] f.

transmission; broadcast
transmitować [trans-mee-to-
-vaćh] v. transmit; broadcast
transparent [trans-pa-rent] m.
(marching) slogans; banner
transport [trans-port] m. transport; haulage; consignment
tranzyt [tran-zit] m. transit
tranzytowy [tran-zi-to-vi] adj. m.
transit-; through (traffic etc.)
trapez [tra-pez] m. trapeze
trapić [tra-peećh] v. molest;
pester; worry; annoy; bother
trasa [tra-sa] f. route; (bus) line
trasa podróży [tra-sa po-droo-
-zhi] f. itinerary
tratować [tra-to-vaćh] v.
trample; tread down
tratwa [trat-va] f. raft; float
trawa [tra-va] f. grass
trawić [tra-veećh] v. digest
trawienie [tra-vye-ńe] n.
digestion; consumption
trawnik [trav-ńeek] m. lawn
trąba [trown-ba] f. trumpet;
trunk (elephant); tornado;
twister; horn; whirlwind; ninny
trąba wodna [trown-ba vod-na]
f. waterspout; wind spout
trąbić [trown-beećh] v. bugle;
toot; hoot; roar; proclaim
trąbka [trownb-ka] f. horn; bugle
trącać [trown-caćh] v. jostle;
elbow; tip; knock; nudge;
strike; touch; nudge
trącić [trown-ćheećh] v.
jostle; smell; be fusty; be out
of date; border on (stupidity)
trąd [trownd] m. leprosy
trel [trel] m. trill
trelować [tre-lo-vaćh] v. trill
trema [tre-ma] f. stage fright
trener [tre-ner] m. coach; trainer
trening [tre-ńeeng] m. training
trenować [tre-no-vaćh] v. train;
coach; practice (shooting)
trepanacja [tre-pa-nats-ya] f.
trepanation
trepki [trep-kee] pl. sandals
tresować [tre-so-vaćh] v. train;
tame; drill; break in (horses)
tresura [tre-soo-ra] f. taming;
training (of animals)

treściwy [treśh-ćhee-vi]
adj. m. concise; substantial;
meaty; pithy; terse; brief; rich

treść [treśhćh] f. contents;
jist; substance; essence; pith;
marrow; tenor; purview; plot

trębacz [tran-bach] m. trumpeter

trędowaty [tran-do-va-ti] adj. m.
leprous; leper

triumfować [tree-oom-fo-vaćh]
v. triumph; achieve triumphs;
prevail; exult; jubilate; crow

trochę [tro-khan] adv. a little bit;
a few; some; awhile; a spell

trociny [tro-ćhee-ni] pl.
sawdust (of wood); scraps (of
writings, poetry, etc.)

trofea [tro-fe-a] pl. trophies

trojaki [tro-ya-kee] adj. m.
threefold; triple; treble; triplex

troje [tro-ye] num. three

troki [tro-kee] pl. straps

trolejbus [tro-ley-boos] m.
trolley-bus

tron [tron] m. throne; the throne

trop [trop] m. track; trace

tropić [tro-peećh] v. track

tropikalny [tro-pee-kal-ni] adj. m.
tropical; of the tropics

troska [tros-ka] f. care; anxiety;
worry; concern; solicitude

troskać się [tros-kaćh śhan] v.
care and worry about; be
concerned; take care

troskliwość [tros-klee-vośhćh]
f. thoughtfulness; care; heed

troskliwy [tros-klee-vi] adj. m.
careful; attentive; thoughtful

troszczyć się [trosh-chićh
śhan] v. care; be anxious
about; take care; look after

trotuar [tro-too-ar] m. sidewalk;
pavement (for pedestrians)

trójbarwny [trooy-barv-ni] adj. m.
tricolor; three-colored

trójca [trooy-tsa] f. trinity

trójka [trooy-ka] f. three

trójkąt [trooy-kownt] m. triangle;
set square

trójnasób [trooy-na-soop] three
times as much

trójnik [trooy-ńeek] m. three-
-way (pipe) connection; "T"

(tee) joint; "Y" joint; twye; tee

truchtem [trookh-tem] adv. by
jogging; by trot; at a trot

trucizna [troo-ćheez-na] f.
poison; venom

truć [trooćh] v. poison; bother
(slang); molest; worry

trud [troot] m. pains; toil

trudnić się [trood-ńeećh
śhan] v. occupy oneself; be
engaged; do (for a living)

trudno [trood-no] adv. with
difficulty; too bad; hard

trudność [trood-nośhćh] f.
difficulty; hardship handicap

trudny [trood-ni] adj. m. difficult;
hard; tough; laborious

trudzić [trood-dźheećh] v.
trouble; disturb; cause trouble

trujący [troo-yown-tsi] adj. m.
poisonous; toxic; poison-

trumna [troom-na] f. coffin

trunek [troo-nek] m. drink

trup [troop] m. corpse; cadaver

trupiarnia [troo-pyar-ńa] f.
mortuary; morgue

truskawka [troos-kav-ka] f.
strawberry

truteń [troo-teń] m. drone

trwać [trvaćh] v. last; persist;
stay; remain; linger on

trwały [trva-wi] adj. m. durable

trwanie [trva-ńe] n. duration

trwoga [trvo-ga] f. awe; fright

trwonić [trvo-ńeećh] v. waste;
squander; trifle away; fritter
away (money, time, energy,
opportunity, etc.)

trwożliwy [trvozh-lee-vi] adj. m.
timid; fearful; shy

trwożny [trvozh-ni] adj. m.
anxious; fearful; timid; shy

trwożyć [trvo-zhićh] v. startle;
frighten; scare; be frightened

tryb [trib] m. manner; mode;
mood; gear; procedure; course

trybuna [tri-boo-na] f. tribune;
stand; speaker's platform

trybunał [tri-boo-naw] m. tribunal

trychina [tri-khee-na] f. trichina;
trichinosis

trygonometria [tri-go-no-metr-ya]
f. trigonometry

tryk [trik] m. ram; trick
trykot [tri-kot] m. tricot
trykotaże [tri-ko-ta-zhe] pl. hosiery; knittings
trykotowy [tri-ko-to-vi] 1. adj. m. tricot; made of tricot
trykotowy [tri-ko-to-vi] 2. adj. m. knitted (goods, fabric, wear
trylion [tri-lyon] m. trillion
tryskać [tris-kaćh] v. spurt; spout; gush; jet; squirt; flow; eject; stream; burst forth
trywialny [tri-vyal-ni] adj. m. trivial; vulgar; coarse; trite
trzask [tshask] m. crack; bang
trzaska [tshas-ka] f. chip (wood)
trzaskać [tshas-kaćh] v. crack; bang; smash; shatter; knock; hit; strike; whack; crush
trząść [tshownśhćh] v. shake
trzcina [tshćhee-na] f. cane; reed (of bamboo etc.)
trzcina cukrowa [tshćhee-na tsook-ro-va] f. sugar cane
trzcinowy [tshćhee-no-vi] adj. m. cane (chair); made out of cane; reedy (area)
trzeba [tshe-ba] v. imp. ought to; one should; it is necessary
trzebić [tshe-beećh] v. clear; gut; geld; cut down; destroy
trzeci [tshe-ćhee] num. third
trzeć [tshećh] v. rub; grate
trzepaczka [tshe-pach-ka] f. whisk; beater; carpet beater
trzepać [tshe-paćh] v. hit dust out; beat (carpet); slap
trzepnąć [tshep-nownćh] v. hit; strike; spank; slap; wag; flip; flit off; smack
trzepotać [tshe-po-taćh] v. flap; flutter; flicker; toss
trzeszczeć [tshesh-chećh] v. crack; crackle; creak; crunch; rustle; decrepitate; jabber
trzewia [tshe-vya] pl. bowels; guts; intestines; entrails
trzewik [tshe-veek] m. shoe; slipper; skid; trig
trzeźwieć [tsheźh-vyećh] v. sober up; bring back to consciousness
trzeźwość [tsheźh-vośhćh] f. sobriety; level-headedness
trzeźwy [tsheźh-vi] adj. m. sober; clear headed; level headed; wide awake
trzęsawisko [tshan-sa-vees-ko] n. bog; swamp; quagmire; slough
trzęsienie ziemi [tshan-śhe-ńe źhe-mee] n. earthquake
trzmiel [tshmyel] m. bumblebee
trznadel [tshna-del] m. yellow bunting; yellow hammer; bunting
trzoda [tsho-da] f. f. herd; flock; heard (of swine, pigs, etc.)
trzon [tshon] m. handle; hilt; core; main part; trunk; stem
trzonek [tsho-nek] m. shaft; shank; handle (of a hammer, axe, etc.); helve
trzonowy ząb [tsho-no-vi zownb] m. molar; grinder
trzpień [tshpyeń] m. pin
trzpiot [tshpyot] m. giddy; gay
trzustka [tshoost-ka] f. pancreas; sweetbread
trzy [tshi] num. three
trzydziestokrotny [tshi-dźhes-to--krot-ni] adj. m. thirty-fold
trzydziestoletni [tshi-dźhes-to--let-ńee] adj. m. thirty year old (man, oak, etc.)
trzydziesty [tshi-dźhes-ti] num. thirtieth
trzydzieści [tshi-dźheśh-ćhee] num. thirty; 30
trzykrotny [tshi-krot-ni] adj. m. threefold
trzylampowy [tshi-lam-po-vi] adj. m. three-lamp
trzyletni [tshi-let-ńee] adj. m. three year old (boy, car, etc.)
trzymać [tshi-maćh] v. hold; keep; cling; clutch; hold on to
trzynasty [tshi-nas-ti] num. thirteenth; 13th
trzynaście [tshi-naśh-ćhe] num. thirteen; 13
trzypiętrowy [tshi-pyant-ro-vi] adj. m. three-story high (house)
trzysta [tshis-ta] num. three hundred; 300

tu [too] adv. here; in here
tuba [too-ba] f. tube; horn
tubka [toob-ka] f. small tube
tuberkuliczny [too-ber-koo-leech-
-ni] adj. m. tuberculous
tubylczy [too-bil-chi] adj. m.
native; indigenous; local
tubylec [too-bi-lets] m. native;
aboriginal; local inhabitant
tucznik [tooch-ńeek] m. porker
tuczyć [too-chićh] v. fatten
tulejka [too-ley-ka] f. socket
tulić [too-leećh] v. hug; fondle
tulipan [too-lee-pan] m. tulip
tułacz [too-wach] m. wanderer;
vagrant; exile; homeless
wanderer
tułaczka [too-wach-ka] f.
homeless wandering;
wandering life
tułać się [too-waćh śhan] v.
wander; be homeless; be in
exile
tułów [too-woov] m. torso
tum [toom] m. cathedral; minster
tuman [too-man] m. 1. dust
-cloud; mint; 2. dummy;
nitwit; duffer; addle-head
tunel [too-nel] m. tunnel
tupać [too-paćh] v. stamp
one's foot; tramp
tupet [too-pet] m. nerve;
chutzpa; self-assurance;
impudence; nerve; cheek
tur [toor] m. bison; aurochs
turbina [toor-bee-na] f. turbine
turecki [too-rets-kee] adj. m.
Turkish (saddle; fashion etc.)
turkawka [toor-kav-ka] f.
turtledove; wild dove
turkot [toor-kot] m. rumble;
rattle
turkotać [toor-ko-taćh] v.
rumble; bump along; rattle
turkus [toor-koos] m. turquoise
turniej [toor-ńey] m. tournament
turysta [too-ris-ta] m. tourist
turystyczny [too-ris-tich-ni] adj.
m. tourist; touring-
tusz [toosh] m. 1. shower; hit;
2. India ink; mascara
tusza [too-sha] f. corpulence
tuszować [too-sho-vaćh] v. 1.

draw with ink; 2. cover up;
hush up; stifle (a scandal etc.)
tutaj [too-tay] adv. here
tutejszy [too-tey-shi] adj. m.
local (custom, man); of this
place; of our (place, country)
tuzin [too-źheen] m. dozen
tuż [toosh] adv. near by; close
by; just before; just after
tuż obok [toosh o-bok] adv. next
too; near by; close by
twardnieć [tvard-ńećh] v.
harden; stiffen; fix; bind
twardość [tvar-dośhćh] f.
hardness; stiffness; severity
twardy [tvar-di] adj. m. hard
twarożek [tva-ro-zhek] m.
cottage cheese; small cottage
cheese; curds
twaróg [tva-rook] m. cottage
cheese curds; cottage cheese
twarz [tvash] f. face;
physiognomy; aspect
twarzowy [tva-zho-vi] adj. m.
becoming; facial (bone etc.)
twierdza [tvyer-dza] f. fortress;
stronghold; citadel
twierdzący [tvyer-dzown-tsi] adj.
m. affirmative (answer etc.)
twierdzenie [tvyer-dze-ńe] n.
affirmation; theorem; assertion
twierdzić [tvyer-dźheećh] v.
assert; maintain; affirm; say
twornik [tvor-ńeek] m. armature
tworzyć [tvo-zhićh] v. create;
form; compose; produce;
make; bring to life
tworzywo sztuczne [tvo-zhi-vo
shtooch-ne] n. plastic
twój [tvooy] pron. yours; your
twór [tvoor] m. creation; piece
of work; origination; outgrowth; composition
twórca [tvoor-tsa] m. creator;
author; maker; originator
twórczość [tvoor-chośhćh] f.
creation; output; production
twórczy [tvoor-chi] adj. m.
creative; originative; formative
ty [ti] pron. you (familiar form)
tyczka [tich-ka] v. pole; perch
tyczyć się [ti-chićh śhan] v.
concern; regard; refer to

tyć [tić] v. grow fat
tydzień [ti-dźheń] m. week
tyfus [ti-foos] m. typhus
tygiel [ti-gel] m. crucible
tygodnik [ti-god-ńeek] m.
weekly (magazine etc.)
tygodniowy [ti-god-ńo-vi]
adj. m. weekly (pay etc.)
tygrys [ti-gris] m. tiger; type of
German tank in World War II
tygrysica [ti-gri-śhee-tsa] f.
tigress
tyka [ti-ka] f. perch; pole
tyka miernicza [ti-ka myer-ńee-
-cha] f. surveyor's rod
tykać [ti-kаćh] v. touch; affect;
tick; strike; call by first name
tykwa [tik-va] f. pumpkin
tyle [ti-le] adv. so much; so
many; that much (was done)
tylekroć [ti-le-kroćh] adv. so
many times; that many times
tylko [til-ko] adv. only; but; just
tylko co [til-ko tso] adv. just
now; a moment ago; this instant; just a minute ago
tylna straż [til-na strash] f. rear
guard
tylny [til-ni] adj. m. back; hind
(leg etc.); rear (light etc.)
tył [tiw] m. back; rear; stern
tym lepiej [tim le-pyey] adv. so
much better
tymczasem [tim-cha-sem] adv.
meantime; during; at the time
tymczasowo [tim-cha-so-vo] adv.
provisionally; temporarily
tymczasowy [tim-cha-so-vi] adj.
m. temporary; provisional
tynk [tink] m. plaster (work)
tynkować [tin-ko-vаćh] v.
plaster; rough cast (a wall)
tynktura [tin-ktoo-ra] f. tincture;
tinge; light color
typ [tip] m. type; model; guy
typowy [ti-po-vi] adj. m. typical;
standard (article etc.)
tyrada [ti-ra-da] f. tirade
tyran [ti-ran] m. tyrant; bully
tyrania [ti-ra-ńya] f. tyranny
tyrański [ti-rań-skee] adj. m.
tyrannical; tyrannous; bullying
tysiąc [ti-śhownts] num.

thousand; 1,000
tysiąclecie [ti-śhownts-le-ćhe]
n. millennium
tysiącletni [ti-śhownts-let-ńee]
adj. m. millinery
tysięczny [ti-śhanch-ni] num.
thousandth; 1,000th
tytan [ti-tan] m. titan; titanium;
demon (of work etc.)
tytaniczny [ti-ta-ńeech-ni]
adj. m. titanic; huge
tytoniowy [ti-to-ńo-vi] adj. m.
tobacco; of tobacco leaves
tytoń [ti-toń] m. tobacco
tytularny [ti-too-lar-ni] adj. m.
titular; nominal
tytuł [ti-toow] m. title
tytułowa strona [ti-too-wo-va
stro-na] f. title page
tytułować [ti-too-wo-vаćh] v.
entitle; address; style as a...

U

u [oo] adj. mbeside; at; with; by;
on; from; in; (idiomatic)
u boku [oo bo-koo] exp.: at
one's side (to have a helper, a
sabre...)
ubarwić [oo-bar-veećh] v. color
ubawić się [oo-ba-veećh śhan]
v. have fun; have a good
laugh
ubezpieczać [oo-bez-pye-chаćh]
v. insure; secure; protect
ubezpieczalnia [oo-bez-pye-chal-
-ńa] f. health insurance
center; insurance company
ubezpieczenie [oo-bez-pye-che-
-ńe] n. insurance; protection
ubezpieczenie życia [oo-bez-pye-
-che-ńe zhi-ćha] n. life
insurance; life assurance
ubezpieczenie społeczne
[oo-bez-pye-che-ńe
spo-wech-ne] n. social
security insurance
ubiec [oo-byets] v. run; pass
ubiegać się [oo-bye-gаćh

śhan] v. solicit; compete for

ubiegły [oo-**byeg**-wi] adj. m.
past; last (year, week etc.)

ubierać [oo-bye-raćh] v. dress

ubijaczka [oo-bee-**yach**-ka] f.
stamper; compactor; kitchen
whisk; stamping machine

ubijać [oo-bee-yaćh] v. stamp;
churn; chip; kill; pack; ram

ubijać interes [oo-bee-yaćh
een-**te**-res] v. strike a bargain;
strike a deal

ubikacja [oo-bee-**kats**-ya] f.
toilet; rest room; powder
room; men's room; W.C.

ubiór [oob-yoor] m. attire; grab

ubliżać [oo-blee-zhaćh] v.
insult; offend; affront

ubliżający [oo-blee-zha-**yown**-tsi]
adj. m. offensive; insulting;
disparaging

uboczny produkt [oo-**boch**-ni **pro**-
-dookt] m. byproduct

ubogi [oo-**bo**-gee] adj. m. poor

ubolewać [oo-bo-**le**-vaćh] v.
deplore; feel sympathy for

ubolewanie [oo-bo-le-va-**ńe**] n.
regret; lamentation; sympathy

uboźeć [oo-**bo**-zhećh] v.
become poor; become
impoverished

ubój [oo-booy] m. slaughter

ubóstwiać [oo-**boost**-vyaćh] v.
idolize; love; be crazy about

ubóstwo [oo-**boost**-vo] n.
poverty; destitution;
meagerness

ubóść [oo-boośhćh] v. gore

ubrać [oob-raćh] v. dress

ubranie [oob-ra-ńe] n. clothes;
decoration; putting in a fix

ubytek [oo-bi-tek] m. decrease

ubytek krwi [oo-bi-tek **krvee**]
blood loss

ubywać [oo-bi-vaćh] v. retire;
go; lessen; reduce; decrease

ucałować [oo-tsa-**wo**-vać] v.
kiss (somebody good night,
good-bye, etc.)

ucho [oo-kho] n. ear; handle;
(needle) eye; ring (of anchors)

uchodzić [oo-kho-dźheećh] v.
go away; flee; pass (for)

uchodźca [oo-**khodźh**-tsa] m.
refugee; displaced person

uchować [oo-**kho**-vaćh] v.
save; preserve; save; retain;
keep; rear

uchronić [oo-khro-ńeećh] v.
guard; preserve; protect; keep

uchwalać [oo-khva-laćh] v.
pass a law; resolve; decide

uchwała [oo-**khva**-wa] f.
resolution; vote; law

uchwycić [oo-khvi-ćheećh] v.
grasp; catch; seize; see; get

uchwyt [**ookh**-vit] m. handle

uchwytny [oo-**khvit**-ni] adj. m.
graspable; palpable; audible

uchybiać [oo-khib-yaćh] v. fail;
offend; transgress

uchybienie [oo-khi-**bye**-ńe] n.
offense; transgression; insult

uchylać [oo-khi-laćh] v. put
aside; half-open; set ajar

uciążliwy [oo-ćh**own**-zhlee-vi]
adj. m. burdensome; heavy

ucichać [oo-ćhee-khaćh] v.
calm down; be hushed; abate

uciecha [oo-ćhe-kha] f. joy

ucieczka [oo-ćhech-ka] f.
escape; flight; desertion;
recourse

ucieleśnić [oo-ćhe-**leśh**-
-ńeećh] v. embody; personify

uciekać [oo-ćhe-kaćh] v. flee

uciemiężać [oo-ćhe-m**yan**-
-zhaćh] v. oppress; burden;
tread down

ucierać [oo-ćhe-raćh] v. wipe
off; grind; grate; level; pound

ucierpieć [oo-ćher-pyećh] v.
suffer from; be hard hit by;
sustain a loss of

ucieszny [oo-ćhesh-ni] adj. m.
funny; comical; droll; amusing

ucieszyć [oo-ćhe-shićh] v.
gladden; please; gratify;
delight; give joy; amuse

ucinać [oo-ćhee-naćh] v. cut
off; clip; curtail; break off

ucisk [oo-ćheesk] m. oppression

uciskać [oo-ćhees-kaćh] v.
press down; pinch; oppress;
hurt; compress; screw down

uciszyć [oo-ćhee-shićh] v.

silence; quiet; still; soothe; lull

uciułać [oo-ćhoo-waćh] v.
scrape together; save; put
aside; store up (money, etc.)

uczcić [ooch-ćheećh] v. honor;
dignify; celebrate; do the
honor of; commemorate

uczciwy [ooch-ćhee-vi] adj. m.
honest; upright; straight

uczelnia [oo-chel-ńa] f. school;
college; academy; university

uczenie [oo-che-ńe] n. learning;
teaching; adv. learnedly

uczennica [oo-chen-ńee-tsa] f.
schoolgirl; (girl) pupil

uczeń [oo-cheń] m. schoolboy

uczepić [oo-che-peećh] v. hang
on; hitch; hook; attach; fasten

uczesać [oo-che-saćh] v. comb
(hair); brush hair; dress hair

uczesanie [oo-che-sa-ńe] n.
hairdo; hairstyle; coiffure

uczestniczyć [oo-chest-ńee-
-ćhićh] v. take part in; share
in; participate in

uczestnik [oo-chest-ńeek] m.
participant; (sport) competitor

uczęszczać [oo-chansh-chaćh]
v. frequent; attend (concerts);
go to (school...)

uczony [oo-cho-ni] m. scientist;
learned; erudite; scholarly man

uczta [ooch-ta] f. feast; banquet

uczucie [oo-choo-ćhe] n. feeling

uczuciowy [oo-choo-ćho-vi] adj.
m. sensitive; emotional;
sentimental

uczuć [oo-choochć] v. feel;
realize; become aware of

uczyć [oo-chićh] v. teach; train

uczyć się [oo-chićh śhan] v.
learn; study; take lessons

uczynek [oo-chi-nek] m. deed

uczynić [oo-chi-ńeećh] v. do;
make (sb. rich; happy)

uczynność [oo-chin-nośhćh]
f. kindness; helpfulness

uczynny [oo-chin-ni] adj. m.
obliging; helpful; cooperative

udany [oo-da-ni] adj. m.
successful; put-on; sham

udar słoneczny [oo-dar swo-
-nech-ni] m. sunstroke

udaremnić [oo-da-rem-ńeećh]
v. frustrate; foil; upset; defeat

udawać [oo-da-vaćh] v.
pretend; imitate

udawać się [oo-da-vaćh śhan]
v. go; succeed; manage; pan
out; make for

udeptać [oo-dep-taćh] v. tread
down; beat a path; tread on

uderzać [oo-de-zhaćh] v. hit

uderzenie [oo-de-zhe-ńe] n.
blow; stroke; hit; bump;
impact; slap; percussion

udo [oo-do] n. thigh

udobruchać [oo-do-broo-khaćh]
v. appease; win over; coax

udogodnić [oo-do-god-ńeećh]
v. facilitate; improve

udoskonalenie [oo-dos-ko-na-le-
-ńe] n. perfection;
improvement

udoskonalić [oo-dos-ko-na-
-leećh] v. perfect; improve

udostępnić [oo-dos-tanp-
-ńeećh] v. give access; put
within reach; facilitate

udowodnić [oo-do-vod-ńeećh]
v. prove; demonstrate;
substantiate; evidence

udowodnienie [oo-do-vod-ńe-
-ńe] n. evidence; proof;
demonstration

udręka [ood-ran-ka] f. anguish;
torment; distress; worry

udusić [oo-doo-śheećh] v.
strangle; smother; stifle;
throttle; suffocate; stew

udział [oo-dźhaw] m. share;
part; quota; participation

udziałowiec [oo-dźha-wo-vyets]
m. shareholder; partner

udzielać [oo-dźhe-laćh]v. give;
grant; furnish; apply

udzielenie [oo-dźhe-le-ńe] n.
giving; granting; dispensing

ufać [oo-faćh] v. trust; confide;

ufność [oof-nośhćh] f.
confidence; trust; reliance

ufny [oof-ni] adj. confident;
trustful; hopeful; reliant;
sanguine

ufundować [oo-foon-do-vaćh]
v. found; set up; endow;

establish; make a gift
uganiać się [oo-ga-ńaćh
śhan] v. chase after; seek
(graces, job, etc.)
ugaszczać [oo-gash-chaćh] v.
entertain; treat; feast; treat to
uginać [oo-gee-naćh] v. bend
down; deflect; bow before
ugłaskać [oog-**was**-kaćh] v.
tame; humor; conciliate; coax
ugniatać [oog-ńa-taćh] v.
press down; exert pressure;
pinch; crush; oppress
ugoda [oo-go-da] f. agreement
ugodowiec [oo-go-do-vyets] m.
compromiser; advocate of
conciliation
ugodowy [oo-go-do-vi] adj. m.
conciliatory; amicable
ugodzić [oo-go-dźheećh] v.
hit; hire; come to terms
ugór [oo-goor] m. fallow
ugryźć [oog-riśhćh] v. bite
off; bite; sting
ugrzęznąć [oo-gzhanz-nownćh]
v. stick; be stuck; get bogged
uiszczenie [oo-eesh-che-ńe] n.
payment (of a bill, rent etc.)
uiścić [oo-eeśh-ćheećh] v.
pay up (a debt); pay; remit (a
sum); discharge (a debt)
ujadać [oo-ya-daćh] v. yelp;
bark; quarrel; wrangle
ujarzmić [oo-yazh-meećh] v.
subdue; enslave; enthrall;
subjugate; oppress
ujawniać [oo-yav-ńaćh] v.
reveal; disclose; expose;
unmask; show; lay open
ująć [oo-yownćh] v. conceive;
deduct; seize; grasp; lessen;
catch hold of; clasp; detain
ujednolicić [oo-yed-no-lee-
-ćheećh] v. standardize;
unify; make uniform
ujemny [oo-yem-ni] adj. m.
negative (value etc.);
unfavorable; detrimental
ujeżdżać [oo-yezh-dzhaćh] v.
break in (a horse); smooth (a
road by the wheels of cars)
ujeźdźalnia [oo-yezh-dzhal-ńa]
f. riding school; manege

ujęcie [oo-**yan**-ćhe] n. grasp
ujma [ooy-ma] f. detraction
ujmować [ooy-mo-vaćh] v.
seize restrain; embrace;
apprehend; express
ujmujący [ooy-moo-**yown**-tsi]
adj. m. winsome; engaging;
prepossessing
ujrzeć [ooy-zhećh] v. see;
glimpse; get a sight of
ujście [ooyśh-ćhe] n.
escape;(river) mouth;
withdrawal; retreat; outlet;
issue; vent (to indignation)
ukamienować [oo-ka-mye-**no**-
-vaćh] v. stone sb; stone to
death; lapidate
ukazać [oo-**ka**-zaćh] v. show
(appear); exhibit; reveal
ukąsić [oo-**kown**-śheećh] v.
bite; sting; bite off
ukąszenie [oo-**kown**-**she**-ńe] n.
bite; sting
uklęknąć [oo-**klank**-nownćh] v.
genuflect; kneel down
układ [ook-wat] m. scheme;
agreement; disposition;
system; arrangement
układać się [ook-**wa**-daćh
śhan] v. lay down; negotiate;
settle down; pan out
układanka [oo-kwa-dan-ka] f.
jigsaw puzzle; building blocks
układny [ook-**wad**-ni] adj. m.
polite; urbane; affable;
mannerly; courteous
ukłon [ook-won] m. bow
(greeting); salute
ukłonić się [oo-**kwo**-ńeećh
śhan] v. bow (to sb); tip
one's hat; greet
ukłucie [oo-**kwoo**-ćhe] n. prick;
sting; sharp pain; prod; twinge
ukochać [oo-ko-khaćh] v. take
a fancy; grow fond of; hug
ukochana [oo-ko-kha-na] adj. f.
beloved; darling; pet (female)
ukochany [oo-ko-kha-ni] adj. m.
beloved; darling; pet (male)
ukoić [oo-ko-eećh] v. soothe
ukojenie [oo-ko-ye-ńe] n. relief;
consolation; alleviation
ukończyć [oo-koń-chićh] v.

complete; finish; end (school etc.); bring to an end

ukos [oo-kos] m. slant; incline

ukośny [oo-kośh-ni] adj. m. oblique; sloping; skew; diagonal; sidelong (glance)

ukracać [oo-kra-tsać] v. curb; subdue; reform; check; put an end; suppress; daunt sb

ukradkiem [oo-krad-kem] adv. stealthily; by stealth; furtively

ukraiński [ook-ra-eeń-skee] adj. m. Ukrainian; of Ukraine

ukrajać [oo-kra-yać] v. cut off

ukręcić [ook-ran-ćheećh] v. twist off; roll up; wrench off

ukrop [ook-rop] m. boiling water; feverish bustle

ukrócić [ook-roo-ćheećh] v. repress; curb; reform; put an end to

ukrycie [ook-ri-ćhe] n. hiding place; hideaway; hideout; cover

ukrywać [oo-kri-vać] v. hide; cover up; conceal; hold back

ukryty [ook-ri-ti] adj. m. hidden; concealed; put out of sight

ukrywać [ook-ri-vać] v. hide

ukształtować [ook-shtaw-to-vać] v. shape; fashion; cast

ukształtowanie [oo-kshtaw-to-va-ńe] n. configuration; formulation; form; shape

ukuć [oo-kooćh] v. hammer out

ul [ool] m. beehive; hive

ulać [oo-lać] v. pour off; cast (metal); pour off water

ulatać [oo-la-tać] v. fly off

ulatniać się [oo-lat-ńać śhan] v. evaporate; volatile; vanish; melt away; leak; escape; cease; disappear

ulatywać [oo-la-ti-vać] v. fly away; leak (vapors, odors, smells); rise in the air

uleczalny [oo-le-chal-ni] adj. m. curable; remediable; medicable

uleczenie [oo-le-che-ńe] n. cure; successful recovery

uleczyć [oo-le-chićh] v. heal

ulegać [oo-le-gać] v. yield

uległy [oo-leg-wi] adj. m.

submissive; docile; compliant

ulepszać [oo-lep-shaćh] v. improve; better; ameliorate

ulepszenie [oo-lep-she-ńe] n. improvement; amelioration

ulewa [oo-le-va] f. rainstorm

ulewać [oo-le-vaćh] v. pour off; cast (metals); pour (water)

ulga [ool-ga] f. relief; solace

uleżeć się [oo-le-zhećh śhan] v. mellow; settle; lie quiet

ulica [oo-lee-tsa] f. street

uliczka [oo-leech-ka] f. lane

ulicznica [oo-leech-ńee-tsa] f. prostitute; streetwalker

ulicznik [oo-leech-ńeek] m. gamin; guttersnipe; nipper

ulitować się [oo-lee-to-vaćh śhan] v. have pity; take pity

ulotka [oo-lot-ka] f. handbill; leaflet; throwaway

ultimatum [ool-tee-ma-toom] n. ultimatum; final offer (demand)

ultrafioletowy [ool-tra-fyo-le-to-vi] adj. m. ultraviolet

ulubieniec [oo-loo-bye-ńets] favorite; darling; pet

ulubiony [oo-loo-byo-ni] adj. m. beloved; favorite; pet

ulżyć [ool-zhićh] v. relive

ułamać [oo-wa-maćh] v. break off; be broken off; come off

ułamek [oo-wa-mek] m. fraction; fragment; mathematical fraction

ułamkowy [oo-wam-ko-vi] adj. m. fractional (number,report etc.)

ułan [oo-wan] m. uhlan (Polish light cavalryman (lancer)

ułaskawić [oo-was-ka-veećh] v. pardon (a condemned person)

ułaskawienie [oo-was-ka-vye-ńe] n. pardon; reprieve

ułatwić [oo-wat-veećh] v. facilitate; simplify; make easier

ułatwienie [oo-wat-vye-ńe] n. facilitation; simplification

ułomność [oo-wom-nośhćh] f. deformity; defect; frailty

ułomny [oo-wom-ni] adj. m. disabled; defective; lame;

faulty

ułożony [oo-wo-**zho**-ni] adj. m.
arranged; well-mannered; set

umacniać [oo-**mats**-ńаćh] v.
strengthen; fortify; secure

umaczać [oo-ma-chaćh] v. dip;
wet; soak; sop; have hand in

umarły [oo-**mar**-wi] adj. m.
deceased; dead

umartwiać [oo-**mart**-vyaćh] v.
mortify (a person)

umarzać [oo-ma-zhaćh] v.
amortize; discontinue; remit

umawiać się [oo-**mav**-yaćh
śhan] v. make a date (or
plan); appoint; fix (a price)

umeblować [oo-meb-**lo**-vaćh] v.
furnish; fit out; fit up

umeblowanie [oo-meb-lo-va-ńе]
n. furniture; furnishings

umiar [oom-yar] m. moderation

umiarkowany [oo-myar-ko-**va**-ni]
adj. m. moderate; temperate

umieć [oo-myećh] v. know-
-how; be able to

umiejętność [oo-mye-**yant**-
-nośhćh] f. science; skill;
know-how; art of; knack of

umiejscowić [oo-myey-**stso**-
-veećh] v. locate; assign a
place; fix a place

umierać [oo-mye-raćh] v. die

umieszczać [oo-**myesh**-chaćh]
v. place; put; set; insert; seat

umilać [oo-mee-laćh] v. make
pleasant; add charm; give
charm; beguile (the time)

umilknąć [oo-meelk-**nownćh**] v.
fall silent; cease talking

umiłowany [oo-mee-**wo**-va-ni]
adj. m. beloved; favorite; dear

umizgać się [oo-meez-gaćh
śhan] v. flirt; woo; court;
ogle sb; make love (to sb)

umizgi [oo-meez-gee] pl. flirting;
courtship; love making

umniejszać [oo-**mńey**-shaćh] v.
diminish; lessen; belittle; abate

umocnić [oo-mots-ńeećh] v.
strengthen; fortify; beef up

umocnienie [oo-mots-ńe-ńe] n.
consolidation; fortification

umocować [oo-mo-**tso**-vaćh] v.

fasten; hitch; fix; secure

umorzyć [oo-mo-zhićh] v.
absolve; amortize; extinguish

umowa [oo-**mo**-va] f. contract

umowny [oo-**mov**-ni] adj. m.
contractual; conventional

umożliwić [oo-mozh-lee-veećh]
v. make possible; enable

umówić = **umawiać**

umundurowanie [oo-moon-doo-
-ro-va-ńe] n. uniforms;
uniform

umyć [oo-mićh] v. wash up

umykać [oo-mi-kaćh] v. run
away; escape; take flight

umysł [oo-misw] m. mind;
intellect; brain; spirit

umysłowy [oo-mis-**wo**-vi] adj. m.
mental; intellectual; brain

umyślnie [oo-**miśhl**-ńe] adv. on
purpose; specially; purposely

umyślny [oo-**miśhl**-ni] adj. m.
intentional; deliberate; special

umywać się [oo-mi-vaćh **śhan**]
v. wash up; have a wash; be
fit for comparison

umywalnia [oo-mi-**val**-ńa] f.
washroom; washstand

unaocznić [oo-na-och-ńeećh]
v. make evident; visualize

unarodowić [oo-na-ro-do-veećh]
v. nationalize; put to state
control; make national

unarodowienie [oo-na-ro-do-**vye**-
-ńe] nationalization

uncja [oon-tsya] f. ounce

unia [ooń-ya] f. union

unicestwić [oo-ńee-**tses**-
-tveećh] v. annihilate;
frustrate; destroy entirely

unicestwienie [oo-ńee-tses-**tvye**-
-ńe] n. annihilation; frust-
ration; complete destruction

uniemożliwić [oo-ńe-mozh-lee-
-veećh] v. make impossible

unieruchomić [oo-ńe-roo-**kho**-
-meećh] v. immobilize; tie up

unieszkodliwić [oo-ńe-shkod-
-lee-veećh] v. render harmless

unieść [oo-ńeśhćh] v. lift up

unieważnić [oo-ńe-**vazh**-
-ńeećh] v. annul; void;
cancel; repeal; abrogate

unieważnienie [oo-ńe-vazh-ńe-
-ńe] n. annulment; invali-
dation; nullification
uniewinnić [oo-ńe-**veen**-
-ńeećh] v. acquit; exculpate;
excuse; clear of charge
uniewinnienie [oo-ńe-veen-ńe-
-ńe] n. acquittal
uniezależnić [oo-ńe-za-**lezh**
-ńeećh] v. make independent
uniform [oo-**ńee**-form] m.
uniform
unikać [oo-**ńee**-kaćh] v. avoid;
shun; steer clear; abstain from
unikat [oo-**ńee**-kat] m. unique
item; rare specimen; curiosity
uniwersalny [oo-ńee-ver-**sal**-ni]
adj. m. universal; versatile
uniwersytet [oo-ńee-ver-**si**-tet]
m. university
uniżać się [oo-**ńee**-zhaćh
śhan] v. humble oneself; be
servile
uniżony [oo-ńee-**zho**-ni] adj. m.
humble; servile; cringing
unormować [oo-nor-mo-vaćh]
v. normalize; regulate;
regularize
unosić [oo-no-**śheećh**] v. carry
up; lift off; bear (a weight)
unowocześnić [oo-no-vo-
-**cheśh**-ńeećh] v. modernize
uodpornić [oo-od-**por**-ńeećh] v.
immunize; harden; inure
uogólnić [oo-o-**gool**-ńeećh] v.
generalize (rules, observations)
uogólnienie [oo-o-gool-ńe-ńe] n.
generalization
uosabiać [oo-o-**sa**-byaćh] v.
personify; embody; typify
uosobienie [oo-o-so-bye-ńe] n.
personification; embodiment
upadać [oo-pa-daćh] v. fall
down; collapse; topple over
upadek [oo-pa-dek] m. fall; drop
upadłość [oo-pad-**wośhćh**] f.
bankruptcy; insolvency
upadły [oo-**pad**-wi] adj. m. fallen;
bankrupt; insolvent
upajać [oo-pa-yaćh] v. elate;
intoxicate; fuddle; make drunk
upalny dzień [oo-**pal**-ni **dźheń**]
m. hot day; very hot day

upał [oo-paw] m. (intense) heat
upaństwowić [oo-pań-**stvo**-
-veećh] v. nationalize;
socialize
upaństwowienie [oo-pań-stvo-
-**vye**-ńe] n. nationalization
uparty [oo-**par**-ti] adj. m.
stubborn; obstinate; pigheaded
upatrywać [oo-pa-**tri**-vaćh] v.
look for; suspect; perceive
upełnomocnić [oo-pew-no-**mots**-
-ńeećh] v. give powers (of
attorney); empower;
commission
upewnić [oo-**pev**-ńeećh] v.
assure; reassure; make sure
upić się [oo-peećh **śhan**] v.
get drunk; be intoxicated
upierać się [oo-**pye**-raćh **śhan**]
v. persist; insist; stick to
upinać [oo-**pee**-naćh] v. fasten
on; pin up; tie (one's hair)
upiór [oop-yoor] m. ghost
upiorny [oo-**pyor**-ni] adj. m.
ghostly; weird; nightmarish;
ghastly; horrible; dreadful
upłynnienie [oo-pwin-**ńe**-ńe] n.
make fluid; flux; liquefaction
upływ [oop-wiv] m. run off;
(blood) loss; lapse; expiration
upływać [oo-**pwi**-vaćh] v. flow
away; pass; lapse; go by; flow
upłynąć [oo-**pwi**-nownćh] v.
elapse; pass; expire; sail away
upodobać [oo-po-do-baćh] v.
take a liking; take to; fancy
upodobanie [oo-po-do-ba-ńe] n.
liking; fancy; predilection for
upodobnić się [oo-po-**dob**-
-ńeećh **śhan**] v. assimilate;
conform to; become like
upoić [oo-po-eećh] v.
intoxicate; make drunk; elate
upojenie [oo-po-**ye**-ńe] n.
inebriation; rapture;
intoxication; ecstasy
upokorzenie [oo-po-ko-**zhe**-ńe] n.
humiliation; abasement
upokorzyć [oo-po-**ko**-zhićh] v.
humiliate; make eat crow;
abase; mortify; hurt the pride
upominać [oo-po-**mee**-naćh] v.
admonish; warn; scold; rebuke

upominek [oo-po-**mee**-nek] m.
gift; souvenir; present; token
uporać się [oo-**po**-raćh **śhan**]
v. get over; cope with; settle;
negotiate; handle; manage
uporczywy [oo-por-**chi**-vi] adj. m.
stubborn; obstinate; severe
uporządkować [oo-po-zhownd-
-ko-vaćh] v. put in order; tidy
up; put straight; regulate
uposażenie [oo-po-sa-zhe-ńe] n.
pay; allowance; salary; wages
uposażyć [oo-po-**sa**-zhićh] v.
endow; give allowance
upośledzenie [oo-po-śhle-**dze**-
-ńe] n. handicap (mental,
physical, etc.); wrong
upośledzony [oo-po-śhle-dzo-ni]
adj. m. feebleminded; deprived
upoważnić [oo-po-**vazh**-ńeećh]
v. authorize; commission;
entitle; empower; qualify for
upoważnienie [oo-po-vazh-**ńe**-
-ńe] n. authorization; full
powers; warrant; authority
upowszechniać [oo-pov-**shekh**-
-ńaćh] v. put into general
use; spread; disseminate
upór [oo-poor] m. obstinacy
upragniony [oo-prag-**ńo**-ni] adj.
m. desired; longed for
upraszać [oo-**pra**-shaćh] v.
request; beg; beseech
uprawa [oo-**pra**-va] f. culture;
cultivation; agriculture; tillage
uprawiać [oo-**prav**-yaćh] v.
cultivate; till (the soil)
uprawnić [oo-**prav**-ńeećh] v.
entitle; qualify; legalize
uprawniony [oo-prav-**ńo**-ni] adj.
m. entitled; qualified
uprosić [oo-pro-**śh**eećh] v. get
by begging; persuade; ask to
do; request; entreat
uprościć [oo-**prośh**-ćheećh]
v. simplify; reduce; cancel
uprowadzić [oo-pro-**va**-
-dźheećh] v. abduct; kidnap;
lead away; take prisoner
uprzątać [oo-pzhown-taćh] v.
clean up; tidy up; put away;
clear; remove; kill
uprząż [oop-zhownsh] f. harness

(horse); gear of draught
animals
uprzedni [oo-pzhed-ńee] adj. m.
previous; prior; foregoing
uprzedzać [oo-pzhe-dzaćh] v.
anticipate; warn; have bias
uprzedzenie [oo-pzhe-dze-ńe] n.
anticipation; prejudice; notice
uprzedzony [oo-pzhe-**dzo**-ni] adj.
m. prejudiced; forewarned
uprzejmość [oo-pzhey-
-**mośh**ćh] f. polite kindness;
courtesy; affability; favor
uprzejmy [oo-**pzhey**-mi] adj. m.
kind; polite; nice; suave;
affable; complaisant; bland
uprzemysłowić [oo-pzhe-mi-
-**swo**-veećh] v. industrialize
uprzemysłowienie [oo-pzhe-mi-
-swo-**vye**-ńe] n. industria-
lization; development of
industry
uprzykszać się [oo-**pzhik**-zhićh
śhan] v. get fed up with
uprzystępnić [oo-pzhis-**tanp**-
-ńeećh] v. facilitate; make
available; make accessible
uprzytomnić [oo-pzhi-**tom**-
-ńeećh] v. make realize;
impress upon (sb); perceive
uprzywilejowany [oo-pzhi-vee-le-
-yo-**va**-ni] adj. m. privileged
upuścić [oo-**poośh**-ćheećh]
v. let fall; let drop; bleed
upychać [oo-pi-khaćh] v. staff;
pack tight; cram; ram; fill
urabiać [oo-**rab**-yaćh] v. fashion
uraczyć [oo-ra-chićh] v. treat
uradować [oo-ra-do-vaćh] v.
gladden; delight; rejoice
uradzić [oo-ra-dźheećh] v.
agree; decide upon a method;
resolve to do; contrive
uran [oo-ran] m. uranium
urastać [oo-ras-taćh] v. grow
uratować [oo-ra-to-vaćh] v.
save; salvage; rescue
uraz [oo-ras] m. injury; complex;
resentment; grudge
uraza [oo-ra-za] f. grudge;
rancor; soreness; ill feeling
urazić [oo-ra-źheećh] v. hurt;
offend; wound sb's feelings

urągać [oo-**rown**-gaćh] v. insult
uregulować [oo-re-goo-lo-vaćh]
v. settle; put in order; pay
urlop [oor-lop] m. leave;
furlough; vacation; holiday
urna [oor-na] f. urn; ballot; box
uroczy [oo-ro-chi] adj. m.
charming; enchanting; delightful; captivating; ravishing
uroczystość [oo-ro-**chis**-
-tośhćh] f. celebration;
festivity; feast; ceremony
uroczysty [oo-ro-**chis**-ti] adj. m.
solemn; ceremonial; festive
uroda [oo-**ro**-da] f. beauty;
loveliness; attraction; charm
urodzaj [oo-**ro**-dzay] m. good
harvest; abundance; harvest;
crop; good yield; yield
urodzajny [oo-ro-**dzay**-ni] adj. m.
fertile; fecund
urodzenie [oo-ro-**dze**-ńe] n. birth
urodzić [oo-**ro**-dźheećh] v.
give birth; breed; bear; yield a
rich crop; be delivered
urodziny [oo-ro-**dźhee**-ni] n.
birthday; birth; birthday party
uroić [oo-**ro**-eećh] v. imagine
urojenie [oo-ro-**ye**-ńe] n. fiction;
fancy; illusion; delusion; dream
urojony [oo-ro-**yo**-ni] adj. m.
imaginary; abstract; fictitious
urok [oo-rok] m. charm; spell
uronić [oo-**ro**-ńeećh] v. shed;
drop; let fall; lose; shed; miss
urozmaicenie [oo-roz-ma-ee-**tse**-
-ńe] n. variety; diversity;
change; variation
urozmaicić [oo-roz-ma-**ee**-
-ćheećh] v. diversity; vary;
while away; beguile the time
uruchomić [oo-roo-**kho**-meećh]
v. start; put in motion; set
going; impel; launch; initiate
urwać [oor-vaćh] v. tear off;
pull off; wrench away; deduct
urwis [oor-vees] m. urchin
urwisko [oor-**vees**-ko] n.
precipice; crag; cliff; steep
rock
urwisty [oor-**vees**-ti] adj. m.
steep; precipitous; abrupt
urywek [oo-ri-vek] m. fragment

urząd [oo-**zhownt**] m. office
urządzać [oo-**zhown**-dzaćh] v.
arrange; settle; set up
urządzenie [oo-**zhown-dze**-ńe] n.
furniture; installation; gear
urzec [oo-zhets] v. enchant;
bewitch; fascinate; cast a
spell; charm; captivate
urzeczywistnić [oo-zhe-chi-
-**veest**-ńeećh] v. make real;
fulfill; carry into effect
urzeczywistnienie [oo-zhe-chi-
-**veest-ńe**-ńe] n. realization
urzędnik [oo-**zhand**-ńeek] m.
official; white-collar worker
urzędowanie [oo-zhan-do-**va**-ńe]
n. office hours; clerical duties
urzędowy [oo-**zhan**-do-vi] adj. m.
official (document,capacity..)
urzynać [oo-**zhi**-naćh] v. cut off
usadowić się [oo-sa-do-veećh
śhan] v. sit or settle down
uschły [oos-khwi] adj. m. dried
up; withered; wasted away
usiąść [oo-**śhown**śhćh] v. sit
down; take one's seat; perch;
take a seat; alight
usidłać [oo-**śheed**-waćh] v.
entrap; ensnare; enmesh;
inveigle; entangle
usilny [oo-**śheel**-ni] adj. m.
strenuous; intense; pressing
usiłować [oo-śhee-**wo**-vaćh] v.
strive; try hard; attempt
usiłowanie [oo-śhee-wo-**va**-ńe]
n. attempt; effort; endeavor
uskarżać się [oos-**kar**-zhaćh
śhan] v. complain (against sb
or sth); grumble (about..)
uskutecznić [oo-skoo-**tech**-
-ńeećh] v. bring about;
effect; perform
usłuchać [oo-**swoo**-khaćh] v.
follow order (advice); obey
usługa [oo-**swoo**-ga] f. service;
favor; good turn; help
usługiwać [oo-swoo-**gee**-vaćh]
v. wait on; serve; attend
usłużyć [oo-**swoo**-zhićh] v. do
a service; do a good turn
usnąć [oo-**snownćh**] v. fall
asleep; go to sleep
uspokoić [oo-spo-**ko**-eećh] v.

calm down; soothe; set at
ease; pacify; tranquilize
uspołecznić [oos-po-**wech**-
-ńeećh] v. induce to socialize; civilize; collectivize
usposobić [oos-po-**so**-beećh] v.
dispose; predispose; incline
usposobienie [oos-po-so-**bye**-ńe]
n. disposition; temper; mood
usprawiedliwić [oos-pra-vyed-
-lee-veećh] v. justify; explain
usprawiedliwienie [oos-pra-vyed-
-lee-**vye**-ńe] n. excuse;
apology; plea; reason;
justification; vindication
usprawnić [oos-**prav**-ńeećh] v.
rationalize; make efficient
usta [**oos**-ta] n. mouth; lips
ustalenie [oo-sta-**le**-ńe] n.
determination; settlement
ustalić [oo-sta-**leećh**] v.
determine; settle; fix; set
ustały [oo-sta-wi] adj. m. settled
(fluid); tired (man, horse)
ustanawiać [oo-sta-**na**-vyaćh]
v. constitute; enact; set up
ustanowienie [oo-sta-no-**vye**-ńe]
n. instituting; establishing
ustatkować się [oo-stat-ko-
-vaćh **śhan**] v. settle down
ustawa [oo-sta-va] f. law; rule
ustawać [oo-**sta**-vaćh] v.
cease; be weary; hardly stand
ustawiać [oo-**stav**-yaćh] v.
arrange; place; put; set up
ustawiczny [oo-sta-**veech**-ni] adj.
m. constant; continual
ustawienie [oo-sta-**vye**-ńe] n.
disposition; installation
ustawodawca [oo-sta-vo-**dav**-tsa]
m. legislator
ustawodawstwo [oo-sta-vo-**dav**-
-stvo] n. legislation
usterka [oo-ster-ka] f. defect
ustęp [oos-tanp] m. rest-room;
paragraph; passage
ustępliwy [oos-tan-plee-vi] adj.
m. yielding; compliant
ustępować [oos-tan-po-vaćh]
v. yield; withdraw; recede;
cease; retreat; surrender
ustępstwo [oos-tanp-stvo] n.
concession; meeting half way

ustnik [**oost**-ńeek] m.
mouthpiece
ustny [**oost**-ni] adj. m. oral;
verbal; spoken
ustosunkowany [oo-sto-soon-ko-
-va-ni] adj. m. influential
ustrój [**oos**-trooy] m. structure;
government system; organism
ustrzec [**oos**-tzhets] v. guard;
avoid; safeguard; protect from
usunięcie [oo-soo-**ńan**-ćhe] n.
removal; withdrawal
usuwać [oo-**soo**-vaćh] v. clear
away; remove; dismiss; retire
usychać [oo-si-khaćh] v. wither
usypać [oo-si-paćh] v. pile up;
pour out; pour off (sand etc.)
usypiać [oo-sip-yaćh] v. put to
sleep; lull to sleep; send to
sleep; anaesthetize
uszanować [oo-sha-**no**-vaćh] v.
respect; spare (life etc.)
uszanowanie [oo-sha-no-**va**-ńe]
n. respect; respects
uszczelka [oosh-**chel**-ka] f.
gasket; seal; packing
uszczeiniać [oosh-**chel**-ńaćh]
v. pack; caulk; stop (a leak
etc.); make water-tight; seal
uszczęśliwić [oosh-chan-**śhlee**-
-veećh] v. make happy;
delight; overwhelm with joy
uszczerbek [oosh-**cher**-bek] m.
harm; damage; loss; detriment
uszczuplić [oosh-**choop**-leećh]
v. curtail; reduce; lessen
uszczypliwy [oosh-chip-lee-vi]
adj. m. sarcastic; biting
uszko [oosh-ko] m. (small) ear;
(needle) eye; ravioli
uszkodzenie [oosh-ko-**dze**-ńe] n.
damage; injury; impairment
uszkodzić [oosh-ko-**dźheećh**]
v. damage; injure; impair; spoil
uszny [oosh-ni] adj. m. ear
uścisk dłoni [**oośh**-ćheesk
dwo-ńee] m. handshake
uścisnąć [oośh-**ćhees**-
-**nownćh**] v. embrace; grasp;
hug; squeeze (hand)
uśmiać się [**oośh**-myaćh
śhan] v. laugh heartily; have
a good laugh; sneer

uśmiech [oośh-myekh] m.
smile; (silly) smirk; simper
uśmiechać się [oośh-mye-
-khać **śhan**] v. smile; give a
smile; simper; grin; sneer
uśmiercić [oośh-**myer**-
-ćheećh] v. kill; put to death
uśmierzyć [oośh-**mye**-zhićh]
v. calm down; mitigate; pacify; alleviate; soothe; still
uśpić [oośh-peećh] v. put to
sleep; anesthetize; etherize
uświadomić [oośh-vya-**do**-
-meećh] v. instruct; initiate;
realize; inform; indoctrinate
uświadomienie [oośh-vya-do-
-mye-ńe] n. consciousness;
information; indoctrination
uświetnić [oośh-**vyet**-ńeećh]
v. give prestige; add splendor
utaić [oo-ta-eećh] v. conceal
utajony [oo-ta-**yo**-ni] adj. m.
secret; latent; potential
utalentowany [oo-ta-len-to-**va**-ni]
adj. m. talented; gifted
utarczka [oo-**tarch**-ka] f.
skirmish; encounter; squabble
utarg [oo-tark] m. receipts; take;
takings; sales (daily, etc.)
utargować [oo-tar-**go**-vaćh] v.
make a bargain; realize
utarty [oo-**tar**-ti] adj. m. usual;
well-worn; wide spread
utęsknienie [oo-**tans**-**kńe**-ńe] n.
longing; earnest desire
utknąć [oot-k**nown**ćh] v. get
stuck; stall; stick fast; get to
a stop; come to a dead stop
utlenić [oo-**tle**-ńeećh] v.
oxidize (metals) peroxide
(hair); become oxidized
utłuc [oot-woots] v. pound;
bruise; crush; pestle; mash
(potatoes etc.); grind
utonąć [oo-to-**nown**ćh] v. be
drowned; sink; be lost
utopia [oo-**top**-ya] f. Utopia
utopić [oo-to-peećh] v. sink;
drown (an animal etc.)
utorować [oo-to-ro-vaćh] v.
clear a path; show the way
utożsamić [oo-tozh-**sa**-meećh]
v. identify with

utracić [oo-tra-**ćheećh**] v.
loose (health, job, etc.);
waste; forfeit a right etc.
utracjusz [oo-**trats**-yoosh] m.
spendthrift; squanderer
utrapienie [oo-trap-**ye**-ńe] n.
worry; torment; nuisance
utrata [oo-**tra**-ta] f. loss
utrącać [oo-**trown**-tsaćh] v.
chip; knock of; blackball
utrudniać [oo-**trood**-ńaćh] v.
make difficult; hinder
utrudnienie [oo-trood-**ńe**-ńe] n.
difficulty; hindrance
utrwalić [oo-**trva**-leećh] v.
make permanent; fix; record
utrzymanie [oo-tzhi-ma-ńe] n.
living; upkeep; board; support
utuczyć [oo-**too**-chićh] v.
fatten; grow fat; fatten up
utulić [oo-**too**-leećh] v.
comfort; console; nestle
(one's head in sb's lap etc.)
utwierdzić [oo-**tvyer**-dźheećh]
v. confirm; fix; set; consolidate; strengthen
utworzenie [oo-tvo-**zhe**-ńe] n.
formation; initiation; creation
utworzyć [oo-**tvo**-zhićh] v.
create; form; compose; initiate
utwór [oot-voor] m. work;
composition; production;
work; creation; formation
utyć [oo-tićh] v. become fat
utykać [oo-ti-kaćh] v. limp
utylitarny [oo-ti-lee-**tar**-ni] adj. m.
utilitarian; useful
utyskiwać [oo-tis-**kee**-vaćh] v.
complain; grumble (at, about)
uwaga [oo-**va**-ga] f. attention;
remark; notice; heed; note;
exp.: caution!; look out!
uwalniać [oo-**val**-ńaćh] v. set
free; rid; let off; dismiss
uważać [oo-va-zhaćh] v. pay
attention; be careful; mind;
take care; look after; watch
out; consider; reckon
uważny [oo-**vazh**-ni] adj. m.
careful; attentive; watchful
uwiąd [oov-**yownt**] m. atrophy
uwiązać [oo-**vyown**-zaćh] v.
attach; bind; tie; fasten

uwidocznić [oo-vee-doch-
-ńeećh] v. make evident;
show; expose
uwiecznić [oo-**vyech**-ńeećh] v.
perpetuate; immortalize
uwielbiać [oo-**vyel**-byaćh] v.
adore; worship; admire
uwielbienie [oo-vyel-bye-ńe] n.
adoration; admiration; worship
uwierać [oo-**vye**-raćh] v. (shoe)
pinch; rub; hurt
uwierzytelnić [oo-vye-zhi-**tel**-
-ńeećh] v. legalize; certify;
attest
uwierzytelnienie [oo-vye-zhi-tel-
-ńe-ńe] n. certification; ac-
creditation; authentication
uwięzić [oo-**vyan**-źheećh] v.
imprison; throw into prison
uwijać się [oo-**vee**-yaćh **śhan**]
v. be busy; bustle about;
hurry up; spin; whirl; dance
uwikłać [oo-**veek**-waćh] v.
entangle; involve; get
entangled; get trapped
uwłaczać [oov-**wa**-chaćh] v.
belittle; insult; outrage; affront
uwłosiony [oo-vwo-**śho**-ni] adj.
m. hairy; hirsute; pilose
uwodziciel [oo-vo-**dźhee**-ćhel]
m. seducer (of women);
inveigler
uwodzić [oo-**vo**-dźheećh] v.
seduce (men or women)
uwolnić [oo-**vol**-ńeećh] v. free
uwolnienie [oo-vol-ńe-ńe] n.
liberation; rescue; acquittal
uwydatnić [oo-vi-**dat**-ńeećh] v.
accentuate; set off; bring out
uwypuklić [oo-vi-pook-leećh] v.
accentuate; set off; protrude
uwzględnić [oovz-**gland**-ńeećh]
v. consider; comply; acquiesce
uwzględnienie [oovz-gland-ńe-
-ńe] n. allowance for;
compliance with; regard to
uzależnić [oo-za-lezh-ńeećh] v.
make dependent; subordinate
uzasadnić [oo-za-**sad**-ńeećh] v.
substantiate; justify; motivate
uzasadnienie [oo-za-sad-ńe-ńe]
n. justification; motive
uzbrajać się [ooz-bra-yaćh

śhan] v. arm oneself; equip
oneself (with tools, weapons)
uzbrojenie [ooz-bro-**ye**-ńe] n.
arming; armament; weapons
uzda [ooz-da] f. bridle
uzdolnić [ooz-dol-ńeećh] v.
enable; qualify; capacitate
uzdolnienie [ooz-dol-ńe-ńe] n.
talent; gift; aptitude
uzdolniony [ooz-dol-**ńo**-ni]
adj. m. gifted; talented;
capable; apt
uzdrawiać [ooz-**dra**-vyaćh] v.
heal; cure; bring back to
health; reorganize; sanify
uzdrowisko [ooz-dro-**vees**-ko] n.
health resort
uzębienie [oo-z**an**-**bye**-ńe] n.
dentition; toothing (of gears..)
uzgadniać [ooz-**gad**-ńaćh] v.
reconcile; coordinate; adjust
uziemienie [oo-źhe-**mye**-ńe] n.
grounding; earth
uzmysłowić [ooz-mi-**swo**-
-veećh] v. visualize; convey
(meaning); demonstrate
uznawać [ooz-na-vaćh] v.
acknowledge; do justice;
confess; recognize; admit
uznanie [ooz-na-ńe] n.
recognition; admission;
approval; esteem; regard
uzupełniać [oo-zoo-**pew**-ńaćh]
v. complete; fill up; make up
uzurpator [oo-zoor-**pa**-tor] m.
usurper (who takes and holds
power, position etc. by force)
uzyskać [oo-**zis**-kaćh] v. obtain;
gain; get; acquire; secure
użerać się [oo-zhe-raćh **śhan**]
v. fight over; quarrel; wrangle
użyczać [oo-**zhi**-chaćh] v.
grant; give; lend; spare; impart
użyć [oo-zhićh] v. use; exert;
take (medicine); profit; employ
użyteczny [oo-zhi-**tech**-ni]
adj. m. useful; serviceable;
helpful; effective
użytek [oo-**zhi**-tek] m. use
użytkownik [oo-zhit-**kov**-ńeek]
m. user (of apartment etc.)
używać [oo-**zhi**-vaćh] v. use;
enjoy; exercise a right; make

use; exert (strength etc.)

używalność [oo-zhi-**val**-noshch] f. use; enjoyment; utilization; usufruct

używalny [oo-zhi-**val**-ni] adj. m. usable; in working order

używany [oo-zhi-**va**-ni] adj. m. used; second-hand; worn

użyźniać [oo-zhizh-ńach] v. fertilize; enrich (the soil)

W

w [v] prep. in; into; at

we [ve] prep. in; into; at

wabić [va-beech] v. lure

wabik [va-beek] m. decoy; lure

wachlarz [vakh-lash] m. fan; range or diversity (of questions, subjects etc.)

wada [va-da] f. fault; defect; flaw

wadliwy [wad-lee-vi] adj. m. faulty; defective; imperfect

wafel [va-fel] m. wafer; cornet

waga [va-ga] f. weight; balance; pair of scales; importance

wagary [va-ga-ri] pl. skipping school; playing truant; the wag

wagon [va-gon] m. car; wagon

wagon restauracyjny [va-gon res-taw-ra-tsiy-ni] dining car

wahać się [va-khach shan] v. hesitate; sway; rock; swing

wahadło [va-kha-dwo] n. pendulum (swinging backwards and forwards)

wahadłowy [va-khad-wo-vi] adj. m. rocking; swinging; oscillatory; pendular

wakacje [va-kats-ye] pl. vacation; holidays; taking a holiday; taking a vacation

walać [va-lach] v. soil; stain; dirty; roll; draggle; wallow

walc [valts] m. waltz

walcować [val-tso-vach] v. roll;

flatten; mill; laminate

walczyć [val-chich] v. fight; vie; straggle; be in conflict; contend; wage war; combat

walec [va-lets] m. cylinder; roller

waleczność [va-lech-noshch] f. bravery; valor; gallantry; courage; prowess

waleczny [va-lech-ni] adj. m. valiant; brave; gallant; courageous

walić [va-leech] v. demolish; hit; pile; bring down; beat

walijski [va-leey-skee] adj. m. Welsh; of Wales

walizka [va-leez-ka] f. suitcase; valise; portmanteau

walka [val-ka] f. struggle; fight; war; battle; wrestling

walny [val-ni] adj. m. general; complete; decisive; signal; outstanding; eminent

walor [va-lor] m. value; quality

waluta [va-loo-ta] f. currency

wał [vaw] m. 1. rampart; dike; bank; 2.shaft; arbor; billow

wałach [va-wakh] m. gelding

wałek [va-wek] m. roller; shaft; cylinder; rolling pin; wad; roll

wałęsać się [va-wan-sach shan] v. rove; loaf; idle about

wałkoń [vaw-koń] m. loafer; do nothing; idler

wałkować [vaw-ko-vach] v. roll out; roll up; mangle; debate; thresh out

wampir [vam-peer] m. vampire

wandal [van-dal] m. vandal

wanienka [va-ńen-ka] f. little tub; bathtub; laboratory dish

wanna [van-na] f. bath tub

wapienny [va-pyen-ni] adj. m. limy; limestone; calcareous

wapień [va-pyeń] m. limestone

wapno [vap-no] n. lime

wapń [vapń] m. calcium

warcaby [var-tsa-bi] pl. checkers; draughts (game)

warchlak [varkh-lak] m. boar-cub; young wild boar; piglet

warchoł [var-khow] m. brawler; discord sower; squabbler

warczeć [var-chech] v. growl

warga [var-ga] f. lip; labium
wariant [var-yant] m. variant
wariactwo [var-yats-tvo] n.
   madness; piece of folly; folly
wariat [var-yat] m. lunatic;
   insane; madman; fool; crazy
   man; crank
wariować [var-yo-vaćh] v. go
   insane; rave; go mad; be mad
warkocz [var-koch] m. braid
warkot [var-kot] m. growl; whirr;
   throb; rattle; drone
warowny [va-rov-ni] adj. m.
   fortified; made into a fortress
warować [va-ro-vaćh] v. fortify
warstwa [vars-tva] f. layer;
   stratum; coat; coating; class
warstwowy [var-stvo-vi] adj. m.
   laminar; stratified; foliated
warsztat [varsh-tat] m.
   workshop; workbench;
   (weaver's) loom
warsztatowy [var-shta-to-vi] adj.
   m. workshop- (equipment etc.)
warta [var-ta] f. watch; guard
wartki [vart-kee] adj. m. rapid;
   fast (current); animated
wartko [vart-ko] adv. fast;
   rapidly; impetuously
warto [var-to] adv. it's worth
   (while); it's proper; it's worth
   one's while; it pays
wartościowy [var-tośh-ćho-vi]
   adj. m. valuable; precious
wartość [var-tośhćh] f. value;
   worth; quality; power;
   magnitude
wartownik [var-tov-ńeek] m.
   guard; sentry; sentinel
warunek [va-roo-nek] m.
   condition; requirement; term;
   stipulation; circumstance
warunkowy [va-roon-ko-vi] adj.
   m. conditional; contingent;
   provisory
warzączhew [va-zhown-khev] v.
   ladle
warzyć [va-zhićh] v. cook;
   brew; boil; nip; turn sour
warzywa [va-zhi-va] pl.
   vegetables; pot herbs; true
   garden produce
warzywny [va-zhiv-ni] adj. m.

vegetable; vegetable (garden)
wasz [vash] pron. your; yours
waśnić [vaśh-ńeećh] v. saw
   discord (among men or
   women) quarrel
waśń [vaśhń] f. quarrel
wata [va-ta] f. cotton wool
watować [va-to-vaćh] v. pad;
   quilt; wad (a jacket etc.)
wawrzyn [vav-zhin] m. laurel
waza [va-za] f. vase; soup
   tureen; tureenful
wazelina [va-ze-lee-na] f.
   vaseline; petrolatum
wazon [va-zon] m. flower pot
ważki [vazh-kee] adj. m. grave;
   weighty; ponderable
ważny [vazh-ni] adj. m.
   important; valid; significant
ważyć [va-zhićh] v. weigh
ważyć się [va-zhićh śhan] v.
   dare; weigh oneself; poise;
   venture; rock oneself
wąchać [vown-khaćh] v. smell
wągr [vowngr] m. blackhead;
   scolex; comedo; tapeworm
   larva; pig measles
wąs [vowns] m. moustache;
   whisker; barb; tentacle
wąski [vown-skee] adj. m.
   narrow; tight (fitting); narrow-
   (gage); bottle-neck
wąskotorowa kolej [vowns-ko-
   -to-ro-va ko-ley] f. narrow
   gauge railroad
wątek [vown-tek] m. weft; plot
wątły [vownt-wi] adj. m. frail
wątpić [vownt-peećh] v. doubt
wątpliwy [vownt-plee-vi] adj. m.
   doubtful; open to doubt; toss-
   up; questionable; precarious
wątroba [vown-tro-ba] f. liver
wątróbka [vown-troob-ka] f. liver
   (dish); (calf's) liver
wąwóz [vown-voos] m. ravine;
   gorge; gully; canyon; defile
wąż [vownsh] m. snake; hose
wbiec [vbyets] v. run in; run up
wbijać [vbee-yaćh] v. hammer
   in; drive into; thrust into
wbrew [vbref] prep. in spite of;
   in defiance; against
wbudować [vboo-do-vaćh] v.

build in; incorporate

w bród [v broot] adv. 1.in abundance; 2. fording (river)

wcale [vtsa-le] adv. quite

wcale nie [vtsa-le ńe] not at all (exp); not in the least

wchłaniać [vkhwa-ńaćh] v. absorb; soak up; take in; soak in; incept; imbibe

wchodzić [wkho-dźheećh] v. enter; get in; set in; climb

w ciągu [v ćhown-goo] adv. during; while; in time of

wciągać [vćhown-gaćh] v. pull in; drag in; inhale; implicate

wciąż [vćhownsh] adv. continually; constantly; persistently; as ever

wcielać [vćhe-laćh] v. incorporate; embody; merge; incarnate; personify

wcielenie [vćhe-le-ńe] n. incarnation; embodiment; merger; incorporation

wcierać [vćhe-raćh] v. rub in

wcięcie [vćhan-ćhe] n. incision notch; narrow waist; low cut neck; dent; indentation

wciskać [vćhees-kaćh] v. press in; squeeze in; wedge; cram; push in; thrust in

w czas [v chas] on time

wczasy [vcha-si] pl. vacations

wczesny [vches-ni] adj. m. early; in the small hours

wcześnie [vcheśh-ńe] adv. early; at an early date

wczoraj [vcho-ray] adv. yesterday; during yesterday

wczoraj wieczorem [vcho-ray vye-cho-rem] adv. last night

wczuwać się [vchoo-vaćh śhan] v. sympathize; get in spirit; understand

wdarcie [vdar-ćhe] n. invasion

wdawać się [vda-vaćh śhan] v. 1.intervene; 2.associate

wdech [vdekh] m. aspiration

wdowa [vdo-va] f. widow

wdowiec [vdo-vyets] m. widower

w dół [v doow] adv. down; downwards; downstairs; (go)

lower; (move) lower

wdrapać się [vdra-paćh śhan] v. climb up; shin up (a tree)

wdrażać [vdra-zhaćh] v. train; implant; accustom to; enter upon; initiate; break in

wdychać [vdi-khaćh] v. breathe; inhale; breathe in; imbibe

wdzierać się [vdźhe-raćh śhan] v. break in; struggle up a hill; force one's way

wdziewać [vdźhe-vaćh] v. put on (clothes); slip on; take (the veil, the habit)

wdzięczność [vdźhanch-nośhćh] f. gratitude; thankfulness; indebtedness

wdzięczny [vdźhanch-ni] adj. m. grateful; thankful; graceful; cute; neat; charming

wdzięk [vdźhank] m. grace; charm; attraction

według [ved-wook] prep. according to; after; along; near; next to; in accordance

wegetacja [ve-ge-tats-ya] f. vegetation; bare existence

wegetarianin [ve-ge-tar-ya-ńeen] m. vegetarian (man on a meatless diet)

wegetować [ve-ge-to-vaćh] v. exist barely; vegetate

wejrzeć [vey-zhećh] v. glance in; look in; get an insight; inspect; take a look inside

wejrzenie [vey-zhe-ńe] n. glance in; (eye) expression; insight

wejście [veyśh-ćhe] n. entrance; way in; admission ticket; entry

wejściowy [veyśh-ćho-vi] adj. m. entrance- (door, gate, opening, etc.)

wejść [veyśhćh] v. enter; get in; step in; walk in; go in

weksel [vek-sel] m. loan note

welon [ve-lon] m. veil

wełna [vew-na] f. wool

wełniany [vew-ńa-ni] adj. m. woolen; worsted; wool- (blanket, fabric, etc.)

weneryczna choroba [ve-ne-rich-

-na kho-**ro**-ba] f. venereal
disease
wenezuelski [ve-ne-zoo-el-skee]
adj. m. Venezuelan; of
Venezuela
wentyl [**ven**-til] m. vent; valve
wentylacja [ven-ti-lats-ya] f.
ventilation; ventilation system
wentylator [ven-ti-la-tor] m.
ventilator; ventilating-fan
weranda [ve-ran-da] f. porch
werbel [**ver**-bel] m. ruffle; drum
-call; drumbeat; drum
werbować [ver-bo-vaćh] v.
enlist; recruit; canvas
werbunek [ver-boo-nek] m. draft;
recruitment; enlisting;
recruiting
wersja [**ver**-sya] f. version
werwa [**ver**-va] f. verve; zip; pep
weryfikować [ve-ri-fee-ko-vaćh]
v. verify; confirm
wesele [ve-se-le] n. wedding
wesołość [ve-so-wośhćh] f.
joy; gaiety; glee; hilarity
wesoły [ve-so-vi] adj. merry;
gay; jolly; gleeful; funny
wespół [**ves**-poow] adv.
together; jointly; all together
westchnienie [vest-khñe-ñe] n.
sigh (of relief etc.)
wesz [**vesh**] louse
wet za wet [vet za vet] exp. tit
for tat; retaliate
weteran [ve-te-ran] m. veteran
weterynarz [ve-te-ri-nash] m.
vet; veterinary; farrier
wetknąć [vet-knownćh] v.
stick in; slip in; tuck away;
stuff; insert; shove
wewnątrz [vev-nowntsh] prep.
adv. inside; within; intra-
wewnętrzny [vev-nantzh-ni] adj.
m. inner; internal; inward
wezbrać [**vez**-braćh] v. swell
wezbrany [vez-bra-ni] adj. m.
flush; overflowing; swollen
wezwać [**vez**-vaćh] v. call in
wezwanie [vez-va-ñe] n. call
węch [**vankh**] m. smell; nose
wędka [**vand**-ka] f. fishing rod
wędkarz [**vand**-kash] m. angler
wędlina [vand-lee-na] f. meat

products; pork products
wędliniarnia [vand-lee-ñar-ña] f.
pork-butcher's shop
wędrować [van-dro-vaćh] v.
wander; roam; rove; hike
wędrowiec [van-dro-vyets] m.
wanderer; tramp;rover
wędrówka [van-droov-ka] f.
migration; roam; tramp;
wandering; wayfaring
wędzić [van-dzheećh] v.
smoke; cure; meat; bloat fish
wędzidło [van-dźheed-wo] n.
(horse) bit; bridle; curb
wędzonka [van-dzon-ka] f. bacon
węgiel [van-gel] m. coal;
carbon; crayon
węgielny kamień [van-gel-ni ka-
-myeń] m. corner stone;
corner stone
węgieł [van-gew] m. corner;
quoin; coin
węgierski [van-ger-skee] adj. m.
Hungarian; of Hungary
węglan [van-glan] m. carbonate
węglowodan [van-glo-vo-dan] m.
carbohydrate (chemical
compound)
węglowodór [van-glo-vo-door] m.
hydrocarbon; rock oil etc.
węglowy [van-glo-vi] adj. m.
carbonic; coal (bed, seam,
field); carboniferous; carbon-
węgorz [van-gosh] m. eel
węzeł [van-zew] m. knot;
junction; noose; loop; snarl;
hitch; bend; tie; bond
węższy [vanzh-shi] adj. m.
narrower (than)
wgląd [vglownt] m. insight; view
wglądać [vglown-daćh] v. look
into; get an insight; inquire
wgłębiać się [vgwan-byaćh
śhan] v. sink; study; go into
(a matter); dig into
wgryźć się [vgriźhćh śhan]
v. penetrate; get teeth into...
wiać [vyaćh] v. blow; beat it
wiadomo [vya-do-mo] v. (imp.) it
is known; everybody knows
wiadomość [vya-do-mośhćh]
f. news; information; message
wiadomy [vya-do-mi] adj. m.

known; a certain; well known

wiadro [**vya**-dro] n. bucket; pail

wiadukt [**vya**-dookt] m. viaduct

wianek [**vya**-nek] m. flower
crown; wreath; maidenhead

wiara [**vya**-ra] f. faith; belief

wiarogodny [vya-ro-**god**-ni] adj.
m. reliable; credible; veracious

wiarołomny [vya-ro-**wom**-ni] adj.
m. unfaithful; treacherous

wiarus [**vya**-roos] m. veteran (old
guard); old campaigner

wiatr [**vyatr**] m. wind; gale;
breeze; (dog's or horse's) nose

wiatrak [**vyat**-rak] m. windmill

wiatrówka [vya-**troov**-ka] f. air
gun; wind breaker (jacket)

wiąz [**vyowns**] m. elm (Ulmus)

wiązać [**vyown**-zaćh] v.
tie; bind; make into bundles

wiązanie [vyown-**za**-ńe] n. tie;
truss; bond; link; fixation;
weave; bonding; setting

wiązanka [vyown-**zan**-ka] f.
garland; bunch; banquet;
cluster; volley of abuse

wiązka [**vyownz**-ka] f. bundle;
bunch; cluster; beam (of rays)

wibracja [vee-**bra**-tsya] f.
vibration; jarring; jar

wichrować się [vee-**khro**-vaćh
śhan] v. warp; curl

wicher [**vee**-kher] m. windstorm;
gale; strong wind

wichrzyciel [veekh-zhi-ćhel] m.
warmonger; firebrand; instigator; sedition-monger

wichrzyć [**veekh**-zhićh] v. make
trouble; create discord; tousle

wichura [vee-**khoo**-ra] f.
windstorm; gale; strong wind

wichura śnieżna [vi-khoo-ra
śhńezh-na] snowstorm with
a heavy snowfall; blizzard

wić [**veećh**] v. wind; meander;
build nest; curl; m. twig; osier

widelec [vee-**de**-lets] m. fork

widełki [vee-**dew**-kee] pl. fork
(small); forked branch

widełkowaty [vee-dew-ko-**va**-ti]
adj. m. forked; fork shaped

widły [**veed**-wi] pl. pitchfork

widmo [**veed**-mo] n. ghost;

phantom; spectrum; specter

widno [**veed**-no] adv. 1.
evidently; 2. in daylight; in
light (in a room, out of doors)

widnokrąg [veed-no-**krownk**] m.
horizon; sea-line; true horizon

widocznie [vee-doch-**ńe**] adv.
evidently; apparently; clearly

widoczność [vee-doch-
-**nośhćh**] f. visibility; field of
vision (visible space)

widoczny [vee-**doch**-ni] adj. m.
visible; evident; noticeable

widok [**vee**-dok] m. view; sight

widokówka [vee-do-**koov**-ka] f.
picture postcard

widowisko [vee-do-**vees**-ko] n.
show; spectacle; pageant

widownia [vee-**dov**-ńa] f.
audience; theater house;
scene; arena

widz [**veets**] m. spectator

widzenie [vee-**dze**-ńe] n. sight;
vision; visit; hallucination

widzialny [vee-**dźhal**-ni] adj. m.
visible (to the naked eye...)

widzieć [**vee**-dźhećh] v. see

wiec [**vyets**] m. meeting; rally

wieczerza [vye-**che**-zha] f.
supper; Lord's Supper

wieczność [**vyech**-nośhćh] f.
eternity; ages; eternal life

wieczny [**vyech**-ni] adj. m.
eternal; perpetual; endless

wieczorek [vye-**cho**-rek] m.
evening (party); nice evening

wieczorem [vye-**cho**-rem] exp. in
the evening; during the
evening

wieczorny [vye-**chor**-ni] adj. m.
evening- (dress, newspaper)

wieczorowy [vye-cho-**ro**-vi] adj.
m. nightly; evening
(performance)

wieczór [**vye**-choor] m. evening

wieczysty [vye-**chis**-ti] adj. m.
eternal; perpetual;
imperishable

wiedza [**vye**-dza] f. knowledge;
learning; erudition; science

wiedzieć [**vye**-dźhećh] v.
know; be aware; be conscious

wiedźma [**vyedźh**-ma] f. witch

wiejska droga [vyey-ska dro-ga]
f. village road; country road
wiejski [vyey-skee] adj. m.
village; rural; rustic; country
wiek [vyek] m. age; century
wiekowy [vye-ko-vi] adj. m.
secular; ancient; aged;
advanced in years; venerable
wiekuistość [vye-koo-ees-
-tośhćh] f. eternity; all time
wiekuisty [vye-koo-ees-ti] adj. m.
eternal; everlasting
wielbiciel [vyel-bee-ćhel] m.
devotee; admirer; idolator
(ladies' man)
wielbicielka [vyel-bee-ćhel-ka] f.
devotee; idolatress (woman)
wielbłąd [vyel-bwownd] m.
camel; dromedary (or bactrian)
wielce [vyel-tse] adv. very;
greatly; extremely; very much
wiele [vye-le] adj. m. many; a
lot; much; far out; a great
deal; how much?
wielebny [vye-leb-ni] adj. m.
reverend (Father etc.)
Wielkanoc [vyel-ka-nots] f.
Easter
wielkanocny [vyel-ka-nots-ni] adj.
m. Easter; of Easter
wielki [vyel-kee] adj. m. big;
large; great; vast; keen;
mighty; intense; important
wielkoduszny [vyel-ko-doosh-ni]
adj. m. magnanimous; noble-
minded; generous
wielkolud [vyel-ko-lood] m. giant
wielkomiejski [vyel-ko-myey-
-skee] adj. m. metropolitan;
urban; of a large city
wielkość [vyel-ko-śhćh] f.
greatness; size; dimension;
value; quantity; vastness
wielobarwny [vye-lo-barv-ni] adj.
m. multi-color (ed); colorful
wieloboczny [vye-lo-boch-ni] adj.
m. multilateral; polygonal
wielokrążek [vye-lo-krown-zhek]
m. set of pulleys; pulley-block
wielokrotny [vye-lo-krot-ni] adj.
m. repeated; multiple
wieloletni [vye-lo-let-ńee]
adj. m. long; years long; many

years (service...)
wielopiętrowy [vye-lo-pyan-tro-
-vi] adj. m. multi-story
wieloraki [vye-lo-ra-kee] adj. m.
manifold; varied; multiple
wieloryb [vye-lo-rib] m. whale
wielorybnik [vye-lo-rib-ńeek] m.
whaler; whale man; whaling
ship; whaling boat
wielostronny [vye-lo-stron-ni] adj.
m. multilateral; many-sided;
versatile; various
wielozgłoskowy [vye-lo-zgwos-
-ko-vi] adj. m. polysyllabic
wieloznaczny [vye-lo-znach-ni]
adj. m. equivocal; ambiguous
wielożeństwo [vye-lo-zheń-
-stvo] n. polygamy
wieniec [vye-ńets] m. wreath;
garland; crown; chaplet
wieńczyć [vyeń-chićh] v.
crown; garland; wreathe
wieprz [vyepsh] m. hog; pig
wieprzowina [vyep-zho-vee-na] f.
pork (meat)
wieprzowy [vyep-zho-vi] adj. m.
pork; pork's; pig's; hog's;
porcine
wiercenie [vyer-tse-ńe] n.
drilling; perforation; boring
wiercić [vyer-ćheećh] v. bore;
drill; pester; bother
wierność [vyer-nośhćh] f.
fidelity; loyalty; faith; truth
wierny [vyer-ni] adj. m. faithful;
true; loyal; exact
wiersz [vyersh] m. verse; poem
wiertarka [vyer-tar-ka] f. drill
wiertnictwo [vyert-ńeets-tvo] n.
drilling (activity)
wierutny [vye-root-ni] adj. m.
stark (liar); notorious; through-
and-through; rank; arrant; born
wierzący [vye-zhown-tsi] adj. m.
believer; believing Christian
wierzba [vyezh-ba] f. willow
wierzch [vyezhkh] m. top; brim
head; surface; cover; lid
wierzchni [vyezh-khńee] adj. m.
upper; top; outer; outside
wierzchołek [vyezh-kho-wek] m.
top; peak; summit; apex;
vertex; cusp

wierzyciel [vye-zhi-ćhel] m.
creditor; mortgagee; obligee
wierzycielka [vye-zhi-ćhel-ka] f.
creditor (woman)
wierzyć [vye-zhić́h] v. believe;
trust; rely; believe in God
wierzytelność [vye-shi-tel-
-nośhćh] f. debt; claim
wieszać [vye-shaćh] v. hang
wieszadło [vye-shad-wo] v.
hanger; peg; coat-stand
wieszak [vye-shak] m. rack
wieszcz [vyeshch] m. bard; seer;
poet (leading, national)
wieszczy [vyesh-chi] adj. m.
prophetic; visionary
wieś [vyeśh] f. village;
countryside; hamlet; the
villagers
wieść [vyeśhćh] 1. f. news
2. v. lead; conduct; draw;
succeed; stand at the head
wieśniaczka [vyeśh-ńach-ka] f.
countrywoman; peasant
woman
wieśniak [vyeśh-ńak] m.
countryman; villager; yokel;
rustic; peasant
wietrzeć [vyet-zhećh] v. decay
wietrzyć [vyet-zhićh] v.
ventilate; smell; nose; aerate
wietrzenie [vyet-zhe-ńe] n.
ventilation; decay (of rocks)
wiewiórka [vye-vyoor-ka] f.
squirrel; squirrel fur
wieźć [vyeźhćh] v. carry (on
wheels, horse, sledge);
transport; convey; drive
wieża [vye-zha] f. tower; rook
wieżowiec [vye-zho-vyets] m.
skyscraper; high-rise (building)
wieżyczka [vye-zhich-ka] f.
turret; pinnacle; small tower
więc [vyants] conj. now; well;
therefore; so; consequently
więcej [vyan-tsey] adv. more
więdnąć [vyand-nownćh] v.
wither; fade; wilt
więcierz [vyan-ćhezh] m. fishing
net (set taut on hoops)
większość [vyank-shośhćh] f.
majority; the bulk; most
większy [vyank-shi] adj. m.

bigger; larger; greater
więzić [vyan-źheećh] v.
imprison; confine; detain;
restrain; keep locked up
więzienie [vyan-źhe-ńe] n.
prison; confinement; jail; gaol;
restraint
więzień [vyan-źheń] m.
prisoner; convict
więzy [vyan-zi] pl. fetters;
restrains; chains; bonds
wigilia [vee-geel-ya] f. Christmas
Eve; Christmas Eve supper
wiklina [vee-klee-na] f. osier
wikłać [veek-waćh] v. entangle
wikt [veekt] m. board; keep
wilczur [veel-choor] m. wolf dog
wilgoć [veel-goćh] f. humidity
wilgotny [veel-got-ni] adj. m.
moist; humid; damp; wet
wilia [veel-ya] f. see wigilia
wilk [veelk] m. wolf; wolf-skin
wilżyć [veel-zhićh] v. moisten
wina [vee-na] f. guilt; fault
winda [veen-da] f. elevator
winiarnia [vee-ńar-ńa] f.
wine-shop; vine vault; winery
winić [vee-ńeećh] v. accuse;
blame for; fix the blame on
winien [vee-ńen] adj. m.
indebted; owing; guilty; at
fault; in debit
winnica [venn-ńee-tsa] f.
vineyard; vine growing
plantation
winny [veen-ni] adj. m. guilty
winny [veen-ni] adj. m. of wine;
vinous; vine-; winy
wino [vee-no] n. wine; grapevine
winogrono [vee-no-gro-no] n.
grape
winorośl [vee-no-rośhl] f. vine
winowajca [vee-no-vay-tsa] m.
culprit; evildoer; the guilty one
winszować [venn-sho-vaćh] v.
congratulate (on having
success); wish well
wiosenny [vyo-sen-ni] adj. m.
spring- (flowers, month etc.)
wioska [vyos-ka] f. hamlet
wiosło [vyos-wo] n. oar; paddle
wiosłować [vyos-wo-vaćh] v.
row; paddle; pull an oar

wiosna [**vyos**-na] f. Spring (time)
wioślarz [**vyośh**-lash] m.
   oarsman; rower
wiotki [**vyot**-kee] adj. m. limp
wiór [**vyoor**] m. shaving; chip
wir [**veer**] m. whirl; eddy; vortex
wiraż [**vee**-rash] m. curve; bend
wirować [vee-ro-**vać**] v. whirl
wirówka [vee-**roov**-ka] f.
   centrifuge; hydro-extractor
wirtuoz [veer-**too**-os] m.
   virtuoso; maestro; great
   musician etc.
wirus [**vee**-roos] m. virus
wisieć [vee-**śheć**] v. hang;
   sag
wisiorek [vee-**śho**-rek] m.
   pendant
wiśnia [**veeśh**-ńa] f. cherry
   (tree)
wiśniak [**veeśh**-ńak] m. cherry
   -brandy; cherry liqueur
witać [vee-**tać**] v. greet;
   welcome; meet to welcome;
   bid welcome
witamina [vee-ta-**mee**-na] f.
   vitamin (A, B, C, D, E etc)
witryna [vee-**tri**-na] f.
   shop window; glass case
wiza [**vee**-za] f. visa
wizerunek [vee-ze-**roo**-nek] m.
   likeness; image; picture; effigy
wizja [**veez**-ya] f. vision; view
wizyta [vee-**zi**-ta] f. call; visit; be
   on a visit
wizytówka [vee-zi-**toov**-ka] f.
   calling card; visiting card
wjazd [**vyazt**] m. (car) entrance
wjeżdżać [vyezh-**dzać**] v.
   drive in; ride to the top
wkleić [vkle-**eeć**] v. stick in
wklęsłodruk [vklan-**swo**-drook]
   m. copper plate print
wklęsły [**vklans**-wi] adj. m.
   concave; hollow; sunken
wkład [**vkwat**] m. input; deposit;
   investment; outlay; inset
wkładać [vkwa-**dać**] v. put in
w koło [**v ko**-wo] adv. round; in
   circles; over and over again
wkoło [**vko**-wo] prep. round;
   about in circles
wkraczać [vkra-**chać**] v.

   appear; step in; invade;
   intervene; enter; stalk
wkradać się [vkra-**dać śhan**]
   v. steal in; slip in; creep in
wkrapiać [vkrap-**yać**] v. put
   drops in; beat up
wkręcać [**vkran**-tsać] v. screw
   in; drive in; push into a job
wkroczyć [vkro-**chić**] v. enter
   (formally); appear; invade
wkrótce [**vkroot**-tse] adv. soon
wkupić się [vkoo-**peeć śhan**]
   v. buy way in; pay one's
   footing
wlać [**vlać**] v. pour in
wlatywać [vla-ti-**vać**] v. fly in;
   rush in; dart in; run in
wlec [**vlets**] v. drag; tow
wlepić [vle-**peeć**] v. 1. paste
   in; 2. glare at; stare at
wlewać [vle-**vać**] v. pour in
wleźć [**vleźhć**] v. crawl in;
   climb up; barge in; step in
wliczenie [vlee-**che**-ńe] n.
   inclusion; counting in
wliczyć [**vlee**-chić] v. count
   in; reckon in; include
w lot [**v lot**] adv. in a flash;
   quickly; in a harry
wlot [**vlot**] m. inlet; intake
wlot kuli [**vlot koo**-lee] m. bullet
   entry
władać [**vwa**-dać] v. rule;
   wield (pen etc.); manage
władca [**vwad**-tsa] m. ruler
władny [**vwad**-ni] adj. m.
   sovereign; having the
   authority (or power)
władza [**vwa**-dza] f. authority
włamać się [vwa-**mać śhan**]
   v. break in; burglarize
włamanie [vwa-ma-**ńe**] n.
   burglary; house breaking
włamywacz [vwa-mi-**vach**] m.
   burglar; housebreaker;
   pick-lock
własnoręcznie [vwa-sno-**ranch**-
   -ńe] adv. personally; with
   one's hand; with one's own
   hand; of one's own hand
własność [**vwas**-nośhć] f.
   property; characteristic feature
własnowolny [vwas-no-**vol**-ni]

adj. m. spontaneous; voluntary

własny [vwas-ni] adj. m. own;
very own; of one's own

właściciel [vwaśh-ćhee-ćhel]
m. proprietor; holder; owner

właściwy [vwaśh-ćhee-vi]
adj. m. proper; right; suitable;
due; adequate; becoming; fit

właściwość [vwaśh-ćhee-
-vośhćh] f. propriety;
characteristic; feature

właśnie [vwaśh-ńe] adv.
exactly; just so; precisely;
very; just as; just now; just
then; only just; quite so

właz [vwas] m. manhole; hatch

włazić [vwa-żheećh] v. crawl
in; barge in; step in; go deep

włączać [vw<u>own</u>-chaćh] v.
include; switch on; plug in

włącznie [vw<u>ownch</u>-ńe] adv.
inclusively; inclusive; including

włączenie [vw<u>own</u>-che-ńe] n.
inclusion; merger; incorporation; turning on (lights, motor)

włochaty [vwo-kha-ti] adj. m.
hairy; shaggy; hirsute; woolly

włos [vwos] m. hair; fur

włosień [vwo-śheń] m. trichina

włoski [vwos-kee] adj. m. Italian;
of Italy

włoskowaty [vwos-ko-va-ti] adj.
m. capillary; hairlike (tubes)

włoszczyzna [vwozh-chiz-na] pl.
vegetables; Italian studies

włościanin [vwośh-ćha-ńeen]
m. farmer; peasant; country
man; pl. country-folk

włożyć [vwo-zhićh] v. put in;
put on; clothe; invest

włóczęga [vwoo-chan-ga] m.
tramp; rover; vagrant; roam

włóczka [vwooch-ka] f. yarn

włócznia [vwooch-ńa] f. spear

włóczyć [vwoo-chićh] v. drag

włókienniczy [vwo-kyen-ńee-chi]
adj. m. textile (trade, fiber)

włókniarz [vwook-ńash] m.
weaver; textile worker

włóknisty [vwook-ńees-ti]
adj.m. fibrous; stringy; thready

włókno [vwook-no] n. fiber

wmawiać [vmav-yaćh] v. talk

into; persuade; make believe

wmieszać się [vmye-shaćh
ś<u>han</u>] v. interfere; join; mix;
mingle with; intervene in

wmuszać [vmoo-shaćh] v.
force (upon); press upon

wnet [vnet] adv. soon; directly;
shortly; before long presently

wnęka [vn<u>an</u>-ka] f. niche; recess

wnętrze [v<u>nan</u>-tzhe] n. interior

wnętrzności [vn<u>an</u>tzh-nośh-
-ćhee] pl. bowels; intestines;
entrails

Wniebowzięcie [vńe-bo-v<u>żhan</u>-
-ćhe] n. Assumption

wnieść [vńeśhćh] v. carry
in; put in; infer; gather; bring
in; conclude

wnikać [vnee-kaćh] v.
penetrate; investigate

wnikliwy [vńee-klee-vi] adj. m.
penetrating; discerning; keen;
discriminating; piercing

wniosek [vńo-sek] m.
conclusion; proposition;
suggestion; motion

wnioskodawca [vńos-ko-dav-
-tsa] m. mover; giver or
proposer of a motion

wnioskować [vńos-ko-vaćh] v.
conclude; deduct; infer; gather

wnioskowanie [vńos-ko-va-ńe]
n. conclusion; inference

wnosić [vno-śheećh] v. carry
in; conclude; infer; gather

wnuczka [vnooch-ka] f.
granddaughter

wnuk [vnook] m. grandson

wnyk [vnik] m. snare

woalka [vo-al-ka] f. veil (hat)

wobec [vo-bets] prep. in the
face of; before; towards

woda [vo-da] f. water; froth; bull

wodnisty [vod-ńees-ti] adj. m.
watery; thin; wishy-washy;
weak; aqueous; hydrous

wodno-płatowiec [vod-no-pwa-
-to-vyets] m. hydroplane;
water plane

wodny [vod-ni] adj. m. water-

wodociąg [vo-do-ćh<u>own</u>k] m.
waterworks; water tap

wodolecznictwo [vo-do-lech-

-ńeets-tvo] n. hydrotherapy;
water cure
wodopój [vo-**do**-pooy] m.
watering spot; cow-pond;
horse-pond; water hole
wodorost [vo-do-rost] m.
seaweed; alga
wodorowa bomba [vo-do-ro-va
bom-ba] f. H-bomb
wodospad [vo-do-spat] m.
waterfall; cascade
wodotrysk [vo-do-trisk] m.
fountain; waterspout
wodować [vo-do-vaćh] v.
launch on water; splash down;
alight (on water)
wodowstręt [vo-do-vstr<u>ant</u>] m.
hydrophobia; rabies
wodór [**vo**-door] m. hydrogen
wodza [**vo**-dza] f. rein; hold;
sway; command
wodzić [**vo**-dźheećh] v. lead;
run; be the ringleader
wodzirej [vo-dźhee-rey] m.
dance leader; ringleader; bell-
wether; gang leader
w ogóle [vo-**goo**-le] adv.
generally; on the whole; in the
main; all in all; altogether
wojak [**vo**-yak] m. warrior;
soldier
wojenny [vo-**yen**-ni] adj. m.
military; war; wartime; of war
województwo [vo-ye-**voodz**-tvo]
n. province; voivodeship
wojłok [**voy**-wok] m. felt (thick)
wojna [**voy**-na] f. war; warfare
wojna domowa [**voy**-na do-mo-
-va] f. civil war
wojować [vo-yo-vaćh] v. wage
war; combat; contend
wojowniczy [vo-yov-**ńee**-chi]
adj. m. warlike; aggressive
wojownik [vo-yov-**ńeek**] m.
(tribal) warrior
wojsko [**voy**-sko] n. army; troops
wojskowość [voy-**sko**-
-voshćh] f. military science;
the army; military service
wojskowy [voy-**sko**-vi] adj. m.
military; army (post etc.)
wokalny [vo-**kal**-ni] adj. m. vocal
wokoło [vo-**ko**-wo] adv. all

around; round; about
wola [**vo**-la] f. will; volition
woleć [**vo**-lećh] v. prefer
wolno [**vol**-no] adv. slowly
wolnomyśliciel [vol-no-mi-
-**śhlee**-ćhel] m. freethinker
wolność [**vol**-noshćh] f.
liberty; freedom; independence
wolnościowy [vol-nośh-**ćho**-vi]
adj. m. for liberation
wolny [**vol**-ni] adj. m. free
wolt [volt] m. volt
woltomierz [vol-**to**-myesh] m.
voltmeter
wołać [**vo**-waćh] v. call; cry
wołanie [vo-**wa**-ńe] n. call; cry
wołowina [vo-wo-**vee**-na] f. beef
wonny [**von**-ni] adj. m. fragrant;
aromatic; sweet-smelling
wonieć [**vo**-ńećh] v. scent;
smell; be fragrant
woń [voń] f. fragrance
woreczek [vo-**re**-chek] m. small
bag; pouch; sack; cyst
worek [**vo**-rek] m. bag; sack
wosk [vosk] m. wax
woskować [vos-**ko**-vaćh] v.
wax
wozić [**vo**-źheećh] v. carry (on
wheels); transport; drive; cart
wozownia [vo-**zov**-ńa] f. coach
house; coach storage depot
woźnica [voźh-**ńee**-tsa] m.
coachman; driver; waggoner
wożenie [vo-**zhe**-ńe] n.
transport; transportation;
carriage
wódka [**vood**-ka] fr. vodka
wódz [voots] m. commander;
chief; leader; headman
wójt [vooyt] m. village mayor
wół [voow] m. ox; steer; bullock
wór [voor] m. (big) sack (full)
wówczas [**voov**-chas] adv. then;
that time; at the time
wóz [voos] m. car; cart; wagon
wózek [**voo**-zek] m. (small) car
wpadać [vpa-daćh] v. fall in;
rush in; drop in; run into
wpajać [vpa-yaćh] v. put in
(head); implant; instill
wpatrywać się [vpa-tri-vaćh
śh<u>an</u>] v. stare; look intently

wpełzać [vpew-zaćh] v. crawl in; creep in (into a cave etc.)

wpędzać [vpan-dzaćh] v. drive sb in; bring on sb...(death etc)

wpić się [vpeećh śhan] v. sink into; penetrate; bury (teeth)

wpierw [vpyerv] adv. first

wpis [vpees] m. enrollment

wpisać [vpee-saćh] v. write in

wpisowe [vpee-so-ve] n. registration fee; inscription fee

wplatać [vpla-taćh] v. twine in; weave; braid; intersperse

wplątać [vplown-taćh] v. entangle; implicate; involve

wpłacać [vpwa-tsaćh] v. pay in

wpłata [vpwa-ta] f. payment

wpław [vpwaf] adv. (swim) across

wpływ [vpwif] m. influence; income; effect; impact of

wpływać [vpwi-vaćh] v. flow in; influence; have effect

wpływowy [vpwi-vo-vi] adj. m. influential

w pobliżu [v po-blee-zhoo] adv. near; in the vicinity; close by

w poprzek [v po-pzhek] prep. adv. across; crosswise

wpół [vpoow] adv. in half; halfway; half past; half-; semi-

w pośród [v pośh-root] adv. among; in the midst of

wprawa [vpra-va] f. skill; practice; proficiency

wprawdzie [vprav-dźhe] adv. in truth; to be sure; indeed

wprawić [vpra-veećh] v. set in; train in; insert; put in

wprawny [vprav-ni] adj. m. skillful; trained; experienced

wprost [vprost] adv. directly; straight ahead; outright; simply; in a straight line

wprowadzenie [vpro-va-dze-ńe] n. introduction; initiation

wprowadzać [vpro-va-dzaćh] v. usher; introduce; lead in; put in; walk into; march into

wprzągać [vpzhan-gaćh] v. harness (horse, river, etc)

wprzód [vpshoot] adv. ahead; before; first; in the first place

wpuszczać [vpoosh-chaćh] v. let in; admit; insert; allow to enter; give free passage

wpychać [vpi-khaćh] v. push in

wracać [vra-tsaćh] v. return

wrastać [vras-taćh] v. grow in

wraz [vras] prep. together

wrażenie [vra-zhe-ńe] n. 1. impression; sensation; feeling; thrill; 2. implant; engraft

wrażliwość [vrazh-lee-vośhćh] f. sensitivity; susceptibility; delicacy

wrażliwy [vrazh-lee-vi] adj. m. sensitive; thin-skinned; tender

wreszcie [vresh-ćhe] adv. at last; finally; after all; eventually; last of all

wręcz [vranch] adv. down right

wręczać [vran-chaćh] v. hand in; hand over; deliver

wrodzony [vro-dzo-ni] adj. m. innate; inborn; inbred; congenital

wrogi [vro-gee] adj. m. hostile

wrogość [vro-gośhćh] f. hostility; ill-will; enmity; malevolence

wrona [vro-na] f. crow

wrota [vro-ta] n. gate

wrotki [vrot-kee] pl. roller skates

wróbel [vroo-bel] m. sparrow

wrócić [vroo-ćheećh] v. return

wróg [vrook] m. foe; enemy

wróżba [vroozh-ba] f. omen

wróżbiarz [vroozh-byash] m. fortune-teller; soothsayer

wróżka [vroozh-ka] f. fortune-teller; palmist; fairy

wróżyć [vroo-zhićh] v. tell fortunes; foretell; predict

wryć sie [vrićh śhan] v. dig in; sink in; imbed into

wrzask [vzhask] m. scream; yell

wrzaskliwy [vzhas-klee-vi] adj. m. shrill; piercing; clamorous

wrzawa [vzha-va] f. noise

wrzący [vzhown-tsi] adj. m. boiling; scalding (hot)

wrzątek [vzhown-tek] m. boiling water

wrzeciono [vzhe-ćho-no] n. spindle; verge

wrzeć [vzhećh] v. boil; rage
wrzesień [vzhe-śheń] m.
September
wrzeszczeć [vzhesh-chech] v.
shriek; yell;scream; cry
wrzos [vzhos] m. heather
wrzosowisko [vzho-so-vees-ko]
n. heat; moor
wrzód [vzhoot] m. abscess
wrzucać [vzhoo-tsaćh] v.
throw in; drop in; put in; cast
wsadzać [vsa-dzaćh] v. put in;
plant; stick; lock sb up
wschodni [vskhod-ńee] adj. m.
east; easterly; eastern
wschodzić [vskho-dźheećh] v.
shoot up; rise; sprout
**wschód słońca [vskhoot swoń-
-tsa]** m. sunrise
wsiadać [vśha-daćh] v. get in;
mount; get on board; take
one's seat; mount (a horse)
wsiąkać [vśhown-kaćh] v.
sink in; infiltrate
wskazany [vska-za-ni] adj. m.
advisable; indicated; desirable
wskazówka [vska-zoov-ka] f.
hint; direction; (clock) hand
**wskazujący palec [vska-zoo-
-yown-tsi pa-lets]** m. forefinger
wskazywać [vska-zi-vaćh] v.
point out; show; indicate
wskaźnik [vskaźh-ńeek] m.
index; pointer; indicator; signal
w skos [v skos] adv. slant
wskroś [vskrośh] prep. through
wskutek [vskoo-tek] prep. as a
result; due to; thanks to
wskrzesić [vskzhe-śheećh] v.
resuscitate; revive; wake;
bring back to life; recall
**wspaniałomyślny [vspa-ńa-wo-
-miśhl-ni]** adj. m. magnanimous; generous
**wspaniałość [vspa-ńa-
-wośhćh]** f. splendor; stateliness; grandeur; lordliness
wspaniały [vspa-ńa-wi] adj. m.
superb; glorious; grand; great;
smashing; magnificent; lordly;
gorgeous; luxurious; splendid
wsparcie [vspar-ćhe] n. support
wspierać [vspye-raćh] v.

support; prop up; assist; help
**wspinać się [vspee-naćh
śhan]** v. climb up; toil up hill;
climb mountains; rear
wspomagać [vspo-ma-gaćh] v.
help; aid; assist; succor
wspominać [vspo-mee-naćh] v.
remember; recall; mention
wspornik [vspor-ńeek] m.
cantilever (beam); bracket;
structural support
wspólnik [vspool-ńeek] m.
partner; accomplice; associate
wspólny [vspool-ni] adj. m.
common; joint; combined;
collective; united
**współczesność [vspoow-ches-
-nośhćh]** f. the present time
(day, age); simultaneousness
współczesny [vspoow-ches-ni]
adj. m. contemporary; modern;
present-day (music, writers)
współczucie [vspoow-choo-ćhe]
n. sympathy; compassion; pity
współcznnik [vspoow-chin-ńeek]
m. coefficient; factor
**współdziałać [vspoow-dźha-
-waćh]** v. cooperate; act
jointly; associate; concur
**współistnieć [vspoow-eest-
-ńećh]** v. coexist
**współistnienie [vspoow-eest-ńe-
-ńe]** n. coexistence
współpraca [vspoow-pra-tsa] f.
cooperation; team-work
współrzędna [vspoow-zhand-na]
f. coordinate axis
współudział [vspoow-oo-dźhaw]
m. participation; share
**współwłaściciel [vspoow-
-vwaśh-ćhee-ćhel]** m. joint
owner; joint proprietor
**współzawodnictwo [vspoow-
-za-vod-ńeets-tvo]** m.
competition; rivalry
**współzawodnik [vspoow-za-
-vod-ńeek]** m. competitor;
rival; contestant
współżyć [vspoow-zhićh] v.
get along; live together;
coexist; be in symbiosis
wstawać [vsta-vaćh] v. get up
wstawiać [vsta-vyaćh] v. set in

wstawiać się [vsta-vyaćh
śhan] v. get tipsy; plead for
someone; stand up for
wstąpić [vstown-peećh] v.
step in; drop in; step up; enter
wstążka [vstownzh-ka] f. ribbon
wstecz [vstech] adv. backwards
wsteczny [vstech-ni] adj. m.
reactionary; reverse; backward
wstęga [vstan-ga] f. (large)
ribbon (of a road, of a river);
band; sash; wreath; wisp
wstęp [vstanp] m. entrance;
admission; preface; opening
wstępny [vstanp-ni] adj. m.
introductory; initial; preliminary
wstręt [vstrant] m. aversion
wstrętny [vstrant-ni] adj. m.
hideous; foul; vile; nasty
wstrząs [vstzhowns] m. shock
wstrząsający [vstzhown-sa-
-yown-tsi] adj. m. shocking;
thrilling; startling
wstrzemięźliwość [vstzhe-
-myan-źhlee-vośhćh] f.
moderation; abstinence
wstrzemięźliwy [vstzhe-myan-
-źhlee-vi] adj. m. moderate
wstrzykiwać [vstzhi-kee-vaćh]
v. inject; give a shot
wstrzmać [vstzhi-maćh] v.
stop; abstain; put off; hold
back; delay; suspend; cease
wstyd [vstit] m. shame;
disgrace; dishonor; indecency
wstydliwy [vstid-lee-vi] adj. m.
shy; bashful; timid;
embarrassing; modest
wstydzić się [vsti-dźeećh
śhan] v. be ashamed; blush
for someone; feel shame for
wsunąć [vsoo-nownćh] v. slip
in; put in; insert into; tuck in
wsypa [vsi-pa] f. a bad break;
gaffe; give-away of a plot
wsypać [vsi-paćh] v. pour in;
tell on somebody; pour (grain)
wszakże [vshak-zhe] conj. adv.
yet; however; nevertheless
wszcząć [vshownćh] v. start;
begin; institute; enter (talks)
wszechmocny [vshekh-mots-ni]
adj. m. omnipotent; almighty

wszechnica [vshekh-ńee-tsa] f.
university
wszechstronny [vshekh-stron-ni]
adj. m. universal; versatile
wszechświat [vshekh-śhvyat]
m. universe; cosmos;
macrocosm
wszelki [vshel-ki] adj. m. every;
all; any (possible); whatever
wszerz [vshesh] adv. broadside
wszędzie [vshan-dźhe] adv.
everywhere; on all sides; all
over; far and near
wszystek [vshis-tek] adj. m.
whole; all; ever; the whole
wszywać [vshi-vaćh] v. sew in
wścibski [vśhćheeb-skee] m.
busybody; meddler; snooper
wściekać się [vśhćhe-kaćh
śhan] v. rage; rave; be
furious; become rabid
wścieklizna [vśhćhe-kleez-na]
f. rabies; madness; rabidness;
hydrophobia
wściekłość [vśhćhek-
-wośhćh] f. fury; rage;
tantrums; madness
w ślad [vśhlad] adv. following
in tracks; following closely
wśliznąć się [vśhleez-nownćh
śhan] v. sneak in; slip in
wśród [vśhroot] prep. among
wtaczać [vta-chaćh] v. roll in
wtajemniczyć [vta-yem-ńee-
-chićh] v. initiate; acquaint;
instruct (in the art of...)
wtargnąć [vtarg-nownćh] v.
invade; break into; interrupt
wtedy [vte-di] adv. then
wtem [vtem] adv. suddenly
wtenczas [vten-chas] adv. then;
at that time; at this junction
wtoczyć [vto-chićh] v. roll in
wtorek [vto-rek] m. Tuesday
wtórny [vtoor-ni] adj. m.
secondary; incidental;
repeated; derivative
wtrącać się [vtrown-tsaćh
śhan] v. meddle; cut into;
butt in; add (a remark)
wtyczka [vtich-ka] f. plug
wtykać [vti-kaćh] v. insert
w tył [v tiw] adv. back

wuj [vooy] m. uncle
wujenka [voo-yen-ka] f. aunt
wulgarny [vool-gar-ni] adj. m.
vulgar; coarse; low
wulkan [vool-kan] m. volcano
wulkanizować [vool-ka-ńee-zo-
-vać] v. vulcanize; cure
(rubber)
wwozić [v-vo-źheeć] v.
import; bring into an area
wwóz [v-voos] m. import;
importation
wy [vi] pron. you; you people
wybaczać [vi-ba-chać] v. 1.
forgive; pardon; 2. buckle out
of line; get out of line
wybawca [vi-bav-tsa] m. savior;
rescuer; liberator; redeemer
wybawić [vi-ba-veeć] v. save;
deliver; free; rescue; rid
wybebeszyć [vi-be-be-shić] v.
gut (chicken etc.)
wybić [vi-beeć] v. knock out
(something); strike; cover; kill
wybiec [vi-byets] v. run out
wybieg [vi-byek] m. evasion;
runway; playground; fowl run
wybielić [vi-bye-leeć] v.
whitewash; bleach; coat with
tin; whiten; grow white
wybierać [vi-bye-rać] v.
choose elect; select; pick out;
mine; extract; scoop; excavate
wybierak [vi-bye-rak] m. selector
(a technical term)
wybieralny [vi-bye-ral-ni] adj. m.
elective; eligible
wybitny [vi-beet-ni] adj. m.
prominent; eminent; marked
wybladły [vi-blad-wi] adj. m.
pale; dim; faded; colorless
wybłagać [vi-bwa-gać] v. get
by entreaty; impetrate
wyblakły [vi-blak-wi] adj. m.
faded; dim; dilute; weathered
wyboisty [vi-bo-ees-ti] adj. m.
rough; full of holes; bumpy
wyborca [vi-bor-tsa] m. voter
wyborczy [vi-bor-chi] adj. m.
electoral; election- (precinct...)
wyborny [vi-bor-ni] adj. m.
excellent; prime; choice;
splendid; delicious; exquisite

wyborowy [vi-bo-ro-vi] adj. m.
choice; select; first rate
wybory [vi-bo-ri] pl. election
wybór [vi-boor] m. choice;
option; selection; adoption
wybrany [vi-bra-ni] adj. m.
elected; chosen; selected
wybredny [vi-bred-ni] adj. m.
fastidious; particular; exacting
wybrnąć [vibr-nownć] v. get
out; pull through; wade out
of; clear out of; extricate
wybrukować [vi-broo-ko-vać]
v. pave (a road, a street etc.)
wybryk [vi-brik] m. prank; freak;
antic; whim; frolic; caprice;
extravagance; escapade
wybrzeże [vi-bzhe-zhe] n. coast;
beach; seashore; seacoast
wybrzuszenie [vi-bzhoo-she-ńe]
n. bulge; swelling; knob; belly
wybuch [vi-bookh] m. explosion;
eruption; outbreak; outburst
wybudować [vi-boo-do-vać]
v. build; erect; raise; construct
wycelować [vi-tse-lo-vać] v.
take aim; level a gun at
wychodek [vi-kho-dek] m. privy
wychodzić [vi-kho-dźheeć] v.
get out; walk out; climb out
wychodźca [vi-khodźh-tsa] m.
emigrant; emigre
wychować [vi-kho-vać] v.
bring up; breed; rear; rise;
train; educate
wychowanek [vi-kho-va-nek] m.
pupil; alumnus; ward; foster
child
wychowanie [vi-kho-va-ńe] n.
upbringing; manners;
education; breeding
wychowawca [vi-kho-vav-tsa] m.
tutor; educator; foster father
wychudły [vi-khood-wi] adj. m.
gaunt; skinny; haggard;
emaciated; hollow-cheeked
wychwalać [vi-khva-lać] v.
praise; exalt; extol; speak
highly of; crack up
wychylać [vi-khi-lać] v. stick
out; empty (a glass) ; bend;
incline; lean out; hang out
wychylać się [vi-khi-lać

śhan] v. lean out; stick one's neck out; hang out; appear; be visible

wyciąg [vi-**chown**k] m. extract; elevator; hoist; winch; excerpt

wyciągać [vi-**chown**-gać] v. pull out; stretch out; derive

wycie [vi-**ć**he] n. howl; scream

wycieczka [vi-**ć**hech-ka] f. trip; excursion; outing; ramble; hike

wyciekać [vi-**ć**he-kać] v. leak out; flow out; ooze out; scamper away; exude

wycieńczać [vi-**ć**heń-chać] exhaust; waste; emaciate

wycieńczenie [vi-**ć**heń-**che**-ńe] n. exhaustion; weakness; debility; emaciation

wycieraczka [vi-**ć**he-**rach**-ka] f. wiper; doormat

wycierać [vi-**ć**he-rać] v. wipe; erase; efface; dust; wear out; blow (nose); rub

wycięcie [vi-**ć**han-**ć**he] n. opening; cut; decollete; notch; jag; neck-line; indentation

wycinać [vi-**ć**hee-nać] v. cut out; carve out; fell; cut down

wycisk [vi-**ć**heesk] m. press; squeeze; beating (slang)

wyciskać [vi-**ć**hees-kać] v. squeeze out; impress; wring

wycofać [vi-**tso**-fać] v. withdraw; remove; retract; call off; call back; recall; retire

wycofanie [vi-tso-fa-ńe] n. withdrawal; recall; retirement

wyczerpać [vi-cher-pać] v. exhaust; drain; deplete; scoop

wyczerpanie [vi-cher-pa-ńe] n. exhaustion; depletion; fag; prostration; tiring out

wyczesywać [vi-che-si-vać] v. comb out; dress hair (beard etc.); comb hair

wyczuwać [vi-choo-vać] v. sense; feel; scent; ascertain; perceive by touch

wyczyn [vi-chin] m. feat; stunt

wyczyszczać [vi-chish-chać] v. clean; brush (clothes); clean out; polish; furbish

wyć [vić] v. howl; roar; shriek

wyćwiczony [vić-vee-cho-ni] adj. m. trained; skilled

wydać [vi-dać] v. give away spend; pay; issue; betray

wydajność [vi-day-nośhść] f. yield; productivity; output

wydajny [vi-day-ni] adj. m. productive; effective

wydalać [vi-da-lać] v. dismiss; sack; expel; eliminate; excrete

wydalenie [vi-da-le-ńe] n. expulsion; dismissal

wydanie [vi-da-ńe] n. edition

wydarty [vi-dar-ti] adj. m. torn out; plucked out; snatched out

wydarzać się [vi-da-zhać śhan] v. happen; turn out well; occur; take place

wydarzenie [vi-da-zhe-ńe] n. event; happening; occurrence

wydatek [vi-da-tek] m. expense

wydatkować [vi-dat-ko-vać] v. spend; lay out funds; expend

wydatny [vi-dat-ni] adj. m. prominent; salient; distinct

wydawać [vi-da-vać] v. spend; give the change; give away; publish

wydawca [vi-dav-tsa] m. publisher; editor; publishing house or firm

wydawnictwo [vi-dav-ńeets-tvo] n. publication; publishing house; publishing firm

wydąć [vi-downć] v. expand; puff up; inflate; blow up

wydech [vi-dekh] m. exhalation

wydeptać ścieżkę [vi-dep-tać śhćhezh-kan] beat a path; thread a path (exp.)

wydłubywać [vi-dwoo-bi-vać] v. scrape out; poke; hollow out; extract; pick out

wydłużać [vi-dwoo-zhać] v. prolong; lengthen; elongate

wydma [vid-ma] f. dune; sand dune; snowdrift

wydobrzeć [vi-dob-zheć] v. recover; get better; improve

wydobycie [vi-do-bi-ćhe] n. output; yield; production

wydobywać [vi-do-bi-vać] v. extract; mine; wring; get;

obtain; draw out; excavate
wydostać [vi-**dos**-tać] v. bring
out; extricate; obtain; pull out
wydra [**vi**-dra] f. otter;
vulg.:bitch; hussy; minx; vixen
wydrapać [vi-dra-**pać**] v.
scratch out; erase a stain
wydrapać się [vi-dra-pać
śhan] v. climb up; scramble
up (out); clamber up
wydrążać [vi-**drown**-zhać] v.
hollow out; drill; excavate
wydrwić [**vi**-drveeć] v. jeer;
mock; cheat; gibe; deride
wydrwigrosz [vi-**drvee**-grosh] m.
swindler; fraud; take-in
wydusić [vi-**doo**-śheeć] v.
squeeze out; extort; strangle
wydychać [vi-**di**-khać] v.
breathe out; exhale; emit
wydymać [vi-**di**-mać] v. puff
out; inflate; belly out; blow up
(a balloon); bulge
wydział [vi-**dźhaw**] m.
department; section; division
wydziedziczyć [vi-dźhe-**dźhee**-
-chać] v. disinherit
wydzielać [vi-**dźhe**-lać] v.
emit; detach; distribute;
secrete; give off; exhale
wydzielenie [vi-dźhe-le-**ńe**] n.
secretion; assignment;
elimination; emanation; issue
wydzieliny [vi-dźhe-**lee**-ni] pl.
secreta; excretions; discharge
wydzielony [vi-dźhe-**lo**-ni]
adj. m. emitted; segregated;
allotted; rationed; secreted
wydzierać [vi-**dźhe**-rać] v.
tear out; roar out; blare out;
scramble; vociferate; bellow
wydzierżawić [vi-dźher-**zha**-
-veeć] v. lease; farm out;
rent; let out; take a lease
wydzirżawienie [vi-dźher-
-zha-**vye**-ńe] n. leasing;
renting; farming out
wyegzekwować [vi-eg-zek-**vo**-
-vać] v. exact; enforce;
carry out (a sentence etc.)
wyekwipowanie [vi-ek-vee-po-
-**va**-ńe] n. outfit; equipment
wyelegancieć [vi-e-le-**gan**-

-**ćheć**] v. acquire; elegance;
become elegant
wyeliminowanie [vi-e-lee-mee-no-
-**va**-ńe] n. elimination;
exclusion
wyga [**vi**-ga] m. old experienced
hand; sly fox; old stager
wygadać [vi-ga-**dać**] v. blab
out
wygadany [vi-ga-**da**-ni] adj. m.
glib; eloquent; wordy;
talkative
wyganiać [vi-ga-**ńać**] v.
expel; chase out; turn out
(cattle)
wygarniać [vi-gar-**ńać**] v.
rake out; tell off; say openly;
shoot
wygasać [vi-ga-**sać**] v.
extinguish; expire; go out; die
out
wyginać [vi-**gee**-nać] v. bend
wygląd [vig-**lownd**] m.
appearance; aspect; air; looks;
semblance
wyglądać [vig-**lown**-dać] v.
look out; appear; appear; look
wygładzać [vi-**gwa**-dzać] v.
smooth; level; even; sleek
wygłodzić [vi-**gwo**-dźheeć] v.
starve out; underfeed; famish
wygłosić [vi-**gwo**-śheeć] v.
pronounce; utter; deliver
(speech)
wygnać [**vig**-nać] v. expel;
banish
wygnanie [vig-na-**ńe**] n. exile
wygniatać [vi-**gńa**-tać] v.
press out; squeeze out; extort;
kill
wygoda [vi-**go**-da] f. comfort
wygodny [vi-**god**-ni] adj. m.
comfortable; cozy; handy
wygolony [vi-go-**lo**-ni] adj. m.
clean-shaven; well shaven
wygotować [vi-go-to-**vać**] v.
boil away; distill; prepare
wygórowany [vi-goo-ro-**va**-ni]
adj. m. excessive; stiff (price)
wygrać [**vi**-grać] v. win; score
wygramolić się [vi-gra-mo-
-**leeć** **śhan**] v. scramble up
(out)

wygrana [vi-gra-na] f. winning;
victory; prize; a win

wygryzać [vi-gri-zać] v. 1.bite
out; corrode; 2.drive out by
harassment; oust; bore a hole

wygrzebywać [vi-gzhe-bi-vać]
v. dig out; unearth; rake out

wygrzewać się [vi-gzhe-vać
śhan] v. bask; warm oneself

wygwizdać [vi-gveez-dać] v.
hiss off (stage); whistle away

wyjałowić [vi-ya-wo-veeć] v.
sterilize; exhaust (brain, soil...)

wyjaśnić [vi-yaśh-ńeeć] v.
explain; clear up; elucidate

wyjaśnienie [vi-yaśh-ńe-ńe] n.
explanation; interpretation

wyjawić [vi-ya-veeć] v.
disclose; reveal; bring to light

wyjazd [vi-yazt] m. departure

wyjąkać [vi-yown-kać] v.
stammer out; stutter out;
falter out

wyjątek [vi-yown-tek] m.
exception; excerpt; extract

wyjątkowy [vi-yownt-ko-vi] adj.
m. exceptional; unusual;
unique

wyjechać [vi-ye-khać] v. drive
away;leave; come out with

wyjeżdżać [vi-yezh-dzhać] v.
leave; drive away; set out

wyjmować [viy-mo-vać] v.
take out; remove; extract;
excerpt

wyjście [viyśh-će] n. exit;
way out; departure; egress

wyka [vi-ka] f. vetch; tare

wykadzić [vi-ka-dźheeć] v.
smoke out; fumigate; perfume

wykałaczka [vi-ka-wach-ka] f.
toothpick

wykarczować [vi-kar-cho-vać]
v. grub out; clear; dig up
(trees)

wykaz [vi-kas] m. list; register;
roll; schedule; docket

wykąpać [vi-kown-pać] v.
bathe

wykipieć [vi-keep-yeć] v. boil
over (milk, water, soup etc.)

wyklęty [vi-klan-ti] adj. m.
cursed; excommunicated

wykluczyć [vi-kloo-chić] v.
exclude; expel; shut out;
except

wykład [vik-wat] m. lecture

wykładać [vi-kwa-dać] v.
lecture; lay out; display; cover

wykładnik [vi-kwad-ńeek] m.
exponent; expression; ratio

wykładowca [vi-kwa-dov-tsa] m.
lecturer; instructor

wykłuwać [vi-kwoo-vać] v.
stab out; put out; tattoo; prick
out

wykoleić [vi-ko-le-eeć] v.
derail; lead astray; ditch (a
train)

wykombinować [vi-kom-bee-no-
-vać] v. contrive; think out

wykonać [vi-ko-nać] v.
execute; do; fulfill; carry out;
perform

wykonalny [vi-ko-nal-ni] adj. m.
feasible; workable; realizable

wykonanie [vi-ko-na-ńe] n.
execution; realization;
fulfillment

wykonawczy [vi-ko-nav-chi] adj.
m. executive; executory
(details)

wykończenie [vi-koń-che-ńe] n.
finish; trimming; last touch

wykończyć [vi-koń-chić] v.
finish off; dress; do sb in

wykop [vi-kop] m. excavation;
potato lifting; flying kick

wykopać [vi-ko-pać] v. dig
out

wykopalisko [vi-ko-pa-lees-ko] n.
find (archeological)

wykorzenić [vi-ko-zhe-ńeeć]
v. root out; uproot; eradicate

wykorzystać [vi-ko-zhis-tać] v.
take advantage; exploit; use
up

wykpić [vik-peeć] v. deride

wykraczać [vi-kra-chać] v.
step over; break law;
transgress

wykradać [vi-kra-dać] v. steal;
kidnap; purloin; pilfer; abduct

wykrajać [vi-kra-yać] v. cut
out; carve out; make a low
cut

wykres [vi-kres] m. graph; chart

wykreślić [vi-**kreśh**-leećh] v.
trace; cross out; draw; erase

wykręcać [vi-**kran**-tsaćh] v.
screw out; distort; elude;
twist

wykręt [**vi**-krant] m. shift;
excuse; dodge; quibble

wykrętny [vi-**krant**-ni] adj. m.
shifty; evasive; sophistical

wykroczenie [vi-kro-che-ńe] n.
offense; misdemeanor;
delinquency

wykroić [vi-**kro**-eećh] v. cut out

wykruszyć [vi-**kroo**-shićh] v.
crumble out; shell (corn etc.)

wykryć [**vi**-krićh] v. discover;
detect; reveal (the truth etc.)

wykrztusić [vi-kzhtoo-śheećh]
v. cough up; choke out; hawk
up

wykrzknąć [vi-kzhik-**nown**ćh]
v. call out; shout; cry out

wykształcić [vi-kzhtaw-
-ćheećh] v. educate; train;
shape; form

wykup [**vi**-koop] m. ransom

wykupić [vi-**koo**-peećh] v. buy
up

wykurzać [vi-**koo**-zhaćh] v.
smoke out (foxes, bees, etc.)

wykwintny [vi-**kveent**-ni] adj. m.
elegant; exquisite; urbane

wyleczalny [vi-le-chal-ni] adj. m.
curable; possible to cure

wyleczyć [vi-le-chićh] v. cure

wylew krwi [**vi**-lev **krvee**]
hemorrhage; blood effusion

wylewać [vi-le-vaćh] v. pour
out; overflow; spill; bail out
water

wylęgać [vi-**lan**-gaćh] v. hatch

wylękły [vi-**lank**-wi] adj. m.
frightened; scared; terrified

wyliczać [vi-lee-chaćh] v. count
up; count out; recite

wylosować [vi-lo-**so**-vaćh]
adj. m. draw by lots; toss for

wylot [**vi**-lot] m. flight departure;
nozzle; exhaust; exit

wyludniać [vi-lood-ńaćh] v.
depopulate; desolate;
devastate

wyładować [vi-wa-**do**-vaćh] v.
unload; discharge; cram; pack

wyładowanie [vi-wa-do-**va**-ńe]
n. unloading; discharge

wyłamać [vi-**wa**-maćh] v. break
out; break loose; break away

wyławiać [vi-**wav**-yaćh] v. fish
out; spot out; catch (a sound)

wyłaniać [vi-**wa**-ńaćh] v.
evolve; emerge; show;
appoint; form

wyłączać [vi-**wown**-chaćh] v.
exclude; switch off;
disconnect

wyłącznik [vi-**wown**ch-ńeek] m.
switch; circuit-breaker; cut off

wyłączny [vi-**wown**ch-ni] adj. m.
exclusive; sole; only; entire

wyłudzić [vi-**woo**-dźheećh] v.
coax; beguile; trick; fool

wyłom [**vi**-wom] m. breach; gap

wyłuskać [vi-**voos**-kaćh] v.
husk; scale; fleece; shell; hull;
pod

wymaczać [vi-**ma**-chaćh] v.
soak

wymagać [vi-**ma**-gaćh] v.
require; expect; demand;
need; exact

wymaganie [vi-ma-**ga**-ńe] n.
requirement; demand;
requisite; need; want

wymawiać [vi-**mav**-yaćh] v.
pronounce; reproach; cancel;
express

wymazać [vi-**ma**-zaćh] v. erase;
efface; blot out; smear; use
up

wymiana [vi-**mya**-na] f. exchange

wymiar [**vi**-myar] m. dimension

wymiatać [vi-**mya**-taćh] v.
sweep out; clean out; sweep

wymieniać [vi-**mye**-ńaćh] v.
exchange; convert; replace

wymierać [vi-**mye**-raćh] v. die
out; become extinct
(gradually)

wymierzać [vi-**mye**-zhaćh] v.
aim; measure; assess; survey;
mete out

wymię [**vi**-myan] n. udder

wymijać [vi-**mee**-yaćh] v. pass
by; evade

wymiotować [vi-myo-to-vać]
v. vomit; be sick; spew up
(one's food)

wymogi [vi-mo-gee] pl.
requirements; exigencies;
demands; needs; wants

wymowa [vi-mo-va] f.
pronunciation; significance (of
facts); eloquence

wymowny [vi-mov-ni] adj. m.
eloquent; telltale; telling

wymóc [vi-moots] v. extort;
compel; wring; force; prevail

wymówienie [vi-moov-ye-ńe] n.
notice (to quit or dismiss)

wymówka [vi-moov-ka] f.
reproach; pretext; excuse; put-
off; evasion; rebuke

wymusić [vi-moo-śhić] v.
extort; wring; force; compel

wymuszenie [vi-moo-she-ńe] n.
extortion; blackmail; shake-
down; coercion; constraint

wymykać się [vi-mi-kać
śhan] v. escape; slip away;
sneak out; dodge; steal out

wymysł [vi-misw] m. fiction;
invention; fiction; abuse

wymyślać [vi-miśh-lać] v.
think up; call names; invent;
abuse; devise; contrive

wymyślny [vi-miśhl-ni] adj. m.
clever; ingenious; fanciful;
cunning; sophisticated

wymywać [vi-mi-vać] v. wash
out; rinse; hollow out

wynagradzać [vi-na-gra-dzać]
v. reward; pay; indemnify;
recompense; make up; gratify

wynagrodzenie [vi-na-gro-dze-
-ńe] n. reward; pay; fee;
wages; reward; reparation

wynajdywać [vi-nay-di-vać] v.
find (out); invent; devise

wynajmować [vi-nay-mo-vać]
v. hire; rent; lease out

wynajem [vi-na-yem] m. lease;
rent; hire; letting out

wynalazca [vi-na-laz-tsa] m.
inventor; contriver

wynalazek [vi-na-la-zek] m.
invention; device; contrivance

wynaleźć [vi-na-leźhćh] v.
invent; discover; find

wynaradawiać [vi-na-ra-dav-
-yać] v. denationalize; divest

wynik [vi-ńeek] m. result; score

wyniosłość [vi-ńos-wośhćh]
f. eminence; haughtiness;
prance; rise; swell; knoll

wyniosły [vi-ńos-wi] adj. m.
lofty; high-handed; insolent

wyniszczać [vi-ńeesh-chać]
v. ruin; exhaust; weaken;
devastate; ravage; destroy

wynosić [vi-no-śheećh] v.
carry out; elevate; amount;
wear out; praise; nurse

wynudzać [vi-noo-dzać] v. get
by bothering; bore stiff

wynurzenie [vi-noo-zhe-ńe] n.
emergence; (personal)
outpouring; effusion

wyobraźnia [vi-o-braźh-ńa] f.
imagination; fancy; empty
fancy

wyobrażać [vi-o-bra-zhać] v.
imagine; picture; fancy; conceive; suppose; represent

wyobrażenie [vi-o-bra-zhe-ńe] n.
notion; idea; image; representation; picture; conception

wyodrębniać [vi-od-ranb-ńać]
v. single out; separate; isolate

wyodrębnienie [vi-od-ranb-ńe-
-ńe] n. separation; isolation

wyolbrzymiać [vi-ol-bzhi-
-myać] v. magnify;
exaggerate (very much)

wypaczyć [vi-pa-chić] v. warp

wypad [vi-pat] m. sally; attack

wypadać [vi-pa-dać] v. fall
out; rash out; become; turn
out; happen; occur; work out

wypadek [vi-pa-dek] m. accident;
case; event; chance; instance

wypadkowa [vi-pad-ko-va] f.
resultant (force, affect, etc)

wypakować [vi-pa-ko-vać] v.
unpack; cram; pack tight

wypalać [vi-pa-lać] v. burn;
burn out; burn down; fire

wypaplać [vi-pap-lać] v.
babble out; blurt out (the
truth, secret); spill the beans

wyparcie się [vi-par-ćhe śhan]

n. disclaimer; repudiation
wyparować [vi-pa-ro-vaćh] v.
  evaporate; vanish into thin air
wypatrywać [vi-pa-tri-vaćh] v.
  watch (for); look out; espy;
  descry; strain one's eyes
wypełniać [vi-pew-ńaćh] v.
  fulfill; fill up; while away; fill
  in; perform; execute (a duty)
wypełnienie [vi-pew-ńe-ńe] n.
  fulfillment; execution (of an
  order, etc.); filler
wypędzać [vi-pan-dzaćh] v.
  drive out; expel; discharge;
  dislodge (an enemy, etc.)
wypiekać [vi-pye-kaćh] v. bake
wypierać [vi-pye-raćh] v. oust;
  push out; force our; supplant
wypierać się [vi-pye-raćh
  śhan] v. deny; repudiate;
  disown; abjure; renounce
wypijać [vi-pee-yaćh] v. drink
  (empty); drink to; drink off
wypinać [vi-pee-naćh] v.
  extend; stretch out; show
  one's back side
wypis [vi-pees] m. extract;
  selected passage; selection
wypisywać [vi-pee-si-vaćh] v.
  (write) extract; make out (a
  check); fill in (a form)
wyplątać [vi-plown-taćh] v.
  extricate; disentangle;
  disengage; free from tangles
wyplątany [vi-plown-ta-ni] adj.
  m. dis-embroiled; extricated
wyplenić [vi-ple-ńeećh] v.
  weed out; root out; eradicate
wypluć [vi-plooćh] v. spit out
wypłacać [vi-pwa-tsaćh] v. pay
  out; pay up; pay off; repay
wypłacalny [vi-pwa-tsal-ni] adj.
  m. solvent; sound (financially)
wypłata [vi-pwa-ta] f. pay (day)
wypłoszyć [vi-pwo-shićh] v.
  scare away; drive away (birds
  etc.); rouse (game)
wypłowieć [vi-pwo-vyećh] v.
  fade; discolor
wypłukać [vi-pwoo-kaćh] v.
  rinse; wash out; swill out;
  give a rinse
wypływ [vi-pwiv] m. outflow;

discharge; afflux; leakage
wypływać [vi-pwi-vaćh] v. flow
  out; sail out; swim out; rise
wypocić [vi-po-ćheećh] v.
  sweat out; perspire; be soaked
  in sweat; exude
wypoczynek [vi-po-chi-nek] m.
  rest; repose
wypoczywać [vi-po-chi-vaćh] v.
  rest; have a rest; take a rest
wypogadzać się [vi-po-ga-
  dzaćh śhan] v. clear up;
  cheer up; brighten; uncloud
wypomnieć [vi-pom-ńećh] v.
  reproach; remind; keep
  reminding; upbraid; rebuke
wyporność [vi-por-nośhćh] f.
  displacement; draught;
  buoyancy
wyposażać [vi-po-sa-zhaćh] v.
  equip; endow; fit out; stock
wyposażenie [vi-po-sa-zhe-ńe]
  n. equipment; outfit; wages;
  salary; dowry; furnishings
wyposażyć [vi-po-sa-zhićh] v.
  endow; equip; fit out; stock
wypowiadać [vi-po-vya-daćh]
  v. pronounce; declare; express
wypowiedzenie [vi-po-vye-dze-
  -ńe] n. (discharge) notice;
  (war) declaration; renunciation; utterance; statement
wypożyczać [vi-po-zhi-chaćh]
  v. lend out; borrow from; hire
  to; hire from; lend to
wypożyczalnia [vi-po-zhi-chal-
  -ńa] f. rental business; rental
  agency
wypracowanie [vi-pra-tso-va-ńe]
  n. (school) composition;
  elaboration; essay; exercise
wyprać [vi-praćh] v. wash out
wypraszać [vi-pra-shaćh] v.
  1.plead; pester; 2.show (the
  door); give somebody the
  gate; turn out; forbid
wyprawa [vi-pra-va] f.
  expedition; excursion; outfit;
  tanning; dowry; plaster
wyprawiać [vi-pra-vyaćh] v.
  send; dispatch; tan; plaster;
  give (a party); arrange
wyprężać [vi-pran-zhaćh] v.

stretch out, tense (a muscle
etc.); tauten (a rope, etc.)
wyprostować [vi-pros-to-vaćh]
v. straighten; set straight
wyprowadzać [vi-pro-**va**-dzaćh]
v. lead out; move out; trace
wypróbować [vi-proo-**bo**-vaćh]
v. test; try out; put to test
wypróżniać [vi-proozh-ńaćh]
v. empty; clear out; evacuate
wyprzedawać [vi-pzhe-da-vaćh]
v. sell out; clear out (stock)
wyprzedaż [vi-pzhe-dash] v.
(clearance) sale
wyprzedzać [vi-**pzhe**-dzaćh] v.
pull ahead; outrace; overtake
wyprzęgać [vi-**pzhan**-gaćh] v.
unharness; unhitch (a horse)
wypukły [vi-**pook**-wi] adj. m.
convex; bulging; cambered
wypuścić [vi-**poośh**-ćheećh]
v. let out; set free; let go;
omit; release; launch; lease
out; drop; set free; launch
wypychać [vi-pi-khaćh] v.
oust;push out; stuff; pack; fill;
cram; shove out; crowd; force
wypytywać [vi-pi-ti-vaćh] v.
question; ask questions;
inquire
wyrabiać [vi-ra-byaćh] v.
1. make; form; 2. play pranks
wyrachowany [vi-ra-kho-**va**-ni]
adj. m. scheming; thrifty
wyratować [vi-ra-to-vaćh] v.
rescue; save (a life etc.)
wyraz [**vi**-ras] m. word;
expression; look; term (of
praise, indignation, etc.)
wyraźny [vi-raźh-ni] adj. m.
explicit; clear; distinct
wyrażać [vi-ra-zhaćh] v.
express; say; signify
wyrażenie [vi-ra-zhe-ńe] n.
expression; utterance; phrase;
statement; formulation
wyrąb [vi-**rownp**] m. clearing;
felling; cutting; slash; fell
wyrąbać [vi-r**own**-baćh] v. cut
out (with axe); clear; hack out
wyręczać [vi-**ran**-chaćh] v. help
out; replace; relieve of tasks
wyrobnik [vi-rob-ńeek] m.

day-laborer; workman
wyrocznia [vi-roch-ńa] f. oracle
wyrodny [vi-rod-ni] adj. m.
degenerate; unnatural (son);
base; infamous; villainous
wyrodzić się [vi-ro-dźeećh
śhan] v. degenerate; deteriorate; spring from
wyrok [**vi**-rok] m. sentence;
verdict; judgment; pronouncement (by doctors, etc.)
wyrostek [vi-**ros**-tek] m.
outgrowth; stripling; teenager
wyrośnięty [vi-rośh-**ńan**-ti] adj.
m. grown up; overgrown
wyrozumiały [vi-ro-zoo-**mya**-wi]
adj. m. indulgent; lenient
wyrozumienie [vi-ro-zoo-mye-ńe]
n. sympathetic understanding
wyrób [**vi**-roob] m. manufacture
wyrównać [vi-roov-naćh] v.
equalize; pay up; smooth
wyrównanie [vi-roov-na-ńe] m.
leveling; balancing (accounts)
offset; payment; handicap
wyróżniać [vi-roozh-ńaćh] v.
distinguish; favor; single out
wyruszyć [vi-roo-shićh] v. start
out; set out; march out; sail
away; start on a journey
wyrwać [**vir**-vaćh] v. extract;
tear out; pull out; run away
wyrywki [vi-**riv**-kee] pl. random
wyryć [**vi**-rićh] v. engrave; root
up; dig out; gully; furrow;
incise; carve out; imprint
wyrzec się [vi-zhets **śhan**] v.
renounce; give up; forgo;
repudiate; surrender
wyrzucać [vi-zhoo-tsaćh] v.
expel; throw out; dump;
reproach; remove; eject
wyrzut [**vi**-zhoot] m. reproach
wyrzutnia [vi-zhoot-ńa] f. launch
(ing) pad; chute; launcher
wyrzutek [vi-zhoo-tek] m.
outcast; ruffian; wretch
wyrzynać [vi-zhi-naćh] v. cut
out; carve out; kill; massacre;
slaughter; bang; slap; whack
wysadzić [vi-sa-dźheećh] v.
set out; land; blow up; eject;
plant; disembark; help out

wyschnąć [vis-khn<u>own</u>ćh] v.
dry up; go dry; shrivel up

wysepka [vi-**sep**-ka] f. islet

wysiadać [vi-śha-daćh] v. get
out (from car etc.); go bust;
get off; disembark

wysiadywać [vi-śha-di-vaćh]
v. sit out; hatch out; sit late

wysiedlać [vi-śhed-laćh] v.
expel (from home); resettle;
eject; displace; evacuate

wysilać [vi-śhee-laćh] v. exert

wysiłek [vi-śhee-wek] m. effort

wyskoczyć [vi-**sko**-chićh] v.
jump out; pop up; run out;
bale out; eject; protrude

wyskok [vis-kok] m. 1. fling;
freak; 2. cam; ledge; run out

wyskokowy [vis-ko-**ko**-vi] adj. m.
alcoholic; intoxicating

wyskrobać [vi-**skro**-baćh] v.
scratch out; erase; scratch

wyskubać [vi-**skoo**-baćh] v.
pluck out; pull out (hair etc.)

wysłać [vi-**swaćh**] v. send off;
dispatch; emit; let fly

wysłaniec [vi-**swa**-ńets] m.
messenger; envoy; deputy

wysłowić [vi-**swo**-veećh] v.
express; say; utter; speak

wysłuchać [vi-**swoo**-khaćh] v.
hear out; give a hearing

wysługiwać się [vi-swoo-**gee**-
-vaćh **śhan**] v. lackey; earn
seniority; get worn out

wysmarować [vi-sma-ro-vaćh]
v. smear; lubricate; soil; stain

wysmażony [vi-sma-**zho**-ni] adj.
m. well done (meat);cooked

wysmukły [vi-**smook**-wi] adj. m.
slender; slim and tall

wysoce [vi-**so**-tse] adv. highly

wysoki [vi-**so**-kee] m. tall; high;
soaring; lofty; towering

wysokość [vi-so-**ko**śhćh] f.
height; altitude; level; extent

wysokościomierz [vi-so-ko**śh**-
-ćho-myesh] m. altimeter

wyspa [vis-pa] f. island; isle

wyspać się [vis-paćh **śhan**] v.
sleep enough; sleep off

wyspowiadać się [vis-po-**vya**-
-daćh **śhan**] v. confess

wysrać się [vi-sraćh **śh<u>an</u>**] v.
(vulgar) shit

wyssać [vis-saćh] v. suck out;
suck dry; suck up; trump up

wystarać się [vi-**sta**-raćh
śhan] v. procure; obtain

wystarczyć [vi-**star**-chićh] v.
suffice; do enough; be enough

wystawa [vi-**sta**-va] f. exhibition;
display (window dressing)

wystawać [vi-**sta**-vaćh] v.
stand long time; stick out

wystawca [vi-**stav**-tsa] m.
exhibitor; signer (of check)

wystawiać [vi-**stav**-yaćh] v. put
out; stick out; sign (check);
expose; put up; draw up; rise

wystawienie [vi-sta-**vye**-ńe] n.
exposition; exposure; display

wystąpić [vi-**stown**-peećh] v.
step forward; perform; resign

wystąpienie [vi-**stown**-pye-ńe]
n. withdrawal; appearance

występ [**vi**-stanp] m. protrusion;
(stage) appearance; utterance

występek [vi-**stan**-pek] m.
felony; crime; vice; offense

występny [vi-**stanp**-ni] adj. m.
criminal; immoral; illicit

wystraszyć [vi-**stra**-shićh] v.
frighten away; terrify; scare

wystroić [vi-**stro**-eećh] v. dress
up; trig out; deck out; adorn

wystrzał [vi-stzhaw] m. shot

wystrzegać się [vi-**stzhe**-gaćh
śhan] v. avoid; beware; shun

wystrzelić [vi-**stzhe**-leećh] v.
fire a gun; shoot out; go off

wystrząpić [vi-**stzhan**-peećh] v.
ravel out; fray; unravel

wystygać [vi-**sti**-gaćh] v. cool
off; grow cold; get cold

wysuszyć [vi-**soo**-shićh] v. dry
up; wither; parch; shrivel

wysuwać [vi-**soo**-vaćh] v.
shove forward; protrude; put
out; put up; advance; propose

wyswobodzić [vi-svo-**bo**-
-dźheećh] v. liberate; deliver;
free from something

wysychać [vi-si-khaćh] v. dry
out; get perched; shrivel up

wysypać [vi-si-paćh] v. pour

out (sand); spill; scatter

wysypka [vi-**sip**-ka] f. (skin) rash; eruption; exanthema

wysysać [vi-**si**-sać] v. suck

wyszczególnić [vi-shche-gool- -**ńee**ćh] v. specify; detail out

wyszeptać [vi-**shep**-tać] v. whisper (not vibrating vocal chords); talk furtively

wyszkolić [vi-**shko**-leećh] v. train; school; educate; instruct

wyszpiegować [vi-shpye-go- -vać] v. spy out that...; watch closely and secretly

wyszukać [vi-**shoo**-kać] v. find out; hunt up; search out

wyszukany [vi-shoo-ka-ni] adj. m. choice; unusual; elaborate

wyszydzać [vi-**shi**-dzać] v. scoff at; jeer; deride

wyszynk [vi-shink] m. liquor store; liquor retail on licence

wyszywać [vi-**shi**-vać] v. embroider; make design on fabric with needlework

wyścielać [vi-**śhćhe**-lać] v. pad; line; strew; cushion

wyścig [**viśh**-ćheek] m. race; contest; rivalry; (horse) race

wyśledzić [vi-**śhle**-dźheećh] v. spy out; track out; detect

wyśliznąć się [vi-**śhleez**- -**no**wnćh **śhan**] v. slip out; slide out; wriggle out

wyśmiać [**viśh**-myać] v. laugh at; deride; mock; ridicule

wyśmienity [viśh-mye-**ńee**-ti] adj. m. choice; excellent

wyśpiewać [vi-**śhpye**-vać] v. sing; say; sound praises; squeal during an investigation

wyświadczyć [viśh-**vyad**- -ćhićh] v. do (favor); do (good); do (wrong)

wyświechtany [vi-śhvyekh-ta- -ni] adj. m. well worn; beat up

wyświetlać [viśh-**vyet**-lać] v. clear up; project (film)

wytaczać [vi-ta-chać] v. roll out; set forth; draw; turn

wytargować [vi-tar-go-vać] v. buy by haggling; haggle a lot

wytarty [vi-tar-ti] adj. m. worn

out; thread bare; shabby

wytchnąć [vi-tkhno**wn**ćh] v. rest up; relax; take a rest; have a rest; breathe

wytchnienie [vi-tkh**ńe**-ńe] n. rest; break; relax; truce

wytępić [vi-**tan**-peećh] v. exterminate; eradicate; wipe out; extripate; root out

wytężać [vi-**tan**-zhać] v. strain; exert; put forth

wytknąć [vit-kno**wn**ćh] v. put out; point out; reproach; trace

wytłuc [vi-twoots] v. kill off; break up; ruin; beat up

wytłumaczenie [vi-twoo-ma- -che-ńe] n. explanation; excuse; justification; account

wytłumaczyć [vi-twoo-**ma**- -ćhićh] v. explain; excuse; justify; account for

wytrawny [vi-**trav**-ni] adj. m. experienced; dry (wine); sea- soned; mature; consummate

wytrącać [vi-tro**wn**-tsać] v. knock of; deduct; snatch

wytrwały [vi-trva-wi] adj. m. enduring; persevering; dogged

wytrwanie [vi-trva-ńe] n. endurance; persistence; lasting

wytrwać [vi-trvać] v. last; bear; persevere; endure; stand

wytrych [vi-trikh] m. pick-a-lock; pass-key; skeleton-key

wytrząść [vi-tzho**wn**śhćh] v. shake out; empty; jolt

wytrzebić [vi-tzhe-beećh] v. devastate; exterminate; clear

wytrzeźwieć [vi-tzheźh- -vyećh] v. sober up; get sober; sober down

wytrzymać [vi-tzhi-mać] v. endure; stand; hold out; keep

wytrzymałość [vi-tzhi-ma- -**wo**śhćh] f. endurance; sta- mina; durability; strength

wytrzymały [vi-tzhi-ma-wi] adj. m. enduring; tough; durable

wytworny [vi-tvor-ni] adj. m. exquisite; elegant; stylish

wytwórca [vi-tvoor-tsa] m. producer; manufacturer; maker

wytwórczość [vi-**tvoor-**

-chośhćh] v. productivity;
output; product; producers
wytwórnia [vi-tvoor-ńa] f.
manufacture; factory; plant;
works; (textile) mill
wytyczna [vi-tich-na] f. directive;
guideline; guiding rule
wyuzdanie [vi-ooz-da-ńe] n.
unbridled license; without
restraint; adv. dissolutely
wywiad [vi-vyat] m. interview;
reconnaissance; espionage
wywiązać się [vi-wyown-zaćh
śhan] v. develop; arise;
discharge (duty); result; set in;
perform; implement; evolve
wywierać [vi-vye-raćh] v. exert
wywiercać [vi-vyer-tsaćh] v.
bore out; sink a well; drill a
hole; talk one's head off
wywlekać [vi-vle-kaćh] v. drag
out; tug; bring out; pull out
wywietrzać [vi-vyet-zhaćh] v.
ventilate; air; nose out
wywłaszczać [vi-vwash-chaćh]
v. expropriate; dispossess
wywłaszczenie [vi-vwash-che-
-ńe] n. expropriation; dis-
possession; disseizin
wywnioskować [vi-vńos-ko-
-vaćh] v. infer; draw a
conclusion; imply
wywodzić [vi-vo-dźheećh] v.
lead out; derive; lead nowhere
wywojować [vi-vo-yo-vaćh] v.
fight out; gain by force
wywołać [vi-vo-waćh] v. call;
cause; develop (film); recall
wywozić [vi-vo-źheećh] v.
take away; remove; export
wywód [vi-voot] m. deduction
wywóz [vi-voos] m. export;
removal; disposal; transport
wywracać [vi-vra-tsaćh] v.
overturn; overthrow; reverse;
upset; bring down; knock over
wywyższać [vi-vizh-shaćh] v.
exalt; elevate; extol; rise
wyzbyć się [viz-bićh śhan] v.
get rid of; sell out; get over
wyzdrowieć [vi-zdro-vyećh] v.
recover; get well; recuperate
wyziębić [vi-źhan-beećh] v.

chill; let be cold; cool
wyzionąć [vi-źho-nownćh] v.
expire; give up (the ghost)
wyznaczać [vi-zna-chaćh] v.
mark out; appoint; point out
wyznanie [vi-zna-ńe] n. admission; confession; denomination; declaration; creed
wyznawać [vi-zna-vaćh] v.
profess (certain principles);
declare; hold a belief; confess
wyznawca [vi-znav-tsa] m.
believer; follower; advocate
wyzuć [vi-zooćh] v. deprive;
take off (shoe); strip; divest;
bereave; dispossess; despoil
wyzywać [vi-zi-vaćh] v.
challenge; tempt; call names;
abuse; revile; curse; abuse
wyzwalać [vi-zva-laćh] v.
liberate; free; let loose;
exempt; deliver; emancipate
wyzwolenie [vi-zvo-le-ńe] n.
liberation; release; exemption
wyzwolić [vi-zvo-leećh] v.
liberate; free; release; set free
wyzysk [vi-zisk] m. exploitation;
sweating (of labor)
wyzyskiwacz [vi-zis-kee-vach] m.
exploiter; slave driver
wyż [vizh] m. height; upland;
highland; high pressure area;
peak; atmospheric high
wyżarty [vi-zhar-ti] adj. m. over
-fed; corroded; bloated
wyżej [vi-zhey] adv. higher;
above; (mentioned) above;
(cited) above; higher up
wyżeł [vi-zhew] m. pointer
wyżerać [vi-zhe-raćh] v. eat
away; corrode; erode; eat up
wyżłobić [vi-zhwo-beećh] v.
hollow out; gully; erode;
groove; gutter; channel
wyżłobienie [vi-zhwo-bye-ńe] n.
groove; gully; erosion; channel
wyższość [vizh-shośhćh] f.
superiority; excellence;
predominance
wyższy [vizh-shi] adj. m. higher
(up); taller; superior; top
(floor); preponderant
wyżyć [vi-zhićh] v. use up;

hardly live; make ends meet;
pull through; survive; pull
through; find an outlet for...
wyżyć się [vi-zhićh śhan] v.
live up to; fulfill oneself
wyżymaczka [vi-zhi-mach-ka] f.
wringer (also machine)
wyżymać [vi-zhi-maćh] v.
wring
wyżyna [vi-zhi-na] f. high
ground; upland; summit (of
glory); highland
wyżywić [vi-zhi-veećh] v. feed
wyżywienie [vi-zhi-vye-ńe] m.
food; board; subsistence; diet
wzajemny [vza-yem-ni] adj. m.
mutual; reciprocal; inter-
w zamian [v za-myan] adv. in
exchange; instead; in return
wzbić się [vzbeećh śhan] v.
soar (up); shoot up; rise
wzbogacić [vzbo-ga-ćheećh] v.
enrich; add to; dress; make
rich; make wealthy; treat
wzbraniać [vzbra-ńaćh] v.
forbid; prohibit
wzbroniony [vzbro-ńo-ni] adj. m.
forbidden; prohibited
wzbudzać [vzboo-dzaćh] v.
excite; inspire; arouse; stir
wzburzenie [vzboo-zhe-ńe] n.
agitation; unrest; tumult
wzburzyć [vzboo-zhićh] v. stir
up; agitate; dishevel; convulse
wzdąć [vzdownćh] v. puff out;
inflate; swell; bulge; fan
wzdłuż [vzdwoosh] prep. along
wzdrygać się [vzdri-gaćh
śhan] v. flinch; object;
shudder; boggle; give a start
wzdychać [vzdi-khaćh] v. sigh
wzgarda [vzgar-da] f. contempt
wzgardliwy [vzgard-lee-vi] adj.
m. disdainful; scornful
względność [vzgland-nośhćh]
f. relativity (of understanding)
względny [vzgland-ni] adj. m.
relative; indulgent; kind of
względy [vzglan-di] pl. favors
wzgórze [vzgoo-zhe] n. hill
wziąć [vźhownćh] v. take;
hold; help oneself to; possess
wziernik [vźher-ńeek] m.

peephole; scope; view finder;
spy hole; sight glass
wzięty [vźhan-ti] adj. m.
popular; in demand; in vogue
wzlot [vzlot] m. ascend; rise
wzmacniać [vzmats-ńaćh] v.
reinforce; brace up; fortify
wzmagać [vzma-gaćh] v. intensify; increase; enhance
wzmianka [vzmyan-ka] v.
mention; reference; notice
wzniesienie [vzńe-śhe-ńe] n.
elevation; height; erection
wznieść [vzńeśhćh] v. raise;
elevate; erect; lift; rear
wzniosły [vzńos-wi] adj. m.
lofty; noble; elevated; sublime
wznowić [vzno-veećh] v. renew; resume; reprint; re-edit
wznowienie [vzno-vye-ńe] n.
resumption; come back; renewal; reissue; revival
wzorowy [vzo-ro-vi] adj. m.
exemplary; model; perfect
wzór [vzoor] m. pattern; model;
formula; fashion; standard
wzrok [vzrok] m. sight; vision
wzrost [vzrost] m. growth
-size; height; increase; rise;
stature; increment; gain
wzruszać [vzroo-shaćh] v.
move; touch; affect; thrill; stir
wzruszający [vzroo-sha-yown-tsi]
adj. m. touching; moving;
pathetic; poignant; stirring
wzuć [vzooćh] v. put on (shoe)
wzuwacz [vzoo-vach] m. shoe
horn (for pulling boots)
wzwyż [vzvizh] adv. up;
upwards; more than; above
skok wzwyż [skok vzvizh] m.
high jump
wzywać [vzi-vaćh] v. call; call
in; summon; cite; ask in

Z

z [z] prep. with; off; together

ze [ze] prep. with; off; together; from (the ceiling etc.)

za [za] prep. behind; for; at; by; beyond; over (a wall)

zabarwić [za-bar-veećh] v. stain; dye; tint; color; tinge; tincture; add pigmentation

zabarwienie [za-bar-vye-ńe] n. color(ing); pigmentation; tinge

zabawa [za-ba-va] f. play; fun; party; game; recreation; ball; amusement; pastime; dance

zabawiać [za-bav-yaćh] v. entertain; amuse; divert; dwell; stay; last; take time

zabawka [za-bav-ka] f. toy; trifle

zabawny [za-bav-ni] adj. m. funny; comical; ridiculous

zabezpieczenie [za-bez-pye-che-ńe] n. protection; safety

zabezpieczyć [za-bez-pye-chićh] v. safeguard; secure; protect

zabić [za-beećh] v. kill; slay; slaughter; plug up; nail down; drive into; beat (a card)

zabieg [za-byek] m. measure; procedure; exertions; fuss

zabiegać [za-bye-gaćh] v. strive; try hard; court; woo; fuss over; exert oneself for

zabierać [za-bye-raćh] v. take away; take along; take on (up)

zabierać się [za-bye-raćh śhan] v. clear out; get ready for; start to do; begin;

zabijać [za-bee-yaćh] v. kill; deaden; wear out; exhaust

zabijaka [za-bee-ya-ka] m. bully; blusterer; swaggerer; hector

zabity [za-bee-ti] adj. m. killed; dead; out-and-out; thorough

zabliźniać [za-bleeźh-ńaćh] v. form cicatrize; scar up

zabłądzić [za-bwown-dźheećh] v. go astray; get lost; stray

zabłąkany [za-bwown-ka-ni] adj. m. lost; stray (bullet, man, steer, etc)

zabłocić [za-bwo-ćheećh] v. get muddy; muddy (shoes etc)

zabobon [za-bo-bon] m. superstition; belief in omens, stars, the supernatural, etc.

zaboleć [za-bo-lećh] v. ache

zaborca [za-bor-tsa] m. invader

zabójca [za-booy-tsa] m. killer

zabójczy [za-booy-chi] adj. m. murderous; seductive; lethal

zabójstwo [za-booy-stvo] n. killing; murder; homicide

zabór [za-boor] m. annexed territory; annexation; rape (of Belgium, Austria etc.)

zabraniać [za-bra-ńaćh] v. forbid; prohibit; interdict

zabrudzać [za-broo-dzaćh] v. dirty; soil; make a mess (of something); make grimy

zabudować [za-boo-do-vaćh] v. build over; build upon; close

zabudowania [za-boo-do-va-ńa] pl. (farm) buildings; (town, factory, etc.) buildings

zaburzenie [za-boo-zhe-ńe] n. disorder; rout; agitation

zabytek [za-bi-tek] m. relic; monument (of art, nature etc.)

zachcianka [zakh-ćhan-ka] f. fad; fancy; caprice; passing whim; megrim; crotchet

zachęta [za-khan-ta] f. encouragement; stimulus; incentive; spur; urge

zachłanność [za-khwan-nośhćh] f. greed; rapacity; cupidity; excessive desire

zachłysnąć się [za-khwis-nownćh shan] v. choke; swallow a bad way

zachmurzyć [za-khmoo-zhićh] v. cloud; become gloomy; overcloud; overcast

zachmurzenie [za-khmoo-zhe-ńe] n. cloudiness; clouds; gloom; gloominess; nebulosity

zachodzić [za-kho-dźheećh] v. call on; occur; arise; become; set; creep from behind; drop in; reach (a place); go far

zachodni [za-khod-ńee] adj. m. western; westerly

zachorować [za-kho-ro-vaćh] v. get sick; fall ill; be taken ill

zachowanie [za-kho-va-ńe] n. behavior; maintenance; retention; manners; behavior

zachowawczy [za-kho-**vav**-chi]
adj. m. conservative
zachowywać [za-kho-**vi**-vać]
v. preserve; maintain; keep;
stick to; reserve for
zachowywać się [za-kho-**vi**-
-vać **śhan**] v. behave; last;
survive; go on; remain
zachód [za-khoot] m. west;
the West; sunset; pains;
trouble; endeavor
zachód słońca [za-khoot swoń-
-tsa] m. sunset
zachrypnięty [za-khrip-**ńan**-ti]
adj. m. hoarse; of a hoarse
voice of a person
zachwalać [za-khva-lać] v.
praise; crack up; boost; cry up
zachwiać [zakh-vyać] v. rock;
shake; unsettle (balance etc.)
zachwycać [za-khvi-tsać] v.
fascinate; charm; delight;
enchant; rouse admiration
zachwyt [zakh-vit] m.
fascination; rapture;
enchantment; ecstasy
zaciąg [za-**ćhownk**] m.
recruitment; levy; draft;
conscription; call-up
zaciągać [za-**ćhown**-gać] v.
recruit; drag to; run in debt
zaciekać [za-ćhe-kać] v. leak;
stain; run down; fill (up)
zaciekawić [za-ćhe-ka-veeć]
v. interest; puzzle; intrigue
zaciekawienie [za-ćhe-ka-**vye**-
-ńe] n. interest; curiosity
zaciekły [za-ćhek-wi] adj. m.
stubborn; bitter; rabid; stiff
zaciemnić [za-ćhem-ńeeć] v.
obscure; dim; darken; black
out (windows, etc.); cloud
zacieniać [za-ćhe-ńać] v.
shade; darken; throw shade
zacierać [za-ćhe-rać] v.
efface; erase; hush up; cover
up; obliterate; rub off
zacieśniać [za-ćheśh-ńać]
v. tighten up; narrow; limit
zacięty [za-ćhan-ti] adj. m.
obstinate; stubborn; dogged
zacinać [za-ćhee-nać] v.
notch; cut; lash; hack; taper;

set (teeth, lips); whip
zaciskać [za-ćhees-kać] v.
tighten; clench; squeeze; clasp
zacisze [za-ćhee-she] n. retreat
zacny [zats-ni] adj. m. worthy;
good; upright; respectable
zacofany [za-tso-fa-ni] adj. m.
backward; old fashioned
zaczaić się [za-cha-eeć śhan]
v. lie in ambush; lurk; hide
zaczarować [za-cha-ro-vać] v.
enchant; bewitch; cast a spell
zacząć [za-**chown**ć] v. start;
begin; fire away; go ahead
zaczepiać [za-chep-yać] v.
hook on; accost; touch upon
zaczepny [za-chep-ni] adj. m.
aggressive; offensive;
provocative; truculent
zaczerpać [za-cher-pać] v.
scoop up; dip up; draw; lade
zaczerwienić [za-cher-**vye**-
-ńeeć] v. redden; blush;
flush; color, paint, dye red
zaczynać [za-chi-nać] v. start;
begin; cut (into a new loaf)
zaćmienie [zaćh-mye-ńe] n.
eclipse; obfuscation
zad [zad] m. posterior; rump
zadać [za-dać] v. give; put;
deal; associate; treat with
zadanie [za-da-ńe] n. task;
charge; assignment; problem;
job; work; stint; duty
zadatek [za-da-tek] m. earnest
money; down payment; installment; advance payment
zadławić [za-dwa-veeć] v.
choke; strangle; throttle
zadłużyć się [za-**dwoo**-zhićh
śhan] v. run into debt; incur
debts; run up bills
zadłużenie [za-dwoo-zhe-ńe] n.
debts; indebtedness; liabilities
zadowalający [za-do-va-la-**yown**-
-tsi] adj. m. satisfactory; fair
zadowolić [za-do-**vo**-leeć] v.
satisfy; gratify; please; suffice
zadowolony [za-do-vo-lo-ni] adj.
m. satisfied; content; pleased
zadra [za-dra] f. silver; splinter
(in one's finger, etc.)
zadrapać [za-dra-pać] v.

scratch open; make a scratch
zadrasnąć [za-**dras**-nownćh] v.
scratch; graze (arm, leg, etc.)
wound (sb's pride etc.);
zadrażnić [za-**drazh**-ńeećh] v.
irritate; embitter; inflame
zadrgać [zadr-gaćh] v. twitch;
vibrate; tremble; flicker
zadrwić [za-drveećh] v. sneer
zaduch [za-dookh] m. bad air;
stuffy air; stink; fustiness; fug
zaduma [za-doo-ma] f. meditation; reverie; musing; wist-
fulness; pensiveness
ządusić [za-doo-śheećh] v.
throttle; smother; choke;
strangle; suffocate
Zaduszki [za-doosh-kee] n. All
Souls' Day (Catholic holiday)
zadymka [za-dim-ka] f.
snowstorm; blizzard
zadyszany [za-di-sha-ni] adj. m.
breathless; panting
zadzierać [za-dźhe-raćh] v.
tear open; turn up; quarrel
zadzierżysty [za-dźher-**zhis**-ti]
adj. m. defiant; perky
zadziwiać [za-dźheev-yaćh] v.
astonish; amaze; astound
zadzwonić [za-dzvo-ńeećh] v.
ring; ring up; ring for
zagadka [za-gad-ka] f. puzzle;
riddle; crux; problem; quiz
zagadnienie [za-gad-ńe-ńe] n.
problem; question; issue
zagajnik [za-gay-ńeek] m. grove;
shrubbery; scrub; coppice;
copse; growth of young trees
zagiąć [za-gyownćh] v. bend
zaginiony [za-gee-ńo-ni] adj. m.
lost; missing (person)
zaglądać [za-glown-daćh] v.
peep; look up; look into
zagłada [za-gwa-da] f. extinction;
extermination; annihilation
zagłębić [za-gwan-beećh] v.
plunge; sink; dip; immerse
zagłodzić [za-gwo-dźheećh] v.
starve to death; starve out
zagłuszać [za-gwoo-shaćh] v.
silence; jam; drown out; stifle
zagmatwać [za-gmat-vaćh] v.
entangle; confuse; embroil

zagniewany [za-gńe-**va**-ni]
adj. m. angry; cross; sore; in a
huff; in (high) dudgeon
zagospodarowywać [za-gos-po-
-da-ro-**vi**-vaćh] v. make
property productive; bring into
cultivation; manage (an estate)
zagotować [za-go-**to**-vaćh] v.
boil; start boiling; flare up
zagrabić [za-**gra**-beećh] v. rake
over; grab; seize; carve out
zagradzać [za-**gra**-dzaćh] v.
bar; fence; obstruct; intercept
zagranica [za-gra-ńee-tsa] f.
foreign countries;outside world
zagraniczny [za-gra-ńeech-ni]
adj. m. foreign; foreign (trade,
sojourn abroad, etc.)
zagrażać [za-**gra**-zhaćh] v.
threaten; impend; be imminent
zagroda [za-**gro**-da] f. farm house
with yard; enclosure
zagrodzić [za-**gro**-dźeećh] v.
fence in; bar; enclose; fence
around; obstruct; intercept
zagrożony [za-gro-**zho**-ni] adj. m.
threatened; endangered
zagrzebać [za-**gzhe**-baćh] v.
bury (in the grave,in the
past...); place alone
zagrzewać [za-**gzhe**-vaćh] v.
heat; warm up; animate;
inspirit; rouse; cheer
zahaczać [za-**kha**-chaćh] v.
hook (up, on, with); question;
accost; find fault; clasp
zahamować [za-kha-mo-vaćh]
v. restrain; put brakes on;
stop; check a motion
zaimek [za-ee-mek] m. pronoun
zainteresowanie [za-een-te-re-so-
-va-ńe] n. interest; concern
zaiste [za-**ees**-te] adv. truly;
indeed; very true; verily; yea
zajadać [za-ya-daćh] v. enjoy
eating; gorge; eat heartily
zajadły [za-yad-wi] adj. m. fierce;
rabid; bitter; unrelenting
zajazd [za-yazt] m. motel; inn;
zając [za-yownts] m. hare
zająć [za-yownćh] v. occupy
zajechać [za-ye-khaćh] v. drive
up; block; stump; pull in; stink

zajęcie [za-yan-ćhe] v. interest;
occupation; work; trade
zajmować [zay-mo-vaćh] v.
occupy; replace; displace
zajmujący [zay-moo-yown-tsi]
adj. m. interesting; absorbing
zajście [zayśh-ćhe] n. incident
zakalec [za-ka-lets] m. slack-
baked bread (or cake)
zakatarzony [za-ka-ta-zho-ni] adj.
m. suffering from a cold
zakatować [za-ka-to-vaćh] v.
flog to death; torture to death
zakaz [za-kas] m. prohibition
zakazić [za-ka-źheećh] v.
infect; contaminate; poison;
pollute; spread a disease
zakazywać [za-ka-zi-vaćh] v.
forbid; ban; suppress; prohibit;
forbid to do something
zakaźny [za-kaźh-ni] adj. m.
infectious; contagious
zakąska [za-kowns-ka] f. snack
zaklęcie [za-klan-ćhe) n. spell;
curse; incantation; charm;
entreaty; entreaties
zakład pogrzebowy [za-kwat po-
gzhe-bo-vi] m. funeral parlor
zakład [za-kwat] m. plant; shop;
institute; bet; wager; fold
zakładać [za-kwa-daćh] v.
found; initiate; put on; lay
zakładka [za-kwad-ka] f. fold;
bookmark; tuck; pleat; splice
zakładnik [za-kwad-ńeek] m.
hostage (for ransom etc.)
zakłamanie [za-kwa-ma-ńe] n.
hypocrisy; mendacity; pretense of virtue; dissimulation
zakłopotanie [za-kwo-po-ta-ńe]
n. embarrassment; confusion
zakłócać [za-kwoo-tsaćh] v.
disturb; unsettle; ruffle
zakłuwać [za-kwoo-vaćh] v.
stab to death; prick; stick (a
pig); cause a stabbing pain
zakochać się [za-ko-khaćh
śhan] v. fall in love; become
infatuated; become a lover of
zakochany [za-ko-kha-ni] adj. m.
a person in love; infatuated;
an enumerated man
zakomunikować [za-ko-moo-

-ńee-ko-vaćh] v.
communicate; let know;
convey a message; notify
zakon [za-kon] m. monastic
order; convent; sisterhood
zakonnica [za-kon-ńee-tsa] f.
nun; religious (woman)
zakonnik [za-kon-ńeek] m. monk
zakończenie [za-koń-che-ńe] n.
end; ending; termination; tip
zakopać [za-ko-paćh] v. bury
zakorkować [za-kor-ko-vaćh] v.
plug up; cork up; jam (the
traffic, a movement, etc.)
zakorzenić się [za-ko-zhe-
-ńeećh śhan] v. get roots
in; take roots; strike roots;
become deep-rooted
zakorzeniony [za-ko-zhe-ńo-ni]
adj. m. rooted; deep rooted
zakradać się [za-kra-daćh
śhan] v. creep; steal; sneak
zakrapiać [za-krap-yaćh] v. put
drops in; sprinkle; have a
drink; instil (in one's eyes)
zakres [za-kres] m. range; field;
scope; domain; sphere; realm
zakreślić [za-kreśh-leećh] v.
outline; mark off; encircle
zakręcić [za-kran-ćheećh] v.
turn; twist; turn off; curl
zakręt [za-krant] m. curve; bend
turn; twist; (street) corner
zakrętka [za-krant-ka] f.
turnbuckle; cap; nut; latch
zakrwawić [za-krva-veećh] v.
stain with blood; draw blood
zakryć [za-krićh] v. cover; hide
zakrzątnąć się [za-kzhownt-
-nownćh śhan] v. get busy;
bustle; try one's best; bestir
oneself; start bustling
zakrztusić [za-kzhtoo-śheećh]
v. choke (on food, fish bone)
zakrzywić [za-kzhi-veećh] v.
bend; bend down; bend back
zaksięgować [za-kśhan-go-
-vaćh] v. post; enter in the
books; to book (an item)
zakup [za-koop] m. purchase
zakurzony [za-koo-zho-ni] adj. m.
dusty; covered with dust
zakuty [za-koo-ti] adj. m.

shackled; chained; thick-head-
ed; crass; grossly stupid
zakwitnąć [za-kveet-nownch]
v. blossom out; go moldy
zalążek [za-lown-zhek] m. germ;
ovule; seed; origin; embryo
zalecać [za-le-tsaćh] v.
recommend; advise; enjoin;
counsel; prescribe; court; woo
zaledwie [za-led-vye] adv. barely;
scarcely; merely; but; only just
zalegać [za-le-gaćh] v. be
behind (in paying); lie useless;
fill (a space); surge
zaległy [za-leg-wi] adj. m.
unpaid; overdue; unfulfilled;
unaccomplished (duty, task)
zalepić [za-le-peećh] v. glue
up; paste up; gum up; paste
over; seal up; putty up
zalesienie [za-le-śhe-ńe] n.
forestation; afforestation
zaleta [za-le-ta] f. virtue;
advantage; quality; good point
zalew [za-lev] m. flood; bay;
invasion; deluge; lagoon
zalewać [za-le-vaćh] v. pour
over; flood; submerge; swarm;
spill; inundate; invade
zależeć [za-le-zhećh] v. depend on; be relative to
zależny [za-lezh-ni] adj. m.
dependent; contingent; subordinate; conditioned (by)
zaliczać [za-lee-chaćh] v.
include; count in; credit; rate;
accept; number; rate; reckon
zaliczka [za-leech-ka] f. earnest
money; down payment; pay-
ment on account; installment
zalotnica [za-lot-ńee-tsa] f. flirt;
coquette; kitten (slang)
zalotnik [za-lot-ńeek] m. suitor;
wooer; wheedler
zaloty [za-lo-ti] pl. courtship;
wooing; love making
zaludniać [za-lood-ńaćh] v.
populate; bring in population
zaludnienie [za-lood-ńe-ńe] n.
population; population density
załadować [za-wa-do-vaćh] v.
load up; embark; ship (goods)
załagodzić [za-wa-go-dźheećh]

v. mitigate; alleviate; soothe
załamać [za-wa-maćh] v. break
down; collapse; crash; slump
załamanie [za-wa-ma-ńe] n.
break down; (light) refraction
załatwiać [za-wat-vyaćh] v.
settle; transact; deal; dispose
załączać [za-wown-chaćh] v.
enclose; connect; annex; plug
in; include; subjoin
załącznik [za-wownch-ńeek] m.
enclosure; attachment; annex
załoga [za-wo-ga] f. crew;
garrison; staff; personnel
założenie [za-wo-zhe-ńe] n.
layout; foundation; assumption
założyciel [za-wo-zhi-ćhel] m.
founder; initiator; promoter
zamach [za-makh] m. attempt;
swing; sweep; coup d'etat;
spar; sparring motion
zamaczać [za-ma-chaćh] v.
steep; dip; wet; soak; drench
zamarzły [za-mar-zwi] adj. m.
frozen; frozen over; frozen to
death; frozen stiff; congealed
zamarznąć [za-mar-znownćh]
v. freeze up; freeze over;
freeze to death; congeal
zamaskować [za-mas-ko-vaćh]
v. mask; conceal; hide;
disguise; camouflage
zamaszysty [za-ma-shis-ti] adj.
m. brisk; vigorous; dashing;
swinging; sprawling; heavy
zamawiać [za-ma-vyaćh] v.
reserve; order (goods); book (a
seat); engage (workers)
zamazać [za-ma-zaćh] v. smear
over; soil up; daub; blur (a
picture); blur (outlines)
zamącić [za-mown-ćheećh] v.
ruffle (a water surface));
disturb; make turbid; stir
zamążpójście [za-mownzh-
-pooy-śhćhe] n. marriage
zamek [za-mek] m. lock; castle
zamek błyskawiczny [za-mek
bwis-ka-veech-ni] m. zipper
zamęt [za-mant] m. confusion;
disarray; muddle; welter
zamężna [za-manzh-na] adj. f.
married (woman in married

state); f. married woman
zamiana [za-mya-na] f. exchange
zamianować [za-mya-no-vać]
v. nominate; appoint; design
zamiar [za-myar] m. purpose
zamiast [za-myast] prep. instead
of; in place; in lieu
zamiatać [za-mya-tać] v.
sweep; brush with a broom
zamieć [za-myeć] f.
violent snowstorm; blizzard;
snow in a windstorm
zamiejscowy [za-myeys-tso-vi]
adj. m. out of town; coming
from an other place
zamienić [za-mye-ńeeć] v.
change; convert; replace;
swap; turn into; exchange
zamienny [za-myen-ni] adj. m.
exchangeable; interchangeable
zamierać [za-mye-rać] v. die
out; fade out; wither; die
away; decay; waste away
zamierzać [za-mye-zhać] v.
intend; mean; propose; think
zamierzenie [za-mye-zhe-ńe] n.
aim; purpose; plan; project
zamieszać [za-mye-shać] v.
stir up; blend; mix up; involve
zamieszanie [za-mye-sha-ńe] n.
confusion; disarray; turmoil;
stir; commotion; welter; to-do
zamieszkać [za-myesh-kać] v.
take up residence; put up; live
zamieszkiwać [za-myesh-kee-
-vać] v. inhabit; reside;
occupy; live; settle; put up
zamilknąć [za-meel-known̄ć]
v. became silent; be hushed
zamiłowanie [za-mee-wo-va-ńe]
n. predilection; fondness;
liking; relish; passion
zamknąć [zam-known̄ć] v.
close; shut; lock; wind up;
fence in; surround; clasp
zamoczyć [za-mo-chić] v.
wet; soak; steep; drench; dip;
submerge; moisten
zamorski [za-mor-skee] adj. m.
overseas; from overseas
zamożny [za-mozh-ni] adj. m.
rich; wealthy; affluent; well-to-
-do; well-off; (man) of means

zamówić [za-moo-veeć] v.
order; reserve; commission;
book; engage; charm away
zamówienie [za-moo-vye-ńe] n.
order; commission (a work of
art); custom order
zamrażać [za-mra-zhać] v.
freeze; chill; refrigerate
zamroczyć [za-mro-chić] v.
dim; gloom; confuse; darken;
cloud; bewilder; muddle
zamsz [zamsh] m. chamois;
suede; shammy-leather
zamulić [za-moo-leeć] v. fill
with slime; silt up (a harbor)
zamurować [za-moo-ro-vać] v.
brick over; brick up; wall up
zamydlić [za-mid-leeć] v. soap
over; pull the wool over eyes
zamykać [za-mi-kać] v. shut;
conclude; close (the view etc.)
zamysł [za-misw] m. design
zamyślać się [za-miśh-lać
śh*an*] v. contemplate; muse;
ponder; plan; intend
zamyślenie [za-mi-śhle-ńe] n.
reverie; pondering; meditation
zanadto [za-nad-to] adv. too
much; excess; more than
enough; beyond measure
zaniechać [za-ńe-khać] v.
give up; wave; desist from
zanieczyścić [za-ńe-chiśh-
-ćheeć] v. soil; dirty; litter;
grime; pollute; contaminate
zaniedbanie [za-ńed-ba-ńe] n.
neglect; negligence; sloppiness
zaniemóc [za-ńe-moots] v.
become ill; fall ill; get sick
zaniemówić [za-ńe-moo-veeć]
v. become speechless (dumb)
zaniepokoić [za-ńe-po-ko-eeć]
v. alarm; upset; disturb
zaniepokojenie [za-ńe-po-ko-ye-
-ńe] n. anxiety; alarm; uneasiness; concern; disquiet
zanieść [za-ńeśhć] v. carry
zanik [za-ńeek] m. wane
atrophy; disappearance
zanikać [za-ńee-kać] v.
disappear; vanish; decay;
wither; fade away; die out
zanim [za-ńeem] conj. before

zanocować [za-no-**tso**-vać] v.
stay over night; put up at
zanotować [za-no-to-vać] v.
note; write down;take down
zanurzyć [za-**noo**-zhić] v. dip
zaocznie [za-och-**ńe**] adv. in
absence; (judgement or sentence) by default
zaognić [za-og-**ńeeć**] v.
inflame; irritate; excite; kindle
zaokrąglić [za-o-**krowng**-leeć]
v. round off; make even
zaopatrzenie [za-o-pa-**tzhe**-ńe] n.
supplies; equipment; provision
zaopatrzyć [za-o-pa-**tzhić**] v.
provide; equip; supply; fit out;
furnish; stock; affix (a seal)
zaorać [za-o-rać] v. plough
over(a field etc.); plough up
zaostrzyć [za-os-**tzhić**] v.
sharpen; whet; tighten
(restrictions); stimulate (the
appetite); intensify
zaoszczędzić [za-osh-**chan**-
-**dźheeć**] v. save; spare
(trouble); put (money) by
zapach [**za**-pakh] m. smell;
aroma; flavor; odor; stench
zapadać [za-pa-dać] v. fall in;
sink; set in; drop; settle
zapakować [za-pa-ko-vać] v.
pack up; stow away; pack off
zapalczywy [za-pal-**chi**-vi] adj. m.
hotheaded; impetuous
zapalenie [za-pa-le-ńe] n.
ignition; inflammation (of the
skin); setting fire
zapaleniec [za-pa-le-ńets] m.
fanatic; enthusiastic; hot head
zapalić [za-pa-leeć] v. switch
on light; set fire; animate
zapalniczka [za-pal-**ńeech**-ka] f.
(cigarette) lighter
zapalnik [za-pal-**ńeek**] m. fuse
zapalny [za-pal-ni] adj. m.
inflammable; combustible;
ardent; impetuous
zapał [za-paw] m. enthusiasm
zapałka [za-**paw**-ka] f. match
zapamiętać [za-pa-**myan**-tać]
v. remember; memorize; keep
(something) in mind
zaparcie [za-par-**ćhe**] n.

constipation; denial
zaparzyć [za-pa-zhać] v. draw
(tea); brew; gall; make (tea);
heat (hay, etc.); infuse
zapas [**za**-pas] m. stock; store;
reserve; supply; fund; refill
zapasowy [za-pa-**so**-vi] adj. m.
spare; emergency (door, part,
etc.); reserve (fund, etc.)
zapaść [**za**-paśhćh] v. drop
sink; subside; collapse
zapaśnik [za-**paśh**-ńeek] m.
wrestler; contender
zapatrywać się [za-pa-tri-vać
śhan] v. have an opinion;
consider; stare;take example
zapatrywanie [za-pa-tri-**va**-ńe] n.
opinion; view; slant
zapełniać [za-pew-ńeeć] v. fill
up; stop a gap; fill (a space
etc.); crowd a street
zaperzyć się [za-pe-zhićh
śhan] v. flare up; be testy;
get mad; get on a high horse
zapewne [za-**pev**-ne] adv.
certainly; surely; doubtless; to
be sure; I should think
zapewnić [za-pev-ńeeć] v.
assure; secure; assert
zapewnienie [za-pev-**ńe**-ńe] n.
assurance; protestation;
assertion; affirmation
zapieczętować [za-pye-chan-to-
-vać] v. seal up (a letter);
seal; seal with wax
zapierać się [za-pye-rać
śhan] v. deny; disavow;
resist; repudiate
zapinać [za-pee-nać] v. button
up; fasten; buckle up
zapis [**za**-pees] m. registration;
bequest; record; notation
zapisać [za-pee-sać] v. note
down ; prescribe; enroll;
bequeath; record; write down
zapisek [za-pee-sek] m. note
zaplątać [za-**plown**-tać] v.
entangle; snarl; involve
zaplecze [za-ple-che] n.
hinterland; base (of supplies
etc.); subsidiaries
zapłacić [za-**pwa**-ćheeć] v.
pay; repay; requite; pay off

zapłakany [za-pwa-ka-ni] adj. m.
in tears; tearful; tear stained
zapłata [za-pwa-ta] f. payment
zapłodnić [za-pwod-ńeećh] v.
fertilize; inseminate; fecundate
zapłon [za-pwon] m. ignition
zapobiegać [za-po-bye-gaćh] v.
prevent; avert; ward off; stave
off; take precautions against
zapobiegliwy [za-po-bye-glee-vi]
adj. m. anticipating; thrifty
industrious; thrifty; provident
zapodziać [za-po-dźhaćh] v.
misplace; mislay; get lost
zapominać [za-po-mee-naćh] v.
forget; neglect; unlearn
zapomnienie [za-pom-ńe-ńe] n.
oblivion; forgetfulness
za pomocą [za po-mo-tsown]
adv. by means (of something);
with help (of a tool...)
zapomoga [za-po-mo-ga] f. hand
out; relief; benefit; grant
zapora [za-po-ra] f. dam;
(river) dam; obstacle; barrier;
check; (artillery) barrage
zapotrzebowanie [za-po-tzhe-bo-
-va-ńe] n. demand; order;
requisition; request
zapowiadać [za-po-vya-daćh] v.
announce; forecast; pretend
zapoznać [za-poz-naćh] v.
acquaint; introduce; instruct
zapożyczać [za-po-zhi-chaćh]
v. borrow (an idea, money);
adopt from; take from
zapracować [za-pra-tso-vaćh]
v. earn; get by hard work
zapracowany [za-pra-tso-va-ni]
adj. m. earned; overworked
zapraszać [za-pra-shaćh] v.
invite (to dinner etc.); offer
zaprawa [za-pra-va] f. mortar; v.
seasoning; training; work out
zaprawdę [za-prav-dan] adv.
indeed; to tell you the truth...
zaprawić [za-pra-veećh] v.
season; train; learn; dress;
spice; flavor; dress; train
zaproszenie [za-pro-she-ńe] n.
invitation (to dinner etc.)
zaprowadzić [za-pro-va-
-dźheećh] v. lead in; show

in; establish; initiate
zaprząg [za-pshownk] m. team
zaprzeczać [za-pshe-chaćh] v.
deny; contest; dispute
zaprzeczenie [za-pshe-che-ńe] n.
denial; negation; contradiction
zaprzepaścić [za-pshe-paśh-
ćheećh] v. loose; waste;
miss; bring to ruin; wreck
zaprzestać [za-pshes-taćh] v.
discontinue; stop; cease; quit
zaprzęg [za-pshank] m. team;
cart; harness; yoke (of oxen);
carriage; turn-out; vehicle
zaprzyjaźnić się [za-pshi-yaźh-
ńeećh śhan] v. make friends
zaprzysiąc [za-pshi-śhownts] v.
swear by oath; vow; pledge
zaprzysiężony [za-pshi-śhan-
-zho-ni] adj. m. sworn in;
pledged; fanatic; ardent
zapusty [za-poos-ti] pl. carnival;
Shrovetide (Catholic holiday)
zapuszczać [za-poosh-chaćh] v.
let in (dye); grow (hair);
neglect; let down; sink into
zapychać [za-pi-khaćh] v. stuff;
cram; fill; block; crowd
zapytanie [za-pi-ta-ńe] n.
question; inquiry; query;asking
zapytywać [za-pi-ti-vaćh] v.
ask; question; interrogate
zarabiać [za-rab-yaćh] v. earn
zaradczy [za-rad-chi] adj. m.
preventive; remedial (measure)
zaradny [za-rad-ni] adj. m.
resourceful (man,boy etc.)
zaranie [za-ra-ńe] n. dawning
zarastać [za-ras-taćh] v.
overgrow; cicatrize (a wound)
zaraz [za-ras] adv. at once;
directly; right away; soon
zaraza [za-ra-za] f. infection;
plague; epidemic; pestilence
zarazek [za-ra-zek] m. virus;
germ; microbe; (disease)
bacteria; (microorganism)
zarazem [za-ra-zem] adv. at the
same time; as well; also
zarazić [za-ra-źheećh] v. infect
zarażenie [za-ra-zhe-ńe] n.
infection (with a disease etc.)
zardzewieć [zar-dze-vyećh] v.

rust; get rusty; corrode

zaręczyny [za-ran-chi-ni] n.
betrothal; engagement

zarobek [za-ro-bek] m. gain;
bread; earnings; wages;
livelihood; living

zarobkować [za-rob-ko-vaćh] v.
earn working; earn a living

zarodek [za-ro-dek] m. embryo

zarosły [za-ros-wi] adj. m.
overgrown (with vegetation
etc.); unshaven; shaggy

zarost [za-rost] m. beard; hair

zarośla [za-rośh-la] n. thicket

zarozumiały [za-ro-zoo-mya-wi]
adj. m. conceited; uppish

zarówno [za-roov-no] adv.
equally; as well; alike; both

zarumienić się [za-roo-mye-
-ńeećh śhan] v. blush;
flush; brown; get browned

zaryglować [za-rig-lo-vaćh] v.
bolt a door; bar an entrance

zarys [za-ris] m. sketch; outline;
broad lines; design; draft

zarząd [za-zhownd] m.
management; administration;
board (of directors, trustees)

zarządca [za-zhownd-tsa] m.
administrator; manager

zarządzenie [za-zhown-dze-ńe]
n. administrative order

zarzucać [za-zhoo-tsaćh] v. fill;
give up; reproach; fling; cast

zarzut [za-zhoot] m. reproach;
objection; accusation; blame

zasada [za-sa-da] f. principle;
alkali; base; law; rule; tenet

zasadniczy [za-sad-ńee-chi] adj.
m. fundamental; essential; basic; primary; primordial; vital

zasadzka [za-sadz-ka] f. ambush

zasądzić [za-sown-dźheećh] v.
sentence (to imprisonment);
adjudge to (somebody)

zasępiony [za-san-pyo-ni] adj. m.
gloomy; despondent; dejected

zasiadać [za-śha-daćh] v. take
a seat; sit down; settle down

zasiąg [za-śhank] m. reach;
scope; extent; range; radius

zasięgać rady [za-śhan-gaćh
ra-di] v. consult; seek advice

zasiłek [za-śhee-wek] m.
handout; grant; relief;
subvention; allowance

zaskarżyć [za-skar-zhićh] v.
sue; take legal proceedings

zasklepić się [za-skle-peećh
śhan] v. scab; shut oneself
up (in);seal up; vault; wall up

zaskoczyć [za-sko-chićh] v.
surprise (an enemy); attack
unawares; click; lock

zaskórny [za-skoor-ni] adj. m.
subcutaneous; underground
(water); subsoil (water)

zasłabnąć [za-swab-nownćh] v.
faint; get sick; grow faint;
swoon; weaken; fall ill

zasłać [za-swaćh] v. cover
(bed); strew; litter

zasłona [za-swo-na] f. blind; veil;
screen; curtain; shield

zasłonić [za-swo-ńeećh] v.
curtain shade; shield; cover up

zasługa [za-swoo-ga] f. merit

zasługiwać [za-swoo-gee-vaćh]
v. deserve; be worthy; merit

zasłużony [za-swoo-zho-ni] adj.
m. man of merit; just; fair

zasmucić [za-smoo-ćheećh] v.
sadden; pain; distress; grieve

zasmucony [za-smoo-tso-ni] adj.
m. sad; grieved; distressed

zasnąć [za-snownćh] v. fall
asleep; sleep; drop off to
sleep; fall to sleep

zasobnik [za-sob-ńeek] m.
container; tank; storage tank

zasób [za-soop] m. store;
resource; stock; supply

zaspa [zas-pa] f. snowdrift;
dune; drifted sand; drifted
snow; ridge of drifted snow

zaspać [zas-paćh] v. oversleep

zaspokoić [za-spo-ko-eećh] v.
satisfy (a desire, a demand);
quench; appease; provide

zastanowić się [za-sta-no-
-veećh śhan] v. reflect;
puzzle; ponder; wonder

zastaw [za-stav] m. pawn;
deposit; security; forfeit; lien

zastawić [za-sta-veećh] v.
1.bar; 2.pledge; 3.set a table;

cram a room; lay (snares)
zastąpić [za-st<u>own</u>-peećh] v.
replace; bar passage; do duty
for; supersede; stand for
zastępca [za-st<u>anp</u>-tsa] m.
proxy; substitute; deputy
zastępczo [za-st<u>anp</u>-cho] adv.
replacing; temporary; in lieu
zastępstwo [za-st<u>anp</u>-stvo] n.
replacement; proxy; agency
zastosować [za-sto-**so**-vaćh] v.
adopt (measures, etc.); apply;
employ; make use; bring into
zastosować się [za-sto-**so**-vaćh
śh<u>an</u>] v. comply; toe the line
zastosowanie [za-sto-so-va-ńe]
n. application; use compliance
zastój [za-stooy] m. stagnation
zastraszyć [za-**stra**-shićh] v.
intimidate; cow; bully; browbeat; use undue influence
zastrzał [za-stshaw] m. (knee)
brace; strut; boom; cramp
zastrzec [za-stshets] v. reserve
(for); stipulate; condition
zastrzeżenie [za-stshe-**zhe**-ńe] n.
reservation; qualification
zastrzyk [za-stshik] m. injection;
shot (in the arm); grouting
zastygnąć [za-**stig**-n<u>own</u>ćh] v.
congeal; set; harden; petrify
zasuszyć [za-**soo**-shićh] v. dry
up; wither; shrivel (the skin)
zasuwa [za-**soo**-va] f. bar;(door)
bolt; valve; shutter; damper
zasuwka [za-**soov**-ka] f. small
(door) bolt; damper; valve
zasypać [za-**si**-paćh] v. bury;
cover; add (to soup); fill up
zasypiać [za-**sip**-yaćh] v. cat
nap; doze off; fall asleep
zaszczepiać [za-**shche**-pyaćh]
v. inoculate; graft; instill
zaszczycać [za-**shchi**-tsaćh] v.
honor; dignify; favor; grace
zaszczyt [zash-chit] m. honor;
distinction; privilege; dignity
zaszkodzić [za-**shko**-dźheećh]
v. harm; hurt; damage; injure
zasznurować [za-shnoo-ro-
-vaćh] v. tie up; lace (shoes);
tighten one's stays
zaszyć [za-shićh] v. sew up

zaszyć się [za-shićh **śh<u>an</u>**] v.
hide; burrow; conceal oneself
zaś [zaśh] conj. but; whereas;
and; while; specially
zaślepić [za-**śhle**-peećh] v.
blind; infatuate; blind to facts
zaślepiony [za-śhle-pyo-ni] adj.
m. infatuated; fanatic; blind
zaślubić [za-śhloo-beećh] v.
marry; get married
zaślubiny [za-śhloo-**bee**-ni] pl.
wedding; marriage;nuptials
zaśmiecić [za-**śhmye**-ćheećh]
v. litter (the street, etc.);
clutter up (a room, etc.)
zaśniedziały [za-śhńe-dźha-
-wi] adj. m. rusty; stagnant
zaśrubować [za-śhroo-bo-
-vaćh] v. screw tight; screw
on (a lid); screw up (a case)
zaświadczenie [za-śhvyad-che-
-ńe] n. certificate; affidavit
zaświadczyć [za-śhvyad-
-chićh] v. certify; attest;
witness; record; give evidence
zaświecić [za-**śhvye**-ćheećh]
v. put light on; light up; turn
on light; shed light; shine
zataczać [za-ta-chaćh] v. roll
in; describe (a circle); stagger;
wheel; turn on a lathe
zataić [za-ta-eećh] v. conceal
from; suppress; keep secret;
hold back (one's breath); hide
zatamować [za-ta-mo-vaćh] v.
dam up; stop; block; impede
zatańczyć [za-tań-chićh] v.
dance; perform a dance
zatapiać [za-tap-yaćh] v. flood;
sink; penetrate; inundate; submerge; immerse; scuttle
zatarasować [za-ta-ra-**so**-vaćh]
v. obstruct; block up; bolt
zatarg [za-targ] m. conflict;
clash; dispute; quarrel
zatem [za-tem] adv. then; consequently; therefore; and so
zatemperować [za-tem-pe-ro-
-vaćh] v. sharpen (a pencil)
zatkać [za-tkaćh] v. stop up
clog; clutter; block; chock up
zatlić się [za-tleećh **śh<u>an</u>**] v.
catch fire; start smoldering

zatłoczony [za-two-cho-ni] adj.
m. crowded; crammed; congested; cluttered
zatoka [za-to-ka] f. bay; gulf
zatonąć [za-to-nownch] v. sink
zator [za-tor] m. (traffic) jam
zatracić [za-tra-ćheećh] v.
lose;waste; lose all sense of
zatroskać [za-tros-kaćh] v.
grieve; alarm; make anxious
zatrucie [za-troo-ćhe] n.
poisoning; intoxication; toxaemia (blood poisoning)
zatruć [za-troo-ćh] v. poison
zatrudniać [za-trood-ńaćh] v.
employ; engage; give work;
take on (workers); occupy
zatrzask [za-tshask] m. (door)
latch; (snap) fastener lock
zatrzymać [za-tshi-maćh] v.
stop; retain; detain; arrest;
hold; bring to a stand still
zatwardzenie [za-tvar-dze-ńe] n.
constipation; costiveness
zatwierdzać [za-tvyer-dzaćh] v.
approve; ratify; affirm
zatwierdzenie [za-tvyer-dze-ńe]
n. ratification; approval;
assent; confirmation
zatwierdzić [za-tvyer-dźheećh]
v. ratify; approve; confirm (a
nomination, etc.); validate
zatyczka [za-tich-ka] f. plug
zatykać [za-ti-kaćh] v. stop up;
plug up; insert a plug
zaufać [za-oo-faćh] v. confide
zaufanie [za-oo-fa-ńe] n.
confidence; trust; faith;
reliance (in somebody)
zaufany [za-oo-fa-ni] adj. m.
reliable; confidential; trusted
zaułek [za-oo-wek] m.
alley; back street; lane;
recess; corner; nook
zauważyć [za-oo-va-zhićh] v.
notice; catch sight; remark
zawada [za-va-da] f. obstruction;
nuisance; hindrance; obstacle
zawadiaka [za-vad-ya-ka] m.
bully; blusterer; swashbuckler
zawadzać [za-va-dzaćh] v.
hinder; scrape; touch; be a
drag; scrape against; impede

zawalać [za-va-laćh] v. soil
zawalić [za-va-leećh] v.
collapse; obstruct; bury; cover up; crush; bungle; clutter
zawartość [za-var-tośhćh] f.
contents; subject (of a book)
zawczasu [za-vcha-soo] adv. in
time; in advance; beforehand
zawczoraj [za-vcho-ray] adv. the
day before yesterday
zawdzięczać [za-vdźhan-
-chaćh] v. owe (gratitude); be
indebted (for something)
zawezwać [za-vez-vaćh] v. call;
summon; call in (a doctor etc.)
zawiadomić [za-vya-do-meećh]
v. inform; give notice; let
know; notify; intimate
zawiadomienie [za-vya-do-mye-
-ńe] n. notification; information; notice; intimation
zawiadowca stacji [za-vya-dov-
-tsa stats-yee] m. stationmaster; superintendent
zawiasa [za-vya-sa] f. hinge
zawiązać [za-vyown-zaćh] v.
tie up; bind; set up (a club)
zawieja [za-vye-ya] f. blizzard;
snow-storm; cloud (of dust)
za wiele [za vye-le] adv. too
much; too many (expenses)
za widna [za veed-na] adv. in
day light; before dark
zawierać [za-vye-raćh] v.
contain; include; contract;
conclude; shut; strike up
zawierucha [za-vye-roo-kha] f.
wind storm;gale;(war) clouds
zawieszenie broni [za-vye-she-ńe
bro-ńee] n. armistice; truce;
cessation of hostilities
zawietrzna [za-vyetsh-na] f. lee
side (sheltered from the wind)
zawijać [za-vee-yaćh] v. wrap
up; tuck in; put in a port
zawikłać [za-veek-waćh] v.
complicate; entangle; embroil;
tangle; confuse
zawiły [za-vee-wi] adj. m.
intricate; baffling; knotty; involved; complicated (problem)
zawinąć [za-vee-nownch] v.
wrap; take care of; pack

zawinić [za-**vee**-ńeeć] v. be guilty; commit an offense

zawisły [za-**vees**-wi] adj. m. dependent (on somebody etc.)

zawistnie [za-**veest**-ńe] adv. with envy; jealously

zawistny [za-**veest**-ni] adj. m. envious; jealous

zawiść [za-**veeśhćh**] f. envy

zawitać [za-**vee**-taćh] v. call on; come and see (somebody)

zawlec [za-vlets] v. drag; tug; cloud; (wrap with a mist)

zawodnik [za-**vod**-ńeek] m. competitor (in sport); contestant; participant

zawodowiec [za-vo-do-vyets] m. professional; specialist

zawody [za-**vo**-di] pl. (sport) competition; match; race; game; (sport) event

zawodzić [za-**vo**-dźheećh] v. 1. lead; 2. disillusion; lament

zawołać [za-**vo**-waćh] v. call out for; call; exclaim; shout; cry; cry out for; summon

zawołany [za-vo-**wa**-ni] adj. m. excellent; perfect; born (poet)

zawozić [za-**vo**-źheećh] v. convey; take to; cart; deliver; give rides; carry; drive

zawód [za-voot] m. 1. profession; trade; vocation; craft 2. disappointment; deception

zawór [**za**-voor] m. valve; vent

zawrót głowy [za-vroot **gwo**-vi] m. dizziness;vertigo; giddiness

zawstydzić [za-**vsti**-dźheećh] v. shame; embarrass; overwhelm; put to shame

zawsze [**zav**-she] adv. always; evermore; (for) ever; at all times; for all times; still

zawszyć [**zav**-shićh] v. louse up; infect with lice

zawziąć się [zav-**źhown**ćh **śhan**] v. be obstinate; persist; set on; grow obstinate

zawziętość [zav-**żhan**-tośhćh] f. persistence; obstinacy; keenness; doggedness

zazdrosny [zaz-**dros**-ni] adj. m. jealous; envious; resentful

zazdrość [zaz-**drośhćh**] f. envy; jealousy

zaziębić się [za-**żhan**-beećh **śhan**] v. catch a cold

zaznaczyć [za-**zna**-chićh] v. mark; make a note; state

zaznać [zaz-naćh] v. experience; taste; enjoy; undergo; taste (ill fortune, etc.)

zaznajomić [za-**zna**-yo-meećh] v. acquaint; introduce to

zazwyczaj [za-zvi-chay] adv. usually; generally; ordinarily

zażalenie [za-zha-le-ńe] n. complaint; grievance

zażarty [za-**zhar**-ti] adj. m. fierce; bitter; vehement

zażądać [za-**zhown**-daćh] v. demand; require; order

zażenować [za-zhe-**no**-vaćh] v. shame; embarrass; confuse; abash; disconcert

zażyły [za-**zhi**-wi] adj. m. familiar; intimate; close; chummy; hob-nob (with)

zażywać pigułki [za-zhi-vaćh pee-**goow**-kee] v. take pills

ząb [zownp] m. tooth; fang; prong; cog; indentation

ząb mleczny [zownp mlech-ni] m. milk tooth (of a child etc.)

ząb trzonowy [zownp tsho-**no**-vi] adj. m. molar

ząbkować [**zownb**-ko-vaćh] v. teethe; jag; cut one's teeth

zbaczać [zba-chaćh] v. deviate

zbankrutowany [zban-kroo-to-**va**-ni] adj. m. bankrupt; insolvent

zbawca [zbav-tsa] m. savior

zbawiciel [zba-**vee**-ćhel] m. savior; redeemer; Saviour

zbawicielka [zba-vee-**ćhel**-ka] f. savior; redeemer

zbawić [zba-veećh] v. save; redeem; rescue; take (time)

zbawienie [zba-**vye**-ńe] n. salvation; deliverance; rescue; (spiritual) redemption; a saving

zbesztać [zbesh-taćh] v. scold

zbeszcześcić [zbez-chesh-ćheećh] v. desecrate; defile; profane; reprove sharply

zbędny [zb**and**-ni] m.

superfluous; redundant;
needless; useless

zbieg [zbyek] m. fugitive; con-
fluence; deserter; escapee

**zbieg okoliczności [zbyek o-ko-
-leech-nośh-ćhee]** m. coincidence; an accidental occurrence at the same time

zbiegać [zbye-gaćh] v. run
down (stairs); escape; desert

zbiegowisko [zbye-go-vees-ko] n.
concourse; throng; crowd

zbieracz [zbye-rach] m. collector;
gatherer; (mushroom) picker

zbierać [zbye-raćh] v. gather;
pick; summon; clear; take in

zbieżny [zbyezh-ni] adj. m. con-
vergent; tapering; concurrent

zbijać [zbee-yaćh] v. knock
together; refute; beat down;
knock off; press together

zbiornik [zbyor-ńeek] m. tank;
reservoir; container; receptacle

zbiór [zbyoor] m. harvest;
collection; set; crop; class;
series; aggregation

zbiórka [zbyoor-ka] f. rally;
assembly; meeting; gathering

zbir [zbeer] m. thug; ruffian

zbity [zbee-ti] adj. m. close;
1.beaten up; 2. compact;
dense; firm; close

zblednąć [zbled-nownćh] v.
pale; grow pale; fade; turn
pale; become pale

z bliska [z blees-ka] adv. from
near; close up; from near by

zbliżać [zblee-zhaćh] v. nearby

zbliżyć się [zblee-zhićh śhan]
v. become close; approach; be
near; come up; draw near

zbliżenie [zblee-zhe-ńe] n.
rapprochement; close-up

zbliżony [zblee-zho-ni] adj. m.
approximate; nearing;
congenial; resembling

zbłądzić [zbwown-dźheećh] v.
go astray; make a mistake;
lose trail; wander off; loose
one's way; commit a blunder

zbocze [zbo-che] n. (hill) slope

zboczenie [zbo-che-ńe] n.
deviation; aberration; drift; sag

zbolały [zbo-la-wi] adj. m.
aching; sore; woeful; cheerless; wretched

zboże [zbo-zhe] n. corn; grain

zbój [zbooy] m. bandit; robber

**zbór ewangielicki [zboor e-van-
-ge-leets-kee]** m. Protestant
Church; Evangelical Church

zbratać się [zbra-taćh śhan] v.
fraternize; chum up (with)

**zbroczony krwią [zbro-cho-ni
krvyown]** adj. m. blood-stained

zbrodnia [zbrod-ńa] f. crime

zbrodniarz [zbrod-ńash] m.
criminal; felon; malefactor

zbroić [zbro-eećh] v. arm

zbroja [zbro-ya] f. armor

**zbrojony beton [zbro-yo-ni be-
-ton]** m. reinforced concrete

zbrojownia [zbro-yov-ńa] f.
arsenal; armory; gun room

zbryzgać [zbriz-gaćh] v.
spatter; bespatter; splash

zbrzydnąć [zbzhid-nownćh] v.
grow ugly; lose good looks

zbudować [zboo-do-vaćh] v.
build; rise; erect; lay out

**zbudzić się [zboo-dźheećh
śhan]** v. wake up; awake; be
stirred; be roused

zbujać [zboo-yaćh] v. fool;
hoax; pull one's leg

zburzyć [zboo-zhićh] v.
demolish; ruin; devastate

zbutwieć [zboo-tvyećh] v.
molder; rot; decompose;
decay; spoil; mildew

zbydlęcić [zbi-dlan-ćheećh] v.
bestialize; turn into a brute

zbyt [zbit] adv. too (much)

zbyt wiele [zbit vye-le] adv. too
much; excessively; over

zbyt [zbit] m. sale; market

zbyteczny [zbi-tech-ni] adj. m.
superfluous; needless; odd;
redundant; left over

zbytek [zbi-tek] m. frills; luxury;
pranks; follies; extravagance

zbytni [zbit-ńee] adj. m.
excessive; undue; more than
needed; superfluous

zbytnik [zbit-ńeek] m. rogue

zbywać [zbi-vaćh] v. dispose;

dismiss; put off (with an excuse); sell; lack; want

z czasem [z cha-sem] adv. with time; eventually; later

z dala [z da-la] adv. from far

z daleka [z da-le-ka] adv. from far; from afar; away from

zdalnie [zdal-ńe] adv. remote; from afar; by remote control

zdanie [zda-ńe] n. 1. opinion; judgment; sentence; clause; proposition; 2. giving back

zdanie sprawy [zda-ńe spra-vi] n. report; account; giving account; giving information

zdarzać się [zda-zhaćh śhan] v. happen; take place; occur

zdarzenie [zda-zhe-ńe] n. happening; event; incident

zdatność [zdat-nośhćh] f. fitness; capability; suitability

zdatny [zdat-ni] adj. m. able; fit; apt; suitable (for the purpose)

zdawać [zda-vaćh] v. entrust; submit; turn over; give up; pass (test); hand over

zdawać się [zda-vaćh śhan] 1. seem; 2. surrender; 3. rely

z dawien dawna [z da-vyen dav-na] adv. from way back

z dawna [z dav-na] adv. since a long time; from way back

zdążyć [zdown-zhićh] v. come on time; keep pace; tend

zdechlak [zdekh-lak] m. weakling

zdechły [zdekh-wi] adj. m. peaked; dead (animal); weakly; sickly (person)

zdecydować się [zde-tsi-do-vaćh śhan] v. decide; determine; make up one's mind

zdejmować [zdey-mo-vaćh] v. take off; strip (clothes); remove; snap (a photo)

zdenerwowany [zde-ner-vo-va-ni] adj. m. nervous; excited

zderzak [zde-zhak] m. bumper

zderzenie [zde-zhe-ńe] n. collision; clash; crash; smash-up; conflict (of interest, etc.)

zderzyć się [zde-zhićh śhan] v. collide; clash; run into

zdjęcie [zdyan-ćhe] n. snapshot

zdjęcie rentgenowskie [zdyan-ćhe rent-ge-nov-skye] n. X-ray picture; X-ray photograph

zdmuchiwać [zdmoo-khee-vaćh] v. blow off; blow out; blow away; puff away

zdobić [zdo-beećh] v. decorate

zdobycz [zdo-bich] f. booty; spoils; prey; prize; trophy

zdobyć [zdo-bićh] v. conquer

zdolność [zdol-nośhćh] f. ability; capacity; talent; aptitude; capability

zdolny [zdol-ni] adj. m. clever; able; capable; fit; competent

zdołać [zdo-waćh] v. be able

zdrada [zdra-da] f. treason

zdradliwy [zdrad-lee-vi] adj. m. treacherous; tricky; unsafe

zdradzać [zdra-dzaćh] v. betray

zdrajca [zdray-tsa] adj. m. traitor informer; turncoat; renegade;

zdrapać [zdra-paćh] v. scratch off; scrape off; loosen up

zdrętwieć [zdrant-vyećh] v. grow numb; stiffen; grow torpid; anchylose

zdrętwienie [zdrant-vye-ńe] n. numbness; stiffness; torpidity

zdrobniały [zdrob-ńa-wi] adj. m. diminutive; grown smaller

zdrojowisko [zdro-yo-vees-ko] n. spa; health resort; baths

zdrowie [zdrov-ye] n. health; good constitution; being well

zdrowotne jedzenie [zdro-vot-ne ye-dze-ńe] n. health food

zdrowy [zdro-vi] adj. m. healthy; sound; mighty; in good health

zdrożny [zdrozh-ni] adj. m. vicious; wicked; wrong; blameworthy; fatigued

zdrój [zdrooy] m. spring; spa

zdrów i cały [zdroov ee tsa-wi] m. safe and sound

zdrzemnąć się [zdzhem-nownćh śhan] .v. doze off; sleep light; catnap; take a nap

zdumienie [zdoo-mye-ńe] n. astonishment; amazement

zdumiony [zdoo-myo-ni] adj. m. astonished; flabbergasted

zdun [zdoon] m. stove fitter

zdwajać [zdva-yaćh] v. double

zdychać [zdi-khaćh] v. die

zdyszany [zdi-sha-ni] adj. m. breathless; panting for breath; out of breath

zdziałać [zdźha-waćh] v. accomplish; achieve; manage to do; do successfully

zdziczeć [zdźhee-chećh] v. grow wild; become savage; turn wild; fall into savagery

zdziecinnieć [zdźhe-ćheen-ńećh] v. grow childish (in old age); grow senile

zdzierać [zdźhe-raćh] v. strip off; fleece; tear down; peel

zdzierstwo [zdźher-stvo] n. exorbitance; extortion

zdziwaczeć [zdźhee-va-chećh] v. become odd; grow whimsical; become freaky

zdziwić [zdźhee-veećh] v. surprise; astonish; make wonder; amaze; cause doubt

zdziwienie [zdźhee-vye-ńe] n. surprise; wonderment; astonishment; sudden surprise

zebra [ze-bra] f. zebra

zebrać [ze-braćh] v. gather; clear; collect; unite; pick

zebranie [ze-bra-ńe] n. meeting

zecer [ze-tser] m. type setter

zechcieć [zekh-ćhećh] v. be willing; feel inclined; choose

zegar [ze-gar] m. clock; meter

zegar słoneczny [ze-gar swo-nech-ni] sundial

zegarek [ze-ga-rek] m. watch

zegarmistrz [ze-gar-meestsh] m. watch-maker; clock-maker; watch-maker's shop

zejście [zeyśh-ćhe] n. descent

zejść [zeyśhćh] v. descent

zejść się [zeyśhćh śhan] v. meet (as prearranged); meet; rendezvous; have a date

zelówka [ze-loov-ka] f. (shoe) sole; bottom surface of a shoe

zelżeć [zel-zhećh] v. lighten up; ease; let up; diminish; abate; give; remit

zemdleć [zem-dlećh] v. faint; pan out; swoon; feel weak

zemsta [zem-sta] f. revenge

zepchnąć [zep-khnownćh] v. push down; drive out; shove down; thrust down

zepsuć [zep-sooćh] v. damage; spoil; worsen; pervert; harm; injure; disarrange; pollute

zepsuty [zep-soo-ti] adj. m. damaged; spoiled; corrupt; bad; perverse; out of order

zerkać [zer-kaćh] v. squint at; peep (into...); take a peep

zero [ze-ro] n. zero; nought; nil

zerwać [zer-vaćh] v. pick off; snap loose; break off; sprain; rip off; burst out; blow off

zerwanie [zer-va-ńe] n. rupture

zeskakiwać [ze-ska-kee-vaćh] v. jump off; dismount; get off

zeskrobywać [ze-skro-bi-vaćh] v. scrape off; erase; scrape clean; scrape away; scratch

zesłać [ze-swaćh] v. deport; send down; send into exile

zesłanie [ze-swa-ńe] n. deportation; exile; penal colony; transportation

zespolić [ze-spo-leećh] v. unite

zespół [ze-spoow] m. team; group; gang; crew; troupe; set; complex; co-operative

zestarzeć się [ze-sta-zhećh śhan] v. grow old; get old; age; stale (news, story)

zestawienie [ze-sta-vye-ńe] n. comparison; balance sheet; list

zestrzelenie [ze-stshe-le-ńe] n. shooting down; downing (of an airplane, of a bird, etc.)

zeszłoroczny [ze-shwo-roch-ni] adj. m. last year's (crop etc.)

zeszpecić [ze-shpe-ćheećh] v. disfigure; make look ugly; deface; mar the beauty of

zeszyt [ze-shit] m. notebook

ześlizgiwać się [ze-śhleez-gee-vaćh śhan] v. glide down; slip; slide down; skid down

zetknąć się [zet-knownćh śhan] v. meet face-to-face; get in touch; come into contact; meet; put in touch

zew [zef] n. call; appeal; slogan

zewnątrz [zev-nowntsh] adv. &
prep. out; outside; outwards;
outdoors; on the surface
zewnętrzny [zev-nantsh-ni] adj.
m. exterior; external; outward
zewsząt [ze-vshownt] adv. from
everywhere; from all points
zez [zes] m. squint; cross-eye
zeznawać [zez-na-vaćh] v.
declare; testify; give evidence
zezować [ze-zo-vaćh] v. squint
zezwalać [zez-va-laćh] v. allow;
give permission; permit
zezwolenie [zez-vo-le-ńe] n.
permission; leave; license
zębaty [zan-ba-ti] adj. m.
toothed; cogged; indented
zębate koło [zan-ba-te ko-wo] n.
cog wheel; gear (wheel)
zęby [zan-bi] pl. teeth; cogs
zgadywać [zga-di-vaćh] v. anticipate; guess; make a guess
zgadzać się [zga-dzaćh śhan]
v. agree; fit in; see eye-to-eye
zgaga [zga-ga] f. heartburn
zganić [zga-ńeećh] v. blame
zgarnąć [zgar-nownćh] v. rake;
together; brush aside
zgasić [zga-śheećh] v. put
out; extinguish; switch off;
dim; stub out (a cigarette)
zgęszczenie [zgan-shche-ńe] n.
condensation; compression
zgiełk [zgewk] m. uproar;
clamor; turmoil; tumult
zgięcie [zgyan-ćhe] n. bend;
fold; inflection; inflexion
zginać [zgee-naćh] v. bend
(over); fold; stoop; bow
zgliszcza [zgleesh-cha] pl.
cinders; ashes; site of fire
zgłaszać [zgwa-shaćh] v.
notify;call for;tender;submit
zgłębiać [zgwan-beećh] v.
probe; sound out; deepen; go
deeply; get to the bottom
zgłodniały [zgwod-ńa-wi] adj. m.
hungry; starving; hungering
zgłosić [zgwo-śheećh] v.
notify; tender; lay a claim
zgłoska [zgwos-ka] f. syllable
zgłupieć [zgwoo-pyećh] v.
grow silly; grow stupid; be

astounded; be astonished
zgnębić [zgnan-beećh] v.
depress; dispirit; oppress;
dishearten; bring to ruin
zgnić [zgńeećh] v. rot; decay;
putrefy; molder; ret
zgnieść [zgńeśhćh] v. crush;
stub out; squash; suppress;
quell; squeeze; crumble
zgnilizna [zgńee-leez-na] f. rot;
corruption; foul smell
zgniły [zgńee-wi] adj. rotten;
foul, corrupt; perverted
zgoda [zgo-da] f. concord;
assent; consent; unity; harmony; approval; reconciliation
zgodnie [zgod-ńe] adv. according; in concert; peaceably;
in unison; in compliance
zgodność [zgod-nośhćh] f.
accord; agreement; unanimity;
consistence; concordance
zgodny [zgod-ni] m. compatible;
good-natured; unanimous
zgoić się [zgo-eećh śhan] v.
heal up; heal over; heal a
wound; become well again
zgon [zgon] m. death; decease
zgorszyć [zgor-shićh] v. horrify;
scandalize; shock; arouse
zgorzkniały [zgosh-kńa-wi] adj.
m. sour; embittered; acrimonious; soured (by misfortune)
zgotować [zgo-to-vaćh] v.
prepare; cook; give (an ovation, a hearty welcome)
z góry [z goo-ri] adv. in advance
zgrabny [zgrab-ni] adj. m. skillful;
clever; deft; smart; neat;
shapely; slick; deft; well-built
zgraja [zgra-ya] f. gang; mob
zgromadzenie [zgro-ma-dze-ńe]
n. assembly; congress; meeting; collection; congregation
zgromadzać się [zgro-ma-dzaćh
śhan] v. assemble; gather
zgroza [zgro-za] f. horror
z grubsza [zgroob-sha] adv.
roughly; approximately
zgryzota [zgri-zo-ta] f. grief
zgryźliwy [zgriźh-lee-vi] adj. m.
sarcastic; peevish; harsh
zgrzać się [zgzhaćh śhan] v.

get hot; sweat; become hot
zgrzebło [zgzheb-wo) n.
horse-comb; harrow; curry-
comb; comb; stirrer
zgrzyt [zgzhit] m. screech; jar
zguba [zgoo-ba] f. loss;
doom; undoing; ruin; destruction; lost (property, object)
zgubić [zgoo-beećh] v. lose;
undo; drop; bring to ruin;
destroy; unmake; fall out of
zgubić się [zgoo-beećh śhan]
v. get lost; get mixed up; be
mislaid; lose one another
zgubny [zagoob-ni] adj. m.
disastrous; fatal; ruinous;
calamitous; pernicious
zgwałcić [zgvaw-ćheećh] v.
rape; violate; force to do
ziarnisty [źhar-ńees-ti] adj. m.
granular; grainy; whole grain
ziarno [źhar-no] n. grain; corn
ziele [źhe-le] n. weed; herb
zieleń [źhe-leń] f. greenery
zielonawy [źhe-lo-na-vi] adj. m.
greenish; of greenish color
zielony [źhe-lo-ni] adj. m. green;
young and inexperienced
(man); raw; sappy; unripe
ziemia [źhem-ya] f. earth; land
ground; native soil; native
land; district; the world
ziemianin [źhe-mya-ńeen] m.
squire; landowner; mortal
ziemianka [źhe-myan-ka] f.
1.dugout; 2. landowner's wife
ziemniak [źhem-ńak] m. potato
ziemski [źhem-skee] adj. m.
earthly; worldly; landed; land
ziewać [źhe-vaćh] v. yawn;
gape; give a yawn
zięba [źhan-ba] f. finch;
chaffinch
ziębić [źhan-beećh] v. cool;
chill; expose to the cold
zięć [źhanćh] m. son-in-law
zima [źhee-ma] f. winter
zimno [źheem-no] n. cold; chill
zimno [źheem-no] adv. coldly
zimny [źheem-ni] adj. m. cold
zimować [źhee-mo-vaćh] v.
hibernate; winter; pass the
winter; survive the winter

zioło [źho-wo] n. herb (mint,
sage, camomile, etc.)
ziszczać [zeesh-chaćh] v.
realize; fulfill; carry out (a
plan); materialize
zjadać [zya-daćh] v. eat; eat
up; have food; ruin; drain
zjadliwy [zya-dlee-vi] adj. m.
biting; caustic; spiteful;
vicious; mordant; malignant
zjawa [zya-va] f. apparition;
ghost; vision; specter;
phantom; a becoming visible
zjawisko [zya-vees-ko] n. fact;
event; phenomenon; vision;
very unusual occurrence
zjazd [zyazt] m. meeting;
coming; descent; downhill
drive or slide; congress
zjednoczenie [zyed-no-che-ńe] n.
union; unification; association
zjeść [zyeśhćh] v. eat up;
devour; eat away (profits, etc)
zjeżdżać [zyezh-dzhaćh] v. ride
down; slide down; make way;
turn off the road; arrive; slip
zlecać [zle-tsaćh] v. order
commission to do; entrust to
do; instruct; charge with
zlecenie [zle-tse-ńe] n.
commission; order; errand;
message; instruction
z ledwością [z led-vośh-
-ćhown] adv. hardly; with
difficulty; with great pains
z lekka [z lek-ka] adv. lightly;
softly; slightly; gently
zlepek [zle-pek] m. agglomerate
zlew [zlef] m. sink; kitchen sink
zlewać [zle-vaćh] v. pour off;
decant; pour together; mix;
flunk; whip; blend (liquids)
zliczyć [zlee-chićh] v. count up;
total; add up; reckon; tot up
zlikwidować [zlee-kvee-do-
-vaćh] v. liquidate; wind up;
destroy; suppress; abolish
zlodowacenie [zlo-do-va-tse-ńe]
n. freezing; glaciation
zlot [zlot] m. rally; flocking in
złagodzenie [zwa-go-dze-ńe] n.
mitigation; softening
złagodzić [zwa-go-dźheećh] v.

mitigate; soothe; lessen;
soften; diminish the severity
złamać [zwa-maćh] v. break;
smash; overcome (resistance)
złamanie [zwa-ma-ńe] n. break;
fracture; prostration; collapse
złazić [zwa-źheećh] v. climb
down; get off; peel off
złączenie [zwown-che-ńe] n.
connection; junction; weld
złączyć [zwown-chićh] v. join;
link; fuse; weld; unite; bind
złe [zwe] n. evil; wrong; ill
zło [zwo] n. evil; devil; harm
złocenie [zwo-tse-ńe] n. gilding
złocić [zwo-ćheećh] v. gild
złoczyńca [zwo-chiń-tsa] m.
evildoer; criminal; malefactor
złodziej [zwo-dźhey] m. thief
złodziejka [zwo-dźhey-ka] f.
1. thief; 2. electrical adapter
złom [zwom] m. scrap; waste
złość [zwośhćh] f. anger;
malice; spite; soreness; resentment; animosity against
złośliwy [zwośh-lee-vi] adj. m.
malignant; spiteful; malicious
złotnik [zwot-ńeek] m.
goldsmith; silversmith
złoto [zwo-to] n. gold; gold work
złoty [zwo-ti] adj. m. golden
złoty [zwo-ti] m. Polish money
unit (originally gold ducat)
złowić [zwo-veećh] v. catch
(an animal, a thief); net; hook
(a fish, a husband, etc.)
złowrogi [zwo-vro-gee] adj. m.
ominous; sinister; portentous
złoże [zwo-zhe] n. stratum; bed
złożony [zwo-zho-ni] adj. m.
complex; multiple; intricate
złuda [zwoo-da] f. illusion
złudny [zwood-ni] adj. m.
illusory; deceptive; illusive
zły [zwi] adj. m. bad; evil; ill;
vicious; cross; poor; rotten
zmagać się [zma-gaćh śhan]
v. struggle with; grapple with
zmaganie [zma-ga-ńe] n.
struggle; strife against
zmarły [zmar-wi] adj. m.
deceased; dead; defunct; the
late (husband, father, etc,)

zmarszczka [zmarshch-ka] f.
wrinkle; crease; fold; pucker
zmartwienie [zmar-tvye-ńe] n.
worry; sorrow; grief; trouble
**zmartwychwstać [zmar-tvikh-
-vstaćh]** v. rise from the dead
**zmartwychwstanie [zmar-tvikh-
-vsta-ńe]** n. resurrection
zmarznąć [zmar-znownćh] v.
freeze; freeze over; be cold
zmawiać się [zma-vyaćh śhan]
v. conspire; plot; arrange;
collude; enter into collusion
zmaza [zma-za] f. stain; blemish;
blot; wet dream; slur
zmazywać [zma-zi-vaćh] v.
wipe out; efface; erase; expiate; wipe off (a stain)
zmęczenie [zman-che-ńe] n.
fatigue; weariness; lassitude
zmiana [zmya-na] f. change;
variation; shift; relay; exchange; alteration; transition
zmiatać [zmya-taćh] v. sweep
up; carry away; dispatch
zmiażdżyć [zmyazh-dzhićh] v.
crush; overwhelm (the enemy)
zmienić [zmye-ńeećh] v. alter; change; modify; vary; exchange; replace; transform
zmierzać [zmye-zhaćh] v. aim;
tend towards; make one's
way; drive at; intend to do
zmierzch [zmyeshkh] m. dusk;
twilight; decline; fall; at dark;
zmierzyć [zmye-zhićh] v.
measure; gauge; take aim;
make for; estimate (a distance); eye up and down
zmieszanie [zmye-sha-ńe] n. mix
up; confusion; embarrassment
zmiłowanie [zmee-wo-va-ńe] n.
mercy; pity; disposition to
forgive or to be kind
zmniejszenie [zmńey-she-ńe] n.
reduction; decrease; relief
zmniejszyć [zmńey-shićh] v.
diminish; lessen; abate; reduce
zmoczyć [zmo-chićh] v. wet;
soak; moisten; drench
zmora [zmo-ra] f. nightmare;
ghost; curse (of war); bane
zmorzyć [zmo-zhićh] v.

overpower; overcome

zmordować [zmor-**do**-vaćh] v.
tire; wear; do in; tire out;
exhaust; tire to death; toil

zmowa [**zmo**-va] f. conspiracy;
collusion; plot; secret deal

zmrok [zmrok] m. dusk; twilight

zmurszały [zmoor-**sha**-wi] adj. m.
mouldy; decaying; crumbling;
rotten; mildew; musty

zmuszać [zmoo-**shać**] v.
coerce; compel; force; oblige;
constrain; make do; get to do

zmykać [zmi-**kać**] v. cut and
run; bolt; scoot off; scurry
away; scamper away

zmylić [zmi-**leć**] v. fool;
mislead; lead into error;
deceive; lose way; outwit

zmysł [zmisw] m. sense;
instinct; knack; aptitude;
consciousness; pl. reason

zmysłowy [zmis-**wo**-vi] adj. m.
sensual; sensory; sense; lewd

zmyślać [zmiśh-**lać**] v. invent; trump up; fake up; cook
up; bluff; fabricate; brag

zmyślony [zmiśh-**lo**-ni] adj. m.
fictitious; invented; unreal

znaczący [zna-**chown**-tsi] adj. m.
significant; emphatic; telling

znaczek [zna-**chek**] m. mark;
stamp; badge; tick

znaczny [**znach**-ni] adj. m.
notable; goodly; prominent

znać [znać] v. know; know
how; adv. apparently

znajdować [znay-**do**-vaćh] v.
find; see; meet; experience

znajomość [zna-**yo**-**mo**śhćh]
f. acquaintance; knowledge

znajomy [zna-**yo**-mi] adj. m. well
acquainted; well-known; well-
known man; familiar

znak [znak] m. mark; sign;
stamp; signal; token; trace

znakomity [zna-ko-**mee**-ti] adj. m.
excellent; illustrious

znalazca [zna-**laz**-tsa] m. finder

znaleźne [zna-**leźh**-ne] n.
finder's reward; finder's share

znamienny [zna-**myen**-ni] adj. m.
significant; characteristic

znamię [zna-my**an**] n. stigma;
mole; trait; birthmark

znany [**zna**-ni] adj. m. noted;
known; famed; familiar; well-
known; notorious; famous

znawca [**znav**-tsa] m. expert

znęcać się [zn**an**-tsaćh śh**an**]
v. torment; harass; ill-treat

znękany [zn**an**-ka-ni] adj. m.
dejected; harassed; wasted

znicz [**źn**eech] m. (holy) fire;
fireside; pilot-light

zniechęcać [źne-kh**an**-tsaćh] v.
discourage; sicken; indispose

zniecierpliwić się [źne-**ćh**er-
-plee-veećh śh**an**] v. grow
impatient; get vexed; lose
patience; become annoyed

znieczulić [źne-**choo**-leećh] v.
anesthetize; deaden; harden

zniedołężniały [źne-do-w**an**-
-zhńa-wi] adj. m. impotent;
decrepit; infirm; disable; feeble
(old man); without force

zniekształcać [źne-**kshtaw**-
-tsaćh] v. deform; disfigure;
distort; put out of shape

zniemczać [**źń**em-chaćh] v.
Germanize; make into a German; force to accept German
identity or citizenship

znienacka [źne-**nats**-ka] adv. all
of a sudden; unawares

znienawidzieć [źne-na-**vee**-
-dźheećh] v. grow to hate;
loathe; come to detest

znieprawić [źne-**pra**-veećh] v.
deprave; demoralize; debauch

zniesienie [źne-**śhe**-ńe] n.
abrogation; abolition; repeal

zniesławienie [źne-swa-**vye**-ńe]
n. defamation; slander

zniewaga [źne-**va**-ga] f. insult

zniewalać [źne-va-**lać**] v.
coerce; rape; captivate; win

znikać [**źń**ee-kaćh] v. vanish

zniewieściały [źne-vyeśh-**ćh**a-
-wi] adj. m. effeminate; sissy

znikąd [źńee-**kownt**] adv. from
nowhere; out of nowhere

znikomy [źńee-**ko**-mi] adj. m.
perishable; negligible; minute

zniszczeć [**źń**eesh-chećh] v.

decay; go to ruin; be worn out
zniszczenie [zńeesh-che-ńe] n.
destruction; ravage; ruin;
havoc; annihilation
zniszczyć [zńeesh-chićh] v.
destroy; ruin; wear out;
ravage; annihilate; waste
zniweczyć [zńee-ve-chićh] v.
annihilate; wreck; lay waste
zniżać [znee-zhaćh] v. lower
zniżka [zneezh-ka] f. reduction;
decline; slump; drop; fall
znosić [zno-śheećh] v. annul;
endure; carry down; ware out
znośny [znośh-ni] adj. m.
tolerable; bearable; so-so; fair
znowu [zno-voo] adv. again;
anew; once again; afresh
znój [znooy] m. toil; sweat
znów [znoof] adv. again; anew
znudzenie [znoo-dze-ńe] n.
boredom; weariness; tedium;
till one is sick and tired
znużenie [znoo-zhe-ńe] n.
weariness; fatigue (people,
metals etc.); oppression
zobaczyć [zo-ba-chićh] v. see
zobojętnić [zo-bo-yant-ńeećh]
v. neutralize; make indifferent
zobojętnieć [zo-bo-yant-ńeećh]
v. grow indifferent; grow
listless; become apathetic
zobowiązać [zo-bo-vyown-
-zaćh] v. oblige; obligate;
bind to do; pin down to do
zobowiązanie [zo-bo-vyown-za-
-ńe] n. obligation; com-
mitment; engagement
zobrazować [zob-ra-zo-vaćh] v.
illustrate; describe; depict
zogniskować [zog-ńees-ko-
-vaćh] v. focus; concentrate
zohydzać [zo-khi-dzaćh] v.
defame; make loathsome; sicken of; render repugnant
zoolog [zo-o-log] m. zoologist
zorza północna [zo-zha poow-
-nots-na] f. aurora borealis
zostać [zos-taćh] v. remain;
stay; become; get to be; be
left; turn (green etc.)
zostawiać [zos-tav-yaćh] v.
leave; abandon; put aside

z powodu [z po-vo-doo] prep.
because of; owing to; due to
z powrotem [z pov-ro-tem] adv.
back; backwards; on the way
back (home, to work, etc.)
zrabować [zra-bo-vaćh] v. rob
z rana [z ra-na] adv. in the
morning; during the morning
zranić [zra-ńeećh] v. wound;
injure; hurt (feelings); mangle
zrastać [zras-taćh] v. grow into
one; fuse; heal up; blend
zrazu [zra-zoo] adv. at first
zrażać [zra-zhaćh] v. set
against; alienate; estrange;
antagonize; discourage
zrąb [zrownp] m. frame (work);
clearing; trunk; shell
zrąbać [zrown-baćh] v, hew;
cut down; hack; chop; pick to
pieces; prang (a target)
zrealizować [zre-a-lee-zo-vaćh]
v. realize; actualize; execute
zredagować [zre-da-go-vaćh] v.
draw up; compose; edit; draft
zresztą [zresh-town] adv.
1. moreover; besides; 2. after
all; though; anyway; in the
end; ah, well, no matter
zręczność [zranch-nośhćh] f.
cleverness; dexterity; skill
zrobić [zro-beećh] v. make; do;
turn; execute; perform
zrodzić [zro-dźheećh] v. give
birth; beget; originate
zrosnąć się [zros-nownćh
śhan] v. grow into one; fuse;
blend; set; heal up; knit
zrozpaczony [zros-pa-cho-ni] adj.
m. desperate; brokenhearted
zrozumiały [zro-zoo-mya-wi] adj.
m. intelligible; understandable
zrozumieć [zro-zoo-myećh] v.
understand; grasp (mentally);
see; make out; comprehend
zrozumienie [zro-zoo-mye-ńe] n.
understanding; sympathy; (legal) sense; mental grasp; comprehension; spirit; sense
zrównać [zroov-naćh] v. level;
make even; align; equalize
zrównoważyć [zroov-no-va-
-zhićh] v. balance; equalize;

equilibrate; compensate for

zróżniczkować [zroozh-ńeech--ko-vaćh] v. differentiate

zryć [zrićh] v. dig up; furrow

zrywać [zri-vaćh] v. rip; tear off; tear down; pick; quarrel

z rzadka [z zhad-ka] adv. rarely

zrządzenie losu [zzhown-dze-ńe lo-soo] n. fate; decree of fate

zrzeczenie się [zzhe-che-ńe śhan] n. resignation; renunciation; renouncement; abdication; relinquishment

zrzeszenie [zzhe-she-ńe] n. association; union

zrzęda [zzhan-da] m. grumbler

zrzucać [zzhoo-tsaćh] v. throw (down); buck off; drop; shed

zrzut lotniczy [zzhoot lot-ńee--chi] m. drop (from plane)

zsiadać [zśha-daćh] v. dismount; descend from; get off

zstąpić [zstown-peećh] v. descend; step down (one time); come down

zstępować [zstan-po-vaćh] v. descent; step down

zsyłać [zsi-waćh] v. deport; exile; send (down); inflict

zsyłka [zsiw-ka] f. deportation

zsypywać [zsi-pi-vaćh] v. heap up; pour off; shoot into

zszyć [zshićh] v. sew together

zubożeć [zoo-bo-zhećh] v. impoverish; grow poor; pauperize; reduce to poverty

zuch [zookh] m. brave fellow

zuchwalstwo [zockh-val-stvo] n. insolence; audacity; cheek; impudence; perkiness

zuchwały [zookh-va-wi] adj. m. insolent; impudent; bold

zupa [zoo-pa] f. soup

zupełny [zoo-pew-ni] adj. m. entire; whole; total; out and out; utter; outright; strict

zużycie [zoo-zhi-ćhe] n. consumption; wear and tear; waste; expenditure (of time)

zużytkować [zoo-zhit-ko-vaćh] v. utilize; use up; exploit

zużyty [zoo-zhi-ti] adj. m. worn out; used up; wasted; trite

zwać [zvaćh] v. call; name

zwalczyć [zval-chićh] v. overpower; overcome; cope; strive; stand against; subdue

zwalić [zva-leećh] v. demolish; fell; collapse; pile up; knock down; tumble down; dump

zwalniać [zval-ńaćh] v. release; loosen; let go; disengage; slow dawn; vacate

zwał [zvaw] m. heap; bank; pile

zwapnienie [zvap-ńe-ńe] n. calcification

zwarcie [zvar-ćhe] n. short (circuit); contraction; infighting adv. densely; closely

zwariować [zvar-yo-vaćh] v. go mad; go crazy; become insane; alter (a composition)

zwarzyć [zva-zhićh] v. boil; nip; frost damage; turn sour; blight

zważać [zva-zhaćh] v. pay attention; weigh (words); consider; give heed; have regard

zważyć [zva-zhićh] v. weigh; consider; give heed; regard

zwąchać [zvown-khaćh] v. smell out; get wind; sniff; scent; nose out; get wind of

zwątpić [zvownt-peećh] v. despair of; lose hope; give up

zwędzić [zvan-dźheećh] v. swipe; sneak; pinch; pilfer

zwęglić [zvang-leećh] v. carbonize; char; get charred

zwęzić [zvan-źheećh] v. narrow down; contract; restrict; confine; reduce width

zwiady [zvya-di] pl. reconnaissance; scouting; reconnoitring; surveying patrol

zwiastować [zvyas-to-vaćh] v. announce; herald; foreshadow

zwiastowanie [zvyas-to-va-ńe] n. Annunciation

zwiastun [zvyas-toon] m. harbinger; herald; omen; forerunner; precursor

związać [zvyown-zaćh] v. bind; fasten; join; tie up; strap; frame; lash together; link

związek [zvyown-zek] m. alliance; connection; bond;

compound; tie; trade union
zwichnąć [zveekh-n<u>ow</u>nćh] v.
strain; dislocate; disjoin;
luxate; warp; ruin (a career)
zwichnięcie [zveekh-ńan-ćhe]
n. dislocation; luxation; sprain
zwiedzać [zvye-dzaćh] v. visit;
see the sights; tour (a
country); see; inspect
zwiedzanie [zvye-dza-ńe] n.
sightseeing; touring
zwierciadło [zvyer-ćhad-wo] n.
mirror; reflection; looking glass
zwierz [zvyesh] n. beast of prey
**zwierzać się [zvye-zhaćh
śh<u>an</u>]** v. disclose a secret;
confide in. ..
zwierzchnik [zvyezh-khńeek] m.
boss; superior; chief; lord;
master; suzerain; feudal lord
**zwierzchnictwo [zvyezh-
-khńeets-tvo]** n. sovereignty;
superior of rank; authority;
supreme power; control
zwierzę [zvye-zh<u>an</u>] n. animal
zwierzyna [zvye-zhi-na] f. game
(animals); game
zwierzyniec [zvye-zhi-ńets] m.
zoo; zoological garden; zodiac
zwieszać [zvye-shaćh] v. hang
low; let hang down; droop;
dangle; hang down
zwietrzeć [zvye-tshećh] v.
decompose; go stale; spoil
zwiewać [zvye-vaćh] v. cut
and run; blow away; run away
zwiędły [zvy<u>an</u>d-wi] adj. m.
withered; wilted; faded
zwiędnąć [zvy<u>an</u>d-n<u>ow</u>nćh] v.
wither (away); wilt; fade
zwiększyć [zvy<u>an</u>k-shićh] v.
increase; magnify; heighten
zwięzły [zvy<u>an</u>z-wi] adj. m.
concise; brief; terse; compact
zwijać [zvee-yaćh] v. roll up;
wind up; coil; twist up; furl
zwilżać [zveel-zhaćh] v.
moisten; wet; dampen (often)
zwilżyć [zveel-zhićh] v.
moisten; wet; dampen (once)
zwinąć [zvee-n<u>ow</u>nćh] v. roll
up; wind up; coil up; twist up;
furl; take in (sails); fold

zwinny [zveen-ni] adj. m. agile;
nimble; deft; dexterous; lis-
some; light-fingered; light
zwisać [zvee-saćh] v. hang
down; droop; dangle; sag;
flag; overhang; beetle
zwlekać [zvle-kaćh] v. delay
zwłaszcza [zvwash-cha] adv.
particularly; chiefly; especially;
most of all; specially
zwłoka [zvwo-ka] f. delay;
respite; lag; postponement
zwłoki [zvwo-kee] n. corpse
zwodzić [zvo-dźheećh] v.
delude; deceive; mislead; let
down; lower
zwolenniczka [zvo-len-ńeech-ka]
f. adherent; follower; advocate
zwolennik [zvo-len-ńeek] m.
adherent; follower; advocate
zwolna [zvol-na] adv. slowly
zwolnieć [zvol-ńećh] v. slow
down; slack off; relax; slacken
zwolnienie [zvol-ńe-ńe] n.
1. dismissal; release; acquittal;
sack; exemption; 2. slowing
zwoływać [zvo-wi-vaćh] v. call
together; assemble; convene
zwój [zvooy] m. roll; reel; coil
zwracać [zvra-tsaćh] v. return;
give back; pay (attention)
zwrot [zvrot] m. 1. turn;
2. restitution; restoration; refund 3. revulsion; 4. phrase
zwrotka [zvrot-ka] f. stanza
zwrotnica [zvrot-ńee-tsa] f.
switch (large) steering
zwrotnik [zvrot-ńeek] m. tropic
zwrotny [zvrot-ni] adj. m.
flexible; returnable; repayable
**zwrócić się [zvroo-ćheećh
śh<u>an</u>]** v. turn (to); give back
zwycięski [zvi-ćh<u>an</u>s-kee]
adj. m. victorious; triumphant;
triumphal; winning (team, etc.)
zwycięstwo [zvi-ćh<u>an</u>s-tvo] n.
victory; triumph; win
zwyciężać [zvi-ćh<u>an</u>-zhaćh] v.
conquer; win; prevail; over-
come; get the upper hand
zwyczaj [zvi-chay] m. custom;
habit; fashion; usage; practice
zwyczajny [zvi-chay-ni] adj. m.

usual; ordinary; common; normal; regular; plain; simple
zwyczajowy [zvi-cha-yo-vi] adj. m. customary; regular; usual
zwykły [zvik-wi] adj. m. common
zwyrodniały [zvi-rod-ńa-wi] adj. m. degenerate; degenerated
zwyrodnienie [zvi-rod-ńe-ńe] n. degeneration; degradation
zwyżka [zvizh-ka] f. rise (of prices); advance (of stocks)
zwyżka cen [zvizh-ka tsen] f. price rise; price increase
zygzak [zig-zak] m. zigzag
zysk [zisk] m. gain; profit
zyskać [zis-kaćh] v. gain; earn
zyskowność [zis-kov-nośhćh] f. profitability; remunerativeness; lucrativeness
zyskowny [zis-kov-ni] adj. m. profitable; lucrative
zza [zza] prep. from behind
zziajać się [zźha-yaćh śhan] v. get out of breath; tire oneself out; become dog-tired
zzielenieć [zźhe-le-ńećh] v. turn green; become green
zziębnąć [zźhanb-nownćh] v. feel cold; be chilled to the bone; become cold
zziębnięty [zźhanb-ńan-ti] adj. m. chilled (to the bone)
zżyć się [zzhićh śhan] v. become familiar (with); grow accustomed (to)
zżymać [zzhi-maćh] v. wring
zżynać [zzhi-naćh] v. cut down; reap (corn with a scythe); mow (the grass etc.)
zżywać się [zzhi-vaćh śhan] v. grow familiar; reconcile

Ź

źdźbło [źhdźhbwo] n. stalk; blade; trifle; a bit; a little
źle [źhle] adj. n. & adv. ill; wrong; badly; falsely; mis-

takenly; improperly; poorly
źrebak [źhre-bak] m. colt
źrebię [źhre-byan] n. foal; colt
źrenica [źhre-ńee-tsa] f. pupil
źródlany [źhrood-la-ni] adj. m. spring (water); of spring
źródło [źhrood-wo] n. spring; source; well; fountain head
źródłosłów [źhhrood-wo-swoof] m. root of a ward; etymology; radical of a word
źródłowy [źhrood-wo-vi] adj. m. original; spring (water)

Ż

żaba [zha-ba] f. frog
żaden [zha-den] pron. none; neither; not any; no one; no-
żagiel [zha-gyel] m. sail
żakiet [zha-kyet] m. jacket
żal [zhal] m. regret; grief; sorrow; remorse; grudge; rancor; compunction; soreness
żalić się [zha-leećh śhan] v. complain; lament; find fault
żaluzja [zha-looz-ya] f. blind
żałoba [zha-wo-ba] f. mourning
żałobny marsz [zha-wob-ni marsh] m. funeral march
żałosny [zha-wos-ni] adj. m. lamentable; wretched; plaintive; piteous; deplorable
żałość [zha-wośhćh] f. grief; desolation; sorrow; deep sorrow; emotional suffering
żałować [zha-wo-vaćh] v. regret; be sorry; mourn
żar [zhar] m. heat; glow; ardor
żarcie [zhar-ćhe] n. swill; dub
żargon [zhar-gon] m. jargon
żarliwość [zhar-lee-vośhćh] f. ardor; zeal; earnestness
żarliwy [zhar-lee-vi] adj. m. ardent; zealous; fervent
żarłoczny [zhar-woch-ni] adj. m. greedy; voracious; gluttonous
żarłok [zhar-wok] m. glutton

żarówka [zha-roof-ka] f. light bulb; electric bulb; bulb

żart [zhart] m. joke; jest; quip

żartować [zhar-to-vaćh] v. joke; make fun; poke fun; trifle; jest; make sport

żarzyć [zha-zhićh] v. glow; anneal; incandesce

żąć [zhownćh] v. mow; cut; reap (corn with a sickle)

żądać [zhown-daćh] v. demand; require; exact; stipulate; postulate; claim

żądanie [zhown-da-ńe] n. demand; claim (for damages); requirement; stipulation

żądło [zhownd-wo] n. sting; (snake) fang; dart

żądny [zhownd-ni] adj. m. eager (for); anxious; greedy; avid (of fame, honors, etc.)

żądny przygód [zhownd-ni pzhi-goot] adventurous (man)

że [zhe] conj. that; then; as

żebrać [zhe-braćh] v. beg

żebraczka [zhe-brach-ka] f. beggar; pauper (girl, woman)

żebrak [zhe-brak] m. beggar (men); pauper; mendicant

żebranina [zhe-bra-ńee-na] f. beggary; begging; alms

żebro [zhe-bro] n. rib; fin

żeby [zhe-bi] conj. so as; in order that; if; may; if only

żeglarski [zhe-glar-skee] adj. m. nautical; seaman's (life etc.)

żeglarstwo [zhe-glar-stvo] n. sailing; navigation; seamanship

żeglarz [zhe-glash] m. seaman; sailor; mariner; seafarer

żeglować [zhe-glo-vaćh] v. sail; navigate (the seas, the ocean)

żeglowny [zhe-glov-ni] adj. m. navigable (river, canal, etc.)

żegluga [zhe-gloo-ga] f. navigation; shipping; sailing

żegnać [zheg-naćh] v. bid farewell; bless; bid good-bye; see off; bid farewell

żelatyna [zhe-la-ti-na] f. jelly

żelazko [zhe-laz-ko] n. press-iron; cutting iron; edger

żelazny [zhe-laz-ni] adj. m. iron

żelazo [zhe-la-zo] n. iron; armor

żelazobeton [zhe-la-zo-be-ton] m. reinforced concrete

żelaztwo [zhe-las-tvo] n. scrap iron; hardware; iron junk

żelbet [zhel-bet] m. reinforced concrete; ferro-concrete

żeliwo [zhe-lee-vo] n. cast iron

żenić [zhe-ńeećh] v. marry

żenować [zhe-no-vaćh] v. embarrass; disconcert; nonplus

żeński [zheń-skee] adj. m. female; feminine; women's

żer [zher] m. food; prey; feeding

żerdka [zherd-ka] f. (small) perch

żerdź [zherdźh] f. perch; rod

żłobek [zhwo-bek] m. crib

żłobić [zhwo-beećh] v. channel; erode; furrow; groove

żłób [zhwoop] m. trough; crib

żmija [zhmee-ya] f. viper; adder; poisonous snake

żmudny [zhmood-ni] adj. m. uphill; toilsome; strenuous

żniwiarka [zhńee-vyar-ka] f. harvester; reaper

żniwo [zhńee-vo] n. harvest

żołądek [zho-wown-dek] m. stomach; belly; the abdomen

żołądź [zho-wowndźh] f. acorn

żołd [zhowd] m. (soldier's) pay

żołdactwo [zhow-dats-tvo] n. soldiery; the soldiery

żołnierz [zhow-ńesh] m. soldier

żona [zho-na] f. wife

żonaty [zho-na-ti] adj. m. married; family man

żółć [zhoowćh] f. bile

żółciowy [zhoow-ćho-vi] adj. m. gall; peevish; harsh; biting

żółknąć [zhoow-knownćh] v. turn yellow; become yellow

żółtaczka [zhoow-tach-ka] f. jaundice; the yellows

żółtawy [zhoow-ta-vi] adj. m. yellowish; nankeen; sallow

żółtko [zhoowt-ko] n. yolk

żółty [zhoow-ti] adj. m. yellow

żółto-blady [zhoow-to-bla-di] adj. m. yellow-pale; sallow

żółw [zhoowf] m. turtle; tortoise

żółwi krok [zhoow-vee krok] m. snail's pace; turtle's gait

żrący [zhrown-tsi] adj. m.
corrosive; caustic; biting

żubr [zhoobr] m. (European-
-Polish) bison; aurochs

żuchwa [zhookh-va] f. jawbone

żuć [zhooćh] v. chew up;
chew; masticate; manducate

żucie [zhoo-ćhe] n. chewing;
mastication; (the) chew;
chewing up

żuk [zhook] m. beetle; dung
beetle

żulik [zhoo-leek] m. swindler;
rogue; cheat; street urchin

żuławy [zhoo-wa-vi] pl.
marshlands; lowlands; fertile
lowlands (river delta)

żupa [zhoo-pa] f. salt-works

żupan [zhoo-pan] m. old Polish
costume; (hist.) district chief

żur [zhoor] m. soup of
fermented meal; sour soup

żuraw [zhoo-rav] m. crane;
gantry; water-crane

żurawina [zhoo-ra-vee-na] f.
cranberry; cranberry shrub

żurnal [zhoor-nal] m. fashion
magazine (for women or men)

żużel [zhoo-zhel] m. slag; cinder;
scoria; clinker; cinder track

żużlobeton [zhoo-zhlo-be-ton] m.
slag concrete

żwawo [zhva-vo] adj. m. briskly;
alertly; apace; jauntily

żwawy [zhva-vi] adj. m. brisk;
quick; lively; spry; sprightly

żwir [zhveer] m. gravel

życie [zhi-ćhe] n. life; pep;
upkeep; lifetime; animation

życiodajny [zhi-ćho-day-ni] adj.
m. life-giving; vivifying

życiorys [zhi-ćho-ris] m.
biography; life history

życzenie [zhi-che-ńe] n. wish;
desire;request; greeting

życzliwy [zhich-lee-vi] adj. m.
favorable; friendly; kindly

żyć [zhićh] v. be alive; live;
exist; subsist; get along

Żyd [zhid] m. Jew; Hebrew

żydowski [zhi-dov-skee] adj. m.
Jewish; Judaic; Yiddish

żydostwo [zhi-dos-tvo] n. Jewry

Żydówka [zhi-doov-ka] f. Jewess

żyjący [zhi-yown-tsi] adj. m.
living; pl. the living

żyjątko [zhi-yownt-ko] n.
animalcule; tiny animal

żylak [zhi-lak] m. varix

żylakowy [zhi-la-ko-vi] adj. m.
varicose; of varicose vein

żylasty [zhi-las-ti] adj. m.
venous; stringy; sinewy

żyletka [zhi-let-ka] f. (razor)
blade; safety razor blade

żyła [zhi-wa] f. vein; seam; core;
strand; streak; lode; string

żyłka [zhiw-ka] f. vein; streak

żyrafa [zhi-ra-fa] f. giraffe

żyrant [zhi-rant] m. endorser

żyrować [zhi-ro-vaćh] v.
endorse; sign as payee

żytni [zhit-ńee] adj. m. rye

żytniówka [zhit-ńoov-ka] f. corn
vodka; gin; rye vodka

żyto [zhi-to] n. rye

żywcem [zhiv-tsem] adv. alive

żywe srebro [zhi-ve sreb-ro] n.
mercury; restless person

żywica [zhi-vee-tsa] f. resin

żywiec [zhi-vyets] m. cattle for
slaughter; live bait

żywić [zhi-veećh] v. feed;
nourish; cherish; feel; foster

żywioł [zhi-vyow] m. element

żywiołowy [zhi-vyo-wo-vi] adj.
m. elemental; spontaneous;
impulsive; impetuous

żywność [zhiv-nośhćh] f.
food; provisions; eatables;
victuals; (animal) fodder

żywo [zhi-vo] adv. quickly;
briskly; exp. make it snappy!

żywopłot [zhi-vo-pwot] m. hedge

żywość [zhi-vośhćh] f. animation; liveliness; vivacity; vitality; intensity; vigor; esprit

żywot [zhi-vot] m. life; womb;
belly; life (of a saint)

żywotnie [zhi-vot-ńe] adv.
vitally; exuberantly; luxuriantly

żywotność [zhi-vot-nośhćh]
f. vitality; liveliness; vivacity

żywotny [zhi-vot-ni] m. vital

żywy [zhi-vi] adj. m. alive; lively;
vivid; intense; gay; brisk; live;

acute; keen; bright
żyzność [zhiz-nośhćh] f.
   fertility; fruitfulness; richness
żyzny [zhiz-ni] adj. m. fertile;
   generous (soil); fruitful; fat;
   fecund; rich

Pogonowski
Phonetic Notation

PRONUNCIATION AS IN COMMON, EVERYDAY SPEECH

Complete Phonetics
for
English and Polish Speakers

POGONOWSKI PHONETIC NOTATION
POLISH PRONUNCIATION
FOR ENGLISH SPEAKERS

Pronunciation related to familiar English sounds
Pronunciation explained with speech organ diagrams

GUIDE TO PRONUNCIATION
AS IN COMMON, EVERYDAY SPEECH

The phonetic transcription follows all
entries. It is subdivided into syllables.

In multi-syllable words the stressed syllables
are printed in bold letters.

Polish vowels are pure and consist of one
sound only.

Polish vowels are never drawled as happens
often in English.

Schematic Ellipse of the
Tip of the Tongue Positions
Of Six Basic Polish Vowels

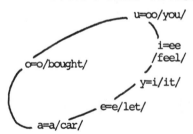

Polish nasalized vowels "ą" and "ę" are discussed on the next page.

Polish vowels:

A, a   as in: father, car;
                          in the phonetic guide: a

E, e, as in: let, met, get;   -"-   : e

I, i, as in: feel, keel;   -"-   : ee

O, o, as in: bought, not;   -"-   : o

U, u, as in: hook, too;   -"-   : oo

Y, y, as in: it, big, bib;   -"-   : i

The two *Polish nasalized vowels* can not be exactly described by English sounds.

The two Polish nasalized vowels:

Ą, ą, shown in the phonetic guide as: <u>own</u> =
                French sound of "on."
it is a single nasalized sound composed of:
a clear "o" as in "bought" followed by "w"
        and the ending with a trace of "n"

Ę, ę, shown in the phonetic guide as: <u>an</u> =
                French sound of "un."
it is a single nasalized sound composed of:
a clear "e" as in "pen" and the ending with
                a trace of "n"

POLISH CONSONANTS

Most Polish consonants are to be read as in English. However, voiced consonants become unvoiced at the end of any Polish word and immediately in front or behind of any unvoiced cosonat.

There are *no silent* Polish letters, except "c" in "ch" pronounced as [kh].

UNVOICED CONSONANTS: (without sounding the vocal cords)	VOICED CONSONANTS: (with sounding the vocal cords)
p = p	b = b
t = t	d = d
k = k	g = g
k in kie = k̲	g in gie = g̲
f = f	w = v
s = s	z = z
ś = śh	ź = źh
sz = sh	ż = zh
(sz = sh	rz = zh)
c = ts	dz = dz
ć = ćh	dź = dźh
cz = ch	dż = dzh
h & ch = kh	
l = l	

GLIDES:	NASALS:
r = r	m = m
j = y	n = n
ł = w	n & ni = ń

PRONUNCIATION OF POLISH CONSONANTS SPELLED OR VOICED DIFFERENTLY THAN IN ENGLISH

cz = ch in the phonetic guide - it is pronounced exactly like "ch" in English.

sz = sh in the phonetic guide - it is pronounced exactly like "sh" in English.

szcz = shch pronounced exactly like in "fresh cheese" in English.

h & ch = kh pronounced like in Scottish "loch."

ń & ni = n with an apostrophe - a nasal consonant as in "onion," or Spanish "n" as in "manana". It also occurs in Polish when "n" is followed by the vowel "i."

ni = ń when the "i" is followed by a vowel

ni = ń + "ee" when the "i" is followed by a consonant.

j = y - a gliding consonant - pronounced exactly like "y" in the English word "yes."

ł = w - a gliding consonant - pronounced like "w" in English.

r = r - a gliding consonant - it is trilled with the tip of the tongue.

g = g - in Polish it is always pronounced as in the English word "good."

gie = g underlined indicates a trace of an "e" sound after "g" and before the sound of "e" as in "let."

kie = k underlined indicates a trace of an "ee" sound after "k" and before the "e" sound, as in "pet."

PRONUNCIATION OF POLISH PALATAL CONSONANTS

Polish palatal consonants are pronounced by touching the upper palate with the tongue. They are:

ć = ch with an apostrophe over the "c"

ci = ć when the "i" is followed by a vowel

ci = ć + "ee" when the "i" is followed by a consonant

ć is pronounced like "t" in nature.

dź = dźh with an apostrophe over the "z" - pronounced like "dz" while touching the tooth ridge.

dż = dzh - pronounced like "dzh" while touching the upper palate.

ś = śh with an apostrophe over the "s" - pronounced like "sh" while touching the tooth ridge.

si = ś when the "i" is followed by a vowel

si = ś + "ee" when the "i" is followed by a consonant

ź = źh with an apostrophe over the "z" - pronounced like "zh" while touching the upper palate.

zi = ź when the "i" is followed by a vowel

zi = ź + "ee" when the "i" is followed by a consonant

(ż = rz) = zh (note: a dot over the "z"). It is pronounced like the "s" in measure.

ść = śhćh with apostrophes over "s" and "c" - two consonants produced by touching the ridge of the teeth ridge with the tongue while pronouncing each consonant separately.

SPEECH ORGAN DIAGRAM
for Polish palatal consonants
not used in the English language.

Explosives: air compressed behind lips and teeth, then
suddenly released: dź, dzi, [dźh]
and ć, ci, [ćh]
Fricatives: air flow with a continuous friction:
ź, zi, [źh], and ś, si, [śh].
The tip of the tongue is at the tooth ridge.

POLISH SOUND "R"
is fluttered and may be pronounced
like the Scottish "r"

Mouth is slightly open; tip of the tongue is raised;
it vibrates on the exhaling impulse and strikes the
tooth-ridge; sides of the tongue touch back teeth.
The tongue does not glide as far back as is needed
in the English "r."

**ZAPIS FONETYCZNY POGONOWSKIEGO
WYMOWA ANGIELSKA DLA POLAKÓW
ENGLISH PRONUNCIATION FOR POLES**

Pronunciation related to familiar Polish sounds
Pronunciation explained with speech organ diagrams.

**Uproszczona wymowa wyrażona zapisem polskim
i wytłumaczona przekrojami narządów mowy.**

Nie ulega wątpliwości, że zapoznanie się z językiem angielskim w dużej mierze polega na zapoznaniu się z angielskimi dzwiękami, których wiele różni się od wymowy polskiej.
Akcent, rytm i intonacja mają zasadnicze znaczenie w porozumiewaniu się.

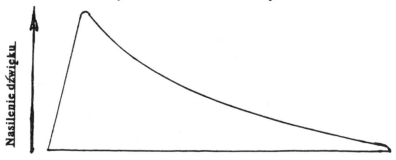

Często angielskie wyrazy można graficznie przedstawić powyższym wykresem dzwięku, intonacji, oraz akcentu (nacisku). Często początek słowa jest wymawiany w silniejszy sposób a następnie dźwięk *zamiera* ku końcowi słowa. Jednocześnie wymowa słów musi być jak najbardziej *swobodna*.

Należy unikać wszelkiego zmuszania się do mówienia w sposób sztuczny i nienaturalny.

Szkice narzadów mowy są pomocne w nauce wymowy słów angielskich. Ilustrują one różnice w używaniu narządów mowy przez mówiących po polsku i po angielsku. Ważne jest żeby pamiętać że przecinek u góry oznacza akcent na następującą po nim zgłoskę. Przecinek u dołu oznacza akcent słabszy, drugorzędny. Litery polskiego alfabetu są zastosowane jako podstawa znaków fonetycznych. Dwukropek zwiększa długość samogłoski.

Przy szkicach narządów mowy pokazane są angielskie samogłoski na obwodzie schematycznej elipsy ilustrującej pozycje języka. Oprocz dwunastu angielskich samogłosek, trzy postawowe dwugłoski angielskie zaznaczone są wewnątrz elipsy między początkową i końcową samogłoską dwugłoski. Początkowa część dwugłoski jest silniejsza niż końcowa. Cechą samogłosek angielskich, w przeciwieństwie do polskich, jest ich skłonność do przybierania dźwięków przejściowych i stawania się dwugłoskami. Trzeba pamiętać że w języku angielskim oznakowanie fonetyczne samogłosek może być tylko przybliżone. Zwłaszcza "e" fonetyczne jest mniej wyraźne niż po polsku. Samogłoska w końcówce, jak np. "nal" lub "bel" jest w fonetycznej wersji pominięta tak, że wymowa tych końcówek wymaga użycia dźwięku naturalnego zbliżonego do polskiego "y".

SPÓŁGŁOSKI ANGIELSKIE

Lista spółgłosek angielskich jest uzupełniona szkicami narządów mowy w układach odpowiadających dźwiękom, których się nie używa w języku polskim. Spółgłoski "seplenione" oznaczone literami "th" są jednymi z trudniejszych dźwięków angielskich. Jest ich pięć. Są one oznaczone podkreśleniem: s, t, d, dz, z. Wymowa ich jest wytłumaczona przy pomocy szkiców narządów mowy.

Angielskie "r" przypomina słabe rzężenie i jest inaczej a zarazem dużo słabiej wymawiane niż polskie "r". Angielskie "r" nie może być wymówione samodzielnie, jedynie przed lub po samogłosce.

Zmiękczone angielskie "n" [n] jak w "sing" [syn] różni się od polskiego "ń", które jest bliższe dźwiękowi w angielskim słowie "new" [ńju]. Zapis fonetyczny [n] zawiera w sobie ślad następującego dźwięku "g" lub "k."

Angielskie "h" jest prawie nieme w porównaniu do polskiego "h". Język i usta są w pozycji do następnego dźwięku i tylko lekkie tchnienie zaznacza dźwięk angielski "h."

Angielska przejściowa spółgłoska "w" [ł] jest niemożliwa do wypowiedzenia samodzielnie. Usta zaokrąglone w pozycji jak do "u," przejściowy dzwięk bliski jest polskiemu "ł." Usta i język szybko przechodzą do układu dla następującej samogłoski. W zapisie fonetycznym "ou" wymawia się jak "oł" a dźwięk "au" jak "ał."

Poza omówionymi powyżej, spółgłoski angielskie i polskie nie różnią się.

Większość angielskich współgłosek czyta się tak samo jak w języku polskim.

Dźwięczne spółgłoski na końcu słów angielskich pozostają dźwięczne w przeciwieństwie do polskich.

SPÓŁGŁOSKI
BEZDŹWIĘCZNE:

(bez dźwięku
strun głosowych)

SPÓŁGŁOSKI
DŹWIĘCZNE:

(z dźwiękiem
strun głosowych)

p = p	b = b
t = t	d = d
k & q = k	g = g
x = ks	
f = f	w = v
th = t̲ & s̲	th = d̲, d̲z̲ & z̲
s = s	z = z
sh = sz	zh = ż
c = ts	dz = dz
ch = cz	dzh = dż
hw = hł (why = hłaj)	l = l
h = prawie nieme	

GŁOSKI
PRZEJŚCIOWE:

GŁOSKI
NOSOWE:

r = r	m = m
y = j	n = n
w = ł	ng & nk = n̲

PRZEKRÓJ NARZĄDÓW MOWY
ANGIELSKI DŹWIĘK "TH"

Angielska "sepleniona" spółgłoska "th": koniec i przód języka szeroko spłaszczony, widzialny między zębami; ciągły przelot powietrza między zębami i wargami.

Głoska bezdźwięczna: [s̱] bath [ba:s̱]
      [ṯ] thank [ṯaenk]

Głoska dźwięczna: [ḏ] those [ḏouz]
  [dẕ] they [dẕej]
  [ẕ] bathing [bejẕyng]

ANGIELSKI DŹWIĘK "R"

Andielska spółgłoska "r": usta nieco otwarte; koniec języka uniesiony wklęsłym podgięciem ku tyłowi, nie dotyka podniebienia; boki języka dotykają zębów; wymowa możliwa tylko w przejściu od lub do samogłski -- przypomina lekkie rzężenie.

SCHEMATYCZNA ELIPSA POZYCJI KOŃCA JĘZYKA DLA DWUNASTU SAMOGŁOSEK ANGIELSKICH (WYMOWA AMERKAŃSKA)

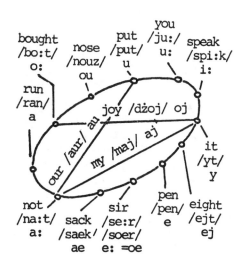

Trzy podstawowe dwugłoski angielskie -- diphtongs ['dyfto<u>n</u>s] -- są zaznaczone wewnątrz schematycznej elipsy pozycji końca języka przy wymawianiu dwunastu samogłosek angielskich.

STRUNY GŁOSOWE CZYLI FAŁDY GŁOSOWE VOCAL CHORDS OR RATHER VOCAL FOLDS

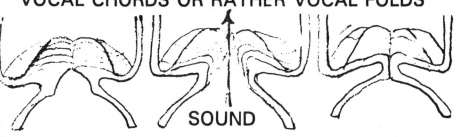

SOUND

PRODUCTION OF HUMAN VOICE

ENGLISH-POLISH

A

a [ej] art. jeden; pewien; pierwsza litera angielskiego alfabetu; pierwszej kategorii

A-O'k [ej okej] zupełnie gotów

aback [e'baek] adv. wstecz; w tył; do tyłu; nazad

abandon [e'baendon] v. opuszczać; porzucić; zarzucić; zaniechać; oddać się

abandonment [e'baendonment] s. opuszczenie; brak pohamowania; zrezygnowanie z

abashed [e'baeszt] adj. speszony; zmieszany (czymś)

abate ['ebejt] v. osłabiać; zmniejszać; mitygować; uciszyć; osłabić; anulować

abbey ['aebi] s. opactwo

abbreviate [e'bry:wjejt] v. skrócić; skracać

abbreviation [e'bry:wjejszyn] s. skrót; skrócenie; skracanie

ABC ['ej'bi:'si] alfabet

abdicate ['aebdykejt] v. zrzekać się (stanowiska); abdykować

abdomen ['aebdomen] s. brzuch

abduct [aeb'dakt] v. uprowadzić; uprowadzać; porwać; porywać (kogoś, coś)

abhor [eb'ho:r] v. mieć odrazę

abide, abode, abode [e'bajd, e'boud, e'boud]

abide [e'bajd] v. znosić; obstawać; dotrzymywać; czekać (na coś); trwać

ability [e'bylyty] s. zdolność

abject ['aebdżekt] adj. podły; nędzny, nikczemny, skrajny

abjure [eb'dżuer] v. poprzysiąc

able ['ejbl] adj. zdolny; zdatny; utalentowany; poczytalny

abnormal [aeb'no:rmel] adj. anormalny; nieprawidłowy

aboard [e'bo:rd] adv. na pokładzie; na statku; w

pociągu; w tramwaju, etc.

abode [e'boud] v. był posłuszny

abode [e'boud] s. mieszkanie; v. proszę zobaczyć: abide

abolish [e'bolysz] v. obalić; znieść; znosić; obalać

abolition [aebe'lyszyn] n. obalenie (ustawy, etc.); zniesienie (zwyczaju, etc.)

A-bomb ['ejbom] s. bomba atomowa; bomba jądrowa

abominable [e'bomynebl] adj. ohydny; wstrętny; obrzydliwy

abortion [e'bo:rszyn] s. przerwanie ciąży; poronienie

abound [e'baund] v. obfitować

about [e'baut] adv. naokoło; około; dookoła; po (czymś); o; wobec (kogś); przy

about [e'baut] prep. o; przy; odnośnie; naokoło; wokoło

about to [e'baut tu] gotów do

above [e'baw] adv. powyżej; w górze; wyżej; na górze

above [e'baw] prep. nad; ponad

above [e'baw] adj. powyższy

abrasive [e'brejsyw] adj. ścierny; s. scierniwo

abreast [e'brest] adv. obok; rzędem; ramię przy ramieniu

abridge [e'brydż] v. skrócić

abroad [e'bro:d] adv. zewnątrz; za granicą; za granicę; w dal

abrogate ['aebrogejt] v. obalić; unicestwić; odwoływać; znosić (ustawę, zarządzenie etc.)

abrupt [e'brapt] adj. nagły; lapodarny; szorstki; urwany; ostry; os-chły; obcesowy

abscess ['aebses] s. wrzód; ropień (na skórze, etc.)

absence ['aebsens] s. brak; (czyjaś) nieobecność; niestawiennictwo (roztargnienie)

absent ['aebsent] adj. nieobecny; v. być nieobecnym

absent-minded ['aebsent-'majndyd] adj. roztargniony

absolute ['aebselu:t] adj. absolutny; zupełny; czysty (alkohol) nieodwołalny; prawdziwy

absolutely ['aebselu:tly] adv. absolutnie; oczywiście

absolve [eb'zolv] v. rozgrzeszyć;
darować; uwolnić; oczyś-
cić; zwolnić; zwalniać
absorb [eb'zorb] v. chłonąć;
wchłonąć; tłumić; absorbować; złagodzić (uderzenie)
abstain [eb'stejn] v. powstrzymywać się (od czegoś);
być abstynentem; pościć
abstention [eb'stenszyn] s.
wstrzymanie się (od jedze-nia);
powstrzymywanie sie
abstinence ['aebstynens] s.
wstrzemięźliwość; pow-
strzymywanie abstynencja
abstract ['aebstraekt] adj.
oderwany; abstrakcyjny; s.
abstrakcja; streszczenie; v.
streszczać; abstrahować; odrywać; ukraść; sprzątnąć;
wyabstrahować; wydobyć
absurd [eb'se:rd] adj. absurdalny;
bezsensowny; niedorzeczny
abundance [e'bandens] s.
obfitość; znaczna ilość; dostatek; zasobność
abundant [e'bandent] adj. obfity;
liczny; bogaty; zasobny (w
coś); płodny (urodzajny)
abuse [e'bju:s] s. nadużycie;
obelga; [e'bju:z] v. obrażać;
nadużywać; lżyć; obrzucać
obelgami (przekleństwami)
abyss [e'bys] n. otchłań;
przepaść; głębia; pierwotny
chaos (we wszechświecie)
acacia [e'kejsze] s. akacja
academic [,aeke'demyk] adj.
akademicki; jałowy; s. uczony
academy [e'kaedemy] s. akademia; uniwersytet
accelerate [aek'selerejt] v.
przyspieszać; przyśpieszyć
accelerator [aek'selerejter] s.
przyspieszacz; gaźnik; akce-
lerator; katalizator
accent ['aeksent] s. wymowa;
akcent; [aek'sent] v. ak-
centować; uwydatniać; da-
wać nacisk; znakować
accept [ek'sept] v. akceptować;
zgadzać się na; zechcieć
wziąć (przyjąć); uznać

acceptable [ek'septebl] adj. do
przyjęcia (możliwy); znośny;
zadawalający; mile widziany
access ['aekses] s. dostęp
accessible [aek'sesybl] adj.
dostępny; przystępny
accession [aek'seszyn] s.
wstąpienie; dostęp; dojście;
przystąpienie; objęcie (urzędu)
accessory [aek'sesery] s. dodatek; adj. dodatkowy; uboczny; pomocniczy (w zbrodni)
access road ['aekses roud] droga
dojazdowa (do miasta, etc.)
accident ['aeksydent] s. traf;
wypadek; katastrofa; awaria
accidental [,aeksy'dentl] adj.
przypadkowy; nieważny; mało
znaczący; uboczny
acclimatize [e'klajmetajz] v.
(za)aklimatyzować
accommodate [e'komedejt] v.
przystosować; pogodzić; zakwaterować; wygodzić; wy-
świadczyć (pysługą); za-
łagodzić (spór, etc.)
accommodation [e,kome'dejszyn]
s. wygoda; dostosowanie;
kwatera; pogodzenie się;
ugoda; kompromis; usługa
accompaniment
[e'kampenyment] s.
towarzyszenie; akom-
paniament; dodatki
accompany [e'kampeny] v.
towarzyszyć; odprowadzać;
akompaniować
accomplice [e'komplys] s.
współsprawca; współwinny
accomplish [e'kamplysz] v.
dokonać; spełnić; zre-
alizować; udoslonalić
accomplished [e'kamplyszt] adj.
utalentowany; znakomity;
wykończony; z ogładą;
skończony (artysta itp.)
accomplishment
[e'kamplyszment] s.
osiągnięcie; realizacja;
dokonanie; wykonanie; ogłada
accord [e'ko:rd] s. zgoda; v.
uzgadniać; dać; licować
according [e'ko:rdyng] prep.

według; zależnie od
accordingly [e'ko:rdyngly] adv.
odpowiednio; więc; zatem
accost [e'kost]v. zaczepić
(kogoś); zagadnąć (kogoś);
przystąpić do kogoś
account [e,kaunt] s. rachunek;
sprawozdanie; v. wyliczać;
wytłumaczyć; uważać; oce-
niać; być odpowiedzialnym
account for [e'kaunt fo:r] v. dać
powód; wytłumaczyć
accountant [e'kauntent] s.
księgowy, księgowa
accounting [e'kauntyng] s.
księgowość
accumulate [e'kju:mju,lejt] v.
gromadzić; zbierać; piętrzyć
accuracy ['aekjuresy] s.
ścisłość; dokładność;
celność (strzału)
accusative [e'kju:zetyw] s.
biernik (gramatyka)
accusation [aekju:zejszyn] s.
oskarżenie; winienie (kogoś);
posądzenie (o coś)
accuse [e'kju:z] v. oskarżać
accused [e'kju:zd] adj.
oskarżony; oskarżona
accustom [e'kastem] v.
przyzwyczajać; przyzwyczaić
accustomed [e'kastemd] adj.
przyzwyczajony (do); zwykły;
przywykły; zwyczajny
ace [ejs] s. as; oczko (in cards)
ache [ejk] s. ból; v. boleć
achieve [e'czi:w] v. dokonać;
osiągnąć (cel); zdobywać
(sławę); dochodzic (do)
achievement [e'czi:wment] s.
osiągnięcie; wyczyn; zdobycz
aching ['ejkyng] adj. bolący
acid ['aesyd] adj. kwaśny; s.
kwas; kwaśna substancja
acid trip ['aesyd tryp]
halucynacje po narkotyku
acknowledge [ek'nołłydż] v.
uznać; potwierdzić; przy-
znać (się); nagrodzić
acknowledgement
[ek'nołłydżment] s.
przyznanie; potwierdzenie;
uznanie; dowód uznania

acoustics [e'ku:styks] pl.
akustyka
acquaint [e'kłejnt] v.
zaznajomić; zapoznać;
zapoznawać (kogoś)
acquaintance [e'kłejntens] s.
znajomość; znajomy
acquiesce [,aekły'es] v. zgadzać
się; przyzwalać (bez oporu);
przychylić się (do prośby)
acquire [e'kłajer] v. nabywać
acquisition [,aekły'zyszyn] s.
nabytek; nabycie; zdobycz
acquit [e'kłyt] v. zwolnić;
wywiązać się; spławić; uniewinnić (kogoś); uiścić
acquittal [e'kłytl] s. zwolnienie;
uiszczenie; wywiązanie się
acre [ejker] s. akr; morga amery
-kańska; 4047 m. kwadr.
acrid ['aekryd] adj. żrący; ostry;
cierpki; kwaskowaty
acrimonious [,aekry'mounjes]
adj. szorstki; zjadliwy; cierpki;
zgorzkniały; tetryczny
acrobat ['aekrebaet] s. akrobata
across [e'kros] adv. w poprzek;
na krzyż; prep. przez; na
przełaj; po drugiej stronie
(rzeki, ulicy, itp.)
act [aekt] v. czynić; działać;
postępować; s. czyn; akt;
uczynek; akt sztuki; uchwała
(parlamentu); ustawa
action ['aekszyn] s. działanie;
czyn; akcja; ruch; proces
active ['aektyw] adj. czynny;
obrotny; rzutki; ożywiony;
żywy; ożywiony; bujny
activity [aek'tywyty] s.
działalność; czynność;
ożywienie; ruch
actor ['aekter] s. aktor
actress ['aektrys] s. aktorka
actual ['aekczuel] adj. istotny;
faktyczny; bieżący; obecny
actually ['aekczuely] adv.
rzeczywiście; obecnie; istotnie; faktycznie; nawet
acute [e'kju:t] adj. ostry;
przynikliwy; bystry
ad [aed] s. ogłoszenie (reklama)
(pot. od advertisement)

adapt [e'daept] v. dostosować; przerobić; przystosować; dostrajać; nadawać się (do)
adaptation ['aedaep'tejszyn] s. przystosowanie; dostrojenie
add [aed] v. dodać; doliczyć
addict [aedykt] s. nałogowiec; v. oddawać; poświęcać się
addicted [e'dyktyd] adj. nałogowy; nałogowo poświęcający się (czemuś)
addition [e'dyszyn] s. dodawanie; dodatek; (in addition = ponadto)
additional [e'dyszynl] adj. dodatkowy; dalszy
address [e'dres] s. adres; mowa; odezwa; v. zwracać się; adresować (do); skierować (prośbą); przemawiać
addressee [,aedre'si:] s. adresat; adresatka (listu itp.)
adequate ['aedykłyt] s. stosowny; dostateczny; kompetentny; właściwy; trafny
adhere [ed'hjer] v. lgnąć; należeć; trzymać; przylegać
adhesion [ed'hi:żyn] s. lepkość; zrost; przyleganie; przywieranie do czegoś
adhesive [ed'hi:syw] adj. lepki; przylegający; s. plaster
adjacent [e'dżejsent] adj. przyległy; sąsiedni
adjective ['aeddżyktyw] s. przymiotnik; adj. dodatkowy
adjoin [e'ddżoyn] v. stykać się; sąsiadować; dołączać
adjourn [e'ddże:rn] v. odraczać; przesuwać; przerywać; zakończyć (obrady itp.)
adjust [e'ddżast] v. dostosowywać; uregulować; nastawić; pogodzić
administer [ed'mynyster] v. dawać; sprawować; administrować; zarządzać
administration [ed,myny'strejszyn] s. zarząd; rząd; administracja; ministerstwo; wymiar (kary itp.)
administrative [ed'mynystrejtyw] adj. administracyjny

administrator [ed'mynystrejtor] s. zarządca; administrator
admirable ['aedmerebl] adj. godny podziwu; zachwycający
admiral ['aedmyrel] s. admirał
admiration [aedmy'rejszyn] s. podziw; zachwyt; przedmiot podziwu (zachwytu)
admire [ed'majer] v. podziwiać
admirer [ed'majrer] s. wielbiciel; wielbicielka (kogoś,czegoś)
admissible [ed'mysybl] adj. dopuszczalny; do przyjęcia
admission [ed'myszyn] s. wstęp; dostęp; przyznanie; uznanie; (dopływ); bilet wstępu
admission ticket [ed'myszyn'tykyt] bilet wstępu
admit [ed'myt] v. wpuszczać; uznać; przyjmować; dopuścić (do); przyznać (rację)
admittance [ed'mytens] s. dostęp; przyjęcie; przyznanie się; wstęp; dopuszczenie
admonish [ed'monysz] v. upominać; ostrzegać; pouczać; strofować; namówić
ado [e'du] s. wrzawa; kłopot; trudności; grymasy; ceregiele; narzekania; fochy
adolescence [,aede'lesns] s. młodość (pokwitanie - dojrzałość); wiek młdzieńczy
adolescent [,aede'lesnt] adj. młodociany; dorastający
adopt [e'dopt] v. adoptować; przyjmować; akceptować; usynawiać; przybierać
adoption [e'dopszyn] s. adopcja; adaptacja; przyjęcie; przysposobienie; akceptacja; wybór; zastosowanie (pomysłu itp.)
adorable [e'do:rebl] adj. godny uwielbienia; bardzo miły
adoration [,aede:rejszyn] s. uwielbienie; wielka miłość
adore [e'do:r] v. czcić; uwielbiać; bardzo lubić; kochać; oddawać cześć
adorn [e'do:rn] v. zdobić; upiększać; być ozdobą
adrift [e'dryft] adv. na fali; na wodzie bez steru; zdany na

laskę losu
adult ['aedalt] adj. dorosły;
dojrzały; s. osoba dorosła
adulterate [e'dalterejt] v.
fałszować (żywność itp.);
podrabiać; zatruwać
adultery [e'daltery] s.
cudzołóstwo
advance [ed'waens] v. iść
(posuwać się) naprzód; po-
śpieszać; awansować;
przedkładać; popierać; pożyczać; adj. wysunięty;
wcześniejszy; w przodzie
advanced [ed'waenst] adj.
postępowy; światły; wysu-
nięty naprzód; stary; przedwczesny; czołowy; późny
advanced reservation [ed'waenst
rezerwejszyn] rezerwacja z
góry zamówiona (załatwiona)
advantage [ed'waentydż] s.
korzyść; pożytek; przewaga
advantageous [,aedwaen'tej-
dżes] adj.korzystny; zyskowny
adverb ['aedwe:rb] s. przysłówek
(oznaczający czas, sposób ...)
adversary ['aedwersery] s.
przeciwnik; wróg; oponent
adverse ['aedwe:rs] adj. wrogi;
przeciwny; szkodliwy; niechętny; niekorzystny
advertise ['aedwertajz] v.
ogłaszać; reklamować
advertisement ['edwertysment]
s. ogłoszenie; reklama
advertising ['aedwertajzyng] s.
reklama; ogłoszenie handlowe
advice [ed'wajs] s. rada;
informacje; porada; pouczenie
advisable [ed'wajzebl] adj.
wskazany; rozsądny; ostrożny
advise [ed'wajz] v. radzić;
powiadamiać; pouczać
adviser [ed'wajzer] s. doradca;
radca (prawny etc.)
advocate ['aedwekejt] v.
zalecać; bronić; s. rzecznik;
orędownik; adwokat (ka)
aerial ['eerjel] adj. powietrzny; s.
antena (radiowa etc.)
aeronautics [eere'no:tyks] pl.
aeronautyka; lotnictwo

aeroplane ['eereplejn] s. samolot
aesthetic [i:st̲etyk] adj.
estetyczny; wrażliwy na
piękno (sztukę itp.)
afar [e'fa:r] adv. daleko; z daleka
affair [e'feer] s. sprawa; interes;
romans; przedsięwzięcie
affect [e'fekt] v.
1. wpływać; oddziaływać;
wzruszać; 2, dotyczyć; udawać (ar-tystę, uczucia itp.)
affected [e'fektyd] adj.
dotknięty; przejęty; sztuczny
affection [e'fekszyn] s. uczucie;
przywiązanie; choroba; mi-
łość; afekt (do)
affectionate [e'fekszynyt] adj.
czuły; kochający; tkliwy (dla);
przywiązany (do)
affidavit [aef'ydejwyt] s.
poręczenie pod przysięgą
affinity [e'fynyty] s.
pokrewieństwo (z kimś);
przyciąganie; powinowactwo
affirm [e'fe:rm] v. potwierdzać;
zapewniać; zaręczać (że)
affirmation [,aefe:r'mejszyn] s.
twierdzenie; oświadczenie;
zapewnienie; zatwierdzenie
(wyroku w sądzie)
affirmative [e'fe:rmetyw] adj.
pozytywny; twierdzący
afflict [e'flykt] v. gnębić
affliction [e'flykszyn] s.
przygnębienie; choroba; ból;
cierpienie; schorzenie
affluence ['aefluens] s. dostatek;
bogactwo; obfitość; natłok
affluent ['aefluent] 1. adj. zamożny; 2. s. dopływ (rzeki)
afford [e'fo:rd] v. zdobyć się;
dostarczyć; stać na coś
affront [e'frant] v. znieważać
aficionado ['efisienado] s.
entuzjasta (walki byków etc.)
aflame [e'flejm] adv. w ogniu; w
podnieceniu; w zapale
afraid [e'frejd] adj.
przestraszony; wyrażający
rezerwę; w strachu (przed)
African ['aefryken] adj.
afrykański
Afro ['aefro] s. (niby) styl

afrykański (uczesania, ubioru)
after ['a:fte:r] prep. po; za;
odnośnie; według; poniekąd
after all ['a:fte: o:l] prep. jednak;
przecież; mimo wszystko
after that ['a:fte: daet]
następnie; potem; po; za
afternoon ['a:fte:rnu:n] s.
popołudnie; adj. popołudniowy
afterwards ['aftełerdz] adv.
później; potem; następnie
again [e'gen] adv. ponownie;
znowu; na nowo; więcej;
ponadto; nadto; jeszcze
again and again [e'gen end
e,gen] wciąż; ciągle
against [e'genst] prep. przeciw;
wbrew; na; pod; na wypadek
age [ejdż] s. wiek; stulecie;
czasy; epoka; v. starzeć się
aged ['ejdżyd] adj. stary;
sędziwy; wiekowy; w po-
deszłym wieku; zniszczony
age ten [ejdż ten] w wieku lat
dziesięciu; dziesięć lat
agency ['ejdżensy] s. ajencja;
działanie; pośrednictwo
agenda [e'dżenda] s. agenda;
lista; porządek dzienny
agent ['ejdżent] s. pośrednik;
ajent; czynnik; przedstawiciel
aggravate ['aegrewejt] v.
pogarszać; rozjątrzać; denerwować; działać na nerwy
aggression [e'greszyn] s.
napaść; agresja; agresyw-
ność; napastliwość
aggressive [e'gresyw] adj.
napastliwy; zaczepny; agre-
sywny; napastniczy
aggressor [e'grese:r] s.
napastnik; agresor
aghast [e'gaest] adj. przerażony;
ogłupiały; skonsternowany
agile ['aedżyl] adj. zwinny;
obrotny; zręczny; ruchliwy
agitate ['aedżytejt] v. poruszać;
miotać; agitować; wzruszać
agitation [,aedżytejszyn] s.
poruszenie; agitacja; ruch;
podniecenie; wzruszenie
agitator ['aedżytejter] s. agitator;
mieszadło; trzęsarka

agnostic ['aegnostyk] s.
agnostyk; adj. agnostyczny
ago [e'gou] adv. przed; ... temu
agonize ['aegenajz] v. męczyć
się; (za) dręczyć się
agony ['aegeny] s. śmiertelna
męka; katusze; spazm; agonia
agree [e'gri:] v. godzić się;
zgadzać się; uzgadniać
agree about [e'gri: e'baut] v.
zgadzać się co do ...
agree to [e'gri: tu] zgadzać się
(na); wyrażać zgodę (na)
agreeable [e'gri:ebl] adj. zgodny;
miły; chętny; sympatyczny
agreement [e'gri:ment] s. zgoda;
umowa; porozumienie; układ
agricultural [,aegry'kalczeral] adj.
rolniczy; rolny
agriculture [,aegry'kalczer] s.
rolnictwo; uprawa ziemi
agriculturist [,aegry'kalczeryst] s.
rolnik
ague ['ejgju:] s. febra; dreszcze;
malaria; zimnica
ahead [e'hed] adv. naprzód;
dalej; na przedzie; z przodu
aid [ejd] s. pomoc; pomocnik; v.
pomagać; subwencjonować
aide [ejd] s. asystent; pomocnik
AIDS [ejdz] s. nabyta strata
odporności prowadząca do
zapadniecia na raka, zapalenie
płóc, itd. (Acquired Immune
Defficieny Syndrome)
ailing ['ejlyng] s. choroba
aim [ejm] s. zamiar; cel; v.
celować (w coś); mierzyć;
wymierzyć; zamierzać; skierować; dążyć (do czegoś)
aimless ['ejmlys] adj. bezcelowy
air [eer] s. 1. powietrze; 2. mina;
postawa; wgląd; nastrój
air [eer] v. 1. wietrzyć;
2. obnosić się; nadawać
air base ['eerbejs] s. baza
lotnicza (wojskowa)
air brake ['eer,brejk] s. hamulec
na sprężone powietrze
air-conditioning [,eer-
-ken'dyszynyn] s. klimatyzacja
air compressor [,eer-kem'presor]
s. sprężarka (powietrza)

aircraft ['eer-kra:ft] s. samolot;
lotnictwo (wiedza, flota etc.)
aircraft carrier ['eer-kra:ft
'kaerje:r] s. lotniskowiec
airfield ['eer-fi:ld] s. lotnisko (do
startowania i lądowania)
air force ['eer fo:rs] s. lotnictwo
(wojskowe); siły lotnicze
airline ['eerlajn] s. linia lotnicza
(system transportu lotniczego)
airmail ['eermejl] s. poczta
lotnicza; przesyłka lotnicza
airplane ['eerplejn] s. samolot
airport ['eerpo:rt] s. lotnisko
air raid ['eerejd] atak lotniczy
air show ['eerszou] pokaz
lotniczy (samolotów, lotów)
airsickness ['eersyknys] s.
choroba powietrzna
airtight ['eertajt] adj.
hermetyczny
air traffic ['eer-traefyk] ruch
lotniczy (samolotów, poczty,
pasażerów; ładunków itp.)
airway ['eerłej] linia lotnicza
airy ['eery] adj. przewiewny
aisle [ajl] s. przejście; nawa
boczna (kościoła)
ajar [e'dża:r] adv. uchylony; pół
otwarty; nieco otwarty
akin [e'kyn] adj. pokrewny
alacrity [e'laekryty] s. ochota;
gotowość (do); żwawość;
skwapliwość (do czegoś)
alarm [e'la:rm] s. popłoch;
strach; sygnał alarmowy;
trwoga; v. alarmować;
trwożyć; płoszyć
alarm clock [e'la:rm,klok] s.
budzik (zegar alarmowy)
alas ! [e'laes] excl. niestety
alcohol ['aelkehol] s. alkohol;
spirytus (ziemniaczany itp.)
alcoholic [,aelke'holyk] s.
alkoholik; adj. alkoholowy
alcove ['aelkouw] s. altanka;
alkowa; nisza; wnęka
alder ['o:lder] s. olcha; olsza
ale [ejl] s. piwo (gorzkie,
angielskie lub amerykańskie)
alert [e'le:t] adj. czujny; raźny;
żwawy; s. alarm; pogotowie
algae ['aeldżi:] pl. glony; algi

alias ['ejliaes] adv. inaczej; alias;
vel; s. pseudonim (autora itp.)
alibi ['aelybaj] s. alibi; wymówka;
v. usprawiedliwiać się
alien ['ejljen] adj. obcy
alienate ['ejljenejt] v.
odstręczać; odrywać (się);
zrażać; wyobcować (się)
alike [e'lajk] adj. jednakowy;
podobny; adv. tak samo;
jednako; podobnie; zarówno;
także; jednakowo
alimony ['aelimeny] s. alimenty
alive [e'lajw] adj. żywy; żyjący;
ożywiony; pełen życia
all [o:l] adj. & pron. cały;
wszystek; każdy (człowiek);
adv. całkowicie; w pełni;
zupełnie; s. wszystko
all of us [o:l ow as] my
wszyscy; my wszyscy razem
all at once [o:l at łans] wszyscy
na raz; wszyscy jednocześnie
all the better [o:l dy bete:r] tym
lepiej; tym bardziej
all told [o:l told] wszystkiego
razem; razem wziąwszy
alleged [e'ledżd] adj. rzekomy
alleviate [e'li:wjejt] v. łagodzić;
zmniejszać; złagodzić
alley ['aely] s. aleja; przejście;
zaułek; boczna ulica; tor
alliance [e'lajens] s. związek;
sojusz; powinowactwo; sko-
ligacenie; przymierze
allot [e'lot] v. przydzielać;
losować; wyznaczać; wya-
sygnować (na coś, kogoś)
allotment [e'lotment] s. przydział;
działka; asygnata; asygnacja
allow [e'lau] v. pozwalać;
użyczać; uznawać; uwzględniać; przyzwalać (na coś)
allow for [e'lau fo:r] v.
uwzględniać; dawać (czas)
allowance [e'lauens] s. przydział;
pozwolenie; kieszonkowe
alloy ['aeloj] s. stop; próba;
domieszka; stop kilku metali
all-round [o:l-raund] adj.
wszechstronny; uniwersalny
allude [e'lu:d] v. robić aluzje
allure [e'lju:] v. wabić; kusić;

oczarować; nęcić; znęcić;
zwabić; zwabiać (kogoś)
allusion [e'lu:żyn] s. aluzja
(do czegoś); przymówka (do);
przytyk; napomknienie (o)
ally [e'laj] v. sprzymierzać się;
łączyć; połączyć; skoligacić
ally ['aelaj] s. sprzymierzeniec;
sojusznik (wojskowy itp.)
almighty [o:l'majty] adj.
wszechmogący; ogromny;
straszliwy; wszechmocny
almond [am'end] s. migdał
almost ['o:lmoust] adv. prawie;
niemal; jak gdyby; o mało;
ledwo; zaledwie; ledwie
almost never ['o:lmoust 'newer]
prawie nigdy; rzadko kiedy
alms [a:mz] s. jałmużna
aloft [e'loft] adv. wysoko; hen;
w górze; w górę; do góry
alone [e'loun] adj. sam;
samotny; w pojedynkę; sam
jeden; jedyny; osamotniony
along [e'lo:ng] adv. naprzód;
wzdłóż; razem z sobą
alongside [e'lo:ngsajd] adv.
obok; wzdłóż; przy (molu,
burcie, chodniku, itp.)
aloof [e'lu:f] adv. z dala; na
uboczu; z daleka; na dystans
aloud [e'laud] adv. głośno
alphabet ['aelfebyt] s. alfabet
already [o:l'redy] adv. już;
(dużo) wcześniej; poprzednio;
uprzednio; wcześniej niż
also [o:lsou] adv. także; również
altar ['o:lter] s. ołtarz
alter ['o:lter] v. zmieniać
(styl, użytek, itp.); poprawiać; odmienić; przemienić
alteration [o:lte'rejszyn] s.
zmiana; poprawka; przemiana
alternate ['o:lternejt] v. zmieniać
się (kolejno); brać kolejno
alternate ['o:lternyt] adj. co
drugi; na zmianę; kolejny
alternating current [o:lter-
-nejtyn'karent] prąd zmienny
alternative [ol-ter'netyw] 1.
s. alternatywa (wybór) 2. adj.
alternatywny (dający wybór)
although [o:lzou] conj. chociaż

altitude ['aeltytju:d] s.
wysokość (nad poziomem
morza); wysokie miejsce
altogether [o:lte'gedze:r] adv.
zupełnie; całkowicie
aluminum [e'lumynem] s.
aluminium (metal)
alumna [e'lamne] s. była
studentka; była wychowanka
alumnus [e'lamnes] s. były
student uczelni (uniwersytetu);
były wychowanek (szkoły)
always ['o:lłejz] adv. stale;
zawsze; ciągle; wciąż
am [aem] v. (ja) jestem
amass [e'maes] v. gromadzić
amateur ['aemecze:r] s.
miłośnik; amator; dyletant
amaze [e'mejz] v. zdumiewać;
zadziwiać; wprawić (wpra-
wiać kogoś) w zdumienie
amazement [e'mejzment] s.
zdumienie; osłupienie
amazing [e'mejzyng] adj.
zdumiewający; zadziwiający
ambassador [aem'baesede:r] s.
ambasador; przedstawiciel
amber ['aembe:r] s. bursztyn
ambient ['aembient] adj.
otaczający (coś, kogoś)
ambiguous [aem'bygjues] adj.
dwuznaczny; mętny; nie wyraźny; nie jasny; zagadkowy
ambition [aem'byszyn] s.
ambicja; chęć wybicia się
ambitious [aem'byszes] adj.
(bardzo) ambitny; żądny
ambulance ['aembjulens] s.
ambulans; wóz pogotowia
ambush ['aembusz] s. zasadzka
amen [ej'men] amen; tak jest!
amend [e'mend] v. poprawiać
amendment [e'mendment] s.
poprawa; ulepszenie (czegoś);
uzupełnienie; zmiana
amends [e'mendz] s.
odszkodowanie (za); zadośćuczynienie (za krzywdę)
American [e'meryken] s.
Amerykanin; adj. amerykański
amiable ['ejmjebel] adj. miły;
uprzejmy; sympatyczny
amicable ['aemykebl] adj.

polubowny; przyjacielski
amid [e'myd] prep. wśród;
pośród; między; pomiędzy
amidst [e'mydst] prep. wśród;
pośród; między; pomiędzy
amiss [e'mys] adv. na opak;
błędnie; źle; niefortunnie
ammo ['aemou] s. amunicja
ammunition [,aemju'nyszyn] s.
amunicja (proch, kule itp.)
amnesty [aemnysty] s.
ułaskawienie; amnestia
among [e'mang] prep. wśród;
pomiędzy; między; pośród
amongst [e'mangst] prep.
wśród; pomiędzy; między;
pośród; w otoczeniu
amount [e'maunt] v. wynosić;
s. suma; kwota; wynik
amount to [e'maunt tu] v.
wynosić (w sumie)
ample ['aempl] adj. rozległy;
dostatni; hojny; suty; obfity
amplifier ['aemplyfajer] s.
wzmacniacz; amplifikator
amplify ['aemplyfy] v.
rozszerzać (bardziej); wzmacniać; przesadzać; rozwinąć
amplitude ['aemplytju:d] s.
amplituda; wielkość; zasięg;
zakres; obfitość
amply ['aemply] adv. obszernie;
szeroko; zupełnie (całkiem,
więcej niż) wystarczająco
amulet ['aemjulyt] s. amulet
amuse [e'mju:z] v. bawić;
ubawić; śmieszyć (kogoś);
zabawić; rozśmieszać
amusement [e'mju:zment] s.
rozrywka; zabawa
amusing [e'mju:zyng] adj. zabawny; śmieszny; pocieszny
an [aen; en] art. jeden; jakiś
anemia [e'ni:mja] s. anemia
anesthetic [e'nystetyk] s.
środek znieczulający
analogous [e'naeleges] adj.
analogiczny; zbieżny
analogy [e'naeledży] s.
podobieństwo; analogia
analysis [e'naelysys] s. analiza
analyze [e'naelajz] v.
analizować; rozpatrywać;

zanalizować (szczegółowo)
anathema [e'naetyma] s. klątwa
anatomize [e'naetemajz] v.
rozbierać; anatomizować
anatomy [e'naetemy] s. ana-
tomia (budowa organizmów)
ancestor ['aensester] s. przodek
ancestry ['aensestry] s.
przodkowie; starożytność
rodu; antenaci rodu
anchor ['aenker] s. kotwica
anchovy ['aenczewy] s. sardela
ancient ['ejnszent] adj.
starodawny; stary; sędziwy;
wiekowy; s. osoba stara
and [aend; end] conj. i; coraz
anecdote ['aenyk,dout] s.
dykteryjka; anegdota
anew [e'nju] adv. na nowo
angel ['ejndżl] s. anioł
anger ['eanger] s. gniew; złość;
v. gniewać; irytować
angina [aendżajna] s. angina
angle ['aengl] s. kąt; narożnik;
kątówka; v. kluczyć
Anglican ['aenglyken] adj.
anglikański (kościół)
Anglo-Saxon [aenglou-saeksen]
adj. anglo-saski (język itp.)
angry [aengry] adj. zagniewany
anguish [aengłysz] s. udręka;
męka; udręczenie; boleść;
ból (fizyczny, psychiczny)
angular ['aengjuler] adj. kanciasty; narożny; kątowy; gra-
niasty; szczupły; bez wdzięku
animal ['aenyml] s. zwierzę;
stworzenie; adj. zwierzęcy
animate ['aenymejt] v. ożywiać;
adj. ożywiony; żywy
animated cartoon ['aenymejtyd
'ka:rtu:n] film rysunkowy;
kreskówka (filmowa)
animation [,aeny'mejszyn] s.
ożywianie; ożywienie; ży-
wość; natchnienie
animosity [,aeny'mosyty] s.
uraza; niechęć; animozja
ankle ['aenkl] s. kostka u stopy;
staw między stopą i łydką
annex ['aeneks] v. przyłączać;
wcielać; s. przybudówka; załącznik (do czegoś)

annihilate [ə'najelejt] v.
unicestwić; niszczyć; niweczyć; zniszczyć zupełnie
anniversary [‚aeny've:rsery] s.
rocznica; adj doroczny (obchód tego samego zdarzenia)
annotation ['aene'tejszyn] s.
waga; komentarz; przypis
announce [ə'nauns] v.
zapowiadać; ogłaszać (pu-
blicznie); oznajmiać (coś)
announcement [ə'naunsment] s.
zapowiedź; zawiadomienie
announcer [ə'naunser] s.
1. zapowiadacz; 2. (radio)
speaker; konferansjer
annoy [ə'noj] v. dokuczać;
drażnić; nękać (stale); trapić; martwić (ciągle)
annoyance [ə'nojens] s. udręka;
przykrość; irytacja; kłopot
annoyed [ə'nojd] adj.
rozgniewany; rozdrażniony;
strapiony; skłopotany
annual ['aenjuel] adj. coroczny;
s. rocznik; jednorocznik
annuity [ə'njuyty] s. renta
roczna; renta dożywotnia
annul [ə'nal] v. unieważniać;
anulować; skasować; pozbawić (czegoś); kasować
anodyne ['aenedajn] s. anodyna;
środek od bólu, łagodzący
anomalous [ə'nomeles] adj.
nienormalny; nietypowy
anonym ['aenenym] s. anonim
anonymous [ə'nonymes] adj.
bezimienny; anonimowy
another [ə'nadzer] adj. & pron.
drugi; inny; jeszcze jeden
another time [ə'nadzer‚tajm]
kiedy indziej; innym razem
answer ['aenser] s. odpowiedź
answer for ['aenser fo:r] v.
odpowiadać za (przed kimś)
ant [aent] s. mrówka
antagonist [aen'taegenyst] s.
przeciwnik; przeciwniczka
antagonize [aen'taego'najz] v.
zrażać; narażać; zwalczać
antelope ['aentyloup] s. antylopa
anterior [aen'tierjer] adj.
poprzedni; uprzedni; w przo-

dzie; wcześniejszy; przed-
anthem ['aentem] s. hymn
narodowy (religijny)
anti ['aenty] pre. przeciw-
anti-aircraft ['aentaj'e:rkra:ft] adj.
przeciwlotniczy (obronny)
antibiotic ['aentybajotyk] s.
antybiotyk (przeciw bakteriom)
antic ['aentyk] adj. dziwaczny;
groteskowy; s. figiel; dziwac-
twa; błazeństwo; głupi kawał
anticipate [aen'tysypejt] v.
przewidywać; uprzedzać
anticipation [aen'tysypejszyn]
s.uprzedzenie; przewidywanie;
przyśpieszenie; oczekiwanie
anticlimax ['aenty'klajmaeks] s.
rozczarowanie; zawód; spadek
anticyclone [‚aenty'sajkloun] s.
antycyklon; wyż (atmosf.)
antidote ['aentydout] s. odtrutka;
antydotum (zapobiegające złu)
antifreeze ['aentyfri:z] s.
mieszanka niemarznąca
antiknock ['aentynok] s.
mieszanka przeciwstukowa
antipathy [aen'typety] s. odraza;
niechęć (do kogoś)
antiquated ['aentykłejtyd] adj.
przestarzały; staroświecki
antique [aen'ti:k] adj. stary;
starożytny; staromodny
antiquity [aen'tykłyty] s.
starożytność; zabytki
antiseptic [aenty'septyk] adj.
antyseptyk; przeciwgnilny
antlers ['aentlerz] pl. rogi (np.
jelenia); rozgałęzione rogi
anvil ['aenwyl] s. kowadło
anxiety [aeng'zajety] s.niepokój;
troska; obawa; pragnienie
anxious ['aenkszes] adj.
zaniepokojony; zabiegający;
pragnący (usilnie czegoś)
anxious about ['aenkszes e'baut]
troskliwy o ...; niepokojący
się o ...; zabiegający o ...
anxious for ['aenkszes fo:r]
pragnący bardzo czegoś
anxious to ['aenkszes tu]
pragnący żeby; mający
ochotę na; chcący (czegoś)
any ['eny] pron. jakikolwiek;

któryś; jakiś; żaden; lada;
byle; jakaś; któraś; żadna
any farther ['eny fa:<u>rdz</u>er] trochę
dalej; nieco (jeszcze) dalej
any more ['eny mo:r] trochę
więcej; teraz; obecnie
anybody ['eny'body] pron. ktoś;
ktokolwiek; każdy; nikt
anyhow ['enyhau] adv. w każdym razie; jakkolwiek
anyone ['enyłan] pron.
ktokolwiek; każdy; ktoś; nikt
anything ['eny<u>tyn</u>g] pron. coś;
cokolwiek; wszystko (oprócz);
nic; cokolwiek bądź
anything else ['eny<u>tyn</u>g els]
jeszcze coś; coś więcej
anyway ['enyłej] adv. w każdym
razie; jakkolwiek; byle jak
anywhere ['enyhłeer] adv.
gdziekolwiek; byle gdzie;
nigdzie; (colloq.) at all
apart [e'pa:rt] adv. osobno;
niezależnie; na boku; od siebie
apart from [e'pa:rt,from]
niezależnie od ...; poza;
oprócz; prócz; inny niż
apartment [e'pa:rtment] s.
mieszkanie; izba; pokój
apartment house [e'pa:rtment
,haus] blok mieszkalny;
kamienica (czynszowa)
apathetic [aepe'<u>t</u>etyk] adj.
apatyczny; obojętny; bez
uczuć; nieczuły; bierny
ape [ejp] s. małpa (bezogonowa);
v. małpować; naśladować
(ruchy etc.); błaznować
apex ['ejpeks] s. szczyt; czubek;
wierzchołek; kulminacja
apiary ['ejpjery] s. pasieka
apiece [e'pi:s] adv. na osobę; od
sztuki; za sztukę; każdy
aplomb [e'plom] s. pewność
siebie; opanowanie; zimna
krew (wobec trudności)
apologize [e'poledżajz] v.
usprawiedliwiać; przepraszać
apology [e'poledży] s.
usprawiedliwienie; obrona
(ideologii etc.); przeprosiny
apoplexy ['aepepleksy] s.
apopleksja; udar

apostle [e'posl] s. apostoł
apostolic [,aepe'stolyk] adj.
apostolski; papieski
apostrophe [e'postrefy] s.
apostrof; apostrofa
appall [e'po:l] v. przerażać
apparatus [aepe'rejtes] s. aparat;
urządzenie; przyrząd; organ
apparent [e'paerent] adj. jawny;
pozorny; oczywisty; widoczny
appeal [e'pi:l] v. apelować;
odwoływać się (do wyższej
instancji); uciekać się do
appeal to [e'pi:l tu] v. zwracać
się do ...; zwracać się z
apelem; apelować do ...
appear [e'pier] v. ukazywać się;
zjawiać się; pokazywać się
appearance [e'pierens] s.
(zewnętrzny) wygląd; pozór;
wystąpienie; zjawienie się
appease [e'pi:z] v. łagodzić;
uśmierzać; zaspakajać; ulegać (prośbom); ugłaskać
append [e'pend] v. dołączać;
doczepiać; dodawać; zawieszać; przyczepić
appendicitis [ependy'sajtys] s.
zapalenie wyrostka robaczko-
wego (ślepej kiszki)
appendix [e'pendyks] s. dodatek;
uzupełnienie; ślepa kiszka
appetite ['aepitajt] s. apetyt
appetizing ['aepitajzing] adj.
apetyczny; smakowity
applaud [e'plo:d] v. oklaskiwać;
klaskać; bić brawo; przy-
klasnąć; (po)chwalić
applause [e'plo:z] s. aplauz;
oklaski; poklask; pochwała;
aprobata; klaskanie
apple ['aepl] s. jabłko
apple-pie ['aeplpaj] s. placek
jabłkowy; szarlotka
applesauce ['aepl so:s] s. puree
z jabłek; (slang) nonsens
apple tree ['aepltri:] s jabłoń
appliance [e'plajens] s. przyrząd;
urządzenie; akcesoria
applicant ['aeplykent] s. petent;
zgłaszający się; kandydat
application [,aeply'kejszyn] s.
podanie; użycie; zasto-

-sowanie; przykładanie;
pilność; sposób używania
apply [e'plaj] v. używać;
stosować; odnosić się; naciskać; być pilnym; prosić o
apply for [e'plaj fo:r] v. starać
się o ...; wnosić podanie o
apply to [e'plaj tu] v. zwracać
się do ...; zgłaszać się do (o
coś); stosować się
appoint [e'point] v. mianować;
wyznaczać; ustanawiać;
ustalić (datę, miejsce etc.)
appointment [e'pointment] s.
nominacja; oznaczenie czasu i
miejsca; umówione spotkanie
apportion [e'po:rszyn]
v. wyznaczyć; wydzielać;
przydzielać; wydać udziały
appraise [e'prejz] v. oceniać;
szacować; ustalić cenę
appreciate [e'pri:szjejt] v. cenić
wysoko; zyskiwać na war-
tości; ocenić; oszacować;
docenić; dobrze myśleć o
appreciation [e'pri:szjejszyn] s.
ocena; uznanie; wzrost
wartości; zrozumienie
czegoś; uznanie (jakości)
apprehend [,aepry'hend] v.
ująć; pojmać; rozumieć
apprehension [,aepry'henszyn] s.
obawa; pojęcie; aresztowanie;
lęk; zrozumienie; wrażenie
apprehensive [,aepry'hensyw]
adj. obawiający się; pojętny
apprentice [e'prentys] s.
czeladnik; uczeń; terminator
apprenticeship [e'prentsszyp] s.
termin; nauka rzemiosła
approach [e'proucz] v. zbliżać
się; podchodzić; s. dostęp
approach road [e'proucz,roud]
droga (rampa) dojazdowa
appropriate [e'prouprjejt] adj.
właściwy; odpowiedni; stosowny; przywłaszczyć sobie
appropriation [e'prouprejszyn] s.
asygnowanie; przywłasz-
czenie; przeznaczenie; kredyty;
przejęcie na własność
approval [e'pru:wel] s. aprobata;
uznanie; zatwierdzenie

approximate [e'proksymyt] adj.
zbliżony; przybliżony; mniej
więcej; v. zbliżać (się); być
około; przybliżać (coś)
apricot ['ejprykot] s. morela
April ['ejprel] s. kwiecień
apron ['ejpren] s. fartuch; płyta
przednia; przedpole
apropos [aepre'pou] adv. do tego
celu; w związku z tym
apt [aept] v. mieć skłonność
apt to [aept tu] v. być
skłonnym do ...; często coś
robić; być zdolnym
aquarium [e'kłerjem] s. akwarium
aquatic [e'kłaetyk] adj. wodny
aquatic sports [e'kłaetyk sports]
sporty wodne (żeglarstwo)
aqueduct ['aekłydakt] s.
wodociąg; akwedukt (rzym-ski
wraz z budowlą)
aquiline ['aekłylajn] adj. orli
Arabic [ae'rebyk] adj. arabski
arable ['aerebl] adj. orny
arbitrary ['a:rbytrary] adj.
dowolny; samowolny
arbor ['a:rber] s. altanka; wał
napędowy; oś maszyny; drzewo (krzaki) cieniste
arc [a:rk] s. łuk
arc lamp [a:rk lemp] lampa
łukowa (jarzeniowa)
arcade [a:r'kejd] s. arkada;
podcienie; przejście kryte
arch [a:rcz] s. łuk; sklepienie;
podbicie; v. tworzyć łuk
arch [a:rcz] adj. chytry;
wierutny; arcy...; figlarny
archaeologist [a:rky'oledżyst] s.
archeolog; badacz wykopalisk
archeology [a:rky'oledży] s.
archeologia
archaic [a:rkejyk] adj. archaiczny;
przestarzały; staroświecki
archangel ['a:rkejndżel] s.
archanioł; anioł wysokiej rangi
archbishop ['a:rczbyszep] s.
arcybiskup
archer ['a:rczer] s. łucznik
archery ['a:rczery] s. łucznictwo
(jako sztuka); łuki i strzały
architect ['a:rkytekt] s. architekt;
twórca; budowniczy

architecture ['a:rkytekczer] s.
architektura; styl budowy
archives ['a:rkajwz] pl. archiwa;
archiwum (miejsce i zbiory)
archway ['a:rczłej] s. sklepione
przejście; brama; łuk
arctic ['a:rktyk] adj. arktyczny;
polarny; bardzo zimny
ardent ['a:rdent] adj. rozpalony;
prażący; płonący; gorliwy
ardor ['a:rder] s. żar;
żarliwość; gorliwość; zapał
arduous ['a:rdżues] adj.
mozolny; wytrwały; stromy;
żmudny; wymagający wysiłku
are [a:r] v. są; jesteś; jesteście
area ['e:rje] s. obszar; zakres;
powierzchnia; teren; okolica;
strefa; część (domu, lasu)
Argentine ['a:rdżentajn] adj.
argentyński; z Argentyny
argot ['a:rgou] s. żargon
(złodziei, włóczęgów etc.)
argue ['a:rgju:] v. wykazywać;
rozumować; spierać się;
rozpatrywać; dowodzić;
udowadniać; kłócić się
argument ['a:rgjument] s.
argument; dowód; sprzeczka;
spór; debata; podsumowanie
argumentation [,a:rgjumen
'tejszyn] s. roztrząsanie;
argumentacja; rozumowanie;
debata; proces argumentacji
arid ['aeryd] adj. suchy; jałowy;
oschły; wypalony; spieczony
arise, arose, arisen [e'rajz;
e'rouz; e'ryzn]
arise [e'rajz] v. powstawać;
wstawać; wynikać; nada-
rzyć się; stać się
aristocrat ['aeryste,kraet] s.
arystokrata; arystokratka
arithmetic ['aeryt'metyk] s.
rachunki; arytmetyka; adj.
arytmetyczny; rachunkowy
ark [a:rk] s. arka; skrzynia
arm [a:rm] s. ramię; odnoga;
konar; rękaw; poręcz
arm [a:rm] s. broń (rodzaj);
uzbrojenie; v. uzbroić; opan-
cerzyć; nastawiać (zapłon);
przygotowywać się do walki

armament ['a:rmement] s.
uzbrojenie; zbrojenia; siły
zbrojne; wyposażenie wojska
armament race ['a:rmement,rejs]
wyścig zbrojeń
armchair [,a:rm'cze:r] s. fotel
armistice ['a:rmystys] s.
zawieszenie broni; rozejm
armor ['a:rmer] s. zbroja;
opancerzenie; v. zbroić w
płyty pancerne; opancerzać
armored car ['a:rmerd,ka:r]
samochód pancerny
arm-twisting ['a:rm'tłystyn]
napór na (kogoś); (wykrę-
canie ręki); nagabywanie
kogoś; narzucanie się
arms ['a:rmz] pl. broń;
uzbrojenie; herby; herb
arms race ['a:rmz,rejs] s.
wyścig zbrojeń
army ['a:rmy] s. wojsko; armia
aroma [e'roume] s. aromat
arose [e'rouz] v. powstał; wstał;
wynikł; zob. arise
around [e'raund] prep. dookoła;
naokoło; wokoło; adv. wokół;
tu i tam; około; wszędzie
arousal [e'rauzel] s. pobudzenie
do czynu (działania)
arouse [e'rauz] v. pobudzić;
budzić; wzniecać (uczucia)
arraign [e'rejn] v. pozwać;
oskarżyć; atakować pogląd
arrange [e'rejndż] v. układać;
szykować; porządkować;
ustalać; komponować
arrangement [e'rejndżment] s.
układ; ułożenie się; urządzenie; zaaranżowanie; porządek; szyk; plan; układ
array [e'rej] v. szykować;
przybrać; rozmieszczać; s.
szyk (bojowy); szereg; uszeregowanie; wystawa; strój
arrears [e'rierz] pl. zaległości;
długi; zaległe płace (płatności)
arrest [e'rest] s. areszt;
aresztowanie; zatrzymanie; v.
aresztować; zatrzymywać (i
sprawdzić); wstrzymywać;
przyciągać (uwagę etc.)
arrival [e'rajwel] s. przyjazd;

przybysz; rzecz nadeszła
arrive [e'rajw] v. przybyć;
dojść; osiągnąć; wspólnie
ustalać; zdobyć sławę etc.
arrive at [e'rajw,aet] v. dojść
do ...; wspólnie ustalać
arrogance ['aeregens] s.
zarozumiałość; buta;
arogancja; wyniosłość
arrogant ['aeregent] adj. butny;
arogancki; wyniosły
arrow ['aerou] s. strzała
arrow head ['aerou hed] s. grot
arse [a:rs] s. vulg. rzyć; zadek;
dupa; dupsko
arsenal ['a:rsynl] s. arsenał
arsenic ['a:rsnyk] s. arszenik;
arsen (pierwiastek chemiczny);
['a:rsenyk] adj. arsenowy
arson ['a:rsen] s. podpalenie
(zbrodnia); podpalenie
art [a:rt] s. sztuka; chytrość;
zręczność; rzemiosło; fortel
arterial [a:r'tyrjal] adj. tętniczy;
magistralny; artaryjny
arterial road [a:r'tyrjal,roud]
magistrala; główna szosa
artery [a:rtery] s. arteria; tętnica;
arteria ruchu; magistrala
artful ['a:rtful] adj. chytry;
zręczny; pomysłowy; dow-
cipny; sprytny; cwany
artichoke ['a:rty,czouk] s.
karczoch (jarzyna)
article ['a:rtykl] s. rodzajnik;
artykuł; warunek; paragraf
(dokumentu); temat
articulate [a:rtykjulejt] v.
wyrażać jasno; artykułować;
adj. artykułowany; wyraźny;
łączony stawami; wygadany
artifact [,a:rty'faekt] s. wytwór
ludzkiej ręki (jakikolwiek)
artificial [,a:rty'fyszel] adj.
sztuczny; udany; symulowany
artillery [a:r'tylery] s. artyleria
artisan ['a:rtyzaen] s.
wysokiej klasy rzemieślnik
artist ['a:rtist] s. artysta; artystka
artiste [a:r'ty:st] s. artysta;
odtwórca; artysta estradowy
artless ['artlys] adj. niewinny;
niedołężny; szczery; otwarty

as [aez; ez] adv. pron. conj. jak;
tak; co; jako; jaki; skoro;
żeby; choć; z (dniem, rokiem)
as ... as [ez ... ez] tak jak
as far as [ez fa:r ez] co do
as many [ez meny] tak wiele
as well [ez łel] również
as well as [ez łel ez] jak także;
tak jak; jak również
as for [ez fo:r] co się tyczy
asbestos [aez'bestes] s. azbest
ascend [e'send] v. piąć się;
iść w górę; wznosić się;
wracać w przeszłość; wstępować (na tron); wsiąść na
ascension [e'senszyn] s.
wznoszenie się; święcenie
Wniebowstąpienia
ascent [e'sent] s. wzlot; wzrost;
stok; postęp; wchodzenie
ascertain [aeser'tejn] v.
stwierdzać; ustalać; konstatować; upewniać się
ascetic [e'setyk] s. asceta; adj.
ascetyczny; surowo odmawia-
jący sobie; ograniczający się
ascribe [e'skrajb] v. przypisywać; przypisać (coś
komuś); przydzielić do
aseptic ['eseptyk] adj. jałowy;
wyjałowiony; aseptyczny
ash [aesz] s. popiół; jesień
ashamed [e'szejmd] adj.
zawstydzony; zażenowany
ashamed of [e'szejmd ow] adj.
wstydzący się czegoś
ash can [aesz kaen] wiadro na
śmieci; wiadro na popiół
ashen ['aeszen] adj. popielaty
ashes ['aeszyz] pl. popioły
ashore [e'szo:r] adv. na brzeg;
na brzegu; na ląd; na lądzie
ash tray ['aesztrej] s. popielniczka (dla palaczy)
Ash Wednesday [,aesz'łenzdy]
Środa Popielcowa
Asian [,ejż,jen] adj. Azjata;
Azjatka; azjatycki; azjatycka
Asiatic [,ejży'atyk] adj. azjatycki
aside [e'sajd] adv. na stronę; na
stronie; na boku; na uboczu
aside from [e'sajd,from] adv.
oprócz; z wyjątkiem; poza;

prócz; w rezerwie; w zapasie
asinine ['aesynajn] adj. ośli;
głupi (jak osioł); idiotyczny
ask [ae:sk] v. pytać; zapytywać; prosić; zapraszać
ask a question ['ae:sk ej'kłesz-
czyn] v. stawiać pytanie; pytać; dowiadywać się o ...
ask to dinner ['ae:sk tu'dyner]
zapraszać na obiad
ask for ['ae:sk fo:r] prosić o ...
askance [as'kaens] adv. z ukosa;
zezem; niepewnie; podejrzliwie
askew [es'kju:] adv. krzywo;
skośnie; z ukosa; adj. krzywy
aslant [e'sla:nt] adv. ukośnie;
skośnie; na ukos; w poprzek
asleep [e'sli:p] adv. we śnie;
adj. śpiący; zdrętwiały;
ścierpły; nudny; martwy
asparagus [es'paereges] s.
szparag (jarzyna)
aspect ['aespekt] s. aspekt;
wygląd; wyraz; faza; postać;
strona; mina; przejaw; strona
(fasada) domu; zapatrywanie
aspen ['aespen] s. osika; osina
asphalt ['aesfalt] s. asfalt
aspire [es'pajer] v. dążyć;
marzyć; wzdychać do; mieć
aspiracje; być ambitnym
aspire after [es'pajer'a:fter]
aspirowć; dążyć do (cze-
goś); mieć aspiracje żeby ...
ass [aes] s. osioł; wulg. dupa
assail [e'sejl] v. napadać (brutalnie); przystąpować; atakować (argumentami); uderzać
assailant [e'sejlent] s. napastnik
assassin [e'saesyn] s. morderca
(najęty); zamachowiec
assassinate [e'saesynejt] v.
zamordować (podstępnie);
dokonać zamachu (na ...)
assassination [e,saesy'nejszyn]
s. morderstwo; zabójstwo;
zamach; skrytobójstwo
assault [e'sa:lt] s. napad; atak;
zgwałcenie; v. atakować; bić
assemblage [e'semblydż] s.
zebranie; zbiór; zmontowanie
assemble [e'sembl] v. zbierać;
montować; nagromadzać;

złożyć; wpasować (w coś)
assembly [e'sembly] s. zebranie;
zbiórka; montaż; legislatura
assembly line [e'sembly,lajn]
taśma montażowa; linia mon-
tażowa (w fabryce etc.)
assent [e'sent] s. zgoda; pogodzenie się; v. zgadzać się;
uznawać; wyrażać zgodę
assent to [e'sent tu] v. zgadzać
się na coś; zatwierdzać coś
assert [e'se:rt] v. twierdzić;
upominać się; dowieść; stawiać się; potwierdzić
assess [e'ses] v. szacować;
oceniać; wymierzać; opodatkować; nałożyć podatek na;
określić wysokość podatku
assets ['aesets] pl. własności;
aktywa (ściągalne); wartościowi pracownicy
assign [e'sajn] v. przydzielać;
ustalać; odnosić; przekazywać; przypisywać (do pracy)
assignment [e'sajnment] s.
przydzielenie; przypisanie;
przekazanie; przydział; podział
assimilate [e'symylejt] v.
upodabniać; wcielać; wchłaniać; asymilować; przyswajać sobie; strawić
assist [e'syst] v. pomagać;
brać udział; być przy
assistance [e'systens] s. pomoc
(pieniężna); asysta; wsparcie
assistant [e'systent] s. asystent;
pomocnik; adj. pomocniczy
assizes [e'sajzyz] pl. okresowe
sesje sądu (wyjazdowe) w
Anglii (ich czas i miejsce)
associate [e'souszjejt] s. towarzysz; wspólnik; partner;
sprzymierzeniec; rzecz zwią-
zana z czymś; część (cze-
goś); v. łączyć; obcować;
kojarzyć; brać do spółki; adj.
towarzyszący (podrzędny)
association [e,souszy'ejszyn] s.
łączenie; współpraca; kojarzenie; przyłączenie się;
związek; organizacja
assort [e'so:rt] v. sortować;
dobierać; obcować; klasy-

-fikować; porządkować
assorted [e'so:rtyd] adj. dobrany;
posortowany; mieszany
assortment [e'so:rtment] s.
asortyment; wybór; sortowanie; klasyfikacja
assume [e'sju:m] v. zakładać;
obejmować; przybierać; przypuszczać; wdziewać; udawać; przedsiębrać; brać
assumption [e'sampszyn] s.
założenie; przypuszczenie;
przybranie; objęcie (władzy);
udawanie; symulowanie
assurance [e'szu:rens] s.
zapewnienie; pewność; zaufanie; ubezpieczenie
assure [e'szu:r] v. zapewniać;
ubezpieczać; zabezpieczać
assured [e'szu:rd] adj. pewny
(siebie); s. ubezpieczony
asthma [aesma] s. dusznica;
astma; dychawica (chroniczna)
astigmatic [,aestyg'maetyk] adj.
astygmatyczny
astir [e'ste:r] adv. poruszony; w
ruchu; na nogach; ożywiony
astonish [es'tonysz] v. zadziwiać; zdumiewać; zdziwić;
wprawić w zdumienie
astonished [es'tonyszt] adj.
zdumiony; bardzo zdziwiony
astonishment [es'tonyszment] s.
zdumienie; zdziwienie
astray [es'trej] adv. na błędną
drogę; na bezdrożu; na
manowce; w błąd
astride [es'trajd] adv. okrakiem;
rozstawionymi nogami
astringent [es'tryndżent] adj.
ściągający; surowy; wstrzymujący; s. środek wstrzymujący
astrodome ['aestre,doum] s.
astrokopuła (nad stadionem
sportowym)
astrologer [es'troledżer] s.
astrolog
astronomer [es'tronemer] s.
astronom
astronaut ['aestreno:t] s.
astronauta; kosmonauta
astute [es'tu:t] adj. bystry;
przebiegły; wnikliwy

asunder [e'sander] adv.
oddzielnie; na boki; na strony
asylum [e'sajlem] s. azyl (polityczny etc.); schronisko; przytułek; schronienie
at [aet; et] prep. w; na; u; przy;
pod; z; za; do; o; po
ate [ejt] v. jadłem; jadłeś; jadł
etc.; zob. eat
athlete ['eatli:t] s. atleta; siłacz;
sportowiec; wyczynowiec
athletic ['aet'letyk] adj.
atletyczny; sportowy
athletics [aet'letyks] pl. atletyka;
sport; wychowanie fizyczne
Atlantic [et'laentyk] adj.
atlantycki; s. Atlantyk
atlas ['aetles] s. atlas
atmosphere ['aetmesfier] s.
atmosfera; otoczenie; nastrój
atoll ['aetol] s. atol
atom ['aetem] s. atom
atom bomb ['aetem bom] s.
bomba atomowa
atomic [e'tomyk] adj. atomowy
atomic age [e'tomyk ejdż] epoka
atomowa; era atomowa
atomic pile [e'tomyk pajl] stos
atomowy; stos jądrowy
atomic weight [e'tomyk łejt]
ciężar atomowy
atomize ['aetemajz] v. rozbijać
na atomy; rozpylać
atomizer ['aetemajzer] s.
rozpylacz (cieczy, płynu)
atone [e'toun] v. odpokutować;
okupić; załagodzić
atrocious [e'trouszes] adj.
potworny; okropny; skandaliczny; bardzo okrutny; zły
atrocity [e'trosyty] s.
okrucieństwo; okrutny czyn;
ohyda; (colloq.) obrzydliwość
attach [e'taecz] v.
przywiązywać; przyczepiać;
przydzielać; łączyć;
przymocowywać; nalepiać
attachment [e'taeczment] s.
załącznik; przymocowanie;
więź; przywiązanie
attack [e'taek] v. napadać;
atakować; s. atak; uderzenie
attempt [e'tempt] v. usiłować;

czynić zamach; próbować; s.
próba; usiłowanie; zamach
attend [e'tend] v. uczęszczać;
leczyć; obsługiwać; towa-
rzyszyć; iść razem
attendance [e'tendens] s.
obsługa; opieka; uczęszczanie
attendant [e'tendent] s. obecny;
służący; adj. towarzyszący
attention [e'tenszyn] s. uwaga;
uprzejmość; troska; opieka
attentive [e'tentyw] adj.
uważny; gorliwy; uprzejmy;
pilny; przywiązany
attest [e'test] v. poświadczyć;
stwierdzać; zalegalizować
attic ['aetyk] s. poddasze;
attyka; strych
attitude ['aetitu:d] s. postawa;
ustosunkowanie się; poza
attorney [e'te:rny] s. pełnomocnik; adwokat; prawnik
attract [e'traekt] v. przyciągać;
zwabić; być pociągającym;
zdobywać uznanie; urzekać
attraction [e'traekszyn] s.
przyciąganie; powab; urok;
atrakcja; siła przyciągania
attractive [e'traektyw] adj.
pociągający; przyciągający;
miły; urzekający
attribute ['aetrybju:t] s. przymiot;
cecha; właściwość
attribute [e'trybju:t] v.
przypisywać komuś (cze-
muś); odnosić do czegoś
attrition [e'tryszyn] s.
wyniszczenie; ścieranie;
skrucha; zużycie; starcie
auburn ['o:bern] adj. (barwa)
kasztanowa; złotobrązowa
auction ['o:kszyn] s. licytacja;
(publiczna) aukcja
auction off ['o:kszyn of] v.
licytować; sprzedawać na
licytacji; wystawiać na
(publiczną) licytację
audacious [o:'dejszes] adj.
odważny; śmiały; zuchwały
audacity [o:'daesyty] s.
śmiałość; odwaga; zuchwa-
łość; bezczelność
audible ['o:dybel] adj. słyszalny;

odbierany słuchem
audience ['o:djens] s. słuchacze
publiczność; audiencja
audit ['o:dyt] s. sprawdzenie
rachunków; rozliczenie; v.
kontrolować rachunki
aught [a:t] s. coś; nic; zero
August ['o:gest] s. sierpień
august ['o:gast] adj. wyniosły;
dostojny; majestatyczny
aunt [aent] s. ciotka; wujenka;
stryjenka
aurora [o:'ro:re] s. brzask;
jutrznia; jutrzenka; zorza
polarna; (rzymska bogini)
austere [o:s'tier] adj. surowy;
poważny; prosty; czysto użytkowy; bez ozdób; ponury
austerity [o:s'teryty] s.
surowość; powaga; prosto-
ta; srogość; charakter czysto
użytkowy; zaciskanie pasa
Australian [o:s'trejljen] adj.
australijski; s. Australijczyk
Austrian ['o:strjen] adj.
austriacki; s. Austriak
authentic [o:'tentyk] adj.
autentyczny; prawdziwy
author ['o:ter] s. autor; pisarz;
sprawca; twórca (dzieł etc.)
authoritative [o:'torytejtyw] adj.
stanowczy; miarodajny
authority [o:'toryty] s. władza;
autorytet; znaczenie; powaga;
moc rozkazywania; urząd
authorize ['o:terajz] v. upoważniać; zatwierdzać; dać
prawo (urząd); aprobować
authorship ['o:terszyp] s.
autorstwo; zawód pisarza
autobiography ['o:tebaj'ogrefy] s.
autobiografia
autograph ['o:tegraef] s. podpis;
autograf; podpis własny
automat ['o:temaet] n. automat;
automatem na monety do
sprzedaży (porcji) jedzenia
automatic [,o:te'maetyk] adj.
automatyczny; machinalny
automation [,o:te'mejszyn] s.
automatyzacja; robotyzacja
automobile ['o:temeby:l] s.
samochód; auto; sl. wóz

autumn ['o:tem] s. jesień
auxiliary [o:g'zyljery] adj.
pomocniczy; pomocny
avail [e'wejl] v. pomagać;
znaczyć; być przydatny
available [e'wejlebl] adj.
dostępny; osiągalny
avalanche ['aewelaencz] s.
lawina; v. spadać lawiną
avarice ['aewerys] s. chciwość;
skąpstwo; sknerstwo
avaricious [,aewe'ryszes] adj.
chciwy na pieniądze; skąpy
avenue ['aewynju:] s. bulwar;
aleja; ulica; dojazd; dojście
average ['aewerydż] adj. przeciętny; średni; s. średnia;
wartość średnia; przeciętna; v. osiągać średnio; obliczać średnią; wypośrodko-
wywać; pracować przecięt-
nie, w średnim tempie
averse [e'we:rs] adj. niechętny;
czujący odrazę; przeciwny
aversion [e'werżyn] s. odraza;
niechęć; powód odrazy
avert [e'we:rt] v. odwracać (np.
myśli, oczy); oddalić (cios)
aviation [,ejwy'ejszyn] s. lotnictwo; aeronautyka
aviator ['ejwyejter] s. lotnik
avid ['ewyd] adj. chciwy;
zachłanny; bardzo chętny
avoid [e'woyd] v. unikać;
uchylać się; stronić
avow [e'wau] v. wyznawać
avowal [e'wauel] s. wyznanie;
przyznanie się; zeznanie
await [e'łejt] v. czekać;
oczekiwać; być w ocze-
kiwaniu; być zagrożonym
awake; awoke; awoke [e'łejk;
e'łouk; e'łouk]
awake [e'łejk] v. budzić się;
otwierać oczy na ...; adj.
czujny; przebudzony; na jawie
awaken [e'łejkn] v. budzić;
uświadamiać komuś (ko-
goś); adj. czynny; obudzony
award [e'ło:rd] v. przysądzać;
wyznaczać; s. nagroda;
zapłata; grzywna sądowa
aware [e'łeer] adj. świadomy

away [e'łej] adv. precz; z dala
awe [o:] s. lęk; nabożna cześć
awful ['o:ful] adj. straszny;
budzący lęk i szacunek
awhile ['ehłajl] adv. na krótko;
przez chwilę; na chwilę; na
króciutko; na krótki czas
awkward ['o:kłerd] adj. niezgrabny; niezdarny; kłopotliwy; nieporęczny; zakłopotany; trudny
(do prowadzenia); niewygodny
awning ['o:nyng] s. dach z
płótna; markiza; zasłona; stora
awoke [e'łouk] v. zbudzony;
proszę zobaczyć: awake
awry [e'raj] adv. skośnie;
krzywo; na opak; adj. krzywy;
błędny; opaczny; wypaczony
ax [aeks] s. siekiera; topór; v.
obcinać siekierą; redukować
axe [aeks] = ax
axes [aeksyz] pl. osie; siekiery
axis ['aeksys] s. oś; ośka
axle ['aeksel] s. oś (koła); ośka
(łącząca tylnie koła wozu)
azimuth ['aezymet] s. azymut
azure ['aeżer] s. błękit; lazur;
adj. błękitny; lazurowy

B

b [bi] b; druga litera alfabetu
angielskiego
babble ['baebl] v. paplać;
gadać; s. paplanina; gadanina
babe [bejb] s. niemowlę
baboon [be'bu:n] s. pawian
baby ['bejby] s. niemowlę
baby carriage ['bejby kaerydż] s.
wózek dziecinny
babyhood ['bejbyhud] s. wiek
niemowlęcy; niemowlęctwo
bachelor ['baeczeler] s. niezamężna; nieżonaty; stopień
uniwersytecki (najniższy); osoba posiadająca ten stopień
back [baek] s. tył; grzbiet; v.
cofać się; wycofać się

backbone ['baekboun] s. kręgosłup; stos pacierzowy
back-door ['baek'do:r] s. tylne
drzwi; adj. zakulisowy; potajemny; adv. od tyłu; tajemnie
backfire ['baek'fajer] s. wybuch
odwrotny; zawiść; v. spalić
na panewce; wypalać zapo-
biegawczo (małe połacie lasu)
background ['baekgraund] s. tło;
dalszy plan; przeszłość
back number ['baeknamber] s.
zaległy numer; stare wydanie
pisma (gazety, dziennika etc.)
back-seat ['baek'si:t] s. tylne
siedzenie (miejsce); wycofanie
się z akcji, działalności
backstairs ['baeksteerz] s. tylne
schody; adj. zakulisowy
backstroke ['baek'strouk] s.
pływanie na plecach; rzut
odbity od lewa w tenisie
back-tire ['baek'tajer] s. tylna
opona samochodowa (slang)
backward ['baekłerd] adj. tylny;
zacofany; zapóźniony
backwards ['baekłerds] adv. w
tyle; odwrotnie; do tyłu
back wheel ['baekhłil] s. tylne
koło (samochodu; ciężarówki)
bacon ['bejkn] s. słonina; wędzony i solony boczek; bekon
bacon and eggs ['bejkn end egz]
jajka z boczkiem
bacterium [baek'tierjem] s. bak-
teria; mikroorganizm
bacteria [baek'tjerie] pl. bakterie
bad [baed] adj. zły; niedobry;
przykry; sfałszowany; słaby;
zdrożny; niewłaściwy
bade [baed] v. proponował;
oferował cenę; kazał; zob. bid
badge [baedż] s. odznaka; oznaka (członkostwa, rangi etc.)
badger ['baedżer] s. borsuk; v.
zadręczać (narzekaniem)
badly ['baedly] adv. źle; bardzo;
w zły sposób; sl. świetnie
badly wounded ['baedly'łu:ndyd]
ciężko ranny; ciężko zraniony
badminton ['baedmynten] s. rodzaj tenisa (piłka z piórkiem)
bad mouth ['baedmous] v. ob-

mawiać; oczerniać; stawiać
(kogoś) w złym świetle
baffle ['baefl] v. udaremniać;
łudzić; niweczyć; skonfun-
dować; s. przegroda
bag [baeg] s. torba; worek;
sl. babsztyl; upodobanie;
v. pakować; zwędzić
baggage ['baegydż] s. bagaż
baggage check ['baegydż,czek]
kwit bagażowy
baggy ['baegy] adj. workowaty
bag-pipe ['baegpajp] s. kobza
bail [bejl] s. kaucja; poręka
bail out [bejl'ałt] v. zwolnić za
kaucją; wywinąć się z opresji
bailiff ['bejlyf] s. woźny
sądowy (powiatowy); ko-
mornik; rządca majątku
bait [bejt] s. przynęta; pokusa
bake [bejk] v. piec; wypalać
baker ['bejker] s. piekarz
bakery [bejkery] s. piekarnia
baking powder ['bejkyn,pałder]
proszek do pieczenia
balance ['baelens] s. waga
(przyrząd); bilans; równowaga;
v. równoważyć; bilansować;
wahać się; przeciwdziałać
balcony ['baelkeny] s. balkon
bald [bo:ld] adj. łysy; jawny
bale [bejl] s. zwój płótna; bela;
snop (siana); v. zob. bail
balk [bo:k] v. opierać się;
przeszkadzać; zniechęcać; s.
belka; miedza; zawada
ball [bo:l] s. 1. piłka; pocisk;
kłębek; kula (ziemska); 2. bal;
zabawa taneczna; gra
ballad ['baeled] s. ballada;
pieśń (sentymentalna, opi-
sowa, zwykle anonimowa)
ballast ['baelest] s. balast; v.
obciążać balastem
ball-bearing ['bo:lbearyn] łożysko
kulkowe (też jedna z kulek)
ballet ['baelej] s. balet; zespół
baletowy (tancerzy)
ball game ['bo:lgejm] s. rozgrywka w piłkę; sl. położenie
ballistic [be'lystyk] adj. balis-
tyczny (swobodnie spadający)
balloon [be'lu:n] s. balon

ballot ['baelet] s. (tajne)
głosowanie; kartka do głosowania; v. tajnie głosować
ballot box ['baeletboks] s. urna
wyborcza
ball-point pen ['bo:l-point-pen] s.
kulkowy pisak; długopis
balm [ba:m] s. balsam
balmy ['ba:my] adj. błogi; bal-
samiczny; łagodzący
balustrade [,baeles'trejd] s.
poręcz; balustrada
bamboo [baem'bu:] s. bambus
ban [baen] s. zakaz; klątwa; v.
zabraniać; wyjąć spod prawa
banana [be'na:ne] s. banan
band [baend] s. szajka; kapela;
zespół muzyczny; taśma; v.
wiązać się; przepasywać
opaską; zrzeszać (w celu)
bandage ['baendydż] s. bandaż;
v. bandażować; obandażo-
wać; nakładać bandaże
bandit ['baendyt] s. bandyta
bandmaster ['baend,ma:ster] s.
kapelmistrz
bandstand [baendstaend] s.
estrada (zwykle na dworze)
bang [baeng] s. huk; zryw;
uciecha; bęc; v. trzaskać;
walnąć (z wielkim hukiem)
banish ['baenysz] v. wygnać;
usunąć; wykluczać; wypę-
dzać; pozbywać się (kogoś)
banishment ['baenyszment] s.
wygnanie; banicja
banisters ['baenystez] pl.
banistry (schodów); poręcze
banjo ['baendżou] s. rodzaj
gitary okrągłej, pokrytej skórą
bank ['baenk] s. brzeg; łacha;
nasyp; skarpa; bank; stół roboczy; rząd; nachylenie toru;
zasób; zbiór; wał przeciw-
powodziowy; v. prowadzić
bank; składać w banku; piętrzyć; pochylać; sl. polegać;
obwałowywać; pochylić jezdnię
bank bill ['baenk,byl] s. banknot
banker ['baenker] s. bankier
banking ['baenkyng] s. bankowość; transakcje banku
banknote ['baenknout] s.

banknot; papierowy pieniądz
bank-rate ['baenkrejt] s. stopa
dyskontowa; stopa procentowa (obciążająca pożyczki)
bankrupt ['baenkrept] s. bankrut
banner ['baener] s. chorągiew;
transparent; tytuł (czołowy)
banns [baenz] pl. zapowiedzi
banquet ['baenkłyt] s. bankiet
baptism ['baeptyzem] s. chrzest
baptize ['baeptajz] s. chrzcić
bar [ba:r] s. belka; drąg; rogatka;
krata; bariera; v. zagradzać;
hamować; prep. oprócz
bar [ba:r] s. izba adwokacka,
sądowa; adwokatura; bar; bufet z wyszynkiem; szynkwas
barb [ba:rb] s. haczyk; docinek;
kolec; skaza (na odlewie);
szew; cierń; grot
barbarian [ba:r'baerjen] s. barbarzyńca; adj. barbarzyński
barbed wire ['ba:rbd,łajer] drut
kolczasty (do zasieków etc.)
barber ['ba:rber] s. fryzjer
(męski); golibroda
barbershop ['ba:rber,szop] s.
zakład fryzjerski (męski)
barbiturate [ba:r'buczeret] lek
uspakajający; nasenny lek
bare [beer] adj. nagi; goły; łysy;
v. obnażać; odkrywać
barefoot ['beerfut] adj. & adv.
boso; bosy; bosa
bareheaded ['beerhedyd] adj. z
gołą głową; bez czapki
barely ['beerly] adv. ledwie;
otwarcie; ubogo; zaledwie
bargain ['ba:rgyn] s. ubicie targu;
dobre (okazyjne) kupno; v. targować się (o cenę); spodziewać się; dobijać targu
barge [ba:rdż] s. barka; v.
pakować się; trynić się
bark [ba:rk] s. kora drzewna;
szczeknięcie; barka rzeczna; v.
zdzierać korę; garbować
korę; szczekać; pyskować;
kaszleć; warkliwie mówić;
wyszczekać; zakaszleć
barley ['ba:rly] s. jęczmień
barmaid ['ba:rmejd] s. bufetowa;
kelnerka; szynkarka

barn [ba:rn] s. stodoła; stajnia; obora; wozownia; remiza

barometer [be:romyter] s. barometr; ciśnieniomierz

barracks ['baereks] pl. koszary; baraki; budynki koszarowe

barrel ['baerel] s. beczka; lufa; rura; cylinder; walec; bęben

barren ['baeren] adj. jałowy; wyczerpany; nieurodzajny; pustynny; niewydajny; nudny; nudzący; pozbawiony (czegoś)

barricade [,baery'kejd] s. barykada; v. barykadować się

barrier ['baerjer] s. zapora; zastawa; rogatka; ogrodzenie

barrister ['baeryster] s. adwokat; adwokatka; obrońca; obrończyni (głównie w Anglii)

barrow ['baerou] s. taczki

bartender ['ba:rtender] s. barman; bufetowy; bufetowa; barmanka; sprzedający wódkę

barter ['ba:rter] v. wymieniać; handlować; s. handel wymienny (bez pieniędzy)

base [bejs] s. podstawa; nasada; adj. podły; nędzny; niski

baseball ['bejsbo:l] s. (sport) palant amerykański (grany piłką i maczugą)

baseless ['bejslys] adj. bezpodstawny; nieuzasadniony

basement ['bejsment] s. suterena; piwnica; podziemie

bashful ['baeszful] adj. wstydliwy; nieśmiały; trwożliwy; lękliwy

basic ['bejsyk] adj. podstawowy; zasadniczy; zasadowy

basin ['bejsn] s. miednica; zbiornik; dorzecze; zagłębie

basis ['bejsys] pl. fundamenty; podstawy; podłoże; grunt; zasada; główna część

bask [baesk] v. wygrzewać się na słońcu (plażować); wylegiwać się; pławić się

basket ['ba:skyt] s. kosz; koszyk; v. wrzucać do kosza

basketball ['ba:skytbo:l] s. koszykówka (gra); piłka do koszykówki

bass [bejs] s. bas (głos, śpiewak, instrument)

bass [baes] s. okoń; łyko lipowe (sandałowe); okoń morski lub rzeczny

bastard ['baesterd] s. bękart; nieślubne dziecko; adj. nieślubny; nędzny; kiepski

baste [bejst] v. fastrygowć; polewać tłuszczem pieczeń

bat [baet] s. nietoperz; maczuga; kij; v. mrugać; hulać (slang)

bath [ba:s] s. kąpiel; łazienka

bathe [bejz] v. kąpać; moczyć; rosić; przemywać; wykąpać

bathing [bejzyng] s. kąpanie

bathing cap ['bejzyngkaep] czepek kąpielowy

bathing suit ['bejzyng sju:t] strój kąpielowy; kostium kąpielowy

bathing trunks ['bejzyng tranks] spodenki kąpielowe

bathrobe ['ba:zroub] s. płaszcz kąpielowy (z frotte)

bathroom ['ba:zru:m] s. łazienka; ubikacja; ustęp; klozet

bath towel ['ba:z tałel] ręcznik kąpielowy (z frotte)

bathtub ['ba:ztab] s. wanna

baton ['baeton] s. buława; pałka; batuta; pałeczka dyrygenta

battalion [be'taeljen] s. batalion; taktyczny pododdział pułku

batter ['baeter] v. tłuc; walić

battered ['baeterd] adj. pobity

battery ['baetery] s. bateria (elektryczna lub armat); komplet; pobicie; zestaw armat

battle ['baetl] s. bitwa; walka

battleship ['baetlszyp] s. okręt wojenny (opancerzony)

baulk [bo:k] s. przeszkoda; rozczarowanie; v. przeszkadzać; zob. balk

bawl [bo:l] v. wrzeszczeć; drzeć się; krzyczeć; zwymyślać; głośno szlochać

bay [bej] adj. czerwono-brązowy; gniady (koń); s. wawrzyn; laur (drzewo); pl. laury

bay [bej] s. zatoka; wnęka; przęsło; v. ujadać; wyć

bay window ['bej'łyndoł] okno

we wnęce (alkowie)
bazaar [be'za:r] s. bazar
be; was; been [bi:; łoz; bi:n]
be [bi:] v. być; żyć; trwać;
dziać się; istnieć; stawać
się; zdarzać się; pozostawać
be reading [bi:'ry:dyn] czytać
właśnie; być w trakcie
czytania (gazety etc.)
beach [bi:cz] s. brzeg; plaża
beachhead ['bi:czhed] s.
przyczółek (nad wodą)
beach-wear ['bi:człe:r] s. odzież
plażowa; kostiumy; płaszcze
beacon ['bi:ken] s. sygnał
(ogniowy); latarnia morska
bead [bi:d] s. paciorek; koralik;
v. nawlekać korale; perlić
się; ozdabiać paciorkami
beak [bi:k] s. dziób; belfer
beam [bi:m] s. belka; dźwigar;
promień; radosny uśmiech;
v. promieniować; nadawać
sygnał; rozpromieniać się
bean [bi:n] s. fasola; bób;
ziarnko; łeb; animusz
bear; bore; borne [beer; bo:r;
bo:rn]
bear [beer] s. niedźwiedź; v.
dźwigać; ponosić; znosić;
podtrzymywać; trzymać się;
rodzić; mieć (potomstwo);
nosić się; zachowywać się
beard [bierd] s. broda (zarost)
bearer ['beerer] s. nosiciel;
okaziciel (legitymacji);
zwiastun; karawaniarz
bearing ['beeryng] s. zachowanie; wzgląd; wspornik;
rodzenie; łożysko
beast [bi:st] s. bestia; bydlę
beastly ['bistly] adj. bydlęcy;
potworny; sl. przykry; niemiły; adv. straszliwie; okrutnie
beast of prey ['bi:st ow prej] s.
drapieżnik (mięsożerny)
beat; beat; beaten[bi:t; bi:t;
bi:tn]
beat [bi:t] v. bić; bić się;
ubijać; tłuc; trzepotać; zbić;
kuć; karać biciem (batem)
beat it ! ['bi:t,yt] excl. precz!;
wynoś się!; wynoście się!

beaten ['bi:tn] adj. ubity;
wydeptany (przemarszem, ko-
pytami); wyczerpany; znany
beatnik [bi:tnyk] s. nonkonformista; (-tka)
beautiful ['bju:teful] adj. piękny;
cudny; wspaniały; świetny
beautify ['bju:tyfaj] v.
upiększać; upiększyć
beauty ['bju:ty] s. piękność;
piękno; uroda; piękna kobieta
beauty parlor ['bju:ty'pa:rler]
salon kosmetyczny
beaver ['bi:wer] s. bóbr;
przedsiębiorczy człowiek
because [bi'ko:z] conj. dlatego;
że; gdyż; adv. z powodu
beckon ['beken] v. skinąć;
nęcić; s. skinienie
become; became; become
[bi'kam; bi'kejm; bi'kam]
become [bi'kam] v. stawać się;
nadawać się; zostawać
kimś (czymś); pasować do
becoming ['bikamyng] adj.
stosowny; odpowiedni;
twarzowy; właściwy
bed [bed] s. łoże; łożysko;
klomb; grządka; ławica;
podkład; nocleg
bedclothes ['bedklouz] s. pościel; prześcieradła; kołdry
bedding ['bedyng] s. pościel
bed linen ['bed,lynyn] s. pościel;
bielizna pościelowa
bedridden ['bed,rydn] adj.
obłożnie chory; złożony
chorobą; nie mogący wstać z
łóżka; przykuty do łóżka
bedroom ['bedrum] s. sypialnia
bedside ['bedsajd] przy łożu
bedsore ['bedso:r] s. odleżyna
bed spread ['bed'spred] s.
narzuta wierzchnia na łóżko
bedtime ['bedtajm] s. pora do
spania; pora snu
bee [bi:] s. pszczoła
beech [bi:cz] s. buk; adj.
bukowy; z drzewa bukowego
beef [bi:f] s. wołowina; siła;
narzekanie; wyrzekanie (slang)
beefsteak ['be:f'stejk] s. befsztyk
(do smażenia lub pieczenia)

beefy ['bi:fy] adj. krzepki;
flegmatyczny; muskularny
beehive ['bi:hajw] s. ul
beekeeper ['bi:kiper] s.
pszczelarz; hodowca pszczół
beeline ['bi:lajn] s. najkrótsza
droga; linia powietrzna
been [bi:n] v. były; zob. be
beer [bier] s. piwo
beet [bi:t] s. burak
beetle ['bi:tl] s. tłuczek; ubijak;
v. ubijać; wystawać; zwisać
beetroot ['bi:tru:t] s. burak
befall [by'fo:l] v. zdarzać się
(komuś); przydarzać się (komuś); przytrafiać się
before [by'fo:r] adv. przedtem;
dawniej; z przodu; na przedzie
beforehand [by'fo:rhend] adv.
uprzednio; przedtem; z góry
befriend [by'frend] v. zaprzy-
jaźniać się; wspomagać
beg [beg] v. prosić; żebrać
began [by'gaen] v. zaczęty;
proszę zobaczyć: begin
beget; begot; begotten [by'get;
by'got; by'gotn]
beget [by'get] v. płodzić;
rodzić; powodować; wywo-
ływać; stawać się ojcem
beggar ['beger] s. żebrak
begin; began; begun [by'gyn;
by'gaen; by'gan]
begin [by'gyn] v. zaczynać
zapoczątkować; rozpocząć
beginner [by'gyner] s.
początkujący; nowy (człowiek)
beginning [by'gynyng] s.
początek; rozpoczęcie
begun [by'gan] v. p.p.
proszę zobaczyć: begin
behalf [by'hae:f] s. w imieniu
kogoś; poparcie dla kogoś;
w czyimś interesie; dla
behave [by'hejw] v. zachowywać się; prowadzić się
behavior [by'hejwjer] s.
postępowanie; zachowanie się
behind [by'hajnd] adv. w tyle; z
tyłu; do tyłu; prep. za; poza;
s. tyłek; pupa
being ['by:yng] s. byt; istnienie;
istota (ludzka)

belated [by'lejtyd] adj.
spóźniony; zapóźniony;
późny; opóźniony
belch [belcz] v. zionąć; odbijać
się; s. bekanie; buchanie; huk;
odbijanie się
belfry ['belfry] s. dzwonnica
Belgian ['beldżen] adj. belgijski
belief [by'li:f] s. wiara; wierzenie;
zaufanie; przekonanie
believe [by'li:w] v. wierzyć;
sądzić; mieć przekonanie;
zakładać; uważać
believer [by'li:wer] s. wyznawca;
wierzący; zwolennik
bell [bel] s. dzwon; dzwonek
belligerent [by'lydżerent] adj.
wojujący; wojowniczy; wojenny; s. strona walcząca
bellow ['belou] v. ryczeć; s. ryk;
ryczenie; porykiwanie
bellows ['belouz] s. miech;
płuca; przedmiot podobny do
miecha; dmuchawa
belly ['bely] s. brzuch; żołądek
belong [bylong] v. należeć
belongings [bylongynz] pl.
rzeczy; bagaż; przynależności
beloved [by'lawd] adj. ukochany;
drogi; s. kochana osoba
below [by'lou] adv. niżej; w
dole; na dół; pod spodem;
prep. poniżej; pod; w piekle
belt [belt] s. pas; pasek; strefa;
v. bić pasem; opasywać
bench [bencz] s. ława; ławka;
stół; terasa; miejsce sędziego
bend; bent; bent [bend; bent;
bent]
bend [bend] s. zgięcie; krzywa;
v. giąć; wyginać; przeginać;
zginać; naginać
beneath [by'ni:s] prep. pod; pod
spodem; na dół; poniżej
benediction [,beny'dykszyn] s.
błogosławieństwo
benefactor [,beny'faekter] s.
dobroczyńca; dobrodziej
beneficent [bi'nefysent] adj.
dobroczynny
beneficial [,beny'fyszel] adj.
pożywny; korzystny; zbawienny; dobroczynny

benefit ['benyfyt] s. korzyść;
dobrodziejstwo; pożytek;
zasiłek; dobro
benevolent [by'newelent] adj.
dobroczynny; życzliwy;
łaskawy
bent [bent] s. sitowie; skłonność; zgięcie; adj. skłonny;
zgięty; zdecydowany; uparty;
wygięty; wykrzywiony
benzene ['benzi:n] s. benzen
benzine ['benzi:n] s. (lekka)
benzyna (do czyszczenia)
bequeath [by'kłys] v. zostawiać
w spadku; przekazać potom-
ości; zapisać w testamencie
bequest [by'kłest] s. zapis;
spadek; spuścizna; legat
bereave; bereft; bereaved
[by'ri:w; by'reft; by'ri:wd]
bereave [by'ri:w] v. pozbawiać;
odzierać; wyzuwać; osiero-
ić; porwać
bereft [by'reft] adj. osierocony;
pozbawiony; wyzuty
beret ['berej] s. beret
berry ['bery] s. jagoda; ikra
berth [be:rs] s. koja; łóżko;
stoisko; miejsce postoju statku
beseech; besought; besought
[by'si:cz; by'so:t; by'so:t]
beseech [by'si:cz] v. błagać;
upraszać; zaklinać
beside [by'sajd] adv. poza tym;
ponadto; inaczej; prep. obok;
przy; w pobliżu; w porównaniu; na równi z ...
besides [by'sajdz] adv. prócz
tego; poza tym; prep. oprócz;
poza; ponadto; w dodatku
besiege [by'si:dż] v. oblegać
best [best] adj. & adv. najlepszy;
najlepiej; v. okpiwać
best wishes [best'łyszys]
najlepsze życzenia
best of all [best,ow'o:l]
najlepszy; najlepiej; a najlepiej
bestow [by'stou] v. podarować;
składać; nadawać; użyczać;
darzyć; obdarzyć
bet [bet] s. zakład; v. zakładać
się; iść o zakład
betray [by'trej] v. zdradzić;

mylić; zawodzić; dawać
dowód; świadczyć
betrayal [by'trejel] s. zdrada
betrayer [by'trejer] s. zdrajca
better ['beter] adv. lepiej; lepszy;
v. poprawić; przewyższyć;
prześcignąć; prześcigać
better than ['beter dzaen] exp.
więcej (slang); ponad; lepiej
between [by'tłi:n] prep. między;
adv. w pośrodku; tymczasem
beverage ['bewerydż] s. napój
beware [by'łe:r] v. strzec się
beware of the dog [by'łe:r ow dy
dog] strzec się psa; zły pies
bewilder [by'łylder] v. zmieszać
(kogoś); oszałamiać
bewilderment [by'łylderment] s.
zaczarowanie; oszołomienie;
chaos; dezorientacja
bewitch [by'łycz] v. zaczarować; oczarować; ująć
(kogoś czymś)
beyond [by'jond] adv. & prep.
za; poza; dalej niż; nad;
ponad; dalej (położony etc.)
bias ['bajes] s. uprzedzenie;
fałsz; kierunek; ukos; odchylenie; v. skłonić; nachylić;
uprzedzić; usposabiać
biased ['bajest] adj. stronniczy;
uprzedzony; nastawiony
bib [byb] s. śliniak; v. popijać
Bible ['bajbl] s. Biblia
bicycle ['bajsykl] s. rower
bid [byd] v. oferować cenę;
licytować; kazać; s. oferta
na licytacji; stawka; zaproszenie; odzywka; zapowiedź
bid farewell [,byd'fa:rłel] v.
żegnać się (z kimś); pożegnać kogoś
bier [bjer] s. mary (pod trumną)
big [byg] adj. & adv. duży;
wielki; ważny; głośny; godny
big business [byg'byznys] wielkie
interesy; wielkie korporacje
big wig [byg łyg] s. wielka
szyszka; ważniak; gruba ryba
bigamy ['bygemy] s. bigamia;
dwużeństwo
bigness ['bygnys] s. wielkość;
duży rozmiar; grubość

bigot ['byget] s. bigot; bigotka;
świątoszek; zapaleniec
bigoted ['bygetyd] adj. zajadły;
sfanatyzowany
bike [bajk] s. rower
bilateral [baj'laeterel] adj.
dwustronny; obustronny
bile [bajl] s. żółć; zgorzknia-
łość; tetryczność
bilious ['byljes] adj. żółciowy;
zrzędny; popędliwy; tetryczny
bill [byl] s. dziób; pika; cypel
bill [byl] s. rachunek; kwit; afisz;
plakat; v. ogłaszać; afi-
szować; oblepiać afiszami
billboard ['byl,bo:rd] s. tablica
ogłoszeniowa
billfold ['byl,fould] s. portfel (na
dokumenty i pieniądze)
billiards ['byljerdz] s. bilard
billion ['byljen] s. tysiąc
milionów (USA); miliard
bill of exchange ['byl,ow
'eksczendż] weksel
billow ['bylou] s. bałwan; kłąb;
v. piętrzyć; falować; bał-
wanić się
bin [byn] s. skrzynia; paka; v.
pakować; chować do skrzyni
bind [bajnd] v. wiązać; zobowiązywać; opatrywać; oprawiać; obszywać; uwiązać
binding ['bajndyng] adj. wią-
żący; s. połączenie; oprawa
(książki); oprawianie; wiązanie; obszycie; zaciskanie
binoculars [bajnokjulez] pl.
lornetka (polowa, teatralna)
biography [baj'ogrefy] s.
biografia; opis życia i
działalności
biology [baj'oledży] s. biologia
birch [be:rcz] s. brzoza
bird [be:rd] s. ptak; dziwak
bird of passage ['be:rd ow
paesydż] przelotny ptak
bird of prey ['be:rd ow prej]
drapieżny ptak
bird's eye view ['be:rds aj,wju]
widok z lotu ptaka
birth [be:rt] s. urodzenie
birth control ['be:rt kon,troul]
kontrola urodzin

birthday ['be:rtdej] s. urodziny;
początek czegoś
birthday party ['be:rtdej pa:rty]
przyjęcie urodzinowe
birthplace ['be:rt-plejs] miejsce
urodzenia
biscuit ['byskyt] s. bułka;
sucharek lekkostrawny
bishop ['byszep] s. biskup
bison ['bajsn] s. bizon
bit [byt] s. wędzidło; ostrze;
wiertło; ząb; szczypta; odrobina; kawałek; 12 1/2 centów;
moment; krótki czas; najpros-
tsza informacja w komputerze
jak: "tak" lub "nie"
bitch [bycz] s. suka; wulg.
kurwa
bite; bit; bitten [bajt; byt; bitn]
bite [bajt] v. gryźć; kąsać;
docinać; dokuczać; s. po-
karm; przynęta; ukąszenie;
ciętość; lekki posiłek; odrobina czegoś do jedzenia
bitter ['byter] adj. gorzki; ostry;
zły; zgorzkniały; przykry
blab [blaeb] v. paplać; gadać;
s. plotkarz; plotkarka; gaduła
black [blaek] adj. czarny; ponury;
s. murzyn; v. czernić
blackberry ['blaekbery] s. jeżyna
blackbird ['blaekbe:rd] s. kos
blackboard ['blaekbo:rd] s.
tablica (szkolna)
blacken ['bleakn] v. czernić
black eye ['blaekaj] s. podbite
oko
blackhead ['blaekhed] s. wągier
blackmail ['blaekmejl] s. szantaż;
wymuszenie; v. szantażować
black-market ['blaek ma:rkyt] s.
czarny rynek
blackout ['blaekaut] s. za-
ciemnienie (miasta, okien)
black pudding ['blaek'pudyng] s.
kaszanka; kiszka
blacksmith ['blaeksmys] s. kowal
(wiejski)
bladder ['blaeder] s. pęcherz
blade [blejd] s. źdźbło; liść;
ostrze; płetwa; klinga; wesołek
blame [blejm] s. wina; nagana;
v. łajać; ganić; winić

blame for ['blejm for] v. winić za (coś)

blameless ['blejmlys] adj. bez winy; niewinny

blank [blaenk] adj. biały; pusty; czysty; nie wypełniony; s. puste miejsce; nie wypełniony formularz; ślepak

blanket ['blaenkyt] s. koc wełniany; ciepły koc

blasphemy ['blaesfymy] s. bluźnierstwo; pogarda dla Boga

blast [bla:st] s. wybuch; podmuch; odgłos eksplozji; prąd powietrza; v. wysadzić w powietrze; detonować; niszczyć; przeklinać; uderzać

blast furnace ['bla:st,fe:rnys] s. wielki piec hutniczy

blatant ['blejtent] adj. krzykliwy; ryczący; przesadny

blaze [blejz] s. błysk; płomień; wybuch; v. płonąć

bleach [bli:cz] v. wybielać

bleak [bli:k] adj. ponury; smutny; wystawiony do wiatru

blear [blier] adj. mętny; zamglony; niewyraźny

bleat [bli:t] v. beczeć

bleed; bled; bled [bli:d; bled; bled]

bleed [bli:d] v. krwawić

blemish ['blemysz] s. plama; wada; skaza; v. zniekształcić; splamić; poplamić; pobrudzić; zepsuć; być skazą

blend; blent; blent [blend; blent; blent]

blend [blend] v. mieszać się; łączyć się; s. mieszanina

bless [bles] v. błogosławić; udzielić błogosławieństwa

bless my soul ['bles,maj'so:l] excl. o Boże!

blessed ['blesyd] adj. błogosławiony; święty; kojący

blessing ['blesyng] s. błogosławieństwo; aprobata; dobra rzecz; dar boski; szczęście

blew [blu:] v. zob. blow

blight [blajt] s. zniszczenie; zaraza; v. niszczyć

blind [blajnd] adj. ślepy; v.

oślepić; s. zasłona

blind alley ['blajnd,alej] ślepa ulica

blindfold ['blajnd,fould] adj. & adv. na ślepo; z zawiązanymi oczami; na oślep; v. zawiązywać oczy; s. zasłona oczu

blink [blynk] v. mrugać; s. błysk oka; mignięcie; migotanie

bliss [blys] s. radość; błogość

blithe ['blajz] adj. wesoły

blizzard ['blyzerd] s. śnieżyca; zawieja; zadymka; zamieć

bloat [blout] v. nadymać; nabrzmiewać; uwędzić; wędzić

bloater ['blouter] s. śledź wędzony; pikling

block [blok] s. blok; kloc; zeszyt; przeszkoda; v. tamować; wstrzymywać; tarasować; zatykać; zablokować; blokować; tamować

block up ['blokap] v. zablokować; zablokowywać; zamurować; zatkać

blockade [blo'kejd] s. blokada; v. blokować; robić zator

blonde [blond] s. blondynka

blood [blad] s. krew; ród; pokrewieństwo

bloodshed ['bladszed] s. rozlew krwi

bloodshot ['bladszot] adj. nabrzmiały krwią; zaszły krwią

blood vessel ['blad,wesl] s. naczynie krwionośne

bloody ['blady] adj. krwawy

bloom [blu:m] s. kwiecie; v. kwitnąć; rozkwitać

blooming [blu:myng] adj. kwitnący; przeklęty (slang)

blossom ['blosem] v. kwitnąć; s. kwiecie; kwiat

blot [blot] s. plama; v. plamić

blot out ['blot aut] v. wymazać; usunąć; wykreślać; zamazywać; ukrywać

blotter [bloter] s. bibularz; rejestr aresztowań; suszka

blotting paper ['blotyng,pejper] bibuła; suszka

blouse [blauz] s. bluza

blow; blew; blown [blou; blu; błołn]

blow [blou] s. silny cios; nagły atak; nagłe nieszczęście; szok; dmuchnięcie; podmuch; rzut; rozkwit; v. dmuchać; zakwitać; rozkwitać; popychać podmuchem; wybuchać; stapiać; trąbić; chwalić się; rozrzutnie wydawać pieniądze; popełniać błąd; odchodzić; rozbić; rozwalić

blow drier ['blou,drajer] s. suszarka do włosów

blow gun ['blou,gan] s. rura do strzelania pneumatycznego; pistolet pneumatyczny

blowout ['blou'aut] s. rozerwanie opony; libacja; bankiet

blowup ['blou'ap] s. eksplozja; wybuch gniewu; sprzeczka; powiększona fotografia

blue [blu:] adj. niebieski; błękitny; siny; ponury; v. farbować na niebiesko; pomalować na niebiesko; s. błękit; lazur

bluebell ['blu:bel] s. dzwonek (kwiat)

blues [blu:s] pl. smutek; przygnębienie; smutne piosenki

bluff [blaf] s. oszustwo; nabieranie; blaga; bluff; adj. szorstki; stromy; v. wprowadzać w błąd; bluffować

bluish ['blu:ysz] adj. niebieskawy

blunder ['blander] s. ciężki błąd; v. popełniać błąd (gafę)

blunt [blant] adj. tępy; nieczuły; v. stępić; przytępić

blur [ble:r] s. plama; v. zatrzeć; splamić; zamazać

boar [bo:r] s. dzik; odyniec

board [bo:rd] s. deska; władza naczelna; tablica; rada; pokład

boarder ['bo:rder] s. pensjonariusz; pasażer; stołownik

boardinghouse ['bo:rdyng,haus] s. pensjonat

boarding school ['bo:rdyng,sku:l] s. szkoła z internatem

boardwalk ['bo:rd łok] s. chodnik z desek

boast [boust] v. chwalić się; s. samochwalstwo; przechwałki

boat [bout] s. łódź; statek

boat race ['bout,rejs] s. regaty; wyścigi łodzi

bob [bob] v. kiwać sie; krótko strzyc; szturchnąć; s. wisiorek; kłąb włosów; wahadło; pion; szturchnięcie

bobby ['boby] s. angielski policjant

bobsled ['bob sled] s. bobslej; sanki z kierownicą etc.

bodice ['bodys] s. stanik

bodily ['bodyly] adj. & adv. osobiście; fizycznie; całkowicie; gremialnie; cieleśnie

body ['body] s. ciało (ludzkie, fizyczne, astralne); karoseria; korpus; grupa; gromada; ogół

bodyguard ['bodyga:rd] s. straż przyboczna; ochrona osobista

bog [bog] s. bagno; moczary

boil [bojl] v. wrzeć; kipieć; gotować; s. wrzenie; czyrak

boil over ['bojl,ouwer] v. wygotować; wygotować się

boiled eggs ['bojld egs] gotowane jajka

boiler ['bojler] s. kocioł

boisterous ['bojsteres] adj. hałaśliwy; niesforny; burzliwy; gwałtowny; porywisty

bold [bould] adj. śmiały; zuchwały; zauważalny; wyraźny; wyrazisty

bolster ['boulster] s. miękka podkładka; poduszka; v. miękko podeprzeć

bolt [boult] s. zasuwa; bolec; piorun; wypad; rygiel; ucieczka; v. zasuwać; rzucić się; wypaść; czmychać

bomb [bom] s. bomba; v. bombardować; atakować bombami; adj. bombowy

bombard [bom'ba:rd] v. bombardować (artylerią lub bombami)

bond [bond] s. więź; obligacja

bone [boun] s. kość; ość

bonfire ['bonfajer] s. płonący stos; ognisko (obozowe etc.)

bonnet ['bonyt] s. czapka
(damska); czepek
bonny ['bony] adj. piękny; ładny
bonus ['bounes] s. premia
bony ['bouny] adj. kościsty
book [buk] s. książka; rejestr;
v. księgować; rezerwować;
aresztować; rejestrować
booked up ['bukt ap] adj.
wyprzedany; pełny
bookcase ['bukkejs] s. półka na
książki; biblioteczka
booking clerk ['bukyn,klerk] s.
kasjer kolejowy
booking office ['bukyn,ofys]
biuro biletowo-rezerwacyjne
bookkeeper ['buk,ki:per] s.
księgowy; księgowa
bookkeeping ['buk,ki:pyng] s.
księgowość
booklet ['buklyt] s. książeczka
bookseller ['buk,seler] s. księgarz
book shop ['bukszop] s.
księgarnia
bookstore ['buksto:r] s.
księgarnia
bookworm ['buk,łerm] s. mól
książkowy
boom [bu:m] s. huk; nagła
zwyżka; bom; bariera; v.
zwyżkować; podbijać ceny
boomerang ['bu:meraeng] s.
bumerang; v. działać jak
bumerang
boor [bu:r] s. prostak; gbur;
chłop; prostaczka
boost [bu:st] v. forsować;
podnosić znaczenie; za-
chwalać; wzmacniać; rozrek-
lamować; podsadzić (kogoś)
boot [bu:t] s. but; cholewa
booth [bu:s] s. budka; stragan
booty ['bu:ty] s. łup; zdobycz
booze ['bu:z] s. alkohol pitny
border ['bo:rder] s. granica;
brzeg; rąbek; lamówka; skraj;
kresy; v. obrębiać; graniczyć; oblamować; obszyć
bore [bo:r] v. wiercić; drążyć;
nudzić; zanudzać; s. otwór;
nudy; nudziarz; natręt; rzecz
nieznośna; nudziarstwo
bore [bo:r] v. zob. bear

born [bo:rn] adj. urodzony
borough ['be:rou] s. miasteczko
borrow ['borou] v. (za)pożyczać
bosom ['busem] s. (łono) pierś
boss [bo:s] s. szef; v. rządzić
botany ['boteny] s. botanika
botch [bocz] s. fuszerka;
łatanina; partactwo; v.
partaczyć; fuszerować
both [bous] pron. & adj. obaj;
obydwaj; obie; obydwie; oboje
bother [bodzer] s. kłopot; v.
niepokoić; dokuczać; drę-
czyć; zawracać głowę
bother about [,bodzer e'baut] v.
kłopotać się czymś
bottle ['botl] s. butelka
bottom ['botem] s. dno; spód;
dolina; głąb; dolna część;
adj. dolny; spodni; podstawowy; v. sięgać dna; wstawiać dno; osiągać dno
bough [bau] s. konar; gałąź
bought [bo:t] v. zakupiony; zob.
buy (zakupiony, przekupiony)
boulder ['boulder] s. głaz
bounce [bauns] v. odbijać się;
podskakiwać; odskoczyć;
blagować; s. gwałtowne
odbicie; odskok;
samochwalstwo; chełpliwość
bound [baund] s. granica; adj.
będący w drodze; v. gra-
niczyć; być zobowiązanym
boundary [baundry] s. linia
graniczna; adj. graniczny
boundless [baundlys] adj.
bezgraniczny; niezmierzony
bountiful ['bauntyful] adj. obfity;
hojny; szczodry
bouquet [bu:'kej] s. bukiet
kwiatów; zapach (wina)
bout [baut] s. okres; runda;
próba sił; atak (choroby)
bow [bau] s. łuk; kabłąk;
smyczek; ukłon; v. zginać
się; kłaniać się; wygiąć w
kabłąk; schylić się
bowels ['bauelz] pl. trzewia;
wnętrzności; kiszki
bower ['bauer] s. altana; chatka;
kotwica przednia
bowl [boul] s. miska; czerpak;

box 329 break down

stadion; szala; v. grać kulami
(w kręgla); toczyć koło
box [boks] s. skrzynka; pudełko;
loża; boks; v. pakować;
oddzielać; uderzać pięścią
boxer ['bokser] s. pięściarz;
bokser
boxing ['boksyng] s. boks;
pięściarstwo
box office ['boks,ofys] s. kasa w
teatrze; kasa biletów wstępu
boy [boj] s. chłopak; służący
boycott ['bojkot] s. bojkot; v.
bojkotować
boyfriend ['boj-frend] s.
przyjaciel (dziewczyny);
kochanek
boyhood ['bojhud] s. wiek chłopięcy; dzieciństwo chłopca
boyish ['bojysz] adj. chłopięcy
boy-scout ['boj-skaut] s. harcerz
bra [bra:] s. biustnik; stanik;
biustonosz
brace [brejs] s. klamra; korba;
podpora; wiązanie; kleszcze;
v. wzmacniać; krzepić; podpierać; spiąć klamrą; związać; ścisnąć; napiąć
brace up [brejs ap] v. wytężyć
się; zebrać siły; orzeźwić
bracelet ['brejslyt] s. bransoletka;
kajdanek
bracket ['braekyt] s. wspornik;
ramię; nawias; grupa; klamra;
podpórka; konsola; v. brać w
nawiasy; grupować
brag [braeg] v. chełpić się
braggart ['braegert] s. samo-
chwała; pyszałek; bufon;
fanfaron
braid [brejd] s. warkocz; wstążka; plecionka; v. pleść;
opasywać; obszywać
brain [brejn] s. mózg; rozum
brain wave ['brejn,łejw] s.
świetny pomysł; świetna
myśl; natchnienie
brake [brejk] s. hamulec
bramble ['braembel] s. krzak
jagody; krzak jeżyny; jeżyna
branch [bra:ncz] s. gałąź;
odnoga; filia; v. odgałęziać
się; zbaczać; rozwidlać się

brand [braend] s. głownia;
żagiew; wypalony znak na
skórze; piętno; żelazne
narzędzie do wypalania znaku;
znak własności; znak fir-
mowy; marka towaru; pochodzenie towaru; gatunek towaru; v. naznaczać; piętnować; wryć (w pamięć)
brand new [,braen'nju] adj.
nowiutki; nowiusieńki; jak
spod igły
brandy ['braendy] s. wódka ze
spirytusu winnego
brass [braes] s. mosiądz; spiż;
ranga; starszyzna; instrumenty
dęte; forsa; pieniądze; czelność; śmiałość; przedmio-
ty z mosiądzu
brass band [,braes'baend] s.
kapela dęta; orkiestra dęta
brassiere [bre'zier] s. biustnik;
stanik; biustonosz
brat [braet] s. brzdąc; bachor
brave [brejw] adj. dzielny; odważny; śmiały; v. stawiać
czoło; odważyć się
brazen ['brejzn] adj. mosiężny;
brązowy; bezczelny; bez-
wstydny; cyniczny
Brazilian [bre'zyljen] adj.
brazylijski; s. Brazylijczyk
breach [bry:cz] s. naruszenie;
wyłom; zerwanie; niedotrzy-
manie; v. przełamać (się);
zrobić wyłom; przerwać się
bread [bred] s. chleb; forsa
(slang); środki utrzymania
bread and butter [bred-en-bater]
chleb z masłem; środki
utrzymania
breadth [breds] s. szerokość;
rozmach; szerokość poglą-
dów; rozpiętość (skrzydeł)
break; broke; broken [brejk;
brouk; brouken]
break [brejk] v. łamać; rujnować; przegrywać; potłuc; urwać; s. załamanie;
wyłom; nagła zmiana; wada
break away ['brejk ełej] v.
oderwać (się); uciekać
break down ['brejk dałn] v.

załamać (się); s. zaparcie się;
upadek; rozbiór; awaria
break in ['brejkyn] v. włamać
(się); wtargnąć; wtrącić się
break off ['brejkof] v. urwać;
odłamać; zerwać stosunki
break out ['brejkaut] v. wyrwać
(się); pokryć się pryszczami
break up ['brejkap] v. połamać
(się); rozpadać się; rozejść
się; rozebrać; rozdrobnić
breakable ['brejkebel] adj.
kruchy; łamliwy; łatwy do
zbicia, stłuczenia
breakfast ['brekfest] s.
śniadanie; v. jeść śniadanie
breast [brest] s. pierś
breaststroke ['brest,strouk]
pływanie żabką
breath [bres] s. oddech;
tchnienie; dech; oddychanie;
powiew; podmuch
breathe [bri:z] v. oddychać;
tchnąć; żyć; dać wy-
tchnąć; powiewać; na-
tchnąć; wionąć; szepnąć
breathing ['bri:zyng] s. oddech;
wytchnienie; adj. żywy
breathless [breslys] adj. bez
tchu; zasapany; zadyszany;
zziajany
bred [bred] zob. breed;
wychowany
breeches ['bry:czyz] pl. spodnie
do jazdy konnej; bryczesy
breed; bred; bred [bri:d; bred;
bred]
breed [bri:d] v. rodzić;
rozmnażać; hodować; pło-
dzić; s. chów; rasa; ród;
plemię; ród ludzki
breeder ['bri:der] s. hodowca;
rozsadnik (choroby); roz-
płodnik; reproduktor
breeding [bri:dyng] s. hodowla;
obejście; dobre wychowanie
breeze [bri:z] s. wietrzyk; zwada;
podmuch wiatru; v. wiać;
śmigać; odejść; oszukać
brevity ['brewyty] s. zwięzłość;
krótkość; krótkotrwałość
brew [bru:] v. warzyć (piwo);
knuć; s. napój uwarzony;

preparat; warzenie; parzenie;
odwar; napar
brewery [bru:ery] s. browar
bribe [brajb] v. dawać łapówkę;
przekupywać; s. łapówka
bribery ['brajbery] s.
przekupstwo; łapownictwo;
korupcja
brick [bryk] s. cegła; kostka; adj.
ceglany; v. obmurować; zamurować (okno; drzwi etc.)
bricklayer ['bryk,lejer] s. murarz
brickwork ['bryklork] s.
murowanie; wykonana robota
murarska
brickyard ['brykja:rd] s. cegielnia
bridal ['brajdel] adj. ślubny;
weselny; s. ślub; wesele
bride [brajd] s. panna młoda
bridegroom ['brajdgru:m] s. pan
młody; nowożeniec
bridesmaid ['brajdzmejd] s.
druhna; drużka
bridge [brydż] s. most; mostek;
brydż; grzbiet; v. łączyć
mostem; zapełnić lukę
bridgehead ['brydżhed] s. przyczółek mostowy; przyczółek
bridle ['braidl] s. uździenica;
uzda; cuma; cugiel; wodza; v.
kiełznać; powściągać; opanowywać; okiełznać
bridle path ['brajdl,pas] s.
ścieżka do jazdy konnej
brief [bri:f] s. streszczenie;
zestawienie; odprawa; krótkie
majtki; v. zwięźle streścić;
pouczyć; informować; zro-
bić odprawę; mówić krótko;
adj. krótkotrwały; treściwy;
zwięzły; krótki
briefcase ['bri:f,kejs] s. teczka
brigade [bry'gejd] s. brygada
bright [brajt] adj. jasny;
świetny; bystry; adv. jasno
brighten ['brajtn] v. rozjaśnić;
błyszczeć; promieniować
brightness [brajtnys] s.
jasność; światło; blask;
żywość
brilliance ['bryljens] s. blask;
wielkie zdolności; świet-
ność; jasność; blichtr

brilliancy ['bryljensy] s. świetność; blichtr; połysk; jasne
światło; blask; jasność
brilliant ['bryljent] adj.
lśniący; błyszczący; świetny; wybitny; znakomity
brim [brym] s. brzeg (naczynia);
rondo (kapelusza); v.
napełniać po brzegi
brimful ['brym'ful] adj. pełen po
brzegi; przepełniony
bring; brought; brought [bryng;
bro:t; bro:t]
bring [bryng] v. przynosić;
przyprowadzać; powodować;
zmusić (się); ściągnąć
bring an action ['bryng an
'aekszyn] v. wszczynać
działanie, akcję
bring about ['bryng e'baut] v.
uskutecznić; wywoływać;
dokonać; spowodować
bring forth ['bryng,fo:rs] v.
ujawniać; wywoływać; uro-
dzić; wydawać na świat
bring in ['bryng yn] v.
wprowadzać; przynosić;
wydawać (wyrok etc.)
bring up [bring ap] v. poruszyć;
przynieść na górę; przy-
sunąć; wychowywać
brink [brynk] s. skraj; brzeg
brisk [brysk] adj. żywy; raźny;
rześki; trzaskający; wesoły
bristle ['brysl] s. szczecina
British ['brytysz] adj. brytyjski; s.
Anglik; Brytyjczyk
brittle ['brytl] adj. kruchy
broach [broucz] v. żłobić;
zaczynać; poruszać; s.
szydło; rożen; iglica
broad [bro:d] adj. szeroki; z
rozmachem; wyraźny; obszerny; rozległy; s. szeroka
płaszczyzna; wulg. kobieta;
adv. szeroko; z akcentem
broadcast ['bro:dka:st] s.
transmitować; rozsiewać;
szerzyć; s. transmisja
broad-minded ['bro:d'majndyt]
adj. pobłażliwy; z otwartą
głową; tolerancyjny
brochure ['broszjuer] s. broszura

broke [brouk] adj. złamany; bez
grosza; zob. break
broken [brouken] adj. połamany;
zepsuty; zob. break
broker [brouker] s. pośrednik;
ajent; makler; taksator;
handlarz narkotyków
bronchia ['bronkje] pl. oskrzela
bronchitis ['bron'kajtys] s.
bronchit
bronze [bronz] s. brąz; spiż; adj.
brązowy; spiżowy; v. brązo-
wać; brązowieć
brooch [broucz] s. brosza; spinka
brood [bru:d] s. wyląg; potomstwo; v. wysiadywać; tkwić;
rozmyślać ponuro; być
pogrążonym w myślach
brook [bruk] s. potok; strumyk;
v. ścierpieć
broom [bru:m] s. miotła; v.
zamiatać; wymiatać; ob-
miatać
broth [bros] s. rosół; bulion
brothel ['brodzel] s. burdel
brother ['bradzer] s. brat
brotherhood ['bradzer,hud] s.
braterstwo; związek
zawodowy
brothers and sisters ['bradzers
,en'systers] rodzeństwo
brotherly ['bradzerly] adj.
braterski
brought [bro:t] adj. przyniesiony;
zob. bring
brow [brau] s. brew; czoło;
nawis; szczyt; brzeg (prze-
paści); pomost; kładka
brown [braun] adj. brunatny;
brązowy; palony; kasztano-
waty; pakunkowy (papier); v.
brązowieć; opalać się;
przyrumieniać (mięso)
brown paper ['braun,pejpe:r] s.
papier pakunkowy
brown sugar [braun 'szuger] s.
melasa
bruise [bru:z] s. siniak; stłuczenie; v. tłuc; otłuc; posinia-
czyć; połamać kości; ranić;
zgnieść; wyklepać
brunette [bru:'net] s. brunetka
brush [brasz] s. szczotka;

pędzel; draśnięcie; v.
szczotkować; otrzepać;
pędzlować
brush up ['brasz ap] v.
wygładzić; odświeżyć;
zgarnąć szczotką
Brussels sprouts ['brazls,spraut]
s. brukselka (jarzyna)
brutal ['bru:tl] adj. brutalny;
zmysłowy; zwierzęcy
brutality [bru:'taelyty] s.
brutalstwo; brutalność
brute [bru:t] s. bydlę; zwierzę
ludzkie; adj. tępy; brutalny;
bezduszny; bydlęcy; nieokrzesany; zwierzęcy
bubble ['babl] s. bąbel; bańka;
kipienie; wrzenie; v. kipieć;
burzyć się; wydzielać bańki;
musować; bulgotać
buck [bak] s. kozioł; fircyk;
dolar; adj. rogowy; męski;
zwykły (szeregowy); v. skakać narowiście; opierać sie
bucket ['bakyt] s. wiadro;
czerpak (koparki); tłok; miska
buckle ['bakl] v. spinać; łączyć;
wichrować; s. spinka; kla-
merka; sprzączka
buckle on ['bakl on] v. poza-
pinać się; zapiąć pas;
przypiąć
buckskin ['bakskyn] s. wypra-
wiona skóra koźla (sarnia)
bud [bad] s. pączek; zawią-
zek; zarodek; v. pączkować;
wyrastać; być w zarodku;
rozwijać się; dobrze
zapowiadać się
Buddhist ['budyst] s. buddysta
buddy ['bady] s. bliski kolega
budget ['badżyt] s. budżet; v.
budżetować; asygnować
buffalo ['bafelou] s. bawół
buffer ['bafer] s. bufor; zderzak;
odbój
buffet ['bafyt] s. bufet; cios;
kułak; szturchaniec; raz;
uderzenie
buffet ['befej] s. niski kredens;
dania barowe
bug [bag] s. owad; pluskwa;
defekt; amator; insekt; robak

bugle ['bju:gl] s. róg (do
trąbienia); v. trąbić; zatrąbić
build; built; built [byld; bylt; bylt]
build [byld] v. budować;
rozbudowywać; stworzyć;
wznosić
builder ['bylder] s. budowniczy
building ['byldyng] s. budowla
built [bylt] adj. zbudowany; zob.
build
bulb [balb] s. cebula; żarówka
bulge [baldż] v. wzdymać;
wybrzuszać; wydymać; wy-
trzeszczać; s. wypukłość;
wzdęcie; wzdymanie się;
wybrzuszenie; przewaga
bulk [balk] s. masa; kolos;
większość; cielsko; wielka
ilość (towaru); v. groma-
dzić; komasować
bulky ['balky] adj. wielki; otyły;
ciężki; masywny; nieporęczny
bull [bul] s. byk; duży samiec;
głupstwo; nonsens = bull-shit
[bul-szyt] (wulg.)
bullet ['bulyt] s. kula (nabój)
bulletin ['buletyn] s. komunikat;
biuletyn
bulletin board ['buletyn,bo:rd] s.
tablica na ogłoszenia
bullion ['buljen] s. złoto i srebro
w sztabach
bully ['buly] v. dręczyć;
tyranizować; s. awanturnik;
kłótnik; najęty drab; adj.
byczy; żywy; wesoły; świetny; kapitalny
bum [bam] s. włóczęga; nierób;
popijawa; zadek; v. włóczyć
się; cyganić; pić; adj. marny
bumblebee ['bambl-bi:] s. trzmiel
bump [bamp] v. zderzyć się;
łupnąć; odbić z łomotem;
nabić guza; s. zderzenie;
grzmotnięcie; guz; wybój;
wstrząs; uderzenie; wy-
pukłość; zdolności
bumper ['bamper] s. zderzak;
pełny kielich; rekord
bun [ban] s. ciastko drożdżowe;
kok (włosów)
bunch [bancz] s. pęk; banda;
zgraja; guz; v. składać w

pęki; skupiać się; kulić się

bunch of grapes ['bancz,ow grejps] kiść (gałązka) winogron; pęk winogron

bundle ['bandl] s. tłumok; wiązka; v. pakować (w tobół)

bundle up ['bandl,ap] v. zawinąć się; zebrać; zbierać

bungalow ['bangelou] s. domek letni parterowy

bungle ['bangl] s. partactwo; v. partaczyć; bałaganić

bunion ['banjen] s. zapalenie stawu w stopie (bolesny guz)

bunk ['bank] s. koja; banialuki

bunk bed ['bank,bed] s. łóżko piętrowe; łóżko do podnoszenia

bunny ['bani] s. królik; truś

buoy [boj] s. boja; znak pływający; pława; v. znaczyć bojami

buoyant ['bojent] adj. utrzymujący się na powierzchni wody; pławny; sprężysty; pogodny

burden ['be:rdn] s. brzemię; ciężar; obowiązek; v. obciążać; przygniatać; obładowywać

bureau ['bjurou] s. komoda; biuro; sekretarzyk; urząd

bureaucracy [bju'rokresy] s. biurokracja

burglar [be:rgler] s. włamywacz

burglary ['be:rglery] s. włamanie (zwłaszcza w nocy)

burial ['berjel] s. pogrzeb

burly ['be:rly] adj. krzepki; tęgi; duży i silny

burn; burnt; burnt [be:rn; be:rnt; be:rnt]

burn [be:rn] v. palić; płonąć; zapalić; poparzyć; wypalać; s. oparzelizna; dziura wypalona; oparzenie

burner ['be:rner] s. palnik

burning ['be:rnyng] s. palenie

burnt [be:rnt] v. spalony; zob. burn (przypalony, opalony ...)

burst; burst; burst [be:rst; be:rst; be:rst]

burst [be:rst] v. rozsadzać;

rozrywać; s. wybuch; pęknięcie; salwa; zryw; szał; grzmot; hulanka

burst of laughter ['be:rst ,ow'lafter] wybuch śmiechu

burst into flames ['be:rst ,yntu'flejms] buchać ogniem

burst into tears ['be:rst ,yntu'tiers] wybuchnąć płaczem; zalać się łzami

bury ['bery] v. pochować; zagrzebać; pogrzebać; chować; zakopywać

bus [bas] s. autobus

bush [busz] s. krzak; gąszcz

bushel ['buszel] s. korzec (8 galonów); v. przerabiać

bushy ['buszy] adj. nastroszony; krzaczasty; gęsty

business ['byznys] s. interes; zajęcie; sprawa; przedsiębiorstwo; transakcja; handel; adj. handlowy; urzędowy

business hours ['byznys,aurs] godziny urzędowe

business letter ['byznys,leter] oficjalny list

businesslike ['byznys,lajk] adj. rzeczowy; solidny; poważny; praktyczny; dokładny

businessman ['byznysman] s. przedsiębiorca; człowiek interesów; handlowiec

business trip ['byznys,tryp] podróż służbowa

businesswoman ['byznys'łumen] s. kobieta interesu; właścicielka przedsiębiorstwa

bus stop ['bas-stop] s. przystanek autobusowy

bust [bast] s. popiersie; biust; v. rujnować; psuć; rozwalić; niszczyć; bankrutować; wybuchnąć

bustle ['basl] v. krzątać się; zapędzać do pracy; s. rozgardiasz; krzątanina; bieganina

busy ['byzy] adj. zajęty; skrzętny; wścibski; ruchliwy

busybody ['byzy,body] adj. wścibski; złośliwy; plotkarz; intrygant

but [bat] adv. conj. prep. lecz;
ale; jednak; natomiast; tylko;
inaczej niż; z wyjątkiem
but for ['bat fo:r] exp. oprócz;
bez; gdyby nie
but now ['bat nau] exp. dopiero
teraz; dopiero w tej chwili
but once ['bat lans] exp. tylko
raz; chociaż tylko raz
butcher ['buczer] s. rzeźnik; kat;
v. zarzynać; mordować;
masakrować; brutalnie
zabijać; partaczyć
butt [bat] 1. s. drzewce; kolba;
nasada; niedopałek papierosa;
pośladki; cel; przedmiot kpin;
ofiara; tarcza; v. bóść; trącać; przytykać; 2. s. styk;
zetknięcie; uderzenie głową
(bykiem)
butt in ['bat yn] v. wtrącać się;
przerywać rozmowę
butter ['bater] s. masło; v.
smarować masłem; przy-
chlebiać
buttercup ['baterkap] s. jaskier
butterfly ['baterflaj] s. motyl; adj.
motyli
buttocks ['bateks] pl. pośladki
button ['batn] s. guzik; przycisk
dzwonka; v. zapinać
button up ['batn ap] v. zapinać
się; zapinać na guziki
buttonhole ['batnhoul] s. dziurka
od guzika; v. zmuszać do
słuchania
buttress ['batrus] s. podpora
buxom ['baksem] adj. dorodny;
okazały; pełny (biust); ładna
(babka)
buy; bought; bought [baj; bo:t;
bo:t]
buy [baj] v. kupować; przekupić; okupić
buyer [bajer] s. nabywca
buzz [baz] s. brzęczenie; v.
brzęczeć; przelatywać nisko
buzzard ['bazed] s. myszołów
by [baj] prep. przy; koło;
co(dzień); przez; z; po; w
(nocy); o; według
by myself ['baj majself] ja sam
by and large ['baj end 'la:rdż]

adv. ogólnie mówiąc; ogólnie
biorąc
by twos ['baj,tuz] dwójkami
by the dozen ['baj dy 'dazn]
tuzinami
by the end ['baj dy ,end] przy
końcu; ku końcowi; z koń-
cem; pod koniec
by land ['baj,laend] lądem
by bus ['baj,bas] autobusem
by day ['baj,dej] za dnia
by-and-by ['baj-end-baj] s.
przyszłość; adv. wnet; po
chwili
bye-bye! ['baj'baj] excl. pa !
by-election [,baj-e'lekszyn] s.
wybory uzupełniające
bygone ['bajgon] adj. miniony;
przestarzały; s. zdarzenia
minione
bygones ['bajgonz] pl.
przeszłość; dawne urazy;
dawne zatargi
bylaw ['bajlo:] s. przepis;
zarządzenie (miejscowe etc.)
by-name ['bajnejm] s. przydomek
bypass ['baj-pas] s. droga
dojazdowa; objazd; v. ob-
jeżdżać; ominąć
by-product [,baj-'prodact] s.
produkt uboczny
byroad [,baj-'roud] s. boczna
droga; droga drugorzędna
bystander [,baj-'stander] s.
przygodny widz
bystreet [,baj-'stri:t] s. boczna
ulica (drugorzędna)
byte ['bajt] s. osiem bitów (zob.
"bit"); 256 układów jednostek
informacji; informacja
wyrażająca literę w tekscie;
zakodowanie jednej litery;
odczytanie kodu jednej litery;
jakakolwiek liczba jest
zazwyczaj oznaczona w
komputerze grupą "baytów;"
jeden "byte" może zapisać w
pamięci komputera cyfrę od
zera do 255
byway ['baj-łej] s. boczna droga;
boczne przejście
byword ['baj-,łe:rd] s.
przysłowie; przydomek

(pogardliwy)
by work ['baj-,łe:rk] s. praca
uboczna poza zajęciem
głównym

C

c [si:] litera "c"; trzecia litera
alfabetu angielskiego
cab [kaeb] s. taksówka;
dorożka-szoferka; budka
maszynisty
cabaret [,kaebe'rej] s. lokal
taneczny; kabaret; serwis na
tacy
cabbage ['kaebydż] s. kapusta
cabin ['kaebyn] s. kabina;
chatka; prymitywnie zbudowany domek
cabinet ['kaebynyt] s. szafka;
rada ministrów; adj. tajny
cabinetmaker ['kaebynyt,mejke:r]
s. stolarz meblowy
cable ['kejbl] s. przewód; lina;
depesza; v. depeszować;
umocowywać liną; przesyłać
kablem
cable-car ['kejbl,ka:r] s. wóz
linowy; kolejka linowa
cabman ['kaebmen] s.
taksówkarz
cabstand ['kaeb staend] s. postój
taksówek
cackle ['kaekl] v. gdakać;
gęgać; chichotać; s. gda-
kanie; gęganie; chichot
cacti ['kaektaj] pl. kaktusy
cactus ['kaektes] s. kaktus
cad [kaed] s. ordynus; cham
cafe ['kaefej] s. kawiarnia; kawa;
restauracja; bar
cafeteria [,kaefy'tierja] s.
restauracja samoobsługowa
cage [kejdż] s. klatka; kosz; v.
zamykać w klatce
cake [kejk] s. ciastko; kostka
(mydła); smażony placek (z
ryby)

cake tin ['kejk,tyn] s. forma na
ciastko
calamity [ke'laemyty] s.
nieszczęście; klęska; niedola
calculate ['kaelkjulejt] v.
rachować; sądzić; oceniać
calculation [,kaelkju'lejszyn] s.
liczenie; ostrożność
calendar ['kaelynder] s.
kalendarz; terminarz
calf [kaef] s. cielak; łydka
caliber ['kaelyber] s. średnica
wewnętrzna; kaliber; wzorzec;
sprawdzian
call [ko:l] v. wołać; wzywać;
telefonować; odwiedzać; zawijać do portu; wyzywać; s.
krzyk; wezwanie; apel; powołanie; wizyta; nazwanie;
żądanie; sygnał
call for help ['ko:l,fo:r help]
wołanie o pomoc; wzywanie
pomocy
call names ['ko:l,nejmz] przezywać; wyzywać; ubliżać
call back ['ko:l,baek]
odtelefonować; odwołać z
powrotem
call at ['ko:l,aet] odwiedzać
call for ['ko:l,fo:r] żądać;
chodzić po coś (żeby
otrzymać)
call on ['ko:l,on] odwiedzać
(kogoś); prosić o
wypowiedź
call up ['ko:l,ap] telefonować
wywoływać (duchy etc.)
caller ['ko:ler] s. gość;
odwiedzający; adj. rześki;
świeży
calling ['ko:lyng] s. zawód;
powołanie; zatrudnienie; fach
callous ['kaeles] adj. stwardniały;
nieczuły; zrogowaciały
calm [ka:m] adj. spokojny; cichy;
opanowany; s. spokój; cisza;
opanowanie; v. uspokajać;
uciszać; uciszyć się
calm down ['ka:m,dałn] v.
uciszyć się; uspokoić się
calorie ['kaelery] s. kaloria
calves [ka:wz] pl. cielaki; łydki
camber ['kaember] v. wyginać;

s. wygięcie; wypukłość (jezdni)

came [kejm] v. przyszedł; zob. come

camel ['kaemel] s. wielbłąd

camera ['kaemere] s. aparat fotograficzny; prywatna izba

camomile ['kaemoumajl] s. rumianek

camouflage ['kaemufla:ż] s. maskowanie; v. maskować (wojsk.)

camp [kaemp] s. obóz; v. obozować; rozlokowywać w namiotach

camp out [kaemp aut] v. obozować w namiocie

campaign [kaem'pejn] s. kampania; akcja; v. odbywać kampanię; agitować

camp bed ['kaemp‚bed] s. łóżko polowe; łóżko składane

camper ['kaemper] adj. obozujący; s. wóz lub przyczepa do obozowania; mieszkalny wóz (turystyczny)

camping ['kaempyng] s. obozowanie; życie obozowe

camping ground ['kaempyng ‚graund] s. obozowisko; miejsce do obozowania

campus ['kaempes] s. teren uniwersytecki lub szkolny

can [kaen] s. puszka blaszana; ustęp; v. móc; konserwować; wyrzucać; umieć; zdołać; potrafić

Canadian [ke'nejdjen] adj. kanadyjski; s. Kanadyjczyk

canal [ke'nael] s. kanał; kanalik

canard [kae'na:rd] s. kaczka dziennikarska; plotka

canary [ke'nery] s. kanarek

cancel ['kaensel] v. znosić; kasować; odwoływać; skreślać; anulować

cancer ['kaenser] s. rak (choroba); nowotwór

candid ['kaendyd] adj. szczery; bezstronny; otwarty

candidate ['kaendydyt] s. kandydat; kandydatka

candied ['kaendyd] adj.

pocukrzony; lukrowany

candle ['kaendl] s. świeca

candlestick ['kaendlstyk] s. świecznik; lichtarz

candy ['kaendy] s. cukierki; lukier; cukier lodowaty

cane [kejn] s. trzcina; laska; pałka; v. chłostać; wyplatać trzciną; ukarać trzciną

canned [kaend] adj. zakonserwowany w puszce

cannery [kaenery] s. fabryka konserw

cannibal ['kaenybel] s. ludożerca; adj. ludożerczy

cannon ['kaenen] s. działo

cannot ['kaenot] v. nie móc (od can not); nie potrafić

canoe [ke'nu:] s. czółno; kajak; łódka; v. pływać kajakiem; wiosłować

canopy ['kaenepy] s. baldachim; okap; firmament; sklepienie

cant ['kaent] s. żargon; frazes

can't [ka:nt] v. nie móc (od can); nie potrafić

canteen [kaen'ti:n] s. manierka; menażka; kantyna

canvas ['kaenwes] s. płótno impregnowane

canvass ['kaenwes] s. badanie; zapobieganie; v. zabiegać; badać; starać się o głosy

cap [kaep] s. czapka; pokrywa; wieko; kapiszon; beret

cap [kaep] v. wkładać czapkę lub nakrywkę; wieńczyć; zakładać spłonkę; zakasować; nakrywać

capability [‚kaepe'bylyty] s. zdolność; zdatność; możliwość

capable ['kejpebl] adj. zdolny

capacity [ke'paesyty] s. zdolność; kompetencja; pojemność; właściwość; nośność; objętość

cape [kejp] s. 1. peleryna; 2. przylądek

caper [kejper] v. wywijać kozły; s. hołubiec; sus; skok

capital ['kaepytl] s. stolica; kapitał; adj. główny;

zasadniczy; stołeczny; fatalny
capital crime ['kaepytl,krajm] s.
morderstwo
capitalism ['kaepytlyzem] s.
kapitalizm
capital letter ['kaepytl,leter] s.
duża litera
capital punishment ['kaepytl
'panyszment] kara śmierci
capricious [ke'pryszes] adj.
kapryśny
capsize [kaep'sajz] v. wywracać
(statek) dnem do góry
capsule ['kaepsju:l] s. kapsułka;
torebka; pochewka; kabinka
captain ['kaeptyn] s. kapitan;
naczelnik; v. dowodzić
caption ['kaepszyn] s. nagłówek;
napis; poświadczenie; aresztowanie; pojmanie
captivate ['kaeptywejt] v. ująć;
czarować; urzekać; zniewa-
lać; oczarować
captive ['kaeptyw] s. jeniec
captivity ['kaeptywyty] s.
niewola
capture ['kaepczer] s.
owładnięcie; łup; zdobycz; v.
pojmać; owładnąć
car [ka:r] s. samochód; wóz
caravan ['kaerewaen] s.
karawana; wóz kryty;
przyczepka mieszkalna
carbohydrate ['ka:rbe'hajdrejt] s.
węglowodan
carbon ['ka:rben] s. węgiel;
kopia (kalka)
carbon dioxide ['ka:rben daj
'oksajd] s. CO_2; dwutlenek
węgla
carbon paper ['ka:rben,pejper] s.
kalka
carburetor ['ka:rbjurejter] s.
gaźnik
car carrier [ka:r-'kaerjer] s. wóz
do przewozu aut
carcass ['ka:r-kes] s. ścierwo;
padlina; szkielet
card ['ka:rd] s. karta; bilet;
pocztówka; legitymacja; atut
cardboard ['ka:rdbo:rd] s.
tektura; adj. tekturowy
card box ['ka:rdboks] s. karton

cardigan ['ka:rdygen] s. wełniana
kurta (kamizelka)
cardinal ['ka:rdynl] adj. główny;
s. kardynał
card index ['ka:rd yndeks] s.
kartoteka
car papers [ka:r pejpers] s.
dokumenty samochodowe
care [keer] s. opieka; troska;
ostrożność; zgryzota; dozór;
uwaga; niepokój
care of [keer ow] c/o; adres (u
kogoś)
care for [keer fo:r] v. dbać o
kogoś; lubić; kochać; mieć
ochotę; przepadać za
career [ke'rier] s. kariera; zawód;
tok; pęd; bieg; v. cwałować
carefree [keerfri:] adj. beztroski
careful [keerful] adj. ostrożny;
troskliwy; dbały; pieczołowity
careless [keerles] adj. niedbały;
nieuważny; nieostrożny
caress [ke'res] s. pieszczota; v.
pieścić; popieścić
caretaker ['keertejker] s.
dozorca; stróż
careworn ['keerło:rn] s.
zgnębiony kłopotami
carfare ['ka:rfeer] s. opłata za
jazdę
cargo ['ka:rgou] s. ładunek
caricature [,kaeryke'czjuer] s.
karykatura; v. karykaturować
car mechanic [ka:r-my'kaenyk] s.
mechanik samochodowy
carnation [ka:r'nejszyn] 1. s. &
adj. ciemno-czerwony; cielisty;
2. goździk ogrodowy
carnival ['ka:rnywel] s. karnawał;
zapusty
carnivorous [ka:r'nyweres] adj.
mięsożerny
carol ['kaerel] s. kolęda; v.
kolędować
carp [ka:rp] s. karp; v. czepiać
się; ganić; przycinać
car parking ['ka:r-pa:rkyng] s.
parking samochodowy
carpenter ['ka:rpynter] s. cieśla;
stolarz
carpet ['ka:rpyt] s. dywan; v.
wyścielać dywanem

carriage ['kaerydż] s. wagon;
powóz; postawa; kareta; chód
carrier ['kaerjer] s. firma
przewozowa; nośnik; tragarz;
rozsadnik (zakażenia);
lotniskowiec; okaziciel
carrion ['kaerjen] s. padlina
carrot ['kaeret] s. marchewka
carry ['kaery] v. nosić; wozić;
zanieść; unosić
carry off ['kaery,of] v.
uprowadzić; zabrać;
zdobywać (nagrodę)
carry on ['kaery,on] v.
kontynuować; wytrwać;
awanturować się
carry out ['kaery,aut] v.
wykonać; przeprowadzić;
spełnić
cart ['ka:rt] s. wóz
cartel ['ka:rtel] s. kartel
carter ['ka:rter] s. woźnica
cart horse ['ka:rt,hors] s. koń
pociągowy
carton ['ka:rten] s. karton
cartoon [ka:r'tun] s. karykatura;
v. rysować karykatury
cartoonist [ka:r'tunyst] s.
karykaturzysta
cartridge ['ka:rtrydż] s. nabój
cartwheel ['ka:rt-hłi:l] s. kołodziej
carve ['ka:rw] v. rzeźbić;
krajać; cyzelować; pociąć
na części
carver ['ka:rwer] s. snycerz
carving ['ka:rwyng] s. rzeźba
cascade [kaes'kejd] s.
wodospad; v. spadać jak
wodospad
case [kejs] s. 1. wypadek;
sprawa; dowód; 2. skrzynia;
pochwa; torba; 3. sprawa
sądowa; v. zamykać w
pochwie; otaczać czymś;
oszalować; oprawić
casement ['kejsment] s. rama
okienna; okno z kwaterami
cash [kaesz] s. gotówka;
pieniądze; v. spieniężać;
inkasować; płacić (gotówką)
cash on delivery [kaesz on
dy'lywery] zapłata przy
odbiorze; C.O.D.

cashier [kae'szjer] s. kasjer
cash register [kaesz 'redżyster]
s. kasa (zmechanizowana)
casing ['kejsyng] s. 1. powłoka;
pochwa; 2. obudowa; oprawa;
3. łuska; 4. opancerzenie
cask [kaesk] s. beczułka
casket [kaeskyt] s. trumna; urna;
szkatuła
cassock ['kaesek] s. sutanna
cast; cast; cast [ka:st; ka:st;
ka:st]
cast [ka:st] s. rzut; odlew; gips;
odcień; v. rzucać; łowić;
odlewać; powalić; dzielić
role teatralne
castaway ['ka:st,e'łej] s.
wyrzutek; rozbitek
cast down [ka:st dałn] adj.
przygnębiony; v. de-
prymować
caste [ka:st] s. kasta
cast iron [ka:stajren] s. żeliwo
castle ['ka:sl] s. zamek
castor oil ['ka:ster,ojl] s. olej
rycynowy
cast steel ['ka:st,sti:l] s. lana stal
casual ['kaeżuel] adj. przypadkowy; niedbały; dorywczy;
nie planowany; niechlujny
casualty ['kaeżuelty] s.
wypadek; ofiara wypadku;
lista strat; nieszczęście
cat [kaet] s. kot; jędza
catalog ['kaetelog] s. katalog
catamaran [,kaeteme'raen] s.
dwu-czółnowa łódź
cataract ['kaeteraekt] s.
katarakta; ulewa; wodospad
catarrh [ke'ta:r] s. katar
catastrophe [ka'taestrefy] s.
katastrofa
catch; caught; caught [kaecz;
ko:t; ko:t]
catch [kaecz] v. łapać; łowić;
ujmować; słyszeć; wybuch-
nąć; nabawić się; usidlić;
uchwycić; s. łup; połów
catch cold [kaecz kold] v.
zaziębiać się
catch fire [kaecz fajer] v.
zapalać się
catch up [kaecz ap] v. dogonić

catching [kaeczyng] adj.
zaraźliwy; s. tryby; uchwyt;
zazębienie
category ['kaetygery] s.
kategoria
cater ['kejter] v. dostarczać
żywności; obsługiwać
caterpillar ['kaetepyler] s. gąsienica (traktora, czołgu)
cathedral [ke'ti:drel] s. katedra
Catholic ['kaetelyk] adj. katolicki;
s. katolik
cattle [kaetl] s. bydło rogate
caucus ['ko:kes] s. tajne narady
partyjne; klika
caught [ko:t] złapany; zob. catch
cauldron ['ko:ldren] s. kocioł
cauliflower ['kaulyflauer] s.
kalafior
cause [ko:z] s. przyczyna;
sprawa; racja; motywacja;
proces; powód; v. spowodować; być przyczyną
causeless [ko:zles] adj.
przypadkowy; bezpodstawny
caustic ['ko:styk] adj. żrący;
gryzący; złośliwy; do-
kuczliwy; uszczypliwy
caution ['ko:szyn] s. ostrożność; przezorność; roztropność; uwaga; v. ostrzegać
cautious ['ko:szes] adj. ostrożny;
rozważny; roztropny; uważny
cavalry ['kaewelry] s. kawaleria
cave [kejw] s. pieczara; jaskinia;
v. zapadać się; drążyć
cavern ['kaewen] s. jama;
jaskinia; grota; pieczara
cavity ['kaewyty] s. wklęsłość;
dziura (w zębie); dół; jama;
wydrążenie
cease [sy:s] v. ustawać;
przestawać; położyć kres
ceaseless [sy:slys] adj.
bezustanny; ciągły; nie-
przerwany
cedar ['si:der] s. cedr
cede [si:d] v. ustąpić; cedować
ceiling ['sy:lyng] s. sufit; pułap;
górna granica
celebrate ['selybrejt] v.
święcić; uczcić; sławić;
obchodzić

celebrated ['selybrejtyd] adj.
sławny; słynny; głośny
celebration ['selybrejszyn] s.
obchód; odprawianie; święcenie; celebrowanie
celebrity ['sylebryty] s. sławna
osoba; sława; znakomita
osobowość
celery ['selery] s. seler (jarzyna)
celibacy ['selybesy] s.
bezżeństwo; celibat
cell [sel] s. cela; komórka
cellar ['seler] s. piwnica
Celtic [keltyk] adj. celtycki
cement [sy'ment] s. cement; v.
cementować; kleić; utwierdzać; spoić; złączyć
cemetery ['semytry] s. cmentarz
censor ['sensor] s. cenzor
censorship ['senserszyp] s.
cenzura
censure ['senszer] s. nagana;
krytyka; v. krytykować
cent [sent] s. cent
centenary [sentynery] adj.
stuletni; s. stulecie; setna
rocznica
centennial ['sen'tenjel] s.
stulecie; adj. stuletni
center ['senter] s. ośrodek;
centrum; v. ześrodkowywać;
centrować; skupiać się
centigrade ['sentygrejd] adj.
stustopniowy (termometr)
centimeter ['sentymi:ter] s.
centymetr
central ['sentral] adj. środkowy;
czołowy; s. centrala
Central Europe ['sentral juerop]
Europa Środkowa
central heating ['sentrel hi:tyng]
centralne ogrzewanie
centralize ['sentrelajz] v.
centralizować; ześrod-
kowywać
century ['senczury] s. stulecie
cereals ['syerjelz] pl. zboża
cerebral ['serybrel] adj. mózgowy
ceremonial [,sery'mounjel] adj.
ceremonialny; s. rytuał; ceremoniał; ceremonialność
ceremonious [,sery'mounjes] adj.
drobiazgowy; ceremonialny

ceremony ['serymeny] s.
ceremonia; v. sztywno się
zachowywać
certain ['se:rtyn] adj. niejaki;
pewien; pewny; ustalony;
jakiś
certainly ['se:rtnly] adv. na
pewno; oczywiście; bez-
względnie
certainty ['se:rtynty] s.
pewność; pewnik; rzecz
pewna
certificate [se'rtyfykyt] s.
świadectwo; poświadczenie;
dyplom; metryka; v. za-
świadczać; dyplomować
certify ['se:rtyfaj] v.
zaświadczać; zapewniać;
uznawać za
certitude ['se:rtytju:d] s.
pewność; przeświadczenie
chafe [czejf] v. trzeć; otrzeć;
irytować; s. tarcie; otarcie;
irytacja; rozdrażnienie; złość
chaff [cza:f] s. 1. sieczka;
2. żart; naciąganie; v.
wyśmiewać żartobliwie;
naciągać
chagrin ['szaegryn] s. smutek;
rozczarowanie; v. upokarzać;
rozczarowywać boleśnie
chain [czejn] s. łańcuch;
syndykat; trust; v. wiązać na
łańcuchu; mierzyć; uwiązać;
zakuć
chair [czeer] s. krzesło; stołek;
fotel; katedra; v. prze-
wodniczyć; sadzać na
krześle
chair lift ['czeerlyft] s. wyciąg
linowy
chairman ['czeermen] s.
przewodniczący; prezes
chalk [czo:k] s. kreda; v. pisać
kredą
challenge ['czaelyndż] s.
wyzwanie; zadanie; v. wy-
zywać; zarzucać; wzywać;
korcić; prowokować; rzucać
wyzwanie
chamber ['czejmber] s. izba;
komora; sala; pokój; v.
wydrążyć

chambermaid ['czejmbermejd] s.
pokojowa
chameleon [ke'my:ljen] s.
kameleon
chamois ['szaemła:] s. giemza;
ircha; zamsz
champagne ['szaem'pejn] s.
szampan
champion ['czaempjen] s. mistrz;
obrońca; v. bronić; walczyć
o ...; popierać; adj.
przewyższający wszystkich
championship ['czaempjenszyp]
s. mistrzostwo
chance [cza:ns] s. okazja;
przypadek; szczęście; szansa;
ryzyko; adj. przypadkowy;
przygodny; v. zdarzać się;
ryzykować; próbować; przytrafić się; natknąć się
chancellor [cza:seler] s. kanclerz;
pierwszy sekretarz
(ambasady); najwyższy sędzia
chandelier [szaendy'ljer] s.
żyrandol; świecznik
change [czejndż] s. zmiana;
wymiana; drobne; v. zmienić;
przebierać (się); wymieniać;
rozmieniać (na drobne)
change one's mind ['czejndż
‚łans'majnd] zmienić czyjeś
zdanie (przekonania etc.)
change trains ['czejndż,trejns] v.
przesiąść się (na kolei)
changeable ['czejndżebl] adj.
zmienny; ulegający zmianom
channel ['czaenl] s. kanał;
koryto; łożysko; v. żłobić;
przesyłać drogą (urzędową)
chaos ['kejos] s. chaos
chap [czaep] s. chłop; chłopiec;
człek; v. pękać; powodować
pęknięcia (warg); zary-
sowywać
chapel ['czaepel] s. kaplica
chaplain ['czaeplyn] s. kapelan
chaps [cza:ps] pl. skórzane
nogawice (kowboja); ochra-
niacze (chaparillos)
chapter ['czaepter] s. rozdział;
oddział; v. dzielić na rozdziały
character ['kaerykter] s.
charakter; typ; cecha;

reputacja; moralność; facet;
znak; usposobienie
characteristic ['kaerykterystyk]
adj. charakterystyczny;
typowy; s. cecha; własność;
właściwość
characterize ['kaerykterajz] v.
charakteryzować (opisywać)
charge [cza:rdż] s. ciężar;
ładunek (naboju, baterii); obowiązek; piecza; podopieczny;
zarzut; opłata; należność;
koszt; szarża; godło; v. ładować; nasycać; obciążać;
żądać; liczyć sobie; oskarżać; atakować; szarżować
charge account [cza:rdż e'kaunt]
s. otwarty kredyt (w banku)
charge card [cza:rdż 'kard] s.
karta kredytowa do zakupów
chariot ['czaerjet] s. wóz;
rydwan
charitable ['czaerytebl] adj.
litościwy; dobroczynny
charity ['czaeryty] s. miłosierdzie; dobroczynność
charm [cza:rm] s. czar; urok;
amulet; urok; wdzięk; v.
czarować; oczarować
charming [cza:rmyng] adj.
czarujący
chart [cza:rt] s. wykres; mapa
morska; v. robić wykres;
wytyczać; pokazywać (jak)
charmless [cza:rmlys] adj. bez
wdzięku
charter [cza:rter] s. statut;
przywilej; dyplom; akt nadania
prawa do ...; v. nadawać; zakładać na statutach; wynajmować statek lub samolot
charter plane [cza:rter plejn] s.
wynajęty grupowo samolot
charwoman ['cza:rłumen] s.
sprzątaczka; dochodząca;
sprzątaczka; posługaczka
chase 1. [czejs] s. pościg;
pogoń; polowanie; łowy;
teren polowania; v. gonić;
ścigać; polować; wyganiać
chase 2. [czejs] s. łożysko;
wgłębienie; wykop; v. żłobić
chasm ['kaezem] s. otchłań

chaste [czejst] adj. czysty;
niewinny; nieskażony;
cnotliwy
chastity ['czaestyty] s.
niewinność; prostota;
dziewictwo
chat [czaet] s. pogawędka;
awędzenie; v. gawędzić; gadać; rozmawiać
chatter [czaeter] v. szczebiotać;
klapać; s. szczebiot; klapanie;
klekot; paplanie; terkot
chatterbox [czaeterboks]
s.trajkotka; gaduła; pleciuga
chauffeur ['szoufer] s. zawodowy kierowca; przenośny
piecyk
cheap [czi:p] adj. tani; marny
cheapen [czi:pen] v. tanieć;
obniżać wartość; spadać
na cenie
cheat [czi:t] s. oszust; oszustka;
v. oszukiwać; zdradzać (w
małżeństwie); okpiwać
check [czek] s. wstrzymanie;
przerwa; sprawdzenie; czek;
kwit; szach; adj. szachownicowy; kontrolny; pod-
kreślony; v. hamować;
sprawdzać; zakreślać;
nadawać; zgadzać się;
szachować; ganić; kryty-
kować; opanowywać
check in [czek yn] v.
wmeldowywać się (w pracy,
w wojsku, w hotelu, etc.)
check out [czek aut] v.
wymeldowywać się; zapłacić
za hotel
checked [czekt] adj. w kratkę
checkroom [czekrum] s.
przechowalnia (bagażu);
szatnia
cheek [czi:k] s. policzek;
bezczelne gadanie; śmia-
łość; v. mówić bezczelnie
do kogoś; stawiać się
cheeky ['czi:ky] adj. bezczelny;
zuchwały; pełen tupetu; z
tupetem; impertynencki
cheer [czier] s. brawo; hurra;
radość; jadło; v. krzyczeć;
rozweselać; dodawać otuchy

cheer on ['czier on] v.
zachęcać; zagrzewać;
dodawać otuchy
cheer up ['czier'ap] v.
pocieszać; nabrać otuchy;
rozpogodzić
cheerful ['czierful] adj. pogodny;
wesoły; ochoczy;
rozweselający
cheerless ['czierlys] adj. ponury;
smutny; przybity
cheery ['cziery] adj. wesoły;
radosny; pogodny
cheese ['czi:z] s. ser
chef [czef] s. kuchmistrz
chemical ['kemykel] adj.
chemiczny; s. substancja
chemiczna
chemicals ['kemykels] pl.
chemikalia; leki; lekarstwa
chemise [sze'mi:z] s. damska
koszula luźna i długa
chemist ['kemyst] s. chemik;
aptekarz
chemistry ['kemystry] s. chemia
cheque [czek] s. czek (poza
USA)
chequered ['czekerd] adj.
kratkowany; urozmaicony;
burzliwy
cherish ['czerysz] v. lubić;
tulić; żywić (uczucie);
miłować
cherry ['czery] s. czereśnia;
wiśniowy kolor; vulg.
prawiczka; adj. wiśniowy;
vulg. prawiczy; czerwony
chess [czes] s. szachy
chess-board [czes-bo:rd] s.
szachownica
chess man ['czesmen] s. figurka
szachowa
chest [czest] s. skrzynia;
komoda; pierś; płuca; kufer;
skrzynka
chestnut ['czesnat] s. kasztan
chest of drawers ['czest
,ow'dro:ers] s. komoda
chew [czu:] v. żuć;
przeżuwać; besztać;
gderać; s. żucie; tytoń do
żucia; prymka
chewing gum ['czu:yng,gam] s.

guma do żucia
chewy [czu:y] adj. nadający się
do żucia
chicken ['czykyn] s. kurczę; adj.
tchórzliwy; bojący się
chicken out ['czykyn aut] v.
stchórzyć; ustąpić ze
strachu
chide; chid; chidden [czajd; czyd;
czydn]
chide [czajd] v. łajać; droczyć
się; skarżyć; besztać
chicken pox ['czykyn poks] s.
ospa wietrzna
chief [czy:f] s. wódz; szef; adj.
główny; naczelny
chilblain ['czylblejn] s.
odmrożenie (zob. frost bite)
child [czajld] s. dziecko
childish ['czajldysz] adj.
dziecinny
childless ['czajldlys] adj.
bezdzietny
childlike ['czajldlajk] adj.
dziecięcy; jak dziecko
children ['czyldren] pl. dzieci
chill [czyl] s. chłód; dreszcz; v.
studzić; mrozić; oziębiać
chilly [czyly] adj. chłodny; adv.
chłodno; zimno
chime ['czajm] s. dzwony
grające; rytm; kurant; v. bić
w dzwony; wydzwaniać;
rymować; zabrzmieć
chimney ['czymny] s. komin;
wylot; szkło lampy naftowej
chimney sweeper ['czymny
,sli:per] s. kominiarz;
kominiarski
chin [czyn] s. broda; podbródek;
v. podciągać brodę do
drążka
china ['czajna] s. porcelana
chinese ['czaj'ni:z] adj. chiński;
Chinese s. Chińczyk
chink ['czynk] 1. s. brzęk; v.
pobrzękiwać; brzęczeć; 2. s.
szpara; szczelina; v. zapychać
szpary
chip [czyp] s. drzazga; odłamek;
skrawek; v. otłuc; obijać;
dokuczać; nabierać; ciosać;
ćwierkać; piszczeć; nogę

podstawiać; złuszczać się;
odłupać
chirp [czy:rp] s. świergot; v.
ćwierkać; szczebiotać
chisel ['czyzl] s. dłuto; przecinak;
v. ciąć; rzeźbić; oszukać
chivalrous ['czywelres] adj.
rycerski
chivalry ['czywelry] s. rycerstwo;
rycerskość
chive [czajw] s. szczypiorek
chlorine ['klo:ry:n] s. chlor
chloroform ['klo:refo:rm] s.
chloroform; v. maczać w
chloroformie; usypiać
chloroformem
chock [czok] s. klin; v. osadzać
na klinach; adv. szczelnie;
ciasno; mocno; w pełni
chocolate ['czoklyt] s. czekolada;
adj. czekoladowy (kolor etc.)
choice [czojs] s. wybór;
wybranka; adj. wyborowy;
doborowy
choir ['kłajer] s. chór
choke [czouk] v. dusić;
zadusić; tłumić; dławić; s.
duszenie; dławik; gardziel;
przewężenie; odgłosy
duszenia; zawór
choke down [czouk dałn] v.
dławić; zmniejszać gardziel
choke up [czouk ap] v. zatykać
(rurę); zadławić (motor etc.)
choose; chose; chosen [czu:z;
czouz; czouzn]
choose [czu:z] v. wybierać;
woleć; postanowić; obrać;
zadecydować
chop [czop] v. rąbać; obcinać;
s. rąbnięcie; kotlet; krótka fala
chop down [czop dałn] v.
powalić (drzewo etc.);
ściąć; zrąbać
chord [ko:rd] s. struna; cięciwa;
struna głosowa
chorus ['ko:res] s. chór; v.
mówić chórem; śpiewać
chórem
chose [czouz] v. wybrał; zob.
choose
chow [czau] s. jadło (slang)
Christ [krajst] Chrystus

christen ['krisn] v. ochrzcić
Christian ['krystjen] adj.
chrześcijański; s. chrześcijanin (slang: cywilizowany)
Christianity [krys'czaenyty] v.
chrześcijaństwo
Christian name ['krystjen,nejm]
s. imię (inne niż nazwisko)
Christmas ['krysmas] s. Boże
Narodzenie
Christmas Day ['krysmas dej]
Dzień Bożego Narodzenia
Christmas Eve ['krysmas i:w]
wilia; wigilia Bożego
Narodzenia
chromium ['kroumjem] s. chrom
chronic ['kronyk] adj. chroniczny;
straszliwy (ból)
chronicle ['kronykl] s. kronika
chronological [krone'lodżykel]
adj. chronologiczny
chubby ['czaby] adj. pucołowaty;
pyzaty; mały i gruby
chuck [czak] v. rzucać;
gdakać; klinować; cmokać;
zwężać strumień wody w
rurze s. zawór wodny; klin
chuckle [czakl] v. chichotać; s.
chichot; zduszony śmiech
chum [czam] v. przyjaźnić się
blisko; s. serdeczny kolega;
współlokator
church [cze:rcz] s. kościół
churchyard ['cze:rcz,ja:rd] s.
cmentarz; dziedziniec kościelny; adj. cmentarny
churn [cze:rn] v. robić masło;
kłócić się; burzyć się;
kotłować się; pienić się; s.
maślnica; maślniczka; bańka
na mleko
chute [szu:t] s. koryto zrzutowe;
spadek; wodospad; zsyp; ryn-
na; spadochron; tor zjeżdżalni
dla dzieci
chutzpah [hucpa] s. nachal-
ność; śmiałość; tupet (po
nowohebrajsku)
cider ['sajder] s. wino z jabłek
cigar [sy'ga:r] s. cygaro
cigarette [sige'ret] s. papieros
cigarette lighter [sy'gae'ret'lajter]
s. zapalniczka

cinder ['synder] s. popiół; żużel;
v. spalać na żużel
Cinderella [,synde'rele] s.
kopciuszek; Kopciuszek
cinder track ['synder-traek] s.
bieżnia żużlowa; tor żużlowy
cinécamera ['syni-'kaemere] s.
aparat filmowy
cinema ['syneme] s. kino
cinema projector ['syneme
,prodżekter] s. rzutnik filmowy
cipher ['sajfer] s. cyfra; szyfr;
zero; monogran; v. szyfrować; rachować
circle ['se:rkl] s. koło; krąg;
obwód; v. otaczać; kręcić
się w koło; opasywać; krążyć; okrążać
circuit ['se:rkyt] s. obwód;
okrężna; okólna (podróż)
circular ['se:rkjuler] s. okólnik;
adj. okrągły; kolisty
circulate ['se:rkjulejt] v. krążyć;
cyrkulować; puszczać w
obieg; być w obiegu
circulation ['se:rkjulejszyn] s.
krążenie; obrót; nakład
circumference [se'rkamfyrens] s.
obwód (koła etc.)
circumcision [se:rkem'syżyn] s.
obrzezanie; obcięcie napletka
circumscribe [,se:rkem'skrajb] v.
opisywać; zakreślać
circumstance ['se:rkemstaens] s.
okoliczności; szczegóły
circus ['se:rkes] s. cyrk; okrągły
plac; rondo; desant (sl.)
cistern ['systern] s. zbiornik na
wodę; cysterna
citation [saj'tejszyn] s. cytat;
przytoczenie; wzmianka
pochwalna; pochwała
cite [sajt] v. cytować;
przytaczać; pozywać;
wymieniać w komunikacie;
pozywać do sądu
citizen ['sytyzn] s. obywatel
citizenship ['sytyzenszyp] s.
obywatelstwo; cnoty oby-
watelskie
city ['syty] s. (wielkie) miasto;
centrum finansowe; ośrodek
city center ['syty,senter] s.

centrum miasta
city guide ['syty'gajd] s. plan
miasta; przewodnik po
mieście
city hall ['syty,ho:l] s. zarząd
miasta; magistrat
civics ['sywyks] s. nauka praw i
obowiązków obywatela
civil ['sywl] adj. społeczny;
uprzejmy; obywatelski; cywilny (kodeks)
civilian [sy'wyljen] adj. cywilny;
s. cywil; obywatel
civility [sy'wylyty] s.
uprzejmość; grzeczność
civilization [,sywylaj'sejszyn] s.
cywilizacja; całość kultury
civilize ['sywylajz] v.
cywilizować; ucywilizować
civil marriage ['sywl'maerydż] s.
ślub cywilny
civil rights ['sywl,rajts] s. prawa
obywatelskie
civil service ['sywl'se:rwys] s.
służba państwowa
civil war ['sywl,ło:r] s. wojna
domowa
clack [klaek] v. klekotać;
gdakać; s. klekot; wieko
clad [klaed] adj. odziany; zob.
clothe
claim [klejm] v. żądać;
twierdzić; s. żądanie; twierdzenie; działka; skarga; zażalenie; dług
claimant [klejment] s. rościciel;
pretendent; adj. pilny; rażący
clammy ['klaemy] adj. mokro-
-lepki; wiligotny i zimny
clamor ['klaemer] s. zgiełk;
krzyk; v. krzyczeć; robić
wrzawę; wymuszać krzykiem
clamorous ['klaemeres] adj.
zgiełkliwy; krzykliwy
clamp [klaemp] s. klamra; zacisk;
v. zaciskać (jak) klamrą
clan [klaen] s. klan; szczep
szkocki; v. tworzyć klikę
clandestine [klaen'destyn] adj.
potajemny; skryty; tajny
clang [klaeng] s. dźwięk;
szczęk; klekot; v.
dźwięczeć; szczękać; kle-

kotać; rozbrzmiewać; brzękać; dzwonić
clank [klae<u>nk</u>] s. chrzęst; brzęk;
v. brzękać; chrzęścić
clap [klaep] s. huk; klaskanie; v.
łopotać; oklaskiwać; klepać
claret ['klaeret] s. czerwone
wino; bordo; slang: krew
clarify ['klaeryfaj] v. wyjaśniać;
rozjaśniać; oczyszczać
clarity ['klaeryty] s. czystość;
jasność; przejrzystość;
klarowność
clash [klaesz] s. brzęk; starcie;
v. brzęczeć; ścierać się;
kolidować; uderzać w coś
clasp [klaesp] s. klamra; uchwyt;
okucie; v. spinać; ściskać
clasp knife ['klaesp-najf] s.
scyzoryk; kozik; nóż składany
class [klaes] s. klasa; lekcja;
rocznik; grupa; kurs; kategoria; v. klasyfikować;
segregować; sortować
classmate ['kla:s,mejt] s. kolega
szkolny
classroom ['kla:s,ru:m] s. klasa
(w szkole); sala szkolna
class struggle [,kla:s'stragl] s.
walka klas w społeczeństwie
classic ['klaesyk] s. klasyk;
studia klasyczne; adj. klasyczny; uznany autorytet;
klasyk
classical ['klaesykel] adj.
klasyczny; typowy; huma-
nistyczny
classification [klaesyfy'kejszyn]
s. klasyfikacja; klasyfikowanie
classify ['klaesyfaj] s.
klasyfikować; sortować;
zaklasyfikować
clatter ['klaeter] v. brzęczeć;
klapać; s. brzęk; łoskot; gwar
clause [klo:z] s. klauzula; zdanie;
punkt umowy
claw [klo:] s. pazur; szpon; łapa;
kleszcze; v. drapać; wy-
drapać; łapać w szpony
clay [klej] s. glina; sl. trup
clean [kli:n] adj. czysty;
wyraźny; zgrabny; adv.
całkiem; zupełnie; po prostu;

v. oczyścić; opróżniać; ogo-
łocić; wygrać; uprzątnąć;
dużo zyskać (sl.)
clean out ['kli:n aut] v.
oczyścić; opróżniać;
wyczyścić
clean up ['kli:n ap] v.
posprzątać; wygrać; zrobić
na czysto; robić porządek
cleaner ['kli:ner] s. czyściciel;
oczyszczalnik; właściciel
pralni; pralnia chemiczna
cleaning ['kli:ny<u>ng</u>] s.
czyszczenie; sprzątanie;
porządki
cleanliness ['klenlynys] s.
czystość; zamiłowanie do
czystości
cleanly ['klenly] adj. czysty; adv.
czysto; schludnie
cleanness ['kli:nnys] s.
czystość; zamiłowanie do
czystości
cleanse [klenz] v. czyścić;
zmywać (grzechy);
oczyszczać
clear [klier] adj. jasny; czysty;
bystry; adv. jasno; wyraźnie;
z dala; zupełnie; dokładnie; s.
wolna przestrzeń
clear away ['klier,ełej] v. usunąć
(przeszkodę etc.)
clear up ['klier,ap] v. wyjaśnić
clear-cut ['klier,kat] adj.
wyraźny; czysty; poprawny
clearing ['kliery<u>ng</u>] s.
karczowisko; rozrachunek;
obrachunek
clearly ['klierly] adv. wyraźnie;
jasno; oczywiście
cleave; cleft; cleft [kli:w; kleft;
kleft]
cleave [kli:w] v. 1. łupać;
pękać; rozdwajać; 2.
trzymać się wiernie; nie
odstępować
clef [klef] s. klucz (muzyczny)
cleft [kleft] s. szczelina;
pęknięcie; zob. cleave
clemency ['klemensy] s.
miłosierdzie; łagodność
(klimatu etc.)

clench [klencz] v. ściskać; zaciskać; zewrzeć się; ubić (targu); s. uścisk; zaciśnięcie; zagięcie

clergy ['kle:rdży] s. duchowieństwo; kler

clergyman ['kle:rdżymen] s. duchowny; ksiądz; pastor

clerical ['klerykel] adj. urzędniczy; duchowny; biurowy

clerk [kla:rk] s. subiekt; urzędnik; pisarz; ekspedient

clever ['klewer] adj. zdolny; sprytny; zręczny; pomysłowy; uprzejmy

click [klyk] v. szczękać; cmokać; trzaskać; dopiąć swego; wygrać; s. trzask; zatrzask; klamka; mlaśnięcie; klekot; brzęk

client ['klajent] s. klient

cliff [klyf] s. urwisko; stroma ściana; ściana skalna

climate ['klajmyt] s. klimat

climax ['klajmaeks] s. szczyt; zakończenie; v. stopniować; szczytować; kulminować

climb [klajm] s. wspinaczka; miejsce wspinania; v. piąć się; wspinać; wzbijać się; wdrapać się

climb up [klajm ap] v. wspinać się w górę; wdrapywać się

climber [klajmer] s. taternik; karierowicz; pnącze (roślina)

clinch [klyncz] v. zaciskać; zaginać; zanitować; zakończyć

cling; clung; clung [klyng; klang; klang]

cling [klyng] v. trzymać się; chwytać się; czepiać się; trwać

clinic ['klynyk] s. klinika; poradnia; adj. kliniczny

clink [klynk] s. dzwonienie; ciupa; v. dzwonić (kluczami etc.)

clip [klyp] 1. s. sprzączka; v. spinać; 2. s. strzyżenie; nożyce; v. strzyc; orżnąć

clippings ['klypyns] pl. wycinki (z gazet); okrawki; obrzynki

cloak [klouk] s. płaszcz; maska; v. okryć płaszczem; wdziewać

clock [klok] s. zegar ścienny

clockwise ['klokłajz] adj. (obrót) w prawo wg. zegarka

clod [klod] s. gruda; ziemia; gamoń; v. obrzucać grudkami ziemi

clog [klog] s. kłoda; chodak; v. zatykać; zapychać; zawadzać

cloister ['klojster] s. krużganek; klasztor

close [klouz] v. zamykać; zatykać; zakończyć; zwierać; zgodzić się; s. zakończenie; koniec; miejsce ogrodzone; adv. szczelnie; blisko; prawie; adj. zamknięty; skąpy; gęsty; bliski; ścisły; ekskluzywny

close to ['klous tu] przy; tuż obok

close by ['klous baj] obok

close dawn ['klouz dałn] v. zamykać; kończyć (działalność etc.)

close in [klouz yn] v. nadchodzić; ogarniać; okrążyć; otoczyć

closet ['klozyt] s. pokoik; klozet; kredens

close-up ['klousap] s. zdjęcie zbliżone; zbliżenie

closing time ['klouzyng,tajm] s. koniec pracy; zamknięcie (sklepu); koniec urzędowania

clot [klot] s. skrzep; v. ścinać się; skrzepnąć; zsiadać się

cloth [klos] s. materiał; szmata; szafa; obrus; sukno; żagiel

cloth-bound [klos baund] s. oprawny w płótno

clothe [klouz] s. materiał; sukno; v. przywdziewać; zamaskować

clothes [klouz] pl. ubranie; pościel; pranie; odzież; ubiór

clothes brush ['klouz,brasz] s. szczotka do ubrań

clothes hanger ['klouz,hanger] s.

wieszak do ubrań
clothesline ['klous̱,lajn] s. sznur na bieliznę do suszenia
clothespin ['klouẕ,pyn] s. spinacz do bielizny
clothing [klouzyng̱] s. odzież; osłona; bielizna; odzienie
cloud [klaud] s. chmura; obłok; zasępienie; tuman; kłąb dymu; v. chmurzyć; sępić; rzucać cień; ufarbować
cloudy ['klaudy] adj. chmurny; posępny; zamglony; mętny
clove [klouw] s. goździk; ząbek czosnku; zob. cleave
clover [klouwer] s. koniczyna
clown [klaun] s. błazen; prostak; v. błaznować; wygłupiać się
club [klab] s. klub; pałka; kij; v. bić pałką; zbijać; łączyć; zrzeszać; stowarzyszać się
clue [klu:] s. klucz; ślad; wątek; v. informować (o wątku)
clumsy ['klamzy] adj. niezgrabny; nietaktowny; niekształtny
clung [klang̱] v. przywarty; zob. cling
cluster ['klaster] s. grono; kiść; pęk; kupka; v. tworzyć pęki; skupiać się; zbierać się
clutch [klacz] s. chwyt; szpon; sprzęgło; v. trzymać się kurczowo
clutch pedal ['klacz,pedl] s. pedał sprzęgła
coach [koucz] s. wóz pasażerski; trener; v. jechać wozem; trenować; uświadamiać; pouczać
coagulate [kou'aegjulejt] v. stężać; skrzepnąć; koagulować
coal [koul] s. węgiel
coal-field ['koul'fi:ld] s. zagłębie węglowe
coalition [,koue'lyszyn] s. związek; koalicja; przymierze
coal mine [koul-majn] s. kopalnia węgla
coal pit ['koul-pyt] s. kopalnia węgla; szyb kopalniany
coarse [ko:rs] adj. pospolity; gruboziarnisty; szorstki

coast [koust] s. brzeg; v. jechać bez napędu; płynąć brzegiem
coast-guard ['koustga:rd] s. straż przybrzeżna
coat [kout] s. marynarka; surdut; powłoka; v. okrywać; pokrywać warstwą; powlekać (farbą)
coat hanger ['kouthaeng̱er] s. wieszak (do ubrania)
coating [koutyng̱] s. powłoka; warstwa; pokrycie
coat of arms ['kout ow,a:rms] s. herb; godło
coax [kouks] v. namówić pochlebstwem; udobruchać; przymilać się; wycyganiać; wyczarowywać (z butelki)
cob [kob] s. głąb; kucyk; łabędź samiec; kaczan; kutwa; bochenek
cobra ['koubre] s. kobra
cobweb ['kobłeb] s. pajęczyna
cock [kok] s. kogut; kurek; kran; kutas (wulg.); v. postanowić; nastroszyć; napiąć; odwodzić; podnieść; zadzierać; wznieść
cock-and-bull ['koken'bul] exp. o żelaznym wilku
cockchafer ['kok,czejfer] s. chrząszcz
cockle ['kokl] s. kąkol; piecyk
cockpit ['kokpyt] s. kokpit; kabina; arena do walki kogutów
cockroach ['kokroucz] s. karaluch
cocksure ['kokszuer] adj. pewny siebie; zarozumiały
cocktail ['koktejl] s. cocktail
coco ['koukou] s. palma kokosowa; kokos
cocoa ['koukou] s. kakao
coconut ['koukenat] s. orzech kokosowy
cocoon [ke'ku:n] s. kokon; oprzęd
cod [kod] s. dorsz; sztokfisz; wątłusz; v. wystrychnąć na dudka
coddle ['kodl] v. podgotować;

pieścić; tuczyć; zepsuć
code [koud] s. kodeks; szyfr; v.
szyfrować; pisać szyfrem
cod-liver oil ['kod,lywer ojl] s.
tran (lekarski)
coerce [kou'e:rs] przymusić;
zniewalać
coexist ['kouyg'zyst] v.
współistnieć; koegzystować
coexistence ['kouyg'zystens] s.
współistnienie; współżycie
coffee ['kofy] s. kawa
coffee bean ['kofy-bi:n] s. ziarno
kawy
coffee mill ['kofy-myl] s. młynek
do kawy
coffeepot ['kofy-pot] s.
maszynka do kawy
coffin ['kofyn] s. trumna
cogwheel ['kog-hłil] s. koło
zębate; tryb
coherence [kou'hierens] s. sens;
spoistość; związek logiczny
coherency [kou'hierensy] s.
sens; zwartość; spójność
coherent [kou'hierent] adj.
logiczny; zwarty; spoisty
cohesive [kou'hi:syw] adj.
spoisty; zwarty; kleisty
coiffure [kła:'fjuer] s. fryzura;
styl uczesania
coil [kojl] s. zwój; cewka; lok; v.
zwijać; skręcać; wić się
coin [koyn] s. moneta; v. bić
monety; spieniężać; ukuć
(nowe pojęcie); tłoczyć
coinage [koynydż] s. bicie
monety; monety; system
monetarny; wymysł; nowe
słowo
coincide [kouyn'sajd] v. zbiegać
się; pokrywać się;
przystawać do siebie;
pasować
coincidence [kou'ynsydens] s.
zbieg okoliczności;
zgodność; przystawanie;
zgodność faktów
coke [kouk] s. koks; kokaina;
Coca-Cola; v. koksować
cold [kould] s. zimno;
przeziębienie; adj. zimny;
chłodny; mroźny

cold storage room [kould-
-storedż,ru:m] chłodnia
colic ['kolyk] s. kolka (w
brzuchu); ostry ból w brzuchu
collaborate [ke'laeberejt] v.
współpracować;
kolaborować
collaboration [ke'laeberejszyn] s.
współpraca; kolaboracja
collapse [ke'laeps] s. załamanie
się; upadek; runięcie;
zawalenie się; v. załamać się;
upaść; opaść; zawalić się;
załamywać
collapsible [ke'laepsebl] adj. składany (mebel, stół, łóżko etc.)
collar ['koler] s. kołnierz; szyjka;
pierścień; obroża; chomąto;
piana (na piwie); v. wkładać
obrożę; pojmać; ująć
collarbone ['koler-boun] s.
obojczyk
colleague ['koli:g] s. kolega (po
fachu); współpracownik
collect ['ke'lekt] v. zbierać;
odbierać; inkasować
collected ['ke'lektyd] adj.
skupiony; opanowany;
spokojny
collection ['ke'lekszyn] s. zbiór;
kolekcja; inkaso;
zainkasowane pieniądze
collective ['ke'lektyw] adj.
zbiorowy; wspólny; s.
kolektyw
collector ['ke'lektor] s. inkasent;
poborca; zbieracz
college ['kolydż] s. uczelnia;
kolegium; zrzeszenie;
akademia
collegiate [ke'ly:dżiet] adj.
uniwersytecki; studencki;
kolegialny; kolegiacki
collide [ke'lajd] v. zderzyć się;
kolidować; wejść w kolizję
colliery ['koljery] s. kopalnia
węgla
collision [ke'lyżen] s. zderzenie;
kolizja
colloquial [ke'loukłjel] adj.
potoczny (język); familiarny
colon ['koulen] s. grube jelito;
dwukropek

colonel ['ke:nl] s. pułkownik
colonial [ke'lounjel] adj.
  kolonialny; s. mieszkaniec
  kolonii
colonialism [ke'lounjelyzem] s.
  kolonializm
colonist ['kolenyst] s. osadnik;
  mieszkaniec kolonii
colonize ['kolenajz] v. osiedlać;
  kolonizować
colony ['koleny] s. kolonia
color ['kaler] s. barwa; farba;
  koloryt; v. barwić; farbować;
  koloryzować; rumienić się
color bar ['kaler ba:r] s.
  oddzielenie ras
colored ['kaleret] adj. barwny;
  kolorowy
colorful ['kalerful] adj. pstry;
  barwny; żywy; kolorowy
coloring ['kaleryng] s. koloryt;
  kolorowanie; rumieńce
colorless ['kalerlys] adj.
  bezbarwny; nudny; monotonny
color-line ['kalerlajn] s. przedział
  rasowy
color print ['kaler,prynt] s.
  chromodruk
colt [koult] s. źrebak
column ['kolem] s. kolumna;
  stos; trzon; szpalta; formacja
coma ['koume] s. omdlenie;
  koma; śpiączka; ogon
  (komety)
comb [koum] s. grzebień;
  grzbiet (fali); v. czesać;
  kłębić się
combat ['kombet] s. walka; v.
  zwalczać; walczyć
combatant ['kombetent] adj.
  walczący; s. kombatant;
  bojownik
combination [komby'nejszyn] s.
  kombinacja; zespół; związek
combine [kembajn] v. połączyć;
  powiązać; skombinować;
  łączyć w sobie
combine-harvester [kembajn-
  -'ha:rwyster] s. kombajn
combustible [kem'bastebl] adj.
  palny; s. paliwo; materiały
  pędne; opał; adj. popędliwy
combustion [kem'bastszyn] s.

spalanie; zapłon
come; came; come [kam; kejm;
  kam]
come [kam] v. przybyć;
  pochodzić; wynosić; dziać
  się; być
come about ['kam,e'baut] v.
  zdarzyć się; stać się;
  odwracać się
come across ['kam,e'kros] v.
  natknąć się; dać się
  przekonać
come along ['kam,e'long] v.
  pośpieszyć się; nadejść
come around ['kam,e'raund] v.
  zmienić zdanie; odwiedzić
come at ['kam,et] v. podejść;
  dotrzeć; przyjść o
  (czwartej...)
come by ['kam,baj] v. dojść do
  czegoś; minąć; nabyć
come for ['kam,for] v. przyjść
  po coś
come loose ['kam,luz] v.
  obluźniać się
come off ['kam,of] v. odpaść;
  odlecieć; puszczać; mieć
  miejsce
come on ['kam,on] v. chodźże;
  przestań; daj spokój
come round ['kam,raund] v.
  zmienić zdanie; przechytrzyć;
  obejść
come to see ['kam tu si:] v.
  odwiedzić; przyjść z wizytą
come up to ['kam ap tu] v.
  podejść do ...; wejść na
  sam (szczyt)
come-and-go ['kam-en-'go] s.
  bieganina; ruch tam i z
  powrotem
comeback ['kam-'baek] s.
  powrót; bystra odpowiedź;
  poprawa
comedian [ke'mi:djen] s. komik
comedy ['komydy] s. komedia
comer ['kamer] s. przybysz
comet ['komyt] s. kometa
comfort ['kamfert] s. wygoda;
  pociecha; v. pocieszać;
  czynić wygodnym; dodawać
  otuchy
comfortable ['kamfertebl] adj.

wygodny; zadowolony;
spokojny
comforter ['kamferter] s.
pocieszyciel; kołdra; smoczek
comical ['komykel] adj. zabawny;
śmieszny; komiczny
comic strips ['komyk,stryps] s.
seryjne obrazkówki; kreskówki
comma ['kome] s. przecinek
command [ke'maend] v.
rozkazywać; kazać;
rozporządzać; panować nad;
dowodzić; s. rozkaz; nakaz;
komenda; dowództwo
commander [ke'maender] s.
dowódca; komendant; kapitan
(fregaty)
commander-in-chief [ke'maender
yn'czi:f] głównodowodzący
commandment [ke'maendment]
s. przykazanie (boskie)
commend [ke'mend] v. chwalić;
zalecać; polecać opiece
commendable [ke'mendebl] adj.
chwalebny; godny polecenia
comment ['koment] s.
objaśnienie; v. robić uwagi
krytyczne lub złośliwe;
wypowiadać zdanie
comment on ['koment on] v.
komentować; oceniać
(utwór)
commentary ['komentery] s.
komentarz; uwaga; notatka
commentator ['komentejter] s.
komentator; sprawozdawca
commerce ['kome:rs] s. handel
commercial [ke'me:rszel] adj.
handlowy; s. ogłoszenie (w
radio ...)
commissar ['komy'sa:r] s.
komisarz w b. ZSRR
commission [ke'myszyn] s.
zlecenie; misja; urząd; v.
delegować; powierzać;
objąć; zlecać; zamianować;
upoważniać
commissioner [ke'myszener] s.
delegat; pełnomocnik;
komisarz rządowy; członek
komisji rządowej
commit [ke'myt] v. powierzać;
przekazywać; odsyłać;

popełniać; wciągać;
zobowiązywać się; oddawać
w opiekę; zamykać w (domu
wariatów); obiecywać
commitment [ke'mytment] s.
zobowiązanie; dopuszczenie
się; przekazanie;
zaangażowanie się
committee [ke'myti:] s. komitet;
komisja; opiekun (umysłowo
chorego)
commodity [ke'modyty] s.
towar; rzecz przydatna;
artykuł handlu
common ['komen] adj. wspólny;
publiczny; ogólny; pospolity;
zwyczajny; prosty
**Common Wealth of Independent
States** ['komen łels ow
,yndy'pendet stejc] s.
Wspólnota Niezależnych
Państw
commoner ['komener] s.
człowiek z gminu; nie
szlachcic
common law marriage ['komen,
,lo:'maerydż] pożycie na
wiarę
common market ['komen'
ma:rkyt] wspólny rynek (Zach.
Europa)
commonplace ['komen-plejs] s.
banał; adj. banalny; oklepany
common sense ['komen,sens]
zdrowy rozsądek
commonwealth ['komen,łels] s.
wspólnota; rzeczpospolita
commotion [ke'mouszyn] s.
zamieszki; tumult; poruszenie
commune ['komju:n] s. gmina;
komuna; v. obcować;
rozmawiać
communicate [ke'mju:ny,kejt] v.
dzielić się; komunikować
się; łączyć się; przenosić
(ciepło, zimno etc.)
communication [ke,mju:ny
'kejszyn] s. łączność;
komunikacja; porozumiewanie
się; zakomunikowanie
communicative [ke'mju:nykejtyw]
adj. otwarty; rozmowny;
towarzyski; przystępny

communion [ke'mju:njen] s.
obcowanie; uczestnictwo;
wspólnota; komunia; wyznanie
wiary
communism ['komju,nyzem] s.
komunizm; ruch
komunistyczny
communist ['komjunyst] s.
komunista; adj. komunistyczny
community [ke'mju:nyty] s.
środowisko; społeczność;
gmina; kolektyw; wspólnota;
koło; zakon
commute [ke'mju:t] v.
zamieniać; zastępować;
łagodzić; dojeżdżać do
pracy; brać bilet okresowy
comose ['koumous] adj.
włochaty; puszysty; włóknisty
compact [kem'paekt] adj. gęsty;
zbity; zwarty; v. ubijać;
zbijać; zagęszczać; s.
puderniczka
compact ['kempaekt] s. ugoda;
porozumienie; puderniczka;
samochód średniej wielkości
(USA)
companion [kem'paenjen] s.
towarzysz; (coś) do pary
companionship [kem'
paenjenszyp] s. koleżeństwo;
towarzystwo
company ['kampeny] s.
towarzystwo; załoga; goście;
partnerzy; spółka; kompania;
trupa teatralna
comparable ['komperebl] adj.
porównywalny; wytrzymujący
porównanie
comparative [kem'paeretyw] adj.
porównawczy; względny;
stosunkowy; s. stopień
wyższy (przymiotnika)
compare [kem'peer] v.
porównywać; dawać się
porównać; stopniować
(gram.)
comparison [kem'paeryson] s.
porównanie; zestawienie
compartment [kem'pa:rtment] s.
przedział; przegroda; komora
wodoszczelna
compass ['kampes] s. kompas;

busola; obwód; obręb; cyrkiel;
zasięg; v. obchodzić;
otaczać; ogarniać; osiągać;
dopiąć
compassion [kem'paeszyn] s.
litość; współczucie
compassionate [kem'paeszynyt]
adj. litościwy; v. litować się
compatible [kem'paetebl] adj.
zgodny; licujący; do
pogodzenia
compatriot [kem'paetryet] s.
rodak; ziomek; rodaczka
compel [kem'pel] v. zmuszać;
wymuszać (coś); wzbudzać
compensate ['kompen,sejt] v.
wyrównywać; nagradzać;
wypłacić odszkodowanie;
kompensować
compensation [,kompen'sejszyn]
s. rekompensata;
wynagrodzenie;
odszkodowanie; wyrównanie
compete [kem'pi:t] v.
konkurować; rywalizować;
ubiegać się
compete for [kem'pi:t,fo:r] v.
(o coś) współzawodniczyć;
współubiegać się;
prześcigać się
competence ['kompytens] s.
fachowość; kwalifikacja;
uzdolnienie; zasobność;
dobrobyt
competent ['kompytent] adj.
właściwy; kwalifikowany;
odpowiedni; kompetentny
competition [,kompy'tyszyn] s.
konkurencja; konkurs; zawody;
współzawodnictwo; turniej
competitor [kem'petyter] s.
rywal; konkurent;
współzawodnik;
współzawodniczka; rywalka
compile [kem'pajl] v. zbierać;
zestawiać; kompilować
complacent [kem'plejsnt] adj.
zadowolony (z siebie, ze
świata); błogi
complain [kem'plejn] v. żalić
się; narzekać; skarżyć;
wnosić zażalenie; wnosić
skargę

complaint [kem'plejnt] s. skarga;
zażalenie; dolegliwość
complete [kem'pli:t] adj.
całkowity; zupełny; kompletny;
v. uzupełniać; udoskonalić;
ukończyć; wypełnić
(formularz)
completion [kem'pli:szyn] s.
ukończenie; uzupełnienie;
udoskonalenie; spełnienie
(woli, testamentu)
complex [kem'pleks] adj.
złożony z dwu lub więcej
części; zawiły;
skomplikowany; s. połączona
grupa (np. budynków;
impulsów, itd.); obsesja
complexion [kem'plekszyn] s.
cera; płeć; postać; aspekt
(charakter); wygląd
complicate ['komply,kejt] v.
wikłać; splatać;
komplikować
complicated ['kemlpy,kejtyd] adj.
skomplikowany; powikłany
compliment ['komplyment] s.
komplement; gratulacje;
ukłony; uszanowanie; v.
mówić komplementy;
gratulować
complimentary ['komply'mentery]
adj. pochlebny; okazowy;
grzecznościowy
comply [kem'plaj] v.
zastosować się; spełnić;
podporządkować się;
uczynić zadość;
przestrzegać
comply with [kem'plaj,łys] s.
spełniać; przestrzegać
czegoś
component [kem'pounent] s.
składnik; część składowa;
siła składowa; adj. składowy
compose [kem'pouz] v. składać;
układać; tworzyć;
komponować; skupiać
(myśli); uspokoić;
załagodzić; uspakajać się
composed [kem'pouzd] adj.
opanowany; spokojny;
stateczny
composer [kem'pouzer] s.

kompozytor; kompozytorka
composition [,kempe'zyszyn] s.
skład; układ; ugoda;
wypracowanie; budowa;
usposobienie
composure [kem'poużer] s.
spokój; opanowanie; zimna
krew; przytomność umysłu
compote ['kompout] s. kompot
(z puszki); kompotiera
compound [kom'paund] adj.
złożony; sprężony; s. związek
(chem.); mieszanka; złożenie;
v. mieszać; składać;
powiększać; łączyć;
zawrzeć; załatwić
comprehend [,kompry'hend] v.
pojmować; rozumieć;
zawierać
comprehensible [,kompry
'hensebl] adj. zrozumiały;
pojętny
comprehensive [,kompry
'hensyw] adj. obszerny;
szeroki; rozumowy;
wyczerpujący; ogólny;
wszechstronny
compress [kem'pres] v.
ściskać; streszczać; s.
kompres; okład
comprise [kem'prajz] v.
włączać; obejmować;
składać się
compromise ['kompre,majz] s.
kompromis; ugoda;
kompromitacja; narażenie; v.
załatwić ugodowo;
kompromitować
compulsion [kem'palszyn] s.
przymus; siła przymusu
compulsory [kem'palsery] adj.
przymusowy; przymuszający
compunction [kem'pankszyn] s.
skrucha; żal za grzechy
computation [,kompju'tejszyn] s.
obliczenie; kalkulacja
computer [kem'pju:ter] s.
kalkulator; komputer;
przelicznik
comrade ['komraed] s. kolega;
druh; współpracownik
comradeship ['komraedszyp] s.
koleżeństwo; braterstwo

con [kon] adv. (głosować)
przeciw; v. wkuwać (lekcje);
oszukiwać; w błąd
wprowadzać; s. aresztant;
skazaniec
concave ['kon'kejw] adj.
wklęsły; wklęśnięty
conceal [ken'si:l] v. taić;
ukrywać; przemilczać;
zataić
concede [ken'si:d] v.
przyznawać; ustępować;
poddawać się
conceit [ken'si:t] s. próżność;
zarozumiałość; mniemanie;
koncept
conceited [ken'si:tyd] adj.
próżny; zarozumiały
conceivable [ken'si:webl] adj.
wyobrażalny; zrozumiały
conceive [ken'si:w] v.
wymyślić; wyobrażać;
rozumieć; ujmować; zajść
w ciążę; pojąć; redagować
concentrate ['konsentrejt] v.
skupiać się; stężać; s.
roztwór
concentration ['kensentrejszyn]
s. skupienie (się); stężenie;
koncentracja; skoncentrowanie
conception [ken'sepszyn] s.
pomysł; poczęcie (dziecka);
początek
concern [ken'se:rn] s. interes;
troska; związek; v. tyczyć
się; dotyczyć; obchodzić;
niepokoić się o ...; wchodzić
w grę
concerned [ken'se:rnd] adj.
zainteresowany; zaaferowany;
strapiony; niespokojny
concert ['konsert] s. koncert;
porozumienie; v. ułożyć;
ukartować; porozumieć się
concession [ken'seszyn] s.
koncesja; ustępstwo;
przyzwolenie
conciliate [ken'syly,ejt] v.
zjednywać; jednać; godzić;
łagodzić; pogodzić;
udobruchać
conciliatory [ken'syljeto:ry] adj.
pojednawczy

concise [ken'sajs] adj. zwięzły;
treściwy; krótki i węzłowaty
conclude [ken'klu:d] v.
zakończyć; zawierać;
wnioskować; postanawiać;
kończyć się
conclusion [ken'klu:żyn] s.
zakończenie; wynik;
postanowienie; wniosek;
konkluzja; zawarcie układu;
wynik ostateczny
conclusive [ken'klu:syw] adj.
rozstrzygający; dowodny
concord ['konko:rd] s. zgoda;
jedność; harmonia; v.
zgadzać się
concrete ['konkri:t] s. beton;
konkret; adj. rzeczywisty;
realny; zwarty; stały;
konkretny; specyficzny;
betonowy
concur [ken'ke:r] v. zgadzać
się; schodzić się;
współdziałać
concurrence [ken'ke:rens] s.
zgodność; zbieżność;
zgoda
concussion [ken'kaszyn] s.
wstrząs (mózgu); uderzenie
condemn [ken'dem] v. potępiać;
skazywać; krytykować;
wybrakować
condemnation [,kendem'nejszyn]
s. potępienie; skazanie
condense [ken'dens] v.
kondensować; zgęszczać;
streszczać
condenser [ken'denser] s.
kondensator; skraplacz
condescend [,kondy'send] v.
zniżać się; raczyć;
zezwalać; zachowywać się z
wyższością
condition [ken'dyszyn] s. stan;
warunek; zastrzeżenie;
poprawka; v.
uwarunkowywać;
zastrzegać; naprawiać;
przygotowywać;
przyzwyczajać;
klimatyzować
conditional [ken'dyszynl] adj.
warunkowy; uzależniony;

zależny
condole [ken'doul] v. składać
kondolencje; współczuć;
ubolewać
condolence [ken'doulens] s.
wyrazy współczucia;
kondolencje
condom [kan'dem] s.
prezerwatywa; kondon
conduct [kon'dakt] s.
prowadzenie; sprawowanie;
prowadzenie się; sprawowanie
się; kierownictwo; v.
prowadzić; wieść;
przewodzić; dyrygować;
dowodzić
conduction [kon'dakszyn] s.
przewodzenie (fiz.)
conductor [kon'dakter] s.
kierownik; przewodnik;
dyrygent; przewód;
odgromnik; piorunochron
cone [koun] s. stożek; szyszka;
v. nadawać kształt stożka
confection [ken'fekszyn] s.
sporządzanie; konfitura;
słodycze; konfekcja (damska)
confectioner [ken'fekszyner] s.
cukiernik; właściciel cukierni
confectionery [ken'feksznery] s.
cukiernia; wyroby cukiernicze
confederacy [ken'federesy] s.
konfederacja; sojusz; związek;
spisek; sprzysiężenie
confederate [ken'federyt] adj.
sprzysiężony; v. jednoczyć;
spiskować; knuć;
sprzymierzać
confederation [ken,fede'rejszyn]
s. sprzymierzenie;
skonfederowanie; konfederacja
confer [ken'fe:r] v. naradzać
się; nadawać; przyznawać
conferee [,konfe'ri:] s. uczestnik
konferencji; nagrodzony
conference ['konferens] s.
narada; liga; zebranie; zjazd
confess [ken'fes] v. wyznać;
przyznać się; spowiadać się
confession [ken'feszen] s.
wyznanie; spowiedź;
przyznanie się; religia
confessor [ken'feser] s.

spowiednik; ksiądz spowiednik
confide [ken'fajd] v. ufać
(komuś); zwierzać się;
powierzać
confidence ['konfydens] s.
zaufanie; bezczelność;
pewność; ufność;
zwierzenie; śmiałość
confident ['konfydent] adj.
dufny; bezczelny; przekonany
confidential [,konfy'denczel] adj.
tajny; poufny; zaufany;
poufały; intymny
confine ['konfajn] v. ograniczać;
odosabniać; s. kres; granica
confinement [kon'fajnment] s.
uwięzienie; ograniczenie;
odosobnienie; połóg; poród
confirm [ken'fe:rm] v.
potwierdzać; zatwierdzać;
umacniać; bierzmować;
utwierdzać; pokrzepić
confirmation [,konfer'mejszyn] s.
potwierdzenie; zatwierdzenie;
bierzmowanie; pokrzepienie
confiscate ['konfyskejt] v.
konfiskować; skonfiskować
conflagration [,konfle'grejszyn] s.
pożar; pożoga
conflict ['konflykt] s. zatarg;
starcie; konflikt; kolizja
conform [kon'fo:rm] v.
dostosować; upodabniać;
dostrajać
conformity [kon'fo:rmyty] s.
zgodność; dostosowanie się
confound [kon'faund] v.
mieszać; zawieść;
pokrzyżować; poplątać
confound it! [kon'faund,yt] exp.
do licha!; niech to diabli
wezmą!
confront [ken'frant] v. stawiać
czoło; konfrontować;
unaocznić
confuse [ken'fju:z] v. zmieszać
(kogoś, siebie); wikłać;
gmatwać
confusion [ken'fju:żyn] s. nieład;
zamieszanie; bałagan; chaos
congeal [ken'dżi:l] v. mrozić;
ścinać; marznąć;
zakrzepnąć

congestion [ken'dżestczyn] s.
przeludnienie; przeciążenie
(ruchu); przekrwienie

conglomerate [ken'glomerejt] v.
skupiać; zlewać w jedną
masę

congratulate [ken'graetju,lejt] v.
gratulować; składać
(komuś) gratulacje;
pogratulować

congratulation [ken,
graetju'lejszyn] s. gratulacje;
gratulowanie; gratulacja

congregate ['kongry,gejt] adj.
zbiorowy; v. skupiać; zbierać
(się); gromadzić (się)

congregation [,kongry'gejszyn] s.
zbieranie; zgromadzenie

congress ['kongres] s. zjazd;
zebranie; parlament USA

conjecture [ken'dżekczer] s.
domysł; przypuszczenie; v.
przypuszczać; mniemać

conjugal ['kondżugel] adj.
małżeński

conjugate ['kondżu,gejt] v.
odmieniać się; kopulować;
parzyć się; adj. połączony

conjugation [,kondżu'gejszyn] s.
koniugacja; zespalanie się;
kopulacja; odmiana
czasownika

conjunction [ken'dżankszyn] s.
zbieg; związek; skojarzenie;
spójnik; połączenie

conjunctive mood [ken'
dżanktyw,mu:d] s. tryb
łączący

conjure [kan'dżuer] v. zaklinać;
błagać; robić sztuczki

conjure ['kandżer] v. czarować

conjurer ['kandżerer] s.
czarownik; magik; kuglarz

connect [ke'nekt] v. łączyć;
wiązać; mieć połączenie

connected [ke'nektyd] adj.
zwarty (logiczny);
ustosunkowany

connection(xion) [ke'nekszyn] s.
połączenie; pokrewieństwo

connive [ke'najw] v. pobłażać;
tolerować nadużycie; być w
zmowie

connoisseur ['kony':ser] s.
znawca; fachowiec

conquer ['konker] v. zdobyć;
zwyciężyć; pokonać

conqueror ['konkerer] s.
zdobywca; zwycięzca

conquest ['konkłest] s. podbój;
zdobycie; zawojowanie

conscience ['konszyns] s.
sumienie; świadomość zła i
dobra

conscientious [,konszy'enszes]
adj. sumienny; skrupulatny

conscious ['konszes] adj.
przytomny; świadomy;
naumyślny

consciousness ['konszysnys] s.
świadomość; całość
myśli i uczuć

conscript ['konskrypt] s. & adj.
poborowy; s. rekrut; v.
rekwirować; brać do wojska

consecrate ['konsy,krejt] v.
poświęcać; adj.
poświęcony

consecutive [ken'sekjutyw] adj.
kolejny; nieprzerwany;
skutkowy

consensus [ken'senses] s.
zgoda; jednomyślność

consent [ken'sent] s. zgoda; v.
zgadzać się; przyzwalać

consequence ['konsykłens] s.
wynik; znaczenie;
konsekwencja

consequently ['konsykłently] adv.
a zatem; przeto; tym samym;
w skutek tego; więc

conservative [ken'se:rwatyw]
adj. ostrożny; zachowawczy;
konserwatywny; s.
konserwatysta; środek
konserwujący

conserve [ken'se:rw] v.
konserwować; zachowywać;
zabezpieczać; s. konserwa
owocowa

consider [ken'syder] v.
rozważać; rozpatrywać;
uważać; szanować; mieć
wzgląd; sądzić

considerable [ken'syderebl] adj.
znaczny; adv. znacznie

considerate [ken'syderyt] adj.
myślący; uważający;
troskliwy

consideration [ken,syde'rejszyn]
s. wzgląd; rozważanie;
warunek; uprzejmość;
rekompensata

consign [ken'sajn] v. przekazać;
powierzać; złożyć do
(banku, grobu ...)

consignment [ken'sajnment] s.
przesyłka; powierzenie

consist [ken'syst] v. składać
się; polegać; zgadzać się

consistency [ken'systensy] s.
konsystencja; solidność;
stałość; zgodność;
logiczność

consistent [ken'systent] adj.
zgodny; stały; konsekwentny

consolation [,konse'lejszyn] s.
pocieszenie; pociecha;
ukojenie

console [ken'soul] v. pocieszać;
s. konsola; wspornik; podpora

consolidate [ken'solydejt] v.
utwierdzać; scalać;
jednoczyć

consonant ['konsenent] s.
spółgłoska; adj. spółgłoskowy;
zgodny; harmonijny

conspicuous ['ken'spykjues] adj.
widoczny; zwracający uwagę

conspiracy [ken'spyresy] s. spise
k; konspiracja; zmowa; umowa

conspirator [ken'spyreter] s.
spiskowiec; konspirator

conspire [ken'spajer] v.
konspirować; spiskować;
uknuć

constable ['kanstebl] s. policjant;
posterunkowy

constant ['konstent] adj. stały;
trwały; s. liczba stała

consternation [,konste:r'nejszyn]
s. przerażenie; osłupienie

constipation [,konsty'pejszyn] s.
zatwardzenie; zaparcie

constituency [ken'stytjuensy] s.
okręg wyborczy; wyborcy

constituent [ken'stytjuent] adj.
składowy; s. wyborca;
część; składowa; element

constitute ['konsty,tju:t] v.
stanowić; ustanawiać;
wyznaczać

constitution [,konsty'tju:szyn] s.
statut; konstytucja; struktura;
założenie; układ psychiczny

constitutional [,konsty'tu:szenl]
adj. zasadniczy; istotny;
zdrowotny; s. przechadzka dla
zdrowia

constrain [ken'strejn] v.
wymuszać; zmuszać;
ograniczać; więzić;
zniewalać; przymuszać

constraint [ken'strejnt] s.
przymus; skrępowanie;
ograniczenie swobody
(ruchów)

construct [ken'strakt] v.
budować; tworzyć; rysować
(figury geom.)

construction [ken'strakszyn] s.
budowa; konstrukcja; układ;
konstruowanie; ujęcie;
interpretacja

constructive [ken'straktyw] adj.
twórczy; konstruktywny

consul ['konsel] s. konsul

consular ['konsjuler] adj.
konsularny

consulate ['konsjulyt] s.
konsulat; uprawnienia konsula

consulate general ['konsjulut
'dżeneral] s. konsulat
generalny

consult [ken'salt] v. radzić się;
informować się

consultation [,konsel'tejszyn] s.
porada; konsultacja

consultative [ken'saltetyw] adj.
doradczy; konsultatywny

consume [ken'sju:m] v.
spożywać; zużywać;
trawić; niszczyć; marnieć;
uschnąć

consumer [ken'sju:mer] s.
konsumer; spożywca;
odbiorca

consummate [ken'samyt] adj.
doskonały; wielkiej miary;
skończony

consummate ['konsemejt] v.
spełniać małżeństwo

consumption [ken'sampszyn] s.
zużycie; suchoty; pylica
contact ['kontaekt] s.
styczność; stosunki;
znajomości; v. kontaktować;
porozumiewać się; stykać
się; zetknąć się
contact lenses ['kontaekt,lenzys]
pl. szkła kontaktowe
contagious [ken'tejdżes] adj.
zaraźliwy; zakaźny;
udzielający się
contain [ken'tejn] v. zawierać;
opanowywać się; wiązać;
hamować
container [ken'tejner] s.
zasobnik; zbiornik; naczynie
contaminate [ken'taemynejt] v.
zakazić; skalać;
deprawować
contamination [ken'
taemynejszyn] s. konta-
minacja; zakażenie; skażenie;
ujemny wpływ
contemplate ['kontemplejt] v.
oglądać; rozważać; liczyć
się z (czymś); medytować;
planować
contemplation ['kontemplejszyn]
s. oglądanie; kontemplacja;
rozważanie; planowanie;
medytacja
contemplative ['kontemplejtyw]
adj. kontemplacyjny;
zamyślony
contemporary [ken'temperery]
adj. & s. współczesny
(rówieśnik)
contempt [ken'temt] s. pogarda;
lekceważenie; obraza (sądu
etc.)
contemptible [ken'temtebl] adj.
godny pogardy, lekceważenia
contemptuous [ken'temtjues]
adj. pogardliwy; nadęty;
lekceważący
contend [ken'tend] v. spierać
się; walczyć; rywalizować;
upierać się
content 1. [ken'tent] adj.
zadowolony; s. zadowolenie;
v. zadowalać
content 2. ['kontent] s.

zawartość; treść; obję-
tość; pojemność; po-
wierzchnia; kubatura; istota
contented [ken'tentyd] adj.
zadowolony; zaspokojony
contents ['kontents] s.
zawartość (pojemnika, książki); treści
contest ['kontest] s. rywalizacja;
spór; v. walczyć; spierać
się; ubiegać; kwestionować
context ['kontekst] s. kontekst
continent ['kontynent] s.
kontynent; część świata
continental ['kontynentl] adj.
kontynentalny; s. mieszkaniec
kontynentu
continual [ken'tynjuel] adj.
ciągły; powtarzający się; stały
continuance [ken'tynjuens] s.
ciągłość; trwanie; przebieg;
ciąg dalszy; odroczenie; pobyt
continuation [ken'tynju'ejszyn] s.
kontynuacja; ciąg dalszy
continue [ken'tynju:] v.
kontynuować; ciągnąć dalej;
trwać; ciągnąć się;
odroczyć; upierać się
continuous [ken'tynjues] adj.
nieprzerwany; stały; ciągły
contort [ken'to:rt] v. skręcać;
wykrzywiać; zwichnąć;
przekrzywić
contour ['kontuer] s. zarys;
kontur; warstwica; v.
konturować
contraceptive [,kontre'septyw] s.
środek zapobiegający zapłod-
nieniu; środek antykoncepcyjny; adj. antykoncepcyjny
contract ['kontraekt] s. umowa;
układ; kontrakt; obietnica
contract [ken'traekt] v.
ściągać; kurczyć; zobo-
wiązywać
contractor [ken'traekter] s.
przedsiębiorca (budowlany
etc.); kontrahent
contradict [,kontre'dykt] v.
zaprzeczać; posprzeczać się
contradiction [,kontre'dykszyn] s.
sprzeczność; zaprzeczenie
contradictory [,kontre'dyktery]

adj. sprzeczny; przekorny;
kłótliwy; zaprzeczający
contrary ['kontrery] adj.
przeciwny; s. przeci-
wieństwo; adv. w przeci-
wieństwie
contrariwise ['kontrery,łajz] adv.
odwrotnie; natomiast
contrast [ken'traest] v.
przeciwstawiać; kontras-
tować; s. kontrast;
przeciwieństwo
contribute [ken'trybjut] v.
przyczynić się; dostarczyć;
współdziałać; zasłużyć się
contribution [,kontry'bju:szyn] s.
przyczynek; wkład; ofiara;
kontrybucja; datek; wsparcie
contributor [ken'trybjuter] s.
ofiarodawca; współpracownik
(pisarz); współpracowniczka
contrite [ken'trajt] adj.
skruszony; pełen skruchy
contrivance [ken'trajwens] s.
pomysł; sztuczka; fortel;
wynalazek; wynalazczość;
pomysłowość
contrive [ken'trajw] v.
wymyślić; wynaleźć;
doprowadzić do czegoś;
zaplanować; wykombinować
control [ken'troul] v. sprawdzać;
rządzić; kontrolować; opanować; s. kontrola; sterowanie; regulowanie; ster;
władza
controller [ken'trouler] s.
kontroler; regulator; zarządca
controversial [,kentre'we:rżel]
adj. sporny; sprzeczający się
controversy ['kontre,we:rsy] s.
spór; kłótnia; polemika;
dysputa
contuse [ken'tju:z] v. stłuc;
kontuzjować
convalesce [,konwe'les] v.
wyzdrowieć i odzyskać siły
convalescence [,konwe'lesens] s.
wyzdrowienie
convalescent [,konwe'lesnt] s.
rekonwalescent; ozdrowieniec
convenience [ken'wi:njens] s.
wygoda; korzyść;

dogodność
convenient [ken'wi:njent] adj.
wygodny; łatwy do
osiągnięcia
convent ['konwent] s. zakon
convention [ken'wenszyn] s.
zjazd; zgromadzenie; układ;
umowa; konwent; zebranie
conventional [ken'wenszynl] adj.
zwyczajowy; konwencjonalny;
umowny; powszechnie stosowany; klasyczny
conversation [,konwer'sejszyn] s.
rozmowa; konwersacja
converse [ken'we:rs] v.
rozmawiać; obcować; pro-
wadzić rozmowę
converse ['konwe:rs] s.
rozmowa; adj. odwrotny; s.
rzecz odwrotna
conversion [ken'we:rżyn] s.
odwrócenie; przemiana;
nawrócenie; przeistoczenie
convert [ken'we:rt] v. zmieniać;
nawracać; przekształcać;
odwracać; przemieniać; przystosować
convert ['konwert] s. neofita
convertible [ken'we:rtybl] adj.
wymienialny; s. otwarty samochód z podnoszonym dachem;
kabriolet
convey [ken'wej] v. przewozić;
przenosić; przesyłać; przekazywać; komunikować;
zapisywać
conveyance [ken'wejens] s.
przewóz; przenoszenie;
uzmysławianie; pojazd;
przekazanie
conveyor belt [ken'wejer,belt] s.
przenośnik taśmowy
convict ['konwykt] s. skazaniec;
więzień; v. udowadniać;
przekonywać; uznać winnym
conviction [ken'wykszyn] s.
przeświadczenie; przekonanie;
zasądzenie; skazanie
convince [ken'wyns] v.
przekonać; przekonywać
convoy ['konwoj] s. konwój;
eskorta; straż
convoy [kon'woj] v.

konwojować
convulsion [ken'walszyn] s.
drgawki; wstrząs; konwulsje
convulsive [ken'walsyw] adj.
konwulsyjny; niepohamowany
cook [kuk] s. kucharz;
kucharka;v. gotować;
preparować
cookbook [kuk'buk] s. książka
kucharska
cooking [kukyng] s. gotowanie
cool [ku:l] adj. chłodny; oziębły;
spokojny; v. chłodzić; stu-
dzić; ochłonąć; s. chłód
cooler ['ku:ler] s. chłodnica;
element chłodzący; więzienie
coolness ['ku:lnys] s. chłód;
zimna krew; opanowanie;
spokój
co-op [kou'op] s. spółdzielnia
cooperate [kou'operejt] v.
współpracować; współ-
działać
cooperation [kou,ope'rejszyn] s.
współpraca; współdziałanie;
kooperacja; spółdzielczość
cooperative [kou,ope'rejtyw] adj.
spółdzielczy; uspołeczniowy;
uczynny; współpracujący
cooperator [kou'ope,rejter] s.
współpracownik; spółdzielca
coordinate [kou'o:rdynejt] adj.
współrzędny; współrzędna
cop [kop] s. policjant (slang); v.
złapać; wygrać; buchnąć;
nakryć; porwać; ukraść
(slang)
copartner [kou'pa:rtner] s.
uczestnik; wspólnik;
udziałowiec (we wspólnym
interesie)
cope ['koup] v. uporać; dawać
sobie radę; pokrywać;
borykać się; zwieńczać; s.
kapa; peleryna
copilot ['kou'pajlot] s. kopilot;
zastępca pilota
copious ['koupjes] adj. obfity;
suty; bogaty; płodny;
obfitujący
copper ['koper] s. miedź; v.
miedziować; s. (slang) glina;
policjant; miedziak; kocioł z

miedzi
copy ['kopy] v. kopiować;
przepisywać; naśladować;
s. kopia; odpis; odbitka;
egzemplarz; wzór; model;
rękopis do druku
copybook ['kopy,buk] s. zeszyt
copyright ['kopy,rajt] s. prawo
autorskie; v. chronić prawem
autorskim
coral ['korel] s. koral
cord [ko:rd] s. sznur; lina; v.
wiązać; ustawiać w sągi
cordial ['ko:rdżel] adj. serdeczny;
nasercowy; s. lek nasercowy
cordiality [,ko:rdy'aelyty] s.
serdeczność; kordialność
corduroys ['ko:rde,rojz] pl.
sztruksowe spodnie
core [ko:r] s. rdzeń; v. usuwać
rdzeń; wycinać rdzeń
cork [ko:rk] s. korek; v.
korkować
corkscrew ['ko:rk,skru:] s.
korkociąg; adj. w kształcie
korkociągu
corn [ko:rn] s. 1. ziarno; zboże;
kukurydza; 2. nagniotek
corner ['ko:rner] s. róg;
narożnik; kąt; zakręt; v.
zapędzać do kąta; zmuszać;
monopolizować
cornered ['ko:rnerd] adj. rogaty;
schwytany; zapędzony w
ślepą ulicę
cornet ['ko:rnyt] s. kornet;
trąbka (mosiężna)
corn-flakes ['ko:rn,flejks] pl.
płatki z kukurydzy
coronary disease ['korenery
dy'zi:z] s. choroba wieńcowa
coronation [,kore'nejszyn] s.
koronacja
coroner ['korener] s. sędzia
śledczy; lekarz sądowy
(oględziny zwłok)
corporal ['ko:rperel] adj. cielesny;
osobisty; s. kapral
corporation [,ko:rpe'rejszyn] s.
korporacja; zrzeszenie; osoba
prawna zbiorowa
corpse [ko:rps] s. trup; zwłoki
corpulent ['ko:rpjulent] adj. tęgi;

otyły; gruby; tłusty
corral [ke'rael] s. ogrodzenie dla
bydła; tabór; v. zamykać w
ogrodzeniu; łapać; ustawiać
tabor; wpędzać do
ogrodzenia
correct [ke'rekt] adj. poprawny;
v. korygować; karcić;
prostować; leczyć;
naprawiać
correction [ke'rekszyn] s.
poprawka; korekta; kara
correspond [,korys'pond] v.
odpowiadać; korespondować
correspondence [,korys'pondens]
s. zgodność; korespondencja
correspondent [,korys'pondent]
s. korespondent; adj.
odpowiedni; zgodny z;
odpowiadający
corridor ['korydo:r] s. korytarz
corrigible ['korydżybl] adj. dający
się poprawiać; uległy
corroborate [ke'robe,rejt] v.
potwierdzić; potwierdzać
corrode [ke'roud] v. zżerać;
rdzewieć; niszczeć; niszczyć
corrosion [ke'roużyn] s. korozja;
zżeranie; niszczenie
corrugate ['korugejt] v.
marszczyć; fałdować;
karbować
corrugated iron ['korugejtyd
'ajron] s. pofałdowana blacha
corrupt [ke'rapt] adj. zepsuty;
sprzedajny; v. korumpować;
psuć się
corruption [ke'rapszyn] s.
zepsucie; korupcja; rozkład;
fałszowanie
corset ['ko:rsyt] s. gorset;
sznurówka; v. wkładać gorset
cosmetic [koz'metyk] s.
kosmetyk; adj. kosmetyczny
cosmetician [koz'metyszyn] s.
kosmetyczka
cosmonaut ['kozme,no:t] s.
kosmonauta; astronauta (w
USA)
cost; cost; cost [kost; kost;
kost]
cost [kost] v. kosztować; s.
koszt; strata; cena

costly ['kostly] adj. kosztowny;
wspaniały; drogi; cenny
costume ['kostju:m] s. kostium;
strój; przystroić w kostium
cosy ['kouzy] adj. przytulny; v.
przytulić się
cot [kot] s. łóżko składane;
szałas; schronienie
cottage ['kotydż] s. chata;
dworek; domek letniskowy
cottage cheese ['kotydż,czi:z] s.
biały ser krowi z kwaśnego
mleka
cotton ['kotn] s. bawełna; v.
polubić; kapować; adj.
bawełniany
cotton wool ['kotn,łul] s. wata
couch [kaucz] s. tapczan;
posłanie; łóżko; v. rozsiadać
się; mówić
cougar ['ku:ger] s. puma; kuguar
cough [kof] s. kaszel; v.
kaszleć; wykaszleć;
zakaszleć
could [kud] v. mógłby; zob. can
council ['kaunsyl] s. rada;
konsylium; sobór; zarząd
(miejski etc.)
councilor ['kaunsyler] s. radny;
radca; członek zarządu
counsel ['kaunsel] s. rada;
zamysł; radca prawny; v.
radzić; doradzać;
przyjmować radę
count [kaunt] v. liczyć; sądzić;
liczyć się; znaczyć; s.
rachuba; liczenie; suma;
zarzut; hrabia
countdown [kaunt-dałn] s.
liczenie do startu (rakiety)
count in [kaunt yn] v. brać w
rachubę; wliczać; włączyć
count out [kaunt aut] v.
wyliczyć; nie brać w
rachubę
countenance ['kauntynens] s.
mina; wyraz twarzy;
śmiałość; pewność siebie;
animusz; fantazja; v.
zachęcać; popierać;
zatwierdzać; usankcjonować
counter ['kaunter] s. 1. kantor;
lada; licznik; żeton;

2. przeciwieństwo; cios
odbijający; napiętek; adj.
przeciwny; przeciwległy;
podwójny; v. sprzeciwiać się;
reagować; uderzać; adv.
przeciwnie; na przekór; wbrew
(instrukcjom, poleceniom etc.)
counteract [,kaunter'aekt] v.
przeciwdziałać;
neutralizować
counterbalance ['kaunter
,baelens] s. przeciwwaga
counterespionage ['kaunter
'espje,na:ż] s. kontrwywiad
counterfeit ['kaunterfyt] adj.
fałszywy; podrobiony; v.
udawać; fałszować
counterintelligence ['kaunter
yn'tylydżens] s. kontrwywiad
counterpart ['kaunter,pa:rt] s.
odpowiednik; duplikat
countess ['kauntys] s. hrabina;
hrabianka
countless ['kauntlys] adj.
niezliczony; nie do zliczenia
country ['kantry] s. kraj;
ojczyzna; wieś; prowincja
country house ['kantry-'haus] s.
dom wiejski; dom na wsi
countryman ['kantrymen] s.
rodak; wieśniak; człowiek ze
wsi; mieszkańcy wsi
countryside ['kantry,sajd] s.
okolica; krajobraz; ludzie ze
wsi
country town ['kantry,tałn] s.
miasteczko; duża wieś
county ['kaunty] s. powiat;
hrabstwo; adj. powiatowy
couple ['kapl] s. para; v. łączyć;
parzyć się; żenić
coupling ['kaplyng] s. złącze;
skojarzenie; sprzęgło
coupon ['ku:pon] s. odcinek;
kupon wymienny (w sklepie,
banku ...)
courage ['karydż] s. odwaga
courageous [ke'rejdżes] adj.
odważny; śmiały; dzielny;
waleczny
courier ['kurjer] s. posłaniec;
goniec; kurier; agent
turystyczny

course [ko:rs] s. bieg; kierunek;
ruch naprzód; droga; danie;
kolejność; bieżnia; warstwa;
kurs; ciąg; v. gnać; pędzić;
ścigać; uganiać się
court [ko:rt] s. podwórze; hala;
dwór; hotel; sąd; v. zalecać
się; wabić; zabiegać
courteous ['ke:rczjes] adj.
grzeczny; uprzejmy i miły
courtesy ['ke:rtysy] s.
grzeczność; uprzejmość;
kurtuazja; (darmowa) usługa;
gest przez grzeczność; adj.
grzecznościowy
courtly ['ko:rtly] adj. układny;
wytworny; dworski; dostojny
court-martial ['ko:rt'ma:rszel] s.
sąd wojenny; v. sądzić
sądem wojskowym
court of justice
['ko:rt,ow'dżastys] s. sąd
courtroom ['ko:rt,ru:m] s. sala
sądowa (rozpraw)
courtship ['ko:rtszyp] s. zaloty;
umizgi do kobiety
courtyard ['ko:rt,ja:rd] s.
podwórze; dziedziniec
cousin ['kazyn] s. kuzyn;
kuzynka; krewny; cioteczny
brat (siostra)
cover ['kawer] s. koc; wieko;
oprawa; osłona; koperta;
nakrycie (stołu); pokrycie; v.
kryć; pokryć (klacz);
ubezpieczać; dać opis;
nakrywać; rozlać; chować;
przejechać
coverage ['kawerydż] s. pokrycie
ubezpieczeniem; zasięg
radiowy; omówienie w prasie
covering ['kaweryng] s. osłona;
pokrycie (dachu); przykrycie
covert ['kawert] s. schronienie;
adj. ukryty; potajemny;
przebrany
covet ['kawyt] v. pożądać
(cudzego); patrzeć z
zawiścią
covetous [kawytes] adj. chciwy;
pożądliwy; łapczywy;
zawistny
cow [kał] s. krowa; v.

zastraszyć się; przestraszyć
coward ['kauerd] s. tchórz; adj.
tchórzliwy; bojaźliwy
cowardice ['kauerdys] s.
tchórzostwo; tchórzliwość
cowardly ['kauerdly] adj.
tchórzliwy; adv. tchórzliwie
cowboy ['kałboj] s. konny
pastuch; pastuch bydła;
krowiarz
cower ['kauer] v. skulić się;
kucnąć; przykucać na ziemi
cowherd ['kał,he:rd] s. pasterz
bydła; pastuszka
cowhide ['kał,hajd] s. krowia
skóra; skóra wołowa
cowshed ['kał,szed] s. krowia
szopa; obora
cowslip ['kał,slyp] s. pierwiosnek
(kwiat bagienny)
coxcomb ['koks,koum] s. błazen;
fircyk; pajac; głupi
zarozumialec
coxswain ['kok,słejn] s. sternik
na regatach
coy [koj] adj. skromny;
nieśmiały; ostrożny; cichy;
udający
cozy [kouzy] adj. wygodny;
przytulny; s. okrycie czajnika
crab [kraeb] s. krab; rak; (wulg.)
menda; v. łowić kraby;
krytykować; rujnować;
narzekać
crab louse ['kraeb,laus] s. wesz
łonowa
crack [kraek] s. trzask; rysa;
szpara; próba; dowcip; v.
trzaskać; żartować; łupać;
uderzyć; rujnować; spowo-
dować pęknięcie; adj.
wysokiej jakości; doskonały
crack a joke ['kraek e 'dżok] v.
palnąć żart; palnąć kawał
crack a smile ['kraek,e'smajl] v.
(slang) uśmiechnąć się
cracker ['kraeker] s. sucharek;
petarda; łupacz; kłamstwo
crackpot ['kraekpot] s. wariat;
bez piątej klepki (slang)
crackle ['kraekl] v. trzeszczeć;
s. trzeszczenie; pajęczyna;
porcelana zdobiona

cradle ['krejdl] s. kołyska;
kolebka; wywrotka; v. kraść
w kołysce; kołysać; kosić
(kosa z ramą); płukać złoto
craft [kraeft] s. rzemiosło;
branża; sztuka; cech;
podstęp; chytrość;
biegłość; pojazd
craftsman ['kraftsmen] s.
rzemieślnik; mistrz w swoim
zawodzie
crafty ['kra-fty] adj. sprytny;
zręczny; podstępny;
przebiegły
crag [kraeg] s. skała (stroma);
turnia; nawis skalny
cram [kraem] v. tłoczyć;
napychać; opychać;
wytłaczać; wkuwać (się); s.
tłok; ciżba; wkuwanie do
egzaminu; ścisk; kłamstwo;
uczenie się do egzaminu
intensywnie i w pośpiechu
cramp [kraemp] s. skurcz;
klamra; zwornik; v. ściskać;
krępować; ograniczać; adj.
ściśnięty; stłoczony;
nieczytelny; sztuczny;
uchwycomy w imadło
cranberry ['kraenbery] s.
żurawina; brusznica błotna
crane [krejn] s. żuraw; dźwig;
v. podnosić; wyciągać szyję
crank [kraenk] s. korba; dziwak;
bzik; v. puszczać w ruch
(korba); kręcić; wydąbić
crank up ['kraenk,ap] v.
zapuszczać (motor);
uruchomić (motor)
crap [kraep] s. gra w kości;
brednie; bzdury; nonsens
crape [krejp] s. krepa
crash [kraesz] s. huk; łomot;
upadek; katastrofa; ruina;
krach; samodział; v. trzaskać;
huczeć; roztrzaskiwać;
wpaść na ...; adv. z hukiem;
z trzaskiem; z łomotem; z
hałasem
crash helmet ['kraesz,helmyt] s.
kask ochronny (motocyklisty)
crash landing ['kraesz,laendyng]
s. rozbicie się przy lądowaniu

crate [krejt] s. stare pudło; skrzynia; paka; v. pakować w skrzynie; wkładać do pak

crater ['krejter] s. krater

crave [krejw] v. pożądać; pragnąć; prosić usilnie; błagać

crawfish ['kro:fysz] s. rak; v. wycofywać się (rakiem)

crawl [kro:l] v. pełzać; czołgać się; wlec; roić się; s. czołganie; pływanie kraulem; ciarki; basen do hodowli raków

crayfish ['krejfysz] s. rak (rzeczny); rak morski bez kleszczy

crayon ['krejen] s. kredka; rysunek kredką; v. rysować kredką; szkicować; narysować węglem

crazy ['krejzy] adj. zwariowany; pomylony; walący się (np. dom)

crazy about ['krejzy,e'baut] zwariowany na punkcie czegoś

creak [kri:k] v. skrzypieć; trzeszczeć; s. skrzypienie; pisk; zgrzyt; trzask; trzeszczenie; pisknięcie; zgrzytnięcie

cream [kri:m] s. śmietana; śmietanka; krem; v. ustać się; zbierać śmietankę; zabielać

cream cheese ['kri:m,czi:z] s. ser śmietankowy (biały i miękki)

creamy ['kri:my] adj. śmietankowy; jak śmietana

crease ['kri:s] s. fałda; kant (spodni); v. fałdować; plisować; prasować; zmiąć; pomiąć

create [kry:'ejt] v. tworzyć; wywoływać; zapoczątkowywać; powodować

creation [kry'ejszyn] s. stworzenie; kreacja; świat; wszechświat

creative [kry'ejtyw] adj. twórczy; wynalazczy; tworzący

creator [kry'ejter] s. twórca

creature ['kry:czer] s. stwór; istota; kreatura (dominowana)

credentials [kry'denszelz] pl. dokumenty; listy uwierzytelniające (tożsamość posła etc.)

credibility gap [,kredy'bylyty gaep] s. niedowierzanie; luka w zaufaniu; brak zaufania

credible ['kredybl] adj. wiarogodny; wiarygodny

credit ['kredyt] s. kredyt; wiara; autorytet; powaga; uznanie; chluba; v. dawać wiarę; zapisywać na rachunek; zaliczać; przypisywać (coś komuś)

creditable ['kredytebl] adj. zaszczytny; godny pochwały; chlubny

credit card ['kredyt ka:rd] karta kredytowa do zakupów

creditor ['kredyter] s. wierzyciel (handlowy, prywatny etc.)

credulous ['kredjules] adj. łatwowierny; zbyt łatwowierny

creed [kri:d] s. wiara; wierzenia; głębokie przekonania

creek [kri:k] s. potok; zatoka

creep; crept; crept [kri:p; krept; krept]

creep [kri:p] v. pełzać; wkradać się; mieć ciarki; s. pełzanie; ciarki; obsuwanie; poślizg; nędzny typ; pełzanie się

creeper ['kri:per] s. pnącz

cremate [krymejt] v. spalać zwłoki na popiół

crept [krept] v. podpełzał; zob. creep

crescent ['kresnt] s. półksiężyc; rogalik; adj. półksiężycowy; rosnący; przybywający

cress [kres] s. rzeżucha

crest [krest] s. czub; grzebień; grzywa; pióropusz; kita; hełm; klejnot; grzbiet; v. formować grzbiet; osiągnąć szczyt

crestfallen [krest-folen] adj. z opadniętym czubem; speszony; zawstydzony; przygnębiony

crevasse [kry'waes] s. szczelina;

pęknięcie (w lodowcu etc.)
crevice ['krewys] s. szczelina;
rysa; pęknięcie; szpara
crew [kru:] s. załoga; drużyna;
zgraja; zob. crow
crib [kryb] s. żłób z pętami;
stajnia; obora; ciupka; pokoik;
domek; kojec; plagiat; v.
stłaczać; wyposażać w
żłoby; ocembrować;
zwędzić; używać
ściągaczki
cricket ['krykyt] s. świerszcz;
krykiet; v. grać w krykieta
crime [krajm] s. zbrodnia
criminal ['krymynl] s. zbrodniarz;
kryminalista; adj. zbrodniczy;
kryminalny
crimson ['krymzn] s. & adj.
karmazyn(owy); v. zabarwiać
na karmazynowo;
zaczerwieniać się
cringe [kryndż] s. uniżoność;
v. kulić; kurczyć się; kłaniać
się; płaszczyć się (usłużnie)
cripple ['krypl] s. kulawy; kaleka;
v. okulawić; osłabiać; kuleć;
utykać; okaleczyć;
przeszkadzać
crisis ['krajsys] s. przesilenie;
kryzys; krytyczna sytuacja
crises ['krajsi:z] pl. przesilenia;
kryzysy; opały
crisp [krysp] adj. rześki;
chrupki; energiczny; v. robić
kruchym; marszczyć;
kędzierzawić; fryzować;
ufryzować
critic ['krytyk] s. krytyk
recenzent; recenzentka
critical ['krytykel] adj.
krytykujący; krytyczny; trudny
do nabycia; ważny (moment)
criticism ['krytysyzem] s.
krytyka; krytycyzm;
znajdowanie błędów
criticize ['krytysajz] v.
krytykować; ganić;
znajdować błędy
croak [krouk] v. rechotać;
krakać; s. rechot; rechotanie;
krakanie
crochet ['krouszej] v. robić na

szydełku; szydełkować
crockery ['krokery] s. naczynia
gliniane (słoje, dzbany etc.)
crocodile ['krokedajl] s. krokodyl;
adj. krokodylowy
crocus ['kroukes] s. krokus;
szafran (z rodziny irysów)
crook [kruk] s. hak; zagięcie;
krzywizna; kanciarz; v.
krzywić; wyginać; kraść;
kantować
crooked ['krukyd] adj.
zakrzywiony; krzywy;
wypaczony; zgarbiony;
cygański; szachrajski;
oszukańczy; zgięty; wygięty
crop [krop] s. plon; biczysko;
bacik; całość; przycinanie;
krótko strzyżone włosy;
ucinek; v. strzyc; skubać;
zbierać; zasiewać; obrodzić;
wyłaniać się; uprawiać
ziemię; obradzać
crop up ['krop ap] v. nagle
zjawiać się; wyskoczyć
nagle
cross [kros] s. krzyż;
skrzyżowanie; mieszaniec;
kant; cygaństwo; v. żegnać
się; krzyżować; przecinać
coś; iść w poprzek;
przekreślać; udaremnić; adj.
poprzeczny; skośny;
krzyżujący; przeciwny;
gniewny; opryskliwy
cross out ['kros,aut] v.
wykreślać; skreślać;
przekreślać
cross-examination ['kros-
-ig'zaemynejszyn] s.
przesłuchanie; badanie (w
śledztwie)
crossing ['krosyng] s.
skrzyżowanie; przejście lub
przejazd na drugą stronę
(rzeki itp.)
crossroads ['krosroudz] pl.
rozstaje; skrzyżowanie dróg
crossword puzzle ['krosłord-'pazl]
s. krzyżówka
crouch [kraucz] v. kulić się;
kurczyć; przysiąść;
gotować się do skoku

crow [krou] s. kruk; wrona;
pianie; wesoły pisk; v. piać;
piszczeć wesoło; krzyczeć z
radości
crowbar ['krouba:r] s. drąg;
lewar; łom (do podważania
etc.)
crowd [kraud] s. tłum; tłok;
banda; mnóstwo; v. tłoczyć;
natłoczyć; napierać;
wpychać; śpieszyć;
przepełniać
crowded ['kraudyd] adj.
zatloczony; zapchany;
przeludniony
crown [kraun] s. korona;
wieniec; v. wieńczyć;
koronować
crucial ['kru:szel] adj.
decydujący; przełomowy;
krytyczny
crucifixion [,kru:sy'fykszyn] s.
ukrzyżowanie; krucyfiks
crucify [kru:syfaj] v.
ukrzyżować; torturować;
znęcać się
crude [kru:d]adj. surowy;
szorstki; niepożyty; obskurny
cruel [kruel] adj. okrutny
cruelty ['kruelty] s.
okrucieństwo; znęcanie się
(nad kimś)
cruet ['kru:yt] s. flaszeczka;
ampułka; buteleczka (na ocet
etc.)
cruise [kru:z] v. krążyć; lecieć;
podróżować; s. wycieczka
morska; przejażdżka; rejs
crumb [kram] s. okruch; (slang)
drań; v. kruszyć; drobić;
dodawać okruszyn; obtoczyć
(w bułce)
crumble ['kramb] v. kruszyć
(się)
crumple ['krampl] v. zmiąć;
zmarszczyć; załamywać się
crumple up ['krampl,ap] v.
pomiąć; zawalić się;
załamać się
crunch [krancz] v. miażdżyć;
chrupać; s. chrupanie;
chrzęst; kłopotliwa sytuacja
crunchy [kranchy] adj.

chrupiący; chrzęszczący;
kłopotliwy
crusade [kru:'sejd] s. wyprawa
krzyżowa; iść z krucjatą
crusader [kru:'sejder] s.
krzyżowiec; aktywny działacz
crush [krasz] v. kruszyć;
miażdżyć; miąć; s.
miażdżenie; tłok; ciżba;
zadurzenie się
crusher [kraszer] s. łamacz;
miażdżarka; druzgocący cios
crust [krast] s. skorupa; skóra;
v. zaskorupiać (się)
crutch [kracz] s. kula; podpórka;
laska; v. podpierać się
cry [kraj] s. krzyk; płacz; wrzask;
okrzyk; hasło; v. krzyczeć;
płakać; urągać; ujadać
cry-baby ['kraj,bejby] s. mazgaj;
beksa; płaksa (dziecinna)
crying ['krajyng] s. wołanie;
płacz; adj. płaczący;
skandaliczny
cry of rage ['kraj,ow'rejdż] s.
krzyk szału (wściekłości)
crypt [krypt] s. krypta
crystal ['krystl] s. kryształ;
szkiełko od zegarka; adj.
kryształowy
crystalline ['krystelajn] adj.
krystaliczny; kryształowy
crystallize ['krystelajz] v.
krystalizować się
cub [kab] s. szczenię (dzikiego
zwierza); zuch; młodzik
cube [kju:b] s. sześcian; kostka;
(slang) facet; v. podnosić do
sześcianu; obliczać
kubaturę; formować w
sześciany
cube root ['kju:b,ru:t] s.
pierwiastek sześcienny
cubicle ['kju:bykl] s. pokoik;
mała sypialnia; małe
mieszkanie
cuckoo ['kuku] s. kukułka;
głuptas; kukanie; dureń
cucumber ['kju:kamber] s.
ogórek
cuddle ['kadl] s. tulić; pieścić;
kulić się; gnieździć się
cudgel ['kadżel] s. pałka; bić

pałką, kijem
cue [kju:] s. wskazówka; nastrój;
ogonek (do sklepu); kij
bilardowy; warkocz; v. dać
wskazówkę
cuff [kaf] s. mankiet; kajdanki; v.
bić pięścią; uderzać;
kułakować; potarmosić;
szturchać
cuff links ['kaf,lynks] pl. spinki
do mankietów
culminate ['kalmynejt] v.
szczytować; kulminować
culmination [,kalmy'nejszyn] s.
kulminacja; punkt szczytowy
culprit ['kalpryt] s. oskarżony;
winowajca; winowajczyni
cultivate ['kaltywejt] v.
uprawiać; rozwijać;
kultywować; pielęgnować;
spulchniać
cultivation [,kalty'wejszyn] s.
uprawa; kultura;
kultywowanie; kultura
duchowa
cultivator ['kaltywejter] s.
plantator; kultywator; rolnik
cultural ['kalczerel] adj.
kulturalny; kulturowy
culture ['kalczer] s. kultura;
uprawa; v. uprawiać;
hodować; kształcić;
hodować bakterie
cultured ['kalczerd] adj.
kulturalny; oczytany;
wykształcony
cumulative ['kju:mjulejtyw] adj.
łączny; kumulacyjny;
skumulowany; kumulujący się
cunning ['kanyng] s. chytrość;
przebiegłość; adj. chytry;
przebiegły; miły; ładny
cup [kap] s. kubek; kielich;
czasza; filiżanka; v.
wgłębiać; stawiać bańki
cup board ['kaberd] s. kredens;
szafka; półka na kubki
cupola ['kju:pele] s. kopuła; piec
kopułowy; żeliwiak
cur [ke:r] s. kundel; szelma
curable ['kjuerebl] adj. uleczalny;
wyleczalny
curate ['kjueryt] s. wikary

curb [ke:rb] s. krawężnik;
łańcuszek; wędzidło; oszczep;
twarda spuchlizna; v.
okiełznać; hamować;
ograniczać
curd [ke:rd] s. twaróg; tłuszcz
curdle [ke:rdl] v. ścinać;
zsiadać się; formować w
grudki
cure [kjuer] s. kuracja; lek;
lekarstwo; v. uleczyć;
wyleczyć; zaradzić;
wykurować
cure-all ['kjuero:l] s. panaceum;
lek na wszystkie dolegliwości
curfew ['ke:rfju:] s. godzina
policyjna; capstrzyk
curio ['kjuerjou] s. okaz;
osobliwość; unikat;
rzadkość
curiosity [,kjur'josyty] s.
ciekawość; osobliwość
curl [ke:rl] s. kędzior; lok; pukiel;
skręt; spirala; wir; v. kręcić;
skręcać; zwijać; marszczyć;
złościć; skulić się
curling iron ['ke:rlyng,ajren] s.
rurki do fruzowania
curl up ['ke:rl ap] v. zwinąć
(się)
curly ['ke:rly] adj. kędzierzawy;
kręty; falujący; kręcony
currant ['karent] s. porzeczka;
rodzynek bez pestki
currency ['karensy] s. waluta;
obieg; potoczność;
popularność
current ['karent] adj. bieżący;
obiegowy; obiegający;
powszechnie znany; panujący
(pogląd); s. prąd; bieg; nurt;
tok; strumień; natężenie
prądu
curriculum [ke'rykjulem] s. plan
studiów; program nauki
curriculum vitae [ke
'rykjulem,wajti:] s. życiorys
curse [ke:rs] s. przekleństwo;
klątwa; v. przeklinać;
wyklinać; kląć; bluźnić;
złorzeczyć
cursed [ke:rsyd] adj. przeklęty;
cholerny; adv. paskudnie;

cholernie; po diable
curt [ke:rt] adj. krótki; zwięzły;
lakoniczny; szorstki; suchy
curtail [ke:r'tejl] v. obcinać;
skracać; zmniejszać;
uszczuplać
curtain ['ke:rtn] s. zasłona;
firanka; kurtyna; v. zasłaniać
curtsy ['ke:rtsy] s. dyg; v.
dygać; złożyć głęboki ukłon
curve [ke:rw] s. krzywa;
krzywizna; krzywka; wyginać
(się); wykrzywiać (się);
zakręcać
cushion ['kuszyn] s. poduszka
custody ['kastedy] s. opieka;
nadzór; areszt; przetrzymanie
custom ['kastem] s. zwyczaj;
klientela; zrobiony na
zamówienie; nawyk; stałe
zaopatrywanie się
customary ['kastemery] adj.
zwyczajny; zwyczajowy; s.
zbiór praw
customer ['kastemer] s. klient
customhouse ['kastem-haus] s.
komora celna; urząd celny
custom-made ['kastem-mejd] adj.
zrobiony na zamówienie
customs ['kastemz] pl. cło
customs clearance ['kastemz
klierenz] s. odprawa celna
customs declaration ['kastemz
,dekle'rejszyn] s. deklaracja
celna (przy przekraczaniu
granicy etc.)
customs examination ['kastemz
ig,zamy'nejszyn] s. rewizja
celna (bagażu, towarów etc.)
cut; cut; cut [kat; kat; kat]
cut [kat] s. cięcie; przecięcie;
wycięcie; ścięcie; odrzynek;
krój; styl (krawiecki); wykop;
drzeworyt; v. ciąć; zaciąć;
skaleczyć; ranić; krajać;
kroić; przycinać; kosić;
rżnąć; rzeźbić; szlifować;
wycinać; obcinać; uciąć;
ścinać
cut down ['kat,dałn] v. obniżać;
redukować; wyciąć w pień
(wroga)
cut in ['kat,yn] v. wtrącać się

cut off ['kat,of] v. odcinać;
przerywać (dopływ);
wydziedziczać
cut out ['kat,aut] v. wykroić;
przestać; zaprzestać (palić);
wyciąć; wyrżnąć
cut up ['kat,ap] v. posiekać;
skrytykować; wypatroszyć;
siec; rozciąć
cute [kju:t] adj. miły; ładny;
chytry; sprytny; ciekawy;
bystry
cuticle ['kju:tykl] s. naskórek
cuticle scissors ['kju:tykl-'syzez]
s. nożyczki od naskórka
cutlery ['katlery] s. wyroby
nożownicze; sztućce
cutlet ['katlyt] s. kotlet (bity);
kotlet mielony (mięsny, rybi)
cut-off ['katof] s. odcięcie;
skrót; wyłącznik; wycinek;
zawór (wodny; parowy;
gazowy etc.)
cutout ['kat aut] = cut-off
cutpurse ['kat pe:rs] s.
rzezimieszek; kieszonkowiec;
opryszek
cutter ['kater] s. kuter;
przecinek; przykrawacz;
odcinacz; kamieniarz; mistrz
kamieniarski
cutting ['katyng] adj. bolesny;
przenikliwy; cięty; s. sadzonka
cutthroat ['kat,trout] s. zbój;
bandyta; adj. zbójecki;
bandycki; morderczy;
bezlitosny
cycle [sajkl] s. cykl; okres;
obieg; rower; v. jechać na
rowerze; obiegać cyklicznie
(tam i nazad, w koło itp.)
cyclist ['sajklyst] s. rowerzysta;
rowerzystka; cyklista;
cyklistka
cyclone ['sajkloun] s. cyklon
cylinder ['sylynder] s. walec;
(maszyny do pisania); cylinder;
bęben (rewolweru etc.)
cynic ['synyk] s. cynik
cynical ['synykel] adj. cyniczny
(pomysł, program, człowiek)
cynicism ['syny,syzem] s.
cynizm

cypress ['sajprys] s. cyprys
cyst [syst] s. cysta; torbiel
czar [za:r] s. car; (od nafty,
sportu, walki z narktukami,
komisarz generalny USA)
Czech [czek] adj. czeski
Czechoslovak ['czekou,slouwaek]
adj. czechosłowacki

D

d [di] czwarta litera alfabetu
angielskiego; oznaczenie centa
dab [daeb] v. musnąć; klepać;
dotknąć; dziobnąć; s.
muśnięcie; klaps;
stuknięcie; dziobnięcie; plama;
bryzg; odrobina
dabble ['daebl] v. moczyć;
babrać; pluskać (się);
interesować (się)
dabbler ['daebler] s. amator;
amatorka; dyletant; dyletantka
dachshund ['daekshund] s.
jamnik; a. jamniczy; jamnika
dad [daed] s. tato; tatuś
daddy ['daedy] s. tatuś
daffodil ['daefedyl] s. żółty
narcyz; żonkil; adj. bladożółty
daffy ['daefy] adj. zwariowany
daft ['daeft] adj. pomylony;
głupkowaty; zwariowany
dagger ['daeger] s. sztylet;
odsyłacz; v. sztyletować
daily ['dejly] adj. codzienny; adv.
codziennie; s. dziennik
dainty ['dejnty] adj. wyszukany;
wyborowy; delikatny;
gustowny; miły; wybredny
daiquiri ['daikery] s. rum z
sokiem cytrynowym, cukrem i
lodem (po amerykańsku)
dairy ['deery] s. mleczarnia
dairyman ['deerymen] s.
mleczarz; właściciel mleczarni
daisy ['dejzy] s. stokrotka; ładny
okaz (człowieka)
dale [dejl] s. dolina

dally ['daely] v. marudzić;
igrać; flirtować; tracić czas
dam [daem] s. tama; zapora
damage ['daemydż] s. szkoda;
uszkodzenie; odszkodowanie;
(slang) koszt; v. uszkodzić;
ponieść szkody; uwłaczać
dame [dejm] s. dziewczyna;
kobieta; pani (starsza)
damn [daem] v. potępiać;
przeklinać; adj. przeklęty
damnation [daem'nejszyn] s.
potępienie (kogoś, czegoś;
excl. psiakrew; cholera; a
niech to piorun trzaśnie!
damp [daemp] v. zwilżyć;
skropić; stłumić; ostudzić;
amortyzować; butwieć; s.
wilgoć; czad; przygnębienie;
zwątpienie; depresja
dampen ['daempen] v.
wilgotnieć; zwilgotnieć;
zwilżyć; ostudzić
dance [da:ns] s. taniec; zabawa
taneczna; v. tańczyć;
skakać; kazać tańczyć;
huśtać; kręcić się
dancer ['da:nser] s. tancerz;
tancerka; baletnica
dancing ['da:nsyng] s. taniec;
adj. tańczący; do tańca
dandelion ['daendylajon] s.
mniszek lekarski; mlecz
dandruff ['daendref] s. łupież
danger ['dejndżer] s.
niebezpieczeństwo; groźba
dangerous ['dejndżeres] adj.
niebezpieczny; groźny; niepewny (grunt, interes etc.)
dangle ['daengl] v. dyndać;
bujać; kręcić się; nadskakiwać (komuś, koło kogoś)
Danish [dejnysz] adj. duński
dapper ['daeper] adj. wytworny;
elegancki; dobrze ubrany;
zwinny; fertyczny
dare [deer] v. śmieć; ważyć
się; wyzywać; s. wyzwanie
daring ['deeryng] adj. śmiały;
śmiałość; odwaga
dark [da:rk] adj. ciemny; ponury;
s. ciemność; mrok; cień;
murzyn; tajemniczość; brak

ninformacji; niewiedza
dark-brown ['da:rk braln] adj.
ciemno-brązowy
darken [da:rkn] v. zaciemniać
darkness ['da:rknys] s.
ciemność; ciemnota; mrok;
śniadość (cery); ciemności
darling ['da:rlyng] s. kochanie;
ulubieniec; adj. kochany;
ulubiony; ukochany
darn [da:rn] v. cerować; s. cera;
adj. (slang) przeklęty
dart [da:rt] s. żądło; szybki ruch;
oszczep; zryw; v. pędzić;
rzucać; wybuchać; strzelać
dash [daesz] v. roztrzaskać;
rzucać się; rzucić (czymś)
pędzić; popisywać się;
zakropić; opryskać;
niweczyć (coś); mieszać;
onieśmielać (kogoś); odbić;
naszkicować; s. uderzenie;
zderzenie; plusk; barwna
plama; szczypta; przymieszka;
myślnik; kreska; pęd; skok;
rozmach; popęd; popis
dash-board ['daeszbo:rd] tablica
rozdzielcza; zestaw zegarów
(lotniczych, samochodowych
etc.); błotnik (samochodowy)
dashing [daeszyng] adj. dziarski;
z werwą; z rozmachem
data ['dejte] pl. dane; podstawa
odniesienia; dane liczbowe
data processing ['dejte
'prousesyng] s. przetwarzanie
danych (na komputerze)
date [dejt] v. datować (list)
nosić datę; chodzić z kimś;
s. data; spotkanie; randka;
umówienie się; termin; palma
daktylowa; daktyl
date from ['dejt,from] data z ...
(dnia, miejsce, miasto etc.)
dative case ['dejtyw,kejs] s.
trzeci przypadek; celownik
datum ['dejtem] s. dana (fakt;
szczegół); punkt wyjściowy
daub [do:b] v. babrać; mazać;
oblepiać; s. tynk; polepa;
plama; kicz sknocony; gips
daughter ['do:ter] s. córka
daughter-in-law ['do:ter,yn lo:] s.

synowa, (żona syna)
dawdle ['do:dl] v. próżniaczyć;
mitrężyć; wałkonić się
dawdle away ['do:dl,a'łej] v.
marnować czas; tracić czas
dawn [do:n] v. świtać;
zaświtać; dnieć; jaśnieć;
s. świt; brzask; zaranie;
zdanie sobie sprawy
day [dej] s. dzień; doba
daybreak ['dejbrejk] s. świt;
brzask; świtanie
day by day ['dej,baj dej] exp.
dzień w dzień; dzień po dniu
daydream ['dejdri:m] s. marzenie;
sen na jawie; v. marzyć; budować zamki na lodzie
day in day out ['dej,yn'dej aut]
exp. codziennie; dzień w
dzień (robić to samo, etc.)
daylight ['dejlajt] s. światło
dzienne; biały dzień
day nursery ['dej,ne:rsery] s.
żłobek (dzienny)
day off ['dej of] s. dzień wolny
days to come ['dejs,tu kam] exp.
przyszłość (niedaleka)
day's work ['dejz,łe:rk] s.
dniówka; dzienna praca
daytime ['dejtajm] s. dzień od
świtu do zmroku
daze [dejz] v. oszałamiać;
otumaniać; oślepiać; s.
oszołomienie; otumanienie
dazzle [daezl] v. oślepiać;
olśniewać; zamaskować; s.
oślepiający blask
dead [ded] adj. & s. zmarły;
martwy; wymarły; matowy
dead body [ded'body] s. zwłoki
dead center ['ded'senter] s.
punkt martwy, zwrotny
deaden ['deden] v. zabijać siły,
uczucia etc.; tłumić; osłabiać; stępiać; zmartwieć;
złagodzić (cios); obumrzeć;
pozbawiać blasku, połysku,
zapachu; znieczulać
dead end ['dedend] s. ślepa
(ulica, ostateczny konic)
deadline ['dedlajn] s.
nieprzekraczalny termin; ostateczna granica (czegoś)

deadlock ['dedlok] s. impas;
martwy punkt; v. powo-
dować impas (zastój)
deadly [dedly] adj. śmiertelny;
adv. śmiertelnie; nieludzko
deadweight ['dedłejt] s. ciężar
własny (urządzenia); kula u
nogi; kamień u szyi
deaf [def] adj. głuchy
deafen [defn] v. ogłuszać
deafening [defnyng] adj.
ogłuszający (hałas)
deal; dealt; dealt [di:l; delt; delt]
deal [di:l] v. zajmować się;
traktować o; załatwiać
(coś); przestawać z (kimś);
postępować; handlować;
rozdzielać (karty); s. ilość;
sprawa; sporo; wiele
deal with ['di:l łyt] v.
postępować z ...; mieć do
czynienia (z kimś, czymś)
dealer ['di:ler] s. kupiec;
handlarz; rozdający karty
dealing ['di:lyng] s.
postępowanie z; stosunki;
transakcje; konszachty
dealt [delt] zob. deal
dean [di:n] s. dziekan
dear [dier] adj. kochany; drogi
dear Sir ['dier,se:r] exp.
Szanowny Panie; Drogi Panie
dear me! [dier mi] exp. ojej! mój
Boże! czyżby! ależ nie!
death [des] s. śmierć; zgon
deathly [desly] adj. śmiertelny;
trupi; adv. śmiertelnie;
grobowo; trupio
debar ['dyba:r] v. wykluczać;
zabraniać (komuś); za-
kazywać (komuś czegoś)
debase [dy'bejs] v. obniżać;
poniżać; fałszować; upadlać
debate [dy'bejt] v. roztrząsać;
rozważać; debatować; s.
debata; spór; rozprawa
debauchery ['dy'bo:czery] s.
rozpusta; wyuzdanie; roz-
wiązłość; rozwiązłe życie
debit ['debyt] s. debet;
obciążenie rachunku
debrief [dy'bri:f] s. przesłuchania
po (akcji); v. przesłuchiwać

po (akcji wojskowej etc.)
debris ['dejbri:] pl. gruzy
debt [det] s. dług
debtor ['deter] s. dłużnik;
dłużniczka (czyjaś)
decade ['dekejd] s.
dziesięcioletni okres
decadence ['dekejdens] s.
dekadencja; chylenie się ku
upadkowi; schyłek; upadek
decapitate [dy'kaepytejt] v.
ścinać głowę; pozbawić
wodza (przywództwa)
decay [dy'kej] v. gnić;
rozpadać się; psuć się; s.
upadek; ruina; zanik; rozkład;
gnicie; uwiąd; niszczenie
decease [dy'si:s] v. umierać; s.
zgon; śmierć; zejście
deceased [dy'si:st] adj. zmarły;
s. nieboszczyk; nieboszczka
deceit [dy'si:t] s. oszukaństwo;
podstęp; złuda; fałsz
deceitful [dy'si:tfel] adj.
kłamliwy; zwodniczy; oszukańczy; podstępny; fałszywy
deceive [dy'si:w] v. okłamywać;
zwodzić; łudzić; zawodzić
deceiver [dy'si:wer] s.
oszukaniec; zwodziciel; kłamca
decelerate [dy:'selerejt] v.
zwalniać szybkość (cze-
goś); zmniejszać szybkość
December [dy'sember] s.
grudzień (mieśiąc)
decency ['di:snsy] s.
przyzwoitość; obyczajność;
dobre obyczaje
decent ['di:sent] adj. przyzwoity;
porządny; skromny; znośny
deception [dy'sepszyn] s.
łudzenie; okłamywanie; podstęp; zawód; szachrajstwo
oszukanie; oszukaństwo
decide [dy'sajd] v. rozstrzygać;
postanawiać; decydować się
(na coś); zadecydować;
skłaniać się (ku czemuś)
decided [dy'sajdyd] adj.
zdecydowany; stanowczy; definitywny; kategoryczny
decimal ['desymel] adj.
dziesiętny (system, ułamek);

s. ułamek dziesiątny
decipher [dy'sajfer] v.
odcyfrować (depeszą, etc.);
rozszyfrować; rozwiązać
decision [dy'syżyn] s.
rozstrzygnięcie (czegoś);
postanowienie (o czymś); decyzja; zdecydowanie; stanowczość; wygrana na punkty;
ustalenie; rezolutność
decisive [dy'sajsyw] adj.
decydujący; rozstrzygający;
zdecydowany; stanowczy
deck [dek] s. pokład; pomost;
podłoga; talia; v. pokrywać
pokładem; przystrajać
deck chair ['dek czeer] s. leżak
(do opalania się na statku)
declaration [dekle'rejszyn] s.
deklaracja; zapowiedź;
oświadczenie (oficjalne)
declare [dy'kle:r] v. deklarować;
oświadczać; zeznawać; wy-
powiadać (wojnę); ogłaszać
(coś); uznawać (za niewin-
nego); stwierdzać; wykazać;
dawać (coś) do oclenia
declension [dy'klenszyn] s.
deklinacja (gram.); przypad-
kowanie; odchylenie; upadek
decline [dy'klajn] v. uchylać
(się); pochylać (się); skłaniać
(się); iść ku schyłkowi; opadać; obniżać; podupadać;
marnieć; słabnąć; zanikać;
zamierać; przypadkować; odrzucać (propozycją etc.); s.
schyłek; utrata; spadek
declivity [dy'klywyty] s.
pochyłość; spadzistość;
stok (góry etc.); skłon
decode [dy'koud] v. rozszyfrować; rozszyfrowywać
decorate ['dekerejt] v. ozdabiać;
odznaczać; udekorować; odnowić; upiększać (coś)
decompose [,dy:kem'pouz] v.
rozkładać (się); rozłożyć (na
części etc.); gnić
decoration [,deke'rejszyn] s.
ozdoba; odznaczenie; medal
decorative [,deke'rejtyw] adj.
ozdobny; dekoracyjny

decorator ['dekerejter] s.
dekorator; architekt wnętrz
decoy ['dy:koj] s. wabik;
przynęta; v. wabić (w pułapkę, w sidła); usidlać; zwabiać; wciągać w pułapkę; zaciągać sidła (na lisy etc.)
decrease ['dy:kri:s] v.
zmniejszać; słabnąć; ob-
niżać; s. zmniejszenie;
spadek (cen, wartości etc.)
decree [dy'kri:] s. dekret;
rozporządzenie; wyrok rozwodowy; postanowienie o se-
paracji; zrządzenie (losu); v.
zarządzać; rozporządzać; nakazywać (coś) dekretem
decrepit [dy'krepyt] adj.
zgrzybiały; wyniszczony
decry [dy'kraj] v. potępić;
okrzyczeć; zohydzić; obgadać; oczernić (kogoś)
dedicate ['dedykejt] v.
dedykować; poświęcać; in-
augurować; przeznaczyć na
dedication ['dedykejszyn] s.
dedykacja; poświęcenie; otwarcie; przeznaczenie
deduce [dy'du:s] v.
wnioskować; dedukować;
wywodzić (rodowód etc.)
deduct [dy'dakt] v. potrącać;
odciągać (kwotę etc.); odejmować; odtrącać (kogoś)
deduction [dy'dakszyn] s.
potrącenie; odciągnięcie;
wnioskowanie; wniosek; wydedukowanie; wywód
deed [di:d] s. czyn; wyczyn; akt;
v. przekazywać aktem (własność); przekazywać (ko-
muś) pieniądze etc.
deep [di:p] adj. głęboki; s.
głębia; adv. głęboko
deepen ['di:pn] v. pogłębiać
deep-freeze ['di:p,fri:z] s.
(głębokie) zamrożenie
deeply ['di:ply] adv. głęboko
deep-rooted ['di:p'ru:tyd] adj.
głęboko zakorzeniony
deer [dier] s. jeleń; sarna; łoś;
łania; daniel; renifer
deface [dy'fejs] v. szpecić;

zniekształcać; zacierać
defame [dy'fejm] v. zniesławić
defeat [dy'fi:t] v. pokonać;
pobić (przeciwnika); uni-
cestwić; udaremnić; unie-
możliwić; unieważnić prawnie; s. klęska; udaremnienie
defect [dy'fekt] s. brak; wada;
błąd; defekt; skaza; man-
kament; przywara; v. od-
paść; skłonić do odstęp-
stwa; odstąpić (od czegoś)
defective [dy'fektyw]
adj. wadliwy; wybrakowany
defence [dy'fens] = defense
defend [dy'fend] v. bronić
defendant [dy'fendent] s.
pozwany; oskarżony; obrońca
defender [dy'fender] s. obrońca
(w prawie i sporcie)
defensive [dy'fensyw] adj.
obronny; defensywny (układ);
s. defensywa; (być) w defen-
sywie; stanowisko obronne
defense [dy'fens] s. obrona
defenseless [dy'fenslys] adj.
bezbronny (człowiek etc.)
defer [dy'fe:r] v. odraczać;
ustępować; ulegać; mieć
wzgląd; skłaniać się (przed)
defiant [dy'fajent] adj.
zbuntowany; nieufny; bun-
towniczy; prowokujący
deficiency [dy'fyszynsy] s. brak;
niedobór; należność nie-
zapłacona; niedostatek; słabość (natury człowieka etc.)
deficit ['defysyt] s. deficyt;
niedobór; nadwyżka rozchodu
defile ['dy:fail] v. kalać;
plugawić; brukać; bez-
cześcić; iść szeregami; defilować; s. wąwóz; przełęcz
define [dy'fajn] v. określać;
definiować; zakreślać (granice); precyzować (coś)
definite ['defynyt] adj.
określony; wyraźny; pewny;
jasny; prostolinijny; okreś-
lający; sprecyzowany
definition [,defy'nyszyn] s.
określenie; definicja; ostrość (konturów, obrazu etc.);

czystość; oznaczenie
definitive [dy'fynytyw] adj.
ostateczny; definitywny; stanowczy; rozstrzygający; kon-
kluzywny; definiujący
deflate [dy'flejt] v. wypuszczać
powietrze (z dętki); zmniejszać (obieg, znaczenie etc.)
deform [dy'fo:rm] v. szpecić;
zniekształcać; oszpecać
deformed [dy'fo:rmd] adj.
ułomny; szpetny; zniekształ-
cony; zdeformowany
defrost ['dy:frost] v. odmrozić
defunct ['dy'fankt] adj. zmarły;
zlikwidowany; już nie istniejący; wymarły; rozwiązany
defy [dy'faj] v. stawiać czoło;
rzucać wyzwania (by zrobić,
wykazać); przeciwstawiać
degenerate [dy'dżeneryt] adj.
zwyrodniały; s. degenerat
degrade [dy'grejd] v. poniżać;
obniżać; wyrodnieć; spod-
leć; upadlać; znieważać
degree [dy'gri:] s. stopień (np.
naukowy, ciepła etc.)
dejected [dy'dżektyd] adj.
przygnębiony; zgaszony
(człowiek); zdeprymowany;
strapiony (złą wieścią)
dejectedly [dy'dżektydly] adv. z
przygnębieniem; z niechęcią
delay [dy'lej] v. odraczać;
opóźniać; zwlekać; s. od-
roczenie; zwłoka; opóźnienie
delegate ['delegejt] s. zastępca;
wysłannik; v. delegować;
udzielać delegacji; zlecać
(władzę); udzielać (władzy,
pełnomocnictwa komuś)
delegation [,dely'gejszyn] s.
delegacja; grupa delegatów
deliberate [dy'lyberejt] adj.
rozmyślny; spokojny; powolny; umyślny; [dy,ly'berejt] v.
rozmyślać; rozważać (coś);
obradować; naradzać się
delicacy ['delykesy] s.
delikatność; smakołyk; takt
delicate ['delykyt] adj. delikatny;
wyśmienity; taktowny
delicatessen [,delyka'tesn] s.

sklep z delikatesami
delicious [dy'lyszes] adj.
rozkoszny; bardzo smaczny
delight [dy'lajt] s. rozkosz; v.
zachwycać się; rozkoszować
się (czymś); lubować się
delightful [dy'lajtful] adj.
zachwycający; czarujący; czarowny; niezapomniany
delinquency [dy'lynkłensy] s.
zaniedbanie; wina; przestępstwo; niepłacenie należności;
przestąpczość; wykroczenie
delinquent [dy'lynkłent] a. winny;
zaniedbany; zalegający z zapłatą (podatkiem); s. winowajca; przestępca (nieletni);
osoba zalegająca etc.
deliver [dy'lywer] v. doręczać;
zdawać; wydawać; wygłaszać; zadawać; uwalniać;
ratować; wybawić; wyzwolić; podawać; oddawać
deliverance [dy'lywerens] s.
uwolnienie; wygłoszenie
deliverer [dy'lywerer] s. zbawca;
oswobodziciel; wybawca
delivery [dy'lywery] s. dostawa;
wydawanie; wygłaszanie;
podanie; poród; przekazanie
deluge ['delju:dż] s. potop
delusion [dy'lu:żyn] s. urojenie;
zwodzenie; ułuda; iluzja
delusive [dy'lu:syw] adj. złudny;
oszukańczy; bałamutny;
zwodniczy; iluzoryczny
demand [dy'ma:nd] s. zadanie;
popyt; v. zadać; dopytywać
się; wymagać; domagać się
demeanor [dy'mi:ner] s.
zachowanie się; postępowanie; postawa (wobec)
demented [dy'mentyd] adj.
obłąkany; oszalały; umysłowo
chory; opętany
demi- ['demy] pref. pół-
demilitarized ['dy:mylyterajzd]
adj. zdemilitaryzowany
demise [dy'majz] s. zgon;
przekazanie spadku; v.
przekazywać (coś) testamentem lub zgonem
demobilize [dy:,moubylajz] v.

demobilizować (wojsko etc.);
zdemobilizować (żołnierzy)
democracy [dy'mokresy] s.
demokracja (równość praw)
democrat ['dymokreat] s.
demokrata; demokratka
democratic [,deme'kraetyk] adj.
demokratyczny
demolish [dy'molysz] v. burzyć;
niszczyć; obalać (teorię);
demolować; zburzyć (coś)
demon ['di:men] s. diabeł;
demon; doskonały zawodnik
sportowy, gracz, tenisista
demonstrate ['demenstrejt] v.
wykazywać; udowadniać;
demonstrować; urządzać
manifestację etc.
demonstration [,demen'strejszyn]
s. wykazywanie; okazywanie;
demonstracja; zademonstrowanie; manifestacja
demonstrative [dy'menstrejtyw]
adj. wylewny; dowodowy;
wskazujący (coś); dowodzący (czegoś); ekspansywny
demurrage [dy'me:rydż] s.
przestój; opłata za postojowe
den [den] s. nora; jaskinia;
ustronie; cicha pracownia
denial [dy'najel] s. zaprzeczenie;
odmowa; wyparcie się
denomination [dynomy'nejszyn]
s. nazwa; miano; określenie;
wyznanie (rel.); kategoria
denounce [dy'nauns] v.
oskarżać; donosić; wypowiadać; denuncjować
dense [dens] adj. gęsty; zwarty;
tępy (człowiek); niepojętny
density ['densyty] s. gęstość;
zwartość; głupota; tępota;
spoistość; szczelność
dent [dent] s. wgłębienie; wrąb;
wklęśnięcie; sl. znaczenie; v.
szczerbić; wyginać
dental ['dentl] adj. zębowy;
dentystyczny; stomatologiczny
dentist ['dentyst] s. dentysta;
dentystka; stomatolog
denture [denczer] s. (sztuczne)
uzębienie; szczęka
deny [dy'naj] v. zaprzeczyć;

odrzucić; odmawiać; wypierać się; dementować; przeczyć (czemuś); odmówić
depart [dy'pa:rt] v. odjeżdżać;
odbiegać; robić dygresję;
zejść (zs swiata); odejść
department [dy'pa:rtment] s.
wydział; ministerstwo; dział
department store [dy'pa:rtment
,sto:r] s. dom towarowy
departure [dy'pa:rczer] s. odjazd;
rozstanie; odchylenie
depend on [dy'pend on] v.
polegać na ...; zależeć od
depend upon [dy'pend,apon] v.
być zależnym od ...; być na
utrzymaniu (kogoś)
depends [dy'pends] v. zależy
deplorable [dy'plo:rebl] adj.
godny pożałowania; opłakany
deplore [dy'plo:r] v. ubolewać;
boleć nad ...; wyrażać ubolewanie, żal, współczucie
depolarize [dy'poulerajz] v.
depolaryzować; rozwiać
(czyjeś) złudzenia
depopulate [dy'popjulejt] v.
wyludniać; pustoszyć; wy-
ludniać się; opustoszyć
deport [dy'po:rt] v. zsyłać;
deportować (złoczyńcę);
zsyłać; zachowywać się
depose [dy'pouz] v. składać;
zeznawać; usunąć (z tronu)
deposit [dy'pozyt] s. osad;
warstwa; kaucja; depozyt; v.
składać do depopzytu; osadzać; deponować; nawar-
stwiać; złożyć (jaja ...)
depositor [dy'pozyter] s.
depozytor; deponent
depot [depou] s. stacja kolejowa;
skład; remiza; kadra
depraved [dy'prejwd] adj.
zdeprawowany; zepsuty
moralnie; deprawowany
depreciate [dy'pry:szy,ejt] v.
obniżać wartość; de-
waluować; ujmować znacze-
nie; ujemnie mówić (o kimś)
depress [dy'pres] v.
przygnębiać; deprymować;
spychać w dół (ceny); zni-

żać (cenę etc.); martwić
depressed [dy'prest] adj.
przygnębiony; przygnieciony;
zmartwiony; zatroskany; prrzy-
płaszczony; zahamowany
depression [dy'preszyn] s.
przygnębienie; depresja
deprive [dy'prajw] v. odzierać;
wykluczać; umartwiać się;
pozbawiać; odwołać (z urzędu etc.); odbierać
depth [deps] s. głębokość;
głębia; głębina; dno (nędzy)
deputy ['depjuty] s. zastępca;
deputowany; poseł; wice-
derail [dy'rejl] v. wykoleić (się)
(czyjś plan, zamiar etc.)
derange [dy'rejndż] v.
pomieszać; rozstrajać; psuć;
zakłócać; powodować obłęd;
wprowdzić (nieład, chaos)
deride [dy'rajd] v. wyśmiewać
derision [dy'ryżyn] s.
szyderstwo; pośmiewisko;
drwina; wyszydzanie kogoś
derisive [dy'rajsyw] adj. kpiący;
ironiczny; wart śmiechu
derive [dy'rajw] v. uzyskiwać;
czerpać; wywodzić; wypro-
wadzić (ród); pochodzić (z)
derogatory [dy'rogeto:ry] adj.
pomniejszający; uszczupla-
jący; uwłaczający; szkodliwy
descend [dy'send] v. zejść;
spaść; zstępować z; zni-
żać się; pochodzić (od); opadać; zwalić się (na kogoś)
descendant [dy'sendent] s.
potomek (przodka, rodziny,
grupy, narodu, etc.)
descent [dy'sent] s. zejście;
spadek; pochodzenie; nagły
atak; lądowanie; obniżka
describe [dys'krajb] v.
opisywać; określać; prze-
rysowywać; dawać rysopis
description [dy'skrypszyn] s.
opis; sposób opisywania
desegregate [dy'segrygejt] v.
(Am,) znieść podział rasowy
desert ['desert] adj. pustynny;
pusty; s. pustynia; pustkowie
desert [dy'ze:rt] v. porzucać;

opuszczać; dezerterować; s.
zasłużenie; zasługa; nagroda;
zasłużona kara (opinia)
deserted [dy'ze:rted] adj.
opuszczony; bezludny
deserter [dy'ze:rter] s. dezerter;
dezerterka; zbieg; zbiegła
desertion [dy'ze:rszyn] s.
opuszczenie; dezercja;
porzucenie (kogoś, czegoś)
deserve [dy'ze:rw] v.
zasługiwać na ...; mieć
zasługi wobec (kogoś)
design [dy'zajn] s. zamiar; plan;
szkic; v. pomyśleć; za-
mierzać; przeznaczać; projektować; zamyślać; uplano-
wać; kreślić; szkicować
designate ['dezygnejt] v.
wyznaczać; określać; za-
mianować; desygnować
designer [dy'zajner] s. projektant;
konstruktor; rysownik;
intrygant; projektodawca;
autor; autorka; kreślarz
desirable [dy'zajerebl] adj.
pożądany; pociągający; atrak-
cyjny; celowy; mile (dobrze)
widziany; wskazany
desire [dy'zajer] v. pożądać;
pragnąć; życzyć sobie
desirous [dy'zajeres] adj. żądny;
pragnący czegoś; spragniony
desk [desk] s. biuro; referat;
pulpit; ambona; ławka szkolna
desk set ['desk set] s. zestaw
przyborów do pisania
desolate ['deselyt] adj.
opuszczony; posępny; wyludniony; zdewastowany
desolate ['deselejt] v.
pustoszyć; wyludniać;
opuszczać; (z)dewastować
desolation [,dese'lejszyn] s.
wyludnienie; spustoszenie;
pustka; żałość; strapienie
despair [dys'peer] s. rozpacz
despairingly [dys'peeryngly] adv.
rozpaczliwie; beznadziejnie
desperate ['desperyt] adj.
rozpaczliwy; beznadziejny;
beznadziejny; zaciekły
desperation [,despe'rejszyn] s.

rozpacz; desperacja
despise [dys'pajz] v. pogardzać;
gardzić; (z)lekceważyć
despite [dys'pajt] s. przekora;
złość; prep. pomimo; wbrew;
na przekór (komuś; czemuś)
despond [dys'pond] v.
przygnębiać się; stracić
otuchę; s. przygnębienie
despondent [dys'pondent] adj.
przygnębiony; zniechęcony
despot ['despot] s. despota;
despotka; władca absolutny
dessert [dy'ze:rt] s. deser;
legumina; ciastka
destination [desty'nejszyn] s.
miejsce przeznaczenia
destine ['destyn] v. przeznaczać
(z góry); przeznaczyć
destiny ['destyny] s.
przeznaczenie (wypadków, ludzi); (nieunikniony) los
destitute ['destytju:t] adj. bez
środków; całkowicie pozbawiony środków; w nędzy
destroy [dy'stroj] v. burzyć;
niweczyć; zabijać; zgładzać
destroyer [dy'strojer] s.
kontrtorpedowiec; niszczyciel
destruction [dys'trakszyn] s.
zniszczenie; ruina; zguba;
zagłada (powód, środki etc.)
destructive [dy'straktyw] adj.
niszczycielski; s. niszczyciel
detach [dy'taecz] v. odczepić;
odłączyć; odpiąć; odwią-
zać; odkomenderować; od-
lepiać (coś); urwać (z)
detached [dy'taeczt] adj.
odosobniony; obojętny; niezależny (od); na dystans
detail ['di:tejl] s. szczegół;
wyszczególnienie; v. wyłuszczać; przydzielać do zadań
detain [dy'tejn] v. wstrzymywać; więzić (kogoś);
przeszkadzać (komuś)
detect [dy'tekt] v. wykrywać;
wyśledzić; przychwycić na
detection [dy'tekszyn] s.
wykrywanie; wyśledzenie
detective [dy'tektyw] s.

detektyw; adj. detek-
tywistyczny; śledczy
detention [dy'tenszyn] s.
areszt; więzienie; zatrzymanie;
przetrzymanie; opóźnienie
deter [dy'te:r] v. odstraszać od;
pohamować; onieśmielać
detergent [dy'te:rdżent] s. & adj.
czyszczący (środek)
deteriorate [dy'tierjerejt] v.
psuć; marnieć; tracić na
wartości; pogarszać się
determination [dyte:rmy'nejszyn]
s. określenie; postanowienie;
ustalenie; orzeczenie; wygaśnięcie (umowy); dawkowanie
determine [dy'te:rmyn] v.
rozstrzygać; określać; postanawiać; ustalać; zdefi-
niować; zadecydować (o)
determined [dy'te:rmynd] adj.
zdecydowany; stanowczy;
zdeterminowany (człowiek)
deterrent [dy'terent] adj.
odstraszający; s. (czynnik)
odstraszający; środek
zaradczy (zapobiegawczy)
detest [dy'test] v. nienawidzić;
czuć wstręt; nie cierpieć
detestable [dy'testebl] adj.
wstrętny; nienawistny;
obmierzły; znienawidzony
detonate ['detounejt] v.
wybuchać; powodować
gwałtowny wybuch (czegoś)
detour ['dy:tuer] s. objazd
devaluation [,dy:waelju'ejszyn] s.
dewaluacja; zdewaluowanie
detriment ['detryment] s. ujma;
szkoda; uszczerbek; krzywda
devaluate ['dy:waelju:ejt] v.
dewaluować; obniżać war-
tość; zdewaluować (coś)
devastate ['dewestejt] v.
pustoszyć; niweczyć (coś);
dewastować; zniweczyć
develop [dy'welop] v. rozwijać
(się); wywoływać (zdjęcia)
development [dy'welepment] s.
rozwój; rozbudowa; osiedle;
wywołanie (filmu); ewolucja
deviate ['di:wyejt] v. zbaczać;
odchylać; schodzić z drogi

device [dy'wajs] s. plan; pomysł;
urządzenie; dewiza; hasło;
środek (wiodący do celu)
devil ['dewl] s. czart; diabeł
devilish ['dewlysz] adj.
szatański; diabelski; demo-
niczny; adv. diabelsko
devise [dy'wajz] v. zapisać
(komuś); wymyślać; wyna-
leźć; obmyślać; knuć
devoid [dy'woyd] adj.
pozbawiony (czegoś); próżny;
czczy; wolny (od czegoś)
devote [dy'wout] v. poświęcać; ofiarować; odda-
wać się; przeznaczyć (na)
devoted [dy'wouted] adj. oddany (komuś, czemuś); przywiązany (do kogoś, czegoś)
dew [dju:] s. rosa; świeżość;
powiew; v. rosić; zraszać
dew point ['dju:point]
temperatura powstawania rosy
dexter ['dekster] a. prawy
dexterity [deks'teryty] s.
zręczność; bystrość;
sprawność (ciała, umysłu)
dexterous ['deksteres] s.
zręczny; zwinny; sprawny
diabetes [,daje'by:ty:z] s.
cukrzyca; choroba cukrowa
diagnose ['dajeg,nouz] v.
rozpoznać (chorobę)
diagonal [daj'aegnl] adj.
przekątny; skośny; s.
przekątnia; przekątna
diagram ['dajegraem] s. wykres;
schemat; diagram; plan
dial ['dajel] s. tarcza numerowa
(zwł. zegarowa); v. mierzyć;
nakręcać (numer telefonu)
dial tone ['dajel,toun] s. sygnał
połączenia (telefonicznego)
dialect ['dajelekt] s. gwara;
narzecze; dialekt
dialogue ['dajelog] s. rozmowa;
dialog (na scenie etc.)
diameter [dai'aemyter] s.
średnica; długość średnicy
diamond ['dajemend] s. diament;
romb; a. diamentowy; romboidalny; s. boisko do gry w
palanta amerykańskiego

diaper ['dajeper] s. pieluszka;
wzór romboidalny; v. przewijać; ozdabiać (coś) w romby
diaphragm ['dajefraem] s.
przepona; membrana; przesło-
na; damska prezerwatywa
diarrhea [daje'rye] s. biegunka
diary ['daiery] s. dziennik
dice [dajs] v. grać w kości;
kratkować; pl. od die = kostka do gry (towarzyskiej)
dictate [dyk'tejt] s. nakaz; v.
dyktować; narzucać (wolę)
dictation [dyk'tejszyn] s. dyktat;
dyktowanie; wyraźny nakaz
dictator [dyk'tejter] s. dyktator;
dyktujący dyktando; dyktujący
na głos (tekst, list etc.)
dictatorship [dyk'tejterszyp] s.
dyktatura; władza nieograni-
czona (dyktatora, partii)
dictionary ['dykszeneeri] s.
słownik; mała encyklopedia
did [dyd] v. zrobić; zob. do
die [daj] v. umierać; zdechnąć;
zginąć; s. matryca; sztanca;
proszą zobaczyć: pl. dice
die-hard ['daj-ha:rd] adj. twardy;
nieustępliwy; s. zagorzały
bojownik (szermierz etc.)
diet ['dajet] v. dieta; zjazd; sejm;
v. trzymać na diecie
differ ['dyfer] v. różnić się;
niezgadzać się (z opinią etc.);
miećinną opinię (o czymś)
difference ['dyferens] s. różnica;
sprzeczka; nieporozumienie
different ['dyferent] adj.
różny; odmienny; niezwykły
difficult ['dyfykelt] adj. trudny;
ciężki; niełatwy (do)
difficulty ['dyfykelty] s.
trudność; przeszkoda
diffident ['dyfydent] adj.
(bardzo) nieśmiały; bez wiary
we własne siły; bez zaufania
do siebie samego
diffuse [dy'fju:z] adj. rozwlekły;
rozproszony; v. rozlewać;
szerzyć; rozpraszać
dig; dug; dug [dyg; dag; dag]
dig [dyg] v. kopać; ryć; ro-
umieć; ocenić; bawić się;

kuć się; grzebać się; s.
szarpnięcie; przytyk; kujon;
szturchnięcie; docinek
digest [dy'dżest] v. trawić;
przetrawiać; s. streszczenie;
skrót; przegląd; zbiór praw
digestible [dy'dżestebl] adj.
strawny; łatwy do strawienia
(przyswojenia czegoś))
digestion [dy'dżestszyn] s.
trawienie; wygotowanie
diggings ['dygynz] s. kopalnia
(złota); mieszkanie
dignified ['dygnyfajd] adj. dostojny; godny; (człowiek) pełen godności (dostojeństwa)
dignity ['dygnyty] s. godność;
dostojeństwo; powaga; tytuł;
zaszczyt; stanowisko; ranga
digress ['daj'gres] v. zbaczać;
odbiegać od rzeczy (tematu)
digs [dygz] s. mieszkanie; pokój;
buda; melina (złodziejska)
dihedral [daj'hi:drel] adj. m. (o
kącie) dwuścienny
dike [dajk] s. tama; grobla; rów;
v. osuszać rowem; otamo-
wać; ochronić tamą
dilapidated [dy'laepydejtyd] adj.
zniszczony; walący się
dilate [daj'lejt] v. rozszerzać;
rozwodzić się; rozciągać
diligence ['dylydżens] n.
pilność; przykładanie się do
pracy; pracowitość
diligent ['dylydżent] adj. pilny;
przykładający się do pracy
dill [dyl] s. koper ogrodowy
dill-pickle ['dyl,pykl] s. kiszony
ogórek; ogórek z koperkiem
dilute [daj'lju:t] v. rozpuszczać;
rozcieńczać; rozrzedzać; adj.
rozpuszczony; rozcieńczony;
rozrzedzony; rozwodniony;
wypłukany; wybladły; spłowiały; wyblakły; wyjałowiony
dim [dym] v. przyćmić;
zaciemnić; zamglić; adj.
przyćmiony; blady; zamazany;
niewyraźny; nikły; ciemny
dime [dajm] s. dziesięciocentowa
moneta (Stany Zjednoczone)
dimension [dy'menszyn] s.

wymiar; rozmiar; wielkość
diminish [dy'mynysz] v.
zmniejszać; zwężać (coś);
uszczuplać; niknąć; maleć
diminutive [dy'mynjutyw] adj. &
s. drobniutki; zdrobniały;
zdrobnienie; malutka kobieta
dimple ['dympl] s. dołek (w
twarzy); v. robić dołki; mieć
dołki (w twarzy etc.)
dine [dajn] v. jeść obiad;
jeść; mieć na obiedzie
diner [dajner] s. stołówka;
wagon restauracyjny; osoba
jedząca; restauracja
dining car ['dajny̲n̲g,ka:r] s.
wagon restauracyjny
dining room ['dajny̲n̲g,ru:m] s.
jadalnia; pokój jadalny
dinner ['dyner] s. obiad
dinner-jacket ['dyner,dżaekyt] s.
smoking (tuxedo)
dinner-party ['dyner,pa:rty] s.
przyjęcie; obiad proszony
dip [dyp] v. zanurzać; czerpać;
farbować; pogrążać; płu-
kać; nachylać się; opadać;
zamoczyć; wykąpać (coś
w czymś s. zanurzenie; zamoczenie; rozczyn; nachylenie;
obniżenie; łojówka; sos do
maczania; skok do wody
diphtheria [dyf̲t̲eria] s. dyfteryt;
błonica (choroba)
diploma [dy'plouma] s. dyplom
diplomacy [dy'ploumesy] s.
dyplomacja; takt
diplomat ['dyplemaet] s. dy-
plomata; człowiek taktowny
diplomatic [,dyple'maetyk] adj.
dyplomatyczny; taktowny
direct [dy'rekt] v. kierować;
kazać; zarządzić; dowodzić;
zaadresować; nakierować;
wymierzać; polecić; dyrygować; adj. prosty; bezpośredni; otwarty; szczery; wyraźny; adv. wprost; prosto; bezpośrednio; otwarcie
direct current [dy'rekt'karent] s.
prąd stały (elektryczny)
direction [dy'rekszyn] s.
kierunek; kierowanie; kierow-

nictwo; zarząd; wskazówka;
administracja; adres
directions [dy'rekszyns] pl.
instrukcje; przepisy; przepis
directly [dy'rektly] adv.
bezpośrednio; wprost; od
razu; zaraz; skoro tyklo;
natychmiast; dokładnie
director [dy'rektor] s. dyrektor;
reżyser; celownik; kierownik;
zarządzający; nadzorca
directory [dy'rektery] s. książka
adresowa, telefoniczna (lub
przepisów); skorowidz
dirigible ['dyrydżebl] adj. & s.
sterowy; sterowiec
dirt [de:rt] s. brud; błoto;
świństwo; ziemia; język
plugawy; mówienie osz-
czerstw; plotki; śmieci
dirt-cheap [de:rt'czi:p] adv. za
bezcen; adj. bardzo tani; tani
jak barszcz; śmiesznie tani
dirty [de:rty] adj. brudny;
sprośny; podły; wstrętny
disability [,dyse'bylyty] s.
inwalidztwo; niemoc; niemożność; niezdolność (do)
disabled [dys'ejbld] s. kaleka;
inwalida wojenny
disadvantage [dysed'wa:ntydż]
s. niekorzyść; wada; strata;
szkoda; niekorzystne położenie; v. szkodzić; zaszkodzić (komuś w czymś))
disadvantageous [dysaedwa:n
tejdżes] adj. niekorzystny;
szkodliwy; ujemny
disagree [dyse'gri:] v. nie
zgadzać się; różnić się; nie
służyć (jedzenie, klimat)
disagreeable [,dyse'gri:ebl] adj.
nieprzyjemny; niemiły
disagreement [,dyse'gri:ment] s.
niezgoda; różnica
disallow [,dyse'lau] v. nie
pozwalać; nie dopuszczać
disappear [,dyse'pier] v. znikać;
zapodziewać się; przepaść
disappearance [,dyse'pierens] s.
zniknięcie; zanik; zginięcie
disappoint [dyse'point] v.
zawieść; rozczarować; nie

spełnić (oczekiwań, nadzieii)
disappointment [dyse'pointment]
s. zawód; rozczarowanie
disapproval [dyse'pru:wel] s.
potępienie; niechęć; dez-
aprobata; niepochwalenie
disapprove [dyse'pru:w] v.
potępiać (kogoś, coś); ganić; źle widzieć (kogoś);
disarm [dys'a:rm] v. rozbroić;
unieszkodliwić (kogoś);
odebrać broń (komuś)
disarmament [dys'a:rmement] s.
rozbrojenie; a. rozbrojeniowy
disarrange ['dyse'rejndż] v.
rozstrajać; dezorganizować
disarray [,dyse'rej] v.
wprowadzać nieład; roz-
strajać; s. nieład; zamieszanie; bałagan; niekompletny
strój; wywracać; rozebrać
disaster [dy'za:ster] s.
nieszczęście; klęska (żywio-
łowa etc.); katastrofa
disastrous [dy'za:stres] adj.
katastrofalny; zgubny; fatalny
disband [dis'baend] v.
rozpuścić (wojsko); pójść
w rozsypkę; rozbiegać się
disbelief ['dysby'li:f] s. niewiara;
niedowierzanie; nieufność
disbelieve ['dysby'li:w] v. nie
wierzyć; niedowierzać
disc [dysk] s. krążek; tarcza;
płyta; dysk; płyta gramofonowa; krążek (metalowy etc.)
discard [dys'ka:rd] v. wyrzucać;
(coś niepotrzebnego); odrzucać; zarzucać; zaniechać
discard ['dyska:rd] s. odrzucenie;
odrzucona (rzecz lub osoba);
odpadek; rzecz wybrakowana
discern [dy'se:rn] v. rozróżniać;
odróżniać; rozpoznawać
discharge [dys'cza:rdż] v.
rozładować; odciążać; zwalniać; wypuścić; wystrzelić;
s. rozładowanie; wystrzał;
zwolnienie; wydzielina; odpływ (czegś); odchody; ropa
(z wrzodu, z rany etc.)
disciple [dy'sajpl] s. uczeń;
wyznawca; jeden z apostołów

discipline ['dyscyplyn] s. dyscyplina; karność; v. karać;
ćwiczyć; musztrować
disc-jockey [dysk'dżoki] s.
nadający przez radio muzykę z
płyt; (disc jockey)
disclaim [dys'klejm] v. wypierać
się (czegoś); rezygnować (z
czegoś); zrzekać się
disclose [dys'k-ouz] v.
odsłaniać; ujawniać; wyjawiać; odkryć; odsłonić (coś)
discolor [dys'kaler] v. odbarwiać
discomfort [dys'kamfert] s.
niewygoda; niepokój; v.
sprawiać niewygody lub złe
samopoczucie; krępować; żenować; deranżować kogoś
discompose [,dyskem'pouz] v.
zaniepokoić; niepokoić; mieszać; zmieszać (kogoś)
disconcert [,dysken'ser:t] v.
żenować; krzyżować plany
disconnect ['dyske'nekt] v.
odłączyć; oderwać; odcze-
pić; odhaczyć (od czegoś)
disconnected ['dyske'nektyd]
adj. bez związku; bezładny;
rozłączony; chaotyczny
disconsolate [dys'konselyt] adj.
niepocieszony; posępny
discontent ['dysken'tent] s.
niezadowolenie; adj. niezadowolony; v. wywoływać niezadowolenie; wywoływać rozgoryczenie (czyjeś)
discontented ['dysken'tentyd]
adj. niezadowolony; rozgo-
ryczony; zniecierpliwiony
discontinue ['dysken'tynju:] v.
zaprzestawać; przerywać;
ustawać; zakończyć (coś);
zaniechać (czegoś)
discord ['dysko:rd] s. niezgoda;
różnica; dysonans; niesnaski
discordance ['dysko:rdens] s.
niezgodność; dysonans
discotheque ['dyskoutek] s.
dyskoteka; nocny lokal z
muzyką z płyt do tańca
discount ['dyskaunt] s.
dyskonto; rabat; odjęcie; v.
potrącać; odliczać; nie da-

wać wiary (komuś, czemuś)
discourage [dys'karydż] v.
zniechęcać (do czegoś); odstraszać; być przeciwnym
discover [dys'kawer] v.
wynaleźć; odkryć; odsła-
niać; (nagle) zobaczyć
discoverer [dys'kawerer] s.
odkrywca; wynalazca
discredit [dys'kredyt] v.
dyskredytować; przynosić
ujmę; pozbawiać zaufania; s.
utrata zaufania i dobrego
imienia; niewiara (w coś); zła
opinia (o kimś, o czymś)
discreet [dys'kri:t] a. rozsądny;
dyskretny; z rezerwą
discrepancy [dys'krepensy] s.
sprzeczność; rozbieżność
discretion [dys'kreszyn] s.
swoboda decyzji; rozwaga;
powściągliwość; dyskrecja
discriminate [dys'krymynejt] v.
odróżniać; dyskryminować;
robić różnicę; wyróżniać
discriminate against [dys'
krymynejt e'gejnst]
wprowadzać dyskryminację
w stosunku do (kogoś)
discrimination [dys,krymy
'nejszyn] s. odróżnienie;
niejednakowe traktowanie
discuss [dys'kas] v.
dyskutować (o); roztrząsać
(coś); debatować (o czymś)
discussion [dys'kaszyn] s.
dyskusja; debata; debaty
disdain [dy'dejn] s. pogarda;
wzgarda; v. gardzić (kimś,
czymś); lekceważyć
disease [dy'zi:z] s. choroba
diseased [dy'zi:zd] adj. chory;
schorzały; cierpiący na ...
disembark ['dysym'ba:rk] v.
wyładować; wysiadać; lądować (samolotem, statkiem)
disengage ['dysen'gejdż] v.
odczepiać; wyłączać; odwikłać; rozłączyć; odhaczyć
disengaged ['dysyn'gejdżd] adj.
wolny; nie zajęty; zwolniony
disentangle ['dysyntaengl] v.
wyplątać; rozplątać; wywik-

łać (się); rozwikłać (coś)
disfavor ['dys'fejwer] s. niełaska;
dezaprobata; v. odnosić się
nieprzychylnie; z niechęcią
traktować; dezaprobować
disfigure [dys'fyger] v.
zniekształcić; zeszpecić
disgrace [dys'grejs] s. hańba;
niełaska; v. hańbić; zniesławić; pozbawiać łaski; narobić (komuś, sobie) wstydu
disgraceful [dys'grejsfel] adj.
haniebny; hańbiący; sromotny; niecny; shameless
disguise [dys'gajz] v. przebierać;
ukrywać; maskować; zata-
ić; s. charakteryzacja; udawanie; pozory; zamaskowanie;
maska; nadanie pozorów
disgust [dys'gast] s. odraza;
wstręt; obrzydzenie; v.
budzić odrazą, wstręt, obrzydzenie, rozgoryczenie, oburzenie (na kogoś, na coś)
disgusting [dys'gastyng] adj.
wstrętny; obrzydliwy; oburzający; odrażający (czymś)
dish [dysz] s. półmisek; naczynie; potrawa; danie; v. nakładać; podawać; drążyć; ok-
piwać; nakładać na półmisek
dishes ['dyszyz] pl. statki;
naczynia; smaczne potrawy
dish-cloth ['dysz,klos] s. ścierka
do wycierania talerzy
disheveled [dy'szeweld] adj.
rozczochrany; zaniedbany
dishonest [dys'onyst] adj.
nieuczciwy; (człowiek) nie
godny zaufania (czyjegoś)
dishonesty [dys'onysty] s.
nieuczciwość; nieuczciwy
postępek; oszustwo
dishonor [dys'oner] s. hańba;
dyshonor; niehonorowanie;
hańbiący czyn; v. hańbić
dishonorable [dys'onerebl] adj.
haniebny; podły; (człowiek)
bez czci i wiary
dishwasher ['dysz,łoszer] s.
pomywacz; pomywaczka
dish-water [dysz,ło:ter] s. pomyje
disillusion [,dysy'lu:żyn] s.

rozczarowanie; otrzeźwienie
disincline [,dysyn'klajn] v.
zniechęcać; mieć niechęć
disinclined [,dysyn'klajnd] adj.
zniechęcony; źle usposobiony
disinfect [,dysyn'fekt] v.
odkażać; zdezynfekować
disinfectant [,dysyn'fektent] s.
środek odkażający
disinherit ['dysyn'heryt] v.
wydziedziczyć; wydziedzi-
czać (kogoś z czegoś)
disintegrate [dys'yntegrejt] v.
rozpadać (się); rozkładać
(się); rozdrobnić (coś)
disinterested [dys'yntrystyd] adj.
bezinteresowny; nie zainteresowany; obiektywny
disjoint [dys'dżoint] v.
rozłączać; rozdzielać;
zwichnąć; rozerwać
disk [dysk] s. krążek; tarcza;
płyta gramofonowa; dysk
dislike [dys'lajk] v. nie lubić;
mieć odrazę; s. odraza;
niechęć; awersja; wstręt
dislocate ['dyslekejt] v.
zwichnąć; przesunąć;
zatrącić (porządek etc.)
disloyal [,dys'lojel] adj.
niewierny; nielojalny; zdradziecki (wobec kogoś etc.)
dismal ['dyzmel] adj.
nieszczęsny; ponury; posępny
dismantle [dys'maentl] v.
rozmontowywać; ogołacać;
odzierać; rozbroić; pozbawiać; demontować (coś)
dismay [dys'mej] s. trwoga;
przestrach; v. przerażać; kon-
sternować; skonsternować
dismember [dys'member] v.
rozczłonkować; rozebrać na
części; dokonać rozbioru
dismiss [dys'mys] v. odprawiać;
zwalniać; odsuwać od siebie;
przenieść w stan spoczynku
dismissal [dys'mysel] s.
zwolnienie; dymisja; rozejście
się; pożegnanie; pozbycie się
dismount ['dys'maunt] v.
zsiadać z konia; wyjmować z
oprawy; wysadzać z siodła

disobedience [dyse'bi:djens] s.
nieposłuszeństwo; opór
disobedient [dyse'bi:djent] adj.
nieposłuszny; oporny
disobey [,dyse'bej] v. nie
słuchać; być nieposłusznym
disoblige [,dyse'blajdż] v.
lekceważyć; bagatelizować
disorder [dys'o:rder] s.
nieporządek; zamieszki;
zaburzenie; nieład; zamęt
disorderly [dys'o:rderly] adj.
nieporządny; niesforny;
gorszący; burzliwy; bezładny
disown [dys'oun] v. wypierać
się; zaprzeczać; nie uznawać
disparage [dys'paerydż] v.
poniżać; ubliżać; dyskre-
dytować; uwłaczać; lekce-
ważyć; mówić ubliżająco (o)
dispassion [dys'paeszyn] s.
beznamiętność; obiektywizm
dispassionate [dys'paeszynyt]
adj. beznamiętny; obiektywny
dispatch [dys'paecz] s. wysyłka;
wysyłanie; sprawność; szybkość; szybkie załatwianie; v.
wysyłać; załatwiać; dobijać
(ranne zwierzę, człowieka)
dispel [dys'pel] v. rozwiewać
(obawy); rozpędzać (chmury)
dispensable [dys'pensebl] adj.
zbędny; niekonieczny; możliwy do uchylenia (ślub)
dispense [dys'pens] v.
wydzielać; wymierzać; wy-
dawać; udzielać; sporzą-
dzać (lekarstwo w aptece)
dispense with [dys'pens łys] v.
pomijać; obyć się (bez)
disperse [dys'pe:rs] v.
rozpraszać; rozpędzać; rozjeżdżać się; rozsiewać; płoszyć; rozszczepić (światło)
displace [dys'plejs] v. prze-
mieszczać; wypierać; usu-
wać; przełożyć; przekładać
display [dys'plej] v. wystawiać;
popisywać się; s. wystawa;
popis; pokaz (czegoś); parada
displease [dys'pli:z] v. urażać;
drażnić; gniewać; dotykać;
oburzać (kogoś); irytować

displeased [dys'pli:zd] adj. urażony; zirytowany; niezadowolony; obrażony; poirytowany
displeasure [dys'pleżer] s.
niezadowolenie; gniew; irytacja (na kogoś, na coś)
disposal [dys'pouzel] s. rozkład;
zbyt; sprzedaż; przekazanie;
rozporządzenie; niszczenie
dispose [dys'pouz] v. rozmieszczać; rozporządzić; pozbyć
się (czegoś); sprzedać
(coś); usunąć; niszczyć;
nakłaniać; usposabiać (do)
disposed [dys'pouzd] adj.
skłonny; usposobiony (dobrze,
pogodnie, wesoło, źle etc.)
disposition [dys'pouzyszyn] s.
skłonność; pociąg; zarządzenie; dyspozycje; rozporządza-
nie; popęd; żyłka (do czegś)
disproportionate [,dyspre
'po:rsznyt] adj. nieproporcjonalny; niewspółmierny
dispute [dys'pju:t] s. spór;
kłótnia; v. sprzeczać się;
kłócić się; kwestionować
disqualify [dys'kłolyfaj] v.
dyskwalifikować
disquiet [dys'kłajet] v.
niepokoić; s. niepokój; adj.
niespokojny; zaniepokojony
disregard [,dysry'ga:rd] v.
pomijać; lekceważyć; s. lekceważenie (kogoś, czegoś)
disrepute [,dysry'pju:t] s.
niesława; hańba; zła reputacja
disrespectful [,dysry'spektfel]
adj. niegrzeczny; niedelikatny
disrupt [dys'rapt] v. rozrywać;
rozdzierać; przerwać; obalić
dissatisfaction ['dyssaetys
'faekszyn] s. niezadowolenie
dissatisfied [dys,satys'fajd] adj.
niezadowolony (z czegoś)
dissension [dy'senszyn] s.
waśń; niezgoda; swary
dissent [dy'sent] s. różnica;
rozbieżność zdań; odstęp-
stwo; v. różnić się (w zapa-
trywaniach, opiniach etc.)
dissimilar ['dy'symyler] adj.
niepodobny; różny

dissipate [dy'sypejt] v. rozpraszać; marnować; trwo-
nić; marnotrawić; rozgonić;
hulać; zabawić się
dissociate [dy'souszjejt] v.
rozłączać (się)(od); zrywać
(z kimś, z czymś)
dissolute ['dyselu:t] adj.
rozwiązły; rozpustny
dissolution [,dys'elu:szyn] s.
rozkład; zanik; rozpuszczenie;
rozwiązanie (spółki etc.);
śmierć; zgon; rozpad
dissolve [dy'zolw] v. rozpuszczać; rozkładać; niszczyć; rozwiązywać; zani-
kać; skasować (bilet)
dissuade [dy'słejd] v. odradzać;
odwodzić (kogoś); wyper-
swadować (komuś, coś)
distance ['dystens] s.
odległość; odstęp; oddalenie;
v. zdystansować (się) (od)
distant ['dystent] adj. daleki;
odległy (od); powściągliwy; z
rezerwą (wobec); nie widzący
distaste [,dys'tejst] s. niesmak;
niechęć; odraza; awersja
distasteful [,dys'tejstful] adj.
odstręczający; wstrętny; przykry; odrażający (od siebie)
distend [dys'tend] v. rozdymać;
rozszerzać; nabrzmiewać;
rozdąć; nadać; nadymać
distill [dy'styl] v. przekraplać;
(prze)destylować; przesą-
czać (coś); kapać (czymś)
distinct [dys'tynkt] adj. odmienny (od kogoś, czegoś);
odrębny; wyraźny; dobitny
distinction [dys'tyn̲kszyn] s.
rozróżnienie; wyróżnienie się;
wytworność; podział (na); individual style, character
distinctive [dys'tyn̲ktyw] adj.
odróżniający się; charakterystyczny; wyróżniający się
distinguish [dys'tyn̲głysz] v. dostrzec; rozróżniać; klasyfikować; zauważyć; odznaczyć
distinguished [dystyn̲głyszt] adj.
wybitny; znakomity; dystyngowany; odznaczający się

distort [dys'to:rt] v. wykrzywiać; wykręcać; przekrę-
cać; fałszywie przedstawiać;
zniekształcać (fakty etc.)

distract [dys'traekt] v. odrywać;
rozproszyć; oszołomić

distracted [dys'traektyd] adj.
oszalały; w rozterce; skłopotany; roztargniony; rozproszony (przez kogoś, coś)

distraction [dys'traekszyn] s.
dystrakcja; roztargnienie; rozrywka; rozterka; szaleństwo;
zamieszanie; odwrócenie
uwagi (czyjejś od czegoś)

distress [dys'tres] s. męka;
strapienie; niedostatek;
potrzeba; niebezpieczeństwo

distressed [dys'trest] adj.
umęczony; udręczony; w
niedoli; dotknięty nędzą

distribute [dys'trybju:t] v.
udzielać; rozmieszczać; rozdać; rozprowadzać (ludzi)

distribution [dys'trybju:szyn] s.
rozdział; podział; dystrybucja;
roznoszenie; a. rozdzielczy

district ['dystrykt] s. okręg;
powiat; dystrykt; dzielnica;
rejon (kaju, państwa)

distrust [dys'trast] s.
nieufność; niedowierzanie; v.
nie ufać; niedowierzać; podejrzewać (kogoś o coś)

disturb [dys'te:rb] v.
przeszkadzać; niepokoić;
zakłócać; mącić; zaburzyć;
denerwować (kogoś)

disturbance [dys'te:rbens] s.
zakłócenie; zaburzenie; poruszenie; burda; awantura; rozruchy; wstrząs; niepokoje

disuse [dys'ju:z] s. zarzucenie;
nieużywanie (kogoś, czegoś)

ditch [dycz] s. rów; v. kopać;
drenować; utknąć w rowie;
rzucać (do morza samolot)

dive [dajw] v. nurkować;
zanurzać się; skakać z trampoliny do wody; s. nurkowanie; zanurzenie; melina; lot
nurkowy samolotu; pikowanie
samolotem; (licha) knajpa

diver ['dajwer] s. nurek; skoczek
z trampoliny; ptak nurkujący

diverge [daj'we:rdż] v. rozchodzić się; odchylać się; zbaczać (z drogi, na bok etc.);
odbiegać (od); rozbiegać się

diverse [daj'we:rs] adj.
odmienny; rozmaity; inny;
zmienny; urozmaicony

diversion [daj'we:rżyn] s.
odchylenie (od) objazd; rozrywka; dywersja (wojskowa)

diversion [dy'we:rżyn] s. zboczenie; dywersja; rozrywka;
odwrócenie uwagi; oderwanie
uwagi (od kogoś, od czegoś)

diversity [daj'we:rsyty] s.
rozmaitość (poglądów etc.);
różnorodność; urozmaicenie

diversity [dy'we:rsyty] s.
odmienność (charakterów);
różnorodność; rozmaitość

divert [daj'we:rt] v. odwracać
(uwagę); odrywać; rozer-
wać (się); rozbawić; bawić

divide [dy'wajd] v. dzielić;
rozdzielać; oddzielać; różnić

divide by [dy'wajd,baj] v. dzielić
przez (liczbę, mianownik)

divine [dy'wajn] adj. boski; boży;
v. wróżyć; przepowiadać

diving ['dajwyng] s. skakanie z
trampoliny; pikowanie w locie

divinity [dy'wynyty] s. bóstwo;
boskość; teologia

divisible [dy'wyzebl] adj.
podzielny (przez, na etc.)

division [dy'wyżyn] s. podział;
rozdział; dzielenie; dział;
wydział; oddział; dywizja

divorce [dy'wo:rs] s. rozwód;
rozdzielenie; v. rozwodzić się;
oddzielać; a. rozwodowy

dizzy ['dyzy] adj. wirujący;
oszołomiony; zawrotny; oszo-
łomiający v. oszłomiać

do [du:] v. czynić; robić;
wykonać; zwiedzać; przyrządzać; spełniać obowiązek

do away ['du,ełej] v. znieść;
pozbyć się; zabić (kogoś);
skasować (mecz, lot etc.)

do not ['du not] = **don't** [dont]
nie (rób); nie (idź); nie (stój)
do in ['du,yn] v. uwięzić; zlikwidować; zabić; wykończyć
do up ['du,ap] v. przerobić;
odnowić; upiększyć się
zmęczyć; upudrować etc.
do well [,du'łel] v. mieć się
dobrze; powodzić się; być w
(bardzo) dobrej sytuacji
do without [,du'łysout] v. obywać się bez; obyć się bez
do you know? [du: ju nou] expr.
czy pan wie? czy pani zna?
czy pan słyszał? czy wiesz?
docile ['dousajl] adj. uległy;
posłuszny; pojętny; skory do
nauki; potulny; giętki;
łagodny; podatny (do czegoś)
dock [dok] s. dok; basen; molo;
miejsce oskarżonego; v.
umieścić w doku; cumować
przy molu (w porcie)
dockyard [dokja:rd] s. stocznia
doctor ['dakter] s. lekarz; doktor
(medycyny, filozofii etc.)
doctorate ['dokteryt] s. doktorat
doctrine ['daktryn] s. doktryna
document ['dokjument] s.
dokument; v. poprzeć dokumentami; udokumentować
documentary [,dokju'mentery] s.
adj. dokumentalny (film etc.)
dodge [dodż] v. uchylić;
uniknąć; zwodzić; s. unik;
kruczek; sztuczka; odskok;
kiwanie (w grze w piłkę etc.)
doe [dou] s. łania; pl. does
[douz] łanie
does [daz] v. on czyni; robi;
proszę zobaczyć: do
dog [dog] s. pies; samiec;
klamra; uchwyt; sl. facet
dog-catcher [dog'kaeczer] s.
rakarz; oprawca; hycel
dogged ['dogyd] adj. uparty;
zawzięty; wytrwały
doggie ['dogi] s. psina
dogma ['dogme] s. dogmat
dog-tired ['dog'tajerd] adj.
skonany; ledwo żywy ze zmęczenia; bardzo zmęczony
doings ['du:yngs] pl. sprawki;

uczynki; wyprawiania; psoty
dole [doul] s. zasiłek; zapomoga;
smutek; v. mało dawać
doll [dol] s. lalka; (slang)
dziewczyna; v. wystroić się
dollar ['doler] s. dolar
dollish ['dolysz] adj. lalkowaty;
lalkowata; lalusiowaty
dolorous ['douleres] adj. smętny;
żałosny; zbolały; boleściwy
dolphin ['dolfyn] s. delfin
domain [de'mejn] s. dziedzina;
majątek ziemski; posiadłość;
zakres (władzy, wpływów)
dome [doum] s. kopuła;
sklepienie; v. nakrywać
sklepieniem (kopułą)
domestic [de'mestyk] adj.
domowy; krajowy; domatorski;
s. służący; służąca
domesticate [de'mestykejt] v.
oswajać; zadomowić
domicile ['domysajl] s. miejsce
zamieszkania; v. osiedlać;
zamieszkać na stałe
dominate ['domynejt] v.
dominować; górować; prze-
wyższać; panować; mieć
zwierzchnictwo (nad)
domination ['domynejszyn] s.
władza; panowanie; przewaga
domineer [,domy'nier] v.
dominować; rządzić się; rozkazywać; tyranizować; panoszyć się (nad otoczniem etc.)
domineering [,domy'nieryng] adj.
tyranizujący; apodyktyczny;
despotyczny; władczy
donate [dou'nejt] v. podarować
donation [dou'nejszyn] s.
darowizna; donacja; dar
done [dan] adj. zrobiony; uczy-
niony; proszę zobaczyć: do
donkey ['donky] s. osioł
donor ['douner] s. donator;
dawca (krwi etc.); darujący
doom [du:m] s. zguba; zły los;
śmierć; potępienie; przeznaczenie; v. potępiać; skazać na zgubę; przesądzać
Doomsday ['du:mzdej] s. dzień
sądu ostatecznego
door [do:r] s. drzwi; brama

door handle ['do:r,haendl] s.
klamka do drzwi (do bramy)
doorkeeper ['do:r,ki:per] s.
dozorca; portier; odźwierny
doorknob ['do:r,nob] s. klamka
doormat ['do:r,maet] s.
wycieraczka (przy drzwiach)
doorway ['do:r,łej] s. wejście
dope [doup] s. maź; lakier;
narkotyk; informacja (poufna);
głupiec (slang); naiwniak; v.
narkotyzować; zaprawiać;
fałszować; sfałszować
dormitory ['do:rmytry] s. dom
studencki; sypialnia
dose [dous] s. dawka; dodatek;
dawkowanie; v. dawkować
(lekarstwo); mieszać; fałszować (wino alkoholem);
leczyć; dozować; wydzielać
dot [dot] s. kropka; punkt; v.
kropkować; rozsiewać
dote [dout] v. wariować;
kochać przesadnie; mówić
od rzeczy; dziecinnieć
double ['dabl] adj. podwójny;
dwukrotny; dwojaki; fałszywy;
v. podwajać; adv. podwójnie;
w dwójnasób; dwojako
double up ['dabl,ap] v. składać
się we dwoje; zsuwać się
(razem); przybiegać; dzielić
pokój (na dwie osoby)
double bed ['dabl,bed] podwójne
łóżko (podwójnej szerokości)
double-breasted ['dabl,brestyd]
adj. dwurzędowy (płaszcz);
dwurzędowa (marynarka)
double-decker ['dabl-'deker] s.
dwupokładowiec; dwupoklado-
wy (statek, okręt, dom etc.)
double-park ['dabl-'pa:rk] v.
parkować podwójnie na jezdni przy chodniku)
double-room ['dabl,ru:m] s. pokój
dwuosobowy (w hotelu etc.)
doubt [daut] s. wątpliwość;
niedowierzanie; v. wątpić;
powątpiewać; niedowierzać
doubtful ['dautful] adj. wątpliwy;
niepewny; niezdecydowany
doubtless ['dautlys] adv.
niewątpliwie; bez wątpienia

douche [du'sz] s. natrysk
dough [dou] s. ciasto; (slang)
forsa; pieniądze
doughnut ['dounat] s. pączek (z
dziurą w środku
dove [daw] s. gołąb(ica)
down [dałn] s. wydma; puch;
meszek; puszek; piórka
down [dałn] adv. na dół; niżej;
nisko; v. obniżać; poniżać;
przewrócić; strącić; połknąć
downcast ['dałnka:st] adj.
przybity; przygnębiony; ze
spuszczonymi oczyma
downfall ['dałnfo:l] s. upadek;
klęska; ruina; zguba
downhill ['dałn'hyl] adj.
opadający; s. spadek; adv. na
dół; z góry na dół
downpour ['dałnpo:r] s. ulewa
downright ['dałnrajt] adv.
zupełnie; całkowicie; gruntownie; wprost; wręcz; stanowczo; adj. zupełny; szczery;
otwarty; uczciwy; jawny
downstairs ['dałn'steerz] adv. na
dół; w dole; na dole; pod nami
downtown ['dałntałn] s. centrum
miasta; adv. w śródmieściu;
w centrum; adj. śródmiejski
downwards ['dałnłodz] adv. w
dół; ku dołowi; na dół; z góry
downy ['dałny] adj. puszysty;
(slang) chytry; falisty; puchaty
dowry ['dałry] s. posag; wiano;
dar wrodzony; talent (do)
doze [douz] s. drzemka; v.
drzemać; zdrzemnąć się
dozen ['dazn] s. tuzin
drab [draeb] s. & adj. brudno-
-brunatny; nudny; szary; monotonny; brudas; prostytutka;
flądra v. puszczać się
draft [dra:ft] s. szkic; brulion;
zarys; przekaz; pobór; rysunek; ciąg w kominie; v.
szkicować; projektować; rysować; odkomenderować
draftsman ['dra:ftsmen] s.
kreślarz (techniczny);
rysownik; projektodawca
drag [draeg] v. wlec; ciągnąć;
s. pogłębiarka; pojazd; wle-

czenie (po); opór czołowy
dragon ['draegen] s. smok
dragonfly ['draegenflaj] s. ważka
drain [drejn] v. odwadniać; wysączać; ociekać; osuszać;
wuczerpać; s. dren; spust;
ściek; rów odwadniający
drainage ['drejnydż] s.
odwadnianie; wody ście-
kowe; obszar odpływowy
(rzeki, strumienia etc.)
drainpipe ['drejnpajp] s. dren
drake [drejk] s. kaczor
drama ['dra:ma] s. dramat
dramatic [dre'maetyk] adj.
dramatyczny; jak w sztuce;
żywy; uderzjący; frapujący
drank [draenk] s. pijak; pijany;
proszę zobaczyć: drink
drape [drejp] v. upinać; spadać
fałdami; drapować; s. kotara
drastic ['draestyk] adj. dra-
astyczny; gwałtowny; surowy
draught [draeft] s. przeciąg;
ciąg (w kominie); haust; łyk;
dawka; zanurzenie statku;
wyporność; adj. pociągowy
draw; drew; drawn [dro:; dru:;
dro:n]
draw [dro:] v. ciągnąć; pociągać (skutki etc); wyciągać;
przyciągać (uwagę); odcią-
gnąć; czerpać (pociechę);
wdychać; ściągać (wodze);
spuszczać (wodę); napinać
(łuk); mieć wyporność;
wlec; rysować; kreślić
draw near [dro:nier] v. zbliżać
się; przybliżać się (do)
drawback [dro:baek] s. strona
ujemna; przeszkoda; wada
etc.; v. cofać się (draw back)
draw up [dro:,ap] v. podciągać
(się); redagować; zbliżać
się; zrównać się; ustawiać
drawer ['dro:er] s. szuflada;
kreślarz; rysownik; bufetowy
drawers ['dro:ers] pl. kalesony;
majtki (damskie, dziecięce ...)
drawing ['dro:yng] s. rysunek
drawing pen ['dro:yng,pen] s.
grafion; piórko kreślarskie
drawing room ['dro:yng,ru:m] s.

salon; wagon salonowy
drawn [dro:n] adj. nierozstrzygnięty; ciągniony; wychudzony; wyciągnięta (szabla
etc.); proszę zobaczyć: draw
drawn-out [dro:n aut] adj.
przewlekły; przeciągający się;
wyciągnięty (z pochwy etc.)
dread [dred] s. strach; postrach;
lęk; v. bać się bardzo; lękać
się; adj. straszny; straszliwy
dreadful [dredful] adj. przeraźliwy; okropny; straszny; sl.
bardzo zły, irytujący etc.
dream; dreamt; dreamt [dri:m;
dremt; dremt]
dream [dri:m] v. śnić; marzyć;
s. sen; marzenie; mrzonka;
urojenie; miła nadzieja
dreamt [dremt] v. mieć sen,
marzenie (o); zob. dream
dreamy ['dri:my] adj. kojący;
marzycielski; mglisty; niewyraźny (obraz); sl. wspaniały
dreary ['dryery] adj. posępny;
ponury; smętny; melancholijny
dregs [dregz] pl. osady; męty
drench [drencz] v. zmoczyć;
przemoczyć; s. ulewa
dress [dres] s. ubiór; strój; szata;
suknia; v. ubierać; stroić;
opatrywać; czyścić; cze-
sać; przyprawiać; wykań-
czać; wyprawiać; wygarbo-
wać; przygotować (do)
dress down ['dres dałn] v.
besztać; czyścić (konia)
dress up ['dres,ap] v. stroić
dressing ['dresyng] s. przyprawa;
opatrunek; nawóz; ubiór
dressing-case ['dresyng,kejs] s.
neseser (z kosmetykami etc.)
dressing-gown ['dresyn-gołn] s.
podomka; szlafrok
dressing-room ['dresyng,ru:m] s.
garderoba; ubieralnia; umywalnia; (schowek z ubraniami)
dressing-table ['dresyng,tejbl] s.
toaleta (mebel z lustrem etc.)
dressmaker ['dresmejker] s.
krawiec damski; krawcowa
drew [dru:] zob. draw
dribble ['drybl] v. kapać; ślinić

się; wolno toczyć; odbijać
(piłkę); dryblować; s. kapanie; ciekncą ślina (dziecka)
drift [dryft] s. dryf; znoszenie;
bierność; prąd; dążność;
treść; zamieć; zaspa; na-
nos; v. dryfować; znosić;
plątać się; nanosić; płynąć
z prądem; być biernym
drill 1. [dryl] s. świder;
wiertarka; dryl; musztra; v.
wiercić; świdrować; ćwi-
czyć; musztrować; drążyć;
sortować (wagony etc.)
drill 2. [dryl] s. rowek do siania;
siewnik rzędowy; rząd; v.
siać; obsadzać w rowkach
drink; drank; drunk [drynk;
draenk; drank]
drink [drynk] v. pić; przepijać;
s. napój; woda (morze)
drinking water ['drynkyng,ło:ter]
s. woda pitna (do picia)
drip [dryp] v. kapać; ociekać;
ciec; s. kapanie; okap; piła
(sl.); nudziara; kapka; kropla
(płynu, cieczy, wody etc.)
drip-dry ['dryp,draj] s. bielizna
nie wymagająca prasowania
(schnąca na wieszaku etc.)
dripping ['drypyng] s. tłuszcz
spod pieczeni; adj. kapiący;
ociekający; przemoczony
drive; drove; driven [drajw;
drouw; drywn]
drive [drajw] v. pędzić; gnać;
wieźć; powozić; prowa-
dzić; napędzać; jechać;
wbijać; drążyć; s. przejażd-
ka; obława; napęd; droga; dojazd; energia; pościg (za)
drive at [drajw et] v. kierować
(dyskusją, rozmową ku ...)
drive out ['drajw, aut] v.
wyjeżdżać (z garażu); wy-
pędzać; wuganiać (kogoś)
drive-in ['drajw,yn] s. obsługa w
samochodzie, w banku, jadłodajni etc.; kino; sklep; poczta
drive-in movies [drajw,yn
mu:wiz] kino do oglądania siedząc w (swoim) samochodzie
driven [drywn] v. napędzany;

proszę zobaczyć: drive
driver [drajwer] s. kierowca
driving license ['drajwyng
,lajsens] s. prawo jazdy
drizzle ['dryzl] s. mżący deszcz;
mżawka; kapuśniaczek; v.
mżyć; adj. mżący (deszcz)
drone [droun] s. truteń;
buczenie; brzęczenie; dudnią-
cy mówca; v. zbijać bąki;
buczeć; dudnić (monotonnie)
droop [dru:p] v. opadać;
zwisać; zwieszać (głowę);
omdlewać; s. zwis; spadek
(tonu); utrata (otuchy)
drop [drop] v. kapać; ciec;
upuszczać; spadać; opadać;
s. kropla; cukierek; spadek
(temperatury, terenu etc.); łuk;
kieliszek; zniżka; kotara; upadek; uskok; obniżenie
drop in ['drop,yn] v. wpaść do
kogoś; wejść na chwilę
dropout [dropaut] s. osoba
przerywająca (studia, gimnazjum lub szkołę wstępną)
drove [drouw] zob. drive
drown [draun] v. tonąć; topić;
tłumić; głuszyć; zagłuszać
drowsy ['drauzy] adj. senny;
śpiący; ospały; na pół
śpiący; usypiający (kogoś)
drudge [dradż] s. niewolnik;
popychadło; v. harować
drug [drag] s. lek; lekarstwo; v.
narkotyzować; przesycać
drug-addict ['drag,aedykt] s.
narkoman; narkomanka
drugstore ['drag,stor] s. apteka;
drogeria (z kosmetykami etc.)
drum [dram] s. bęben; v.
bębnić; zwoływać bębnie-
niem; zjednywać (poparcie)
drummer ['dramer] s. dobosz
drunk [drank] adj. pijany;
proszę zobaczyć: drink
drunkard ['drankerd] s. pijak;
pijaczka (nałogowa)
drunken driving ['dranken
'drajwyng] s. kierowanie po
pijanemu (samochodem etc.)
dry [draj] adj. suchy; wytrawny
(wino); v. osuszać; suszyć;

zeschnąć; wyjaławiać; wy-
cierać; konserwować (mięso)
dry up [draj,ap] v. wycierać;
wysychać; zapomnieć (co
mówić); zaniemówić
dry-clean ['draj kli:n] v.
oczyścić chemicznie (sucho)
dry goods ['drajgudz] pl.
materiały do szycia; konfekcja
dual ['dju:el] adj. podwójny;
dwoisty; dwudzielny; wspólny
duchess ['daczys] s. księżna
duck [dak] s. kaczka; unik; v.
zanurzyć; zrobić unik (przed
kimś, czymś); nurkować
duct [dakt] s. przewód; kanał
dud [dad] s. (slang) poroniony
pomysł; safanduła; nieuk;
niewypał; strach na wróble;
adj. niezdolny; przegrany
dude [d(j)u:d] s. elegancik;
laluś; turysta; goguś;
wycieczkowicz (na wsi)
dude ranch ['du:d,ra:ncz] ranczo
wakacyjne (dla mieszczuchów)
due [dju:] adj. należny; płatny;
należyty; adv. w kierunku na
(wschód); s. to co się należy;
należności; opłata; składka
due to ['dju:,tu] exp. z powodu
duel ['dju(:)el] s. pojedynek
dug [dag] 1. s. cycek; wymię;
proszę zobaczyć: dig
dug 2. [dag] s. dójka
dugout ['dagaut] s. ziemianka;
łódź drążona; okop; schron
duke [dju:k] s. książę
dull [dal] adj. tępy; głuchy;
ospały; ociężały; niemrawy;
nudny; ponury; ciemny; nie-
ostry; v. tępić; tłumić
duly ['dju:ly] adv. właściwie;
należycie; punktualnie; we
właściwy sposób; słusznie
dumb [dam] adj. niemy; milczący; głupi; v. odbierać mowę
dumbfounded [dam'faundyd] adj.
osłupiony; osłupiały; oniemiały
dummy ['damy] s. imitacja;
makieta; atrapa; sl. bałwan;
manekin; dureń; głupiec; niemowa; adj. udany; pozorny;
sztuczny; podstawiony; symu-

lujący; imitowany; na niby
dump [damp] s. śmietnisko;
hałda; magazyn; v. zwalać;
rzucać; zarzucać (towarem)
dun [dan] s. wierzyciel; inkasent
długów; bezwzględne żądanie
zapłaty; v. (wielokrotnie) napastować o spłatę długu; adj.
ciemnobrązowy; szarobrązowy
dune [dju:n] s. wydma; diuna
dung [dang] s. nawóz; gnój;
bagno moralne; v. nawozić;
użyźniać ziemię; gnoić
dungeon ['dandżen] s. loch;
baszta; v. więzić w lochu lub
baszcie zamkowej etc.
dupe [du:p] s. ofiara; łatwo
wystrychnięty na dudka; v.
oszukać; okpić; nabrać
duplicate ['dju:plykyt] adj.
podwójny; s. duplikat; w dwu
egzemplarzach; v. podwajać;
duplikować (niepotrzebnie)
duplicity [dju:'plysyty] s.
dwulicowość; fałszywość;
podstęp; fałsz; obłuda
durable ['djuerebl] adj. trwały
duration [dju'rejszyn] s. trwanie;
czas trwania (czegoś)
duress [dju'res] s. przymus
during ['djueryng] prep. podczas;
w czasie; w ciągu; przez; za
dusk [dask] s. zmierzch; mrok;
cień; adj. ciemny; mroczny;
v. zaćmić; zamroczyć
dust [dast] s. pył; kurz; prochy;
pyłek; v. odkurzać; trzepać;
kurzyć się; posypywać
dust bowl [dast,boul] s. kraj
suszy i zamieci piaskowych
dust-cover ['dast,kawer] s.
obwoluta; pokrowiec od kurzu
duster ['daster] s. odkurzacz;
wiatr z kurzem; zmiotka
dust-pan ['dast,paen] s.
śmietniczka; łopatka na
śmieci, odpadki etc.
dust-storm ['dast,sto:rm] s.
wicher z tumanami kurzu
dusty ['dasty] adj. zakurzony;
pokryty kurzem; suchy; nudny; nieciekawy; niewyraźny
Dutch [dacz] adj. holenderski; w

niełasce; skąpy; niemiecki
duty ['dju:ty] s. powinność;
   obowiązek; szacunek; służba;
   uległość; cło; podatek od
   sprzedaży; funkcja; obowiązki
dwarf [dło:rf] s. karzeł;
   krasnoludek; adj. karłowaty; v.
   pomniejszać; karleć; skar-
   leć; skarłowacieć; zmniejszać wzrost (wymiar)
dwell; dwelt; dwelt [dłel; dłelt;
   dłelt]
dwell [dłel] v. mieszkać; zatrzymywać się; rozwodzić się (o
   czymś); przeciągać (rozmowę); zwlekać; przystanąć
dwelling [dłelyng] s. mieszkanie;
   pomieszczenie mieszkalne
dwelt [dłelt] v. mieszkał ...;
   proszę zobaczyć: dwell
dwindle [dłyndl] v. maleć;
   topnieć; marnieć; kurczyć
   się; tracić znaczenie; poniej-
   szać (coś); zwyrodnieć
dye [daj] v. barwić; farbować;
   s. barwa; barwnik; farba
dying ['dajyng] v. umierający;
   zanikający; zob. die
dyke [dajk] s. grobla; rów; tama;
   v. ogroblić; ochronić tamą
dynamic [daj'naemyk] adj.
   dynamiczny; energiczny; z
   wigorem; z energią (siłą)
dynamics [daj'naemyks] s.
   dynamika (sił fizycznych
   działających razem w ruchu)
dynamite ['dajne,majt] s.
   dynamit; v. wysadzać (w
   powietrze) dynamitem
dynamo ['dajne,mou] s. dynamo
dynasty ['dajnesty] s. dynastia
dysentery ['dysnetry] s.
   czerwonka; dyzenteria (krwawa i ostre bóle brzucha)

E

e [i:] piąta litera angielskiego

alfabetu
each [i:cz] pron. każdy (z dwu
   lub więcej); za (sztukę)
each other ['i:cz,odzer] siebie;
   nawzajem (dwie osoby); sobie
eager ['i:ger] adj. gorliwy; ostry;
   żądny; ożywiony pragnieniem;
   żywy; niecierpliwy; pragnący
eagerness ['i:gernys] s.
   gorliwość; skwapliwość;
   pochopność; pragnienie
eagle ['i:gl] s. orzeł; a. orli
ear [ier] s. ucho; słuch; kłos
   (zboża); adj. uszny; dotyczący
   uszu (leczenia uszu etc.)
eardrum ['ierdram] s. bębenek
   ucha; błona bębenkowa (ucha)
early ['e:rly] adj. wczesny; adv.
   wcześnie; przedwcześnie
earn [e:rn] v. zarabiać (pracą, etc.); zasługiwać; zapracować; zdobywać (sławę)
earnest ['e:rnyst] adj. poważny;
   gorliwy; nie żartujący; s. zadatek (dowód kupna domu)
earnings ['e:rnynz] pl. zarobki
earphone ['ierfoun] s. słuchawka;
   loki ułożone na uszach
earring ['ieryng] s. kolczyk
earshot ['ier,szot] w zasięgu
   głosu; w zasięgu słuchu
earth [e:rs] s. ziemia; świat;
   gleba; planeta ziemska
earthen ['e:rsen] adj. ziemisty;
   gliniany; wypiekany z gliny
earthenware ['e:rsen,łe:r] s.
   wyroby garncarskie (z gliny)
earthly ['e:rsly] adj. ziemski
earthquake ['e:rs,kłejk] s.
   trzęsienie ziemi
earthworm ['e:rs,łe:rm] s.
   (glista); dżdżownica
ease [i:z] v. łagodzić; uspokoić
   (się) odciążyć; ostrożnie ruszać; s. spokój; wygoda; beztroska; ulga (od); łatwość
easel ['i:zl] s. sztaluga
easily ['i:zyly] adv. łatwo; lekko;
   swobodnie; bez trudności
east [i:st] s. wschód; adj.
   wschodni; adv. na wschód
Easter ['i:ster] s. Wielkanoc

eastern ['i:stern] adj. wschodni;
ku wschodowi; ze wschodu
eastward ['i:stłerd] adv. ku
wschodowi; na wschód; adj.
wschodni (wiatr, kierunek)
easy [i:zy] adj. łatwy; beztroski;
wygodny; adv. łatwo; swo-
bodnie; lekko; s. odpoczynek
easy chair ['i:zy,czeer] s. fotel
(klubowy, wygodny) miękki
eat; ate; eaten [i:t; ejt; i:tn]
eat [i:t] v. jeść (posiłek)
eat up ['i:t,ap] v. wyjeść
eaten [i:tn] adj. zjedzony;
proszę zobaczyć: eat
eau-de-Cologne ['oudeke'loun] s.
woda kolońska (pachnąca)
eaves [i:wz] pl. okap (dachu)
eavesdropping ['i:wzdropyng] s.
podsłuchiwanie (rozmowy)
ebb-tide ['ebtajd] s. odpływ w
morze; v. odpływać (jak
morze, ocean etc.)
ebony ['ebeny] s. heban
eccentric [ik:sentryk] adj.
dziwaczny; s. ekscentryk;
dziwak; mimośród; dziwaczka
ecclesiastic [ik,ly:zi'aestyk] adj.
kościelny; s. duchowny
echo ['ekou] s. echo; v. odbijać
się echem; powtarzać za
kimś (czyjeś słowa); odbijać
głos (od powierzchni)
eclipse [i'klyps] s. zaćmienie; v.
zaciemniać; zaćmiewać
ecology [i'koledży] s. ekologia;
związek między środowis-
kiem a organizmem (część
biologii i inżynierii)
economic [,i:ke'nomyk] adj.
ekonomiczny; gospodarczy
economical [,i:ke'nomykel] adj.
oszczędny; ekonomiczny
economics [,i:ke'nomyks] pl. nauka o ekonomii (gospodarce)
economist [i'konemyst] s.
ekonomista; specjalista od
działania gospodarki
economize [i'kone,majz] v.
oszczędzać; zmniejszać
wydatki i marnotrawstwo;
gospodarować oszczędnie;
używać (coś) wydajnie

economy [i'konemy] s. ekonoomia; gospodarka; gospodarowanie; zapobiegliwość
economy class [i'konemy,kla:s]
s. druga klasa (w pociągu,
samolocie); klasa turystyczna
ecstasy ['ekstesy] s. zachwyt;
ekstaza; uniesienie; siódme
niebo; wielka radość
eddy ['edy] s. wir; v. wirować
edelweiss ['ejdl,wajs] s. szarotka
(kwiat górski, tatrzański)
edge [edż] s. ostrze; krawędź;
kraj; v. ostrzyć; obszywać;
wyślizgać się; przysuwać
po trochu; posuwać bokiem
edging ['edżyng] s. brzeg;
obszywka; lamówka; skraj
edgy ['edży] adj. nerwowy;
podniecony; o ostrych kantach
edible ['edybl] adj. jadalny
edict ['i:dykt] s. edykt; dekret
edifice ['edyfys] s. budowla;
gmach (duży i imponujący)
edifying ['edyfajyng] adj.
pouczający, poprawiający
(zwłaszcza moralnie)
edit ['edyt] v. redagować;
wydawać; zarządzać gazetą
edition [i'dyszyn] s. wydanie;
nakład (książki, gazety etc.)
editor [e'dyter] s. redaktor;
wydawca; pisarz "od redakcji"
editorial [,edy'to:rjel] s. artykuł
od redakcji (wydawcy); adj.
redakcyjny; redaktorski
educate ['edju:kejt] v. kształcić;
wychowywać (w szkole);
płacić za szkołę
education [,edju'kejszyn] s.
wykształcenie; nauka; oświata; nauczanie (formalne);
wychowanie; tresura; wiedza
educational [,edju'kejszenl] adj.
kształcący; wychowawczy
educator ['edju,kejter] s. wychowawca; wychowawczyni
eel [i:l] s. węgorz (ryba)
effect [i'fekt] s. skutek; wynik; wrażenie; wpływ; zancze-
nie; powodowanie; v. wykonywać; spełnić; powodować
effects [i'fekts] pl. ruchomości;

dobytek (osobiste); manatki
effective [i'fektyw] adj. skuteczny; wydajny; rzeczywisty;
imponujący; wchodzący w życie; będący w mocy (w sile)
effeminate [i'femynyt] adj.
zniewieściały; nie męski;
słaby; delikatny; wrażliwy
effervescent [,efer'wesnt] adj.
musujący; kipiący (pęcherzmi
powietrza); tryskający życiem
efficacy ['efykesy] s.
skuteczność; dawanie porządnych wyników (skutków etc.)
efficiency [i'fyszency] s.
wydajność; skuteczność;
sprawność (przy minimum
nakładów, wysiłków i strat)
efficient [i'fyszent] adj.
skuteczny; wydajny; sprawny
effigy ['efydży] s. wizerunek;
podobizna; czyjaś kukła
effort ['efert] s. wysiłek;
usiłowanie; wyczyn; próba;
popis; wynik pracy i wysiłków
effusive [i'fju:syw] adj. wylewny;
wylany; ekspansywny; nie-
powstrzymany; wulkaniczny
egg [eg] s. jajko; v. zachęcać;
namawiać; podbechtać; podniecać (kogoś czymś)
egg-cup ['eg,kap] s. kieliszek na
jajko; kieliszek do jaj
egghead ['eg,hed] s.
intelektualista (nieżyciowy)
egoism ['egou,yzem] s. egoizm
egress ['i:gres] s. wyjście;
wyjazd; uchodzenie; wypływ
Egyptian [i'dżypszen] adj. egipski
eiderdown ['ajder,dałn] s. kaczy
puch; kołdra; pierzyna
eight [ejt] num. osiem; s.
ósemka; ośmioro; ośmiu
(wioślarzy, sportowców)
eighteen ['ejt'i:n] num.
osiemnaście; osiemnaścioro;
osiemnastka (w drużynie etc.)
eightfold ['ejt,fould] num.
ośmiokrotny; adv. ośmio-
krotnie; osiem razy (robić)
eighty ['ejty] num. osiemdziesiąt;
s. osiemdziesiątka
either ['ajdzer] pron. każdy (z

dwu); obaj; obie; oboje; jeden
lub drugi; adv. także; też
either ... or ['ajdzer ... o:r] albo
...albo (jeden albo drugi)
ejaculate [i'dżaekju,lejt] v.
zawołać; krzyknąć nag- le;
wytrysnąć (nasienie)
eject [i'dżekt] v. wyrzucać (się);
eksmitować; usuwać
elaborate [i'laebe,rejt] v.
opracować; adj. wypracowany; staranny; skomplikowany
elapse [i'laeps] v. minąć;
przeminąć; przemijać
elastic [i'laestyk] adj. sprężysty;
rozciągliwy; elastyczny; s.
guma; gumka (do majtek ...)
elated [i'lejtyd] adj. podniecony;
uniesiony; entuzjastyczny;
(bardzo) dumny, szczęśliwy
elbow ['elboł] s. łokieć; zakręt;
kolanko; v. szturchać;
przepychać się; zakręcać
elbow grease ['elboł,gri:s] s.
ciężka praca; wysiłek
elder ['elder] s. człowiek starszy;
adj. starszy (z dwóch);
należący do starszyzny
elderly ['elderly] adj. podstarzały;
starszy; starszawy
eldest ['eldyst] adj. najstarszy
(syn w rodzeństwie etc.)
elect [i'lekt] v. wybrać;
postanawiać; decydować;
adj. wybrany (ale jeszcze nie
na stanowisku); wyborowy
election [i'lekszyn] s. wybór;
wybory (głosowaniem)
elector [i'lekter] s. wyborca
(uprwniony) elektor; członek
kolegium wyborczego
electric [i'lektryk] adj.
elektryczny; przyciągający jak
bursztyn; elektryzujący
electrical engineer [e'lektry
kel,endży'nier] s. inżynier
elektryk (dyplomowany)
electric chair [i'lektryk,cze:r] s.
krzesło elektryczne (do
egzekucji w Ameryce w USA)
electrician [ilek'tryszen] s.
elektryk (monter) (instalator)
electricity [ilek'trysyty] s.

elektryczność; prąd elektryczny; energia elektryczna
electrify [i'lektryfaj] v.
elektryfikować; elektryzować
electrocute [i'lektrekju:t] v.
uśmiercić prądem elektrycznym (wykonac egzekucją)
electron [i'lektron] s. elektron
elegance ['elygens] s. elegancja
elegant ['elygent] adj. elegancki;
dostojny; doskonały
element ['elyment] s. żywioł;
pierwiastek; część składowa; ogniwo; część podstawowa; składnik; element
elemental [,ely'mentl] adj.
żywiołowy; zasadniczy; elementarny; podstawowy; konieczny; pierwotny
elementary [,ely'mentery] adj.
elementarny; zasadniczy;
niepodzielny; pierwiastkowy
elementary school [,ely'mentery
sku:l] s. szkoła powszechna
elephant ['elyfent] s. słoń
elevate ['ely,wejt] v. podnosić;
unosić; wynosić (wzwyż)
elevation [ely'wejszyn] s.
wysokość; godność; fasada (domu); podwyższenie
elevator ['ely,wejter] s. winda;
dźwig; wyciąg; spichlerz
eleven [i'lewn] num. jedenaście;
s. jedenastka; jedenaścioro
eleventh [i'lewnt] num.
jedenasty; jedenastka
eligible ['elydżebl] adj. nadający
się; odpowiedni na wybór
eliminate [i'lymy,nejt] v. usuwać; wydzielać; pozbywać
się; nie brać pod uwagę;
opuszczać; wyeliminować
elimination [i,lymy'nejszyn] s.
eliminacja; pozbycie się
elk [elk] s. łoś (rogacz)
ell [el] s. łokieć (miara)
ellipse [i'lyps] s. elipsa
elm [elm] s. wiąz (drzewo)
elongate [i'longejt] v. wydłużać
się; adj. wydłużony
elope [i'loup] v. uciekać z
ukochanym (potajemnie)
eloquence ['eloukłens] s.

elokwencja; krasomówstwo
eloquent ['elokłent] adj.
elokwentny; wymowny (też w
piśmie); kroasowówczy
else [els] adv. inaczej; bo
inaczej; w przeciwnym razie;
poza tym; jeszcze; jeśli nie;
(będziesz) adj. różny; inny
elsewhere [els'hłer] adv. gdzie
indziej; w innym miejscu
elude [i'lu:d] v. ujść; wymknąć się; obejść prawo;
uchylić się; ukrywać się
elusive [ilu:syw] adj.
nieuchwytny; wymykający się
emanate ['eme,nejt] v. wydobywać; pochodzić; wydzielać się; emanować
emancipate [i'maens,ypejt] v.
wyzwolić; wyemancypować
embalm [im'ba:lm] v. zabalsamować; napełnić aromatem
embankment [im'baenkment] s.
nasyp; grobla; nabrzeże
embargo [em'ba:rgou] s. zakaz
handlowania, wjazdu, wyjazdu
embark [im'ba:rk] v. ładować
(się); wsiadać (na statek);
załadować (wojsko, towar);
rozpoczynać; przedsięwziąć
embark upon [im'ba:rk e'pon] v.
rozpoczynać; przedsięwziąć
embarrass [im'baeres] v. zakłopotać; wikłać; przeszkadzać; powodować zadłużenie; zażenować; skrępować
embarrassing [im'baeresyng] adj.
żenujący; kłopotliwy;
krępujący; zawstydzający
embarrassment [im'baeresment]
s. zakłopotanie; powikłanie;
skrępowanie; zaaferowanie
embassy ['embesy] s. ambasada
embed [im'bed] v. osadzić; sadzić; wmurować; wryć; zalać; wkopać; wbijać w coś
embedded [im'bedyd] adj.
osadzony; wsadzony; wryty;
wmurowany; wbity; wkopany
embellish [im'belysz] v.
upiększać; ozdabiać; podkolorowywać; dekorować; poprawić (opowiadanie etc.)

embers ['emberz] pl. niewygasłe węgle; żar; palące się polana

embezzle [ym'bezl] v. sprzeniewierzać (własność cudzą); zdefraudować (pieniądze)

embitter [im'byter] v. rozgoryczać; zatruwać; pogarszać; rozjątrzać (kłótnię)

emblem ['emblem] s. godło; wzór; symbol; emblemat

embody [im'body] v. wcielać; uosabiać; zawierać; włączać; ucieleśniać (coś)

embolden [im'boulden] v. ośmielać; rozzuchwalać; dodać (komuś) śmiałości

embolism [embelyzem] s. zator

embrace [im'brejs] v. uścisnąć się; obejmować; przystępować; imać się; korzystać z; s. uścisk; objęcie; włączenie (do jakiejś kategorii)

embroider [im'brojder] v. hafhaftować; wyszywać; upiększać (ubarwiać) opowiadanie

embroidery [im'brojdery] s. haft; hafciarstwo; upiększanie (ubarwianie) opowiadania

embryo ['embry'ou] s. płód; zarodek; embrion; adj. zarodkowy; nierozwinięty

emerald ['emereld] s. szmaragd

emerge [y'me:rdż] v. wynurzać się; wyłaniać; wyniknąć; nasunąć się (komuś coś); wyłonić się z wody (z morza); wyjść na jaw; wynikać z; nabawiać (kłopotów komuś)

emergency [y'me:rdżensy] s. nagła potrzeba; stan wyjątkowy; stan pogotowia

emergency brake [y'me:rdżensy ,brejk] s. ręczny hamulec w samochodzie (zapasowy)

emergency call [y'me:rdżensy ,kol] s. wzywanie pogotowia

emergency exit [y'me:rdżensy ,eksyt] s. wyjście zapasowe

emergency landing [y'me:r dżensy,laendyng] s. przymusowe lądowanie (samolotu)

emigrant ['emygrent] s. wychodźca; emigrant; adj. wychodźczy; emigracyjny

emigrate ['emygrejt] v. emigrować; wywędrować; przeprowadzać się (dokądś)

emigration [,emy'grejszyn] s. emigracja; wychodźctwo

emigre ['emygrej] s. emigrant (polityczny); adj. emigracyjny

eminent ['emynent] adj. dostojny; wybitny; wyniosły; wysoki; znakomity; sławny

eminently ['emynently] adv. szczególnie; wybitnie; wysoce

emit [y'myt] v. wydawać; wysyłać (światło, fale radiowe, ciepło, opinie); wypuszczać (banknoty); nadawać przez radio (audycję); emitować

emotion [y'mouszyn] s. wzruszenie; emocja; uczucie (miłości, strachu, gniewu, oburzenia, współczucia etc.)

emotional [y'mouszynel] adj. emocjonalny; poruszający uczucia (czyjeś); uczuciowy

emperor ['emperer] s. cesarz

emphasis ['emfesys] s. nacisk; emfaza; uwypuklenie; uwydatnienie; siła wyrażenia; wzmocnienie akcentu (na)

emphasize ['emfesajz] v. podkreślać; kłaść nacisk; uwypuklać; uwydatniać coś

emphatic [ym'faetyk] adj. dobitny; wyraźny; stanowczy; emfatyczny; mówiący z naciskiem; zdecydowany; niedwuznaczny; wymowny; znaczący

empire ['empajer] s. cesarstwo; imperium; adj. empirowy

emplacement [ym'plejsment] s. umiejscowienie; stanowisko

employ [ym'ploj] v. zatrudniać; używać; zajmować się; poświęcać (czas); posługiwać się; zastosować coś

employee [,emploj'i:] s. pracownik; siła (robocza)

employer [em'plojer] s. szef; pracodawca; pracodawczyni

employment [ym'plojment] s. zatrudnienie; używanie;

zajęcie; praca (najemna)
employment agency [ym'ploj ment'ejdżensy] agencja pośrednictwa pracy; biuro zatrudnienia bezrobotnych
empower [ym'pałer] v. upełnomocnić; upoważniać; umożliwiać (coś, komuś)
empress ['emprys] s. cesarzowa
emptiness ['emptynys] s. pustka
empty ['empty] adj. pusty; próżny; gołosłowny; bezsensowny; czczy; v. wypróżniać; wysypywać; wylewać brudy
emulate ['emjulejt] v. rywalizować; współzawodniczyć
enable [y'nejbl] v. umożliwiać; upoważniać; dawać możność; upoważniać (kogoś)
enact [y'naekt] v. postanawiać; uchwalać; grać (rolę); odgrywać (sztukę); uprawomocnić; wydawać zarządzenia; zagrać role (na scenie)
enamel [y'naemel] s. emalia; szkliwo (na zębach etc.)
encase [yn'kejs] v. wsadzać do pochwy; oprawiać; obramować; wpakowywać; pokryć
enchant [yn'czaent] v. zaczarować; oczarować (kogoś czymś); zachwycać (czymś)
encircle [yn'se:rkl] v. otaczać; okalać; okrążać; okrążyć; otoczyć (armie wroga etc.)
enclose [yn'klouz] v. ogradzać; zamykać; dołączać; załączać; zawierać (w sobie); okrążyć (wroga); opasać
enclosure [yn'kloużer] s. ogrodzenie; załącznik; płot
encore! [en'ko:r] s. bis! (zagrać, zaśpiewać na bis); bisowanie
encounter [yn'kaunter] s. spotkanie; potyczka; pojedynek; v. natknąć się (na trudności); spotkać się; potykać się (niespodziewanie); mieć utarczkę; utarczka
encourage [yn'ka:rydż] v. zachęcać; ośmielać; popierać; dodawać odwagi; pomagać; udzielać poparcia

encouragement [yn'ka:rydżment] s. zachęta; ośmielenie; popieranie; dodanie odwagi komuś
encroach [yn'kroucz] v. wdzierać się; naruszać; wkraczać na cudze; targnąć się na cudze (mienie, własność etc.)
encumber [yn'kamber] v. krępować; tarasować; obarczać; zawadzać; utrudniać; obciążać (kogoś długami etc.)
end [end] s. koniec; cel; skrzydłowy w piłce nożnej; v. kończyć (się); skończyć; dokończyć; położyć kres
endanger [yn'dejndżer] v. nanarażać, wystawiać kogoś na niebezpieczeństwo
endear [yn'dier] v. czynić drogim, lubianym; przymilać się; zdobywć serce (czyjeś)
endeavor [yn'dewer] v. starać się; usiłować; dążyć; zabiegać o; s. usiłowanie; wysiłek; dążenie do; zabiegi o; próba
ending ['endyng] s. zakończenie; końcówka (wyrazu)
endless ['endlys] adj. nie kończący się; nieskończony; bezustanny; ustawiczny; bezkresny; wieczny; ciągły
endorse [yn'do:rs] v. potwierdzać; popierać; żyrować; podżyrować; notować na odwrocie; indosować coś
endow [yn'dał] v. uposażyć; wyposażyć; ufundować; zapisywać; obdarzyć kogoś
endurance [yn'djuerens] s. wytrzymałość; cierpliwość
endure [yn'djuer] v. znosić (ból; bez skargi); cierpieć; wytrzymać; przetrwać; ostać się; trwać; ścierpieć
enema ['enyme] s. lewatywa
enemy ['enymy] s. wróg; przeciwnik; adj. wrogi; nieprzyjacielski; przeciwny
energetic [,ene:r'dżetyk] adj. energiczny; z wigorem
energy ['enerdży] s. energia
enervate ['ene:rwejt] v. osłabiać (nerwowo, na zdrowiu); wy-

czerpywać; pozbawiać (sił)
enervate [y'ne:rwyt] adj. słaby;
bez energii; wyczerpany
enfold [yn'fould] v. zawijać;
obejmować; zapakowywać
enfranchise [yn'fraenczajz] v.
wyzwalać; nadawać prawo
wyborcze; uwalniać; uwłasz-
czać (niewolników etc.)
engage [yn'gejdż] v. zajmować;
angażować; skłaniać; ścierać się; zaręczyć; zobowiązywać się; nawiązać (walkę)
engaged [yn'gejdżd] adj. zajęty;
zaręczony; włączony
engagement [yn'gejdżment] s.
zobowiązanie; zaręczyny
engine ['endżyn] s. silnik;
parowóz; maszyna; motor
engine-driver ['endżyn,drajwer]
s. maszynista (kolejowy)
engineer [,endży'nier] s. inżynier; v. planować; zręcznie
prowadzić: budowę, operacje
engineering [,endży'nieryng] s.
technika; mechanika; inżynieria; zarząd dróg, maszyn
engine trouble ['endżyn'trabl] s.
zepsucie silnika (samochodo-
wego); kłopot z silnikiem
English ['ynglysz] adj. angielski
(język, mowa); angielszczyzna
english ['ynglysz] v. uderzyć
piłką fałszem; zanglizować;
zangielszczyć; s. fałsz; pod-
kręcona piłka (w tenisie)
engorge [yn'go:rdż] v. pożerać
engrave [yn'grejw] v. rytować;
ryć; grawerować; wyryć;
wyrytować (napis, litery,
wzór, płaskorzeźbę etc.)
engraving [yn'grejwyng] s.
sztych; rytownictwo; grawiura
engross [yn'grous] v. za-
absorbować sobą; pochła-
niać; monopolizować (roz-
mowę, całkowitą uwagę itd.)
engulf [yn'galf] v. pochłonąć w
przepaść; porwać w odmęt
enigma [y'nygme] s. zagadka
enjoin [yn'dżoyn] v. nakazywać;
zarządzać; zakazywać; rozkazywać; zalecać; zabraniać

enjoy [yn'dżoj] v. cieszyć się;
rozkoszować; mieć (przyjemność, użytek); posiadać
enjoyment [yn'dżojment] s.
uciecha; rozkosz; przyjemność; posiadanie, korzy-
stanie z uprawnień etc.
enlarge [yn'la:rdż] v. powiększać; poszerzać; rozdąć;
rozwijać; zwalniać z ciupy
enlargement [yn'la:rdżment] s.
powiększenie; poszerzenie
enlighten [yn'lajtn] v. oświecać; oświetlać; objaśniać
enlist [yn'lyst] v. zaciągać (się);
werbować (do wojska); mobilizować kogoś dla sprawy
enliven [yn'lajwn] v. ożywiać
enmesh [yn'mesz] v. wplatać
(w sieć); usidlać; usidlić
enmity ['enmyty] s. wrogość;
nieprzyjaźń; nienawiść
enormous [y'no:rmes] adj.
olbrzymi; ogromny; kolosalny
enough [y'naf] adj., s. & adv.
dosyć; dość; na tyle; nie
więcej; wystarczająco
enounce [y'nauns] v. ogłaszać;
wymawiać; wypowiadać;
wymówić; wygłaszać mowę
enquire [yn'kłajer] v. pytać o;
dowiadywać się o; rozpytywać się (o coś, o kogoś)
enquiry [yn'kłajry] s. pytanie;
śledztwo; zapytanie; badania
enrage [yn'rejdż] v. rozwścieczać; doprowadzać (czymś,
kogoś) do wściekłości
enraged [yn'rejdżd] adj. rozwścieczony; rozwścieczona
enrapt [yn'raept] adj. zachwycony; pogrążony w zachwycie
enrapture [yn'raepczer] v. zachwycać; oczarowywać (ko-
goś); porywać publiczność
enrich [yn'rycz] v. wzbogacać;
użyźniać; ozdobić; popra-
wić jakość; ozdabiać
enrol(l) [yn'roul] v. zaciągać
(się); zapisywać (się)
ensue [yn'su:] v. wynikać;

nastąpować po kimś, po czymś; wypływać (z)
ensure [yn'szuer] v. zabezpieczać; zapewniać; zagwarantować; asekurować
entangle [yn'taengel] v. gmattwać; wplątać; zmieszać; komplikować; powikłać
enter ['enter] v. wchodzić; wpisywać; penetrować; wkładać; wstępować;
enter into ['enter,yntu] v. wdawać się; brać udział w; zawierać (układ z kimś)
enter upon ['enter,apon] v. wchodzić w posiadanie; przystępować do tematu; zaczynać (pertraktacje etc.)
enterprise ['enterprajz] s. przedsięwzięcie; przedsiębiorstwo; przedsiębiorczość; zadanie; inicjatywa
enterprising ['enterprajzyng] adj. przedsiębiorczy; ryzykujący
entertain [,enter'tejn] v. zabawiać; przyjmować; rozerwać (towarzystwo); żywić (podejrzenia); nosić się; brać pod uwagę; ugościć
entertainer [,enter'tejner] s. artysta (kabaretowy)
entertainment [,enter'tejnment] s. rozrywka; zabawa; uciecha
enthusiasm [yn'tju:zjaezem] s. zapał; entuzjazm do
enthusiast [yn'tju:zaest] s. entuzjasta; zapaleniec
enthusiastic [yn'tu:zy'aestyk] adj. entuzjastyczny; zapalony
entice [yn'tajs] v. znęcić; zwabić, kusić (nagrodą)
entire [yn'tajer] adj. cały; całkowity; nietknięty
entirely [yn'tajerly] adv. całkowicie; jedynie; wyłącznie; kompletnie; niepodzielnie
entitle [yn'tajtl] v. uprawniać; tytułować; nazwać; nadawać coś; upoważniać do
entity ['entyty] s. byt; istnienie; jednostka; istota
entrails ['entrejlz] pl. jelita; wnętrzności; wnętrze ziemi

entrance ['entrens] s. wejście; wstęp (za opłatą); dostęp; wjazd; pozwolenie wstępu
entrance [,en'traens] v. przejmować; wprawiać w trans; zachwycać (kogoś)
entrance fee ['entrens,fi:] opłata za wstęp; bilet wstępu
entreat [yn'tri:t] v. błagać
entreaty [yn'tri:ty] s. błaganie; usilna prośba; modlitwa
entrust [yn'trast] v. powierzać
entry ['entry] s. wejście; wpis; hasło (słownika); uczestnik wyścigu; wkroczenie; wstęp
entry permit ['entry,per'myt] pozwolenie wejścia, wjazdu
enumerate [y'nju:merejt] v. wliczać; sporządzać wykaz
envelop [yn'welep] v. owijać; otaczać; ogarniać; okryć (całkiem); ukryć; objąć
envelope ['enweloup] s. koperta; otoczka; teczka (papierowa)
envenom [yn'wenem] v. zatruwać; zaognić; podsycić
enviable ['enwjebl] adj. godzien zazdrości; godny pożądania
envious [enwjes] adj. zazdrosny; zawistny; pełen zazdrości
environment [ynwajerenment] s. otoczenie; środowisko
environmental pollution [yn'wajerenmentel pel'u:szyn] zanieczyszczenie środowiska
environs [yn'wajerenz] s. okolice podmiejskie; przedmieścia
envoy ['enwoj] s. wysłannik
envy ['enwy] s. zawiść; zazdrość; przedmiot zazdrości; niezadowolenie z powodzenia drugiego człowieka
epic ['epyk] adj. epicki; s. epos
epidemic [,epy'demyk] s. epidemia; adj. epidemiczny
epidermis [,epy'de:rmys] s. naskórek; skóra (powierzchnia)
epilepsy ['epylepsy] s. epilepsja; padaczka (choroba)
epilogue ['epylog] s. epilog
episode ['epysoud] s. epizod
epitaph ['epytaef] s. napis na grobie (ku pamięci zmarłego)

epoch [i:'pok] s. epoka (czyjaś)
equal ['i:kłel] adj. równy; jednaki;
jednakowy; jednostajny; zrównoważony; równy (stanem); v.
równać się; dorównywać komuś; wyrównywać (coś)
equality [i'kłolyty] s. równość
equalize [i'kłelajz] v. wyrównywać; równać; zrównywać
(się); (s)kompensować (coś)
equanimity [,i:kłe'nymyty] s.
opanowanie; spokój ducha;
równowaga psychiczna
equate [i'kłejt] v. równać;
przyrównywać do; stawiać
na równi (z kimś, z czymś)
equation [i'kłejżyn] s. równanie;
równoważenie; bilansowanie
equator [i'kłejter] s. równik
equilibrium [,i:kły'lybrjem] s.
równowaga; stan równowagi
equip [i'kłyp] v. wyposażać;
zaopatrywać; uzbrajać; ekwipować (kogoś w coś)
equipment [i'kłypment] s. wyposażenie; ekwipunek; sprzęt
equitable ['ekłytebl] adj. słuszny;
sprawiedliwy; godziwy
equivalent [i'kłylwelent] adj.
równowartościowy; równo-
znaczny; równej wielkości; s.
równoważnik; równowar-
tość; równoważność
era ['yere] s. era (historyczna)
erase [y'rejz] v. wycierać; wy-
mazywać; zatrzeć; zacierać;
wytrzeć; wyskrobać (coś)
erect [y'rekt] adj. prosty; wy-
prężony; sztywny; najeżony;
nastroszony; zadarty; pionowy; v. budować; stawiać
erection [y'rekszyn] s. podniesienie; wyprostowanie; najeże-
nie; erekcja; budowla; montaż
erosion [y'roużyn] s. wyżeranie;
żłobienie; erozja; nadżerka
ermine ['e:rmyn] s. gronostaj
erotic [y'rotyk] adj. erotyczny;
miłosny; s. erotyk; erotoman;
wiersz erotyczny
err [e:r] v. błądzić; być w
błędzie; grzeszyć; zgrzeszyć
errand ['erand] s. posyłka;

zlecenie; cel; sprawunek
erratic [y'raetyk] adj. błędny;
nieobliczalny; dziwny; s.
dziwak; ekscentryk
erroneous [y'rounjes] adj.
błędny; mylny; fałszywy
error ['erer] s. błąd; pomyłka
erudite ['erudajt] adj. uczony; s.
erudyta (b. oczytany etc.)
erupt [y'rapt] v. wybuchać;
wyrzucać; przerzynać (się);
wysypywać się; wybuchać
lawą; mieć wysypkę skórną
eruption [y'rapszyn] s. wybuch;
przerzynanie się; wysypka
escalation [,eske'lejszyn] s.
wzmożenie; rozszerzenie się
escalator ['eskelejter] s. ruchome
schody; ruchoma skala płac
(wg kosztów utrzymania etc.)
escape [ys'kejp] s. ucieczka; wyciekanie; wychodzenie; ocalenie; v. wymknąć się; zbiec;
wyjść cało; uchodzić; ratować się ucieczką
escort ['esko:rt] s. eskorta;
konwój; mężczyzna towarzyszący kobiecie; kawaler; v.
eskortować; kowojować
escort [i'sko:rt] v. eskortować
especial [ys'peszel] adj. szczególny; wyjątkowy; specjalny;
główny; osobliwy (przypadek)
especially [ys'peszely] adv.
szczególnie; zwłaszcza
espionage [,espje'na:dż] s.
wywiad; szpiegostwo; szpiegowanie; śledzenie kogoś
esprit [es'pri:] s. żywość;
życie; dowcip; duch; poczucie
humoru; duma (zespołowa)
espy [ys'paj] v. spostrzegać;
wyśledzić; wykombinować
essay ['esej] s. esej; szkic
literacki; próba; v. próbować;
wypróbować; poddać próbie
essence ['esens] s. esencja;
istota czegoś; wyciąg;
treść; istotna treść; sedno
sprawy; olej; ekstrakt
essential [y'senszel] adj. niezbędny; istotny; zasadniczy;
zupełny; podstawowy; konie

czny; eteryczny; s. cecha
istotna, nieodzowna, zasad-
nicza; rzecz podstawowa
establish [ys'taeblysz] v. zakładać; osądzać; ustalać;
wprowadzać; udowodnić;
ufundować; ustanawiać
establishment [ys'taeblyszment]
s. założenie; osadzenie;
ustalenie; ustanowienie;
zakład; gospodarstwo; koła
rządzące; organizacja
państwowa lub wojskowa;
firma; przedsiębiorstwo
estate [ys'tejt] s. majątek; stan
majątkowy; położenie w życiu
estate tax [ys'tejt,taeks] s.
podatek spadkowy, od nie-
ruchomości (majątkowy)
esteem [ys'ti:m] v. cenić;
szanować; poważać; s. po-
ważanie; szacunek; dobra
opinia; wielkie uznanie
estimate ['estymejt] v. oceniać;
szacować; s. szacunek;
kosztorys; ocena; opinia;
oszacowanie; obliczenie
estimation [,esty'mejszyn] s.
szacowanie; poważanie;
szacunek; zdanie; mniemanie;
sąd
estrange [ys'trejndż] v.
odstręczać; zrażać;
zniechęcać
estray [ys'trej] s. stworzenie
bezpańskie, zgubione
estuary ['estjuery] s. ujście
(rzeki) do morza (oceanu)
eternal [y'ternl] adj. wieczny;
odwieczny; bez początku i
końca
eternity [y'ternyty] s.
wieczność; trwanie bez
końca i odpoczynku
ether ['i:ter] s. eter
ethics ['etyks] pl. etyka
ethnic ['etnyk] adj. etniczny;
pogański; odrębny
zwyczajami i językiem
etymology [,ety'moledży] s.
etymologia; pochodzenie i
rozwój słów
eulogy ['ju:ledży] s. mowa;

pochwała (pogrzebowa)
eunuch ['ju:nek] n. eunuch;
rzezaniec; człowiek
wykastrowany
European [,ju:re'pi:en] adj.
europejski; s. Europejczyk
evacuate [y'waekjuejt] v.
ewakuować; opróżniać;
wypróżniać; wydalać;
usuwać; wycofywać się
evacuation [y,waekju'ejszyn] s.
ewakuacja; wypróżnienie (się)
evade [y'wejd] v. ujść;
uniknąć; obchodzić;
wymykać się; wykręcać się;
pomijać
evaluate [y'waeljuejt] v.
obliczać; oceniać;
analizować
evaporate [y'waeperejt] v.
parować; ulatniać się;
poddawać parowaniu;
wyparować; umrzeć
evasion [y'wejżyn] s. uniknięcie;
wymknięcie się; obejście;
wykręt; oszustwo
(podatkowe)
evasive [y'wejsyw] adj.
wykrętny; wymijający;
nieuchwytny
eve [i:w] s. wilia; wigilia
even ['i:wen] adj. równy;
jednolity; parzysty; adv.
nawet; v. równać;
wyrównać; zemścić się;
wygładzać; ujednostajnić
even-handed ['i:wen,haendyd]
adj. sprawiedliwy; bezstronny
evening ['i:wnyng] s. wieczór
evening dress ['i:wnyn,dres] s.
strój wieczorowy
evening paper ['i:wnyn'pejper]
gazeta wieczorna
evensong ['i:wensong] s.
nieszpory; pieśń wieczorna
event [y'went] s. wydarzenie;
możliwość; wynik; rezultat;
zawody (sportowe);
konkurencja
eventful [y'wentful] adj.
burzliwy; pamiętny; pełen
wydarzeń
eventual [y'wenczuel] adj. w

końcu pewny
eventually [y'wenczuely] adv. w
   końcu na pewno
ever ['ewer] adv. w ogóle;
   niegdyś; kiedyś; jak tylko; ile
   tylko; kiedykolwiek; jeszcze
   wciąż
ever after [,ewer'after] do tego
   czasu; już od tego czasu
ever since [,ewer'syns] od tego
   czasu; od kiedy (był etc.)
everlasting [,ewerlastyng] adj.
   wieczny; ciągły; nieustanny
evermore ['ewer'mo:r] adv.
   zawsze; na zawsze; na wieki
every ['ewry] adj. każdy;
   wszelki; co (dzień, noc, rano)
every other day ['ewry,odzer,dej]
   co drugi dzień
everybody ['ewrybody] pron.
   każdy; wszyscy (ludzie)
everyday ['ewrydej] adj.
   codzienny; powszedni; zwykły
everyone ['ewryłan] pron. każdy;
   wszyscy; każda rzecz
everything ['ewrytyng] pron.
   wszystko (co jest etc.)
everywhere ['ewryhłer] adv.
   wszędzie; gdziekolwiek
evidence ['ewydens] s. znak;
   dowód; świadectwo;
   oczywistość; jasność; v.
   świadczyć; dowodzić
   (czegoś); manifestować
evident ['ewydent] adj.
   oczywisty; widoczny; jawny;
   jasny
evil ['i:wl] adj. zły; fatalny
evildoer ['i:wl-duer] s. złoczyńca
evince [y'wyns] v. wykazywać;
   okazywać (życzenia);
   przejawiać
evoke [y'wouk] v. wywoływać;
   wydobywać; zdobywać
   (odpowiedź)
evolution [,ewe'lu:szyn] s.
   rozwój; ewolucja; rozwinięcie
   (się); pierwiastkowanie
evolve [y'wolw] v. rozwijać;
   wypracowywać; wytwarzać
   (ciepło etc.); rozwijać się
   stopniowo
ewe [ju:] s. owca

ex- [eks] pref. były; była; prep.
   bez; ze; s. (litera) "x"
exacerbate [eks'aeserbejt] v.
   drażnić; pogorszyć;
   irytować
exact [yg'zaekt] adj. dokładny;
   ścisły; v. wymagać;
   ściągać; egzekwować;
   wymuszać
exactitude [yg'zaektytju:d] s.
   ścisłość; dokładność;
   punktualność
exactly [yg'zaektly] adv.
   dokładnie; ściśle; właśnie;
   zgadza się; punktualnie; ostro
exactness [yg'zaektnys] s.
   dokładność; precyzja
exaggerate [yg'zaedżerejt] v.
   przesadzać; wyolbrzymiać
exaggeration [yg'zaedże'rejszyn]
   s. przesada; wyolbrzymienie
exalt [yg'zo:lt] v. wywyższać;
   podnosić; wychwalać;
   chwalić
exam [yg'zaem] s. egzamin
   (slang); klasówka; egzamin w
   szkole lub na uniwersytecie
examination [yg,zaemy'nejszyn]
   s. egzamin; badanie; rewizja
examine [yg'zaemyn] v. badać;
   sprawdzać; egzaminować;
   rozpatrywać; rewidować;
   przesłuchiwać;
   przeprowadzać śledztwo
example [yg'za:mpl] s. przykład;
   wzór; precedens
exasperate [yg'za:sperejt] v.
   rozjątrzać; rozgoryczać;
   pogarszać; powodować
   rozpacz
excavate ['ekskewejt] v. kopać;
   odkopać; wykopać; drążyć;
   pogłębiać; wybierać (ziemię)
exceed [yk'si:d] v.
   przewyższać; celować;
   przekraczać
exceedingly [ek'si:dyngly] adv.
   niezmiernie; nadzwyczajnie
excel [yk'sel] v. przewyższać;
   wybijać się; celować (w
   czymś)
excellence [yk'selens] s.
   wyższość; doskonałość;

zaleta
excellent [yk'selent] adj.
doskonały; wyborny; świetny;
celujący
except [yk'sept] conj. chyba że;
żeby; oprócz; poza; wyjąwszy
except [yk'sept] v. wykluczać;
wyłączać; prep. z wyjątkiem;
pominąwszy; wyjąwszy;
chyba że
exception [yk'sepszyn] s.
wyjątek; wyłączenie; zarzut;
obiekcja
exceptional [yk'sepszenl] adj.
nadzwyczajny; wyjątkowy
excess [yk'ses] s. nadmiar;
nadwyżka; a. nadmierny; nad-
excess fare [yk'ses,fe:r] s.
dopłata do biletu
excessive [yk'sesyw] adj.
nadmierny; zbytni;
nieumiarkowany
excess luggage [yk'ses,lagydż]
nadwyżka bagażu
exchange [yks'czendż] s.
wymiana; zamiana; giełda;
centrala telefoniczna; v.
wymienić; zamienić (się); a.
wymienny; walutowy
excitable [yk'sajtebl] adj.
pobudliwy; pobudzający;
podniecający
excite [yk'sajt] v. pobudzać;
podniecać; prowokować
excited [yk'sajtyd] adj.
podniecony; zdenerwowany
excitement [yk'sajtment] s.
podniecenie; zdenerwowanie
exciting [yk'sajtyng] adj.
emocjonujący; pasjonujący
exclaim [yks'klejm] v. zawołać;
wykrzyknąć; zaprotestować
exclamation [,ekskla'mejszyn] s.
okrzyk; krzyk; wykrzyknik
exclamation mark [,ekskla
'mejszyn,ma:rk] wykrzyknik
exclude [yks'klu:d] v.
wykluczać; wydalać;
usuwać
exclusion [yks'klu:żyn] n.
wykluczenie; wydalenie;
usunięcie; wyłączenie
exclusive [yks'klu:syw] adj.

modny; wykluczający;
wyłączny; jedyny;
ekskluzywny
excursion [yks'ker:żyn] s.
wycieczka; dygresja; a.
wycieczkowy
excuse [yks'kju:z] v.
usprawiedliwiać;
przepraszać; darować;
zwalniać; s.
usprawiedliwienie; wymówka;
pretekst
excuse me [yks'kju:z,mi]
przepraszam; przepraszam
pana
excusable [iks'kju:zebl] adj.
usprawiedliwiony; wybaczalny
execute ['eksykju:t] v. wykonać
(wyrok, plan); stracić
(skazańca); nadawać
ważność
execution [,eksy'kju:szyn] s.
wykonanie; egzekucja;
stracenie
executive [yg'zekjutyw] adj.
wykonawczy; s. władza
wykonawcza; stanowisko
kierownicze
exemplary [yg'zemplery] adj.
wzorowy; przykładny;
przykładowy; wymierzony dla
odstraszenia
exempt [yg'zempt] v. zwalniać;
adj. wolny; zwolniony; s.
osoba zwolniona; człowiek
zwolniony
exercise ['eksersajz] s.
ćwiczenie; wykonywanie
(zawodu); korzystanie; v.
ćwiczyć; używać;
wykonywać; spełniać;
pełnić
exercise book ['eksersajz,buk] s.
zeszyt (szkolny)
exert [yg'ze:rt] v. wytężać
(się); wysilać (się);
wywierać (nacisk, wpływ
etc.) zabiegać
exertion [yg'ze:rszyn] s.
wytężenie; wysiłek;
wywieranie
exhale [eks'hejl] v. wyziewać;
wydychać; zionąć; parować

exhaust [yg'zo:st] v. wydychać;
wyczerpywać; wyciągać;
wypróżniać; odgazować; s.
wydech; wydmuch; rura
wydechowa; opróżnianie (z
powietrza); aspirator; rura
wydechowa (auta)

exhaust fumes [yg'zo:st,fjums]
gazy wydechowe (z motoru)

exhaustion [yg'zo:stszyn] s.
wyczerpanie; opróżnienie;
zużycie; pochłonięcie;
zmęczenie

exhaust-pipe [yg'zo:st,pajp] s.
rura wydechowa (w aucie)

exhibit [yg'zybyt] s. wystawa;
pokaz; eksponaty; v.
wystawiać; okazywać;
pokazywać; wykazywać;
popisywać się czymś;
przedkładać; mieć wystawę

exhibition [,eksy'byszyn] s.
wystawa; wystawianie;
pokazywanie; pokaz;
widowisko; popis

exhibitor [yg'zybyter] s.
wystawca; wystawczyni

exile ['eksajl] s. wygnanie;
tułaczka; emigracja;
wygnaniec; v. wygnać na
banicję

exist [yg'zyst] v. istnieć; być;
żyć; egzystować; zdarzać
się

existence [yg'zystens] s.
istnienie; byt; egzystencja

existent [yg'zystent] a.
istniejący; będący; znajdujący
się

exit ['eksyt] s. wyjście;
odejście; ujście; wylot;
swobodne wyjście; v.
wychodzić; kończyć (slang);
schodzić ze sceny

exit visa ['eksyt,wyza] s. wiza
wyjazdowa

exorbitant [yg'zo:rbytent] adj.
wygórowany; nadmierny;
przesadny

exotic [eg'zotyk] adj.
egzotyczny; s. egzotyk;
egzotyczna roślina;
egzotyczny wyraz

expand [yks'paend] v.
rozszerzać; powiększać;
wzrastać; rozprężać;
rozwijać; rozruszać;
rozpościerać; powiększać

expanse [yks'paens] s. bezmiar;
rozległa przestrzeń; ekspansja

expansion [yks'paenszyn] s.
rozszerzanie; rozprężanie się;
ekspansja; rozpościeranie;
rozwijanie (się); ilość
ekspansji

expansive [yks'paensyw] adj.
rozszerzalny; rozległy;
rozprężalny; obszerny;
wylewny

expect [yks'pekt] v. spodziewać
się; przypuszczać; zgadywać

expectation [,ekspek'tejszyn] s.
oczekiwanie; nadzieja; widoki;
prospekt; przewidywanie

expedient [yks'pi:djent] adj.
celowy; wygodny;
oportunistyczny; korzystny; s.
środek; zabieg; sposób;
wybieg; fortel

expedition [,ekspy'dyszyn] s.
wyprawa; ekspedycja;
sprawność; szybkość;
pośpiech; marsz do akcji

expel [yks'pel] v. wypędzać;
wydalać; usuwać; wyrzucać

expend [yks'pend] v. wydawać;
zużywać; poświęcać czas

expense [yks'pens] s. koszt;
wydatek; rachunek; strata;
ofiara

expensive [yks'pensyw] adj.
drogi; kosztowny; wysoko
wyceniony

experience [yks'pierjens] s.
doświadczenie; przeżycie; v.
doświadczać; doznawać;
poznać (coś); przeżywać;
przechodzić

experienced [yks'pierjenst] adj.
doświadczony; doznany

experiment [yks'peryment] s.
próba; eksperyment;
doświadczenie; v.
eksperymentować; robić
doświadczenia

expert ['ekspe:rt] s. biegły;

ekspert; znawca; adj. biegły;
światły; mistrzowski;
wykonany przez eksperta
expiration [,ekspi'rejszyn] s.
wygaśnięcie; upłynięcie;
wydech; wyzionięcie ducha;
śmierć
expire [yks'pajer] v. wygasać;
upływać; wydychać;
wyzionąć ducha; umierać;
kończyć się
explain [yks'plejn] v. wyjaśnić;
objaśnić; wytłumaczyć
explanation [,eks'plaenejszyn] s.
wyjaśnienie; wytłumaczenie
explicable ['eksplykebl] adj.
dający się wyjaśnić
explicit [yks'plysyt] adj. jasny;
wyraźny; szczery; otwarty;
definitywny; wygadany
explode [yks'ploud] v.
wybuchać; eksplodować;
demaskować (fałsz); obalić
(teorię etc.)
exploit [yks'ploit] v. użytkować;
eksploatować; wyzyskiwać
exploit ['eksploit] s. wyczyn
exploration [,eksplo:'rejszyn] s.
oszukiwanie; badanie
explore [yks'plo:r] v. badać;
sondować; wybadać;
przebadać
explorer [yks'plo:rer] s. badacz;
sonda; odkrywca; odkrywczyni
explosion [yks'ploużyn] s.
eksplozja; wybuch (kłótni etc.)
explosive [yks'plousyw] s.
materiał wybuchowy; adj.
wybuchowy; mogący
wybuchnąć
exponent [yks'pounent] adj.
interpretujący; s. eksponent;
wyraziciel; interpretator;
wykładnik (potęgi);
przedstawiciel
export [yks'po:rt] v. wywozić;
eksportować; s. wywóz;
eksport; towar wywozowy;
wywożenie
expose [yks'pouz] v. wystawiać
(na wpływ); poddawać
(czemuś); odsłaniać;
demaskować; eksponować;

naświetlać; narażać
(dziecko); zrobić zdjęcie
expose [,ekspou'zej] s.
zdemaskowanie; odsłonięcie
skandalu
exposition [,ekspe'zyszyn] s.
wystawa; wykład;
przedstawienie; wyjaśnienie;
opis; naświetlenie;
ekspozycja; porzucenie
(dziecka)
exposure [yks'poużer] s.
wystawienie (na zimę etc.);
ujawnienie; zdemaskowanie;
naświetlenie; jedno zdjęcie na
filmie
exposure-meter [yks'poużer
'mi:ter] s. światłomierz
expound [yks'paund] v.
wykładać; wyjaśnić
szczegółowo; przedstawić
express [yks'pres] s. ekspres;
przesyłka pośpieszna; adj.
wyraźny; umyślny;
dokładny; adv. pośpiesznie;
ekspresem
expression [yks'preszyn] s.
wyrażenie; wyraz; ekspresja;
ton; wydawanie; wytłoczenie;
zwrot; wyciśnięcie;
wyżymanie
expressive [yks'presyw] adj.
wyrażający; wyrazisty;
ekspresyjny; pełen wyrazu
expressly [yks'presly] adv.
wyraźnie; kategorycznie;
naumyślnie; specjalnie;
formalnie
express way [yks'pres,łej] s.
droga przelotowa (bez
skrzyżowań
jednopoziomowych)
expulsion [yks'palszyn] s.
wydalenie; wyrzucenie;
wypędzenie; wygnanie;
wyparcie
exquisite ['ekskłyzyt] adj.
wyborowy; wyborny;
wyśmienity; nadzwyczajny;
ostry; przeszywający; s.
laluś; goguś; pięknis
extent ['ekstent] adj. pozostały;
jeszcze istniejący

extemporaneous [eks,tempe
'rejnjes] adj. zaimprowizowany
extend [yks'tend] v. wyciągać
(się); rozciągać (się);
przeciągać (się); rozszerzać
(się); dawać i udzielać;
przedłużać; powiększać;
rozpościerać się
extendible [yks'tendybl] adj.
rozszerzalny; rozciągalny
extension [yks'tenszyn] s.
rozciąganie; wyciąganie;
rozwinięcie; przedłużenie;
zasięg; rozmiar; zakres;
skrzydło (domu)
extensive [yks'tensyw] adj.
obszerny; rozległy;
ekstensywny
extent [yks'tent] s. obszar;
rozmiar; zasięg; miara;
stopień; wysokość;
oszacowanie
extenuate [yks'tenjuejt] v.
zmniejszać; łagodzić
exterior [eks'tierjer] s.
powierzchowność; wygląd
zewnętrzny; strona
zewnętrzna; fasada
exterminate [yks'te:rmynejt] v.
tępić (np. pogląd);
wyniszczyć
external [eks'te:rnal] adj.
zewnętrzny; zagraniczny
extinct [yks'tynkt] adj. wygasły;
zgasły; zanikły; wymarły
extinguish [yks'tyngłysz] v.
zgasić; zagasić; niszczyć;
unicestwić; umierać; tępić
extirpate ['ekster,pejt] v.
wykorzeniać; plewić; tępić
extol [yks'tol] v. wysławiać;
wynosić pod niebiosa
extort [yks'tort] v. wymuszać;
zdzierać (pieniądze);
wydrzeć
extra ['ekstre] adj. specjalny;
dodatkowy; luksusowy;
nadzwyczajny; ponad normę;
adv. nadzwyczajnie;
dodatkowo; s. dodatek;
dopłata; rzecz szczególnie
dobra; statysta
extra charge ['ekstre,cza:rdż] s.

dopłata; nadpłata
extract ['ekstraekt] s. wyciąg;
ekstrakt; wyjątek; wypis
extract [yks'traekt] v.
wyciągać; wydobywać;
wypisywać
extraction [eks'traekszyn] s.
wyciągnięcie; wydobycie;
wyrwanie (zęba);
pochodzenie; ród
extradite ['ekstredajt] v.
wydawać (przestępcę przez
granicę) do miejsca zbrodni
extraordinary [yks'tro:rdnery] adj.
niezwykły; nadzwyczajny
extravagance [yks'traewygens]
s. przesada; rozrzutność;
nieumiarkowanie; głupstwo;
niedorzeczność;
ekstrawagancja
extravagant [yks'traewegent]
adj. rozrzutny; przesadny;
zwariowany; wygórowany;
szalony
extravaganza [yks,traewe
'gaenze] s. ekstrawagancja;
fantazja
extreme [yks'tri:m] adj. skrajny;
krańcowy; najdalszy; ostatni;
s. kraniec; ostateczna granica;
ostateczność; skrajność
extremity [yks'tremyty] s.
koniec; kraniec; skrajność;
krańcowość; kończyna;
krytyczne położenie; potrzeba;
ostateczność
extrude [yks'tru:d] v. wypierać;
wyrzucać; przeciągać lub
ciągnąć odlew; wytłoczyć
exuberant [yg'zju:berent] adj.
wybujały; pełen życia;
kwitnący; wylewny; płodny;
obfity
exult [yg'zalt] v. triumfować;
unosić się radością
eye [aj] s. oko; wzrok; v.
patrzeć
eyeball ['ajbo:l] s. gałka oczna w
oczodołach za powiekami
eye to eye ['aj,tu'aj] exp. oko w
oko
eyebrow ['ajbrau] s. brew
eyeglasses ['ajgla:sys] pl.

okulary; lupy; monokle
eyelash ['ajlaesz] s. rzęsa
eyelid ['ajlyd] s. powieka
eyesight ['aj-sajt] s. wzrok
eyewash ['ajłosz] s. woda do
oczu; mydlenie oczu (slang)
eyewitness ['aj'łytnes] s.
świadek naoczny

F

f [ef] szósta litera angielskiego
alfabetu; stopień "f" failure =
niedostatecznie
fable [fejbl] s. bajka
fabric ['faebryk] s. tkanina;
materiał; osnowa; szkielet;
budowa; wytwór; a. sukienny
fabricate ['faebrykejt] v.
tworzyć; wymyślać;
zmyślać; montować;
wyssać z palca; sfałszować
fabulous ['faebjules] adj.
bajeczny; legendarny;
fantastyczny
facade [fe'sa:d] s. fasada
face [fejs] s. twarz; oblicze;
mina; grymas; czelność;
śmiałość; powierzchnia lica;
prawa strona; obuch; v.
stawiać czoła; stanąć
wobec; napotykać; stać
frontem do ...; wykładać
powierzchnię; oblicować
face-lifting ['fejs-lyftyng] v.
operacyjnie usuwać
zmarszczki
facet ['faesyt] s. ścianka
(brylantu)
facetious [fe'si:szes] adj.
żartobliwy; krotochwilny
facilitate [fe'sylytejt] v.
ułatwiać; udogadniać;
uprzystępniać
facility [fe'sylyty] s. łatwość;
zręczność; udogodnienia;
układność; swada;
zgodność

facsimile [faek'simily] s.
dokładna reprodukcja; kopia
fact [faekt] s. fakt; stan
rzeczywisty; podstawa
twierdzenia
factor ['faekter] s. czynnik;
współczynnik; część;
okoliczność
faculty ['faekelty] s. zdolność;
władza; wydział; fakultet;
grono profesorskie; dar; zmysł
fad [faed] s. moda; kaprys;
konik; bzik; chwilowa moda;
dziwactwo
fade [fejd] v. więdnąć;
blednąć; zanikać; płowieć;
pełznąć
fail [feil] v. chybić; zawodzić;
nie udać się; brakować;
bankrutować; omieszkać;
słabnąć; załamać się;
zamierać; zepsuć się
failure ['fejljer] s. niepowodzenie;
brak; upadek; zawał (serca);
niezdara; stopień
niedostateczny; pechowiec
faint [fejnt] adj. słaby; omdlały;
bojaźliwy; s. omdlenie; v.
mdleć; słabnąć; zasłabnąć
fair [feer] adj. piękny; jasny;
uczciwy; honorowy; czysty;
pomyślny; niezły; adv. prosto;
honorowo; pomyślnie;
pięknie; v. wypogadzać się;
wygładzać; przepisywać na
czysto; s. targ; targi; jarmark;
targowisko
fairly ['feerly] adv. słusznie;
uczciwie; całkowicie; zupełnie;
dość; rzetelnie; wręcz; po
prostu
fair play ['feer'plej] szlachetne
postępowanie; czysta gra
fairness ['feernys] s. piękność;
jasność; sprawiedliwość;
bezstronność; uczciwość;
uroda
fairy ['feery] s. czarodziejka; adj.
zaczarowany; czarodziejski
fairy-tale ['feerytejl] s. bajka
faith [fejs] s. wiara; zaufanie;
wierność; wyznanie;
słowność

faithful ['fejsful] adj. wierny;
uczciwy; sumienny;
skrupulatny
faithless ['fejslys] adj. niewierny;
wiarołomny; zdradziecki
fake [fejk] v. fałszować;
oszukiwać; podrabiać; s.
fałszerstwo; oszustwo; kant;
lipa; szwindel
falcon ['fo:lken] s. sokół
fall; fell; fallen [fo:l; fel:; fo:len]
fall [fo:l] v. padać; opadać;
wpadać; marnieć; zdarzać
się; przypadać; s. upadek;
spadek; jesień; opad; schyłek;
obniżka
fall back ['fo:l,baek] v.cofać się
fall ill ['fo:l,yl] v. zachorować;
rozchorować się
fall in love ['fo:l,yn'law] v.
zakochać się
fallout ['fo:lałt] s. skutek
uboczny; pył radioaktywny;
wrażenie na publiczności i
prasie (z wypowiedzi, planów)
fall out ['fo:l,ałt] v. poróżnić
się; rozejść się! (komenda)
fall short ['fo:l,szo:rt]
nieosiągnąć;
niewywiązywać się
fallen ['fo:len] upadły; zob. fall
false [fo:ls] adj. fałszywy;
kłamliwy; adv. zdradliwie;
fałszywie
falsehood ['fo:lshud] s. fałsz;
kłamstwo; nieprawda;
kłamliwość
falsify ['fo:lsyfaj] v. fałszować
przekręcać; kłamać;
zawodzić; podrabiać;
oszukać
falter ['fo:lter] v. chwiać się;
wahać się; potykać się;
jąkać się; s. chwiejność;
jąkanie
fame [fejm] s. sława; wieść;
fama
famed [fejmd] adj. sławny;
znany; głośny; słynący z
familiar [fe'myljer] adj. zażyły;
poufały; znany; obeznany
familiarity [fe,myly'aeryty] s.
zażyłość; poufałość;

obeznanie; znajomość
familiarize [fe'myljerajz] v.
obeznać; obznajomić;
oswoić; spoufalić;
spopularyzować
family ['faemyly] s. rodzina; adj.
rodzinny
family name ['faemyly,nejm] s.
nazwisko
family tree ['faemyly,tri:] s.
drzewo genealogiczne
famine ['faemyn] s. głód; klęska
głodu; ogólne braki
wszystkiego
famish ['faemysz] v. głodzić;
wygłodnieć; głodować;
morzyć głodem
famous ['fejmes] adj. znany;
sławny; znakomity; świetny;
nie byle jaki
fan [faen] v. wachlować;
rozdmuchiwać; wiać;
rozpościerać; wywiewać; s.
wachlarz; wentylator; wialnia;
żagiel i śmigło (wiatraka);
entuzjasta; miłośnik; kibic; a.
wachlarzowaty
fanatic [fe'naetyk] adj. zagorzały;
fanatyczny; s. fanatyk
fanciful ['faensyful] adj.
dziwaczny; kapryśny;
fantastyczny; zmyślony;
wyszukany; fantazyjny
fancy ['faensy] s. urojenie;
złudzenie; fantazja; kaprys;
humor; pomysł; chętka; a.
pstry
fancy dress ball ['faensy'dres
,bo:l] s. bal kostiumowy
fancy-free ['faensy,fri:] adj.
wolny od trosk; nie zakochany
fancy work ['faensy,łe:rk] s.
robótki ręczne
fang [faeng] s. ząb jadowity;
kieł; sztyft; korzeń; v. dławić
pompę
fantastic [faen'taestyk] adj.
fantastyczny; s. fantasta
fantasy ['faentsy] s. fantazja;
wyobraźnia; kaprys
far [fa:r] adv. daleko
far away ['fa:r,ełej] adv. hen;
daleko; adj. daleki; odległy

far from ['fa:r,from] adv.
bynajmniej; daleko od
fare [feer] s. pasażer; bilet
pasażerski; pożywienie;
potrawa; v. być w położeniu;
mieć się; wieść się; czuć
się; odżywiać się; jadać;
podróżować
farewell [,feer'łel] s. pożegnanie;
adj. pożegnalny; v. żegnaj; do
widzenia
farfetched [,fa:r'feczt] adj.
przesadny; naciągany;
wyszukany; nierozsądny
far-flung [,fa:r'flang] adj. szeroko
rozrzucony; rozgałęziony;
zakrojony na szeroką skalę
farm [fa:rm] s. ferma;
gospodarstwo rolne; kolonia
hodowlana; v. uprawiać;
dzierżawić; wydzierżawiać;
wynajmować;
poddzierżawiać; prowadzić
gospodarstwo
farmer ['fa:rmer] s. rolnik;
farmer; dzierżawca; hodowca
farmhand ['fa:rm,haend] s.
parobek; robotnik rolny
farmhouse ['fa:rm,haus] s.
dworek; gospodarski dom
mieszkalny
farming ['fa:rmyng] s. rolnictwo;
gospodarka rolna; dzierżawa
farm worker [,fa:rm'łe:rker] s.
robotnik rolny; parobek
farmyard ['fa:rm,ja:rd] s.
podwórze fermy; podwórze
gospodarskie na fermie
farsighted ['fa:r'sajtyd] adj.
przewidujący; dalekowidz;
dalekowzroczny
farther ['fa:rdzer] adj. dalszy;
adv. dalej; ponadto; poza tym;
prócz tego
farthest ['fa:rdzest] adj.
najdalszy; adv. najdalej;
najpóźniej
fascinate ['faesynejt] v.
urzekać; czarować;
fascynować; hipnotyzować
zachwycić
fascination [,faesy'nejszyn] s.
urok; czar; oczarowanie;

olśnienie
fascist ['faeszyst] s. faszysta;
adj. faszystowski;
faszystowska
fashion ['faeszyn] s. moda;
fason; kształt; wzór; sposób;
v. kształtować; fasonować;
modelować; urabiać
fashionable ['faesznebl] adj.
modny; s. człowiek wytworny
fast [faest] adj. szybki;
przytwierdzony; mocny;
twardy; zwodniczy; adv.
mocno; pewnie; trwale; v.
pościć; s. post
fasten ['faesn] v. umocować;
zamykać; przymocować
fastener ['faesner] s.
przymocowanie (np.
gwóźdź); spinacz; zatrzask;
zasuwka
fastidious [fes'tydjes] adj.
wybredny; grymaśny;
wymagający
fat [faet] s. tłuszcz; tusza; adj.
tłusty; tuczny; głupi; tępy;
urodzajny; zyskowny
fatal ['fejtl] adj. fatalny;
śmiertelny; nieuchronny
fate ['fejt] s. los; przeznaczenie;
zguba; fatum; v. los rządzi ...
father ['fa:dzer] s. ojciec
fatherhood ['fa:dzerhud] s.
ojcostwo; starszeństwo (w
służbie)
father-in-law ['fa:dzerynlo:] s.
teść; ojciec męża lub żony
fatherland ['fa:dzerlaend] s.
ojczyzna; ojczysty kraj
fatherly ['fa:dzerly] adj.
ojcowski; jak ojciec; dobrotliw
fathom ['faedzem] s. sążeń
fathomless ['faedzemlys] s.
bezdenny; niezgłębiony
fatigue [fe'ti:g] s. zmęczenie
(człowieka lub materiału);
służba porządkowa; v.
trudzić; męczyć
fatten ['faetn] v. tuczyć; tyć;
użyźniać ziemię; utyć;
utuczyć
fattening ['faetnyng] adj.
tuczący

fatty ['faety] adj. tłuszczowy; s. tłuścioch; grubas

faucet ['fo:syt] s. kurek (od wody); czop; tuleja

fault ['fo:lt] s. błąd; wada; wina; uskok; usterka; brak; defekt

faultless ['fo:ltlys] adj. bezbłędny; nienaganny; doskonały

faulty ['fo:lty] adj. wadliwy; nieprawidłowy; nieścisły; błędny

favor ['fejwer] s. łaska; uprzejmość; upominek; v. sprzyjać; zaszczycać; faworyzować

favorable ['fejwerebl] adj. życzliwy; łaskawy; sprzyjający; korzystny (dla kogoś, czegoś)

favorite ['fejweryt] s. ulubieniec; faworyt; adj. ulubiony

fawn [fo:n] v. ocielić; łasić się; przymilać (się); płaszczyć się (przed kimś); s. jelonek; sarenka; adj. brunatny; płowy

FAX ['faeks] s. elektroniczna transmisja kopii dokumentów; system przesyłania kopii dokumentów przez telefon (zob. facsimile)

fear [fier] s. strach; obawa; v. bać się; obawiać się

fearful ['fierful] adj. okropny; straszny; wystraszony; bojaźliwy; bojący się; pełen strachu

fearless ['fierlys] adj. nieustraszony; bardzo odważny

feasible ['fi:zebl] adj. wykonalny; możliwy do przeprowadzenia

feast [fi:st] s. święto; odpust; biesiada; v. ucztować; sycić się; ugaszać pragnienie

feat [fi:t] s. wyczyn; czyn (bohaterski); (dokazana) sztuka

feather ['fedzer] s. pióro; v. zdobić piórami

featherbed ['fedzerbed] s. piernat; pierzyna; lekka praca

feathered ['fedzerd] adj. upierzony; pokryty piórami

feathery ['fedzery] adj. puchaty; miękki jak puch; leciutki

feature ['fi:czer] s. cecha; rys; atrakcja; film długometrażowy; v. cechować; odgrywać

February ['februery] s. luty

fed [fed] adj. karmiony; zob. feed

federal ['federel] adj. związkowy; federalny

federation [,fede'rejszyn] s. federacja; konfederacja

fee [fi:] s. opłata; wpisowe; należność; honorarium; v. płacić honorarium; płacić wpisowe

feeble ['fi:bl] adj. słaby

feed; fed; fed [fi:d; fed; fed]

feed [fi:d] v. karmić; paść; zasilać; s. pasza; obrok; zasilacz; posuw

feeder [fi:der] s. boczna (droga); dopływ; przewód zasilający

feel; felt; felt [fi:l; felt; felt]

feel [fi:l] v. czuć (się); odczuwać; macać; dotykać

feel well ['fi:l,łel] v. czuć się dobrze; być zdrowym

feel bad ['fi:l,baed] v. czuć się źle

feeler ['fi:ler] s. macka; sonda; próbny balon; szperacz

feeling ['fi:lyng] s. dotyk; uczucie; odczucie; poczucie; takt; wrażliwość; adj. wrażliwy; czuły; współczujący; szczery; wzruszony

feet [fi:t] pl. stopy; nogi

feign [fejn] v. udawać; symulować; znaleźć wymówkę

fell [fel] v. ścinać (drzewo); zob. fall

felloe ['felou] s. dzwono (koła)

fellow ['felou] s. towarzysz; człowiek; chłop; gość; facet; odpowiednik; wykładowca; adiunkt

fellow being ['felou bi:yng] s. bliźni

fellow citizen ['felou'sytyzen] s.

współobywatel
fellowship ['felouszyp] s. udział;
wspólnota; związek;
towarzystwo; przyjaźń; cech
felon ['felen] s. przestępca; adj.
okrutny; zły; zbrodniczy
felony ['feleny] s. przestępstwo;
zbrodnia
felt [felt] czuły; zob. feel
felt [felt] s. wojłok; filc
female ['fi:mejl] s. kobieta;
niewiasta; samica; adj.
żeński; kobiecy; wewnętrzny
(gwint)
feminine ['femynyn] adj. żeński;
kobiecy; zniewieściały; s.
rodzaj żeński; a. rodzaju
żeńskiego
fen [fen] s. bagno; trzęsawisko;
nizina bagienna
fence [fens] s. płot; ogrodzenie;
szermierka; v. ogrodzić;
fechtować się; odpowiadać
wykrętnie
fencing ['fensyng] s. szermierka;
płot; ogrodzenie; paserstwo
fend for ['fend,fo:r] v.
zaspokajać potrzeby;
utrzymywać
fend off ['fend,of] v. odbijać;
odparowywać; chronić;
ochraniać
fender ['fender] s. błotnik;
zderzak; zasłona
fennel ['fenel] s. koper
ferment ['fe:rment] s. ferment;
ermentacja; v. wywoływać
fermentację; podniecać;
fermentować
fermentation [,fe:rmen'tejszyn] s.
fermentacja; ferment
fern [fe:rn] s. paproć
ferocity [fe'rosyty] s. dzikość;
okrucieństwo; srogość
ferry ['fery] v. przeprawiać
promem; kursować; s. prom
ferryboat ['ferybout] s. prom
fertile ['fe:rtajl] adj. żyzny;
płodny; zapłodniony;
obfitujący
fertility [fer'tylyty] s. żyzność;
płodność; urodzajność
fertilize ['fe:rtylajz] v. użyźniać

nawozić; zapładniać;
zapylać
fertilizer ['fe:rtylajzer] s. nawóz
sztuczny
fervent ['fe:rwent] adj. żarliwy;
gorący; płomienny; gorliwy
fester ['fester] v. jątrzyć (się);
ropieć; gnić; s. ropiejąca
rana; mały wrzód; ropniak;
zajad
festival ['festewel] adj.
świąteczny; odświątny; s.
święto
festive ['festyw] adj. uroczysty;
wesoły; radosny; biesiadny
festivity [fes'tywyty] s.
wesołość; zabawa;
uroczystość
fetch [fecz] v. iść po coś;
przynieść; przywieźć; s.
odległość
fetish [fet'ysz] s. fetysz
fetter ['feter] v. skuć; spętać
feud [fju:d] s. lenno; waśń
rodowa; wojna między
klanami
feudal ['fju:dl] adj. feudalny
fever ['fy:wer] s. gorączka
feverish ['fy:werysz] adj.
gorączkowy;
rozgorączkowany
few [fju:] adj. & pron. mało;
kilka; niewielu; nieliczni; kilku;
kilkoro
fiance [fi'a:nsej] s. narzeczony(a)
fib [fyb] s. kłamstwo; v.
cyganić; okładać; s. cios;
uderzenie
fiber ['fajber] s. włókno; siła
ducha; charakter; łyko;
budowa
fibrous ['fajberes] adj. włóknisty;
łykowaty
fickle ['fykl] adj. zmienny;
niestały; płochy; wietrzny
fiction ['fykszyn] s. fikcja;
urojenie; beletrystyka; wymysł
fictitious [fyk'tyszes] a. fikcyjny;
urojony; fałszywy
fiddle ['fydl] v. grać na
skrzypcach; baraszkować; s.
skrzypce
fiddler ['fydler] s. skrzypek;

skrzypaczka
fidelity [fy'delyty] s. wierność;
dokładność; ścisłość
fidget ['fydżyt] v. wiercić się;
niepokoić się; s. niepokój;
człowiek niespokojny
fidgety ['fydżyty] adj. wiercący
się; niespokojny; niecierpliwy
field [fi:ld] s. pole; boisko;
drużyna; dziedzina; v.
ustawiać na boisku;
zatrzymać (piłkę);
poprowadzić do akcji
field-events ['fi:ld,ywents] pl.
lekkoatletyka
field-glasses ['fi:ld,glasys] pl.
lornetka polowa
field-gun ['fi:ld,gan] s. działo
polowe
fiend ['fy:nd] s. zły duch; szatan;
demon; nałogowiec;
zagorzalec
fierce [fiers] adj. dziki; srogi;
zażarty; wściekły; zawzięty;
nieopanowany; gwałtowny
fiery ['fajery] adj. ognisty;
płomienny; palący; zapalny;
burzliwy; popędliwy;
choleryczny
fife [fajf] s. piszczałka; v. grać
na piszczałce (na fujarce)
fifteen ['fyf'ti:n] num.
piętnaście; piętnaścioro;
piętnastka
fifteenth ['fyf'ti:nt] num.
piętnasty; jedna piętnasta
część
fiftieth ['fyftjet] num.
pięćdziesiąty; jedna
pięćdziesiąta
fifty ['fyfty] num. pięćdziesiąt
fig [fyg] s. figa; strój
fight; fought; fought [fajt; fo:t;
fo:t]
fight [fajt] s. walka; bitwa;
zapasy; bój; duch do walki;
mecz bokserski; v. walczyć
(przeciw lub o coś); bić się
fighter ['fajter] s. bojownik;
zapaśnik; samolot myśliwski
figurative ['fygjurejtyw] adj.
obrazowy; przenośny;
symboliczny

figure ['fyger] s. kształt; postać;
wizerunek; cyfra; wzór; v.
figurować; liczyć;
rachować; oznaczać cenami;
wyobrażać; przedstawiać
figure out ['fyger,aut] v.
obliczać; wynosić; składać
się na
figure skating ['fyger,skejtyng] s.
jazda figurowa na łyżwach
filament ['fylement] s. włókno;
nitka; drucik jarzeniowy; żyła
mineralna
file [fajl] s. rejestr; archiwum;
seria; pilnik; v. archiwować;
defilować; piłować pilnikiem;
wnosić (podanie, skargę);
iść rzędem (rzędami);
maszerować
fill [fyl] v. napełniać;
plombować ząb; osadzać; s.
wypełnienie; napicie i
najedzenie do syta; nasyp;
ładunek; porcja
fill in ['fyl,yn] v. zapełniać;
wypełniać (formularze,
blankiety)
fill up ['fyl,ap] v. wypełniać;
zapełniać; nabierać benzyny
fillet ['fylyt] s. wstążki; zraz
zawijany; dzwonko; v.
przepasywać; wycinać filety
fillet ['fylej] v. dzielić na
dzwonka; wycinać dzwonka
filling ['fylyng] s. nadziewka;
plomba; wątek; zapas
benzyny
filing station ['fylyng,st'ejszyn] s.
stacja benzynowa
filly ['fyly] s. źrebica; koza;
młoda dziewczyna; dzierlatka
film [fylm] s. powłoka; błona;
warstwa; film; mgiełka;
bielmo; v. pokrywać błoną;
filmować
filter ['fylter] s. filtr; sączek; v.
filtrować; przeciekać
filth [fyls] s. brud; plugastwo
filthy ['fylsy] adj. brudny;
plugawy; niegodziwy;
sprośny
fin [fyn] s. płetwa; v. obcinać
płetwy; ruszać płetwami

finagle ['fy'nejgl] v. oszukiwać;
wyłudzać; nabierać
final ['fajnl] adj. końcowy;
ostateczny; s. finał (sport,
egzamin etc.); coś
ostatecznego
finally ['fajnly] adv. w końcu;
wreszcie; na końcu;
ostatecznie
finance [faj'naens] s. finanse;
skarbowość; v. finansować;
udzielać pożyczki
financial [faj'naenszel] adj.
pieniężny; finansowy
financier [,fynaen'sjer] s.
finansista; v. spekulować;
sprzeniewierzać pieniądze
finch [fyncz] s. łuszczak; ptak z
krótkim dziobem
find; found; found [fajnd; faund;
faund]
find [fajnd] v. znajdować;
konstatować; dowiedzieć się
find out ['fajnd,aut] v. wykryć;
wynaleźć; dowiedzieć się
finder ['fajnder] s. znalazca;
odkrywca; wizjer; dalekomierz
finding ['fajndyng] s. odkrycie;
stwierdzenie; dane; wniosek
fine [fajn] adj. piękny; misterny;
czysty; przedni; wyszukany;
dokładny; adv. świetnie;
wspaniale; s. grzywna; kara;
v. ukarać grzywną
finery ['fajnry] s. szyk; elegancja;
strojny ubiór
finger ['fynger] s. palec; kciuk;
v. przebierać w palcach;
wskazywać palcem; brać
palcami
finger nail ['fynger,nejl] s.
paznokieć
finger print ['fynger,prynt] odcisk
palca
finish ['fynysz] s. koniec;
wykończenie; v. kończyć;
skończyć; wykończyć;
dokończyć
finite ['fajnajt] adj. skończony;
ograniczony; końcowy
Finnish ['fynysz] adj. fiński
fir [fe:r] s. jodła; jedlina
fire ['fajer] s. ogień; pożar

fire alarm ['fajer,e'la:rm] s.
sygnał pożarowy; alarm
pożarowy
firearm ['fajera:rm] s. broń palna
(armaty, strzelby etc.)
firebug ['fajer,bag] s. świetlik;
robaczek świętojański
fire brigade ['fajerbry,gejd] s.
straż pożarna
fire department ['fajer
,dy'pa:rtment] s. miejska straż
pożarna; straż ogniowa
fire engine ['fajer'endżyn] s. wóz
straży ogniowej (pompa)
fire escape ['fajerys,kejp] s.
wyjście zapasowe; schody
zapasowe
fire extinguisher ['fajer
yks,tyngłyszer] s. gaśnica
fireman ['fajermen] s. strażak
fireplace ['fajer-plejs] s. kominek;
palenisko
fireproof ['fajerpru:f] adj.
ogniotrwały; ognioodporny
fireside ['fajersajd] s. przy
kominku; kominek; ognisko
domowe
firewood ['fajerłud] s. drzewo
opałowe; drewno opałowe
fireworks ['fajerłe:rks] pl. ognie
sztuczne; hałaśliwe sceny
firm [fe:rm] s. firma; adv.
mocno; adj. pewny;
stanowczy; trwały; v. ubijać;
osadzać (mocno); umacniać
się
firmness ['fe:rmnys] s. stałość;
trwałość; stanowczość;
jędrność; moc; energia
first ['fe:rst] adj. pierwszy; adv.
najpierw; po raz pierwszy;
początkowo; na początku
first of all ['fe:rst,ow'o:l] przede
wszystkim; najpierw
first aid ['fe:rst,ejd] pierwsza
pomoc; doraźna pomoc;
opatrunek
first aid kit ['fe:rst,ejd kyt]
podręczna apteczka; zestaw
pierwszej pomocy
(opatrunków etc.)
firstborn ['fe:rstbo:rn] adj.
pierworodny (syn, dziecko)

first class ['fe:rst'klas] s.
pierwsza klasa; a. najlepszej
jakości
first-class ['fe:rst'klas] adj.
pierwszorzędny; wspaniały
first floor ['fe:rst flo:r] s. parter;
w Anglii pierwsze piętro
first hand ['fe:rst,haend] adj.
bezpośredni; z pierwszej ręki
firstly ['fe:rstly] adv. po
pierwsze; najpierw
first name ['fe:rst,nejm] s. imię
(chrzestne)
first-rate ['fe:rst,rejt] adj.
pierwszorzędny; adv.
pierwszorzędnie; bardzo
dobrze
firth [fe:rs] n. odnoga morska;
zatoka (zwłaszcza w Szkocji)
fish [fysz] s. ryba; v. łowić ryby
fish-bone ['fyszboun] s. ość
fisherman ['fyszemen] s. rybak
fishery ['fyszery] s.
rybołówstwo; teren połowu
lub hodowli
fishing ['fyszyng] s.
wędkarstwo; rybołówstwo;
połów
fishing line ['fyszyng,lajn] s.
linka; żyłka od wędki
fishing rod ['fyszyng,rod] s.
wędka
fishing tackle ['fyszyng,taekl] s.
sprzęt rybacki
fishmonger ['fyszmanger] s.
handlarz ryb; sklep z rybami
fission ['fyszyn] s. dzielenie;
rozbicie (atomu);
rozszczepienie; rozerwanie
fissure ['fyszer] s. szczelina;
pęknięcie; v. rozszczepiać;
pękać; łupać (się)
fist [fyst] s. pięść; v. uderzać
fit [fyt] s. atak (choroby, gniewu
etc.); krój; dopasowanie; adj.
dostosowany; odpowiedni;
nadający się; gotów; zdatny;
dobrze leżący; v. sprostać;
dobrze leżeć; przygotować
się
fit on [fyt on] v. przymierzać
fit out [fyt aut] v. zaopatrywać;
s. wyposażenie; umeblowanie

fitness ['fytnys] s.
stosowność; kondycja;
trafność (uwagi);
przyzwoitość
fitter ['fyter] s. monter; krawiec
dokonujący przymiarek;
ślusarz
fitting ['fytyng] s. okucie;
oprawa; przymiarka; adj.
odpowiedni; właściwy;
trafny; stosowny
five [fajw] num. pięć; pięcioro;
piąta (godzina); piątka (numer
obuwia)
fix [fyks] v. umocować;
przyczepiać; ustalać;
utkwić; zgęszczać; tężeć;
krzepnąć; urządzić kogoś
(źle); usytuować;
zaaranżować wynik
(zapasów); s. kłopot; dylemat;
położenie nawigacyjne (statku,
samolotu etc.)
fix up [fyks,ap] v. naprawić;
uporządkować; ulokować
(kogoś)
fixed [fykst] adj. trwały; stały;
nieruchomy; niezmienny
fixedly ['fyksydly] adv. stale;
trwale; uporczywie
fixture ['fyksczer] s. urządzenie
przymocowane
fizz [fyz] s. syk; napój musujący;
v. syczeć; musować
flabbergast ['flaebergaest] v.
zdumieć; odebrać mowę (ze
zdumienia); oszołamiać
flabby ['flaeby] adj. zwiotczały;
obwisły; miękki; słaby;
niedbały; bez charakteru
flag [flaeg] s. flaga; chorągiew;
lotka; v. wywieszać flagę;
sygnalizować
flagstone ['flaeg,stoun] s. płyta
brukowa; płyta chodnikowa
flak [flaek] s. artyleria
przeciwlotnicza (niemiecka)
flake [flejk] s. płatek; łuska;
iskra; v. prószyć;
odpryskiwać łuszczyć;
padać płatkami
flake off ['flejk,of] v. złuszczyć
(się); odpadać płatkami

flame [flejm] s. płomień;
miłość; v. zionąć;
błyszczeć; płonąć; opalać;
migotać; być podnieconym

flank [flaenk] s. bok; flanka; v.
flankować; strzec flanki

flannel ['flaenl] s. flanela; v.
wycierać flanelą; ubierać we
flanelę (lekka wełna)

flap [flaep] s. trzepot; klapnięcie;
klapa; poła; płat; pokrywa; v.
trzepotać; zwisać; klapnąć;
uderzyć czymś płaskim

flare [fleer] v. błyszczeć;
sygnalizować; popisywać
się; rozszerzać się; s. jasny
płomień

flare up [fleer ap] s. wybuch;
błysk; v. wybuchnąć
(gniewem, płomieniem);
reagować gwałtownie

flash [flaesz] s. błysk; blask; adj.
błyskotliwy; fałszywy;
gwarowy; v. zabłysnąć;
sygnalizować; pędzić;
mknąć; wysyłać
(natychmiastowo
wiadomości)

flashbulb ['flaeszbalb] s.
żarówka (do zdjęć); flesz

flashlight ['flaeszlajt] s. latarka
(elektryczna)

flashy ['flaeszy] adj. błyskotliwy
(chwilowo); jaskrawy;
krzykliwy

flask [flaesk] s. flaszka; flakon;
kolba; opleciona flaszka wina

flat [flaet] adj. płaski; płytki;
nudny; równy; stanowczy;
oczywisty; matowy;
bezbarwny; adv. płasko;
stanowczo; dokładnie; s.
płaszczyzna; równina;
mieszkanie; przedziurawiona
dętka; v. rozpłaszczyć;
matować

flatten ['flaetn] v. spłaszczyć
(się); matowieć; wietrzeć;
równać

flatter ['flaeter] v. pochlebiać

flattery ['flaetery] s.
pochlebstwo; schlebianie
komuś

flavor ['flejwer] s. smak; zapach;
v. dawać smak; mieć
posmak

flaw [flo:] s. skaza; rysa;
pęknięcie; v. psuć; pękać

flawless ['flo:les] adj. bez skazy;
(przedstawienie) bez usterek

flax [flaeks] s. len

flaxen [flak'sn] adj. płowy; lniany

flea [fli:] s. pchła

fled [fled] zob. flee

fledgling ['fledżlyng] s. świeżo
opierzony ptak; żółtodziób

flee; fled; fled [fli:; fled; fled]

flee [fli:] v. uciekać; pierzchać

fleece [fli:s] s. runo; wełna;
czupryna; puch; v. strzyc;
skubać; pokrywać puchem

fleet [fli:t] s. flota; park
pojazdów; v. mknąć;
przemknąć; mijać; adj.
płytki; adv. płytko

flesh [flesz] s. ciało; miąższ

fleshy ['fleszy] adj. mięsisty;
tłusty; cielesny; zmysłowy

flew [flu:] zob. fly

flexible [fl'eksybl] adj. giętki;
gibki; układny; obrotny;
elastyczny; łatwo
przystosowujący się;
ustępliwy; poddający się

flick [flyk] s. przytyk;
śmignięcie; smuga; v.
śmignąć; trzepnąć; rzucać
się; trzepotać się; zapalać
zapalniczkę

flicker ['flyker] s. mig; miganie;
drganie; trzepot; v. migać;
drgać; trzepotać; machać;
lekko się poruszać

flier ['flajer] s. lotnik; ulotka;
pośpieszny pociąg etc.

flight [flajt] s. lot; przelot;
ucieczka; kondygnacja
schodów

flight engineer ['flajt,endży'nier]
s. mechanik pokładowy

flimsy ['flymzy] adj. cienki;
wątły; słaby (papier,
wymówka ...)

flinch [flyncz] v. uchylać się;
cofać się; drgać; s. unik

fling; flung; flung [flyng; flang;

flang]
fling [flyng] v. rzucać (się);
powalić; wypaść; wierzgać
fling open ['flyn,oupen] v.
rozewrzeć (gwałtownie)
flint [flynt] s. krzemień;
krzesiwo; kamyk do
zapalniczki
flip [flyp] v. prztykać; rzucać;
wyprztykiwać; s. prztyk
flippant ['flypent] adj.
niepoważny; impertynencki
flipper ['flyper] s. płetwa nożna;
graba; łapa; błona pławna
flirt [fle:rt] v. flirtować;
machać; s. flirciarz; flirciarka;
machnięcie (raptowne)
flirtation [,fle:r'tejszyn] s. flirt;
powierzchowny romans
flit [flyt] v. biegać; fruwać;
wyjechać; poruszać się
zwinnie
float [flout] v. unosić się;
pływać na powierzchni;
spławiać; puszczać w obieg;
lansować; s. pływak; tratwa;
platforma na kołach; gładzik
do tynku; niezdecydowany
ruch
flock [flok] s. trzoda; stado;
tłum; v. tłoczyć się; iść
tłumem; gromadzić się
floe [flou] s. kra (lodowa)
flog [flog] v. chłostać; smagać;
bić; biczować się
flood [flad] s. powódź; wylew;
potok; v. zalewać nawadniać
floodlights ['flad,lajts] pl.
reflektory (szeroko-stożkowe)
flood tide ['fladtajd] s. przypływ
(morza); fala powodziowa
floor [flo:r] s. podłoga; dno
floor cloth ['flo:rklo:s] s. szmata
do podłogi; linoleum
floor lamp ['flo:r,laemp] s. lampa
stojąca na podłodze
floor show ['flo:r,szou] s.
przedstawienie kabaretowe
flop [flop] s. klapanie; klapa;
fiasko; v. klapnąć; załamać
się; zrobić klapę; a.
dziadowski
florist ['floryst] s. kwiaciarz;

kwiaciarka; hodowca kwiatów
flounder ['flaunder] s. flądra;
brnięcie; v. brnąć; brodzić;
błądzić; wystękać (mowę)
flour [flauer] s. mąka; v. mleć
na mąkę; dodawać mąki
(posypywać)
flourish ['flarysz] s. fanfara;
wymachiwanie; v. kwitnąć;
zdobić kwiatami;
wymachiwać
flow [flou] s. strumień; prąd;
przepływ; dopływ; v. płynąć;
lać się; zalewać; ruszać się
płynnie
flower [flauer] s. kwiat; v.
kwitnąć; być w rozkwicie
flown [floun] zob. fly
fluctuate ['flaktjuejt] v. falować;
wahać się; być
niezdecydowanym
flu [flu:] s. grypa; influenca
fluent ['fluent] adj. płynny; biegły
i wymowny (mówca, pisarz)
fluff [flaf] s. puch; v. trzepać;
knocić
fluffy ['flafy] adj. puszysty; lekki
fluid ['flu:yd] s. płyn; adj.
płynny; płynnie poruszający
się
flung [flang] zob. fling
flunk [flank] v. oblać (egzamin);
spalić (ucznia); nie zdać;
zawalić
flurry ['fle:ry] s. wichura; ulewa;
śnieżyca; podniecenie;
rozgardiasz; v. oszałamiać;
denerwować; wprowadzać
zamieszanie
flush [flasz] v. rumienić się;
napełniać; spłukiwać; s.
rumieniec; rozkwit; blask; adj.
wylewający się; krzepki;
rumiany; równy; etc.; adv.
równo; prosto; gładko; pełno;
poziomo; sowicie (wyposażać
w pieniądze)
fluster ['flaster] s. podniecenie;
niepokój; v. podniecać;
oszałamiać; kręcić się
flute [flu:t] s. flet; rowkowanie
flutter ['flater] s. trzepotanie;
dygotanie; niepokój; v.

trzepotać; drzeć; dygotać;
płoszyć; powodować
trzepotanie
flux [flaks] s. prąd; przepływ;
potok; płynność; krwotok;
przypływ; pasta do lutowania
fly [flaj] s. mucha; klapka
fly; flew; flown [flaj; flu; floun]
v. latać; lecieć; powiewać;
uciekać; przewozić
samolotem; puszczać
(latawca)
fly across [,flaj e'kros] v.
przelatywać (przez)
flyblown ['flaj-bloun] adj.
popstrzony przez muchy
fly into a rage ['flaj,yntu ej'rejdż]
v. wpaść w pasję
flyer ['flajer] s. lotnik
flying ['flajyng] adj. latający;
lotny; lotniczy; krótkotrwały;
samolotowy; pośpieszny
flying boat ['flajynbout] s.
hydroplan (do wodowania)
flying buttress ['flajyn,batrys] s.
łuk przyporowy
flying machine ['flajyng,meszi:n]
s. samolot
flying time ['flajyng,tajm] s. czas
przelotu; czas lotu
fly weight ['flaj,łejt] s. waga
musza (112 funtów lub mniej)
flywheel ['flajhłi:l] s. koło
zamachowe (do regulowania
szybkości)
foal [foul] s. źrebię
foam [foum] s. piana; v. pienić
się; a. pianowy; piankowy
foamy ['foumy] adj. pieniący się;
pienisty; spieniony
focus ['foukes] s. ognisko;
ogniskowa; v. skupiać;
ogniskować; koncentrować;
ześrodkowywać
fodder ['foder] s. pasza
foe [fou] s. wróg; przeciwnik
fog [fog] s. mgła; v. otumaniać
foggy ['fogy] adj. mglisty
foible ['fojbl] s. słabostka; lekka
słabość charakteru;
słabość; wątłość
foil [fojl] s. folia; tło; floret; trop;
ślad; v. udaremnić; zacierać

(ślad); niweczyć
fold [fould] s. fałda; zagięcie;
zagroda (owiec); v. składać;
zaginać (się); splatać;
zamykać owce (w owczarni);
fałdować
folder ['foulder] s. składana
teczka; broszura; falcownik
folding ['fouldyng] adj. składany;
rozsuwany; s. fałd; fałda
folding boat ['fouldyng bout]
składana łódź (turystyczna)
folding chair ['fouldyng,czeer]
składane krzesło (kampingowe)
foliage ['fouljydż] s. listowie;
liście (rosnące); ulistnienie
folk [fouk] s. ludzie; krewni; lud;
rasa; adj. ludowy;
folklorystyczny
folklore ['fouklo:r] s. folklor
folksy ['fouksy] adj. towarzyski;
prosty; ludzki
folk song ['fouksong] s. pieśń
ludowa (regionalna etc.)
follow ['folou] v. iść za;
następować za; śledzić;
rozumieć (kogoś); wnikać;
gonić; wynikać
follower ['folouer] s. stronnik;
zwolennik; uczeń; pomocnik
following ['folouyng] s.
zwolennicy; adj. następujący;
następny; s. orszak; świta;
posłuch; autorytet
folly ['foly] s. szaleństwo
foment [fou'ment] v. podżegać;
podsycać; nagrzewać;
pobudzać
fond [fond] adj. kochający;
czuły; łatwowierny; głupio
czuły
fondle ['fondl] v. pieścić
fondness ['fondnys] s. czułość;
miłość; zamiłowanie; pociąg
food [fu:d] s. żywność;
strawa; pokarm; jedzenie; a.
żywnościowy; odżywczy
fool [fu:l] s. głupiec; głuptas;
błazen; v. błaznować;
wyśmiewać; oszukiwać;
okpiwać; partaczyć
foolhardy ['fu:l,ha:rdy] adj.
szaleńczy; wariacki;

lekkomyślny; nieroztropny;
gwałtowny
foolish ['fu:lysz] adj. głupi
foolishness ['fu:lysznys] s.
głupota; głupstwo; bzdura;
nonsens
foolproof ['fu:l,pru:f] adj.
niezawodny; nie do zepsucia
foot [fut] s. stopa; dół; spód;
miara (30.5 cm); piechota; v.
płacić
foot the bill ['fut,ty'byl] v.
zapłacić rachunek
football ['fut,bo:l] s. piłka nożna;
futbol; piłka do nożnej
foot brake ['fut,brejk] s. hamulec
nożny w (samochodzie)
foothills ['fut,hylz] pl. podgórze
(przy łańcuchu górskim)
foothold ['fut,hould] s. oparcie
(dla nóg); miejsce gdzie
można stanąć; pewna
pozycja
footing ['futyng] s. fundament;
ostoja; podstawa; położenie
footpath ['futpas] s. ścieżka dla
pieszych; chodnik
footprint ['futprynt] s. ślad
stopy
footstep ['fut,step] s. odgłos
kroku; ślad; długość kroku
for [fo:r] prep. dla; zamiast; z;
do; na; żeby; że; za; po; co
do; co się tyczy; jak na;
mimo; wbrew; po coś; z
powodu; conj. ponieważ;
bowiem; gdyż; albowiem;
dlatego że
for two years ['fo:-tu-je:rs] przez
dwa lata
forbade [fe:r'bejd] zob. forbid
forbear; forbore; forborne
[fo:'beer; fe'bo:r; fe'bo:rn]
forbear ['fo:r'beer] v. znosić
cierpliwie; powstrzymywać
(się); s. wyrozumiałość;
przodek
forbid; forbade; forbidden
[fer'byd; fe:r'bejd; fer'bydn]
forbid [fer'byd] v. zakazywać;
zabraniać; nie dopuszczać;
uniemożliwiać; nie pozwalać
forbidding [fe'rbydyng] adj.

odpychający; posępny; ponury
forbore [fer'bo:r] zob. forbear
forborne [fer'bo:rn] zob. forbear
force [fo:rs] s. siła; moc; potęga;
sens; v. zmuszać; pędzić;
wpychać; forsować
forced landing ['fo:rst,laendyng]
przymusowe lądowanie
forceps ['fo:rsyps] pl. kleszcze;
szczypce; szczypczyki
forcible ['fo:rsybl] adj.
gwałtowny; przymusowy;
przekonywujący; mocny;
dosadny; bezprawny
ford [fo:rd] v. przeprawiać się
brodem; s. bród (płytkie
miejsce)
fore [fo:r] adj. przedni; adv. na
przedzie; s. przednia część
foreboding [fo:r'boudyng] s.
przeczucie (złego); złe
przeczucie
forecast ['fo:r-ka:st] v.
przewidywać; s.
przewidywanie
forefather ['fo:r,fa:dzer] s.
przodek; antenat
forefinger ['fo:rfynger] s. palec
wskazujący
forefoot ['fo:r-fut] s. przednia
noga (zwierzęcia)
foregone [fo:r'gon] adj.
przesądzony; miniony
foreground ['fo:rgraund] s.
pierwszy plan (obrazu)
forehead ['fo:ryd] s. czoło
foreign ['foryn] adj. obcy;
obcokrajowy; cudzoziemski
foreign currency [,foryn'karensy]
s. obca waluta
foreigner ['foryner] s.
cudzoziemiec; cudzoziemka;
obcokrajowiec
foreign policy ['foryn,polysy]
polityka zagraniczna
foreign trade ['foryn,trejd] handel
zagraniczny
foreleg ['fo:rleg] s. przednia noga
(zwierzęcia)
foreman ['fo:rmen] s. majster;
sztygar; starszy przysięgły
foremost ['fo:r,maust] adj.
główny; przedni; adv. przede

wszystkim; w pierwszym
rzędzie
forenoon ['fo:rnu:n] s.
przedpołudnie; a.
przedpołudniowy
foresee ['fo:rsi:] v.
przewidywać; przewidzieć;
wiedzieć z góry
foresight ['fo:rsajt] s.
przezorność; przewidywanie;
muszka celownika (przy
strzelbie etc.)
forest ['foryst] s. las; v.
zalesiać; a. leśny; w lesie
forester ['foryster] s. leśniczy;
leśnik; ptak leśny; ćma
leśna
forestry ['forystry] s. leśnictwo;
lasy; wiedza o lesie
foretaste ['fo:rtejst] s.
przedsmak; zapowiedź tego
co ma nastąpić
foretell; foretold; foretold [fo:rtel;
fo:'tould; fo:'tould]
foretell [fo:rtel] v.
przepowiadać; zapowiadać;
wróżyć
forever [fe'rewer] adv. wiecznie;
na zawsze; ustawicznie
foreword ['fo:rłe-rd] v.
przedmowa; przedsłowie;
słowo wstępne
forfeit ['fo:rfyt] s. grzywna; fant;
zastaw; utrata; v. stracić (w
skutek konfiskaty); utracić
forge ['fo:rdż] s. kuźnia; huta;
v. kuć; fałszować; posuwać
się z trudem; wykuwać sobie
przyszłość
forgery ['fo:rdżery] s.
fałszerstwo; podrobiony
dokument
forget; forgot; forgotten [fer'get;
fer'got; fer'gotn]
forget [fer'get] v. zapominać;
pomijać; przeoczyć;
zaniedbać
forgetful [fer'getful] adj.
zapominający; zapominalski;
niepomny
forget-me-not [fer'getmyna:t] s.
niezapominajka
forgive; forgave; forgiven

[fer'gyw; fer'gejw; fer'gywn]
forgive [fer'gyw] v. przebaczać;
darować; odpuszczać
forgiveness [fer'gywnys] s.
przebaczenie; darowanie;
wybaczenie
forgiving [fer'gywyng] adj.
wyrozumiały; pobłażliwy
forgo [fo:r'gou] v.
powstrzymywać się;
obchodzić się bez czegoś;
zrzekać się czegoś
forgot [fer'got] zob. forget
fork [fo:rk] s. widły; widelec;
widełki; v. rozwidlać (się);
brać na widły; spulchniać
(ziemię)
forlorn [fer'lo:rn] adj.
zapuszczony; opuszczony;
beznadziejny; rozpaczliwy;
niepocieszony
form [fo:rm] v. formować (się);
kształtować (się); utworzyć
(się); organizować (się);
wytworzyć; s. forma; kształt;
postać; formuła; formułka;
formularz; blankiet; styl; układ
formal ['fo:rmel] adj. formalny;
urzędowy; oficjalny; s. strój
wieczorowy
formation ['fo:rmejszyn] s.
formacja; szyk; układ;
tworzenie (się); kształtowanie
formowanie (się);
powstawanie; budowa
formative ['fo:rmetyw] adj.
formujący; kształtujący;
tworzący (się); słowotwórczy
former ['fo:rmer] adj. & pron.
oprzedni; były; miniony;
dawny; s. formierz; giser;
wzornik
formerly ['fo:rmerly] adv.
dawniej; przedtem; poprzednio
formidable ['fo:rmydebl] adj.
straszny; potężny; ogromny
formulate ['fo:rmjulejt] v.
formułować; wyrażać;
redagować
fornicate ['fo:rnykejt] v.
cudzołożyć; spółkować bez
ślubu
forsake; forsook; forsaken

[fer'sejk; fer'suk; fer'sejken]
forsake [fer'sejk] v. opuszczać;
porzucać; poniechać;
zaprzeć się
fort [fo:rt] s. fort
forth [fo:rs] adv. naprzód; dalej;
wobec; na zewnątrz etc.
forthcoming [fo:rs'kamyng] adj.
zbliżający się; nadchodzący
forthwith ['fo:rs'tys] adv.
bezzwłocznie; natychmiast
fortieth ['fo:rtyjes] num.
czterdziesty; czterdziesta
(część)
fortify ['fo:rtyfaj] s. wzmacniać;
fortyfikować; umacniać
fortnight ['fo:rtnajt] s. dwa
tygodnie (czternaście nocy)
fortran ['fo:rtraen] = formula
translation, język dla
programów na komputery
fortress ['fo:rtrys] s. twierdza;
forteca; warownia
fortunate ['fo:rcznyt] adj.
szczęśliwy; pomyślny;
udany
fortunately ['fo:rcznytly] adv. na
szczęście; szczęśliwie
fortune ['fo:rczen] s. szczęście;
los; majątek; traf; ślepy los
forty ['fo:rty] num. czterdzieści;
czterdziestka; czterdzieścioro
forward ['fo:rterd] adj. przedni;
naprzód; postępowy;
wczesny; chętny; gotowy; v.
przyśpieszać; ekspediować;
s. napastnik (w sporcie); gracz
w ataku
forwards ['fo:rterds] adv.
naprzód; dalej; adj. frontowy;
śmiały
foster-child ['foster,czajld] s.
wychowanek; wychowanka
fought [fo:t] zob. fight
foul [faul] adj. zgniły; plugawy;
wstrętny; adv. nieuczciwie;
wbrew regułom; s.
nieuczciwość; v. zawalać
(się); zabrudzić (się);
plugawić się; kalać
found [faund] v. 1. uzasadniać;
zakładać; odlewać; 2. zob.
find

foundation [faun'dejszyn] s.
podstawa; założenie;
fundament; fundacja;
podwalina
founder ['faunder] s. odlewnik;
założyciel; v. zatonąć;
przepaść; okulawić;
zatopić
foundling ['faundlyng] s.
podrzutek; znajda
fountain ['fauntyn] s. fontanna;
źródło; wodotrysk; pijalnia
fountain-pen ['fauntyn,pen] s.
wieczne pióro
four [fo:r] num. cztery; czwórka;
czworo
fourscore ['fo:rskor] nom.
osiemdziesiąt
four-stroke engine ['fo:r,strok
'endżyn] motor cztero-
taktowy
fourteen ['fo:rti:n] num.
czternaście; czternaścioro;
czternastka
fourth ['fo:rs] num. czwarty
fourthly [fo:rsly] adv. po
czwarte; na czwartm miejscu
fowl [faul] s. drób; ptaki
fox [foks] s. lis; v. przechytrzyć
fraction ['fraekszyn] s. ułamek;
część; odłam; frakcja
fracture ['fraekczer] s. złamanie;
v. złamać; łamać się
fragile ['fraedżajl] adj. kruchy;
łamliwy; słabowity; wątły
fragment ['fraegment] s.
fragment; urywek; odłamek;
okruch
fragrance ['frejgrens] s. zapach;
woń; aromat
fragrant ['frejgrent] adj.
pachnący; aromatyczny;
wonny
frail [frejl] adj. kruchy; wątły;
lekkomyślny; s. kosz;
plecionka
frailty ['frejlty] s. słabość;
wątłość; chwila słabości
frame ['frejm] s. oprawa; rama;
struktura; szkielet; v.
oprawiać; kształtować;
wrabiać
frame of mind ['frejm,ow'majnd]

s. nastrój; nastawienie
psychiczne; usposobienie do
czegoś
frame-house ['frejm,haus] s.
drewniany dom (typowy w
USA)
framework ['frejm,łe:rk] s.
struktura; zrąb; szkielet;
wiązanie
franchise ['fraenczajz] s.
przywilej; prawo do
prowadzenia filii lub firmy, do
głosowania
frank [fraenk] adj. szczery;
otwarty; v. wysyłać bez
opłaty
frankness ['fraenknys] s.
szczerość; otwartość
frantic ['fraetyk] adj. wariacki;
szalony; zapamiętały
fraternal [fre'te:rnl] adj. braterski;
bratni; bracki
fraternity [fre'te:rnyty] s.
braterstwo; korporacja
studencka
fraud [fro:d] s. oszustwo; oszust
fray [frej] v. strzępić; wycierać;
s. bójka; burda
freak [fri:k] s. kaprys; wybryk;
potwór; a. fantazyjny
freckle ['frekl] s. pieg; v.
pokrywać piegami;
powodować piegi
free [fri:] adj. wolny; bezpłatny;
nie zajęty; v. uwolnić;
wyzwolić; oswobodzić; adv.
wolno; swobodnie; bezpłatnie
free and easy ['fri:,end'i:zy] adj.
beztroski; bez ceremonii
freedom ['fri:dem] s. wolność;
swoboda; nieskrępowanie;
prawo do
freemason ['fri:,mejsn] s. mason;
wolnomularz
free port ['fri:,port] s.
wolnocłowy port
freethinker ['fri:tynker] s.
wolnomyśliciel;
wolnomyślicielka
freeway ['fri:łej] s. szosa
przelotowa wielopasmowa
freewheel ['fri:hłi:l] s. wolne koło
(np. od roweru)

freeze; froze; frozen [fri:z; frouz;
frouzn]
freeze [fri:z] v. marznąć;
zamarznąć; krzepnąć;
przymarznąć; mrozić;
wyrugować (konkurenta)
freezing point ['fri:zyn,point] s.
punkt zamarzania
freight [frejt] s. przewóz; fracht;
v. przewozić; frachtować
statek; adj. towarowy (pociąg)
freighter ['frejter] s. frachtowiec;
statek towarowy
French [frencz] adj. francuski
frenzy ['frenzy] s. szał;
szaleństwo; v. doprowadzać
do szału
frequency ['fri:kłensy] s.
częstość; częstotliwość
frequent ['fri:kłent] adj. częsty;
rozpowszechniony; v.
uczęszczać; odwiedzać;
bywać
fresh [fresz] adj. świeży; nowy;
zuchwały; niedoświadczony;
adv. świeżo; niedawno;
dopiero co
freshman ['freszmen] s. student
pierwszego roku
freshness ['fresznys] s.
świeżość; zuchwałość;
zuchwalstwo
freshwater ['fresz,ło:ter] adj.
słodkowodny; s. słodka woda
fret [fret] v. gryźć się;
niepokoić się; s.
rozdrażnienie; niepokój;
zdenerwowanie; irytacja
fretful ['fretful] adj.
rozdrażniony; drażliwy;
nerwowy; wzburzony
friar ['frajer] s. mnich; zakonnik;
biała plamka
friction ['frykszyn] s. tarcie;
ścieranie się; ucieranie
Friday ['frajdy] s. piątek
fridge [frydż] s. lodówka (slang)
fried [frajd] adj. smażony
friend [frend] s. znajomy;
znajoma; przyjaciel; kolega;
klient
friendly ['frendly] adj. przyjazny;
przychylny; życzliwy

friendship ['frendszyp] s.
przyjaźń osobista; dobra
znajomość; znajomość
powierzchowna; stosunki
koleżeńskie lub handlowe
fright [frajt] s. strach;
przerażenie; strach na wróble
frighten ['frajtn] v. straszyć
frightened ['frajtnd] adj.
przestraszony; zastraszony;
wylękniony
frightful ['frajtful] adj. straszny;
przerażający; straszliwy;
alarmujący; nieprzyjemny;
wstrętny
frigid ['frydżyd] adj. zimny;
lodowaty; oziębły; zimna
(kobieta)
frill [fryl] v. plisować; s.
falbanka; pl. fochy; fanaberie;
niepotrzebne ozdóbki
fringe [fryndż] v. frędzla;
obrąbek; v. obrębiać;
obramowywać; ograniczać;
wystrzępić
frisk [frysk] v. brykać s. sus;
podskok; skok; v. rewidować
frisky ['frysky] adj. rozbrykany;
ożywiony; samowolny
fro [frou] exp. to and fro; tu i
tam; tam i z powrotem
frock [frok] s. sukienka; habit;
mundur; surdut; anglez
frog [frog] s. żaba; strzałka
(w kopycie konia); vulg.
Francuz
frolic ['frolyk] s. wybryk; figiel;
swawola; v. dokazywać;
swawolić; figlować; adj.
rozbawiony; swawolny;
figlarny
frolicsome ['frolyksem] adj.
figlarny; swawolny;
rozbawiony
from [from] prep. od; z; przed
(zimnem); że; (ponieważ;
żeby)
from under [from ander] prep.
spod (czegoś)
from ... to [from ... tu] exp. stąd
... dotąd; od ... do
front [frant] s. przód; front;
czoło; adj. przedni; frontowy;

czołowy; v. stawiać czoło;
stać frontem; konfrontować
front-door ['frant,do:r] s. główne
drzwi wejściowe
frontier ['frantjer] s. granica; a.
pograniczny
front-page ['frant,pejdż] s.
strona tytułowa; a. sensacyjny
front tire ['frant,tajer] s. przednia
opona (samochodu)
front-wheel ['frant,hłi:l] s.
przednie koło (wozu)
front wheel drive ['frant,hłi:l
'drajw] s. napęd na przednie
koła (auta etc.)
frost [frost] s. mróz; przymrozek;
oziębłość; v. zmrozić;
oszronić
frostbite ['frost,bajt] s.
odmrożenie (nosa, ręki, stopy)
frosted ['frostyd] adj. matowy;
oszroniony; matowy odcień
frosty ['frosty] adj. mroźny;
oszroniony; lodowaty
froth [froš] s. piana; szumowiny;
v. pienić się; ubijać białko
frothy ['frošy] adj. spieniony
frown [fraun] v. marszczyć
brwi; s. zachmurzone czoło;
wyraz dezaprobaty;
niezadowolona mina
froze [frouz] zob. freeze
frozen food ['frouzn,fu:d] s.
mrożonki; mrożona
żywność
frugal ['fru:gel] adj. oszczędny;
tani; skromny (posiłek etc.)
fruit [fru:t] s. owoc; v.
owocować; a. owocowy
fruitcake ['fru:t,kejk] s.
świąteczne ciasto z
kandyzowanymi owocami i
orzechami
fruitful ['fru:tful] adj. owocny;
owocujący; zyskowny;
wydajny
fruitless ['fru:tlys] adj.
bezowocny; bezpłodny;
nieudany
frustrate [fra'strejt] v.
udaremnić; zniechęcić;
zawieść
fry [fraj] v. smażyć; s. narybek

frying pan [frajyn,paen] s.
patelnia
fuel [fjuel] s. paliwo; opał
fugitive ['fju:dżytyw] s. zbieg;
adj. zbiegły; przelotny
fulfill [ful'fyl] v. spełnić;
wykonać; dokonać;
skończyć
fulfillment [ful'fylment] s.
spełnienie; wykonanie;
dokonanie; wypełnienie;
wysłuchanie
full [ful] adj. pełny; pełen;
zapełniony; całkowity;
kompletny; cały; adv. w pełni;
całkowicie
full board ['ful'bo:rd] s. pełne
utrzymanie; wikt i opierunek
full moon ['ful'mu:n] s. pełnia
księżyca
fullness [ful'nys] s. pełność;
dokładność;
drobiazgowość
full-time ['ful'tajm] adj.
pełnoetatowy; całkowicie
zajęty
fumble ['fambl] v. szperać;
partaczyć; s. gmeranie;
partactwo; niezdarność;
niezdarne zagranie
fume [fju:m] v. dymić; kopcić;
s. dym (ostry); wyziew
(przykry); gazy spalinowe;
zapach; woń; napad gniewu;
wybuch gniewu
fun [fan] s. uciecha; zabawa;
wesołość; śmiech; powód
do wesołości
in fun ['yn,fan] adv. żartem
make fun [mejk fan] v.
dokuczać; kpić;
wyśmiewać się
function ['fankszyn] v. działać;
funkcjonować; s. działanie;
funkcja; praca; obowiązek;
impreza; uroczystość;
czynność
functionary ['fanksznery] s.
urzędnik; funkcjonariusz
fund [fand] s. fundusz
fundamental [,fande'mentel] adj.
podstawowy; s. zasada;
podstawa; nakaz

funeral ['fju:nerel] s. pogrzeb;
adj. pogrzebowy; żałosny
funereal [fju'njerjel] adj. żałobny;
pogrzebowy
funicular railway [fju'nykjuler
,rejłłej] kolejka linowa
funk ['fank] s. strach; trema;
tchórz (człowiek); v. mieć
pietra; zlęknąć się;
stchórzyć
funky ['fanky] adj. tchórzliwy
funnel ['fanl] s. lej; lejek; komin
(maszyny parowej etc.)
funny ['fany] adj. zabawny;
śmieszny; dziwny;
humorystyczny
fur [fe:r] s. futro; v. okładać
furious ['fjuerjes] adj. wściekły;
rozjuszony; gwałtowny;
zaciekły
furl [fe:r] v. składać (się);
złożyć (się); s. zwitek;
zawinięcie
furnace ['fe:rnys] s. piec
(centralny); palenisko; piekło
furnish ['fe:rnysz] v. zaopatrzyć;
dostarczyć; umeblować;
wyposażyć; uzbrajać;
meblować
furniture ['fe:rnyczer] s.
umeblowanie; urządzenie
furrier ['farjer] s. kuśnierz
furrow ['farou] s. bruzda;
zmarszczka; koleina; v. orać;
przeorać; ryć; zryć; pruć;
żłobić
further ['fe:rdzer] adv. dalej;
dodatkowo; adj. dalszy;
dodatkowy; v. pomagać;
ułatwiać; posuwać naprzód;
sprzyjać; popierać
further more ['fe:rdzermo:r] adv.
ponadto; oprócz tego; w
dodatku
furtive ['fe:rtyw] adj. skryty;
potajemny; ukradkowy;
skradający się
furuncle ['fjuerankl] s. czyrak
fury ['fjuery] s. szał; furia; pasja;
gwałtowna siła; jędza;
megiera; siła burzy; siła wiatru
fuse [fju:z] v. stopić; s.
zapalnik; bezpiecznik; korek

fuselage ['fju:zyla:ż] s. kadłub
(samolotu) bez skrzydeł i
ogona
fusion ['fju:żen] s. stopienie;
spawanie; zlewanie się
fuss [fas] v. niepokoić;
denerwować; krzątać się; s.
wrzawa; zamieszanie;
krzątanina
fussy ['fasy] adj. grymaśny;
hałaśliwy; nieznośny;
zrzędny
futile ['fju:tajl] adj. daremny;
bezskuteczny; próżny
future ['fju:tczer] s. przyszłość;
adj. przyszły (czas ...)
fuzzy ['fazy] adj. kędzierzawy;
kręty; puszysty; niewyraźny;
zamazany (obraz, pojęcie etc.)

G

g [dżi:] siódma litera
angielskiego alfabetu
gab [gaeb] s. gadanie (slang)
gable ['gejbl] s. szczyt (dachu);
trójkąt płaszczyzn dachu
gad-fly ['gaedflaj] s. giez; bąk;
osoba zaczepna jak giez
gag [gaeg] s. knebel; v.
kneblować; nałożyć
kaganiec; zamknąć debatę;
oszukiwać
gage [gejdż] s. wskaźnik;
miara; rękojmia; v. mierzyć;
oceniać; zestawiać; sądzić
gaiety ['gejety] s. wesołość
gaily ['gejly] adv. wesoło
gain [gejn] s. zysk; zarobek;
korzyść; v. zyskiwać;
zdobywać; pozyskiwać;
wygrywać; osiągać; mieć
korzyść; wyprzedzać
gait [gejt] s. chód; bieg (konia)
gaiter ['gejter] s. kamasz; getr
galaxy ['gaeleksy] s. galaktyka;
plejada; rój
gale [gejl] s. poryw wiatru;

sztorm; wybuch śmiechu;
zefir
gall [go:l] s. żółć; złość;
gorycz; tupet; otarcie; v.
urazić
gallant ['gaelent] s. bawidamek;
galant; adj. piękny; dzielny;
waleczny; szarmancki
gallery ['gaelery] s. arkady;
galeria; krużganek; balkon;
chór
galley ['gaely] s. galera; kuchnia
na statku; szufelka
galley proof ['gaely,pru:f] s.
odbitka na korektę
(szczotkowa)
gallon ['gaelen] s. miara płynu
(ok. 4,5 litra)(am. gal. = 3,78 l)
gallop ['gaelep] v. galopować;
s. galop; cwał; galopada
gallows ['gaelouz] s. szubienica;
kobylica; szelki; a.
szubieniczny
galore [ga'lo:r] s. mnóstwo; adv.
w bród; bardzo wiele
gamble ['gaembl] s. hazard;
ryzyko; v. uprawiać hazard;
ryzykować; igrać;
spekulować
gambler ['gaembler] s. gracz-
-hazardzista; ryzykant
gambol ['gaembel] v.
podskakiwać; s. podskok;
skok
game [gejm] s. gra; zabawa;
zawody; sztuczki; machinacje;
adj. dzielny; odważny;
kulawy; v. uprawiać hazard
gamekeeper ['gejm,ki:per] s.
gajowy; leśnik
gander ['gaender] s. gąsior
gang [gaeng] s. banda; szajka;
grupa; v. łączyć się w bandę
gangster ['gaengster] s.
gangster; bandyta
gangway ['gangłej] s. przejście;
kładka; chodnik w kopalni
gaol = jail [dżejl] s. więzienie;
ciupa; v. uwięzić; wsadzać
do więzienia
gaoler = jailer ['dżejler] s.
dozorca więzienny; strażnik
więzienny

gap [gaep] s. szpara; luka;
otwór; przerwa; odstęp;
wyrwa; przełęcz; wyłom

gape [gejp] v. gapić się;
ziewać; s. ziewanie; gapienie
się

garage [gaera:dż] s. garaż; v.
garażować; zagarażować

garbage ['ga:rbydż] s. odpadki;
śmieci; bezwartościowe
publikacje

garden ['ga:rdn] s. ogród; v.
uprawiać ogród

gardener ['ga:rdner] s. ogrodnik

gardening ['ga:rdenyng] s.
ogrodnictwo (warzywne,
kwiatowe etc.)

gargle ['ga:rgl] v. płukać gardło;
s. płyn do płukania gardła

garland ['ga:rlend] s. girlanda

garlic ['ga:rlik] s. czosnek

garment ['ga:rment] s. część
ubrania; szaty; v. odziewać

garnish ['ga:rnysz] v. ozdabiać;
s. ozdoba; przybranie
(potraw); upiększenia literackie

garret ['gaeret] s. poddasze;
strych; mansarda; sl. łeb

garrison ['gaerysn] s. załoga;
garnizon; v. garnizonować

garter ['ga:rter] s. podwiązka

gas [gaes] s. gaz; benzyna

gaseous ['gejzjes] adj. gazowy

gash [gaesz] v. skaleczyć się; s.
szrama; skaleczenie; blizna

gasket ['gaeskyt] s. uszczelka

gas-meter ['gaes,mi:ter] s.
gazomierz; zegar gazowy

gasoline ['gaesely:n] s. gazolina;
benzyna

gasp [ga:sp] v. ciężko dyszeć;
sapać; s. ciężki oddech

gas station ['gaes,stejszyn] s.
stacja benzynowa

gas-stove ['gaes'stouw] s.
kuchenka gazowa; kuchnia
gazowa

gate [gejt] s. brama; furtka;
wrota; szlaban; ilość
publiczności; wpływy kasowe
ze wstępu

gateway ['gejtłej] s. przejście;
wjazd; brama wjazdowa

gather ['gaedzer] v. zbierać;
wnioskować; wzbierać;
narastać

gather speed ['gaedzer spi:d]
nabierać szybkości;
rozpędzać się

gathering ['gaedzeryng] s.
zebranie; nagromadzenie;
ropień

gaudy [go:dy] adj. jaskrawy;
krzykliwy; s. obchód
(uroczysty)

gauge [gejdż] s. wskaźnik;
miara; skala; v. kalibrować;
oceniać; szacować;
oszacować

gaunt [go:nt] adj. chudy;
nędzny; wycieńczony;
ponury; posępny

gauze ['go:z] s. gaza; siateczka;
mgiełka; gaza metalowa

gave [gejw] zob. give

gay [gej] adj. wesoły; jaskrawy;
pstry; rozpustny; s. pederasta;
pedzio; pedał

gaze [gejz] s. spojrzenie; v.
przyglądać się;
przypatrywać się

gaze at [gejz aet] v. wpatrywać
(się) w kogoś, w coś

gear [gier] v. włączyć (napęd);
s. przybory; bieg; układ

gear change ['gier,czeindż]
zmiana biegów

gearbox ['gier,boks] s. skrzynka
biegów; skrzynia biegów

gearing ['gieryng] s. przekładnia;
mechanizm napędowy

gear wheel ['gier-hłi:l] s. tryb;
koło zębate

geese [gi:s] pl. gęsi

gem [dżem] s. klejnot; perła

gender ['dżender] s. rodzaj;
płeć; wytwór; potomstwo

general ['dżenerel] adj. ogólny;
powszechny; generalny;
naczelny; główny; nieścisły;
ogólnikowy; s. generał; wódz

generalize ['dżenerelajz] v.
uogólniać; mówić ogólnikami

generally ['dżenerely] adv.
ogólnie; zazwyczaj;
powszechnie; najczęściej; w

ogóle
generate ['dżenerejt] v. rodzić;
 wytwarzać; płodzić;
 wywoływać
generation ['dżenerejszyn] s.
 powstawanie; pokolenie
generator ['dżenerejter] s.
 prądnica; sprawca; generator
generosity [,dżene'rosyty] s.
 szczodrość;
 wspaniałomyślność
generous ['dżeneres] adj. hojny;
 wielkoduszny; suty; obfity;
 bogaty; żyzny; mocny;
 krzepiący
genial ['dżi:njel] adj. wesoły;
 łagodny; miły; jowialny;
 ożywczy
genitive [dżenytyw] s. (gram.)
 dopełniacz; adj. wesoły;
 łagodny
genius [dżi:njes] s. geniusz;
 duch; talent; duch epoki etc.
genocide ['dżenousajd] s.
 ludobójstwo (systematyczne
 mordowanie)
gentle ['dżentl] adj. łagodny;
 delikatny; subtelny; stopniowy
gentleman ['dżentlmen] s. pan;
 człowiek honorowy;
 dżentelmen
gentlemanly ['dżentlmenly] adj.
 dżentelmeński; honorowy
gentleness ['dżentlnys] s.
 łagodność; delikatność
gentlewoman ['dżentl,łumen] s.
 szlachcianka; dama; dama
 dworu
gentry ['dżentry] s.
 ziemiaństwo; szlachta;
 światek
genuine ['dżenjuyn] adj.
 prawdziwy; autentyczny;
 szczery
geography [dży'ogrefy] s.
 geografia; fizyczne cechy
 rejonu
geologist [dży'oledżyst] s.
 geolog
geology [dży'oledży] s. geologia
geometry [dży'omytry] s.
 geometria
germ [dże:rm] s. zarodek;

zarazek; nasienie; pączek
German ['dże:rmen] adj.
 niemiecki (język, człowiek); s.
 Niemiec
germinate ['dże:rmynejt] v.
 kiełkować; rozwijać się
gerund [dżerend] s. rzeczownik
 odsłowny (z końcówką "ing")
gestation ['dżes'tejszyn] s. ciąża
gesticulate ['dżes'tykjulejt] v.
 gestykulować; mówić na
 migi
gesture ['dżesczer] s. gest
get; got; got [get; got; got]
get [get] v. dostać; otrzymać;
 nabyć; zawołać; łupać;
 przynieść; zmusić; musić;
 mieć; dostać się; wpływać;
 wsiadać
get about [,get e'baut] v.
 poruszać się; rozchodzić się
get along [,get e'long] v. dawać
 sobie radę; współpracować
get away [,get e'łej] v. uciec;
 odejść; wyjeżdżać;
 oderwać się
get in [,get'yn] v. wejść;
 wsiąść
get off [,get'of] v. wysiąść
get on [,get'on] v. wdziewać;
 posuwać się; robić dalej
get out [,get'aut] v. wysiąść;
 wyjmować; wyciągać;
 wynosić się
get to [,get'tu] v. dotrzeć;
 przyjść; musieć; być
 zmuszonym
get together [,get te'gedzer] v.
 zebrać się; s. zebranie
get up [,get'ap] v. wstać;
 zbudzić się
get-up ['getap] s. wygląd; ubiór
get ready [,get'redy] v.
 przygotować (się);
 przygotowywać się
get to know ['get,tu'nou] v.
 zapoznać się (bliżej)
geyser ['gajzer] s. gejzer
ghastly ['ga:stly] adj. ohydny;
 upiorny; blady; adv. okropnie
gherkin ['ge:rkyn] s. korniszon
ghost [goust] s. duch; cień;
 widmo

ghostly ['goustly] adj. upiorny

giant ['dżajent] s. olbrzym

gibbet ['dżybyt] s. szubienica

gibe ['dżajb] s. kpina; drwina; v. kpić; szydzić; wyśmiewać

giblets ['dżyblyts] pl. podróbki (np. kurze); podroby

giddy ['gydy] adj. zawrotny; mający zawrót głowy; roztrzepany; v. przyprawiać o zawrót głowy

gift [gyft] s. dar; upominek; talent; uzdolnienie; a. darowany

gifted ['gyftyd] adj. utalentowany; mający naturalne zdolności

gigantic [dżaj'gantyk] adj. olbrzymi; gigantyczny; kolosalny

giggle ['gygl] s. chichot; v. chichotać; głupio śmiać się

gild [gyld] v. złocić; pozłocić; nadać lepszego wyglądu

gill [gyl] s. skrzela; wąwóz; potok; jedna czwarta galona

gilt [gylt] adj. pozłacany; s. złocenie; pozłocenie

gin [dżyn] s. jałowcówka

ginger ['dżyndżer] s. imbir

ginger bread ['dżyndżer,bred] s. piernik; przesadne dekoracje

gingerly ['dżyndżerly] adj. ostrożny; delikatny; adv. ostrożnie; delikatnie; nieśmiało

gipsy ['dżypsy] s. cygan

giraffe [dży'ra:f] s. żyrafa

gird; girt; girt [ge:rd; ge:rt; ge:rt]

gird [ge:rd] v. opasać; kpić; s. kpina

girder ['ge:rder] s. dźwigar; belka; wzdłużnik

girdle ['ge:rdl] s. pas; v. opasać; okrążyć; opasywać lekkim gorsetem

girl [ge:rl] s. dziewczyna; ukochana

girlfriend [ge:rl'frend] s. przyjaciółka; dobra znajoma; kochanka

girlhood ['ge:rlhud] s. wiek dziewczęcy; dziewczęta (kraju etc.)

girl scout ['ge:rl skaut] s. harcerka

girl's name ['ge:rls,nejm] s. panieńskie nazwisko

girt [ge:rt] zob. gird

girth [ge:rt] s. popręg; obwód

gist [dżyst] s. treść; istota; sedno; esencja; osnowa; sens; główna treść

give; gave; given [gyw; gejw; gywn]

give [gyw] v. dać; dawać; być elastycznym; zawalić się; ustąpić; s. elastyczność; ustępstwo pod naciskiem

give away [,gyw e'łej] v. wydawać; zdradzać; wydawać córkę

give in [,gyw'yn] v. ustępować; podawać (nazwisko); uznawać w końcu

give up [,gyw'ap] v. poddać się; ustąpić; zaniechać; dać za wygraną

give way [,gyw'łej] v. zrobić miejsce; ustąpić; obsunąć się

glacier ['glaesjer] s. lodowiec

glad [glaed] adj. rad; wesoły; radosny; dający radość; ochoczy

gladly ['glaedly] adv. z przyjemnością; chętnie; właściwie

gladness ['glaednys] s. wesołość; pogoda ducha; przyjemność

glamorous ['glaemeres] adj. czarujący; wspaniały; fascynujący

glance [gla:ns] v. spojrzeć; ześliznąć się; błyszczeć; połyskiwać; s. rzut oka; błysk; połysk; rykoszet; odbicie się

glance at ['glan:s et] v. spojrzeć na (coś); rzucić spojrzenie

gland [glaend] s. gruczoł

glare [gleer] v. błyskać; razić; wlepiać wzrok; s. błysk; blask

glass [gla:s] s. szkło; szklanka; lampka; kieliszek; szyba etc.

glasses ['gla:sys] pl. okulary; szkła

glassy ['gla:sy] adj. szklisty; szklany; przezroczysty; bez wyrazu

glaze [glejz] v. szklić; oszklić

glazier ['glejzjer] s. szklarz

gleam [gli:m] s. połysk; v. połyskiwać; zjawić się nagle

glee [gli:] s. wesele; radość

glen [glen] s. dolina (zaciszna)

glib [glyb] adj. gładki; żwawy; płynny; wygadany (zanadto)

glide ['glajd] s. poślizg; szybowanie; v. ślizgać się; szybować; powodować poślizg

glider ['glajder] s. szybowiec

glimmer ['glymer] v. migotać; słabo świecić; s. słabe światło; migotanie; słabe postrzeganie

glimpse [glymps] s. mignięcie; przelotne spojrzenie; v. ujrzeć w przelocie; zerknąć

glint [glynt] s. błysk; odblask; v. błysnąć; zamigotać

glisten ['glysn] s. połysk; v. połyskiwać; lśnić; iskrzyć się

glitter ['glyter] v. świecić się; błyszczeć; s. połysk; blask; pretensjonalność

gloat ['glout] v. napawać się; źle patrzeć; pożerać oczami

gloat over ['glout,ower] v. napawać się (cudzym nieszczęściem); unosić się

globe [gloub] s. globus; kula ziemska; jabłko królewskie; gałka

gloom [glu:m] s. smutek; mrok; przygnębienie; v. zasmucać (się); zaciemniać (się); posępnieć

gloomy ['glu:my] adj. ponury; mroczny; posępny; przygnębiony

glorify ['glo:ryfaj] v. chwalić; wychwalać; gloryfikować

glorious ['glo:rjes] adj. sławny; wspaniały; przepiękny; chlubny

glory ['glo:ry] s. chwała; sława; v. szczycić się; chlubić się; chwalić się; chełpić się

gloss [glos] s. połysk; v. polerować; interpretować (błędnie)

glossary ['glosery] s. słownik (przy tekście); glosariusz

glossy [glosy] adj. lśniący

glove [glaw] s. rękawiczka

glow [glou] v. żarzyć się; pałać; s. jarzenie; zapał; żarliwość; łuna; rumieniec; jasność

glowworm ['glou,łe:rm] s. robaczek świętojański

glue [glu:] s. klej; v. kleić; zalepiać; wlepiać (oczy); zlepić

glutton ['glatn] s. żarłok

gluttonous ['glatnes] adj. żarłoczny; jedzący zbyt dużo

gluttony ['glatny] s. żarłoczność; zwyczaj jedzenia za dużo

glycerine [,glyse'ry:n] s. gliceryna

gnarled ['na:rld] adj. sękaty; wykrzywiony; węzłowaty

gnash [naesz] v. zgrzytać zębami jak w złości

gnat [naet] s. komar; owad

gnaw [no:] v. gryźć; wgryzać; ogryzać; nękać (stałym bólem)

gnome [noum] s. gnom; chochlik; zdanie wyrażające myśl ogólną; przysłowie; sentencja

go; went; gone [gou; łent; gon]

go [gou] v. iść; chodzić; jechać; stać się; być na chodzie

go about [,gou e'baut] v. zająć się (czymś); afiszować się

go along [,gou e'long] v. towarzyszyć; zgadzać się; iść sobie

go away [,gou e'łej] v. iść precz; odchodzić; wyjeżdżać

go back [,gou'bek] v. wracać; cofać się; sięgać wstecz

go by [,gou'baj] v. mijać

go on [,gou'on] v. iść naprzód; ciągnąć dalej; kontynuować

go out [,gou'aut] v. wychodzić (z kimś); gasnąć; bywać (u ludzi)

go through [,gou'tru] v. przechodzić; brnąć przez; przebrnąć

go under [,gou'ander] v. tonąć; ulegać; zniknąć; umrzeć

goad [goud] s. kolec; bodziec; v. popędzać; drażnić; prowokować; doprowadzać do zrobienia

goal [goul] s. cel; meta; bramka

goalie [gouli] s. bramkarz

go-between [,gouby'tły:n] s. pośrednik; stręczyciel

goblet ['goblyt] s. kieliszek; czara; puchar; kielich na nóżce

goblin ['goblyn] s. chochlik

god [god] s. Bóg; bożek; bóstwo

godchild ['godczajld] s. chrześniak; chrześniaczka

goddess ['godys] s. bogini

godfather ['god,fadzer] s. ojciec chrzestny; v. trzymać do chrztu

godless ['godlys] adj. bezbożny; grzeszny; niegodziwy; nikczemny

godmother ['god,madzer] s. matka chrzestna

goggles ['goglz] pl. okulary ochronne; gogle; okrągłe okulary

going ['gouyng] s. chodzenie; jazda; tempo; adj. ruchliwy; istniejący

going rate ['gouyn,rejt] bieżący kurs (dolara, oprocentowania)

gold [gould] s. złoto; adj. złoty

gold digger ['gould,dyger] poszukiwacz złota; naciągaczka

golden ['gouldn] adj. złoty

gold-plated ['gould,plejtyd] s. plater złoty; adj. platerowany

goldsmith ['gould,smys] s. złotnik

golf [golf] s. golf; v. grać w golfa

golf course ['golf,ko:rs] s. pole golfowe

gondola ['gondele] s. gondola (np. balonu); otwarty, niski wagon towarowy

gone [gon] v. zob. go

good [gud] adj. dobry; s. dobro; pożytek; zaleta; wartość; better ['beter] lepszy; best [best] najlepszy

good at it ['gud,et'yt] dobry w tym; dobrze to robi

good-bye [,gud'baj] s. do widzenia; pożegnanie

good-for-nothing ['gudfe:r ,nasyng] s. nicpoń; hultaj; łobuziak

good-looking ['gud'lukyng] adj. przystojny; ładny

good-natured ['gud'nejczerd] adj. dobroduszny; poczciwy

goodness ['gudnys] s. dobroć

good will ['gud'łyl] s. dobra wola; wartość reputacji firmy

goose [gu:s] s. gęś; pl. geese [gi:s] gęsi; gęsie mięso; dureń

gooseberry ['gusbery] s. agrest

gooseflesh ['gu:sflesz] s. gęsia skórka (z zimna, strachu etc.)

gopher ['goufer] s. suseł; v. grzebać; ryć; plądrować gospodarkę

gore [go:r] v. bóść; klinować; s. klin w krawiectwie; posoka

gorge ['go:rdż] s. wąwóz; żarłoczność; treść żołądka; przejedzenie; gardziel; v. obżerać się; pożerać; połykać; opychać się

gorgeous ['go:rdżes] adj. wspaniały; okazały; suty; ozdobny; wystawny; cudowny

gospel ['gospel] s. ewangelia

gossip ['gosyp] s. plotka; plotkarz; plotkarka; v. plotkować; pisać popularne artykuły

got [got] zob. get

Gothic ['gotyk] adj. gotycki

gotten ['gotn] = got; zob. get

gourd [go:rd] s. bania; tykwa
gourmet ['guermej] n. smakosz
gout [gaut] s. gościec; podagra
govern ['gawern] v. rządzić;
kierować; dowodzić;
trzymać w ryzach
governess ['gawernys] s.
guwernantka; nauczycielka;
instruktorka
government ['gawernment] s.
rząd; ustrój; okręg; a.
rządowy
governor ['gawerner] s.
gubernator; zarządca;
naczelnik; szef
gown [gaun] s. suknia; toga; v.
układać togę; ubierać suknię
grab [graeb] v. łapać;
zagarniać; grabić; s. łapanie;
chwyt; zagarnięcie; porwanie
grace [grejs] s. łaska; wdzięk;
przyzwoitość; v. czcić;
ozdabiać; dodawać wdzięku;
zaszczycić
graceful ['grejsful] adj. pełen
wdzięku; wdzięczny; łaskawy
gracious ['grejszes] adj. łaskawy;
miłosierny; exp. goodness
gracious! ['gudnys'grejszes]
Boże miłosierny
grade [grejd] s. stopień; klasa;
nachylenie; v. stopniować;
dzielić na stopnie;
cieniować; równać teren;
niwelować; profilować
grade crossing ['grejd'krosyng] s.
skrzyżowanie dróg; przejazd
przez tory (jednopoziomowy)
grade school ['grejd'sku:l] s.
szkoła podstawowa
gradient ['grejdjent] s.
nachylenie; stopień
nachylenia
gradual ['graedżuel] adj.
stopniowy; po trochu
graduate ['graedżuejt] s.
absolwent; v. stopniować;
ukończyć studia; adj.
podyplomowy (kurs)
graduation [,graedżu'ejszyn] s.
ukończenie wyższych
studiów; stopniowanie;
cechowanie; podziałka

graft [gra:ft] v. szczepić;
dawać łapówkę;
przeszczepiać; s. szczepienie;
łapówka; przeszczep; szufla
(pełna ziemi)
grain [grejn] s. ziarno; zboże;
odrobina; grań; włókno; słój;
v. granulować; ziarnować
gram [graem] s. gram; 1/28 uncji
grammar ['graemer] s. gramatyka
grammar school ['graemer-,sku:l]
s. szkoła podstawowa
grammatical [gre'maetykel] adj.
gramatyczny (poprawny)
gramme [graem] s. gram (ang.)
gramophone ['graemefoun] s.
patefon; gramofon
grand [graend] adj. wielki;
główny; wspaniały; świetny;
okazały; (slang): 1000
dolarów; całkowity
grandchild ['graen,czajld] s.
wnuk
granddaughter ['graen,do:ter] s.
wnuczka
grandeur ['graendżer] s.
wielkość; dostojność;
okazałość; wspaniałość;
majestat; blask; pompa
grandfather ['graend,fa:dzer] s.
dziadek
grandma ['graenma:] s. babcia
grandmother ['graen,madzer] s.
babka
grandpa ['graenpa:] s. dziadzio
grandparents ['graen,paerents]
pl. dziadkowie
grandson ['graensan] s. wnuk
grandstand ['graen'staend] s.
główna trybuna; v.
popisywać się
granny ['graeny] s. babunia
grant [gra:nt] v. nadawać;
udzielać; uznawać; zgadzać
się na; przekazywać; s.
pomoc; przekazanie tytułu
własności; darowizna
granulated ['graenjulejtyd] adj.
ziarnisty; rozdrobniony;
granulowany
grape [grejp] s. winogrona
grapefruit ['grejp-fru:t] s.
grejpfrut (owoc lub drzewo)

grape-sugar ['grejp,szuger] s.
cukier gronowy
grapevine ['grejp-wajn] s.
winorośl; poczta pantoflowa;
szeptanka; źródło kaczek
prasowych
graph [graef] s. wykres; krzywa
graphic ['graefyk] adj. graficzny;
plastyczny; obrazowy
(dosadny)
grasp [gra:sp] v. łapać;
chwytać; pojmać;
pojmować; dzierżyć; s.
chwyt; uchwyt; pojęcie;
panowanie; zrozumienie;
kontrola
grass [gra:s] s. trawa; (slang):
marijuana; "pot"; haszysz
grasshopper ['gra:s,hoper] s.
konik polny (z czterema
skrzydłami)
grass widower ['gra:s,łydouer] s.
słomiany wdowiec
grate [grejt] s. krata; ruszt; v.
trzeć; ucierać; zgrzytać;
skrzypieć; irytować; być
irytującym
grateful ['grejtful] adj.
wdzięczny; dobrze widziany
grater ['grejter] s. tarko; tarło;
raszpla; tarnik do drzewa
gratification [,graetyfy'kejszyn] s.
zaspokojenie; wynagrodzenie;
gratyfikacja; łapówka
gratify ['graetyfaj] v. dogadzać;
uprzyjemniać; zadawalać;
przekupywać; wynagradzać
grating ['grejtyng] s. krata; adj.
zgrzytliwy; ochrypły
gratis ['grejtys] adv. gratis;
bezpłatnie; adj. bezpłatny;
gratisowy; darmowy
gratitude ['graetytju:d] s.
wdzięczność (za pomoc etc.)
gratuitous [gre'tjuites] adj.
bezpłatny; niepotrzebny
gratuity [gre'tjuity] s. napiwek;
zasiłek przy zwolnieniu
grave ['grejw] s. grób; adj.
poważny; v. wyryć; wryć;
wykopać
gravel ['grawel] s. żwir; piasek;
v. posypywać żwirem;

kłopotać
graveyard ['grejwja:rd] s.
cmentarz; nocna zmiana w
pracy
gravitation [,graewy'tejszyn] s.
ciążenie (ciał); grawitacja
gravity ['graewyty] s. siła
ciężkości; ciężkość;
powaga (np. sytuacji); ciężar
(gatunkowy)
gravy ['grejwy] s. sos mięsny;
sok; dodatkowy zysk; osobista
korzyść
gray [grej] adj. szary; zob. grey;
v. szarzeć; s. szary kolor
graze [grejz] v. paść; drasnąć;
s. draśnięcie; muśnięcie;
odarcie
grazing land ['grejzyng,laend] s.
pastwisko; pastwiska
grease [gri:s] s. tłuszcz; smar; v.
brudzić; smarować;
nasmarować smarem
(samochód etc.)
grease gun ['gri:s,gan] s.
smarownica wtryskowa;
towotnica
greasy ['gri:sy] adj. tłusty; śliski
great [grejt] adj. wielki; duży;
świetny; znakomity;
wspaniały; zamiłowany;
doniosły
greatcoat ['grejt'kout] s. palto;
płaszcz; opończa
great grandchild ['grejt'graend
,czajld] s. prawnuk
great grandfather ['grejt'graend
fa:dzer] s. pradziadek
great grandmother ['grejt'graend
madzer] s. prababka
greatness ['grejtnys] s.
wielkość; ogrom;
wielkoduszność; powaga
greed [gri:d] s. chciwość;
zachłanność; żądza (władzy)
greedy [gri:dy] adj. chciwy;
zachłanny; łakomy; łapczywy;
żądny; żarłoczny; spragniony
Greek [gri:k] adj. grecki;
(niezrozumiały); s. język
grecki; Grek
green [gri:n] adj. zielony;
naiwny; młody;

niedoświadczony; świeży; s.
zieleń; zielenina; trawnik; v.
zielenić; naciągać
greenback ['gri:nbaek] s. (slang)
dolar (banknot)
greenhorn ['gri:nhorn] s.
nowicjusz; żółtodziób
greenhouse ['gri:nhaus] s.
cieplarnia
greenish ['gri:nysz] adj.
zielonkawy
greet ['gri:t] v. kłaniać się;
pozdrawiać; ukazać się;
dojść do (uszu);
zaprezentować się
greeting ['gri:tyng] s.
pozdrowienie; powitanie;
pozdrowienia
grew [gru:] zob. grow
grey [grej] adj. szary; siwy; s.
szarość; v. szarzeć; siwieć
(ortografia brytyjska)
greyhound ['grejhaund] s. chart
(wysoki, chudy, szybki pies)
grid [gryd] s. krata; sieć; siatka;
sieć wysokiego napięcia
grief [gri:f] s. zmartwienie;
zgryzota; smutek; żal
grievance ['gri:wens] s. uraza;
krzywda; skarga; zażalenie
grieve [gri:w] v. martwić;
krzywdzić; smucić;
zasmucić
grievous ['gri:wes] adj.
dręczący; przykry; ciężki;
smutny
grill [gryl] s. rożen; krata;
potrawa z rusztu; v. smażyć
na rożnie; przesłuchiwać
grim [grym] adj. srogi; ponury;
okrutny; groźny; odrażający
grimace [gri'mejs] s. grymas; v.
grymasić
grime [grajm] s. brud; v. brudzić
(sadzą, smarem etc.)
grimy ['grajmy] adj. brudny;
wysmarowany; zatłuszczony
grin [gryn] v. szczerzyć zęby;
uśmiechać się; s. uśmiech
grind; ground; ground [grajnd;
graund; graund]
grind [grajnd] v. ostrzyć;
toczyć; mleć; zgrzytać;

trzeć; harować; s. mlenie;
harówka; kujon; ciężka
rutyna; kucie się
grindstone ['grajnd,stoun] s.
kamień szlifierski; harówka
grip [gryp] s. uchwyt; trzonek;
rękojeść; rączka; łapka;
uścisk dłoni; władza; moc;
wywieranie wrażenia;
opanowanie (tematu); v.
chwycić; złapać; mocno
trzymać w rękach;
opanować sytuację; ująć
rozumem
gripes [grajps] pl. kolka
gristle ['grysl] s. chrząstka
grit [gryt] s. żwir; piasek;
odwaga; wytrzymałość;
charakter; v. zgrzytać;
skrzypieć; posypywać
groan [groun] s. jęk; v. jęczeć
grocer ['grouser] s. właściciel
sklepu spożywczego
groceries ['grouserys] pl. towary
spożywcze
grocery ['grousery] s. sklep
spożywczy; artykuł
spożywczy
groin [grain] s. pachwina
groom [grum] s. parobek; pan
młody; v. obrządzać;
przygotowywać do objęcia
stanowiska
groove [gru:w] s. bruzda; rowek;
rutyna; v. żłobić; rowkować;
nacinać zwojnik; gwintować
grope [group] v. szukać po
omacku; iść po omacku;
iść na ślepo
gross [grous] adj. gruby;
ordynarny; prostacki;
całkowity; hurtowy; tłusty;
niesmaczny; spasły; wybujały;
s. 12 tuzinów; v. uzyskać
brutto ...
ground [graund] s. grunt; ziemia;
podstawa; podłoże; teren; dno
(morza); osad; powód;
przyczyna; dno; v. 1. osiąść
na mieliźnie; uziemiać;
gruntować; zagruntować; 2.
zob. grind
ground control ['graund,ken

'troul] kontrolna stacja (lotów)
ground crew ['graund,kru:] s.
załoga, ekipa na ziemi
ground floor ['graund,flo:r] s.
parter (bliski poziomu gruntu)
ground glass ['graund,glas] s.
tłuczone szkło
groundhog ['graundhog] s.
świstak (amerykański)
groundless ['graundlys] adj.
bezpodstawny; gołosłowny
groundnut ['graundnat] s.
orzeszek ziemny
ground staff ['graund,staf] s.
personel naziemny (lotnictwa)
groundwork ['graundłerk] s.
podstawa; podłoże; zasada;
fundament; tło; osnowa;
kanwa (utworu)
group [gru:p] s. grupa; v.
grupować; rozsegregowywać
na grupy
grove [grouw] s. gaj
grow; grew; grown [grou; gru:;
groun]
grow [grou] v. rosnąć; stawać
się; dojrzewać; hodować;
sadzić
growl [graul] s. ryk; pomruk;
warczenie; v. mruknąć;
warknąć; burczeć; warczeć;
odburknąć; gderać;
mrukliwie odpowiadać
grown [groun] v. zob. grow
grown-up ['groun,ap] adj.
dorosły; s. człowiek dorosły
growth [grous] s. rozwój;
wzrost; uprawa; narośl;
porost; przyrost
grub [grab] v. karczować;
dłubać; harować; wcinać
(jedzenie)
grubby [graby] adj. brudny;
niechlujny; robaczywy
grudge [gradż] v. żałować;
skąpić; zazdrościć; mieć
niechęć; s. żal; uraza;
niechęć
gruel [gruel] s. kaszka; kleik; v.
wymęczyć; zadawać bobu
(komuś)
gruesome ['gru:sem] adj.
okropny

gruff [graf] adj. burkliwy;
gburowaty; ochrypły; gruby
(głos)
grumble ['grambl] v. narzekać;
utyskiwać; gderać; skarżyć
się; s. narzekanie; pomruk;
szemranie
grumbler ['grambler] s. zrzęda
grunt [grant] s. kwik; v.
kwiczeć; chrząkać;
wymruczeć
guarantee [,gaeren'ti:] v.
gwarantować; poręczać; s.
poręczyciel; poręka; rękojmia
guarantor [,gaeren'to:r] s.
poręczyciel; poręczycielka
guard [ga:rd] v. pilnować;
chronić; s. strażnik; opiekun;
obrońca; bezpiecznik
guard against ['ga:rd,e'genst] v.
zabezpieczać się przed ...
guardhouse ['ga:rdhaus] s.
wartownia; tymczasowy
areszt
guardian ['ga:rdjen] s. opiekun;
kustosz; adj. opiekuńczy
guardianship ['ga:rdjenszyp] s.
opieka; opiekuństwo; kuratela
guess [ges] v. zgadywać;
przypuszczać; myśleć; s.
zgadywanie; przypuszczenie;
zgadnięcie
guest [gest] s. gość
guest house ['gesthaus] s.
pensjonat; osobny domek dla
gości
guest room ['gestru:m] s. pokój
gościnny; gościnna sypialnia
guidance ['gajdens] s.
kierownictwo; poradnictwo;
kierowanie
guide [gajd] s. przewodnik;
doradca; v. wskazywać
drogę; prowadzić
guidebook ['gajdbuk] s.
przewodnik (książka) dla
turystów
guild [gyld] s. cech; związek
guildhall ['gyld'ho:l] s. dom
cechowy; ratusz; dom
związkowy
guile [gajl] s. oszustwo
guileless ['gajllys] adj. szczery;

otwarty (w postępowaniu)
guilt [gylt] s. wina; przestępstwo
guiltless ['gyltlys] adj. niewinny;
wolny od zarzutu
guilty ['gylty] adj. winny
guinea pig ['gynypyg] s. świnka
morska; przedmiot
eksperymentów
guitar [gy'ta:r] s. gitara
gulf [galf] s. zatoka; przepaść;
wir; v. pochłaniać
gull [gal] s. mewa; v. oszukiwać
gullet [galyt] s. przełyk; gardło;
gardziel
gully ['galy] s. wąwóz; ściek;
kanał; v. żłobić; wyżłobić;
poryć
gulp [galp] s. łyk; duży kęs
gulp down ['galpdałn] v. łukać;
dławić się; hamować łzy
gum [gam] s. dziąsło; guma; v.
kleić; wydzielać żywicę
gun [gan] s. strzelba; armata;
pistolet; działo; wystrzał
armatni
gunpowder ['gan,pałder] s. proch
strzelniczy; proch armatni
gurgle ['ge:rgl] v. bulgotać;
bełkotać; s. bulgotanie;
szemranie
gush [gasz] s. ulewa; wylew; v.
tryskać; lać się; wytrysnąć
gust [gast] s. podmuch; wybuch
gut [gat] s. kiszka; v. patroszyć;
wypalić wnętrze (domu)
guts [gats] pl. wnętrzności
gutter ['gater] v. wyżłobić;
okapywać; s. rynna;
rynsztok; rów; wyżłobienie;
adj. rynsztokowy; brukowy
(dziennik)
guy [gaj] s. facet; człek; cuma;
v. cumować; uwiązać
gym [dżym] s. sala
gimnastyczna; gimnastyka
(przedmiot w szkole)
gymnasium [dżym'nejzjem] s.
sala gimnastyczna; hala
sportowa
gymnastics [dżym'naestyks] s.
gimnastyka; ćwiczenia
fizyczne
gynecologist [,gajny'koledżyst]

s. ginekolog
gypsy ['dżypsy] s. cygan;
cyganka; cyganeria; język
cygański
gyrate [,dżaje'rejt] v. wirować;
kręcić się (wzdłuż koła lub
spirali)

H

h [ejcz] ósma litera angielskiego
alfabetu (prawie niema)
haberdasher ['haeberdaeszer] s.
kupiec galanteryjny; szmuklerz
habit ['haebyt] s. zwyczaj; nałóg;
usposobienie;
przyzwyczajenie; habit; v.
odziewać się
habitation [,haeby'tejszyn] s.
miejsce zamieszkania;
zamieszkiwanie
habitual [he'bytjual] adj. zwykły;
nałogowy; zwyczajny
hack [haek] v. siekać; rąbać;
kopać; kaszleć; s. szrama;
motyka; szkapa; najemnik;
taksówka; adj. wynajęty;
spowszedniały; banalny;
oklepany; szablonowy
hacksaw ['haekso:] s. piła do
metalu (z drobnymi zębami)
had [haed] zob. have
haddock ['haedek] s. łupacz
h(a)emorrhage ['hemerydż] s.
krwotok; mieć krwotok
hag [haeg] s. wiedźma;
czarownica; brzydka, zła
kobieta
haggard ['haegerd] adj.
wynędzniały; strapiony;
wychudły
hail [hejl] s. grad; powitanie; v.
grad pada; witać;
pozdrawiać; zawołać; walić
jak gradem
hair [heer] s. włos; włosy
hairbrush ['heerbrash] s.
szczotka do włosów

haircut ['heerkat] s. ostrzyżenie; styl ostrzyżenia włosów

hairdo ['heerdu:] s. uczesanie; fryzura; styl uczesania

hairdresser ['heer,dreser] s. fryzjer damski

hair dryer ['heer,drajer] s. suszarka do włosów (elektryczna)

hairless ['heerlys] adj. bezwłosy; łysy; wyłysiały

hairpin ['heerpyn] s. szpilka do włosów

hairy [heery] adj. włochaty

half [ha:f] s. połowa; adj. pół; adv. na pół; po połowie

half an hour ['ha:f,en'aur] s. pół godziny

half brother ['ha:f,bradzer] s. przyrodni brat

half-breed ['ha:f,bri:d] s. mieszaniec

half time ['ha:f'tajm] s. przerwa; pół etatu; a. półetatowy

halfway ['ha:f'łej] adv. w pół drogi; w połowie drogi

hall [ho:l] s. sień; sala; hala; dwór; gmach publiczny; westybul

halloo! [he'lu:] excl. okrzyk w celu zwrócenia uwagi; v. krzyczeć; wołać

halo ['hejlou] s. nimb; aureola

halt [ho:lt] v. zatrzymać; utykać; kuleć; wahać się; s. postój; przystanek; utykanie

halter ['ho:lter] s. kantar pastewny; stryczek; v. nakładać kantar

halve [ha:w] v. przepołowić; podzielić się po połowie

ham [haem] s. szynka

hamburger ['haembe:rger] s. siekany kotlet wołowy; bułka z siekanym kotletem wołowym

hamlet ['haemlyt] s. wioska; sioło; malutka wieś

hammer ['haemer] s. młotek; v. bić młotkiem; walić

hammock ['haemok] s. hamak

hamper ['haemper] v. zawadzać; krępować; s. kosz z wiekiem

hamster ['haemster] s. chomik

hand [haend] s. ręka; dłoń; pismo; v. podać; zwijać; pomagać; a. podręczny; przenośny

hand back ['haend,baek] v. oddać; podać do tyłu

hand down ['haend,dałn] v. przekazać; dać w spadku; podać w dół

hand in ['haend,yn] v. wręczyć

hand over ['haend,ouwer] v. wręczyć; podać; dostarczyć

handbag ['haendbaeg] s. damska torebka

handbill ['haendbyl] s. ulotka

handbook ['haend-buk] s. podręcznik; poradnik

hand brake ['haend,brejk] s. hamulec ręczny

handcuff ['haendka:f] s. kajdany; v. zakuwać w kajdany

handful ['haendful] s. garść; garstka; kłopotliwa osoba

handicap ['haendykaep] s. przeszkoda; upośledzenie; trudność

handicraft ['haendykra:ft] s. rzemiosło; rękodzieło (tkactwo, etc.)

handkerchief ['hendkerczy:f] s. apaszka; chustka do nosa

handle ['haendl] s. trzonek; rękojeść; uchwyt; sposób; v. dotykać; manipulować; traktować; załatwiać; dać radę; handlować; zarządzać; kontrolować

handlebar ['haendlba:r] s. kierownica od (roweru)

hand luggage ['haend,lagydż] s. bagaż ręczny

handmade ['haend'mejd] adj. ręcznie zrobiony

handrail ['haend,rejl] s. poręcz; bariera; balustrada

handshake ['haend,szejk] s. uścisk dłoni (w pozdrowieniu, targu)

handsome ['haensem] adj. przystojny; szczodry; znaczny (datek)

handwork ['haend,łe:rk] s. robota

ręczna; praca fizyczna
handwriting ['haend,rajtyng] s.
pismo; charakter pisma
handy ['haendy] adj. zręczny;
wygodny; bliski; pod ręką
hang; hung; hung [haeng; hang;
hang]
hang [haeng] v. wieszać;
powiesić; rozwiesić;
wywiesić; zwisać; s.
nachylenie; pochyłość;
powiązanie; orientacja
hang around ['haeng e'raund] v.
wałęsać się; obijać się
hang out ['haeng'aut] v.
wywieszać; wychylać się
hang up ['haeng,ap] v. zaczepić
sie; powiesić słuchawkę;
opóźniać (pracę);
wstrzymywać
hangar ['haenger] s. hangar
hang-glider ['haeng'glajder] s.
lotnia; skrzydło Rogali
hangings ['haenynz] s. kotary;
portiery; draperie; obicia;
firanki
hang loose ['haen,lu:z] v. być
rozluźniony w akcji
(sportowej); zwisać
swobodnie
hangover ['haeng,ouwer] s.
(slang) kac; przeżytek
hanky-panky ['haenky-'paenky]
s. hokus-pokus; też:
rozwiązłość
haphazard ['haep'haezerd] s. los
szczęścia; przypadek; adj.
przypadkowy; dorywczy; adv.
przypadkowo; na chybił trafił
happen ['haepen] v. zdarzać
się; trafić się; przypadkowo
być (gdzieś); mieć
(nie)szczęście
happen on ['haepen,on] v.
przypadkiem spotkać;
natknąć się na
happening ['haepenyng] s.
wydarzenie; wypadek;
zdarzenie
happily ['haepyly] adv.
szczęśliwie; na szczęście;
trafnie
happiness ['haepynys] s.

szczęście; zadowolenie;
radość
happy ['haepy] adj. szczęśliwy;
zadowolony; właściwy
(wybór); mądra (rada);
radosny
happy-go-lucky ['haepy,gou'laky]
adj. beztroski
harass ['haeres] v. niepokoić;
trapić; dręczyć; nękać
harbor ['ha:rber] s. przystań;
port; v. gościć; dawać
schronienie; zawijać do portu
harelip ['heer'lyp] s. zajęcza
warga
hard [ha:rd] adj. twardy; surowy;
trudny; ciężki; ostry; adv.
usilnie; wytrwale; ciężko; z
trudem; siarczyście
hard by ['ha:rd,baj] adv. blisko;
tuż obok; w pobliżu
hard up ['ha:rd,ap] v. być w
kłopotach pieniężnych
hard of hearing [ha:rd,ow
'hieryng] adj. głuchawy
harden ['ha:rdn] v. twardnieć;
uodparniać; stabilizować
hardheaded ['ha:rd'hedyd] adj.
trzeźwy; praktyczny; twardy
człowiek
hardhearted ['ha:rd'ha:rtyd] adj.
nieczuły; niemiłosierny
hardly ['ha:rdly] adv. ledwie;
zaledwie; prawie; z trudem;
surowo; chyba nie; rzadko
hardness ['ha:rdnys] s.
twardość; wytrzymałość;
odporność
hardship ['ha:rdszyp] s.
trudność; trudy; męka; znój
hardware ['ha:rdłeer] s. wyroby
żelazne; towary żelazne
hare [heer] s. zając; królik
harebell ['heer-bel] s. dzwonek
okrągłolistny
hark [ha:rk] v. słuchaj; uważaj;
odejdź; słuchaj uważnie
harm [ha:rm] s. szkoda;
krzywda; v. szkodzić;
krzywdzić
harmful ['ha:rmful] adj.
szkodliwy; szkodzący;
zadający ból

harmless ['ha:rmlys] adj.
nieszkodliwy; niewinny
harmonious [ha:rmounjes] adj.
harmonijny; melodyjny; zgodny
harmonize ['ha:rmenajz] v.
uzgadniać; harmonizować
harmony ['ha:rmeny] s. harmonia
(dźwięków, ludzi); zgoda
harness ['ha:rnys] s. uprząż; v.
zaprzęgać; zużytkować
(wiatr ...)
harp [ha:rp] s. harfa; v. gadać
w kółko; grać na harfie
harpoon [ha:'rpu:n] s. harpun; v.
ugodzić harpunem
harrow ['haerou] s. brona; v.
bronować; dręczyć;
szarpać; ranić; pustoszyć;
niszczyć
harsh [ha:rsz] adj. szorstki;
żrący; ostry; cierpki; przykry;
surowy; nieprzyjemny
hart [ha:rt] s. rogacz (dorosły)
(powyżej pięcioletni)
harvest ['ha:rwyst] s. żniwa;
zbiory; zbiór; urodzaj; plony; v.
zbierać (zboże); zbierać
(plony); sprzątać z pól
harvester ['ha:rwyster] s.
żniwiarz; żniwiarka
(mechaniczna)
has [haez] (on, ona, ono) ma;
zob. have
hash [haesz] s. siekane mięso;
v. siekać; knocić;
przemieszać
haste [hejst] s. pośpiech
hasten [hejstn] v. przyśpieszać;
spieszyć; być szybkim
hasty ['hejsty] adj. pośpieszny;
prędki; porywczy; niecierpliwy
hat [haet] s. kapelusz
hatch [haecz] v. wysiadywać;
wylęgać; wykluwać; knuć;
zakreskować; s. wyląg; łuk;
drzwiczki; śluza; kreska
hatchet ['haeczyt] s. toporek
hatchet man ['haeczyt,men] s.
człowiek przeprowadzający
czystkę (odrabiający brudną
robotę)
hate [hejt] s. nienawiść; v.
nienawidzieć; nie znosić

hateful ['hejtful] adj.
nienawistny; zasługujący na
nienawiść
hatred ['hejtryd] s. nienawiść
haughtiness ['ho:tynys] s.
pyszność; hardość;
zarozumialstwo
haughty ['ho:ty] adj. hardy;
pyszny; zarozumiały;
wzgardliwy
haul [ho:l] s. wleczenie;
holowanie; ładunek; połów;
zysk; v. wlec; ciągnąć;
holować; wozić;
transportować; taszczyć
haunch [ho:ncz] s. biodro z
udem
haunt [ho:nt] v. nawiedzać; s.
miejsce często odwiedzane;
melina; spelunka; legowisko
have; had; had [haew; haed;
haed]
have [haew] v. mieć;
otrzymać; zawierać; nabyć;
musieć
have-not ['haew,nat] adj. nie
posiadający; biedny
have on ['haew on] v. mieć na
sobie; być ubranym w
have to do ['haew,tu'du] v.
musieć (coś) robić
haven ['hejwn] s. przystań;
port; v. dawać schronienie;
wprowadzać do portu
havoc ['haewek] s. spustoszenie
hawk [ho:k] s. jastrząb; packa;
chrząknięcie; v. polować z
jastrzębiem; sprzedawać na
ulicy; chrząkać głośno
hawthorn ['ho:torn] s. głóg
hay [hej] s. siano
haycock ['hejkok] s. stóg siana
hay-fever ['hej'fi:wer] s.
uczulenie; katar sienny
hayloft ['hej-loft] s. strych na
siano (w stodole etc.)
hayrick ['hejryk] s. stóg siana
haystack ['hejsta:k] s. stóg siana
(w polu, na łące etc.)
hazard ['haezerd] s. przypadek;
traf; ryzyko; v. ryzykować
hazardous ['haezerdes] adj.
ryzykowny; hazardowny;

niebezpieczny
haze [hejz] s. lekka mgła
hazel ['hejzl] s. leszczyna; kolor
orzechowy
hazel-nut ['hejzl-nat] s. orzech
laskowy
hazy ['hejzy] adj. mglisty;
zamglony; nieco podchmielony
H-bomb ['ejcz bom] s. bomba
wodorowa
he [hi:] pron. on
head [hed] s. głowa; łeb; szef;
naczelnik; nagłówek; szczyt;
v. prowadzić; kierować (się)
head over heels ['hed,ouwer
hi:ls] do góry nogami; na łeb
na szyję; panicznie; w panice
headache ['hedejk] s. ból głowy
headgear ['hedgi:r] s. nakrycie
głowy; ubiór głowy
heading ['hedyng] s. nagłówek
headland ['hedlend] s. przylądek
(daleko wysunięty w morze)
headlights ['hedlajts] pl. główne
światła samochodu
headline ['hedlajn] s. nagłówek
(w gazecie); wiadomość w
skrócie
headlong ['hedlong] adv. na łeb
na szyję; na złamanie karku;
na oślep; głową w przód
headmaster ['hedma:ster] s.
dyrektor (szkoły)
heads or tails ['heds,o:r'tejlz]
orzeł czy reszka
headphones ['hedfouns] pl.
słuchawki (radiowe,
gramofonowe)
headquarters ['hed'kło:terz] pl.
kwatera główna; główne biuro
headstrong ['hedstrong] adj.
zawzięty; uparty;
bezwzględny
headway ['hedłej] s. postęp
heal [hi:l] v. leczyć; łagodzić;
uspakajać; wyleczyć się
heal up ['hi:l,ap] v. zagoić
health [hels] s. zdrowie
health resort [hels ry'zo:rt] s.
uzdrowisko
healthy ['helsy] adj. zdrowy;
potężny; spowodowany
zdrowiem

heap [hi:p] s. kupa; gromada; v.
gromadzić; ładować na stos;
obsypywać dużą ilością
hear; heard; heard [hier; he:rd;
he:rd]
hear [hier] v. słyszeć; usłyszeć;
słuchać; dowiedzieć się
heard [he:rd] zob. hear
hearing ['hieryng] s. słuch;
posłuch; przesłuchanie;
rozprawa; zasięg głosu;
słyszenie
hearsay ['hiersej] s. pogłoska
hearse [he:rs] s. karawan
heart [ha:rt] s. serce; odwaga;
otucha; sedno; symbol serca
heartbreaking ['ha:rtbrejkyng]
adj. rozdzierający serce
heartburn ['ha:rtbe:rn] s. zgaga;
pieczenie w żołądku
hearth [ha:rs] s. palenisko
heartless ['ha:rtlys] adj. nieczuły;
bez serca
heart transplant ['ha:rt,traens
'pla:nt] przeszczepienie serca
hearty ['ha:rty] adj. serdeczny;
szczery; otwarty; pożywny;
obfity; solidny; dobry; krzepki;
rześki
heat [hi:t] s. gorąco; upał; żar;
ciepło; uniesienie; pasja;
popęd płciowy (zwierząt)
heater ['hi:ter] s. grzejnik; piec
heath [hi:s] s. wrzos; wrzosiec;
wrzosowisko
heathen [hi:zen] adj. pogański;
s. poganin; ciemniak
heather ['hedzer] s. wrzos
heating ['hi:tyng] s. ogrzewanie
heave; hove; hove [hi:w; houw;
houw]
heave [hi:w] v. unosić;
dźwigać; podważać;
nabrzmiewać; wyciągać;
sapać; s. dźwignięcie;
przesunięcie
heaven ['hewn] s. niebo; raj;
niebiosa
heavenly ['hewnly] adj. niebieski;
niebiański; boski
heaviness ['hewynys] s.
ciężkość; ociężałość
heavy ['hewy] adj. ciężki; duży;

ponury; zrozpaczony
heavy-handed ['hewy'haendyd]
adj. niezgrabny; nietaktowny;
bezwzględny
heavy traffic ['hewy'traefyk]
ciężki ruch (np. kołowy)
heavyweight ['hewyłejt] s. waga
ciężka
hectic ['hektyk] adj. gorący;
dziki; niszczący;
rozgorączkowany
hedge [hedż] s. płot; żywopłot;
ogrodzenie; zapora;
ubezpieczenie; v. ogradzać;
wykręcać się; ubezpieczać
się w spekulacji
hedgehog ['hedżhog] s. jeż;
świnka morska
heed [hi:d] s. troska; dbałość;
uwaga; wzgląd; ostrożność;
v. uważać; baczyć
heedful ['hi:dful] adj. uważny;
ostrożny
heedless ['hi:dlys] adj. niedbały;
nieostrożny; nieuważny
heel [hi:l] s. pięta; obcas;
przechył; łajdak; v. dotykać
piętą; podbijać obcas;
zaopatrywać; przechylać się;
tupać obcasem
he goat ['hi:gout] s. kozioł
heifer ['hefer] s. jałówka
height [hajt] s. wysokość;
wzniesienie; wyniosłość;
szczyt; najwyższa granica
heighten [hajtn] v. podnosić;
podwyższać; powiększać
heinous ['hejnes] adj. potworny;
ohydny; nienawistny; haniebny
heir [eer] s. spadkobierca;
dziedzic; następca
heiress ['eerys] s.
spadkobierczyni; następczyni;
dziedziczka (majątku, tytułu)
held [held] zob. hold
helicopter ['helykopter] s.
śmigłowiec; helikopter
hell [hel] s. piekło; psiakrew!
miejsce nędzy i okrucieństwa
hello ['he'lou] excl. halo!
cześć! czołem! dzień dobry!
helm [helm] s. ster; v. sterować
helmet ['helmyt] s. hełm; kask

help [help] v. pomagać;
usługiwać; nakładać
(jedzenie); s. pomoc;
pomocnik; robotnik
helper ['helper] s. pomocnik
helpful ['helpful] adj. pomocny;
przydatny; użyteczny
helping ['helpyng] s. porcja
(jedzenia); udzielanie pomocy
helpless ['helplys] adj. bezradny;
bez pomocy; słaby
helplessness ['helplysnys] s.
bezradność; słabość
helter-skelter ['helter'skelter]
adv. łapu-capu; na łeb na
szyję; s. popłoch; bezładny
pośpiech (w bałaganie)
hem [hem] s. brzeg; obrąbek;
chrząkanie; v. obrębiać;
otoczyć; pochrząkiwać;
wahać się
hem in ['hem,yn] v. okrążyć;
zamknąć; obrąbić
hemisphere ['hemysfier] s.
półkula (zachodnia,
wschodnia, etc.)
hemline ['hemlajn] s. obrąbek
spódnicy
hemlock ['hemlek] s. szalej;
cykuta jadowita; drzewo tsuga
hemp [hemp] s. konopie; adj.
konopny (sznur etc.)
hemstitch ['hemstycz] s.
mereżka; v. mereżkować
(ozdobnie)
hen [hen] s. kura; kwoka; baba
hence [hens] adv. stąd; odtąd; a
więc; przeto; dlatego
henceforth [hens'fo:rs] adv.
odtąd; na przyszłość; od
teraz
hen coop ['henku:p] s. kurnik
hen house ['henhaus] s. kurnik
henpecked ['henpekt] s.
pantoflarz; adj. będący pod
pantoflem
her [he:r] pron. ją; jej; adj. jej;
(należący) do niej
herald ['hereld] s. zwiastun; v.
zwiastować; wprowadzać
heraldry ['hereldry] s. heraldyka;
pompa; ceremonia
herb [he:rb] s. zioło

(jednoroczne)

herd [he:rd] s. trzoda; stado;
pastuch; v. iść stadem;
zganiać w stado; paść;
popędzać stadem

herdsman ['he:rdzmen] s.
pasterz; pastuch

here [hier] adv. tu; tutaj; oto

here you are [,hier'ju:,a:r] exp. tu
pan ma! proszę bardzo!

hereafter ['hier'a:fter] adv.
odtąd; poniżej; potem; w
życiu pozagrobowym; s.
przyszłość; przyszłe życie

hereby ['hier'baj] adv. przez to;
w ten sposób; skutkiem tego;
w pobliżu

hereditary [hy'redytery] adj.
dziedziczny; odziedziczony;
tradycyjny; przekazany
dziedzicznie

herein ['hier'yn] adv. tutaj; tam
że; wobec tego; w tych
warunkach; w tym (rozdziale)

hereof ['hier'of] adv. tego; o
tym; w odniesieniu do tego

heresy ['herysy] s. herezja

heretic ['heretyk] s. heretyk;
heretyczka

hereupon ['hiere'pon] adv.
potem; skutkiem tego; o tym

herewith ['hier'łys] adv.
niniejszym; w ten sposób

heritage ['herytydż] s.
spuścizna; spadek;
dziedzictwo

hermit ['he:rmyt] s. pustelnik;
odludek; eremita; pustelnica

hero ['hierou] s. bohater

heroic ['hierouyk] adj.
bohaterski; heroiczny; epicki;
bardzo wymowny; podniosły

heroine ['hierouyn] s. bohaterka

heroism ['hierouyzem] s.
bohaterstwo (w czynach i
cechach)

heron ['heren] s. czapla

herring ['heryng] s. śledź

hers [he:rz] pron. jej

herself [he:r'self] pron. ona
sama; ona sobie; ja sama

hesitate ['hezytejt] v. wahać
się; być niepewnym;

zatrzymać się

hesitation [,hezytejszyn] s.
wahanie; v. być
niezdecydowanym

hew; hewed; hewn [hju:; hju:d;
hju:n]

hew [hju:] v. rąbać; ciosać;
kuć; wyrąbywać (ścieżkę)

hewn [hju:n] zob. hew

hey [hej] excl. hej! ejże!

heyday ['hejdej] s. pełnia;
rozkwit; świetny nastrój

hi [haj] excl. hej! (pozdrowienie);
cześć! czołem!

hiccup; hiccough ['hykap] s.
czkawka; v. mieć czkawkę

hid [hyd] zob.hide

hidden [hydn] zob. hide

hide; hid; hidden [hajd; hyd;
hydn]

hide [hajd] v. chować;
ukrywać; s. kryjówka; skóra
(zwierzęca)

hide-and-seek ['hajd,en si:k] exp.
zabawa w chowanego

hideous ['hydjes] adj. ohydny;
wstrętny; paskudny;
odrażający

hiding ['hajdyng] s. kryjówka;
skórobicie; lanie; manto

hiding place ['hajdyng'plejs] s.
kryjówka; melina

hi-fi ['haj'faj] = high fidelity ['haj
fy'delyty] wiernie
odtwarzający dźwięk (aparat)

high [haj] adj. wysoki; wyniosły;
silny; cienki (głos)

highbrow ['hajbrau] s.
intelektualista; a. intelektualny

high diving ['hajdajwyng] s.
skakanie z wieży do wody

high jump ['hajdżamp] s. skok
wzwyż (w sporcie)

highlands ['hajlend] s. podgórze;
góry; górzysty kraj

highlights ['hajlajts] pl. główne
punkty (np. programu)

highly ['hajly] adv. wysoko;
wysoce; wielce; zaszczytnie

highness ['hajnys] s. wysokość
(tytuł); wyniosłość

high-pitched ['haj'pyczt] adj.
wysoki; ostry; cienki (głos);

spadzisty; stromy (dach)
high-powered ['haj'pałerd] adj.
potężny
high-pressure ['haj'preszer] adj.
wysokiego ciśnienia;
nachalny
highroad ['haj'roud] s. szosa;
główna droga
high-school ['haj'sku:l] s.
gimnazjum; szkoła średnia
high-strung ['haj'strang] adj.
nerwowy; napięty; wrażliwy
high-tide ['haj'tajd] s. przypływ
highway ['haj'łej] s. szosa
highwayman ['haj,łejmen] s.
rozbójnik
hijack ['hajdżaek] v. rabować;
grabić
hike [hajk] v. włóczyć się;
wędrować; wyciągać do
góry; s. wycieczka; podwyżka
hilarious [hy'leerjes] adj. wesoły;
hałaśliwie wesoły
hill [hyl] s. górka; pagórek;
kopiec; v. sypać kopiec
hillbilly ['hylbyly] s. prowincjusz
hillside ['hyl'sajd] s. stok
hilly ['hyly] adj. pagórkowaty;
górzysty
hilt [hylt] s. rękojeść; garda
him [hym] pron. jego; go; jemu;
mu
himself [hym'self] pron. się;
siebie; sobie; sam; osobiście;
we własnej osobie
hind [hajnd] s. parobek; łania;
adj. tylni; zadni
hinder ['hynder] v.
przeszkadzać;
powstrzymywać
hind leg ['hajnd,leg] s. tylnia
noga
hindrance ['hyndrens] s.
przeszkoda; zawada;
zawadzanie
hindsight ['hajnd,sajt] s.
zrozumienie co trzeba było
zrobić
hinge [hyndż] s. zawiasa; v.
obracać; zależeć; zawiesić
na zawiasach; wisieć na
zawiasach
hinny [hyny] s. muł (z oślicy i

ogiera); v. rżeć
hint [hynt] s. aluzja; przytyk;
wskazówka; v. napomknąć;
dać do zrozumienia; zrobić
aluzję
hinterland ['hynter,laend] s.
zaplecze; daleki teren
hip [hyp] s. biodro; naroże;
dachu; chandra; adj.
biodrowy; współczesny;
stylowy
hip to [hyp,tu] adj.
poinformowany o (slang)
hippie [hypi:] s. nonkonformista;
adj. zbuntowany przeciw
tradycji (wyobcowany)
hippopotamus [hype'potemes] s.
hipopotam
hire [hajer] s. najem; opłata za
najem; v. najmować;
wynajmować; dzierżawić;
odnajmować
hire out ['hajer aut] v.
wynajmować (się do pracy,
na służbę ...)
hire purchase ['hajer'pe:rczys]
wynajem - zakup na raty
his [hyz] pron. jego
hiss [hys] v. syczeć; gwizdać;
s. syk; gwizd; głoska sycząca
historian [hys'to:rjen] s. historyk;
historyczka
historic [hys'toryk] adj.
historyczny; sławny w historii
history ['hystory] s. historia;
dzieje; przeszłość (znana)
hit [hyt] s. uderzenie; przytyk;
sukces; sensacja; v. uderzyć;
utrafić; natrafić; zabić
hit and run ['hyt,en'ran] adj.
uciekający od wypadku
(drogowego); walczący
podjazdowo; dorywczy i
niepewny
hit man ['hytmen] s. najemny
zabójca; najemny morderca
hit or miss [hyt o:r mys] adv. na
chybił trafił; przypadkiem
hit upon ['hyte'pon] v. natrafić
(na coś, na kogoś)
hitch [hycz] s. zaciśnięcie;
węzeł; przeszkoda;
szarpnięcie; uchwyt; służba

(wojskowa); v. doczepić;
uczepić; pociągnąć;
szarpnąć; przywiązać;
zaczepić się; ciągnąć
szarpiąc
hitchhike ['hycz,hajk] v. jechać
autostopem
hitchhiker ['hycz,hajker] s.
jadący autostopem
hither ['hydzer] adv. dotąd; tutaj;
adj. bliżej
hitherto ['hydzer'tu] adv.
dotychczas; do tej pory
hive [hajw] s. ul; rojowisko; v.
umieszczać w ulu; wchodzić
do ula; zbierać do ula
hoard [ho:rd] v. gromadzić;
zbierać; s. zapas; zbiór; skarb
hoarfrost ['ho:r'frost] s. szron
(na trawie, włosach etc.)
hoarse [ho:rs] adj. zachrypnięty;
v. zachrypnąć; mieć
chrapliwy głos
hoax [houks] v. bujać;
nabierać; s. bujda; kaczka;
kawał
hobble ['hobl] s. pęta; utykanie;
v. utykać; kuleć; pętać
hobby ['hoby] s. hobby; pasja
(np. filatelistyka)
hobbyhorse ['hobyho:rs] s. konik
na kiju do zabawy (na
biegunach)
hobgoblin ['hob,goblyn] s.
skrzat; chochlik
hobnob ['hobnob] v. być za pan
brat; blisko się zadawać
hobo ['haubou] s. włóczęga
hock [hok] s. pęcina; v.
zastawić (się) w lombardzie
hockey ['hoky] s. hokej
hoe [hou] s. motyka; graca; v.
gracować; okopywać
motyką
hog [hog] s. wieprz; człowiek
zachłanny; v. łapać dla siebie;
jechać środkiem; wyginać
łukowato w środku;
zagarniać sobie
hoist [hojst] s. dźwig; wyciąg;
v. wyciągać ładunek w górę;
wywieszać (flagę);
podciągać do góry

hold; held; held [hould; held;
held]
hold [hould] v. trzymać;
posiadać; zawierać;
powstrzymywać; uważać;
obchodzić; wytrzymywać;
trwać; s. chwyt; pauza;
pomieszczenie; więzienie;
twierdza; silny wpływ; uchwyt
hold back ['hould,baek] v.
powstrzymać; zataić;
wahać się
hold on ['hould,on] v. trzymać
się; wytrzymywać;
powstrzymać
holdup ['hould'ap] s.
zatrzymanie; zator; napad
rabunkowy
holder ['houlder] s. właściciel;
posiadacz; uchwyt
holding ['houldyng] s.
posiadłość; portfel akcji;
dzierżawa; uchwyt; ujęcie;
trzymanie
hole [houl] s. dziura; nora; dołek;
v. dziurawić; przedziurawiać;
przekopywać (tunel)
holiday ['holedy] s. święto;
wakacje; urlop; adj. wesoły;
radosny
holiday maker ['holedy,mejker] s.
wczasowicz; letnik; turysta;
wycieczkowicz; letniczka
holler ['holer] v. wrzeszczeć;
krzyczeć (po prostacku)
hollow ['holou] s. dziupla; dziura;
kotlina; dolina; adj. wklęsły;
dziurawy; fałszywy; głuchy;
pusty; czczy; głodny;
nieszczery; adv. pusto
hollow out ['holou,aut] v.
drążyć; wydrążyć; żłobić
holly ['holy] s. ostrokrzew
holy ['holy] adj. święty
homage ['homydż] s. hołd
home [houm] s. dom; ojczyzna;
kraj; schronisko; bramka; adj.
domowy; rodzinny; krajowy;
wewnętrzny; ojczysty
homeless ['houmlys] adj.
bezdomny; bez dachu nad
głową
homely ['houmly] adj. swojski;

pospolity; nieładny; prosty; skromny; niewybredny; niewyszukany

homemade ['houm'mejd] adj. domowego wyrobu; krajowy

homesick ['houm-syk] adj. stęskniony za domem rodzinnym; stęskniony za (czymś swoim)

homesickness ['houm,syknys] s. nostalgia; tęsknota za domem

home team ['houm-ti:m] s. drużyna miejscowa (sportowa)

home trade ['houm-trejd] s. handel wewnętrzny

homewards ['houmłedz] adv. ku domowi (ojczyźnie); do domu

homework ['houmłerk] s. zadanie domowe; odrabianie lekcji

homicide ['homy,sajd] s. zabójca; zabójstwo

honest ['onyst] adj. uczciwy; prawy; przyzwoity; szczery; adv. naprawdę

honesty ['onesty] s. zacność; prawość; rzetelność; uczciwość

honey ['hany] s. miód; słodycz

honeycomb ['hany,koum] s. (woskowy) plaster pszczeli; v. dziurawić; przenikać

honeymoon ['hany,mu:n] s. miodowy miesiąc; v. spędzić miodowy miesiąc

honk [honk] s. krzyk gęsi; głos trąbki, klaksonu; v. trąbić; (slang: wymyślać)

honorary ['onerery] adj. honorowy (np. urząd); bezpłatny

honor ['oner] s. cześć; uczciwość; cnota; tytuł sędziego; v. czcić; zaszczycać; honorować

honorable ['onerebl] adj. czcigodny; uczciwy; szanowny; honorowy; zaszczytny; poważany

hood [hud] s. kaptur; kapturek; maska; buda; v. zaopatrywać w kaptur; przykrywać

hoodlum ['hu:dlem] s. opryszek; chuligan; łobuz

hoodwink ['hudłynk] v. oczy mydlić; zmylić; zawiązywać oczy

hoof ['hu:f] s. kopyto; v. kopać; iść; tańczyć; iść pieszo

hook [huk] s. hak; v. zahaczyć; zakrzywić (się); złapać (męża)

hoop [hu:p] s. obręcz; v. otaczać obręczą;wykrzyknąć

hooping-cough ['hu:pyng-kof] s. koklusz; krztusiec; zob. whooping cough

hoot [hu:t] s. hukanie; odgłosy niezadowolenia; v. hukać gwizdać; wyć; trąbić; wygwizdać

hooves [hu:wz] pl. kopyta

hop [hop] s. chmiel; skok; potańcówka; v. podskakiwać; poderwać (się); przeskakiwać

hope [houp] s. nadzieja; v. mieć nadzieję; spodziewać się; ufać; żywić nadzieję

hopeful ['houpful] adj. pełen nadziei; ufny; obiecujący; rokujący nadzieję

hopeless ['houplys] adj. beznadziejny; rozpaczliwy; zrozpaczony; zdesperowany

horde [ho:rd] s. horda; gromada

horizon [he'rajzen] s. horyzont; widnokrąg; warstwa oznaczona

horizontal [,hory'zontel] adj. poziomy; horyzontalny; widnokręgowy; s. płaszczyzna pozioma; poziom równy i płaski

horn [ho:rn] s. róg; trąbka; syrena; kula (siodła); v. bóść; przebóść; wmieszać się

hornet ['ho:rnyt] s. szerszeń

horny ['ho:rny] adj. rogowy; zrogowaciały; rogaty; jak róg

horoscope ['hore,skoup] s. horoskop

horrible ['horebl] adj. straszny; okropny; szokujący; paskudny

horrid ['horyd] adj. straszny; ohydny; odrażający; paskudny

horrify ['horyfaj] v. przerażać;
oburzać; ciężko szokować

horror ['horer] s. groza; wstręt;
odraza; przerażenie; dreszcz

horse ['ho:rs] s. koń; konnica;
jazda; kozioł z drzewa

horseback ['ho:rs,baek] s. grzbiet
koński; adv. konno

horsefly ['ho:rs,flaj] s. giez

horsehair ['ho:rs,heer] s. włosie
końskie; sztywna tkanina

horseman ['ho:rsmen] s.
jeździec

horse opera ['ho:rs'opera] s. film
kowbojski (nie-realistyczny)

horseplay ['ho:rs,plej] s.
ordynarna zabawa (brutalna)

horsepower ['ho:rs,pałer] s. koń
mechaniczny = 746 watów

horse race ['ho:rs,rejs] s.
wyścigi konne

horseradish ['ho:rs,raedysz] s.
chrzan; adj. chrzanowy

horseshoe ['ho:rs,szu] s.
podkowa; a. w kształcie
podkowy

horticulture ['ho:rty,kaltczer] s.
ogrodnictwo

hose [houz] s. pończochy; wąż
do podlewania (wiedza i
praktyka)

hosiery ['haouzery] s. trykotaże;
pończochy

hospitable ['hospytebl] adj.
gościnny; szczodry dla gości

hospital ['hospytl] s. szpital;
lecznica; a. szpitalny

hospitality [,hospy'taelyty] s.
gościnność

host [houst] s. gospodarz;
żywiciel; chmara; czereda;
tłum

hostage ['hostydż] s. zakładnik;
zastaw; zakładniczka

hostel ['hostel] s. dom
studencki; bursa; zajazd

hostess ['houstys] s. gospodyni;
stewardesa; fordanserka

hostile ['hostajl] adj. wrogi;
nieprzyjemny; antagonistyczny

hostility [hos'tylyty] s.
wrogość; stan wojny; ostra
opozycja

hot [hot] adj. gorący; palący;
pieprzny; ostry; nielegalny;
świeży; pobudliwy; adv.
gorąco

hotbed ['hot,bed] s. inspekty;
wylęgarnia; siedlisko;
rozsadnik

hot dog ['hot,dog] s. kiełbaska w
bułce; kiełbaska smażona

hotel [hou'tel] s. hotel

hothead ['hot,hed] s. człowiek
zapalczywy; raptus; a.
porywczy

hothouse ['hot,haus] s.
cieplarnia; oranżeria

hot-pants [,hot'paents] exp.
obcisłe damskie szorty; vulg.
panna puszczalska

hot water bottle [hot'ło:ter'botl]
s. gorąca butelka

hound [haund] s. ogar; łajdak; v.
tropić; szczuć; podjudzać

hour ['auer] s. godzina; pora

hourly ['auerly] adj. cogodzinny;
adv. co godzinę; ustawicznie;
z godziny na godzinę

house [haus] s. dom; zajazd;
teatr; widzowie; v. gościć;
dawać pomieszczenie;
mieszkać

housekeeper ['haus,ki:per] s.
najęta gosposia; pomoc
domowa

housekeeping ['haus,ki:pyng] s.
gospodarka domowa

housemaid ['haus,mejd] s.
pokojówka; pomoc domowa

housewife ['haus,łajf] s.
gospodyni (nie pracująca poza
domem)

housework ['haus,łe:rk] s. prace
domowe; sprzątanie i
gotowanie

housing ['hauzyng] s.
pomieszczenie; kolonia;
osłona; pokrywa; czaprak;
obudowa

hove [houw] zob. heave

hover ['hower] v. unosić się;
kręcić się; być w
niepewności; s. stan
niepewności; unoszenie się;
wahanie się; przywieranie

how [hau] adv. jak; jak? sposób
how do you do ['hau,du'ju:du]
exp.: dzień dobry! dobry
wieczór! (jak się pan(i) ma ?)
how are you ['hau,a:r'ju] exp.:
jak się pan(i) ma?
how about ['hau,e'baut] exp.:
może? pozwolisz? etc.
how much ['hau,macz] exp.: ile?
how many ['hau,meny] exp.: ile?
ilu? jak wielu?
how much is it? ['hau,macz'yz
,yt] ile to kosztuje?
however [hau'ewer] adv.
jakkolwiek; jednak; niemniej
howl [haul] s. wycie; ryk; v.
wyć; wyganiać (gonić)
wrzaskiem
howler ['hauler] s. gruby błąd
hub [hab] s. piasta; ośrodek;
slang: mąż; środek
(rozgrywki)
hubbub ['habbab] s. zgiełk;
gwar; awantura; wrzawa;
tumult
hubby ['haby] s. mężulek (slang)
huckleberry ['hakelbery] s.
borówka amerykańska (krzak
i jagoda)
huddle together ['hadl,tu'gedzer]
v. przytulać się; tulić się
huddle up ['hadl,ap] v. skulić
się; zwinąć się w kłębek
hue [hju:] s. barwa; odcień
hug [hag] s. uścisk; chwyt
zapaśniczy; v. ściskać;
przyciskać; tulić (się);
uściskać
huge [hju:dż] adj. ogromny
hull [hal] s. łuska; kadłub; v.
łuszczyć; godzić w kadłub
hullabaloo ['halebelu:] s.
harmider; zgiełk; wrzawa;
gwar
hullo [he'lou] excl. hola! halo!
hum [ham] v. nucić; buczeć;
mruczeć; chrząkać; s.
pomruk; chrząkanie; wahanie
się; blaga
human ['hju:men] adj. ludzki; s.
istota ludzka
humane ['hju:mejn] adj. ludzki;
humanitarny; litościwy

humanitarian [hju,maeny'teerjen]
adj. humanitarny; s. filantrop
humanity [hju'maenyty] s.
ludzkość; rasa ludzka; cechy
ludzkie; dobre uczynki
humble ['hambl] adj. pokorny;
uniżony; skromny; v.
upokarzać; poniżać;
poniżyć
humbleness ['hamblnys] s.
pokora; bezpretensjonalność
humbug ['hambag] s. oszustwo;
blaga; bujda; oszust; blagier;
v. blagować; oszukiwać;
nabierać; wyłudzać
opowiadaniem bredni
humdrum ['hamdram] adj. nudny;
banalny; monotonny; s.
szarzyzna; banalność;
nudziarz
humidity [hju'mydyty] s. wilgoć;
wilgotność (powietrza etc.)
humiliate [hju'myly,ejt] v.
upokarzać; poniżać;
martwić
humiliation [hju,:myly,ejszyn] s.
upokorzenie; poniżenie
humility [hju'mylyty] s.
skromność; pokora ducha
humming-bird ['hamyng,byrd] s.
koliber
humor ['hju:mer] s. humor;
nastrój; kaprys; wesołość; v.
dogadzać; zaspakajać;
zadowalać; ustępować;
dostosować się do
zachcianek etc.
humorous ['hju:meres] adj.
śmieszny; pocieszny; pełen
humoru; zabawny; komiczny
hump [hamp] s. garb; v. garbić
się; wyginać w łuk
humpback ['hampbaek] s. garbus
hunchback ['hancz,baek] s.
garbus; garb na plecach
hundred ['handred] num. sto; s.
setka; niezliczona ilość
hundredth ['handredt] num.
setny; jedna setna
hundredweight ['handred,łejt] s.
cetnar angielski
hung [hang] zob. hang
Hungarian [han'geerjen] adj.

węgierski; s. Węgier
hunger ['hanger] s. głód; v.
głodować; łaknąć; głodzić
hunger strike ['hanger-strajk] s.
strajk głodowy
hungry ['hangry] adj. głodny;
zgłodniały; pożądliwy; ubogi;
jałowy; nieurodzajny; łaknący
hunt [hant] s. polowanie; teren
łowiecki; v. polować; gonić;
przeszukiwać; szukać
hunter ['hanter] s. myśliwy
hunting ['hantyng] s. polowanie;
adj. myśliwski
hunting ground ['hantyng
,graund] s. teren myśliwski
huntsman ['hantsmen] s.
myśliwy; łowca
hurdle ['he:rdl] s. opłotki; v.
porać się; skakać przez
płotki; grodzić; przebijać się
hurdler ['he:rdler] s. zawodnik
wyścigów (z płotkami)
hurdle race ['he:rdl,rejs] s.
wyścigi (z płotkami; przez
płotki)
hurl [he:rl] s. rzut; v. rzucać
hurrah [he'ra:] excl.: hura!
hurray [he'rej] excl.: hura! v.
krzyczeć hura (z radości)
hurricane ['haryken] n. huragan;
orkan tropikalny
hurried ['haryd] adj. pośpieszny
hurry ['hary] s. pośpiech
hurry up! ['hary,ap] v. śpiesz
się! ruszaj się!
hurt; hurt; hurt [he:rt; he:rt;
he:rt]
hurt [he:rt] v. ranić; kaleczyć;
urazić; uszkodzić; boleć;
dokuczać; s. skaleczenie;
rana; szkoda; krzywda; uraz;
uszkodzenie; ból; ujma; ranka
husband ['hazbend] s. mąż; v.
gospodarować oszczędnie;
wydawać za mąż
husbandry ['hazbendry] s.
rolnictwo; uprawa; hodowla
hush [hasz] s. cisza; spokój;
milczenie; v. cicho! sza!
uciszyć się; milczeć;
tuszować (coś); ululać;
załagodzić

hush up ['hasz,ap] v. siedzieć
cicho; zatuszować (coś)
husk [hask] s. łuska; v.
łuszczyć; wyłuszczać;
złuszczać
husky ['hasky] adj. krzepki;
suchy; zachrypnięty;
łuszczasty; s. pies eskimoski;
język eskimoski
hustle ['hasl] s. pośpiech;
krzątanina; bieganina;
popychanie; v. śpieszyć się;
krzątać się; popychać;
pchać się; szturchać;
popędzać; wypchnąć
hut [hat] s. chata; barak;
chałupa; v. mieszkać w
chałupie
hutch [hacz] s. skrzynia; klatka;
domek; kurnik; chlewik; v.
wkładać coś do skrzyni
hybrid ['hajbryd] s. mieszaniec;
adj. mieszany; mieszanego
pochodzenia
hydrant ['hajdrent] s. hydrant
hydraulic ['haj'dro:lyk] adj.
hydrauliczny
hydro ['hajdrou] adj. wodo-;
wodoro-; wodny
hydrocarbon ['hajdrou'ka:rben] s.
węglowodór
hydrochloric acid [,hajdrou'klo:
ryk,asyd] s. kwas solny
hydrogen ['hajdrydżen] s. wodór
hydrogen bomb ['hajdrydżen
,bom] s. bomba wodorowa
hydroplane ['hajdrou,plejn] s.
wodnopłatowiec; ślizgacz
hyena [haj'y:ne] s. hiena
hygiene ['hajdżi:n] s. higiena
hymn [hym] s. hymn; v.
śpiewać hymn; chwalić
hymnem
hyphen ['hajfen] s. łącznik; v.
używać łącznika
hypnotize ['hypne,tajz] v.
hipnotyzować
hypocrisy [hy'pokresy] s.
hipokryzja; udawanie cnoty
hypocrite ['hypekryt] s.
hipokryta; obłudnik; obłudnica
hypocritical [,hypou'krytekl] adj.
obłudny; hipokrytyczny;

dwulicowy; udający cnotę
hypodermic [,hajpe'de:rmyk] adj.
podskórny (zastrzyk)
hypothesis [haj'potysys] s.
hipoteza; niesprawdzona teoria
hysterectomy [,histe'rektemy] s.
wycięcie macicy
hysteria [hys'tyerje] s. histeria;
wybuch podniecenia
hysterical [hys'terykel] adj.
histeryczny; podlegający
histerii
hysterics [hys'teryks] pl. atak
histerii
hysterotomy [,histe'rotemy] s.
operacja macicy

I

I [aj] pron. ja; dziewiąta litera
angielskiego alfabetu
I-beam ['aj,bi:m] s. belka
dwuteówka (stalowa)
ice [ajs] s. lód; lody; v.
zamrażać; mrozić; lukrować
Ice Age ['ajsejdż] s. epoka
lodowa; epoka lodowcowa
iceberg ['ajsbe:rg] s. góra
lodowa (na morzu)
ice-cream ['ajskri:m] s. lody
icicle ['ajsykl] s. sopel
ice floe ['ajs-flou] s. kra
icing ['ajsyn] s. lukier
icon ['ajkon] s. ikona
icy ['ajsy] adj. lodowaty
idea [aj'die] s. idea; pojęcie;
pomysł; wyobrażenie; myśl;
plan
ideal [aj'diel] adj. idealny; s.
ideał; model doskonały
idealize [aj'dielajz] v.
idealizować; wyidealizować
identical [aj'dentykel] adj. taki
sam; identyczny;
tożsamościowy; zupełnie
podobny
identification [ajdentyfy'kejszyn]
s. utożsamienie; identyfikacja;

stwierdzenie tożsamości
identification papers [aj,dentyfy
'kejszyn'pejpers] s. dowód
tożsamości; dowód osobisty
identify [aj'dentyfaj] v.
utożsamić; identyfikować
identity [aj'dentyty] s.
tożsamość; identyczność
identity card [aj'dentyty ka:rd] s.
dowód osobisty
ideological [,ajdye'lodżykel] adj.
ideologiczny
idiom ['ydjem] s. wyrażenie
zwyczajowe; wyrażenie
idiomatyczne; dialekt; typowy
styl
idiot ['ydjet] s. idiota; dureń
idiotic [,ydy'otyk] adj. idiotyczny;
bardzo głupi
idle ['ajdl] adj. niezajęty;
bezczynny; jałowy; zbyteczny;
leniwy; pusty; czczy; v.
próżnować; być na wolnym
biegu; być bez pracy; obijać
się
idle away ['ajdl,e'łej] v.
marnować (czas); roztrwonić
czas
idleness ['ajdlnys] s.
bezczynność; lenistwo;
próżniactwo; daremność;
bezpodstawność
idol ['ajdl] s. bożyszcze; bałwan;
posąg bożka
idolize ['ajdelajz] v. ubóstwiać;
uwielbiać; bałwochwalić
idyll ['ydyl] s. sielanka; idylla;
opis raju na wsi (w poezji)
if [yf] conj. jeżeli; jeśli; gdyby;
o ile; czy; żeby (tylko)
iffy [yffy] adj. wątpliwy (slang)
igloo ['iglu:] s. eskimoska chata
kopulasta ze śniegu
ignite [yg'najt] v. zapalić
ignition [yg'nyszyn] s. zapłon;
zapalenie; elektryczny zapłon
ignition key [yg'nyszyn,ki:] s.
klucz do zapłonu (w aucie)
ignoble [yg'noubl] adj. nędzny;
podły; haniebny; niecny;
marny; niegodziwy; niskiego
pochodzenia
ignorance ['ygnerens] s.

nieświadomość; ignorancja;
nieuctwo; ciemnota;
obskurantyzm
ignorant ['ygnerent] adj.
nieświadomy; ciemny; bez
wykształcenia; zdradzający
ignorancję
ignore [yg'no:r] v. pomijać;
lekceważyć; odrzucać; nie
zważać
ill [yl] adj. zły; chory; słaby;
lichy; s. zło; adv. źle; nie
bardzo; kiepsko; niepomyślnie
ill-advised ['yled'wajzd] adj.
nierozsądny; nierozważny
ill-affected ['yle'fektyd] adj. źle
usposobiony; nieżyczliwy
ill-bred ['yl'bred] adj. źle
wychowany; grubiański
illegal [y'li:gel] adj. bezprawny;
nielegalny; samowolny;
przeciw prawu i ustawom
illegible [y'ledżybl] adj.
nieczytelny; źle napisany
(wydrukowany)
illegitimate [,yly'dżytymejt] adj.
bezprawny; nieprawny;
nieprawowity; nieślubny
ill-fated ['yl-fejtyd] adj. fatalny;
nieszczęśliwy; nieszczęsny
ill-humored ['yl'hju:merd] adj. w
złym humorze
illicit [y'lysyt] adj. bezprawny;
niedozwolony; niewłaściwy
illiterate [y'lyteryt] s. analfabeta;
adj. niepiśmienny
ill-judged ['yl'dżadżd] adj.
nierozważny; nierozsądny
ill-mannered ['yl'maenerd] adj.
źle wychowany; grubiański
ill-natured ['yl'nejczerd] adj. zły;
złośliwy; opryskliwy
illness ['ylnys] s. choroba
illogical [y'lodżykel] adj.
nielogiczny; nierozsądny
ill-tempered ['yl'temperd] adj. w
złym humorze; zły; kłótliwy
ill-timed ['yl'tajmd] adj. nie na
czasie; niefortunny
ill-treat ['yl'tri:t] v. maltretować;
znęcać się (nad kimś)
illuminate [y'lju:mynejt] v.
oświetlać; oświecać;

uświetniać
illumination [y'lju:my'nejszyn] s.
oświecenie; oświecanie;
uświetnianie; rozjaśnienie
illusion [y'lu:żyn] s. złudzenie;
iluzja; złuda
illusive [y'lu:syw] s. złudny;
iluzyjny; iluzoryczny;
zwodniczy
illusory [y'lu:sery] adj. złudny;
iluzoryczny; zwodniczy
illustrate ['yles,trejt] v.
wyjaśniać; ilustrować
illustration [,yles'trejszyn] s.
lustracja; ilustrowanie
illustrative ['yles,trejtyw] adj.
objaśniający; ilustrujący
(przykład, zdarzenie etc.)
illustrious [y'lastrjes] adj.
znakomity; wybitny; sławny
ill will ['yl'łyl] s. niechęć
image ['ymydż] s. wizerunek;
obraz; wcielenie; v.
wyobrażać; odzwierciedlać;
ucieleśniać; dawać obraz
(wyobrażenie)
imagery ['ymydżery] s.
wizerunki; podobizny; gra
wyobraźni; porównanie przez
przykłady
imaginable [y'maedżynebl] adj.
wyobrażalny; możliwy; do
pomyślenia
imaginary [y'maedżynery] adj.
urojony; zmyślony;
nierzeczywisty
imagination [y,maedży'nejszyn]
s. wyobraźnia; fantazja;
urojenie; tworzenie nowych
pomysłów
imagine [y'maedżyn] v.
wyobrażać sobie;
przypuszczać; myśleć
imbecile ['ymby,syl] adj.
upośledzony; głupi;
niedorozwinięty; cherlawy; s.
człowiek upośledzony;
imbecyl (niedorozwinięty)
imitate ['ymytejt] v.
naśladować; małpować;
imitować; wzorować się
imitation [,ymy'tejszyn] s.
naśladowanie;

naśladownictwo; imitacja;
falsyfikat; podróbka
immaterial [,yme'tierjel] adj.
nieistotny; bezcielesny; błahy
immature [,yme'tjuer] adj.
niedojrzały; niewyrobiony;
niedorosły
immeasurable [y,meżerebl] adj.
niezmierzony; ogromny;
bezmierny
immediate [y'mi:djet] adj.
bezpośredni;
natychmiastowy; pilny; nagły
immediately [y'mi:djetly] adv.
natychmiast; bezpośrednio
immense [y'mens] adj. olbrzymi;
ogromny; świetny; kapitalny
immerse [y'me:rs] v. zanurzać;
pogrążać; ochrzcić przez
zanurzenie
immigrant ['ymygrent] s.
imigrant; adj. imigrujący;
osadniczy
immigrate ['ymygrejt] v.
imigrować; przywędrować;
sprowadzać osadników
immigration [,ymy'grejszyn] s.
imigracja; urząd imigracyjny
imminent ['ymynent] adj.
nadchodzący; groźny;
nadciągający; bliski
immobile [y'moubajl] adj.
nieruchomy; przytwierdzony
na stałe
immoderate [y'moderyt] adj.
nieumiarkowany;
niepohamowany; nadmierny
immodest [y'modyst] adj.
nieskromny; bezczelny;
zuchwały
immoral [y'morel] adj.
niemoralny; nieetyczny;
rozpustny
immorality [ym'e-ral'ety] s.
rozpusta; niemoralność
immorality [,yme'raelyty] s.
niemoralność; rozpusta
immortal [y'mo:rtl] adj.
nieśmiertelny; wiekopomny
immortality [,ymo:r'taelyty] s.
nieśmiertelność
immovable [y'mu:webl] adj.
nieruchomy; niezmienny;

nieczuły; nieugięty;
niewzruszony
immune [y'mju:n] adj. odporny;
uodporniony; wolny (od
przepisów)
imp [ymp] s. skrzat; diablik
impact ['ympaekt] v. wgniatać;
s. zderzenie; uderzenie;
wpływ; wstrząs; kolizja;
działanie
impair [ym'peer] v. uszkadzać;
osłabiać; nadwyrężać;
umniejszać
impart [ym'pa:rt] v. dawać;
udzielać; zakomunikować
impartial [ym'pa:rszel] adj.
bezstronny; sprawiedliwy
impartiality ['ym,pa:rszy'aelyty]
s. bezstronność;
sprawiedliwość
impassable [ym'pa:sebl] adj.
nieprzebyty; nie do przebycia
impassive [ym'paesyw] adj.
niewzruszony; obojętny;
nieczuły
impatience [ym'pejszens] s.
zniecierpliwienie;
niecierpliwość; irytacja (z
powodu czegoś)
impatient [ym'pejszent] adj.
niecierpliwy; zniecierpliwiony;
palący się do; podrażniony
impeach [ym'pi:cz] v.
zakwestionować; podawać
w wątpliwość; oskarżyć;
postawić w stan oskarżenia
impediment [ym'pedyment] s.
przeszkoda; utrudnienie
impend [ym'pend] v. grozić;
zbliżać się; zagrażać (z
bliska)
impenetrable [ym'penytrebl] adj.
nieprzenikniony; niedostępny;
niezgłębiony; nie do przebycia
imperative [ym'peretyw] adj.
stanowczy; rozkazujący;
konieczny; naglący; niezbędny
imperceptible [,ym-pe'rseptebl]
adj. niedostrzegalny;
nieuchwytny
imperfect [ym'pe:rfykt] adj.
niedoskonały; niedokończony;
wadliwy; niezupełny;

niedokonany
imperial [ym'pierjel] adj. cesarski;
imperialny; dostojny;
rozkazujący; majestatyczny
imperialism [ym'pierjelyzem] s.
imperializm (budowanie
imperium)
imperil [ym'peryl] v. zagrażać;
narazić na
niebezpieczeństwo
imperiuos [ym'pierjes] adj.
władczy; naglący; nakazujący
imperishable [ym'peryszebl] adj.
niezniszczalny;
nieprzemijający; trwały;
wieczysty
impermeable [ym'pe:rmiebl] adj.
nieprzemakalny;
nieprzenikniony;
nieprzepuszczający
impersonal [ym'pe:rsenl] adj.
nieosobowy; nieosobisty
impersonate [ym'pe:rsenejt] v.
wcielać; uosabiać;
odgrywać kogoś;
personifikować
impertinence [ym'pe:rtynens] s.
niestosowność;
impertynencja;
niewłaściwość; natręctwo;
nietakt
impertinent [ym'pe:rtynent] adj.
niestosowny; impertynencki;
bezczelny; natrętny; bez
związku
imperturbable [,ympe:r'te:rbebl]
adj. niewzruszony; spokojny
impervious [ym'pe:rwjes] adj.
nieprzepuszczalny;
niedostępny
impetuous [ym'petjues] adj.
popędliwy; porywczy;
gwałtowny
implacable [ym'plekebl] adj.
nieubłagany; nieprzejednany
implant [ym'pla:nt] v.wszczepić;
wpoić; zaszczepić
implement ['ymplyment] s.
narzędzie; środek; sprzęt; v.
uzupełniać; urzeczywistniać;
wykonać; uprawomocniać;
spełniać
implicate ['ymplykejt] v.

uwikłać; owijać; włączać;
wplątać; wmieszać
implication [,ymply'kejszyn] s.
uwikłanie; włączenie; sugestia
implicit [ym'plysyt] adj.
rozumiejący się sam przez się;
niezaprzeczalny; domniemany;
ślepy
implore [ym'plo:r] v. błagać
impromptu ym'promptju:] adj.
improwizowany; nie
przygotowany; powiedziany z
głowy; adv. bez
przygotowania; z głowy
imply [ym'plaj] v. zawierać w
sobie; mieścić; sugerować;
zakładać; nasuwać wniosek
impolite [,ympo'lajt] adj.
nieuprzejmy; niegrzeczny
import [ym'po:rt] s. import;
treść; v. oznaczać;
importować; przywozić z
zagranicy; a. importowy
import ['ympo:rt] s. treść;
znaczenie; ważność;
doniosłość
importance [ym'po:rtens] s.
znaczenie; ważność;
doniosłość
important [ym'po:rtent] adj.
ważny; znaczący; doniosły
importation [,ympo:r'tejszyn] s.
przywóz; importowanie
importune [ym'po:rtju:n] v.
dokuczać; żądać
natarczywie; narzucać się;
naprzykrzać się
impose [ym'pouz] v. nadawać;
narzucać; oszukiwać;
imponować; nakładać
obowiązek
impose upon [,ym'pouz e'pon] v.
narzucać się komuś;
okpiwać
imposing [ym'pouzyng] adj.
imponujący; wspaniały;
okazały
impossibility [ym,posy'bylyty] s
niemożliwość
impossible [ym'posybl] adj.
niemożliwy (do zrobienia,
zniesienia)
impostor [ym'poster] s. oszust

(podszywający się); szarlatan
impotence ['ympotens] s.
niemoc; zniedołężnienie
(płciowe); nieudolność;
niesprawność
impotent ['ympotent] s. bezsilny;
impotent; nieudolny
impracticable [ym'praektykebl]
adj. niewykonalny; krnąbrny
impregnate ['ympregnejt] v.
zapładniać; impregnować;
nasycać; wpoić; zaszczepić;
nasiąkać
impress [ym'pres] v. odcisnąć;
wycisnąć; robić wrażenie; s.
odcisk; odbicie; piętno
impression [ym'preszyn] s.
wrażenie; druk; odbicie;
nakład
impressive [ym'presyw] adj.
robiący wrażenie; uderzający;
podniosły; wstrząsający;
frapujący
imprint [ym'prynt] v. odbijać;
wpajać; wydrukować;
wbijać w pamięć; wyryć w
pamięci
imprint ['ymprynt] s. odbicie;
nadruk; odcisk; piętno; znak
firmowy
imprison [ym'pryzn] v. uwięzić
imprisonment [ym'pryznment] s.
uwięzienie (kara więzienia)
improbable [ym'probebl] adj.
nieprawdopodobny
improper [ym'proper] adj.
niewłaściwy; nieprzyzwoity;
zdrożny
improve [ym'pru:w] v.
poprawić; udoskonalić;
ulepszać (jakość)
improvement [ym'pru:wment] s.
poprawa; udoskonalenie;
wykorzystanie (sposobności)
improvise ['ymprowajz] v.
improwizować; sklecić na
poczekaniu
imprudent [ym'pru:dent] adj.
nierozsądny; nieopatrzny;
nierozważny; nieoględny;
niebaczny
impudence ['ympjudens] s.
bezwstyd; bezczelność;

tupet
impudent ['ympjudent] adj.
bezwstydny; bezczelny;
zuchwały; z tupetem
impulse ['ympals] s. impuls;
poryw; popęd; pęd; siła
napędowa; bodziec
impulsive ['ympalsyw] adj.
impulsywny; porywczy;
pobudliwy
impunity [ym'pju:nyty] s.
bezkarność; swoboda od
skutków (kary)
impure [ym'pjur] adj. nieczysty;
zanieczyszczony
impute [ym'pju:t] v. oskarżać;
przypisywać (zbrodnię, błąd)
in [yn] prep. w; we; na; za; po;
do; u; nie-
in and out ['yn,end'aut] exp.: na
wylot; wchodzić i wychodzić
in a week ['yn,ej'ti:k] exp.: za
tydzień; w ciągu tygodnia
in my opinion ['yn,maj e'pynjen]
exp.: według mnie; moim
zdaniem
in order that ['yn,o:rder'daet]
exp.: ażeby; w celu; po to
żeby
in pairs ['yn,peers] exp.: parami
in Shakespeare ['yn,Szekspir] u
Szekspira; w sztukach
Szekspira
inability [,yne'bylyty] s.
niezdolność; niemożność
inaccessible [ynaek'sesybl] adj.
niedostępny; nieprzystępny
inaccurate [yn'aekjuryt] adj.
nieścisły; niedokładny
inactive [yn'aektyw] adj.
bezczynny; bierny; obojętny;
inertny
inadequate [yn'aedykłyt] adj.
nieodpowiedni;
niewystarczalny
inadmissible [,yned'mysebl] adj.
niedopuszczalny; nie do
przyjęcia
inadvertent [,yned'we:rtent] adj.
nieuważny; niedbały;
nierozmyślny; mimowolny;
nieumyślny
inalterable [yn'o:lterebl] adj.

niezmienny
inanimate [yn'aenymyt] adj.
martwy; nieożywiony;
bezduszny; nieorganiczny
inappropriate [,yne'prouprjyt] adj.
niewłaściwy; niestosowny
inapt [yn'aept] adj. niezdatny
inarticulate [,yna:r'tykjulyt] adj.
nieartykułowany; niewyraźny;
niemy; słabo mówiący
inasmuch [,ynez'macz] adv. o
tyle; ponieważ; wobec tego;
że; skoro; zważywszy; jako
inasmuch as [,ynez'macz,aez]
adv. gdyż; o tyle że; o tyle o
ile; zważywszy
inattentive [,yne'tentyw] adj.
nieuważny; nie uważający
inaudible [yn'o:debl] adj.
niesłyszalny; nieuchwytny dla
ucha
inaugural [y'no:gjurel] adj.
inauguracyjny
inaugurate [y'no:gjurejt] v.
otwierać uroczyście;
inaugurować; uroczyście
zapoczątkowywać
inborn ['yn'bo:rn] adj. wrodzony;
przyrodzony; z natury
incalculable [yn'kaelkjulebl] adj.
nieobliczalny; nieprzewidzialny
incapable [yn'kejpebl] adj.
niezdolny; nie będący w
stanie
incapacitate ['ynke'paesytejt] v.
czynić niezdatnym;
dyskwalifikować; uznać za
niezdatnego
incapacity [,ynke'paesyty] s.
niezdolność; nieudolność
incarnate [yn,ka:rnejt] adj.
wcielony; v. wcielać;
ucieleśniać (się); być
wcieleniem
incautious [yn'ko:szes] adj.
nierozważny; niebaczny
incendiary [yn'sendjery] adj.
zapalający; podżegający; s.
podpalacz; podżegacz
incense ['ynsens] s. kadzidło
incense [yn'sens] v.
rozwścieczać; doprowadzać
do szału

incertitude [yn'se:rtytju:d] s.
niepewność; niepokój
incessant [yn'sesnt] adj.
ustawiczny; bezustanny; stały
incest ['ynsest] s. kazirodztwo;
adj. kazirodczy
inch [yncz] s. cal (2.54 cm); v.
posuwać cal po calu
incident ['ynsydent] s. zajście;
wydarzenie; incydent; adj.
padający; związany;
prawdopodobny
incidental [,ynsy'dentl] adj.
przypadkowy; uboczny;
drugorzędny
incidentally [,ynsy'dently] adv.
przypadkowo; ubocznie;
nawiasem mówiąc;
mimochodem; przy
sposobności
incinerate [yn'synerejt] v. palić;
spopielić; palić na popiół
incise [yn'sajz] v. naciąć;
wyryć; wyrzeźbić;
wygrawerować
incision [yn'syżyn] s. nacięcie;
cięcie; ciętość; bystrość;
ostrość
incisive [yn'sajsyw] adj.
przenikliwy; ostry; tnący;
bystry; sieczny; zjadliwy;
wcinający się
incisor [yn'sajzer] s. siekacz
(ząb); każdy z przednich
zębów między kłami
incite [yn'sajt] v. zachęcać;
podburzać; podżegać;
namawiać
inclement [yn'klement] adj.
surowy; ostry (klimat etc.)
inclination [ynkly'nejszyn] s.
skłonność; nachylenie;
pociąg
incline [yn'klajn] v. mieć
skłonność; pochylać się
inclose [yn'klous] v. ogrodzić;
załączyć; włączyć;
zamknąć
include [yn'klu:d] v. zawierać;
włączać; wliczać (w cenę);
obejmować
inclusive [yn'klu:syw] adj.
włączony; obejmujący; adv.

włącznie
incoherent [,ynkou'hierent] adj.
bez związku;
nieskoordynowany
income ['ynkam] s. dochód
income tax ['ynkam,taeks] s.
podatek dochodowy
incoming ['yn,kamyng] adj.
nadchodzący; następujący;
przyrastający; s. przybycie;
dochód
incomparable [yn'komperebl] adj.
niezrównany; nie do
porównania; nieporównywalny
incompatible [,ynkem'paetebl]
adj. niezgodny; sprzeczny
incompetent [yn'kompytent] adj.
niekompetentny; nieudolny
incomplete [,ynkem'pli:t] adj.
niezupełny; nieukończony
incomprehensible [yn,kompry
'hensebl] adj. niepojęty;
niezrozumiały
inconceivable [,ynken'si:webl]
adj. niepojęty;
niprawdopodobny
inconclusive [,ynken'klu:syw]
adj. nieprzekonywujący;
nierozstrzygający; nie
decydujący
inconsequent [yn'konsykłent]
adj. bez związku;
niekonsekwentny; nielogiczny
inconsiderable [,ynken'syderebl]
adj. nieznaczny; niepokaźny
inconsiderate [,ynken'syderyt]
adj. bezwzględny;
nierozważny
inconsistent [,ynken'systent] adj.
niejednolity; niekonsekwentny;
niezgodny; bez związku
inconsolable [,ynken'soulebl] adj.
niepocieszony; nieutulony
inconstant [yn'konstent] adj.
zmienny; niestały; nieregularny
inconvenience [,ynken'wi:njens]
s. niewygoda; kłopot; v.
niepokoić; przeszkadzać;
sprawiać kłopot;
deranżować
inconvenient [,ynken'wi:njent]
adj. niewygodny; niedogodny;
kłopotliwy; uciążliwy

incorporate [yn'korperejt] v.
jednoczyć; wcielać;
zrzeszać; [yn'ko:rperyt] adj.
zrzeszony
incorporated [yn'ko:rperejtyd]
adj. zarejestrowany;
zalegalizowany; wcielony;
złączony
incorrect [,ynke'rekt] adj.
niepoprawny; nieścisły;
błędny
incorrigible [yn'korydżybl] adj.
niepoprawny; nie do
poprawienia
increase [yn'kri:s] v. wzrastać;
zwiększać się; pomnażać
się; wzmagać się;
rozmnażać się; ['ynkri:s] s.
wzrost; przyrost; podwyżka;
mnożenie się
increasingly [yn'kri:syngly] adv.
coraz więcej; coraz bardziej;
coraz to; wciąż
incredible [yn'kredebl] adj. nie do
wiary; niewiarygodny;
nieprawdopodobny; nie do
pomyślenia
incredulous [yn'kredjules] adj. nie
incriminate [yn'krymynejt] v.
obwiniać; oskarżać;
pomawiać; objąć (kogoś)
oskarżeniem
incubator ['ynkjubejter] s.
wylęgarka; inkubator
incur [yn'ke:r] v. narażać się;
ponieść; zaciągać; natknąć
się na
incurable [yn'kjuerebl] adj.
nieuleczalny; s. człowiek
nieuleczalnie chory
indebted [yn'detyd] adj. dłużny;
zobowiązany; wdzięczny;
zawdzięczający
indecency [yn'di:sensy] s.
nieskromność;
nieprzyzwoitość
indecent [yn'di:sent] adj.
nieprzyzwoity; obrażający
moralność
indecision [,yndy'syżyn] s.
chwiejność;
niezdecydowanie
indecisive [,yndy'sajsyw] adj.

nierozstrzygnięty;
niezdecydowany; chwiejny;
nie rozstrzygający
indecisiveness [,yndy'sajsywnys]
s. chwiejność;
niezdecydowanie
indeed [yn'di:d] adv. naprawdę;
istotnie; rzeczywiście;
faktycznie; wprawdzie; co
prawda; właściwie
indefatigable [,yndy'faetygebl]
adj. niestrudzony;
niezmordowany
indefinite [yn'defynyt] adj.
nieokreślony; niewyraźny;
nie sprecyzowany
indelible [yn'delybl] adj.
niezatarty; trwały; nie do
zmazania
indelicate [yn'delykyt] adj.
niedelikatny; nietaktowny;
niestosowny
indemnify [yn'demnyfaj] v.
dawać odszkodowanie;
zabezpieczać przed (np.
szkodą); powetować
indemnity [yn'demnyty] s.
odszkodowanie;
zabezpieczenie przed ...;
wynagrodzenie
indent [yn'dent] v. naciąć;
wyciąć; wyrżnąć; zamówić;
zawierać umowę; tłoczyć; s.
wgłębienie; nacięcie;
karbowanie
indent ['yndent] s. wcięcie;
nacięcie; karbowanie;
zamówienie
independence [,yndy'pendens] s.
niezależność;
niepodległość;
niezależność materialna
independent [,yndy'pendent] adj.
niepodległy; niezależny
(materialnie); osobny;
oddzielny
indescribable [,yndys'krajbebl]
adj. nieopisany; nie do
opisania (poza możliwościami
opisania)
indeterminate [,yndy'te:rmynyt]
adj. nieokreślony;
niewyraźny

index ['yndeks] s. wskaźnik;
indeks; v. umieszczać w
spisie (indeksie); robić indeks
Indian ['yndjen] adj. indiański;
hinduski
Indian Summer ['yndjen'samer]
exp.: słoneczne dni w jesieni;
babie lato
India-rubber ['yndje'raber] s.
guma (naturalna, elastyczna)
indicate ['yndykejt] v.
wskazywać; stwierdzać;
wymagać
indication [,yndy'kejszyn] s.
wskazówka; wskazanie; znak
indicative [yn'dyketyw] adj.
oznajmiający; dowodzący
indicator ['yndykejter] s.
wskaźnik; indykator; licznik
indict [yn'dajt] v. oskarżyć
indictment [yn'dajtment] s.
oskarżenie; akt oskarżenia
indifference [yn'dyferens] s.
obojętność; nieistotność;
błahość
indifferent [yn'dyfrent] adj.
obojętny; mierny; błahy;
neutralny
indigent ['yndydżent] adj. ubogi;
biedny; s. biedak; biedaczka
indigestible [,yndy'dżestebl] adj.
niestrawny; źle strawny
indigestion [,yndy'dżestczyn] s.
niestrawność
indignant [yn'dygnent] adj.
oburzony (na
niesprawiedliwość ...)
indignation [,yndyg'nejszyn] s.
oburzenie
indirect [,yndy'rekt] adj.
pośredni; okrężny;
nieuczciwy
indiscreet [,yndys'kri:t] adj.
nierozważny; niedyskretny
indiscretion [,yndys'kreszyn] s.
nierozwaga; niedyskrecja;
uchybienie (słowem, czynem)
indiscriminate [,yndys'krymynyt]
adj. bezkrytyczny; pomieszany
indispensable [,yndys'pensebl]
adj. nieodzowny; niezbędny;
konieczny; niezastąpiony
indisposed [,yndys'pouzd] adj.

niezdrów; niedysponowany;
niechętny; bez zapału;
niedomagający
indisposition [,yndyspe'zyszyn] s.
niedyspozycja; niechęć;
odraza; dolegliwość;
niedomaganie
indisputable [,yndys'pju:tebl] adj.
bezsporny; niezaprzeczalny
indistinct [,yndys'tynkt] adj.
niewyraźny; niejasny; mętny
individual [,yndy'wydjuel] adj.
pojedynczy; odrębny; s.
jednostka; osobnik; okaz;
człowiek
individualist [,yndy'wydjuelyst] s.
indywidualista; indywidualistka
indivisible [,yndy'wyżebl] adj.
niepodzielny; nieskończenie
mały
indolence ['yndelens] s. lenistwo;
opieszałość; próżniactwo
indolent ['yndelent] adj. leniwy;
opieszały; obojętny;
niebolesny
indomitable [yn'domytebl] adj.
nieposkromiony; nieugięty
indoor ['yndo:r] adj. domowy;
wewnętrzny; pokojowy;
zakładowy
indoors ['yndo:rz] adv. w domu;
pod dachem; do domu; do
mieszkania
indorse [yn'do:rs] v. potwierdzić
(podpisem)
induce [yn'dju:s] v. skłonić;
namówić; powodować;
wnioskować; pobudzić;
nakłonić
induct [yn'dakt] v. wprowadzać;
tworzyć; brać do wojska
indulge [yn'daldż] v. pobłażać;
znosić; ulegać; dogadzać;
używać sobie; dawać upust;
zaspokajać
indulgence [yn'daldżens] s.
dogadzanie; nałóg; oddawanie
się; pobłażanie; odpust;
uleganie
indulgent [yn'daldżent] adj.
pobłażliwy; ulegający;
folgujący
industrial [yn'dastrjel] adj.

przemysłowy (towar, robotnik)
industrial area [yn'dastrjel'eerje]
s. teren przemysłowy
industrial city [yn'dastrjel'syty] s.
miasto przemysłowe
industrialist [yn'dastrjelyst] s.
przemysłowiec
industrialize [yn'dastrjelajz] v.
uprzemysławiać
industrious [yn'dastrjes] adj.
skrzętny; pilny; pracowity
industry ['yndastry] s. przemysł;
pilność; pracowitość;
skrzętność; gałąź
przemysłu; właściciele i
zarządcy przemysłu
ineffective [,yny'fektyw] adj.
bezskuteczny; niesprawny
inefficient [,yny'fyszent] adj.
niewydajny; niesprawny
inequality [,yny'kłolyty] s.
nierówność;
niewystarczalność;
zmienność (krajobrazu);
niestałość
inert [y'ne:rt] adj. bezwładny;
ociężały; obojętny; opieszały
inertia [y'ne:rszja] s. inercja;
bezwład; ociężałość
inestimable [yn'estymebl] adj.
nieoceniony; bezcenny
inevitable [yn'ewytebl] adj.
nieunikniony; nieuchronny
inexact [,ynyg'zaekt] adj.
nieścisły; niedokładny
inexcusable [,ynyks'kju:zebl] adj.
niewybaczalny;
nieusprawiedliwiony; nie do
darowania
inexhaustible [,ynyg'zo:stebl] adj.
niewyczerpany; nieprzebrany;
niestrudzony; bez dna
inexpensive [,ynyks'pensyw] adj.
niedrogi; niekosztowny; tani
inexperience [,ynyks'pierjens] s.
niedoświadczenie; brak
wprawy
inexplicable [yn'eksplykebl] adj.
niewytłumaczalny;
niewyjaśniony; zagadkowy
inexpressible [,yneks'presebl]
adj. niewysłowiony;
niewyrażalny; niewymowny

inexpressive [,ynyks'presyw] adj.
bez wyrazu
infallible [yn'faelebl] adj.
nieomylny; niezawodny;
niechybny; bezbłędny; zawsze
słuszny
infamous ['ynfemes] adj.
haniebny; niesławny;
hańbiący; podły
infamy ['ynfemy] s. hańba;
niesława; podłość; utrata
praw obywatelskich
infancy ['ynfensy] s.
niemowlęctwo; dzieciństwo
infant ['ynfent] s. niemowlę;
dziecko; noworodek; a.
dziecinny
infantile ['ynfentajl] adj.
dziecięcy; infantylny;
niemowlęcy
infantry ['ynfentry] s. piechota
(wojsko)
infatuated with [yn'faetjuejtyd
łys] adj. szalejący za ...;
rozkochany w ...; nierozsądnie
zakochany
infect [yn'fekt] v. zakazić;
zarazić; zatruwać
infection [yn'fekszyn] s.
zakażenie; zarażenie; zaraza
infectious [yn'fekszes] adj.
zakaźny; zaraźliwy;
infekcyjny
infer [yn'fe:r] v. wnioskować;
zawierać w sobie pojęcie
inference ['ynferens] s. wniosek;
konkluzja; domniemanie
inferior [yn'fierjer] adj. niższy;
podrzędny; pośledni
inferior to [yn'fierjer,tu] adj.
ustępujący; gorszy
inferiority [yn,fiery'oryty] s.
niższość; poczucie
niższości
infernal [yn'fe:rnel] adj. piekielny;
diabelski; szatański
infest [yn'fest] v. nawiedzać;
trapić; być utrapieniem
infidelity [,ynfy'delyty] s.
niewiara; niewierność
infiltrate ['ynfyltrejt] v. wsiąkać;
przesiąkać; przenikać
infinite ['ynfynyt] adj.

**nieskończony; bezgraniczny;
niezliczony; ogromny;
bezkresny**
infinitive [yn'fynytyw] s.
bezokolicznik; adj.
nieokreślony
infinity [yn'fynyty] s.
nieskończoność
infirm [yn'fe:rm] adj. słaby;
niedołężny; dotknięty
niemocą
infirmary [yn'fe:rmery] s. szpital;
lecznica; izba chorych
infirmity [yn'fe:rmyty] s. niemoc;
słabość; zniedołężnienie
inflame [yn'flejm] v. zapalić;
rozognić; pobudzać;
zagrzewać
inflammable [yn'flaemebl] adj.
zapalny; pobudliwy; palny
inflammation [,ynfle'mejszyn] s.
zapalenie; zaognienie
inflammatory [yn'flaemeto:ry]
adj. podżegający; zapalny
inflate [yn'flejt] v. nadąć;
rozdąć; powodować inflację
inflation [yn'flejszyn] s. inflacja;
nadymanie; nadmuchanie;
zwyżka cen
inflect [yn'flekt] v. zginać;
skrzywić; odmienić; naginać
inflection [yn'flekszyn] s. fleksja;
modulacja; końcówka;
wygięcie; nadgięcie;
odchylenie
inflexible [yn'fleksebl] adj.
sztywny; nieugięty;
nieelastyczny
inflict [yn'flykt] v. żądać;
narzucać; zsyłać (na kogoś)
infliction [yn'flykszyn] s. zadanie
(ciosu); narzucanie;
przykrość; nieszczęście;
strapienie
influence ['ynfluens] s. wpływ;
v. wywierać wpływ;
oddziaływać
influential [,ynflu'enszel] adj.
wpływowy (polityk etc.)
influenza [,ynflu'enza] s. grypa;
influenca
inform [yn'fo:rm] v.
powiadomić; nadawać;

donosić; ożywić
inform against [yn'fo:rm e'genst]
v. donosić na (kogoś)
information [,ynfer'mejszyn] s.
wiadomość; wiedza;
objaśnienie; informacja;
doniesienie
information desk [,ynfer'mejszyn
,desk] punkt informacyjny (w
banku, hotelu, na wystawie)
information officer [,ynfer
'mejszyn 'ofyser] oficer
informacyjny (w banku etc.)
informative [yn'fo:rmetyw] adj.
objaśniający; pouczający
informer [yn'fo:rmer] s.
donosiciel; konfident;
konfidentka
infuriate [,yn'fjuerjejt] v.
rozwścieczać; rozjuszać
infuse [yn'fju:z] v. wlewać;
zalewać; zaparzać; dodać
(odwagi)
ingenious [yn'dżi:njes] adj.
pomysłowy; dowcipny
(pomysł)
ingenuity [,yndży'njuyty] s.
pomysłowość;
oryginalność; dowcip
ingot ['yngot] s. sztaba
ingratiate [yn'grejszjejt] v.
wkradać się w łaski czyjeś
ingratitude [yn'graetytju:d] s.
niewdzięczność
ingredient [yn'gri:djent] s.
składnik (mieszanki etc.)
ingress ['yngres] s. wejście
inhabit [yn'haebyt] v.
zamieszkiwać; mieszkać
inhabitable [yn'haebytebl] adj.
mieszkalny (godny
zamieszkania)
inhabitant [yn'haebytent] s.
mieszkaniec; mieszkanka
inhale [yn'hejl] v. wdychać;
zaciągać się (dymem);
wziewać
inherent [yn'hierent] adj.
nieodłączny; właściwy;
wrodzony
inherit [yn'heryt] v. dziedziczyć;
być spadkobiercą
inheritance [yn'herytens] s.

spadek; spuścizna;
dziedzictwo
inhibit [yn'hybyt] v.
wstrzymywać; wzbraniać;
zakazywać
inhibition [,ynhy'byszyn] s.
zakaz; zahamowanie;
wstrzymanie
inhospitable [yn'hospytebl] adj.
niegościnny
inhuman [yn'hju:men] adj.
nieludzki; okrutny; brutalny
initial [y'nyszel] adj.
początkowy; v. znaczyć
własnymi inicjałami
initiate [y'nyszjejt] v.
zapoczątkować;
wprowadzać; zainicjować;
wtajemniczać; s. nowicjusz
initiation [y,nyszy'ejszyn] s.
wprowadzenie;
zapoczątkowanie
initiative [y'nyszjejtyw] s.
inicjatywa; adj. początkowy
inject [yn'dżekt] v. wstrzyknąć
injection [yn'dżekszyn] s.
zastrzyk; wstrzyknięcie; a.
wtryskowy
injudicious [,yndżu'dyszes] adj.
nierozważy; nieroztropny
injure ['yndżer] v. zranić;
uszkodzić; krzywdzić;
zepsuć
injurious [yn'dżuerjes] adj.
szkodliwy; krzywdzący;
obelżywy; przynoszący ujmę;
obraźliwy
injury ['yndżery] s. szkoda;
krzywda; rana; uszkodzenie
injustice [yn'dżastys] s.
niesprawiedliwość; krzywda
ink [ynk] s. atrament; tusz
inkling ['ynklyng] s. wzmianka;
podejrzenie; przypuszczenie
ink-pot ['ynk,pot] s. kałamarz
inland ['ynlend] s. wnętrze kraju;
adj. w głębi kraju;
wewnętrzny; adv. w głębi; w
głąb kraju; w głębi kraju
inlet ['ynlet] s. wstawka; zatoka;
wlot; wejście; a. wlotowy
inmate ['ynmejt] s. mieszkaniec;
lokator; współ-(więzień etc.)

inmost ['ynmoust] adj. głęboko
utajony; skryty; najtajniejszy
inn [yn] s. gospoda; oberża
innate ['y'nejt] adj. wrodzony
inner ['yner] adj. wewnętrzny
innermost ['ynermoust] adj.
głęboko ukryty; najskrytszy
inner tube ['yner,tju:b] s. dętka
(samochodowa, rowerowa)
innkeeper ['yn,ki:per] s.
oberżysta; właściciel zajazdu
innocence ['ynesns] s.
niewinność; naiwność;
prostoduszność
innocent ['ynesynt] adj.
niewinny; naiwny;
nieszkodliwy; niemądry; s.
prostaczek; niewiniątko;
głuptas
innovation [,ynou'wejszyn] s.
innowacja; wprowadzenie
zmian
innuendo [,ynju'endou] s.
insynuacja
innumerable [y'nju:merebl] adj.
niezliczony; bez liku
inoculate [y'nokjulejt] v.
szczepić; wpajać; oczkować
rośliny
inoffensive [,yne'fensyw] adj.
nieszkodliwy; spokojny;
obojętny
inopportune [yn'oper,tju:n] adj.
niewczesny; nie w porę; nie
na czas; nieodpowiedni
inpatient ['ynpejszent] s. pacjent
leżący w szpitalu
inquest ['ynkłest] s. śledztwo
inquire [yn'kłajer] v. pytać się;
dowiadywać się; dociekać
inquiry [yn'kłajry] s. badanie;
zasięganie informacji;
śledztwo; poszukiwanie;
ankieta; wywiad
inquisitive [yn'kłyzytyw] adj.
badawczy; ciekawski;
wścibski
insane [yn'sejn] adj. chory
umysłowo; zwariowany; bez
sensu
insanity [yn'saenyty] s. obłęd
insatiable [yn'sejszjebl] adj.
nienasycony; niezaspokojony;

chciwy
insatiate [yn'sej'szjyt] adj.
nienasycony; niezaspokojony
inscribe [yn'skrajb] v. wpisać;
napisać; umieszczać na
liście
inscription [yn'skrypszyn] s.
napis; dedykacja
insect ['ynsekt] s. owad
insecure [,ynsy'kjuer] adj.
niepewny; niezabezpieczony
insemination [yn,semy'nejszyn]
s. zapłodnienie; zasianie
insensible [yn'sensybl] adj.
nieświadomy; bez zmysłów;
w stanie omdlenia;
niedostrzegalny
insensitive [yn'sensytyw] adj.
nieczuły; niewrażliwy
inseparable [yn'seperebl] adj.
nierozłączny; nieodstępny
insert [yn'se:rt] v. wstawiać;
wkładać; s. wkładka;
wstawka
insertion [yn'se:rszyn] s.
wkładka; wstawka; włożenie;
wstawienie; przyczep;
przyczepienie
inshore [yn'szo:r] adv. blisko
brzegu; przy brzegu; adj.
przybrzeżny; bliski brzegu
inside ['ynsajd] s. wnętrze; adj.
wewnętrzny; adv. wewnątrz
inside [yn'sajd] adv. wewnątrz
inside out ['ynsajd'aut] exp.: na
lewą stronę (np. marynarki)
insidious [yn'sydjes] adj.
podstępny; zdradziecki;
zdradliwy
insight ['ynsajt] s. wgląd;
intuicja; wnikliwość
insignificant [,ynsyg'nyfykent]
adj. mało znaczący; błahy
insincere [,ynsyn'sier] adj.
nieszczery; zwodniczy;
dwulicowy
insinuate [yn'synjuejt] v.
insynuować; podsuwać;
sugerować
insipid [yn'sypyd] adj. mdły;
tępy; bez sensu; głupi; ckliwy
insist [yn'syst] v. nalegać;
nastawać; utrzymywać;

obstawać
insist on [yn'syst,on] v.
domagać się; upierać się;
nastawać
insolent ['ynselent] adj.
bezczelny; zuchwały; butny;
wyniosły
insoluble [yn'soljubl] adj.
nierozpuszczalny; nie do
rozwiązania
insolvent [yn'solwent] adj.
niewypłacalny; s. bankrut;
bankrutka
insomnia [yn'somnja] s.
bezsenność (nie normalna)
insomuch [,ynsou'macz] adv. o
tyle; do tego stopnia; tak
dalece
inspect [yn'spekt] v. oglądać;
doglądać; mieć nadzór;
badać
inspection [yn'spekszyn] s.
przegląd; oglądanie; inspekcja;
doglądanie; sprawdzanie;
kontrola
inspector [yn'spekter] s.
inspektor; nadzorca; kontroler
inspiration [,ynspe'rejszyn] s.
natchnienie; wdech;
wdychanie
inspire [yn'spajer] v. natchnąć;
podsunąć; zainspirować;
wdychać
instability [ynste'bylyty] s.
niestałość; chwiejność;
nietrwałość
install [yn'sto:l] v. instalować;
wprowadzać na stanowisko
installation [,ynsto:'lejszyn] s.
instalacja; wprowadzenie na
stanowisko; zamontowanie
instal(l)ment [yn'sto:lment] s.
część całości; rata
instance ['ynstens] s. wypadek;
przykład; v. przytaczać
przykład
instant ['ynstent] adj. nagły;
natychmiastowy; bieżący; s.
moment; chwila (szczególna)
instantaneous [,ynsten'tejnjes]
adj. natychmiastowy;
momentalny; zdarzający się w
momencie

instantly [yn'stently] adv.
natychmiast; momentalnie
instead [yn'sted] adv. zamiast
tego; natomiast; w miejsce
instead of [yn'sted,ow] adv.
zamiast (kogoś, czegoś)
instigate ['ynstygejt] v.
podżegać; podjudzać;
prowokować
instigator ['ynstygejter] s.
podżegacz; prowokator;
poduszczyciel
instil(l) [yn'styl] v. wsączać;
wpajać (uczucia etc.);
wkraplać
instinct ['ynstynkt] s. instynkt;
adj. tchnący (czymś); pełen
instinctive [yn'stynktyw] adj.
instynktowny; odruchowy
institute ['ynstytju:t] s. instytut;
v. zakładać; ustanawiać;
zarządzać (śledztwo etc.)
institution [,ynsty'tju:szyn] s.
instytucja; ustanowienie
instruct [yn'strakt] v. uczyć
instruction [yn'strakszyn] s.
pouczenie; nauka; instrukcja
instructive [yn'straktyw] adj.
pouczający; kształcący
instructor [yn'strakter] s.
nauczyciel; wykładowca;
instruktor
instructress [yn'straktrys] s.
nauczycielka; instruktorka
instrument ['ynstrument] s.
instrument; przyrząd;
dokument
insubordinate [,ynseb'o:rdnyt]
adj. niesforny; nieposłuszny
insufferable [yn'saferebl] adj.
nieznośny; nie do zniesienia
insufficient [,ynse'fyszent] adj.
niedostateczny; nieodpowiedni
insulate ['ynsjulejt] v. izolować;
oddzielać; odosabniać
insult ['ynsalt] s. zniewaga
insult [yn'salt] v. lżyć;
znieważać; uchybiać;
zelżyć
insupportable [,ynse'po:rtebl]
adj. nie do zniesienia;
nieznośny; nieuzasadniony
insurance [yn'szuerens] s.

ubezpieczenie; a.
ubezpieczeniowy
insurance policy [yn'szuerens
'polysy] s. polisa
ubezpieczeniowa; polisa
asekuracyjna
insure [yn'szuer] v. ubezpieczać
(się); asekurować;
zabezpieczać
insurmountable [,ynse:r
'mauntebl] adj. niepokonany
insurrection [,ynse'rekszyn] s.
powstanie; insurekcja
intact [yn'taekt] adj. nietknięty;
nieuszkodzony
integrate ['yntygrejt] v. scalić;
uzupełniać; całkować
integrity [yn'tegryty] s.
uczciwość; rzetelność;
czystość; prawość;
niepodzielność
intellect ['yntylekt] s. rozum;
umysł; rozsądek; wybitne
umysły
intellectual [,ynty'lekczuel] adj.
intelektualny; umysłowy; s.
intelektualista; inteligent
intelligence [yn'telydżens] s.
inteligencja; informacja;
wywiad; wiadomości; nowiny
intelligent [yn'telydżent] adj.
inteligentny; łatwo uczący się
intelligentsia [yn'tely'dżencja] s.
inteligencja (warstwa
ludności kraju)
intelligible [yn'telydżybl] adj.
zrozumiały; jasny; wyraźny
intemperate [yn'temperyt] adj.
nieumiarkowany; bez umiaru
intend [yn'tend] v. zamierzać;
przeznaczać; mieć na myśli
intense [yn'tens] adj. napięty;
usilny; gorliwy; wytężony;
uczuciowy
intensify [yn'tensyfaj] v. wzmóc;
wzmocnić; napiąć;
wzmagać
intensity [yn'tensyty] s.
intensywność; wzmożenie;
natężenie
intensive [yn'tensyw] adj.
intensywny; wzmożony; silny;
wzmacniający

intent [yn'tent] s. plan; zamiar;
adj. uważny; zamierzający;
zajęty; pochłonięty;
zdecydowany
intent on [yn'tent on] adj.
pochłonięty; zajęty czymś
intention [yn'tenszyn] s. zamiar;
cel; zamierzenie (czynu)
intentional [yn'tenszenel] adj.
umyślny; celowy; zamierzony
inter [yn'te:r] v. grzebać
intercede [,ynte:r'si:d] v.
wstawiać się; orędować
intercept ['ynte:rsept] v.
przechwycić; przejąć;
przerwać; udaremnić;
podsłuchać
intercession [,ynter'seszyn] s.
wstawiennictwo;
orędownictwo
interchange [,ynte:r'czejndż] s.
wzajemna wymiana; v.
wymieniać się; zmieniać się
intercourse ['ynterko:rs] s.
stosunek; obcowanie;
spółkowanie
interdict [,ynter'dykt] s. zakaz; v.
zakazywać; zabraniać
interest ['yntryst] s.
zainteresowanie; ciekawość;
odsetki; interes; procent; v.
zainteresować
interested ['yntrystyd] adj.
zaciekawiony; zainteresowany
interesting ['yntrystyng] adj.
ciekawy; interesujący
interfere [,ynter'fier] v. wtrącać
się; wdawać się; kolidować;
zakłócać; dokuczać
interfere with [,ynter'fier,tys] v.
mieszać się do kogoś
interference [,ynter'fierens] s.
wtrącanie się; zakłócenie
interior [yn'tierjer] adj.
wewnętrzny; środkowy; s.
wnętrze; głąb kraju; głąb
duszy (serca)
interior decorator [yn'tierjer
'dekerejter] s. architekt
wnętrz; sprzedawca mebli
interjection [,ynter'dżekszyn] s.
okrzyk; wykrzyknik
interlude [ynter'lu:d] s. przerwa;

antrakt
intermarriage ['ynter'maerydż] s.
małżeństwo w obrębie
własnego rodu, szczepu,
plemienia
intermediary [,ynter'mi:diery] adj.
pośredni; pośredniczący; s.
pośrednik; pośredniczka;
średnie stadium; pośrednia
forma; pośredni produkt;
agent
intermediate [,ynter'mi:djet] adj.
pośredni; środkowy; średni;
s. pośrednik; v.
pośredniczyć
intermingle [,ynter'myngl] v.
mieszać (się); pomieszać
(się)
intermission [,ynter'myszyn] s.
przerwa; pauza; antrakt
intermittent [,ynter'mytent] adj.
przerywany; niemiarowy
intern [yn'te:rn] v. internować;
odbywać praktykę lekarską
intern ['ynte:rn] s. praktykant
lekarski w szpitalu
internal ['ynte:rnl] adj.
wewnętrzny; krajowy;
domowy
international [,ynter'naeszenl]
adj. międzynarodowy; s.
międzynarodówka; zawody
międzynarodowe; zawodnik
międzynarodowy
interpose [,ynter'pouz] v.
wstawać; wtrącać (się);
przerywać
interpret [yn'ter:pryt] v.
tłumaczyć i objaśniać;
interpretować; rozumieć
(opacznie etc.)
interpretation [yn,te:rpry'tejszyn]
s. interpretacja; tłumaczenie;
sposób zrozumienia
interpreter [yn'te:rpryter] s.
tłumacz (ustny)
interrogate [yn'teregejt] v.
wypytywać; przesłuchiwać
interrogation [yn,tere'gejszyn] s.
przesłuchanie; pytanie
interrogative [,ynte'rogetyw] adj.
pytający (np. ton)
interrupt [,ynte'rapt] v.

przerywać; zasłaniać (widok)
interruption [,ynte'rapszyn] s.
przerwa (w czynności etc.)
intersect [,ynte:r'sekt] v.
przecinać (się); pokrzyżować
(się)
intersection [,ynter'sekszyn] s.
przecinanie się; skrzyżowanie
interval ['ynterwel] s. odstęp;
przerwa; antrakt; okres
(pogody)
intervene [,ynter'wi:n] v.
wdawać się; interweniować;
zdarzyć się; zajść; być
między (dwoma etc.)
intervention [,ynter'wenszyn] s.
interwencja; wdanie się
interview ['ynterwju:] s. wywiad;
rozmowa; v. mieć wywiad;
widzieć się z kimś (dla
wywiadu)
interviewer ['ynterwju:er] s.
przeprowadzający wywiad
intestines [yn'testynz] pl.
wnętrzności; jelita
intimacy ['yntymesy] s.
zażyłość; intymność;
poufałe stosunki (płciowe);
poufałość
intimate ['yntymyt] adj. zażyły;
wewnętrzny; intymny; v.
zawiadamiać; dawać do
zrozumienia; s. serdeczny
przyjaciel
intimation [,ynty'mejszyn] s.
zawiadomienie; danie do
zrozumienia; napomknięcie;
znak (czegoś)
intimidate [yn'tymydejt] v.
zastraszyć; onieśmielić
into ['yntu:] prep. do; w; na
intolerable [yn'tolerebl] adj.
nieznośny; nie do zniesienia
intolerant [yn'tolerent] adj.
nietolerancyjny; nie znoszący
czegoś (cudzych przekonań)
intoxicate [yn'toksykejt] v. upić;
upajać; odurzać się
intransitive [yn'traensytyw] adj.
& s. nieprzechodni
intrepid [yn'trepyd] adj.
nieustraszony; śmiały;
odważny

intricate ['yntrykyt] adj. zawiły;
trudny do zrozumienia
intrigue [yn'tri:g] s. intryga;
potajemna miłość; v.
intrygować; potajemnie
utrzymywać stosunek
miłosny; zaciekawiać
introduce [,yntre'dju:s] v.
wprowadzać (coś lub
kogoś); przedstawiać;
rozpoczynać; wsuwać;
wysuwać; wkładać;
zapoznawać
introduction [,yntre'dakszyn] s.
wstęp; wprowadzenie;
włożenie; wsunięcie;
przedstawienie (kogoś);
przedmowa; innowacja etc.
introductory [,yntre'daktery] adj.
wstępny; wprowadzający
intrude [,yn'tru:d] v. wpychać
(się); wciskać (się); wedrzeć
(się); narzucać (się) (komuś)
intruder [yn'tru:der] s. natręt;
intruz; nieproszony gość
intrusion [yn'tru:żyn] s.
wciśnięcie (się); wepchnięcie
(się); narzucanie (się); wdarcie
(się) w cudze prawa
intuition [,yntju'yszyn] s. intuicja;
przeczucie; wyczucie
inundate ['ynan,dejt] v.
zalewać; zatopić;
zasypywać (prośbami)
inutile [yn'ju:tyl] adj.
niepotrzebny; bezcelowy;
bezużyteczny
invade [yn'wejd] v. najeżdżać;
wdzierać się; zalewać;
owładać; ogarnąć;
wtargnąć
invader [yn'wejder] s.
najeźdźca; okupant
invalid [yn'weli:d] s. chory;
inwalida; kaleka; człowiek
słaby
invalid [yn'waelyd] adj.
nieważny; nieprawomocny
invalidate [yn'waelydejt] v.
unieważniać (prawnie etc.)
invaluable [yn'waeljuebl] adj.
bezcenny; nieoceniony
invariable [yn'weeryebl] adj.

niezmienny; stały;
równomierny
invariably [yn'w-eryebly] adv.
niezmiennie; stale;
równomiernie
invasion [yn'wejżyn] s. inwazja;
najazd; wdarcie się
invective [yn'wektyw] s.
inwektywa; obelga; napaść
(słowna); obelżywe słowa
invent [yn'went] v. wynaleźć;
wymyślić; zmyślić (coś na
kogoś)
invention [yn'wenszyn] s.
wynalazek; wymysł;
zmyślenie
inventive [yn'wentyw] adj.
pomysłowy; wynalazczy
inventor [yn'wentor] s.
wynalazca (w nauce,
mechanice etc.)
inverse [yn'we:rs] adj. odwrotny;
s. odwrotność (czegoś)
inversion [yn'we:rżyn] s.
odwrócenie; inwersja;
homoseksualizm; wynicowanie
invert [yn'we:rt] v. odwrócić;
przestawić; s.
homoseksualista
inverted commas [yn'we:rtyd
'komes] cudzysłów
invest [yn'west] v. inwestować;
wyposażać; oblegać;
obdarzać
investigate [yn'westygejt] v.
badać; prowadzić
dochodzenie
investigation [yn,westy'gejszyn]
s. badanie; dochodzenie;
śledztwo; rozpatrzenie;
dociekanie
investigator [yn'westygejtor] s.
badacz; agent (prokuratury)
investment [yn'westment] s.
inwestycja; lokata; oblężenie;
osaczenie; obleczenie
invincible [yn'wynsebl] adj.
niepokonany; niezwyciężony
inviolable [yn'wajelebl] adj.
nienaruszalny; nietykalny;
niepogwałcony; niezniszczalny
invisible [yn'wyzybl] adj.
niewidoczny; niewidzialny

invitation [,ynwy'tejszyn] s.
zaproszenie (pisemne, słowne)
invite [yn'wajt] v. zapraszać;
wywoływać; ściągać;
nęcić; zachęcać; prosić o
(radę)
invoice ['ynwois] s. faktura; v.
fakturować
invoke [yn'wouk] v. wzywać;
odwoływać się; wywoływać
involuntary [yn'wolentery] adj.
mimowolny; nieumyślny;
bezwiedny (czyn, ruch etc.)
involve [yn'wolw] v. gmatwać;
wikłać; mieszać;
komplikować; obejmować;
wymagać
invulnerable [yn'walnerebl] adj.
nie do zranienia;
nienaruszalny; nie do zdobycia
inward ['ynłerd] adj.
wewnętrzny; adv. wewnątrz;
w sercu etc.
inwards ['ynłerds] adv.
wewnątrz; w duchu; w myśli
iodine ['ajoudi:n] s. jod
I.O.U. = **I owe you** ['ajou'ju:] s.
kwit; skrypt dłużny
irascible [y'raesybl] adj. gniewny;
popędliwy; wybuchowy; skory
do gniewu
irate [aj'rejt] adj. rozgniewany;
zirytowany; zły; wściekły
iridescent [,yry'desnt] adj.
mieniący się; tęczowy
iris ['ajerys] s. tęczówka
Irish ['ajerysz] adj. irlandzki; s.
Irlandczyk
irk [e:rk] v. drażnić; być
przykrym; męczyć
irksome [e:rksem] adj.
nieprzyjemny; przykry
iron ['ajern] s. żelazo; żelazko;
(pistolet; rewolwer); adj.
żelazny; v. zakuwać;
prasować
ironic(al) [aj'ronyk(el)] adj.
ironiczny; drwiący;
uszczypliwy
ironing ['ajernyng] s. prasowanie
(bielizna etc.)
ironmonger ['ajern,manger] s.
handlarz wyrobów żelaznych;

właściciel sklepu żelaznego
iron mold ['ajern,mould] s. plama
od rdzy
ironworks ['ajernłe:rks] s. huta
żelaza; przetwórnia żelaza
irony ['ajereny] s. ironia
irradiate [y'rjedjejt] v.
oświetlać; naświetlać;
oświecać; rozjaśniać;
rozpromieniać
irrational [y'raesznel] adj.
nieracjonalny; nierozumny;
niewymierny; s. liczba
niewymierna
irreconcilable [y'rekesajlebl] adj.
nieprzejednany; nie dający się
pogodzić (z wiarą etc.)
irrecoverable [,yry'kawerebl] adj.
niepowetowany; nie do
odzyskania; stracony
bezpowrotnie
irredeemable [,yry'di:mebl] adj.
niewymienny; beznadziejny;
nieodwracalny; nieodkupny
irrefutable [y'refjutebl] adj.
niezbity; nieodparty
irregular [y'reguler] adj.
nieregularny; nierówny;
nieporządny; nielegalny;
nieprawidłowy
irrelevant [y'relywent] adj.
nieistotny; niestosowny;
oderwany; od rzeczy; nie do
rzeczy
irremovable [,yry'mu:webl] adj.
nieusuwalny; nie do pokonania
irreparable [y'reperebl] adj.
niepowetowany; nie do
naprawienia
irreplaceable [,yry'plejsebl] adj.
niezastąpiony; nie do
zastąpienia
irrepressible [,yry'presybl] adj.
niepohamowany; nieodparty
irreproachable [,yry'proczebl] adj.
nienaganny; bez zarzutu
irresistible [,yry'zystybl] adj.
nieodparty; porywający;
gwałtowny
irresolute [y'rezelu:t] adj.
niezdecydowany; chwiejny
irrespective [,yrys'pektyw] adj.
niezależny; adv. niezależnie;

bez względu na ...; bez
szacunku
irresponsible [,yrys'ponsybl] adj.
nieobliczalny;
nieodpowiedzialny
irretrievable [,yry'tri:webl] adj.
bezpowrotnie stracony
irreverent [y'rewerent] adj.
lekceważący; uchybiający
irrevocable [y'rewokebl] adj.
nieodwołalny; nie do
odwołania
irrigate ['yrygejt] v. nawadniać;
przepłukiwać; odświeżać
irritable ['yrytebl] adj. drażliwy;
wrażliwy; nerwowy;
przewrażliwiony; skory do
gniewu
irritate ['yrytejt] v. denerwować;
irytować; drażnić;
rozdrażniać; unieważniać
prawnie
irritation [,yry'tejszyn] s. irytacja;
rozdrażnienie
is [yz] v. jest; zob. be
island ['ajlend] s. wyspa;
wysepka (na bruku)
isle [ajl] s. wyspa; v. żyć na
wyspie; zrobić (jak) wyspę
isn't ['yznt] = is not; exp.: nie
jest (w domu etc.)
isn't it? ['yznt yt] nieprawda?
czy nie prawda?
isolate ['ajselejt] v. odosabniać;
izolować; osamotniać
isolated ['ajselejtyd] adj.
odosobniony; osamotniony
isolation [,ajse'lejszyn] s.
odosobnienie; izolacja;
wyodrębnienie; osamotnienie
issue ['yszu:] s. wydanie;
przydział; zeszyt; spór;
problem; argument; wynik;
koniec; ujście; wyjście;
wypływ; potomstwo;
upuszczenie; dochód; v.
wysyłać; wypuszczać;
wydawać; dawać w wyniku;
wychodzić; pochodzić;
emitować
isthmus ['ysmes] s. przesmyk;
międzymorze; cieśń; węzina
it [yt] pron. to; ono

Italian [y'taeljen] adj. włoski
italics [y'taelyks] pl. kursywa;
pismo pochyłe
itch ['ycz] s. swędzenie;
świerzb; chętka; v. czuć
swędzenie; swędzić; mieć
ochotę
item ['ajtem] s. pozycja; punkt
programu; artykuł;
wiadomość; adv. podobnie;
także; też dotyczy
itemize ['ajte,majz] v.
wyszczególniać (rachunek,
spis)
itinerary [aj'tynerery] s.
marszruta; szlak; przewodnik;
adj. podróżny; drogowy
its [yts] pron. jego; jej; swój
itself [yt'self] pron. się; siebie;
sobie; sam; sama; samo
ivory ['ajwery] s. kość
słoniowa; klawisz fortepianu;
biel kremowa; adj. z kości
słoniowej; biały
ivy ['ajwy] s. bluszcz

J

J [dżej] dziewiąta litera
angielskiego alfabetu
jab [dżaeb] s. szturchaniec;
dźgnięcie; v. szturchać;
dźgać
jack [dżaek] s. lewarek;
dźwignia; przyrząd; walet;
flaga; gniazdo elektr.; złącze
jack up ['dżaek,ap] v. podnieść
lewarkiem; wyśrubowanie
(cen)
jackal [dżaeko:l] s. szakal;
sługus; harować na kogoś
jackass ['dżaekaes] s. osioł;
dureń; bałwan; menda;
niedojda
jackdaw ['dżaekdo:] s. kawka
jacket [dżaekyt] s. marynarka;
żakiet; kurtka; okładzina;
obwoluta; osłona;

v.okrywać; nakładać
okładzinę; wkładać do teki
jack-in-the-box ['dżaek-yn-dy
-boks] s. figura wyskakująca z
pudełka; typ ognia sztucznego
jack-nife ['dżaeknajf] s.
scyzoryk; nóż składany
jack-of-all-trades ['dżaek,ow'o:l
,trejds] majster do
wszystkiego; majster klepka
jackpot ['dżaek,pot] s. główna
wygrana; pula
jackscrew [dżaekskru:] s. lewar
śrubowy (podnośnik)
jag [dżaeg] s. ostry występ;
zadarcie; nacięcie;
podniecenie; popijawa;
zabawa; v. poszarpać;
postrzępić; ząbkować
jagged [dżaegyd] adj.
postrzępiony; wyszczerbiony;
szczerbaty
jaguar [dżaegjuer] s. jaguar
jail [dżejl] s. ciupa; więzienie; v.
więzić; uwięzić (kogoś)
jam [dżaem] s. tłok; zator;
korek; zła sytuacja; v.
stłoczyć; zablokować;
zaciąć; zagłuszyć
janitor ['dżaenitor] s. portier;
dozorca; sprzątacz biurowy
January ['dżaenjuery] s.
styczeń; a. styczniowy
(dzień etc.)
Japanese [,dżaepe'ni:z] adj.
japoński; s. Japończyk
jar [dża:r] s. słój; słoik; zgrzyt;
kłótnia; drganie; v. zgrzytać;
drażnić; wstrząsać; kłócić
się; trząść; razić
jaundice ['dżo:ndys] s.
żółtaczka; v. powodować
zazdrość (żółtaczkę)
javelin ['dżaewlyn] s. oszczep
jaw [dżo:] s. szczęka; v.
ględzić; gadać; wstawiać
mowę
jaw-bone ['dżo:boun] s. kość
szczękowa; v. nakłaniać
słowami (pod presją)
jay [dżej] s. sójka; dudek;
pleciuga; gaduła (arogancki)
jay-walker ['dżej,ło:ker] s.

nieprawidłowo przechodzący
jezdnię; roztrzepaniec
jazz [dżaz] s. muzyka jazzowa;
(slang) mowa lub czyny
oceniane lekceważąco; v.
grać w stylu jazzu; adj.
zgrzytliwy; krzykliwy
jazz it up ['dżaz,yt'ap] exp.
ożyw to; popraw to; przystrój
to
jazz up ['dżaz,ap] v. (slang)
ożywiać; upiększać;
ulepszać (coś)
jazzy [dżazy] adj. w stylu jazz'u;
podobny do jazz'u; (slang)
żywy, ostentacyjny
jealous ['dżeles] adj. zazdrosny;
baczny (nadzór); zawistny
jealousy ['dżelesy] s. zazdrość;
zawiść; wybuch zazdrości
jeep [dżi:p] s. łazik; samochód
terenowy (silnie zbudowany)
jeer [dżier] s. kpina; szyderstwo;
drwina; v. drwić; kpić;
wykpiwać (ordynarnie i
złośliwie)
jelly ['dżely] s. galareta; kisiel; v.
zgalarecieć; robić galaretę
jellyfish ['dżelyfysz] s. meduza;
człowiek słabej woli
jeopardize ['dżepe,dajz] v.
narazić na
niebezpieczeństwo
jerk [dże:rk] s. szarpnięcie;
skręt; skurcz; pchnięcie; bzik;
frajer; v. szargać; targać;
pchnąć; rzucać się;
wzdrygać się
jerky ['dże:rky] adj. urwany;
trzęsący; bzikowaty;
spazmatyczny
jersey ['dże:rzy] s. sweter
jest [dżest] s. żart; dowcip;
zabawa; pośmiewisko; v.
żartować; dowcipkować;
przekomarzać się
jester ['dżester] s. błazen;
trefniś; błazen nadworny
jet [dżet] s. strumień; wytrysk;
płomień; dysza; rozpylacz;
odrzutowiec; v. tryskać; a.
czarny jak smoła
jet engine [,dżet'endżyn] s.

motor odrzutowy
jet-lag ['dżet,laeg] s. ujemny efekt zmiany czasu na pasażera samolotu odrzutowego
jet plane ['dżet,plejn] s. samolot odrzutowy; odrzutowiec
jet-propelled ['dżet-pre,peld] adj. odrzutowy
jet set ['dżet,set] s. złota młodzież; prominenci
jetty [dżety] s. grobla; molo; adj. czarny jak smoła
Jew [dżu:] s. Żyd
jewel ['dżu:el] s. klejnot; drogi kamień; ozdabiać klejnotami; osadzać na kamieniach (zamontować)
jeweler ['dżu:eler] s. jubiler; właściciel sklepu jubilerskiego
jewelry ['dżu:elry] s. klejnoty; biżuteria; kosztowności
Jewess ['dżuys] s. Żydówka (członkini narodu żydowskiego); żydówka (wyznawczyni religii mojżeszowej)
Jewish ['dżu:ysz] adj. żydowski; hebrajski; judaistyczny; w stylu żydowskim; s. Yidysz, język żydowski
Jewry ['dżuery] s. Żydzi; Zydostwo; getto
Jewishness ['dżu:ysznys] s. żydowskość; żydowskie cechy
jibe [dżajb] v. zgadzać się; pasować (do czegoś); harmonizować
jiffy ['dżyfy] s. mig; chwileczka; momencik; sekundka
jiggle ['dżygl] v. kołysać; lekko huśtać; wstrząsać zrywnie
jig [dżyg] s. skoczny taniec; osadzarka; prowadnica
jig is up [dżyg yz ap] exp. beznadziejna sytuacja; koniec
jigsaw ['dżyg,so:] s. laubzega; włośnica
jigsaw puzzle ['dżyg,so:'pazl] s. składanka
jilt [dżylt] v. porzucić uwiedzionewgo lub

uwiedzioną s. kokietka; uwodzicielka
jimmy ['dżymy] s. krótki łom do podważania; v. otwierać podważając
jingle ['dżyngl] v. brzękać; szczękać; dzwonić; s. brzęk; szczęk; wierszyk (rymy); dzwonek
jingo ['dżyngou] s. szowinista; szowinistka
jingoism ['dżyngou'yzem] s. dżyngoism; szowinizm
jink [dżynk] v. unikać; wymknąć się; oszukiwać; s. unik; kiwnięcie (kogoś)
jitters ['dżyterz] s. pl. zdenerwowanie; trema
job [dżob] s. robota; zajęcie; zadanie; posada; v. pracować; robić; handlować; wynajmować
job [dżob] v. ukłuć; dźgnąć; dziobnąć; s. dźgnięcie; praca; dziobnięcie; zadanie; robota; fach
jobless ['dżoblys] adj. bezrobotny; bez pracy
job-work ['dżobłerk] s. praca na akord (zob. piece-work)
jockey ['dżoky] s. dżokej; v. oszukać; nabrać; pchać się na pozycję
jocular ['dżokjuler] adj. wesoły; żartobliwy; krotochwilny
jocularity [,dżokju'laeryty] s. wesołość; żartobliwość; żarty; krotochwilność; figlarność
jocund ['dżoukend] adj. wesoły
jog [dżog] s. potrącenie; poruszenie; trucht; róg; występ; v. potrącać; poruszać; przebiedować; biec truchtem; telepać się
jog-trot ['dżog'trot] s. trucht; a. monotonny; jednostajny
join [dżoyn] v. łączyć; przyłączać się; przytykać się do; spotykać się; brać udział
joiner ['dżojner] s. stolarz
joint [dżoynt] v. spajać; łączyć; ćwiartować;

kantować; s. spojenie; fuga;
złącze; zestawienie; zawiasa
francuska; część; lokal;
melina; a. wspólny;
połączony; dzielący się z
kimś
joint stock ['dżoynt,stok] adj.
akcyjny (bank); udziałowy
joke [dżouk] s. żart; dowcip;
figiel; v. żartować z kogoś;
dowcipkować; wyśmiać;
zadrwić
joker ['dżouker] s. żartowniś;
dowcipniś; gość; facet;
dżoker; pułapka; trudność
jolly ['dżoly] adj. wesoły; miły;
podochocony; adv. szalenie;
bardzo; v. przychlebiać;
nabierać; zachęcać;
mitygować; ugłaskać
jolt [dżoult] v. wstrząsać;
podrzucać; s. wstrząs;
podrzucenie; szarpnięcie;
podskok
jostle ['dżosl] v. rozpychać
(się); roztrącać; szarpać się;
walczyć (z kimś); s.
pchnięcie; starcie;
szturchnięcie; tłok; ścisk
jot down ['dżot,dałn] v. zapisać
naprędce; zanotować
pośpiesznie
journal ['dże:rnl] s. dziennik;
czasopismo; czop; oś w
łożysku
journalism ['dże:rnlyzem] s.
dziennikarstwo
journey ['dże:rny] v.
podróżować; s. podróż;
jazda; wycieczka
journeyman ['dże:rnymen] s.
czeladnik (nauczony rzemiosła)
jovial ['dżouwjel] adj. wesoły;
jowialny; pełen dobrego
humoru
joy [dżoj] s. radość; uciecha
joyful ['dżojful] adj. radosny;
wesoły; zadowolony (bardzo)
joyous ['dżojes] adj. = joyful
jubilant ['dżu:bylent] adj.
triumfujący; rozradowany
jubilee ['dżu:byli:] s. jubileusz;
wielka radość; a.

jubileuszowy
judge [dżadż] v. sądzić;
osądzać; rozsądzać; s.
sędzia; znawca; znawczyni;
człowiek biegły w ocenach
judgment ['dżadżment] s. sąd;
sądzenie; wyrok; rozsądek;
opinia; ocena; decyzja
judicial [dżu'dyszel] adj. sądowy;
sędziowski; bezstronny;
krytyczny; sądownie
zrzeszony
judicious [dżu'dyszes] a.
rozsądny; rozumny;
wykazujący rozum
jug [dżag] s. dzbanek; koza;
ciupa; v. gotować; wsadzać
do kozy, ciupy; dusić
(potrawkę)
juggle ['dżagl] v. żonglować;
cyganić; robić sztuczki; s.
kuglarstwo; żonglerka
juggler ['dżagler] s. kuglarz;
żongler; oszust; kanciarz
jugglery ['dżaglery] s.
kuglarstwo; podstęp;
oszukaństwo; żonglerka
juice [dżu:s] s. sok; treść;
benzyna; elektryczność; v.
wyciskać sok; doić
juicy ['dżu:sy] adj. soczysty;
jędrny; barwny; deszczowy
juke-box ['dżuk,boks] s.
automat-gramofon (na
monety)
July [dżu:laj] s. lipiec
jumble ['dżambl] s. pomieszać;
kotłować; s. mieszanina;
galimatias; bigos; trzęsąca
jazda
jumble-sale ['dżambl,sejl] s.
wyprzedaż wysortowanych
towarów (często dobroczynna)
jump [dżamp] s. skok; sus;
podskok; wyskok; v. skakać;
podskoczyć; wskoczyć;
wyskoczyć; wyprzedzać;
podnosić cenę; wykoleić;
poderwać się; rzucać się
jumper ['dżamper] s. skoczek;
typ sukni (bez rękawów)
jumpy ['dżampy] adj. nerwowy;
zmienny; nierówny; kapryśny

junction ['dżankszyn] s.
połączenie; złącze; stacja
węzłowa; węzeł;
skrzyżowanie (dróg)
juncture ['dżankczer] s.
połączenie; stan rzeczy;
krytyczna chwila; chwila;
przesilenie
June [dżu:n] s. czerwiec
jungle ['dżangl] s. dżungla;
gąszcz zarośli, lian etc.
junior ['dżu:njer] s. junior;
młodszy; student trzeciego
roku (USA); a. młodszy; z
młodszych
junk ['dżank] s. złom; szmelc;
narkotyki; v. wyrzucać
junkie ['dżanki] s. narkoman
jurisdiction [‚dżurys'dykszyn] s.
wymiar sprawiedliwości;
sądownictwo; zasiąg władzy
jurisprudence [‚dżurys'pru:dens]
s. prawoznawstwo
juror ['dżuerer] s. sędzia
przysięgły; ławnik;
zaprzysiężony; juror
jury ['dżuery] s. sąd
przysięgłych; sąd konkursowy
just [dżast] adj. sprawiedliwy;
słuszny; dokładny; adv.
właśnie; po prostu; zaledwie;
przecież; dokładnie; moment
wcześniej; ściśle; równie;
tak samo
just now ['dżast‚nał] exp.:
właśnie teraz; przed chwilą
justice ['dżastys] s.
sprawiedliwość; słuszność;
sędzia (pokoju, sądu
najwyższego)
justification [‚dżastyfy'kejszyn]
s. uzasadnienie;
usprawiedliwienie; wykazanie
justify ['dżastyfaj] v.
usprawiedliwić;
wytłumaczyć; umotywować;
uzasadnić; dać dowody
justly ['dżastly] adv. słusznie;
poprawnie; właściwie;
sprawiedliwie
jut [dżat] s. występ; v.
wystawać
jut out ['dżat‚aut] v. wystawać;

sterczeć (na zewnątrz);
występować
juvenile ['dżu:wynajl] adj.
małoletni; nieletni; s.
wyrostek; młodzik; podrostek
juvenile court ['dżu:wynajl‚ko:rt]
s. sąd dla nieletnich
juvenile delinquent ['dżu:wynajl
‚dy'lynkłent] s. młodociany
przestępca
juxtaposition [‚dżakstepe'zyszyn]
s. zestawienie; bezpośrednie
sąsiedztwo (tuż obok)

K

k [kej] jedenasta litera
angielskiego alfabetu
kangaroo [‚kaenge'ru:] s. kangur;
a. samosądny; nielegalny
kayak ['kajaek] s. kajak; a.
kajakowy
keel [ki:l] s. stępka; kil; v.
wywracać do góry stępką
keen [ki:n] adj. ostry; dotkliwy;
żywy; cięty; serdeczny;
gorliwy; zapalony; bystry;
przenikliwy; wrażliwy; czuły
keen on ['ki:n‚on] adj. palący się
do ...; czujący miętę
keep; kept; kept [ki:p; kept;
kept]
keep [ki:p] v. dotrzymywać;
przestrzegać; dochować;
obchodzić; strzec; pilnować;
utrzymywać; prowadzić;
trzymać (się);
powstrzymywać się;
mieszkać; kontynuować; s.
utrzymanie; jedzenie; wikt;
umocnienie
keep away ['ki:p‚e'łej] v.
trzymać się z daleka;
odstraszać
keep back ['ki:p‚baek] v.
powstrzymać; nie zbliżać się
keep down ['ki:p‚dałn] v.
trzymać w ryzach; tłumić;

kulić się; utrzymywać na niskim poziomie

keep in ['ki:p,yn] v. zatrzymywać; nie wychodzić; pozostawać; nie pokazywać się

keep off ['ki:p,of] v. nie dopuszczać; trzymać się z dala

keep on ['ki:p,on] v. kontynuować; iść dalej; nudzić; męczyć

keep on doing ['ki:p,on'du:yng] v. robić dalej; nie przestawać; nie dawać spokoju; nudzić

keep out ['ki:p,ałt] v. nie wchodzić; trzymać się na uboczu; nie pozwolić wejść; odpędzać

keep talking ['ki:p'to:kyng] v. mówić dalej; kontynuować rozmowę

keep time ['ki:p'tajm] v. być punktualnym; zapisywać czas pracy

keep to oneself ['ki:p,tu'łanself] v. trzymać się na uboczu; żyć w odosobnieniu

keep up ['ki:p,ap] v. dotrzymywać; utrzymywać w porządku; nie dawać iść spać; trzymać się w dobrym stanie; czuwać

keep up with ['ki:p,ap'łys] v. śledzić; dotrzymywać (kroku)

keeper ['ki:per] s. opiekun; dozorca; strażnik; konserwator; klamra; kotwica magnesu; skobel

keeping ['ki:pyng] s. opieka; zgoda; harmonia; a. do przechowywania

keepsake ['ki:psejk] s. upominek; pamiątka od kogoś

keg [keg] s. beczułka; 100 funtów

kennel ['kenl] s. psiarnia; psia buda; ściek; v. trzymać w budzie; mieszkać w norze

kept [kept] v. zob. keep

kerb stone ['ke:rb,stoun] s.

krawężnik (ang.) zob. curb

kerchief ['ke:rczyf] s. chustka (na głowę); chustka do nosa

kernel ['ke:rnl] s. jądro; ziarno; sedno sprawy; istotna rzecz

ketchup ['keczap] s. sos pomidorowy (gotowy) do mięsa

kettle ['ketl] s. kocioł; czajnik; imbryk na herbatę

kettledrum ['ketl,dram] s. bęben kocioł (półkolisty) miedziany

key [ki:] s. klucz; klawisz; klin; ton; rafa; wysepka; v. stroić; zamykać kluczem lub zwornikiem; adj. ważny; kontrolujący

keyboard ['ki:bo:rd] s. klawiatura (maszyny do pisania etc.)

keyhole ['ki:houl] s. dziurka od klucza (w drzwiach etc.)

keynote ['ki:nout] s. nuta kluczowa; myśl przewodnia

keystone ['ki:stoun] s. zwornik; zasada; główna część

kick [kyk] s. kopniak; kopnięcie; wierzgnięcie; wykop; strzał; odrzut; skarga; narzekanie; przyjemność; uciecha; krzepa; miłe podniecenie; opór; v. kopać; wierzgać; skrzywić się; protestować; opierać się

kickback ['kykbaek] s. łapówka za kontrakt; dawanie łapówki

kick downstairs ['kykdałn'steerz] v. degradować; zrzucać ze schodów (kopniakiem)

kick-off ['kykof] s. rozpoczęcie meczu; pierwszy strzał

kick out ['kyk aut] v. wyrzucić; wykopać; pozbyć się

kick the bucket ['kyk,dy'bakyt] v. umrzeć; odwalić kitę; wyciągnąć nogi; wykitować

kid [kyd] s. koźlę; dzieciak; smyk; młodzik; blaga; bujda; v. urodzić koźlę; bujać; nabierać; żartować; dcwcipkować

kid glove ['kydglaw] s. rękawiczka; a. balowy; delikatny

kidnap ['kydnaep] v. porywać;
uprowadzać; ukraść dziecko
kidnapper ['kydnaeper] s.
porywacz (dziecka, zakładnika)
kidney ['kydny] s. nerka; rodzaj;
a. w kształcie nerki
kidney bean ['kydny,bi:n] s.
fasola szparagowa; piesza
kill [kyl] v. zabijać; uśmiercać;
wybić; zatrzymać (piłkę,
motor); ścinać (piłkę); s.
upolowane zwierzę; zabicie;
mord
killjoy ['kyldżoj] s. człowiek
psujący innym zabawę lub
humor
kill time [,kyl'tajm] v. zabijać
czas; marnować czas
killer ['kyler] s. zabójca;
morderca; narzędzie śmierci
kiln [kyln] s. piec do wypalania
lub wysuszania cegieł etc.
kilogram(me) ['kylougraem] s.
kilogram; a. kilogramowy
kilometer ['kyle,mi:ter] s.
kilometr; a. kilometrowy
kilt [kylt] s. spódniczka męska
(szkocka); v. podkasać;
plisować pionowo
kin [kyn] s. rodzina; krewni; ród;
adj. spokrewniony; pokrewny
kind [kajnd] s. rodzaj; jakość;
gatunek; charakter; natura;
adj. grzeczny; uprzejmy;
życzliwy; łagodny;
wyrozumiały
kindergarten ['kynder,ga:rtn] s.
przedszkole (do sześciu lat
wieku)
kindhearted ['kajnd'ha:rtyd] adj.
dobrotliwy; współczujący
kindle ['kyndle] v. rozpalić;
rozżarzyć; rozniecać;
podniecać; zapalać się
kindly ['kajndly] adv. uprzejmie;
życzliwie; adj. dobry;
dobrotliwy; życzliwy
kindness ['kajndnys] s. dobroć;
uprzejmość; łaskawość;
życzliwość; życzliwy
postępek
kindred ['kyndryd] s. krewni;
pokrewieństwo; adj.

pokrewny
king [kyng] s. król
kingdom ['kyngdom] s.
królestwo; monarchia; świat
(roślin etc.)
king-size ['kyngsajz] adj. wielki;
duży; królewskich wymiarów
kingly ['kyngly] adj. królewski
kinsman ['kynzmen] s. krewny;
powinowaty (mężczyzna)
kipper ['kyper] s. śledź
wędzony; ryba suszona; v.
suszyć; wędzić i solić;
zasuszać (ryby)
kiss [kys] s. całus; v. całować;
pocałować; lekko dotknąć
kit [kyt] s. przybory; narzędzia;
wyposażenie; zestaw;
komplet; torba; bagaż;
cebrzyk; kubeł; komplet
(narzędzi)
kitchen ['kyczn] s. kuchnia
kitchenette ['kyczynet] s.
kuchenka (mała w kawalerce)
kite [kajt] s. latawiec; v.
szybować
kitten ['kytn] s. kotek
knack [naek] s. spryt; sztuczka;
chwyt; dryg; talent
knapsack ['naepsaek] s. plecak
knave [nejw] s. łajdak; łotr;
szelma; walet; naciągacz;
kanalia
knavery ['nejwery] s. łajdactwo;
szelmostwo; niegodziwość
knead ['ni:d] v. miesić; gnieść;
masować; kształtować
(charakter)
knee ['ni:] s. kolano; v. klękać
kneecap ['ni:kaep] s. rzepka
(kolana)
knee-deep ['ni:di:p] adj. po
kolana
knee-jerk ['ni:dże:rk] s. odruch
kolanowy; automatyczna
reakcja
kneel; knelt; knelt [ni:l; nelt; nelt]
kneel [ni:l] v. klękać
knelt [nelt] zob. kneel
knew [nju:] zob. know
knickerbockers ['nikerbokers] s.
pumpy; krótkie spodnie spięte
pod kolanami

knickknack ['niknaek] s. cacko;
fatałaszek; przysmaczek
knife [najf] s. nóż; v. krajać;
kłuć nożem; zakłuć;
zadźgać nożem
knight [najt] s. rycerz; v.
nadawać szlachectwo;
nobilitować
knit; knit; knit [nyt; nyt; nyt]
knit [nyt] v. robić na drutach;
dziać; marszczyć (brwi);
łączyć; ściągać;
powodować zrośnięcie
(kości); spajać (cementem)
knitting [nytyng] s. dzianie;
trykotarstwo; dziewiarstwo
knives [najwz] pl. noże; pl. od
knife
knob [nob] s. guzik; guz; gałka;
sęk; uchwyt; pokrętło; rączka
knock [nok] s. stuk; uderzenie;
pukanie; v. stukać; pukać;
zapukać; uderzyć; zderzyć;
szturchać; zderzyć się
knock down ['nok,dałn] v.
powalić; obniżać cenę;
rozkręcać
knock out ['nok,aut] v.
nokautować; wybijać;
wymęczyć
knock over ['nok,ower] v.
przewracać; przewrócić
knocker ['noker] s. kołatka na
drzwiach; malkontent;
opukiwacz
knot [not] s. węzeł; kokarda;
sęk; zgrubienie; dystans
morski 1853 m; v. wiązać;
zawiązywać; komplikować;
motać
knotty ['noty] adj. węzłowaty;
sękaty; zawiły; zagadkowy
know; knew; known [nou; nju:
noun]
know [nou] v. wiedzieć; umieć;
znać; móc odróżniać;
poznać
know-how ['nouhau] s.
umiejętność; znajomość
rzeczy
knowingly ['nouyngly] adj.
świadomie; naumyślnie;
chytrze

knowledge ['noulydż] s. wiedza;
nauka; znajomość; zasięg
wiedzy
knowledgeable ['nolydżebl] adj.
dobrze poinformowany; mądry
knuckle ['nakl] s. staw palca;
kastet; uderzać kośćmi
palców
kosher ['kouszer] adj. koszerny;
v. koszerować (mięso)
kotow ['kou,tał] = kowtow
kowtow ['koł,tał] v. bić czołem;
płaszczyć się; s. ukłon
starochiński czołem do ziemi
Kraut [kraut] adj. szkopski
(niemiecki); kapuściany
kudos ['kju:dos] s. nagroda lub
uznanie za znaczne
osiągnięcie; sława (slang)
Ku Klux Klan ['kju:,kluks'klaen]
s. rasistowska tajna
organizacja w USA przeciw
Murzynom, Żydom i katolikom
kulak [ku:'la:k] s. zamożny
chłop; kułak

L

l [el] dwunasta litera alfabetu
angielskiego; klauzura; kolanko
(rury); kątownik
lab [laeb] s. (slang) laboratorium;
a. laboratoryjny
label ['lejbl] s. nalepka; etykieta;
naklejka; przezwisko; v.
przylepiać etykiety (na coś,
komuś); przezywać
labor ['lejber] s. praca; robota;
trud; mozół; wysiłek; klasa
robotnicza; poród; v. ciężko
pracować; mozolić się;
borykać się; łudzić się;
brnąć; opracować;
rozwodzić się; rodzić;
szczegółowo opracować
laboratory [lae'boretery] s.
laboratorium; pracownia
laborious [le'bo:rjes] adj.

pracowity; mozolny;
wypracowany; ciężko
pracujący
labor union ['lejber'ju:njen] s.
związek zawodowy
laborer ['lejberer] s. robotnik
płatny na godzinę (fizyczny)
laborite ['lejberajt] s. członek
partii pracy (w Anglii)
lace [lejs] s. sznurówka;
sznurowadło; koronka; v.
sznurować; przetykać;
koronkować; urozmaicać;
chłostać; zakrapiać (wódkę);
młócić; bić; walić
lack [laek] s. brak; niedostatek;
v. brakować; nie mieć
czegoś; być bez czegoś
laconic [le'konyk] adj.
lakoniczny; zwięzły; treściwy
lacquer ['laeker] s. lakier; v.
lakierować; emaliować
lad [laed] s. chłopak; chłopiec
ladder ['laeder] s. drabina; v.
pruć; rozpruć; puszczać
oczka
ladder proof ['laeder,pru:f] adj.
nie prujące się (np.
pończochy); nie puszczający
oczek
laden ['lejdn] adj. obciążony;
obarczony; pogrążony (w
smutku)
lading ['lejdyng] s. fracht;
załadowanie; ładunek (statku)
ladle ['lejdl] s. warząchew;
czerpak; chochla; v. czerpać;
nalewać warząchwią
(czerpakiem)
lady ['lejdy] s. pani; dama
lady killer ['lejdy,kyler] s.
pożeracz serc niewieścich
ladylike ['lejdylajk] adj.
wytworny; zniewieściały
lag [laeg] s. zaleganie;
opóźnienie; zwłoka; v.
zalegać; wlec się z tyłu; nie
nadążać
lag behind ['laeg,by'hajnd] v.
pozostawać w tyle; zalegać
lager ['la:ger] s. wystałe piwo
lagoon [le'gu:n] s. laguna
laid [lejd] zob. lay

lain [lejn] zob. lie
lair [leer] s. barłóg; legowisko;
szałas; v. iść na legowisko
lake [lejk] s. jezioro; a. jeziorny
lamb [laem] s. jagnię; baranina
lame [lejm] adj. kulawy; ułomny;
v. okulawić; okaleczyć
lament [le'ment] s. lament;
biadanie; v. lamentować;
biadać; opłakiwać;
narzekać; ubolewać;
zawodzić; być w żałobie
lamentable ['laementebl] adj.
opłakany; godny ubolewania;
żałosny; wyrażający
ubolewanie
lamentation [,laemen'tejszyn] s.
lament; biadanie; lamentacja
lamp [laemp] s. lampa; latarka;
kaganek; v. świecić;
oświetlać; gapić się;
zobaczyć; widzieć
lamppost ['laemp,poust] s. słup
latarniany; latarnia uliczna
lamp shade ['laempszejd] s.
abażur
lance [la:ns] s. lanca; lansjer;
lancet; v. kłuć; przebijać
lancą lub lancetem; rozcinać
land [laend] s. ląd; ziemia; grunt;
kraj; v. wyciągać na ląd;
wyładować; zdobyć (np.
nagrodę)
landholder ['laend,houlder] s.
właściciel ziemski;
dzierżawca
landing ['laendyng] s. lądowanie;
pomost; przystań; półpiętrze
landing field ['laendyng,fi:ld] s.
lotnisko polowe; lądowisko
landing gear ['laendyng,gier] s.
podwozie (z kołami -
samolotu)
landing stage ['laendyng, stejdż]
s. pomost pływający;
wyładunek
landlady ['laend,lejdy] s.
właścicielka domu, hotelu
etc.; gospodyni (pensjonatu)
landlord ['laend,lo:rd] s.
właściciel domu

czynszowego; gospodarz
odnajmujący pokój
landmark ['laendma:rk] s. punkt
orientacyjny; słup graniczny
landowner ['laend,ołner] s.
właściciel ziemski
landscape ['laendskejp] s.
krajobraz; v. kształtować
teren i ogród (upiększać)
landslide ['laendslajd] s.
osuwisko; lawina głazów
landslip ['laendslyp] s. osuwisko;
obsunięcie się ziemi
lane [lejn] s. tor; uliczka; szlak;
przejście; linia ruchu
kołowego; trasa (samolotu)
language ['laengłydż] s. mowa;
język mówiony i pisany
languid ['laengłyd] s. ospały;
omdlały; słaby; ociężały;
powolny; rozmarzony; tęskny
languish ['laengłysz] v.
omdlewać; marnieć; ginąć z
tęsknoty; mieć wyraz zadumy
languor ['laenger] s. omdlenie;
osłabienie; ociężałość;
ospałość; tęsknota;
rozmarzenie; powolność;
brak wigoru; słabość
lank [laenk] adj. mizerny;
wysoki; chudy; wychudzony;
prosty; gładki; długi i płaski
lanky ['laenky] adj. wychudzony;
wysoki i chudy
lanolin ['laenolyn] s. lanolina
lantern ['laentern] s. latarnia
lap [laep] s. łono; podołek; poła;
okrążenie; zanadrze; dolinka;
chlupotanie; lura; v. spowijać;
otulać; zakładać (jak
dachówki); wystawać;
chłeptać; chlupotać;
chlupać
lapel [le'pel] s. klapa (płaszcza)
dochodząca kołnierza
lapse [laeps] s. lapsus; upływ;
okres; omyłka; v. potknąć
się; odstąpić; omylić się;
upłynąć; stracić ważność;
minąć; przechodzić;
pogrążyć się w stan ...
larceny ['la:rseny] s. kradzież
larch [la:rcz] s. modrzew

lard [la:rd] s. smalec; v.
szpikować; naszpikowywać;
ozdabiać cytatami
larder ['la:rder] s. spiżarnia
large [la:rdż] adj. wielki; rozległy;
obfity; hojny
largely ['la:rdżly] adv. znacznie;
hojnie; suto; w dużym
stopniu; w dużej ilości;
głównie
lark [la:rk] s. skowronek;
zabawa; uciecha; v. figlować;
żartować; przeskakiwać
larva ['la:rwa] s. larwa
larynx ['laerynks] s. krtań
lascivious [le'sywjes] adj.
lubieżny; wzbudzający
lubieżność
lash [laesz] s. bicz; uderzenie;
nagana; rzęsa; v. chłostać;
machać; walić; pędzić;
uwiązać
lass [laes] s. dziewczyna;
dziewczę; młoda kobieta
lasso [lae'su:] s. lasso; v.
chwytać na lasso
last [laest] adj. ostatni; ubiegły;
ostateczny; adv. po raz
ostatni; ostatnio; wreszcie; w
końcu; v. trwać;
wytrzymać; wystarczyć;
długo służyć; s. koniec; kres;
wytrzymałość; kopyto
szewskie; ostatnie dziecko
last but one ['laest,bat'łan] exp.:
przedostatni
lasting ['la:styng] adj. stały;
trwały; długotrwały
lastly [la:stly] adv. w końcu; na
końcu; w konkluzji;
ostatecznie
last night ['laest,najt] exp.:
wczoraj wieczór
last name ['laest,nejm] s.
nazwisko
latch [laecz] s. zasuwka; rygiel;
zatrzask; v. zamykać na
zasuwkę, rygiel lub zatrzask
latch onto ['laecz,ontu] v.
uczepić się kogoś
late [lejt] adj. & s. późny;
spóźniony; były; zmarły; adv.
późno; poniewczasie;

niegdyś
lately ['lejtly] adv. ostatnio
later on ['lejter,on] adv. później; potem; dalej
lath [laes] s. łata; deseczka; v. pokrywać łatami (do tynkowania)
lathe [lejz] s. tokarnia; koło garncarskie; v. toczyć (na tokarni); obrabiać (na obrabiarce)
lather ['laedzer] s. piana; mydliny; v. mydlić (brodę); zapienić (się); prać; łoić
Latin ['laetyn] adj. łaciński; s. łacina; łacinnik
latitude ['laetytju:d] s. szerokość (geograficzna); szerokość poglądów; zakres; rozmiary; wolność; swoboda (np. działania); tolerancja
latter ['laeter] adj. drugi; końcowy; schyłkowy; ostatni
latterly ['laeterly] adv. ostatnio; niedawno; później
lattice ['laetys] s. kratownica; v. kratować; ułożyć w kratę
laudable ['lo:debl] adj. chwalebny; godny pochwały
laugh [laef] v. śmiać się; zaśmiać się; roześmiać się
laugh at ['laef,et] v. wyśmiewać; uśmiać się (z czegoś)
laugh away ['laef,e'łej] v. zbyć śmiechem
laugh off ['laef,of] v. obrócić w żart; pokryć zmieszanie śmiechem
laughter ['laefter] s. śmiech
launch [lo:ncz] v. puszczać w ruch; spuszczać na wodę; miotać; rzucać; zadawać; wydawać; s. szalupa; spuszczenie na wodę (statku, okrętu etc.)
launching pad ['lo:nczyng,paed] s. wyrzutnia (rakiet)
launderette [lo:n'dret] s. pralnia samoobsługowa
laundry ['lo:ndry] s. pralnia; bielizna do prania
laurel ['lorel] s. wawrzyn; laur; v.

wieńczyć wawrzynem
lava ['la:we] s. lawa
lavatory ['laewetery] s. umywalnia; ustęp; umywalka
lavender ['laewynder] s. lawenda; v. wkładać lawendę w bieliznę; a. lawendowy
lavish ['laewysz] adj. hojny; suty; rozrzutny; v. nie szczędzić (pieniędzy, miłości)
law [lo:] s. prawo; ustawa; reguła; sądy; posłuszeństwo prawu
lawful ['lo:ful] adj. legalny; słuszny; prawowity; z prawego łoża; prawnie uznany
lawless ['lo:lys] adj. bezprawny; łamiący prawo; rozpustny
lawn [lo:n] s. trawnik; murawa
lawn mower ['lo:n,mołer] s. kosiarka do strzyżenia trawy
lawsuit ['lo:sju:t] s. proces (sądowy); sprawa sądowa
lawyer ['lo:jer] s. prawnik; adwokat; radca prawny
lax [laeks] adj. luźny; nieszczelny; niedbały; nieścisły; mający rozwolnienie; wolny
laxative ['laeksetyw] adj. & s. przeczyszczający (środek)
laxity ['laeksyty] s. luźność; nieścisłość; niedokładność; niedbalstwo; rozwiązłość
lay; laid; laid [lej; lejd; lejd]
lay [lej] v. kłaść; uspokajać; układać; skręcać (się); zaczaić się; spać z kimś; s. położenie; układ; spanie (z kimś); adj. świecki; laicki; niefachowy; lay- zob. lie
layout ['lejout] s. rozkład; plan; założenie; układ
lay out ['lej,aut] v. układać; projektować; powalić; (slang) zabić; wydatkować; wyłożyć
lay up ['lejap] v. zbierać; gromadzić; przechowywać
layer ['lejer] s. warstwa; odkład; kura niosąca; zakładający się;

pokład
layman ['lejmen] s. człowiek
  świecki; laik
lazy ['lejzy] adj. leniwy;
  próżniaczy; ociężały
lead [led] s. ołów; v. pokrywać
  ołowiem; obciążać ołowiem
lead; led; led [li:d; led; led]
lead [li:d] v. prowadzić;
  kierować; dowodzić;
  naprowadzać; nasunąć;
  namówić; dyrygować;
  przewodzić; s. kierownictwo;
  przewodnictwo; przewaga;
  prym; wskazówka; przykład;
  powodzenie
leaden ['ledn] adj. ołowiany;
  ciężki; ociężały; ponury; szary
leader ['li:der] s. przywódca;
  lider; przewodnik; prowadzący
leadership ['li:der,szyp] s.
  przywództwo; kierownictwo;
  przewodnictwo; umiejętność
  przewodzenia
leading ['li:dyng] adj.
  kierowniczy; naczelny;
  główny; s. kierownictwo;
  prowadzenie; przewodnictwo;
  przywództwo
leaf [li:f] s. liść; kartka; pl.
  leaves [li:wz]
leaflet [li:flyt] s. listek; ulotka
  (często złożona)
league [li:g] s. liga; związek;
  mila; v. łączyć (się) w ligę
leak [li:k] s. dziura; otwór;
  przeciekanie; v. cieknąć;
  przeciekać; wyciekać
  (sekrety); wysączać;
  zaciekać
leakage [li:kydż] s. przeciekanie
  (sekretów); wyciekanie
  (pieniędzy); rozproszenie
leaky ['li:ky] adj. dziurawy;
  nieszczelny; cieknący;
  niedyskretny; nie
  dochowujący sekretu
lean; leant; leant [li:n; lent; lent]
lean [li:n] v. nachylać (się);
  pochylać (się); opierać (się)
  (o coś); adj. chudy; s. chude
  mięso; nachylenie;
  skłonność

leant [lent] v. zob. lean
leap; leapt; leapt [li:p; lept; lept]
leap [li:p] v. skakać;
  przeskoczyć; s. skok;
  podskok
leapt [lept] v. zob. leap
leap-year ['li:pje:r] s. rok
  przestępny
learn; learnt; learnt [le:rn; le:rnt;
  le:rnt]
learn [le:rn] v. uczyć się;
  dowiadywać się; zapamiętać
learned ['le:rnyd] adj. uczony
learner ['le:rner] s. uczący się;
  uczeń; uczennica
learning ['le:rnyng] s. nauka;
  wiedza; erudycja;
  umiejętności
learnt [le:rnt] v. zob. learn
lease [li:s] s. dzierżawa; v.
  dzierżawić; wydzierżawić
leash [li:sz] s. smycz
least [li:st] adj. najmniejszy; adv.
  najmniej; w najmniejszym
  stopniu; s. najmniejsza rzecz;
  drobnostka najmniej ważna
leather ['ledzer] s. skóra; adj.
  skórzany; v. pokrywać skórą;
  oprawiać w skórę; sprać
  (rzemieniem)
leave; left; left [li:w; left; left]
leave [li:w] v. zostawiać;
  opuszczać; odchodzić;
  odjeżdżać; pozostawiać; s.
  pożegnanie; urlop; pozwolenie
leaven [lewn] s. drożdże
leaves [li:wz] pl. liście; zob. leaf
lecture ['lekczer] s. wykład;
  nagana; v. wykładać;
  udzielać nagany; przemawiać
  do sumienia
lecturer ['lekczerer] s.
  wykładowca (na uczelni, w
  klasie etc.)
led [led] v. zob. lead
ledge [ledż] s. występ; stopień;
  półka; gzyms; listwa; rafa
lee [li:] s. strona zawietrzna;
  osłona; adj. zawietrzny;
  osłonięty
leech [li:cz] s. pijawka
leek [li:k] s. por
leer [lier] s. spojrzenie z ukosa;

v. łypać okiem znacząco
(chytrze, złośliwie,
pożądliwie)
left [left] adj. lewy; adv. na
lewo; s. lewa strona; zob.
leave
left-hand ['left,haend] s. lewa
ręka; adj. lewoskrętny;
lewostronny
left-handed ['left'haendyd] s.
mańkut; adj. leworęki;
niezgrabny; wątpliwy;
nieszczery
left side ['left,sajd] s. lewa
strona (drogi, samochodu etc.)
leg [leg] s. noga; nóżka;
podpórka; odcinek; kończyna;
udziec
legacy [legesy] s. spadek;
spuścizna; dziedzictwo; zapis
legal ['li:gel] adj. prawny;
prawniczy; ustawowy; legalny
legation [li'gejszyn] s. poselstwo
(włącznie z posłem)
legend ['ledżend] s. legenda
legendary ['ledżendery] adj.
legendarny; tradycyjny
legible ['ledżebl] adj. czytelny;
łatwo czytelny
legion ['li:dżen] s. legion; legia;
wojsko; wielka ilość;
mnóstwo; tłumy; mnogość
legislation [,ledżys'lejszyn] s.
prawodawstwo;
ustawodawstwo
legislative ['ledżysletyw] adj.
prawodawczy; ustawodawczy
legislator ['ledżyslator] s.
prawodawca; poseł do
parlament (sejmu, senatu etc.)
legitimate [ly'dżytymyt] adj.
ślubny; prawowity; słuszny;
uzasadniony; logiczny;
rozsądny
leg-pull ['legpu:l] s. kawał; żart;
sztuczka; naciąganie
leisure ['li:żer] s. wolny czas;
swoboda od zajęć; wolne
chwile
leisurely ['li:żerly] adv.
swobodnie; bez pośpiechu;
adj. mający czas; spokojny;
robiony w wolnym czasie

lemon ['lemen] s. cytryna;
tandeta; adj. cytrynowy; z
cytryn
lemonade ['lemenejd] s.
lemoniada (z soku
cytrynowego etc.)
lend; lent; lent [lend; lent; lent]
lend [lend] v. pożyczać;
użyczać; udzielać
length [lenks] s. długość
lengthen ['lenksen] v.
przedłużać; wydłużać (się);
podłużać
lengthwise ['lensłajz] adv. adj.
wzdłuż; na długość
lenient ['li:njent] adj.
wyrozumiały; łagodny
lens [lenz] s. soczewka;
obiektyw; lupa
lent [lent] s. post; zob. lend
leopard ['leperd] s. lampart
leper ['leper] s. trędowaty;
trędowata
leprosy ['lepresy] s. trąd
less [les] adj. mniejszy; adv.
mniej; s. coś mniejszego;
prep. bez; nie tak dużo (wiele)
lessen [lesn] v. zmniejszać (się);
maleć; pomniejszać
lesser [leser] adj. mniejszy
lesson [lesn] s. lekcja; nauczka;
urywek z Biblii; wykład
lest [lest] conj. ażeby nie; że
let; let; let [let; let; let]
let [let] v. zostawić;
wynajmować; dawać;
puszczać; pozwalać
let alone ['let,e'loun] v.
zostawić w spokoju; dać
spokój
let down ['let,dałn] v. robić
zawód; spuszczać;
opuszczać; upokorzyć;
odmawiać pomocy
let go ['let,gou] v. wypuszczać;
zwalniać; pozwolić odejść
let know ['let,nou] v.
zawiadomić; donieść;
powiadomić
let up ['let,ap] v. zelżeć;
złagodnieć; s. zelżenie
lethal ['li:sel] adj. śmiertelny;
zgubny; śmiercionośny

letter ['leter] s. litera; list;
czcionka; v. drukować;
oznaczać literami;
kaligrafować
letter-box ['leter,boks] s.
skrzynka pocztowa
letter-carrier ['leter'kaerjer] s.
listonosz
lettuce ['letys] s. sałata
(głowiasta); liście sałaty
leukemia [lju'ki:mie] s. białaczka;
leukemia
level ['lewl] s. poziom;
płaszczyzna; równina;
poziomnica; adj. poziomy; adv.
poziomo; równo; v.
zrównywać; celować
level crossing ['lewl'krosyng] s.
skrzyżowanie dróg (kolizyjne)
w jednej płaszczyźnie
lever ['li:wer] s. dźwignia;
lewar; v. podważać;
podnosić dźwigiem
(lewarem)
levity ['lewyty] s.
lekkomyślność
levy ['lewy] v. pobierać;
nakładać (podatek); s. pobór
lewd [lu:d] adj. zmysłowy;
lubieżny; pożądliwy; sprośny
liability [,laje'bylyty] s.
odpowiedzialność;
obowiązek; obciążenie;
zadłużenie; ryzyko
liable ['lajebl] adj.
odpowiedzialny; podlegający;
podatny; skłonny; narażony;
mający widoki
liable to ['lajebl,tu] adj. skłonny
do ...; adv. łatwo (zgnije)
liaison [ly'ejzo:n] s. łączność;
związek; romans (nielegalny)
liar ['lajer] s. kłamca; łgarz
libation [laj-bej'szyn] s. libacja
libel ['lajbel] s. paszkwil;
oszczerstwo; zniesławienie
(publiczne w piśmie, filmie
etc.); v. zniesławiać
liberal ['lyberel] s. liberał; a.
liberalny; hojny; tolerancyjny
liberate ['lyberejt] v. uwalniać;
zwalniać; wyzwalać
liberation ['lyberejszyn] s.

uwalnianie; oswobodzenie
liberator ['lyberejter] s.
oswobodziciel; wyzwoliciel
liberty ['lyberty] s. wolność;
swoboda; nadużywanie
wolności
librarian [laj'breerjen] s.
bibliotekarz
library ['lajbrery] s. biblioteka;
księgozbiór
lice [lajs] pl. wszy; zob. louse
license(ce) ['lajsens] s. licencja;
pozwolenie; upoważnienie;
swoboda; rozpusta; v.
upoważniać; udzielać
pozwolenia; nadużywać
wolności
licensee [,lajsen'si:] s. posiadacz
zezwolenia; koncesjonariusz;
właściciel licencji
lichen ['lajken] s. liszaj
lick [lyk] s. liźnięcie; odrobina;
cios; raz; wybuch; energia; v.
lizać; polizać; wylizać; bić;
smarować
licking ['lykyng] s. (slang) bicie;
pobicie; młocka
lid [lyd] s. wieko; powieka;
pokrywa; nakrywka;
przykrywka
lie; 1. lay; lain [laj; lej; lejn]
lie [laj] v. leżeć; s. układ;
położenie; konfiguracja;
legowisko
lie; 2. lied; lied [laj; lajd; lajd]
lie [laj] s. kłamać; s. kłamstwo;
łgarstwo; fałsz
lie down ['laj,dałn] v. kłaść się;
położyć się; nie reagować
lie in ['laj,yn] v. być w połogu;
leżeć w (łóżku)
lie over ['laj,ouwer] v. być
odroczonym; zostać przez
noc
lieutenant [lef'tenant; lu:tenant]
s. porucznik
life [lajf] s. życie; życiorys; zob.
pl. lives
life assurance ['lajfe'szuerens] s.
ubezpieczenie na życie
life belt ['lajfbelt] s. pas
ratunkowy
lifeboat ['lajfbout] s. łódź

ratunkowa
lifeguard ['lajfga:rd] s. ratownik
life insurance ['lajn,yn'szuerens]
s. ubezpieczenie na życie
life jacket ['lajfdżaekyt] s. kurta
ratownicza; kamizelka
ratunkowa
lifeless ['lajflys] adj. bez życia;
martwy; zamarły; wymarły
lifelike ['lajflajk] adj. jak żywy
(człowiek, osoba, stworzenie)
life sentence ['lajf,sentens] s.
kara dożywocia (wyrok)
life-style ['lajfstajl] s. styl życia;
modła życia; sposób życia
lifetime ['lajf,tajm] s. życie; całe
życie
lift [lyft] s. dźwig; winda;
przewóz; podniesienie;
wzniesienie; v. podnieść;
dźwignąć; podnosić się;
kraść; spłacić (np. dom);
kopnąć; buchnąć;
awansować
lift-off ['lyft,of] s. start lotu (np.
rakiety)
ligament ['lygement] s. ścięgno
ligature ['lygeczuer] s.
przywiązanie; ligatura;
podwiązanie; bandaż; nić
chirurgiczna
light; lit; lit [lajt; lyt; lyt]
light [lajt] s. światło;
oświetlenie; ogień; adj.
świetny; jasny; łatwy; lekki;
błahy; słaby; beztroski;
niefrasobliwy; lekkomyślny;
v. świecić; oświecać;
zapalać; ujawniać;
poświęcić; rozjaśnić;
przyświecić; wsiadać;
zsiadać; wpaść; wyjechać;
adv. lekko
lightheaded ['lajt'hedyd] adj.
lokkomyślny; majaczący;
roztargniony
light up ['lajtap] v. zaświecić;
rozjaśnić; oświecić
lighten ['lajtn] v. ulżyć; zelżyć;
oświecać; rozjaśnić się;
błysnąć; błyskać się
lighter ['lajter] s. zapalniczka;
latarnik; lampiarz

lighthouse ['lajthaus] s. latarnia
morska
lighting ['lajtyng] s. oświetlenie;
oświetlanie
light-minded ['lajt'majndyd] adj.
lekkomyślny; roztargniony
lightness ['lajtnys] s. jasność;
lekkość; łagodność;
łatwość; lekkomyślność
lightning ['lajtnyng] s.
błyskawica; piorun; a.
błyskawiczny
lightning rod ['lajtnyng,rod] s.
piorunochron; odgromnik
lightweight ['lajt-łejt] s. waga
lekka; adj. lekkiej wagi; błahy;
(127 do 135 funtowy bokser)
light-year ['lajt,je:r] s. rok
świetlny (ok. $6x10^{12}$ mil =
$10x10^{12}$ km)
lignite ['lygnajt] s. węgiel
brunatny; lignit
like [lajk] v. lubieć; upodobać
sobie; (chcieć); mieć
zamiłowanie, ochotę; adj.
podobny; analogiczny;
typowy; adv. podobnie; w ten
sam sposób; s. drugi taki sam;
rzecz podobna; conj. jak; tak
jak; po; w ten sposób; niby
to; niczym
like that ['lajk'dzaet] adv. tak; w
ten sposób; właśnie tak
likelihood ['lajklyhud] s.
prawdopodobieństwo
likely ['lajkly] adj. możliwy;
prawdopodobny; odpowiedni;
nadający się; obiecujący; adv.
pewnie; prawdopodobnie
likeness ['lajknys] s.
podobieństwo; podobizna;
pozory
likewise ['lajkłajz] adv. także;
również; podobno; podobnie;
w ten sam sposób; też
liking ['lajkyng] s. sympatia;
upodobanie; zamiłowanie
lilac ['lajlek] s. bez; adj. lila;
liliowy; blado siny
lily ['lyly] s. lilia; a. jak lilia
lily of the valley ['lyiy,ow'dy
,waely] s. konwalia
limb [lym] s. kończyna; konar;

brzeg; krawędź; ramię; noga;
skrzydło
lime 1. [lajm] s. wapno; v.
wapnić; adj. wapienny
lime 2. [lajm] s. lipa; cytrus
(dzika cytryna); a. cytrusowy
limelight ['lajmlajt] s. światło
wapienne; światło
reflektorów; widok publiczny
limestone ['lajmstoun] s.
wapień; a. z wapienia
limey ['lajmy] s. (slang)
Brytyjczyk (wulg.) zwłaszcza
marynarz
limit ['lymyt] s. granica; kres; v.
ograniczać; ustalać granice
limitation [,lymy'tejszyn] s.
ograniczenie; zastrzeżenie;
prekluzja; przedawnienie
limited liability ['lymytyd
,laje'bylyty] s. ograniczona
odpowiedzialność
limp [lymp] adj. wiotki; bez sił;
osłabiony; v. kuleć; chromać
line [lajn] s. linia; kreska; bruzda;
lina; sznur; przewód; granica;
zajęcie; zainteresowania;
szereg; rząd; linka; v.
liniować; wyścielać; podbić
podszewką; służyć za
podszewkę
lineup ['lajnap] s. uszeregowanie;
rząd; ustawianie w rząd
line up ['lajnap] v. ustawić w
rząd; uszeregować
lineaments ['lynjements] pl. rysy
twarzy; cechy szczególne
linear ['lynjer] adj. liniowy;
linijny; wąski i długi
linen ['lynyn] s. płótno; bielizna;
adj. lniany; płócienny
linen closet ['lynen'klozyt] s.
schowek na bieliznę
liner ['lajner] s. samolot
pasażerski; statek pasażerski
linger ['lynger] v. ociągać się;
zwlekać; pozostawać w tyle;
marudzić; tkwić; wlec życie
lingerie ['le:nżeri] s. damska
bielizna; damskie artykuły
bieliźniane
lining ['lajnyng] s. podszewka;
podkład; okładzina;

zawartość
link [lynk] s. ogniwo; więź;
spinka; 20,1 cm; połączyć;
zczepiać; związać; sprzęgać
links [lynks] pl. wydmy; boisko
golfowe; wydmy piaszczyste
lion [lajon] s. lew; a. lwi; lwie
lioness [lajonys] s. lwica
lip [lyp] s. warga; brzeg; ostrze;
bezczelne gadanie; v. dotykać
wargami; mruczeć
lipstick ['lypstyk] s. kredka do
warg; pomadka do ust
liquid ['lykłyd] s. płyn; adj.
płynny; niestały; nieustalony
liquor ['lyker] s. napój
alkoholowy; sok; odwar;
bulion
liquorice ['lykorys] s. lukrecja
lisp [lysp] v. seplenić; seplenić
jak niemowlę; s. seplenienie
list [lyst] s. lista; spis; listwa;
krawędź; v. wciągać na
listę; obramowywać;
przechylać (się); pochylać
(się); s. pochylenie; przechył
listen ['lysen] v. słuchać;
usłuchać; przysłuchiwać się
listen in ['lysen,yn] v.
podsłuchiwać; posłuchać
(radia etc.)
listen to ['lysen,tu] v. usłuchać
kogoś (czyjejś rady)
listener ['lysener] s. słuchacz
listless ['lystlys] adj. apatyczny;
obojętny; zobojętniały; bierny
(z powodu choroby)
lit [lyt] zob. light
liter ['li:ter] s. litr
literal ['lyterel] adj. literalny;
dosłowny; prozaiczny;
literowy; rzeczowy (umysł)
literary ['lyterery] adj. literacki;
obeznany w literaturze
literature ['lyter`eczer] s.
literatura; piśmiennictwo
lithe [lajs] adj. giętki; gibki;
łatwo gnący się
litter ['liter] s. śmieci;
podściółka; barłóg; v.
śmiecić; podścielać;
urodzić szczeniaki;
porozrzucać niechlujnie

litter bin ['lyter,byn] s. śmietnik; kosz na śmieci
little ['lytl] adj. mały; niski; nieduży; adv. mało; niewiele
little bit ['lytl,byt] adv. trochę; bardzo mało; troszeczkę
little one ['lytl,łan] s. dziecko; dziecina; dzieciątko
little by little ['lytl,baj'lytl] exp. po trochu; stopniowo; pomału; pomalutku
live [lyw] v. żyć; mieszkać; przeżywać; przetrwać; ocalić
live [lajw] adj. żywy; żyjący; ruchliwy; energiczny
live on ['lyw,on] v. żyć z czegoś; żyć czymś
live wire ['lajw'łajer] s. przewód pod napięciem
livelihood ['lajwly,hud] s. utrzymanie; środki do życia
lively ['lajwly] adj. żywy; wesoły; ożywiony; żwawy; gorący; rześki; pełen życia; jaskrawy
liver ['lywer] s. wątroba; wątróbka; a. wątroby
livery ['lywery] adj. wątrobiany; chory na wątrobę; opryskliwy; s. liberia; utrzymanie konia; wynajem (wozów)
lives [lajws] pl. żywoty; zob. life
livestock ['lajwstok] s. żywy inwentarz; zwierzęta domowe
livid ['lywyd] adj. siny; wściekły; posiniaczony
living ['lywyng] s. życie; utrzymanie; tryb życia
living room ['lywyn,ru:m] s. salon; bawialnia; pokój
lizard ['lyzerd] s. jaszczurka
load [loud] s. ładunek; waga; ciężar; obciążenie; v. ładować; załadować; naładować; obciążać; nasycać; fałszować
load up ['loud,ap] v. brać ładunek; opychać się
loader ['louder] s. ładowniczy; maszyna do ładowania
loading ['loudyng] s. ładunek; ładowanie; a. ładunkowy

(pomost)
loaded words ['loudyd,łe:rds] s. słowa tendencyjne (niesprawiedliwe) (uwłaczające)
loaf [louf] s. bochenek; głowa (cukru); pl. loaves [louwz]; v. wałęsać się; marnować czas
loafer ['loufer] s. włóczęga; łazik; próżniak; nieróbj; wałkoń; wygodny bucik sportowy
loam [loum] s. gleba ilasta; ił; zaprawa gliniana (murarska)
loan [loun] s. pożyczka; v. pożyczać
loath [lous] adj. niechętny
loathe [lous] v. nienawidzieć; czuć wstręt
loathsome ['loussem] adj. wstrętny; obrzydliwy; ohydny
loaves [louwz] zob. loaf
lobby ['loby] s. przedpokój; kuluar; v. urabiać senatora lub posła na czyjąś korzyść (przekupywać)
lobbyist ['lobyst] s. interwencjonalista kuluarowy (często oficjalnie rejestrowany w USA); lobbyista
lobe [loub] s. płat (np. płucny)
lobster ['lobster] s. homar
local ['loukel] adj. lokalny; miejscowy; s. oddział związku zawodowego
locality [lou'kaelyty] s. okolica; miejscowość; strefa; rejon
localize ['lokelajz] v. umiejscowić; lokalizować
locate ['loukejt] v. umieścić; znaleźć; osiedlić się
located ['lokejtyd] adj. zamieszkały; umieszczony; znaleziony
location ['loukejszyn] s. położenie; ulokowanie; miejsce zamieszkania; miejsce zaznaczone
loch [lok] s. jezioro; wąska zatoka (zwłaszcza w Szkocji)
lock [lok] s. zamek; zamknięcie; śluza; lok; v. zamykać (na klucz); przechodzić śluzę

lock in ['lokyn] v. zamykać (wewnątrz); otaczać (górami)
locker ['loker] s. szafka; kabina; skrzynia; schowek
lock out ['lokaut] v. wykluczać; s. lokaut (lockout)
locksmith ['loksmys] s. ślusarz
locomotive ['louke,moutyw] s. lokomotywa; adj. ruchomy
locust ['loukest] s. szarańcza; akacja
lodge [lodż] s. chata; loża; kryjówka; domek myśliwski; nora; v. przenocować; zdeponować; umieszczać; wnosić (skargę etc.)
lodger ['lodżer] s. lokator
lodging ['lodżyng] s. mieszkanie (tymczasowe,wynajęte etc.)
loft [loft] s. strych; poddasze; chór; v. podbić piłkę golfową
lofty ['lofty] adj. wzniosły; wyniosły; wysoki; dumny; hardy
log [log] s. kłoda; kloc; log; dziennik operacyjny (statku, szybu); v. wycinać drzewa; ciąć na kłody; wciągać do dziennika okrętowego etc.
logbook ['logbuk] s. dziennik pokładowy; książka raportowa
log cabin ['log,kaebyn] s. chata (z belek) (z okrąglaków)
logic ['lodżyk] s. logika
logical ['lodżykel] adj. logiczny; rozumujący poprawnie
loin [loin] s. lędźwie; polędwica; comber; krzyże; biodra
loiter [lojter] v. marudzić; wałęsać się; guzdrać; mitrążyć; kręcić się podejrzanie
loll [lol] v. rozwalać się; opierać się niedbale; wywieszać (język psa); zwisać
loneliness ['lounlynys] s. samotność; osamotnienie; odludność
lonely ['lounly] adj. samotny
lonesome ['lounsom] adj. osamotniony; odludny
long [long] adj. długi;

długotrwały; v. tęsknić; pragnąć (czegoś); adv. długo; dawno
long ago [,long'egou] adv. dawno temu; adj. dawno miniony
long before ['long,befor] adv. dużo wcześniej; znacznie wcześniej
long since ['long,syns] adv. dawno temu; od dawna
long distance call ['long'dystans ,kol] s. telefon międzymiastowy; rozmowa międzymiastowa
longing ['longyng] s. pragnienie; tęsknota; ochota; adj. tęskny
long jump ['long,dżamp] s. skok w dal
longshoreman ['long,szo:rmen] s. doker; robotnik portowy
long-sighted ['lon'sajtyd] adj. dalekowzroczny; przewidujący
long spun ['lon'span] a. rozwlekły
long-term ['lon'term] adj. długoterminowy; długofalowy
long-winded ['lon'łyndyd] adj. gadatliwy; długo mówiący; (koń) ze zdrowymi płucami
look [luk] s. spojrzenie; wygląd; v. patrzeć; wyglądać
look after ['luk,a:fter] v. doglądać; opiekować się (kimś)
look around ['luk,e'raund] v. rozglądać się; poszukiwać wzrokiem
look at ['luk,et] v. patrzeć na (kogoś, coś)
look for ['luk,fo:r] v. szukać
look forwards ['luk fo:rłerds] v. oczekiwać; cieszyć się
look into ['luk,yntu] v. badać; wglądać
look on ['luk,on] v. przypatrywać się; przyglądać się; kibicować
look out ['luk,aut] v. być w pogotowiu; mieć się na baczności; uważać; wyjrzeć; wyszukać
look over ['luk,ouwer] v.

przeglądać; przejrzeć
look up ['luk,ap] v. szukać;
odwiedzać; patrzeć w górę
looker-on ['luker'on] s. widz;
przyglądający się; kibic
looking-glass ['lukynglas] s.
lustro; zwierciadło
lookout ['luk,aut] s. widok;
uwaga; czaty; czujność
loom [lu:m] s. krosna; warsztat
tkacki; v. wynurzać się;
zagrażać; grozić;
zamajaczyć
loop [lu:p] s. pętla; węzeł; supeł;
v. robić pętlę, kokardę;
podwiązywać; splatać (się)
loophole ['lu:p,houl] s. strzelnica;
droga ucieczki (od podatków);
wykręt; luka; furtka
loose [lu:s] adj. luźny;
rozluźniony; obluźniony;
wolny; na wolności; rzadki;
sypki; rozwiązły; s. upust; v.
luzować; obluźniać;
zwalniać
loosen ['lu:sn] v. rozluźniać
(się); obluźniać (się);
rozwalniać; leczyć
zatwardzenie
loot [lu:t] s. łupy; (nadużycia
urzędnika); v. plądrować;
szabrować
lop [lop] v. obcinać; ciąć;
zwisać; plątać się; wałęsać
się; s. ścięcie; obcięte
(gałęzie)
lop off ['lop,of] v. obciąć
lope [loup] v. biec susami;
pędzić krótkim galopem; s.
krótki galop; sus
lord [lo:rd] s. pan; władca;
magnat; Bóg; v. grać pana;
nadawać tytuł lorda
lorry ['lory] s. ciężarówka;
platforma; lora; przyczepa
lose; lost; lost [lu:z; lost; lost]
lose [lu:z] v. stracić; schudnąć;
zgubić; zabłądzić;
niedosłyszeć; spóźnić się;
przegrać; być pokonanym,
pozbawionym
loss [los] s. strata; utrata; zguba;
ubytek; szkoda; kłopot

lost [lost] adj. stracony;
zgubiony; zob. lose
lot [lot] s. doba; las; losowanie;
udział; działka; parcela; grupa;
zespół; partia; sporo; wiele; v.
parcelować; dzielić;
losować; adv. bardzo dużo
loth [lous] adj. niechętny;
wstrętny; z ciężkim sercem
lotion ['louszyn] s. płyn
(leczniczy)
lottery ['lotery] s. loteria
lotto ['lotou] s. loteryjka
loud [laud] adj. głośny;
smrodliwy; krzykliwy; adv. na
cały głos; głośno; w głośny
sposób
loudspeaker ['laud'spi:ker] s.
głośnik; megafon
lounge [laundż] v. próżnować;
wylegiwać; łazić; s. lokal;
salonik; hall; włóczęga; wolny
krok; wygodna kanapa
louse [laus] s. wesz; pl. lice
lousy ['lauzy] adj. zawszony;
wstrętny; dobrze zaopatrzony
(slang)
lout ['laut] s. gbur; prostak
love [law] s. kochanie; miłość;
lubienie; ukochana; ukochanie;
gra na zero; v. kochać; lubić;
być przywiązanym; pieścić;
umizgać się
love-affair ['lawefeer] s. romans;
przygoda miłosna; osobiste
troski w sprawach miłosnych
loveless ['lawlys] adj.
niekochany; nie kochający;
bez miłości; nie kochany
przez nikogo
lovely ['lawly] adj. śliczny;
uroczy; rozkoszny; przyjemny
(bardzo)
lovemaking ['law,mejkyng] s.
zaloty; umizgi; spółkowanie
lover ['lawer] s. kochanek;
miłośnik; amator czegoś
loving ['lawyng] adj. kochający;
s. kochanie; miłość
low [lou] s. ryk (bydła); v.
ryczeć; adj. niski; niewysoki;
słaby; przygnębiony; cichy;
podły; mały; adv. nisko;

niewysoko; słabo; skromnie;
cicho; szeptem; marnie; podle
lower ['louer] adj. niższy; dolny;
młodszy; adv. niżej; v.
obniżać; zniżać; spuszczać;
poniżyć; ściszyć;
zmniejszyć; osłabić; opadać;
spadać; ryczeć (jak bydło)
low-grade ['lougrejd] adj.
niskoprocentowy; niskiej
jakości; kiepski; tandetny
lowland ['loulend] pl. nizina; adj.
nizinny
lowly ['louly] adj. skromny; adv.
skromnie; bez pretensji
low-necked ['lou,nekyd] adj.
dekoltowany (głęboko)
low-pressure ['lou'preszer] s.
niskie ciśnienie; adj.
niskoprężny; pod niskim
ciśnieniem
low tide ['lou'tajd] s. odpływ
(morza)
loyal [lojel] adj. lojalny; wierny
(krajowi, ideałem etc.)
loyalty ['lojelty] s. lojalność;
wierność
lozenge ['lozyndż] s. romb;
tabletka; pastylka
lubber ['laber] s. niezdara;
niedołęga; niezdarny marynarz
lubricant ['lu:brykent] s. smar;
adj. smarujący; smarowniczy
lubricate ['lu:brykejt] v.
smarować; oliwić; robić
śliskim
lubrication ['lu:brykejszyn] s.
smarowanie; oliwienie
lubricity [lu:'brysyty] s.
smarowność; lubieżność
lucid ['lu:syd] adj. świecący;
jasny; błyszczący; klarowny;
przezroczysty; czysty;
oczywisty
luck [lak] s. los; traf; szczęście;
szczęśliwy traf; powodzenie
luckily ['lakyly] adv. na
szczęście; szczęśliwie
luckless ['laklys] adj.
niefortunny; nieszczęśliwy
lucky ['laky] adj. szczęśliwy
lucky fellow ['laky'felou] s.
szczęściarz

ludicrous ['lu:dykres] adj.
śmieszny; nonsensowny;
absurdalny; komicznie głupi
lug [lag] v. wlec; pociągać;
przytłaczać; s. wleczenie;
szarpanie; ucho; uchwyt
luggage ['lagydż] s. bagaż;
walizki
luggage carrier ['lagydż'kaerjer]
s. bagażowy
luggage rack ['lagydż'raek] s.
półka na walizki
luggage slip ['lagydż'slyp] s.
kwit bagażowy
luggage van ['lagydż'waen] s.
wóz bagażowy
lukewarm ['lu:kło:rm] adj.
ciepławy; letni; obojętny;
oziębły; niezainteresowany
lull [lal] v. ukołysać; uciszyć;
uśmierzyć; s. cisza; zastój
lullaby ['lalebaj] s. kołysanka
lumbago [lam'bejgou] s.
lumbago; ischias
lumbar ['lamber] adj. lędźwiowy
lumber ['lamber] s. budulec
(drewniany); rupiecie; graty; v.
zwalać; wycinać; ciężko
stąpać; poruszać się
ociężale
lumberjack ['lamber'dżaek] s.
drwal (przygotowujący do
tartaku)
lumber mill ['lambermyl] s. tartak
luminous ['lu:mynes] adj.
świetlny; jasny; świecący;
wyjaśniający; zrozumiały
lump [lamp] s. bryła; gruda;
masa; hurt; guz; niezdara;
niedołęga; v. zwalać;
gromadzić; dojść do ładu;
zcierpieć; znosić
lump of ['lamp,ow] s. kawałek
lump sugar ['lamp,szu:ger] s.
gruda cukru
lump sum ['lamp,sam] s. suma
całościowa
lunar ['lu:nar] adj. księżycowy;
mierzony ruchem księżyca
lunar module ['lu:nar,modjul] s.
kapsuła do lądowania na
Księżycu
lunatic ['lu:netyk] s. wariat

(chory umysłowo); lunatyk;
adj. obłąkany; zwariowany
lunch [lancz] s. obiad
(popołudniowy); v. jeść
obiad; gościć obiadem
lunch-hour ['lancz'auer] s.
przerwa obiadowa (w
południe)
lung [lang] s. płuco
lunge [landż] s. wypad;
pchnięcie; v. pchnąć; zrobić
wypad; spowodować wypad
lurch [le:rcz] v. opuszczać w
potrzebie; słaniać się na
nogach; przechylać się; s.
nagłe przechylenie się (na
bok); trudna sytuacja
lure [ljuer] s. przynęta; wabik;
urok; powab; v. kusić;
nęcić; wabić; przywabiać
lurk [le:rk] v. czaić się; s. czaty;
ukrycie
luscious ['laszes] adj. słodziutki;
ckliwy; soczysty
lush [lasz] adj. bujny; soczysty;
miękki i pełen soku
lust [last] s. żądza; lubieżność;
namiętność; pożądliwość;
v. pożądać (namiętnie)
luster ['laster] s. blask; połysk;
świecznik; świetność; v.
glansować; wyświecać
lusty ['lasty] adj. krzepki; pełen
wigoru (młodzieńczego)
lute [lu:t] s. lutnia; glina; v.
lepić gliną; kitować
luxate ['laksejt] v. zwichnąć
(np. nogę, staw)
luxuriant [lag'zjuerjent] adj.
wybujały; płodny; kwiecisty
(styl); bogato zdobiony
luxurious [lag'żjuerjes] adj.
zbytkowny; luksusowy;
zmysłowy
luxury ['lakszery] s. zbytek;
luksus; rozkosz; a. od zbytku
lying ['lajyng] adj. kłamliwy; zob.
lie; s. kłamstwo; adj. leżący;
zob. lie; s. leżenie; posłanie;
pozycja leżąca
lying-in [,lajyng'yn] adj.
położniczy; połogowy; s.
połóg

lymph [lymf] s. limfa;
szczepinka; wysięk; serum;
(czysta woda)
lynch [lyncz] v. zlinczować; s.
linczowanie; zabijanie bez
wyroku
lynx [lynks] s. ryś
lyre ['lajer] s. lira
lyric ['lirik] adj. liryczny; s. słowa
pieśni; poemat liryczny; tekst
piosenki
lysol ['lajsol] s. lizol

M

m [em] trzynasta litera alfabetu
angielskiego; cyfra rzymska:
1000
ma'am [maem] s. pani (madam)
mac [maek] s. nieprzemakalny
materiał (płaszcz) mackintosh
macaroni ['maeka;rouny] s.
makaron rurkowaty
machine [me'szi:n] s. maszyna;
machina (polityczna); v.
obrabiać maszynowo; adj.
maszynowy
machine-made [me'szi:nmejd]
adj. maszynowy; maszynowo
robiony
machine-gun [me'szi:ngan] s.
karabin maszynowy
machinery [me'szi:nery] s.
maszyneria; aparat
machinist [me'szi:nyst] s.
maszynista (np. tokarz,
szwaczka)
macho [ma:czou] s. bardzo
męski mężczyzna (slang)
mack [maek] s. zob. mac
mackintosh ['maekyntosz] s.
zob. mac
mad [maed] adj. obłąkany;
szalony; zły; wściekły; v.
doprowadzać do obłędu; być
obłąkanym
madam ['maedem] s. pani;
(panienka); (w zwrocie: proszą

pani)
madcap ['maedkaep] s.
narwaniec
madden ['maedn] v.
rozwścieczać; szaleć;
wściekać się; wariować
made [mejd] v. zrobiony; zob.
make; (wykombinowany,
fabryczny)
madman ['maedmen] s. wariat;
szaleniec; furiat; obłąkaniec
madness ['maednys] s. obłęd;
obłąkanie; furia;
wściekłość; wścieklizna;
szał; szaleństwo
magazine [maege'zi:n] s.
czasopismo; magazynek (na
kule); skład broni dla wojska
maggot ['maeget] s. dziwactwo;
chimera; larwa
magic ['maedżyk] s. magia; adj.
magiczny; działający jak magia
magician [me'dżyszyn] s.
czarodziej; magik
magistrate ['maedżystrejt] s.
sądownik; stróż prawa
magnanimous [maeg'neanymes]
adj. wielkoduszny
magnet ['maegnyt] s. magnes
magnetic [maeg'netyk] adj.
magnetyczny; przyciągający
magnificence [maeg'nyfysns] s.
wspaniałość; świetność;
okazałość
magnificent [maeg'nyfysnt] adj.
okazały; wspaniały
magnify ['maegnyfaj] v.
powiększać; potęgować;
wyolbrzymiać
magpie ['maegpaj] s. sroka;
gaduła
mahogany [me'hogeny] s.
mahoń; z mahoniu
maid [mejd] s. dziewczyna;
dziewka; panna; służąca
maiden ['mejden] s. dziewczyna;
panna; adj. panieński;
dziewiczy; świeży; nowy
maidenly ['mejdenly] adj.
dziewczęcy; panieński
maiden name ['mejden,nejm] s.
nazwisko panieńskie
mail [mejl] s. poczta; kolczuga;

v. wysyłać pocztą
mailbag ['mejl,baeg] s. worek
pocztowy
mailbox ['mejl,boks] s. skrzynka
pocztowa
mailman [mejlmen] s. listonosz
mail-order house ['mejl,order
,haus] s. firma sprzedająca
przez pocztę (z katalogu)
maim [mejm] v. okaleczyć
main [mejn] s. główny
(przewód); adj. główny;
najważniejszy
mainland ['mejnlaend] s.
kontynent (w odróżnieniu od
bliskich wysp)
mainly ['mejnly] adv. głównie;
przeważnie; po większej
części
main road ['mejnroud] s. główna
droga; główna szosa
main street ['mejn,stri:t] s.
główna ulica
maintain [men'tejn] v.
utrzymywać (w dobrym
stanie); trzymać (pozycję);
podtrzymywać;
zachowywać; twierdzić;
mieć na utrzymaniu; bronić;
pomagać
maintenance ['mejntenens] s.
utrzymanie; utrzymywanie;
poparcie; wyżywienie
maize [mejz] s. kukurydza
majestic [medżestyk] adj.
majestatyczny
majesty ['maedżysty] s.
majestat; godność;
wielkość
major ['mejdżer] s. major;
pełnoletni; przedmiot
kierunkowy specjalizacji; adj.
większy; główny; ważniejszy;
pełnoletni; starszy; v.
specjalizować się w studiach
majorette ['mejdżeret] s.
tancerka na defiladach i w
przerwach meczów w USA
majority [me'dżoryty] s.
większość; a.
większościowy
major road ['mejdżer,roud] s.
główna droga; ważniejsza

droga
make; made; made [mejk; mejd; mejd]
make [mejk] v. robić; tworzyć; sporządzać; powodować; wynosić; doprowadzać; ustanawiać; starać się; postanowić etc.
make a bed [mejk e bed] exp. pościelić łóżko
make-believe ['mejk,by'li:w] s. udawanie; pozory
make off ['mejkof] v. uciec; uciekać; gwizdnąć coś komuś
make up ['mejkap] v. uzupełnić; wynagrodzić; sporządzić; zmontować; ucharakteryzować
makeup ['mejkap] s. makijaż; charakteryzacja; układ (graficzny); stan (kogoś, czegoś)
make up your mind ['mejk,ap'jo:r ,majnd] exp.: zdecyduj się (czego chcesz, co wolisz, na co nasz ochotę, gdzie jedziesz, etc.)
maker ['mejker] s. wytwórca; sprawca; producent; fabrykant; konstruktor; (Maker = Bóg)
makeshift ['mejkszyft] s. namiastka; urządzenie prowizoryczne; adj. prowizoryczny
malady ['maeledy] s. choroba
male [mejl] s. mężczyzna; samiec; adj. męski; samczy; wewnętrzny; obejmowany
malediction [,maely'dikszyn] s. przekleństwo; złorzeczenie
malefactor ['maelyfaekter] s. złoczyńca; zbrodniarz
malevolent [me'lewelent] adj. niechętny; wrogi
malice ['maelys] s. złośliwość; zła wola; zły zamiar
malicious [me'lyszys] adj. złośliwy; zły; powodowany złością
malignant [me'lygnent] adj. złośliwy; zjadliwy

malnutrition ['maelnju'tryszyn] s. niedożywienie
malt [mo:lt] s. słód; v. słodować; adj. słodowy; scukrzony
maltreat [mael'tri:t] v. poniewierać; maltretować
mamma [me'ma:] s. mama; gruczoł mlekowy
mammal [me'ma:l] s. ssak; a. ssakowy
man [maen] s. człowiek; mężczyzna; mąż; v. obsadzać (np. załogą); pl. men [men]
manacle ['maenekl] s. kajdany; v. zakuwać w kajdany
manage ['maenydż] v. kierować; zarządzać; posługiwać się; obchodzić się; opanowywać; poskramiać; radzić sobie
manageable ['maenydżebl] adj. do pokierowania (możliwy, łatwy)
management ['maenydżment] s. zarząd; kierownictwo; dyrekcja; posługiwanie się; obchodzenie się; sprawne zarządzanie
manager ['maenydżer] s. kierownik; zarządzający; gospodarz
manageress ['maenydżeres] s. kierowniczka
mandate ['maendejt] s. mandat; pełnomocnictwo do sprawowania funkcji pochodzącej z wyboru; pismo władzy wyższej; grzywna; rozkaz; komenda; wola wyborców przekazana wybranemu reprezentantowi
mandatory ['maendetery] adj. zawierający mandat; nakazany przez władze; obowiązujący; obowiązkowy
mane [mejn] s. grzywa
maneuver [me'nu:wer] s. manewr; v. manewrować; manipulować
manger ['mejndżer] s. żłób; koryto

mangle ['maengl] s. magiel; v. maglować; poszarpać; pokaleczyć; poprzekręcać

manhood ['maenhud] s. męskość; ludność męska; wiek męski

mania ['mejnje] s. bzik; obłęd; mania; zbytni entuzjazm; szał

maniac ['mejnjaek] s. maniak; szaleniec; adj. umysłowo chory

manifest ['maenyfest] adj. jawny; oczywisty; v. manifestować; ujawniać; s. manifest okrętowy (szczegółowa lista ładunku)

manifold ['maenyfould] adj. różnorodny; wieloraki; wielokrotny; v. powielać (tekst)

manipulate [me'nypjulejt] v. manipulować; umiejętnie, zręcznie pokierować (niesprawiedliwie)

mankind [,maen'kajnd] s. ludzkość; rodzaj ludzki

mankind ['maenkajnd] pl. mężczyźni; cały rodzaj męski

manly ['maenly] adj. dzielny; mężny; męski; adv. po męsku

manner ['maener] s. sposób; zwyczaj; zachowanie (się); wychowanie; maniera; procedura; rodzaj

manoeuvre [me'nu:wer] s. manewr; v. manewrować (pisownia brytyjska)

man-of-war ['maenew'ło:r] s. okręt wojenny; uzbrojony statek

manor ['maener] s. dwór; rezydencja (w Anglii: duży majątek)

man power ['maen,pałer] s. siła robocza; rezerwy ludzkie

mansion ['maenszyn] s. rezydencja; pałac; duży dwór

manslaughter ['maen,slo:ter] s. zabójstwo (bez premedytacji)

mantelpiece ['maentlpi:s] s. gzyms kominka (obramowanie)

manual ['maenjuel] s. podręcznik; manuał; adj.

ręczny; ręcznie zrobiony

manufacture [,maenju'faekczer] v. wyrabiać; s. sposób; produkcja; produkt (zwłaszcza masowy)

manufacturer [,maenju'faek,czerer] s. wytwórca; producent; fabrykant; przedsiębiorstwo wytwórcze

manure [me'njuer] s. nawóz; v. nawozić (gnój)

manuscript ['maenjuskrypt] s. rękopis; adj. ręcznie pisany

many ['meny] adj. dużo; wiele

many-sided ['meny'sajdyd] adj. wielostronny; wieloboczny; wszechstronny

map [maep] s. mapa; plan; v. planować; robić mapę

maple ['mejpl] s. klon

marble ['ma:rbl] s. marmur; kulka do zabawy; adj. marmurowy; v. marmurkować (np. papier)

March [ma:rcz] s. marzec

march [ma:rcz] s. marsz; v. maszerować

mare [meer] s. klacz; kobyła

margarine ['ma:rdże,ri:n] s. margaryna

margin ['ma:rdżyn] s. margines; brzeg; krawędź; nadwyżka; rezerwa

marine [me'ri:n] adj. morski; s. marynarka; żołnierz piechoty desantowej (USA)

mariner ['maeryner] s. marynarz; żeglarz

maritime ['maerytajm] adj. morski

mark [ma:rk] s. marka (pieniądz); ślad; znak; oznaczenie; nota; cenzura; cel; uwaga; v. oznaczać; określać; notować; zwracać uwagę

marked [ma:rkt] adj. wybitny; wyraźny; znaczny

mark out ['ma:rk,aut] v. wyznaczać; wytyczać (np. granicą)

market ['ma:rkyt] s. rynek; zbyt; targ; v. robić zakupy; sprzedawać na targu

marketing ['ma:rkytyng] s.

organizowanie rynku;
handlowanie
market-place ['ma:rkytplejs] s.
rynek; plac targowy
marksman ['ma:rksmen] s.
strzelec (doborowy)
marmalade ['ma:rmelejd] s.
marmolada (pomarańczowa)
marmot ['ma:rmet] s. świstak
marriage ['maerydż] s.
małżeństwo (skojarzenie); a.
ślubny
marriageable ['maerydżebl] adj.
na wydaniu; odpowiedni do
małżeństwa
marriage certificate [,maerydż
,ser'tyfykyt] s. świadectwo
ślubu
married ['maeryd] adj. żonaty;
zamężna; małżeński; ślubny
married couple ['maerys,kapl] s.
& adj. para małżeńska
marrow ['maerou] s. szpik
(kostny); dynia
marry ['maery] v. poślubić;
udzielać ślubu; ożenić (się);
brać ślub; pobierać się;
wychodzić za mąż
marsh [ma:rsz] s. moczary;
bagno; błota; a. bagienny
marshal ['ma:rszel] s. marszałek;
mistrz ceremonii; komisarz
policji; v. uszykować;
(uroczyście); przetaczać
wagony; uporządkować;
uszykować
marshy ['ma:rszy] adj. bagnisty;
bagienny; błotnisty
marten ['ma:rtyn] s. kuna
martial ['ma:rszel] adj. wojenny;
wojowniczy; wojskowy
martyr ['ma:rter] s. męczennik;
v. zamęczać; zadręczać
marvel ['ma:rwel] s. cudo; cud;
v. podziwiać; dziwić się
marvelous ['ma:rwyles] adj.
cudowny; zdumiewający
mascot ['maesket] s. maskotka
masculine ['maeskjulyn] adj.
męski; płci męskiej
mash [maesz] s. zacier; papka;
mieszanka; v. warzyć; tłuc na
papkę; umizgać się

mashed potatoes ['maeszt,pe
'tejtous] s. gniecione ziemniaki
mask [ma:sk] s. maska; v.
zamaskować; maskować
mason ['mejsn] s. murarz;
kamieniarz; v. wymurować;
murować
masonry ['mejsnry] s.
murarstwo; obmurowanie;
kamieniarstwo
masque [ma:sk] s. maskarada;
pantomima (amatorska)
mass [maes] s. msza; masa;
rzesza; v. gromadzić;
zrzeszać
massacre ['maeseker] s.
masakra; v. masakrować;
urządzić rzeź
massage ['maesa:ż] s. masaż; v.
masować; zrobić masaż
massif ['maesyw] s. masyw
(górski); zwarta roślinność
massive ['maesyw] adj.
masywny; ciężki; zwarty;
bryłowaty
mast [ma:st] s. maszt
master ['ma:ster] s. mistrz;
nauczyciel; pan; gospodarz;
szef; kapitan statku; panicz; v.
panować; kierować;
nabywać (np. wprawy);
owładnąć
master key ['ma:sterki:] s.
wytrych
masterly ['ma:sterly] adj.
mistrzowski
master of ceremony ['ma:ster
,ow sere'mouny] s. mistrz
ceremonii
masterpiece ['ma:sterpi:s] s.
arcydzieło
master-ship ['ma:sterszyp] s.
mistrzostwo; władza;
panowanie; zwierzchnictwo
mastery ['ma:stery] s. władza;
panowanie; mistrzostwo
mat [maet] s. mata; v. plątać;
adj. matowy (bez połysku)
match [maecz] s. zapałka; lont;
mecz; dobór; małżeństwo; v.
swatać; współzawodniczyć;
dobierać; dorównywać
matchless ['maeczlys] adj.

niezrównany; nie mający
równego
matchmaker ['maecz,mejker] s.
swat; swatka; aranżujący
mecze
mate [mejt] s. kolega; małżonek;
samiec; pomocnik; v. łączyć
ślubem; parzyć (się);
pobierać się; zadawać mata
(w szachach)
material [me'tierjal] s. materiał;
tworzywo; tkanka; adj.
materialny; cielesny
maternal [me'te:rnl] adj.
macierzyński; matczyny
maternity [me'te:rnyty] s.
macierzyństwo; adj.
położniczy
maternity hospital [me'te:rnyty
'hospytl] s. szpital położniczy
mathematician [,maetyme
'tyszyn] s. matematyk
mathematics [,maety'maetyks] s.
matematyka
math [maes] s. matematyka
(slang)
matriculate [me'trykjulejt] v.
immatrykulować; zdawać
wstępny egzamin (uniw.);
zapisać się na ...
matrimony ['maetrymeny] s.
małżeństwo; akt ślubu
matron ['mejtren] s. matrona;
kobieta zamężna; (gospodyni)
matter ['maeter] s. rzecz;
treść; materiał; substancja;
sprawa; kwestia; v. znaczyć;
mieć znaczenie; odgrywać
rolę
matter-of-fact ['maeter,ow'faekt]
adj. rzeczowy; praktyczny
mattress ['maetrys] s. materac
mature [me'tjuer] adj. dojrzały;
płatny; v. dojrzewać; stawać
się płatnym (np. pożyczka)
maturity [me'tjueryty] s.
dojrzałość; termin płatności
mauve [mouw] s. kolor różowo-
liliowy; adj. różowo-liliowy
maw [mo:] s. żołądek; wole
maxim ['maeksym] s. maksyma
maximum ['maeksymem] s.
maksimum

May [mej] s. maj
may [mej] v. być może; might
[majt] mógłby
maybe ['mejbi:] adv. być może;
może być; możliwe że
may I? ['mej aj] czy mogę?
may-bug ['mejbag] s. chrabąszcz
mayor [meer] s. burmistrz
maypole ['mejpoul] s. słup do
tańca "gaik", 1-go maja
maze [mejz] s. labirynt;
gmatwanina; v. w błąd
wprowadzić; oszołomić;
dezorientować; mieszać
mazurka [me'ze:rke] s. mazur;
mazurek
me [mi:] pron. mi; mnie; mną;
(slang) ja
meadow ['medou] s. łąka
meager ['mi:ger] adj. chudy;
cienki; skromny; nie
obradzający
meal [mi:l] s. posiłek; grubo
mielona mąka; czas posiłku
mealtime ['mi:l-tajm] s. pora
posiłku (ustalona zwyczajem)
mealy ['mi:ly] adj. mączysty;
nieszczery; słodziutki; obleśny
mean; meant; meant [mi:n;
ment; ment]
mean [mi:n] v. myśleć;
przypuszczać; znaczyć; s.
przeciętna; średnia; środek;
adj. ubogi; nędzny; podły;
marny; skąpy; tandetny
meaning ['mi:nyng] s. znaczenie;
sens; treść; adj. znaczący;
mający zamiar
meaningless ['mi:nynglys] adj.
bez sensu; bez znaczenia
meant [ment] przeznaczony; zob.
mean
meantime ['mi:n'tajm] adv.
tymczasem; w tym samym
czasie
meanwhile ['mi:n,hłajl] adv.
tymczasem
measles ['mi:zlz] s. odra
measure ['meżer] s. miara;
miarka; środek; zabieg;
sposób; v. mierzyć; mieć
rozmiar; oszacować; być ...
wzrostu

measureless ['meżerlys] adj.
bezmierny; nieskończony
measurement ['meżerment] s.
wymiar; miara; mierzenie
meat [mi:t] s. mięso; danie
mięsne; treść (książki etc.)
mechanic [my'kaenyk] s.
mechanik; rzemieślnik;
technik
mechanical [my'kaenykel] adj.
mechaniczny
mechanics [my'kaenyks] s.
mechanika
mechanism ['mekenyzem] s.
mechanizm; maszyneria
mechanize ['mekenajz] v.
zmechanizować
medal ['medl] s. medal
meddle ['medl] v. wmieszać się;
wtrącać się w cudze sprawy
mediate ['my:djejt] adj.
pośredni; v. pośredniczyć;
zapośredniczyć; doprowa-
dzić pośrednictwem do ...
mediator ['my:djejtor] s.
rozjemca; mediator
medical ['medykel] adj. lekarski;
medyczny
medical certificate ['medykel
,sertyfykyt] s. świadectwo
lekarskie
medicated ['medykejtyd] adj.
leczony; zaprawiony
substancją leczniczą
medicinal [me'dysynl] adj.
leczniczy; lekarski; medyczny
medicine ['medysyn] s.
medycyna; lek; lekarstwo; v.
leczyć lekarstwami
medieval [,medy'i:wel] adj.
średniowieczny
mediocre ['my:djouker] adj.
mierny; średni; przeciętny
meditate ['medytejt] v.
obmyślać; rozmyślać;
medytować
meditation [,medy'tejszyn] s.
rozmyślanie; planowanie
meditative ['medytejtyw] adj.
zadumany; zamyślony;
medytacyjny; kontemplacyjny
Mediterranean [,medyter'rejnjen]
adj. śródziemnomorski

medium ['mi:djem] s. środek;
średnia; przewodnik; środek
obiegowy; środowisko;
rozpuszczalnik; sposób;
środkowa droga; adj. średni;
adv. średnio
medley ['medly] s. mieszanina;
pstrokacizna; rozmaitości
meek [mi:k] adj. potulny;
łagodny; skromny; bez wigoru
meet; met; met [mi:t; met; met]
meet [mi:t] v. spotykać;
zbierać się; gromadzić; iść
na kompromis; zgadzać się;
zaspokajać; s. spotkanie;
zbiórka; miejsce spotkania;
spotkanie sportowe; zawody
(na bieżni etc.)
meet with ['mi:t,łys] v. spotkać
się z (kimś); doświadczyć
meeting ['mi:tyng] s. spotkanie;
połączenie się; posiedzenie;
zgromadzenie; wiec; zawody;
konferencja; pojedynek
melancholy ['melenkely] s.
melancholia; adj. smutny;
melancholijny; zasmucający;
ponury
mellow ['melou] adj. słodki;
miękki; soczysty; uleżały;
złagodzony (wiekiem);
łagodny; wesoły; pogodny;
podchmielony; dojrzały; miły;
świetny; przyjemny; v.
dojrzewać; zmiękczać;
uleżeć się; łagodnieć;
łagodzić
melodious [my'loudjes] adj.
melodyjny; harmonijny
melody ['meledy] s. melodia;
piosenka
melon ['melen] s. melon
melt [melt] s. stop; stopienie;
topnienie; wytop; v. topić;
topnieć; roztapiać (się);
rozpuszczać; przetapiać;
odlewać; wzruszyć;
roztkliwiać
melting point ['meltyng'point] s.
temperatura topnienia
member ['member] s. członek;
człon (odróżniający się)
membership ['memberszyp] s.

członkostwo; przynależność;
skład członkowski
membrane ['membrejn] s. błona;
przepona; membrana
memoir ['memła:r] s. pamiętnik;
życiorys; autobiografia
memorable ['memerebl] adj.
pamiętny; znaczny
memorial [my'mo:riel] s. pomnik;
memoriał; petycja; posąg (na
pamiątkę)
memorize ['memerajz] v.
zapamiętywać; uczyć się na
pamięć
memory ['memery] s. pamięć;
wspomnienie
men [men] pl. mężczyźni;
robotnicy; zob. man
menace ['menes] s. groźba;
zagrożenie; v. grozić;
zagrażać
mend [mend] s. naprawa;
naprawka; v. reperować;
zaszyć
menial ['mi:njel] s. sługa;
służalec; adj. czarno-roboczy;
służalczy; służebny
menopause ['mene.po:z] s.
przekwitanie; klimakterium
menstruation [,menstru'ejszyn] s.
menstruacja; miesiączka;
period
mental ['mentl] adj. umysłowy;
pamięciowy; psychiatryczny;
s. (slang) umysłowo chory
mental hospital ['mentl'hospytl]
s. szpital psychiatryczny
mentality [men'taelyty] s.
umysłowość; mentalność
mention ['menszyn] v.
wspominać wymieniać;
nadmieniać; wzmiankować;
s. wzmianka
menu ['menju:] s. jadłospis
meow [mi:'au] v. miauczeć jak
kot
mercantile ['me:rkentajl] adj.
handlowy; kupiecki
mercenary ['me:rsynery] adj.
najemny; wyrachowany; s.
najemnik; żołnierz najemny
merchandise ['me:rczendajz] s.
towar(y); v. handlować

merchant ['me:rczent] s. kupiec;
handlowiec; adj. handlowy;
kupiecki
merciful ['me:rsyful] adj.
miłosierny; litościwy
merciless ['me:rsylys] adj.
bezlitosny; niemiłosierny
mercurial [me:r'kjuerjel] adj.
rtęciowy; żywy; bystry;
rozgarnięty; zmienny
mercy ['me:rsy] s. miłosierdzie;
litość; łaska; rzecz
pomyślna
mercy killing ['me:rsy'kylyng] s.
eutanazja; zabójstwo z litości
mere [mjer] adj. zwykły;
zwyczajny; nie więcej niż
merely ['mjerly] adv. tylko;
jedynie; zaledwie; po prostu
merge [me:rdż] v. roztapiać
(się); zlewać; łączyć (się)
merger ['me:rdżer] s. połączenie;
zlanie się; fuzja
meridian [me'rydjen] s. południk;
zenit; szczyt; adj. południowy;
szczytowy
merit ['meryt] s. zasługa; zaleta;
odznaczenie; v. zasługiwać
meritorious [,mery'to:rjes] adj.
chwalebny; zasłużony
mermaid ['me:rmejd] s. rusałka;
syrena
merriment ['meryment] s.
uciecha; radość; wesołość
merry ['mery] adj. wesoły;
radosny; podochocony;
odświętny; podchmielony
merry-go-round ['merygou,raund]
s. karuzela
merry-making ['mery,mejkyn] s.
zabawa; uciecha; weselenie
się
mesh [mesz] s. siatka; sieć;
układ siatkowy; v. łapać w
sieć; zazębiać; wplątać
mess [mes] s. nieporządek;
bałagan; bród; świństwo;
paskudztwo; paćka; papka;
zupa; bigos; posiłek wspólny;
stołówka; wspólny stół; v.
zababrać; zapaskudzić;
zabrudzić; zabałaganić;
pokpić; sfuszerować; obijać

się; bawić; dawać jeść
(posiłek); stołować się
(wspólnie)
mess up [,mes'ap] v. zepsuć;
zaprzepaścić; sknocić;
zagmatwać; pobrudzić;
zabałaganić
message ['mesydż] v.
wiadomość; orędzie; morał;
wypowiedź; v.
komunikować; podawać;
posłać
messenger ['mesyndżer] s.
posłaniec; zwiastun
messy ['mesy] adj. kłopotliwy;
zapaskudzony; sfuszerowany;
brudny; upaćkany; niechlujny
met [met] v. zob. meet
metal [metl] s. metal; v.
pokrywać metalem; a.
metalowy
metallic [my'taelyk] adj.
metaliczny; metalowy;
metalurgiczny
meteor ['mi:tjer] s. meteor
meteorology [,mi:tjero'ledży] s.
meteorologia
meter ['mi:ter] s. metr; licznik; v.
mierzyć; a. metrowy
method ['meted] s. metoda;
metodyka; metodyczność;
sposób
methodical [me'todykel] adj.
metodyczny; systematyczny
meticulous [my'tykjules] adj.
drobiazgowy; szczegółowy;
drobnostkowy; pedantyczny
metric system ['metryk'system]
s. system metryczny
metropolitan [,metre'polyten] adj.
wielkomiejski; metropolitalny;
s. mieszkaniec metropolii;
metropolita (duchowny)
mew [mju:] v. miauczeć;
pierzyć się
Mexican ['meksyken] adj.
meksykański; s. Meksykanin;
Meksykanka
miaow [mi:'au] v. miauczeć
mica ['maike] s. mika; łuszczyk
mice [majs] pl. myszy; zob.
mouse
micron ['majkron] s. mikron

microphone ['majkrefoun] s.
mikrofon
microscope ['majkreskoup] s.
mikroskop
mid [myd] adj. środkowy; prep.
w; podczas; pośród; między-
midday ['myddej] adj.
południowy; s. południe
mid summer [,myd'samer] exp.:
w środku lata
middle ['mydl] s. środek; kibić;
stan; adj. środkowy; v.
składać w środku; kopać na
środek
middle aged ['mydl'ejdżd] adj. w
średnim wieku
Middle Ages ['mydl'ejdżys] s.
średniowiecze
middle class ['mydl,kla:s] s.
klasa średnia; klasa
średniozamożna; a. ze
średniozamożnej klasy
middle name ['mydl,nejm] s.
drugie imię
middle sized ['mydl,sajzd] adj.
średniej wielkości; średni
middleweight ['mydl,łejt] s. waga
średnia; adj. średniej wagi
(148 do 160 funtów)
middling ['mydlyng] adj. średni;
przeciętny; adv. średnio
midge ['mydż] s. muszka
midget ['mydżyt] s. karzełek;
maleństwo; adj. miniaturowy
midland ['mydlend] s. środek
kraju; adj. leżący w środku
kraju; w głębi kraju
midmost ['mydmoust] adj.
leżący w samym środku;
prep. pośród
midnight ['mydnajt] s. północ;
adj. północny; o północy
midway ['myd'łej] s. połowa
drogi; adv. w połowie drogi
midwife ['mydłajf] s. położna;
akuszerka
might [majt] s. moc; potęga; v.
mógłby; zob. may
mighty ['majty] adj. potężny;
adv. bardzo; wielce
migrate ['maj,grejt] v.
wędrować; przesiedlać się
migratory ['maj,gretery] adj.

wędrowny (ptak etc.)
mild [majld] adj. łagodny;
powolny; potulny; słaby;
delikatny
mildew ['myldju:] s. pleśń; v.
pleśnieć; rdzewieć (o
zbożu)
mildly ['majldly] adv. łagodnie;
umiarkowanie; oględnie
mildness ['majldnys] s.
łagodność; nieostrość
mile [majl] s. mila; 1,609 km
mil(e)age ['majlydż] s. milaż;
odległość w milach
milestone ['majlstoun] s. kamień
milowy
military ['mylytery] adj.
wojskowy; pl. wojskowy;
wojsko
milk [mylk] s. mleko; v. doić
(krowy); wykorzystać;
eksploatować; podsłuchiwać
(telefon)
milkmaid ['mylk,mejd] s. dojarka;
mleczarka
milkman ['mylkmen] s. mleczarz
milk-shake ['mylkszejk] s.
mieszany napój mleczny
milksop ['mylksop] s.
maminsynek; fajtłapa; oferma;
niedołęga
milky ['mylky] adj. mleczny;
zniewieściały; koloru mleka
mill [myl] s. młyn; huta; fabryka;
(1/1000); walcownia;
krawędź ząbkowana; v.
mleć; frezować; pilśnić;
kręcić się
miller ['myler] s. młynarz
millet ['mylyt] s. proso
milliner ['mylyner] s. modniarka;
modystka
million ['myljen] num. milion
millionaire ['myljeneer] s. milioner
millionth ['myljent] num.
milionowy; jedna milionowa
(część)
milt [mylt] s. mlecz rybi; v.
zapładniać ikrę
mimic ['mymyk] s. naśladowca;
imitator; v. naśladować;
małpować; adj.
naśladowniczy; udany;

mimiczny; zmyślony; fikcyjny
mince [myns] v. siekać; mówić
bez ogródek; cedzić (słowa);
drobić nogami; s. siekane
mięso; nadzienie mięsne
mincing ['mynsyng] adj.
mizdrzący się; afektowany;
sztucznie zachowujący się
(wykwintny)
mind [majnd] s. umysł; pamięć;
zdanie; opinia; postanowienie;
zamierzenie; v. pamiętać;
zważać; przejmować się;
baczyć; mieć coś
przeciwko; być posłusznym
mind your own business ['majnd
,jo:'ołn'byznys] pilnuj swego
nosa; nie wtrącaj się
minded ['majndyd] adj.
nastawiony na; skłonny do;
gotów; gotowy
mindful ['majndful] adj. pomny;
dbały; uważający; troskliwy
mindless ['majndlys] adj.
nierozumny; niedbały; nie
uważający
mine [majn] pron. mój; moje;
moja; s. kopalnia; podkop;
mina; bomba; v. kopać;
podkopywać; eksploatować;
minować
miner ['majner] s. górnik
mineral ['mynerel] s. mineralny;
adj. zawierający minerały
mingle ['myngl] v. mieszać się;
przyłączać się (do innych)
miniature ['mynjeczer] s.
miniatura; adj. miniaturowy
minimum ['mynymem] s.
minimum; adj. minimalny;
najmniejszy
mining ['majnyng] s. górnictwo;
adj. górniczy; kopalniany
miniskirt ['myny,ske:rt] s.
spódnica (mini) (b. krótka)
minister ['mynyster] s.
duchowny; minister; v.
stosować; przyczyniać się;
udzielać; pomagać
ministry ['mynystry] s.
duszpasterstwo; kler;
duchowieństwo;
ministerstwo; gabinet

ministrów; służba; pomoc;
posługa
mink ['mynk] s. norka; adj. z
norek; z futer norek
minor ['majner] adj. mniejszy;
mało ważny; młodszy;
nieletni; s. człowiek
niepełnoletni
minority [maj'noryty] s.
mniejszość;
niepełnoletniość
minster ['mynster] s. katedra;
kościół klasztorny
minstrel ['mynstrel] s. bard;
śpiewak przebrany za
murzyna
mint [mynt] s. mięta; mennica;
majątek; źródło; v. bić
pieniądze; wymyślać;
tworzyć; kuć
minute ['mynyt] s. minuta;
chwilka; notatka; v.
szkicować; protokołować;
[maj'nju;t] adj. szczegółowy;
bardzo mały; znikomy
miracle ['myrekl] s. cud; a.
cudowny
miraculous [my'raekjules] adj.
cudowny; nadprzyrodzony
mirage ['myra:dż] s. miraż;
fatamorgana; złudzenie
wzrokowe
mire ['majer] s. muł; błoto;
bagno; v. grzęznąć (w
trudnościach); zabłocić się
mirror ['myrer] s. zwierciadło; v.
odzwierciedlać
mirth [me:rs] s. wesołość;
radość; uciecha (pełna
śmiechu)
miry ['majry] adj. błotnisty;
mulisty; bagnisty
mis- [mys] przedrostek: nie; źle;
(błędnie) nie-; źle-
misadventure ['mysed'wenczer]
s. niepowodzenie; zła
przygoda
misanthrope ['myzentroup] s.
mizantrop; wróg ludzkości
misapply ['myse'plaj] v.
nadużyć; źle zastosować
misapprehend ['mys,aepry'hend]
v. nie pojąć; źle zrozumieć

misbehave ['mysby'hejw] v.
nieodpowiednio zachowywać
się
miscalculate ['mys'kaelkjukejt] v.
przeliczyć się; przerachować
się
miscarriage [mys'kaerydż] s.
poronienie; omyłka;
niepowodzenie
mischief ['mysczyf] s. szkoda;
krzywda; psota; utrapienie;
złośliwość; figiel;
figlarność; licho; szkodnik;
bieda; niezgoda
mischievous ['mysczywes] adj.
szkodliwy; niegodziwy;
niesforny; niegrzeczny; psotny
misdeed ['mys'di:d] s.
przestępstwo; zły czyn
(karygodny)
misdemeano(u)r ['mysdy'mi:ner]
s. wykroczenie; złe
sprawowanie
miser ['majzer] s. sknera;
chciwiec; skąpiec; kutwa
miserable ['myzerebl] adj.
nędzny; chory; marny;
żałosny
miserably ['myzerebly] adv.
nędznie; marnie; żałośnie
misfortune [mys'fo:rczen] s.
nieszczęście; pech; zły los
misgiving [mysgywyng] s. złe
przeczucie; obawa;
powątpiewanie
misguide [,mys'gajd] v.
wprowadzać w błąd;
sprowadzać na manowce
mishap ['myshaep] s. (mały,
niepoważny) wypadek
(niepowodzenie)
misinform ['mysyn'form] v. źle
informować; zwieść z drogi
misjudge ['mys'dżadż] v. źle
osądzić; źle ocenić; mieć
fałszywe mniemanie; nie
doceniać
mislay [mys'lej] v. zatracić; zob.
lay; zagubić; zapodziać
mislead [mys'li:d] v.
wprowadzać w błąd; zob.
lead; zbałamucić
mismanage [,mys'maenydż] v.

źle prowadzić; źle
pokierować

misplace [,mys'plejs] v.
zatracić; położyć nie na
miejscu

misprint [,mys'prynt] v. błędnie
wydrukować; s. omyłka
drukarska; błąd drukarski

mispronounce ['myspre'nauns] v.
błędnie wymawiać; źle
wymawiać

misrepresent ['mysrepry'zent] v.
przekręcić; błędnie
przedstawić; fałszywie
przedstawić

Miss [mys] s. panna; panienka

miss [mys] v. chybić; nie
trafić; nie znaleźć; nie
dostać; brakować; tęsknić;
zacinać się; s. pudło;
niepowodzenie; opuszczenie;
chybienie

miss out ['mys,aut] v.
wypuścić (słowo); chybić;
nie dostać

missile ['mysajl] s. pocisk;
rakieta; adj. nadający się do
rzucania (oszczep, rakieta etc.)

missing ['mysyng] adj.
nieobecny; brakujący;
zaginiony

mission ['myszyn] s. misja;
delegacja; v. wysłać z misją;
zakładać misje; a. misyjny

missionary ['myszynery] s.
misjonarz; adj. misjonarski

misspelling ['mys'spelyng] s.
błąd ortograficzny

mist [myst] s. lekka mgiełka; v.
zachodzić parą (mgiełką)

mistake [mys'tejk] s. omyłka;
nieporozumienie; v. pomylić
(się) (co do faktu lub
człowieka); źle zrozumieć;
mylić się

mistaken [mys'tejken] adj.
mylny; błędny; pomylony; nie
mający zrozumienia sytuacji

mistakenly [mys'tejknly] adv.
błędnie; pomyłkowo;
nierozsądnie

Mister ['myster] s. pan
(używane z nazwiskiem);

skrót Mr. (bez nazwiska
niegrzecznie!)

mistletoe ['mysltou] s. jemiołka;
jemioła; liście jemioły

mistress ['mystrys] s. kochanka;
nauczycielka; [myzys] s. pani;
(skrót Mrs.); zob. Mister

mistrust [mys'trast] v.
podejrzewać; nie ufać; s.
niedowierzanie; nieufność

misty ['mysty] adj. mglisty;
zamglony; niejasny;
nieokreślony

misunderstanding ['mysande:r
'staendyng] s. nieporozumienie

misuse ['mys'ju:z] v.
nadużywać; źle używać;
['mys'ju:s] s. nadużycie; złe
użycie

mite [majt] s. molik; kruszyna;
drobiazg; grosz (wdowi);
berbeć; mała sumka
pieniędzy

mitigate ['mytygejt] v. koić;
uśmierzać; łagodzić;
łagodnieć; ukoić; złagodzić

mitten ['mytn] s. rękawiczka bez
palców; (slang) rękawica
bokserska (zimowa etc.)

mix [myks] v. mieszać;
obcować; współżyć; s.
mieszanka; mieszanina;
zamieszanie

mix-up ['myks'ap] s.
gmatwanina; plątanina;
zamieszanie; bójka

mixed up with ['mykst'ap,tys]
adj. zamieszany (w coś)

mixture ['myksczer] s.
mieszanka; mieszanina;
mikstura

moan [moun] s. jęk; v. jęczeć;
lamentować; mówić jęcząc

moat [mout] s. fosa; rów; v.
opasywać fosą

mob [mob] s. tłum; motłoch;
banda; v. napastować;
atakować tłumnie; stłoczyć
się

mobile ['moubajl] adj. ruchomy;
ruchliwy; zmienny; s. rzeźba -
kompozycja wisząca
(abstrakcyjna)

mock [mok] v. wykpić;
przedrzeźniać; zmylić;
stawiać czoło; żartować z
kogoś; s. kpiny;
przedrzeźnianie;
naśladownictwo; adj.
fałszywy; udany; pozorny
mockery ['mokery] s. kpiny;
śmiech; pośmiewisko;
pokrzywianie się
mode [moud] s. sposób; tryb;
moda; rzecz modna (lub
zwyczajowa)
model ['modl] s. model; wzór;
modelka; manekin; v.
modelować
moderate ['moderyt] adj.
umiarkowany; średni; s.
człowiek umiarkowany (w
poglądach etc.)
moderate ['moderejt] v.
powściągać; uspokoić (się);
prowadzić (zebranie)
moderation [,mode'rejszyn] s.
umiarkowanie; umiar; spokój
modern ['modern] adj.
współczesny; nowoczesny;
nowożytny
modernize ['modernajz] v.
unowocześnić (się);
modernizować
modest ['modyst] adj. skromny
modesty ['modysty] s.
skromność
modification [,modyfy'kejszyn] s.
modyfikacja; łagodzenie z
lekka
modify ['modyfaj] v.
modyfikować; zmieniać
częściowo; łagodzić
modulate ['modjulejt] v.
modulować; regulować;
dostosowywać
module ['modju:l] s. moduł;
kabina (astronauty)
moist [mojst] adj. wilgotny
moisten [mojsen] v. wilgnąć;
zwilżać (sobie usta etc.);
wilgotnieć
moisture ['mojsczer] s. wilgoć;
wilgotność; lekkie
zamoczenie
molar [mouler] s. trzonowy

(ząb); adj. trzonowy
molasses [me'laesyz] s. pl.
melasa; ciemny, gęsty syrop z
trzciny cukrowej
mole [moul] s. kret; grobla;
molo; znamię; brodawka etc.
molecule ['molykju:l] s. molekuła;
cząsteczka
molest [mou'lest] v.
napastować; dokuczać;
molestować; naprzykrzać się
mollify ['molyfaj] v. łagodzić;
miękczyć; mięknąć;
uśmierzać
moment ['moument] s. chwila;
moment; waga; znaczenie;
motyw; powód; doniosłość;
ważność
momentary ['moumentery] adj.
chwilowy; mijający; lada
chwila
monarch ['monerk] s. monarcha;
król; duży motyl tropikalny
monarchy ['monerky] s.
monarchia
monastery ['monestery] s.
klasztor (głównie męski);
miejsce zamieszkania mnichów
(zakonnic)
Monday ['mandy] s.
poniedziałek; a.
poniedziałkowy
monetary ['manytry] adj.
monetarny; pieniężny;
walutowy
money ['many] s. pieniądze
money-order ['many,o:rder] s.
przekaz pieniężny
monger ['manger] s. handlarz;
przekupień; kupiec
monk [mank] s. mnich
monkey [manky] s. małpa
(ogoniasta); v. dokazywać;
małpować; wygłupiać się
monkey business ['manky
'byznys] s. małpie figle
(dokuczliwe)
monkey wrench ['manky'rencz]
s. francuski klucz
(dostosowywalny)
monolog(ue) ['monelog] s.
monolog; a. monologowy
monopolize [me'nopelajz] v.

monopolizować; skupiać na sobie uwagę wszystkich etc.
monopoly [me'nopely] s. monopol
monotonous [me'notnes] adj. monotonny; jednolity
monotony [me'notny] s. monotonia
monster ['monster] s. potwór; adj. olbrzymi; potworny; okrutny
monstrous ['monstres] adj. potworny; ogromny; okrutnie zły
month [mant] s. miesiąc
monthly ['mantly] adj. miesięczny; adv. miesięcznie; co miesiąc; na miesiąc; s. miesięcznik
monument ['monjument] s. pomnik
moo [mu:] v. ryczeć; s. ryk (krowy)
mood [mu:d] s. humor; nastrój; (gram.) tryb; usposobienie
moody [mu:dy] adj. ponury; mający humory; markotny
moon [mu:n] s. księżyc; a. księżycowy
moonlight ['mu:nlajt] s. światło księżyca; v. mieć kilka posad równocześnie
moonlit ['mu:nlyt] adj. oświetlony księżycem
moonshine ['mu:nszajn] s. światło księżyca; alkohol pędzony nielegalnie lub przemycony
Moor [muer] adj. mauretański; s. Maur
moor [muer] s. otwarty teren łowiecki; wrzosowisko; bagno; trzęsawisko; v. cumować; umocować; przybijać do brzegu
moorings ['mueryns] pl. kotwica martwa; miejsce przycumowania
moose [mu:s] s. łoś amerykański
mop [mop] s. szmata do podłóg; grymas; v. wycierać; zgarniać; robić miny;

spuścić manto
moral ['morel] s. morał; pl. moralność; adj. moralny; obyczajny
morale [me'rael] s. nastrój; duch (w wojsku, narodzie)
morality [me'raelyty] s. moralność; moralizowanie; etyka
moralize ['morelajz] v. umoralniać; moralizować
morass [me'raes] s. moczary; bagno; mokradła; grzązawiska
morbid ['mo:rbyd] adj. chorobliwy; chorobowy; niezdrowy; schorzały
more [mo:r] adv. bardziej; więcej; adj. liczniejszy; dalszy
morel [mo'rel] s. (grzyb) smardz; psianka; a. psiankowaty
more or less ['mo:r,or'les] adv. mniej więcej; w przybliżeniu
moreover [mo:'rouwer] adv. co więcej; prócz tego; nadto; poza tym
morgue [mo:rg] s. morga (na zwłoki); kostnica; a. kostnicy
morning ['mo:rnyng] s. rano; poranek; przedpołudnie
morose [mo'rous] adj. ponury; zasępiony; przygnębiony; markotny
morphine ['mo:rfi:n] s. morfina; a. morfinowy
morsel ['mo:rsel] s. kęs; kąsek; kawałek; smakołyk; v. dzielić na kawałki; rozdrabniać; rozparcelowywać
mortal ['mo:rtl] s. śmiertelnik; adj. śmiertelny; straszny
mortality [mo:'rtaelyty] s. śmiertelność; liczba ofiar
mortar ['mo:ter] s. moździerz; zaprawa murarska; v. tynkować; kłaść zaprawą; strzelać z moździerza; związać zaprawą
mortgage ['mo:rgydż] s. hipoteka; v. hipotekować
mortician [mo:r'tyszen] s. przedsiębiorca pogrzebowy
mortification [mo:rtyfy'kejszyn] s. upokorzenie; umartwianie

się; wstyd; gangrena
mortify ['mo:rtyfaj] v.
zamierzać; ranić (uczucia);
upokarzać; umartwiać (się);
powściągać; zgangrenować
mortuary ['mo:rtjuery] s.
trupiarnia; kostnica; a.
pogrzebowy
mosaic [mou'zejyk] s. mozaika;
adj. mozaikowy; mojżeszowy
mosque [mosk] n. meczet
mosquito [mes'ki:tou] s. komar;
moskit; a. moskitowy
moss [mos] s. mech; v.
pokrywać mchem
(torfowiskiem)
most [moust] adj. największy;
najliczniejszy; adv. najbardziej;
najwięcej; s. największa
ilość; maksimum
mostly ['moustly] adv.
przeważnie; głównie; po
największej części
moth [mos] s. ćma; mól
moth-eaten ['mos,i:tn] adj.
zjedzony przez mole;
przestarzały
mother ['madzer] s. matka; v.
matkować
mother country ['madzer'kantry]
s. ojczyzna; kraj rodzinny
motherhood ['madzer,hud] s.
macierzyństwo
mother-in-law ['madzer,yn'lo:] s.
teściowa
motherly ['madzerly] adj.
macierzyński
mother tongue ['madzer,tang] s.
język ojczysty
motif [mou'ti:f] s. motyw
(artystyczny); główny temat
motion ['mouszyn] s. ruch;
wniosek; stolec; v. kierować
skinieniem, znakiem; skinąć
na kogoś znaczącym gestem
motionless ['mouszenlys] adj.
bez ruchu; unieruchomiony
motion picture ['mouszyn
'pykczer] s. film ruchomy
motivate ['moutywejt] v.
uzasadniać; pobudzać
kogoś; zachęcać
motive ['moutyw] s. motyw;

podnieta; adj. napędowy;
poruszający
motor ['mouter] s. motor; adj.
ruchowy; mechaniczny;
samochodowy; v. jeździć;
przewozić samochodem;
prowadzić wóz
motorbike ['mouter,bajk] s.
motocykl; rower z motorkiem
motorboat ['mouter,bout] s.
motorówka; łódź motorowa
motorcycle ['mouter,sajkl] s.
motocykl
motorcyclist ['mouter,sajklyst] s.
motocyklista
motoring ['mouteryng] s. jazda
samochodem; automobilizm
motorist ['mouteryst] s.
automobilista; kierowca
motorize ['mouterajz] v.
motoryzować; zmotoryzować
mottle ['motl] s. cętka; plama; v.
cętkować; nakrapiać;
upstrzyć
motto [motou] s. motto; dewiza
mould [mould] s. pleśń;
ziemia; modła; forma; v.
pleśnieć; odlewać;
kształtować; urabiać
moulder ['moulder] v. gnić;
próchnieć; niszczyć się;
kruszyć się; zgłupieć; s.
odlewacz
mouldy ['mouldy] adj.
spleśniały; zgniły; stęchły;
przeżyty; nudny
moult [moult] v. linieć; s.
linienie
mound [maund] s. hałda; kopiec
mount [maunt] s. oprawa;
podstawa; wierzchowiec; v.
stanąć (na); wsiąść (na
konia); podnieść; wchodzić;
oprawić; osadzić;
wyposażyć; zmontować;
wyreżyserować
mountain ['mauntyn] s. góra;
sterta; adj. górski; górzysty
mountaineer [,maunty'nier] s.
góral; alpinista
mountainous ['mauntynes] adj.
górzysty; olbrzymi; zawrotny
mourn [mo:rn] v. być w żałobie;

opłakiwać; pogrążać się w smutku
mournful ['mo:rnful] adj. żałobny; ponury; przygnębiony
mourning ['mo:rnyng] s. żałoba
mouse [maus] s. mysz; pl. mice [majs]; podbite oko; v. myszkować
moustache [mos'ta:sz] s. wąsy
mouth [maus] s. usta; ujście; wylot; v. mówić przesadnie (z patosem)
mouth [mous] v. deklamować; brać w usta; robić złą minę
mouthful ['mausful] s. pełne usta; kęs; dźwięk trudny do wymówienia; ważne słowa; dużo czegoś; v. powiedzieć do rzeczy
mouthpiece ['mauspi:s] s. ustnik; rzecznik; kiełzno
mouthwash ['mausłosz] s. woda do ust; płukanka do ust
move [mu:w] s. ruch; pociągnięcie; krok; zmiana mieszkania; przeprowadzka; v. ruszać się; posuwać; przesuwać; postępować; przeprowadzać się; wzruszać; nakłonić; zwracać się; wnosić; zrobić ruch; działać
move in ['mu:wyn] v. wprowadzać się; wtargnąć; wejść
move on ['mu:w,on] v. jechać dalej; iść dalej; ruszyć (w drogę)
move out ['mu:w,aut] v. wyprowadzać się; wynieść się
movement [mu:wment] s. ruch; poruszenie; przemieszczenie; mechanizm; wypróżnienie
movies ['mu:wyz] s. (slang) kino; film niemy; film
moving ['mu:wyng] adj. ruchomy; wzruszający; s. przeprowadzka
moving violation ['mu:wyn, waje'lejszyn] przestępstwo drogowe w czasie jazdy (autem)

mow; mowed; mown [moł; mołd; mołn]
mow [moł] v. kosić (trawę)
mower ['mołer] s. kosiarz
mown [mołn] v. zob. mow
Mr. [myster] s. pan (używane z nazwiskiem)
Mrs. [mysyz] s. zamężna pani (używane z nazwiskiem)
much [macz] adj. & adv. wiele; bardzo; dużo; sporo; niemało
much too much [,macz'tu,macz] exp.: dużo za dużo; zbyt dużo
mucus ['mju:kes] s. śluz
mud [mad] s. błoto; brud
muddle ['madl] v. nurzać się; mącić; bełtać; mieszać; brnąć; wikłać się; s. powikłanie; trudne położenie; nieład; zamęt
muddle through ['madl,tru:] v. przebrnąć; wybrnąć z kłopotów
muddy ['mady] adj. zabłocony; błotnisty; mętny; v. błocić; mącić
muff [maf] s. zarękawek; fuszerka; fuszer; v. fuszerować
muffle [mafl] v. tłumić; owinąć; otulić; s. pysk (przeżuwaczy, gryzoni)
muffler ['mafler] s. tłumik; szal; rękawica bokserska; szalik
mug [mag] s. dzban; kubek; gęba
mulberry ['malbery] s. morwa
mule [mju:l] s. muł (zwierzę)
mull [mal] v. rozmyślać; pokpić; sfuszerować; zagrzać i zaprawić (np. piwo); s. bałagan; muślin; przylądek; tabakiera
mullion ['malion] s. pręt; drążek okienny; słupek okienny
multiple ['maltypl] s. wielokrotna; adj. wielokrotny; złożony
multiplication [,maltyply'kejszyn] s. mnożenie; rozmnażanie się
multiplication table [,maltyply 'kejszyn tejbl] s. tabliczka

mnożenia

multiply ['maltyplaj] s. mnożyć (się); rozmnażać się; pomnożyć

multitude ['maltytju:d] s. mnóstwo; tłum; pospólstwo; mnogość

mumble ['mambl] s. mruknięcie; bąknięcie; v. mruknąć; bąknąć; żuć bezzębnymi dziąsłami; mamrotać

mummy ['mamy] s. mumia; miazga; brunatny barwik; mamusia

mumps ['mamps] s. (choroba) świnka; zapalenie ślinianki

munch [mancz] v. chrupać; schrupać

municipal [mju:'nysypel] adj. miejski; samorządowy; komunalny

municipality [mju:,nysy'paelyty] s. zarząd miasta; miasteczko

mural ['mjuerel] s. malowidło ścienne; fresk; adj. ścienny

murder ['me:rder] s. mord; morderstwo; v. mordować; paskudzić (rolę)

murderer ['me:rderer] s. morderca

murderess ['me:rderys] s. morderczyni

murderous ['me:rderes] adj. morderczy; śmiercionośny

murmur ['me:rmer] s. mruczenie; pomruk; pomrukiwanie; szmer; szmeranie; sarkanie; v. mruczeć; szmerać

muscle ['masl] s. mięsień; muskuł; v. pchać się na siłę

muscle bound ['masl,baund] adj. z zerwanym mięśniami

muscular ['maskjuler] adj. mięśniowy; krzepki; muskularny; wykonany muskułami etc.

muse [mju:z] v. dumać; s. zaduma

museum [mju:'zjem] s. muzeum

mush [masz] s. papka; kulesza (z kukurydzy); v. iść po śniegu

mushroom ['maszrum] s. grzyb; pieczarka polna; dorobkiewicz;

v. zbierać grzyby; rozszerzać się (jak grzyby po deszczu)

music ['mju:zyk] s. muzyka; nuty; konsekwencje postąpku (slang)

musical ['mju:zykel] adj. muzyczny; muzykalny; s. komedia lub film muzyczny

music hall ['mju:zykho:l] s. teatr rewiowy

musician ['mju:zyszen] s. muzyk (zawodowy)

music stand ['mju:zyk,staend] s. pulpit (na nuty)

musk [mask] s. piżmo

musket ['maskyt] s. muszkiet

muskrat ['mask,raet] s. piżmoszczur; futro piżmoszczura

Muslim ['muslym] adj. muzułmański; s. muzułmanin

muslin ['mazlyn] s. muślin

musquash ['maskłosz] s. (muskrat) piżmowiec; piżmoszczur

mussel ['masl] s. małż

must [mast] s. moszcz winny; stęchlizna; szał; v. musieć; adj. konieczny; nieodzowny

mustache ['mastasz] s. wąsy

mustard ['masterd] s. musztarda

muster ['master] v. musztrować; zbierać (się); s. przegląd; zebranie; zbiór; apel; zebrani

muster in ['master,yn] v. zaciągać się do wojska (powołać)

muster out ['master,aut] v. zwalniać z wojska

musty ['masty] adj. stęchły; zapleśniały; zbutwiały; przestarzały

mute [mju:t] adj. niemy; v. tłumić

mutilate ['mju:tylejt] v. okaleczyć; psuć; okroić (tekst książki)

mutineer [,mju:ty'nier] s. buntownik; winny buntu

mutinous ['mju:tynes] adj. buntowniczy; zbuntowany

mutiny ['mju:tyny] s. bunt; v. buntować

mutter ['mater] v. mamrotać;
mruczeć; szemrać (przeciw);
szeptać; pomrukiwać; s.
mamrot; pomruk; szemranie;
narzekanie
mutton ['matn] s. baranina; a.
barani
mutton chop ['matn,czop] s.
kotlet barani
mutual ['mju:tjuel] adj.
wzajemny; wspólny;
obustronny
muzzle ['mazl] s. wylot lufy;
pysk; kaganiec; v. nakładać
kaganiec (psu, dziennikarzowi)
my [maj] pron. mój; moje; moja;
moi
myelitis [,maje'lytys] s. zapalenie
rdzenia pacierzowego
myriad ['myryed] s. krocie; roje;
10000; miriada; adj.
niezliczony; wielostronny
myrrh [me:r] s. mirra
myrtle ['me:rtl] s. mirt
myself [maj'self] pron. ja sam;
sam osobiście; siebie; sobie
mysterious [mys'tierjes] adj.
tajemniczy; niezgłębiony
mystery ['mystery] s. tajemnica;
tajemniczość; misterium
mystify ['mystyfaj] v.
wprowadzać w błąd;
okrywać tajemnicą
myth [mys] s. mit; postać
mityczna; bajka; mistyfykacja
mystic ['mystyk] s. mistyk; adj.
mistyczny; tajemniczy

N

n [en] czternasta litera
angielskiego alfabetu
nab [naeb] v. capnąć; złapać;
przydybać; aresztować;
przyłapać
nag [naeg] v. gderać;
dokuczać; dręczyć; s.
szkapa; kucyk; konik

nail [nejl] s. gwóźdź;
paznokieć; pazur; v.
przybijać; utkwić (wzrok);
ujawnić (kłamstwo);
przygwoździć; chwytać
naive [na:'i:w] adj. naiwny
naked ['nejkyd] adj. nagi; goły;
goła (prawda etc.); obnażony
name [nejm] s. imię; nazwa;
nazwisko; v. nazywać;
mianować; wymieniać;
naznaczyć (datę)
nameless ['nejmlys] adj.
bezimienny; nieznany;
niesłychany; nieopisany;
anonimowy
namely ['nejmly] adv.
mianowicie; właśnie; żeby
(wyjaśnić)
nanny ['naeny] s. niańka; koza
nanny-goat ['naeny,gout] s. koza
(żywicielka, mlekodajna)
nap [naep] v. drzemać;
zdrzemnąć się; s. drzemka;
meszek; puch; włos;
stroszenie meszku
nape [nejp] s. kark
nappy ['naepy] adj. mocny;
podchmielony; puszysty; v.
napój; piwo; półmisek;
serwetka
narcosis [na:r'kousys] s.
narkoza; uśpienie
narkotykami
narcotic [na:r'kotyk] adj.
narkotyczny; s. narkotyk;
narkoman
narrate [nae'rejt] v. opowiadać
(coś); opowiedzieć
narration [nae'rejszyn] s.
opowiadanie; opowieść
narrative ['naeretyw] adj.
narracyjny; s. opowiadanie
narrator [nae'rejter] n. narrator;
opowiadający; opowiadacz
narrow ['naerou] adj. wąski;
ciasny; ograniczony; s.
przesmyk; cieśnina; v.
zwężać; ścieśniać;
kurczyć się; zmniejszać się;
redukować do ...
narrow-minded ['naerou
'majndyd] s. ciasny;

ograniczony

nasty ['na:sty] adj. obrzydliwy;
wstrętny; nieznośny;
groźny; brudny;
nieprzyzwoity

nation ['nejszyn] s. naród; kraj;
państwo

national ['naeszenl] adj.
narodowy; państwowy; s.
członek narodu; obywatel;
ziomek

nationality [,naesze'naelyty] s.
narodowość; obywatelstwo

nationalize ['naesznelajz] v.
upaństwowić; nadawać
obywatelstwo (imigrantom)

native ['nejtyw] adj. rodzinny;
krajowy; miejscowy;
wrodzony; naturalny; prosty;
s. tubylec; autochton;
człowiek miejscowy

native language ['nejtyw
'laengłydż] s. ojczysty język

nativity [ne'tywyty] s.
narodzenie

natural ['naeczrel] adj. naturalny;
przyrodniczy; przyrodzony;
doczesny; fizyczny; przyrodni;
pierwotny; nieślubny; dziki; s.
biały klawisz (pianina);
kasownik (muzyczny)

naturalize ['naeczerelajz] v.
naturalizować (się);
aklimatyzować (się); robić
naturalnym; przyswajać
sobie; pozbawiać cech
nadprzyrodzonych

naturally ['naeczrely] adv.
naturalnie; z przyrodzenia;
oczywiście

natural-science ['naeczerel
'sajens] s. przyroda; nauka
przyrody; przyrodoznawstwo

nature ['nejczer] s. natura;
przyroda; usposobienie; rodzaj

naught [no:t] s. nic; zero

naughty ['no:ty] adj.
niegrzeczny; nieposłuszny;
nieprzyzwoity

nausea ['no:sje] s. nudność;
mdłość; choroba morska;
obrzydzenie; wstręt; chęć
wymiotowania

nauseating ['no:sjejtyng] adj.
obrzydliwy; przyprawiający o
mdłości, wymioty etc.

nautical ['no:tykel] adj.
marynarski; morski

nautical mile ['no:tykel,majl] s.
mila morska; 1853 m

naval ['nejwel] adj. morski

naval base ['nejwel,bejz] s. baza
morska (wojskowa)

nave [nejw] s. 1. nawa;
2. piasta (u koła)

navel ['nejwel] s. pępek
(ośrodek)

navigable ['naewygebl] adj.
spławny; żeglowny; sterowny;
przydatny do żeglugi

navigate ['naewygejt] s.
żeglować; kierować (np.
balonem)

navigation [,naewy'gejszyn] s.
żegluga; podróż morska;
nawigacja

navigator ['naewygejter] s.
żeglarz; nawigator

navy [nejwy] s. marynarka
wojenna; granatowy kolor

nay [nej] adv. nie; nawet; co
więcej; s. sprzeciw

near [nier] adj. bliski; dokładny;
v. zbliżać się; adv. blisko;
prawie; oszczędnie

nearby ['nier'baj] adj. pobliski;
sąsiedni; adv. w pobliżu

nearly ['nierly] adv. prawie;
blisko; oszczędnie; nie całkiem

nearness ['niernys] s. bliskość

nearsighted ['nier-sajtyd] s.
krótkowzroczny

neat [ni:t] adj. schludny;
zgrabny; proporcjonalny

neatness ['ni:tnys] s.
schludność; prostota;
porządek; gustowność;
dobre proporcje

necessary ['nesysery] adj.
konieczny; potrzebny;
wynikający

necessitate [ny'sesytejt] v.
wymagać; czynić
koniecznym

necessity [ny'sesyty] s.
potrzeba; konieczność;

artykuł pierwszej potrzeby;
niedostatek; los; zrządzenie
losu
neck [nek] s. szyja; kark; szyjka;
przesmyk; v. pieścić się
necklace ['neklys] s. naszyjnik
neck-tie ['nektaj] s. krawat
née [nej] z domu (nazwisko
panieńskie)
need [ni:d] s. potrzeba;
trudność; bieda; v.
potrzebować; musieć;
cierpieć biedę
needful [ni:dful] adj.
potrzebujący; potrzebny;
konieczny
needle ['ni:dl] s. igła; v. kłuć
needless ['ni:dlys] adj.
niepotrzebny; zbyteczny;
zbędny
needy ['ni:dy] adj. będący w
potrzebie, w biedzie etc.
negate [ny'gejt] v. zaprzeczać;
negować; anulować
negation [ny'gejszyn] s.
zaprzeczenie; odmowa; niebyt
negative ['negetyw] adj.
przeczący; negatywny;
odmowny; ujemny; s.
zaprzeczenie; odmowa; forma
przecząca; wartość ujemna;
negatyw; v. sprzeciwić się;
odrzucać (np. plan)
neglect [ny'glekt] v.
zaniedbywać; nie zrobić; s.
zaniedbanie; pominięcie;
lekceważenie
negligent ['neglydżent] adj.
niedbały; opieszały;
nieuważny
negotiate [ny'gouszjejt] v.
pertraktować; omawiać;
załatwiać; przezwyciężać;
przebić się przez; uporać
się; przekazać lub sprzedać
negotiation [ny,gouszy'ejszyn] s.
pertraktacje; omawianie w
celu osiągnięcia porozumienia
neigh [nej] s. rżenie; v. rżeć
neighbor ['nejber] s. sąsiad
neighborhood ['nejberhud] s.
sąsiedztwo; sąsiedzi; okolica
neighboring ['nejberyng] adj.

sąsiedni; sąsiadujący
neither ['ni:dzer] pron. & adj.
żaden (z dwóch); ani jeden ani
drugi; ani ten ani tamten; conj.
też nie; jeszcze nie
neither ... nor ['ni:dzer ... no:r]
exp. ani ... ani
neon ['ni:en] s. neon; a.
neonowy
neon sign ['ni:en,sajn] s. reklama
neonowa
nephew ['nefju:] s. siostrzeniec;
bratanek
nerve [ne:rw] s. nerw; siła;
energia; odwaga; opanowanie;
zuchwalstwo; tupet;
czelność; v. dodawać sił,
odwagi
nervous ['ne:rwes] adj. nerwowy
nervousness ['ne:rwesnys] s.
nerwowość; zdenerwowanie
nest [nest] s. gniazdo; wyląg; v.
budować; gnieździć się
nestle ['nesl] v. skulić; stulić
się; przytulić się; urządzić
się
nestle down ['nesl,daln] v.
usadawiać się (wygodnie)
nestle close up to ['nesl'klouz
,ap'tu] v. przytulić się (do
kogoś lu czegoś)
net [net] adj. czysty; netto; s.
siatka; sieć; v. łowić siecią;
trafić w siatkę; zarobić na
czysto (na sprzedaży etc.)
nettle ['netl] s. pokrzywa; v.
parzyć pokrzywą; drażnić;
irytować; docinać (komuś);
dopiekać
network ['net,łe:rk] s. sieć (np.
elektryczna)
neurosis [njue:rousys] s.
nerwica; zaburzenia
psychiczne
neuter ['nju:ter] adj. nijaki;
neutralny; bezstronny;
bezpłciowy; s. człowiek
bezstronny; rodzaj nijaki
neutral ['nju:trel] adj. bezstronny;
neutralny; obojętny; pośredni;
nieokreślony; bezpłciowy; s.
państwo neutralne
neutrality [nu'traelyty] s.

neutralność; obojętność
neutralize ['ny:trelajz] v.
neutralizować;
unieszkodliwiać; zobojętniać
neutron ['nu:tron] s. neutron
never ['newer] adv. nigdy; chyba
nie; wcale; ani nawet
nevermore ['newer'mo:r] adv.
nigdy więcej; przenigdy
nevertheless [,newerty'les] adv.
niemniej; jednak; pomimo tego
new [nju:] adj. nowy; świeży;
nowoczesny; adv. znowu; na
nowo
newborn ['nju:,bo:rn] adj. nowo
urodzony; s. noworodek
newcomer [nju:'kemer] adj.
nowoprzybyły; s. przybysz
news [nju:z] s. nowiny;
wiadomości; aktualności;
zdarzenia
newscast ['nju:z,ka:st] s.
nadawanie wiadomości
newspaper ['nju:s,pejper] s.
dziennik (gazeta); tygodnik
newsreel ['nju:sri:l] s. kronika
filmowa
newsstand ['nju:staend] s. kiosk
z gazetami
new year ['nju:je:r] s. nowy rok;
pierwszy stycznia
New Year's Eve ['nju:,je:rs'i:w]
s. Sylwester (31 grudnia)
next [nekst] adj. następny;
najbliższy; sąsiedni; adv.
następnie; potem; z kolei; tuż
obok; prep. obok; najbliżej
next but one ['nekst,bat'lan] adj.
przedostatni
next day ['nekst,dej] exp.:
następnego dnia
next door ['nekst,do:r] adj. (dom)
obok; sąsiedni (budynek)
next to ['nekst,tu] prep. obok
nibble at ['nydl,et] v. obgryzać;
nadgryzać; brać (przynętą);
s. ogryzanie; dziobanie
nice [najs] adj. miły;
sympatyczny; przyjemny;
uprzejmy; ładny; wybredny;
dokładny
nicely ['najsly] adv. przyjemnie;
miło; grzecznie; ściśle;

dokładnie; skrupulatnie
nicety ['najsyty] s. delikatność;
subtelność; zawiłość;
drobiazgowość;
dokładność; drobny
szczegół; małe rozróżnienie;
precyzja; akuratność
niche [nycz] s. nisza; v. chować
(się) w niszy
nick [nyk] s. karb; otłuczenie;
moment; v. karbować;
podcinać; przecinać; trafić;
natrafić; odgadnąć;
oszukać; złapać; otłuc
nickel ['nykl] s. nikiel; 5 centów
USA; v. niklować
nick-nack ['nyk,naek] (= knickknack) ozdóbka; świecidełko
nickname ['nyknejm] s.
zdrobniałe imię; przezwisko; v.
nazywać zdrobniale;
przezywać
niece [ni:s] s. siostrzenica;
bratanica
niggard ['nyged] s. sknera; adj.
żałujący (czegoś); skąpiący
night [najt] s. noc; wieczór
night cap ['najtkaep] s. kieliszek
przed snem; czepek do spania;
szklanka wina przed snem
nightclub ['najtklab] s. nocny
lokal (rozrywkowy)
nightgown ['najtgaln] s. damska
koszula nocna; nocny ubiór
nightingale ['najtyngejl] s.
słowik; a. słowiczy; słowika
nightly ['najtly] adv. co noc; w
nocy; adj. nocny; jak noc
nightmare ['najtmeer] s.
koszmar; przerażające
doświadczenie
night school ['najtsku:l] s. szkoła
wieczorowa
nightshirt ['najtsze:rt] s. koszula
nocna
nighty ['najty] s. koszulka nocna
(dziecinna, kobieca)
nil [nyl] s. nic; zero
nimble ['nymbl] adj. zwinny;
zgrabny; bystry; żywy;
żwawy
nine [najn] num. dziewięć; s.
dziewiątka; dziewięcioro

ninepins ['najnpynz] pl. kręgle
nineteen ['najn'ti:n] num.
dziewiętnaście;
dziewiętnastka
nineteenth ['najn'ti:ns] num.
dziewiętnasty; dziewiętnasta
część
ninetieth ['najntys] num.
dziewięćdziesiąty
ninety ['najnty] num.
dziewięćdziesiąt;
dziewięćdziesiątka
ninth ['najns] num. dziewiąty
ninthly ['najnsly] adv. po
dziewiąty (raz)
nip [nyp] v. uszczypnąć;
przychwycić; odszczepić;
stłumić; zmrozić; buchnąć;
ukraść; popędzić; polecieć;
ucinać; niszczyć; s.
ukąszenie; uszczypnięcie
nip off ['nypof] v. zmykać;
odszczepić się
nipple ['nypl] s. brodawka
sutkowa; smoczek; złącze
gwintowane rury; wzniesienie;
pagórek; bańka; złącze;
nasuwka
niter ['najter] s. saletra
nitrogen ['najtrydżen] s. azot
no [nou] adj. nie; żaden; adv.
nie; bynajmniej; nic; wcale nie;
s. odmowa; sprzeciw
no one ['nou,łan] adj. żaden; ani
jeden; nikt (w ogóle)
nobility [nou'bylyty] s.
szlachetność; szlachta
noble [noubl] adj. szlachetny;
szlachecki; wspaniały;
wielkoduszny; s. szlachcic
nobleman [noublmen] s.
szlachcic
nobody ['noubedy] s. nikt;
człowiek bez znaczenia
nod [nod] v. skinąć głową;
ukłonić się; drzemać
przyzwalać skinieniem; być
nachylonym
noise ['nojz] s. hałas; zgiełk;
wrzawa; szum; odgłos; szmer;
v. rozgłaszać coś; rozgłosić
noiseless ['nojzlys] adj. cichy;
bezszelestny; niehałaśliwy

noisy ['nojzy] adj. hałaśliwy;
krzykliwy; wrzaskliwy
nomadic ['noumaedyk] adj.
wędrowny; koczowniczy;
wędrujący
nominal ['nomynl] adj.
nominalny; imienny;
symboliczny; tylko z nazwy
nominate ['nomynejt] v.
mianować; wyznaczać;
obierać
nomination [,nomy'nejszyn] s.
nominacja
nominative ['nomynetyw] s.
mianownik (gram.); ta sprawa
(sądowa)
non- [non] prefix nie-; bez-
nonalcoholic ['non,aelke'holyk]
adj. bezalkoholowy
noncommissioned ['nonke
'myszend] adj. bez rangi
oficerskiej (podoficer)
noncommittal ['nonke'mytl] adj.
wymijający; nie
zobowiązujący (się)
nonconducting ['nonken'daktyng]
adj. nieprzewodzący
nonconformist ['nonken'fo:rmyst]
s. dyskontent; nonkonformista
nondescript ['nondyskrypt] adj.
nieokreślony; s. człowiek
nieokreślony (trudny do
opisania)
none [non] pron. nikt; żaden;
nic; adv. wcale nie; bynajmniej
nie
nonexistence [,nony'ksystens] s.
niebyt; nieistnienie
nonfiction [,non-'fykszyn] s.
reportaże; opowieść
prawdziwa; opisy faktów (w
dziennikach etc.)
nonsense ['nonsens] s.
niedorzeczność; nonsens;
głupstwo
nonskid ['nonskyd] adj.
przeciwślizgowy; nie
ślizgający się (samochód,
opona etc.)
nonsmoker ['non'smouker] s.
osoba niepaląca; przedział dla
niepalących (w pociągu etc.)
nonstop ['non'stop] adj.

bezpośredni; bez lądowania;
bez postoju; nieprzerwany (lot)

nonunion ['non'ju:njen] adj. nie
należący do związku
zawodowego; nie uznający
związku zawodowego

nonviolence ['non'wajelens] s.
(polityka) bez gwałtów

noodle ['nu:dl] s. makaron;
kluska; cymbał;pała; głupek;
łeb

nook [nuk] s. kącik; zakątek

noon [nu:n] s. południe

noose [nu:s] s. pętla; stryczek;
sidła; lasso; v. usidlić; zrobić
pętlę

nor [no:r] conj. też nie

norm [no:rm] s. norma; wzorzec;
standard

normal ['no:rmel] adj. normalny;
prostopadły; prawidłowy; s.
stan normalny; prostopadła

normalize ['no:rmelajz] v.
normalizować; unormować

Norman ['no:rmen] adj.
normański; s. Normandczyk;
Normandka

north [no:rs] adv. na północ; s.
północ; adj. północny

northeast [no:rs'i:st] adj.
północno-wschodni

northerly ['no:rdzerly] adj.
północny; adv. na północ

northerner ['no:rdzerner] s.
człowiek z północnych stanów

northward ['no:rslerd] adj.
północny; adv. na północ

northwest ['no:rs'łest] adj.
północno-zachodni; adv. na
północny-zachód; s. północny-
zachód

Norwegian [no:rłi:dżen] adj.
norweski; s. Norweg

nose [nouz] s. nos; węch; wylot;
dziób; v. węszyć; pocierać
nosem; wtykać nos

nosegay ['nouzgej] s. wiązanka;
bukiet

nostril ['noustryl] s. nozdrze;
chrapy; dziura w nosie

nosy ['nouzy] adj. wścibski;
śmierdzący; aromatyczny;
stęchły; cuchnący; s. nosacz

wielki

not [not] adv. nie; ani (jeden)

not a [not ej] adv. żaden

notable ['noutebl] adj.
znakomity; sławny; wybitny;
s. dostojnik; wybitny człowiek

notary public ['noutery'pablyk] s.
notariusz

notation [nou'tejszyn] s.
znakowanie; notacja; symbol

notch [nocz] s. nacięcie; karb;
przełęcz; v. nacinać;
karbować; rowkować; s.
krok (dalej)

note [nout] s. nuta; znak;
znamię; uwaga; notatka;
banknot; v. zapisywać;
zauważać

note down ['nout'dałn] v.
zanotować; zapisywać

notebook ['noutbuk] s. zeszyt;
notatnik; notes; notesik

noted ['noutyd] adj. znany;
znakomity; wybitny

notepaper ['nout,pejper] s. papier
listowy; blok

noteworthy ['nout,łe:rsy] adj.
godny uwagi; wybitny;
osobliwy

nothing ['nasyng] s. nic;
drobiazg; adv. nic; nie; w
żaden sposób; bynajmniej nie;
wcale nie

nothing but ['nasyng'bat] s. nic
tylko ... (coś najlepszego)

notice ['noutys] v. zauważyć;
spostrzec; traktować
grzecznie; powiadamiać; s.
zawiadomienie; uwaga;
recenzja; spostrzeżenie

noticeable ['noutysebl] adj.
godny uwagi; widoczny

notification [,noutyfy'kejszyn] s.
zawiadomienie; zgłoszenie

notify [noutyfaj] v. zawiadomić

notion ['nouszyn] s. pojęcie;
wyobrażenie; zamiar;
wrażenie

notorious ['nou'to:rjes] adj.
notoryczny; osławiony; jawny

notwithstanding [,noutlys
'staendyng] adv. jednakże;
niemniej; mimo; prep. pomimo

(tego); mimo
nought [no:t] s. nic; zero
noun [naun] s. rzeczownik
nourish ['narysz] v. żywić;
karmić; utrzymywać
nourishing ['naryszyng] adj.
pożywny; pokrzepiający
nourishment ['naryszment] s.
pokarm; pożywienie;
żywienie; karmienie;
żywność; jedzenie
novel ['nowel] s. powieść;
opowieść; nowela; adj.
nowy; nowatorski; osobliwy;
oryginalny
novelist ['nowelyst] s.
powieściopisarz
novelty ['nowelty] s. nowość;
innowacja; oryginalność
November [nou'wember] s.
listopad; adj. listopadowy
novice ['nowys] s. nowicjusz;
neofita; początkujący
now [nał] adv. teraz; obecnie;
dopiero co; otóż; a więc; s.
teraźniejszość; chwila
obecna; chwila dzisiejsza
now and again ['nał,ende'gejn]
exp.: od czasu do czasu
now and then ['nał,end'dzen]
exp.: nieraz; od czasu do
czasu; czasem; co jakiś czas
nowadays ['nałe,dejz] adv.
obecnie; dzisiaj; s. obecne
czasy; dzisiejsze czasy
nowhere ['nouhłer] adv. nigdzie;
s. niepowodzenie etc.
no way [nołej] adv.
bynajmniej; wcale nie
noxious ['nokszes] adj.
szkodliwy; niezdrowy
(moralnie etc.)
nozzle ['nozl] s. dysza;
rozpylacz; dziób; wylot (rury)
nuclear ['nu:kli:er] adj. jądrowy;
o napędzie nuklearnym
nuclear fission ['nu:kli:er'fyszyn]
s. rozszczepienie jądra
nuclear power plant ['nu:kli:er
'pałer'pla:nt] s. elektrownia
atomowa
nuclear reactor ['nu:kli:er
,ri:'aekter] s. reaktor nuklearny

nucleus ['nu:kljes] s. jądro
nude [nju:d] adj. nagi; goły; nie
ważny (prawnie); s. człowiek
nagi; nagość; akt
nudge [nadż] v. trącać lekko; s.
trącenie łokciem
nugget ['nagyt] s. bryłka; złoty
samorodek
nuisance ['nju:sns] s. zawada;
naruszenie porządku
publicznego; osoba
sprawiająca zawadę
null and void ['nal,end'woid]
exp.: nieważny; bez
znaczenia; unieważniony; nic
nie znaczący
numb [nam] adj. ścierpły;
zdrętwiały; odrętwiały; v.
drętwieć; odurzać;
paraliżować; zdrętwieć
number ['namber] s. liczba;
numer; ilość; v. liczyć;
numerować; wyliczać;
zaliczać
numberless ['namberlys] adj.
niezliczony; bez numeru
number plate ['namber'plejt] s.
płyta z numerem rejestracji
samochodu, motoru etc.
numeral ['nju:merel] adj.
liczbowy; cyfrowy; s.
liczebnik; cyfra (pisana,
mówiona etc.)
numerous ['nju:meres] adj.
liczny; obfity; liczebny;
rytmiczny
nun [nan] s. zakonnica; mniszka
nunnery ['nanery] s. zakon
żeński
nuptials ['napszels] pl.
zaślubiny; gody; wesele;
ślub
nurse [ne:rs] s. pielęgniarka;
pielęgniarz; mamka; osłona; v.
pielęgnować; leczyć;
opiekować się; żywić;
podsycać; szanować;
obejmować; karmić; pić
powoli; (piersią) niańczyć
nursery ['ne:rsery] s. pokój
dziecinny; żłobek; przedszkole;
ochronka; wylęgarnia; szkółka
(roślin, drzewek)

nursery school ['ne:rsery'sku:l] s.
przedszkole
nursing bottle ['ne:rsyng'botl] s.
flaszka do karmienia
nursing home ['ne:rsyn'houm] s.
przytułek - lecznica dla starych
i kalekich; dom zdrowia
nut [nat] s. orzech; bzik; dziwak;
nakrętka; zakrątka; v. szukać
i zbierać orzechy
nutcracker ['natkraeker] s.
dziadek do orzechów
nutmeg ['natmeg] s. gałka
muszkatołowa
nutria ['nju:trje] s. nutria (futro);
nutrie
nutrient ['nju:trjent] adj.
pożywny; odżywczy; s.
odżywka
nutriment ['nju:tryment] s.
środek odżywczy; jedzenie;
pokarm
nutrition [nju'tryszyn] s.
odżywianie; pokarm; nauka o
diecie
nutritious [nju'tryszes] adj.
pożywny; odżywczy
nuts ['nats] adj. (slang)
zwariowany; głupi;
zwariowany na punkcie
czegoś; bardzo zakochany;
excl.: (wyrażające) wstręt,
szyderstwo, lekceważenie
nutshell ['natszel] s. łupka od
orzecha; istota rzeczy; sama
treść (w paru słowach)
nutty ['naty] adj. orzechowy;
pomylony; zbzikowany;
dziwaczny; zwariowany;
pikantny; zakochany
nuzzle ['nazl] v. wsadzać nos
(w coś); ryć; węszyć;
wtulać się (twarzą w czyjeś
ramię); pocierać nosem lub
ryjem
nylon ['najlon] s. nylon;
pończochy nylonowe
nymph [nymf] s. nimfa
nymphomania [,nymfe'mejnia] s.
nimfomania (kobieca
nieposkromiona żądza
miłości; chorobliwy stan
podniecenia erotycznego

kobiety;) snębica
nymphomaniac [,nymfe'menjek]
s. nimfomanka; adj. typowy
dla nimfomanki

O

o [ou] piętnasta litera
angielskiego alfabetu; zero
oak [ouk] s. dąb; a. dębowy
oar [o:r] s. wiosło; v. wiosłować
oarsman ['o:rzmen] s. wioślarz
oasis [ou'ejsys] s. oaza; zielone i
żyzne miejsce wśród
pustynnej okolicy
oat [out] s. owies
oatmeal ['outmi:l] s. owsianka
oath [ous] s. przysięga;
przekleństwo;
świętokradztwo etc.
obedience [e'bi:djens] s.
posłuszeństwo
obedient [e'bi:djent] adj.
posłuszny
obey [e'bej] v. słuchać; być
posłusznym (rozsądkowi etc.)
obituary [e'bytjuery] s. nekrolog;
adj. pośmiertny; żałobny
object ['obdżykt] s. przedmiot;
rzecz; cel; śmieszny człowiek;
dopełnienie; v. zarzucać coś;
być przeciwnym; sprzeciwiać
się
objection [eb'dżekszyn] s.
zarzut; sprzeciw; przeszkoda;
trudność; wada; niechęć
objective [eb'dżektyw] s. cel;
obiektyw; adj. przedmiotowy;
obiektywny; rzeczywisty
obligation [obly'gejszyn] s.
zobowiązanie; obowiązek;
obligacja; dług (wdzięczności)
oblige [e'blajdż] v.
zobowiązywać; spełniać
prośbę
obliging [e'blajdżyng] adj.
uprzejmy; uczynny; usłużny
oblique [e'bli:k] adj. pośredni;

ukośny; skośny; kręty;
nieszczery; potajemny; v. iść
na ukos
obliterate [e'blyterejt] s.
zacierać; zamazywać;
wykreślić; zniszczyć;
skasować (znaczek etc.)
oblivion [e'blywjen] s.
zapomnienie; niepamięć
oblivious [o'blywjes] adj.
zapominający; niepomny;
nieświadomy; dający
zapomnienie
oblong ['oblong] adj. podłużny;
s. podłużny przedmiot
oboe ['oubou] s. obój (instr.
muzyczny)
obscene [ob'si:n] adj. sprośny;
nieprzyzwoity; niemoralny
obscure [eb'skjuer] adj. ciemny;
skromny; niejasny; ukryty;
nieznany; v. zaciemniać;
przyciemniać; zaćmiewać
obsequies ['obsykłyz] pl. pogrzeb
observance [eb'ze:rwens] s.
obrzęd; zwyczaj;
przestrzeganie; szacunek;
poszanowanie; rytuał
observant [eb'ze:rwent] adj.
uważny; postrzegający;
spostrzegawczy; bystry;
czujny
observation [,obzer'wejszyn] s.
obserwacja; spostrzeżenie;
uwaga; spostrzegawczość
observatory [eb'ze:rweto:ry] s.
obserwatorium; punkt
obserwacyjny
observe [eb'ze:rw] v.
obserwować; przestrzegać;
obchodzić; zauważać;
wypowiedzieć uwagę;
zbadać
observer [eb'ze:rwer] s.
obserwator; człowiek
przestrzegający praw
obsess [eb'ses] v. opętać;
prześladować; nie dawać
spokoju; nawiedzać
obsession [eb'seszyn] s. obsesja;
opętanie; natręctwo
(myślowe)
obsolete ['obseli:t] adj.

przestarzały; szczątkowy;
zarzucony
obstacle ['obstekl] s. przeszkoda;
zawada
obstetrics [ob'stetryks] s.
położnictwo
obstinacy ['obstynesy] s. upiór
obstinate ['obstynyt] adj. uparty;
uporczywy; zawzięty;
wytrwały
obstruct [eb'strakt] v. tamować;
zagradzać; zasłaniać;
wstrzymywać; wywoływać
zator; zawadzać
obtain [eb'tejn] v. uzyskać;
trwać; panować;
obowiązywać
obtainable [eb'tejnebl] adj.
osiągalny (do nabycia etc.);
możliwy do nabycia
obtrusive [eb'tru:syw] adj.
natarczywy; natrętny
obvious ['obwjes] adj.
oczywisty; rzucający się w
oczy
occasion [e'kejżyn] s.
sposobność; okazja; powód
occasional [e'kejżenl] adj.
przypadkowy; okazyjny;
okolicznościowy; rzadki
Occident ['oksydent] s. Zachód
(jako kultura, ekonomia etc.) -
całość geograficzna
occult [o'kalt] adj. tajemny
occupant ['okjupent] s.
mieszkaniec; posiadacz
(faktyczny)
occupation [,okju'pejszyn] s.
okupacja; zawód; zajęcie;
zajmowanie; zamieszkiwanie
occupy ['okjupaj] v. okupować;
zajmować (się czymś);
zatrudniać
occur [e'ke:r] v. zdarzać się;
przychodzić na myśl;
pojawiać się; dziać się;
trafić się
occurrence [e'karens] s.
wydarzenie; przypadek;
występowanie
ocean ['ouszen] s. ocean; a.
oceaniczny
o'clock [e'klok] adv. na zegarze;

według zegara
October [ok'touber] s.
październik; a.
październikowy
ocular ['okjuler] adj. oczny;
naoczny; na oko; okiem; s.
okular
oculist ['okjulyst] s. okulista
odd [od] adj. nieparzysty;
dziwny; dziwaczny;
zbywający; pozostały;
dodatkowy; od pary
odds [ods] pl. szanse; fory;
nadwyżka; różnica; drobne
szczegóły; spór; nierówność
(w grze); sprzeczność
odds-and-ends ['ods,end'ends]
exp.: resztki; rupiecie
oddity ['odyty] s. osobliwość;
dziwak; dziwactwo; dziwna
rzecz
odor ['ouder] s. odór; woń;
ślad; reputacja; sława;
posmak
of [ow] prep. od; z; o; w
of Cracow [ow'Krakau] exp.: z
Krakowa (pochodzeniem etc.)
of charity [ow'czaeryty] exp.: z
miłosierdzia
off [of] adv. od; z; na boku;
precz; z dala; przy; prep. z
dala
offshore [of'szo:r] adv. przy
wybrzeżu; adj. od lądu (na
morze)
offense [e'fens] s. obraza;
zaczepka; przekroczenie;
ofensywa
offend [e'fend] v. obrażać;
razić; występować przeciw
(np. prawu); zawinić;
wykroczyć
offender [e'fender] s. winowajca;
przestępca; strona winna
offensive [e'fensyw] adj.
obraźliwy; drażniący;
przykry; cuchnący; zaczepny;
s. ofensywa; postawa
zaczepna
offer ['ofer] s. oferta; propozycja
(np. ślubu); v. ofiarować
(się); oświadczyć (się);
oferować; nastręczyć się;

nadarzyć się; występować z
propozycją
offering ['oferyng] s. ofiara
office ['ofys] s. biuro; urząd;
obowiązek; służba
urzędowania; posada; funkcja;
stanowisko; gabinet
officer ['ofyser] s. urzędnik;
oficer; policjant; v. obsadzać
kadrą; dowodzić; kierować
official [e'fyszel] s. urzędnik; adj.
urzędowy; oficjalny
officious [e'fyszes] adj.
narzucający się; natrętny;
gorliwy; nieurzędowy;
nieoficjalny
offish ['ofysz] adj. chłodny;
sztywny; z rezerwą;
nieprzystępny
offset [o':fset] s. offsetowy
druk; gałąź; odgałęzienie;
odrośl; potomek;
wyrównanie; kompensata; v.
wynagradzać; rozrastać się
offspring ['o:fspryng] s.
potomek; wynik; potomstwo
often ['o:fn] adv. często
oh! [ou] excl. och! ach!
oil [ojl] s. oliwa; olej; ropa; nafta;
farba olejna; v. oliwić
smarować; przetapiać;
pochlebiać
oilcloth ['ojlklos] s. cerata
oily ['ojly] adj. oleisty; olejny;
tłusty; obleśny; służalczy
ointment ['oyntment] s. maść
O.K., okay ['ou'kej] adv. w
porządku; tak; adj. b. dobry;
s. zgoda; v. zaaprobować
(coś)
old [ould] adj. stary;
staroświecki; doświadczony;
były; s. dawne czasy; dawno
temu
old age ['ould,ejdż] s. starość
old-age ['ould ejdż] adj. dawny;
stary; starczy
old-fashioned ['ould'faeszend]
adj. staromodny; staroświecki
old-time ['ould,tajm] adj. dawny
old town ['ould,tałn] s.
starówka; stare miasto
olive ['olyw] s. oliwka; drzewo

oliwne; (kolor) oliwkowy;
oliwa stołowa
olive-branch ['olywbra:ncz] s.
gałązka oliwna
Olympic Games [ou'lympyk,
gejms] pl. igrzyska olimpijskie
ombudsman [om'bu:dz,men] s.
rzecznik ludu - załatwia skargi
na biurokratów
omelet(te) ['omlyt] s. omlet
omen ['oumen] s. omen;
wróżba; znak; v. być
wróżbą; być znakiem
ominous ['omynes] adj.
złowieszczy; źle wróżący
omission [e'myszyn] s.
opuszczenie; zaniedbanie
omit [ou'myt] v. opuszczać;
pomijać; zaniedbywać
omnipotent [om'nypetent] adj.
wszechmocny; wszechmogący
omniscient [om'nysjent] adj.
wszechwiedzący
on [on] prep. na; ku; przy; nad;
u; po; adv. dalej; przed siebie;
naprzód; przy sobie
on and on ['on,end'on] exp.:
coraz dalej; bez końca; wciąż
on demand [,on dy'ma:nd] exp.:
na żądanie
on the street ['on,dy'stri:t] exp.:
na ulicy
on to ['ontu] exp.: na; do
once [łans] adv. raz; nagle;
naraz; zaraz; kiedyś;
niegdyś; dawniej; s. raz; conj.
raz; gdy; skoro; od razu;
zarazem etc.
one [łan] num; jeden; adj.
pierwszy; pojedynczy; jedyny;
pewien; s. dowcip; kieliszek;
jedynka; pron. ten; który;
ktoś; niejaki
one Adams ['łan,aedems] exp.:
pewien Adams; niejaki Adams
one day ['łan,dej] exp.: pewnego
dnia; kiedyś; niegdyś
one by one ['łan,baj'łan] adv.
pojedynczo; jeden za drugim
one another [,łan e'nadzer] adv.
jeden drugiego; wzajemnie
oneself [łan'self] pron. się;
siebie; sobie; sam; osobiście;

samodzielnie; samotnie
one-sided ['łan'sajdyd] adv.
jednostronny
one-up-manship ['łan-,ap-
'menszyp] s. "wyścig"
nerwów (w zatargu etc.)
one-way ['łan,łej] adj.
jednokierunkowy (ruch)
onion ['anjen] s. cebula
onlooker ['onluker] s. widz
only ['ounly] adj. jedyny;
jedynak; adv. tylko; jedynie;
ledwo; dopiero; conj. tylko że;
cóż z tego, kiedy ...
onward ['onłerd] adj. naprzód; ku
przodowi; adv. naprzód; dalej;
dalej naprzód
ooze [u:z] v. sączyć się;
wydzielać się; ciec; s. szlam;
muł; wyciek; rzadkie błoto
opaque [ou'pejk] adj.
nieprzezroczysty; matowy;
mętny; niejasny; s. rzecz
matowa, nieprzezroczysta
open ['oupen] adj. otwarty;
rozwarty; dostępny;
wystawiony; jawny;
odsłonięty; wakujący; wolny;
v. otworzyć; zwierzyć się;
umożliwić; rozpoczynać;
rozchylić; udostępnić
open air ['oupen,eer] s. świeże
powietrze; wolna przestrzeń
opener ['oupener] s. otwieracz
(np. puszek); przyrząd do
otwierania
open-handed ['oupn'haendyd]
adj. szczodry; hojny
open-hearted ['oupn,ha:rtyd] adj.
szczery; serdeczny
opening ['oupnyng] s. otwór;
wylot; otwarcie; początek;
zbyt; adj. początkowy;
wstępny
openly ['oupnly] adv. otwarcie;
szczerze; publicznie; bez
ogródek; po prostu; wprost
(powiedzieć)
open-minded ['oupn'majndyd]
adj. z otwartą głową; bez
przesądów; bezstronny
opera ['opere] s. opera
opera glasses ['operegla:sys] s.

lornetka (teatralna)

operate ['operejt] v. działać;
zadziałać; oddziałać;
pracować; operować (kimś,
kogoś); wywoływać;
prowadzić; kierować;
obsługiwać; spekulować

operation [,ope'rejszyn] s.
działanie; czynności;
operacja; obsługiwanie; akcja

operative ['operejtyw] adj.
skuteczny; działający;
praktyczny; operacyjny; s.
pracownik; agent; mechanik;
robotnik; detektyw; agent
wywiadu

operator ['operejter] s. operator;
pracownik; obsługujący
maszynę; telefonista;
kierownik; przemysłowiec;
finansista; spekulant

opinion [e'pynjen] s. pogląd;
opinia; zdanie; zapatrywanie;
sąd

opponent [e'pounent] s.
przeciwnik; oponent; adj.
przeciwny; przeciwległy

opportunity [,oper'tju:nyty] s.
sposobność; okazja

oppose [e'pouz] v.
przeciwstawiać; sprzeciwiać
się

opposed [e'pouzd] adj.
przeciwny; przeciwdziałający

opposite ['epezyt] adj.
przeciwny; przeciwległy;
odmienny; adv. naprzeciwko;
naprzeciw; s. przeciwieństwo;
odwrotność

opposition [,ope'zyszyn] s.
sprzeciw; opór; opozycja;
przeciwstawienie (się);
przeciwieństwo; a.
opozycyjny

oppress [e'pres] v. przygniatać;
uciskać; ciemiężyć; gnębić;
nużyć; męczyć

oppression [e'preszyn] s. ucisk

oppressive [e'presyw] adj.
uciążliwy; dręczący;
gnębicielski; ciężki; duszny;
deprymujący

opt [opt] v. wybierać z dwu

alternatyw; optować na rzecz
czegoś

optical ['optykel] adj. optyczny;
wzrokowy; pomocny w
widzeniu

optician [op'tyszen] s. optyk

optimism ['optymysem] s.
optymizm; pogodny pogląd na
życie

optimize ['optymajz] v. używać
najwydajniej, najsprawniej

option ['opszyn] s. możność
wyboru; opcja; wybór; v.
wybrać alternatywę

or [o:r] conj. lub; albo; czy; ani;
inaczej; czyli; s. złoto; adj.
złoty

or else ['o:rels] exp.: bo jak nie
...; w przeciwnym razie

oral ['o:rel] adj. ustny; doustny;
s. egzamin ustny

orange ['oryndż] s. pomarańcza;
adj. pomarańczowy

orangeade ['oryn'dżejd] s.
oranżada (z pomarańcz,
cukru)

orator ['oreter] s. mówca

orbit ['o:rbyt] s. orbita; oczodół;
v. latać na orbicie (ziemi,
słońca etc.)

orchard ['o:rczerd] s. sad

orchestra ['o:rkystra] s. orkiestra

ordain [o:r'dejn] v. wyświęcać;
mianować; nakazywać;
przeznaczać; zarządzać;
nakazać

ordeal [o:r'di:l] s. ciężka próba;
ciężkie doświadczenie

order ['o:rder] s. rozkaz;
zlecenie; zarządzenie; przekaz;
porządek; szyk; układ; stan;
zakon; order; obrzęd;
zamówienie; zadanie; v.
rozkazywać; zamawiać;
komenderować; zarządzać;
wyświęcać; porządkować

orderly ['o:rderly] s. posługacz;
ordynans; adj. adv. porządny;
czysty; dokładny; skromny;
spokojny; dyżurny

ordinal ['o:rdynl] s. liczebnik
porządkowy; adj. porządkowy

ordinary ['o:rdnry] adj.

zwyczajny; zwykły;
przeciętny; pospolity; typowy;
s. rzecz zwykła, codzienna,
przeciętna
ore [o:r] s. ruda; kruszec; a.
kruszcowy; rudowy
organ ['o:rgen] s. narząd; organ;
organy; czasopismo
organic ['o:rgaenyk] adj.
organiczny;
usystematyzowany
organization [,o:rgenaj'zejszyn] s.
organizacja; organizowanie;
struktura; zrzeszenie
organize ['o:genajz] v.
organizować; zrzeszyć;
nadawać ustrój
organizer ['o:genajzer] s.
organizator
orgasm ['o:rgaesem] s. orgazm;
punkt kulminacyjny aktu
seksualnego; paroksyzm
orgy ['o:rdży] s. orgia
Orient ['o:rjent] adj. orientalny;
wschodni; s. Wschód (bliski)
orient ['o:rjent] v. orientować;
ukierunkowywać; ustawiać
origin ['orydżyn] s. pochodzenie;
początek; źródło; geneza
original [e'rydżynel] adj.
oryginalny; początkowy; s.
oryginał; dziwak
originality [e,rydży'naelyty] s.
oryginalność
originate [e'rydżynejt] v.
zapoczątkować; powstawać
ornament ['o:rnament] s.
ozdoba; v. ozdabiać;
upiększać
ornamental [,o:rne'mentl] adj.
ozdobny; dekoracyjny;
zdobniczy; upiększający
orphan ['o:rfen] s. sierota; adj.
sierocy; osierocony
orphanage ['o:rfenydż] s.
sierociniec; sieroctwo
orthodox ['o:tedoks] adj.
prawowierny; prawosławny
oscillate ['osylejt] v. drgać;
wahać się; oscylować
osmose ['osmous] s. osmoza;
prznikanie równoważące obie
strony (membrany, przedziału)

ostentatious [,osten'tejszes] adj.
ostentacyjny; wystawny;
okazały
ostracize ['ostre'sajz] v.
wykluczać z towarzystwa;
skazywać na wygnanie
ostrich ['ostrycz] s. struś
other ['adzer] pron. inny; drugi;
adv. inaczej; odmiennie
otherwise ['adzerłajz] adv.
inaczej; poza tym; skądinąd
ought [o:t] v. powinien; trzeba
żeby; należy; zobowiązany
ounce [auns] s. uncja; odrobina;
lampart; 1/16 funta
our ['aur] adj. nasz
ours ['auerz] pron. nasz
ourselves [auer'selwz] pl. pron.
my; my sami; (dla) nas etc.
oust [aust] v. usuwać;
wypierać; wyrzucać;
wywłaszczać
out [aut] adv. na zewnątrz;
precz; poza; na dworze; poza
domem; nieobecnym (być)
out-and-out [auten'aut] adj.
całkowity; adv. całkowicie
out of ['autow] adv. z; bez;
poza; nie (modne, rozsądne)
outbalance [aut'baelens] v.
przeważyć; przewyższać
outbid [aut'byd] v.
przelicytować; dać więcej
(niż inny)
outbreak ['autbrejk] s. wybuch
(np. wojny, epidemii)
outburst ['autbe:rst] s. wybuch
(np. gniewu, wulkanu)
outcast ['autka:st] s. wyrzutek;
wygnaniec; adj. wygnany
outcome ['autkam] s. wynik;
rezultat; konsekwencje
outcry ['autkraj] s. okrzyk;
wrzawa; silny protest
outdoors ['aut'do:rz] adj. na
wolnym powietrzu; s. wolna
przestrzeń; adv. zewnątrz
(domu)
outer ['auter] adj. zewnętrzny
outermost ['auter'moust] adj.
najbardziej zewnętrzny
outfit ['autfyt] s. wyposażenie;
drużyna; zespół; towarzystwo;

zestaw narzędzi; v.
wyposażyć; zaopatrywać;
wyekwipować

outgoing ['aut,gouyng] adj.
odchodzący; odjeżdżający;
przyjazny; komunikatywny;
towarzyski

outgrow [aut'grou] v.
przerastać; wyrastać z ...;
wyróść (z roli)

outing ['autyng] s. wycieczka
(na otwarte morze, do lasu
etc.); wypad

outlast [aut'la:st] v. przetrwać
(coś, kogoś); wytrwać
dłużej

outlaw ['aut-lo:] v. zakazywać;
wyjmować spod prawa; s.
przestępca; banita; notoryczny
kryminalista

outlet ['autlet] s. wylot; rynek
zbytu; wyjście; ujście

outline ['autlajn] s. zarys; szkic;
v. konturować; szkicować;
przedstawiać (plany etc.)

outlive [aut'lyw] v. przeżyć;
przetrwać; wytrwać dłużej

outlook ['autluk] s. widok;
pogląd; obserwacja; widoki
(na przyszłość); czaty

outnumber [aut'namber] v.
przewyższać liczebnie; być
liczniejszym

out-of-date [autew'dejt] adj.
przestarzały; niemodny

outpatient ['aut,pejszent] s.
pacjent dochodzący (z domu)

output ['autput] s. wydajność;
wydobycie; moc; produkcja

outrage ['autrejdż] s. gwałt;
zniewaga; v. gwałcić;
znieważać; urągać
(zdrowemu rozsądkowi)

outrageous [aut'rejdżes] adj.
wołający o pomstę; bezecny;
gwałtowny; skandaliczny;
obrażający

outright [aut'rajt] adj. całkowity;
zupełny; stanowczy;
bezpośredni; adv. od razu;
całkowicie; zupełnie; otwarcie

outrun [aut'ran] v. przegonić;
prześcignąć

outside ['aut'sajd] s. okładka;
fasada; strona zewnętrzna; na
dworze; adj. zewnętrzny; inny
niż; adv. zewnątrz; oprócz; z
wyjątkiem; poza (czymś)

outside on the right ['aut'sajd
'on,dy'rajt] exp.: na zewnątrz
po prawej

outsider ['aut'sajder] s. człowiek
obcy; niewtajemniczony; laik;
obcy zawodnik

outsize ['autsajz] s. wielkość
nietypowa, za duża

outskirts ['aut,ske:rts] s. krańce;
kraj; peryferie

outspoken [aut'spouken] adj.
szczery; otwarcie
wypowiedziany, bez ogródek,
prosto w oczy

outspread [aut'spred] adj.
rozpostarty; rozpowszechniony

outstanding ['autstaendyng] adj.
wybitny; wyróżniający się;
otwarty; niezałatwiony;
zaległy; wystający; sterczący

outstretched [aut'streczt] adj.
rozpostarty; wyciągnięty

outward ['autlerd] adj.
zewnętrzny; powierzchowny;
pozorny; cielesny; s. strona
zewnętrzna; wygląd
zewnętrzny; adv. na zewnątrz

outweigh [aut'łej] v. przeważyć

outwit [aut'łyt] v. przechytrzyć

oval ['ouwel] s. owal; adj.
owalny; owalnego kształtu

oven ['own] s. piekarnik; piec

over ['ouwer] prep. na; po; w;
przez; ponad; nad; powyżej;
adv. na drugą stronę; po
powierzchni; całkowicie; od
początku; zbytnio; znowu; raz
jeszcze (odrabiać zadanie
etc.)

over again ['ouwer,e'gejn] adv.
na nowo; jeszcze raz

over-and-over ['ouwer,end
'ouwer] adv. w kółko

overall ['ouwero:l] adj. ogólny;
wszystko obejmujący; s.
kombinezon roboczy

overboard ['ouwerbo:rd] adv.
(zaniechać) za burtę

(wyrzucić)

overburden [,ouwe'rbe:rden] v.
przeładowywać; s. ciężar
pokładów (np. nad kopalnią);
nadmiar ciężaru; ciężar
warstw

overcast ['ouwerka:st] adj.
zachmurzony; mroczny;
ponury; obrębiony; v.
mroczyć; chmurzyć (się);
obrębiać

overcharge [,ouwer'cza:rdż] v.
przeciążać; zdzierać
(pieniądze); stawiać za
wysokie ceny

overcoat ['ouwerkout] s. płaszcz

overcome [,ouwer'kam] v.
pokonać

overcrowd [,ouwer'kraud] v.
zatłoczyć; przepełniać

overdo [,ouwerdu:] v.
przeciążać; przesadzać;
przegotowywać; niszczyć
przesadą; robić za dużo

overdraw [,ouwer'dro:] v.
wyczerpać (konto);
przesadzać; pisać czeki bez
pokrycia

overdue [,ouwer'dju:] adj.
zaległy; zapóźniony (pociąg)

overestimate [,ouwer'esty,mejt]
v. przeceniać; s. za wysoka
ocena; zbyt duże oczekiwania

overflow [,ouwer'flou] v.
przepełniać; przelewać; s.
wylew; przelew; kanał
przelewowy etc.

overgrow [,ouwer'grou] v.
obrastać; przerastać; rosnąć
nadmiernie; róść zbyt szybko

overhang ['ouwer'haeng] v.
zwisać; sterczeć; zagrażać;
s. występ; zwis; nawis
(dachu); występ (skały); zwis
(skalny etc.)

overhaul [,ouwer'ho:l] v.
gruntownie naprawić;
gruntownie zbadać; s.
gruntowny remont

overhead ['ouwer'hed] s.
wydatki administracyjne; adv.
powyżej; na górze; adj. górny

overhear [,ouwer'hier] v.

usłyszeć przypadkiem;
podsłuchać

overheat ['ouwerhi:t] v.
przegrzać; s. nadmierne
gorąco; przegrzanie

overjoyed [,ouwer'dżojd] adj.
nieposiadający się z radości

overlap [,ouwer'laep] v.
zachodzić na siebie; s.
zachodzenie (na siebie)

overload [,ouwer'loud] v.
przeładować; s. nadmierny
ciężar; przeciążenie (dachu)

overlook [,ouwer'luk] v.
przeoczyć; puszczać płazem;
mieć widok z góry;
nadzorować; wybaczyć; s.
widok z góry; nadzór

overlord ['ouwerlo:rd] s. suzeren;
samodzierżca

over-night ['ouwer'najt] adv.
przez noc; poprzedniego
wieczora; adj. nocny; na noc

overpass [,ouwer'pa:s] s.
skrzyżowanie wiaduktem;
przejazd wiaduktem; v.
przecinać; przekraczać;
przewyższać;
przezwyciężać; pomijać (w
kolejce etc.)

overrate ['ouwer'rejt] v.
przeceniać; spodziewać się
zbyt dużo

overrule [,ouwer'ru:l] v.
opanować; uchylać;
odrzucać; unieważniać;
zmieniać czyjeś
postanowienie

overrun [,ouwer'ran] v.
najechać; zalewać;
przelewać; s. przekraczanie
ceny umówionej

overseas ['ouwer'si:z] adv. za
morzem; do krajów
zamorskich; adj. zamorski

oversee ['ouwer'si:] v.
dozorować; doglądać

overseer ['ouwer'si:er] s.
nadzorca

overshadow ['ouwer'szaedou] v.
przyćmiewać; zaćmiewać

oversight ['ouwersajt] s.
przeoczenie

oversleep ['ouwer'sli:p] v.
zaspać; przespać
over-strain ['ouwer'strejn] v.
przemęczać s. przeciążenie;
przemęczenie
overtake ['ouwer'tejk] v.
doganiać przeganiać;
zaskoczyć
overthrow ['ouwer'srou] v.
przywrócić; obalić; pobić; s.
obalenie
overtime ['ouwertajm] s. godziny
nadliczbowe; adv.
nadprogramowo; adj.
nadprogramowy; v.
prześwietlić;
przeeksponować
overtone ['ouwertoun] s.
niedomówienie; sugestia;
akcent; główna nuta
overture ['ouwer,tjuer] s.
rozpoczęcie rokowań;
propozycja; uwertura; v.
proponować
overturn [,ouwer'te:rn] v.
wywracać; obalać; s.
przewracanie; przewrót;
podbój
overweight [,ouwer'łejt] s.
nadwaga; dodatkowa waga;
otyłość; adj. ponad normalną
wagę
overwhelm [,ouwer'hłelm] v.
przygniatać przywalać;
zalewać; rujnować; ogarniać
overwork ['ouwer'łe:rk] v.
przepracowywać się;
przeciążać pracą; zmuszać
do za ciężkiej pracy;
przemęczać się; s. nadmierna
praca
ovulate ['ouwjulejt] v.
jajeczkować; wytwarzać jaja
owe [oł] v. być winnym;
zawdzięczać
owing ['ołyng] adj. dłużny;
należny; prep. z powodu;
skutkiem
owing to ['ołyng,tu] prep.
ponieważ
owl [aul] s. sowa
own [ołn] v. mieć; posiadać;
przyznawać (się); adj.

własny; rodzony
owner ['ołner] s. właściciel
ownership ['ołnerszyp] s.
własność; posiadanie
ox [oks] s. wół; pl. oxen
oxen ['oksen] pl.woły; zob. ox
oxide ['oksajd] s. tlenek
oxidation [oksy'dejszyn] s.
utlenianie; oksydacja
oxidize [oksydajz] v. utleniać
oxygen [oksydżen] s. tlen
oyster ['ojster] s. ostryga
ozone ['ouzoun] s. ozon

P

p [pi:] szesnasta litera
angielskiego alfabetu
pa [pa:] s. tato
pace [pejs] s. krok; chód; v.
kroczyć; mierzyć krokami;
ustalać rytm kroku; ćwiczyć
krok (np. konia); przebywać
(drogą); chodzić (tam i z
powrotem)
pacer ['pejser] s. regulator rytmu
(serca, kroku etc.)
pacific [pe'syfyk] adj. spokojny;
pokojowy
pacify ['paesyfaj] v. uspakajać;
zaspokajać
pack [paek] s. pakunek; tłumok;
tobół; stek; sfora; okład; kupa;
v. pakować; opakować;
owijać; stłoczyć; napychać;
objuczyć; zbierać w stado
pack up ['paek,ap] v. spakować
package ['paekydż] s. pakunek;
paczka
package deal ['paekydż'di:l] s.
przyjęcie złożonej propozycji
bez zmian
packer ['paeker] s. pakier;
przedsiębiorca od pakowania
artykułów spożywczych;
maszyna do pakowania
packet ['paekyt] s. pakiet; v.
zawijać

packing ['paekyng] s.
pakowanie; opakowanie;
uszczelka; okładzina; tampon
packthread ['paektred] s. szpagat
pact [paekt] s. pakt; układ
pad [paed] s. wyściółka; notes;
blok (papieru); bibularz; łapa;
podkładka; v. wyścielać;
wywoływać; rozdymać
padding ['paedyng] s. obicie;
wyściółka; podbicie;
podszycie; rozwadnianie
tekstu
paddle ['paedl] s. wiosełko
kajakowe; v. wiosłować
paddock ['paedek] s. wybieg
(koński)
padlock ['paedlok] s. kłódka; v.
zamykać na kłódkę
pagan ['pejgen] s. poganin; adj.
pogański
page [pejdż] s. stronica; karta;
paź; goniec
pageant ['paedżent] s. widowisko (np. historyczne)
paid [pejd] adj. zapłacony;
płatny; zob. pay
pail [pejl] s. wiadro
pain [pejn] s. ból; cierpienie;
trud; starania; v. zadawać
ból; boleć; dolegać
painful ['pejnful] adj. bolesny;
przykry
painless [pejnlys] adj. bezbolesny
paint [pejnt] s. farba; szminka; v.
malować
paintbrush ['pejntbrasz] s. pędzel
painter ['pejnter] s. malarz
painting ['pejntyng] s.
malarstwo; obraz
pair [peer] s. para; parka; stadło;
v. dobierać do pary;
stanowić parę
pajamas [pe'dża:mez] pl. piżama
pal [pael] s. kumpel; druh;
przyjaciel
palace ['paelys] s. pałac
palate ['paelyt] s. podniebienie
pale [pejl] s. pal; granica; adj.
blady; v. otaczać palami;
blednąć; spowodować
blednięcie
pallor ['paeler] s. bladość

palm [pa:m] s. palma; dłoń;
piędź; v. ukrywać w dłoni;
dotykać dłonią
palpitation [,paelpy'tejszyn] s.
palpitacja; mocne bicie serca;
kołatanie serca; drżenie;
dygotanie
pamper ['paemper] v.
rozpieszczać; przekarmiać;
zbyt pobłażać
pamphlet ['paemflyt] s. broszura
natury polemicznej na tematy
bieżące, kontrowersyjne etc.
pan [paen] s. patelnia; rondel;
rynka; szalka; panewka; gęba;
kra; v. gotować na patelni;
udawać się; krytykować
pancake ['paen,kejk] s.
naleśnik; adj. płaski
pane [paen] s. szyba; krata;
ścianka; płaszczyzna
panel ['paenl] s. tafla; otoczyna;
płyta; wstawka; tablica
(rozdzielcza); komitet; lista
(przysięgłych, lekarzy etc.);
czaprak
pang [paeng] s. ostry ból; męka;
wyrzuty (sumienia etc.)
panhandler [,paen'haendler] s.
kwestarz; ksiądz z tacą
panic ['paenyk] s. panika;
popłoch; v. wpaść w panikę;
wywoływać panikę; poddać
się panice
pan-Slavism ['paen'sla:wyzem] s.
panslawizm
pansy ['paensy] s. bratek
pant [paent] s. zadyszka; v.
sapać; dyszeć
panther ['paenter] s. pantera
panties ['paentyz] pl. majtki
(damskie)
pantry ['paentry] s. spiżarnia
pants [paents] pl. spodnie;
kalesony
panty hose ['paenty'houz] s.
rajstopy; pończochy z
majtkami
pap [paep] s. papka; bzdury;
sutka; brodawka piersiowa
papa ['pa:pe] s. papa; tata
paper ['pejper] s. papier; gazeta;
tapeta; rozprawa naukowa;

papierowe pieniądze; adj.
papierowy; rzekomy; v.
zawinąć w papier;
tapetować
paper-back ['pejper,baekt] adj. w
papierowej okładce; s.
kieszonkowe wydanie książki
paper bag ['pejper,baeg] s. torba
papierowa
paper-hanger ['pejper,haenger] s.
tapeciarz
paper-hangings ['pejper
,haengyngs] pl. tapety
paper money ['pejper'many] s.
papierowe pieniądze
paperweight ['pejper,łejt] s.
przycisk
par [pa:r] s. stan równości;
norma
parable ['paerebl] s.
przypowieść
parachute ['paere,szu:t] s.
spadochron
parachutist ['paere,szu:tyst] s.
spadochroniarz
parade [pe'rejd] s. parada;
pochód; rewia; defilada; v.
popisywać się; obnosić się
(z czymś)
paradise ['paere,dajs] s. raj; adj.
rajski
paragraph ['paere,gra:f] s. ustęp;
odnośnik; notatka; v. dzielić
na ustępy; pisać notatkę
parallel ['paere,lel] adj.
równoległy; odpowiedni
(czemuś); s. równoległa;
równoleżnik; porównanie; v.
być równoległym; kłaść
równolegle; zestawiać;
znaleźć odpowiednik
paralyze ['paere,lajz] v.
paraliżować; porażać
paralysis [pe'raelysys] s. paraliż
paramount ['paere,maunt] adj.
główny; najważniejszy;
kapitalny; najwyższy
parasite ['paere,sajt] s. pasożyt
parcel ['pa:rsl] s. paczka; działka;
v. dzielić; pakować w paczki
parch ['pa:rcz] v. wysuszać
(się); prażyć; cierpieć z
pragnienia

parchment ['pa:rczment] s.
pergamin
pardon ['pa:rdn] s. ułaskawienie;
przebaczenie; v. przebaczać;
darować; ułaskawiać
pardon me ['pa:rdn,mi:] exp.:
przepraszam
pardonable ['pa:rdnebl] adj.
wybaczalny
pare [peer] v. obcinać; obierać;
obskrobać
parent ['peerent] s. ojciec;
matka; rodziciel; rodzicielka
parental [pe'rentl] adj.
rodzicielski
parenthesis [pe'rentysys] s.
nawias
parentheses [pe'renty,si:s] pl.
nawiasy
parings ['peerynz] pl. łupiny;
obrzynki
parish ['paerysz] s. parafia
parishioner [pe'ryszener] s.
parafianin
park [pa:rk] s. park; postój
samochodów; v. parkować
parking ['pa:rkyng] s. postój
samochodów; parkowanie
parking garage ['pa:rkyng
'gaera:ż] s. garaż parkingowy
parking lot ['pa:rkyn,lot] s. plac
parkingowy
parking meter ['pa:rkyn'mi:ter] s.
licznik do płacenia za parking
(na ograniczony czas)
parking ticket ['pa:rkyn'tykyt] s.
mandat karny za złe
parkowanie lub za
niezapłacenie
parkway ['pa:rkłej] s.
czteroliniowa szosa
przedzielona roślinnością
parliament ['pa:rlyment] s.
parlament
parliamentary [,pa:rly'mentery]
adj. parlamentarny
parlor ['pa:rler] s. salon; sala;
pokój (przyjęć)
parquet ['pa:rkej] s. parkiet; v.
wyłożyć parkietem
parrot ['paeret] s. papuga; v.
powtarzać jak papuga
parsley ['pa:rsly] s. pietruszka; a.

pietruszkowy
parry ['paery] v. parować;
odpierać; s. odparcie
parson ['pa:rsn] s. proboszcz
parsonage ['pa:rsnydż] s.
plebania
part [pa:rt] s. część; ustęp;
udział; rola; strona; przedział
(włosów); v. rozchodzić (się);
rozdzielać; dzielić; pękać;
robić (przedział); wyjeżdżać;
adj. mniejszy niż całość
partake [pa:r'tejk] v. brać udział;
dzielić coś z kimś; zob. take
partaken [pa:r'tejkn] v. zob.
partake
partial ['pa:rszel] adj. stronniczy;
częściowy; mający słabość
do ...; niepełny
partiality [,pa:rszy'aelyty] s.
stronniczość; upodobanie
participant [pa:r'tysypent] s.
uczestnik; adj. uczestniczący
participate [pa:r'tysypejt] v.
brać udział
particle ['pa:rtykl] s. cząstka;
odrobina; partykuła
particular ['per'tykjuler] adj.
szczególny; szczegółowy;
specjalny; prywatny;
grymaśny; dokładny;
uważny; dziwny;
niezwyczajny; ostrożny; s.
szczegół; fakt
particularity [per,tykju'laeryty] s.
osobliwość;
szczegółowość;
drobiazgowość;
wybredność
particularly [per,tykju'laerly] adv.
osobliwie; szczególnie
particulars [per'tykjulers] s. dane
osobiste
parting ['pa:rtyng] s. przedziałek
(włosów); rozstanie; rozdział;
pożegnanie; rozdroże; zgon
partition [pa:r'tyszyn] s. podział;
rozbiór; rozdział; v. dzielić;
przegradzać
partition off [pa:rtyszyn,of] v.
oddzielać
partly ['pa:rtly] adv. częściowo;
po części; poniekąd

partner ['pa:rtner] s. wspólnik
partnership ['pa:rtnerszyp] s.
spółka
partook [pa:r'tuk] v. zob. partake
partridge ['pa:trydż] s.
kuropatwa
part-time ['pa:rt,tajm] adv. na
niepełnym etacie; na
niepełnym czasie; adj.
niepełnoetatowy
party ['pa:rty] s. partia; przyjęcie
towarzyskie; towarzystwo;
grupa; strona; uczestnik;
osobnik
pass [pa:s] s. przełęcz; odnoga
rzeki; przepustka; wypad;
bilet; umizg; sztuczka; v.
przechodzić; mijać; pomijać;
zdać; przekazać; wymijać;
wyprzedzać; przeprowadzić;
przewyższać; spędzać;
puszczać w obieg; podawać;
odchodzić; umierać; dziać
się; krążyć
pass away ['pa:se,łej] v.
odchodzić; umierać
pass by ['pa:s,baj] v. mijać;
pomijać
pass for ['pa:s,fo:r] v. udawać
(kogoś)
pass out ['pa:s,aut] v. zemdleć;
umrzeć; wyjść
pass round ['pa:s,raund] v.
podawać w koło (np.
gościom)
pass through ['pa:s,tru] v.
przechodzić (przez, na
wskroś)
passable ['paesebl] adj. nadający
się do przebycia; (stopień)
dostateczny; znośny
passage ['paesydż] s. przejście;
przejazd; przeprawa; przelot;
upływ; korytarz; urywek
tekstu
passenger ['paesyndżer] s.
pasażer; pasażerka
passer-by ['pa:ser'baj] s.
przechodzień
passion ['paeszyn] s.
namiętność; pasja; Męka
Pańska; stan bierny
passionate ['paeszenyt] adj.

namiętny; porywczy;
zapalczywy; żarliwy; ognisty
passive ['paesyw] adj. bierny; s.
strona bierna
passport ['pa:s,po:rt] s. paszport
password ['pa:s,ło:rd] s. hasło
past [pa:st] adj. przeszły;
miniony; ubiegły; prep. za;
obok; po; przed; adv. obok; s.
przeszłość; czas przeszły
paste [pejst] s. pasta; ciasto; klej
mączny; klajster; masa;
makaron; uderzenie (slang); v.
przylecieć; oblepiać; obić
(kogoś)
pasteboard ['pejst,bo:rd] s.
karton; tektura; adj.
tekturowy; kartonowy; lichy
pastime ['pa:s,tajm] s. rozrywka
(po pracy etc.)
pastry ['pejstry] s. wyroby
cukiernicze; ciastka
pastry shop ['pejstry szop] s.
sklep wyrobów cukierniczych
past tense ['pa:st tens] s. czas
przeszły (gram.)
pasture ['pa:sczer] s. pastwisko
pat [paet] s. głaskanie; klepanie;
krążek (np. masła); v.
pogłaskać; poklepać;
pochwalić (kogoś); adv.
trafnie; w sam raz; adj. trafny;
biegły; na czasie; zupełnie
właściwy
patch [paecz] s. łata; plama;
skrawek; pólko; zagon;
grządka; klapka (na oko);
przepaska; v. łatać; załatać;
szyć z łat; sztukować;
naprawić; skleić; załagodzić
patch pocket ['paecz,pokyt] s.
naszywana kieszeń
patchwork ['paecz,łe:rk] s.
łatanina; szachownica
pate [pejt] s. slang: głowa; łeb;
pała; szczyt głowy
patent ['paetnt] s. patent; v.
opatentować; a.
patentowany; opatentowany;
oczywisty
patent ['pejtnt] adj. jasny;
otwarty; oczywisty; chroniony
patentem

patent-leather ['paetnt'le_dz_er] s.
skóra lakierowana
paternal [pe'te:rnl] adj. ojcowski;
po ojcu
paternity [pe'te:rnyty] s.
ojcostwo; pochodzenie po
ojcu; autorstwo (książki,
planu etc.)
path [pa:s] s. ścieżka; tor;
droga ruchu; zob. paths
pathetic [pe'_t_etyk] adj. żałosny;
smutny; uczuciowy;
wzruszający; rozrzewniający
paths [pa:_s_z] pl. ścieżki; tory;
drogi ruchu
patience ['pejszens] s.
cierpliwość; pasjans
patient ['pejszent] adj. cierpliwy;
wytrwały; s. pacjent;
pacjentka; chory; chora
patio ['pa:ti:o] s. ogródek
wewnętrzny; taras
patriarch ['pejtry,a:rk] s.
patriarcha
patriot ['pejtryet] s. patriota
patriotic [,paetry'otyk] adj.
patriotyczny
patriotism ['paetrye,tyzem] s.
patriotyzm
patrol [pe'troul] v. patrolować;
s. patrolowanie; patrol
patrolman [pe'troulmen] s.
policjant (drogowy USA)
patron ['pejtren] s. klient;
opiekun; patron
patronage ['paetrenydż] s.
opieka; poparcie; klientela;
rozdawanie posad;
protekcjonalność; przywileje;
posady
patronize ['paetre,najz] v.
popierać; protegować;
traktować protekcjonalnie
patsy ['paecy] s. oferma przez
wszystkich zawsze
nadużywana
patter ['paeta] s. stukot; trajkot;
trajkotanie; gwara; klepanie;
szybka recytacja; żargon; v.
stukać; bębnić; trajkotać;
klepać (np. pacierze);
odklepywać; kłapać; gadać
pattern ['paetern] s. próbka;

wzór; układ; materiał na
suknię lub ubranie (USA);
zespół; cechy
charakterystyczne; ślady kul
(na tarczy); v. wzorować;
modelować; ozdabiać
wzorami
paunch ['pa:ncz] s. (duży)
brzuch; żołądek krowy
paunchy ['pa:nczy] adj.
brzuchaty; z wydatnym
brzuchem
pause [po:z] s. przerwa; pauza;
v. robić przerwę; wahać się
pave [pejw] v. brukować;
torować drogę
pavement ['pejwment] s. bruk;
posadzka; materiał do
brukowania
pavement-cafe ['pejwment
'kaefej] s. kawiarnia za
stolikami na chodniku
paw [po:] s. łapa; (slang) tatuś;
v. uderzać łapą lub kopytem;
miętosić w łapach; macać
(poufale)
pawn [po:n] s. zastaw; fant;
pionek; v. zastawiać; dawać
w zastaw
pawnbroker ['po:n,brouker] s.
lichwiarz pożyczający pod
zastaw; właściciel lombardu
pawnshop ['po:n-szop] s.
lombard; sklep zastawniczy
pay; paid; paid [pej; peid; peid]
pay [pej] v. płacić; zapłacić;
wynagradzać; udzielać
(uwagi); dawać (dochód);
opłacać (się); s. płaca;
zapłata; pobory;
wynagrodzenie; adj. płatny
(np. automat telefoniczny);
opłacalny
pay back ['pej baek] v. zwrócić
dług; odpłacać
payday ['pej dej] s. dzień
wypłaty
pay down ['pej dałn] v. dawać
zadatek; płacić pierwszą ratę
gotówką
pay for ['pej,fo:r] v. płacić (za
coś)
pay in ['pej,yn] v. wpłacać

pay off ['pej,of] v. spłacać
pay out ['pej,aut] v.
wydatkować; wypuszczać
linę (na statku); wypłacać;
płacić
pay up ['pej,ap] v. wyrównywać
(dług); zapłacić
payable ['pejebl] adj. płatny;
dochodowy; opłacający się
payee ['pej'i:] s. odbiorca
płatności
payer ['pejer] s. płatnik
payment ['pejment] s.
płatność; wypłata; zapłata
pea [pi:] s. groch; ziarnko grochu
peace [pi:s] s. pokój; pojednanie;
spokój
peaceful ['pi:sful] adj. spokojny;
pokojowy
peach [pi:cz] s. brzoskwinia;
wspaniała rzecz, dziewczyna,
człowiek; v. (slang) sypać;
donosić (na kogoś)
peacock ['pi:,kok] s. paw; v.
pysznić się jak paw; chodzić
jak paw; paradować
peak [pi:k] s. (ostry) szczyt;
wierzchołek; daszek (u
czapki); szpic; garb (krzywej)
peak hour ['pi:k'auer] s. godzina
szczytu ruchu
peal [pi:l] s. huk; łoskot; bicie w
dzwony; huczny śmiech;
zespół dzwonów; v. huczeć;
bić w dzwony; grać (coś)
hucznie
peanut ['pi:nat] s. orzeszek
ziemny; drobnostka; a.
drobny; prowincjonalny
pear [peer] s. gruszka
pearl [pe:rl] s. perła
peasant ['pezent] s. chłop;
wieśniak; adj. chłopski
peat [pi:t] s. torf
peat bog ['pi:t'bog] s. torfowisko
pebble ['pebl] s. kamyk; otoczak;
v. granulować; obrzucać
kamykami
peck [pek] v. dziobać; wcinać
(jedzenie); dziobnąć;
cmoknąć (męża); stukać;
wydziobać; dłubać;
odziobać; s. dziobnięcie;

cmok; ślad dziobania
peculiar [py'kju:ljer] adj.
szczególny; dziwny; osobliwy;
charakterystyczny; dziwaczny
peculiarity [py'kju:li'aeryty] s.
właściwość; cecha;
osobliwość; dziwaczność
pedal ['pedl] s. pedał; nuta
pedałowa; v. pedałować;
naciskać pedał; ['pi:dl] adj.
pedałowy; nożny
peddle ['pedl] v. sprzedawać po
domach; być domokrążcą;
wydzielać po trochu
peddler ['pedler] s. domokrążca
pedestal ['pedystl] s. piedestał;
podstawa; v. stawiać na
piedestał
pedestrian [py'destrjen] adj.
pieszy; przyziomny;
prozaiczny; s. piechur; pieszy
człowiek
pedestrian crossing [py'destrjen
'krosyng] s. przejście dla
pieszych; zebra; pasy
pedigree ['pedygri:] s. rodowód;
drzewo genealogiczne
peddlar ['pedler] s. przekupień;
handlarz
peek ['pi:k] v. podglądać
peel [pi:l] s. skóra; skórka; łupa;
v. obierać; zdzierać;
łuszczyć się; (slang)
rozbierać (się)
peep [pi:p] v. zerkać;
podglądać; wynurzać (się);
wychodzić niepostrzeżenie
peeping Tom ['pi:pyng,tom] s.
podglądający natręt
peer [pier] s. równy (komuś)
stanem, pochodzeniem etc.
peerless ['pierlys] adj.
niezrównany
peevish ['pi:wysz] adj. drażliwy;
zły; gniewny; zirytowany
peg [peg] s. czop; kołek;
zatyczka; szpunt; v.
zakołkować; przymocować
kołkami
pelican ['pelyken] s. pelikan
pelt [pelt] s. futro; kanonada;
grzmocenie; pośpiech; v.
ostrzeliwać; obrzucać;

obsypywać gradem; rzucać
zniewagi; obsypywać
zniewagami; walić
pelvis ['pelwys] s. miednica; a.
miedniczny
pen [pen] s. pióro; kojec;
ogrodzenie; schron; (slang)
więzienie; v. pisać; układać
list; zamykać w ogrodzeniu
penal ['pi:nl] adj. karny; karalny
penalty ['penlty] s. kara
penalty kick ['penlty,kik] s. karny
strzał (do bramki)
penance ['penens] s. pokuta
pence [pens] pl. grosze; zob.
penny
pencil ['pensl] s. ołówek; v.
rysować; pisać
pencil sharpener ['pensl'sza:rp-
ner] s. strugaczka do ołówka
pendant ['pendent] s. wisiorek;
proporzec; adj. wiszący;
zwisający; nierozstrzygnięty;
toczący się; do
rozstrzygnięcia
pending ['pendyng] adj.
niezałatwiony; będący w toku;
wiszący; prep. aż do; podczas
penetrate ['peny,trejt] v.
przenikać; przepajać;
przedostawać się przez;
wtargnąć; zanurzyć
penetration [,peny'trejszyn] s.
penetracja; przenikanie;
przenikliwość
pen friend ['penfrend] s. znajomy
z listów
penguin ['pengłyn] s. pingwin
penholder ['pen,houlder] s.
piórnik; obsadka; stojak na
pióro
penicillin [,peny'sylyn] s.
penicylina
peninsula [py'nynsjule] s.
półwysep
penitent ['penytent] s. żałujący
grzesznik; pokutnik; adj.
żałujący; skruszony
penitentiary [,peny'tenszery] s.
więzienie; adj. karany
więzieniem; poprawczy
penknife ['pen,najf] s. scyzoryk
pennant ['penent] s. proporzec

penniless ['penylys] adj. w nędzy; bez grosza

penny ['peny] s. cent; grosz; pl. pennies ['penyz]; Br. pl. pence [pens]

penny-worth ['penyłe:rs̲] s. wartość centa; exp.: za centa

pen pal [pen pael] s. znajomy (a) z listów

pension ['penszyn] s. renta; emerytura; pensjonat; v. wyznaczać pensję; pensjonować

pension off ['penszyn,of] v. przenosić na emeryturę

pensioner ['penszener] s. emeryt; emerytka; rencista; rencistka

pensive ['pensyw] adj. zamyślony

penthouse ['pent,haus] s. mieszkanie z ogrodem na szczycie budynku; przybudówka na dachu

people ['pi:pl] s. ludzie; ludność; lud; v. zaludniać

pep [pep] s. animusz; werwa; wigor; adj. ożywiony; wesoły; dowcipny; dodający animuszu

pep pills ['pep,pyls] pl. pigułki podniecające

pep up ['pep,ap] v. ożywić; dodać animuszu

pepper ['peper] s. pieprz; papryka; v. pieprzyć; kropić; zasypywać kulami; dać lanie

per [pe:r] prep. przez; za; na; według; co do; za pośrednictwem

perceive [per'si:w] v. uświadamiać sobie; odczuć; dostrzegać; spostrzegać

percent [per'sent] s. odsetek; od sta

percentage [per'sentydż] s. odsetek; procent; od sta

perceptible [per'septebl] adj. dostrzegalny

perception [per'sepszyn] s. spostrzeganie; percepcja

perch [pe:rcz] s. okoń; grzęda; żerdź; pręt; v. siedzieć na grzędzie; sadzać na grzędzie

percussion [per'kaszyn] s. uderzenie; zderzenie; bicie (bębna)

peremptory [per'emptery] adj. stanowczy; apodyktyczny; ostateczny; nieodwołalny

perfect ['pe:rfykt] adj. doskonały; zupełny; v. udoskonalić; wykończyć

perfect tense ['perfykt'tens] s. gram. czas przeszły dokonany

perfection [per'fekszyn] s. doskonałość; szczyt; wykończenie; udoskonalenie

perforate ['pe:rferejt] v. przedziurawiać; dziurkować; przenikać; przebijać się

perform [per'fo:rm] v. wykonywać; odgrywać; spełniać; występować

performance [per'fo:rmens] s. przedstawienie; wyczyn; wykonanie; spełnienie

performer [per'former] s. wykonawca

perfume ['pe:rfju:m] s. perfuma; zapach; [pe'rfju:m] v. perfumować

perhaps [per'haeps, praeps] adv. może; przypadkiem

peril ['peryl] s. niebezpieczeństwo; ryzyko; v. narazić na niebezpieczeństwo

perilous ['peryles] adj. niebezpieczny; ryzykowny

period ['pieried] s. okres; period; menstruacja; kropka; kres; pauza; miesiączka; a. stylowy

periodic [,piery'odyk] adj. okresowy; periodyczny

periodical [,piery'odykel] s. czasopismo; periodyk; adj. okresowy; periodyczny

perish ['perysz] v. zgiąć; niszczyć; nękać; trapić; gnębić; ginąć (przedwczesną śmiercią)

perishable ['peryszebl] adj. zniszczalny; s. łatwo psujący się towar

perjury ['pe:rdżery] s. krzywoprzysięstwo; złamanie

obietnicy

perm [pe:rm] s. trwała ondulacja

permanent ['pe:rmenent] adj.
trwały; permanentny

permanent wave ['pe:rmenent
‚łejw] s. trwała ondulacja

permeable ['pe:rmjebl] adj.
przepuszczalny; przenikalny

permission [per'myszyn] s.
pozwolenie; zezwolenie

permit [per'myt] s. pisemne
zezwolenie; pozwolenie; v.
pozwalać; zezwalać;
dopuszczać

pernicious [pe:rnyszes] adj.
szkodliwy; zgubny

perpendicular [‚pe:rpen'dykjuler]
adj. prostopadły; s.
prostopadła; pion

perpetual [per'petjuel] adj.
wieczny; wieczysty; trwały;
dożywotni

persecute ['pe:rsy‚kju:t] v.
prześladować

persecution [‚pe:rsy'kju:szyn] s.
prześladowanie

persecutor ['pe:rsy‚kju:ter] s.
prześladowca

persevere [‚pe:rsy'wier] v.
wytrwać

persist [pe'rsyst] v. obstawać;
wytrwać; upierać się

persistence [per'systens];
persistency [per'systency] s.
wytrwałość; uporczywość;
trwałość

persistent [per'systent] adj.
wytrwały; uporczywy; trwały

person ['pe:rson] s. osoba;
człowiek

personage ['pe:rsonydż] s.
osobistość; ważny człowiek

personal ['pe:rsenel] adj.
osobisty; robiący osobiste
uwagi; s. wiadomość
osobista

personality [‚pe:se'naelyty] s.
osobowość;
powierzchowność; postawa;
indywidualność; pl.
wycieczki (uwagi) osobiste

personify [pe:r'sony‚faj] v.
uosabiać; personifikować

personnel [‚pe:rse'nel] s.
personel

personnel manager [‚pe:rse'nel
'maenydżer] s. kierownik
oddziału personalnego;
personalny

perspiration [‚pe:rspy'rejszyn] s.
pocenie się; pot

perspire [‚pe:r'spajer] v. pocić
się; wypacać się

persuade [pe:r'słejd] v.
przekonywać; namawiać

persuasion [pe:r'słejżyn] s.
perswazja; przekonywanie;
namawianie; przekonanie;
wyznanie; wierzenie

persuasive [pe:r'słejsyw] adj.
przekonywujący; s. motyw;
pobudka (do czegoś)

pert [pe:rt] adj. śmiały;
arogancki; (slang) żwawy

pertain [per'tejn] v. należeć do
czegoś; być właściwym
czemuś; odnosić się;
wchodzić w zakres

pertinent ['pe:rtynent] adj.
stosowny; trafny; słuszny;
odnoszący się do czegoś lub
kogoś

perusal [pe'ru:zal] s.
przestudiowanie; dokładne
przeczytanie

peruse [pe'ru:z] v. czytać
uważnie; studiować (np.
twarz)

pervade [per'wejd] v. przenikać;
owładnąć; ogarniać; szerzyć
się

perverse [per'we:rs] adj.
przewrotny; przekorny;
wyuzdany

pesky ['pesky] adj. (slang)
dokuczliwy; natrętny; cholerny

pessimism ['pesy‚myzem] s.
pesymizm; spodziewanie się
najgorszego

pest [pest] s. plaga; zaraza

pet [pet] s. faworyt; ulubieniec
(np. pies); adj. ulubiony; v.
(slang) pieścić; być w złym
nastroju; gniewać się;
migdalić; wypieścić

petal ['petl] s. płatek

petition [py'tyszyn] s. petycja;
prośba; podanie; v. prosić;
wnosić podanie
petrify ['petry,faj] v. zamieniać
(się) w kamień; powodować
kostnienie
petroleum [py'trouljem] s. ropa
naftowa; olej skalny
pet shop ['petszop] s. sklep
zwierzątek pokojowych
petticoat ['petykout] s. halka;
spódniczka; kobieta; adj.
kobiecy
petty ['pety] adj. drobny
petty cash [,pety'kaesz] s.
gotówka podręczna
pew [pju:] s. ławka (kościelna)
pewter ['pju:ter] s. stop cyny z
ołowiem; naczynie cynowe
pharmacy ['fa:rmesy] s. apteka;
farmacja
phase [fejz] s. faza (np.
rozwojowa); aspekt
pheasant ['feznt] s. bażant
philanthropist [fy'laentrepyst] s.
filantrop; filantropka
philatelist [fy'laetelyst] s.
filatelist; filatelistka
philologist [fy'loledżyst] s.
filolog; lingwista;
językoznawca
philology [fy'loledży] s. filologia;
językoznawstwo; lingwistyka
philosopher [fy'losefer] s. filozof
philosophize [fy'lose,fajz] v.
filozofować
philosophy [fy'losefy] s. filozofia
phlegm [flem] s. flegma; śluz;
plwocina; spokój
phone [foun] s. telefon (slang)
phonetic [fou'netyk] adj.
fonetyczny
phony ['founy] adj. fałszywy;
udawany; s. rzecz fałszywa,
podrabiana; ktoś udający
photo ['foutou] s. fotka;
fotografia; v. fotografować
photograph ['foute,gra:f] s.
fotografia; zdjęcie; v.
fotografować
photographer [fe'togrefer] s.
fotograf; fotografik
photography [fe'tegrefy] s.

fotografia; fotografika
phrase [frejz] s. wyrażenie;
zwrot; v. wyrażać;
wypowiadać wyrażeniami lub
słowami
physical ['fyzykel] adj. fizyczny;
cielesny
physician ['fyzyszyn] s. lekarz
physicist ['fyzysyst] s. fizyk
physics ['fyzyks] s. fizyka
physique [fy'zi:k] s. budowa
ciała; rozwój; wygląd fizyczny;
kondycja; siła muskularna
piano [py'aenou] s. fortepian;
pianino
pick [pyk] v. wybierać;
dorabiać; kopać;
krytykować; dłubać;
obierać; zbierać; usuwać;
oskubać; wydziobać;
kraść; okradć; s. kilof;
dłuto; wybór; czółenko; nitka
pick-off ['pyk,of] v. zedrzeć;
wystrzelać pojedynczo
(wrogów)
pick out ['pyk,aut] v. wybrać;
dobrać; doszukiwać się
pick over ['pyk,ouwer] v.
przebierać; wybrać co lepsze
pick up ['pyk,ap] v. podnosić;
brać; nauczyć się; zarabiać;
odnaleźć; odzyskać;
przyjść do siebie; poznać
się; s. adapter; lekka
ciężarówka
picket ['pykyt] s. palik; kół;
pikieta; posterunek; v.
rozstawiać pikiety strajkowe;
służyć jako pikieta;
zabezpieczać pikietami
pickle ['pykel] s. kiszony ogórek;
marynata; kłopot; łobuz; v.
marynować; kisić;
wytrawiać
pickpocket ['pyk,pokyt] s.
złodziej kieszonkowy;
kieszonkowiec
picnic ['pyknyk] s. piknik;
majówka; v. brać udział w
pikniku, majówce, posiłku na
dworze
pictorial [pyk'to:rjel] adj.
obrazowy; ilustrowany;

malowniczy; malarski; s.
(czaso)pismo ilustrowane;
ilustracja (trzywymiarowa)
techniczna
picture ['pykczer] s. obraz; film;
rysunek; rycina; portret;
widok; v. odmalowywać;
przedstawiać; opisywać;
wyobrażać sobie; dawać
obraz czegoś
picturesque [,pykcze'resk] adj.
malowniczy; żywy i przyjemny
pie [paj] s. placek; szarlotka;
pasztet; pasztecik; (ptak)
sroka
piece [pi:s] s. kawałek; część;
sztuka; moneta; utwór; v.
łączyć; zeszyć; łatać;
naprawiać
piecework ['pi:s,łe:rk] s. robota
na akord
pier [pier] s. pomost ładunkowy;
molo; falochron; filar (np.
mostu)
pierce [piers] v. przewiercać;
wnikać; przedziurawiać;
przebijać; przedostawać się
piercing [piersyng] adj.
przeszywający; ostry;
rozdzierający; przenikający
piety ['pajety] s. pobożność
pig [pyg] s. wieprz;
świnia;prosię; v. prosić się
pigeon ['pydżyn] s. gołąb; v.
oszukiwać
pigeon-hole ['pydżyn,houl] s.
przegródka; v. umieszczać w
przegródkach
pigheaded ['pyg'hedyd] adj.
uparty; głupi
pigskin ['pyg,skyn] s. świńska
skóra; (slang) piłka; siodło
pigtail ['pyg,tejl] s. warkocz
pike [pajk] s. rogatka; dzida;
pika; szpic; ostrze; szczupak
pile [pail] s. stos; sterta; kupa;
pal; słup; puszek; meszek;
włos; v. układać w stos;
gromadzić na kupę; stawiać
w kozły
pile up ['pail,ap] v. walić na
kupę; s. zwalenie na kupę
piles [pailz] pl. hemoroidy

pilfer ['pylfer] v. ukraść;
zwędzić; buchnąć
pilgrim ['pylgrym] s. pielgrzym
pilgrimage ['pylgrymydż] s.
pielgrzymka
pill [pyl] s. pigułka; tabletka
pillar ['pyler] s. filar; słup;
podpora
pillbox ['pylboks] s. bunkier;
pudełeczko na pigułki;
kapelusz
pillion ['pyljen] s. tylne siodełko
(np. na motocyklu)
pillory ['pylery] s. pręgierz; v.
stawiać pod pręgierzem
pillow ['pylou] s. zagłówek;
jasiek; poduszka; podkładka;
v. spoczywać; opierać (np.
głowę)
pillowcase ['pylou,kejs] s.
poszewka
pillow slip ['pylou,slyp] s.
poszewka
pilot ['pajlet] s. pilot; sternik; v.
pilotować; sterować;
przeprowadzić
pimp [pymp] s. stręczycielka;
alfons; v. stręczyć
pimple ['pympl] s. pryszcz;
wągier
pin [pyn] s. szpilka; sztyft;
sworzeń; kołek; kręgiel; v.
przyszpilić; przymocować
pincers ['pynserz] pl. kleszcze;
obcęgi
pinch [pyncz] v. szczypać;
gnieść; cisnąć; przycisnąć;
przyskrzynić; krępować;
dokuczać; doskwierać;
podważać łomem; s.
uszczypnięcie; szczypta; łom;
(slang) aresztowanie; obława;
kradzież
pinch bar ['pyncz ba:r] s. łom (ze
stopką)
pine [pajn] s. sosna; ananas; v.
usychać
pineapple ['pajnaepl] s. ananas
pinion ['pynjen] s. kółko zębate;
wrzeciono zębate; wał
przekładni; koniec pióra; lotka;
v. podcinać (skrzydła);
pętać; przywiązywać

pink [pynk] s. różowy kolor;
radykał (komunizujący);
goździk; v. urazić do
żywego; przekłuwać
pinnacle ['pynekl] s. szczyt;
wieżyczka; v. zwieńczać;
postawić na szczycie;
stanowić szczyt
pint [pajnt] s. półkwarcie; 0.47
litra; 1/8 galona
pioneer [,paje'nier] s. pionier;
saper; v. torować drogę
pious [pajes] adj. pobożny
pip [pyp] s. pestka; oczko;
gwiazdka; ziarnko; punkcik;
pypeć; dźwięk gwizdka; v.
piszczeć; wykluwać się;
pobić; trafić; postrzelić
pipe [pajp] s. rura; rurka;
przewód; piszczałka; (slang)
łatwizna; drobiazg; v.
doprowadzać rurami;
włączyć; połączyć;
prowadzić dźwiękiem fujarki;
grać na fujarce; grać na
kobzie; gwizdać; piszczeć
pipeline ['pajp,lajn] s. rurociąg;
(slang) informator; v.
przesyłać rurociągiem
piper [pajper] s. kobziarz
pipes [pajps] s. kobza
pirate [pajeryt] s. korsarz; pirat;
statek piracki; maruder; v.
grabić; uprawiać korsarstwo;
wydawać bezprawnie
(książki)
piss [pys] v. szczać (wulg.) s.
szczyny (wulg.)
piss off [pys'of] v. wkurzyć;
irytować (wulg.)
pistol ['pystl] s. pistolet
piston ['pysten] s. tłok
pit [pyt] s. dół; jama; kopalnia;
pestka; v. puszczać do walki;
robić dołki; wkładać do dołu;
wyjmować pestki
piston-stroke ['pysten,strouk] s.
suw tłoka
pitch [pycz] v. rozbijać (obóz);
umieszczać; rzucać;
ustawiać; chwiać się;
upaść ciężko; kołysać (na
fali); przechylać; wybierać;

ostro pracować; rzucać się
na ...; smołować; s. stopień;
najwyższy punkt; wzniesienie;
wzdłużne kołysanie statku;
spadek dachu; odstęp między
(falami, zębami kół etc.); skok
(uzwojenia, śruby); smoła
pitcher ['pyczer] s. dzban;
rzucający piłkę
piteous ['pytjes] adj. żałosny;
nędzny
pitfall ['pytfo:l] s. pułapka;
wilczy dół
pith [pys] s. miękisz; rdzeń;
tężyzna; moc; v. wyjmować
rdzeń; przecinać rdzeń w
celu zabijania bydła (w rzeźni)
pitiable ['pytjebl] s. żałosny;
godny pożałowania
pitiful ['pytyful] adj. litościwy;
żałosny; nędzny
pitiless ['pytylys] adj. bezlitosny
pity ['pyty] s. litość;
współczucie; szkoda; v.
litować się; współczuć;
żałować kogoś
pivot ['pywet] s. czop; oś;
ośrodek; v. obracać się jak
na osi
pivotal ['pywetel] s. adj.
centralny; kardynalny;
kluczowy; decydujący
placard ['plaeka:rd] s. afisz;
plakat; [ple'ka:rd] v. rozlepiać
plakaty
place [plejs] s. miejsce;
miejscowość; plac; ulica;
dom; mieszkanie; zakład;
krzesło; posada; v.
umieszczać; położyć;
ulokować; dać stanowisko;
pokładać; powierzyć;
określać
placid ['plaesyd] adj. łagodny;
spokojny
plagiarism ['plejdżje,ryzem] s.
plagiat; popełnienie plagiatu
plague [plejg] s. plaga; dżuma;
zaraza; v. dręczyć
plaice [plejs] s. płastuga
pospolita
plaid [plaed] s. sukno; pled w
kratę; rysunek w kratę

plain [plejn] adj. wyraźny;
prosty; gładki; szczery; płaski;
równy; adv. jasno; szczerze;
s. równina

plainclothes man ['plejn,kloźmen]
s. tajny policjant

plaintiff ['plejntyf] s. powód
(zaskarżający); powódka

plaintive ['plejntyw] adj. żałosny;
płaczliwy

plait [plejt] s. plecionka;
warkocz; fałda; zakładka; v.
pleść; splatać; fałdować

plan [plaen] s. plan; v.
planować; zamierzać

plane [plejn] s. płaszczyzna;
równina; poziom; samolot; płat
(skrzydła); strug; wiórnik;
gładzik; platan (owoc); v.
ślizgać; ześlizgiwać się;
heblować

planet ['plaenyt] s. planeta

plank ['plaenk] s. deska; tarcica;
punkt programu (politycznego
w USA); v. pokrywać
deskami

plank down ['plaenk,daln] v.
wybulić gotówkę

plant ['pla:nt] s. roślina;
fabryka; zakład; wtyczka;
(slang) oszustwo; włamanie;
kant; v. zasadzać; zakładać;
umieszczać; pozorować;
ukrywać; wtykać; sadzić
(rośliny)

plantation [plaen'tejszyn] s.
plantacja

planter ['pla:nter] s. plantator;
maszyna do sadzenia;
skrzynka na kwiaty

plaque [plaek] s. tablica
(pamiątkowa); odznaka

plaster ['pla:ster] s. tynk;
wyprawa wapienna;
przylepiec; v. tynkować;
wyprawiać; powlekać;
zalepiać; oblepiać

plaster cast ['pla:ster,ka:st] s.
odlew gipsowy; opatrunek
gipsowy

plaster of Paris ['pla:ster of
'paerys] s. gips

plastic ['plaestyk] s. plastyk;

sztuczne tworzywo; adj.
plastyczny; giętki

plastics ['plaestyks] s. tworzywa
sztuczne

plate [plejt] s. talerz; danie;
płyta; taca; tafla; v.
platerować; opancerzać

platform ['plaet,fo:rm] s.
platforma; podium; trybuna;
rampa; program polityczny

platinum ['plaetynem] s. platyna

platter ['plaeter] s. półmisek

plausible ['plo:zebl] adj. pozornie
słuszny, prawdziwy, uczciwy;
obłudnie przymilny

play [plej] s. gra; zabawa;
sztuka; v. grać; bawić się;
zagrać; udawać

play back ['plej,baek] v.
reprodukować; przegrywać

playboy ['plej,boj] s. lekkoduch

player ['plejer] s. gracz; muzyk;
aktor; zawodnik

playful ['plejful] adj. wesoły;
żartobliwy; figlarny; filuterny;
swawolny; rozbawiony;
zabawny; rozbrykany;
ożywiony

playground ['plej,graund] s.
boisko; park

playhouse ['plej,haus] s. teatr

playmate ['plej,mejt] s.
towarzysz zabaw (dziecinnych,
intymnych)

play-off ['plejof] s. rozgrywka
poremisowa

play off ['plej,of] v. rozgrywać
partię poremisową

plaything ['plejtyng] s. zabawka

playwright ['plej,rajt] s.
dramaturg

plea [pli:] s. usprawiedliwienie;
wywód; apel; prośba

plead [pli:d] v. bronić; błagać;
powoływać się

plead guilty ['pli:d'gylty] v.
przyznawać się do winy

pleasant ['plesnt] s. przyjemny;
miły; wesoły

please [pli:z] v. podobać się;
zadowalać

please! [pli:z] v. proszę

pleased [plizd] adj. zadowolony

pleasing ['pli:zyng] adj.
przyjemny; miły
pleasure ['pleżer] s.
przyjemność; adj.
rozrywkowy
pleat [pli:t] s. fałda; v. plisować
pledge [pledż] v. zobowiązywać
(się); zastawiać; s. zastaw;
gwarancja; przyrzeczenie
plenipotentiary [,plenype
'tenszery] s. pełnomocnik; adj.
pełnomocny
plentiful ['plentyful] adj. obfity;
liczny
plenty ['plenty] s. obfitość;
mnóstwo; adv. zupełnie; aż
nadto; adj. obfity; liczny;
obszerny
pliable ['plajebl] adj. giętki
pliers ['plajerz] pl. szczypce
plight [plajt] s. trudności; stan;
położenie; przyrzeczenie; v.
ręczyć; dawać słowo
plod [plod] v. mozolić się;
ślęczeć; s. harowanie; kucie
plod along ['plod,e'long] v. wlec
się; mozolić się; trudzić się
plot [plot] s. osnowa; fabuła;
spisek; działka; wykres; mapa;
v. knuć; spiskować; nanosić
na mapę; planować; dzielić
plough [plau] s. pług; v. orać
plow [plau] s. pług; v. orać
plowshare ['plau-szeer] s.
lemiesz
pluck [plak] v. wyrwać;
zerwać; szarpnąć
pluck up courage ['plak,ap
'karydż] exp.: zdobyć się na
odwagę
plucky ['plaky] adj. śmiały;
odważny
plug [plag] s. czop; zatyczka;
kurek; reklama; świeca
(silnika); v. zatykać
plug up ['plag,ap] v. zatykać
plum [plam] s. śliwka; rodzynka;
gratka; adv. pionowo
plumage ['plu:mydż] s.
upierzenie
plumb [plam] adj. pionowy;
zupełny; adv. pionowo;
prosto; dokładnie; zupełnie; s.

pion murarski; sonda; v.
pionować; sondować
plumber ['plamer] s. hydraulik
plumbing ['plambyng] s.
instalacja wodociągowo-
ściekowa budynku
plume [plu:m] s. pióro;
pióropusz; v. ozdabiać
piórami; czyścić pióra
plummet ['plamyt] s. pion
murarski; v. spadać pionowo
plump [plamp] adj. pulchny; tęgi;
stanowczy; otwarty; v.
tuczyć; tyć; wypełniać (się);
ciężko upaść; upuścić;
rzucić; popierać w wyborach
masowym głosowaniem; adv.
prosto; nagle; ciężko; s.
upadek
plum pudding ['plam'pudyng] s.
budyń świąteczny
plunder ['plander] s. grabież;
rabunek; łup; v. plądrować;
łupić grabić
plunge [plandż] v. pogrążać
(się); zanurzać (się);
wpadać; spadać; s. skok do
wody; pływalnia
plunk [plank] v. brząkać;
wybulić; ciskać; rzucać;
upaść ciężko; szarpać
(struny); strzelić do kogoś;
s. brzęk; adv. z brzękiem;
prościutko; s. sl. dolar
pluperfect ['plu:pe:rfykt] adj.
zaprzeszły; s. czas zaprzeszły;
plusquamperfectum
plural ['pluerel] s. liczba mnoga;
adj. pluralny; mnogi
plus [plas] prep. plus; więcej;
adj. dodatni; dodatkowy; s.
znak plus; dodatek
plush [plasz] s. plusz; adj.
pluszowy; okazały
ply [plaj] v. uprawiać gorliwie;
używać czegoś; zasypywać
(np. pytaniami); kursować po
...; s. warstwa; grubość;
skłonność; pasmo
plywood ['plaj,łud] s. sklejka;
dykta
pneumatic [nju'maetyk] adj.
pneumatyczny

pneumonia [nju'mounje] s.
zapalenie płuc
poach [poucz] v. uprawiać
kłusownictwo; grzęznąć;
rozrabiać; udeptywać;
rozmiękać; gotować jajko na
miękko bez skorupki
poached egg ['pauczt,eg] s. jajko
gotowane na miękko bez
skorupki
poacher ['pouczer] s. kłusownik
pocket ['pokyt] s. kieszeń;
dziura (powietrzna); v.
wkładać do kieszeni
pocketbook ['pokyt,buk] s.
portfel
pocketknife ['pokyt,najf] s.
scyzoryk
pocket money ['pokyt,many] s.
kieszonkowe
pod [pod] s. strączek; kokon;
stadko; obsada; v. rodzić
strączki; łuszczyć; spędzać
razem
poem [pouim] s. wiersz; poemat
poet [pouyt] s. poeta
poetess ['pouytys] s. poetka
poetic [pou'etyk] adj. poetyczny;
poetycki; poetycznie piękny
poetry ['pouytry] s. poezja
pogrom ['pougrem, pe'grom] s.
pogrom
poignant ['pojnent] adj.
przejmujący; uszczypliwy;
cięty; ostry; dotkliwy;
wzruszający
point [point] s. punkt; ostry
koniec; szpiczaste narzędzie;
przylądek; kropka; pointa;
cecha; sedno; sens; v.
zaostrzać; celować;
wskazywać; punktować;
kropkować; dowodzić;
dążyć; pokazywać
point at ['point,aet] v.
wycelować; wskazać
point of view ['point,ow'wju:] s.
punkt widzenia
point out ['point,aut] v.
wskazywać; uwydatnić
point to ['point,tu] v. wskazać
kierunek (kogoś, coś)
pointed ['pointyd] adj. spiczasty;

ostry; cięty; zjadliwy
point-blank ['point'blaenk] adj.
(strzelać) na wprost;
bezpośredni;
bezceremonialny; bez ogródek;
adv. bezpośrednio; z bliska;
wprost; bez ogródek; w
prostej linii; bez zastanowienia
się
pointer ['pointer] s. wskaźnik;
wskazówka
pointless ['poyntlys] adj. tępy;
bez sensu; bez znaczenia
poise [pojz] s. równowaga;
postawa; swoboda; stan
zawieszenia; stan
niepewności; v.
równoważyć; ważyć w
rękach; zawisnąć w
powietrzu; być
przygotowanym do ataku
poison ['pojzn] s. trucizna; v.
truć; zatruć; zakazić
poisonous ['pojznes] adj. trujący;
jadowity; szkodliwy
poke [pouk] v. wtykać;
wpychać; szturchać;
dłubać; sterczeć; wtrącać
się; plątać
poker ['pouker] s. pogrzebacz;
poker
polar ['pouler] adj. polarny
polar bear ['pouler beer] s. biały
niedźwiedź
Pole [poul] s. Polka; Polak
pole [poul] s. biegun; słup;
żerdź; dyszel; maszt
pole jump ['poul dżamp] s. skok
o tyczce
police [pe'li:s] s. policja; v.
rządzić; pilnować;
utrzymywać porządek
policeman [pe'li:smen] s.
policjant
police officer [pe'li:s,ofyser] s.
policjant
police station [pe'li:s,stejszyn] s.
komisariat
policewoman [pe'li:s,łumen] s.
policjantka
policy ['polysy] s. polityka
rządzenia; polityka
postępowania; mądrość

polityczna; polisa
ubezpieczeniowa
polio ['pouljou] s. polimyelitis
[,poliou,maje'lajtis] paraliż
dziecięcy; choroba Haine-
Medina
Polish ['poulysz] adj. polski
(język, obywatel etc.)
polish ['polysz] v. polerować;
gładzić; pochlebiać;
nabierać połysku; s. pasta (do
butów); połysk; politura; polor
polite [pe'lajt] adj. grzeczny;
uprzejmy; kulturalny
politeness [pe'lajtnys] s.
grzeczność; ogłada; kultura;
uprzejmość
political [pe'lytykel] adj.
polityczny
politician [,poly'tyszyn] s.
polityk; politykier
politics ['polytyks] s. polityka
poll [poul] s. głosowanie;
rejestrowanie głosów; wyniki
głosowania; lista; wykaz; lokal
wyborczy; urny wyborcze;
ankieta; głowa; tył głowy;
obuch; v. oddawać głosy;
obliczać głosy; rejestrować;
dostawać głosy; strzyc
włosy; obcinać rogi
pollen ['polyn] s. pył kwiatowy
pollute [pe'lju:t] v.
zanieczyszczać; skazić
pollution [pe'lju:szyn] s.
skażenie; zanieczyszczenie
pomp [pomp] s. pompa
pompous ['pompes] adj.
napuszony; nadęty;
pompatyczny
pond [pond] s. staw
ponder ['ponder] v. rozważać;
rozmyślać; przemyśliwać;
dumać; zastanawiać się;
zadumać się
ponderous ['ponderes] adj.
ciężki; niezgrabny
pontoon [pon'tu:n] s. ponton
pony ['pouny] s. kuc; bryk; v.
odpisywać; ściągać;
zrzynać
poodle ['pu:dl] s. pudel (pies)
pool [pu:l] s. kałuża; sadzawka;

pływalnia; v. składać się
razem; zbierać się w grupę
poor [puer] adj. biedny; ubogi;
lichy; marny; słaby; kiepski;
nędzny; skromny
poorhouse ['puer,haus] s.
przytułek
poorly ['puerly] adv. licho;
kiepsko; skąpo; skromnie;
biednie; ubogo; adj. niezdrów
pop [pop] s. trzask; puknięcie;
strzał; napój musujący;
lombard; tatuś (slang); v.
strzelać; pukać; nagle
wyrzucać; nagle wsadzać;
skakać; wściekać się
popcorn ['pop,ke:rn] s. sucha
prażona kukurydza
pop in ['pop,yn] v. wskoczyć
pop out ['pop,aut] v.
wyskoczyć
pope [poup] s. papież
poplar ['popler] s. topola
poppy ['popy] s. mak
popular ['popjuler] adj. ludowy;
rozpowszechniony; popularny
(tani)
popularity [,popju'laeryty] s.
popularność
populate ['popjulejt] v. zaludniać
population ['popjulejszyn] s.
ludność
populous ['popjules] adj. ludny;
gęsto zaludniony
porch [po:rcz] s. weranda;
ganek; portyk
porcupine ['po:rkjupajn] s. jeż;
jeżozwierz; kolczatka
pore [po:r] v. rozmyślać;
ślęczeć; wpatrywać się; s.
por (skóry)
pore over ['po:r,ouwer] v.
rozmyślać nad czymś;
ślęczeć (nad książką);
zagłębiać się
pork [po:rk] s. wieprzowina
porous ['po:res] adj. porowaty
porpoise ['po:rpes] s. morświn;
ssak morski
porridge ['porydż] s. owsianka
port [po:rt] s. port; przystań;
otwór; otwór ładunkowy;
postawa; trzymanie się;

prezentowanie (broni); wino porto; lewa burta; sterowanie w lewo

portable ['po:rtebl] adj. przenośny; polowy

porter ['po:rter] s. tragarz; kolejarz od sypialnego wagonu

portion ['po:rszyn] s. część; porcja; udział; posag; los; v. dzielić; przydzielać

portion out ['po:rszyn,aut] v. wydzielać; wyposażać

portly ['po:rtly] adj. dostojny; godny; tęgi; postawny; okazały

portrait ['po:rtryt] s. portret

pose [pouz] v. pozować; upozować; stawiać (np. problem); kłopotać (zapytaniem); s. poza

posh [posz] adj. elegancki; szykowny; v. wyelegantować się

position [pe'zyszyn] s. położenie; stanowisko; postawa; twierdzenie; umieszczenie; v. umieszczać; ulokować

positive ['pozetyw] adj. pozytywny; stanowczy; ustanowiony; zupełny; dodatni; pozytywistyczny; s. znak dodatni; wartość dodatnia; pozytyw

possess [pe'zes] v. posiadać; opanować; opętać; przepajać

possessed [pe'zest] adj. opętany

possession [pe'zeszyn] s. posiadanie; posiadłość; własność; dobytek; opanowanie

possessor [pe'zeser] s. posiadacz; właściciel

possibility [pose'bylyty] s. możliwość; możność; ewentualność

possible ['posebl] adj. możliwy; ewentualny

possibly ['posebly] adv. może; w ogóle możliwe; możliwie

post [poust] s. słup; posada; posterunek; poczta; v. ogłaszać; wywieszać;

zalepiać plakatami

postage ['poustydż] s. opłata pocztowa

postage stamp ['poustydż ,staemp] s. znaczek pocztowy

postal ['poustel] adj. pocztowy

postal order ['poustel'o:rder] s. przekaz pocztowy

postcard ['poust,ka:rd] s. pocztówka

post code ['poust,koud] = zip--code [,zyp'koud] pocztowy numer kierunkowy

poste restante ['poust'resta:nt] s. list lub przesyłka do odebrania na poczcie

poster ['pouster] s. plakat

posterity [po'teryty] s. potomność

post-free ['poust'fri:] adj. wolny od opłaty pocztowej

posthumous ['post,jumes] adj. pośmiertny

postman ['poustmen] s. listonosz

postmark ['poust,ma:rk] s. stempel pocztowy

postmaster ['poust,ma:ster] s. naczelnik poczty

post office ['poust,ofys] s. poczta

post office box ['poust,ofys 'boks] s. skrytka pocztowa

postpaid ['poust,pejd] s. opłata pocztowa z góry uiszczona

postpone [poust'poun] v. odłożyć; odroczyć; odwlekać

postscript ['pous,skrypt] s. dopisek; postscriptum

posture ['posczer] s. postawa; stan; położenie; v. przybrać postawę; pozować

postwar ['poust'ło:r] adj. powojenny

posy ['pouzy] s. bukiet

pot [pot] s. garnek; imbryk; czajnik; nocnik; doniczka; wazonik; rondel; dzban; kocioł; kufel; słój; puchar; więcierz; łuza; szklanka; haszysz; v. wsadzać do garnka; polować; strzelać

potato [po'tejtou] s. ziemniak

potent ['potent] adj. potężny;
skuteczny; jurny
potion ['pouszyn] s. dawka;
napój
potter ['poter] s. garncarz; v.
grzebać się; włóczyć się;
łazić
potter about ['poter,e'baut] v.
włóczyć się
pottery ['potery] s. wyroby
gancarskie; gancarstwo
potty ['poty] adj. marny; lichy;
błahy; łatwy; stuknięty;
pomylony; zbzikowany
pouch [paucz] s. worek; torba;
brzuszysko; ładownica;
sakiewka; v. nadawać formę
worka; łykać
poulterer ['poulterer] s. handlarz
drobiu
poultice ['poultys] s. okład; v.
kłaść okład
poultry ['poultry] s. drób
pounce [pauns] s. szpon; nagły
atak z góry; v. rzucać się na
coś; trybować;
pumeksować; posypywać
(rysunek) proszkiem
(kolorowym)
pound [paund] s. funt (pieniądz,
waga); stuk; tupot; uderzenie;
tłuczenie; walnięcie;
ogrodzenie; magazyn; areszt;
v. tłuc; walić; tupać;
biegać; więzić; zamykać
pour [po:r] v. wysypać;
posypać; lać; polać; wylać;
rozlać; nalać
pour out ['po:r,aut] v. wysypać;
wylać
pout [paut] v. dąsać się;
wydymać; s. wydęcie warg;
kwaśna mina
poverty ['powerty] s. bieda;
ubóstwo
powder ['pałder] s. proch; pył;
puder; proszek; v.
posypywać; pudrować;
proszkować
powder room ['pałder,ru:m] s.
toaleta damska
power ['pałer] s. potęga; moc;
energia; siła; własność;

władza; mocarstwo; v.
napędzać; wspomagać;
dostarczać energii
power brake ['pałer,brejk] s.
serwohamulec; wspomagany
hamulec
powerful ['pałerful] adj. potężny;
mocny
powerless ['pałerlys] adj.
bezsilny
power plant ['pałer,plaent] s.
siłownia
power station ['pałer,stejszyn] s.
elektrownia
powwow ['pał,łał] v. naradzać
się co do taktyki; leczyć; s.
sejmik Indian; odprawa
oficerska; czarownik indiański
practicable ['praektykebl] adj.
wykonalny; możliwy do
przeprowadzenia
practical ['praektykel] adj.
praktyczny
practice ['praektys] s. praktyka;
ćwiczenie; v. praktykować;
uprawiać; ćwiczyć
practise ['praektys] v. = practice
practitioner [praek'tyszener] s.
zawodowiec; praktykujący
lekarz
prairie ['preery] s. preria
praise [prejz] s. pochwała; v.
chwalić; sławić
praiseworthy ['prejz,łe:rsy] adj.
chwalebny; godny pochwały
pram [praem] s. ręczny wózek
prance [praens] v. stawać dęba;
tańczyć; paradować;
hasać; kazać koniowi
stawać dęba
prank [praenk] s. psota; figiel; v.
wystroić; popisywać się
prattle ['praetl] v. paplać; s.
paplanina
prawn ['pro:n] s. krewetka; v.
łowić krewetki
pray [prej] v. modlić się;
prosić; błagać
prayer ['prejer] s. modlitwa;
prośba
prayer book ['prejer,buk] s.
modlitewnik; książka do
nabożeństwa

pre- [pri:-] prefix. przed-; z góry
preach [pri:cz] v. głosić; kazać; wygłaszać
preacher [pri:czer] s. kaznodzieja; pastor
precarious [pry'keeries] adj. niepewny; nieubezpieczony; dowolny
precaution [pry'ko:szyn] s. przezorność; środek ostrożności
precede [pry:'si:d] v. poprzedzać; mieć pierwszeństwo
precedence [pry'si:dens] s. pierwszeństwo; nadrzędność
precedent [pry'si:dent] adj. uprzedni; poprzedzający
precedent ['presydent] s. precedens
precept ['pry:sept] s. nakaz; przykazanie; nauka moralna; reguła
precinct ['pry:synkt] s. okrąg (wyborczy); obręb; granice
precious ['preszes] adj. drogi; cenny; afektowany; wyszukany; wspaniały; adv. bardzo; niezwykle
precipice ['presypys] s. przepaść
precipitate [pry'sypytejt] s. opad; osad; v. przyspieszać (zdarzenia); skraplać (się); rzucać; spadać
precipitation [pry,sypy'tejszyn] s. opady; przyspieszanie; pochopność; upadek; strącanie
precipitous [pry'sypytes] adj. przepaścisty; spadzisty
precis ['prejsi:] s. skrót; v. robić skrót
precise [pry'sajs] adj. dokładny; wyraźny; v. precyzować; wyszczególniać
precision [pry'syżyn] s. precyzja; dokładność
precocious [pry'kouszes] adj. przedwczesny; przedwcześnie rozwinięty; kwitnący
preconceived ['pry:ken'si:wd]

adj. uprzedzony do; powzięty z góry
predatory ['predetery] adj. łupieżczy; grabieżczy; drapieżny
predecessor ['pry:dyseser] s. poprzednik; przodek
predetermine ['pry:dy'te:rmyn] v. z góry ustanowić; z góry określić; z góry zadecydować
predicament [pry'dykement] s. kłopot; kłopotliwe położenie
predicate ['predy,kejt] v. opierać się na czymś; łączyć się z czymś; przypisywać czemuś; orzekać o czymś; mieścić pojęcie czegoś; ['predykt] s. cecha; orzecznik; adj. orzeczeniowy; dopełnienie orzeczenia
predict [pry'dykt] v. przepowiadać
prediction [pry'dykszyn] s. przepowiednia
predisposition ['pri:dyspe,zyszyn] s. skłonność; predyspozycja
predominant [pry'domynent] adj. przeważający; panujący; górujący
predominate [pry'domynejt] v. górować; przewyższać
preface ['prefys] s. przedmowa; wstęp
prefect ['pry:fekt] s. prefekt
prefer [pry'fe:r] v. woleć; przedkładać; dawać awans
preferable ['preferebl] adj. lepszy
preferably ['preferebly] adv. raczej
preference ['preferens] s. pierwszeństwo; uprzywilejowanie; możność wyboru; rzecz bardziej lubiana, upodobana
preferment [pry'fe:rment] s. wybór; awans
prefix ['pry:fyks] s. przedrostek; prefiks; tytuł przed nazwiskiem; v. umieszczać przedrostek; umieszczać na wstępie
pregnancy ['pregnensy] s. ciąża

pregnant ['pregnent] adj.
brzemienny; doniosły;
sugestywny; płodny; ciężarna
(kobieta)
prejudice ['predżudys] s.
uprzedzenie; szkoda; v.
uprzedzać się do kogoś;
szkodzić (komuś);
rozpowszechniać uprzedzenie
prejudiced ['predżudyst] adj.
uprzedzony; mający
uprzedzenie
preliminary [pry'lymynery] adj.
wstępny; przygotowawczy; s.
wstęp
prelude ['prelju:d] s. wstęp;
preludium; v. grać preludium;
dawać wstęp do czegoś
premature [,preme'tjuer] adj.
przedwczesny; przedwcześnie
dojrzały
premeditate [pry'medy,tejt] v.
obmyślać; rozważać
premier ['premjer] adj. pierwszy;
najważniejszy; premier; prezes
rady ministrów
premises ['premysys] pl. lokal;
obejście
premium ['pri:mjem] s. nagroda;
premia
preoccupied [pry:'okju,pajd] adj.
pochłonięty; zaabsorbowany
preparation [,prepe'rejszyn] s.
przygotowywanie;
przyrządzanie
prepare [pry'peer] v.
przygotowywać (się);
szykować (się); przyrządzać
prepay ['pry'pej] v. opłacać z
góry
preposition [,prepe'zyszyn] s.
przyimek
prepossess [,pry:po'zes] v.
wpoić; usposobić; natchnąć
prepossessing [prype'zesyng]
adj. miły; sympatyczny
preposterous [pry'posteres] adj.
niedorzeczny; absurdalny
prerequisite [pry'rekłyzyt] adj. &
s. (warunek) wstępny;
podstawowy
prescribe [prys'krajb] v.
przepisać; nakazać;

zaordynować
prescription [prys'krypszyn] s.
nakaz; przepis; recepta
presence ['presens] v.
obecność
presence of mind
['prezens,ow'majnd] v.
przytomność umysłu
present ['preznt] s. upominek;
prezent; teraźniejszość; adj.
obecny; niniejszy;
teraźniejszy; v. stawiać się;
nadarzyć się
present tense ['presnt,tens] s.
czas teraźniejszy
presentation [,prezen'tejszyn] s.
przedstawienie; ofiarowanie;
podarek; darowanie;
przedłożenie
presentiment [pry'zentyment] s.
przeczucie
presently ['prezently] adv.
wkrótce; niebawem; zaraz
preservation [,preze:r'wejszyn] s.
zachowanie; ochrona;
zabezpieczenie
preserve [pry'ze:rw] v.
zachowywać; chronić;
przechowywać;
konserwować; ochraniać; s.
konserwa; rezerwat
preside [pry'zajd] v.
przewodniczyć
president ['prezydent] s.
prezydent
press [pres] s. prasa; dzienniki;
tłocznia; druk; drukarnia;
nacisk; tłok; ścisk; pośpiech;
v. cisnąć; ściskać;
przyciskać; ciążyć;
pracować; naglić; narzucać;
wciskać; tłoczyć
press in ['pres-yn] v. wciskać
pressing ['presyng] adj. naglący;
natarczywy
pressure ['preszer] s. ciśnienie;
napór; parcie
prestige [pres'ty:dż] s. prestiż
(szacunek i uznanie)
presumable [pry'zju:mebl] adj.
przypuszczalny
presume [pry'zju:m] v.
przypuszczać;

wykorzystywać (kogoś);
ośmielać się
presumedly [pry'zju:mydly] adv.
przypuszczalnie
presuming [pry'zju:my̱ng] adj.
zarozumiały
presumption [pry'zampszen] s.
przypuszczenie; założenie;
zarozumiałość
presumptuous [pry'zamptjues]
adj. zarozumiały
presuppose [pry'se:pouz] v.
przypuszczać; zakładać z
góry; stawiać warunek
pretend [pry'tend] v. udawać;
pretendować
pretender [pry'tender] s.
pretendent
pretense [pry'tens] s. udawanie;
pozór; pretensja;
pretensjonalność
pretension [pry'tenszyn] s.
aspiracje; roszczenie;
pretensjonalność; pretensja
preterite ['preteryt] adj. przeszły;
s. czas przeszły
pretext ['pry:tekst] s. pretekst;
pozór
pretext [pry'tekst] v. wymawiać
się; powoływać się
pretty ['pryty] adj. ładny; adv.
dość; dosyć
prevail [pry'wejl] v. przeważać;
brać górę; przekonać;
panować (np. zwyczaj)
prevalent ['prewelent] adj.
panujący; przeważający
prevent [pry'went] v. zapobiec;
powstrzymywać
prevention [pry'wenszyn] s.
zapobieganie; środek
zapobiegający
preventive [pry'wentyw] adj.
zapobiegawczy; prewencyjny
previous ['pry:wjes] adj.
poprzedni; wcześniejszy od
...; przedwczesny; nagły;
pochopny
previous to ['pry:wjes,tu] adv.
przed czymś
previously ['pry:wjesly] adv.
wcześniej
prewar ['pri:'ło:r] adj.

przedwojenny
prey [prej] s. zdobycz; łup;
ofiara; v. grabić; trawić
price [prajs] s. cena; koszt; v.
wyceniać
priceless ['prajslys] adv.
bezcenny; nieoceniony
prick [pryk] s. ukłucie; (wulg.)
penis; v. kłuć; przekłuwać
prick up one's ears
[pryk,ap'łans,eerz] v.
nadstawiać uszu; postawić
uszy
prickle ['prykl] s. kolec; cierń; v.
ukłuć; jeżyć się
prickly ['prykly] adj. kolczasty
pride [prajd] s. duma; pycha;
ambicja; chluba; v. być
dumnym z czegoś; chełpić
się; pysznić się
priest [pri:st] s. kapłan;
duchowny
prim [prym] adj. sztywny;
pedantyczny; sztuczny;
wyszukany; przesadny
primarily ['prajmeryly] adv.
głównie; przede wszystkim
primary ['prajmery] adj. główny;
zasadniczy; pierwotny; s.
wybór kandydatów (USA)
primary school ['prajmery,sku:l]
s. szkoła podstawowa
prime ['prajm] adj. pierwszy;
najważniejszy; główny; v.
przygotować
prime minister ['prajm-'mynyster]
s. premier
primer ['prajmer] s. elementarz;
podręcznik (elementarny)
primitive ['prymytyw] adj.
prymitywny; pierwotny
primrose ['prymrous] s.
pierwiosnek
prince ['pryns] s. książę
princess [pryn'ses] s. księżna;
księżniczka
principal ['prynsepel] adj.
główny; s. kierownik;
zleceniodawca; kapitał;
sprawca
principality [prynsy'paelyty] s.
księstwo
principle ['prynsepl] s. zasada;

reguła; podstawa; źródło;
składnik

prink [pry<u>nk</u>] v. stroić się;
muskać się

print [prynt] s. ślad; odcisk;
druk; pismo; fotka; v.
wycisnąć; wytłoczyć;
wydrukować; być w druku;
drukować się; odbić

printed matter ['prynted'maeter]
v. druki; materiały drukowane

printer ['prynter] s. drukarz

printing ['prynty<u>ng</u>] s. druk;
drukowanie; nakład; a.
drukarski

printing ink ['prynty<u>ng</u>,y<u>nk</u>] s.
farba drukarska

printing office ['prynty<u>n</u>,ofys] s.
drukarnia

prior ['prajer] adj. wcześniejszy;
ważniejszy; s. przeor

prior to ['prajer,tu] adv. przed
czymś; wcześniej od
czegoś

priority ['praj'oryty] s.
pierwszeństwo;
starszeństwo; priorytet

prison ['pryzn] s. więzienie

prisoner ['pryzner] s. więzień

privacy ['prajwesy] s.
odosobnienie; samotność;
utrzymanie w dyskrecji
(tajemnicy); życie prywatne,
intymne, osobiste

private ['prajwyt] adj. prywatny;
tajny; ukryty; s. szeregowiec;
(private parts = genitalia)

private hotel ['prajwyt,hou'tel] s.
pensjonat

privation [praj'wejszyn] s.
prywacja; niedostatek

privilege ['prywylydż] s.
przywilej; prawdziwa
satysfakcja

privileged ['prywylydżd] adj.
uprzywilejowany; zaszczycony

prize [prajz] v. podważyć;
zajmować; cenić; s. nagroda;
premia; wygrana; łup; a.
kapitalny

prizefighter ['prajz,fajter] s.
zawodowy bokser

prizewinner ['prajz,łyner] s.

laureat; zdobywca nagrody

pro [prou] s. zawodowiec
(slang); adv. za; dla; prep. pro
(forma etc.)

probability [proba'bylyty] s.
prawdopodobieństwo; widoki;
szanse

probable ['probebl] adj.
prawdopodobny; wiarygodny;
mający szanse

probation [pro'bejszyn] s. okres
próbny; próba; zawieszenie
kary

probe [proub] s. sonda; v.
sondować; zagłębiać się;
badać w śledztwie

problem ['problem] s. problem;
zadanie; zagadnienie; a.
problemowy

procedure [pre'si:dżer] s.
postępowanie; procedura
(sądowa)

proceed [pre'si:d] v. iść dalej;
postępować; kontynuować;
zaskarżać

proceed from [pre'si:d,from] v.
wychodzić z ...; iść dalej z
...

proceedings [pre'si:dy<u>ng</u>s] pl.
sprawozdanie (z sesji etc.)

proceeds ['prosi:dz] pl. zysk;
dochody; przychód (ze
sprzedaży)

process ['prouses] s. przebieg;
proces; postęp; v. obrabiać;
przerabiać; załatwiać;
procesować; poddawać
procesowi; mleć

procession [pre'seszyn] s.
pochód; procesja;
kontynuowanie; prowadzenie
dalej; dalszy rozwój

proclaim [pre'klejm] v.
proklamować; ogłaszać;
zakazywać; wskazywać;
wprowadzać ograniczenia

proclamation [,prokle'majszyn] s.
proklamacja; obwieszczenie

procrastinate [pre'kraesty,nejt] v.
zwlekać; odkładać na
później

procure [pre'kjuer] v. postarać
się; stręczyć do nierządu

prodigal ['prodygel] adj.
marnotrawny; s. marnotrawca;
utracjusz
prodigious [pre'dydżes] adj.
niezwykły; cudowny; olbrzymi
prod [prod] v. szturchać; kłuć;
drażnić; popędzać; s.
dźgnięcie; bodziec; szpikulec
prodigy ['prodydży] s. dziwo;
cud; genialne dziecko etc.
produce ['produ:s] s. produkty;
plony; wynik; produkcja;
wydajność; wydobycie;
produkty rolne
produce [pre'dju:s] v.
wytwarzać; produkować;
dostarczać; wydobywać;
wystawiać; okazywać
producer ['produ:ser] s.
wytwórca (filmowy);
producent
product ['predakt] s. produkt;
wynik; iloczyn; wytwór
(natury etc.)
production [pre'dakszyn] s.
wytwórczość; wydobycie;
produkcja; utwór; produkty; a.
produkcyjny
productive [pre'daktyw] adj.
wydajny; produktywny;
produkcyjny; urodzajny; żyzny
profess [pre'fes] v. twierdzić;
zapewniać; udawać;
wyznawać; uprawiać
(zawód); być profesorem
professed [pre'fest] adj. jawny;
rzekomy; zawodowy
profession [pre'feszyn] s. zawód;
wyznanie; zapewnienie;
oświadczenie; śluby zakonne
professional [pre'feszenl] s.
zawodowiec; adj. zawodowy;
fachowy; należący do
wolnego zawodu
professor [pre'feser] s. profesor;
wyznawca; nauczyciel (tańca)
proficiency [pre'fyszensy] s.
biegłość; sprawność
proficient [pre'fyszent] adj.
biegły; sprawny; s. mistrz;
biegły; znający (obcy język);
fachowiec
profile ['proufajl] s. profil; szkic

biograficzny; v. przedstawiać
z profilu; profilować
profit ['profyt] s. zysk; dochód;
korzyść; pożytek; v.
korzystać; być korzystnym;
przydawać się; mieć zyski
profitable ['profytebl] adj.
korzystny; intratny; zyskowny
profiteer [,profy'tier] v.
paskować; spekulować; s.
paskarz; spekulant (na
czarnym rynku etc.)
profound [pro'faund] adj.
głęboki; gruntowny; s.
otchłań
profusion [pro'fju:żyn] s.
obfitość; rozrzutność;
nadmiar
prognoses [prog'nousi:z] pl.
prognozy; rokowania
prognosis [prog'nousys] s.
prognoza; rokowanie
program ['prougraem] s.
program; plan; audycja;
przedstawienie; v. planować
progress ['prougres] s. postęp;
bieg; rozwój; kolejne etapy
etc.
progress [pre'gres] v. robić
postępy; iść naprzód; być
w toku
progressive [pre'gresyw] adj.
postępowy; stopniowy; s.
postępowiec
prohibit [pro'hybyt] v.
zakazywać; zabraniać
prohibition [,prouy'byszyn] s.
zakaz; prohibicja
project ['prodżekt] s. projekt;
plan; przedsięwzięcie;
schemat
project [pro'dżekt] v.
projektować; miotać;
rzutować; sterczeć;
wystawać; wyświetlać (na
ekranie)
projection [pro'dżekszyn] s. rzut;
planowanie; projektowanie;
rzutowanie; wystawanie;
projekcja; wyświetlanie
projector [pro'dżekter] s. rzutnik;
aparat projekcyjny
proletariat [,proule'teerjet] s.

proletariat; robotnicy przemysłowi

prolific [pre'lyfyk] adj. płodny

prologue ['proulog] s. prolog

prolong [prou'long] v. przedłużać; wydłużać; prolongować (spłaty)

promenade [,promy'nejd] s. przechadzka; przejażdżka; deptak; promenada; v. przechadzać się

prominent ['promynent] adj. wydatny; wybitny; sterczący; wystający; wyróżniający się; sławny

promiscuous [pre'myskjues] adj. mieszany; różnorodny; niewybredny w stosunkach płciowych

promise ['promys] s. obietnica; przyrzeczenie; v. obiecywać; przyrzekać; zaręczać; zapewniać; robić obietnice; zapowiadać się

promising ['promysyng] adj. obiecujący; rokujący nadzieje

promontory ['promento:ry] s. przylądek; wyrostek

promote [pre'mout] s. popierać; promować; awansować; (slang) oszukiwać; kombinować

promoter [pre'mouter] s. organizator; krzewiciel; inspirator

promotion [pre'mouszyn] s. popieranie; ułatwienie; awans; promowanie; lansowanie

prompt [prompt] adj. szybki; natychmiastowy; v. nakłaniać; pobudzać; podpowiadać; suflerować; adv. punktualnie; co do minuty

prompter ['prompter] s. sufler (w teatrze); podżegacz

promptly ['promptly] adv. natychmiast; z miejsca; bezzwłocznie; punktualnie

prone [proun] adj. leżący twarzą w dół; stromy; skłonny

prong [prong] s. ząb (wideł); róg; v. kłuć; przebijać;

zaopatrywać w zęby

pronoun ['prounaun] s. zaimek

pronounce [pre'nauns] v. oświadczać; wymawiać; mieć wymowę; wypowiadać się

pronto ['prontou] adv. (slang) prędko; już; natychmiast; zaraz

pronunciation [pra,nansy'ejszyn] s. wymowa; zapis fonetyczny

proof [pru:f] s. dowód; próba (np. złota); sprawdzian; wypróbowanie; korekta; próbna odbitka; adj. odporny; wypróbowany; sprawdzony; nieprzemakalny

prop(up) ['prop,ap] v. podpierać; s. podpórka; ostoja; oparcie

propagate ['prope,gejt] v. rozmnażać (się); rozszerzać; propagować; przekazywać

propagation [,prope'gejszyn] s. rozmnażanie się; propagowanie

propel [pre'pel] v. napędzać; poruszać; pędzić

propeller [pre'peler] s. śmigło; śruba (okrętowa)

proper ['proper] adj. właściwy; własny; przyzwoity

properly ['properly] adv. właściwie; słusznie; przyzwoicie

property ['property] s. własność; właściwość; cecha; nieruchomość

prophecy ['profysy] s. proroctwo

prophet ['profyt] s. prorok; apostoł

proportion [pre'po:rszyn] s. proporcja; stosunek; rozmiar; część; v. dostosowywać; rozdzielać; dawkować; dozować

proportional [pre'po:rsznl] adj. proporcjonalny (do czegoś)

proposal [pre'pouzel] s. propozycja; projekt; oświadczyny

propose [pre'pouz] v. proponować; przedkładać; zamierzać

proposition [,prope'zyszyn] s.
propozycja; sąd; zagadnienie;
twierdzenie; v. robić
nieprzyzwoite propozycje
proprietary [pre'prajetery] adj.
należący; będący własnością
prywatną; s. właściciel;
własność
proprietor [pre'prajeter] s.
właściciel; posiadacz;
gospodarz
propulsion [pre'palszyn] s.
napęd; bodziec; popędzanie
prose [prouz] s. proza; v. nudzić
prosecute ['prosy,kju:t] v.
ścigać prawnie; prowadzić
(np. studia); nie zaniedbywać;
pilnować
prosecution [,prosy'kju:szyn] s.
oskarżenie
prosecutor ['prosy,kju:ter] s.
prokurator; oskarżyciel
prospect ['prospekt] s. widok;
perspektywa; ewentualny
klient; potencjalne złoża; v.
przeszukiwać (okolice);
próbnie eksploatować
kopalnię; szukać złota etc.;
badać (teren etc.)
prospective [pres'pektyw] adj.
przyszły; ewentualny
prospectus [pres'pektes] s.
prospekt (nowego
przedsiębiorstwa)
prosper ['prosper] v.
prosperować; sprzyjać
powodzeniu
prosperity [pros'peryty] s.
dobrobyt; powodzenie;
koniunktura; pomyślność
prosperous ['prosperes] adj.
mający powodzenie;
kwitnący; pomyślny;
zamożny
prostate [pros'tejt] s. prostata;
gruczoł krokowy
prostitute ['prosty,tu:t] s.
prostytutka; v. prostytuować
(się); adj. wszeteczny;
rozpustny
prostrate ['prostrejt] v. powalić
(np. ze zmęczenia); adj.
leżący twarzą w dół;

powalony; wyczerpany;
bezsilny; kłaniający się;
leżący plackiem
protect [pre'tekt] v. chronić;
bronić; ochraniać;
zabezpieczać
protection [pre'tekszyn] s.
ochrona; opieka; protekcja; list
żelazny; wymuszanie
pieniędzy przez grożenie
gwałtem
protective [pre'tektyw] adj.
ochronny; zapobiegawczy
protector [pre'tekter] s. opiekun;
protektor; ochraniacz
protest [pro'test] v.
protestować; zapewniać;
oponować
protest ['proutest] s. protest
protestant ['protystent] s.
ewangelik; protestant
protestation [proutes'tejszyn] s.
uroczyste zapewnienie;
protest; zaprotestowanie
protocol ['proute,kol] s.
początkowa forma
dokumentu; protokół
dyplomatyczny; etykieta
prototype ['proute,tajp] s.
prototyp; model
protract [pre'traekt] v.
przeciągać; przedłużać;
wystawiać; przedstawiać w
skali
protrude [pre'tru:d] v.
wystawać; wysuwać;
sterczeć
proud [praud] adj. dumny;
napawający dumą; piękny;
szczęśliwy
prove [pru:w] v. udowadniać;
wykazać (się);
uprawomocnić; poddawać
próbie; okazywać się
proverb ['prowe:rb] s.
przysłowie; przypowieść
proverbial [pre'we:rbjel] adj.
przysłowiowy
provide [pre'wajd] v.
zaopatrywać;
przygotowywać; postarać
się; sprzyjać; postanowić;
zaplanować

provide for [pre'wajd,fo:r] v.
zaopatrywać (kogoś)
provided that [pre'wajdyd,daet]
exp.: pod warunkiem że ...; o
ile
providence ['prowydens] s.
opatrzność; oszczędność;
przezorność; skrzętność
province ['prowyns] s.
prowincja; zakres; dziedzina
provincial [pre'wynszel] adj.
zaściankowy; prowincjonalny;
s. człowiek z prowincji
provision [pro'wyżyn] s.
klauzula; dostawa;
przygotowanie się; (pl.)
prowianty; v. prowiantować;
zaopatrywać w żywność;
zaprowiantować
provisional [pro'wyżenl] adj.
prowizoryczny; tymczasowy
provocation [,prowe'kejszyn] s.
prowokacja; rozdrażnienie;
podniecenie; spowodowanie
provocative [pro'woketyw] adj.
prowokujący; zaciekawiający;
drażniący; wyzywający
provoke [pre'wouk] v.
prowokować podniecać;
pobudzać; wywoływać;
podżegać; jątrzyć
prowl [praul] v. grasować; s.
grasowanie (po łup)
proxy ['proksy] s. zastępstwo;
pełnomocnik
prude [pru:d] s. świętoszka
prudence ['pru:dens] s. rozwaga;
roztropność; ostrożność
prudent ['pru:dent] s. rozważny;
roztropny; ostrożny
prudish ['pru:dysz] adj.
pruderyjny; przesadnie
skromny
prune [pru:n] s. śliwka
(suszona); v. obcinać (np.
gałązki); oczyszczać (z
czegoś)
psalm [sa:m] s. psalm
pseudonym ['sju:de,nym] s.
pseudonim; fikcyjne nazwisko
psyche ['sajki:] s. dusza; duch;
umysł (zwierciadło odchylone)
psychiatrist [saj'kajetryst] s.

psychiatra
psychiatry [saj'kajetry] s.
psychiatria
psychological [,sajke'lodżykel]
adj. psychologiczny
psychologist [saj'koledżyst] s.
psycholog
psychology [saj'koledży] s.
psychologia
pub [pab] s. Br. knajpa
puberty ['pju:berty] s.
dojrzałość płciowa
public ['pablyk] s. publiczność;
adj. publiczny; obywatelski
publication [,pably'kejszyn] s.
opublikowanie; ogłoszenie;
publikacja; wydanie książki
public house ['pablyk,haus] s.
szynk; oberża
publicity [pab'lysyty] s. rozgłos;
reklama; a. reklamowy
publish ['pablysz] v.
publikować; wydawać;
ogłaszać; rozgłaszać;
wydawać drukiem
publisher ['pablyszer] s.
wydawca; nakładca
publishing house
['pablyszyng,haus] s. firma
wydawnicza
pudding ['pudyng] s. budyń
puddle ['padl] s. kałuża
puff [paf] v. pykać; sapać;
dmuchać; reklamować;
pudrować; s. puszek;
pyknięcie; dmuchnięcie; blaga
reklamowa; pierzyna; kłąb
dymu; zwój włosów
puff paste ['paf,pejst] s.
francuskie ciasto
puffy ['pafy] adj. dychawiczny;
nadęty; pękaty; napuszony;
otyły; porywisty
pull [pul] v. pociągnąć;
szarpnąć; wyrwać;
wyciągać; przeciągać;
wiosłować; ściągnąć
pull down ['pul,dałn] v.
spuścić; rozbierać (np.
budynek); osłabiać; ściągać
(storę etc.)
pull for ['pul,fo:r] v. popierać
pull in ['pul,yn] v. wciągać

pull off ['pul,of] v. ściągać;
zdobywać; potrafić; zdołać;
stanąć
pull out ['pul,aut] v. wyrwać;
wycofać; s. wycofanie się
pulley ['puli] s. bloczek; blok
krążkowy; v. podnosić
bloczkiem
pullover ['pul,ouwer] s. pulower
pulp [palp] s. miazga; miąższ;
papka; v. rozcierać na miazgę
pulpit ['pulpyt] s. ambona;
kazalnica; kaznodzieja; kazanie
pulpy ['palpy] adj. papkowaty;
miąższowy
pulsate [pal'sejt] v. tętnić;
pulsować; drgać; trząść
się
pulse [pals] s. tętno; puls; v.
tętnić; pulsować
pulverize ['palwerajz] v.
proszkować (się); rozpylać;
ścierać w proch; zemleć na
proch
pump [pamp] v. pompa; lakierek;
v. pompować; pytać
uporczywie
pump gun ['pamp,gan] s.
strzelba (do repetowania)
pumpkin ['pampkyn] s. dynia
pun [pan] s. gra słów
(dwuznacznych); v. robić
kalambury
punch [pancz] s. uderzenie
(pięścią); poncz; przebijak;
krzepa; siła; sztanca; kułak;
rozmach; v. dziurkować;
tłoczyć; walić; szturchać
punctual ['panktjuel] adj.
punktualny; punktowy
punctuate ['panktju,ejt] v.
przestankować; przerywać
punctuation [,panktju'ejszyn] s.
interpunkcja
punctuation mark [,panktju
'ejszyn ma:rk] s. kropka; znak
przestankowy
puncture ['pankczer] s. przebicie;
punkcja; v. przekłuwać;
przedziurawiać; przebić
pungent ['pandżent] adj. kłujący;
ostry; cierpki; zjadliwy;
gryzący; sarkastyczny;

pikantny
punish ['panysz] v. karać; dać
bobu
punishment ['panyszment] s.
kara; sromotna klęska (na
boisku)
pupil ['pju:pl] s. źrenica; uczeń;
wychowanek; małoletni;
niepełnoletni
puppet ['papyt] s. kukiełka;
marionetka; a. kukiełkowy;
marionetkowy
puppet show ['papyt,szou] s.
występy marionetek
puppet state ['papyt,stejt] s.
państwo marionetkowe
puppy ['papy] s. szczenię;
szczeniak; piesek;
zarozumialec
purchase ['pe:rczes] s. zakup;
kupno; dźwignia; v. kupić;
okupić; nabywać; podnosić
(np. kotwicą); sprawiać sobie
purchaser [pe:rczeser] s.
nabywca; kupujący
pure [pjuer] adj. czysty; zupełny;
szczery; niewinny; nie
zepsuty; zwykły; czystej krwi
purgative ['pe:rgetyw] adj.
przeczyszczający; s. środek
na przeczyszczenie
purgatory ['pe:rgetery] s.
czyściec; adj. oczyszczający
purge [pe:rdż] v. przeczyszczać;
oczyścić; usuwać; dawać
na przeczyszczenie;
oczyszczenie; czystka; środek
przeczyszczający; rafinowanie;
klarowanie
purify ['pjuery,faj] v. oczyszczać
(się); klarować; rafinować
purity ['pjueryty] s. czystość
purloin [pe:rloyn] v. okraść;
ściągać; porwać
purple ['pe:rpl] s. purpura; adj.
purpurowy; v. robić
purpurowym; robić
szkarłatnym
purpose ['pe:rpes] s. cel; zamiar;
skutek; decyzja; wola; v.
zamierzać; mieć na celu;
planować
purposeful ['pe:rpesful] adj.

celowy; znaczący; rozmyślny;
zdecydowany; stanowczy
purposeless ['pe:rpeslys] adj.
bezcelowy; bezsensowny;
daremny; próżny (wysiłek
etc.)
purposely ['pe:rpesly] adv.
naumyślnie; celowo;
rozmyślnie
purr [pe:r] v. mruczeć;
pomrukiwać; s. mruczenie;
pomruk
purse [pe:rs] s. sakiewka;
torebka damska; kiesa;
nagroda; v. ściągać (się);
marszczyć (czoło)
pursue [per'sju:] v. ścigać;
tropić; iść dalej; uprawiać
(np. zawód); działać wg
planu; prześladować;
kontynuować; towarzyszyć;
spełniać (obowiązek)
pursuer [per'sju:er] s. ścigający;
prześladowca; dążący do
czegoś
pursuit [per'sju:t] s. pościg;
pogoń; zawód; zajęcie;
rozrywka
pursy [pe:rsy] adj. dychawiczny;
wydęty; otyły; ściągnięty
purvey [pe:r'wej] v. dostarczyć;
zaopatrywać; być dostawcą
purveyor [pe:rwejer] s. dostawca
pus [pas] s. ropa
push [pusz] s. pchnięcie; suw;
nacisk; wypad; wysiłek;
energia; dryg; bieda; kryzys;
zdecydowanie; v. pchać;
posunąć; szturchnąć;
nakłonić; dopingować;
odpychać; spychać;
pomiatać; robić karierę;
ponaglać
push along ['pusz,e'long] v. iść
dalej; ciągnąć się dalej;
jechać dalej; spieszyć się
push around ['pusz,e'raund] v.
pomiatać kimś
pusher ['puszer] s. popychacz
(uliczny); sprzedawca
narkotyków
puss [pus] s. kociak;
dziewczyna; (slang) gęba; kot

(tygrys)
pussycat ['pusy,kaet] s. kociak;
pliszka; (wulg.) narząd płciowy
żeński
put; put; put [put; put; put]
put [put] v. kłaść; stawiać;
umieszczać; wsadzać;
pouczać; przedkładać;
ujmować; wystawiać;
dodawać; wlewać;
szacować; nakładać;
opierać; składać; narażać;
wypychać (np. kule); zanosić
(np. prośby); s. rzut; adj.
nieruchomy (pozostający na
miejscu)
put back ['put,baek] v.
przestawić do tyłu; odłożyć
z powrotem
put down ['put,dałn] v. położyć;
stłumić; spuścić w dół;
zapisywać
put forth ['put,fo:rs̲] v.
wydobyć; wytężyć (siły);
wydawać (pismo)
put off ['put,of] v. odłożyć;
odroczyć; zbywać;
odwieść; pozbyć się
put on ['put,on] v. wdziewać;
przybierać; tyć; udawać;
dodawać
put out ['put,aut] v. zwichnąć;
zgasić; wytężyć (się);
produkować; wydawać;
wysunąć (rękę etc.)
put together [,put'tuge̲dzer] v.
łączyć; montować;
powiązać; zbierać (myśli);
kojarzyć; zliczyć
put up ['put,ap] v. ustawiać;
wywieszać; cierpieć;
wetknąć; schować;
dźwigać do góry; ustawić
putrefy ['pju:try,faj] v. gnić;
ropieć; ulegać zepsuciu
putrid ['pju:tryd] adj. zgniły;
zepsuty; cuchnący;
śmierdzący; wstrętny;
obrzydliwy
putty ['paty] s. kit; szpachlówka;
v. szpachlować; zakitować
putty knife ['paty,najf] s.
szpachla

puzzle ['pazl] s. zagadka;
łamigłówka; zakłopotanie; v.
intrygować; wprawiać w
zakłopotanie; odgadnąć;
wymyślić
puzzler ['pazler] s. łamigłówka
pajamas [pe'dże:mes] pl. piżama
pyramid ['pyremyd] s. piramida;
ostrosłup; v. zarabiać na
spekulacji; wznosić (się)
piramidalnie; budować jak
piramidę
python ['pajsen] s. pyton

Q

q [kju:] siedemnasta litera
alfabetu angielskiego (q. =
kwarta)
quack [kłaek] s. znachor;
szarlatan; kwakanie; v.
uprawiać znachorstwo;
gadać jak szarlatan; kwakać
quad [kłod] (skrót) s. kwadrat;
czworokąt
quadrangle [kło'draengl] s.
czworokąt
quadruped ['kładru,ped] adj.
czworonożny
quadruple [kło'drupl] adj.
czterokrotny; cztery razy
większy; czterokrotnie
większy
quadruplets [kło'dru:plets] s.
czworaczki
quail [kłejl] s. przepiórka; v.
drżeć przed czymś
quaint [kłejnt] adj. malowniczy;
trochę dziwaczny
quake [kłejk] s. trzęsienie (ziemi);
v. trząść się (np. z zimna, ze
strachu etc.)
quaky [kłejky] adj. trzęsący się;
grząski
qualification [,kłolyfy'kejszyn] s.
warunek; określenie;
kwalifikacja; uzdolnienie (do
pracy)

qualified ['kłolyfajd] adj.
wykwalifikowany;
uwarunkowany; kwalifikujący
się
quality ['kłolyty] s. jakość;
gatunek; właściwość; zaleta
qualm [kło:m] s. mdłości;
nudności; obawa; wyrzuty;
skrupuły
quandary ['kłondery] s.
zakłopotanie; kłopot; dylemat
quantity ['kłontyty] s. ilość;
wielkość; hurt; obfitość
quarantine ['kłorenti:n] s.
kwarantanna; v. izolować
quarrel ['kło:rel] s. kłótnia;
zerwanie; spór; sprzeczka; v.
kłócić się; sprzeczać się;
zerwać z sobą; robić
wyrzuty
quarrelsome ['kłorelsem] adj.
kłótliwy; swarliwy
quarry ['kłory] s. kamieniołom;
kopalnia odkrywkowa; łup;
zdobycz; płytka; szybka; v.
łamać; wygrzebywać;
wydobywać; eksploatować;
szperać (za wiadomościami)
quart [kło:rt] s. jedna czwarta
galonu (0.946 l.); kwarta piwa
quarter ['kło:ter] v.
ćwiartować; kwaterować;
rozpłatać; stacjonować; s.
ćwierć; ćwiartka; kwadrans;
kwartał; kwatera; 25 centów
(moneta); kwadra (księżyca);
dzielnica; mieszkanie; strona
świata; czynniki wpływowe;
(pl.) sfery (rządzące); kwartał
quarterly ['kło:terly] adj.
kwartalny; adv. kwartalnie; s.
kwartalnik; pismo kwartalne
quartet(te) [kło:r'tet] s. kwartet;
czwórka
quarto ['kło:rtou] s. format
ćwiartkowy
quartz [kłe:rts] s. kwarc
quash [kło:sz] v. unieważnić;
zdławić; stłumić; zgnieść
quasi ['kła:zy] conj. prawie;
niemal; jak gdyby; niby;
poniekąt
quaver ['kłejwer] s. drżenie

głosu; tryl; v. drżeć; drgać;
wibrować; trelować
quavery ['kłejwery] adj. drżący
quay [ki:] s. molo; nadbrzeże
queasy ['kłi:zy] adj. przeczulony;
mdlejący; grymaśny;
wrażliwy
queen [kłi:n] s. królowa;
królówka
queen bee ['kłi:n,bi:] s. królowa
pszczoła
queer [kłir] adj. dziwny;
dziwaczny; nieswój;
podejrzany; fałszywy; s.
pederasta; v. zepsuć;
wpakować w złą sytuację;
mdlić
quench ['kłencz] v. gasić;
tłumić; nagle oziębiać
(metal)
querulous ['kłerules] adj.
narzekający; zrzędny;
płaczliwy
query ['kłiery] s. zapytanie;
pytajnik; znak zapytania; v.
pytać; kwestionować
quest [kłest] s. poszukiwanie;
śledztwo; v. szukać
question ['kłesczyn] s. pytanie;
zagadnienie; kwestia;
wątpliwości; v. wypytywać;
przesłuchiwać; badać;
kwestionować; pytać się;
przeegzaminować
questionable ['kłesczenebl] adj.
wątpliwy (moralnie); sporny;
niepewny; niejasny
question mark ['kłesczyn,ma:rk]
s. znak zapytania
questionnaire [,kłejstje'neer] s.
kwestionariusz
queue [kju:] s. warkocz; ogonek;
kolejka; v. czekać w kolejce;
czekać w ogonku
queue up ['kju:,ap] v. ustawiać
się w kolejce
quibble ['kłybl] s. kruczek; v.
szukać wykrętów
quibbler ['kłybler] s. krętacz;
matacz
quick [kłyk] adj. prędki; szybki;
bystry; pomysłowy; żywy;
lotny; rudonośny; adv.

szybko; chyżo; v.
przyspieszać; ożywiać (się);
zwiększać szybkość
quicken ['kłyken] v.
przyspieszać;
pobudzać; ożywiać się;
wrócić do życia
quickie divorce ['kłyky dy'wo:rs]
s. rozwód błyskawiczny (w
stanie Newada; w Meksyku
etc.)
quickly ['kłykly] adv. szybko;
prędko; z pośpiechem
quickness ['kłyknys] s.
prędkość; ostrość
quicksand ['kłyk,saend] s.
grząski piasek
quicksilver ['kłyk,sylwer] s.
rtęć; żywe srebro
quick-tempered ['kłyk'temperd]
adj. porywczy
quick-witted ['kłyk'łytyd] adj.
bystry; rozgarnięty
quid [kłyd] s. funt szterling;
prymka; kawałek do żucia
quiet ['kłajet] adj. spokojny;
cichy; s. spokój; cisza; v.
uspokoić (się); uciszyć (się);
uspokajać; ściszyć;
ucichnąć
quiet down ['kłajet dałn] v.
uspokajać; przyciszyć;
ucichnąć
quietness ['kłajetnys] s. spokój;
cisza; łagodność;
skromność
quietude [kłajetju:d] s. spokój
(ducha)
quill [kłyl] s. lotka; dutka; kolec;
szpulka; pióro
quilt [kłylt] s. pikowana kołdra;
pikowana narzuta; v.
pikować; watować; robić
kołdry; zszywać; sprawić
lanie
quince [kłyns] s. pigwa
quinine ['kłajnajn] s. chinina
quintal ['kłyntl] s. cetnar; kwintal
quintuple ['kłyntjupl] adj.
pięciokrotny
quintuplets ['kłyntjuplyts] pl.
pięcioraczki
quit [kłyt] v. przestać; odejść;

odjechać; zabrać się;
wyprowadzać się;
opuszczać; porzucać;
rezygnować; adj. wolny;
uwolniony

quite [kłajt] adv. całkowicie;
zupełnie; raczej; wcale

quiver ['kływer] s. kołczan;
drżenie; drganie; v. drżeć;
drgać; trzepotać skrzydłami

quixotic ['kłyks,otyk] s. marzyciel
w stylu Don Kichota

quiz [kłyz] s. klasówka; egzamin;
badanie; przesłuchiwanie;
kawał; v. egzaminować;
badać; przesłuchiwać;
przeglądać; kpić

quota ['kłouta] s. udział;
kontyngent; norma

quotation [kłou'tejszyn] s.
cytata; cytowanie; notowanie;
przytaczanie (bieżącej ceny)

quotation marks
[kłou'tejszyn,ma:rks] pl.
cudzysłów

quote [kłout] v. cytować;
przytaczać; umieszczać w
cudzysłowie; notować;
podawać kurs; powoływać
się na kogoś

quotient ['kłouszent] s. iloraz

R

r [a:r] osiemnasta litera
angielskiego alfabetu

rabbi ['raebaj] s. rabin

rabbit ['raebyt] s. królik

rabble ['raebl] s. motłoch

rabid ['raebyd] adj. wściekły;
szalony; rozjuszony;
rozzłoszczony

rabies ['raebi:z] s. wścieklizna;
wodowstręt

raccoon [ra'ku:n] s. pracz
pospolity

race [rejs] s. rasa; plemię;
szczep; ród; rodzaj; bieg;

gonitwa; wyścigi; prąd;
kanał; v. ścigać (się); gonić
(się); pędzić; iść w zawody

racer ['rejser] s. wyścigowiec

racial ['rejszel] adj. rasowy

racing ['rejsy<u>ng</u>] adj.
wyścigowy; s. wyścigi; biegi

racist ['rejsyst] s. rasista

rack [raek] s. ruina; zagłada;
zniszczenie; koło tortur;
wieszak; drabina stajenna;
półka; stojak; zębatka; szybki
kłus; v. niszczeć; łamać
kołem; torturować; cedzić;
szarpać; męczyć; dręczyć

racket ['raekyt] s. rakieta; rak;
zabawa; hulanka; awantura;
hałas; afera; granda;
nieuczciwe interesy; kant; v.
hałasować; hulać;
bumblować; zabawiać się;
awanturować się

racketeer [,raeky'tier] s.
szantażysta; opryszek; v.
szantażować; robić grandę

racoon [re'ku:n] s. szop

racy ['rejsy] adj. typowy; cięty;
żywy; dosadny; aromatyczy;
pikantny; nieprzyzwoity

radar ['rejder] s. radar

radiance ['rejdjens] s.
promieniowanie; blask;
promienność

radiant ['rejdjent] adj.
promieniujący; promienny;
rozpromieniony; rzucający
promienie

radiate ['rajdyejt] v.
promieniować (ciepłem,
światłem etc.)

radiation [,redy'ejszyn] s.
promieniowanie; źródło
promieniowania

radiator ['rejdy'ejter] s. grzejnik;
kaloryfer; chłodnica
(samochodowa); radiowa
antena nadawcza;
radioaktywna substancja
wydzielająca promienie

radical ['raedykel] s. pierwiastek;
radykał; adj. zasadniczy;
radykalny; podstawowy;
pierwiastkowy; korzeniowy

radio ['rejdjou] s. radio; adj.
radiowy; v. nadawać przez
radio; wysyłać drogą radiową
radioactive ['rejdjou'aektyw] adj.
radioaktywny;
promieniotwórczy
radio set ['rejdjou,set] s. aparat
radiowy; odbiornik radiowy
radiotherapy ['rejdjou-'terepy] s.
radioterapia
radish ['raedysz] s. rzodkiewka
radius ['rejdjes] s. promień
raffle ['raefl] s. loteria fantowa;
rupiecie; v. sprzedawać na
loterii; kupować los
raft [raeft] s. tratwa; (slang)
mnóstwo; v. spławiać na
tratwie; robić tratwę
rafter [raefter] s. krokiew
rag [raeg] s. szmata; łachman;
łupek; dachówka; v. (slang)
besztać; dokuczać
rage [rejdż] v. szaleć;
wściekać się; s. szał;
wściekłość; namiętność
ragged [raegyd] adj. szmatławy;
obdarty; podarty; poszarpany;
kosmaty; zapuszczony;
zaniedbany; wadliwy;
chropowaty
raid [rejd] s. obława; nalot;
najazd; v. urządzać obławę;
najeżdżać; dokonywać
napadu
rail [rejl] s. poręcz; szyna; kolej;
listwa; erekcja (slang); v.
ogradzać poręczami; kłaść
szyny; przewozić koleją;
drwić; gorzko narzekać;
pomstować
rail in ['rejl,yn] v. przywozić
koleją (materiały, towar)
rail off ['rejl,of] v. wywozić
koleją (ludzi, towary etc.)
railing ['rejlyng] s. sztachety;
ogrodzenie; poręcz; balustrada
railroad ['rejlroud] s. kolej; v.
przewozić koleją; przepychać
pospiesznie (np. ustawę);
(slang) wpakować niesłusznie
do więzienia
railway ['rejłłej] s. kolej; tor
kolejowy; tor na szynach

railway man ['rejłłej,men] s.
kolejarz
rain [rejn] s. deszcz; v. pada
deszcz; spadać deszczem
rainbow ['rejn,boł] s. tęcza
raincoat ['rejnkout] s. płaszcz
nieprzemakalny
rainfall ['rejn,fo:l] s. opad; ilość
opadów
rainproof ['rejn,pru:f] adj.
nieprzemakalny
rainy ['rajny] adj. deszczowy;
dżdżysty; mokry od deszczu
rainy day ['rejny,dej] exp.:
czarna godzina
raise [rejz] v. podnosić;
wskrzeszać; wznosić;
wynosić; hodować;
wychowywać; wysuwać;
wytaczać; wzniecać;
zrywać; wywoływać;
budzić; zbierać (np.
fundusze); wydobywać;
przerywać (np. oblężenie);
znosić (zakaz); s. podwyżka
(płac); podwyższenie
raisin ['rejzyn] s. rodzynek
rake [rejk] v. grabić;
przegrzebać; grzebać;
ostrzeliwać (wzdłuż);
obrzucać wzrokiem;
nachylać do tyłu; uganiać
się za zwierzyną; s. grabie;
grabki; rozpustnik
rake-off ['rejk,of] s. nielegalna
prowizja; łapówka
rake out ['rejk,aut] v.
wygrzebywać; wygarniać
(popiół etc.)
rakish ['rejkisz] adj. zgrabny;
rozpustny; hulaszczy;
(pozornie) szybki (okręt) (z
wyglądu)
rally ['raely] v. zbierać (się);
skupiać (się); przyjść do
siebie; ochłonąć; okrzepnąć;
ulegać poprawie (giełda);
żartować z kogoś; s.
zbiórka; wiec; okrzepnięcie;
ożywienie walki bokserskiej;
wymiana ciosów; poprawa
(koniunktury)
ram [raem] s. tryk; baran; taran;

tłok; dźwig hydrauliczny;
bijak; v. uderzyć; zderzyć
się; ubijać; wtłaczać; bić
taranem; upychać; ugniatać;
najechać; zanudzać
ramble ['raemb] v. włóczyć się;
przechadzać się; piąć się
(np. o bluszczu); mówić bez
związku; odbiegać od tematu;
s. wędrówka
ramify ['raemyfaj] v. rozgałęziać
(się); s. odgałęzienie (się)
ramp [raemp] s. rampa; v.
rzucać się; stawać na
tylnych łapach; opadać
pochyło; szaleć
rampart [raempa:rt] s. wał;
szaniec; v. umacniać
(szańcem)
ramshackle ['raem-szaekl] adj.
zrujnowany; walący się; w
ruinie
ran [raen] v. zob. run
ranch [raencz] s. rancho
(gospodarstwo hodowlane); v.
prowadzić rancho (farmę
etc.)
rancher ['raenczer] s. właściciel
rancha
rancid ['raensyd] adj. zjełczały
(tłuszcz, oliwa etc.)
rancor ['raenker] s. uraza;
zajadłość; zawziętość;
złość
rancorous [raenkeres] adj.
urażony; złośliwy
random ['raendem] adj. na chybił
trafił; przypadkowy; pierwszy
lepszy; nieplanowany
rang [raeng] v. zob. ring
range [rejndż] s. skala; zasięg;
rozpiętość; nośność;
strzelnica; pasmo; obszar;
wędrówka; pastwisko; piec
kuchenny; v. ustawiać;
układać; klasyfikować;
wędrować; nastawiać
teleskop; mieć zasięg;
wstrzeliwać się; ciągnąć
się; zaliczać się; rozciągać
się; sięgać; nieść
range finder ['rejndż‚fajnder] s.
dalekomierz; odległościomierz

ranger [rejndżer] s. strażnik
leśny; policjant; komandos;
wędrowiec; desantowieć etc.
rank [raenk] s. ranga; stan;
stanowisko; v. ustawiać
rzędem; układać;
klasyfikować; zaszeregować;
przewyższać rangą; mieć
rangę; adj. wybujały; zjełczały;
śmierdzący; zupełny;
jaskrawy; obrzydliwy;
sprośny; wierutny
ransack ['raensaek] v.
przetrząsać; plądrować;
grzebać
ransom ['raensem] s. okup;
zwolnienie za okupem; v.
wykupić; zwalniać za
okupem
rant [raent] v. deklamować z
patosem; s. tyrada;
bombastyczna mowa
rap [raep] v. dać klapsa;
stukać; krytykować; s.
klaps; kołatanie; nagana;
zarzut; skazanie na więzienie;
odrobina
rapacious [re'pejszes] adj.
drapieżny; chciwy
rape [rejp] s. zgwałcenie
(kobiety); zniewolenie;
spląndrowanie; uprowadzenie;
v. gwałcić (kobietę);
uprowadzać; plądrować;
pogwałcić neutralność
rapid ['raepyd] adj. prędki;
szybki; bystry; stromy
rapidity ['raepydyty] s.
szybkość; bystrość; rwący
nurt (rzeki)
rapids ['raepyds] pl. progi (na
rzece); wodospad
rapt [raept] adj. zaabsorbowany;
zachwycony; urzeczony;
oczarowany
rapture ['raepczer] s. zachwyt;
uniesienie; wzięcie żywcem
do nieba
rare [reer] adj. rzadki;
niedopieczony (np. kotlet); na
pół surowy; niedosmażony;
adv. rzadko
rarity ['reeryty] s. rzadkość

rascal ['raeskal] s. hultaj; łobuz;
adj. hulatajski
rascally ['raeskely] adj. hultajski;
łobuzerski
rash [raesz] s. wysypka skórna;
ulewa; powódź; adj.
pochopny; popędliwy;
nieprzemyślany
rasher ['raeszer] s. płatek (np.
szynki)
rasp [raesp] s. raszpla; pilnik;
zgrzytanie; v. drapać;
skrobać; drażnić; chrapliwie
mówić
raspberry [ra:zbery] s. malina
rat [raet] s. szczur; łamistrajk;
donosiciel; v. polować na
szczury; zdradzać; donosić;
zaprzedawać
rats [raets] pl. szczury; bzdura
rate [rejt] s. stopa; stosunek;
proporcja; wysokość;
poziom; szybkość; cena;
stawka; opłata; podatek;
stopień; klasa; v. szacować;
oceniać; ustalać; zaliczać;
opodatkować; zasługiwać;
besztać; wymyślać
rate of exchange ['rejt of
yks'czejndż] s. kurs wymiany
rate of interest [,rejt of 'yntryst]
s. stopa procentowa
rather ['raedzer] adv. raczej;
chętniej; dość; nieco; do
pewnego stopnia; poniekąd;
zamiast
ratify ['raetyfaj] v. zatwierdzać;
ratyfikować
ration ['raeszyn] s. przydział;
porcja; racja; v. racjonować;
sprzedawać na kartki
rational ['raeszynl] adj. rozumny;
rozsądny; racjonalny;
wymierny; sensowny
rationalize ['raeszyne,lajz] v.
racjonalizować;
usprawiedliwiać
rattle ['raetl] v. grzechotać
szczękać; brzęczać; stukać;
trzaskać; terkotać; paplać
wiersze; s. grzechotanie;
terkot; stuk; paplanina; gaduła
rattler ['raetler] s. grzechotnik

rattlesnake ['raetl,snejk] s.
grzechotnik
ravage ['raewydż] s.
spustoszenie; zniszczenie; v.
pustoszyć; niszczyć;
plądrować
rave [rejw] v. bredzić;
majaczyć;
szaleć; wściekać się; wyć;
zachwycać się; s. wrzask;
wycie; zaślepienie; przesadna
pochwała (entuzjastyczna)
raven ['rejwn] s. kruk; adj.
kruczy; ['raewen] s. grabież;
łup; v. pożerać; szukać łupu;
mieć szalony apetyt
ravenous ['raewynes] adj.
wygłodniały; zgłodniały;
żarłoczny; drapieżny
ravine [re'wi:n] s. parów; jar;
wąwóz
raving ['rejwyng] adj. bredzący;
szalony; porywający (np.
pięknością); s. atak furii;
bredzenie; majaczenie
ravish ['raewysz] v. porywać
(kobietę); gwałcić (kobietę)
raw [ro:] adj. surowy; otwarty
(np. rana); wrażliwy;
nieokrzesany; brutalny;
nieprzyzwoity; s. gołe ciało;
surówka; v. ocierać (skórę)
ray [rej] s. promień; promyk;
(ryba) płaszczka; v.
promieniować; naświetlać;
prześwietlać; wysyłać
promienie (światła etc.)
rayon ['rejon] s. sztuczny jedwab
raze [rejz] v. zburzyć; zatrzeć;
otrzeć (skórę)
razor ['rejzer] s. brzytwa
razor blade ['rejzer'blejd] s.
żyletka; ostrze brzytwy
re [ri:] prep. w sprawie; tyczy;
dotyczy; przedrostek: znowu;
od nowa
reach [ri:cz] v. osiągać;
wyciągnąć (np. rękę);
dosięgnąć; dotrzeć;
docierać; sięgnąć; s.
sięgnięcie; zasięg; połać;
przestrzeń; pobliże; granice
reach out ['ri:cz,aut] v.

wyciągnąć (ręką etc.)
react [ri:'aekt] v. reagować;
oddziaływać; przeciwdziałać
reactor [ri:'aekter] s. reaktor (np.
jądrowy)
read; read; read [ri:d; red; red]
read [ri:d] v. czytać;
tłumaczyć; interpretować
read out ['ri:d,aut] v. wydalać
kogoś; wyczytywać
readout ['ri:daut] s. odczyt
wyników komputera
read to [ri:d tu] v. czytać
komuś
reader ['ri:der] s. czytelnik;
korektor; czytanka; wypisy;
recenzent (wydawnictwa)
readily ['redyly] adv. łatwo;
chętnie; ochoczo; bez trudu
readiness ['redynys] s.
gotowość; pogotowie;
obrotność; ciętość;
przytomność umysłu
reading ['ri:dyng] s. czytanie;
oczytanie; interpretacja;
lektura; czytelnictwo; adj.
czytający
readjust ['ri:e'dżast] v.
dopasować na nowo
ready ['redy] adj. gotów;
gotowy; przygotowany; adv.
w przygotowaniu; gotowy; v.
przygotowywać
ready-made ['redy'mejd] s.
konfekcja; adj. gotowy
ready-to-wear ['redy,tu'łeer] s.
odzież fabrycznej produkcji
reaffirm ['ry:eferm] v.
potwierdzić (ponownie)
real [ryel] adj. rzeczywisty;
realny; istotny; prawdziwy;
autentyczny; faktyczny
real estate ['ryel,es'tejt] s.
nieruchomość; realność
realism ['ryelyzem] s. realizm
realistic ['ryelystyk] s. adj.
realistyczny
reality [ry'aelyty] s.
rzeczywistość; realizm;
prawdziwość
realization [,ryelaj'zejszyn] s.
realizacja; spełnienie;
wykonanie; spieniężenie;

uświadomienie sobie
realize ['ry:e,lajz] v.
urzeczywistnić; realizować;
uprzytamniać; zdawać sobie
sprawę; uzyskiwać;
zdobywać (majątek)
really ['ryely] adv. rzeczywiście;
naprawdę; doprawdy;
faktycznie; istotnie
realm [relm] s. królestwo;
dziedzina; sfera; zakres
realpolitik [rej'a:lpouly'tyk] s.
polityka egoistyczna
realtor ['ryelter] s. pośrednik
sprzedaży nieruchomości
realty ['ryelty] s. nieruchomość
reap [ry:p] v. żąć; zbierać
plony, owoce pracy etc.
reaper ['ry:per] s. żniwiarz;
żniwiarka
reappear ['ry:e'pier] v. zjawić
się ponownie; znowu ukazać
się
rear [rier] s. tył; tyły; ustęp; v.
stawać dęba; hodować;
wychowywać; wznosić (się);
wybudować; wystawiać
rear guard ['rier,ga:rd] s. tylna
straż
rear-light ['rier,lajt] s. tylne
światło samochodu
rearm ['ry:'a:rm] v. ponownie
uzbrajać
rearmament ['ry:'a:rmement] s.
remilitaryzacja
rearmost [rie:r,moust] adj.
końcowy; ostatni
rear-view mirror ['rier,wju:'myrer]
s. (tylne) lusterko w
samochodzie (do sprawdzania
ruchu za samochodem)
rearrange ['ry:erejndż] v.
przestawić; zmieniać
(porządek); poprawić (fryzurę
etc.)
rearwards ['rierłedz] adv. wstecz;
ku tyłowi; na tył
reason ['ri:zn] s. rozum; powód;
uzasadnienie; motyw;
przesłanka; rozsądek; v.
rozumować; rozważać;
wnioskować; rozprawiać;
przekonywać; dowodzić

reason out ['ri:zn,aut] v.
przemyślać; wyrozumować;
dociekać
reason with ['ri:zn,łys] v.
przekonywać kogoś
reasonable ['ri:znabl] adj.
rozumny; rozsądny;
umiarkowany; słuszny;
racjonalny
reassure [,ry:a'szuer] v.
zapewniać; upewniać;
ubezpieczać na nowo;
uspakajać; przywracać
zaufanie; upewniać na nowo
reassuring [,ry:a'szueryng] adj.
uspakajający
rebate [ry'bejt] s. rabat; zwrot
(części kwoty); v. udzielać
rabatu; potrącać (z
rachunku); zamortyzować
przytępiać
rebel ['rebel] s. buntownik; v.
buntować się; adj.
zbuntowany; buntowniczy
rebellion [ry'beljen] s. bunt;
powstanie
rebellious [ry'beljes] adj.
zbuntowany; buntowniczy;
niesforny; oporny
rebirth [ry'be:rs] s. odrodzenie;
odżywanie
re-book ['ry:buk] v. zamawiać
na nowo (program teatralny,
bilety lotnicze etc.)
rebound [ry'baund] s. odbicie;
odskok; rykoszet; v.
odskakiwać; odbijać (się)
(sobie na kimś)
rebuff [ry'baf] s. ofuknięcie;
odrzucenie; v. ofuknąć; dać
odprawę; odesłać z kwitkiem
rebuild ['ry:byld] v.
odbudowywać;
przebudowywać
rebuke [ry'bju:k] s. nagana; v.
upominać; łajać
recall [ry'ko:l] v. odwoływać;
przypominać (sobie);
wycofywać; cofać
(obietnicę); s. nakaz powrotu
recap ['ry:kaep] s. opona
ponownie gumowana; v.
ponownie wulkanizować

opony; powtarzać dla
podsumowania
recapture ['ri:'kaepczer] v.
odzyskać; s. odzyskanie
recede [ry'si:d] v. cofać się;
oddalać się; mdleć; słabnąć
receipt [ry'si:t] s. pokwitowanie;
odbiór; recepta
receive [ry'si:w] v. otrzymywać;
dostawać; odbierać;
przyjmować (np. gości)
receiver [ry'si:wer] s. odbiornik
(radiowy); słuchawka
(telefoniczna); odbiorca;
syndyk; zarządca upadłości
recent ['ri:snt] adj. niedawny;
świeży; nowy
recently ['ri:sntly] adv.
niedawno; świeżo; ostatnio;
współcześnie
reception [ry'sepszyn] s.
przyjęcie; odbiór; recepcja
reception desk [ry'sepszyn,desk]
s. biuro do przyjmowania
interesantów; portiernia; biuro
przyjęć
receptionist [ry'sepszynyst] s.
recepcjonistka; sekretarka
przyjmująca klientów; portier
recess [ry'ses] s. przerwa
(między lekcjami); ferie;
wgłębienie; nisza; wnęka; v.
odraczać; wkładać do wnęki;
robić wnęką; rozjeżdżać się
na ferie
recession [ry'seszyn] s.
cofnięcie; recesja
(gospodarcza); wgłębienie;
wnęka; kryzys; zastój
recipe ['rysypy] s. przepis;
recepta
recipient [ry'sypjent] adj.
odbiorczy; s. odbiorca;
zdobywca nagrody; osoba
obdarowana
reciprocal [ry'syprekel] adj.
wzajemny; odwrotny; s.
odwrotność (w matematyce)
recital [ry'sajtl] s.
przedstawienie; opowiadanie;
recytacja; koncert;
deklamowanie utworu
recite [ry'sajt] s. recytować

wiersz; wyliczać
reckless ['reklys] adj.
(niebezpiecznie) lekkomyślny;
nie uważający; na oślep;
wariacki; brawurowy;
szaleńczy; zuchowaty
reckon ['reken] v. liczyć;
sądzić; myśleć że; polegać
na
reckon up ['reken,ap] v. zliczać;
zsumować; podsumowywać
reckon with ['reken,tys] v.
liczyć się (z kimś)
reckoning ['rekenyng] s.
obliczanie (położenia);
rachuba; obrachunek;
kalkulacja; rozliczenie
reclaim [ry'klejm] v. odzyskiwać
(pod uprawę); użyźniać;
przerabiać odpadki;
wyprowadzać z (zaniedbania,
błędu etc.); zażądać zwrotu;
dochodzić
recline [ry'klajn] v. kłaść się;
wyciągać się; złożyć (np.
głowę); spoczywać na pół
leżąc
recognition [,rekeg'nyszyn] s.
rozpoznanie; uznanie;
pozdrowienie; dowód uznania
recognize ['rekeg,najz] v.
rozpoznawać; pozdrowić;
uznawać; przyznawać;
udzielać (głosu)
recoil [ry'kojl] v. wzdrygać się;
cofać się; kopać (np. kolbą);
odskoczyć; odbijać; s.
odskok; odrzut; odbicie;
wzdrygnięcie się
recollect [reke'lekt] v.
wspominać; przypominać
sobie; zbierać na nowo;
przypominać sobie z trudem
recollection [,reke'lekszyn] s.
wspomnienie; pamięć
recommend [reke'mend] v.
polecać; zalecać; dobrze
świadczyć
recommendation
[,rekemen'dejszyn] s.
polecenie; zlecenie
recompense ['rekem,pens] v.
odpłacać; dawać

odszkodowanie; s.
wynagrodzenie;
zadośćuczynienie;
odszkodowanie; rekompensata
reconcile ['rekensajl] v. godzić
(sprzeczności); zażegnać
(spór); pojednać; pogodzić
się
reconciliation [,reken,syly'ejszyn]
s. pojednanie; pogodzenie
reconsider [,ri:ken'syder] v.
ponownie rozważyć;
reasumować
reconstruct [,ri:ken'strakt] v.
odbudowywać; odtwarzać
reconstruction ['ri:ken'strakszyn]
s. rekonstrukcja; odbudowa
record ['ryko:rd] v. zapisywać;
notować; rejestrować;
zaznaczać; nagrywać; s.
zapiska; archiwum; rejestracja;
dokument; przeszłość
(czyjaś); pamięć o kimś;
nagranie; rekord
recorder [ry'ko:rder] s.
rejestrator; aparat zapisujący;
pisak; pisarz archiwista
record holder ['reko:rd,houlder]
s. rekordzista; mistrz
recording ['reko:rdyng] s.
nagranie (płyta)
record player ['reko:rd,plejer] s.
adapter
recourse [ry'ko:rs] s. uciekanie
się (ratunek)
recover [ry'kawer] v. odzyskać;
nadrabiać; powetować sobie;
uzyskać przywracać;
wyzdrowieć; ochłonąć;
przyjść do siebie
recovery [ry'kawery] s.
odzyskanie (pozycji);
wyzdrowienie; poprawa
(gospodarcza)
recreation [,rekry'ejszyn] s.
rozrywka; zabawa;
odtworzenie
recruit [ry'kru:t] s. rekrut;
poborowy; v. werbować;
uzupełniać (stan zatrudnienia)
rectangle ['rektaengl] s.
prostokąt; a. prostokątny
rectify ['rektyfy] v. prostować

(np. błąd); poprawiać (np. plan); usuwać (np. nadużycia)

rector ['rekter] s. proboszcz; rektor

rectory ['rektery] s. probostwo

recur [ry'ke:r] v. powtarzać się; przypominać się; nawiązywać do czegoś (wielokrotnie)

recurrent [ry'karent] adj. powracający; nawracający

recycle [,ry'sajkl] v. puścić w obieg drugi raz; używać wielokrotnie

red [red] adj. czerwony; s. czerwień; lewicowiec; komunista; radykał (skrajny); forsa (sl.)

red-bait ['redbejt] v. oskarżać o komunizm (USA)

red-blooded ['red,bladyd] adj. męski; krzepki; jurny

redden ['reden] v. zaczerwienić się; zarumienić się

reddish ['redysz] adj. czerwonawy

redeem [ry'di:m] v. wykupywać; okupywać; wybawiać; zbawiać; odkupić; zamienić; kompensować

redemption [ry'dempszyn] s. wykup; okupienie; odkupienie; wybawienie; umorzenie; zbawienie

red-handed ['red'haendyd] adj. splamiony krwią; exp.: na gorącym uczynku

red letter day ['red'leter,dej] s. dzień specjalny; dzień świąteczny

redouble [ry'dabl] v. podwoić (się); zwijać się

reduce [ry'dju:s] v. zmniejszać (się); chudnąć; redukować; ograniczać; obniżać; dostosowywać; sprowadzać; doprowadzać; rozcieńczać; osłabiać; odtleniać; wytapiać

reduction [ry'dakszyn] s. zmniejszenie; redukcja; obniżka; sprowadzenie; dostosowanie; odtlenienie; wytapianie

redundant [ry'dandent] adj. niepotrzebny; zbędny; zbyteczny

reed [ri:d] s. trzcina; słoma; fujarka; strzała; płocha tkacka; stroik (muzyczny)

reeducation ['ry:edju'kejszyn] s. przeszkolenie ponowne

reef [ri:f] s. rafa; skała podwodna; ref; v. refować

reek [ri:k] s. odór; para; dym; v. śmierdzieć; parować; dymić; wędzić; ociekać (krwią)

reel [ri:l] s. szpula; cewka; rolka; chwianie się; kręcenie się; v. nawijać; odwijać; rozwijać; recytować; chwiać się; zataczać się; kręcić się; dostawać zawrotu głowy; dawać zawrót głowy; zachwiać się na nogach

reel off ['ri:l,of] v. odwijać

reel up ['ri:l,ap] v. nawijać

reelect ['ri:y'lekt] v. ponownie wybierać

reenter ['ri:'enter] v. ponownie wchodzić (w posiadanie etc.)

reentry ['ri:'entry] s. ponowne wejście; rewindykacja

re-establish [,ry:ys'taeblysz] v. ponownie: zakładać; ustanawiać; ustalać; wprowadzać

refer [ry'fe:r] v. odsyłać; powiązywać; skierować; odwoływać; cytować; odnosić się; dotyczyć; powoływać się

referee [refe'ri:] s. sędzia sportowy; rozjemca; v. sędziować

reference ['refrens] s. odsyłacz; odnośnik; odwoływanie się; aluzja; informacja; referencja; stosunek; związek; wgląd; przelotna wzmianka

reference book ['referens,bu:k] s. tekst podręczny; podręcznik

reference library ['referens laj'brery] s. biblioteka

podręczna naukowo-
informacyjna
referendum [,refe'rendem] s.
referendum
refill [ry:'fyl] s. ponowne
napełnienie; wypełnienie;
nowy zapas; v. ponownie
napełniać, wkładać,
zapełniać etc.
refine [ry'fajn] v. oczyszczać;
rafinować; wysubtelniać;
rozprawiać subtelnie
refinement [ry'fajnment] s.
rafinowanie; wyrafinowanie;
subtelność; wytworność
refinery [ry'fajnery] s. rafineria
reflect [ry'flekt] v. odbijać;
odzwierciedlać; rozmyślać;
zastanawiać się;
krytykować; przynosić
(zaszczyt, ujmę)
reflection [ry'flekszyn] s. odbicie;
odzwierciedlenie; odbicie
światła; zarzut; rozwaga;
namysł; wzmianka; pomysł;
wstyd
reflex ['ry:fleks] s. odruch;
refleks; odbicie;
odzwierciedlenie; adj.
refleksyjny; odbity; wygięty;
v. poddawać refleksom;
wyginać wstecz
reflexive [ry'fleksyw] adj.
odbijający; pełen zadumy;
refleksyjny
reform [ry'fo:rm] v.
reformować; poprawiać;
usuwać; ulegać reformie; s.
reforma; poprawa
reformation [,refer'mejszyn] s.
reformacja; poprawa
reformer [ry'fo:rmer] s.
reformator (moralności,
warunków etc.)
refract [ry'fraekt] v. załamywać
światło; wyginać promień
światła
refractory [ry'fraektery] adj.
oporny; uporczywy; krnąbrny;
odporny; ogniotrwały
refrain [ry'frejn] v.
powstrzymywać się; s. refren
refresh [ry'fresz] v. odświeżyć;

wzmacniać; pokrzepiać
refreshment [ry'freszment] s.
odpoczynek; wytchnienie;
odświeżenie; zakąska
refrigerator [ry'frydże,rejter] s.
lodówka; chłodnia
refuel ['ry:'fjuel] v. zaopatrzyć
w paliwo; dodać paliwa
refuge ['refju:dż] s. schronienie;
azyl; przytułek; v. schronić
się
refugee [,refju'dżi:] s. zbieg;
uchodźca; uciekinier
refund [ry'fand] s. zwrot; spłata;
v. zwracać pieniądze
refusal [ry'fju:zel] s. odmowa;
prawo opcji; wbijanie do oporu
refuse [ry'fju:z] v. odmawiać;
odrzucać; adj. odpadowy; s.
odpadki; rupiecie
refute [ry'fju:t] v. zbijać (np.
twierdzenie)
regain [ry'gejn] v. odzyskać;
wrócić (do zdrowia)
regal ['ry:gel] adj. królewski
regard [ry'ga:rd] v. spoglądać;
zważać; uważać; dotyczyć;
s. wzgląd; spojrzenie;
szacunek; uwaga;
pozdrowienia; ukłony
regarding [ry'ga:rdyng] prep.
odnośnie; co się tyczy; w
sprawie
regardless [ry'ga:rdlys] adv. w
każdym razie; adj. nie
zważający; bez względu (na
kłopoty etc.); nie licząc się (z
wydatkami)
regard of [ry'ga:rd,ow] exp.: co
się tyczy; w sprawie etc.
regent ['ri:dżent] s. regent;
opiekun; członek zarządu
regime [ry'żi:m] s. ustrój; reżym;
tryb życia; system; rządy
regiment ['redżyment] s. pułk;
zastęp; v. organizować;
koszarować; wcielać do
pułku
region ['ri:dżen] s. okolica; sfera;
rejon; obszar; dzielnica
register ['redżyster] v.
rejestrować; zapamiętywać;
wysyłać polecony list;

prowadzić rejestr;
wstrzeliwać się; wyrażać
minami
registered letter
['redżysterd,leter] s. list
polecony
registration [,redżys'trejszyn] s.
rejestracja; meldunek; ilość
zarejestrowana
regret [ry'gret] s. ubolewanie;
żal; v. żałować czegoś
regrettable [ry'gretebl] adj.
godny ubolewania
regular ['regjuler] adj. regularny;
stały; zawodowy; poprawny;
przepisowy; s. regularny
(żołnierz, ksiądz etc.); stały
gość; wierny partyjniak
regularity [,regju'laeryty] s.
regularność;
systematyczność
regulate ['regjulejt] v.
regulować; przystosowywać
do wymogów
regulation [,regju'lejszyn] s.
przepis; regulowanie; adj.
przepisowy; zwykły
rehearsal [ry'he:rsel] s. próba;
powtarzanie
rehearse [ry'he:rs] v. odbywać
próbę; powtarzać
reign [rejn] v. panować;
władać; s. władza;
panowanie
rein [rejn] v. kierować wodzami;
trzymać na wodzach
reins [rejns] pl. wodze
reindeer ['rejn,dier] s. renifer
reinforce [,ri:yn'fors] v.
wzmocnić; popierać; dodać
sił
reject [ry'dżekt] v. odrzucić;
odpalić; zwracać; ['rydżekt]
s. wybrakowany towar;
niezdatny do wojska; coś
odrzuconego
rejection [ry'dżekszyn] s.
odrzucenie; odmowa;
wybrakowany towar; oblanie
studenta; odkosz
rejoice [ry'dżojs] v. radować;
cieszyć się; weselić się
rejoicing [ry'dżojsyng] s.

radość; uradowanie; adj.
uradowany
rejoin ['ri:dżoyn] v. ponownie
łączyć (się); zestawiać
połamane części;
odpowiadać na zarzut
relapse [ry'laeps] s. nawrót;
pogorszenie; v. ponownie
popadać; zapadać z
powrotem
relate [ry'lejt] v. opowiadać;
referować; łączyć się
related [ry'lejtyd] adj. bliski;
spokrewniony;
spowinowacony; związany;
pokrewny; powinowaty
relation [ry'lejszyn] s.
sprawozdanie; opowiadanie;
stosunek; związek;
pokrewieństwo;
powinowactwo; krewny
relationship [ry'lejszynszyp] s.
stosunek; pokrewieństwo;
powinowactwo; zależność
relative ['reletyw] adj. względny;
stosunkowy; podrzędny;
zależny; dotyczący; adv.
odnośnie; w sprawie; s.
krewny; zaimek względny
relax [ry'laeks] v. odprężać
(się); osłabnąć; rozluźniać
się; łagodnieć; odpoczywać
relaxation [,ry:laek'sejszyn] n.
odprężenie; odpoczynek;
rozrywka; złagodzenie
relay [ry'lej] s. bieg rozstawny;
wzmacniacz; v. przekazywać;
zmieniać (tor); kłaść na
nowo
relay race [ry'lej,rejs] s. bieg
rozstawny; bieg sztafetowy
release [ry'li:z] v. wypuszczać;
uwalniać; zwalniać; s.
zwolnienie; uwolnienie;
puszczenie (do druku); spust;
wyzwalacz; wypuszczenie
(filmu)
relent [ry'lent] v. łagodnieć;
mięknąć; dać się wzruszyć
relentless [ry'lentlys] adj.
nieugięty; bezlitosny;
nieprzejednany; nieustępliwy;
srogi

relevant ['relewent] adj. istotny; trafny; na miejscu; należący do rzeczy

reliability [ry,laje'byłyty] s. rzetelność; solidność; pewność

reliable [ry'lajebl] adj. pewny; solidny; rzetelny

reliance [ry'lajens] s. zaufanie; otucha

reliant [ry'lajent] adj. ufny w siebie; liczący na kogoś; zależny od czegoś

relic ['relyk] n. zabytek; relikwie; pozostałość; resztka

relief [ry'li:f] n. odprężenie; ulga; urozmaicenie; zapomoga; pomoc; zmiana (np. warty); płaskorzeźba; uwypuklenie

relieve [ry'li:w] v. nieść pomoc, ulgę; ulżyć (sobie); oddać mocz; ożywić; zmieniać wartę; zluzować; uwypuklić (na tle czegoś); uwydatnić

religion [ry'lydżyn] s. religia; obrządek; wyznanie; zakon

religious [ry'lydżes] adj. pobożny; religijny; zakonny; s. zakonnik; zakonnica

relinquish [ry'lynkłysz] v. porzucać; wyrzekać się czegoś; zaniechać; zrzekać się; rezygnować; wypuścić coś z rąk

relish ['relysz] s. smak; posmak; przyprawa; przysmak; urok; zamiłowanie; v. smakować w czymś; czynić smaczniejszym; przyprawiać; mieć dobry smak; być przyjemnym; dodawać smaku

reluctance [ry'laktens] s. niechęć; opór (magnetyczny); wstręt

reluctant [ry'laktent] adj. niechętny; oporny

rely on [ry'laj,on] v. polegać na czymś lub kimś; liczyć na

remain [ry'mejn] v. pozostawać

remains [ry'mejns] pl. pozostałości; resztki; przeżytki; zwłoki; szczątki

remainder [ry'mejnder] s. reszta;

pozostałość; remanent

remand [ry'maend] v. odsyłać (do niższej instancji lub więzienia); s. odesłanie do więzienia; człowiek odesłany z powrotem

remark [ry'ma:rk] v. zauważyć; zrobić uwagę; s. uwaga

remarkable [ry'ma:rkebl] adj. wybitny; godny uwagi

remedy ['remydy] s. lekarstwo; środek; rada; v. leczyć; zaradzać; naprawiać

remember [ry'member] v. pamiętać; przypominać; pozdrawiać; modlić się za kogoś; mieć w pamięci

remembrance [ry'membrens] s. wspomnienie; pamiątka; pamięć; pozdrowienie; ukłony

remind [ry'majnd] v. przypominać coś komuś; przypomnieć

reminder [ry'majnder] s. przypomnienie; upomnienie; ponaglenie; ktoś przypominający

reminiscent [,remy'nysnt] adj. przypominający; wspominający; pełen wspomnień

remiss [ry'mys] adj. niedbały; ospały; niechlujny

remit [ry'myt] s. przekazywać (pieniądze); darować (dług); odpuszczać (grzechy); odsyłać; przywracać; łagodzić; łagodnieć; słabnąć

remittance [ry'mytens] s. przesyłka pieniężna; wypłata

remnant ['remnent] s. resztka; pozostałość; ślad czegoś

remodel [ry'modl] v. przerabiać; odnowić; przemodelować

remonstrate ['remenstrejt] v. protestować

remorse [ri'mo:rs] s. wyrzuty sumienia; skrupuły

remorseless [ri'mo:rslys] adj. bezlitosny; nieskruszony

remote [ry'mout] adj. odległy; zdalny; mało prawdopodobny; obcy

removal [ry'mu:wl] s. usunięcie; przeprowadzka

remove [ry'mu:w] v. usuwać; przewozić; zdejmować; przeprowadzać się; opuszczać; s. przeprowadzka; odległość; stopień; oddalenie

remover [ry'mu:wer] s. usuwacz (plam); środek do usuwania

renaissance [ry'nesens] s. odrodzenie; renesans; a. renesansowy

rend; rent; rent [rend; rent; rent]

rend [rend] v. drzeć; targać; wydzierać; urągać; rozdzierać

render ['render] v. uczynić; zrobić; oddawać; okazywać; składać; wydawać; płacić; odpłacać; oczyszczać; wytapiać; tynkować; s. odpłata (np. w naturze); pierwsza warstwa tynku

rendezvous ['ra:ndy,wu:] s. randka; umówione spotkanie; miejsce spotkań

renew [ry'nu:] v. odnawiać; ponawiać; wznawiać; odświeżać; prolongować

renewal [ry'nu:el] s. odnowienie (np. kontraktu)

renounce [ry'nauns] v. zrzekać się; zrezygnować; wyrzekać się; wypowiadać; odstępować; nie uznawać

renovate [ry'nowejt] v. odnowić; naprawić

renown [ry'naun] s. sława; rozgłos; pogłoska

renowned [ry'naund] adj. sławny

rent 1. [rent] v. zob. rend

rent 2. [rent] s. komorne; czynsz; renta; najem; rozdarcie; szczelina; rozłam; parów; v. wynajmować; dzierżawić; pobierać czynsz; być wynajmowanym

rental ['rentl] s. czynsz; komorne; wypożyczanie; adj. czynszowy

rental agency ['rentl'ejdżensy] s. biuro wynajmu (narzędzi,

mieszkań etc.)

rent free ['rent'fri:] adj. wolny od opłaty czynszowej

repair [ry'peer] v. pójść; uczęszczać; naprawiać; reperować; remontować; powetowć; wynagrodzić; s. naprawa; remont; stan

repair shop [ry'peer,szop] s. warsztat naprawy

reparation [repa'rejszyn] s. naprawa; remont; odszkodowanie

repartee [repa:r'ti:] s. riposta; cięta odpowiedź; odcinanie się

repay [ry:'pej] v. spłacić; zwrócić; wynagrodzić; odwzajemnić się; oddać

repeat [ry:'pi:t] v. powtarzać (się); repetować; odbijać się; robić powtórkę; robić ponownie; odtwarzać; s. powtórka; powtórzenie; powtórne zamówienie; a. powtórny; wielokrotny

repel [ry'pel] v. odpierać; odrzucać; odtrącać; budzić odrazą, niechęć, wstręt etc.

repent [ry'pent] v. żałować

repentance [ry'pentens] s. skrucha; żal

repentant [ry'pentent] adj. żałujący; pełen skruchy

repetition [,repy'tyszyn] s. powtórzenie; powtórka

replace [ry'plejs] v. zastępować; zwracać oddawać; umieszczać z powrotem; przywrócić; wymienić

replacement [ry'plejsment] s. zastępstwo; zastępca; zastąpienie; wymiana (części)

replenish [ry'plenysz] v. ponownie napełniać; wypełniać; uzupełniać

replay [ry'plej] v. ponownie rozgrywać; ['ry:plej] s. ponowna rozgrywka

reply [ry'plaj] v. odpowiadać; s. odpowiedź

report [ry'po:rt] v. opowiadać; meldować; dawać

sprawozdanie; zdawać
sprawę; pisać sprawozdanie;
referować; s. raport;
sprawozdanie; komunikat;
opinia; huk; wybuch; pogłoska
reporter [ru'po:rter] s.
dziennikarz; sprawozdawca;
reporter
repose [ry'pouz] s. odpoczynek;
spokój; v. odpoczywać;
spoczywać; polegać;
opierać; pokładać
represent [,repry'zent] v.
przedstawiać;
reprezentować; wyobrażać;
grać (kogoś)
representation [,repryzen'tejszyn]
s. przedstawicielstwo;
reprezentacja; przedstawienie;
wyobrażenie
representative [,repry'zentetyw]
adj. przedstawiający;
reprezentujący; wyobrażający;
s. przedstawiciel; reprezentant
(poseł na sejm)
repress [ry'pres] v. tłumić;
hamować; powstrzymywać;
poskromić
reprieve [ry'pri:w] v. zawieszać;
odraczać; dawać odroczenie;
s. odroczenie; darowanie;
zmiana kary (śmierci)
reprimand ['reprymaend] v.
karcić; udzielać nagany; s.
nagana
reproach [ry'proucz] v. robić
wyrzuty; wymawiać; s.
wyrzut; zarzut; wymówka
reproachful [ry'prouczful] adj.
pełen wyrzutu
reproduce [,rypre'du:s] v.
odtwarzać; reprodukować;
rozmnażać; wznawiać
reproduction [,ri:pre'dakszyn] s.
reprodukcja; rozmnażanie się;
płodzenie
reproof [ry'pru:f] s. nagana
reprove [ry'pru:w] v. ganić
reptant ['reptent] adj. pełzający
reptile ['reptajl] s. gad; płaz;
gadzina; adj. pełzający;
gadzinowy
republic [ry'pablyk] s. republika;

rzeczpospolita
republican [ry'pablyken] adj.
republikański; s. republikanin
repugnance [ry'pagnens] s.
odraza; niechęć;
niezgodność; sprzeczność
repugnant [ry'pagnent] adj.
odrażający; oporny;
sprzeczny; niezgodny
repulse [ry'pals] v. odpierać;
odrzucać; odtrącać; s.
odparcie; odrzucenie; odmowa
repulsive [ry'palsyw] adj.
odrażający; wstrętny;
odpychający; budzący odrazą
reputable ['repjutebl] adj.
szanowany; zaszczytny
reputation [,repju'tejszyn] s.
reputacja; sława; dobre imię
repute [ry'pju:t] s. reputacja;
sława; v. uważać za coś
request [ry'kłest] s. prośba;
życzenie; żądanie;
zapotrzebowanie; v. prosić o
pozwolenie; upraszać;
poprosić o przysługę
require [ry'kłajer] v. żądać;
nakazywać; wymagać; być
wymaganym
required [ry'kłajerd] adj.
obowiązkowy; wymagany;
żądany
requirement [ry'kłajerment] s.
wymaganie; żądanie; potrzeba
requisite ['rekłyzyt] adj.
wymagany; s. rzecz
konieczna, potrzebna; rekwizyt
requisition [,rekły'zyszyn] s.
żądanie; nakaz;
zapotrzebowanie; v.
wydawać zapotrzebowanie;
zapotrzebowywać;
rekwirować; zażądać
dostaw
requite [ry'kłajt] v.
odwzajemniać się;
wynagradzać; zemścić się
rescue ['reskju:] v. ratować;
wybawiać; odbijać z
więzienia; s. ratunek; odbicie
z więzienia; odebranie
przemocą
research [ry'se:rcz] s.

poszukiwanie; badanie
researcher [ry'se:rczer] s. badacz
(naukowy etc.); badaczka
resemblance [ry'zemblens] s.
podobieństwo
resemble [ry'zembl] v. być
podobnym (z wyglądu)
resent [ry'zent] v. czuć urazę
resentful [ry'zentful] adj.
urażony; obrażony; zawzięty
resentment [ry'zentment] s.
uraza; złość; oburzenie;
obraza
reservation [,rezer'wejszyn] s.
zastrzeżenie; zarezerwowanie;
miejsce zarezerwowane;
rezerwat (np. indiański);
rezerwa; zapas; ograniczenie
reserve [ry'ze:rw] v. odkładać;
zastrzegać; rezerwować; s.
rezerwa; zapas; rezerwat;
zastrzeżenie; warunek
reserved [ry'ze:rwd] adj.
zarezerwowany;
powściągliwy; pełen rezerwy;
z rezerwą; zastrzeżony
reservoir ['reserwła:r] s. zbiornik;
zbiór; pokład kopalniany; v.
składać w zbiorniku
reside [ry'zajd] v. mieszkać;
tkwić; spoczywać w;
osadzać się
residence ['rezydens] s. miejsce
zamieszkania; pobyt (stały)
residence permit
['rezydens,per'myt] s. prawo
pobytu
resident ['rezydent] s. stały
mieszkaniec; adj. zamieszkały;
umiejscowiony; zamieszkujący
residue ['rezydju:] s. reszta;
pozostałość; reszta
spadkowa
resign [ry'zajn] v. zrzekać się;
wyrzekać się; godzić się z
losem
resignation [,rezyg'nejszyn] s.
dymisja; zrzeczenie się;
wyrzeczenie się; pogodzenie
się (z losem)
resigned [ry'zajnd] adj.
zrezygnowany; w stanie
spoczynku

resin ['rezyn] s. żywica; v.
zaprawiać żywicą
resist [ry'zyst] v. opierać się;
stawiać opór; być opornym;
powstrzymywać się
resistance [ry'zystens] s. opór;
sprzeciw; wytrzymałość;
odporność; opornica; a.
oporowy
resistant [ry'zystent] adj.
odporny; opierający się; s.
coś lub ktoś odporny,
opierający się
resolute ['rezelu:t] adj. rezolutny;
śmiały; zdecydowany
resolution [,rese'lu:szyn] s.
uchwała; postanowienie;
rezolucja; śmiałość;
rozłożenie; rozwiązanie;
rozkład (sił)
resolve [ry'zolw] s.
postanowienie; decyzja;
stanowczość; v. rozkładać;
rozwiązywać; uchwalać;
decydować; postanawiać;
usuwać; przemieniać;
skłaniać
resolved [ry'solwd] adj.
zdecydowany; śmiały
resonance ['resnens] s.
oddźwięk; odgłos; rezonans
resonant ['reznent] adj.
rezonujący; rozbrzmiewający
resort [ry'zo:rt] v. uciekać się;
uczęszczać; s. uzdrowisko;
uczęszczanie; ucieczka;
uciekanie się; ratunek;
wyjście
resort to [ry'zo:rt,tu] v. uciekać
się do ...
resound [ry'zaund] v.
rozbrzmiewać; odbijać;
opiewać; obiegać;
wypowiadać się; odbijać się
echem
resource [ry'so:rs] s. zasoby;
środki; bogactwa;
zaradność; pomysłowość;
zasoby naturalne
resourceful [ry'so:rsful] adj.
zaradny; pomysłowy
respect [rys'pekt] v. szanować;
dotyczyć; zważać; s.

wzgląd; szacunek; poważanie;
związek; łączność;
pozdrowienia
respectable [rys'pektebl] adj.
chwalebny; godny szacunku;
poważny; pokaźny
respectful [rys'pektful] adj. pełen
szacunku
respectfully [rys'pektfuly] adv. z
poważaniem; z uszanowaniem
respecting [rys'pektyng] prep.
odnośnie do ...
respective [rys'pektyw] adj.
odpowiedni; poszczególny
respectively [rys'pektywly] adv.
odpowiednio; każdemu z
osobna; kolejno
respiration [,respy'rejszyn] s.
oddech; oddychanie
respite ['respajt] s. wytchnienie
(krótkie); odroczenie; v.
odraczać (stracenie);
przynosić (krótką) ulgę
resplendent [rys'plendent] adj.
błyszczący silnie; jasny
respond [rys'pond] v.
odpowiadać; reagować; być
czułym
respondent [rys'pondent] adj.
odpowiadający; wrażliwy; s.
pozwany; obrońca
response [rys'pons] s.
odpowiedź; odzew; reakcja;
oddźwięk; odezwanie się
responsibility [rys,ponse'byłyty]
s. odpowiedzialność
responsible [rys'ponsebl] adj.
odpowiedzialny (wobec, przed)
rest [rest] s. odpoczynek;
spokój; przerwa; przystanek;
podpórka; pomieszczenie;
schronienie; reszta; v.
spoczywać; odpoczywać;
dawać odpoczynek;
uspokoić; być spokojnym;
podpierać się; polegać
restaurant ['resterent] s.
restauracja; jadłodajnia
restful ['restful] adj. spokojny;
uspokajający; wypoczęty
restless ['restlys] adj.
niespokojny; bezsenny;
niesforny

restlessness ['restlysnys] s.
niepokój; zniecierpliwienie
restoration [,reste'rejszyn] s.
odnowienie; rekonstrukcja;
restytucja; odtworzenie
restore [rys'to:r] v. przywracać;
uleczyć; odnawiać;
restaurować; restytuować;
zwracać; rekonstruować;
odtwarzać
restrain [rys'trejn] v.
powstrzymywać;
powściągać; krępować;
ograniczać; trzymać w
ryzach
restraint [rys'trejnt] s.
skrępowanie; uwięzienie;
zamknięcie w szpitalu
psychiatrycznym;
wstrzemięźliwość; umiar
restrict [rys'trykt] v. ograniczać
do; zamykać (w granicach)
restriction [rys'trykszyn] s.
ograniczenie
rest room ['rest,rum] s. ustęp;
toaleta
result [ry'zalt] s. rezultat; wynik;
v. wynikać; dawać w
wyniku; wypływać;
pochodzić
result in [ry'zalt,yn] v. kończyć
się na
resultant [ry'zaltent] adj.
wynikający; (np. siła)
wypadkowa
resume [ry'zju:m] v. wznawiać;
ponownie podejmować;
obejmować; zajmować;
odzyskiwać; ciągnąć dalej;
streszczać; odzyskać
resumption [ry'zampszyn] s.
wznowienie; odzyskanie;
podjęcie na nowo; powrót do
czegoś
resurrection [,reze'rekszyn] s.
odżycie; zmartwychwstanie;
wskrzeszenie; wznowienie
(zwyczaju)
retail ['ri:tejl] s. detal; adj.
detaliczny; v. sprzedawać
detalicznie; szczegółowo
opowiadać; adv. detalicznie
retailer [ri:'tejler] s. sklepikarz;

detalista; plotkarz
retain [ry'tejn] v. zatrzymywać;
zapamiętywać; zgodzić (do
pracy); zachowywać
(tradycje)
retaliate [ry'taeliejt] v.
odwzajemnić się; brać
odwet
retaliation [ry,taely'ejszyn] s.
odwet; zemsta; odpłata
retard [ry'ta:rd] v. opóźniać;
zwalniać; zahamować;
wstrzymywać
retell ['ri:'tel] v. ponownie
opowiedzieć; powtórzyć
retention [ry'tenszyn] s.
zatrzymanie (np. moczu);
zdolność zatrzymywania;
pamięć
retinue ['retynu:] s. orszak;
świta; czeladź; poczet
(dostojnika)
retire [ry'tajer] v. wycofywać
(się); iść na spoczynek;
pensjonować; s. sygnał
odwrotu
retired [ry'tajerd] adj.
emerytowany; ustronny;
odosobniony
retirement [ry'tajerment] s.
przejście w stan spoczynku;
ustronie; odosobnienie;
wycofanie (weksla); odwrót
retort [ry'to:rt] v. odpłacać się;
odcinać się; odparować;
ripostować; s. retorta;
riposta; odwet; odwrócenie
(oskarżenia); cięta odpowiedź
retrace [ry'trejs] v. odtworzyć;
przypomnieć sobie; badać
początek
retrace [ry:'trejs] v. ponownie
liniować; kopiować
retract [ry'traekt] v. cofnąć się;
odwołać; chować się;
wciągać (się) (pazury)
retreat [ry'tri:t] v. cofać się; s.
odwrót; wycofanie się w
zacisze; kryjówka;
odosobnienie; przytułek;
ustronie
retribution [,retry'bju:szyn] s.
odpłata; kara; nagroda

retrieve [ry'tri:w] v. odzyskać;
powetować; odszukać;
uratować; uprzytomnić
sobie; aportować; s.
odzyskanie; odszukanie;
powetowanie; uratowanie;
ruch wsteczny (powrotny)
retrospect ['retrespekt] s.
spojrzenie wstecz; rozważanie
przeszłości; v. rzucać okiem
wstecz; nawiązywać do
(przeszłości); patrzeć w
przeszłość
retrospective ['retrespektyw] adj.
retrospektywny; działający
wstecz; z mocą retroaktywną
return [ry'te:rn] v. wracać;
przynosić dochód; złożyć
(zeznanie); obracać w ...;
oddawać; odwzajemnić;
odpowiedzieć; wybrać; s.
powrót; nawrót; dochód; zysk;
zwrot; rewanż; sprawozdanie
(np. podatkowe)
return flight [ry'te:rn,flajt] s. lot
powrotny
return ticket [ry'te:rn,tykyt] s.
powrotny bilet
reunification ['ri:ju:nyfy'kejszyn]
s. ponowne zjednoczenie
reunion ['ri:'ju:njen] s. zjazd;
ponowne połączenie; zebranie
revaluation [ri:'wael'juejszyn] s.
ponowna ocena;
przewartościowanie (po
ponownej ocenie)
revaluate [ri:'waelju':ejt] v.
ponownie ocenić;
przewartościować (dom w
celach podatkowych)
revamp [ry:'waemp] v.
przerobić; reorganizować;
rewidować; okapować
(buty); odnowić
reveal [ry'wi:l] v. ujawniać;
objawiać; odsłaniać; s. rama
okna w karoserii
revel ['rewl] s. zabawa; hulanka;
v. hulać; używać sobie
revelation [,rewy'lejszyn] s.
ujawnienie; objawienie;
odsłonięcie; rewelacja;
odkrycie

revenge [ry'wendż] s. zemsta;
mściwość; v. pomścić;
zemścić się (za zniewagą,
krzywdę etc.)

revengeful [ry'wendżful] adj.
mściwy

revenue ['rewy,nu:] s. dochód (z
podatków)

revenue office ['rewy,nu:'ofys] s.
urząd podatkowy (finansowy)

revere [ry'wier] v. czcić;
odnosić się z czcią

reverence ['rewerens] s. cześć;
szacunek; wielebność

reverend ['rewerend] adj.
czcigodny; wielebny; s.
duchowny

reverse [ry'we:rs] s.
odwrotność; rewers; tył;
niepowodzenie; wsteczny
bieg; adj. odwrotny;
przeciwny; wsteczny; v.
odwracać; zmieniać
kierunek; obalać (np. przepis)

reverse gear [ry'we:rs,gier] s.
wsteczny bieg (w
samochodzie)

reverse side [ry'we:rs,sajd] s.
odwrotna strona

review [ry'wju:] v. przeglądać;
pisać recenzje; przeglądać w
myśli; dokonywać przeglądu;
s. recenzja; przegląd; rewia;
ponowny przegląd

reviewer [ry'wju:er] s. recenzent;
krytyk

revile [ry'wajl] v. wyzywać;
wymyślać; przezywać

revise [ry'wajz] v. przejrzeć;
zrewidować; przerabiać

revision [ry'wyżyn] s. rewizja;
przejrzane wydanie; przeróbka

revival [ry'wajwel] s. ożywienie;
odżywanie; powrót do życia;
powrót do stanu
użyteczności

revive [ry'wajw] v. wskrzeszać;
przywracać do życia;
wznawiać; ożywiać;
odżywać; wracać do
przytomności

revolt [ry'woult] s. bunt;
powstanie; v. buntować się;

wzdrygać się; mieć odrazę;
budzić odrazę

revolution [,rewe'lu:szyn] s.
obrót; rewolucja

revolutionary [,rewe'lu:sznry] adj.
rewolucyjny; s. rewolucjonista

revolutionist [,rewe'lu:szynyst] s.
rewolucjonista

revolutionize [,rewe'lu:szn,ajz] v.
zrewolucjonizować;
wywoływać rewolucją

revolve [ry'wolw] v. obracać;
krążyć; obracać się;
obmyślać

revolving [ry'wolwyng] adj.
obrotowy

reward [ry'ło:rd] s. nagroda;
wynagrodzenie; v.
wynagradzać

rheumatism ['ru:metyzem] s.
reumatyzm; gościec stawowy

rhubarb ['ru:ba:rb] s. rabarbar;
(slang) kłótnia

rhyme [rajm] s. rym; v.
rymować się

rhythm ['rytm] s. rytm

rhythmic ['rytmyk] adj.
rytmiczny; miarowy

rib [ryb] s. żebro; żeberko;
wręga; v. żeberkować;
nabierać; wyśmiewać;
droczyć się; płytko orać

ribbed [rybd] adj. żebrowany

ribbon ['ryben] s. taśma; pasek;
strzęp; wstążka; v. drzeć na
strzępy, paski; ozdabiać
wstążką; wić się wstęgą

rice [rajs] s. ryż

rich [rycz] adj. bogaty;
kosztowny; suty; obfity;
tuczący; pożywny; soczysty;
mocny (zapach); pełny; tłusty
(np. pokarm); pocieszny
(zdarzenie)

riches ['ryczyz] pl. bogactwo;
bogactwa

richness ['rycznys] s. bogactwo;
pełnia

rick [ryk] s. stóg; v. ustawiać w
stogi; stawiać stóg

rickets ['rykyts] s. choroba
angielska; krzywica; rachityzm

rickety ['rykyty] adj. chwiejny;

koślawy; rachityczny
rid; rid; ridded [ryd; ryd; 'rydyd]
rid [ryd] v. uwalniać się od ...;
oczyszczać się; pozbywać
się
ridden ['rydn] v. zob. ride
riddle ['rydl] s. zagadka; v.
zadawać zagadki; mówić
zagadkami; rozwiązywać
zagadki
ride; rode; ridden [rajd; roud;
'rydn]
ride [rajd] v. pojechać; jechać
(też statkiem); jeździć;
tyranizować; wozić; nosić;
dokuczać; s. przejażdżka;
jazda; nabieranie (kogoś);
droga
rider ['rajder] s. jeździec;
dżokej; poprawka; dodatek;
klauzula; ciężarek
przesuwany; nasadka;
poprawka na dokumencie
ridge [rydż] s. grzbiet (też góry);
krawędź; kalenica; pasmo
górskie; wał; skiba; grobla; v.
pokrywać skibami; robić
krawędzie; marszczyć
ridicule ['rydy,kju:l] v.
wyśmiewać się; s. kpiny
ridiculous [ry'dykju:les] adj.
śmieszny; bezsensowny
riding ['rajdyng] s. konna jazda;
adj. jadący; do konnej jazdy
rife [rajf] adj. częsty;
rozpowszechniony; pełen
riff-raff [ryf-raf] pl. motłoch;
swołocz
rifle [rajfl] s. karabin; gwintówka;
gwint; strzelec; v. gwintować
(lufę); strzelać; ograbić;
okraść; pokrzyżować
rift [ryft] s. szczelina; różnica
zdań; v. rozszczepiać się;
pęknąć; popękać
rig [ryg] v. zaopatrywać;
klecić; montować; stroić;
robić kanty; manipulować
ceny; s. sprzęt (wiertniczy);
wóz z koniem; kostium;
machlojka
right [rajt] adj. prawa; prawy;
poprawny; prawoskrętny;

prosty (też kąt); właściwy;
słuszny; dobry; odpowiedni;
prawidłowy; w porządku;
zdrowy; adv. w prawo; na
prawo; prosto; bezpośrednio;
bezzwłocznie; dokładnie;
słusznie; dobrze; s. prawa
strona; prawo; dobro;
słuszność; sprawiedliwość;
pierwszeństwo; v.
naprostować; naprawić;
sprostować; odpłacać;
mścić; usprawiedliwiać
right ahead ['rajt,e'hed] exp.:
wprost; na wprost; przed
siebie
right away ['rajt,e'łej] exp.:
zaraz; natychmiast; już teraz
righteous ['rajtszes] adj.
sprawiedliwy; prawy; słuszny
rightful ['rajtful] adj. słuszny;
sprawiedliwy; prawowity;
należny z prawa; prawy
right-hand ['rajt,haend] adj.
praworęki; położony na prawo
right-handed ['rajt-'haendyd] adj.
praworęczny; dostosowany do
prawej ręki; idący wg. ruchu
zegara; obracający się w
prawo (gwint etc.)
right of way ['rajt,ow'łej] exp.:
prawo pierwszeństwa na
drodze; prawo przejazdu;
grunt pod drogą (kolej) (pod
szosą etc.)
rightist ['rajtyst] s. prawicowiec;
adj. prawicowy
rightly ['rajtly] adv.
sprawiedliwie; słusznie;
poprawnie; właściwie; na
miejscu
rigid ['rydżyd] adj. sztywny;
nieugięty; surowy;
nieustępliwy
rigor ['ryger] s. rygor;
surowość; zesztywnienie
rigorous ['rygeres] adj. surowy;
rygorystyczny
rim [rym] s. brzeg; krawędź;
obręcz; powierzchnia wody
(przy żeglowaniu); v. robić
krawędź; posuwać wzdłuż
krawędzi; dawać oprawę (do

okularów)

rind [rajnd] s. kora; łupina;
skórka (owocu, sera, etc.); v.
zdzierać (korę, jarzynę)

ring [ryng] s. pierścień;
obrączka; kółko; koło; zmowa;
szajka; słój; arena; ring
(bokserski); v. otaczać;
kołować; krajać w kółko

ring; rang; rung [ryng; raeng;
rang]

ring [ryng] v. dzwonić;
dźwięczeć; brzmieć;
rozbrzmiewać; wydzwaniać;
telefonować; wybijać czas
na zegarze kontrolnym;
sprawdzać monetę
dźwiękiem; s. dzwonek;
dzwony; dźwięk; brzęk;
telefonowanie

ring off ['ryng,of] s. skończyć
rozmowę telefoniczną

ring the bell ['ryng,dy'bel] v.
dzwonić (do drzwi etc.)

ring up ['ryng,ap] v. wybijać
kwotę (na kasie
rejestracyjnej); zatelefonować
(do kogoś)

ringleader ['ryng,li:der] s.
prowodyr; herszt

rink [rynk] s. ślizgawka; tor
jazdy na wrotkach; boisko do
gry w kule

rinse [ryns] s. płukać s.
wypłukanie

rinse out ['ryns,aut] v.
wypłukać; przepłukiwać

riot ['rajot] s. zgiełk; zamęt;
rozruchy; bunty; rozpusta;
hulanka; rozprężenie; orgia; v.
buntować się; robić
rozruchy, zamieszki; hulać;
używać sobie; uprawiać
rozpustę

riotous ['rajetes] adj.
buntowniczy; rozpustny;
hulaszczy; hałaśliwy; bujny;
oporny; niesforny

rip [ryp] v. odrywać; zrywać;
łupać; rozpruwać; piłować
wzdłuż; pękać; pędzić; s.
rozprucie; rozpustnik; hulaka;
szkapa; rzecz nie warta nic;

wir; wzburzona powierzchnia
wody

ripe [rajp] adj. dojrzały

ripen ['rajpn] v. dojrzewać;
przyspieszać dojrzewanie

ripeness ['rajpnys] s. dojrzałość

ripple ['rypl] s. zmarszczki (na
wodzie); fale (na włosach);
falowanie; grzebień do lnu; v.
marszczyć; falować;
rozczesywać; rozwodzić się

rise; rose; risen [rajz; rouz; 'ryzn]

rise [rajz] v. podnieść się;
stanąć; wstawać; powstać;
buntować się; wzbierać;
wzbijać się; wzmagać się;
sprostać; s. wschód;
wznoszenie się; podwyżka;
wzrost; powodzenie;
początek; stopień

risen ['ryzn] v. zob. rise

riser [rajzer] s. osoba wstająca;
pionowy przewód (też rura);
podstawka stopnia (na
schodach)

rising ['rajzyng] s. wzniesienie;
powstanie; zmartwychwstanie;
bąbel; pryszcz; zaczynanie
ciasta; adj. podnoszący się;
wzrastający; wschodzący

risk [rysk] s. ryzyko;
niebezpieczeństwo; v.
narażać się; ryzykować;
ponosić ryzyko

risky ['rysky] adj. niebezpieczny;
ryzykowny; pikantny;
drastyczny

rite [rajt] s. obrządek; obrzęd
(ślubny); rytuał

rival ['rajwel] s. rywal;
współzawodnik; v.
rywalizować

rivalry ['rajwelry] s. rywalizacja;
współzawodnictwo

river ['rywer] s. rzeka

river boat ['rywer,bout] s. statek
rzeczny; łódź rzeczna

riverside ['rywer,sajd] s. brzeg
rzeki

rivet ['rywyt] s. nit; v. nitować;
utkwić; przykuć

rivulet ['rywjulyt] s. rzeczułka;
mały strumień; mały potok

road [roud] s. droga; kolej; reda; v. topić

road hog ['roud,hog] s. pirat drogowy (lekceważący przepisy)

road map ['roud,maep] s. mapa drogowa; mapa samochodowa

roadside ['roud,sajd] s. bok drogi; adj. przydrożny

road sign ['roud,sajn] s. znak drogowy

roam [roum] v. włóczyć się; s. włóczęga; wędrówka

roar [ro:r] v. ryczeć; huczeć; s. ryk; huk (armat); ryk (śmiechu)

roars of laughter ['ro:rs,ow'lafter] exp.: wybuchy śmiechu

roast [roust] v. piec; opiekać; przypiekać; wypalać; ośmieszać; krytykować ostro; s. pieczeń; pieczenie; kpiny; krytyka ostra; adj. pieczony

roast beef ['roust,bi:f] s. pieczeń wołowa

roast meat ['roust,mi:t] s. pieczone mięso

rob [rob] v. grabić; rabować; ograbić; pozbawiać (czegoś)

robber ['rober] s. rabuś

robbery ['robery] s. rabunek

robe [roub] s. podomka; suknia; szata; płaszcz kąpielowy; toga; v. przyodziewać; przyoblekać

robin ['robyn] s. drozd; rudzik

robot ['roubot] s. robot

robust ['roubast] adj. krzepki; trzeźwy; szorstki; hałaśliwy; ciężki; silny; mocny

rock [rok] s. kamień; skała; farba; kołysanie; taniec (rock and roll); pl. kostki lodu w napoju; v. kołysać się; bujać się; huśtać się; wstrząsać; wypłukiwać piasek; płukać (się); a. kamienny; skalisty

rocker ['roker] s. biegun; łyżwa holenderka

rocket ['rokyt] s. rakieta; v. wznosić się

rocket power ['rokyt'pałer] s. napęd rakietowy

rocketry ['rokytry] s. broń rakietowa; technika rakietowa

rocking chair ['rokyng,czeer] s. krzesło na biegunach

rocky ['roky] adj. skalisty; chwiejny; kamienisty; skalny

rod [rod] s. pręt; drąg; wędka; (pręt = 5.029m)

rode [roud] v. zob. ride

rodent ['roudent] s. gryzoń

roe [rou] s. sarna; łania; ikra we wnętrzu ryby; sperma ryby

rogue [roug] s. łobuz; łajdak; psotnik; słoń samotnik

roguish ['rougysz] adj. psotny; figlarny; łobuzerski

role [roul] s. rola

roll [roul] s. rolka; zwój; zwitek; rulon; bułka; rożek; spis; wykaz; rejestr; lista; wokanda; wałek; walec; wałek; kołysanie (się); werbel; huk; v. toczyć; wałkować; tarzać; grzmieć; dudnić; rozlegać się; zataczać beczkę; toczyć koło; wręcić; obracać; wymawiać "r"; rozwałkowywać; wałkować

roll up ['roul,ap] v. zawinąć (rękawy); kłębić się; podjeżdżać; skumulować (się)

roller ['rouler] s. wałek; rolka; kółko; długa tocząca się fala; narzędzie do wałkowania

roller coaster ['rouler'kouster] s. kolejka wysokogórska; wesołe miasteczko

roller-skate ['rouler'skejt] s. wrotka

rolling mill ['roulyn,myl] s. walcownia

Roman ['roumen] adj. rzymski

romance [rou'maens] s. romans średniowieczny; powieść miłosna; sprawa miłosna; adj. romański; v. romansować; koloryzować; przesadzać; pisać romanse

romantic [rou'maentyk] adj. romantyczny; s. romantyk

romp [romp] s. urwis; zbytki; swawole; figle; igraszki; v. figlować; dokazywać; uganiać; łatwo wygrać (wyścigi)

rompers ['rompers] pl. kombinezon do zabawy dla dziecka

roof [ru:f] s. dach; v. pokrywać dachem

roof over ['ru:f,ouwer] v. pokrywać dachem

rook [ruk] s. gawron; szuler; wieża (w szachach); v. ograć; oszukać; zdzierać skórę

room [rum] s. pokój; miejsce; mieszkanie; izba; wolna przestrzeń; sposobność; powód; v. dzielić pokój lub mieszkanie; mieszkać lub odnajmować pokój

room-mate ['rum,mejt] s. współmieszkaniec; współlokator

roomy ['rumy] adj. przestronny; obszerny

roost [ru:st] s. grzęda; v. siedzieć na grzędzie

rooster [ru:ster] s. kogut

root [ru:t] s. korzeń; nasada; podstawa; istota; źródło; sedno; pierwiastek; v. posadzić; zakorzenić; ryć; szperać; wygrzebywać; popierać; dopingować

root out ['ru:t,aut] v. wykorzenić; wyrwać z korzeniami

rope [roup] s. sznur; powróz; lina; stryczek; v. związać; przywiązać; łapać na lasso; ogradzać sznurami; ciągnąć na linie; przyciągać; zdobywać; obśliznąć

rope off ['roup,of] v. ogradzać linami

rose [rous] s. róża; kolor różowy; rozetka; v. zaróżowić; zob. rise

rosy ['rouzy] adj. różowy

rot [rot] s. zgnilizna; rozkład; zepsucie; głupstwa; brednie; motylica; v. gnić; butwieć; rozkładać się

rotary ['routery] adj. rotacyjny; obrotowy

rotate ['routejt] v. obracać (się); kolejno zmieniać (się); wirować; adj. kółkowy

rotation [rou'tejszyn] s. rotacja; ruch obrotowy; obracanie (się); płodozmian; ciągła wymiana; kolejne następstwo

rotor ['router] s. wirnik

rotten ['rotn] adj. zgniły; zepsuty; zdemoralizowany; lichy; kiepski; marny; chory na motylicę; do niczego; do chrzanu

rotund [rou'tand] adj. okrągły; zaokrąglony; szumny; przysadkowy

rough [raf] adj. szorstki; chropowaty; ostry; nierówny; wyboisty; nieokrzesany; brutalny; drastyczny; cierpki; nieprzyjemny; nieociosany; surowy; gruby; burzliwy; gwałtowny; hałaśliwy; ciężki; pobieżny; przybliżony; prymitywny; wstępny; szkicowy; adv. ostro; szorstko; grubiańsko; z grubsza; s. nierówny teren; stan naturalny - nieobrobiony; hacel; chuligan; v. być szorstkim; szorstko postępować; hartować (się); jeżyć (się); burzyć (się); szlifować z grubsza; pasować z grubsza; obrabiać z grubsza; szkicować; przebiedować; ujeżdżać (konia); robić coś z grubsza; podkuwać hacelami

roughness ['rafnys] s. szorstkość; grubiaństwo; chamstwo

rough-neck ['rafnek] s. członek obsługi szybu; łobuz; brutal; chuligan

round [raund] adj. okrągły; zaokrąglony; kolisty; okrężny; tam i nazad; kulisty; sferyczny; adv. wkoło; kołem;

dookoła; prep. dookoła; s.
koło; obwód; kula; obrót;
krąg; bieg; cykl; ciąg; zasiąg;
seria; objazd; obchód; runda;
zaokrąglenie; pasmo (np.
trudności); przechadzka; v.
zaokrąglać; wygładzać;
okrążyć; obchodzić;
opływać
round off ['raund,of] v.
zaokrąglać
round out ['raund,aut] v.
zaokrąglać się; tyć
round up ['raund,ap] v. spędzać
(bydło)
round-up ['raund'ap] s.
spędzanie bydła
roundabout ['raundebaut] adj.
okrężny; s. rondo; karuzela
round trip ['raund,tryp] s. podróż
tam i nazad
rouse [rauz] v. pobudzić;
wzniecać; ruszyć; ożywiać;
podsycać; wyrywać;
wypłoszyć; obudzić się;
otrząsnąć się
roustabout ['rauste,baut] s.
robotnik portowy; robotnik
przemysłu naftowego
route [ru:t] s. droga; trasa;
marsz; szlak
routine [ru:'ti:n] s. rutyna; tok
zajęć
rove [rouw] v. wałęsać się;
błądzić wzrokiem; łowić;
skręcać włókno; s.
niedoprzęd
rover ['rouwer] s. wędrowiec;
włóczęga; korsarz; pirat
row [roł] s. szereg; rząd; jazda
łodzią; v. wiosłować
row [rał] s. zgiełk; hałas; kłótnia;
bójka; burda; nagana; bura; v.
besztać; pokłócić się
row-boat ['roł,bout] s. łódź
wiosłowa
rower ['rołer] s. wioślarz
rowing boat ['rołyngbout] s.
łódź wiosłowa
royal ['rojel] adj. królewski
royalty ['rojelty] s.
królewskość; honorarium
autorskie

rub [rab] v. trzeć; potrzeć;
wytrzeć; wycierać; głaskać;
nacierać; s. tarcie; nacieranie
rub down ['rab,dałn] v.
nacierać; wcierać
rub in ['rab,yn] v. wcierać;
wytykać
rub off ['rab,of] v. zetrzeć
rub out ['rab,aut] v. wymazać
rubber ['raber] s. guma;
masażysta; pl. kalosze; v.
pokrywać gumą; odwracać
(głowę)
rubberneck ['raber,nek] s.
ciekawski; turysta; gapa
rubber plant ['raber,plaent] s.
kauczukowa roślina
rubbish ['rabysz] s. śmieć;
gruz; tandeta; nonsens;
brednie; głupstwa; bzdury
rubble ['rabl] s. gruz; rumowisko
skalne; kamień łamany
ruby ['ru:by] s. rubin
rucksack ['ruksaek] s. plecak
rude [ru:d] adj. szorstki;
niegrzeczny; ostry; surowy;
prosty; pierwotny; nagły;
gwałtowny; krzepki
ruder ['rader] s. ster
ruddy ['rady] adj. rumiany;
czerstwy; czerwony; v.
rumienić się
ruff [raf] s. kołnierz; kreza;
batalion; bojownik; bicie
atutem; v. przebić atutem
ruffian ['rafjen] s. zbój; łotr
ruffle ['rafl] s. kreza; żabot;
mankiet koronkowy; kłopot;
zamieszanie; marszczenie; v.
marszczyć (powierzchnię);
rozwiewać; rozczochrać;
nastroszyć; wzburzyć (się)
rug [rag] s. pled; kilim; dywan
rugby ['ragby] s. (sport) rugby
ruin [,ruyn] s. ruina; v. rujnować
(się); zniszczyć (się)
rule [ru:l] s. przepis; prawo;
reguła; zasada; rządy;
panowanie; postanowienie;
miarka; linijka; v. rządzić;
panować; kierować;
orzekać; postanawiać;
liniować

rule out ['ru:l,aut] v. wykluczać
ruler ['ru:ler] s. władca; liniał;
linijka
rum [ram] s. rum; adj. dziwny
rumble ['rambl] v. dudnić;
grzmieć; turkotać; s. huk;
grzmot; dudnienie; tylne
miejsce w pojeździe na bagaż
lub służącego
ruminant ['ru:mynent] adj.
przeżuwający; s. przeżuwacz
rummage ['ramydż] s. szperanie;
przetrząsanie; wyprzedaż
resztek; v. wygrzebać;
przetrząsać
rumor ['ru:mer] s. pogłoska;
słuchy; v. puszczać pogłoski
rump [ramp] s. zad; kuper;
comber; kadłub
rumple ['rampl] v. zmiąć;
zmiętosić; mierzwić;
czochrać
run; ran; ran [ran; raen; raen]
run [ran] v. biec; biegać;
pędzić; spieszyć się;
jechać; płynąć; kursować;
obracać się; działać;
funkcjonować; pracować;
uciekać; zbiec; prowadzić;
toczyć się; wynosić (sumę);
rozpływać się; łzawić;
głosić; spotykać; narzucać
się; molestować; zderzyć
się; sprzeciwiać się; wpaść
etc.; s. bieg; przebieg;
bieganie; rozbieg; rozpęd;
przebieg; passa; sekwens;
okres; seria; ciąg; dostęp;
wybieg; pastwisko; zjazd; tor
run about ['ran,e'baut] v. biegać
tu i tam; s. wędrowiec; adj.
wędrowny
run across ['ran,e'kros] v.
spotkać przypadkowo
run after ['ran,aefter] v. gonić
run away ['ran,e'łej] v. uciekać;
ponieść
run down ['ran,dałn] v.
przejechać; wyczerpać;
wytropić
run in ['ran,yn] v. wpaść na ...;
dotrzeć
run off ['ran,of] v. uciekać;

recytować; drukować
run out ['ran,aut] v. skończyć
się; wygasnąć; drukować
run over ['ran,ouwer] v.
przejechać; przepełniać
run up ['ran,ap] v. dobiec;
dojść do ...; dodać;
wyśrubować; s. dochodzenie
do celu
rung [rang] s. poprzeczka;
szczebel; szprycha; v. zob.
ring
runner ['raner] s. goniec;
biegacz; posłaniec; woźny;
akwizytor; łopatka;
obsługujący maszynę;
chodnik; przemytnik; płoza;
łożysko ślizgowe; wałek
running ['ranyng] adj. bieżący;
biegający; będący w biegu;
cieknący; ropiejący; w ruchu;
ruchomy; ciągły; nieustanny;
pochyły; nieprzerwany; s.
bieg; wyścig; kandydowanie;
funkcjonowanie; ropienie;
kierownictwo
running board ['ranyng,bo:rd] s.
stopień; pomost
runway ['ran,łej] s. bieżnia (do
lądowania); tor (jezdny)
rupture ['rapczer] s. złamanie;
zerwanie; przepuklina; v.
przerywać; zrywać;
poderwać się (mieć
przepuklinę)
rural ['ruerel] adj. wiejski
ruse [ru:z] s. podstęp
rush [rasz] v. pędzić; poganiać;
ponaglać; rzucać się na
coś; przeskakiwać; wysyłać
pospiesznie; zdobywać
szturmem; zdzierać
(pieniądze); słać sitowiem; s.
pęd; ruch; pośpiech; napływ;
atak; intensywny popyt;
sitowie
rush hour ['rasz,auer] s. godzina
szczytu; chwila uderzenia
Russia [rasz'e] s. Rosja
Russian ['raszyn] adj. rosyjski; s.
Rosjanin
rust [rast] s. rdza (zbożowa); v.
rdzewieć; niszczyć się

rust-eaten ['rast,i:tn] adj.
zardzewiały
rustic ['rastik] adj. wiejski;
prostacki; s. wieśniak;
prostak
rustle ['rasl] v. szeleścić;
kraść bydło; krzątać się; s.
szelest
rusty ['rasty] adj. zardzewiały;
zaniedbany; wyszły z wprawy;
podniszczony
rut [rat] s. koleina; bruzda; utarty
szlak; rutyna; nawyk; rowek;
wyżłobienie; ruja; bokowisko;
rykowisko
ruthless ['ru:tlys] adj. bezlitosny;
bezwzględny; niemiłosierny
rutted ['ratyd] adj. rozjeżdżony;
wyjeżdżony
rutty ['raty] adj. wyjeżdżony
rye [raj] s. żyto; żytniówka
rye whisky ['raj,hłysky] szkocka
żytnia wódka

S

s [es] dziewiętnasta litera
alfabetu angielskiego
's skrót: is, has, us
saber ['sejber] s. szabla; pałasz;
v. ciąć; ranić; ścinać
sable ['sejbl] s. soból; czerń;
adj. czarny; sobolowy (z futer)
sabotage ['saebeta:ż] s.
sabotaż; v. sabotować
sabre ['sejber] s. szabla; zob.
saber
saccharin ['saekeryn] s.
sacharyna
sack [saek] s. worek; torebka;
sak; luźny płaszcz;
plądrowanie; v. pakować do
worków; zwalniać z pracy;
plądrować
sacrament ['saekrement] s.
sakrament
sacred ['sejkryd] adj.
poświęcony; nienaruszalny

sacrifice ['saekryfajs] s. ofiara;
wyrzeczenie (się); v.
ofiarowywać; poświęcać;
wyrzekać się w zamian za
coś innego
sacrilegious [,saekry'lydżes] adj.
świętokradzki
sad [saed] adj. smutny; bolesny;
posępny; ponury; okropny
sadden ['saedn] v. zasmucać
(się); posmutnieć
saddle ['saedl] s. siodło; v.
siodłać; obarczać; wkładać
ciężar (komuś) (na kogoś)
sadness ['saednys] s. smutek
safe [sejf] adj. pewny;
bezpieczny; s. schowek
bankowy; kasa pancerna;
spiżarnia wietrzona; (slang):
kondon
safeguard ['sejfga:rd] v.
ochraniać; zabezpieczać;
gwarantować; s.
zabezpieczenie; gwarancja
safety ['sejfty] s.
bezpieczeństwo;
zabezpieczenie; bezpiecznik;
adj. dający bezpieczeństwo
safety belt ['sejfty,belt] s. pas
bezpieczeństwa (np. w
samochodzie)
safety lock ['sejfty,lok] s. zamek
bezpieczeństwa
safety pin ['sejfty,pyn] s. agrafka
safety razor ['sejfty,rejzer] s.
maszynka do golenia się
żyletkami (które się wymienia
po użyciu)
safety-valve ['sejfty,waelw] s.
klapa bezpieczeństwa; zawór
bezpieczeństwa
sag [saeg] v. obwisać; zwisać;
wyginać (się); przechylać
się; spadać w cenie; s. zwis;
wygięcie; spadek (ceny)
sagacity [se'gaesyty] s.
rozwaga; mądrość;
roztropność; bystrość
said [sed] v. zob. say
sail [sejl] s. żagiel; podróż
morska; v. żeglować;
kroczyć okazale; sterować
okrętem; bawić się modelem

statku
sail-boat ['sejl,bout] s. żaglówka
sailing-ship ['sejlyng,szyp] s.
statek żaglowy
sailor ['sejlor] s. żeglarz;
marynarz
saint [sejnt] s. & adj. święty
sake [sejk] s. czyjeś dobro;
wzgląd
salad ['saeled] s. sałatka
salary ['saelery] s. pensja;
pobory; wynagrodzenie
sale [sejl] s. sprzedaż;
wyprzedaż
saleslady ['sejls'lejdy] s.
sprzedawczyni
salesman ['sejlsmen] s.
sprzedawca
sales manager [,sejls'maenydżer]
s. kierownik działu sprzedaży
saliva [se'lajwa] s. ślina
sallow ['saelou] adj. ziemisty;
blady; żółtawy; v. dawać
żółtawy odcień; s. iwa
(wierzba)
sally ['saely] s. wypad;
wycieczka z oblężenia;
docinek (cięty)
sally out ['saely,aut] v.
wyruszać w podróż
salmon ['saemen] s. łosoś; adj.
łososiowy; łososiowego koloru
saloon [se'lu:n] s. bar; szynk;
sala (zabaw); salon (na
okręcie)
salt [so:lt] s. sól; adj. słony; v.
solić
saltcellar ['so:lt,seler] s.
solniczka
salt-free ['so:lt,fri:] adj. bezsolny;
pozbawiony soli
salty ['so:lty] adj. słony
salutation [,saelju:'tejszyn] s.
pozdrowienie; przywitanie
salute [se'lu:t] s. pozdrowienie;
salutowanie; honory
wojskowe; salwa (powitalna);
v. pozdrowić; powitać;
salutować; odbierać
defiladę; przejść przed
kompanią honorową
salvation [sael'wejszyn] s.
zbawienie; ratunek;

wybawienie
salve [sa:w] v. natrzeć;
złagodzić; uspokoić; s.
maść; balsam
same [sejm] adj. ten sam; taki
sam; jednostajny; monotonny;
adv. tak samo; identycznie;
bez zmiany; pron. to samo
sample ['sa:mpl] s. próbka;
wzór; v. próbować; dawać
próbki
sanatorium [,saene'to:rjem] s.
sanatorium
sanctify ['saenkty,faj] v.
uświęcać; poświęcać
sanctimonious [,saenkty
'mounjes] adj.
świętoszkowaty
sanction ['saenkszyn] v.
usankcjonować; s. sankcja
sanctuary ['saenkczuery] s.
przybytek; azyl
sand [saend] s. piasek; v.
posypywać piaskiem;
obrabiać papierem ściernym
sandal ['saendl] s. sandał;
rzemyk; v. wkładać sandały;
przywiązywać rzemykiem
sandwich ['saendłycz] s.
kanapka; sandwicz; v.
wkładać (między)
sandy ['saendy] adj. piaskowy;
piaskowego koloru
sandy beach ['saendy,bi:cz] s.
plaża
sane [sejn] adj. zdrowy na
umyśle; rozsądny; normalny
sang [saeng] v. zob. sing
sanitarium [,saeny'teerjem] s.
sanatorium
sanitary ['saenytery] adj.
higieniczny; zdrowy
sanitary napkin ['saenytery
'naepkyn] s. podpaska
higieniczna
sanitation [,saeny'tejszyn] s.
higiena; kanalizacja;
urządzenia sanitarne
sank [saenk] v. zob. sink
Santa Claus [,saenta'klo:z] s.
Dziadek Mróz; Święty Mikołaj
sap [saep] s. żywica; sok;
głupiec; kujon; nudziarstwo;

sapa; podkopywanie; v.
wyciągać soki; usuwać biel
z drzewa; podkopywać;
podmywać; kopać sapę

sappy ['saepy] s. soczysty; pełen
wigoru; energiczny

sarcasm ['sa:rkaezem] s.
sarkazm

sardine [sa:r'di:n] s. sardynka

sash [saesz] s. szarfa; rama
okienna do pionowego
suwania okien; v. instalować
ramy okienne

sash window ['saesz'łyndou] s.
suwane okno

sat [saet] v. zob. sit

Satan ['sejtn] s. szatan

satchel ['saeczel] s. torba z
rzemieniami na plecy

satellite ['saete,lajt] s. satelita

satin ['saetyn] s. atłas; adj.
atłasowy; v. satynować
(papier)

satire ['saetajer] s. satyra

satirize ['saety,rajz] v.
wykpiwać; wyśmiewać;
satyryzować

satisfaction [,saetys'faekszyn] s.
zadowolenie; satysfakcja;
spłacenie długu; zaspokojenie

satisfactory [,saetys'faektery]
adj. zadowalający; odpowiedni

satisfy ['saetys,faj] v.
zaspokoić; uiścić; spełnić;
zadowalać; odpowiadać;
przekonywać

Saturday ['saeterdy] s. sobota

sauce [so:s] s. sos; kompot; v.
przyprawiać jedzenie;
nagadać komuś; stawiać
się

sauce-box ['so:s,boks] s.
impertynent; zuchwalec

saucepan ['so:spen] s. patelnia;
rondel

saucer ['so:ser] s. spodek

saunter ['so:nter] s. przechadzka;
v. przechadzać się; chodzić
powolnym krokiem

sausage ['sosydż] s. kiełbasa

save [sejw] v. ratować;
oszczędzać; zachowywać
pozory; zbawiać; uniknąć;

zyskiwać (czas); prep.
oprócz; wyjąwszy; poza;
pominąwszy; conj. że; poza
tym; chyba że; z wyjątkiem

save for a car ['sejw,fo:r'ej,ka:r]
exp.: oszczędzać na
samochód

saver ['sejwer] s. osoba
oszczędzająca; przedmiot
oszczędzający (np. czas)

saving ['sejwyng] adj.
zbawienny; oszczędny; prep.
wyjąwszy

savings-bank ['sejwynz'baenk] s.
kasa oszczędności

savior ['sejwjer] s. zbawca;
zbawiciel

savor ['sejwer] s. smak; aromat;
powab; v. mieć smak;
pachnieć; smakować;
nadawać smak

savory ['sejwery] adj. smaczny;
apetyczny; smakowity;
pikantny; aromatyczny

saw; sawed; sawn [so:; so:d;
so:n]

saw [so:] v. zob. see; piłować;
s. piła

sawdust ['so:,dast] s. trociny

sawmill ['so:,myl] s. tartak

Saxon ['saeksn] adj. saksoński;
saski; s. Sas

say; said; said [sej; sed; sed]

say [sej] v. mówić; powiedzieć;
odprawiać; twierdzić

say-so ['sejso] s. prawo decyzji;
zapewnienie; ostatnie słowo

saying ['sejyng] s. powiedzonko;
powiedzenie

scab [skaeb] s. strup; parch;
świerzb; łamistrajk

scaffold ['skaefeld] s.
rusztowanie; platforma;
estrada; szafot; v. stawiać
rusztowanie

scaffolding ['skaefeldyng] s.
rusztowanie

scald [sko:ld] v. oparzyć;
wyparzyć; pasteryzować; s.
oparzenie

scale [skejl] s. skala; podziałka;
układ; drabina; szalka; łuska;
kamień nazębny; v. wyłazić;

wdzierać się; mierzyć
(podziałką); ważyć;
łuszczyć; łuskać; złuszczać
się
scale down ['skejl,dałn] v.
zmniejszać (proporcjonalnie)
scale up ['skejl,ap] v.
powiększać (proporcjonalnie)
scales ['skejls] pl. waga
scalp ['skaelp] s. skalp; skóra na
głowie; v. oskalpować;
złośliwie krytykować
scan [skaen] v. badawczo
przeglądać; skandować;
mieć rytm
scandal ['skaendl] s. skandal;
zgorszenie; oszczerstwo; plotki
scandalous ['skaendeles] adj.
skandaliczny; gorszący;
oszczerczy
Scandinavian [,skaendy'nejwjan]
adj. skandynawski
scant [skaent] adj. skąpy;
ograniczony; ledwo
wystarczający; niedostateczny
scapegoat ['skejp,gout] s. kozioł
ofiarny
scar [ska:r] s. blizna; szrama;
wyrwa; urwisko; v.
pokiereszować (się);
zabliźniać się
scar over ['ska:r,ouwer] v.
zabliźnić
scarce [skeers] adj. rzadki;
niewystarczający
scarcely ['skeersly] adv.
zaledwie; ledwo; z trudem; z
trudnością
scarcity ['skeersyty] s.
niedostatek; niedobór; brak
scare [skeer] s. popłoch; panika;
strach; v. nastraszyć;
przestraszyć; siać popłoch
scare away ['skeere,łej] v.
odstraszać
scarecrow ['skeer,krou] s.
straszydło; strach na wróble
scarf [ska:rf] s. szalik; chustka
na szyję; szarfa
scarfs [ska:rfs] pl. styk; złącza
scarlet ['ska:rlyt] s. szkarłat; adj.
szkarłatny
scarlet fever ['ska:rlyt,fi:wer] s.

szkarlatyna; płonica
scarp [ska:rp] s. skarpa; urwisko
scarred [ska:rd] adj. poznaczony
bliznami; poszarpany
scarves [ska:rwz] pl. zob. scarf;
chusty na szyję; szarfy etc.
scathing ['skejzyng] adj.
kostyczny; zjadliwy; niszczący
scatter ['skaeter] v. rozpraszać
(się); rozsypywać; rozrzucać;
rozwiewać; posypywać;
rozpierzchnąć (się)
scavenge ['skaewyndż] v.
czyścić; oczyszczać;
wyrzucać spaliny; być
zamiataczem ulic
scenario [sy'na:riou] s.
scenariusz; plan zdarzeń
rzeczywistych lub
zmyślonych
scene [si:n] s. scena; miejsce
zdarzeń; widowisko; widok;
obraz; awantura publiczna
scenery [si:nery] s. widok;
krajobraz; dekoracje sceniczne
scent [sent] v. węszyć;
wietrzyć; wydawać zapach;
s. zapach; nos (węch);
perfumy
sceptic ['skeptyk] s. sceptyk;
adj. sceptyczny;
powątpiewający
sceptical ['skeptykel] adj.
sceptyczny; powątpiewający
we wszystko
schedule ['skedżul] s. rozkład
jazdy; wykaz; zestawienie;
tabela; taryfa; harmonogram;
lista; plan; v. planować;
wciągać na listę; naznaczać
wg planu
scheme [ski:m] s. intryga;
podstęp; plan
scholar ['skoler] s. uczony;
stypendysta; uczeń; student
scholarship ['skolerszyp] s.
poziom naukowy; stypendium;
erudycja; systematyczna
wiedza
school [sku:l] s. szkoła; katedra;
nauka; ławica; adj. szkolny; v.
szkolić; kształcić; nauczać;
wyćwiczyć; tworzyć

ławicę; karcić; sprawdzać naukę
schoolboy ['sku:l,boj] s. uczeń
schoolgirl ['sku:l,ge:rl] s. uczennica
schooling ['sku:lyng] s. nauka; szkolenie; wykształcenie
schoolmaster ['sku:l,ma:ster] s. kierownik szkoły
schoolmate ['sku:l,mejt] s. kolega szkolny
school of driving ['sku:l,ow'drajwyng] s. nauka jazdy (samochodem)
schooner ['sku:ner] s. skuner; szklanka na piwo
science ['sajens] s. wiedza; nauka; umiejętność
scientific ['sajentyfyk] adj. naukowy; umiejętny
scientist ['sajentyst] s. uczony; przyrodnik; naukowiec
scissors ['syzez] s. nożyce; nożyczki
scoff [skof] v. szydzić; kpić; drwić; s. pośmiewisko; szyderstwo; kpiny; drwiny
scold [skould] v. besztać; skrzyczeć; obrugać; łajać; złorzeczyć; s. jędza; sekutnica; megiera
scone [skon] s. placek trójkątny z jęczmiennej mąki
scoop [sku:p] v. zaczerpnąć; wygarnąć; wybrać; s. czerpak; szufelka; chochla; kubeł; sensacyjna wiadomość
scooter ['sku:ter] s. skuter; hulajnoga
scope [skoup] s. zasięg; zakres; dziedzina; meta; sposobność; możliwość
scorch [sko:rcz] v. spalić; przypiekać; przypalać; dopiekać; wypłowieć; pędzić samochodem jak szalony; s. poparzenie
score [sko:r] v. zdobyć (punkt); podkreślić; zanotować; zapisać; wygrać; osiągnąć; strzelić bramkę; s. ilość (zdobytych punktów lub bramek); zacięcie; rysa; znak; dwadzieścia
scorn [sko:rn] s. lekceważenie; wzgarda; v. lekceważyć; gardzić; odrzucać z pogardą
scornful ['sko:rnful] adj. pogardliwy (i zagniewany); odrzucający z gniewem i pogardą
Scot [skot] adj. szkocki
Scotch [skocz] adj. szkocki
scot-free ['skot'fri:] adj. cały; nietknięty; niezraniony; gratis; bezpłatny
scoundrel ['skaundrel] s. kanalia; łotr
scour ['skauer] v. podmyć; szorować; przepłukiwać; poszukiwać; grasować; przetrząsać; s. podmycie; przemywanie; przepłukiwanie
scout [skaut] s. harcerz; zwiadowca; v. iść na zwiady; robić rekonesans
scoutmaster ['skaut,ma:ster] s. harcmistrz
scowl [skaul] v. chmurzyć się; patrzeć spode łba; groźnie patrzeć; s. zła mina; groźne spojrzenie; krzywa mina
scramble ['skraembl] s. ubijanie się; gramolenie się; dobijanie się; robienie jajecznicy; v. ubijać się; gramolić się; dobijać się; robić jajecznicę
scrambled eggs ['skraembld,egs] s. jajecznica
scrap [skraep] s. szmelc; odpadki; skrawki; wycinki; bójka; v. wyrzucać na szmelc; odrzucać; wycofać; bić się
scrape [skrejp] s. skrobanie; tarapaty; szurnięcie; ciułanie; draśnięcie; v. skrobać; drasnąć; ciułać; szurnąć
scrape off ['skrejp,of] v. zeskrobać
scrape out ['skrejp,aut] v. wyskrobać
scrape together [skrejp, tu'gedzer] v. uciułać
scrap iron ['skraep,ajern] s. złom

żelazny
scrappy ['skraepy] adj.
niejednolity; bez związku;
fragmentaryczny
scratch [skraecz] s. draśnięcie;
zadrapanie; rozdarcie;
skrobanie; linia startu; adj. do
pisania (np. brulion);
brulionowy; v. drapać (się);
zadrasnąć; gryzmolić;
wydrapać; wykreślić
scream [skri:m] s. krzyk; pisk;
gwizd; kawał; v. krzyczeć
przenikliwie; śmiać się
hałaśliwie i histerycznie
screech [skri:cz] s. zgrzyt; pisk;
skrzypienie; v. zgrzytać;
piszczeć; skrzypieć
screen [skri:n] s. zasłona; osłona;
siatka na komary; ekran; sito;
siewnik; filtr (światła); v.
zasłaniać; osłaniać;
zabezpieczać; wyświetlać;
przesiewać; sortować;
badać; przesłuchiwać;
filmować; izolować
screw [skru:] s. śruba; propeler;
śmigło; zwitek; wyzyskiwacz;
dusigrosz; (slang): stosunek
płciowy; v. przyśrubować;
wyduszać; naciskać;
wykrzywiać; zabałaganić;
obracać się; (slang):
spółkować; wkopać
(kogoś); oszukać
screwdriver ['skru:,drajwer] s.
śrubokręt; wódka z sokiem
pomarańczowym
scribble ['skrybl] s. gryzmoły;
bazgranina; v. gryzmolić;
bazgrać; pisać naprędce
script [skrypt] s. rękopis;
scenariusz
scripture ['skrypczer] s. Pismo
Święte
scroll [skroul] s. zwitek; krzywa;
spirala
scrub [skrab] s. zarośla; zagajnik; karłowate drzewo; pętak;
niepozorny człowiek;
szorowanie; v. szorować;
oczyszczać; adj. lichy; marny;
maławy

scruple ['skrupl] s. skrupuł; v.
wahać się; mieć skrupuły
scrupulous ['skru,pjules] adj.
sumienny; dokładny;
skrupulatny; pedantyczny
scrutinize ['skru:tynajz] v. badać
szczegółowo
scrutiny ['skru:tyny] s. dokładne
badanie
scuff [skaf] s. włóczenie nogami;
wytarte miejsca; v.
powłóczyć nogami;
wycierać; rozrzucać;
porysować; musnąć;
zedrzeć; zdzierać; szurać
scuffle [skafl] s. włóczenie
nogami; szamotanie się;
utarczka; bójka; v. szamotać
się; bić się; powłóczyć
nogami; szurać; zaszurać
sculptor ['skalpter] s. rzeźbiarz
sculpture ['skalpczer] s. rzeźba;
v. rzeźbić
scum [skam] s. szumowiny; v.
zbierać szumowiny;
wytarzać
scurf [ske:rf] s. łupież; strup;
parchy
scurvy ['ske:rwy] s. szkorbut;
adj. podły; nędzny
scuttle ['skatl] s. wiaderko;
szybka ucieczka; właz; v.
pędzić; uciekać; robić
dziury w dnie; zatapiać
scuttlebutt ['skatelbat] s. kadź;
pogłoska
scythe [sajz] s. kosa; v. kosić
sea [si:] s. morze; fala
sea breeze ['si:'bri:z] s. wiatr od
morza
seafarer ['si:,feerer] s. żeglarz;
podróżnik morski
seafood ['si:fu:d] s. potrawy
morskie (ryby, skorupiaki)
sea gull ['si:gal] s. mewa
seal [si:l] s. foka; futro foki;
uszczelka; zagadka; plomba;
pieczątka; piętno; znak; v.
polować na foki;
uszczelniać; plombować;
pieczętować; zalakować
seal up ['si:l,ap] v.
zaplombować; uszczelnić;

zamknąć; zalakować;
zapieczętować

sea level ['si:,lewl] s. poziom
morza

sealskin ['si:lski:n] s. futro z fok

seam [si:m] s. szew; rąbek;
pokład; blizna; szpara;
szczelina; v. łączyć szwami;
pąkać; pokiereszować

seaman ['si:men] s. marynarz;
żeglarz

seamstress ['semstrys] s.
szwaczka

seaplane ['si:,plejn] s. hydroplan

seaport ['si:,po:rt] s. port morski

sea-power ['si:,pałer] s. potęga
morska

search [se:rcz] s. poszukiwanie;
badanie; szperanie; rewizja; v.
badać; dociekać; szukać;
przetrząsać; rewidować

searching ['se:rczyng] adj.
badawczy; przenikliwy

seashore ['si:,szo:r] s. wybrzeże;
brzeg morski

seasick ['si:,syk] adj. chory na
morską chorobę

seaside ['si:'sajd] s. wybrzeże
morskie

season ['si:zn] s. pora roku;
pora; sezon; v. zaprawiać;
przyprawiać; okrasić

seasonable ['si:znebl] adj.
stosowny; odpowiedni;
właściwy na porę roku; w
porę

seasonal ['si:zenl] adj. sezonowy

seasoned ['si:znd] adj.
zaprawiony; wdrożony;
przyprawiony; pikantny;
wystały

seasoning ['si:znyng] s.
przyprawa

season ticket ['si:sn'tykyt] s.
abonament; karta wstępu;
bilet (np. na serię
przedstawień)

seat [si:t] s. siedzenie; ławka;
krzesło; miejsce siedzące;
siedlisko; siedziba; gniazdo; v.
posadzić; usadowić;
wybierać (do sejmu); siąść;
osadzić

seat belt ['si:t,belt] s. pas
ochronny w samolocie lub
samochodzie; pas
bezpieczeństwa

seaward ['si:łerd] adv. ku
(otwartemu) morzu; adj.
skierowany ku morzu

seaweed ['si:łi:d] s. wodorost

seaworthy ['si:,łe:rsy] adj. zdatny
do podróży morskiej (m.in.
wodoszczelny)

secession [sy'seszyn] s. secesja;
oddzielenie się

seclude [sy'klu:d] v. odosabniać
(się)

secluded [sy'klu:dyd] adj.
odosobniony

seclusion [sy'klu:żyn] s.
odosobnienie; ustronie; zacisze

second ['sekend] adj. drugi;
wtórny; powtórny; ponowny;
zastępczy; zapasowy;
drugorzędny; v. poprzeć;
sekundować; s. sekunda;
moment; chwila; drugi;
sekundant; delegat; zastępca

secondary ['sekendery] adj.
drugorzędny; wtórny;
pochodny

secondary school ['sekendery
,sku:l] s. szkoła średnia

second floor ['sekend,flo:r] s.
pierwsze piętro

secondhand ['sekend,haend] adj.
z drugiej ręki; używany

secondly ['sekendly] adv. po
drugie

second-rate ['sekend'rejt] adj.
drugorzędny; lichy; kiepski

secrecy ['si:krysy] s. tajemnica;
skrytość; dyskrecja

secret ['si:kryt] adj. tajny;
tajemny; sekretny; skryty;
ustronny; dyskretny; s.
tajemnica; sekret; pl.
wstydliwe części ciała

secretary ['sekretry] s. sekretarz;
sekretarka; sekretarzyk

secretary of state
['sekretry,ow'stejt] s. minister
spraw zagranicznych USA

secrete [sy'kri:t] v. wydzielać;
ukrywać

secretion [sy'kri:szyn] s.
wydzielina; wydzielanie;
ukrycie
section ['sekszyn] s. część;
wycinek; etap; oddział; grupa;
dział; ustęp; paragraf; sekcja;
przekrój; żelazo profilowe;
przedział; drużyna robocza; v.
dzielić na części; robić
przekrój
sector ['sekter] s. wycinek;
odcinek
secular ['sekjuler] adj. świecki;
wiekowy; stuletni; s. ksiądz
świecki
secularize ['sekjulerajz] s.
sekularyzować
secure [sy'kjuer] v.
zabezpieczać (się);
umacniać; uzyskiwać;
zapewniać sobie; adj.
spokojny; bezpieczny; pewny
security [sy'kjueryty] s.
bezpieczeństwo;
zabezpieczenie; pewność;
zastaw; papier wartościowy;
zbytnia ufność
sedan [sy'daen] s. samochód 4
-osobowy
sedate [sy'dejt] v. uspokajać
(lekarstwami); adj. spokojny;
opanowany; zrównoważony
sedative ['sedetyw] adj. & s.
(środek) uspokajający,
nasenny
sediment ['sydyment] s. osad;
nanos; skała osadowa
seduce [sy'du:s] v. uwodzić
seduction [sy'dakszyn] s.
uwodzenie; pokusa; ponęta;
powab
seductive [sy'daktyw] adj.
kuszący; nęcący
sedulous ['sedjules] adj. pilny;
skrzętny; staranny; skwapliwy
see; saw; seen [si:; so:; si:n]
see [si:] v. zobaczyć; widzieć;
ujrzeć; zauważyć;
spostrzegać; doprowadzić;
odprowadzić; zwiedzać;
zrozumieć; odwiedzać;
przeżywać; dożyć;
uważać; zastanawiać się;

dopilnować
see off ['si:,of] v. odprowadzać
see out ['si:,aut] v. odprowadzić
do drzwi
see through ['si:,tru:] v.
przeprowadzić do końca;
doczekać się końca
see to ['si:,tu:] v. troszczyć się
o...
seed [si:d] v. obsiewać;
obsypywać się; zasiewać;
wybierać; s. nasienie;
zarodek; plemię
seek; sought; sought [si:k; so:t;
so:t]
seek [si:k] v. szukać; starać
się; chcieć; zadać;
nastawać; usiłować;
próbować; przetrząsać;
dążyć
seek out ['si:k,aut] v.
odszukiwać; wykrywać
seem [si:m] v. zdawać się;
robić wrażenie; okazywać
się; mieć wrażenie
seeming [si:myng] adj. pozorny;
widoczny
seemingly ['si:myngly] adv. na
pozór; widocznie
seemly ['si:mly] adj. właściwy;
przyzwoity
seen [si:n] v. zob. see
seep [si:p] v. sączyć się;
wyciekać
seer [sier] s. jasnowidz; prorok;
prorokini
seesaw ['si:so:] s. huśtawka (na
desce); adj. wahadłowy;
huśtawkowy; s. huśtać się;
wahać się; adv. (poruszać
czymś) do góry i na dół
segment ['segment] s. odcinek;
segment; v. podzielić na
części
segregate ['segry'gejt] v.
oddzielać; segregować
segregation ['segry'gejszyn] s.
oddzielenie; segregacja
seize [si:z] v. uchwycić;
złapać; zrozumieć;
owładnąć; skorzystać;
zaciąć się; zatrzeć się;
zablokować się

seizure ['si:zer] s. zagarnięcie;
zawładnięcie; zajęcie; napad;
atak apopleksji; zatarcie;
zablokowanie; atak drgawek
seldom ['seldem] adv. rzadko; z
rzadka
select [sy'lekt] v. wybierać;
wyselękcjonować; adj.
wybrany; doborowy;
ekskluzywny
selection [sy'lekszyn] s. wybór;
dobór; selekcja
self [self] prefix samo;
automatycznie; s. jaźń;
osobowość; własne dobro;
pl. selves [selwz]
self-acting ['self'aektyng] adj.
samoczynny
self-command ['self,ke'ma:nd] s.
spokój; panowanie nad sobą;
opanowanie
self-confidence ['self,konfydens]
s. pewność siebie; tupet
self-conscious ['self'konszes]
adj. nieśmiały; zażenowany
self-control ['self,ken'troul] s.
zimna krew; opanowanie
self-defense ['self,dy'fens] s.
samoobrona
self-employment ['self
,ym'plojment] s.
samozatrudnienie
self-government ['self
'gawenment] s. samorząd;
autonomia
self-interest ['self'yntryst] s.
interesowność; własne
dobro
selfish ['selfysz] adj. samolubny;
egoistyczny
self-made ['self'mejd] adj. przez
samego siebie osiągnięty
self-possessed ['self,pe'zest] adj.
opanowany; spokojny
self-reliant ['self,ry'lajent] adj. na
sobie polegający
self-respect ['self,rys'pekt] s.
poczucie własnej godności
self-righteous ['self'rajczes] adj.
nadmiernie pewny siebie
self-service ['self'se:rwys] s.
samo-obsługa
sell; sold; sold [sel; sould; sould]

sell [sel] v. sprzedawać;
zaprzedawać;
sprzeniewierzyć; wykiwać;
mieć zbyt; być na sprzedaż;
wyprzedawać
sell out ['selaut] v.
wyprzedawać
seller ['seler] s. sprzedawca
selves [selwz] pl. zob. self
semblance ['semblens] s. pozór;
podobieństwo
semen ['si:men] s. nasienie
semester [sy'mester] s. półrocze;
semestr
semicolon ['semy'koulen] s.
średnik
semifinal ['semy'fajnl] s. półfinał
senate ['senyt] s. senat
senator ['seneter] s. senator
send; sent; sent [send; sent;
sent]
send [send] v. posyłać;
wysyłać; nadawać;
transmitować; wystrzeliwać;
sprawiać; wywoływać
send away ['send,e'łej] v.
odprawiać; wypędzać
send for ['send,fo:r] v. zawołać;
zamawiać; kazać przynieść
send in ['send,yn] v. posłać;
nadesłać
send off ['send'o:f] v. wysyłać;
odprowadzać (np. na
lotnisko); pożegnać kogoś
(na stacji)
sender ['sender] s. nadawca;
nadajnik (np. radiowy)
send-off ['send'o:f] s.
pożegnanie
senior ['si:njer] adj. starszy (np.
rangą); s. starszy człowiek;
senior; student ostatniego
roku
sensation [sen'sejszyn] s.
wrażenie; doznanie; uczucie;
sensacja
sensational [sen'sejszenl] adj.
sensacyjny; wrażeniowy
sense [sens] s. zmysł; poczucie;
uczucie (np. zimna);
świadomość (czegoś);
rozsądek; znaczenie; sens; v.
wyczuwać; czuć; rozumieć

senseless ['senslys] adj. bez
sensu; nierozumny;
nieprzytomny
sensibility [,sensy'bylyty] s.
wrażliwość
sensible ['sensybl] adj. rozsądny;
świadomy; przytomny;
wrażliwy; odczuwalny;
poznawalny; sensowny
sensitive ['sensytyw] adj.
wrażliwy; delikatny
sensual ['senszuel] adj.
zmysłowy (też seksualnie)
sensuous ['senszues] adj.
zmysłowy (nie seksualnie)
sent [sent] v. zob. send
sentence ['sentens] s. zdanie;
powiedzenie; wyrok;
sentencja; v. wydawać
wyrok; skazywać
sentiment ['sentyment] s.
sentyment; uczucie; opinia;
zdanie; życzenie;
sentymentalność
sentimental [,senty'mentl] adj.
uczuciowy; sentymentalny
sentimentality
[,senty'ment'aelyty] s.
uczuciowość; czułostko-
wość; sentymentalność
sentry ['sentry] s. posterunek;
wartownik
separable ['seperebl] adj.
rozłączny
separate ['seperejt] v.
rozłączyć; rozdzielić;
oddzielić; oderwać;
odseparować (się);
odgrodzić; rozszczepić
separate ['sepryt] adj. odrębny;
oddzielny; osobny;
indywidualny; poszczególny
separation [,sepe'rejszyn] s.
separacja; rozdzielenie;
oddzielenie; rozłączenie
September [sep'tember] s.
wrzesień
septic ['septyk] adj. septyczny;
zakaźny
sepulcher ['sepelker] s. grób; v.
składać do grobu
sequel ['si:kłel] s. ciąg dalszy;
wynik; następstwo

sequence ['si:kłens] s.
następstwo; kolejność;
porządek; progresja
serene [sy'ri:n] adj. pogodny;
spokojny; s. spokojne morze;
pogodne niebo etc.; v.
rozpogodzić
sergeant ['sa:rdżent] s. sierżant
serial ['sierjel] adj. seryjny;
periodyczny; kolejny;
odcinkowy
series ['sieri:z] s. seria; szereg;
rząd
serious ['sierjes] adj. poważny
sermon ['se:rmen] s. kazanie;
nagana
serpent ['se:rpent] s. wąż
serum ['sierem] s. surowica
servant ['se:rwent] s. służący;
sługa; służąca; urzędnik
(państwowy)
serve [se:rw] v. służyć;
odbywać służbę (też
kadencję, praktykę etc.);
nadawać się; obsłużyć;
podawać; sprzedawać;
dostarczyć; wręczyć;
potraktować; postąpować;
spełniać funkcje; sprawować
urząd; odbywać karę
(więzienia); zaserwować
service ['se:rwys] s. służba;
obsługa; praca; urząd;
zaopatrzenie; instalacja;
uprzejmość; grzeczność;
przysługa; pomoc;
użyteczność; nabożeństwo;
serw; serwis (stołowy);
wręczenie; v. doglądać;
naprawić; kryć (samice)
serviceable ['se:rwysebl] adj.
pożyteczny; użyteczny;
praktyczny; wygodny; mocny;
trwały
service-station ['se:rwys
-'stejszyn] s. stacja obsługi i
sprzedaży benzyny
session ['seszyn] s. posiedzenie;
siedzenie; półrocze
set; set; set [set; set; set]
set [set] v. stawiać; ustawiać;
wstawić; urządzić;
umieszczać; przykładać;

nastawiać; osadzać; wbijać;
wyznaczać; ustalać; sądzić;
nakrywać; składać;
wysadzać (czymś); ścinać
się; okrzepnąć; adj. zastygły;
nieruchomy; zdecydowany;
stały; ustalony; s. seria;
garnitur; skład; komplet;
zespół; grupa; szczepek;
zachód; ustawienie; układ;
twardnienie; gęstość;
rozstęp; oszalowanie
set at ease ['set,et'i:z] v.
uspokoić
set-back ['setbaek] s.
pogorszenie; nawrót;
zahamowanie
set free ['set,fri:] v. uwolnić
set off ['set,of] v. uwydatnić;
wyodrębnić; wystrzelić;
wysadzić; wywołać;
wyruszyć; wyjeżdżać
set out ['set,aut] v. wystawiać;
ozdabiać; wykładać;
wyruszać; zacząć się
set to ['set,tu] v. zabierać się
(do czegoś)
set up ['set,ap] v. ustawiać;
zakładać; zaczynać;
zaopatrywać; rościć;
wysuwać; przywracać;
podnosić; założyć; podawać
się (za kogoś)
settee [se'ti:] s. kanapa; sofa
setting ['setyng] s. otoczenie;
oprawa; ułożenie; układ;
inscenizacja
settle [setl] v. osiedlić (się);
umieścić (się); uregulować;
osadzić (się); ustalić;
rozstrzygnąć; zapłacić (dług);
zamieszkać; usadowić (się);
uspokoić (się); zawierać
(umowę); układać (się)
settle down ['setl,daln] v.
ustatkować się; osiedlić się;
zabrać się do czegoś
settlement ['setlment] s. osiedle;
osada; kolonia; osiadanie;
sedymentacja; załatwienie;
rozstrzygnięcie; ustalenie
settler ['setler] s. osadnik;
kolonista

set-up ['set,ap] s. postawa;
układ; drużyna; dodatki do
alkoholu; (slang): ukartowane
zawody; łatwa sprawa
seven ['sewn] num. siedem; s.
siódemka
seventeen ['sewn'ti:n] num.
siedemnaście; s.
siedemnastka
seventh ['sewent] adj. siódmy
seventy ['sewnty] num.
siedemdziesiąt; s.
siedemdziesiątka
sever ['sewer] v. odrywać;
odłączyć; zrywać; urywać;
rozchodzić się
several ['sewrel] adj. kilku; kilka;
kilkoro
severe [sy'wier] adj. surowy;
srogi; ostry; dotkliwy; bolesny;
zacięty
severity [sy'weryty] s.
surowość; srogość;
ostrość; zaciętość; ciężki
stan
sew; sewed; sewn [sou; soud;
soun]
sew [sou] v. szyć; uszyć
sewage ['sju:ydż] s. ścieki
sewer ['suer] s. kanał ściekowy;
v. kanalizować
sewer ['souer] s. osoba szyjąca
sewerage ['su:erydż] s.
kanalizacja; system
kanalizacyjny
sewing ['souyng] s. szycie
sewing-machine ['souyng
me,szi:n] s. maszyna do
szycia
sewn [soun] v. zob. sew
sex [seks] s. płeć
sex appeal ['sekse'pi:l] s.
atrakcyjność płciowa;
seksapil
sexton ['seksten] s. grabarz
sexual ['sekszjuel] adj.
seksualny; płciowy
Seym [sejm] s. Sejm, parliament
shabby ['szaeby] adj. brudny;
skąpy; odrapany; wytarty;
nędzny; podły
shack [szaek] s. buda; szałas;
dom

shack up ['szaek,ap] v. spędzać
noc z kimś (slang)
shackle ['szaekl] s. kajdany;
klamra; pęta; v. zakuwać;
sczepiać
shade [szejd] s. cień; odcień;
abażur; stora; pl. ustronie;
piwnica na wino; v.
zasłaniać; zamroczyć;
cieniować
shadow ['szaedou] s. cień
(czyjś); v. pokrywać cieniem;
śledzić kogoś
shady ['szejdy] adj. cienisty;
nieczysty; mętny
shaft [szaeft] s. drzewce; trzon;
strzała; promień; wał;
trzonek; dyszel; szyb
shaggy ['szaegy] adj. włochaty;
krzaczasty
shake; shook; shaken [szejk;
szuk; szejken]
shake [szejk] potrząsać;
uścisnąć dłoń; grozić
(palcem); wstrząsać; drżeć;
dygotać; s. dygotanie;
dreszcze; drżenie; potrząsanie
shake-up ['szejkap] s.
otrząśnięcie (się); czystka
(slang)
shaky ['szejky] adj. drżący;
rozklekotany; słaby;
zachwiany; chwiejący się
shale [szejl] s. łupek
shall [szael] v. będę; będziemy;
musisz; musi; muszą (zrobić)
shallow ['szaelou] s. mielizna;
adj. płytki; powierzchniowy; v.
spłycać; płycieć; obniżać
poziom (wody)
sham [szaem] adj. fałszywy;
oszukańczy; sztuczny;
udawany; symulowany;
upozorowany; s. poza;
symulowanie; symulant;
pozór; udawanie; v. udawać;
symulować
shambles ['szaemblz] pl. jatki;
rzeź
shame [szejm] s. wstyd; v.
wstydzić się
shame on you! ['szejm,on'ju:]
exp.: wstydź się!

shameful ['szejmful] adj.
sromotny; haniebny
shameless ['szejmlys] adj.
bezwstydny; bezczelny
shampoo [szaem'pu:] s.
szampon; mycie głowy
szamponem; v. myć
szamponem
shank [szaenk] s. goleń;
trzonek; uchwyt
shape [szejp] v. kształtować;
rzeźbić; modelować;
formułować; wyobrazić; s.
kształt; kondycja; postać;
zjawa; widmo; model
shaped ['szejpt] adj.
ukształtowany
shapeless ['szejplys] adj.
bezkształtny; nieforemny;
niezgrabny
shapely ['szejply] adj. kształtny;
foremny; zgrabny
share [szeer] s. udział; należna
część; lemiesz; v.
rozdzielić; dzielić (się);
podzielać; brać udział
share-holder ['szeer,houlder] s.
akcjonariusz
shark [sza:rk] s. rekin
sharp [sza:rp] adj. ostry; bystry;
pilny; wyraźny; chytry;
dominujący; inteligentny; adv.
punktualnie; szybko; biegiem
sharpen ['sza:rpen] v. ostrzyć;
temperować; obostrzyć;
zaostrzyć
sharpener ['sza:rpner] s.
temperówka; narzędzie do
ostrzenia
sharpness ['sza:rpnys] s.
ostrość; bystrość;
chytrość; pilność
sharp-witted ['sza:rp'łytyd] adj.
bystry; dowcipny; rozgarnięty
shatter ['szaeter] v. gruchotać;
roztrzaskać; niweczyć;
szarpać
shave; shaved; shaven [szejw;
szejwd; szejwn]
shave [szejw] v. golić (się);
oskrobać; strugać; s.
golenie; muśnięcie
shaven [szejwn] v. zob. shave

shaving ['szejwyng] v. golenie;
skrobanie; wiórkowanie; s.
wiór

shawl [szo:l] s. szal

she [szi:] pron. ona

sheaf [szi:f] s. snop; wiązka;
wiązanka; plik; pl. sheaves
[szi:wz]

shear; sheared; shorn [szier;
szierd; szo:rn]

shear [szier] v. ścinać; ucinać;
ostrzyć; s. ścinanie; pl.
nożyce (shears)

sheath [szi:s̲] s. pochwa; futerał;
powłoka; prezerwatywa

sheaves [szi:wz] pl. od sheath

shed [szed] s. szopa; buda; v.
zrzucać; strącać; pozbywać
(się); pogubić; ronić;
przelewać (krew); wydzielać;
promieniować

sheep [szi:p] pl. owce

sheep dog ['szi:p,dog] s.
owczarek

sheepish ['szi:pysz] adj.
bojaźliwy; nieśmiały;
zakłopotany; zbaraniały;
ogłupiały

sheer [szier] v. schodzić z
kursu; skręcać nagle; adj.
zwykły; jawny; czysty;
zwyczajny; stromy;
prostopadły; pionowy;
przejrzysty; przewiewny; lekki;
adv. zupełnie; pionowo;
stromo

sheet [szi:t] s. arkusz;
prześcieradło; gazeta; tafla;
obszar; warstwa; v.
pokrywać prześcieradłem;
okrywać brezentem

sheet iron ['szi:t,ajren] s. blacha
stalowa

shelf [szelf] s. półka; rafa;
mielizna; pl. shelves [szelwz]

shell [szel] s. łupina; skorupa;
powłoka; osłona; pancerz;
muszla; szkielet; łuska; pocisk;
granat; gilza; v. ostrzeliwać z
armat; wyłuskiwać

shellfish ['szel,fysz] s. skorupiak;
mięczak

shelter ['szelter] s. schronienie;
ochrona; osłona; v. chronić;
osłaniać; udzielać
schronienia; zabezpieczać

shelve [szelw] v. odkładać (na
półkę); wkładać do szuflady;
opadać (wzdłuż stoku)

shelves [szelwz] pl. zob. shelf

shepherd ['szeperd] s. pastuch;
pasterz; v. paść;
(pilotować) prowadzić

shield [szi:ld] s. tarcza; osłona;
v. osłaniać; ochraniać

shift [szyft] v. zmieniać (np.
biegi); przesuwać;
przełączyć; zwalić; s.
przesunięcie; zmiana; szychta;
wykręt; wybieg

shiftless ['szyftlys] adj.
niezaradny

shifty ['szyfty] adj. zmienny;
fałszywy; chytry

shilling ['szylyng] s. szyling

shin [szyn] s. goleń; v. kopać
w goleń

shine; shone; shone [szajn; szon;
szon]

shine [szajn] v. zabłyszczeć;
zajaśnieć; oczyścić na
połysk; s. jasność; blask;
(slang): granda; awantura;
sympatia

shingle ['szyngl] s. gont; szyld;
wywieszka; kamyk; v. pokryć
gontami; krótko ostrzyc

shingles ['szynglz] pl. półpasiec

shiny ['szajny] adj. błyszczący;
wypolerowany

ship [szyp] s. okręt; statek;
samolot; v. załadować;
zaokrętować; posyłać

shipment ['szypment] s.
załadunek; przesyłka; fracht

shipowner ['szyp,olner] s.
armator

shipping ['szypyng] s. flota
handlowa; żegluga; załadunek;
usługi żeglugowe; przesyłka;
adj. spedycyjny; okrętowy

shipping company ['szypyng
'kampeny] s. firma okrętowa;
armator

shipwreck ['szyp,rek] s. rozbicie
statku; v. ulec rozbiciu;

spowodować rozbicie statku;
rozbić się
ship-wrecked ['szyp,rekt] s.
rozbitek
shipyard ['szyp,ja:rd] s. stocznia
shire ['szajer] s. hrabstwo
(powiat)
shirk [sze:rk] v. uchylać się;
wymigiwać się; s. nierób;
wymigiwacz
shirt [sze:rt] s. koszula
shirt sleeves ['sze:rt,sli:wz] pl.
rękawy od koszuli; bez
marynarki; adj. prosty;
domowy
shit [szyt] v. wulg.: srać; s.
gówno
shitty ['szyty] adj. wulg.: zasrany
shiv [szyw] s. majcher (slang)
shiver ['szywer] v. drżeć;
trząść się; rozbijać się w
kawałki; s. dreszcz; kawałek
shock [szok] s. wstrząs; cios;
uderzenie; starcie; porażenie;
czupryna; kopka; v.
wstrząsać; gorszyć;
oburzać; porazić
shock absorber ['szok-eb,so:rber]
s. tłumik drgań; amortyzator
shocking ['szokyng] adj.
okropny; wstrętny;
skandaliczny; oburzający;
niestosowny
shoddy ['szody] adj. tandetny
shoe; shod; shod [szu:; szod;
szod]
shoe [szu:] s. but; półbucik;
trzewik; okucie; podkowa;
nakładka (hamulca); obręcz;
nasada; v. obuwać;
podkuwać
shoehorn ['szu:,ho:rn] s. łyżka
do butów; wzuwacz
shoelace ['szu:,lejs] s.
sznurowadło
shoemaker ['szu:,mejker] s.
szewc
shoestring ['szu:,stryng] s.
sznurowadło; bardzo mały
kapitał
shoeshine ['szu:,szajn] s.
czyszczenie butów (na połysk)
shone [szon] v. zob. shine

shook [szuk] v. zob. shake
shoot; shot; shot [szu:t; szot;
szot]
shoot [szu:t] v. strzelić;
wystrzelić; zastrzelić;
rozstrzelać; zrobić zdjęcie;
nakręcić film; mknąć;
przemknąć; spłynąć; rwać;
kiełkować; s. pęd; kiełek;
polowanie; progi; plac zwozu
śmieci
shooter ['szu:ter] s. strzelec;
rewolwer
shooting ['szu:tyng] adj.
mknący; pędzący; strzelający
shooting gallery
['szu:tyng,gaelery] s. strzelnica
shooting-star ['szu:tyng,sta:r] s.
spadająca gwiazda
shooting-party ['szu:tyng,pa:rty]
s. wyprawa łowiecka;
polowanie
shop [szop] s. sklep; pracownia;
warsztat; zakład; v. robić
zakupy
shopkeeper ['szop,ki:per] s.
kupiec; sklepikarz
shoplifter ['szop,lyfter] s. złodziej
sklepowy
shopping center
['szopyng,senter] s. skupisko
sklepów; ośrodek zakupów
shopping mall ['szopyng,mol] s.
skupisko sklepów wzdłuż
krytej hali; pasaż handlowy
shop window ['szop'łyndoł] s.
wystawa
shore [szo:r] s. brzeg; wybrzeże;
podpora; v. podpierać;
podstemplować
shorn [szo:rn] v. zob. shear
short [szo:rt] adj. krótki; niski;
zwięzły; oschły; niecały;
niewystarczający; adv. krótko;
nagle; za krótko; s. skrót;
zwarcie; pl. szorty
shortage ['szo:rtydż] s. brak;
niedobór; deficyt
short circuit ['szo:rt'se:rkyt] s.
krótkie spięcie; zwarcie
shortcoming ['szo:rt'kamyng] s.
wada; niedociągnięcie; brak;
niedobór

shorten ['szo:rtn] v. skracać

shorthand ['szo:rthaend] s. stenografia

shortly ['szo:rtly] adv. wkrótce; niebawem

shortness ['szo:rtnys] s. krótkość; niedobór

shorts ['szo:rts] pl. szorty; kalesony (krótkie)

short story ['szo:rt,sto:ry] s. nowela

short-sighted ['szo:rt'sajtyd] adj. krótkowzroczny; nieprzewidujący

short-term ['szo:rt'term] adj. krótkoterminowy; krótkotrwały

short-winded ['szo:rt'łyndyd] adj. zasapany; krótko mówiący

shot [szot] v. zob. shoot; ładować broń; s. strzał; pocisk; śrut; zastrzyk; docinek; adj. mieniący się

shotgun ['szotgan] s. dubeltówka; śrutówka; strzelba

should [szud] v. tryb warunkowy od shall

shoulder ['szoulder] s. ramię; plecy; łopatka; pobocze; v. brać na ramię; rozpychać się

shout [szałt] s. krzyk; okrzyk; wrzask; v. krzyczeć; wykrzykiwać

shove [szaw] v. popychać; posuwać (coś); s. pchnięcie

shovel ['szawl] s. łopata; szufla; v. przerzucać łopatą lub szuflą

show; showed; shown [szou; szoud; szoun]

show [szou] v. pokazywać; wskazywać; s. wystawa; przedstawienie; pokaz

show around ['szou,e'raund] v. oprowadzać

show off ['szou,o:f] v. popisywać się; paradować; starać się imponować

show up ['szou,ap] v. demaskować; zjawiać się; ukazywać się

show business ['szou'byznyz] s. przemysł widowiskowy

shower ['szaler] s. tusz; prysznic; przelotny deszcz; grad; stek; v. przelotnie kropić; obsypywać; oblewać

shower bath ['szaler,ba:t] s. tusz; prysznic

shown [szołn] v. zob. show

showy ['szoły] adj. ostentacyjny; okazały

shrank [szraenk] v. zob. shrink

shred [szred] s. strzęp; v. ciąć na strzępy

shrew [szru:] s. złośnica; sekutnica; sorek

shrewd [szru:d] adj. przenikliwy (np. obserwator)

shriek [szri:k] v. wrzeszczeć; piszczeć; rechotać; s. wrzask; pisk; gwizd (ostry)

shrill [szryl] adj. ostry; przenikliwy; przeraźliwy; v. rozlegać się przenikliwie; adv. przenikliwie

shrimp [szrymp] s. krewetka; karzełek; v. łowić krewetki

shrine [szrajn] s. przybytek; relikwiarz; v. umieszczać w przybytku

shrink; shrank; shrunk [szrynk; szraenk; szrank]

shrink [szrynk] v. kurczyć (się); wzbraniać (się); wzdrygać się; s. kurczenie się; (slang): psychiatra

shrinkage ['szrynkydż] s. kurczenie się; ubytek na wadze

shrivel ['szrywl] v. kurczyć (się)

shroud [szraud] s. całun; kir; zasłona; płaszcz

Shrovetide ['szrouwtajd] s. (święto) ostatki; zapusty

Shrove Tuesday ['szrouw'tju:zdy] s. tłusty wtorek

shrub [szrab] s. krzew; krzak

shrubbery ['szrabery] s. krzaki

shrubby ['szraby] adj. krzaczasty

shrug [szrag] s. wzruszenie ramion; v. wzruszyć ramionami

shrunken ['szrankn] v. zob.

shrink

shudder ['szader] s. dreszcz; (slang): nudziarz; v. zadrżeć; wzdrygać się

shuffle ['szafl] v. wlec się; powłóczyć; kręcić; tasować; mieszać; s. krok suwany; krętactwo; tasowanie (kart); wleczenie się; szuranie

shun [szan] v. unikać; wystrzegać się; s. baczność; uwaga

shut; shut; shut [szat; szat; szat]

shut [szat] v. zamykać (się); przytrzasnąć; adj. zamknięty

shut down ['szat,dałn] s. zamknięcie; wstrzymanie pracy; v. zamykać; kłaść koniec; zasłaniać; (o zakładzie) stanąć

shut up ['szat,ap] v. pozamykać; zamknąć gębę; zamilknąć; bądź cicho; wulg.: stul pysk!

shutter ['szater] s. okiennica; zasłona; migawka; regulator organów; v. zamykać okiennice

shy [szaj] adj. płochliwy; wstydliwy; nieśmiały; nieufny; ostrożny; skąpy; szczupły; v. płoszyć się; stronić; rzucać; s. rzut (w coś)

shyness ['szajnys] s. skromność; nieśmiałość

shyster ['szajster] s. chytry (polityk) bez zasad; adwokat-krętacz

sick [syk] adj. chory; znudzony; chorowity; skażony zarazkami; chorobowy

sickbed ['sykbed] s. łóżko chorego; łoże boleści

sick benefit ['syk'benefyt] s. zasiłek chorobowy

sicken ['sykn] v. zaczynać chorować; wywoływać obrzydzenie; brzydzić (się)

sickle ['sykl] s. sierp

sick leave ['sykli:w] s. zwolnienie lekarskie; urlop chorobowy

sickly ['sykly] adj. chorowity;

słabowity; niezdrowy; chorobliwy; ckliwy

sickness ['syknys] s. choroba; wymioty; nudności

sick room ['syk-ru:m] s. izba chorych; pokój chorego

side [sajd] s. strona; adj. uboczny; v. stać po czyjejś stronie

side by side ['sajd,baj'sajd] exp.: obok siebie; jeden przy drugim

side arms ['sajda:rmz] pl. broń boczna (np. szable)

sideboard ['sajdbo:rd] s. kredens

sidecar ['sajd,ka:r] s. przyczepa do motocykla

sided ['sajdyd] adj. stronny; mający strony

side dish ['sajd,dysz] s. przystawka

side-kick ['sajdkyk] s. (slang): kompan; pomagier

side road ['sajd,roud] s. boczna droga

side line ['sajd,lajn] v. odsuwać na bok; zapobiegać

sidewalk ['sajd-ło:k] s. chodnik; trotuar

sidewalk café ['sajdło:kaefej] s. kawiarnia na chodniku

side-wards ['sajdłedz] adv. bokiem; w bok

sideways ['sajdłejz] adv. bokiem; na poprzek; adj. boczny

side with ['sajd,łys] v. brać czyjąś stronę

siege [si:dż] s. oblężenie

sieve [syw] s. sito; rzeszoto; przetak; v. przesiewać

sift [syft] v. przesiewać; przebierać; oddzielać; prószyć; posypywać

sigh [saj] s. westchnienie; v. wzdychać

sight [sajt] s. wzrok; widok; celownik; przeziernik

sighted ['sajtyd] adj. spostrzeżony

sightly ['sajtly] adj. dający dobry widok; miły; przyjemny

sightseeing ['sajtsi:yng] s. zwiedzanie; adj. turystyczny

sightseeing tour ['sajtsi:yng,tu:r]

s. zwiedzanie z wycieczką;
wycieczka krajoznawcza
sightseer ['sajtsi:er] s. turysta;
zwiedzający
sign [sajn] s. znak; omen; godło;
napis; wywieszka; szyld;
skinienie; oznaka; objaw;
ślad; znak drogowy; hasło;
odzew; v. znaczyć;
naznaczyć; podpisać;
skinąć
sign up ['sajn,ap] v. zapisywać
się
sign out ['sajn,aut] v.
wypisywać się
signal ['sygnl] s. sygnał; znak; v.
sygnalizować; zapowiadać;
dawać znak
signature ['sygnyczer] s. podpis;
sygnatura; klucz
signature-tune ['sygnyczer,tju:n]
s. oznaczenie tonacji
signboard ['sajnbo:rd] s.
wywieszka; szyld; godło
signet ['sygnyt] s. sygnet;
pieczątka; v. pieczętować
significance [syg'nyfykens] s.
wyraz; ważność; znaczenie
significant [syg'nyfykent] adj.
istotny; znaczący; doniosły;
znamienny; ważny
signification [,sygnyfy'kejszyn] s.
znaczenie
signify ['sygnyfaj] v. znaczyć;
mieć znaczenie; oznaczać;
zaznaczać
signpost ['sajn,poust] s.
drogowskaz
silence ['sajlens] s. milczenie;
cisza; v. nakazywać
milczenie; cicho!
silencer ['sajlenser] s. tłumik
silent ['sajlent] adj. milczący;
cichy; małomówny
silk [sylk] s. jedwab; adj.
jedwabny
silken ['sylkn] adj. jedwabny;
jedwabniczy
silky [sylky] adj. jedwabisty
sill [syl] s. próg; podkład;
parapet
silly ['syly] s. głupiec; adj. głupi;
ogłupiały

silver ['sylwer] s. srebro; v.
posrebrzać; adj. srebrny;
srebrzysty
silvery ['sylwry] adj. srebrzysty
similar ['symyler] adj. podobny
similarity [,symy'laeryty] s.
podobieństwo
simmer ['symer] v. wolno
gotować (się); burzyć się
wewnątrz; s. gotowanie na
wolnym ogniu
simple ['sympl] adj. prosty;
zwykły; naturalny; szczery;
naiwny; głupkowaty;
zwyczajny
simpleton ['symplten] s.
prostaczek; kiep; głuptas
simplicity [sym'plysyty] s.
prostota
simplification [,symplyfy'kejszyn]
s. uproszczenie
simplistic ['symplystyk] adj. zbyt
upraszczający
simplify ['symplyfaj] v.
uprościć; ułatwić
simply ['symply] adv. po prostu
simulate ['symjulejt] v. udawać;
naśladować
simultaneous [symel'tejnjes] adj.
równoczesny; jednoczesny
sin [syn] s. grzech; v. grzeszyć
since [syns] adv. odtąd; potem;
conj. skoro; ponieważ; od
czasu jak
sincere [syn'sier] adj. szczery
sincerely [syn'sierly] adv.
szczerze
sincerity [syn'seryty] s.
szczerość
sinew ['synu:] s. ścięgno
sinews ['synu:s] pl. muskulatura;
siła; moc
sinewy ['synuy] adj. muskularny;
mocny
sinful ['synful] adj. grzeszny
sing; sang; sung [syng; saeng;
sang]
sing [syng] v. śpiewać; wyć;
zawodzić; bzykać; świstać;
opiewać; s. śpiew; świst
singe [syndż] v. opalać;
osmalać
singer ['synger] s. śpiewak

single ['syngl] adj. pojedynczy;
jeden; samotny; szczery;
uczciwy; s. bilet w jedną
stronę; gra pojedyncza; v.
wybierać; wyróżniać
single out ['syngl,aut] v.
wybierać
single-handed ['syngl'haendyd]
adj. adv. w pojedynkę; na
własną rękę; samodzielny;
samodzielnie
single room ['syngl'ru:m] s.
pojedynczy pokój
single ticket ['syngl'tykyt] s.
bilet w jedną stronę
singles bar ['syngls,ba:r] s. bar
dla samotnych
singular ['syngjuler] adj.
osobliwy; niezwykły;
pojedynczy; s. liczba
pojedyncza
singularity [,syngju'laeryty] s.
osobliwość; niezwykłość;
niezwykły człowiek
sinister ['synyster] adj.
zbrodniczy; złowieszczy; lewy
sink; sank; sunk [synk; saenk;
sank]
sink [synk] v. zatonąć; zatopić;
zagłębić (się); opuścić;
obniżyć; pogrążyć; zanikać;
zmaleć; wykopywać;
ukrywać; wyryć;
zainwestować; s. zlew; ściek;
bagno zepsucia
sinking ['synkyng] s. uczucie
mdłości (np. z przerażenia)
sinner ['syner] s. grzesznik
sip [syp] s. łyk; popijanie; v.
popijać
sir [se:r] s. pan; v. nazywać
panem; exp.: proszę pana!
sirloin ['se:rloin] s. polędwica
sister ['syster] s. siostra
sister-in-law ['syster yn,lo:] s.
szwagierka
sit; sat; sat [syt; saet; saet]
sit [syt] v. siedzieć;
przesiadywać; usiąść;
zasiadać; obradować; leżeć;
pozować
sit down ['syt,dałn] v. usiąść

sit up ['syt,ap] v. wyprostować
się siedząc; czuwać; usiąść
prosto
site [sajt] s. miejsce; plac (np.
budowy); położenie; v.
umieszczać
sitting ['sytyng] s. posiedzenie;
sesja
sitting-room ['sytyng,ru:m] s.
bawialnia; salon
situated ['sytjuejtyd] adj.
umieszczony; stojący;
usytuowany
situation [,sytu'ejszyn] s.
położenie; posada; sytuacja
six [syks] num. sześć; s.
szóstka
sixteen ['syks'ti:n] num.
szesnaście; s. szesnastka
sixth [sykst] num. adj. szósty; s.
jedna szósta
sixthly ['sykstly] adv. po szóste
size [sajz] s. wielkość; numer;
format; klajster; krochmal;
rzadki klej; v. sortować wg
wielkości; oceniać
wielkość; nadawać się;
krochmalić; usztywnić klejem
sized-up ['sajzd,ap] adj. oceniony
(co do wielkości, siły lub
ważności)
sizzle ['syzl] v. skwierczeć; s.
skwierczenie
skate [skejt] s. łyżwa; wrotka;
płaszczka; szkapa; pętak;
patałach; v. ślizgać się;
jeździć na wrotkach
skater ['skejter] s. łyżwiarz;
wrotkarz
skeleton ['skelytn] s. szkielet
skeptic ['skeptyk] adj.
sceptyczny; s. sceptyk
sketch ['skecz] s. szkic; skecz;
zarys; v. szkicować;
przedstawić w ogólnych
zarysach (w krótkich
słowach); robić wstępny
rysunek
sketch block ['skecz,blok] s.
szkicownik
sketchbook ['skecz,bu:k] s.
szkicownik
ski [ski:] s. narta; wyrzutnik

bomb; v. jeździć na nartach

skid [skyd] s. deska; płoza; podpórka; klin hamowniczy; poślizg; zarzucenie; v. ślizgać się; zarzucać; umieszczać na płozach; hamować

skier ['ski:er] s. narciarz

skiing ['skiyng] s. narciarstwo; jazda na nartach

ski lift ['ski lyft] s. wyciąg narciarski

skill ['skyl] s. zręczność; wprawa

skilled ['skyld] adj. wykwalifikowany; wykonany fachowo

skillful ['skylful] adj. zręczny; wprawny

skillet ['skylyt] s. patelnia; (slang): draka

skim [skym] v. zbierać (śmietankę); szumować; przebiegać wzrokiem; puszczać po powierzchni; szybować; s. zbieranie; mleko zbierane; adj. zbierany

skimmer ['skymer] s. warząchew; cedzidło

skimp [skymp] v. skąpić

skimpy ['skympy] adj. skąpy; za mały; niewystarczający

skin [skyn] s. skóra; skórka; cera; szawłok; (slang): oszust; v. zdzierać skórę; pokrywać naskórkiem; ściągać z siebie

skin-deep ['skyn'di:p] adj. powierzchowny

skin diver ['skyn'dajwer] s. płetwonurek

skindiving ['skyn'dajwyng] s. sportowe nurkowanie (z płetwami)

skinny ['skyny] adj. chudy; skóra i kości

skip [skyp] v. skakać; przeskakiwać; odskakiwać; pomijać; (slang): uciekać; s. skok; przeskok; kapitan sportowy

skipper ['skyper] s. szyper; kapitan statku; skoczek; kapitan drużyny

skirt ['ske:rt] s. spódnica; poła; wulg.: kobietka; przepona; brzeg; v. jechać brzegiem; obchodzić; leżeć na skraju

skit ['skyt] s. skecz; satyra; mnóstwo

skoal [skoul] excl.: na zdrowie!

skull [skal] s. czaszka

sky [skaj] s. niebo; klimat

skyjack ['skaj,dżaek] s. porwanie samolotu w locie; v. porwać samolot w locie (uprowadzać)

skyjacker ['skaj,dżaeker] s. pirat powietrzny

skylark ['skajla:rk] s. skowronek; v. dokazywać; swawolić

skylight ['skajlajt] s. okno dające górne światło; okno w suficie

skyscraper ['skaj,skrejper] s. drapacz chmur

skyward ['skajłerd] adv. ku niebu

slab [slaeb] s. płytka; v. krajać na płytki (kromki)

slack [slaek] adj. luźny; wolny; rozlazły; opieszały; ospały; leniwy; niedbały; v. zluźniać; zwalniać; popuszczać; zaniedbywać; gasić (np. ogień); s. luźna część; lenistwo; zastój; bezczelność; miał węglowy; zwis; impertynencja

slacken ['slaeken] v. rozluźniać (się); zwalniać; poluźniać (się); popuszczać; zaniedbywać

slacks [slaeks] pl. (luźne) spodnie

slain [slejn] adj. zabity; v. zob. slay

slake [slejk] v. gasić (np. wapno); wywierać (np. zemstą)

slam [slaem] v. zatrzasnąć (się); (slang): krytykować ostro; pobić; s. trzaśnięcie; ostra krytyka; ciupa

slang [slaeng] s. gwara; żargon; slang; adj. gwarowy; żargonowy; v. nawymyślać komuś

slangy [slaengy] adj. gwarowy

slant [sla:nt] s. pochyłość;
skos; tendencja; punkt
widzenia; spojrzenie; adj.
ukośny; v. iść skośnie;
pochylać (się); odchylać
(się); być nachylonym

slap [slaep] s. klaps; plaśnięcie;
v. plasnąć; dać klapsa;
uderzyć; narzucić; adv.
nagle; prościutko; regularnie

slapstick ['slaep,styk] s. laska
arlekina; błazeńska komedia

slash [slaesz] v. pokiereszować;
przeciąć; chłostać; smagać;
walić; ciąć; s. cięcie;
szrama; przecięcie; wyrąb;
odpadki drzewne; porosłe
(krzakami) moczary

slate [slejt] s. łupek; dachówka
łupkowa; tabliczka do pisania;
lista (kandydatów w USA); v.
pokrywać dachówkami;
umieszczać na liście
kandydatów; łajać;
wymyślać; krytykować

slate pencil ['slejt'pensl] s. rysik

slattern ['slaete:rn] s. brudas;
flejtuch; kocmołuch

slaughter ['slo:ter] v. rżnąć;
zabijać; wymordować; s.
ubój; rzeź; masakra

Slav [sla:w] adj. słowiański

slave [slejw] adj. niewolniczy; s.
niewolnik; v. harować

slavery ['slejwery] s.
niewolnictwo

slay; slew; slain [slej; slu:; slejn]

slay [slej] v. zabić; uśmiercać

sled [sled] s. sanie; v. wozić
saniami

sledge hammer ['sledż-haemer]
s. oburęczny młot

sleek [sli:k] adj. gładki; ulizany;
v. gładzić; wygładzać

sleep; slept; slept [sli:p; slept;
slept]

sleep [sli:p] v. spać;
spoczywać; dawać nocleg;
s. sen; spanie; drzemka

sleep off ['sli:p,of] v. odespać

sleeper ['sli:per] s. człowiek
śpiący; dźwigar; potencjalny
przedmiot rozgłosu; truteń;

leń; wtyczka (szpiegowska
etc.)

sleeping-bag ['sli:pyng,baeg] s.
śpiwór

sleeping car ['sli:pyng,ka:r] s.
wagon sypialny

sleeping partner ['sli:pyng
'pa:rtner] s. cichy wspólnik

sleeping pill ['sli:pyng,pyl] s.
pigułka nasenna

sleepless ['sli:plys] adj. bezsenny

sleepwalker ['sli:p,ło:ker] s.
lunatyk

sleepy ['sli:py] adj. śpiący

sleet [sli:t] s. słota; deszcz ze
śniegiem; gołoledź

sleeve [sli:w] s. rękaw; tuleja;
łuska; nasadka; tuba; zanadrze

sleeved ['sli:wd] adj. z rękawami

sleigh [slej] v. saneczkować
(się); jechać saniami

slender ['slender] adj. wysmukły;
szczupły; wiotki; nikły;
skromny; niewielki; słaby

slept [slept] v. zob. sleep

slew [slu:] v. zob. slay

slice [slajs] s. kromka; płatek;
plasterek; kawałek; łopatka
kuchenna; v. krajać na
kromki,
kawałki etc.; przecinać;
wiosłować; wyjmować
łopatką

slick [slyk] adj. gładki; tłusty;
oślizgły; miły; pociągający;
pierwszorzędny; adv. gładko;
prościutko; s. tłusta plama
(na morzu); szerokie dłuto

slicker ['slyker] s. gładki płaszcz
od deszczu; oszust

slid [slyd] v. zob. slide

slide; slid; slid [slajd; slyd; slyd]

slide [slajd] v. suwać (się);
sunąć (się); ślizgać (się); s.
ślizganie się; suwak;
prowadnica ślizgowa;
poślizg; przeźrocze; zrzutnia

slide rule ['slajd,ru:l] s. suwak
logarytmiczny

slight [slajt] adj. wątły; niewielki;
drobny; skromny; nieznaczny;
v. lekceważyć; s.
lekceważenie

slim [slym] adj. szczupły;
wysmukły; słaby; (slang):
chytry; v. wyszczuplać;
odchudzać (się)

slime [slajm] s. szlam; muł; śluz;
płynna smoła ziemna; v.
zamulać; odmulać; zwilżać
(np. śliną)

slimy ['slajmy] adj. mulisty;
zamulony; obleśny; oślizgły

sling; slung; slung [slyng; slang;
slang]

sling [slyng] s. proca; rzut; pętla
(np. do ładowania dźwigiem);
temblak; rzemień do strzelby
itp.; v. rzucać; strzelać z
procy; podnosić na pętli;
zawieszać na (np. rzemieniu)

slinger ['slynger] s. procarz

slinky ['slynky] adj. ukradkowy;
(slang): mający ruchy węża

slip; slipped; slipped [slyp; slypt;
slypt]

slip [slyp] v. pośliznąć (się);
wyśliznąć (się); ześliznąć
(się); popełnić nietakt; zrobić
błąd; przepuścić (np.
okazję); wymknąć się;
zerwać się; zapomnieć;
spuszczać (np. ze smyczy); s.
poślizg; potknięcie; pomyłka;
błąd; przemówienie się; zsuw;
halka; świstek (papieru);
pochylnia

slip off ['slyp,of] v. zdejmować;
rozbierać się; ześlizgiwać
się; spadać

slip on ['slyp,on] v. wdziewać

slip out ['slyp,aut] v. wymknąć
się

slip up ['slyp,ap] s. błąd;
zachwianie się; przemówienie
się; zsuw; ślizg; v. zrobić
błąd; pomylić się; potknąć
się

slipper ['slyper] s. pantofel

slippery ['slypery] adj. śliski;
niebezpieczny; ryzykowny;
nieuczciwy; nieczysty;
drażliwy; delikatny; wykrętny;
chytry

slit; slit; slit [slyt; slyt; slyt]

slit [slyt] v. rozszczepić;

rozedrzeć wzdłuż; s. szpara;
szczelina; rozcięcie

slobber ['slober] s. ślina;
rozczulenie; v. oślinić się;
rozczulić się

slogan ['slougen] s. slogan;
hasło; powiedzonko (np.
reklamowe)

sloop [slu:p] s. slup (łódź)

slop [slop] v. rozlewać;
przepełniać płynem;
rozpryskiwać; s. kałuża;
brudna woda; pomyje; lura

slop over ['slop,ouwer] v.
przelewać się przez wierzch

slope [sloup] s. pochyłość;
spadek; nachylenie;
spadzistość; stok; skarpa;
zbocze; pochylnia; v. być
pochylonym; mieć nachylenie;
nachylać; pochylać;
wałęsać się; łazikować

sloping [sloupyng] adj. pochyły;
skośny

sloppy ['slopy] adj. błotnisty;
pochlapany; zaniedbany;
rozlazły; ckliwy

slot [slot] s. szczelina; rozcięcie;
trop; ślad; v. rozciąć;
naciąć; wyżłobić

sloth [slous] s. lenistwo; leniwiec

slot-machine ['slotme,szi:n] s.
(grający lub sprzedający)
automat na monety

slouch [slaucz] s. przygarbienie;
niedbała postawa; wałkoń; v.
garbić się; iść ociężale;
opuszczać rondo kapelusza

slough [slou] s. bagno;
trzęsawisko

slough [slaw] v. lenieć; zrzucać
skórę

sloven ['slawn] s. niechlujny;
brudas; flejtuch; fuszer;
partacz

slovenly ['slawnly] adj.
niechlujny; partacki

slow [słoł] adj. powolny;
niegorliwy; nieskory;
opieszały; leniwy; tępy;
nudny; adv. wolno; powoli

slow down ['słoł,dałn] v.
zwalniać; przyhamować

slow-motion ['sloł'mouszyn] s.
zwolnione tempo; adv. w
zwolnionym tempie
slow-worm ['sloł,łe:rm]s. padalec
sluggish ['slagysz] adj. ospały;
leniwy; powolny
sluice [slu:s] s. śluza; ściek;
rynna; v. puszczać wodę (ze
stawu etc.); spłukiwać;
zalewać; chlusnąć; spływać
ze śluzy
slums [slamz] s. dzielnica nędzy
slumber ['slamber] v. spać
lekko; drzemać; s. sen;
drzemka; spokój;
bezczynność
slung [slang] v. zob. sling
slush [slasz] s. chlapa; odpadki
tłuszczowe; smar; fundusz z
odpadków; tajny fundusz na
przekupstwo; v. opryskać;
wysmarować; pokrywać
zaprawą
slut [slat] s. flejtuch; kocmołuch;
plucha; pinda; szmata; flądra;
suka
sly [slaj] adj. szczwany; chytry;
filuterny
slyboots ['slajbu:ts] s. urwis;
spryciarz; chytrus (udający
głupiego)
smack [smaek] s. posmak;
odrobina; trzask; mlaśnięcie;
cmoknięcie; klaps;
jednomasztowiec; v. cmokać;
strzelać z bata; dać w pysk;
oblizywać (wargi)
smacking ['smaekyng] adj.
zgrabny; raźny; mocny (wiatr)
small [smo:l] adj. mały; drobny;
niewielki; skromny; ciasny;
nieliczny; nieznaczny;
małostkowy; adv. drobno; na
małą skalę; cicho; s. drobna
rzecz; mała część
small change ['smo:l,czejndż] s.
drobne (pieniądze)
small hours ['smo:l,auers] pl.
bardzo wczesne godziny ranne
smallish ['smo:lysz] adj. małowy
small of the back
['smo:l,ow'dy,baek] s. krzyże
smallpox ['smo:l,poks] s. ospa

smart [sma:rt] adj. dotkliwy;
cięty; zręczny; żwawy;
dowcipny; szykowny; zgrabny;
elegancki; v. piec; palić (np.
w oczy); cierpieć; szczypać;
parzyć; odczuwać boleśnie;
pokutować
smart aleck ['sma:rt,alek] s.
Jędrek-mędrek
smash [smaesz] v. rozbić;
rozwalić; roztrzaskać;
zmiażdżyć; potłuc; palnąć;
rozgromić; upadać;
zbankrutować; ścinać piłkę
smashing ['smaeszyng] adj.
nadzwyczajny; niezwykły
smattering ['smaeteryn] s.
znajomości po łebkach;
wiedza powierzchowna
smear [smier] v. osmarować;
zasmarować; wlepić komuś
smary; s. plama; smar
smell; smelt; smelled [smel;
smelt; smeld]
smell [smel] s. węch; woń;
zapach; odór; smród; v.
pachnieć; trącić; mieć
zapach; śmierdzieć; mieć
powonienie; obwąchiwać;
czuć zapach; zwietrzyć;
zwąchać; poczuć
smelt [smelt] v. zob. smell;
stapiać; wytapiać (metal); s.
stynka (ryba)
smile [smajl] v. uśmiechać się;
s. uśmiech
smite; smote; smitten [smajt;
smout; 'smytn]
smite [smajt] v. uderzać;
porazić; powalić; zabić;
nękać; karać; oczarować
smith [smys] s. kowal
smithy ['smysy] s. kuźnia
smitten ['smytn] v. zob. smite
smock [smok] s. chałat; kitel; v.
ubierać chałat; ozdabiać
rysunkiem szachownicy
smog [smog] s. mgła
zanieczyszczona dymem
(Londyn, Los Angeles)
smoke [smouk] s. dym; palenie;
papieros; v. dymić; kopcić;
wykurzać; wyjawiać;

wykadzać; okadzać;
okopcić; uwędzić;
przypalać; palić (tytoń)
smoke-dried ['smouk,drajd] adj.
wędzony
smoker ['smouker] s. palący;
palacz
smoking ['smoukyng] s. palenie
(tytoniu)
smoking car ['smoukyng,ka:r] s.
wagon dla palących
smoking compartment
['smoukyngkaem,pa:rtment] s.
przedział dla palących
smoky ['smouky] adj. dymiący;
przydymiony; zadymiony;
okopcony
smolder ['smoulder] v. tlić się;
s. tlenie się; dym
smooch [smu:cz] v. brudzić;
walać; całować się;
ściskać się; migdalić się
smooth [smu:s] adj. gładki;
spokojny; łagodny; v. gładzić;
łagodzić; adv. gładko; s.
wygładzenie
smooth down ['smu:s,dałn] v.
wygładzić; uspokajać (się)
smother ['smadzer] v. stłumić;
stłamsić; obcałowywać;
zatuszować; okrywać
smudge [smadż] v. poplamić;
zabrudzić; s. plama; kleks;
brud
smuggle ['smagl] v. przemycać
smuggler ['smagler] s.
przemytnik
smut [smat] v. poplamić; s.
brud z sadzy; sprośności;
tłuste kawały; śnieć
smutty ['smaty] adj. sprośny;
brudny od sadzy
snack [snaek] s. zakąska
snack bar ['snaek,ba:r] s. bufet;
bar
snafu [snae'fu:] v. zabałaganić;
s. bałagan (slang)
snail [snejl] s. ślimak
snake [snejk] s. wąż; v. wić
się; wlec (za sobą); pełzać
jak wąż; przybierać kształt
węża
snap [snaep] v. łapać zębami;

warczeć; błysnąć; urwać;
złamać; chwytać; zapalić
się do; przerwać szorstko;
poprawić się; mieć się na
baczności; zatrzasnąć (się);
strzelać z bicza; pstryknąć;
sfotografować; śpiesznie
załatwiać; machnąć ręką
lekceważąco; s. ugryzienie;
warknięcie; trzask; zatrzask;
dociskacz; zdjęcie; rzecz
łatwa; adj. prosty; łatwy;
doraźny; nagły
snap bolt ['snaep,boult] s.
zatrzask u drzwi
snap fastener ['snaep,fa:sner] s.
zatrzask
snappish ['snaepysz] adj.
zgryźliwy; kostyczny
snappy ['snaepy] adj. zgryźliwy;
kostyczny; żwawy; prędki
snapshot ['snaepszot] s. zdjęcie
migawkowe; strzał na chybił
trafił
snare [sneer] v. usidlać; łapać
w sidła; s. sidła; pułapka
snarl [sna:rl] s. warknięcie;
plątanina; v. warczeć; plątać
(się); zaplątać; robić zator
snatch [snaecz] v. złapać;
wyrwać; s. złapanie; urywek;
strzęp; mig
sneak [sni:k] v. chyłkiem
zakradać się; przemykać się;
zerkać; zwiać; s. podły
tchórz
sneakers ['sni:kers] pl. trzewiki;
trampki
sneer [snier] v. uśmiechać się
szyderczo; kpić; drwić; s.
szyderstwo; szydercze
spojrzenie
sneeze [sni:z] v. kichać; s.
kichnięcie
sniff [snyf] v. prychać;
pociągać nosem; krzywić się
na coś; powąchać;
obwąchać; zwąchać;
wyczuć; s. prychnięcie;
pociągnięcie nosem
sniffle ['snyfl] s. katar;
pociąganie nosem; v.
pociągać nosem

snipe [snajp] s. bekas; strzał z ukrycia; v. z ukrycia: strzelać, trafić, zabić

sniper ['snajper] s. strzelec wyborowy; strzelec z ukrycia

snivel ['snywel] s. śluz z nosa; biadolenie; udawanie; v. smarkać się; skamleć; biadolić; płakać; rozczulać się

snob [snob] s. człowiek wywyższający się

snoop [snu:p] v. myszkować; wścibiać nos; s. szpicel

snoop around ['snu:p,e'raund] v. przemyszkowywać; szpiegować

snooze [snu:z] s. drzemka; v. drzemać; zdrzemnąć się

snore [sno:r] v. chrapać; s. chrapanie

snort [sno:rt] v. parskać; s. parsknięcie

snout [snaut] s. ryj; pysk; morda; wylot

snow [snou] s. śnieg; (slang): kokaina; heroina; v. ośnieżyć; śnieg pada; zasypać śniegiem; pobić na głowę; omamiać

snowball ['snoubo:l] s. kula śnieżna; v. bić się śniegiem; rosnąć jak lawina

snow blindness ['snou'blajndnys] s. śnieżna ślepota

snowdrift ['snou'dryft] s. zaspa śnieżna

snowdrop ['snoudrop] s. śnieżyczka

snow job ['snou,dżob] s. naciąganie pochlebstwami

snow-white ['snou'hłajt] adj. śnieżnobiały

snowy ['snoły] adj. śnieżny; śniegowy

snub [snab] v. ofuknąć; dać po nosie; traktować lekceważąco; nagle zatrzymać; adj. perkaty, zadarty (nos); s. bura; ofuknięcie; ostra odprawa; afront; ucieranie nosa komuś; przywodzenie kogoś do porządku

snuff [snaf] s. tabaka; proszek do zażywania przez nos; zapach; opalony koniec knota; v. zażywać tabakę; pociągać nosem; czyścić koniec knota

snug [snag] adj. przytulny; wygodny; ukryty; v. tulić się; zrobić przytulnym

snuggle ['snagl] v. przytulić się

so [sou] adv. tak; a więc; w takim razie; a zatem; też; tak samo; bardzo to; także; excl.: to tak! no, no!

so far ['sou fa:r] adv. jak dotąd; jak do tej pory

soak [souk] v. moczyć (się); nasycać (się); przenikać; namoknąć; (slang): wyciągać (od kogoś) pieniądze; mocno uderzyć; s. moczenie (się); woda do moczenia; popijawa; zastaw

soap [soup] s. mydło; pochlebstwo; wazelinowanie się (komuś); v. mydlić (się); pochlebiać; adj. mydlany; mydlarski

soap box ['soup,boks] s. skrzynia od mydła; mównica (np. uliczna); v. przemawiać na ulicy, w parku etc.

soap opera ['soup'opere] s. (popołudniowe) przedstawienie radiowe lub telewizyjne pełne małżeńskich kryzysów, tragedii, cierpień, płaskiej czułostkowości i melodramatycznych zakończeń

soar [so:r] v. wznosić się; osiągać wyżyny; iść w górę (np. ceny)

sob [sob] v. łkać; szlochać; s. łkanie; szloch

sober ['souber] adj. trzeźwy; wstrzemięźliwy; stateczny; zrównoważony; rzeczowy; poważny; spokojny; v. trzeźwieć; wytrzeźwieć; wytrzeźwiać; otrzeźwieć; opanować się

sober up ['souber,ap] v.
wytrzeźwieć
sober-minded ['souber,majndyd]
adj. stateczny; zrównoważony
so-called ['sou-ko:ld] adj. tak
zwany
soccer ['soker] s. piłka nożna
sociable ['souszebl] adj.
towarzyski; przyjacielski;
gromadny; stadny
social ['souszel] adj. społeczny;
socjalny; s. zebranie
towarzyskie
social democrat ['souszel
'demekraet] s.
socjaldemokrata
socialism ['souszelyzem] s.
socjalizm
social security
['souszelsy'kjueryty] s.
ubezpieczenia społeczne
socialist ['souszelyst] s.
socjalista; adj. socjalistyczny
social worker ['souszel'łerker] s.
pracownik społeczny;
pracownik urzędu opieki
społecznej
socialize ['souszelajz] v.
upaństwowić; uspołecznić
social welfare ['souszel,łelfeer] s.
opieka społeczna
society [so'sajety] s.
towarzystwo; społeczeństwo;
społeczność; spółka (np.
akcyjna)
sock [sok] s. skarpetka; cios;
szturchaniec; v. cisnąć w
kogoś; uderzyć; walnąć;
adv. prosto (np. w nos)
socket ['sokyt] s. oprawka;
oczodół; zębodół; gniazdko;
wydrążenie
sod [sod] s. darń; darnina;
wulg.: skurwysyn; sodomita
sofa ['soufe] s. kanapa; sofa
soft [soft] adj. miękki; delikatny;
przyciszony; łagodny; słaby;
głupi; wygodny
soft drink ['soft,dry̱nk] s. napój
bezalkoholowy
soft goods ['soft,gu:ds] pl.
tekstylia
soften ['so:fen] v. zmiękczyć;

osłabić; złagodzić;
złagodnieć; zmięknąć
soil [sojl] s. gleba; rola; ziemia;
brud; plama; v. zabrudzić;
powalać; poplamić;
wysmarować
sojourn ['sedże:rn] s. pobyt; v.
przebywać; zatrzymywać
(się)
sold [sould] adj. sprzedany; v.
zob. sell
soldier ['souldżer] s. żołnierz
najemnik; adj. żołnierski; v.
służyć w wojsku
sole [soul] s. podeszwa;
podwalina; zelówka; stopa;
spodek; sola; adj. jedyny;
wyłączny
solemn ['solem] adj. solenny;
uroczysty; poważny
solicit [se'lysyt] v. prosić;
zwracać się (o coś);
nagabywać; ubiegać się;
zwracać (np. uwagę)
solicitor [se'lysyter] s. radca
prawny; akwizytor; agent
firmowy
solicitous [se'lysytes] adj.
pragnący; troszczący się o ...;
niepokojący się
solicitude [se'lysytju:d] s. troska;
pieczołowitość; troskliwość
solid ['solyd] adj. stały;
masywny; lity; trwały; mocny;
rzetelny; solidny; s. ciało stałe;
bryła
solidarity [,soly'daeryty] s.
solidarność
solidity [so'lydyty] s.
masywność; trwałość;
rzetelność
soliloquy [se'lylekły] s. monolog;
mówienie do siebie
solitary ['solytery] adj. samotny;
odosobniony; odludny;
pojedynczy; wyjątkowy; s.
pustelnik; odludek; samotnik
solitude ['solytju:d] s.
samotność; osamotnienie;
odludne miejsce
solo ['soulou] adv. w pojedynkę;
adj. jednoosobowy; s. solo
soloist ['soulouyst] s. solista

soluble ['soljubl] adj.
rozpuszczalny; możliwy do
rozwiązania
solution [so'ljuszyn] s. rozczyn;
roztwór; rozwiązanie
(problemu)
solve [solw] v. rozwiązywać
(np. problemy)
solvent ['solwent] adj.
wypłacalny; rozpuszczający; s.
rozpuszczalnik
somber ['somber] adj. mroczny;
ciemny; posępny; ponury
some [sam] adj. jakiś; pewien;
niejaki; nieco; trochą; kilku;
kilka; kilkoro; niektórzy;
niektóre; sporo; niemało; nie
byle jaki; adv. niemało; mniej
więcej; jakieś; pron.
niektórzy; niektóre; kilku; kilka
some more ['sam,mor] exp.:
nieco więcej
somebody ['sambedy] pron.
ktoś; s. ktoś ważny
someday ['samdej] adv. kiedyś
somehow ['samhał] adv. jakoś;
w jakiś sposób
someone ['samłan] pron. ktoś;
s. ktoś
somersault ['samerso:lt] s. salto;
koziołek
something ['samsyng] s. coś;
coś niecoś; ważna osoba;
adv. trochą; nieco; (slang): co
się zowie
sometime ['samtajm] adj. były;
adv. kiedyś; swego czasu
sometimes ['samtajmz] adv.
niekiedy; czasem; czasami
someway ['sam,łej] adv. jakoś
somewhat ['samhłot] adv. nieco;
do pewnego stopnia; niejako
somewhere ['samhłe:r] adv.
gdzieś
son [san] s. syn
song [song] s. pieśń; śpiew
song-bird ['songbe:rd] s. ptak
śpiewający
song-book ['songbuk] s.
śpiewnik
sonic ['sonyk] adj. dźwiękowy
sonic boom ['sonyk,bu:m] s.
grzmot samolotu

przekraczającego szybkość
dźwięku
son-in-law ['san,ynlo:] s. zięć
sonnet ['sonyt] s. sonet
soon [su:n] adv. wnet;
niebawem; wkrótce; zaraz;
niedługo
sooner ['su:ner] adv. wcześniej;
chętnie
soot [sut] s. sadza; kopeć; v.
brudzić sadzą; użyźniać
sadzą
soothe [su:z] v. uspokajać;
uciszać
soothing ['su:zyng] adj. kojący;
uspokajający; uśmierzający
sooty ['suty] adj. okopcony;
zakopcony; czarny jak sadza
sophisticated [se'fystykejtyd]
adj. wyszukany;
wyrafinowany; wymyślny;
doświadczony
sophomore ['sofemo:r] s. student
drugiego roku
sorcerer ['so:rserer] s.
czarownik; czarodziej
sorceress ['so:rserys] s.
czarodziejka
sorcery ['so:rsery] s. czary
sordid ['so:rdyd] adj. brudny (np.
zysk); nikczemny; podły;
skąpy
sore [so:r] adj. bolesny;
drażliwy; wrażliwy; dotkliwy;
dotknięty; złoszczący się;
zmartwiony; adv. srodze;
bardzo; okrutnie
sore throat ['so:r,trout] s.
zapalenie gardła; angina
sorrow ['sorou] s. zmartwienie;
żal; smutek; narzekanie; v.
martwić się; boleć za ...
sorrowful ['soroful] adj.
smutny; zmartwiony; przykry
sorry ['so:ry] adj. żałujący;
zmartwiony; przygnębiony;
nędzny; marny
sorority [se'ro:ryty] s. korporacja
studentek (w USA)
sort [so:rt] s. rodzaj; gatunek;
sorta; v. sortować
sortie ['so:rty] s. wypad
wojskowy; lot bojowy

so-so ['sou-sou] adj. taki sobie;
adv. tak sobie

sought [so:t] v. zob. seek

soul [soul] s. dusza

soulless ['soullys] adj. bezduszny

sound [saund] s. dźwięk; ton;
szmer; cieśnina wodna;
pęcherz pławny; sonda; v.
dźwięczeć; brzmieć; grać
(na trąbce); bić na alarm;
głosić; opukiwać;
wymawiać; zabierać głos;
chwalić się; sondować;
zanurzać się do dna

soundless ['saundlys] adj.
bezdźwięczny

soundproof ['saundpru:f] adj.
dźwiękoszczelny

sound wave ['saundłejw] s. fala
dźwiękowa

soup [su:p] s. zupa

sour ['sauer] adj. kwaśny;
skwaszony; cierpki; v.
kisnąć; kwasić się;
zniechęcać się

source [so:rs] s. źródło

south [saus] adj. południowy; s.
południe; adv. na południe

southeast ['saus'i:st] s.
południowy wschód; adj.
południowo-wschodni; adv. na
południowy wschód

southern ['sadzern] adj.
południowy; s. południowiec

southernmost [,sadzern'moust]
adj. najbardziej na południe

southward ['sausłerd] adv. ku
południowi; na południe

southwest ['saus'łest] s.
południowy zachód; adj.
południowo-zachodni; adv. na
południowy zachód

southwesterly ['saus'łesterly]
adj. południowo-zachodni

souvenir ['su:wenier] s. pamiątka

sovereign ['sawryn] s. suweren;
władca; adj. suwerenny;
wyniosły; najwyższy

sovereignty ['sawrenty] s.
suwerenność;
zwierzchnictwo; najwyższa
władza

Soviet ['souwjet] adj. sowiecki;
radziecki

sow; sowed; sown [sou; soud;
soun]

sow [sou] v. siać; zasiewać;
posiać

sow [sau] s. maciora; koryto
odlewnicze

sown [soun] v. zob. sow

spa [spa:] s. zdrojowisko; zdrój
mineralny; (USA) sport
zdrowotny za opłatą

space [spejs] s. przestrzeń;
miejsce; obszar; odstęp;
okres; przeciąg (czasu);
chwila; v. robić odstępy;
rozstawiać

spacecraft ['spejs,kra:ft] s.
pojazd międzyplanetarny

spaceship ['spejs,szyp] s. statek
międzyplanetarny (kosmiczny)

space suit ['spejs,sju:t] s.
kombinezon międzyplanetarny

spacious ['spejszes] adj.
przestronny; obszerny

spade [spejd] s. łopata; v.
kopać łopatą

spades [spejdz] pl. piki (w
kartach)

spadework ['spejd-łe:rk] s. praca
przygotowawcza

span; spanned; spanned [spaen;
spaend; spaend]

span [spaen] v. sięgać (np.
przez rzekę); rozciągać się
(np. nad rzeką); obejmować
(pamięcią); mierzyć piędzią;
posuwać się stopniowo;
łączyć brzegi; s. piędź;
rozpiętość; prześwit;
przęsło; przeciąg (czasu);
zasięg; rozciągłość; para;
zaprzęg

spangle ['spaengl] s.
świecidełko; błyskotka; v.
pokrywać świecidełkami;
błyszczeć świecidełkami

spangled ['spaengld] adj. pokryty
(świecidełkami)

Spanish ['spaenysz] adj.
hiszpański

spank ['spaenk] s. klaps; v.
dawać klapsa; popędzać
klapsami; iść kłusem

spanking [spaenkyng] s.
skórobicie; lanie; adj. chyży;
zamaszysty; silny; solidny;
świetny; adv. bardzo (slanı)
spanner ['spaener] s. ściągno
(mostu); klucz do nakrętek;
gąsienica miernikowa
spare [speer] v. oszczędzać;
zaoszczędzić; odstąpować;
obywać się; zachować;
przeznaczać; szanować
(uczucia); szczędzić; adj.
zapasowy; oszczędny;
skromny; drobny; szczupły;
wolny (np. czas); s. część
zapasowa; koło zapasowe
spare time ['speer,tajm] s. wolny
czas
spare tire ['speer,tajer] s. koło
zapasowe
sparing ['speeryng] adj.
oszczędny; wstrzemięźliwy
spark [spa:rk] s. iskra; zapłon;
wesołek; zalotnik; v. iskrzyć
się; sypać iskrami; zapalać
się; dawać początek;
zalecać się; grać galanta
spark plug ['spa:rk,plag] s.
świeca samochodowa
(zapłonowa)
sparrow ['spaerou] s. wróbel
sparse [spa:rs] adj. rzadki; z
rzadka; rozsiany; szczupły
spasm ['spaezem] s. skurcz;
spazm; napad (kaszlu)
spastic ['spaestyk] adj.
skurczowy; spazmatyczny;
chory na paraliż kurczowy
spat [spaet] v. zob. spit; kłócić
się; dawać klapsy; składać
jaja (przez ostrygi); s. jaja
mięczaków; kłótnia; klaps;
lekki cios
spatial ['spejszel] adj.
przestrzenny
spawn [spo:n] s. ikra; skrzek;
nasienie; v. składać (ikrą,
skrzek); wylęgać się;
płodzić; zasiewać grzybnię
spayed [spejd] adj. (samica) z
usuniętymi jajnikami;
bezpłodna; wytrzebiona
speak; spoke; spoken [spi:k;

spou:k; 'spouken]
speak [spi:k] v. mówić;
przemawiać; szczekać na
rozkaz; grać; sygnalizować
do ataku
speak out ['spi:k,aut] v.
wypowiadać (się); mówić
otwarcie; mówić głośno
speak up ['spi:k,ap] v.
wypowiedzieć się bez
osłonek
speaker ['spi:ker] s. mówca;
głośnik; marszałek sejmu;
przewodniczący
spear [spier] s. dzida; włócznia;
oszczep; kopia; oścień;
źdźbło; v. przebijać dzidą;
kłuć; wystrzelić w górę
spearhead ['spierhed] s. ostrze
dzidy; czołówka; v.
prowadzić; być na czele
special ['speszel] adj. specjalny;
wyjątkowy; osobliwy;
dodatkowy; nadzwyczajny; s.
dodatkowy autobus;
nadzwyczajne wydanie;
reklamowa dzienna zniżka
ceny w sklepie
specialist ['speszelyst] s.
specjalista; specjalistka
specialize ['speszelajz] v.
wyspecjalizować (się); wyszczególniać; ograniczać;
precyzować; różniczkować
(się); ograniczać (się)
specially ['speszely] adv.
specjalnie; szczególnie
specialty [,speszy'aelyty] s. 1.
specjalność; specjalna cecha
specialty ['speszelty] s. 2.
fach; specjalizacja; umowa
species ['spi:szi:z] s. gatunek;
rodzaj; postać (czegoś)
specific [spy'syfyk] adj.
(ściśle) określony; wyraźny; gatunkowy; właściwy;
charakterystyczny; swoisty;
specyficzny; szczególny
specify ['spesyfaj] v.
wyszczególniać; precyzo-
wać; konkretyzować; spo-
rządzić specyfikację
specimen ['spesymyn] s. okaz;

przykład; wzór; typ; próba;
numer okazowy
speck [spek] s. plamka; cętka;
punkcik; skaza; pyłek; ziarnko;
odrobina; zdziebło
spectacle ['spektekl] s.
widowisko
spectacles ['spektekls] pl.
okulary
spectacular [spek'taekjuler] adj.
widowiskowy; efektowny;
sensacyjny; okazały; s. film
widowiskowy "wielki"
spectator ['spektejter] s. widz
specter ['spekter] s. widmo;
upiór
speculate ['spekjulejt] v.
spekulować; rozmyślać
nad ...; rozważać
speculation [,spekju'lejszyn] s.
spekulacja; domysł;
rozmyślanie
sped [sped] v. zob. speed
speech [spi:cz] s. mowa;
przemówienie; język;
wymowa; przemowa
speechless ['spi:czlys] adj.
(chwilowo) niemy; oniemiały;
(slang): pijany (kompletnie)
speed; sped; sped [spi:d; sped;
sped]
speed [spi:d] v. pośpieszyć;
popędzić; pędzić; odprawić;
kierować śpiesznie;
popierać (np. sprawę); s.
szybkość; prędkość; bieg
speedboat ['spi:dbout] s.
ślizgacz
speed limit ['spi:d,lymyt] s.
ograniczenie szybkości
speedometer [spi'domyter] s.
szybkościomierz
speed up ['spi:d,ap] v.
przyśpieszyć; s.
przyśpieszenie
speedy ['spi:dy] adj. szybki
spell; spelled; spelt [spel; speld;
spelt]
spell [spel] v. przeliterować
(poprawnie); napisać
ortograficznie; znaczyć;
mozolnie odczytywać;
sylabizować; zaczarować;

urzec; dać (wytchnienie);
odpoczywać; zaczarować;
pracować na zmiany; s.
chwila pracy; chwila; okres;
pewien czas; zaklęcie; czar
spellbound ['spelbaund] adj.
zaczarowany; urzeczony;
oczarowany
spelling ['spelyng] s. pisownia
spelt [spelt] v. zob. spell
spend; spent; spent [spend;
spent; spent]
spend [spend] v. wydawać (np.
pieniądze); spędzać (czas);
zużywać (się);
wyczerpywać; tracić (np.
siły); składać ikrę
spent [spent] v. wyczerpany;
wydany; zob. spend
sperm [spe:rm] s. sperma;
nasienie męskie
spew [spju:] v. wypluwać;
wymiotować; wyrzucać z
siebie
sphere [sfier] s. kula; globus;
ciało niebieskie; sfera (np.
działalności)
spice [spajs] s. wonne korzenie;
pikanteria; v. przyprawiać
korzeniami; dodawać
pikanterii
spick-and-span [spyk'n,span] adj.
nowy; świerzy; porządny i
czysty
spicy ['spajsy] adj. korzenny;
zaprawiony korzeniami;
aromatyczny; pikantny; nieco
nieprzyzwoity; elegancki;
żywy; ostry
spider [spajder] s. pająk
spike [spajk] s. ćwiek; bretnal;
kolec; gwóźdź do szyn;
szpic; ostrze; fanatyk religijny;
kłos; v. przymocowywać
gwoździami; zaostrzać
końce; ranić kolcami;
zagważdżać armatę;
zaprzeczać pogłoskom;
odpierać; zakrapiać
alkoholem; wspinać się na
słup ostrymi okuciami (na
butach)
spiky ['spajky] adj. kolczasty;

wydłużony; ostro
zakończony; fanatyczny
religijnie
spill; spilled; spilt [spyl; spyld;
spylt]
spill [spyl] v. rozlewać (się);
rozsypywać (się); uchylać
żagiel z wiatru; wyśpiewać;
wygadać (się); powiedzieć
wszystko; popsuć sprawę; s.
rozlanie; rozsypanie; ilość
rozlana; ilość rozsypana;
odłamek; zatyczka; upadek;
fidybus do zapalania świec
spilt [spylt] v. zob. spill
spin; spun; spun [spyn; span;
span]
spin [spyn] v. snuć; prząść;
kręcić (się); puszczać bąka;
toczyć na tokarni; łowić ryby
na błyszczkę; zawirować; s.
kręcenie (się); zawirowanie;
ruch wirowy; przejażdżka;
korkociąg (w locie)
spinach ['spynycz] s. szpinak
spinal column ['spajnel'kolem] s.
stos pacierzowy; kręgosłup
spinal cord ['spajnel'ko:rd] s.
rdzeń kręgowy
spindle ['spyndl] s. wrzeciono;
oś; wał; 14400 jardów lnu;
15120 jardów bawełny; v.
mieć kształt wrzecionowaty
spine [spajn] s. kręgosłup;
grzbiet; cierń
spinning mill ['spynyng,myl] s.
przędzalnia
spinster ['spynster] s. stara
panna
spiny ['spajny] adj. ciernisty;
kolczasty; trudny
spiral ['spajerel] s. spirala; adj.
spiralny; v. poruszać się
spiralnie; szybko iść w górę
(np. ceny); nadawać kształt
spirali
spire [spajer] s. iglica; hełm
wieży; zwój; spirala; ostry
szczyt; szpic; pęd; v. strzelać
w górę; nakładać hełm na
wieżę
spirit ['spyryt] s. duch; intelekt;
umysł; zjawa; odwaga;

nastawienie; nastrój; v.
zachęcać; ożywiać;
rozweselać; zabierać
(potajemnie)
spirits ['spyryts] s. spirytus;
alkohol
spirited ['spyrytyd] adj.
ożywiony; z werwą; napisany
z zacięciem
spiritual ['spyryczuel] adj.
duchowy; duchowny;
natchniony; s. murzyńska
pieśń religijna
spit; spat; spat [spyt; spaet;
spaet]
spit [spyt] v. pluć; zionąć;
splunąć; wypluć;
lekceważyć; fuknąć;
parsknąć; mżyć; kropić;
pryskać; nadziewać na
rożen; s. plucie; ślina;
parskanie; mżenie; jaja
owadów; rożen; językowaty
półwysep; głąbokość łopaty
spite [spajt] s. złość; uraz;
złośliwość; v. zrobić na
złość; in spite of = wbrew;
pomimo
spiteful ['spajtful] adj. złośliwy;
mściwy
spittle ['spytl] s. plwocina; ślina
splash [splaesz] v. chlapać;
pryskać; plusnąć;
rozpryskać; upstrzyć; s.
rozprysk; plusk; zakropienie;
plamka; sensacja
splash down ['splaesz,dałn] v.
wodować; s. wodowanie
spleen [spli:n] s. śledziona;
przygnębienie; splin; złość
splendid ['splendyd] adj.
wspaniały; świetny;
doskonały
splendor ['splender] s.
wspaniałość; przepych; blask
splint [splynt] s. łupek; szyna;
patyk; kość piszczelowa; v.
wstawiać w szyny złamaną
kość
splinter ['splynter] s. drzazga;
odłamek
split; split; split [splyt; splyt;
splyt]

split [splyt] v. łupać; pękać; rozszczepiać (się); dzielić; oddzielać (się); odchodzić; s. pęknięcie; rozszczepienie; rozdwojenie; odejście

splitting ['splytyŋg] adj. rozsadzający; ostry; gwałtowny

splutter ['splater] v. pryskać; opryskać; mówić bezładnie; s. pryskanie; szybka gadanina; zgiełk

spoil; spoilt; spoiled [spojl; spojlt; spojld]

spoil [spojl] v. psuć (się); zepsuć (się); (slang): kraść; sprzątnąć; przetrącić

spoils [spojls] pl. łupy (też w polityce)

spoilsport ['spojl'spo:rt] s. psujący zabawę

spoilt ['spojlt] v. zob. spoil

spoke [spouk] v. zob. speak; s. szczebel; szprycha

spoken ['spoukn] v. zob. speak

spokesman ['spouksmen] s. rzecznik

sponge [spandż] s. gąbka; wycior; tampon; pieczeniarz; pasożyt; v. myć gąbką; chłonąć; łowić gąbki; wyłudzać; wsysać; pasożytować

sponger ['spandżer] s. pasożyt; pieczeniarz (slang)

sponge cake ['spandż'kejk] biszkopt

spongy ['spandży] adj. gąbczasty

sponsor ['sponser] s. patron; organizator; gwarant; ojciec chrzestny; v. wprowadzać; być gwarantem; popierać; opłacać (np. program telewizyjny)

spontaneous [spon'tejnjes] adj. spontaniczny; samorzutny; naturalny; odruchowy

spook [spuk] s. zjawa; duch; upiór

spool [spu:l] s. cewka; rolka; szpulka; v. nawijać (na rolkę etc.)

spoon [spu:n] s. łyżka; v. czerpać (łyżką); durzyć się w kimś

spoon out ['spu:n,aut] v. drążyć; nabierać

spoon-fed ['spu:n,fed] adj. rozpieszczony; łyżką karmiony

spoonful ['spu:nful] s. łyżka czegoś

sporadic [spe'raedyk] adj. sporadyczny; rzadki; rzadko zdarzający się

spore [spo:r] s. zarodnik; v. wytwarzać zarodniki

sport [spo:rt] s. sport; zawody; zabawa; rozrywka; sportowiec; (slang): człowiek dobry, elegancki, lubiący zakładać się; v. bawić się; uprawiać sport; obnosić się z czymś; popisywać się; wyśmiewać się

sportive ['spo:rtyw] adj. żartobliwy

sportsman ['spo:rtsmen] s. sportowiec; myśliwy

sporty ['spo:rty] adj. (slang): sportowy; krzykliwy (ubiór); modny

spot [spot] s. plama; skaza; kropka; cętka; plamka; miejsce; lokal; odrobina; punkt; dolar; krótkie ogłoszenie; v. plamić (się); umiejscowić (np. zepsucie); poznawać; wyróżniać; rozmieszczać; adj. gotowy; gotówkowy; dorywczy

spotless ['spotlys] adj. bez skazy

spotlight ['spotlajt] s. reflektor szczelinowy; v. rzucać światło (na coś)

spouse [spauz] s. małżonek; małżonka

spout [spaut] s. wylot; rynna; wylew; dziobek; strumień; pochyłe koryto; v. wyrzucać z siebie płyn; tryskać; chlusnąć; recytować

sprain [sprejn] s. bolesne wykręcenie (nie zwichnięcie); v. wykręcić

sprang [spraeŋg] v. zob. spring

sprat [spraet] s. szprotka
(śledź); v. łowić szproty

sprawl [spro:l] v. rozwalać się;
gramolić się; rozłazić się;
rozrzucać; być rozrzuconym;
s. rozwalenie się; rozłażenie
się; rozkrzewianie się

spray [sprej] s. rozpylony płyn;
krople z rozpylacza; płyn do
rozpryskiwania; spryskiwacz;
grad (kul); gałązka; v.
opryskiwać; rozpryskiwać
(się)

spread; spread; spread [spred;
spred; spred]

spread [spred] v. rozpościerać
(się); rozszerzać (się);
posiać; rozsmarowywać;
rozkładać; pokrywać;
nakrywać; rozklepywać; s.
rozpostarcie; rozpiętość;
zasięg; szerokość; pasta;
narzuta; (slang): smarowidło
na chleb

sprig [spryg] s. gałązka;
latorośl; młokos; szyft; v.
ozdabiać gałązkami

sprightly ['sprajtly] adj. żywy;
dziarski; wesoły

spring; sprang; sprung [spryng;
spraeng; sprang]

spring [spryng] v. skakać;
sprężynować; wypłynąć;
puścić pędy (pąki);
zaskoczyć; spowodować
wybuch; paczyć się;
puszczać oczko; pękać; s.
wiosna; skok; sprężyna;
źródło; zdrój; prężność; adj.
wiosenny; sprężynowy;
źródlany

springboard ['spryng,bo:rd] s.
trampolina; odskocznia

springtime ['spryngtajm] s.
wiosna

sprinkle ['sprynkl] v. posypać;
pokropić; s. deszczyk

sprint [sprynt] s. krótki bieg;
krótki zrywny wysiłek; v. biec
na krótki dystans

sprinter ['sprynter] s. sprinter;
biegacz krótkodystansowy

sprout [spraut] s. pęd; odrośl;

v. puszczać pędy; wyrastać

spruce [spru:s] s. świerk;
smrek; adj. elegancki;
schludny; v. stroić się

sprung [sprang] v. zob. spring

spun [span] v. zob. spin

spur [spe:r] v. pogardliwie
odtrącać; pośpieszyć;
popędzać; s. odtrącenie z
pogardą

sputter ['spater] v. pryskać
(śliną); bełkotać; s.
pryskanie; plwociny; bełkot

spy [spaj] s. szpieg; tajniak;
szpiegowanie; v. szpiegować;
wybadać; czatować;
wypatrzyć

squabble ['skłobl] s. sprzeczka;
v. sprzeczać się

squad [skłod] s. oddział; grupka;
(lotny) patrol; wóz patrolowy;
v. formować grupki

squall [skło:l] s. szkwał; kłopot;
wrzask; v. wiać gwałtownie;
wrzeszczeć

squander ['skłonder] s.
marnotrawstwo; v. trwonić;
marnotrawić

square [skłeer] s. kwadrat;
czworobok (budynków); plac;
kątownik; węgielnica; adj.
kwadratowy; prostokątny;
prostopadły; uporządkowany;
zupełny; uczciwy; v. robić
kwadratowym, prostym;
podnosić do kwadratu;
płacić (dług); adv. w sedno;
rzetelnie; wprost

squash [skłosz] v. ubijać (się);
gnieść (się); miażdżyć; s.
miazga; tłok; rodzaj tenisa;
napój owocowy; mała dynia

squat; squat; squat [skłot; skłot;
skłot]

squat [skłot] v. kucać;
przycupnąć; nielegalnie
koczować na gruncie; adj.
przysadzisty; niski; szeroki; s.
osoba przysadzista; kucki

squeak [skłi:k] v. piszczeć;
skrzypieć; mówić piskliwie;
(slang): zdradzać (sekrety);
sypać; przepychać się z

trudnością; s. pisk; trudne
osiągnięcie czegoś
squeal [skłi:l] v. piszczeć;
kwiczeć; (slang):
awanturować się; sypać;
wydawać (kogoś); s. pisk;
kwik; sypanie (kogoś,
czegoś)
squeamish ['skłi:mysz] adj.
wybredny; pruderyjny;
przesadny; wrażliwy
squeegee ['skłi:dżi:] s. przyrząd
w kształcie litery T do
usuwania wody z mytych szyb
squeeze [skłi:z] v. ściskać;
wyciskać; wygniatać;
wciskać; odciskać;
ścieśnić; s. ucisk; nacisk;
odcisk; tłok; ściśnięcie
squeezer ['skłi:zer] s. wyciskacz
(soku)
squid [skłyd] s. przynęta z
mątwy; kałamarnica (ryba)
squint [skłynt] s. zez; ukośne
spojrzenie; zerknięcie;
skłonność; v. mrużyć oczy;
wysilać wzrok; zezować;
skłaniać się; adj. zezowaty;
zerkający
squirm [skłe:rm] v. wić się (z
bólu); płonąć (ze wstydu);
kręcić się niespokojnie; s.
skręcanie się
squirrel ['skłe:rel] s. wiewiórka
squirt [skłe:rt] v. strzykać;
tryskać; s. strzykawka;
struga; pętak
stab [staeb] v. dźgnąć;
pchnąć; ugodzić; ranić; s.
pchnięcie; dźgnięcie; rana
kłuta
stability [ste'bylyty] s. stałość;
stateczność; stabilność;
równowaga
stabilize ['stejbylajz] v. ustalać;
stabilizować
stable ['stejbl] s. stajnia;
stadnina; v. trzymać konie w
stajni; adj. stały; stanowczy;
trwały
stack [staek] s. stóg; stos;
sterta; komin; kupa; v.
układać w stogi; ustawiać w

kozły; układać podstępnie
przeciwko komuś
stadium ['stejdjem] s. stadion;
faza; stadium (czegoś)
staff [staef] s. laska; drzewce;
sztab; personel; adj.
sztabowy; v. obsadzać
personelem
stag [staeg] s. rogacz; jeleń;
samotny mężczyzna
stage [stejdż] s. scena; stadium;
etap; rusztowanie; pomost;
postój; v. wystawiać;
odegrać (sztukę); urządzać;
inscenizować; adj. teatralny;
sceniczny
stagecoach ['stejdż-koucz] s.
dyliżans
stage-manager ['stejdż
'maenydżer] s. reżyser
stagflation ['staegflejszyn] s.
stagnacja, rosnące bezrobocie
i inflacja jednocześnie
stagger ['staeger] v. zataczać
się; wahać się; chwiać się;
układać w zygzak lub w
odstępach; porażać; s. układ
skośny, zachodzący na siebie
w odstępach lub
zygzakowaty; zataczanie się;
pl. zawroty głowy
staggering ['staegeryng] adj.
przerażający; oszałamiający;
rozbrajający
stagnant ['staegnent] adj.
zastały; stojący; będący w
zastoju
stain [stejn] v. plamić (się);
brudzić; szargać; barwić;
kolorować; farbować;
drukować tapety; s. plama;
barwnik; bejca do drewna
stained ['stejnd] adj. zabarwiony
(np. szkło)
stainless ['stejnlys] adj.
nierdzewny (stal); nieskalany
stair [steer] s. stopień; pl.
schody
staircase ['steer,kejs] s. klatka
schodowa
stairway ['steerłej] s. schody
stake [stejk] s. słup; słupek;
kołek; palik; stawka;

kowadełko blacharskie; v.
przytwierdzać kołkami;
wytaczać; przywiązywać do
słupa; stawiać na coś
stake out ['stejk,aut] v. wziąć
pod obserwację; wyznaczać
granicę
stake-out ['stejkaut] s. zasadzka
(slang)
stale [stejl] adj. stęchły;
nieświeży; zwietrzały;
czerstwy; przestarzały; v.
czuć nieświeżym
stalk [sto:k] v. kroczyć;
podkradać się; podchodzić;
s. (majestatyczny) chód;
podkradanie się;
podchodzenie; wysoki komin;
łodyga; nóżka (kieliszka)
stall [sto:l] v. działać
opóźniająco; zwlekać;
przewlekać; kręcić;
zwodzić; przetrzymywać;
dławić motor; utykać;
grzęznąć; trzymać bydło w
oborze; zaopatrywać w
przegrody; s. stajnia; obora;
stragan; kiosk; przegroda;
komora (w kopalni); (slang):
trik; kruczek
stallion ['staeljen] s. ogier
stalwart ['sto:łłert] s. bojownik
partyjny; adj. dzielny; krzepki;
stanowczy
stammer ['staemer] v. jąkać
się; s. jąkanie się
stamp [staemp] v. stemplować;
wytłaczać; tupać; kruszyć;
wbijać (w pamięć);
przylepiać znaczki pocztowe;
s. stempel; pieczątka;
znaczek; piętno; cecha;
pokrój; tupnięcie; ubijak do
kruszenia (rudy)
stanch [staencz] v. tamować
krwotok; adj. wierny; stały;
krzepki; szczelny
stand; stood; stood [staend;
stud; stud]
stand [staend] v. stać; stanąć;
wytrzymać; znosić;
przetrzymać; zostać;
utrzymywać się; stawiać

opór; znajdować się; być;
postawić; (slang): płacić; s.
stanie; stanowisko; stojak;
trybuna; postój; łan; ława dla
świadków; unieruchomienie;
umywalka
stand back ['staend,baek] v.
stać w tyle; zachowywać
rezerwę
stand by ['staendbaj] v.
popierać; być w stanie
pogotowia
stand off ['staend,of] v. cofać
się
stand-off ['staend,of] s.
nierozegrana (równowaga sił)
stand out ['staend,aut] v.
wyróżniać się;
kontrastować; wytrwać
stand up ['staend,ap] v.
wstawać; powstawać;
stawać w obronie; nie
ustępować; stawiać czoło
standard ['staenderd] s.
sztandar; norma; miernik;
wzorzec; wskaźnik; stopa
(życiowa); próba; słup;
podpórka; adj.
znormalizowany; normalny;
typowy; przeciętny;
wzorcowy; klasyczny; literacki
(język)
standardize ['staenderdajz] v.
normalizować;
dostosowywać do normy;
mierzyć wzorcem;
porównywać z wzorcem
standing ['staendyng] adj.
stojący; na pniu; pionowy;
stały; s. stanie; stanowisko;
znaczenie; poważanie;
reputacja; czas trwania
standing room ['staendyng,ru:m]
s. miejsce stojące
standoffish ['staend'ofysz] adj.
nieprzystępny; trzymający się
z dala
standpoint ['staend,point] s.
punkt widzenia; punkt
obserwacyjny
standstill ['staendstyl] s. zastój;
przerwa; martwy punkt;
unieruchomienie

stank [staenk] v. zob. stink

star [sta:r] s. gwiazda; gwiazdor; gwiazdka; v. ozdabiać gwiazdkami; być gwiazdorem; adj. gwiezdny; występujący w głównej roli

starboard ['sta:rberd] s. prawa burta; v. sterować na prawo

starch [sta:rcz] s. skrobia; sztywność; krochmal; v. nakrochmalić; (slang): siła

starchy ['sta:rczy] adj. nakrochmalony; skrobiowaty; sztywny

stare [steer] v. patrzeć; gapić się; wpatrywać się; zwracać uwagę; s. nieruchomy wzrok; wytrzeszczone oczy; zagapione spojrzenie

stare at ['steer,aet] v. gapić się na ...

stark [sta:rk] adj. sztywny; zupełny; czysty; wierutny; ponury; posępny; adv. zupełnie; całkowicie

starling ['starlyng] s. szpak

starlit ['sta:rlyt] adj. gwiaździsty; oświetlony gwiazdami; wygwieżdżony

starry ['sta:ry] adj. gwiaździsty; usiany gwiazdami; promienny; marzycielski; rozmarzony

star-spangled ['sta:r-spaengld] adj. usiany gwiazdami (flaga USA)

start [sta:rt] v. zacząć; ruszyć; startować; zerwać się; podskoczyć; wyruszyć; zabierać się; uruchamiać; obsuwać; rozpoczynać; wszczynać; s. początek; start; wymarsz; poderwanie się; obsunięcie się; zdobywanie przewagi

starter ['sta:rter] s. starter; rozrusznik; startujący zawodnik; pierwsze danie; kierownik ruchu

startle ['sta:rtl] v. zaskoczyć; zaniepokoić; podrywać; wzdrygać się; przestraszać; s. zaniepokojenie; poderwanie się

startling ['sta:rtlyng] adj. sensacyjny; zdumiewający; niepokojący

starvation [sta:r'wejszyn] s. głód; głodowanie; głodzenie; przymieranie głodem

starve [sta:rw] v. głodować; zagłodzić; przymierać z głodu, zimna; łaknąć; zmuszać (głodem, brakiem)

stash [staesz] v. (slang): chować na potem; s. schowanie; schowek

state [stejt] s. państwo; stan; zajęcie; parada; pompa; ceremoniał; stan prac; adj. państwowy; stanowy; uroczysty; paradny; formalny; v. stwierdzać; wyrażać (też symbolami); określać

state department ['stejt,dy'pa:rtment] s. (w USA) ministerstwo spraw zagranicznych

stately ['stejtly] adj. uroczysty; okazały; adv. uroczyście; okazale

statement ['stejtment] s. wyrażenie; twierdzenie; sprawozdanie; wyciąg; oświadczenie; deklaracja; zeznanie

state room ['stejt,rum] s. prywatny pokój; kabina; przedział

stateside ['stejt,sajd] adj. amerykański; w stanach

statesman ['stejtsmen] s. mąż stanu

statesmanship ['stejtsmenszyp] s. rozum polityczny

static ['staetyk] adj. statyczny; nieruchomy

station ['stejszyn] s. stacja; stanowisko; stan; pozycja życiowa; godność; punkt; stacja telewizyjna, radiowa etc.

stationary ['stejsznery] adj. niezmienny; stały; nieruchomy; pozycyjny

stationery ['stejszn,ery] s. pl. materiały piśmienne; papier listowy

station master ['stejszyn,ma:ster]
s. naczelnik stacji

station wagon ['stejszyn,łaegn]
s. samochód typu kombi

statistics [ste'tystyks] s.
statystyka

statue ['staeczu:] s. posąg

statute ['staetjut] s. ustawa;
prawo; statut; nakaz

staunch [sto:ncz] v. tamować
krwotok; tamponować; adj.
oddany; wierny; zagorzały

stay; stayed; staid [stej; stejd;
stejd]

stay [stej] s. pobyt; zwłoka;
odroczenie; opóźnienie;
zawieszenie; podpora; wanta;
zatrzymanie; przerwa;
wytrzymałość; v. zostać;
przebywać; wytrzymać;
odraczać; kłaść kres;
zaspokajać (głód)

stay away ['stej,ełej] v. trzymać
się z dala

stay up ['stej,ap] v. nie siadać

stay with ['stej,łys] v. mieszkać
u kogoś

stead [sted] s. miejsce; na
miejsce; pożyteczność

steadfast ['sted,fa:st] adj. stały;
nieruchomy; niezachwiany;
niewzruszony; mocny; pewny

steady ['stedy] adj. mocny; silny;
pewny; stały; rzetelny; równy;
stateczny; excl.: powoli!
prosto! naprzód! stój!; v.
dawać równowagę;
odzyskiwać równowagę; s.
podpora; (slang): ukochany

steak [stejk] s. stek; befsztyk;
płat (np. mięsa)

steal; stole; stolen [sti:l; stoul;
stoulen]

steal [sti:l] v. kraść; wykraść;
wejść ukradkiem; zakradać
się; skradać się; s. kradzież;
rzecz ukradziona; rzecz
kupiona prawie, że za darmo;
darmocha (slang)

stealth [stels] s. tajemniczość;
ukradkowość

stealthy ['stelsy] adj. ukradkowy;

tajemny

steam [sti:m] s. para; v.
parować; dymić; płynąć
pod parą; gotować w parze;
umieszczać pod parą

steam up ['sti:m,ap] v. zamglić
(się); zajść mgłą lub parą

steamer ['sti:mer] s. parowiec

steamship ['sti:m,szyp] s.
parowiec

steel [sti:l] s. stal; pręt stalowy;
adj. stalowy; ze stali; v.
pokrywać stalą; hartować

steel works ['sti:l,łe:rks] s.
stalownia

steep [sti:p] v. moczyć się;
rozmiękczać; impregnować;
pogrążyć się; rozpijać się;
adj. stromy;
nieprawdopodobny;
wygórowany; przesadny

steepen ['sti:pn] v. nagle
podnosić ceny; robić
stromym

steeple ['sti:pl] s. strzelista
wieża; ostra wieżyczka

steer [stier] v. sterować;
kierować; prowadzić; s.
wskazówka; młody wół na
mięso

steering wheel ['stieryng,hłi:l] s.
kierownica; koło sterowe

stem [stem] s. pień; łodyga;
szpulka; trzon; trzonek; nóżka;
v. pochodzić; tamować;
powstrzymywać; iść pod
prąd; zwalczać

stench [stencz] s. smród; odór;
fetor

stenographer [ste'negraefer] s.
stenograf; stenografistka

step [step] s. krok; stopień;
takt; szczebel; schodek; v.
stąpać; kroczyć; iść;
tańczyć; podnosić;
wzmagać; przyciskać nogą;
mierzyć (krokami)

stepchild ['step,czajld] s. pasierb

stepfather ['step,fa:dzer] s.
ojczym

stepmother ['step,madzer] s.
macocha

stereo ['steriou] s. stereoskop;

dwugłośnikowe radio-adapter;
adj. stereofoniczny
sterile ['sterajl] adj. wyjałowiony;
jałowy; sterylny; bezpłodny
sterilize ['stery,lajz] v.
wyjałowić; wysterylizować
sterling ['ste:rlyng] s. pieniądz
pełnowartościowy; adj.
solidny; niezawodny
stern [ste:rn] adj. surowy; srogi;
s. rufa; zad; zadek; tył;
pośladki
sternness ['ste:rnys] s.
surowość; srogość
stew [stu:] v. gotować; dusić
(się); martwić się; wkuwać
się; s. potrawa duszona;
kłopot; staw na ryby
steward ['stu:erd] s. zarządca;
ekonom; kelner; v. zarządzać;
być stewardem
stewardess ['stu:erdys] s.
stewardessa
stew pan ['stu:,paen] s. rondel;
garnek
stick; stuck; stuck [styk; stak;
stak]
stick [styk] v. wtykać;
przekłuwać; kłuć; wbijać;
zarzynać; przyklejać;
naklejać; utkwić; utknąć;
ugrzęznąć; przyczepiać (się);
trzymać się (tematu);
oszukiwać; s. pałka; patyk;
laska; kij; tyczka; żerdź
stick out ['styk,aut] v.
wystawiać; sterczeć; zadać
stick to ['styk,tu] v. trzymać się
(tematu); przylepiać
stick up ['styk,ap] v.
terroryzować (bronią); brać
w obronę; podnosić;
przeciwstawiać się
sticky ['styky] adj. lepki; kleisty;
grząski; parny; (slang): marny;
nieprzyjemny
stiff [styf] adj. sztywny; twardy;
kategoryczny; zdrętwiały;
"słony"; wygórowany; trudny;
ciężki; silny; s. (slang): trup;
umrzyk; niedojda; włóczęga;
facet; pedant
stiffen ['styfn] v. usztywniać;

podnieść (wymagania);
zgęszczać; zesztywnieć
stifle [stajfl] v. dusić (się);
tłumić; przygaszać;
tuszować
stile [stajl] s. przełaz; kołowrót;
pionowa rama drzwi
still [styl] adj. spokojny; cichy;
nieruchomy; martwy
(przedmiot); milczący; adv.
jeszcze; jednak; wciąż; dotąd;
niemniej; mimo to; v.
uspokoić (się); uciszyć;
destylować; s. destylarnia
(też wódki)
stillness ['stylnys] s. cisza;
spokój; bezruch
stilt [stylt] s. szczudło
stilted ['styltyd] adj. na
szczudłach; nienaturalny;
sztuczny; na wspornikach
stimulant ['stymjulent] s.
bodziec; podnieta; alkohol;
środek podniecający;
zachęta; adj. pobudzający
stimulate ['stymjulejt] v.
pobudzać; zachęcać
stimulating ['stymjulejtyng] adj.
podniecający; pobudzający
stimulation ['stymjulejszyn] s.
podnieta; zachęta; podniecenie
stimulus ['stymjules] s. bodziec;
zachęta; podnieta
sting; stung; stung [styng;
stang; stang]
sting [styng] v. kłuć; parzyć;
kąsać; szczypać; palić;
rwać; gryźć; s. żądło;
ukłucie; poparzenie; piekący
ból; uszczypliwość;
zjadliwość
stingy ['styndży] adj. skąpy
stink; stank; stunk [stynk;
staenk; stank]
stink [stynk] v. cuchnąć;
śmierdzieć; zasmradzać;
wyganiać smrodem; (slang):
poczuć smród; s. smród
stipulate ['stypjulejt] v.
zażądać; uwarunkować;
zastrzegać w umowie
stir [ste:r] v. ruszać; poruszać;
grzebać; mieszać; wzniecać;

podniecać; s. poruszenie;
podniecenie; ruch; (slang):
więzienie
stirrup ['styrep] s. strzemię;
pocięgiel; okucie do wspinania
się
stitch [stycz] s. szew; ścieg;
oczko; kłucie; v. szyć;
zaszyć; zeszywać
stoat [stout] s. gronostaj;
zaszywać niewidocznym
ściegiem
stock [stok] s. zapas; zasób;
bydło; pień; trzon; kłoda;
łożysko; ród; rasa; surowiec;
kapitał udziałowy; akcje
giełdowe; obligacje; wywar; v.
zaopatrywać;
zagospodarować; zarybiać;
mieć na składzie; adj.
typowy; seryjny; w stałym
zapasie; repertuarowy
stockade [sto'kejd] s. palisada;
częstokół; obóz
stockbroker ['stok,brouker] s.
makler giełdowy
stock exchange
['stok,eks'czejndż] s. giełda
stockholder ['stok,houlder] s.
akcjonariusz; udziałowiec
stocking ['stokyng] s.
pończocha
stocky ['stoky] adj. krępy
stock market ['stok-'ma:rkyt] s.
giełda
stole [stoul] v. zob. steal; s.
stula; etola
stolen ['stouln] v. zob. steal
stolid ['stolyd] adj. obojętny;
flegmatyczny
stomach ['stamek] s. żołądek;
brzuch; apetyt; ochota; v.
jeść; przełykać (obelgą);
znosić
stone [stoun] s. kamień; głaz;
skała; pestka; adj. kamienny;
v. ukamienować; obkładać
(mur) kamieniem; wyjmować
pestki; upijać (się) na umór
stonewall ['stoun-ło:l] v.
odmówić zaciekle
jakiejkolwiek kooperacji
stoneware ['stoun-łeer] s.

naczynia kamionkowe
stony ['stouny] adj. kamienny;
kamienisty; skamieniały;
pestkowy
stood [stud] v. zob. stand
stool [stu:l] s. stołek; sedes;
taboret; stolec; klęcznik;
podnóżek; pniak puszczający
pędy; wabik; v. puszczać
pędy
stoop [stu:p] v. schylać się;
ugiąć się; poniżyć się;
raczyć; garbić się; s.
pochylenie; przygarbione
plecy; weranda; taras (przy
domu)
stooping ['stu:pyng] adj.
przygarbiony
stop [stop] v. zatrzymywać;
powstrzymywać;
wstrzymywać; zatykać;
zaplombować; zagrodzić;
zablokować; zamknąć;
zaprzestawać; nie dopuścić;
stanąć; przestać; exp.:
przestań stój! dosyć tego!;
s. zatrzymanie (się); stop;
postój; przystanek; zatkanie;
zator; zatyczka; zderzak;
ogranicznik
stop by ['stop,baj] v. wstąpić
do kogoś na chwilę
stopover ['stop'ouwer] s.
zatrzymanie się w podróży
stoppage ['stopydż] s.
wstrzymanie; zatrzymanie
(się); zatwardzenie
stopper ['stoper] s. korek;
zatyczka; v. zatykać;
umocować liną
stopping ['stopyng] s. plomba (w
zębie); zatrzymanie; zatkanie
storage ['sto:rydż] s. skład;
przechowywanie;
magazynowanie
store ['sto:r] s. zapas; sklep;
skład; mnóstwo; składnica; v.
magazynować; mieścić w
sobie; zaopatrywać;
wyposażać
store up ['sto:r,ap] v.
zamagazynować; zachować
storehouse ['sto:rhaus] s. skład;

magazyn; skarbnica; kopalnia
storekeeper ['sto:r,ki:per] s.
sklepikarz; kupiec
storey ['sto:ry] (=story) s. piętro
storeyed ['sto:rjed] adj. piętrowy
(angielska pisownia)
storied ['sto:rjed] adj. piętrowy
stork [sto:rk] s. bocian
storm [sto:rm] s. burza; wichura;
sztorm; zawierucha; szturm; v.
szaleć (burza etc.); wpaść
do pokoju; wypaść z pokoju
(jak burza); rzucać gromy;
szturmować; brać szturmem
stormy ['sto:rmy] adj. burzliwy;
zwiastujący burzę
story ['sto:ry] s. opowiadanie;
opowieść; powiastka;
historia; bajka; anegdota;
gawęda; zmyślanie; nowela;
piętro
story teller ['sto:ry,teler] s.
gawędziarz; kłamczuch
stout [staut] adj. dzielny;
krzepki; gruby; s. mocne np.
porto (wino); mocne piwo;
tęga osoba
stove [stouw] s. piec (też
kuchenny); cieplarnia; v. zob.
stave; hodować w cieplarni
stow [stou] v. wypełniać;
układać szczelnie; mieścić;
wsuwać; chować; przesłać
(slang)
stow away ['stou,e'łej] v.
jechać na gapę
stowaway ['stouełej] s. pasażer
na gapę
straggling ['straeglyng] adj.
sporadyczny; rozpościerający
się; rzadki
straight [strejt] adj. prosty;
bezpośredni; celny; szczery;
otwarty; rzetelny; zwykły; s.
prosta linia; prosty odcinek
(toru); adv. prosto; wprost; na
przełaj; po prostu; pod rząd;
należycie; nieprzerwanie;
ciągiem
straightaway ['strejt,ełej] adv.
natychmiast; bez zwłoki
straight ahead ['strejt,ehed] adv.
na wprost

straighten ['strejtn] v.
wyprostować (się); poprawić
(się)
straightforward [strejt'fo:rłerd]
adj. łatwy; jasny; prosty;
prostolinijny; szczery; uczciwy
strain [strejn] v. prężyć;
naprężać; naciągać;
wytężać; odkształcać;
nadużywać; nadwerężać;
przeciążać; robić gwałtowne
wysiłki; cedzić; przecedzać;
s. naprężenie; napięcie;
obciążenie; przemęczenie;
zwichnięcie; nadwerężenie;
wysiłek; odkształcenie; rasa;
odmiana; rys
strainer ['strejner] s. sito;
sączek; cedzidło; rozciągacz;
napinacz
strait [strejt] v. ścieśniać; być
w trudnościach
straited circumstances ['strejtyd,
ser'kamstensys] s. kłopoty
pieniężne
straiten ['strejtn] v. zbiednieć;
zubożeć
strait jacket ['strejt'dżaekyt] s.
kaftan bezpieczeństwa
straits [strejts] pl. cieśnina
morska; kłopoty finansowe;
braki czegoś
strand [straend] s. skręt; zwitek;
pasmo; nitka; warkocz; sznur;
rys; kosmyk; brzeg; plaża; v.
splatać; osadzać na
mieliźnie; osiąść na
mieliźnie
strange [strejndż] adj. obcy;
dziwny; niezwykły; nieznany;
niewprawny
stranger ['strejndżer] s. obcy;
nieznajomy; człowiek
nieobeznany; exp. panie tego!
strangle ['straengl] v. dusić;
trzymać za gardło; zadusić
strap [straep] s. rzemień; pasek;
rzemyk; taśma; uchwyt;
rączka; chłosta; bicie; v. na
pasku umocowywać;
ostrzyć; bić paskiem;
zalepiać plastrem
strategic [stre'ti:dżyk] adj.

strategiczny
strategy ['straetydży] s.
strategia; taktyka
straw [stro:] s. słoma
strawberry ['stro:bery] s.
truskawka
stray [strej] v. zabłądzić;
zabłąkać się; schodzić na
manowce; s. zbłąkane
zwierzę; dziecko bez opieki;
adj. zabłąkany
strays [strejs] pl. zaburzenia
atmosferyczne (np. w radiu)
streak [stri:k] s. smuga; pasek;
pasmo; prążek; rys;
pierwiastek; passa; v.
rysować paski, prążki;
błyskawicznie poruszać się;
wpadać nagle dokądś
streaky ['stri:ky] adj.
prążkowany; w paski;
zmienny; nierówny (slang)
stream [stri:m] s. strumień;
potok; rzeka; struga; prąd; v.
płynąć (strumieniami);
ociekać; tryskać; powiewać
street [stri:t] s. ulica
streetcar ['stri:tka:r] s. tramwaj
strength [strenks] s. moc; siła;
stężenie; natężenie; ilość;
skład (ludzi)
strengthen ['strenksn] v.
wzmocnić (się); wzmagać;
dać przewagę
strenuous [strenjues] adj.
męczący; żmudny; mozolny;
wytężony; zawzięty;
pracowity; energiczny; silny
stress [stres] s. nacisk; akcent;
napór; wysiłek; v. kłaść
nacisk; podkreślać; naciskać
stretch [strecz] v. naciągać
(się); naprężać; napinać;
nadużywać; przeciągać;
rozciągać (się); ciągnąć się;
sięgać; powiesić (kogoś); s.
napięcie; rozciąganie;
przeciąganie się; nadużycie;
połać; okres służby; przeciąg
czasu; prosty odcinek toru;
(slang): pobyt w więzieniu
stretcher ['streczer] s. nosze
strew; strewed; strewn [stru:;

stru:d; stru:n]
strew [stru:] s. posypać;
rozrzucić; porozrzucać
strewn [stru:n] v. zob. strew
stricken ['stryken] v. zob. strike;
adj. dotknięty; nawiedzony;
rażony; udręczony
stride; strode; stridden [strajd;
stroud; strydn]
stride [strajd] v. kroczyć;
przekroczyć; stać okrakiem
(nad czymś); s. krok; rozkrok
strife [strajf] s. spór; walka;
współzawodnictwo
strike; struck; stricken [strajk;
strak; strykn]
strike [strajk] v. uderzać; bić
(monetę); walić; kuć;
wykrzesać; zapalić (zapałkę);
natrafić; zastrajkować;
porzucać robotę; chwytać
(przynętę); s. strajk;
strychulec; wybicie monety;
natrafienie (żyły, np.
złotodajnej); chwycenie
przynęty; nieudane uderzenie
palantem; zwalenie wszystkich
kręgli naraz
strike off ['strajk off] v.
odrapywać; ścinać;
wykreślać; drukować kilka
egzemplarzy
strike out ['strajk‚aut] v.
uderzać na odlew; zacząć;
ukuć; wymyślić
striker ['strajker] s. strajkujący;
młotek (w dzwonku)
striking ['strajkyng] adj.
uderzający
string; strung; strung [stryng;
strang; strang]
string [stryng] v. zawiązać;
przywiązać; zaopatrzyć w
struny; stroić; napinać;
podniecać; powiesić kogoś;
ciągnąć się (klej);
obwieszać; s. sznurek;
szpagat; powróz;
sznurowadło; tasiemka;
cięciwa; struna; żyła; włókno;
rząd; stek (głupstw)
strip [stryp] v. obdzierać;
ogołacać; obnażać;

zdzierać; rozbierać (się);
wydobyć do końca; ścierać
(gwint); ciąć na paski; s.
pasek; skrawek; seria
komiksów
strip-tease ['strypti:z] s.
rozbieranie się na scenie
striped ['strajpt] adj. pasiasty; w
pasy
stripes [strajps] pl. paski; prążki;
naszywki; chłosta; cięgi
strive; strove; striven ['strajw;
strouw; strywn]
strive [strajw] v. starać się;
usiłować; dążyć; borykać
się; zwalczać
striven ['strywn] v. zob. strive
strode [strode] v. zob. stride
stroke [strouk] s. uderzenie;
cios; cięcie; raz; porażenie;
ciąg; pociągnięcie (pióra); rys;
kreska; ruch (wiosła); wysiłek;
suw; skok (tłoka); takt;
głaskanie; v. znaczyć;
przekreślać; nadawać
tempo; głaskać; ugłaskać
stroke of luck ['strouk,ow'lak]
exp.: los szczęścia
stroll [stroul] v. przechadzać
się; spacerować; wędrować;
s. przechadzka
stroller ['strouler] s. spacerowicz;
włóczęga; aktor wędrowny;
wózek (dziecięcy)
strong [strong] adj. mocny; silny;
będący w liczbie ...;
mocarstwowy; potężny;
trwały; solidny; wyskokowy;
przekonywający; ordynarny
strongbox ['strong,boks] s. sejf;
kasa ogniotrwała
strongroom ['strong,rum] s.
skarbiec
strove [strouw] v. zob. strive
struck [strak] v. zob. strike
structure ['strakczer] s. budowa;
struktura; budowla; wiązanie;
splot; v. nadawać kształt
struggle ['stragl] v. szarpać się;
szamotać się; walczyć;
usiłować; s. walka; borykanie
strum [stram] v. rzępolić;
brzdąkać; s. brzdęk;

brzdąkanie
strung [strang] v. zob. string;
adj. napięty
strut [strat] v. kroczyć
majestatycznie; rozpierać; s.
krok majestatyczny; zastrzał;
rozpora
stub [stab] s. pniak; korzeń;
resztka; niedopałek; grzbiet
(biletu); v. karczować; gasić
(papierosa)
stubble ['stabl] s. rżysko;
ściernisko; twardy zarost
stubborn ['stabern] adj. uparty
stuck [stak] v. zob. stick
stud [stad] s. sworzeń;
gwóźdź; guz; trzon; słup;
rozpórka; ogier; stadnina; v.
nabijać (np. gwoździami,
guzami); usiewać
czymś; być rozsianym;
podpierać (słupami)
student ['stu:dent] s. student;
badający coś; znawca
czegoś
studio ['stju:djou] s. studio;
pracownia
studio couch ['stju:djou,kaucz] s.
tapczan
studious ['stu:djes] adj. pilny;
staranny; dbały; wyszukany
study ['stady] s. pracownia;
gabinet; nauka; przedmiot
nauki, starań, troski, zadumy,
marzenia; v. badać;
studiować; dociekać; uczyć
się
stuff [staf] v. napychać;
opychać (się); tuczyć (się);
faszerować; wpychać;
wkuwać; s. materia; materiał;
glina; rzecz; rupiecie (brednie)
stuffing ['stafyng] s. nadzienie;
farsz; nadziewka; wyściółka
stuffy ['stafy] adj. zatęchły;
duszny; ciężki; nudny;
zatkany (nos); (slang): ważny;
tępy; skwaszony; zły;
purytański
stumble ['stambl] v. potykać
(się); utykać; natknąć się;
zawahać (kogoś); mieć
skrupuły; czuć się

dotkniętym; s. potknięcie się
stumble-bum ['stambl,bam] s.
(slang): zawalidroga; próżniak
stumbling block
['stamblyng,blok] s.
przeszkoda; zawada; szkopuł;
trudność
stump [stamp] s. pniak; głąb;
kikut; ogarek; resztka;
niedopałek; kulas; krzykactwo;
agitacja (polityczna); klocek;
przysadkowaty człowiek; v.
karczować; obcinać;
zdumieć (się); agitować;
wyzwać kogoś; chodzić na
protezie
stun [stan] v. ogłuszać;
oszołomić; s. oszołomienie
(uderzenie hukiem)
stung [stang] v. zob. sting
stunk [stank] v. zob. stink
stunning ['stanyng] adj.
nadzwyczajny; szlagierowy;
kapitalny
stupefy ['stu:pyfaj] v. ogłupiać;
odurzać; wprawiać w
osłupienie
stupid ['stu:pyd] adj. głupi;
odurzony; nudny; s. głupiec
stupidity ['stu:pydyty] s. głupota;
głupstwo
stupor ['stu:per] s. osłupienie;
odurzenie; apatia
sturdy ['ste:rdy] adj. krzepki;
dzielny; solidny; s. motylica
stutter ['stater] v. jąkać (się); s.
jąkanie się
sty [staj] s. chlew; burdel;
jęczmień (w oku); v. żyć w
chlewie; trzymać w chlewie
style [stajl] s. styl; maniera;
sposób; fason; wzór; kształt;
rylec; szyjka; tytuł; nazwa;
format; wskazówka; v.
formować stylowo; określać
mianem
stylish ['stajlysz] adj. szykowny;
stylowy; wytworny
suave [sła:w] adj. gładki;
łagodny; uprzejmy
subdivision [,sabdy'wyżyn] s.
dzielnica (miasta, osiedla);
podział

subdue [seb'du:] s. ujarzmiać;
poskramiać; przyciszać;
tłumić; łagodzić; podbijać
subject ['sabdżykt] s. podmiot;
przedmiot; temat; treść;
tworzywo; [sab'dżekt] motyw;
poddany; osobnik; v.
podporządkować; ujarzmić;
podbić; narazić; poddać
czemuś; adj. poddany; uległy;
podległy; narażony; podatny;
podlegający; ujarzmiony; adv.
pod warunkiem; z
zastrzeżeniem; z
uwzględnieniem czegoś
subjective [seb'dżektyw] adj.
subiektywny; podmiotowy
subjunctive mood
[seb'dżanktyw,mu:d] s. tryb
warunkowy
sublime [se'blajm] adj. wzniosły;
wyniosły; podniosły
submachine-gun
['sabme'szi:ngan] s.
(automatyczny) pistolet
maszynowy
submarine [sabme'ri:n] s. łódź
podwodna
submariners [sabme'ri:ners] pl.
załoga łodzi podwodnej
submerge [seb'me:rdż] v.
zalewać; zatapiać; zanurzać
(się); zakrywać
submission [seb'myszyn] s.
uległość; poddanie się;
przedłożenie (opinii)
submissive [seb'mysyw] adj.
uległy
submit [seb'myt] v. poddawać
(się); przedkładać
subnormal [sab'no:rmel] adj.
niżej normy; cofnięty w
rozwoju
subordinate [se'bo:rdnyt] adj.
zależny; podporządkowany; s.
podwładny; [se'bo:rdnejt] v.
podporządkowywać
subordinate clause
[se'bo:rdnyt,klo:z] s. zdanie
podrzędne
subscribe [seb'skrajb] b.
zaprenumerować;
podpisywać (np. obraz);

pisać się na coś; dawać na
cel

subscribe for [seb'skrajb,fo:r] v.
zapisywać się na (nową)
książkę

subscribe to [seb'skrajb,tu] v.
abonować gazetę

subscriber [seb'skrajber] s.
abonent; człowiek popierający

subscription [seb'skrypszyn] s.
prenumerata; przedpłata;
podpisanie; zgoda pisemna;
podpis dołączony

subsequent ['sabsykłent] adj.
następny

subsequently ['sabsykłently] adv.
następnie

subside [seb'sajd] v. klęsnąć;
opadać; osadzać się;
osiadać; uspokajać się

subsidiary [seb'sydjery] adj.
pomocniczy; subsydiowany
(zależny); s. pomocnik

subsidiary company
[seb'sydjery'kampeny] s. firma
zależna od innej firmy

subsidize ['sabsydajz] v.
zasiłkować; zasilać;
opłacać; przekupywać

subsidy ['sabsydy] s. zasiłek
(państwowy); subwencja;
danina

subsist [seb'syst] v. istnieć;
egzystować; utrzymywać się
przy życiu; żyć czymś

subsistence [seb'systens] s.
utrzymanie; istnienie

substance ['sabstens] s. istota;
treść; sens; sedno;
substancja; znaczenie;
rzeczywistość; majątek

substandard [sab'staenderd] adj.
poniżej poziomu; ordynarny
(język)

substantial [sab'staenszel] adj.
materialny; rzeczywisty;
solidny; zasadniczy; ważny;
bogaty; wpływowy;
konkretny; treściwy

substantive ['sabstentyw] adj.
rzeczywisty; niezależnie
istniejący; zasadniczy;
poważny; rzeczownikowy;

wyrażający istnienie; s.
rzeczownik

substitute ['sabstytut] s.
namiastka; zastępca

substitution [,sabsty'tuszyn] s.
zastępstwo; zastąpienie

subtitle ['sabtajtl] s. podtytuł;
napis na filmie

subtle ['satl] adj. subtelny;
delikatny; cienki; rzadki;
chytry; bystry

subtract [sab'traekt] v.
odejmować

suburb ['sabe:rb] s.
przedmieście

suburban [se'be:rben] adj.
podmiejski

subway ['sabłej] s. kolejka
podziemna

succeed [sek'si:d] v. mieć
powodzenie; udawać się;
następować po kimś

success [sek'ses] s. powodzenie;
sukces; rzecz udana; człowiek
mający sukces

successful [sek'sesful] adj.
udały; mający powodzenie

succession [sek'seszyn] s.
następstwo; kolej; kolejność;
sukcesja; spadkobiercy; szereg

successive [sek'sesyw] adj.
kolejny

successor [sek'seser] s.
następca; dziedzic;
spadkobierca

succumb [se'kam] v. ulegać
(pokusie); poddawać się;
umierać

such [sacz] adj. taki; tego
rodzaju; pron. taki; tym
podobny

suck [sak] v. ssać; korzystać;
wyzyskiwać; wchłaniać;
wciągać; (slang): nabierać;
dać się nabrać; podlizywać
się komuś; s. ssanie;
wciąganie; (slang): łyk

suckle ['sakel] v. karmić piersią;
dawać pierś; ssać pierś

suckling ['saklyng] s. osesek;
młode w okresie ssania

sudden ['sadn] adj. nagły

sudden death ['sadn,det] s.

nagła śmierć; rozstrzygnięcie
w następnej rozgrywce
suddenly ['sadnly] adv. nagle;
raptownie; nieoczekiwanie
suds [sadz] pl. mydliny; (slang):
piwo
sue [su:] v. skarżyć;
zaskarżać; pozywać;
upraszać; ubiegać się
suede [słejd] s. zamsz
suet ['su:yt] s. łój; adj. łojowy
suffer ['safer] v. cierpieć;
ucierpieć; ścierpieć; doznać
(czegoś); zostać straconym
suffer from ['safer,from] v. być
chorym (na coś)
sufferable ['saferebl] adj.
znośny
sufferer ['saferer] s. cierpiący
suffice [se'fajs] v. wystarczyć
sufficiency [se'fyszensy] s.
wystarczająca ilość; zapasy
sufficient [se'fyszent] adj.
dostateczny; wystarczający
suffix ['safyks] s. przyrostek
suffocate ['safokejt] v. udusić;
zadusić
sugar ['szuger] s. cukier; słodkie
dziecko; (slang): forsa; v.
słodzić
sugar-cane ['szugerkejn] s.
trzcina cukrowa
suggest [se'dżest] v.
sugerować; proponować;
nasuwać; podsuwać;
poddawać (myśl)
suggestion [se'dżesczyn] s.
sugestia; wskazówka; myśl;
poddawanie; podsuwanie;
ślad (czegoś)
suggestive [se'dżestyw] adj.
przypominający; nasuwający
(myśl); dwuznaczny
suicide [,su:y'sajd] s.
samobójstwo; samobójca; v.
popełnić samobójstwo
suit [su:t] v. dostosować;
odpowiadać; służyć;
wybrać; być odpowiednim;
zadowalać; pasować; s.
garnitur; ubranie; komplet;
skarga; proces; prośba;
zaloty; staranie się; zestaw

suit yourself ['su:tjor,self] exp.:
rób co chcesz
suitable ['su:tebl] adj. właściwy;
stosowny; odpowiedni
suitcase ['su:tkejs] s. walizka
suite [śli:t] s. świta; orszak;
szereg; zestaw (mebli);
apartament; garnitur; komplet;
suita
suitor ['su:ter] s. zalotnik;
petent; pretendent; strona;
konkurent
sulfate ['salfejt] s. siarczan; v.
zakwaszać; zamieniać na
siarczan
sulfur ['salfer] s. siarka; v.
siarkować
sulk [salk] v. być w złym
humorze; s. zły humor;
człowiek w złym humorze
sulky ['salky] adj. w złym
humorze; ponury; s.
jednokonny dwukołowy wózek
sullen ['salen] adj. ponury;
posępny; flegmatyczny;
powolny
sulphur ['salfer] s. siarka; v.
siarkować
sultry ['saltry] adj. parny;
duszny; gwałtowny; gorący;
namiętny
sum [sam] s. suma; w sumie;
rachunek; v. dodawać;
zbierać; podsumowywać
sum up ['sam,ap] v. dodawać;
zbierać; podsumowywać
summarize ['samerajz] v.
streszczać; zbierać;
podsumowywać
summary ['samery] s.
streszczenie; skrót; adj.
pobieżny; doraźny; krótki
summer ['samer] s. lato; v.
spędzać lato
summer resort ['samer ry'so:rt]
s. letnisko
summer school ['samer,sku:l] s.
szkoła w lecie, w czasie
wakacji
summit ['samyt] s. szczyt
summon ['samen] v. wzywać
(oficjalnie); zdobywać się (na
odwagę)

summons ['samens] pl.
wezwanie urzędowe; v.
doręczać wezwanie
urzędowe
sumptuous ['samptjues] adj.
wspaniały; wystawny;
okazały; zrobiony z
przepychem
sun [san] s. słońce; v.
nasłoneczniać (się)
sun-bath ['sanba:s] s. kąpiel
słoneczna (brit.)
sunbathe ['sanbejz] v. opalać
się
sunbeam ['sanbi:m] s. promień
słońca
sunburn ['sanbe:rn] s. opalenizna
Sunday ['sandy] s. niedziela
sundial ['sandajel] s. zegar
słoneczny
sundries ['sandryz] pl. różności;
rozmaitości
sundry ['sandry] adj. różny;
rozmaity
sung [sang] v. zob. sing
sunglasses ['san,gla:sys] pl.
okulary od słońca
sunk [sank] v. zob. sink
sunken ['sanken] v. zob. sink;
adj. zapadnięty; zatopiony;
podwodny
sunny ['sany] adj. słoneczny
sunny side up ['sany,sajd ap]
exp.: jaja sadzone
sunrise ['san-rajz] s. wschód
słońca
sunshade ['sanszejd] s. parasol
od słońca
sunset ['sanset] s. zachód
słońca
sunshine ['sanszajn] s. blask
słońca; pogoda; wesołość
sunstroke ['sanstrouk] s.
porażenie słoneczne
sup [sap] s. łyk; v. częstować
kolacją; zjeść kolację; pić
małymi łykami
super ['su:per] adj.
pierwszorzędny; wspaniały;
kwadratowy; prefix: nad-;
prze-; s. statysta; nadzorca;
szlagier; przebój (filmowy);
najlepszy gatunek

superabundant
['su:per,e'bandent] adj.
nadmierny; przebogaty
superb [se'pe:rb] adj. wspaniały
super-duper [,su:per-'du:per] adj.
(slang): b. dobry; luksusowy;
bardzo elegancki
superficial [,su:per'fyszel] adj.
powierzchowny;
powierzchniowy
superfluous [su'pe:rflues] adj.
zbędny; zbyteczny
super-highway ['su:per'haj,łej] s.
(m. in. 4-pasmowa) autostrada
superhuman [,su:per'hju:man]
adj. nadludzki
superintend [,su:peryn'tend] v.
nadzorować; doglądać;
kierować
superintendent
[,su:peryn'tendent] s.
nadzorca; dozorca;
nadinspektor
superior [su:'pierjer] adj. wyższy;
nieprzeciętny; pierwszorzędny;
przewyższający; lepszy;
nadęty; wyniosły; s.
zwierzchnik; przełożony;
starszy rangą
superiority [su:,pie:ry'oryty] s.
wyższość
superlative [su:'pe:rlatyw] adj.
najwyższy; s. szczyt;
superlatyw; stopień
najwyższy
superman ['su:permen] s.
nadczłowiek
supermarket ['su:per'ma:rkyt] s.
supersam; duży sklep
samoobsługowy
(żywnościowy)
supernatural [,su:per'naeczerel]
adj. nadprzyrodzony
supernumerary
[,su:per'nju:meryry] adj.
nadliczbowy; nieetatowy; s.
statysta
superscription [,su:per'skrypszyn]
s. napis u góry; nadpis; adres;
napis
supersede [sju:per'si:d] v.
zastąpić; wypierać;
zajmować miejsce

supersonic [,su:per'sonyk] adj.
ultradźwiękowy;
ponaddźwiękowy

superstition [su:per'styszyn] s.
zabobon; przesądy

supervise ['su:perwajz] v.
nadzorować; doglądać

supervisor ['su:perwajzer] s.
inspektor; nadzorca

supper ['saper] s. wieczerza;
kolacja

supple ['sapl] adj. giętki; gibki;
v. stawać się gibkim

supplement ['saplyment] s.
dodatek; uzupełnienie; v.
uzupełniać

supplementary [,saply'mentery]
adj. dodatkowy; uzupełniający

supplication [,saply'kejszyn] s.
błaganie; prośba

supplier [se'plajer] s. dostawca

supply [se'plaj] s. zapas;
aprowizacja; zaopatrzenie;
dostarczenie; dostawy;
kredyty; podaż; dopływ;
zasilanie; v. dostarczać;
zaopatrywać; zaradzić;
zastępować

support [se'po:rt] s. utrzymanie;
podtrzymanie; podpora;
poparcie; pomoc; wspornik;
dźwigar; rama; łożysko;
podłoże; ostoja; v.
podtrzymywać; utrzymywać;
podpierać; popierać;
wytrzymywać; znosić;
tolerować

suppose [se'pouz] v.
przypuszczać; zakładać;
sądzić

supposed [se'pouzd] adj.
domniemany; przypuszczalny;
rzekomy

supposedly [se'pouzdly] adv.
rzekomo; przypuszczalnie

supposition [sape'zyszyn] s.
przypuszczenie; domniemanie

suppress [se'pres] v. tłumić;
zgniatać; znosić;
zatrzymywać (krwawienie);
usuwać; taić

suppression [se'preszyn] s.
stłumienie; zgniecenie;

zniesienie; usunięcie;
przemilczenie; zatajenie

suppurate ['sapjurejt] v. ropieć

supremacy [se'premesy] s.
zwierzchnictwo; przewaga;
najwyższa władza; supremacja

supreme [se'pri:m] adj.
najwyższy; doskonały;
ostateczny

surcharge [se:r'cza:rdż] s.
nadpłata; nadmierny ciężar;
dodatkowy ciężar; opłata
(karna); przeładowanie; v.
ściągać opłatę podatkową;
nakładać grzywnę;
przeładować; przedrukować
(znaczek)

sure [szuer] adj. pewny;
niezawodny; niemylny;
bezpieczny; exp.: na pewno!;
zgadza się!; adv. z
pewnością; pewnie; na
pewno; niezawodnie;
niechybnie

sure enough ['szuer,y'naf] adv.
faktycznie

surely ['szuerly] adv. pewnie; z
pewnością

surety ['szuerty] s. ręczyciel;
gwarancja; zabezpieczenie;
kaucja; pewność

surf [se:rf] s. (łamiące się) fale
przybrzeżne

surface ['se:rfys] s.
powierzchnia; v. wypływać
na powierzchnię; wykańczać
powierzchnię

surfboard ['se:rfbo:rd] s.
pojedyncza deska; narta
wodna; v. jeździć na desce
na falach ku brzegowi

surf-riding ['se:rf,rajdyng] s.
zjeżdżanie z fal ku brzegowi

surge [se:rdż] s. gwałtowny
impuls; fala uskokowa;
falowanie; fala; v. nagle
wzbierać; drgać; popuścić;
kołysać; huśtać;
ześlizgiwać się

surgeon ['se:rdżen] s. chirurg

surgery ['se:rdżery] s. chirurgia;
operacja; sala operacyjna

surgical ['se:rdżykel] adj.

chirurgiczny
surly ['se:rly] adj. grubiański;
zgryźliwy
surmise ['se:rmajz] s. domysł; v.
domyślać się czegoś
surmount [ser'maunt] v.
pokonywać; wychodzić na
(górę); przechodzić przez;
pokrywać; wznosić się
surmounted by [ser'mauntyd baj]
adj. pokonany przez
surname ['se:rnejm] s. nazwisko;
przydomek; [se:r'nejm] v.
przezywać; nadawać
przydomek
surpass [se:r'paes] v.
przewyższać; przechodzić
(oczekiwania)
surpassing [se:r'paesyng] adj.
nieprześcigniony;
niezrównany
surplus ['se:rplas] s. nadwyżka;
nadmiar; superata; nadwyżka
produkcyjna; wartość
dodatkowa; adj. stanowiący
nadwyżką; nadwyżkowy;
zbywający
surprise [ser'prajz] s.
niespodzianka; zaskoczenie;
zdziwienie; v. zaskoczyć;
zdziwić; zmuszać; złapać na
gorącym uczynku; adj.
nieoczekiwany;
niespodziewany
surprised [ser'prajzd] adj.
zaskoczony; złapany na
gorącym uczynku
surrender [se'render] s. poddanie
się; wyrzeczenie się; v.
poddawać się; oddawać się;
wyrzekać się czegoś
surround [se'raund] v. otaczać;
okrążać
surroundings [se'raundyngs] pl.
otoczenie
survey [se:r'wej] s. przegląd;
oględziny; inspekcja; pomiary;
plan (topograficzny); opis;
ankieta; statystyka; v.
przeglądać; robić pomiary;
wymierzać; oglądać
surveying [se:r'wejyng] s.
miernictwo

surveyor [se:r'wejer] s.
mierniczy; inspektor celny
survival [ser'wajwel] s.
przeżycie; przeżytek
survive [ser'wajw] v. przeżyć;
dalej żyć
survivor [ser'wajwer] s. człowiek
pozostały przy życiu
susceptible [se'septybl] adj.
wrażliwy; drażliwy; podatny;
dopuszczający
suspect [ses'pekt] v.
podejrzewać kogoś; s. adj.
['saspekt] podejrzany
suspected [ses'pektyd] adj.
podejrzany
suspend [ses'pend] v. zawiesić;
powstrzymać (się chwilowo)
suspended [ses'pendyd] adj.
zawieszony w czynnościach
suspenders [ses'penders] pl.
podwiązki; szelki
suspense [ses'pens] s.
niepewność; zawieszenie;
nierozstrzygnięcie
suspension [ses'penszyn] s.
zawieszenie; zawiesina;
wstrzymanie
suspension bridge [ses'penszyn,
brydż] s. wiszący most
suspicion [ses'pyszyn] s.
podejrzenie; v. podejrzewać
suspicious [ses'pyszes] adj.
podejrzany; nieufny
sustain [ses'tejn] v.
podtrzymywać; dźwigać;
cierpieć; doznawać;
ponosić; potwierdzać;
utrzymywać; uznawać
(słuszność)
sustenance ['sastynens] s.
pożywienie; utrzymanie
swab [słob] s. wycior; wacik
chłonący; ścierka na kiju;
(slang): gamoń; epolet; v.
wycierać; ścierać;
wyszorować
swab up ['słob,ap] v. wytrzeć
swagger ['słaeger] v.
paradować; dumnie chodzić;
chełpić się; pysznić się;
odstraszyć; nakłaniać
strachem

swallow ['słolou] v. połykać (np.
zniewagę); przełykać; dać
się nabrać; odwołać (słowa);
s. przełykanie; łyk; kąs;
przełyk; jaskółka

swam [słaem] v. zob. swim

swamp [słomp] s. bagno; v.
zalewać; pochłaniać;
przysłaniać; grzęznąć

swampy ['słompy] adj. bagnisty;
błotnisty

swan [słon] s. łabędź

swap [słop] v. zamieniać (się);
wymieniać (się); s. zamiana;
wymiana

swarm [sło:rm] s. mrowie;
mnóstwo; rój; v. roić (się);
wyroić; obfitować (w coś);
wspinać się; wdrapywać się

swarthy ['sło:rty] adj. śniady;
smagły

swathe [słejz] v. spowijać; s.
zawinięcie; bandaż

sway [słej] v. kołysać (się);
chwiać (się); zachwiać (się);
rządzić czymś; władać; s.
chwianie się; władza

swear; swore; sworn [słeer;
sło:r; sło:rn]

swear [słeer] v. przysięgać;
poprzysiąc

sweat [słet] s. poty; pot;
harówka; v. pocić się;
pracować ciężko; (slang):
harować; szwejsować;
fermentować;
wyświechtywać monety;
wydzielać (żywicą)

sweat out ['słet,aut] v.
wypacać (się); (slang):
ciężko pracować; wyduszać
z kogoś coś; wyciągać
pieniądze szantażem;
wyciągać odpowiedzi
torturami; odsiadywać
więzienie

sweater ['słeter] s. sweter;
wyzyskiwacz robotników

sweatshop ['słet,szop] s. zakład
wyzyskujący robotników

sweatshirt ['słet,sze:rt] s.
koszula trykotowa

Swedish ['sli:dysz] adj. szwedzki

sweep; swept; swept [sli:p;
słept; słept]

sweep [sli:p] v. zamiatać;
wymiatać; zmiatać;
oczyszczać; wygrywać (np.
wszystkie medale); porywać
(słuchaczy); przewalić się
przez coś (burza, wichura,
powódź); ogarniać;
obejmować; rozciągać się;
sunąć uroczyście; ślizgać
się; śmigać; zwalać (kogoś
z nóg); ostrzeliwać; etc.; s.
zamiatanie; zdobycie;
zagarnięcie; ogołocenie;
śmieci; śmignięcie;
machnięcie; zasięg; robienie
zakrętu; etc.

sweeper ['sli:per] s. zamiatacz;
zamiataczka; zmiotka

sweeping ['sli:pyng] adj. szeroki;
wspaniały; rozległy; daleko
idący

sweepings ['sli:pyngs] pl. śmieci

sweepstake ['sli:pstejk] s.
wyścigi; loteria; nagroda
(zbiorowa) w wyścigach

sweet [sli:t] adj. słodki;
przyjemny; miły; rozkoszny;
dobrze osłodzony; deserowy;
melodyjny; świeży; łagodny;
zakochany

sweeten ['sli:tn] v. słodzić;
osładzać; stawać się
słodkim; (slang): zwiększać
stawkę; zwiększać zastaw

sweetheart ['sli:t-ha:rt] s.
ukochana; ukochany

sweetness ['sli:tnys] s. słodycz

sweet pea ['sli:tpi:] s. groszek
pachnący

swell; swelled; swollen [słel;
słeld; 'słoulen]

swell [słel] v. puchnąć;
wzdymać (się); nadymać
(się); wydymać (się);
rozdymać; wzbierać;
wzrastać; potęgować się; s.
wydęcie; zgrubienie;
nabrzmienie; wzbieranie;
wzburzona fala (morze);
(slang): wytworniak; gruba
ryba

swelling 614 swordfish

swelling ['słelyng] s. spuchlizna;
wzdęcie; obrzęk; wezbranie
(rzeki)

swept [słept] v. zob. sweep

swerve [słe:rw] s. odchylenie;
zboczenie; v. zbaczać;
odchylać (się)

swift [słyft] adj. prędki; rączy;
chyży; żywy; s. nawijak
przędzy; traszka; jaszczurka;
jerzyk

swiftness ['słyftnys] s.
prędkość; chyżość

swim; swam; swum [słym;
słaem; słam]

swim [słym] v. płynąć;
przepłynąć; pływać (w
wyścigach); pławić; ociekać
czymś; unosić się na
powierzchni; iść z prądem;
kręcić się (w głowie); s.
pływanie; nurt (życia); woda
(do pływania); głębia; pęcherz
pławny

swimmer ['słymer] s. pływak

swimming ['słymyng] s. pływanie

swimming pool ['słymyng,pu:l] s.
pływalnia

swimming suit ['słymyng,sju:t] s.
kostium kąpielowy

swindle ['słyndl] s. oszustwo; v.
oszukiwać

swine [słajn] s. świnia

swing; swung; swung [słyng;
słang; słang]

swing [słyng] v. huśtać (się);
kołysać (się); wahać (się);
bujać (się); machać;
wywijać; przerzucać (się) na
coś; porywać (za sobą);
pociągać (za sobą); s.
huśtanie (się); kołysanie (się);
ruch wahadłowy; zmiana
pracy; objazd (terenu); rytm;
przerzucanie się; kołyszący
chód; taniec (swing)

swing bridge ['słyng,brydż] s.
most wahadłowy

swing door ['słyng,do:r] s. drzwi
wahadłowe

swing wheel ['słyng,hłi:l] s. koło
rozpędowe (zamachowe)

swipe [słajp] s. uderzenie; cios z

rozmachu; v. walić z
rozmachem; slang: ukraść;
zwędzić; porwać; walić

swirl [słe:rl] s. wir; wirowanie;
skręt; lok; trąba powietrzna;
kłębiący się dym; zwój
(koronek); upięcie warkocza
dookoła głowy; v. wirować;
kręcić się; unosić się
(wirując)

Swiss [słys] adj. szwajcarski

switch [słycz] s. pręt; zwrotnica;
przekładnia; wyłącznik;
przełącznik; kontakt;
śmignięcie; v. bić prętem;
machać; wyrywać;
zmieniać; przełączać;
włączać (np. światło);
rozłączać (się); wyłączać
(się)

switch off ['słycz,of] v.
wyłączać

switch on ['słycz,on] v. włączać

switchboard ['słyczbo:rd] s.
tablica rozdzielcza; łącznica
(telefoniczna etc.)

swivel ['sływl] s. połączenie
przegubowe (zawiasowe); oś;
v. obracać (się) na połączeniu
zawiasowym

swivel bridge ['sływl,brydż] s.
most obrotowy

swivel chair ['sływl,cze:r] s.
krzesło ruchome (na przygubie
i na kółkach)

swollen ['słoulen] v. zob. swell;
adj. opuchnięty; wzdęty;
wezbrany

swoon [słu:n] v. zemdleć;
omdleć; zamierać; s.
omdlenie

swoop down on ['słu:p,dałn on]
v. zaatakować z góry; runąć
na coś

swoop up ['słu:p,ap] v.
porywać; s. spadnięcie;
porwanie

swop [słop] v. zamieniać;
wymieniać; s. zamiana;
wymiana

sword [so:rd] s. pałasz; szpada;
miecz; szabla; bagnet (slang)

swordfish [so:rd'fysz'] s.

miecznik (ryba)
swordsman ['so:rdzmen] s.
szermierz
swore [sło:r] v. zob. swear
sworn [sło:rn] v. zob. swear; adj.
zaprzysiężony; przysięgły
swum [słam] v. zob. swim
swung [słang] v. zob. swing
sycamore ['sykemo:r] s. jawor;
klon; figowiec
syllable ['sylebl] s. sylaba;
zgłoska
syllabus ['sylebes] s. program
(nauki; kursu)
symbol ['symbel] s. symbol; v.
symbolizować
symbolic [,sym'bolyk] adj.
symboliczny
symbolism ['symbelyzem] s.
symbolizm
symmetric [sy'metryk] adj.
symetryczny
symmetry ['symytry] s. symetria
sympathetic [,sympe'tetyk] adj.
współczujący; życzliwy;
sympatyczny; współbrzmiący;
współczulny; łatwy do
zahipnotyzowania
sympathize ['sympetajz] v.
współczuć; mieć
zrozumienie; sympatyzować z
kimś
sympathy ['sympety] s.
współczucie; solidarność;
sympatia
symphony ['symfeny] s.
symfonia
symposium [sym'pouzjem] s.
sesja; konferencja; sympozjum
symptom ['symptem] s.
symptom; objaw
symptomatic [,sympte'maetyk]
adj. znamienny;
symptomatyczny
synagogue ['synegog] s.
bożnica; bóżnica; synagoga
synchronism ['synkre,nyzem] s.
synchronizm; równoczesność
synchronize ['synkrenajz] s.
działać równocześnie;
synchronizować; pokazywać
jednakowo (czas); uzgadniać
(zegary)

syndic ['syndyk] s. pełnomocnik;
przedstawiciel
synonym ['synenym] s. synonim
synod ['syned] s. synod
synonymous [sy'nonymes] adj.
równoznaczny z czymś
synopsis [sy'nopsys] s.
streszczenie
syntax ['syntaeks] s. składnia
synthesis ['syntysys] s. synteza
syntheses ['syntysi:z] pl. syntezy
synthetic [syn'tetyk] adj.
sztuczny; syntetyczny
synthesize ['synty,sajz] v.
wyciągać syntezę
synthetize ['synty,tajz] v.
wyciągać syntezę
syphilis ['syfylys] s. kiła; syfilis
syphon ['sajfn] s. syfon
syringe ['syryndż] s. strzykawka;
v. strzykać (wodą)
syrup ['syrep] s. syrop
system ['systym] s. system;
układ; metoda; sieć
(kolejowa); organizm
(człowieka); formacja; ustrój
systematic [,systy'maetyk] adj.
systematyczny
systematize ['systyme,tajz] v.
systematyzować
systemic [sys'temyk] adj.
układowy
systole ['systely] s. normalny
rytmiczny skurcz serca
systolic [sys'tolyk] adj.
skurczowy

T

t [ti:] dwudziesta litera alfabetu
angielskiego
tab [taeb] s. patka; wieszak
(przyszyty); język (buta);
naszywka; języczek; ucho;
przywieszka; rachunek;
kontrola; pilnowanie; v.
prowadzić ewidencję;
tabelować; zaopatrywać w

table 616 taint

(języczek lub ucho etc.)
table ['tejbl] s. stół; stolik;
tablica; tabela; tabliczka (np.
mnożenia); płyta; płaskowyż;
blat; v. kłaść na stole;
odraczać (na długo);
wciągać na agendę; adj.
stołowy
tablecloth ['tejbl,klos] s. obrus
tableland ['tejbl-laend] s.
płaskowyż
tablespoon ['tejbl-spu:n] s. łyżka
stołowa (do zupy)
tablespoonful ['tejblspu:nful] s.
pełna łyżka (pół uncji)
tablet ['taeblyt] s. tabletka;
tabliczka (do pisania)
tabloid ['taeb'loid] s. gazeta,
zwykle małego wymiaru,
zawierająca krótkie
ilustrowane, często
sensacyjne, wiadomości
bieżące (przeważnie w
skrócie); gazeta brukowa,
sensacyjna, często płacąca
wysokie wynagrodzenia za
rewelacje skandaliczne; adj.
ściśnięty; prasowany
tabloid journalism ['taeb'loid
'dźe:rne,lysem] s.
wiadomości dziennikarskie
podawane w skrócie;
polowanie na rewelacje
skandaliczne dotyczące
zwykle znanych osobistości
taboo [te'bu:] s. tabu; v.
zakazywać; adj. zakazany
tacit ['taesyt] adj. milczący;
cichy; niemy
taciturn ['taesyte:rn] adj.
małomówny
tack [taek] s. gwóźdź
tapicerski;
papiak; pluskiewka; fastryga;
kurs (polityki); taktyka; stan
lepki; prowiant; żywność;
jedzenie; v. przyczepiać;
przybijać (lekko);
fastrygować; zmieniać kurs;
lawirować; hałasować
tackle ['taekl] s. zestaw
przyborów (do łowienia,
golenia); wielokrążek;

takielunek; złapanie i
trzymanie; v. zewrzeć się;
borykać (się); złapać i
trzymać; zmagać (się); brać
się do czegoś (ostro);
umocowywać; porać (się)
tacky ['taeky] adj. lepki;
niemodny; marny
tact [taekt] s. takt; wyczucie;
dotyk
tactful ['taektful] adj. taktowny
tactics ['taektyks] pl. taktyka
tactile ['taektajl] adj. dotykowy;
dotykalny
tactless ['taektlys] adj.
nietaktowny
tad [taed] s. berbeć
tadpole ['taedpoul] s. kijanka
tag [taeg] s. skuwka; etykieta;
kartka; strzęp; przywieszka;
znaczek tożsamości; marka;
mandat karny (pisany); ucho;
igliczka; wieszadło (przyszyte);
błyszczka; dodatek; morał;
frazes; banał; cytat; refren;
ogon; zabawa w gonionego; v.
przyczepiać: skuwkę, kartkę,
znaczek, markę, ucho,
wieszadło, igliczkę, ogon;
dawać: mandat karny, morał;
bawić się w gonionego;
tańczyć odbijanego;
wymierzać wyrok;
przeznaczać; włóczyć się za
kimś; dołączyć do czegoś
tail [tejl] s. ogon; tył; koniec;
tren; poła; pośladki;
buńczuk; warkocz; świta;
cień (chodzący za kimś); v.
dodawać ogon; obrywać
ogonki; śledzić (krok w
krok); zamykać pochód
tailcoat ['tejl,kout] s. frak
taillight ['tejl,lajt] s. tylne
światło (wozu)
tailor ['tejler] s. krawiec; v. szyć
odzież
tailor-made ['tejlermejd] adj.
uszyty na zamówienie
tail wind ['tejlłynd] s. wiatr w
plecy
taint [tejnt] s. skaza; zaraza;
plama; v. plamić; kazić;

zepsuć; plugawić
taintless ['tejntlys] adj. bez skazy
take; took; taken [tejk; tuk; 'tejkn]
take [tejk] s. brać; wziąć; łapać;chwytać; zdobywać (twierdzę); zajmować (miejsce); rezerwować; zażywać; pić; jeść; odczuwać; rozumieć; pojechać; notować; zrobić (zdjęcie); zadać sobie (trud); dostawać (napadu); przyjmować (radę, karę etc.); mierzyć swoją temperaturę; godzić się (na traktowanie); nabierać (połysku); iść (za przykładem); s. połów; zdjęcie; wpływy (do kasy)
take along [,tejke'loŋg] v. zabrać ze sobą
take down ['tejk,dałn] v. zdejmować; rozmontowywać
take-in ['tejk'yn] s. oszukanie; naciąganie
take off ['tejk,of] v. rozbierać; kasować; małpować; wystartować; odjąć; usunąć
takeoff ['tejkof] s. start; skok; skocznia; karykatura; parodia; naśladowanie; odbicie; lista materiałów
take out ['tejk,aut] v. podejmować (poza domem); wyprowadzać; wynieść; wyrywać; wykupić; odjąć; oddzielić
takeover ['tejkouwer] s. opanowanie firmy przez manipulacje giełdowe lub finansowe
take over ['tejk,ouwer] v. przejmować (firmę); przyjmować (obowiązki); dominować
take up ['tejk,ap] v. ponosić; wchłonąć; wziąć (miejsce); zacząć (uczyć się); zadawać się; brać; ścieśniać; besztać
taken ['tejkn] v. zob. take; adj. zabrany; porwany; zdobyty;

nabrany; oszukany
talc [taelk] s. talk; v. posypywać talkiem
tale [tejl] s. opowiadanie; plotka; wymysł
talent ['taelent] s. talent (do czegoś); dar; uzdolnienie
talk [to:k] v. mówić; rozmawiać; plotkować; namawiać; s. rozmowa; dyskusja; pogadanka; plotka; gadanie; mowa
talkative ['to:ketyw] adj. rozmowny; gadatliwy
talk-to ['to:k,tu] s. bura
tall [to:l] adj. wysoki; (slang): nieprawdopodobny
tall talk ['to:l,to:k] s. przechwałki
tallow ['taelou] s. łój; v. tuczyć; smarować łojem
talon ['taelen] s. szpon; pazur; rygiel; łapa ludzka; palec
tame [tejm] v. oswajać; poskramiać; ujarzmić; okiełznać; łagodzić; przytłumić; upokorzyć
tamper ['taemper] s. ubijak; v. majstrować; manipulować; zmieniać coś nielegalnie
tan [taen] s. opalenizna; kolor (brązowy) brunatny; kora garbarska; v. garbować; opalać się (na słońcu); brązowieć; wyłoić komuś skórę
tangent ['taendżent] adj. styczny; s. styczna; szczegół oderwany; zmiana tematu (od rzeczy); zmiana kierunku rozmowy
tangerine [taendże'ri:n] s. mandarynka
tangle ['taeŋgl] s. plątanina; v. plątać (się); wikłać (się); (slang): pobić się z kimś
tank [taeŋk] s. tank; zbiornik; cysterna; czołg; (slang): więzienie; v. nabierać do zbiornika; (slang): popić sobie
tankard ['taeŋkerd] s. kufel
tanner ['taener] s. garbarz
tantalize ['taentelajz] v. dręczyć (zwodną) nadzieją; łudzić

tantrum ['taentrem] s. napad
złości
tap [taep] v. stukać;
odszpuntować; napoczynać;
robić punkcje; naciąć;
ciągnąć sok;
wykorzystywać; gwintować;
podsłuchiwać (telefon); s.
czop; szpunt; kurek; zawór;
gwintownik; zaczep; odczep
tape [tejp] s. taśma; tasiemka;
tasiemiec; (slang): wódka; v.
wiązać taśmą (przylepcem);
mierzyć; (slang): oceniać
kogoś
tape measure ['tejp,meżer] s.
miara na taśmie (krawiecka)
taper ['tejper] s. stopniowe
zwężanie (się); stożek;
ubytek; osłabianie; stoczek;
świeczka
taper off ['tejper,of] v. zwężać
się stopniowo; cichnąć
stopniowo; kończyć się
spiczasto
tape recorder ['tejp-ry,ko:rder] s.
magnetofon
tape recording ['tejp-ry,ko:rdyng]
s. nagranie na taśmę
tapestry ['taepystry] s. gobelin;
arras; v. zdobić gobelinami
tapeworm ['tejpłe:rm] s. soliter;
tasiemiec
tar [ta:r] s. smoła; dziegieć; ter;
v. smołować; terować
target ['ta:rgyt] s. cel; obiekt;
tarcza strzelnicza; v.
kierować do celu; celować;
ustalać cel
tariff ['taeryf] s. cło; taryfa;
cennik; v. clić wg taryfy;
układać taryfę celną
tarnish ['ta:rnysz] v. matowieć;
przyćmiewać; brudzić (się);
brukać (się); tracić połysk; s.
matowienie; skaza
tart ['ta:rt] adj. cierpki;
zgryźliwy; s. ciastko
owocowe; (slang): kurewka
tartan ['ta:rten] s. materiał w
kratę szkocką
task ['taesk] s. zadanie
(specjalne); lekcja zadana;

przedsięwzięcie; v.
wyznaczać zadanie;
wystawiać na próbę; rugać
task force ['taesk,fo:rs] s. oddział do specjalnego zadania
taskmaster ['taesk,ma:ster] s.
nadzorca (kontrolujący
wykonanie zadania)
tassel ['taesel] s. kutas; kitka; v.
ozdabiać kutasami, kitkami
taste [tejst] s. smak; gust;
posmak; zamiłowanie; v.
smakować; kosztować;
czuć smak; mieć smak;
doznawać (czegoś)
tasteful ['tejstful] adj. gustowny;
w dobrym smaku
tasteless ['tejstlys] adj. bez
gustu; bez smaku
tasty ['tejsty] adj. smakowity;
smaczny
ta-ta [tae'-ta:] exp. do widzenia;
pa! pa!
tattoo [te'tu:] v. bębnić
palcami; tatuować; s.
capstrzyk; tatuaż
taught [to:t] v. zob. teach
taunt [to:nt] v. urągać;
wymyślać komuś;
zwymyślać kogoś; s.
urąganie; wymyślanie; adj.
wysoki (np. maszt)
taut [to:t] adj. napięty;
naprężony; w dobrej formie;
w dobrym stanie
tax [taeks] s. podatek; wysiłek;
ciężar; obciążenie; v.
opodatkować; obarczać;
obciążać; nadwerężać;
sprawdzać; wymagać
wysiłku; zarzucać coś
taxation [taek'sejszyn] s.
opodatkowanie
tax collector ['taekske,lekter] s.
poborca podatkowy
taxi ['taeksy] s. taksówka; v.
jechać taksówką; wieźć
taksówką
taxi driver ['taeksydrajwer] s.
taksówkarz
taximeter ['taeksy,mi:ter] s.
licznik (w taksówce);
taksometr

taxpayer ['taeks,pejer] s.
podatnik
tax return ['taeks,ry'te:rn] s.
podatek (zapłata ze
sprawozdaniem)
tea [ti:] s. herbata; herbatka;
podwieczorek; v. pić i
częstować herbatą
tea-bag ['ti:baeg] s. woreczek
papierowy z herbatą
teach; taught; taught [ti:cz; to:t;
to:t]
teach [ti:cz] v. uczyć; nauczać;
wykładać
teacher ['ti:czer] s. nauczyciel
teacup ['ti:kap] s. filiżanka na
herbatę
teakettle ['ti:,ketl] s. imbryk;
czajnik
team [ti:m] s. zespół; drużyna;
zaprząg; v. zaprzęgać;
jeździć zaprzęgiem
team up ['ti:map] v. łączyć się
razem (do pracy etc.)
teamwork ['ti:młe:rk] s. praca
zespołowa
teapot ['ti:pot] s. mały czajnik
tear; tore; torn [teer; to:r; to:rn]
tear [teer] v. drzeć; targać;
rwać; kaleczyć; wydrzeć
(ranę); pędzić; s. dziura;
rozdarcie; wybuch pasji;
kropla; łza; (slang): hulanka
tea-room ['ti:ru:m]s. herbaciarnia
tease [ti:z] v. drażnić; nudzić;
s. dokuczanie; nudziarstwo
teat [tyt] s. cycek (wulg.:
kobiecy)
technical ['teknykel] adj.
techniczny; formalny;
spekulacyjny
technician [tek'nyszyn] s.
technik
technique [tek'ni:k] s. technika
malowania, rzeźby etc.
tedious ['ti:dies] adj. nudny
teem [ti:m] v. roić się;
obfitować; opróżniać;
wylewać
teen [ti:n] s. szkoda; zgryzota
teenager ['ti:,nejdżer] s.
nastolatek; nastolatka
teens [ti:nz] pl. wiek 12 do 18
lat
teeny ['ti:ny] adj. maleńki
teeth [ti:s] pl. zęby; zob. tooth
teethe [ti:z] v. ząbkować
teetotaler [ti:'toutler] s.
abstynent
telegram ['telygraem] s. telegram
telegraph ['telygra:f] s. telegraf
telephone ['telyfoun] s. telefon;
v. telefonować
telephone booth ['telyfoun,bu:s]
s. kabina telefoniczna
telephone call ['telyfoun,ko:l] s.
rozmowa telefoniczna
telephone directory
['telyfoundy,rektory] s.
książka telefoniczna
telephone exchange ['telyfoun
-eks,czejndż] s. centrala
telefoniczna na zagranicę
telephone kiosk ['telyfoun-kiosk]
s. kiosk telefoniczny
teleprinter ['tely,prynter] s.
dalekopis
telescope ['telyskoup] s.
teleskop
teletypewriter [,tely'tajprajter] s.
dalekopis
televise ['telywajz] v. nadawać
przez telewizję
television ['telywyżyn] s.
telewizja
television set ['telywyżyn,set] s.
telewizor; odbiornik
telewizyjny
televisor ['telywajzer] s.
telewizor
tell; told; told [tel; tould; tould]
tell [tel] v. (o kimś; o czymś):
mówić; opowiadać;
powiedzieć; wskazywać;
pokazywać; kazać; poznać;
sprawdzić; policzyć;
poznawać; wiedzieć;
donieść; oskarżyć;
skarżyć; mieć znaczenie;
odbijać się na kimś;
odróżniać
teller ['teler] s. narrator; kasjer;
liczący głosy
telltale ['teltejl] s. plotkarz;
okoliczność ostrzegawcza;
wskaźnik odchylenia (steru);

aparat sprawdzający,
ostrzegawczy; adj.
ostrzegawczy; wymowny
temper ['temper] s.
usposobienie; humor; gniew;
złość; domieszka;
mieszanka; stan;
hartowność; v. łagodzić;
hartować
temperament ['temprement] s.
temperament; usposobienie;
skala temperowana;
temperatura skali
temperance ['temperens] s.
umiarkowanie;
powściągliwość;
abstynencja;
wstrzemięźliwość
temperate ['temperyt] adj.
umiarkowany; powściągliwy;
wstrzemięźliwy
temperature ['tempereczer] s.
temperatura; ciepłota
tempest ['tempyst] s. burza; v.
zaburzać
tempestuous [tem'pestjues] adj.
burzliwy
temple ['templ] s. świątynia;
skroń; ucho od okularów;
rozciągacz tkacki
temporal ['temperel] adj.
doczesny; czasowy;
skroniowy; s. kość
skroniowa
temporary ['temperery] adj.
chwilowy; tymczasowy
tempt [tempt] v. kusić; nęcić
temptation [temp'tejszyn] s.
pokusa; kuszenie
tempting ['temptyng] adj.
ponętny; nęcący; kuszący
ten [ten] num. dziesięć; s.
dziesiątka
tenacious [ty'nejszes] adj.
wytrwały; nieustępliwy;
trwały; wierny; czepny;
ciągliwy; mocny; spoisty
tenant ['tenent] s. lokator;
dzierżawca; v. zamieszkiwać;
dzierżawić
tend [tend] v. skłaniać się;
zmierzać; służyć; doglądać;
obsługiwać

tendency ['tendensy] s.
skłonność; tendencja
tender ['tender] adj. delikatny;
miękki; kruchy; wrażliwy;
czuły; niedojrzały; młody;
młodociany; uważający;
dbały; łamliwy; drażliwy;
wywrotny; v. oferować;
przedłożyć; założyć; s.
oferta; środek płatniczy;
dozorca; tender; statek
pomocniczy-zaopatrzeniowy
tenderloin ['tenderloin] s.
polędwica
tenderness ['tendernyss] s.
czułość; dbałość;
delikatność
tendon ['tenden] s. ścięgno
tendril ['tendryl] s. wąs; wić
tenement house
['tenyment,haus]
s. dom czynszowy
tennis ['tenys] s. tenis
tennis court ['tenys'ko:rt] s. kort
tenisowy
tense [tens] s. czas (np.
przyszły); adj. naprężony;
napięty
tension ['tenszyn] s. naprężenie;
napięcie; prężność
tent [tent] s. namiot
tentacle ['tentekl] s. macka;
czułek
tenth [tens] adj. dziesiąty
tenthly ['tensly] adv. po
dziesiąte
tepee ['ti:pi:] s. namiot indiański
(stożkowy)
tepid ['tepyd] adj. letni;
ciepławy; bez zapału
term [te:rm] s. okres; czas
trwania; przeciąg; semestr;
kadencja; termin; wyrażenie;
określenie; kres; v.
określać; nazywać
terms [te:rms] pl. warunki
(kontraktu, porozumienia);
stosunki wzajemne
terminal ['te:rmynel] adj.
końcowy; terminowy;
ostateczny; s. zakończenie;
końcówka; uchwyt;
końcowa stacja

terminate ['te:rmynejt] v.
skończyć; zakończyć;
kończyć (się); ograniczać;
upływać; rozwiązywać
(umowę); ustawać;
wygasać; wymawiać pracę
termination [,te:rmy'nejszyn] s.
koniec; wypowiedzenie
(pracy); wygaśnięcie;
zakończenie; końcówka
terminus ['te:rmynes] s.
końcowa
stacja; kres; koniec; granica
termite ['te:rmajt] s. termit
terrace ['teres] s. taras; terasa;
ulica wzdłuż zbocza; v. robić
terasy
terraced ['terest] adj.
uformowany w terasy
terrible ['terybl] adj. straszliwy;
straszny; okropny
terrific [te'ryfyk] adj.
przerażający; (slang):
fantastyczny; pierwszej klasy
terrify ['teryfaj] v. przerażać
territorial [,tery'torjel] adj.
terytorialny
territory ['teryto:ry] s. obszar;
rejon; terytorium bez praw
stanu (np. w USA)
terror ['terer] s. terror;
przerażenie; postrach
terrorize ['tereraiz] v. siać
strach; przerażać;
terroryzować
terse [te:rs] adj. zwięzły;
dosadny
test [test] s. próba; sprawdzian;
test; egzamin; odczynnik;
skorupa; v. sprawdzać;
poddawać próbie;
oczyszczać (metal)
testament ['testement] s.
testament
testify ['testyfaj] v. świadczyć;
dawać świadectwo;
zaświadczać; poświadczać
testimonial [,testy'mounjel] s.
świadectwo (moralności);
polecenie; nagroda w uznaniu
zasług
testimony ['testymouny] s.
świadectwo

testy ['testy] adj. drażliwy;
popędliwy; pobudliwy
tetanus ['tetenes] s. tężec
text [tekst] s. tekst
textbook ['tekstbuk] s.
podręcznik
textile ['tekstail] s. tkanina; adj.
tkacki; tekstylny
texture ['teksczer] s. budowa;
tkanina; struktura; tkanie
than [dzaen] conj. aniżeli; niż;
od
thank [taenk] v. dziękować; s.
podziękowanie; dzięki
thank you ['taenkju:] exp.:
dziękuję
thank you very much
['taenkju:'wery,macz] exp.:
bardzo dziękuję
thankful ['taenkful] adj.
wdzięczny; dziękczynny
thankless ['taenklys] adj.
niewdzięczny
thanks ['taenks] pl.
podziękowanie; dzięki
Thanksgiving Day
['taenksgywyng,dej] s. dzień
święta dziękczynienia (USA)
that [daet] adj. & pron. pl. those
[dzous]; tamten; tamta;
tamto; ten; ta; to; ów; owa;
owo; pl. tamci; tamte; ci; te;
owi; owe; adv. tylu; tyle; conj.
że; żeby; aby; skoro
thatch [taecz] s. strzecha; v.
pokrywać strzechą
thaw [to:] s. odwilż;
rozkrochmalenie się; v. tajać;
odtajać; taje; jest odwilż
the [przed samogłoską dy; przed
spółgłoską de:; z naciskiem
dy:] przyimek określony
rzadko kiedy tłumaczony; ten;
ta; to; pl. ci; te; ten właśnie
etc.; adv. tym; im ... tym
theater ['tieter] s. teatr; kino;
widownia; amfiteatr
theatrical [ti:'aetrykel] adj.
teatralny; sceniczny; aktorski
theatricals [ti:'aetrykels] pl.
przedstawienie (amatorskie)
theatrics [ti:'aetryks] s. sztuka
teatralna

thee [ḏi:] archaiczna forma ty, używana przez kwakrów
theft [ṯeft] s. kradzież
their [ḏzeer] zaimek: ich
theirs [ḏzeers] zaimek dzierżawczy: ich
them [ḏzem] przypadek zależny od they (np.: im, nimi, nich)
theme [ṯi:m] s. temat; zadanie; wypracowanie
themselves [ḏzem'selwz] pl. oni sami; one same
then [ḏzen] adv. wtedy; wówczas; po czym; potem; następnie; później; zatem; zaraz; poza tym; ponadto; conj. a więc; no to; wobec tego; ale przecież; adj. ówczesny; s. przedtem; uprzednio; dotąd; odtąd
theologian [ṯie'loudżjen] s. teolog
theology [ṯi:'oledży] s. teologia
theoretical [ṯie'retykel] adj. teoretyczny
theory [ṯiery] s. teoria
therapy [ṯerepy] s. leczenie; terapia
there [ḏzeer] adv. tam; w tym; co do tego; oto; właśnie; potem; tędy; dlatego; z tego; na to; s. ta miejscowość; to miasto; to miejsce
thereabout [ḏzeerebaut] adv. w tych stronach; gdzieś tam mniej więcej; coś około tego
thereafter [ḏzeera:fter] adv. później; odtąd
there are [ḏzeer'a:r] exp.: są
thereby [ḏzeer'baj] adv. przez to; w ten sposób; skutkiem tego
therefore [ḏzeer,fo:r] adv. dlatego; zatem więc
therein [,ḏzeer'yn] adv. w tym; w nim; w niej
there is [,ḏzeer'ys] exp.: jest
thereupon [ḏzeer,e'pon] adv. skutkiem tego
therewith [,ḏzeer'łys] adv. tym; z tym; w następstwie tego
there you are [,ḏzeer'ju:,a:r]

exp.: proszę; tu jest to!; tu pan to ma! etc.
thermometer [ṯer'momyter] s. termometr
thermos [ṯermos] s. termos
these [ḏi:z] pl. od this
thesis [ṯi:sys] s. teza; praca dyplomowa; pl. theses [ṯi:si:z]
they [ḏzej] pl. pron. oni; one (ci; którzy)
they say [ḏzej sej] exp.: podobno (mówią)
thick [ṯyk] adj. gruby; gęsty; zbity; rzęsisty; stłumiony; niewyraźny; mętny; ponury; tępy; ochrypły; (slang): blatny; spoufalony; s. gruba część; dureń; głuptas; adv. gęsto; grubo; ochryple; tępo
thicken [ṯykn] v. pogrubiać (się); zagęszczać (się)
thicket [ṯykyt] s. gąszcz; gęstwina
thickness [ṯyknys] s. grubość; warstwa; gęstość
thief [ṯi:f] s. złodziej; pl. thieves [ṯi:ws]
thigh [ṯaj] s. udo
thimble [ṯymbl] s. naparstek; końcówka (metalowa liny)
thimbleful [ṯymblful] s. odrobina, naparstek
thin [ṯyn] adj. cienki (sos, głos etc.); rzadki; szczupły; słaby (kolor etc.); (slang): paskudny; v. rozcieńczać; szczupleć; przerzedzać (się)
thine [ṯajn] zob. thy; stara forma: twój; twoje
thing [ṯyng] s. rzecz; przedmiot; uczynek; coś; krzyk mody; warunek; urojenia; przywidzenia; pl. zwierzęta; rzeczy; odzież; ubrania; ruchomości; sytuacja; koniunktura; wszystko; nieruchomości; głupstwa
think; thought; thought [ṯynk; 'ṯo:t; 'ṯo:t]
think [ṯynk] v. myśleć; pomyśleć; zastanawiać się; rozważać; rozmyślać (się); wymyślić; wyobrażać

sobie; uważać za; mieć
zdanie; mieć za; zapomnieć
(rozmyślnie); mieć na myśli;
rozwiązywać; etc.

think over ['tynk'ouwer] v.
przemyśliwać; zastanawiać
się

think up ['tynk,ap] v.
wymyślać; wykombinować;
rozwiązać

third [te:rd] adj. trzeci

third degree [,te:rd dy'gri:] exp.:
trzeci stopień
(przesłuchiwania na policji -
głupi, przykry i męczący)

thirdly ['te:rdly] adv. po trzecie

third party [,te:rd'pa:rty] s.
strona trzecia; osoby trzecie

third-rate ['te:rd'rejt] adj.
trzeciorzędny

Third World ['te:rd'łe:rld] s.
trzeci świat (poza Europą,
Chinami, Indią oraz Ameryką)

thirst ['te:rst] s. pragnienie;
żądza; v. pragnąć

thirsty ['te:rsty] adj. spragniony;
żądny; suchy; wyschnięty;
(slang): ciężki

this [tys] adj. & pron. pl. these
[ti:z] ten; ta; to; tak; w ten
sposób; tyle; obecny; bieżący;
adv. tak; tak daleko; tyle; tak
dużo

thistle ['tysl] s. oset

thorn ['to:rn] s. kolec; cierń;
krzak cierniowy; v. kłuć;
drażnić

thorny ['to:rny] adj. kolczasty;
ciernisty; drażliwy

thorough ['terou] adj. dokładny;
zupełny; całkowity; sumienny;
adv. na wskroś; na wylot

thoroughbred ['te:rou,bred] adj.
rasowy; czystej krwi; s. koń
rasowy

thoroughfare ['te:rou,feer] s.
arteria komunikacyjna;
przejazd; ulica

thoroughly ['te:rouly] adv.
zupełnie; dokładnie;
całkowicie; na wskroś;
sumiennie; gruntownie

those [douz] pl. od that

thou [dau] biblijne: ty

though [tou] conj. chociaż;
choćby; gdyby; adv. jednak;
pomimo tego; przecież

thought [to:t] v. zob. think; s.
myśl; namysł; zastanowienie
się; pomysł; oczekiwanie;
rozwaga; zamiar; pl. zdanie;
pogląd; odrobina; troszkę

thoughtful ['to:tful] adj.
zamyślony; zadumany;
rozważny; uważający; dbały;
uprzejmy; (oryginalnie)
myślący

thoughtless ['to:tlys] adj.
bezmyślny; nieuważający;
nierozważny

thousand ['tauzend] num. tysiąc

thousandth ['tauzendt] adj.
tysięczny

thrash [traesz] s. młócić; walić;
bić; prać; dyskutować; s.
młócenie; walenie

thrashing [traeszyng] s. młocka;
lanie

thread [tred] s. nić; nitka;
przędza; sznurek; wątek;
żyłka; krok (śruby); zwojnik
(nici); gwint; v. nawlekać
(igłą); przetykać; nacinać
gwint (zwojnik); przepychać
się

threadbare [tredbeer] adj.
wytarty; wyświechtany;
wyszarzały

threat [tret] s. groźba; pogróżka

threaten ['tretn] v. grozić;
zagrażać; odgrażać się

threatening ['tretnyng] adj.
grożący; zagrażający; groźny

three [tri:] num. trzy; s. trójka

threefold ['tri:fold] adj. potrójny

threescore ['tri:sko:r] num.
sześćdziesiąt

three-stage ['tri:stejdż] adj.
trójfazowy; trzystopniowy

thresh [tresz] v. młócić;
roztrząsać; obgadać
szczegółowo; omówić
gruntownie; s. młocka

thresher ['treszer] s. młockarnia

threshing ['treszyng] s. młócenie

threshing machine

['treszyng,me'szi:n] s.
młockarnia
threshold ['treszould] s. próg
threw [tru:] v. zob. throw
thrice [trajs] adv. trzykrotnie
thriftless [tryftlys] adj. rozrzutny
thrifty ['tryfty] adj. oszczędny;
rozrastający się; kwitnący
thrill [tryl] v. przejmować (się);
drgać; s. dreszcz; dreszczyk;
drganie; powieść
sensacyjna; szmer (serca)
thriller ['tryler] s. dreszczowiec;
powieść sensacyjna
(kryminalna); sztuka
sensacyjna; opowieść
sensacyjna
thrilling ['trylyng] adj.
podniecający; przejmujący;
sensacyjny
thrive; throve; thriven [trajw;
trouw; trywn]
thrive [trajw] v. dobrze: rosnąć,
chować się, rozwijać się,
miewać się; kwitnąć;
prosperować
thro [tru:] = through
throat [trout] s. gardło; szyja;
wlot; gardziel; wąskie
przejście; v. żłobić;
żłobkować; mówić gardłowo
throb [trob] v. pulsować;
drgać; bić; tętnić; rwać; s.
pulsowanie; drganie; bicie
serca; dreszcz; warkot
maszyny
thrombosis [trom'bousys] s.
skrzep
throne [troun] s. tron; v.
tronować; wprowadzać na
tron
throng [tro:ng] s. tłum; tłok;
rzesza; masa; v. tłoczyć się;
zatłaczać; napierać na
throstle [trosl] s. drozd;
przędzarka
throttle ['trotl] s. gardziel;
dławik; przepustnica; zawór
dławiący; v. dusić;
regulować dławikiem
through [tru:] prep. przez;
poprzez; po; wskroś; na
wylot; ze; z; skutkiem; na

skutek; za; dzięki; z powodu;
adv. na wskroś; na wylot;
adj. przelotowy; bezpośredni;
skończony (np. życiowo)
throughout [tru:'aut] prep.
poprzez; przez cały; od
początku do końca;
wszędzie; całkowicie; adv. na
wskroś
throve [trouw] v. zob. thrive
throw; threw; thrown [trou; tru:;
troun]
throw [trou] v. rzucać; ciskać;
zarzucać; zrzucać; skręcać;
powalić; narzucać;
modelować na kole;
odrzucać; marnować; s. rzut;
ryzyko; szal; narzuta; uskok
throw up ['trou,ap] v.
wymiotować; rzucać w
górę; podrzucać
thrown ['troun] v. zob. throw
thru [tru:] = through
thrum [tram] v. rzępolić;
bębnić; robić z nitek;
odcinać luźne nitki; s.
brzdąkanie; odcięta nitka;
krajka
thrush [trasz] s. drozd; choroba
strzałki kopyta końskiego;
pleśniawka
thrust; thrust; thrust [trast; trast;
trast]
thrust [trast] v. wpychać;
wsadzać; wtykać; wrazić;
pchać (się); przepychać się;
wysuwać (się); szturchać;
przebijać; wepchnąć;
narzucać (się); wtrącać
(się); zadawać pchnięcie;
pchnąć; s. pchnięcie;
dźgnięcie; wypad;
wypchnięcie; nacisk; siła:
napędu, ciągu, pędu; zrzut;
parcie; uwaga; przytyk
thud [tad] s. łomot; łoskot
(głuchy); v. łomotać; upadać
z łoskotem
thug [tag] s. bandyta; zbir
thumb [tam] s. kciuk; duży
palec; władza (domowa);
talent ogrodniczy; zasada
(praktyczna); v. kartkować;

brudzić palcami; niszczyć;
walać; grać niezgrabnie;
prosić o podwiezienie;
wyprosić (gestem)
thumb a lift [tam a lyft] v.
prosić o podwiezienie
(autostopem)
thumbtack ['tam-taek] s.
pinezka; pluskiewka
thump [tamp] s. grzmotnięcie; v.
grzmocić; walić; iść ciężko
thunder ['tander] s. grzmot;
burza; grom; piorun; v.
grzmieć; rzucać gromy;
piorunować; miotać
(groźby)
thunderstorm ['tander-sto:rm] s.
burza z piorunami
thunderstruck ['tander-strak] adj.
rażony piorunem; oszołomiony
Thursday ['te:r-zdej] s. czwartek
thus [tas] adv. tak; w ten
sposób; tak więc; a zatem
thus far ['tas,fa:r] adv. jak dotąd
thus much ['tas,macz] adv. tyle
thwart [tło:rt] v. udaremnić;
pokrzyżować; psuć szyki;
adj. poprzeczny; przeciwny;
niepomyślny; s. poprzeczna
ławka wioślarska
thy [taj] pron. twój; twoje; zob.
thine
tick [tyk] s. kleszcz; tykanie;
moment; wsyp; kredyt;
sprawne działanie; v. tykać;
kupować na kredyt;
sprzedawać na kredyt;
(slang): ustalać sprawne
działanie
tick away ['tyke'łej] v. znaczyć
tykaniem
tick off ['tykof] v. odliczać;
besztać; odfajkować
ticker ['tyker] s. telegraf;
zegarek; serce (slang)
ticket ['tykyt] s. bilet; kwit;
znaczek; wywieszka; lista
kandydatów (USA); v.
zaopatrywać w bilet,
etykietką; umieszczać na
liście kandydatów
ticket office ['tykyt'ofys] s. kasa
biletowa

tickle ['tykl] v. łaskotać;
łechtać; swędzić;
rozśmieszać; bawić;
cieszyć; s. łaskotanie;
łechtanie; swędzenie
tidal wave ['tajdełłejw] s.
olbrzymia fala przypływu
skutkiem trzęsienia ziemi
tide [tajd] s. przypływ i odpływ
morza; fala; okres; v.
przypływać falą; płynąć z
falą; wybrnąć
tidy ['tajdy] adj. schludny;
czysty; niemały; spory; s.
zbiornik na odpadki; pokrowiec
na mebel; v. oporządzić;
sporządzać; oporządzać
(się); porządkować
tie [taj] v. wiązać; zawiązać;
przywiązać; łączyć;
sznurować; remisować;
zawrzeć ślub; unieruchomić;
s. węzeł; krawat; podkład
kolejowy; próg; remis; sznur;
rozgrywka; półbucik
tie up ['taj,ap] v. zawiązywać;
unieruchamiać
tier [tier] s. piętro; rząd; węzeł;
zwój; kondygnacja; rzecz
wiążąca; fartuszek; v.
spiętrzać się (też warstwami)
tiger ['tajger] s. tygrys; jaguar;
kuguar; zawadiaka; pracujący
zapamiętale
tight [tajt] adj. zaciśnięty;
mocny; zwarty; szczelny;
spoisty; obcisły; wąski;
nabity; wstawiony; zalany;
skąpy; niewystarczający;
silny; mocny; uparty; adv.
zwarcie; ciasno; szczelnie;
obciśle; mocno; silnie
tighten ['tajtn] v. zaciskać (się);
uszczelniać; napinać (się)
tightfisted ['tajt-,fystyd] adj.
sknera; kutwa
tight fitting ['tajt-fytyng] adj.
obcisły; opięty
tightrope ['tajt-roup] s. lina
akrobatyczna
tights [tajts] pl. trykot baletnicy,
akrobaty etc.; w Anglii
rajstopy

tigress ['tajgrys] s. tygrysica
tile [tajl] s. dachówka; kafelek; dren; (slang): cylinder; v. pokrywać dachówkami; wykładać kaflami (płytami)
till [tyl] prep. aż do; dopiero; dotychczas; aż; dopóki nie; dotąd; v. uprawiać (ziemię); s. szufladka na pieniądze; kasa podręczna
tilt [tylt] s. przechylenie; przechył; nachylenie; natarcie kopią; plandeka; daszek; v. przechylać (się); nachylać (się); nacierać kopią; (pełnym) pędem lecieć; zaopatrywać w daszek
timber ['tymber] s. drzewo; budulec; drewno; belka; wręga; las; charakter; v. zaopatrywać w budulec; podpierać belką
timberland ['tymber'laend] s. obszar lasu budulcowego
timber-work ['tymberłe:rk] s. konstrukcja drewniana
timber yard ['tymber,ja:rd] s. skład (drzewa) budulca
time [tajm] s. czas; pora; raz; takt; v. obliczać czas zużyty; ustalać czas; wybierać czas; robić we właściwym czasie; nastawiać (przyrząd); regulować (zegar); synchronizować; harmonizować; trzymać takt; excl.: czas! (zamykać lokal etc.)
time and again ['tajm end,e'gen] exp.: ciągle; ustawicznie
time bomb ['tajm,bom] s. bomba zegarowa
timely ['tajmly] adv. na czasie; w porę; adj. aktualny; odpowiedni; właściwy; punktualny
timetable ['tajm,tejbl] s. rozkład jazdy, zajęć etc.
timeless ['tajmlys] adj. wieczny; ponadczasowy (niekończący się)
timid ['tymyd] adj. nieśmiały; bojaźliwy

timidity [ty'mydyty] s. bojaźliwość
timorous ['tymeres] adj. bojaźliwy
tin [tyn] s. cyna; blacha; puszka blaszana; blaszanka; folia cynowa; pieniądze; adj. cynowany; blaszany; dziadowski (kubek); v. cynować
tinfoil ['tynfojl] s. folia metalowa; cynfolia; staniol
tinge [tyndż] s. odcień; lekkie zabarwienie; v. zabarwiać lekko
tingle ['tyngl] s. mrowienie; świerzbienie; kłucie; v. czuć kłucie, mrowienie; kłuć
tinkle ['tynkl] v. dzwonić; brzęczeć; siusiać; s. dzwonienie
tinned [tynd] adj. cynowany
tint [tynt] s. odcień; zabarwienie; v. zabarwiać
tinware ['tynłeer] s. wyroby blaszane
tiny ['tajny] adj. drobny; malusieńki; malutki
tip [typ] s. koniec (np. palca); koniuszek; szczyt; zakończenie; skuwka; okucie; napiwek; poufna informacja; wiadomość; rada; wskazówka; trącenie; przechylenie; skład śmieci; v. wykańczać koniec; okuwać; przechylać (się); ważyć; przewracać (się); dać napiwek; informować (poufnie); trącać lekko; dotykać; uderzać ukosem (piłkę); przeważać
tip off ['typ,of] v. ostrzegać
tip-off ['typof] s. poufne ostrzeżenie; (informacja)
tipster ['typster] s. człowiek udzielający poufnych informacji (o wyścigach etc.)
tipsy ['typsy] adj. podchmielony; pijany; chwiejny; niepewny
tiptoe ['typtou] s. koniec palca u nogi; v. chodzić na palcach; adv. na palcach (u nóg)

tire ['tajer] v. męczyć (się);
nudzić (się); nakładać
obręcz, oponę; przystroić; s.
obręcz; opona; strój

tired ['tajerd] adj. zmęczony;
znużony; znudzony

tireless ['tajerlys] adj.
niestrudzony

tiresome ['tajersem] adj.
męczący; nudny

tissue ['tyszu:] s. tkanka;
tkanina; siatka; bibułka

tissue paper ['tyszu:,pejper] s.
bibułka; papier toaletowy;
papier płótnowany

tit [tyt] s. sikora

tit for tat ['tyt,fo:r'taet] exp.:
wet za wet

titbit ['tytbyt] s. smakołyk

titillate ['tytylejt] s. łechtać

title ['tajtl] s. tytuł; nagłówek;
napis; tytuł rodowy; tytuł
prawny; prawo; czystość
złota w karatach

titled ['tajtld] adj. utytułowany

titter ['tyter] v. chichotać; s.
chichot

tittle-tattle ['tytl-'taetl] v.
plotkować; s. plotkowanie

to [tu:; tu] prep. do; aż do; ku;
przy; w stosunku do; w
porównaniu z; w stosunku jak;
stosownie do; dla; wobec;
względem; za (zależnie od
ustaleń zwyczajowych)

toad [toud] s. ropucha

to and fro ['tu:end'frou] exp.:
tam i z powrotem

toast [toust] s. grzanka; toast; v.
robić grzanki; wznosić toast

tobacco [te'baekou] s. tytoń

tobacconist [te'baekenyst] s.
sprzedawca wyrobów
tytoniowych

toboggan [te'bogen] s. saneczki;
v. sankować się; spadać
(ceny)

today [te'dej] adv. dzisiaj; dziś;
s. dzień dzisiejszy

toddle ['todl] v. dreptać; drobić
nóżkami; s. drobienie
nóżkami; dreptanie; pędrak

toddler ['todler] s. pędrak;

berbeć

to-do [te'du:] s. zamieszanie;
rwetes

toe [tou] s. palec u nogi; nosek;
szpic; stopa wału (tamy);
występ z przodu; przednia
część kopyta; hacel; dno
odwiertu; v. kopnąć;
cerować palec u pończochy;
podporządkować się;
stawać na starcie; stosować
się do linii (też partyjnej);
ukośnie wbijać gwoździe;
krzywo chodzić (palcami zbyt
do wewnątrz lub na zewnątrz)

toffee ['tofi] s. karmelek

together [te'gedzer] adv. razem;
wspólnie; naraz;
równocześnie

toil [tojl] s. znój; mozół; trud; v.
mozolić się; trudzić się;
harować

toilet ['tojlyt] s. ustęp; toaleta;
ubranie; adj. toaletowy

toilet paper ['tojlyt,pejper] s.
papier toaletowy

toils [tojlz] s. sidła; matnia

token ['toukn] s. znak; dowód
autentyczności; symbol;
pamiątka; żeton; bon; adj.
symboliczny; niewiążący

told [tould] v. zob. tell

tolerable ['tolerebl] adj. znośny;
nienajgorszy; dosyć zdrowy

tolerance ['tolerens] s.
tolerancja; luz;
wyrozumiałość

tolerant ['tolerent] adj.
tolerancyjny; wyrozumiały

tolerate ['tolerejt] v. znosić;
tolerować; cierpieć

toleration [,tole'rejszyn] s.
znoszenie; tolerancja;
tolerowanie

toll [toul] s. opłata (np.
telefoniczna); myto: mostowe,
drogowe; miejski podatek;
trybut; danina; dzwonienie; v.
uiszczać opłatę;
wydzwaniać; dzwonić
jednostajnie; wabić
(zwierzynę)

toll bar ['toulba:r] s. szlaban

tollgate ['toulgejt] s. rogatka wjazdowa na płatny most lub autostradę

tomato [te'mejtou] s. pomidor

tomatoes [te'mejtouz] pl. pomidory

tomb [tu:m] s. grób; grobowiec; pochowanie

tombstone ['tu:m,stoun] s. kamień nagrobny; nagrobek

tomcat ['tom'kaet] s. kocur

tomorrow [te'mo:rou] s. & adv. jutro

ton [tan] s. tona (2000 funtów); (slang): mnóstwo

tone [toun] s. ton; normalny stan (np. ciała, organizmu); brzmienie; v. stonować się; stroić; harmonizować

tone down ['toun,dałn] v. złagodzić; stonować

tongs [tonz] s. szczypce; kleszcze; obcęgi

tongue [tan] s. język; mowa; ozór; v. dotykać językiem; łajać; mleć językiem

tonic ['tonyk] adj. wzmacniający; elastyczny; krzepiący; s. środek tonizujący

tonight [te'najt] s. dziś wieczór; dzisiejsza noc; adv. dziś wieczorem; gwara; ubiegłej nocy; wczoraj wieczór

tonnage ['tanydż] s. tonaż; opłata od tony ładunku

tonsil ['tonsel] s. migdałek

tonsillitis [,tonsy'lajtys] s. zapalanie migdałków

too [tu:] adv. tak; także; ponadto; do tego; zbytnio; zanadto; zbyt; za; na dodatek; też

took [tuk] v. zob. take

tool [tu:l] s. narzędzie; obrabiarka; v. obrabiać; oporządzać

tool up ['tu:l,ap] v. oprzyrządzać

tools [tu:ls] pl. przybory; sprzęt

tooth [tu:s] s. ząb; pl. teeth [ti:s] v. uzębiać; wcinać zęby; ząbkować; sczepiać zębami trybów

toothache ['tu:sejk] s. ból zęba

toothbrush ['tu:s,brasz] s. szczotka do zębów

toothless ['tu:slys] adj. bezzębny

toothpaste ['tu:spejst] s. pasta do zębów

toothpick ['tu:spyk] s. wykałaczka

top [top] s. wierzchołek; czubek; szczyt; wierzch; powierzchnia; góra; bocianie gniazdo; przykrywka; bąk; fryga; adj. wierzchni; zewnętrzny; górny; wyższy; najwyższy; szczytowy; maksymalny; v. nakrywać; wieńczyć; uwieńczać; przewyższać; stanowić wierzch; osiągnąć szczyt; ścinać szczyt; przeskoczyć (przez coś); położyć kres; mierzyć wysokość; wznosić się

topaz ['toupez] s. topaz

topic ['topyk] s. temat (rozmowy)

topple ['topl] v. przechylać; wywracać

topple down ['topldałn] v. przewrócić

top-secret ['top'si:kryt] adj. ściśle tajny

topsy-turvy ['topsy'te:rwy] adj. do góry nogami; v. przewracać do góry nogami; s. rozgardiasz; bałagan; galimatias

torch [to:rcz] s. pochodnia; znicz; kaganek; palnik (do lutowania etc.)

tore [to:r] v. zob. tear

torment ['to:rment] s. męka; udręka; [to:r'ment] v. męczyć; dręczyć

torn [to:rn] v. zob. tear

tornado [,to:r'nejdou] s. trąba powietrzna; tornado

torrent ['to:rent] s. potok (rwący); ulewny deszcz; burza

torsion ['to:rszyn] s. skręt; skręcanie

tortoise ['to:rtes] s. żółw (słodkowodny)

torture ['to:rczer] s. tortura;
męka; v. torturować;
męczyć; dręczyć;
wykręcać; przekręcać
tosh [tosz] s. bzdury; brednie;
banialuki (Brit.)
toss [to:s] v. rzucać się;
podrzucać; zarzucać;
podnosić; niepokoić;
kłopotać; przewracać się (w
łóżku); podbijać (piłką);
wypaść z pokoju; kołysać
się na boki; s. rzut; losowanie;
upadek (z konia)
toss about [,to:s e'baut] v.
przewracać się (po czymś)
toss up ['to:s,ap] v.
przewracać; grać w orła i
reszkę
toss-up ['to:sap] s. 50%
prawdopodobieństwa; orzeł
czy reszka?; rzecz wątpliwa
total ['toutel] adj. ogólny;
zupełny; całkowity; totalny;
kompletny; v. zliczać;
wynosić ogółem; (slang):
niszczyć całkowicie (np.
samochód w wypadku)
totalitarian [tou,taely'teerjen] adj.
totalitarny; totalistyczny; s.
totalista
totter ['toter] v. chwiać się;
zataczać się; s. chwianie się;
zataczanie się (dziecka)
touch [tacz] v. dotykać; stykać
(się); wzruszać (się);
poruszać (coś); brać;
wydobywać; zabarwiać;
lekko uszkadzać; cechować;
mierzyć; retuszować;
rąbnąć kogoś na pieniądze
(slang); s. dotyk; dotknięcie;
pociągnięcie; odrobina;
kontakt; lekka choroba; rys;
nuta (np. złości);
obmacywanie; cecha; probierz;
naciąganie na pieniądze
(slang)
touch down ['tacz,dałn] v.
lądować; uzyskiwać 6
punktów
touchdown [taczdałn] s.
lądowanie; gol w futbolu (6

punktów)
touching ['taczyng] adj.
wzruszający; rozrzewniający;
adv. odnośnie (do czegoś)
touchy ['taczy] adj. drażliwy;
obraźliwy; przewrażliwiony
tough [taf] adj. twardy; trudny;
ciężki; łobuzerski; adv. trudno;
s. człowiek: trudny, twardy;
łobuz; chuligan
tour [tuer] s. objazd; wycieczka;
tura; przechadzka; służba
(wojskowa); v. objeżdżać;
obwozić
tourist ['tueryst] s. turysta; klasa
turystyczna
tourist-agency
['tueryst'ejdżensy] s. biuro
podróży
tournament ['tuernement] s.
turniej
tousle ['tauzl] v. szarpać;
mierzwić; czochrać; targać;
s. rozczochrane włosy;
rozczochranie
tout [taut] v. kaptować;
nagabywać; narzucać się; s.
naganiacz; naganianie (np.
klientów)
tow [tou] v. holować; ciągnąć;
s. holowanie; lina holownicza;
przedmiot holowany; włókna
lniane; paździory
towards [to:rdz; 'tołerdz] prep.
ku; w kierunku; dla; w celu;
na (coś)
tow-boat ['toubout] s. holownik
towel ['tauel] s. ręcznik; v.
wycierać ręcznikiem
tower ['tauer] s. wieża; v.
wznosić (się); sterczeć;
wzbijać się
town [tałn] s. miasto
town councilor [,tałn'kaunsyler]
s. radny miejski
town hall ['tałn,ho:l] s. ratusz
tow-rope ['touroup] s. lina
holownicza
toy [toj] s. zabawka; cacko; v.
bawić się; cackać się; robić
niedbale; flirtować (też np. z
pomysłem)
toxic ['toksyk] adj. trujący;

jadowity
trace [trejs] s. ślad; postronek;
drążek przekaźnikowy; v.
iść śladami; kopiować
rysunek; przypisywać
czemuś; wytyczać;
nakreślać; kreślić
track [traek] s. tor; koleina;
ślad; trop; bieżnia; rozstaw
kół; v. śledzić; tropić;
zostawiać ślady; zabłocić;
zawalać; zakładać tor; mieć
rozstęp kół; ciągnąć liną z
brzegu
track down ['traek,dałn] v.
wytropić; wyśledzić;
schwytać
track-and-field events ['traekend
-'fi:ldy'wents] s. lekkoatletyka
track events [traek y'wents] s.
biegi; zawody na bieżni
traction engine
['traekszyn,endżyn] s.
lokomotywa; pociągowy
motor; traktor
tractor ['traekter] s. ciągnik;
traktor
trade [trejd] s. zawód; zajęcie;
rzemiosło; handel; wymiana;
klientela; branża; kupiectwo;
v. handlować; wymieniać;
frymarczyć; przewozić
towary; kupczyć;
przehandlować
trademark ['trejd,ma:rk] s. znak
ochronny; v. przybijać znak
ochronny; rejestrować znak
ochronny
trader ['trejder] s. handlowiec;
statek handlowy; spekulator
giełdowy
trade-union ['trejd'ju:njen] s.
związek zawodowy
trade unionist ['trejd'ju:njenyst]
s. działacz związku
zawodowego
tradition [tre'dyszyn] s. tradycja
traditional [tre'dyszynel] adj.
tradycyjny
traffic ['traefyk] s. ruch (kołowy,
pasażerski, towarowy,
telegraficzny, telefoniczny,
drogowy etc.); handel czymś;

v. frymarczyć; kupczyć
traffic island ['traefyk-ajlend] s.
wysepka na jezdni
traffic jam ['traefyk-dżaem] s.
zator ruchu
traffic lights ['traefyk-lajts] pl.
semafory uliczne
traffic regulation
['traefyk,regju'lejszyn] s.
przepisy ruchu
traffic sign ['traefyk,sajn] s. znak
drogowy
traffic-cop ['traefyk,kop] s.
policjant ruchu (drogowego)
tragedy ['traedżydy] s. tragedia
tragic ['traedżyk] adj. tragiczny
tragical ['traedżykel] = tragic
trail [trejl] v. pociągnąć (się);
powlec (się); holować; wlec
(się); pozostawać w tyle;
iść za tropem; ścigać;
wydeptywać (ścieżką);
nosić (karabin poziomo przy
boku); s. szlak; ścieżka; trop;
ogon; smuga; struga; bruzda;
koleina
trailer ['trejler] s. przyczepa (do
samochodu); przyczepa
towarowa, mieszkalna,
turystyczna etc.; maruder;
pnąca (się) roślina
train [trejn] v. szkolić;
kształcić; przyuczać;
wytresować; ćwiczyć (się);
trenować (się); kierować na
kogoś (np. wzrok); wlec; s.
pociąg; tren; ogon; sznur;
szereg; następstwo; orszak;
świta; porządek; wątek;
łańcuch
trainer ['trejner] s. trener;
instruktor; samolot szkolny
training ['trejnyng] s. zaprawa;
trening; ćwiczenie; szkolenie
trait [trejt] s. cecha
traitor ['trejtor] s. zdrajca
tram [traem] s. tramwaj
tramp [traemp] v. stąpać;
włóczyć się; wędrować
pieszo; iść pieszo; s.
włóczęga; tramp; wędrowiec;
statek (nieregularnej żeglugi)
trample ['traempl] v. deptać

trance [tra:ns] s. trans;
uniesienie; ekstaza
tranquil ['traenkłyl] adj. spokojny
tranquility [traen'kłylyty] s.
spokój
tranquilize ['traenkłylajz] v.
uspokajać
tranquilizer ['traenkłylajzer] s.
środek uspokajający
transact [traen'saekt] v.
załatwiać; pertraktować;
przeprowadzać
transaction [traen'saekszyn] s.
transakcja; przeprowadzenie
sprawy; pl. sprawozdania
naukowe; rozprawy
transalpine [traens'aelpajn] adj.
transalpejski
transatlantic [traenzet'laentyk]
adj. transatlantycki
transcend [traen'send] v.
przewyższać; prześcignąć;
górować
transcribe [traens'krajb] v.
nagrywać na taśmie;
przepisywać
transcript ['traenskrypt] s. kopia;
transkrypcja
transfer [traens'fe:r] v.
przemieścić; przenieść
(się); przewozić; przekazać;
s. ['traensfe:r] przeniesienie;
przewóz; przedruk; przekaz;
przelew; odstąpienie
transferable [traens'fe:rebl] adj.
przenośny
transform [traens'fo:rm] v.
przekształcić; zmienić
postać
transformation
[,traensfer'mejszyn] s.
przekształcenie; przeobrażenie
transfuse [traens'fjuz] v.
przelać; przetoczyć (krew)
transfusion [traens'fjużyn] s.
transfuzja
transgress [traens'gres] v.
naruszyć; zgrzeszyć
transgression [traens'greszyn] s.
naruszenie; grzech;
wykroczenie
transgressor [traens'greser] s.
grzesznik

transient ['traenżent] adj.
przechodni; przejeżdżający;
przelotny
transistor [traen'zyster] s.
tranzystor
transit ['traensyt] s. przejazd;
przelot; przewóz; tranzyt;
teodolit
transition [traen'syszyn] s.
przejście; zmiana
transitive ['traensytyw] adj.
przechodni
translate [traens'lejt] v.
przetłumaczyć; przełożyć
translation [traens'lejszyn] s.
tłumaczenie; przekład
translator [traens'lejter] s.
tłumacz
translucent [traenz'lu:sent] adj.
przeświecający;
półprzeźroczysty
transmission [traenz'myszyn] s.
przekładnia; transmisja
transmit [traenz'myt] v.
przekazywać; nadawać;
transmitować
transmitter [traenz'myter] s.
nadajnik; przekaźnik
transparent [traens'peerent] adj.
przeźroczysty
transpire [traens'pajer] v. pocić
się; wyparować; okazywać
się; zdarzyć się
transplant [traens'pla:nt] v.
przeszczepiać; przesadzać; s.
['traenspla:nt] przesadzanie;
przeszczep
transport [traens'po:rt] v.
przewozić; zachwycać; s.
['traenspo:rt] przewóz;
zachwyt; uniesienie
transportation
[,traenspo:r'tejszyn] s.
przewóz; transport;
deportacja; zesłanie
trap [traep] s. pułapka; potrzask;
sidła; zasadzka; podstęp;
syfon; skała wylewna; (slang):
jadaczka; pl. manatki; v.
złapać w pułapkę;
zaopatrywać w pułapkę;
zatrzymywać (w czymś);
przykrywać czaprakiem;

puszczać rzutki
trap-door ['traep'do:r] s. drzwi
zapadowe; zapadnia
trapeze [tre'pi:z] s. trapez
trapper ['traeper] s. traper;
myśliwy; zastawiający
pułapki; nadzorca szybów
powietrznych w kopalni
trappings ['traepyŋgz] s. ozdoby;
strój ozdobny; czaprak
trash [traesz] s. śmieci; rupieci;
tandeta; odpadki; bzdury;
hołota; v. obdzierać (z liści,
gałązek)
travel ['traewl] v. podróżować
(też za interesem); poruszać
się (części maszyny);
przesuwać się; biec (w
terenie); przechodzić (oczami
po czymś); poruszać się
żwawo; błądzić; s. (daleka)
podróż; ruch (pojazdów); suw
(maszynowy); przesunięcie
travel agency ['traewl'ejdżensy]
s. biuro podróży
traveler ['traewler] s. podróżnik;
wodzik nitkowy; komiwojażer
traveler's check ['traewlers,czek]
s. z góry wykupiony czek do
użytku w podróży
traveling bag ['traewlyŋg,baeg]
s. torba podróżna
traverse [trae'we:rs] v.
przecinać; przesuwać na
bok; przechodzić; omawiać;
pokrzyżować; zaprzeczyć
formalnie; nakierowywać
(działo); obracać (się) jak na
osi
travesty ['traewysty] s.
trawestacja; parodia; v.
trawestować; parodiować
trawl [tro:l] s. włok; włók; trał;
niewód; sieć-worek do
holowania; v. ciągnąć
niewód; łowić niewodem,
włókiem, wędką ciągnioną za
łodzią
trawler ['tro:ler] s. trawler
tray [trej] s. taca; szufladka (też
wkładowa)
treacherous ['treczeres] adj.
zdradziecki; niebezpieczny;

zdradliwy; zawodny; perfidny
treachery ['treczery] s. zdrada;
zdradzieckość;
zdradliwość; perfidia
treacle ['tri:kl] s. syrop; melasa;
sok (drzewny)
tread; trod; trod(den) [tred; trod;
'trodn]
tread [tred] v. deptać; stąpać
(po czymś); nadepnąć;
tłoczyć; wdeptywać; iść
(ścieżką); wydeptać
(ścieżkę); gnieść; s.
stąpanie; krok; podnóżek;
guma opony dotykająca
jezdni; szyna; bieżnik;
podeszwa (dotykająca ziemi);
stopień
treadle ['tredl] s. pedał; v.
pedałować
treadmill ['tredmyl] s. kierat
(cylindryczny ze stopniami)
treason ['tri:zn] s. zdrada
treasure ['treżer] s. skarb; v.
zaskarbiać; cenić; strzec
skarbu
treasurer ['treżerer] s. skarbnik
treasury ['treżery] s. urząd
skarbowy; skarbnica
Treasury Department
['treżery,dy'pa:rtment] s.
ministerstwo skarbu (USA)
treat [tri:t] v. traktować;
potraktować; obchodzić się
z kimś; uważać kogoś za;
brać coś (za żart); leczyć
coś; poddawać działaniu;
pertraktować; fundować
(komuś); s. przyjęcie; uczta;
majówka; poczęstunek;
zabawa; przyjemność;
rozkosz
treatise ['tri:tys] s. traktat;
rozprawa
treatment ['tri:tment] s.
traktowanie; leczenie
treaty ['tri:ty] s. traktat; układ;
umowa
treble ['trebl] adj. potrójny;
wysoki; ostry; przenikliwy;
sopranowy; s. sopran; wysoki
dźwięk; v. potrajać (się)
tree [tri:] s. drzewo; forma;

kopyto; rama siodła; belka;
nadproże; krokiew; szubienica;
v. zapędzić (na drzewo);
wsadzić (na kopyto)
treeless ['tri:lys] adj. bezdrzewny
tree-trunk ['tri:,traŋk] s. pień
trefoil ['trefojl] s. koniczyna
trójlistna; roślina trójlistna;
adj. trójlistny
trellis ['trelys] s. krata; altana; v.
kratować winorośl;
nadawać formę kraty
tremble ['trembl] v. trząść się;
drżeć; dygotać; s. drżenie;
drżączka
tremendous [try'mendes] adj.
straszny; olbrzymi
tremor ['tremer] s. drżenie;
drganie; trzęsienie (ziemi)
tremulous ['tremjules] adj.
drżący
trench [trencz] s. rów; okop;
bruzda; cięcie; rów strzelecki;
v. kopać rów; okopywać się;
kłaść do rowu; żłobić;
ciąć; przecinać;
podkopywać się; graniczyć
trench up ['trencz,ap] v.
wdzierać się (bezczelnie) w
cudze (prawa etc.)
trend [trend] s. dążność;
ogólna tendencja; ogólny
kierunek; v. dążyć; mieć
tendencję; kształtować się;
ciągnąć się
trespass ['trespas] v. wdzierać
się w cudze; nadużywać;
naruszać; wykraczać;
grzeszyć; v. przekroczenie;
wykroczenie; grzech; szkoda
wyrządzona na cudzym
terenie
trespasser ['trespaser] s.
człowiek naruszający przepisy,
prawo (czyjeś)
tress [tres] s. warkocz; v.
zaplatać warkocz
trestle ['tresl] s. kozioł; kobylica;
most filarowy
trial ['trajel] s. próba; proces
sądowy; zmartwienie; zawody
eliminacyjne; adj. próbny;
doświadczalny

trial and error ['trajel end'erer]
exp.: chaotyczne próby (w
nieznane)
triangle ['trajaengl] s. trójkąt
triangular [traj'aengjular] adj.
trójkątny
triangulate [traj'aengulejt] v.
mierzyć (trójkątami) przy
pomocy triangulacji
tribe [trajb] s. plemię; szczep
tribunal [traj'bju:nl] s. trybunał;
sąd
tribune ['trybju:n] s. trybuna;
mównica; gazeta; trybun
(ludu)
tributary ['trybjutery] adj.
pomocniczy; płacący daninę,
haracz; s. dopływ; kraj
płacący daninę
tribute ['trybju:t] s. haracz;
danina
trick [tryk] s. podstęp; chwyt;
sztuczka; sposób; nawyk;
maniera; psota; fortel; (slang):
dziecko; dziewczynka; v.
oszukać; okpić; wyłudzić;
płatać figla; zawodzić;
zaskakiwać
trick up ['tryk,ap] v. wystroić
trickle ['trykl] v. sączyć (się);
przeciekać; przesączyć;
puszczać ciurkiem, kroplami;
s. struga (mała)
tricky ['tryky] adj. podstępny;
chytry; sprytny; trudny;
zawiły; zręczny
tricycle ['trajsykl] s. rower na
trzech kołach
trifle ['trajfl] s. drobiazg;
drobnostka; błahostka;
bagatela; odrobina;
głupstewko; byle co; stop
cyny i ołowiu; biszkopt z
kremem; v. nie brać
poważnie; poflirtować;
baraszkować; paplać;
bagatelizować
trifling ['trajflyŋg] adj. płochy;
błahy; znikomy
trigger ['tryger] s. spust; cyngiel;
zapadka; v. pociągać za
spust; wywoływać; dawać
początek; zaczynać (akcję)

trill [tryl] s. trel; wibrująca spółgłoska; v. wymawiać z wibracją; trząść głosem; trelować; wymawiać wibrująco

trillion ['tryljen] = USA billion ['byljen] num. trylion

trim [trym] v. oporządzać; usuwać niepotrzebne (gałęzie, tłuszcz etc.); przybierać (listwą, taśmą etc.); rozkładać poprawnie ładunek; poprawiać (opinię); być oportunistą; zmyć komuś głowę; dać komuś lanie; wyprowadzić w pole; besztać; rugać; s. stan; forma; nastrój; gotowość; porządek; strój; ozdoby; listwy; taśmy; wstążki do poprawienia wyglądu; dekoracja wystawy; oporządzenie; obcięcie; równowaga lotu; wyposażenie wnętrza (np. samochodu, domu etc.); adj. schludny; porządny; uporządkowany; wysprzątany

trimming ['trymyng] s. ozdoby; uporządkowanie; przystrzyżenie; garnirowanie

Trinity ['trynyty] s. Trójca Św.

trinket ['trynkyt] s. ozdóbka (na suknię); świecidełko; błahostka

trip [tryp] s. podróż; wycieczka; jazda; trans narkomana; potknięcie; podstawienie nogi; zgrabny krok; wyzwalanie zapadkowe lub wychwytowe; błąd; pomyłka; v. potknąć się; iść lekkim krokiem; drobić nóżkami; tańczyć (lekko); pomylić się; podstawiać nogę; złapać na błędzie; wyzwalać; odczepiać kotwicę; przesuwać wychwytem kotwicowym; obracać reje; spuszczać nagle część maszyny

tripe [trajp] s. flaki (też potrawa); byle co;

paskudztwo; lichota

triple [trypl] adj. potrójny; s. potrójna ilość; trójka; v. potrajać (się)

triplets ['tryplyts] pl. trojaczki

tripod ['trajpod] s. trójnóg; statyw

triumph ['trajemf] s. triumf; v. triumfować

triumphal [traj'amfel] adj. triumfalny

triumphant [traj'amfent] adj. zwycięski; triumfalny

trivial ['trywiel] adj. trywialny; błahy; płytki; banalny; znikomy

trod [trod] v. zob. tread

trodden ['trodn] v. zob. tread

trolley car ['troly kar] s. tramwaj; wywrotka (wóz)

trombone [trom'boun] s. puzon

troop [tru:p] s. grupa; gromada; trupa teatralna; rota; pół szwadronu; s. iść gromadą; gromadzić się; formować w roty (pułk)

trophy ['troufy] s. trofeum

tropic ['tropyk] adj. podzwrotnikowy; tropikalny; s. zwrotnik

tropical ['tropykel] adj. tropikalny; gorący; namiętny

trot [trot] s. kłus; trucht; bryk (szkolny); (slang): biegunka

trouble ['trabl] s. kłopot; zmartwienie; zaburzenie; niepokój; trud; dolegliwość; fatyga; bieda; awaria; uszkodzenie; defekt; v. martwić (się); dręczyć (się); dokuczać; niepokoić (się); kłopotać (się)

troublesome ['trablsem] adj. kłopotliwy

trough [trof] s. koryto; rynna; rów (też między falami); niecka; łęk; synklina

trouser leg ['trauzerleg] s. nogawka

trousers ['trauzez] pl. spodnie

trousseau ['tru:sou] s. wyprawa (ślubna)

trout [traut] s. pstrąg; v. łowić pstrągi

truant ['tru:ent] s. wagarowicz;
opuszczający pracę; adj.
próżniacki; wałęsający (się);
v. chodzić na wagary;
opuszczać pracę

truce [tru:s] s. rozejm;
zawieszenie broni

truck [trak] s. ciężarówka;
taczki; wózek; podwozie na
kołach; lora; drobne towary;
warzywa; wymiana; interes;
śmieci; brednie; stosunki z
kimś; v. przewozić wozem;
ładować na wóz; wymieniać
się z kimś; obnosić towar;
utrzymywać stosunki z kimś

truck farm [trak,fa:rm] s.
gospodarstwo warzywne

trudge [tradż] s. trudny marsz;
v. trudzić się marszem;
odbywać z trudem drogę

true [tru:] adj. prawdziwy;
wierny; ścisły; dokładny;
prawdomówny; czysty;
faktyczny; szczery; lojalny;
dobrze dopasowany; s.
prawda; właściwe położenie;
v. regulować; wyregulować;
adv. prawdziwie; dokładnie;
exp.: to jest prawda!

truly ['tru:ly] adv. prawdziwie;
dokładnie

true-blue ['tru:'blu:] adj.
bezkompromisowy;
prawdziwie oddany

trump [tramp] s. atut; as; zuch;
złoty człowiek; trąba; v. bić
atutem; roztrąbić

trump up ['tramp,ap] v. wyssać
z palca; zmyślać (zarzuty);
preparować (zarzuty)

trumpet ['trampyt] s. trąbka;
dźwięk; trębacz; v. grać na
trąbie; trąbić; roztrąbić

truncheon ['tranczen] s. pałka
policjanta; buława marszałka

trunk [trank] s. pień; trzon;
tułów; tors; kadłub; główny
kanał; główna linia; trąba
słoniowa; kufer; bagażnik; pl.
spodnie (krótkie)

trunk line ['trank-lajn] s. linia
międzymiastowa (też

telefoniczna w Anglii)

trunk road ['trank-roud] s. szosa
główna

truss [tras] s. więźba;
wspornik; kratownica;
wiązanie dachowe; wiązka
(siana); pas przepuklinowy; v.
związać (np. dach);
przywiązać; wieszać
(zbrodniarza)

trust [trast] s. pewność;
zaufanie; wiara; nadzieja;
kredyt; opieka; powiernictwo;
trust; v. zaufać; mieć
zaufanie; ufać; wierzyć;
polegać (na pamięci swojej
etc.); powierzać; kredytować

trustful ['trastful] adj. ufny

trusting ['trastyng] adj. ufny;
pełen zaufania

trustworthy ['trast,łe:rty] adj.
godny zaufania; pewny

truth [tru:s] s. prawda;
prawdziwość; rzetelność

truthful ['tru:sful] adj.
prawdomówny; prawdziwy
(np. opis)

truths [tru:zz] pl. prawdy

try [traj] v. próbować;
wypróbować; sądzić;
sprawdzić; kosztować;
doświadczyć; starać się;
męczyć; s. próba; usiłowanie;
wysiłek

trying ['trajyng] adj. przykry;
męczący; nieznośny;
irytujący; ciężki

try on ['traj,on] v. przymierzać

try out ['traj,aut] v.
wypróbowywać

T-square ['ti:,skłeer] s.
węgielnica

tub [tab] s. balia; ceber; kadź;
wanna; kąpiel; łódź
treningowa (wiosłowa);
oszalowanie; v. wsadzać do
wanny; prać; szalować

tube [tju:b] s. rura; wąż; dętka;
tubka; tunel (kolei
podziemnej); v. zamykać w
rurze; zaopatrywać w rury;
nadawać kształt rury

tuberculosis [tju,be:rkje:'lousys]

s. gruźlica

tuck [tak] v. wtykać; wsuwać; podwijać; zawijać (rąbek); otulać; zbierać w fałdy; obrębiać; schować; (slang): pałaszować; wcinać; wieszać (skazańca); s. fałd; fałda; obręb; koncha

tuck in ['takyn] v. otulać (w łóżku)

tuck up ['tak,ap] v. podkasać

Tuesday ['tju:zdy] s. wtorek

tuft [taft] s. pęk; pęczek; kiść; kępa; kitka; bródka; pikowanie; v. robić pęki; dawać pęki; róść pękami; pikować

tug [tag] v. ciągnąć (z trudem); holować; wciągać; s. holownik; gwałtowne pociągnięcie

tug-of-war ['tag,ow'łor] s. przeciąganie liny (próba sił, zawody); zażarta walka o przewagę

tuition [tju'yszyn] s. czesne; nauczanie; lekcje (płatne)

tulip ['tju:lyp] s. tulipan

tumble ['tambl] v. upaść; zwalić (się); potknąć się; zataczać się; kołysać się; huśtać się; wywalić się; gramolić się; rzucać się; biegać na oślep; cisnąć; zwichrzyć; (slang): kapować; iść do łóżka; s. zwalenie; pobicie rekordu; upadek; sztuka akrobatyczna; bałagan

tummy ['tamy] s. żołądek; brzuch (dziecka)

tumor ['tu:mer] s. tumor; obrzęk; guz; nowotwór

tumult ['tu:melt] s. zgiełk; wrzawa; tumult; podniecenie; zaburzenie

tumultuous [tu:'malczues] adj. burzliwy; podniecony; hałaśliwy

tun [tan] s. beczka; kadź (252 galony); v. wlewać do beczki; przechowywać w beczce

tuna ['tu:na] s. tuńczyk

tune [tu:n] s. melodia; nastrój; harmonia; v. stroić; dostroić; harmonizować; nucić

tune in ['tu:n,yn] v. nastawiać (radio etc.)

tune up ['tu:n,ap] v. nastrajać (np. motor)

tunnel ['tanl] s. tunel; nora; v. przekopywać tunel, korytarz, norę; przekopywać się

turbine ['te:rbyn] s. turbina

turbot ['te:rbet] s. skarpturbot (ryba)

turbulent ['te:rbjulent] adj. wzburzony; burzliwy; gwałtowny; buntowniczy

turf [te:rf] s. torf; darń; v. pokrywać darniną; (slang): drałować (piechotą)

Turk [te:rk] s. Turek

turkey ['te:rky] s. indyk; v. mówić bez ogródek

Turkish ['te:rkysz] adj. turecki

Turkish bath ['te:kysz,ba:s] s. parówka; kąpiel parowa; łaźnia

turmoil ['te:rmojl] s. zamieszanie; zgiełk; niepokój; podniecenie

turn [te:rn] v. odwrócić (się); odkręcić (się); przekręcać (się); skręcać (się); zwracać (się); odwracać (się); odpierać (atak); napadać; zmieniać się; nawracać (się); popełniać (zdradą); stawać się (np. katolikiem); wyświadczać; obracać; kierować; robić skręt; wyprawiać; odprawiać; toczyć (na kole); puścić w ruch; okazać się; zdarzać się; zwolnić; wyganiać; wyrzucać etc.; s. obrót; kolej; z kolei; po kolei; tura; zakręt; zwrot; skręt; punkt zwrotny; przełom; kształt; forma; przechadzka; transakcja; wstrząs; atak; przysługa; numer (popisowy); kolejność; postępowanie wobec kogoś

turn away ['te:rn,e'łej] v. odwracać się od; porzucić

turn back ['te:rn,baek] v.

zawrócić (z drogi)
turn down ['te:rn,dałn] v.
odmówić; przyciszać;
odrzucać
turn off ['te:rn,of] v. zakręcić
(kurek); skręcić; wyłączać
(światło); odprawić
turn on ['te:rn,on] v. puszczać
(wodę); włączać (światło);
odkręcać (kurek)
turn out ['te:rn,aut] v. wyrzucać
(za drzwi); wyrabiać;
zwalniać (z pracy)
turn over ['te:rn'ouwer] v.
odwracać; rozważać; mieć
obrót; wydawać (policji);
przekazywać
turn round ['te:rn raund] v.
przekręcać; odwracać;
zmieniać przekonania;
przekabacić
turn to ['te:rn,tu] v. zabrać się
(do czegoś)
turn up ['te:rn,ap] v. odwracać;
zawinąć (rękawy);
podkręcać; przychodzić;
zgłosić się; przytrafić (się)
turncoat ['te:rn,kout] s. zdrajca
turning point ['te:rnyng,point] s.
punkt zwrotny
turnip ['te:rnyp] s. rzepa
turnout ['te:rnaut] s. stawienie
się; ilość obecnych;
ekwipunek
turnover ['te:rn,ouwer] s.
zmiana; kapotaż;
przewrócenie; placek;
przemieszczanie (ludzi, rzeczy)
turnpike ['te:rn,pajk] s. kołowrót;
rogatka; autostrada (płatna)
turnstile ['te:rnstajl] s. kołowrót
(do wchodzenia pojedynczo)
turnup ['te:rnap] s. traf;
zamieszanie; część
wywrócona; coś
podwiniętego; podwinięcie
turpentine ['te:rpentajn] s.
terpentyna; v.
terpentynować; zbierać
terpentynę
turret ['te:ryt] s. wieżyczka;
imak wielonożowy
turtle ['te:rtl] s. żółw (morski)

turtledove ['te:rtl,daw] s.
turkawka
tusk [task] s. kieł; ząb (u brony);
v. bóść; kłuć; rozdzierać
kłami
tutor ['tu:ter] s. nauczyciel
prywatny; korepetytor;
opiekun (studentów); v.
uczyć kogoś; mieć opiekę
nad kimś; powściągać (się);
być korepetytorem; uczyć
się pod nadzorem nauczyciela
tutorial [tu:'torjel] adj.
wychowawczy; opiekuńczy
TV [ti:wi:] s. telewizja
tuxedo [tak'si:dou] s. smoking
(USA)
twang [tłaeng] s. brzęk (struny);
mówienie przez nos; v.
brzęczeć; rzępolić;
brzdąkać; mówić przez nos
tweed [tłi:d] s. materiał wełniany
lub wełniano-bawełniany z
szorstką powierzchnią
tweet [tłi:t] s. ćwierkanie; v.
ćwierkać
tweezers ['tłi:zez] s. szczypczyki
(kosmetyczne itp.)
twelfth [tłelfs] adj. dwunasty
twelve [tłelw] num. dwanaście;
s. dwunastka
twentieth ['tłentyjes] adj.
dwudziesty
twenty ['tłenty] num.
dwadzieścia; s. dwudziestka
twice [tłajs] adv. dwa razy;
podwójnie; dwukrotnie
twiddle ['tłydl] s. obracanie; v.
kręcić; obracać; przebierać
palcami; próżnować
twig [tłyg] v. zrozumieć;
połapać się; spostrzec;
zauważyć; rozpoznawać; s.
gałązka; różdżka
czarodziejska
twilight ['tłajlajt] s. zmrok;
półcień; półmrok; zmierzch
twin [tłyn] s. bliźniak; adj.
bliźniaczy; v. rodzić się jako
bliźnięta; łączyć (się)
ściśle ze sobą
twin-engine ['tłyn'endżyn] adj.
dwumotorowy

twinkle [tłynkl] v. migotać; błyszczeć; mrugać; s. migotanie; błysk; mrugnięcie

twirl [tłe:rl] v. wirować; kręcić (się); s. wirowanie; kręcenie się; zakrętas; piruet

twist [tłyst] v. skręcać (się); zwijać (się); zwichnąć (się); zawirować; wykrzywiać (twarz); przekręcać; pokręcić (się); wić (się); powikłać (się); tańczyć (twista); wykręcać; przewijać się (przez tłum); s. skręt; szpagat; przędza; lina (skręcona); splot; obrót; przekręcenie (znaczenia); zwichnięcie; skłonność; strucla

twitch [tłycz] v. szarpać; wyrwać; wydrzeć; wykrzywić (się); poruszyć się gwałtownie; s. skurcz; szarpnięcie; pociągnięcie (za rękaw); drgawka; tik; drganie (powieki); spazm; kurcz

twitter ['tłyter] v. ćwierkać; świergotać; chichotać; drżeć (ze strachu etc.); s. świergot; chichot; podniecenie; zdenerwowanie

two [tu:] num. dwa; s. dwójka

two-bit ['tu:byt] adj. tandetny; marny; (slang): wart 25 centów; rzecz mała; rzecz bez znaczenia

twofold ['tu:fould] adj. podwójny; adv. podwójnie; dwojako

two-piece ['tu:pi:s] adj. dwuczęściowy

two-stroke ['tu:,strouk] adj. dwutaktowy; dwusuwowy

two-way ['tu:,łej] adj. dwukierunkowy (np. ruch); dwutorowy; dwuwartościowy

type [tajp] s. typ; wzór; przykład; symbol; klasa; okaz; czcionka; kaszta (drukarska); v. pisać na maszynie; ustalać typ; symbolizować; wyznaczać role

typewriter ['tajp,rajter] s. maszyna do pisania

typhoid ['tajfojd] adj. tyfusowy; s. tyfus; dur brzuszny

typhoon [taj'fu:n] s. tajfun; burza (morska) w układzie wielkiego wiru

typhus ['tajfes] adj. tyfusowy

typical ['typykel] adj. typowy; charakterystyczny

typify ['typyfaj] v. uosabiać; stanowić typ; zapowiadać

typist ['tajpyst] s. maszynistka

tyrannical [ty'raenykel] adj. tyrański

tyrannize ['tyrenajz] v. tyranizować

tyranny ['tyreny] s. tyrania

tyrant ['tajrent] s. tyran

U

u [ju:] dwudziesta pierwsza litera alfabetu angielskiego

ubiquity [ju'bykłyty] s. wszechobecność

U-boat ['ju:bout] s. łódź podwodna (niemiecka)

udder ['ader] s. wymię

ugly ['agly] adj. brzydki; paskudny

uhlan ['u:la:n] s. ułan

ulan ['u:la:n] s. ułan

ulcer ['alser] s. wrzód

ultimate ['altymyt] adj. ostateczny; ostatni; końcowy; podstawowy; s. ostateczny wynik; podstawowy fakt

ultimatum [alty'mejtem] s. ultimatum

umbrella [am'brela] s. parasol

umpire ['ampajer] s. sędzia sportowy; rozjemca; v. sędziować; rozstrzygać jako arbiter

unabashed ['ane'baeszt] adj. niespeszony; niezmieszany; nie zbity z tropu

unabated ['an,e'bejtyd] adj. niesłabnący; niezmniejszony

unable ['an'ejbl] adj. niezdolny;
nieudolny

unacceptable ['ane'kseptebl] adj.
nie do przyjęcia

unaccountable ['ane'kauntebl]
adj. niewytłumaczony;
niezrozumiały; dziwny; nie
tłumaczący się nikomu

unaccustomed ['ane'kastemd]
adj. niezwykły; nie
przyzwyczajony

unacquainted ['ane'kłejntyd] adj.
nie obznajomiony

unaffected [,ane'fektyd] adj.
niekłamany; naturalny

unanimous [ju'naenymes] adj.
jednogłośny

unapproachable [,ane'prouczebl]
adj. niedostępny; niezrównany

unarmed ['an'a:rmd] adj.
bezbronny; nie uzbrojony

unashamed ['an,e'szejmd] adj.
bezwstydny

unassisted ['an,e'systyd] adj. nie
wspomagany

unassuming ['an,e'sju:myng] adj.
skromny; bezpretensjonalny

unauthorized ['an'o:terajzd] adj.
nieupoważniony

unavoidable ['an,e'wojdebl] adj.
nieunikniony; niechybny

unaware [,ane'łeer] adj.
nieświadomy;
niepoinformowany

unawares [,ane'łeerz] adv.
nieświadomie; znienacka;
niespodziewanie; nic nie
wiedząc

unbalanced ['an'baelensd] adj.
niezrównoważony

unbar ['an'ba:r] v. odryglować

unbearable [an'beerebl] adj.
nieznośny; nie do
wytrzymania

unbecoming ['an,by'kamyng] adj.
niestosowny; niewłaściwy;
nieodpowiedni; nietwarzowy

unbelievable [,anby'li:webl] adj.
niewiarygodny;
nieprawdopodobny

unbelieving [,anby'li:wyng] adj.
niewierzący; niedowierzający

unbending ['an'bendyng] adj.

nieugięty; niezłomny

unbiased ['an'bajest] adj.
bezstronny

unbidden ['an'bydn] adj.
nieproszony

unborn baby ['an'bo:rn'bejby] s.
przyszłe dziecko; nieurodzone
(jeszcze) dziecko

unbounded [an'baundyd] adj. bez
granic; bezgraniczny

unbroken [an'brouken] adj.
nieprzerwany; niezbity; nie
ujeżdżony (koń)

unbutton ['an'batn] v. odpiąć;
rozpiąć (się)

uncalled-for [an'ko:ld,fo:r] adj.
niewłaściwy; niezasłużony;
niczym nie usprawiedliwiony

uncanny [an'kaeny] adj.
niesamowity

uncared-for ['an'keerd,fo:r] adj.
porzucony; zaniedbany

unceasing [an'si:syng] adj.
bezustanny; nieprzerwany

uncertain [an'se:rtn] adj.
niepewny; wątpliwy

unchallenged [an'czaelyndżd]
adj. niekwestionowany

unchangeable [an'czejndżebl]
adj. stały; niezmienny

unchanged [an'czejndżd] adj.
niezmieniony

unchecked [an'czekt] adj.
niepowstrzymany;
niepohamowany;
nieposkromiony

uncivil ['an'sywyl] adj.
niegrzeczny; nieuprzejmy;
nieokrzesany; grubiański

uncivilized ['an'sywylajzd] adj.
dziki; niecywilizowany;
barbarzyński

uncle ['ankl] s. wujek; stryjek

unclean ['an'kli:n] adj. nieczysty;
plugawy; sprośny

uncommon ['an'komen] adj.
niezwykły; rzadki; adv.
niezwykle; nadzwyczaj

uncommunicative ['an
-ke'mju:nyketyw] adj.
małomówny; skryty;

niekomunikatywny

uncomplaining ['an-kem'plejnyng]
adj. cierpliwy; nienarzekający

unconcern ['anken'se:rn] s.
beztroska; niefrasobliwość;
obojętność

unconcerned ['anken'se:rnd] adj.
obojętny; niefrasobliwy;
beztroski

unconditional ['an-ken'dyszynl]
adj. bezwarunkowy

unconfirmed ['an-ken'fe:rmd] adj.
nie potwierdzony

unconscious [an'konszes] adj.
nieprzytomny; zemdlony;
nieświadomy; s.
podświadomość

unconsciousness
[an'konszesnys] s. omdlenie;
nieprzytomność

unconstitutional
['an,konsty'tju:szynl] adj.
niezgodny z konstytucją

uncontrollable ['an,kon'troulebl]
adj. nieposkromiony;
niepohamowany

unconventional ['an
-ken'wenszynl] adj.
niekonwencjonalny; oryginalny

unconvinced ['an-ken'wynst] adj.
nieprzekonany

unconvincing ['an-ken'wynsyng]
adj. nieprzekonywający

uncouth [an'ku:s] adj.
nieokrzesany; niezręczny;
niezgrabny

uncover [an'kawer] v. odkryć;
demaskować

uncultivated ['an'kaltywejtyd]
adj. nieuprawny; leżący
odłogiem; niekulturalny

uncultured ['an'kalczerd] adj.
niewykształcony; niekulturalny

uncut ['an'kat] daj. nie przecięty;
nie ścinany; nie strzyżony

undamaged ['an'daemydżd] adj.
nieuszkodzony

undated ['an'dejtyd] adj. nie
datowany; bez określonego
terminu

undaunted ['an'do:ntyd] adj.
nieposkromiony; nieustraszony

undecayed ['andy'kejd] adj.

nie
zepsuty; nie zgniły

undecided ['an-dy'sajdyd] adj.
niezdecydowany; niepewny;
nieokreślony;
nierozstrzygnięty

undecisive ['andy'sajsyw] adj.
nieroztrzygnięty; nie
decydujący (Brit.)

undecked ['an'dekt] adj. bez
ozdób; nie ozdobiony (stół,
itd.) (Brit.)

undefeated ['andy'fi:tyd] adj.
niepokonany

undefended ['andy'fendyd] adj.
nie broniony

undefinable ['andy'fajnebl] adj.
nieokreślony

undefined ['andy'fajnd] adj.
nieokreślony; mglisty

undelayed ['andy'lejd] adj.
bezzwłoczny; nie opóźniony;
natychmiastowy (Brit.)

undeniable [,andy'najebl] adj.
niezaprzeczalny

undenominational
['andy,nomy'nejsznl] daj.
bezwyznaniowy; świecki

undependable ['andy'pendebl]
adj. niesolidny; niesłowny;
niewiarogodny

under ['ander] prep. pod;
poniżej; w; w trakcie; zgodnie
z; z; adv. poniżej; pod
spodem; adj. spodni; niższy;
dolny; podrzędni; podwładny

underbid ['ander'byd] v. zob. bid;
składać niższą ofertę w
przetargu

underbrush ['ander,brasz] s.
zarośla; podszycie (lasu)

undercarriage ['ander,kaerydż] s.
podwozie

undercharge ['ander'cza:rdż] v.
za mało policzyć; za słabo
naładować

underclothes ['ander,klouzyz] pl.
bielizna

underclothing ['ander,klouzyng]
s. bielizna

undercooling ['andr,ku:lyng] s.
przechłodzenie; przeziębienie

undercurrent ['ander,karent] s.

prąd pod powierzchnią;
tendencja podstawowa
undercut ['ander'kat] v.
podcinać płace, ceny; s.
polędwica; cios od dołu;
podkop
underdeveloped
[,anderdy'welept] adj.
zacofany; nie wywołany
poprawnie; niedorozwinięty
underdog ['ander'dog] s.
człowiek upośledzony,
przegrywający
underdone ['ander'dan] adj.
półsurowy; niedogotowany
underestimate ['ander'estymejt]
v. niedoceniać; za nisko
oszacować
underfed ['ander'fed] v.
niedożywiony
undergo [,ander'gou] v. zob. go;
doznawać czegoś;
przechodzić coś;
doświadczyć; poddawać się
(operacji)
undergraduate [,ander'graedjuit]
s. student bez stopnia
bachelor
underground ['ander,graund] adj.
podziemny; zaskórny; tajny; s.
kolej podziemna; ruch oporu;
adv. [,ander'graund] pod
ziemią; skrycie; tajnie
undergrowth ['ander-grous̲] s.
poszycie (lasu)
underline ['anderlajn] v.
podkreślać; s. podkreślenie;
podpis pod ilustracją;
zawiadomienie (u spodu afisza
teatralnego) o następnej
sztuce
underling ['ander'lyn̲g] s.
podwładny; sługa
undermine [,ander'majn] v.
podkopywać (zdrowie etc.);
podmywać (brzegi etc.)
undermost ['andermoust] adj.
adv. najniższy; najniższej
rangi; najniżej
underneath [,ander'ni:s̲] adv. pod
spodem; poniżej; na dole; pod
spód
underpants ['ander,paents] s.

kalesony
underpass [,ander'pa:s] s.
przejazd poniżej poziomu;
skrzyżowanie bezkolizyjne;
przejście pod jezdnią
underpay ['ander'pej] v. za mało
płacić
underplay ['ander'plej] v.
pomniejszać; podcinać
underprivileged
['ander'prywylydżd] adj.
upośledzony
underrate ['ander,rejt] v.
niedoceniać
underscore ['ander'skor] v.
podkreślać
undershirt ['andersze:rt] s.
podkoszulek
underside ['ander'sajd] s. spód
undersigned ['ander'sajnd] adj.
(niżej) podpisany
undersized ['ander'sajzd] adj.
zbyt mały; małego wzrostu
undersoil ['ander,sojl] s.
podglebie (Brit.)
understaffed ['ander'sta:ft] adj.
mający zbyt mały personel
understand; understood;
understood [,ander'staend;
,ander'stud; ,ander'stud]
understand [,ander'staend] v.
rozumieć; domyślać się;
orientować się; znać;
wywnioskować; wiedzieć
jak; umieć dobrze
understandable
[,ander'staendebl] adj.
zrozumiały
understanding [,ander'staendyn̲g]
adj. pełen zrozumienia; s.
zrozumienie; warunek;
(wyższa) inteligencja;
porozumienie; rozum
understandingly
[,ander'staendyn̲gly] adv. ze
zrozumieniem;
porozumiewawczo
understate ['ander'stejt] v.
umniejszać; wyrażac się zbyt
słabo
understatement
[,ander'stejtment] s. zbyt
skromne wyrażanie się;

niedomówienie
understood [‚ander'stud] adj.
zrozumiały, umówiony;
domyślny; niedopowiedziany
undertake [‚ander'tejk] v. zob.
take; przedsiębrać;
podejmować się; ręczyć;
zobowiązywać się do
czegoś; być przedsiębiorcą
pogrzebowym
undertaker [‚ander'tejker] s.
przedsiębiorca pogrzebowy
undertaking [‚ander'tejkyng] s.
przedsięwzięcie;
zobowiązanie; obietnica;
przyrzeczenie;
przedsiębiorstwo pogrzebowe
undervalue [‚ander'waelju] v.
niedoceniać; za nisko
szacować
underwaist ['ander‚łejst] s.
kamizelka; bezrękawnik
underwear ['ander‚łeer] s.
bielizna
underweight ['ander‚łejt] s.
niedowaga; adj. nie
doważony; za mało ważący
underwood ['ander‚łu:d] s.
poszycie (lasu) (Brit.)
underworld ['ander‚łe:rld] s.
podziemie; świat podziemny;
pl. antypody
underwrite ['ander-rajt] v. zob.
write; zakontraktować
(ubezpieczenie); podpisać
(się); wydawać (polisę
ubezpieczeniową);
zobowiązywać się
underwriter ['ander-rajter] s.
ajent ubezpieczeniowy
undescribable ['andys'krajbabl]
adj. nie do opisania; nie
dający się opisać
underserved ['andy'ze:rwd] adj.
niezasłużony; niesłuszny (Brit.)
undeserving ['andy'ze:rvyng] adj.
nie zasługujący; bez zasług
undesirable [andy'zajerebl] adj.
niepożądany; niedogodny; s.
człowiek niepożądany
undetected ['andy'tektyd] adj.
niezauważony
undetermined ['andy'te:rmynd]

adj. nieokreślony
undeveloped ['andy'welept] adj.
nierozwinięty; niewywołany
undeviating [an'dy:vj‚ejtyng] adj.
nie zbaczający; prosty;
wierny; niezawodny
undies [andyz] pl. bielizna
(damska i dziecięca)
undifferentiated
['an'dyfe:renszi'ejtyd] adj. nie
zróżnicowany; nie
różniczkowany
undigested ['andaj'dżestyd] adj.
nie strawiony; nie
dopracowany; nie przyswojony
undigestible ['andaj'dżestybl]
adj. niestrawny
undignified [an'dygnyfajd] adj.
niegodny; bez godności
undiluted ['andaj'ljutyd] adj. nie
rozpuszczony; nie
rozwodniony; nie rozrzedzony;
nie rozcieńczony
undiminished [an'dymynszt] adj.
niezmniejszony
undisciplined [an'dysyplind] adj.
niezdyscyplinowany; niekarny
undisclosed ['andys'klouzd] adj.
nie wyjawniony; nieujawniony
undiscovered ['andys'kawerd]
adj. nie odkryty; nie zbadany
undisguised ['andys'gajzd] adj.
nie ukryty; nie maskowany;
nieukrywany
undisposed ['andys'pouzd] adj.
nieskłonny
undisputable ['andys'pju:tebl]
adj. bezsporny
undisputed ['andys'pju:tyd] adj.
bezsporny; niezaprzeczony
undistinguishable
['andys'tyngłyszebl] adj. nie
do rozpoznania;
niedostrzegalny
undisturbed ['andys'te:rbd] adj.
niezakłócony
undivided ['andy'wajdyd] adj.
niepodzielny; cały; całkowity;
nierozdzielony; jednomyślny
undo; undid; undone ['an'du:;
'an'dyd; an'dan]
undo ['an'du:] v. robić
niebyłym; unieważniać;

usuwać; niszczyć;
rujnować; rozpakować;
rozwiązać; otwierać;
rozpinać; przekreślać

undreamt-of ['an'dremt,ow] adj.
nieprawdopodobny; nie do
pomyślenia; niesłychany

undock ['an'dok] v.
wyprowadzać z doku

undone ['an'dan] adj.
niedokończony; nie zrobiony;
rozpięty; rozwiązany; spruty

undreamed [an'dri:md] adj. nie
do pomyślenia;
nieprwadopodobny

undress [an'dres] v. rozbierać
(się); odbandażowywać; s.
negliż; zwykłe ubranie

undressed [an'drest] adj. nie
przyrządzony; chropowaty; nie
opatrzona (rana); rozebrany

undue [an'dju:] adj. przesadny;
nadmierny; postronny;
niewłaściwy; jeszcze
niepłatny (np. rachunek)

undrinkable ['an'drynkebl] adj.
nie (nadający się) do picia

undue ['an'dju:] adj. nadmierny;
przesadny; zbytni; nielegalny;
bezprawny; niewłaściwy; nie
przypadający do zapłaty

unduly ['an'dju:ly] adv.
nadmiernie; przesadnie;
zbytnio; bezprawnie

undutiful [an'dju:tyful] adj.
nieobowiązkowy

undying [an'dajyng] adj.
nieśmiertelny; dozgonny

uneasiness [an'i:zynys] s.
niepokój; zażenowanie;
zakłopotanie

uneasy [an'i:zy] adj. niespokojny;
niepokojący; nieswój;
zażenowany; nieprzyjemny;
krępujący; budzący niepokój

uneatable ['an'i:tebl] adj.
niejadalny; nie (nadający się)
do jedzenia

uneducated [an'edjukejtyd] adj.
niewykształcony; bez
wykształcenia

unemployed [,anem'plojd] adj.
bez pracy; bezrobotny;

niewykorzystany; nie
zużytkowany

unemployment [an'emplojment]
s. bezrobocie

unending [an'endyng] adj.
bezustanny; nie kończący
się; wieczny

unendurable ['anyn'djuerbl] adj.
nie do zniesienia

unentitled ['an-yn'tajtld] adj. nie
upoważniony; bez tytułu

unenviable ['an'enwjebl] adj. nie
do pozazdroszczenia

unequal ['an'i:kłol] adj. nierówny;
nie na wysokości (zadania)

unequaled ['an'i:kłold] adj.
niezrównany

unequivocal ['any'kływokel] adj.
niedwuznaczny; wyraźny;
jasny

unerring ['an'e:ryng] adj.
nieomylny; niezawodny

uneven ['an'i:wen] adj.
nieparzysty; niejednolity;
nierówny

uneventful ['an,y'wentful] adj.
nieurozmaicony; spokojny;
jednostajny

unexpected ['anyks'pektyd] adj.
niespodziewany;
nieoczekiwany

unexperienced ['an-yks'pierienst]
adj. nigdy nie zaznany;
niedoświadczony

unfailing [an'fejlyng] adj.
niezawodny; pewny;
niewyczerpany

unfair [an'feer] adj.
niesprawiedliwy; krzywdzący;
nieuczciwy; nieprzepisowy

unfaithful [an'fejsful] adj.
niewierny; wiarołomny;
nieścisły

unfamiliar ['anfe'myljer] adj.
nieznany; nie obznajomiony;
obcy; słabo zorientowany

unfashionable ['an'faeszenebl]
adj. niemodny

unfasten ['an'fa:sn] v. odczepić
(się); odpiąć (się);
odwiązywać (się);
odryglować (się); rozluźnić
(się)

unfavorable ['an'fejwerebl] adj.
niepomyślny; nieżyczliwy;
niesprzyjający; nieprzychylny
unfeasible [an'fi:sebl] adj.
niewykonalny
unfeeling [an'fi:lyng] adj. bez
uczucia; bez serca; okrutny
unfertile ['an'fe:rtajl] adj.
nieżyzny; nieurodzajny
unfilled ['an'fyld] adj.
niezapełniony; nienapełniony;
nie zajęty; wakujący
unfinished ['an'fynyszt] adj.
niewykończony;
niedokończony
unfit ['an'fyt] adj. nie nadający
się; niezdatny; niezdolny;
nieodpowiedni; v. czynić
niezdolnym do czegoś
unflagging ['an'flaegyng] adj.
niezmordowany; niesłabnący
unflappable ['an'flaepebl] adj. nie
do wytrącenia z równowagi;
beztroski
unflattering ['an'flaeteryng] adj.
niepochlebny
unfold ['an'fould] v. ujawniać
(się); rozwijać (się);
otwierać; odsłonić
unforeseen [,anfer'si:n] adj.
nieprzewidziany;
niespodziewany
unforgettable ['an-fer'getebl] adj.
pamiętny; niezapomniany
unforgivable ['anfe:rgywebl] adj.
nie do darowania;
niewybaczalny
unforgiving ['an-fer'gywyng] adj.
niewybaczający;
nieprzejednany
unforgotten ['an-fer'gotn] adj.
niezapomniany
unfortunate [an'fo:rcznyt] adj.
niefortunny; pechowy;
niepomyślny; nieszczęśliwy
unfortunately [an'fo:rcznytly]
adv. niestety; nieszczęśliwie
unfounded [an'faundyd] adj.
bezpodstawny
unfriendly [an'frendly] adj.
nieprzyjazny; nieprzychylny
unfulfilled ['anful'fyld] adj.
niespełniony

unfurl [an'fe:rl] v. rozwinąć;
rozpościerać
unfurnished [an'fe:rnyszt] adj.
nieumeblowany
ungainly [an'gejnly] adj.
niezdarny; niezgrabny
ungenerous [an'dżeneres] adj.
małostkowy; nie szczodry
ungentle [an'dżentl] adj.
niełagodny
ungodly [an'godly] adj.
bezbożny; grzeszny;
skandaliczny
ungovernable [an'gawernebl] adj.
dziki; niesforny; krnąbrny;
nieopanowany
ungraceful [an'grejsful] adj.
niewdzięczny; nieuprzejmy
ungrateful [an'grejtful] adj.
niewdzięczny
unguarded ['an'ga:rdyd] adj.
niebaczny; nieopatrzny;
nierozważny; niestrzeżony
unhappy [an'haepy] adj.
nieszczęśliwy; pechowy;
zmartwiony; nieudany
unharmed ['an'ha:rmd] adj.
nietknięty
unharness ['an'ha:rnys] v.
wyprzęgać; zdejmować
zbroję etc.
unhealthy [an'helsy] adj.
niezdrowy
unheard-of [an'he:rd,ow] adj.
niesłychany; niebywały;
nieprawdopodobny
unheated [an'hi:tyd] adj.
nieogrzewany
unheeded [an'hi:dyd] adj.
niezauważony; niedostrzeżony
unheeding [an'hi:dyng] adj.
nieuważający;
niedostrzegający
unhesitating [an'hezytejtyng] adj.
nie wahający się
unhinge [an'hyndż] v. zdjąć z
zawiasów; wytrącić z
równowagi
unhitch ['an'hycz] v. odczepić;
wyprząc
unholy [an'houly] adj. bezbożny;
piekielny; niesamowity; nie z
tej ziemi

unhoped-for [an'houpt,fo:r] adj.
niespodziewany;
nieoczekiwany

unhurt [an'he:rt] adj.
nieuszkodzony; bez szwanku

unicorn ['ju:nyko:rn] s.
jednorożec; jednoróg

unidentified ['an-aj'denty,fajd]
adj. niezindentyfikowany;
nieznany

unification [,ju:nyfy'kejszyn] s.
zjednoczenie; scalenie;
ujednolicenie

uniform ['ju:nyfo:rm] adj.
jednolity; równomierny;
jednostajny; s. mundur;
uniform

uniformity ['ju:ny'fo:rmyty] s.
jednolitość; jednostajność;
ujednolicenie; ujednostajnienie

unilateral ['ju:ny'laeterel] adj.
jednostronny

unimaginable [any'maedżynebl]
adj. nie do pomyślenia

unimaginative
[any'maedżynejtyw] adj. bez
wyobraźni; bez polotu

unimportant ['anym'po:rtent] adj.
nieważny; błahy; mało ważny

uninfected ['anyn'fektyd] adj. nie
zarażony

uninformed ['anyn'fo:rmd] adj.
nie poinformowany; nie
powiadomiony

uninhabitable ['anyn'haebytebl]
adj. nie do zamieszkania; nie
do życia

uninhabited ['anyn'haebytyd] adj.
niezamieszkały; pustynny

uninitiated ['any'nyszi,ejtyd] adj.
niewtajemniczony

uninjured ['an'yndżerd] adj. bez
szwanku; nie uszkodzony; bez
obrażeń

uninspired ['anyn'spajerd] adj.
banalny

uninsured ['anyn'szurd] adj.
nieubezpieczony

unintelligible ['anyn'telydżebl]
adj. niezrozumiały

unintentional ['anyn'tenszynl]
adj. mimowolny; nie
zamierzony

uninteresting [an'ynterestyng]
adj. nudny; nieciekawy;
nieinteresujący

uninterrupted [an,ynte'raptyd]
adj. nieprzerwany; ciągły;
bezustanny

uninvited ['anyn'wajtyd] adj.
nieproszony

uninviting ['anyn'wajtyng] adj.
nie zachęcający; odpychający;
nieapetyczny

uninvolved ['an-yn'wolwd] adj.
niezaangażowany

union ['ju:njen] s. połączenie;
złącze; łączność; związek;
zjednoczenie; klub;
małżeństwo; zgoda; łącznik;
złączka; godło

unionist ['ju:njenyst] s.
związkowiec; zwolennik
związku

union Jack ['ju:njen'dżaek] s.
flaga angielska

unique [ju:'ni:k] adj. wyjątkowy;
jedyny; niezrównany; s. unikat

unisex ['ju:ny'seks] adj. styl
(wyrobów) do użytku obu
płci; odzież, przybory
toaletowe, zakład fryzjerski
etc.

unison ['ju:nyzn] adj. zgodnie
(razem)

unit ['ju:nyt] s. jednostka; zespół

unite [ju:'najt] v. łączyć;
jednoczyć; zjednoczyć

united [ju:'najtyd] adj.
połączony; zjednoczony;
łączny

unity ['ju:nyty] s. jedność
(czasu, miejsca, działania
etc.); jednostka; jednolitość;
harmonia; zgoda

universal [ju:ny'we:rsel] adj.
powszechny; ogólny;
uniwersalny

universe ['ju:nywers] s.
wszechświat; świat;
ludzkość; kosmos

university [,ju:ny'wersyty] s.
uniwersytet; wszechnica;
uczelnia

unjust ['an'dżast] adj.
niesprawiedliwy

unjustified ['an'dżasty,fajd] adj.
nieusprawiedliwiony;
nieuzasadniony

unkempt ['an'kempt] adj.
nieuczesany; rozczochrany;
niechlujny

unkind [an'kajnd] adj. niedobry;
okrutny

unknown ['an'noun] adj.
nieznany; niewiadomy

unlabelled [an'lejld] adj. bez
etykiety; nie naznaczony

unlace ['an'lejs] v.
rozsznurować

unlawful ['an'lo:ful] adj.
bezprawny; nielegalny

unlearn ['an'le:rn] v. oduczać
(się); zob. learn

unleash ['an'li:sz] v. spuszczać
ze smyczy; rozpętać (wojnę)

unless [an'les] conj. jeżeli nie;
chyba że

unlike ['an'lajk] adj. niepodobny;
odmienny; prep. odmiennie;
inaczej; w przeciwieństwie

unlikely [an'lajkly] adj.
nieprawdopodobny;
nieoczekiwany; nie rokujący

unlimited [an'lymytyd] adj.
nieograniczony; bezgraniczny;
dowolny

unload ['an'loud] v.
rozładowywać; zrzucać
ciężar

unlock ['an'lok] v. otwierać
zamek; otworzyć

unlocked ['an'lokt] adj. otwarty;
niezamknięty

unlooked-for [an'lukt,fo:r] adj.
nieoczekiwany;
niespodziewany;
nieprzewidziany

unloosen ['an'lu:sn] v.
rozluźnić; rozwiązać;
rozsznurować

unlucky [an'laky] adj. pechowy;
niefortunny; niepomyślny;
nieszczęśliwy

unmanageable [an'maenydżebl]
adj. niesforny; krnąbrny

unmanly [an'maenly] adj.
zniechęcający; odbierający
odwagę; adv. zniechęcająco

unmarried [an'maeryd] adj.
nieżonaty; niezamężna

unmask ['an'ma:sk] v.
zdemaskować; ujawnić

unmelted ['an'meltyd] adj. nie
stopiony; nie stajały; nie
przetopiony

unmendable [an'mendebl] adj.
nie do naprawienia; nie
nadający się do naprawy

unmistakable ['anmys'tejkbl] adj.
niewątpliwy; wyraźny;
niedwuznaczny

unmoved ['an'mu:wd] adj.
niewzruszony

unnamed ['an'nejmd] adj.
bezimienny; anonimowy

unnatural [an'naeczrel] adj.
sztuczny; nienaturalny; wbrew
naturze; nienormalny

unnecessary [an'nesysery] adj.
zbędny; zbyteczny;
niepotrzebny

unnerve [an'ne:rw] v. odbierać
odwagę; denerwować

unnoticed ['an'noutyst] adj.
niezauważony; pominięty

unobtainable ['aneb'tejnebl] adj.
nie do nabycia (otrzymania)

unobstructed ['anob'straktyd]
adj. nie napotykający
przeszkód; nie zasłonięty

unobtrusive ['aneb'tru:syw] adj.
skromny; dyskretny; nie
narzucający się

unoccupied ['an'okjupajd] adj.
wolny; nie zajęty

unoffending ['ane'fendyng] adj.
nieszkodliwy; niewinny

unofficial ['ane'fyszel] adj. nie
urzędowy; nieoficjalny

unopened [an'oupend] adj. nie
otwarty

unopposed ['ano'pouzd] adj. bez
sprzeciwu

unorthodox ['an'o:rto,doks] adj.
nie prawowierny;
nieszablomowy

unpack ['an'paek] v.
rozpakowywać (się)

unpaid ['an'pejd] adj.
niezapłacony; bezinteresowny

unpalatable [an'paeletebl] adj.

niesmaczny
unparalleled [an'paereleld] adj.
niezrównany; niespotykany;
bezprzykładny; niesłychany
unpardonable [an'pa:rdnebl] adj.
niewybaczalny; nie do
darowania
unpenetrable [an'penytrebl] adj.
nie do przebycia; nie do
zrozumienia (Brit.)
unperceived [,anper'si:wd] adj.
niepostrzeżony
unpersuaded ['anper'słejdyd] adj.
nie przekonany
unperturbed ['an-per'te:rbd] adj.
spokojny; nie zaniepokojony;
nie przejmujący się
unpleasant [an'plezent] adj.
nieprzyjemny; przykry; niemiły
unplug [an'plag] v.
odczopować; wyciągnąć z
kontaktu
unpolished ['an'polyszt] adj.
niewyczyszczony;
niewygładzony
unpolluted ['anpe'lu:tyd] adj.
nieskażony; nie
zanieczyszczony
unpopular [an'popjuler] adj.
niepopularny; niemile widziany
unpopularity [,anpopju'laeryty] s.
niepopularność;
nieprzychylne nastawienie; złe
przyjęcie; utrata popularności
unpractical ['an'praektykel] adj.
niepraktyczny; nierealny
unpracticed [an'praektyst] adj.
nie wypraktykowany;
niewprawny
unprecedented [an'presydentyd]
adj. bezprzykładny; bez
precedensu; niesłychany
unprecise ['anpry'sajs] adj.
nieścisły; nie precyzyjny
unprejudiced [an'predżudyst] adj.
bezstronny; nie mający
przesądów
unpremeditated
['anpry:'medytejtyd] adj. bez
premedytacji; nienaumyślny
unprepared ['anpry'peerd] adj.
nieprzygotowany;
nieprzyrządzony

unprincipled [an'prynsepld] adj.
bez skrupułów; niegodziwy
unpreventable ['anpry'wentebl]
adj. nie do uniknięcia;
nieunikniony
unproductive [,anpro'daktyw]
adj. niewydajny; nie
wytwórczy; niepłodny
unprofessional ['anpre'fesznl]
adj. laicki; niezawodowy;
dyletancki; amatorski
unprofitable [an'profytebl] adj.
niepopłatny; niekorzystny;
nierentowny; jałowy
unprotected ['anpro'tektyd] adj.
nie chroniony; bezbronny; nie
zabezpieczony
unproved ['an'pru:wd] adj. nie
udowodniony; nie
wypróbowany
unprovided-for ['an
-pre'wajdyd,fo:r] adj.
niezabezpieczony; bez
środków do życia
unqualified ['an'kłolyfajd] adj.
niewykwalifikowany; bez
kwalifikacji; niesprecyzowany;
nieograniczony (np. zaufanie)
unquestionable [an'kłesczynebl]
adj. bezsporny; niewątpliwy
unquestioned [an'kłesczynd] adj.
niezaprzeczony; niepytany
unravel ['an'raewl] v.
wystrzępić; rozwikłać;
rozwiązać; wyjaśnić
unreal ['an'ryel] adj. nierealny;
zmyślony; iluzoryczny;
wyimaginowany
unreasonable [an'ri:znebl] adj.
nierozsądny; niedorzeczny;
wygórowany (w cenie)
unrefined ['anry'faind] adj.
niesubtelny; niewyrafinowany;
niewykształcony
unreceptive ['anry'septyw] adj.
nieczuły; niepodatny; nie
chłonny; tępy
unreconciled ['an'reken,sajld] adj.
nie pogodzony
unreliable ['anry'lajebl] adj.
niepewny; niesolidny
unrepaid ['anry'pejd] adj. nie
zapłacony

unreserved ['anry'ze:rwd] adj.
otwarty; szczery; bez
zastrzeżeń; całkowity;
niezarezerwowany
unresisting ['anry'zystyng] adj.
nieodporny; nieopierający się
unrest ['an'rest] s. niepokój;
zamieszki; niepokoje
unrestored ['anry'sto:rd] adj. nie
zwrócony; nie odnowiony; nie
przywrócony
unrestrained ['anrys'trejnd] adj.
niepowstrzymany;
niepohamowany;
nieopanowany
unrestricted ['anrys'tryktyd] adj.
nieograniczony
unrig ['an'ryg] v. zdejmować
(żagle); rozbierać (urządzenie)
unripe ['an'rajp] adj. niedojrzały
unrivalled [an'rajweld] adj.
niezrównany;
bezkonkurencyjny
unrobe ['an'roub] v. rozbierać
(się); zdejmować szaty
unroll ['an'roul] v. rozwinąć
(zwój, rolkę)
unruffled [an'rafld] adj.
niezmącony; niezakłócony;
zachowujący równowagę
unruly [an'ru:ly] adj. niesforny
unsaddle ['an'saedl] v.
rozsiodłać; wysadzić z siodła
unsafe ['an'sejf] adj. niepewny;
ryzykowny; niebezpieczny
unsaid ['an'sed] adj. nie
powiedziany; przemilczany
unsalted ['an'so:ltyd] adj. nie
solony
unsanitary ['an'saenytery] adj.
niehigieniczny; szkodliwy;
niezdrowy
unsatisfactory
['an,saetys'faektery] adj.
niezadowalający;
niedostateczny
unsatisfied [an'saetysfajd] adj.
niezadowolony;
niezaspokojony
unsavory ['an'sejwery] adj.
niesmaczny; przykry
unschooled ['an'sku:ld] adj.
nieuczony; nie szkolony;

niewprawny
unscientific ['an,sajen'tyfyk] adj.
nie naukowy; nie zgodny z
nauką
unscrew ['an'skru:] v.
odśrubować; rozśrubować;
odkręcić (gwint)
unscrupulous ['an'skru:pjules]
adj. bez skrupułów;
niegodziwy; bez sumienia
unseal ['an'si:l] v.
rozpieczętowywać; otwierać
unseen [an'si:n] adj. nie
widziany; niewidoczny
unselfish [an'selfysz] adj.
bezinteresowny
unsettled ['an'setld] adj.
zaburzony; zakłócony;
nieustalony; niezapłacony;
rozstrojony
unshaven [an'szejwn] adj.
nieogolony
unshielded ['an'szy:ldyd] adj. nie
chroniony
unshrinkable [an'szrynkebl] adj.
nie kurczący się (w praniu)
unshrinking [an'szrynkyng] adj.
nie wahający się; nie
wzdrygający się
unskillful [an'skylful] adj.
niewprawny; niezręczny
unskilled [an'skyld] adj.
niewprawny;
niewykwalifikowany
unsociable [an'souszebl] adj.
nietowarzyski
unsocial [an'souszel] adj.
niesocjalny; niespołeczny
unsolvable [an'solwebl] adj.
nierozwiązalny;
nierozpuszczalny
unsolved [an'solwd] adj.
nierozwiązany;
nierozpuszczony
unsophisticated
[,anso'fystykejtyd] adj. prosty;
naturalny; prawdziwy
unsound [an'saund] adj.
niezdrowy; spróchniały; słaby;
niepewny; ryzykowny; błędny;
niesolidny
unspeakable [an'spi:kebl] adj.
niewypowiedziany; nie do

opisania
unspoiled [an'spojld] adj.
niezepsuty; nierozpieszczony
(dziecko)
unspoken ['an'spouken] adj. nie
mówiony (np. prawo)
unspoken-for [an'spoukn,fo:r]
adj. niezamówiony
unspoken-of [an'spoukn,ow] adj.
nie omawiany
unstable [an'stejbl] adj.
niepewny; chwiejny;
niezrównoważony
unsteady ['an'stedy] adj.
chwiejny; chwiejący się;
niezdecydowany;
nieustabilizowany; zmienny;
niepewny
unstressed ['an'strest] adj.
nieakcentowany;
niepodkreślony; nieobciążony
unsuccessful ['an-sek'sesful] adj.
nieudany; bez powodzenia;
nieudały; nie mający
powodzenia; bezowocny
unsuitable ['an'sju:tebl] adj.
niewłaściwy; niestosowny;
nieodpowiedni
unsure [an'szuer] adj. niepewny;
zawodny
unsurpassed ['an-ser'pa:st] adj.
nieprześcigniony;
niezrównany
unsuspected ['an-ses'pektyd]
adj. (zupełnie) niepodejrzany
unsuspecting ['an-ses'pektyng]
adj. niczego nie
podejrzewający
unsuspicious ['an-ses'pyszes]
adj. ufny; niepodejrzliwy
unthinkable ['an'tynkebl] adj. nie
do pomyślenia;
nieprawdopodobny
unthinking ['an'tynkyng] adj.
bezmyślny
untidy [an'tajdy] adj. niechlujny;
niestaranny; rozczochrany;
zaniedbany; nie posprzątany
untie [an'taj] v. rozwiązywać
(się); rozsupłać; uwalniać
(się) z więzów; usuwać
(trudności)
until [an'tyl] prep. & conj. do;

dotychczas; dopiero; aż
untimely [an'tajmly] adj. nie w
porę; przedwczesny; nie na
czasie; wczesny; adv.
przedwcześnie; w
nieodpowiedniej chwili
untiring [an'tajeryng] adj.
niezmordowany
unto ['antu:] prep. = to; do; ku;
aż do
untold [an'told] adj.
niewypowiedziany;
nieprzeliczony
untouchable [an'taczebl] adj.
niedotykalny
untouched [an'taczt] adj.
nietknięty; nieskazitelny;
nieczuły
untried [an'trajd] adj.
niewypróbowany
untroubled [an'trabld] adj.
spokojny; beztroski
untrue ['an'tru:] adj.
nieprawdziwy; fałszywy;
niewierny; sprzeniewierzający
się
untrustworthy [an'trast,łe:rzy]
adj. niegodny zaufania;
niepewny
untruth ['an'tru:s] s. nieprawda;
kłamstwo
unused ['an'ju:zd] adj. nie
używany; nie przyzwyczajony;
nie stosowany
unusual [an'ju:żuel] adj.
niezwykły; wyjątkowy
unutterable [an'aterebl] adj.
niewysłowiony;
niewypowiedziany
unvarying [an'weery-yng] adj.
jednostajny; nieurozmaicony;
nie zmieniający (się)
unvoiced [an'woist] adj.
bezgłośny; bezdźwięczny
unwanted [an'łontyd] adj.
niepożądany; niepotrzebny;
zbędny; zbyteczny
unwarranted ['an'łorentyd] adj.
nieusprawiedliwiony;
bezpodstawny
unwholesome ['an'houlsem] adj.
niezdrowy; szkodliwy
unwilling ['an'łylyng] adj.

niechętny

unwind ['an'łajnd] v. zob. wind;
rozwijać (się); odprężać
(się); (slang): odpoczywać
sobie

unwise ['an'łajz] adj. niemądry;
nieostrożny; nieroztropny

unworthy [an'łe:rzy] adj.
niegodny; niegodziwy;
niewart; niezasługujący;
ujemny

unwrap ['an'raep] v. rozwijać
(się); rozpakować; odsłonić
(się); odwijać (się)

unyielding ['an'ji:ldyng] adj.
nieustąpliwy; twardy;
nieugięty

up [ap] adv. do góry; w górę;
wzwyż; w górze; wyżej; na;
tam (gdzie); na górze;
wysoko; aż (do); aż (po); na
(piętro); pod (górę); v.
podnosić; zrywać się;
podbijać (cenę); zaczynać

up-and-about ['apend,e'baut]
exp.: (znowu) na nogach (po
chorobie)

up-and-coming ['ap,end'kamyng]
exp.: (slang): obiecujący;
rzutki; przedsiębiorczy
(człowiek)

up-and-doing ['ap,end'duyng]
exp.: (slang): czynny; ruchliwy

up-and-up ['ap,end'ap] v. być
uczciwym

up to ['ap,tu] adv. aż do

upbeat ['apbi:t] adj.
optymistyczny; pogodny

upbringing ['ap,bryngyng] s.
wychowanie; wychowywanie

uphill ['ap'hyl] adj. wznoszący
(się); stromy; trudny;
uciążliwy; adv. stromo; pod
górę; w górę

upholster [ap'houlster] v. obijać
(meble); wyściełać;
pokrywać; urządzać

upholsterer [ap'houlsterer] s.
tapicer; dekorator

upholstery [ap'houlstry] s.
tapicerstwo; meble
wyściełane

upkeep ['apki:p] s. utrzymanie;

koszty utrzymania

upmanship ['apmen,szyp] s.
wywyższanie się

upon [e'pon] prep. = on; na; po

upper ['aper] adj. wyższy; górny;
wierzchni; s. przyszwa

uppermost ['aper,moust] adj.
najwyższy; adv. na górze; na
górę

uppish ['apysz] adj. (slang):
zadzierający nos do góry

upright ['ap'rajt] adj.
wyprostowany; prosty;
uczciwy; prawy; adv.
pionowo; s. pionowy słup;
podpora; pianino; pozycja
pionowa

uprising [ap'rajzyng] s.
powstanie; wstawanie

uproar ['ap,ro:] s. zgiełk;
wrzawa; harmider; tumult

upset [ap'set] v. zob. set;
przewracać (się);
pokonywać; wzburzać;
rozstrajać; rozkuwać;
pogrubiać; skręcać;
rozklepywać; s. ['ap,set]
wywrócenie (się); porażka;
podniecenie; zaburzenie;
rozstrój; niepokój; bałagan;
sztanca do kucia

upside-down ['apsajd'dałn] adv.
do góry nogami; do góry
dnem; adj. odwrócony do góry
nogami

upstairs ['ap'steerz] adv. na
górę; na górze

upstart ['ap-sta:rt] s. parweniusz

upstream ['ap'stri:m] adv. pod
prąd; w górę rzeki

uptight ['ap'tajt] adj. (slang):
napięty; naprężony (nerwowo)

up-to-date ['ap-tu-'dejt] adj.
bieżący; nowoczesny

upwards ['apłerdz] adv. w górę;
ku górze; na wierzch; wyżej;
powyżej (czegoś)

uranium [ju'rejnjem] s. uran

urbane [e:r'bejn] adj. grzeczny;
układny; wytworny

urchin ['e:rczyn] s. ulicznik;
urwis; łobuz; smyk; jeżowiec;
jeżak; czesak

urge [e:rdż] v. poganiać;
popędzać; ponaglać;
przyśpieszać; nalegać;
pilić; namawiać; s.
pragnienie; impuls; tęsknota;
pociąg; bodziec
urge on ['e:rdż,on] v. namawiać
na coś
urgent ['e:rdżent] adj. pilny;
naglący; gwałtowny;
natarczywy; nalegający
urine ['jueryn] s. mocz; uryna
urn [e:rn] s. urna
usage ['ju:sydż] s. zwyczaj;
praktyka; obchodzenie (się);
używanie (zwrotów, języka
poprawnego)
use [ju:s] s. użytek; używanie;
użycie; posługiwanie;
zastosowanie; pożytek;
korzyść; zwyczaj; praktyka;
obrządek; przyzwyczajenie; v.
używać; korzystać;
wykorzystać; zużywać;
zużyć; wyczerpać;
traktować; obejść się;
mieć zwyczaj
used [ju:zd] adj. przyzwyczajony;
używany; stosowany
useful ['ju:sful] adj. użyteczny;
pożyteczny; dogodny;
wygodny; (slang): doskonały;
sprawny; biegły; zdolny
useless ['ju:zlys] adj.
niepotrzebny; bezużyteczny;
zbyteczny; bezcelowy;
nieużyteczny; do niczego
use up ['ju:z,ap] v. zużyć
(wszystko); wyczerpać (np.
pracą)
usher ['aszer] s. odźwierny;
woźny; bileter;
rozprowadzający na miejsca
(w kinie, w kościele etc.); v.
wprowadzać;
zapoczątkować
usher in ['aszer,yn] v.
wprowadzać do
usherette [,asze'ret] s. bileterka;
rozprowadzająca
usual ['ju:żuel] adj. zwykły;
zwyczajny; normalny;
zwyczajowy; utarty

usually ['ju:żuely] adv. zwykle;
zazwyczaj
usurer ['ju:żerer] s. lichwiarz
usurp [ju:ze:rp] v.
przywłaszczać sobie
usury ['ju:żery] s. lichwa
utensil [ju'tensyl] s. sprzęt;
naczynie; narzędzie
utility [ju'tylyty] s. pożytek;
użyteczność; firma
dostarczająca gaz,
elektryczność lub wodę
ludności w USA
utilize ['ju:tylajz] v. zużytkować;
spożytkować; wykorzystać
utmost ['atmoust] adj.
najwyższy; ostateczny;
skrajny; największy; najdalszy;
ostatni
utter ['ater] adj. całkowity;
zupełny; kompletny;
skończony; skrajny; ostatni;
v. wydawać (głos);
powiedzieć; wypowiedzieć
(hasło itp.); wyrażać;
wystawiać (czeki); podrabiać
(np. dokumenty); puszczać
(w obieg)
utterance ['aterens] s.
wypowiedź; wymowa;
wyrażenie; zeznanie;
oświadczenie
uvula ['ju:wjula] s. języczek
miękkiego podniebienia

V

v [wi:] dwudziesta druga litera
alfabetu angielskiego
vacancy ['wejkensy] s. wolne
mieszkanie; wolne pokoje
motelowe; wakans; próżnia;
pustka; bezczynność
vacant ['wejkent] adj. pusty;
próżny; wolny; wakujący;
bezczynny; bezmyślny;
obojętny
vacate [we'kejt] v. opróżniać;

opuszczać; unieważniać
vacation [we'kejszyn] s. wakacje
; ferie; opróżnienie; zwolnienie
(mieszkania); ewakuacja
vaccinate ['waeksynejt] v.
szczepić
vaccination ['waeksynejszyn] s.
szczepienie
vaccine ['waeksi:n] s.
szczepionka
vacuum ['waekjuem] s. próżnia
vacuum bottle ['waekjuem'botl]
s. termos
vacuum cleaner
['waekjuem'kli:ner] s.
odkurzacz
vacuum flask ['waekjuem,fla:sk]
s. termos
vagabond ['waegebond] adj.
włóczęgowski; wędrowny; s.
włóczęga; nierób; próżniak
vagary ['wejgery] s. kaprys;
chimera; wybryk; dziwactwo
vagina [we'dżajne] s. pochwa
(w anatomii kobiecej)
vague [wejg] adj. niejasny;
niewyraźny; nieokreślony;
nieuchwytny; wymijający;
niezdecydowany
vain [wejn] adj. próżny;
zarozumiały; czczy; pusty;
gołosłowny; daremny;
bezcelowy
valance ['waelens] s. krótka
podłużna zasłona (światła);
rodzaj adamaszku; frędzla;
lamberkin
vale ['wejl] s. dolina;
pożegnanie; excl.: żegnajcie!
valerian [we'lerjen] s. waleriana
valet ['waelyt] s. służący; v.
usługiwać
valiant ['waeljent] adj. dzielny; s.
zuch
valid ['waelyd] adj. słuszny;
ważny; uzasadniony
valley ['waely] s. dolina; koryto
fali; wewnętrzny kąt
płaszczyzn dachu
valor ['waeler] s. dzielność
valuable ['waeljuebl] adj.
wartościowy; cenny;
kosztowny; s. (pl.)

kosztowności; biżuteria
valuables ['waljuebls] pl.
kosztowności
valuation [,walju'ejszyn] s.
oszacowanie; cena
value ['waelju:] s. wartość;
cena; stopień jasności barwy
(w obrazie); v. szacować;
cenić; oceniać
valueless ['waelju:lys] adj.
bezwartościowy
valuer ['waelju:er] s. taksator
valve [waelw] s. zawór; wentyl;
klapa; zastawka
van [waen] s. kryty wóz
(ciężarowy); czoło armii; v.
przewozić krytym wozem;
badać rudę pukaniem
vane [wejn] s. chorągiewka (od
wiatru); łopatka śmigła;
brzechwa bomby; skrzydło
wiatraka
vanguard ['waen,ga:rd] s. straż
przednia; awangarda
vanilla [we'nyle] s. wanilia
vanish ['waenysz] v. znikać;
zanikać
vanity ['waenyty] s. próżność;
pycha; marność; czczość;
toaleta; źródło próżności;
rzecz bez wartości
vanity case ['waenyty,kejs] s.
kosmetyczka
vantage ['waentydż] s.
korzystna pozycja; przewaga
(w tenisie)
vapor ['wejper] s. para; mgła;
opary; v. parować
vaporize ['wejporajz] v.
wyparować; zamieniać się w
parę
vapor [wejpor] s. para; mgła; v.
parować; głędzić
vaporous ['wejperes] adj.
mglisty; zamglony
variable ['weerjebl] adj. zmienny;
niestały; s. zmienny wiatr
variance ['weerjens] s.
rozbieżność; niezgodność
variant ['weerjent] s. odmiana;
wariant; adj. odmienny; różny
variation [,weery'ejszyn] s.
zmiana; odmiana; wariant;

wariacja

varicose vein ['waerykous,wejn]
s. żylak

varied ['waeryd] adj. różnorodny;
różny; urozmaicony

variety [we'rajety] s.
rozmaitość; urozmaicenie;
różnorodność;
wielostronność; teatr
rozmaitości; kabaret; szereg;
odmiana

various ['weerjes] adj. różny;
rozmaity; urozmaicony; wiele;
kilka; kilkakrotnie

varnish ['wa:rnysz] s. pokost;
politura; werniks; polewa; v.
pokostować; werniksować

Varsovian [wa:r'souwjen] adj.
warszawski; s. warszawiak

vary ['weery] v. zmieniać (się);
urozmaicać; różnić się; nie
podzielać zdania

vase [wejz] s. waza; wazon

vat [waet] s. zbiornik; kadź;
cysterna

vault [wo:lt] s. sklepienie;
podziemie; piwnica;
grobowiec; skok o tyczce; v.
przesklepiać; osklepić;
przeskoczyć; skoczyć o
tyczce

vaulting horse ['wo:ltyng,ho:rs]
s. kozioł (przyrząd
gimnastyczny)

veal [wi:l] s. cielęcina

vegetable ['wedżytebl] s. jarzyna

vegetarian [,wedży'teerjen] adj.
jarski; s. jarosz; wegetarianin

vegetate ['wedżytejt] v.
wegetować; rosnąć

vehemence ['wi:ymens] s.
gwałtowność; porywczość;
wybuchowość

vehement ['wi:yment] adj.
gwałtowny; porywczy;
wybuchowy

vehicle ['wi:ykl] s. pojazd;
środek; narzędzie;
przymieszka do farby

veil [wejl] s. welon; woalka;
wstąpienie do klasztoru;
zasłona (maska); chrypka; v.
zasłaniać; ukrywać

vein [wejn] s. żyła (też złota);
usposobienie; natura; nastrój;
wena; v. żyłkować

velocity [wy'losyty] s.
szybkość

velvet ['welwyt] s. aksamit;
delikatna skórka; (slang):
zarobek; forsa; adj. aksamitny

venal ['wi:nl] adj. sprzedajny

vend [wend] v. sprzedawać

vender ['wender] s. (uliczny)
sprzedawca; automat do
sprzedaży

vending machine
['wendyng,me'szi:n] s.
automat do sprzedaży

venerable ['wenerebl] adj.
czcigodny; wielebny

venerate ['wenerejt] v. czcić

venereal [wy'njerjel] adj.
weneryczny; chory
wenerycznie;
przeciwweneryczny; płciowy

Venetian blind
[wy'ni:szyn,blajnd]
s. żaluzja (wenecka)

vengeance ['wendżens] s.
zemsta; pomsta

venison ['wenzn] s. dziczyzna

venom ['wenem] s. jad

venomous ['wenemes] adj.
jadowity

vent [went] s. odwietrznik;
wentyl; otwór wentylacyjny;
rozcięcie w tyle marynarki;
ujście; upust; v. dawać
upust czemuś;
wyładowywać (złość);
rozgłaszać; wietrzyć;
wiercić otwór wentylacyjny

ventilate ['wentylejt] v.
wentylować; wietrzyć;
przedyskutować

ventilator ['wentylejtor] s.
wentylator; wietrznik

ventriloquist [wen'trylokłyst] s.
brzuchomówca

venture ['wenczer] s. ryzyko;
stawka; spekulacja; impreza;
interes; próba; v. odważać
się; ośmielać się;
ryzykować; śmieć; narazić
się

veranda [we'raende] s. weranda
verb [we:rb] s. czasownik; słowo
verbal ['we:rbel] adj. ustny;
słowny; werbalny;
czasownikowy
verbatim [wer'bejtym] adj.
dosłowny; adv. dosłownie
verdict ['we:rdykt] s. wyrok;
werdykt; osąd; orzeczenie
verdure ['we:rdżer] s. zieleń
verge ['we:rdż] s. skraj; brzeg;
krawędź; v. graniczyć;
zbliżać się; chylić się;
skłaniać się
verge on ['we:rdż,on] v.
graniczyć
verification [,weryfy'kejszyn] s.
uwierzytelnienie; sprawdzenie
verify ['weryfaj] v. sprawdzać;
potwierdzać; udowadniać
vermicelli [we:rmy'sely] s. cienki
makaron
vermiform appendix
[we:rmy'fo:rme'pendyks] s.
ślepa kiszka; wyrostek
robaczkowy
vermin ['we:rmyn] s. robactwo;
świat przestępczy
vernacular [we:r'naekjuler] adj.
rodzimy; miejscowy; krajowy;
s. gwara; język rodzinny;
dosadne powiedzenie
versatile ['we:rsetail] adj.
wszechstronny
verse [we:rs] s. wiersz; strofa
versed ['we:rst] adj.
doświadczony; wprawiony (w
czymś)
version ['we:rżyn] s. wersja;
przekład; przekręcenie macicy
vertebra ['we:rtybre] s. krąg
vertebrae ['we:rtybri:] pl. kręgi
vertical ['we:rtykel] adj.
pionowy; szczytowy; s.
pionowa płaszczyzna; linia
very ['wery] adv. bardzo;
absolutnie; zaraz; właśnie;
adj. prawdziwy; sam;
skończony (drań)
vessel ['wesl] s. naczynie;
pojemnik; statek; okręt
vest [west] s. kamizelka; v.
nadawać; przekazać;

przysługiwać komuś;
przypadać komuś; odziewać
w szaty; przykrywać ołtarz
vestry ['westry] s. zakrystia
vet ['wet] s. weterynarz
veteran ['weteran] s. weteran
veterinary ['weterynery] s.
weterynarz
veto ['wi:tou] s. weto; v.
zakładać weto
vex [weks] v. złościć;
dręczyć; dokuczać
vexation [wek'sejszyn] s.
dokuczanie; drażnienie;
zniecierpliwienie; irytacja;
udręka; przykrość;
zaniepokojenie
vexatious [wek'sejszes] adj.
dokuczliwy; irytujący; przykry;
nieznośny
via ['waje] prep. przez; via
vibrate [waj'brejt] v. zadrgać;
zadrżeć; oscylować;
wprawiać w drganie lub ruch
wahadłowy
vibration [waj'brejszyn] s.
drganie; drżenie; wibracja;
oscylacja; ruch wahadłowy
vibrator [waj'brejter] s. wibrator;
oscylator
vibratory [waj'bretery] adj.
wibracyjny; drganiowy;
drgający; migocący
vicar ['wyker] s. wikary;
wikariusz; zastępca;
namiestnik
vice [wajs] imadło; zacisk;
rozpusta; występek; nałóg;
narów; wada; zastępca; v.
zaciskać w imadle
vice-president ['wajs'prezydent]
s. wiceprzewodniczący;
wiceprezydent
vice versa ['wajsy'we:rsa] adv.
odwrotnie
vicinity [wy'synyty] s.
sąsiedztwo; pobliże
vicious ['wy'szes] adj. błędny;
występny; złośliwy; wadliwy;
zepsuty; dokuczliwy;
narowisty; rozpustny
victim ['wyktym] s. ofiara
victor ['wykter] s. zwycięzca

victorian [wyk'to:rjan] adj.
wiktoriański

victorious [wyk'to:rjes] adj.
zwycięski

victory ['wyktery] s. zwycięstwo

victuals ['wytlz] s. żywność;
jedzenie; prowianty; wiktuały

video ['wydjou] s. telewizja; adj.
telewizyjny

video-tape ['wydi:ou,tejp] s.
taśma magnetowidowa; v.
nagrać (obraz i dźwięk) na
taśmie

vie [waj] v. współzawodniczyć;
rywalizować; współubiegać
się

view [wju:] v. oglądać;
rozpatrywać; zbadać;
zapatrywać się; s. obejrzenie;
spojrzenie; wizja; zasięg
wzroku; widok; przegląd
umysłowy; pogląd;
zapatrywanie; intencja; zamiar;
cel; ocena

viewer ['wju:er] s. widz
(telewizyjny etc.)

view-finder ['wju:,fajnder] s.
wizjer

viewpoint ['wju:,pojnt] s. punkt
widzenia; zapatrywanie

vigil ['wydżyl] s. czuwanie;
wigilia

vigilance ['wydżylens] s.
czujność; bezsenność

vigilant ['wydżylent] adj. czujny

vigor ['wyger] s. krzepkość;
tężyzna; rześkość; energia;
siła; moc

vigorous ['wygeres] adj. krzepki;
mocny; jędrny; energiczny

vile [wajl] adj. podły; nędzny;
marny

vilify ['wyly,faj] v. oczerniać;
obmawiać

village ['wylydż] s. wieś

villager ['wylydżer] s. wieśniak
(raczej nieokrzesany)

villain ['wylen] s. łajdak; łotr;
nikczemnik; łobuziak

villainous ['wylenes] adj. łajdacki;
niegodziwy

villainy ['wyleny] s. łajdactwo

vim [wym] s. tężyzna

vincible ['wynsybl] adj.
przezwyciężalny

vindicate ['wyndykejt] v.
oczyszczać z zarzutu,
oskarżenia, podejrzenia;
rehabilitować;
usprawiedliwiać; bronić;
dochodzić; dowodzić

vindication [,wyndy'kejszyn] s.
obrona; windykacja;
usprawiedliwienie;
oczyszczenie się (z zarzutu);
rehabilitacja

vindictive [wyn'dyktyw] adj.
mściwy; karzący

vine [wajn] s. winna latorośl;
winorośl

vinegar ['wynyger] s. ocet; v.
kwasić

vineyard ['wynjerd] s. winnica

vintage ['wyntydż] s. rocznik
wina; winobranie; robienie
wina; model (roczny)

violate ['wajelejt] v. gwałcić;
zgwałcić (kobietę)

violation [,waje'lejszyn] s.
pogwałcenie; zgwałcenie;
gwałt; zbezczeszczenie;
naruszenie (też praw ruchu)

violence ['wajelens] s.
gwałtowność; gwałt;
przemoc

violent ['wajelent] adj.
gwałtowny; niepohamowany;
wściekły

violet ['wajelyt] s. fiołek; adj.
fioletowy (np. promień)

violin [,waje'lyn] s. skrzypce

violinist [,waje'lynyst] s.
skrzypek

viper ['wajper] s. żmija

virgin ['we:rdżyn] s. dziewica

virginity [we:r'dżynyty] s.
dziewictwo

virile ['wyrajl] adj. męski

virility [wy'rylyty] s. męskość;
wiek męski; cechy męskie

virtual ['we:rczuel] adj.
zasadniczy; właściwy;
faktyczny; prawdziwy;
rzeczywisty

virtually ['we:rczuely] adv.
rzeczywiście; faktycznie;

praktycznie biorąc
virtue ['we:rczju:] s. cnota;
prawość; czystość;
skuteczność; siła; moc
virtuoso [,we:rczju'ouzou] s.
wirtuoz; miłośnik-znawca
sztuki
virtuous [,we:rczjues] adj.
cnotliwy; prawy
virulent ['wyrulent] adj. jadowity;
złośliwy; zjadliwy
virus ['wajeres] s. wirus; jad
(chorobowy)
visa ['wi:za] s. wiza; v.
wizować
viscosity [wys'kosyty] s.
lepkość; kleistość
visibility [wyzy'bylyty] s.
widoczność
visible [wyzybl] adj. widoczny;
wyraźny; widzialny
vision ['wyżyn] s. widzenie;
wzrok; wizja; dar
przewidywania; v. okazywać
wizję; mieć wizję
visit ['wyzyt] v. odwiedzać;
wizytować; zwiedzać;
nawiedzać; karać; udzielać
się; gawędzić; s. wizyta;
odwiedziny; pobyt
visitor ['wyzyter] s. gość;
przyjezdny; zwiedzający;
inspektor
vista ['wysta] s. perspektywa;
wizja; widok
visual ['wyżjuel] adj. wzrokowy;
optyczny
visualize ['wyżjuelajz] v.
wyobrażać sobie;
uwidaczniać; uzmysławiać
vital ['wajtl] adj. witalny;
życiowy; żywotny;
zasadniczy; śmiertelny
vitality [waj'taelyty] s.
żywotność; żywość
vitamin ['wajtemyn] s. witamina
vivacious [wy'wejszes] adj.
żywy
vivacity [wy'waesyty] s.
żywość
vivid ['wywyd] adj. żywy
vivify ['wywyfaj] v. ożywiać
vivisection ['wywysekszyn] s.

wiwisekcja
vixen ['wyksen] s. liszka; lisica;
jędza
vixenish ['wyksenysz] adj.
jędzowaty
vocabulary [wou'kaebjulery] s.
słownik (specjalny);
słownictwo
vocal ['woukel] s. samogłoska;
adj. głosowy; wokalny;
głośny; natarczywy
vocalist ['woukelyst] s.
śpiewak; wokalista
vocation [wou'kejszyn] s.
zawód; zamiłowanie;
powołanie; skłonność
vodka ['wodke] s. wódka
vogue [woug] s. moda;
popularność
voice [wois] s. głos; dźwięk
samogłoskowy; strona
(czasownika); v. wymawiać;
wyrażać; dawać wyraz
czemuś; wymawiać
dźwięcznie; udźwięczniać;
pisać partie głosowe do
muzyki; stroić
void [woid] s. próżnia; pustka;
adj. próżny; pusty;
pozbawiony czegoś; wolny
od czegoś; wakujący;
nieważny; v. unieważniać;
wydalać; wypróżniać (się);
oddawać (mocz)
void of ['woid,ow] exp.: bez
volatile ['woletyl] adj. lotny;
ulatniający się; zmienny
volcano [wol'kejnou] s. wulkan
volley ['woly] s. salwa; potok;
odbicie (piłki); wolej; v. dać
salwę; wypuszczać salwę;
podawać wolejem; miotać
potokiem (przekleństw);
lecieć salwą; odbijać w locie
volleyball ['woly,bo:l] s.
siatkówka
volt [woult] s. wolt (elektr.);
wolta; v. robić woltę
voltage ['woultydż] s. napięcie
prądu; woltaż
voluble ['woljubl] adj. gładki;
potoczysty; ze swadą
volume ['wolju:m] s. tom;

objętość; masa; ilość;
pojemność; rozmiar; siła
voluntary ['wolentery] adj.
ochotniczy; dobrowolny; wolą
kontrolowany; spontaniczny;
samorzutny; s. specjalny
wyczyn z wyboru sportowca;
gra solo na organie
volunteer ['wolentier] s. ochotnik
(bezpłatnie pracujący); v.
robić z własnej ochoty;
zgłaszać się na ochotnika;
podejmować coś
dobrowolnie; być ochotnikiem
voluptuous [we'lapczues] adj.
zmysłowy; lubieżny
vomit ['womyt] v. wymiotować;
wyrzucać; pobudzać do
wymiotów; s. wymioty;
środek wymiotny
voodoo ['wu:du:] s. wiara w
czary; czarownik; v.
zaczarować
voracious [we'rejszes] adj.
żarłoczny
voracity [we'raesyty] s.
żarłoczność
vote [wout] s. głos; głosy;
głosowanie; prawo
głosowania; uchwała; wotum
(zaufania); v. głosować;
uchwalać; orzekać;
uznawać powszechnie za
coś
vote down ['wout,dałn] v.
odrzucać w głosowaniu
voting paper ['woutyng'pejper] s.
kartka wyborcza
vouch [waucz] v. ręczyć;
gwarantować; potwierdzać;
zapewnić
voucher ['wauczer] s. dowód
kasowy
vouch for ['waucz,fo:r] v.
ręczyć za kogoś
vouchsafe [waucz'sejf] v.
(łaskawie) raczyć
vow [wau] s. ślub (też
zakonny); przymierze; v.
przysięgać; ślubować;
składać śluby
vowel ['wałel] s. samogłoska
voyage ['wojydż] s. podróż

(statkiem)
voyager ['wojedżer] s. podróżnik
vulcanize ['walkenajz] s.
wulkanizować
vulgar ['walger] adj. ordynarny;
wulgarny; prostacki; gminny;
pospolity; powszechny
vulgarity [wal'gaeryty] s.
wulgarność; wyrażenie
wulgarne
vulnerability [,walnere'bylyty] s.
podatność na zranienie;
wrażliwość na ciosy;
słabość; słaby punkt
vulnerable ['walnerebl] adj.
czuły; wrażliwy; mający słabe
miejsce; narażony na cios;
podatny na zranienie;
niezabezpieczony
vulpine ['walpajn] adj. lisi;
przebiegły; chytry
vulture ['walczer] s. sęp; (slang):
szakal
vying ['wajyn] s. rywalizacja,
współzawodnictwo adj.
współzawodniczący (od
czasownika vie)

W

w ['dablju:] dwudziesta trzecia
litera alfabetu angielskiego
wack [łaek] s. (slang); oryginał;
dziwak; ekscentryk
wacky ['łaeky] adj. (slang):
zwariowany; zdziwaczały;
nieobliczalny
wad [łod] s. tampon; wałek
(zwinięty); wata (w uszach);
przybitka naboju w strzelbie;
(slang): forsa; plik
(banknotów); v. zatykać
(tamponem); watować;
przybijać (nabój); wypychać;
zwijać w wałek
wade [łejd] v. brodzić, brnąć,
przechodzić w bród, torować
sobie drogę

wadding ['łodyng] s. watowanie;
watolina; wata; wełna (do
utykania); podkład; przybitka
waddle ['łodl] v. chodzić
kołysząc się w biodrze jak
kaczka; s. kaczy krok
wade [łejd] v. brodzić; brnąć;
przechodzić w bród; s.
brodzenie
wafer ['łejfer] s. wafel; opłatek;
naklejka urzędowa
(pieczątkowa);
zapieczętowywać naklejką
waffle ['łofl] s. wafel z ciasta
naleśnikowego
waft ['łaeft] v. popychać
(lekko); posuwać; posyłać
(całusa); przepędzać; unosić
(w powietrzu); s. śmignięcie
skrzydła; powiew; podmuch;
tchnienie; przelotne uczucie;
smuga (światła)
wag [łaeg] v. kiwać (ogonem);
poruszać się; wahać się;
chodzić tam i z powrotem;
merdać
wage [łejdż] s. płaca; zarobek;
zapłata; v. prowadzić (np.
wojnę)
wage earner ['łejdż,e:rner] s.
człowiek zarobkujący
wages ['łejdżyz] s. zapłata
wager ['łejdżer] s. zakład; v.
zakładać się o coś
wagon ['łaegen] s. ciężki wóz
(kryty); lora; wóz policyjny;
furgon
wail [łejl] v. zawodzić;
lamentować; opłakiwać; v.
zawodzenie; lament; płacz
wainscot ['łejnsket] s. boazeria;
ozdobne obicie ścian
drzewem
waist [łejst] s. talia; stan; pas;
kibić; stanik; śródokręcie;
zwężenie
waistcoat ['łeistkout] s.
kamizelka
waist-deep ['łejst,di:p] adj. adv.
po pas
wait [łejt] v. czekać;
oczekiwać; czyhać;
czatować; czaić się;

obsłużyć; obsługiwać
kogoś; s. czekanie;
oczekiwanie; zasadzka; czaty
wait on ['łejt,on] v. czekać na;
usługiwać komuś
waiter ['łejter] s. kelner
wait on ['łejton] v. obsługiwać
waiting [łejtyng] s. czekanie;
oczekiwanie; wyczekiwanie;
zasadzka
waiting list [łejtyng,łyst] s. lista
kolejności (kandydatów,
klientów)
waiting room [łejtynrum] s.
poczekalnia
waitings [łejtyns] pl. kolędnicy
waitress [łejtryss] s. kelnerka
wake; woke; woken [łejk; łouk;
łoukn]
wake [łejk] v. obudzić (się); nie
spać; pobudzić; rozbudzić;
wzbudzić; wskrzesić;
czuwać przy (zwłokach); s.
niespanie; czuwanie przy
zwłokach; kilwater; fala w
ślad za statkiem
(motorówką); ślad (po kimś,
po czymś)
wake up ['łejk,ap] v. obudzić
(się); ocknąć się;
oprzytomnieć; zdawać sobie
sprawę; zbudzić
wakeful ['łejkful] adj. czuwający;
bezsenny; czujny
waken ['łejkn] = woken [łouken]
v. zob. wake
waken ['łejkn] v. zbudzić;
obudzić; ożywiać;
wzbudzić; wskrzesić (np.
zmarłego)
walk [ło:k] v. iść; przechadzać
się; chodzić; kroczyć; iść
stępa; jechać stępa; wejść;
zejść; s. chód; krok;
przechadzka; spacer; marsz;
deptak; aleja; odległość
przebyta
walk about ['ło:ke,baut] v.
włóczyć się; łazić
walk along ['ło:ke,long] v.
chodzić sobie
walk away ['ło:ke,łej] v.
odchodzić; (w zawodach):

łatwo wygrywać
walk back ['ło:k,baek] v.
wracać
walk down ['ło:k,dałn] v.
schodzić
walk in ['ło:k,yn] v. wchodzić
walk off ['ło:k,of] v. odchodzić;
zniknąć; ulotnić się (z
czymś)
walk out ['ło:k,aut] v. wyjść;
opuścić
walk over ['ło:k,ouwer] v.
wygrywać łatwo; traktować
pogardliwie
walk up ['ło:k,ap] v. podejść;
wejść na górę
walker ['ło:ker] s. piechur
walkie-talkie ['ło:ky-'to:ky] s.
przenośny, mały odbiornik-
nadajnik radiowy
walking [ło:kyng] s. chodzenie;
marsz; wycieczka piesza; adj.
chodzący; wędrowny
walking papers ['ło:kyn'pejpers]
pl. zwolnienie z pracy na
piśmie
walking stick ['ło:kyng,styk] s.
laska
walking-tour ['ło:kyng,tu:r] s.
wycieczka piesza; zwiedzanie
piechotą
walk-out ['ło:kaut] s. strajk
walk-over ['ło:kouwer] s.
walkower (sport)
wall [ło:l] s. ściana; mur;
przepierzenie; wał; v.
obmurować
wall in ['ło:l,yn] v. otaczać
wall up ['ło:l,ap] v. zamurować
wallboard ['ło:l,bo:rd] s. licówka
(ściany)
wallet ['łolyt] s. portfel
wallop ['łolep] v. walić; łoić;
prać; pobić na głowę;
galopować; łazić ciężko i
niezgrabnie; s. wyrżnięcie
(cios); galop; ruch ciężki i
niezgrabny
wallow ['łolou] v. tarzać się;
kłębić się; kołysać się; s.
tarzanie się
wallpaper ['łol,pejper] s. tapety;
v. tapetować

Wall Street ['łolstri:t] s. ośrodek
finansowy (USA)
walnut ['ło:lnat] s. orzech włoski
walrus ['ło:lres] s. mors
waltz ['ło:ls] s. walc; v.
tańczyć walca; (slang):
ruszać się żwawo
wan [łon] adj. blady; wybladły;
blednąć
wand [łond] s. laseczka;
pałeczka; prąt; buława
wander ['łonder] v. wędrować;
błądzić; błąkać się
wanderer ['łonderer] s.
wędrowiec
wane [łejn] v. zanikać; gasnąć;
s. zanik
wangle ['łaengl] v. (slang):
wycyganić; wyłudzić;
sfałszować; s. krętactwo;
kant
want [ło:nt] s. brak; potrzeba;
niedostatek; niedopatrzenie;
bieda; nędza; v. pragnąć;
chcieć; brakować;
potrzebować; pożądać
want ad [ło:nt, aed] s. drobne
ogłoszenie
want of food [ło:nt ow fu:d] s.
niedożywienie
want in ['o:nt,yn] v. chcieć
wejść
want out ['ło:nt,ałt] v. chcieć
wyjść
wanted ['ło:ntyd] adj.
poszukiwany
wanting ['ło:ntyng] adj.
brakujący; kiepski;
niedokładny; pozbawiony; nie
na poziomie; słaby na
umyśle; prep. bez; mniej;
przy braku
wanton ['łonten] adj. złośliwy;
krzywdzący; bez powodu;
bezmyślny; samowolny;
bezczelny; nieokiełznany;
wyuzdany; lubieżny; bujny;
zbytkowny; s. lubieżnik;
lubieżnica; v. oddawać się
rozpuście; używać sobie;
swawolić; róść bujnie;
trwonić; psocić; figlować;
bawić się

war [łor] s. wojna; v. wojować;
zawojować
warble ['łorbl] v. nucić;
jodłować; s. nucący głos;
nucona pieśń; guz od siodła
na grzbiecie konia; guz
wywołany larwą gza
bydlęcego
ward [ło:rd] s. dzielnica; cela;
sala; oddział; podopieczny;
opieka; kuratela; postawa
obronna; parada; straż; v.
odparowywać (cios);
odsuwać
(niebezpieczeństwo);
umieszczać na oddziale
ward off ['ło:rd,of] v.
odparowywać cios; odsuwać
(zagrożenie)
warden ['ło:rdn] s. dyrektor
więzienia; dozorca; nadzorca;
gatunek twardej gruszki
warder ['ło:rder] s. strażnik
więzienny; posterunek;
buława
ward heeler ['ło:rd,hi:ler] s.
naganiacz partyjny
wardrobe ['ło:droub] s.
garderoba; szafa na ubranie
ware [łeer] s. towar; wyrób;
ceramika; v. uwaga na coś;
trzymać się z dala od
czegoś; excl.: strzeż się!
warehouse ['łeerhaus] s.
magazyn; składnica; dom
składowy; v. magazynować;
składować
warlike ['ło:,lajk] adj.
wojowniczy, wojenny
warm [ło:rm] adj. ciepły; świeży
(trop); bliski znalezienia;
zadomowiony (na posadzie);
zamożny
warm up ['ło:rm,ap] v. ożywiać
(się); podgrzewać (się);
ogrzewać (się); rozgrzewać
(się)
warmup ['ło:rmap] ćwiczenia
rozluźniające (przed
zawodami etc.); zagrzanie się
warmth ['ło:rms] s. ciepło;
serdeczność; zapał
warn [ło:rn] v. ostrzegać;

przypominać; wzywać;
zapowiadać; uprzedzać
warn against [ło:negejnst] v.
ostrzegać przed czymś
warning ['ło:rnyng] adj.
ostrzegawczy; s. ostrzeżenie;
przestroga; znak
ostrzegawczy; wypowiedzenie
(posady)
warp ['ło:rp] v. wypaczyć (się);
zwichrować (się); wykrzywić
(się); spaczyć (się);
przyholowywać do miejsca
utwierdzenia liny lub
łańcucha; użyźniać (przez
zalewanie osadem); s.
spaczenie; wypaczenie;
osnowa; szew skośny; lina
holownicza; osad
warrant ['łorent] v.
usprawiedliwiać; uzasadniać;
gwarantować; s.
upoważnienie; gwarancja;
nakaz prawny (aresztu, rewizji
etc.); pełnomocnictwo dla
adwokatów; patent starszego
podoficera (USA)
warranty ['łorenty] s. gwarancja;
poręka; rękojmia; podstawa;
usprawiedliwienie;
upoważnienie; dokument
sądowy
warren ['ło:ryn] s. królikarnia
warrior ['ło:rjor] s. wojownik;
żołnierz; adj. wojowniczy
wart [ło:rt] s. brodawka;
kurzawka
wary ['łeery] adj. ostrożny
was [łoz] v. zob. be
wash [ło:sz] v. myć (się); prać
(się); oczyszczać; zraszać;
lekko barwić; lawować;
umyć się; sunąć; płynąć z
pluskiem; płukać (rudę); s.
mycie; pranie; płyn
(czyszczący); fale; plusk;
pomyje; lura; wypłukane
miejsce w ziemi; głędzenie;
zaburzenie wody za statkiem;
zaburzenie powietrza za
samolotem; ziemia na tacy
zawierająca złoto;
podmywanie przez fale;

mielizna; kanał wyżłobiony
przez wodę; mielizna
naniesiona wodą; ławowanie;
cienka warstwa metalu;
kilwater; ślad wodny
wash away [ło:sze,łej] v.
spłukać; zmyć; unosić
wash down ['ło:sz,dałn] v.
zmywać strumieniem wody;
popić jedzenie
wash off [ło:sz,of] v. odeprać;
wymywać
wash out ['ło:sz,aut] v.
wupłukiwać (się) (z pieniędzy
etc.)
wash up ['ło:sz,ap] v. zmywać
naczynia; wymyć się
wash and wear ['ło:sz,end'łeer]
s. bielizna i odzież gotowa do
noszenia po praniu bez
prasowania
washbowl ['ło:sz,boul] s.
miednica; umywalka;
umywalnia
washcloth ['ło:sz,klos] s.
zmywak; szmatka do
zmywania
washer ['ło:szer] s. uszczelka;
podkładka; maszyna do prania
washing ['łoszyng] s. mycie;
pranie; przemywanie; woda z
prania; popłuczyny; wypłukane
złoto; wypłukany żwir; bielizna
do prania
washing machine
['ło:szyng,me'szi:n] s. pralka;
maszyna do prania
washing powder ['ło:szyn'pałder]
s. proszek do prania
washing up ['ło:szyng,ap] v.
obmycie się
wash-leather ['ło:sz,ledzer] s.
ircha; zamsz
washout ['ło:szaut] s.
zapadnięcie się; podmycie;
(slang): klapa; niepowodzenie
washtub ['ło:sztab] s. balia
washy ['ło:szy] adj. wodnisty;
rzadki; blady; cienki;
wypłowiały
wasn't = was not
wasp [łosp] s. osa; (slang): biały
-anglosaksonin-protestant

waspish ['łospysz] adj. zjadliwy;
cienki w pasie (jak osa)
wastage ['łejstydż] s. strata;
zużycie
waste [łejst] adj. pustynny;
pusty; nieużyty (ziemia);
opustoszały; wyludniony;
leżący odłogiem; zużyty;
niepotrzebny; zbyteczny;
odpadowy; v. pustoszyć;
psuć; niszczyć (się); stracić
(też zabić); zmarnować;
ginąć; zużywać (się);
zapuścić; zaniedbać; s.
pustynia; marnowanie;
trwonienie; zniszczenie;
ubytek; zużycie; odpady;
bezmiar (np. wody);
zaniedbanie; marnotrawstwo
waste away ['łejst,e'łej] v.
marnieć
wasteful ['łejstful] adj. rozrzutny;
marnotrawny
wastepaper basket ['łejst-pejper
-ba:skyt] s. kosz na śmieci
waste pipe ['łejstpajp] s. rura
odpływowa; rura ściekowa
watch [ło:cz] s. czuwanie;
pilnowanie; czaty; czujność;
wachta; zegarek; oczekiwanie
na coś; wyglądanie czegoś;
v. czuwać; oczekiwać;
czatować; pilnować;
opiekować się; uważać;
mieć na oku; mieć się na
baczności; wyglądać
czegoś; obserwować;
szpiegować; przyglądać się;
patrzyć; oczekiwać
sposobności; śledzić
watch out ['ło:czaut] v.
uważać; strzec się; uwagal;
uważajl
watchdog ['ło:czdog] s. pies
podwórzowy
watchful ['ło:czful] adj. czujny;
baczny
watchmaker ['ło:cz,mejker] s.
zegarmistrz
watchman ['ło:czmen] s. stróż;
dozorca
watchtower ['ło:cz,tauer] s.
stażnica; wieża strażnicza

watchword ['ło:człe:rd] s. hasło;
slogan
watch your step ['ło:cz,jo:r'step]
exp.: uważaj!; pilnuj się!
water [ło:ter] s. woda; wysięk;
przypływ; odpływ; pl. zdrój;
wody lecznicze; ocean; morze;
jezioro; rzeka; v. polewać;
podlewać; pokropić; poić;
iść do wodopoju;
nawadniać; rozwadniać;
rozcieńczać; skrapiać;
łzawić się; ślinić się
water blister ['ło:ter,blyster] s.
pęcherzyk z wodą
waterborne ['ło:ter,born] adj.
przenoszony lub przekazywany
przez wodę
water anchor [ło:ter'aenker] s.
kotwica dryfująca
water bottle ['ło:ter,botl] s.
karafka; manierka
water brush ['ło:ter,brasz] s.
zgaga
water but ['ło:ter,bat] s. zbiornik
na deszczówkę
water cart ['ło:ter,ka:rt] s.
beczkowóz
water closet ['ło:ter'klozet] s.
ustęp
watercolor ['ło:ter'kaler] s.
akwarela
water cool ['ło:ter,ku:l] v.
chłodzić wodą
watercourse ['ło:ter,ko:rs] s.
strumień; rzeka; kanał
watercress ['ło:ter,kres] s.
rzeżucha wodna
water cure ['ło:ter,kjuer] s.
kuracja wodna
water dog ['ło:ter,dog] s. pies
myśliwski aportujący z wody;
(slang): amator pływania etc.
water down [ło:ter,dałn] v.
rozwadniać
waterfall ['ło:ter,fo:l] s.
wodospad
waterfowl ['ło:ter,faul] s.
ptactwo wodne
waterfront ['ło:ter,frant] s.
wybrzeże; doki; dzielnica
portowa
water-gap ['ło:ter,gaep] s.

przełom rzeki
watergate ['ło:ter,gejt] s. śluza
water-gauge ['ło:ter,gejdż] s.
wodowskaz; licznik wodny
water glass ['ło:ter,gla:s] s.
szklanka; naczynie; kubek;
szklany wodowskaz;
przeziernik podwodny
water hammer ['ło:ter,haemer] s.
silny wstrząs wywołany
nagłym zatrzymaniem wody w
rurze
water hen ['ło:ter,hen] s. kurka
wodna
water hole ['ło:terhol] s. stojąca
woda (w suchym łożysku
rzeki); wodopój
water ice ['ło:ter,ajs] s. sorbet
watering place ['ło:teryngplejs] s.
wodopój; kąpielisko;
zdrojowisko
waterless ['ło:terlys] adj.
bezwodny; pozbawiony wody
water level ['ło:ter'lewl] s.
poziom wody
water lily ['ło:ter,lyly] s.
grzybień biały; lilia wodna
waterline ['ło:terlajn] s. linia
zanurzenia statku
waterlogged ['ło:ter,logd] adj.
przesycony wodą
water main ['ło:ter,mejn] s.
główna rura wodociągów
water-man ['ło:termen] s.
przewoźnik; wioślarz
watermark ['ło:terma:rk] s. znak
wodny; wodowskaz; v. robić
znak wodny
watermelon ['ło:ter,melen] s.
arbuz; kawon
water meter ['ło:ter'mi:ter] s.
wodomierz; licznik wodny
water mill ['ło:ter,myl] s. młyn
water moccasin ['ło:ter,mokesyn]
s. żmija wodna w USA
water motor ['ło:ter'mouter] s.
motor wodny
water plane ['ło:ter'plejn] s.
hydroplan
waterpower ['ło:ter'pałer] s. siła
wodna; prawo do używania
wody
water pot ['ło:ter,pot] s.

konewka; polewaczka
waterproof ['ło:ter,pru:f] adj.
  nieprzemakalny; v. robić
  nieprzemakalnym
water-rat ['ło:ter,raet] s. szczur
  wodny
water rate ['ło:ter,rejt] s. opłata
  za wodę; cena wody
water scape ['ło:ter,skejp] s.
  krajobraz morski
watershed ['ło:ter,szed] s. dział
  wodny; (slang): ważna granica
water-ski ['ło:ter,ski:] s. narta
  wodna
water spout ['ło:ter,spaut] s.
  trąba wodna; rynna pionowa
water supply ['ło:terse,plaj] s.
  zaopatrzenie w wodę; sieć
  wodociągowa
water table ['ło:ter,tejbl] s.
  poziom (w ziemi) wody
  zaskórnej
watertight ['ło:ter,tajt] adj.
  wodoszczelny
water tower ['łoter,tauer] s.
  wieża ciśnień
water wave ['ło:ter,łejw] s.
  ondulacja wodna
waterway ['ło:ter,łej] s. droga
  wodna; kanał; rzeka spławna
waterwheel ['ło:ter,hłi:l] s. koło
  (młyńskie) wodne
water witch ['ło:ter,łycz] s.
  różdżkarz
waterworks ['ło:ter,łe:rks] s.
  wodociągi; fontanna
watery ['ło:tery] adj. wodnisty;
  załzawiony; śliniący się;
  wróżący deszcz
watt [łot] s. (electr.) wat
waul [ło:l] miauczeć ostro i
  przeciągle (Brit.)
wave [łejw] s. fala; falistość;
  ondulacja; pokiwanie ręką;
  gest ręką; v. falować;
  ondulować; machać do
  kogoś
wave away ['łejwe'łej] v.
  odprawiać machnięciem ręki
wave back ['łejw,baek] v.
  przywoływać (z powrotem)
  machnięciem ręki
wavelength ['łejw,lenks] s.

długość fali
wave meter ['łejwmi:ter] s.
  falomierz
waver ['łejwer] v. zachwiać
  (się); zamigotać; być
  niezdecydowanym;
  załamywać się; drżeć;
  zawahać się; kołysać się;
  trzepotać się; s. chwianie
  (się)
wavy ['łejwy] adj. falisty;
  sfalowany; drżący; migocący;
  karbowany
wawl ['ło:l] v. wrzeszczeć jak
  kot (Brit.)
wax [łaeks] s. wosk; adj.
  woskowy; v. woskować;
  stawać się
waxen ['łaeksn] adj. woskowy;
  miękki jak wosk
wax paper ['łaeks'pejper] s.
  papier woskowy
waxwork ['łaeksłe:rk] s. figura
  woskowa; v. modelować z
  wosku
waxy ['łaeksy] adj. woskowy;
  woskowaty; (slang):
  wściekły; zły; okrutny
way [łej] s. droga; szlak; trakt;
  przejście; wolna droga;
  odległość; kierunek; strona;
  sposób; zwyczaj; bieg; tok;
  sens; stan; położenie
way back [łej baek] adv. dawno
  temu; daleko w tyle; dawno
waybill ['łejbyl] s. list
  przewozowy; fracht
wayfarer ['łej,feerer] s.
  podróżnik (pieszy)
waylay [łejlej] v. zob. lay;
  zaskoczyć kogoś; czyhać na
  kogoś; czatować
way of life ['łej ow,lajf] s. styl
  życia; sposób życia
way-out ['łej,aut] s. wyjście;
  rozwiązanie; adj. (slang):
  nadzwyczajny; nadzwyczaj;
  dobrze zrobiony; nadzwyczaj
  zdolny; (zob. far-out)
wayside ['łej,sajd] s. skraj drogi;
  adj. przydrożny
way station [,łej'stejszyn] s.
  przystanek

-ways [łejz] (przyrostek) w taki sposób (np. sideways)

wayward ['łejłerd] adj. przewrotny; uparty; kapryśny; nieobliczalny; chimeryczny

we [łi:] pron. my

weak [łi:k] adj. słaby

weaken ['łi:kn] v. osłabiać; słabnąć; rozcieńczać

weak-kneed ['łi:kni:d] adj. słaby

weakling ['łi:klyng] s. słabeusz; cherlak; człowiek słaby; adj. słaby

weakly ['łi:kly] adj. słabowity; adv. słabo

weak-minded ['łi:k,majndyd] adj. słaby na umyśle; słabego charakteru

weakness [łi:knys] s. słabość; słabostka

wealth [łels] s. bogactwo; dobrobyt

wealthy ['łelsy] adj. bogaty

wean [łi:n] v. odłączać od piersi; oduczać; odrywać

weapon ['łepon] s. broń

weaponless ['łepon,les] adj. bezbronny

wear; wore; worn [łeer; ło:r; ło:rn]

wear [łeer] v. nosić; chodzić w czymś; ścierać się; wycierać się; żłobić; zacierać się; przechodzić; mijać; zdzierać; nużyć; męczyć; wyczerpywać; długo trwać; długo służyć; s. noszenie; rzeczy noszone; moda; zużycie; wytrzymałość

wear away ['łeer,e'łej] v. zużywać; wlec się

wear off ['łeer,of] v. zetrzeć (się); zacierać (się); mijać

wear on ['łeer,on] v. wlec się

wear out ['łeer,aut] v. zdzierać (się); wyczerpywać (się)

wearing ['łieryng] adj. przeznaczony do noszenia na sobie

wearisome ['łierysem] adj. męczący; nużący; nudny

weary ['łiery] adj. zmęczony; znużony; znudzony; męczący; nużący; nudny; v. męczyć; nudzić; naprzykrzać się; uprzykrzać sobie

weasel ['łi:zl] s. łasica

weather ['łedzer] s. pogoda; adj. atmosferyczny; odwietrzny; pogodny; v. zwietrzać; okrywać się patyną (śniedzią)

weather-beaten ['łedzer,bi:tn] adj. zahartowany; skołatany przez burze

weather-bound ['łedzer,baund] adj. zatrzymany przez pogodę (statek)

weather bureau ['łedzer,bjuerou] s. instytut meteorologiczny

weather chart ['łedzer,cza:rt] s. wykres meteorologiczny

weathercock ['łedzer,kok] s. chorągiewka na dachu; kurek na dachu; człowiek niestały

weather forecast ['łedz,fo:rka:st] s. komunikat meteorologiczny

weather vane ['łedzer,wejn] s. wiatrowskaz; chorągiewka na dachu

weave; wove; woven [łi:w; łouw; łouwn]

weave [łi:w] v. tkać (tkaninę); knuć (spisek); układać (intrygę, opowiadanie); spleść; splatać; zajmować się tkactwem

weaver ['łi:wer] s. tkacz

weaving ['łi:wyng] s. tkactwo

web [łeb] s. tkanina; sztuka (materiału); stek (kłamstw); pajęczyna; błona (nietoperza); tkanka łączna; usztywnienie

wed [łed] v. zaślubiać; łączyć się; pobrać się; adj. zaślubiony

wedded ['łedyd] adj. zaślubiony; ślubny; oddany (sprawie)

wedding ['łedyng] s. ślub; wesele; adj. ślubny; weselny

wedding ring ['łedyng,ryng] s. obrączka ślubna

we'd [łi:d] = we had; we would; we should

wedge [łedż] s. klin; trójkątny

kawałek (tortu); golfowy kijek
z klinowym zakończeniem; v.
klinować; zaklinować;
rozklinować; łupać
wedge in ['ledż,yn] v. wpychać
(się); wcisnąć (się)
wedge off ['ledż,of] v.
wypychać (się)
wedlock ['ledlok] s. małżeństwo
Wednesday ['lenzdy] s. środa
weed [li:d] s. chwast; zielsko;
cygaro; (slang): chuchro;
cherlak; mizerak; szkapa; v.
pielić; odchwaszczać
weeder ['li:der] s. pielnik;
wypielacz
weed grown ['li:dgroun] adj.
zachwaszczony
weed out ['li:d,aut] v. wypielać;
usuwać
weeds ['li:ds] pl. krepa żałobna;
strój żałobny
weedy ['li:dy] adj.
zachwaszczony; chudy;
wysoki
weed killer ['li:d,kyler] s. trucizna
na chwasty
week [li:k] s. tydzień
weekday ['li:kdej] s. dzień
powszedni
weekend ['li:kend] s. niedziela
oraz części wolne soboty i
poniedziałku; v. spędzać
weekend
weekly ['li:kly] adj. tygodniowy;
adv. tygodniowo; s. tygodnik
weep; wept; wept [li:p; lept;
lept]
weep [li:p] v. płakać;
opłakiwać; zapłakać;
lamentować; cieknąć;
wyciekać; ociekać; s. płacz;
cieknięcie
weeper ['li:per] s. beksa;
płaczek; płaczka; welon
żałobny; krepa żałobna
weep away ['li:pe,lej] v.
wypłakać się
weeping willow ['li:pyng,lylou] s.
wierzba płacząca
weigh [lej] v. ważyć (się);
rozważać; mierzyć;
równoważyć; podnosić

(kotwicą); s. ważenie
weigh in ['lej,yn] v. ważyć
(boksera; dżokeja przed
zawodami)
weigh out ['lej,aut] v. wyważyć
człowieka przed zawodami
weigh up ['lej,ap] v. rozważyć
weigh upon ['lej,apon] v.
przygniatać; ciążyć na kimś
weight [lejt] s. ciężar; waga;
obciążenie; ciężarek;
odważnik; przycisk; grubość
(odzieży); znaczenie;
doniosłość;
odpowiedzialność; v.
obciążać; pogrubiać
sztucznie tkaninę
weight lifting ['lejt lyftyng] s.
(sport) podnoszenie ciężarów
weightless ['lejtlys] adj. lekki;
bez ciężaru
weighty ['lejty] adj. ciężki;
ważki; doniosły; ważny;
poważny; przekonywujący;
rozważony; przemyślany
weir [lier] s. jaz; grobla
weird [lierd] adj. niesamowity;
tajemniczy; nadprzyrodzony;
dziwny; dziwaczny; s. los
welcome ['lekem] exp.: witaj!
witajcie! s. powitanie; adj.
mile widziany; mający
pozwolenie; mogący
korzystać; v. powitać;
witać (z radością)
weld [leld] v. spawać (się);
spajać; zespalać; zgrzewać;
s. spoina; spawanie; spojenie;
miejsce spojenia
welder [lelder] s. spawacz;
spawarka; przyrząd do
spawania
welfare ['lelfeer] s. dobro;
dobrobyt; powodzenie;
pomyślność; szczęście
welfare-state ['lelfeer'stejt] s.
państwo o bardzo wysokich
świadczeniach społecznych
welfare-work ['lelfeer,le:rk] s.
praca społeczna;
społecznictwo; praca
dobroczynna
well; better; best [lel; beter;

best] adv. dobrze; lepiej;
najlepiej
well [łel] s. studnia; otwór
wiertniczy; odwiert; źródło;
klatka (schodowa); adv.
dobrze; należycie; porządnie;
mocno; solidnie; szczęśliwie;
całkiem; wyraźnie; łatwo;
lekko; słusznie; adj. dobry;
zdrowy; zadowalający;
pomyślny; w porządku; exp.:
dobrze! a więc?
well-balanced ['łel'baelenst] adj.
zrównoważony
well-behaved ['łelby'hejwd] adj.
dobrze wychowany
well-being ['łel'bi:yng] s.
dobrobyt; powodzenie;
pomyślność
well-born ['łel'bo:rn] adj. dobrze
urodzony
well-bred ['łel'bred] adj. rasowy;
dobrze wychowany
well-connected ['łel'konektyd]
adj. dobrze skoligacony
well-disposed ['łeldys'pouzd] adj.
życzliwie usposobiony
well done ['łeldan] exp.: brawo!
dobrze zrobione!
well-fed ['łelfed] adj. dobrze
odżywiony
well-founded ['łelfaundyd] adj.
uzasadniony
wellhead ['łel'hed] s. źródło
well-heeled ['łel'hi:ld] adj.
(slang): forsiasty (ma forsę)
Wellingtons ['łelyntenz] s. buty z
wysokimi cholewami (też z
gumy) (Brit.)
well-informed ['łel-ynfo:rmd] adj.
dobrze poinformowany;
wykształcony
well-intended ['łel-'yntendyd] adj.
dobrze pomyślany
well-judged ['łel-'dżadżd] adj.
rozsądny; roztropny; dobrze
pomyślany
well-knit ['łel'nyt] adj. zwarty;
dobrze zbudowany; jędrny
well-known ['łel'nołn] adj. dobrze
znany
well-meant ['łel'ment] adj.
zrobiony w najlepszej intencji

well-nigh ['łel'naj] adv. nieledwie;
o mało co; o mało nie
well-off ['łel'o:f] adj. dobrze
sytuowany; zamożny
well point ['łel'point] s. rura do
usuwania wody podskórnej
(przed kopaniem)
well-read ['łel'red] adj. oczytany
well-sinker ['łel'synker] s.
studniarz
well-spoken ['łel'spouken] adj.
uprzejmy; pięknie mówiący;
dobrze powiedziany
wellspring [łel'spryng] s. źródło
well-timed ['łel'tajmd] adj. na
czasie; odpowiedni
well-to-do ['łel-te'du:] adj.
zamożny; dobrze sytuowany
well-wisher ['łel'łyszer] s.
sympatyk
well-worn ['łel'ło:rn] adj.
wytrwały; wyświechtany;
oklepany; dobrze noszony
welsh [łelsz] adj. walijski; s.
wykręcanie się od płacenia; v.
uciekać nie zapłaciwszy
welter ['łelter] v. falować;
tarzać się; s. falowanie;
powódź; zamęt; kolos; silne
uderzenie
wench [łencz] s. dziewucha;
ulicznica; v. latać za
dziewkami
Wendish [łendysz] adj. łużycki
went [łent] v. zob. go
wept [łept] v. zob. weep
were [łe:r] v. zob. be
we're [łier] = we are
werewolf ['łe:rłuf] s. wilkołak
west [łest] s. zachód; adj.
zachodni; adv. na zachód; ku
zachodowi
westerly ['łesterly] adj. zachodni;
adv. na zachód
western ['łestern] adj. zachodni;
pochodzący z zachodu
westward ['łestłerd] adj.
zachodni; ku zachodowi; na
zachód
wet [łet] adj. mokry; wilgotny;
zmoczony; przemoczony;
słotny; deszczowy; dżdżysty;
(slang): w błędzie; s. wilgoć;

wilgotność; trunek; v.
moczyć (się); zwilżać;
zraszać

wet nurse ['łet,ne:rse] s. mamka;
v. karmić

wether ['ledzer] s. skop
(kastrowany baran)

wet through ['łet'tru:] v.
przemoczyć (na wylot)

we've [łi:w] = we have

whack [hłaek] v. walić;
grzmocić; (slang): dzielić się
czymś; s. walnięcie;
trzaśnięcie; (slang): część;
próba; stan (rzeczy)

whacker ['hłaeker] s. kolor

whacking ['hłaekyng] adj.
kolosalny

whale [hłejl] s. wieloryb; rzecz
wspaniała; v. polować na
wieloryby; (slang): bić

whale-boat ['hłejl,bout] s. łódź
do połowu wielorybów; łódź
strażnicza, ratunkowa

whalebone ['hłejlboun] s. fiszbin

whale-fin ['hłejlfyn] s. fiszbin

whale-oil ['hłejl,ojl] s. tran
wielorybi

whaler ['hłejler] s. statek do
połowu wielorybów

whammy ['hłaemy] s. (slang):
urok (rzucony na kogoś)

whang [hłaeng] s. grzmotnięcie;
huczenie; rzemień; v. walić;
grzmocić; huczeć

wharf [hło:rf] s. przystań
(wyładunkowa); nabrzeże; v.
cumować do wyładunku;
wyładowywać w przystani

wharves [hło:rfs] pl. nabrzeża
wyładunkowe

what [hłot] adj. jaki; jaki tylko;
ten; który; ten ... co; taki ...
jaki; tyle ... ile; pron. co; to
co; coś; excl.: co? czego? jak
to!

what about ['hłote,baut] exp.: a
co z ... ?; co powiesz o ... ?

whatever ['hłot'ewer] adj.
jakikolwiek; pron. cokolwiek;
wszystko co; co tylko; bez
względu; obojętnie co

what for ['hłotfo:r] s. (slang):

bura; lanie; exp.: za co?

what next ['hłot,nekst] exp.: co
dalej?

whatnot ['hłotnot] s. etażerka;
cacka; (slang): cokolwiek;
obojętnie co; wszystko

what's it ['hłotsyt] s. jak się to
nazywa; ten (przedmiot)

whatsoever ['hłotsou'ewer] adj.
jakikolwiek by; cokolwiek by;
co tylko by; pron. wszystko
co tylko

wheat [hłi:t] s. pszenica

wheaten ['hłi:tn] adj. pszeniczny

wheel ['hłi:l] s. koło; kółko; ster;
kierownica; v. obracać (się);
wrócić (się); prowadzić
taczki (rower); wozić
taczkami etc.

wheelbarrow ['hłi:l,baerou] s.
taczki

wheel chair ['hłi:l,czeer] s. fotel
na kółkach

wheeler-dealer ['hłi:ler,di:ler] s.
cwaniak; politykier

wheelwright ['hłi:lrajt] s.
kołodziej

wheeze ['hłi:z] v. sapać; s.
sapanie; (slang): dowcip;
komunał

wheezy ['hłi:zy] adj. sapiący;
zasapany

when [hłen] adv. kiedy; kiedyż;
wtedy; kiedy to; gdy; przy;
podczas gdy; s. czas
(zdarzenia)

whenas [,hłen'aez] conj. kiedy;
podczas gdy

whence [hłens] adv. & conj.
skąd

whenever ['hłenewer] adv. kiedy
tylko; skoro tylko

whensoever ['hłensou'ewer] adv.
skoro tylko; skądkolwiek

where [hłeer] adv. & conj. gdzie;
dokąd

whereabout ['hłeere'baut] adv.
gdzie?

whereabouts ['hłeere'bauts] adv.
zważywszy; gdzie; mniej
więcej; s. miejsce
zamieszkania (pobytu)

whereas ['hłeer'aez] conj.

podczas gdy
whereat ['hłeer,et] conj. podczas gdy
whereby ['hłeer,baj] adv. po czym? po kim? po którym; za pomocą którego? jak? którym
wherefore ['hłeerfo:r] adj. dlaczego; dlatego; z tego powodu
wherefrom [hłeer'fro:m] adv. skąd; z czego
wherein [hłeer'yn] adv. w czym; w którym
whereof [hłeer'ow] adv. z czego; z którego
whereon [hłeer'on] adv. na czym; na którym
wheresoever [,hłeersou'ewer] adv. wszędzie by; dokądkolwiek by; gdzie tylko by
whereupon [,hłeere'pon] adv. na czym; po czym
wherever [,hłeer'ewer] adv. dokądkolwiek; wszędzie; gdzie tylko
wherewith [,hłeer'łyz] adv. (z) czym?
wherewithal [,hłeerły'so:l] s. potrzebne środki (fundusze, przybory)
whet [hłet] v. naostrzyć; zaostrzyć (też apetyt); s. ostrzenie; zakąska
whether ['hłedzer] conj. czy-czy; czy tak, czy owak
whetstone ['hłet,stoun] s. osełka; kamień szlifierski
whey [hłej] s. serwatka
which [hłycz] pron. który; co; którędy; dokąd; w jaki (sposób)
whichever [hłycz,ewer] adj. którykolwiek; jaki; każdy ... jaki; który tylko; pron. którykolwiek; każdy
whichsoever [,hłyczsou'ewer] adj. pron. = whichever (z naciskiem)
whiff [hłyf] s. powiew; podmuch; tchnienie; zapach; dym; lekki wybuch gniewu; v. dmuchać; dymić; palić;

lekko wiać
while [hłajl] s. chwila; pewien czas; po chwili; niebawem; wkrótce; conj. podczas gdy; jak długo; dopóki; póki; natychmiast; chociaż co prawda
while ago [hłajl,egou] adv. jakiś czas temu
whilst [hłajlst] adv. podczas
whim ['hłym] s. kaprys; zachcianka; fantazja; fanaberia; kołowrót górniczy
whimper ['hłymper] v. piszczeć; kwilić; skomleć; skowyczeć; s. kwilenie; skowyt; skamlanie
whimsical ['hłymzykel] adj. kapryśny; dziwaczny; cudaczny
whimsy ['hłymzy] s. kaprys
whim-wham ['hłymhłaem] s. cacko
whine ['hłajn] v. skomleć; jęczeć; powiedzieć jękliwie; s. skomlenie; jęk
whip [hłyp] s. bat; bicz; pomocnik; woźnica; naganiacz; uderzenie biczem; bita śmietana; v. chłostać; zacinać (batem); ubijać (śmietanę); smagać; przyrządzać naprędce; zwyciężyć; zakasować (kogoś); owijać; windować; śmigać; zbierać; wyjechać (pośpiesznie)
whip in ['hłyp,yn] v. zapędzać batem
whip off ['hłyp'o:f] v. zerwać coś; czmychnąć z czymś
whip on ['hłyp'on] v. popędzać batem
whip out ['hłyp,aut] v. wyciągnąć błyskawicznie
whip round ['hłyp,raund] v. odwrócić się znienacka
whip together ['hłyp te'gedzer] v. zganiać batem; zwalać na kupę; montować na gwałt
whipped cream ['hłypt'kri:m] s. bita śmietana
whipper-snapper ['hłyper'snaeper] s. chłystek;

smarkacz
whipping boy ['hłypyng,boj] s.
kozioł ofiarny (chłopak
chłostany za innego)
whipping top ['hłypyng,top] s.
bąk do podbijania
whippy [,hłypy] adj. giętki;
elastyczny
whipsaw [,hłyp'so] s. wąska
piłeczka; v. ciąć piłką;
wygrać podwójnie; pobić
podwójnie
whip-stock [,hłyp'stok] s.
biczysko
whirl [hłe:rl] v. kręcić (się);
wirować; zawirować;
porywać w wir; s. wirowanie;
ruch wirowy; wir; (slang):
próba (czegoś)
whirlpool ['hłe:rl'pu:l] s. wir
whirlwind ['hłe:rl'łynd] s. trąba
powietrzna; wir powietrzny
whirlybird [hłe:rly'be:rd] s.
helikopter (USA)
whirr [hłe:r] v. furkotać;
warkotać; s. furkot; warkot
(maszyny)
whisk [hłysk] s. wiecheć;
śmignięcie; trzepaczka (do
jajek etc.); miotełka; v.
otrzepać; odpędzać;
porywać; szybko odwozić;
przywozić; czmychać;
wymachiwać; śmigać
whisk away ['hłyske'łej] s.
strzepnąć; przewieźć lotem
strzały; czmychnąć
whiskers ['hłyskers] pl. baki;
bokobrody; wąsy
whisky ['hłysky] s. (wódka)
whiskey
whisper ['hłysper] v. szeptać;
mówić cicho; szemrać;
szeleścić; s. szeptanie;
szmer
whistle ['hłysl] v. gwizdać;
świstać; zagwizdać; s.
gwizdanie; gwizd; świst;
gwizdek; gardło
whistle away ['hłysle'łej] v.
pogwizdywać sobie
white [hłajt] adj. biały;
bezbarwny; blady; czysty;

niepokalany; uczciwy;
rzetelny; niewinny; s. biel;
biały (człowiek); białko; białe
wino
white coffee [hłajt'kofi] s. kawa
z mlekiem
white-collar ['hłajt,koler] adj.
zajęci biurowo (urzędnicy etc.)
white elephant [hłajt'elyfent] s.
towary wybrakowane; buble
white collar worker ['hłajt,koler
łerker] s. pracownik umysłowy
white frost ['hłajt'fro:st] s. szron
white-headed ['hłajt'hedyd] adj.
siwowłosy
white heat [hłajt'hi:t] s. biały żar
white lie [hłajt'łaj] s. kłamstwo;
wykręt towarzyski
white paper ['hłajt,pejper] s.
oficjalna publikacja
wykazująca, że rząd ma
zawsze rację (USA)
whiten ['hłajtn] v. wybielać;
pobielać; bielić; zbieleć
whiteness ['hłajtness] s. biel
whitewash [,hłajt'łosz] s. wapno;
wybielanie czegoś lub
kogoś; v. wybielać;
wymywać na czysto;
uniewinnić; usprawiedliwić;
pobić na sucho (na zero)
Whitsuntide ['hłajtsntajd] s.
Zielone Święta (Brit.)
whittle down ['hłytl,dałn] v.
strugać; zestrugać;
wystrugać; obstrugać
whity ['hłajty] adj. białawy
whiz [hłyz] s. świst; (slang):
mistrz; rzecz wspaniała; v.
świstać; suszyć
who [hu:] pron. kto; który
whodunit [hu:danyt] s. (slang):
"kryminał"; powieść
detektywistyczna
whoever [hu:'ewer] pron.
ktokolwiek
whole [houl] adj. cały;
pełnowartościowy; zdrowy; s.
całość
wholehearted ['houl'ha:rtyd] adj.
serdeczny; szczery
whole-hogger ['houl'hoger] s.
człowiek idący na całego

whole length ['houl'le<u>nks</u>] s.
(portret) w całości

wholesale ['houl,sejl] s. hurt;
handel hurtowy; adj. hurtowy;
masowy; adv. hurtem;
masowo

wholesaler ['houl,sejler] s.
hurtownik

wholesale trade ['houlsejl,trejd]
s. handel hurtowy

wholesome ['houlsem] adj.
zdrowy; zdrowotny

whole-time ['houltajm] adj. pełno
-etatowy (czasowy)

whole-wheat ['houl'hłi:t] adj.
pełno-ziarnisty (chleb)

who'll [hu:l] ` = who shall; who
will

wholly ['houly] adv. całkowicie

whom [hu:m] pron. kogo? zob.
who

whoop [hu:p] s. okrzyk (wesoły
np.)

whooping cough ['hu:py<u>n</u>,kof] s.
koklusz

whopping ['hłopy<u>ng</u>] adj. (slang):
ogromny

whore [ho:r] s. wulg.: kurwa;
dziwka; v. kurwić się; gonić
za dziwkami

whose [hu:z] pron. & adj. czyj;
czyja; czyje; którego

why [hłaj] adv. dlaczego; czemu;
czemuż; dlatego; właśnie; s.
przyczyna; powód; exp.: jak
to! właśnie! patrzcie; no
wiesz!; no to co!

why so ['hłaj'sou] adv. dlaczego

wick [łyk] s. knot; tampon

wicked ['łykyd] adj. niegodziwy;
niedobry; frywolny; paskudny;
złośliwy; zły; nikczemny

wickedness ['łykydnys] s.
nikczemność;
niegodziwość

wicker basket ['łyker,ba:skyt] s.
pleciony kosz

wicker chair [łyker,czeer] s.
plecione krzesło

wicket [łykyt] s. furka; kołowrót;
okienko kasowe; bramka; cel;
drzwi na pół wysokości
(otworu)

wide [łajd] adj. szeroki; rozległy;
szeroko otwarty; obszerny;
wielki; pokaźny; znaczny;
duży; daleki; adv. szeroko; z
dala (od czegoś)

wide-awake ['łajde,e'łejk] adj.
czujny; rozbudzony; bystry; z
szeroko otwartymi oczami

widen ['łajdn] v. poszerzyć;
rozszerzać

wideness ['łajdnys] s.
szerokość; rozległość;
bezmiar

wide-open [,łajd'oupen] adj.
szeroko otwarty

widespread [,łajd'spred] adj.
rozprzestrzeniony; szeroko
rozpostarty

widow ['łydou] s. wdowa; v.
wdowieć

widower ['łydouer] s. wdowiec

width [łyd<u>s</u>] s. szerokość

wife [łajf] s. żona; pl. wives
[łajwz]

wig [łyg] s. peruka; v.
zaopatrywać w perukę

wild [łajld] adj. dziki; dziko
rosnący; gwałtowny;
wściekły; szalony; burzliwy;
rozwichrzony; pustynny;
zdziczały; rozwydrzony;
fantastyczny; nierealny;
podniecony; s. pustynia; dziki
teren; adv. na chybił trafił

wildcat ['łajld,kaet] adj.
porywczy; awanturniczy;
nadzwyczajny (np. pociąg); s.
żbik; szyb naftowy na nowym
terenie; awanturnicze
przedsiębiorstwo; spekulacja;
samotna lokomotywa;
porywcza osoba; v. szukać
nafty na niesprawdzonych
terenach

wilderness [łajldernys] s.
pustynia; puszcza; odludzie

wildfire [,łajld'fajer] s.
błyskawicznie
rozprzestrzeniający się ogień;
ogień grecki; błędny ognik

willful ['łylful] adj. rozmyślny;
umyślny; zamierzony;
świadomy; samowolny;

uparty

will [łyl] s. wola; testament; siła woli; v. postanowić; zarządzać; zapisywać (w testamencie); zmuszać; chcieć

willing [‚łylyng] adj. skłonny (coś zrobić); chętny; pełen dobrej woli

willow ['łylou] s. wierzba

willowy ['łyłoły] adj. smukły; gibki; giętki; obfitujący w wierzby

will power ['łyl‚pałer] s. siła woli

willy-nilly ['łyly'nyly] adv. chcąc nie chcąc (Brit.)

will you? ['łyl‚ju:] exp.: czy zrobisz?; czy zechcesz?; czy obiecasz?

wilt [łylt] v. więdnąć; opadać; oklapnąć; powodować zwiędnięcie; opadać z sił; s. więdnięcie; osłabienie; depresja

wily [łajly] adj. chytry

win; won; won [łyn; łon; łon]

win [łyn] v. wygrywać; zwyciężać; zdobywać; zarabiać; osiągać; pozyskać; przedostać się; przezwyciężać; s. wygrana; zwycięstwo

win over [łynouwer] v. pozyskać sobie; przekonać

wince [łyns] v. skrzywić się (z bólu); drgać; s. drgnięcie; skrzywienie

winch [łyncz] s. korba; wyciąg; kołowrót; v. podnosić; wyciągać kołowrotem lub korbą

wind; wound; wound [łajnd; łaund; łaund]

wind [łajnd] v. nawijać; zwijać; zwinąć; owinąć (się); wić (się); zakończyć; [łynd] s. wiatr; podmuch; oddech; dech; zapach; puste słowa; gadanie; v. trąbić; dąć w róg; przewietrzyć; zwietrzyć; poczuć; zmęczyć; dać wytchnąć

windbag ['łyndbaeg] s. czczy gaduła

windfall ['łynd fo:l] s. gratka; owoc zrzucony wiatrem

winding ['łajndyng] adj. kręcony; kręcący się

winding-stairs ['łajndyng‚steers] s. kręcące się schody

wind-instrument [łynd‚ynstrument] s. instrument dęty

windlass [łyndles] s. wyciąg; kołowrót

windmill ['łynmyl] s. wiatrak

wind off [łajnd‚o:f] v. odwinąć (się)

wind up [łajnd‚ap] v. nakręcać (zegar); kończyć (mowę); zamykać (zebranie)

window ['łyndou] s. okno; okienko

window dressing ['łyndou ‚dressyng] s. dekoracja wystawy sklepowej

windowpane ['łyndou‚pejn] s. szyba okienna

window shade ['łyndou‚szejd] s. żaluzja

window shopping ['łyndouszopyng] v. oglądać wystawy (a nie kupować)

window-sill ['łyndou‚syl] s. parapet

windpipe ['łynd‚pajp] s. tchawica

windshield ['łyndszyld] s. szyba ochronna (przednia) w samochodzie

windshield wiper ['łyndszyld'łajper] s. wycieraczka szyby ochronnej

windy ['łyndy] adj. wystawiony na wiatr; wietrzny; gadatliwy

wine ['łajn] s. wino

wine-glass ['łajngla:s] s. kieliszek do wina

wine-press ['łajnpres] s. wytłaczarka do winogron

wing [łyng] s. skrzydło; ramię; kulisa; dywizjon; lot; v. uskrzydlać; przewozić na skrzydłach; przelecieć (przez coś); lecieć; szybować

wing commander ['łyng -ke‚ma:nder] s. dowódca

dywizjonu lotnictwa
(podpułkownik)
wink [¹łynk] v. mrugać (na
kogoś); przymykać oczy; s.
mrugnięcie
winner [¹łyner] s. zdobywca
nagrody; człowiek
wygrywający; laureat
winning [¹łynyng] s. otwór do
wydobywania węgla; adj.
ujmujący; zwycięski
winning post [¹łynyng,poust] s.
meta
winnings [¹łynyngs] pl. wygrana
winsome [¹łynsem] adj.
ujmujący; pociągający
winter [¹łynter] s. zima; adj.
zimowy; v. zimować
winter crop [¹łynter,krop] s.
ozimina
winterize [¹łynterajz] v.
dostosowywać,
przygotowywać do zimy
wintry [¹łyntry] adj. zimowy;
chłodny; obojętny
winy [¹łajny] adj. podchmielony;
winny
wipe [łajp] v. wycierać;
ocierać; ścierać; wymazać;
zamachnąć się; s. starcie;
wytarcie; bicie
wipe away [¹łajpe,łej] v.
wycierać; wymazać
wipe off [¹łajp,o:f] v. zetrzeć
(plamę etc.)
wipe out [¹łajp,aut] v. wytrzeć;
wymazać; wyniszczyć;
zgładzać
wipe up [¹łajp,ap] v. wytrzeć
(podłogę etc.)
wire [łajer] s. drut; przewód;
telegram; kabel; struna
metalowa; sidła; v. drutować;
zadrutować; złapać (w sidła);
założyć przewody (w domu);
zatelegrafować; ciągnąć za
sznurki zakulisowe
wire cutter [¹łajer,kater] s.
szczypce do cięcia drutu
wire haired [¹łajer,heerd] adj.
ostrowłosy (pies)
wireless [¹łajerlys] adj. radiowy;
bez drutu

wiry [¹łajery] adj. twardy;
żylasty; muskularny; druciany
wisdom [¹łyzdem] s. mądrość
wisdom tooth [¹łyzdem,tu:s] s.
ząb mądrości
wise [łajz] s. sposób; adj. mądry;
roztropny
wiseacre [¹łajz,ejker] s. mądrala;
mędrek
wise after [¹łajz,a:fter] adj.
mądry po ...
wisecrack [¹łajzkra:k] s.
dowcipna uwaga; v. robić
dowcipy
wise guy [¹łajzgaj] s. nadęta
wielkość
wise saw [¹łajzso:] s. przysłowie
wish [łysz] v. życzyć (sobie);
pragnąć; chcieć; s.
pragnienie; życzenie; chęć;
powinszowanie; ochota; rzecz
upragniona
wishbone [¹łyszboun] s. kość
widełkowa (ptaków)
wish for [¹łysz fo:r] v. życzyć
sobie (np. pogody)
wishful [¹łyszful] adj. pragnący
wishful thinking [¹łyszful
-tynkyng] s. pobożne życzenie
wish well [¹łysz,łel] v. dobrze
życzyć
wishy-washy [¹łyszy,łoszy] adj.
bez treści; wodnisty;
lurowaty
wisp [łysp] s. wiązka; garść;
pęczek; kosmyk; wstęga
(dymu)
wistful [¹łystful] adj. smutny;
zadumany; pełen tęsknoty
wit [łyt] s. umysł; rozum;
dowcip; człowiek dowcipny;
inteligencja; olej w głowie
witch [łycz] s. czarownica;
czarodziejka; v. zaczarować;
oczarować
witchcraft [¹łycz,kra:ft] s. czary;
czarnoksięstwo
witch doctor [¹łycz,dakter] s.
czarownik; znachor
witchery [¹łyczery] = witchcraft
witch hunt [¹łyczhant] s.
tropienie czarownic; polityczne
głośne śledztwo

(propagandowe) w celu udowadniania działalności wywrotowej

with [łys] prep. z (kimś, czymś); u (kogoś); przy (kimś); za pomocą; (stosownie) do; (cierpliwość) dla

withdraw [łys'dro:] v. zob. draw; cofać (się); wycofywać (się); odwołać (coś); odebrać (ze szkoły); odsuwać (zasłonę)

withdrawal [łys'dro:el] s. wycofanie

wither ['łydzer] v. powodować więdnięcie, usychanie; zabijać (spojrzeniem); usychać; usuwać się (w cień itp.)

withers ['łydzers] pl. kłęby (u konia między łopatkami)

withhold [łys'hould] v. zob. hold; wstrzymywać; odmawiać; wycofać

within [łys'yn] adv. wewnątrz; w domu; u siebie; w (czymś); w duchu; do wnętrza; w obrębie; w odległości (np. mili); w ciągu (np. dnia); w zasięgu (wzroku); s. wnętrze

without [łysaut] prep. bez; poza; na zewnątrz; adv. na zewnątrz; poza domem; s. strona zewnętrzna

withstand [łys'staend] v. zob. stand; opierać się; przeciwstawiać się; być wytrzymałym; wytrzymywać

witling ['łytlyng] s. dowcipniś

witness ['łytnys] s. świadek; widz; świadectwo; v. być świadkiem; świadczyć (też podpisem)

witness box ['łytnys,boks] s. miejsce dla świadka w sądzie (USA)

witness stand ['łytnys,staend] s. miejsce dla zeznawania w sądzie (USA)

witticism ['łytysyzem] s. złośliwy dowcip; dowcipkowanie

witty [łyty] adj. dowcipny

wives [łajwz] pl. żony; zob. wife

wiz [łyz] s. (slang): znawca; mistrz; rzecz wspaniała

wizard ['łyzerd] s. czarownik; czarodziej; adj. czarodziejski; (slang): wspaniały

wo [ło:u] exp.: prrr (na konia, żeby stanął)

wobble ['łobl] v. chwiać się; ruszać się chwiejnie; chodzić chwiejnie; jechać kołysząc się; mówić drżąco; grać drżąco (melodią); drgać; wahać się; być niezdecydowanym

wobbler ['łobler] s. człowiek chwiejny

wobbly [łobly] adj. chwiejący się; chwiejny

woe [łou] s. nieszczęście

woebegone ['łoubi,go:n] adj. nieszczęsny

woeful ['łouful] adj. bolesny; żałosny

woke [łouk] v. zob. wake

woken [łoukn] v. zob. wake

wolf [łulf] s. pl. wolves [łulwz]; wilk; (slang): kobieciarz; v. żreć; pożerać; połykać jak wilk; polować na wilki

wolf down ['łulf,dałn] v. pożerać jak wilk;

wolf-call ['łulf,ko:l] s. (slang): gwizdanie na kobietę (z podziwem, zaczepką etc.)

wolf-cub ['łulf,kab] s. wilczek; wilczę; młodszy harcerz

wolf-dog ['łulfdog] s. wilczur

wolfhound ['łulfhaund] s. wilczur rosyjski lub alzacki

wolfish ['łulfysz] adj. wilczy

wolf skin ['łulf'skyn] s. wilcza skóra (na podłogę etc.); wilczura (okrycie)

wolf whistle ['łulfhłysl] = wolfcall

wolverine [,łulwe'ri:n] s. rosomak; mieszkaniec stanu Michigan

woman ['łumen] s. pl. women ['łymyn]; kobieta; baba; żona; v. mówić per "kobieta";

umieszczać między kobietami
woman doctor ['łumen'dakter] s.
lekarka
womanhood ['łumenhud] s.
kobiety; kobiecość (dojrzała)
womanish ['łumenysz] adj.
babski; zniewieściały
womanize ['łumenajz] v. babieć;
niewieścieć; gonić za
kobietami
womankind ['łumen,kajnd] s.
kobiety; ród niewieści
womanlike ['łumen,lajk] adj.
kobiecy
womanly ['łumenly] adj. kobiecy
womb [łu:m] s. macica; łono;
żywot
women [łymyn] pl. zob. woman
won [łan] v. zob. win
wonder ['łander] s. zdumienie;
cud; v. dziwić się; być
ciekaw; zastanawiać się
wonderful ['łanderful] adj.
cudowny
wonderland ['łanderlaend] s.
kraina cudów (czarów)
wonderment ['łanderment] s.
zdziwienie; zdumienie
wondering ['łanderyng] adj.
zdumiony; niedowierzający
wonder-work ['łanderłe:rk] s. cud
wonder-worker ['łanderłe:rker] s.
cudotwórca
wonder-working ['łanderłe:rkyng]
adj. sprawiający cuda
wondrous ['łandres] adj.
cudowny; adv. cudownie
wont; wont; wonted [łont; łont;
łantyd]
wont [łant] v. przyzwyczajać;
mieć zwyczaj; s. zwyczaj;
przyzwyczajenie
won't [łount] = will not
wonted ['łantyd] adj. zwykły
woo [łu:] v. zalecać się (do
kobiety); umizgać się;
ubiegać się; namawiać do
czegoś
wood [łud] s. drzewo; drewno;
lasek; pl. lasy; puszcza; v.
obsadzać drzewami;
dostarczać drzewo
woodbine ['łudbajn] s. powój

wonny; wiciokrzew pomorski
woodblock ['łudblok] s.
drzeworyt (do odciskania)
wood carving ['łudka:rwyng] s.
drzeworytnictwo
woodchuck ['łudczak] s.
świstak
wood coal ['łudkoul] s. węgiel
drzewny
woodcock ['łudkok] s. słomka
woodcraft ['łudkra:ft] s.
znajomość lasu
woodcraftsman ['łudkra:ftsmen]
s. myśliwy; traper
woodcut ['łudkat] s. drzeworyt
woodcutter ['łudkater] s. drwal;
drzeworytnik
wooded ['łudyd] adj. lesisty;
zalesiony
wooden ['łudn] adj. drewniany;
tępy
wood engraver [,łudyn'grejwer]
s. drzeworytnik
wood engraving
[,łudyn'grejwyng] s.
drzeworytnictwo
wooden head ['łudn,hed] s.
głupiec
woodland ['łudlaend] s. las;
lesisty okręg; adj. lesisty;
leśny
woodman ['łudmen] s. drwal;
leśnik
wood notes ['łudnouts] s.
dźwięki lasu
woodpecker ['łud,peker] s.
dzięcioł
wood pulp ['łud,palp] s. miazga
drzewna
woodruff ['łudraf] s. marzanna
(wonna)
woodshed ['łud,szed] s.
drwalnia; drewutnia
woodsman ['łudsmen] s.
mieszkaniec lasu; drwal
wood sorrel ['łudserel] s.
szczawik zajęczy
woodsy [łudzy] adj. leśny
wood wind ['łud,łynd] s. (dęty)
instrument drewniany
woodwork [łudłe:rk] s. wyroby
drzewne; części drewniane
(np. ramy okien etc.);

drewniana część budowy;
budowa drewniana; stolarka;
ciesiołka
woody ['łudy] adj. lesisty;
drewniany
wooer ['łu:er] s. zalotnik
woof [łu:f] s. wątek
wool [łul] s. wełna (czesana,
strzyżona, zgrzebna);
czupryna; włosy (wełniste);
owcze runo; wełniane rzeczy
wool-ball ['łulbo:l] s. kłąbek
wełny
woolen ['łuln] adj. wełniany; s.
wyrób wełniany
wool fat ['łulfaet] s. lanolina
wool-fell ['łulfel] s. baranica;
skóra owcza
woolgathering ['łul,gaedzeryng]
adj. głupio rozmarzony
(roztargniony); s. głupie
marzycielstwo
woolly ['łuly] adj. wełnisty;
oschły (głos); mętny umysł;
nie soczysty; mączysty;
włóknisty (owoc); zamazany;
(slang): surowy i niekulturalny;
s. wełniana odzież; (slang):
owca
wooly ['łuly] = woolly
woozy ['łu:zy] adj. (slang):
wstawiony; otumaniony;
niezdrów
word [łe:rd] s. słowo; wyraz;
słówko; komplement;
przechwałka; obelga; mowa;
wieść; rozkaz; adv. ustnie;
słownie; adj. słowami
wyrażony; v. wyrazić;
redagować; sformułować;
ubierać w szatę słowną;
przybierać w słowa
wordage ['łe:rdydż] s. ilość
słów
word-blind ['łe:rd,blajnd] adj.
niezdolny do rozumienia pisma
wordbook ['łe:rd,buk] s. słownik
wording ['łe:rdyng] s. ujęcie,
wyrażenie słowami
wordplay ['łe:rd,plej] s. gra słów
word-splitter ['łe:rd,splyter] s.
pedant słowny
word-splitting ['łe:rd,splytyng] s.

sofistyka; dzielenie włosa na
czworo
wordy ['łe:rdy] adj. rozwlekły;
gadatliwy; słowny (wojna
słów)
wore [ło:r] v. zob. wear
work; worked; worked [łe:rk;
łe:rkt; łe:rkt]
work [łe:rk] s. praca; robota;
zajęcie; energia; zadanie;
dzieło; utwór; uczynek; pl.
fabryka; huta; fortyfikacje;
ozdoby; v. pracować;
działać; funkcjonować;
skutkować; oddziaływać;
wywoływać; sprawiać;
wykonywać; kazać robić;
prowadzić; obsługiwać;
poruszać (motor); posuwać
(się); przesuwać (się);
wprawiać w (pasją);
nadawać kształt;
przeprowadzać przez coś;
obrabiać; urabiać (się);
wyszywać; robić robótkę;
(slang): wykorzystywać
(znajomości); drgać; burzyć;
falować; fermentować;
trzeszczeć (statek); źle
działać (maszyna);
wyczerpać się; odrabiać;
wypracować; wytwarzać;
uzyskiwać z trudem;
podniecać (się) stopniowo;
zaznajamiać się z czymś;
mieszać w całości;
dokazywać (cudów);
wywierać (wpływ); urabiać;
fasonować; eksploatować
(kopalnie itp.)
work away ['łe:rke,łej] v.
pracować zawzięcie
work in ['łe:rkyn] v. pasować;
wprowadzać coś
work off ['łe:rko:f] v. pozbywać
się czegoś
work on ['łe:rkon] v. pracować
dalej
work out ['łe:rkaut] v.
przeprowadzać; realizować;
obliczać; rozwiązywać;
wyczerpywać;
wyeksploatować; skończyć;

wynosić (w sumie)
work up ['łe:rkap] v. podniecać
(się); doprowadzać (się);
opracowywać; wyrabiać;
rozwijać; wspinać się;
podnosić (się)
workable ['łe:rkebl] adj. możliwy
(do obróbki, uprawy etc.);
opłacalny; wykonalny; realny;
możliwy do przeprowadzenia;
w stanie używalności
workaday ['łe:rkedej] adj.
codzienny; roboczy;
powszedni
work-basket ['łe:rk,ba:skyt] s.
koszyk z robótką
workbook ['łe:rk,buk] s.
podręcznik ze wskazówkami;
dziennik pracy
workday ['łe:rkdej] s. dzień
roboczy; dzień powszedni
worker ['łe:rker] s. pracownik;
robotnik
workhouse ['łe:rk,haus] s. dom
poprawczy; przytułek
working ['łe:rkyng] adj.
pracujący; pracowniczy;
roboczy; praktyczny;
działający; czynny; ruchomy;
powszedni; s. praca; robota;
działanie; ruch;
roboczodniówka; obróbka
working capital
['łe:rkyng'kaepytl] s. kapitał
obrotowy
working knowledge
['łe:rkyng'nolydż] s. wiedza
praktyczna
working-class ['łe:rkyng'kla:s] s.
klasa robotnicza
working day ['łe:rkyngdej] s.
dzień pracy
working hours ['łe:rkyng,auers]
s. godziny pracy
working load ['łe:rkyng,loud] s.
ciężar użyteczny; nośność
workingman ['łe:rkyng,men] s.
robotnik
working pressure ['łe:rkyng
,preszer] s. ciśnienie robocze
workless ['łe:rklys] adj. & s.
bezrobotny
work-like ['łe:rklajk] adj. dobrze

wykonany; dobrze nastawiony
do pracy
workman ['łe:rkmen] s. pl.
workmen ['łe:rkmen]; robotnik
(fizyczny); fachowiec
workmanship ['łe:rkmanszyp] s.
wykonanie; jakość
wykonania; faktura; twór
work of art ['łe:rk-ow,a:rt] s.
dzieło sztuki
workout ['łe:rkaut] s. trening;
zaprawa; danie komuś szkoły
workroom ['łe:rk'rum] s.
pracownia
works council ['łe:rks'kansl] s.
rada zakładowa
workshop ['łe:rkszop] s.
pracownia; warsztat; zakład;
posiedzenie
worktable ['łe:rktejbl] s. biurko
workup ['łe:rkap] s. podniecenie
(się); powalanie podczas
druku
workwoman ['łe:rkłumen] s. pl.
workwomen ['łe:rkłymyn];
robotnica; pracownica fizyczna
world [łe:rld] s. świat; ziemia;
kula ziemska; sfery; masa;
mnóstwo; zatrzęsienie
czegoś; bezmiar; wielka
ilość; adj. światowy
worldling ['łe:rldlyng] s. człowiek
oddany sprawom doczesnym
worldly ['łe:rldly] adj. światowy;
ziemski; doczesny
world-minded ['łe:rld'majndyd]
adj. oddany sprawom
doczesnym
world old ['łe:rld,old] adj. stary
jak świat
world power ['łe:rld'pałer] s.
potęga światowa; wielkie
mocarstwo
world-series ['łe:rld'sieri:z] s.
mistrzostwa palanta (baseball)
USA
world war ['łe:rld'łor] s. wojna
światowa
world-weary ['łe:rld'łeery] adj.
zmęczony życiem
world-wide ['łe:rld,łajd] adj.
światowy
world wise ['łe:rld,łajz] adj.

obyty; doświadczony

worm [łe:rm] s. robak; robaczek; glista; dżdżownica; gwint; zwojnik; śruba (nie ostra); wężownica; v. wkradać się; wykradać; czołgać się; wyciągać (tajemnicę z kogoś); czyścić (zwierzę) z robaków; czyścić (grządkę) z robaków

worm-eaten ['łe:rm,i:tn] adj. robaczywy; stoczony przez robaki; (slang): przestarzały

worm-fishing ['łe:rm,fyszyn] s. łowienie ryb na robaki

worm gear ['łe:rm,gier] s. przekładnia ślimakowa

wormhole ['łe:rm,houl] s. dziura wygryziona przez robaka

wormseed ['łe:rm,si:d] s. rośliny stosowane przeciw robakom

worm wheel ['łe:rm,hłi:l] s. koło przekładni ślimakowej

wormwood ['łe:rm,łud] s. piołun; (też) przykrość

wormy ['łe:rmy] adj. robaczywy

worn [ło:rn] v. zob. wear; adj. używany; noszony; pomarszczony

worn-out ['ło:rn,aut] adj. zużyty; zniszczony; wynoszony

worried ['łe:ryd] adj. zatroskany; zaniepokojony

worriment [łe:ryment] s. zmartwienie

worrisome [łe:rysem] adj. trapiący; lubiący się martwić

worry [łe:ry] v. dręczyć (się); martwić (się); trapić (się); zadręczać; zamartwiać; naprzykrzać (się); narzucać (się); napastować; kąsać; szarpać zębami; s. zmartwienie; troska; kłopot; kąsanie (zdobyczy przez psa)

worry along ['łe:rye,long] v. uporać się z trudnościami

worry down ['łe:ry,dałn] v. połykać łapczywie

worry out ['łe:ry,aut] v. rozwiązać z wysiłkiem (np. problem)

worse [łe:rs] adj. gorszy (niż:

bad; evil; ill); podniszczony; słabszy; bardziej chory; s. coś gorszego; to co najgorsze; najgorszy stan; najgorszy wypadek; v. pogarszać się; adv. gorzej; bardziej

worsen ['łe:rsn] v. pogorszyć (się)

worship ['łe:rszyp] s. cześć; kult; uwielbienie; nabożeństwo; bałwochwalstwo; v. czcić; wielbić; uwielbiać; brać udział w nabożeństwie

worshipful ['łe:rszypful] adj. pełen czci; czcigodny

worshiper ['łe:rszyper] s. czciciel; wielbiciel

worst [łe:rst] adj. najgorszy; s. coś najgorszego; najgorszy wypadek; adv. najgorzej; najbardziej; (slang): bardzo; v. pokonać; wziąć nad kimś górę; zadać klęskę; pobić

worsted ['łustyd] adj. czesankowy; s. kamgarn; przędza wełniana czesana; czesanka

worth [łe:rs] s. wartość; cena; adj. wart; opłacający się

worthless ['łe:rslys] adj. bezwartościowy

worth seeing ['łe:rs'si:yng] adj. wart widzenia

worthwhile ['łe:rshłajl] adj. wart zachodu; opłacający się

worthy ['łe:rsy] adj. godny; wartościowy; poczciwy; s. godny człowiek; wybitny człowiek (też żartem)

would [łud] v. zob. will (forma warunkowa)

would be ['łud,bi:] adj. rzekomy; niedoszły; adv. rzekomo; niby to

wound [łu:nd] s. rana; v. ranić; zob. v. wind

wounded ['łu:ndyd] adj. ranny; urażony

wove [łouw] v. zob. weave

woven ['łouwn] v. zob. weave

wow [łau] (slang): s. szlagier;

świetna rzecz; v. mieć
powodzenie; wywoływać
zachwyt; excl.: au!; cudownie!
wrack [raek] s. = wreck(age);
chwasty morskie wyrzucone
na brzeg, używane na nawóz
wraith [rejs] s. sobowtór; cień
(duch)
wrangle ['raengl] s. kłótnia;
burda; v. kłócić się; (slang):
pilnować koni
wrangler ['raengler] s. kłótnik;
pastuch koński (kowboj)
wrap; wrapt; wrapt [raep; raept;
raept]
wrap [raep] v. zawijać; owijać;
zapakowywać; spowijać;
otulać się; okrywać (się);
zachodzić na siebie; s. szal;
chusta; okrycie
wrap up ['raepap] v. owijać
(się); pakować
wrapper ['raeper] s. opakowanie;
opaska; obwoluta; banderola;
papierek; bibułka; osłona;
podomka (damska); pakowacz
wrapping ['raepyng] s.
opakowanie
wrapping paper ['raepyng pejper]
s. papier do pakowania
wrapt [raept] v. zob. wrap
wrath [ra:s] s. gniew; oburzenie
wrathful [ra:sful] adj. gniewny
wreak [ri:k] v. wywierać
(zemstę); dawać upust;
wyładować (gniew)
wreath [ri:s] s. wieniec
wreathe [ri:z] v. wieńczyć;
wić się; splatać; spowijać;
pleść się; kłębić się (dym
etc.)
wreck [rek] s. ruina; wrak;
rozbicie się (np. statku);
katastrofa; szczątki (np. na
wodzie); zniszczenie; rozbitek
życiowy; kaleka; wypadek; v.
rozbić (pojazd); zniweczyć
(nadzieje); burzyć; być
rozbitym; spowodować
rozbicie; zrujnować; mieć
wypadek
wreckage ['rekydż] s. rozbicie;
szczątki; gruzy

wrecked ['rekt] adj. rozbity;
zniszczony; zepsuty
wrecking company ['rekyng
'kampeny] s. przedsiębiorstwo
rozbiórki budynków
wrecking service
['rekyng'se:rwys] s. przewóz
zepsutych samochodów
wrecker ['reker] s. sprawca
wypadku; ciężarówka (z
dźwigiem) do przewozu
zepsutych samochodów;
kierowca przewożący zepsute
samochody; przedsiębiorca
rozbiórki budynków;
przedsiębiorca wydobywania
zatopionych statków; człowiek
kradnący szczątki statku;
szkodnik; rozbijacz
małżeństwa
wren [ren] s. strzyżyk
wrench [rencz] s. gwałtowne
skręcenie; ukręcenie;
szarpnięcie; wykręcenie;
zwichnięcie; przekręcenie
(faktów); ból (rozstania); klucz
maszynowy; klucz nasadowy;
klucz nakrętkowy; v.
szarpnąć; skręcić;
wykręcić; zwichnąć (nogę);
przekręcać (fakty); ukręcać
wrench open ['rencz'oupen] v.
odkręcić; otwierać;
odśrubowywać
wrest [rest] v. wykręcać;
wyrywać; przekręcać
(fakty); wydobywać zeznania;
s. wykręcanie; wyrywanie;
klucz do strojenia (harfy)
wrest from ['restfrom] v.
wyrwać komuś
wrestle ['resl] v. mocować się;
zmagać się; borykać się;
walczyć; s. zapasy; walka
wrestler ['resler] s. zapaśnik
wrestling ['reslyng] s.
zapaśnictwo
wrest-pins ['rest,pynz] pl. kołki
na struny fortepianowe
wretch [recz] s. nieszczęśnik;
biedaczysko; biedak; nędzarz;
łajdak; łotr; nikczemnik
wretched ['reczyd] adj.

nieszczęśliwy; pechowy;
biedny; nędzny; marny;
fatalny; ohydny; wstrętny;
nadzwyczajny (łotr)

wrick [ryk] v. lekko zwichnąć;
nadwerężyć; s. zwichnięcie;
lekkie naderwanie

wriggle ['rygl] v. wić się;
wkręcać (się); kręcić;
wywinąć się; s. ruch wijący
się; wicie

wriggle along ['rygle'long] v.
posuwać się wijąc

wriggle in ['rygl,yn] v. wkręcać
się

wriggle out ['ryglaut] v.
wykręcać się

wright [rajt] s. robotnik; twórca

wring; wrung; wrung [ryng;
rang; rang]

wring [ryng] v. wyżymać;
wykręcać; ukręcić (łeb);
przekręcać (słowa); ściskać
(serce); uściskać (ręką);
wymóc (coś na kimś);
zniekształcić; s. wyżymanie;
uścisk; ściskanie; wyżęcie;
wyciśnięcie

wringer [rynger] s. wyżymaczka

wrinkle ['rynkl] s. zmarszczka;
fałda; zmarszczenie; (slang):
ciekawy pomysł; rada; v.
marszczyć (się); być
pomarszczonym; zmiąć (się)

wrinkle up ['rynklap] v.
pomarszczyć

wrinkly [rynkly] adj.
pomarszczony

wrist [ryst] s. przegub; ruch ręki
w przegubie

wristband ['rystbaend] s.
mankiet u koszuli

wristwatch ['ryst,łocz] s. zegarek
na rękę

writ [ryt] s. nakaz pisemny,
prawny

writ for ['ryt,fo:r] s. rozpisanie
(wyborów)

write; wrote; written [rajt; rout;
rytn]

write [rajt] v. pisać; napisać;
zapisać; wypisać;
komponować; wystawiać

(czek); spisywać; sławić
(piórem)

write back ['rajt,baek] v.
odpisywać (komuś)

write down ['rajtdałn] v.
spisywać; notować;
określać (ujemnie)

write home ['rajt,houm] v. pisać
do domu

write-in ['rajt,yn] v. wpisywać;
dopisywać

write-off ['rajt,of] v. odpisywać
(na straty); pisać naprędce

write out ['rajt,aut] v.
wypisywać; sporządzać

write-up ['rajt,ap] v. zapisywać;
opisywać; przesadnie
szacować; pochwalić

writer ['rajter] s. pisarz; niżej
podpisany; powieściopisarz

writhe [rajs] v. wić się (z bólu);
cierpieć (zniewagą); skręcać
się (ze wstydu)

writing ['rajtyng] s. pismo;
utwór; artykuł; pisanie;
piśmiennictwo; sztuka
pisania; praca literacka;
napisana rzecz

writing desk ['rajtyng,desk] s.
biurko; pulpit

writing ink ['rajtyng,ynk] s.
atrament

writing paper ['rajtyng,pejper] s.
papier listowy; papier do
pisania

writing table ['rajtyng,tejbl] s.
biurko

written ['rytn] v. zob. write; adj.
pisany

wrong [ro:ng] adj. zły;
niewłaściwy; błędny; nie w
porządku; mylny;
niekorzystny; niesprawiedliwy;
s. zło; wykroczenie; krzywda;
wina; pomyłka; grzech; strata;
niesprawiedliwość; v.
skrzywdzić; niesłusznie
posądzać; być
niesprawiedliwym; adv.
mylnie; niewłaściwie; błędnie;
źle; zdrożnie; niekorzystnie

wrongdoer ['ro:ng'du:er] s.
krzywdziciel; grzesznik;

winowajca
wrongdoing ['ro:ng'duyng] s.
nadużycia; wykroczenia;
grzechy; przestępstwa
wrongful ['ro:ngful] adj. zły;
krzywdzący; niesprawiedliwy;
bezprawny
wronghead ['ro:ng'hed] v.
przekręcać (słowa etc.)
wrongheaded ['ro:ng'hedyd] adj.
uparty; przewrotny
wrote [rout] v. zob. write
wroth [ro:s] adj. gniewny
wrought [ro:t] v. zob. work
wrought iron ['ro:t'ajern] s. kute
żelazo
wrought-up ['ro:t,ap] adj.
napięty; zdenerwowany
wrung ['rang] v. zob. wring
wry [raj] adj. krzywy; skrzywiony
wryneck ['rajnek] s. zastrzał szyi;
kręcz karku

X

x [eks] dwudziesta czwarta litera
alfabetu angielskiego; rzymska
cyfra 10; niewiadoma
x-bit ['eks,byt] s. krzyżowe
ostrze świdra
x-bracing ['eks,brejsyn] s.
wiązanie krzyżowe
xenon ['zenon] s. ksenon
xenophobia [,zene'foubje] s.
ksenofobia
Xmas ['krysmes] = Christmas
x-ray ['eks'rej] adj.
rentgenowski; v.
prześwietlać; robić zdjęcie
rentgenowskie
x-ray diagnosis
['eks'rej,dajeg'nouzys] s.
rozpoznanie rentgenowskie
x-ray examination
['eks'rej,yg'zaemynejszyn] s.
badanie rentgenowskie
x-ray picture ['eks'rej'pykczer] s.
zdjęcie rentgenowskie

x-ray spectrum ['eks
'rej'spektrem] s. widmo
promieniowania
rentgenowskiego
x-rays ['eks'rejs] pl. promienie
rentgenowskie
xylem ['zajlem] s. drewno
xylograph ['zajlou'graph] s.
drzeworyt
xylophagous [zaj'lofeges] adj.
drewnożerny
xylophone ['zylefoun] s. ksylofon

Y

y [łaj] dwudziesta piąta litera
alfabetu angielskiego
yabber ['jaeber] v. gadać
yacht [jot] s. jacht; v. płynąć
jachtem; urządzać wyścigi
jachtowe
yachting ['jotyng] s. sport
żeglarski
yak [jaek] s. jak; (slang):
gadanie; śmiech; v. gadać;
śmiać się
yam [jaem] s. słodki ziemniak
(amerykański)
yap [jaep] v. ujadać; (slang):
paplać; s. ujadanie;
paplanina; krzykacz; jadaczka
yard [ja:rd] s. jard (91.44 cm);
podwórze; dziedziniec; v.
umieszczać w ogrodzeniu
yardage ['jarrdydż] s. metraż
yard-stick ['jard,styk] s. listewka
do mierzenia, kryterium
yarn [ja:rn] s. włókno; przędza;
historyjka; v. opowiadać
historyjki
yawl [jo:l] s. jolka (łódź); v.
zawyć; s. wycie
yawn [jo:n] v. ziewać; ziąć;
zionąć; s. ziewnięcie;
ziewanie
yawningly ['jo:niynly] adv.
ziewając
Y-axis ['łaj'aeksys] s. oś Y; oś

rzędnych

ye [ji:] pron. wy (biblijne)

yea [jej] adv. tak, zaiste, zaprawdą, ba, nawet; s. głosowanie "tak"

yeah [jej] (slang): tak; excl.: tak!; nie wierzę! ale! czyżby?

year [je:r] s. rok

year-book ['jer:,buk] s. rocznik (statystyczny itd.)

year-long ['jer,lon] adj. trwający od roku

yearly [je:rly] adj. roczny; coroczny; adv. corocznie; s. rocznik; adv. raz na rok

yearn [je:rn] v. tęsknić, zatęsknić

yearning ['jer:nyn] adj. tęskny; s. tęsknota

yearningly ['je:rnynly] adv. tęsknie; z tęsknotą

yeast [ji:st] s. drożdże; ferment; piana; v. fermentować; pienić (się)

yell [jel] v. wrzeszczeć; s. wrzask; dopingowanie

yellow ['jelou] adj. żółty; (slang): tchórzliwy; zawistny; żółty z zazdrości; n. żółty kolor; żółtko; v. żółknąć; powodować żółknięcie

yelp [jelp] s. skowyt; v. skowyczeć

yeoman ['joumen] s. podoficer marynarki; (dawniej) wolny chłop

yep [jep] adv. (slang): tak

yes [jes] adv. tak; v. potakiwać

yes-man [jes'men] s. człowiek potakujący, bez własnego zdania

yesterday ['jesterdy] adv. & s. wczoraj

yet [jet] adv. & conj. dotąd; jeszcze do tej pory; na razie; jak dotąd; jednak; ani też; mimo to

yew [ju:] s. cis

Yiddish [jydysz] s. język żydowski

yield [ji:ld] v. wydawać; dawać; rodzić; przynosić; oddawać (się); porzucać;

ustępować; s. plon; zysk; wydajność

yielding [ji:ldyng] s. wydajność; adj. ustępliwy

yogurt ['jouguert] s. jogurt

yoke [jouk] s. jarzmo; v. zaprzęgać; nakładać jarzmo; (slang): zaskakiwać (przechodnia) w celu rabunku

yolk [jouk] s. żółtko; rodzaj łoju

yonder ['jonder] adj. & adv. tam dalej; tamten

you [ju:] pron. ty; wy; pan; pani; panowie; panie

you'd [ju:d] = you would; you had

you'll [ju:l] = you shall; you will

young [jang] adj. młody; młodzieńczy; młodociany

youngish ['jangysz] adj. młodawy, dość młody

youngster ['jangster] s. dziecko; młodzik

your [ju:r] adj. twój; wasz; pański

you're [jo:r] = you are

yours [juers] pron. twój; wasz; pański (z poważaniem)

yourself [,juer'self] pron. ty sam

yourselves [,juer'selwz] pron. wy sami

youth [ju:s] s. młodość, młodzieniec

youths [ju:dz] pl. młodzież; młodzieniec

youthful ['ju:sful] adj. młody; młodzieńczy

youthfulness ['ju:sfulnys] s. młodość, młodzieńczość

youth-hostel ['ju:s'hostl] s. schronisko młodzieżowe

you've ['ju:w] = you have

Y-shaped ['łaj,szejpt] adj. kształtu litery Y

Yugoslav ['ju:gou'sla:w] adj. jugosłowiański

Yule [ju:l] s. święta Bożego Narodzenia

Yuletide ['ju:l,tajd] s. okres świąt Bożego Narodzenia

Z

soczewka zbliżająca w kamerze filmowej oraz w aparacie fotograficznym

z [i:] dwudziesta szósta litera alfabetu angielskiego

zany ['zejny] adj. pocieszny; błazeński; s. błazen; głupek

zeal [i:l] s. gorliwość

zealous ['zeles] adj. gorliwy

zebra ['zi:bre] s. zebra; (slang): mulat; adj. pręgowany

zenith ['seni̱t] s. zenit; szczyt (sławy)

zero ['zierou] s. zero; v. ustawiać na zero; brać na cel

zest [zest] s. smak; pikanteria; rozkosz; zamiłowanie; v. dodawać pikanterii

zigzag ['zygzaeg] s. zygzak; adj. zygzakowaty; adv. zygzakiem

zigzaggy ['zygzagy] adj. zygzagowaty

zinc [zyṉk] s. cynk; v. cynkować

zip [zyp] s. świst; wigor; v. śmigać; gnać; zapinać zamek błyskawiczny

zip code ['zyp,koud] s. numeracja pocztowa miejscowości

zipper ['zyper] s. zamek błyskawiczny

zippy ['zypy] adj. żywy; zgrabny; pełen werwy

zloty ['zlouty] s. złoty (pieniądz polski)

zodiac ['zoudjaek] s. zodiak

zombie ['zomby] s. bóg-pyton; (slang): bałwan; tuman

zone [zoun] s. strefa; zona; v. opasywać; dzielić na zony

zonal ['zounl] adj. strefowy

zoo [zu:] s. ogród zoologiczny

zoology [zou'oledży] s. zoologia

zoom [zu:m] v. buczeć; wzlatywać; wzbijać się szybko; śmigać; s. poderwanie (samolotu);

How to Use This Dictionary

The Polish-English part of this dictionary contains about 16,000 entries. The large Polish-English dictionaries usually contain some 180,000 entries, which give basic forms only and do not include ending changes, etc. discussed below. The term dictionary entry is used here as defined by the U.S. Bureau of Federal Supply, which indicates that each word variant explained constitutes an entry.

The word choice and translation are updated for current usage in America and Poland. Characteristic idiomatic usages are included. Each entry includes a pronunciation guide for sound and stress. A stress mark is placed over the stressed vowel.

The pronunciation guide, following the listing of all entries in this dictionary, gives also an illustrated discussion of Polish and English sounds and an explanation of the phonetic symbols. For practical reasons, the number of phonetic symbols are expressed in Latin letters only. Special care is given to explain and illustrate the pronunciation of Polish consonants and vowels which do not occur in the English language and vice versa. The information presented stresses whenever possible the familiar pronunciation and meaning in common usage in both languages.

Linguists define the language as a raw material for the creative activity of speaking. It is a rule-governed creativity in which we are creating and understanding sentences within rules of grammar. A grammatical rule is a description of a pattern habitually followed in a given language; changes in pattern render changes in meaning. This is true, of course, in both Polish and English languages.

An active language changes at varying rates but always at a rate faster than its changes in rules of grammar. Grammar has greater stability than syntax and vocabulary. Every language offers a special way of seeing and interpreting. Languages within the same Indo-European group are not simply equivalent.

The abundance of Polish grammatical forms that do not occur in English should be noticed. A multitude of inflectional forms of Polish nouns and adjectives is reflected in their structure and spelling. Changes in endings of nouns and adjectives correspond to their function in a sentence, their gender and number. Thus, Polish declension requires seven ending changes in nouns and adjectives for both singular and plural, in each gender. Polish personal verb forms correspond by gender and number to the subject of the sentence; thus, nine verb endings occur in the present tense alone. Impersonal forms and various moods expand this number. Both the perfect and imperfect of Polish verbs are indicated by structural variation (In informal Polish, the distinction between perfect and imperfect forms is not always carefully observed.). Verbs "dać" and "dawać" and "zabrać" and "zabierać" illustrate the structural difference between perfect and imperfect forms characteristic of the Polish language.

If every possible structural form of every Polish noun, adjective, verb, adverb, etc. inclusive of all ending changes was a dictionary entry, the number of Polish words listed would be in millions. The number of Polish words is further increased by multitudes of augmentative and diminutive forms which give expression to emotional values by word structure. These augmentative and diminutive forms serve to make the meaning of nouns and adjectives precise by often achieving broadening and clarifying. Augmentative and diminutive forms in Polish are often used to express feelings and attitudes both positive and negative. A comparison of a Polish, German and English word may be useful in order to illustrate the relative usage of augmentatives and diminutives. The use of the German word offers a chance to see the transition between Slavic and Germanic languages. In German diminutives and augmentatives we see the influence of the languages of the Elbe River Slavs, the Polabians, the Lusatians and the Czechs as well as the influence of the Polish language./Also see page VII/.

Language:	Basic word:	Augmentative Form:	Diminutive Form:
ENGLISH	BOY	BIG BOY	LITTLE BOY
GERMAN	KNABE	KNAB	KNABCHEN, KNABLEIN
POLISH	CHŁOPIEC	CHŁOPAK CHŁOPACZYSKO CHŁOPCZYSKO ETC.	CHŁOPCZYK CHŁOPACZEK CHLOPTAS CHLOPACZYNA ETC.

It should be noticed that in this example the Polish word "chlopiec" is a diminutive form derived from the Polish word "chlop" which among other meanings stands for a grown man. In the Polish language there is a middle voice of verb inflection not used in English. The middle voice represents the subject as acting on and for itself in a way different than the usual active and passive form common to both the Polish and English languages. The middle voice in Polish describes self-reflectiveness not directly describable in English. The Polish middle voice occurs within the reflexive form of verb followed by "się." The gender of nouns in Polish is structurally indicated in conjugation of verbs (See p.VIII). The designation of gender of the Polish nouns is influenced by the sound of the ending. Thus, inanimate things in the Polish, as in most Indo-European languages, often are of masculine or feminine grammatically designated gender. The Polish word "robota," for example, meaning "work," is of feminine gender because of the ending "a"; a derivative noun "robot" which means a mechanical man or brain is of masculine gender indicated by ending sound of the letter "t." The profound differences between the Polish and English language make literal translation of common expressions usually impossible which is the main cause of the difficulty of learning Polish by English speakers and vice versa. The relative difficulty of learning a foreign language depends on the characteristics of one's own language as illustrated on Table 1, (page VI) showing the relative difficulty of languages for English speakers based on the experience of the Foreign Service Institute (1973).

The Slavic languages, including Polish, are a family of languages evolved directly from the original Indo-European language by relatively undisturbed evolution. Any two of the fourteen Slavic languages are sufficiently similar to allow their speakers to communicate quite effectively if each speaks his own language slowly and explains to the other the words that are not common to both languages. All the Slavic languages have almost the same flexional characteristics with the exception of Bulgarian, which like English lost the declensions. It happened in Bulgaria after the imposition of Greek in place of the Old Slavic liturgical language and during the lengthy Turkish occupation. Polish speakers have to learn to express meaning by word structure within the grammatical rules of flexional changes. The English and Bulgarian speakers achieve logical clarity of meaning by order or position of words. Thus, English and Bulgarian are defined as isolating or position languages. Polish speaker learning English encounters much simpler grammatical forms and basic concepts in the English language than does his English counterpart in Polish. Assuming the same intensity of foreign language teaching program Polish speakers learn English about 20 to 30% faster than vice versa. The English language is mixed so much that it does not have a close sister language. However, what remained in English of the Old Anglo-Saxon grammar, is of Germanic character, even though, to the English speakers today, the Old Anglo-Saxon is a foreign language. Also Germanic is the majority of the high-frequency vocabulary in the modern English. Thus, English is usually classified by the linguists as a Germanic language, even though, the Romance languages, including Latin, contribute to English about half of its vocabulary. Both, Romance and Germanic languages have much simpler grammar than do the Slavic languages with exception of Bulgarian. The Polish language belongs to the inflective group of languages and it utilizes the active voice to a greater extent than does the English language. Numerous diacritical markings in Polish give good correlation of sound to spelling. The difficulties of correlating sound to spelling in English result mainly from the fact that two different sound correlations to the Latin alphabet occurred in Britain, first to the Anglo-Saxon and then to the French (brought with the Norman invasion). Polish pronunciation is rather stable and clear. English vowels are relatively less stable and undergo variations under stress. On the other hand, the voiced consonants that occur at the end of an English word are often pronounced clearly. The word "love," for example, has a clear "v" at the end and not an "f" as it would be pronounced in Polish. In Polish, all consonants that occur at the end of a Polish word are voiceless. The word "woz," for example, is pronounced with an "s" at the end: "voos." Typically, rules of grammar and phonetics in English start with words "often," "sometimes," etc. while in Polish similar rules are stated: "always, with very few exceptions." The foreign words enrich English vocabulary and remain relatively unchanged. In Polish the foreign borrowings are assimilated into declension of nouns (single and plural) and adjectives (both subject to expansion in to augmentative and diminutive forms) and conjugation of verbs (each in perfect and imperfect form) and grammatical forms derived from verbs. The English language is much simpler in this respect because each noun without any change in spelling potentially may be used as a verb and sometimes as an adjective. In Polish the vigorous growth of abstract and scientific terms was based mainly on the indigenous words with parallel foreign borrowings. The Polish language achieves the size of its vocabulary by use of prefixes and suffixes to a much greater extent than does the English language. For example the mystical ancient Indo-European root-word "god," common to both Polish and English is expanded in Polish to over 3,000 structurally different words. Meanings of these words include weather, agreements, disagreements, harmony, adventure, comfort, discomfort, toilet (wy-god-ka), injury, dignity, decency, indecency, mystical union, time measurement, reconciliation, hiring etc.(VII).Total vocabulary in English and Polish is about one half a million words. However the make up of each vocabulary is different. English has some 120,000 root-words or about double the 60,000 root-words that are characteristic of an inflective language such as Polish. A practical dictionary is based on the frequency of use of words. Table II (p. VI) includes the plot of high frequency words as a percent of the words printed on an average English page. Thus knowing 1,000 most frequently used words one would know about 70% of words on an average page; and knowing 5,000 would give 86% and knowing 10,000 would give one about 92% of words on an average English page. The size of a person's vocabulary and the degree of comprehension of a native language learned with age and education is shown approximately on Table III (p. VI).

It is interesting to note that throughout Europe, including Poland, many professional and business people with rudimentary knowledge of English prefer to read factual reports in English, rather than in their native language. English is recognized by them as a methodical, energetic, businesslike and sober language, that is somewhat short on finery and elegance, but flexible and unrestrained by strict rules of grammar and lexicion. Centuries of colonial expansion brought English to all corners of the world where hundreds of millions use it.

English today is a dominant world language, while less than sixty million people know the Polish language. However, the Polish language with its logic, finery and elegance will continue to give a good start to abstract thinkers such as mathematicians, logicians, philosophers, anthropologists, novelists and poets and thus contribute to the pluralistic culture of the world.

TABLE I   RELATIVE DIFFICULTY OF LANGUAGES FOR ENGLISH SPEAKERS
Class time for average student to reach between minimal and working professional proficiency according to Foreign Service Institute (1973).
24 weeks=720 hours: Afrikaans;Danish;Dutch;French;German;Haitian;
Creole;Italian;Norwegian;Spanish;Swedish;Swahili.
38 weeks=1140hours: Bulgarian;Dari:Farsi:Greek:Hindi:Indonesian;
Malay;Urdu.
44 weeks=1320hours: Amharic;Bengali;Burmese;Czech;Finnish;Hebrew;
Hungarian;Cambodian-Khmer;Lao;Nepali:Philipino;Polish;Russian;Ser-
bo-Croatian;Sinhala;Thai;Tamil;Turkish;Vietnamese.
65 weeks=1950hours: Arabic;Chinese;Japanese;Korean.

TABLE II   HIGH FREQUENCY ENGLISH WORDS VS. PERCENTAGE OF WORDS ON
          AN AVERAGE PRINTED PAGE according to H.Kučera and W.N.
Francis"Computational Analysis of Present-day American English"1967.
PERCENTAGE OF WORDS UNDERSTOOD ON AN AVERAGE PRINTED PAGE :

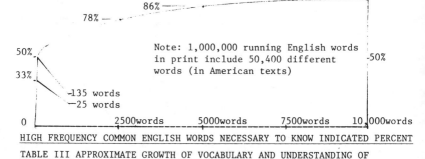

Note: 1,000,000 running English words
in print include 50,400 different
words (in American texts)

HIGH FREQUENCY COMMON ENGLISH WORDS NECESSARY TO KNOW INDICATED PERCENT

TABLE III APPROXIMATE GROWTH OF VOCABULARY AND UNDERSTANDING OF
          WORDS WITH AGE AND EDUCATION IN A NATIVE LANGUAGE
Compare with estimated median vocabulary size for each age group by
K.C.Diller "The Language Teaching Controversy" 1978.

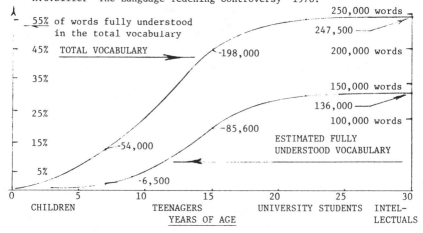

EXAMPLE OF NOUN AND ADJECTIVE DECLENSION IN POLISH LANGUAGE

DOBRY DOM = GOOD HOME, GOOD HOUSE

SINGULAR:

NOMINATIVUS	= MIANOWNIK	DOBRY DOM	GOOD HOME
GENETIVUS	= DOPEŁNIACZ	DOBREGO DOMU	OF A GOOD HOME
DATIVUS	= CELOWNIK	DOBREMU DOMOWI	FOR A GOOD HOME
ACCUSATIVUS	= BIERNIK	DOBRY DOM	A GOOD HOME
INSTRUMENTALIS	=NARZĘDNIK	DOBRYM DOMEM	BY A GOOD HOME
LOCATIVUS	= MIEJSCOWNIK	W DOBRYM DOMU	IN A GOOD HOME
VOCATIVUS	= WOŁACZ	O DOBRY DOMU!	OH! GOOD HOME

PLURAL:

NOMINATIVUS	= MIANOWNIK	DOBRE DOMY (2,3,4)	GOOD HOMES
		DOBRYCH DOMÓW (5...)	GOOD HOMES
GENETIVUS	= DOPEŁNIACZ	DOBRYCH DOMÓW	OF GOOD HOMES
DATIVUS	= CELOWNIK	DOBRYM DOMOM	FOR GOOD HOMES
ACCUSATIVUS	= BIERNIK	DOBRE DOMY (2,3,4)	GOOD HOMES
		DOBRYCH DOMÓW (5...)	GOOD HOMES
INSTRUMENTALIS	=NARZĘDNIK	DOBRYMI DOMAMI	BY GOOD HOMES
LOCATIVUS	= MIEJSCOWNIK	W DOBRYCH DOMACH	IN GOOD HOMES
VOCATIVUS	= WOŁACZ	O DOBRE DOMY!(2,3,4)	OH!GOOD HOMES
		O (PIĘC) DOBRYCH	OH! (FIVE)
		DOMÓW! (5...)	GOOD HOMES

NOTE: (2,3,4) = Small Polish plural of two, three and four.
       (5...) = Large Polish plural of five and more.

DIMINUTIVES: SING.: DOBRY DOMEK - PLUR.: DOBRE DOMKI (2,3,4)
                                              DOBRYCH DOMKÓW (5...)
                 DOBRY DOMECZEK   DOBRE DOMECZKI (2,3,4)
                                       DOBRYCH DOMECZKÓW (5...)
AUGMENTATIVES: SING.:DOBRE DOMISKO PLUR.:DOBRE DOMISKA(2,3,4)
                                             DOBRYCH DOMISK (5...)

EXAMPLE OF CONJUGATION OF A VERB IN THE POLISH LANGUAGE

CZYTAC (chi-tach) = TO READ

- PAST TENSE -

PERFECT FORM = SINGLE TIME COMPLETED OCCURENCE

MASCULINE	"I"	(JA)	CZYTAŁEM	I READ
FEMININE	"I"	(JA)	CZYTAŁAM	
MASCULINE	"YOU"	(TY)	CZYTAŁES	YOU READ
FEMININE	"YOU"	(TY)	CZYTAŁAS	
		(ON)	CZYTAŁ	HE READ
		(ONA)	CZYTAŁA	SHE READ
		(ONO)	CZYTAŁO	IT READ
MASCULINE	"WE"	(MY)	CZYTALISMY	WE READ
FEMININE	"WE"	(MY)	CZYTAŁYSMY	
MASC.PLUR.	"YOU"	(WY)	CZYTALISCIE	YOU READ
FEM. PLUR.	"YOU"	(WY)	CZYTAŁYSCIE	
		(ONI)	CZYTALI	THEY READ
FEM.& NEUTER		(ONE)	CZYTAŁY	

CZYTYWAC (chi-ti-vach)=TO READ (OFTEN)

IMPERFECT FORM = MULTIPLE INCOMPLETE OCCURENCE IN THE PAST

MASCULINE	"I"	(JA)	CZYTYWAŁEM	I USED TO READ
FEMININE	"I"	(JA)	CZYTYWAŁAM	
MASCULINE	"YOU"	(TY)	CZYTYWAŁES	YOU USED TO READ
FEMININE	"YOU"	(TY)	CZYTYWAŁAS	
		(ON)	CZYTYWAŁ	HE USED TO READ
		(ONA)	CZYTYWAŁA	SHE USED TO READ
		(ONO)	CZYTYWAŁO	IT USED TO READ
MASCULINE	"WE"	(MY)	CZYTYWALISMY	WE USED TO READ
FEMININE	"WE"	(MY)	CZYTYWAŁYSMY	
MASC.PLUR.	"YOU"	(WY)	CZYTYWALISCIE	YOU USED TO READ
FEM. PLUR.	"YOU"	(WY)	CZYTYWAŁYSCIE	
		(ONI)	CZYTYWALI	THEY USED TO READ
FEM.& NEUTER		(ONE)	CZYTYWAŁY	

EXAMPLES OF WORDS DERIVED FROM THE VERB "CZYTAC"= TO READ

DOCZYTAC, DOCZYTAC SIE, DOCZYTYWAC, DOCZYTYWAC SIE,
NACZYTAC SIE, NACZYTYWAC SIE, OCZYTAC SIE, ODCZYTAC,
ODCZYTYWAC, POCZYTAC, POCZYTAC SOBIE, POCZYTYWAC, POCZY-
TYWAC SOBIE, PRZECZYTAC, ROZCZYTAC SIE, ROZCZYTYWAC SIE,
WCZYTAC SIE, WCZYTYWAC SIE, WYCZYTAC, WYCZYTYWAC, ZACZY-
TYWAC, SIE, ZACZYTAC SIE describe all the possible ways
and conditions of reading with the exception of "reread-
ing" which can not be translated into Polish in one word.
Besides the twenty three verbs are nouns: CZYTANKA, CZY-
TELNICTWO, CZYTELNIK, CZYTELNIA, CZYTELNOSC, ODCZYT, POCZY-
TALNOSC, NIEPOCZYTALNOSC, POCZYTNOSC, and adjectives as:
CZYTELNY, NIECZYTELNY, OCZYTANY, NIEOCZYTANY, POCZYTALNY,
NIEPOCZYTALNY, POCZYTNY etc.

Angielsko-polska część słownika zawiera około 15,000 haseł.

Jak wiadomo pojęcia i myśli formuje się w poszczególnych językach w różny sposób. Nawet języki należące do tej samej grupy / jak np polski i angielski do grupy indoeuropejskiej/ nie są równoznaczne.

Bogactwo polskich form gramatycznych nie ma odpowiednika w angielskim. Odmiana rzeczowników i przymiotników przez siedem przypadków oraz czasowników przez wszystkie możliwe osoby z odpowiednimi zmianami końcówek, typowymi dla języka polskiego, nie istnieje w angielskim. Język angielski bogatszy jest w wyrażenia zwyczajowo-idiomatyczne; więcej też jest w nim przyimków i zaimków.

Język polski zawiera liczne formy gramatyczne poszczególnych słów i gdyby wprowadzić każdą z nich jako odrębne hasło słownika to takich haseł byłoby kilka milionów.

Polska forma zwrotna zawiera określenia pośrednie między formami czynną i bierną charakterystycznymi dla obu języków. Tej formy nie można dosłownie przetłumaczyć na angielski. Na przykład powiedzenie "wzruszyłem się" nie znaczy dokładnie "I am touched", co równa się polskiemu "jestem wzruszony". "I touched myself" natomiast wcale nie znaczy "wzruszyłem się".

Inną cecha charakterystyczną języka polskiego jest odróżnienie małej liczby mnogiej /2,3 i 4/ od dużej /5 i więcej/: tego rozróżnienia nie ma w języku angielskim.

Ogólnie biorąc język polski ma więcej form rzeczownikowych, przymiotnikowych oraz czasownikowych. W angielskim natomiast prawie każdy rzeczownik bez zmiany pisowni może być użyty jako czasownik a nieraz także jako przymiotnik. Polskie zasady gramatyczne można wyrazić słowami "zawsze z kilkoma wyjątkami", angieskie zasady gramatyczne i fonetyczne są bardziej płynne - mówi się w nich: "często", "czasem" i "nieraz". W angielskim przeważają wyrażenia i fonetyka zwyczajowe.

W części angielsko-polskiej słownika oznaczono formy gramatyczne poszczególnych haseł: rzeczowniki, przymiotniki, czasowniki, przysłówki, zaimki, przyimki i częste zwroty.

Angielskie czasowniki nieregularne podano w trzech podstawo-

X

wych formach /infinitive, past and past participle = bezokolicznik, czas przeszły i imiesłów czasu przeszłego/.

Hasła wybrano z uwzględnieniem słownictwa używanego obecnie
w Polsce i w Ameryce; są wśród nich ważniejsze wyrażenia poto-
czne.

Podano wymowę i akcent.

BIBLIOGRAPHICAL NOTE

The spelling used in this dictionary was checked against standard current dictionaries.

The semantic aspects of phrases was analysed in accordance
with Korzybski's General Semantics. Alfred Korzybski, Polish
philosopher, mathematician and engineer founded in 1938 the
Institute of General Semantics in Lakeland, Connecticut. The
works of Jens Otto Jespersen were used as references for ling-
uistic comments.

Glossary of Menu Terms

Polish cuisine is made for hospitality. It abounds in wonderful hors d'oeuvres, fragrant soups, delightful dishes produced with subtle skill and care integrating native traditions and adaptations from other lands. Polish desserts and sweets are unusually good. They never fail to delight Poles and tourists. There is an abundant variety of very tasty Polish bakery products. Polish cuisine includes distinctive seasonal menus for spring, summer, autumn and winter. Examples of Polish food served in quality restaurants are listed in this glossary of menu terms.

A unique item of daily diet is the Polish bread or "chleb." It is always sold in loaves, has a substantial body and a delicious crust. Fresh Polish bread is bought and consumed daily.

Breakfast or "sniadanie" is served from 6:30 until 10 A.M.; dinner or "objad" is served from 1 until 3:30 P.M.; supper or "kolacja" is served from 6 until 9 P.M. Cafes serve good coffee topped with whipped cream during the day and late into the evening. A small serving of strong coffee is called "pol-czarnej" (half-cup of black).

A variety of excellent pastries are served in the "kawiarnia" (cafe) or "cukiernia" (pastry shop). Food is served in the "restauracja" (restaurant).

"Jadłospis" (menu) will list:
"przystawki" (apetizers);
"zupy" (soups);
"dania" (main courses) including:
"dania miesne" (meats),
"dania jarskie" (vegetarian courses),
"ryby" (fish),
"drób" (poultry or other birds),
"wedliny" (smoked meats and fish, also pates),
"jarzyny" (vegetables),
"sałatki" (salads)
"desery" (desserts) which may include:
"owoce" (fruits),
"kompoty" (compotes),
"ciastka" (cakes),
"torty" (multi-layer torts)
"lody" (ice cream).
Menus will also list:
"napoje" (beverages)
"zakaski" (snacks, usually served with vodka).

"Przystawki" (Appetizers)

"grzyby marynowane" (marinated mushrooms)
"jajka faszerowane po polsku" (stuffed eggs Polish style)
"jajka faszerowane z sosem" (stuffed eggs with sauce)
"jajka faszerowane szynka" (eggs stuffed with ham)
"jajka w sosie chrzanowym" (eggs in horseradiash sauce)
"jajka w sosie musztardowym" (eggs in mustard sauce)
"krokiety z jajka" (egg balls with grated cheese)
"pierozki" (browned onion and mushroom ravioli)
"pierozki z miesem" (dumplings with meat)
"sledzie marynowane" (marinated herring)
"sledzie w smietanie" (herring in sour cream)

"Zakaski" (Snacks, Usually With Vodka)

"wybór kanapek" (canapes Polish style many different snacks)

"Sniadanie" (Breakfast)

"boczek" (bacon)
"bułka" (white bread or roll)
"chleb" (bread made in loafs)
"masło" butter)
"ser bialy" (farmer's cheese)
"ser zółty" (cheese, melted)
"jajka na mieko" (soft boiled eggs)
"jajka po wiedeńsku" (soft boiled eggs with butter)
"jajka sadzone" (fried eggs, sunny side up)
"jajecznica" (scrambled eggs)
"szynka" (ham)
"konfitury" (preserves)
"mleko" (milk)
"dżem" (jam)
"miód" (honey)
"naleśniki z dżemem" (pancakes with jam)
"omlet" (omlette)
"sok z czarnej porzeczki" (black currant juice)
"sok jabłkowy" (apple cider)
"sok pomarańczowy" (orange juice)

"Objad" (Dinner, 1.00-3.30 P.M.)
"Kolacja" (Supper, 6.00-9.00 P.M.
lighter meal served with the same manu as dinner)

"Zupy Gorace" (Soups Served Hot)

"rosól" (comsomes or broth of traditionally seasoned beef or chicken)
"rosól z zoltkiem" (consome with a raw egg yolk)
"rosól z diablotka" (consome with salty biscuit)
"barszcz z pasztecikiem" (beet-root soup)
"barszcz ukraiński z polska kiełbasa" (Ukrainian barshch with Polish sausage)
"barszcz zabielany" barshch with sour cream)
"kapuśniak" (sour cabbage soup)
"krupnik" (barley kasha soup)
"zupa grzybowa" (mushroom soup)
"zupa pomidorowa z ryzem" (tomato soup with rice)
"zupa jarzynowa" (vegetable soup)
"zupa grochowa na wędzonce" (pea and smoked ham soup)
"zupa ziemniaczana" (potato soup)
"zupa chlebowa" (bread soup with egg)
"zupa cytrynowa z ryzem" (lemon soup with rice)
"zupa kminkowa" (caraway seed soup)
"zupa szczawiowa z jajkami" (tart sorrel soup with eggs)
"zupa ogórkowa z koperkiem" (dill picle soup)
"żurek" (sour soup)

"Zupy Zimne" (Cold Soups)

"chłodnik" (cold barshch with cream)
"zupa jabłkowa" (apple soup)
"zupa ogórkowa na barszczu" (barszcz and cucumber soup)
"zupa owocowa" (fruit soup)

"Dania Miesne" (Main Meat Courses)

"baranina" (lamb)
"befsztyk po tatarsku" (Tartar steak)
"bigos" sour cabbage with diced pork, veal, beef, ham, sausage and mushrooms; stewed, then fried
"bite kotlety" (pounded cutlets)
"bite zrazy cielęce" (pounded veal chops)
"boczek pieczony" (baked bacon)
"chuda szynka" (lean ham)
"chude mieso" (lean meat)
"cielecina z papryka" (veal with paprika)

"duszona wołowina z grzybami" (simmered beef with mushrooms)
"flaki" (tripe)
"golonka gotowana" (pig's foot jelly)
"gulasz" (goulash, meat stew)
"gulasz wieprzowy" (pork goulash)
"kiełbasa" (sausage)
"kiełbasa wedzona" (smoked sausage)
"kiszka" (sausage of chopped liver and pork with groats)

XIII

"klops" (meat loaf)
"kłoduny") (meat balls in dough)
"kotlet" (cutlet)
"krokiety" (meat balls)
"królik marynowany" (marinated rabbit)
"krwawa kiszka" (black pudding)
"łopatka barania" (lamb shoulder)
"marynowana baranina" (marinated lamb)
"mielone mięso" (ground meat"
"mózg wieprzowy" (pork brain)
"ozór wołowy" (beef tongue)
"parowki na gorąco" (franks served hot)
"pasztet" (calf's liver, veal and pork meat loaf with bacon, eggs and mushrooms)
"pasztet z watroby" (liver pudding)
"pieczeń barania" (lamb roast)
"pieczeń wolowa duszona" (pot roast of beef)
"potrawka z baraniny" (fricassee of lamb)
"prosię nadziewane" (stuffed piglet)
"rolada mięsna" (meat loaf)
"schab" (loin)
"schabowa pieczeń" (roast loin)
"siekane zrazy" (minced chops)
"smazone mięso" (fried meat)
"szaszłyk" shish kebab
"szynka" (ham)
"szynka gotowana" (cooked ham)
"szynka gotowana, na zimno" (cold cooked ham)
"sztuka miesa" (cooked beef)
"watróbka" (liver)
"wedzone mięso" (smoked meat)
"zeberka" (ribs)
"zrazy baranie" (lamb chops)
"zrazy wieprzowe" (pork chops)

"Drób" (Poultry, Ducks and Geese)

"kura" (hen or chicken)
"kurczak" (spring chiken)
"kurcze pieczone" (baked chicken)
"kaczka" (duck)
"gęs" (goose)
"gołab" (pigeon)
"indyk" (turkey)
"bazant" (pheasant)
"nadziewany indyk" (stuffed turkey)
"paprykarz z kurcząt" (chicken stewed with pepers)
"potrawka z kury" (chiken fricassee)
"smazone kotlety z piersi kury" (chicken brest cutlets)

"Dziczyzna" (Venison)

"dzika gęs" (wild goose)
"dzika kaczka" (wild duck)
"kuropatwa" (partridge)
"pasztet z dziczyzny" (venison meat loaf)
"pieczona dziczyzna" (roast venison)
"potrawka z zająca" (fricassee of hare)
"sarnina" (deer meat)
"udziec sarni" (deer haunch)
"zając" (hare)

"Dania Jarskie" (Vegetarian courses)

"Dania Rybne" (Fishes)

"dorsz w sosie chrzanowym" (cod with horseradish sause)
"gotowany szczupak z sosem chrzanowym" (boiled pike with horseradish sause)
"jesiotr z kwaśną śmietana" (sturgeon with sour cream)
"filet z soli z tartym serem" (fillet of sole with grated cheese)
"karp" (grain fed carp)
"karp w galarecie" (carp in jelly)
"losos w galarecie" (salmon in jelly)
"okon na bialym winie" (perch on white wine)
"okoń z rozna z grzybami" (perch broiled with mushrooms)
"potrawka z ryby z tartym serem" (fricassee of fish with grated cheese)
"pstrąg z pietruszka" (trout with parsley)
"szczupak pieczony z sardelami" (baked pike with anchovies)
"szczupak po zydowsku" pike Jewish style
"wegorz duszony w winie" (eel stewed in wine)

"Jarzyny" (Vegetables)

"brokuly" (broccoli)
"brukiew" (turnips)
"buraczki" (beat dish)
"buraki z rabarbarem" (beets with rhubarb)
"brukselka" (Brussels sprouts)
"chrzan" (horseradish)
"cebula" (onion)
"dania ziemniaczane" (potato dishes)
"dynia" (pumpkin)
"fasola" (beans)
"groszek" (green peas)
"kalafior" (cauliflower)
"kalarepa" (kohlrabi)
"kapusta" (cabbage)
"karczochy" (artichokes)
"kiszona kapusta" (sour cabbage)
"marchewka z groszkiem" (carrots with peas)
"młode ziemniaki" (early potatoes)
"placki zemniaczane" (potato pies or pancakes)
"pomidory" (tomatoes)
"szparagi" (asparagus)
"szparagowa fasola" (string beans)
"szpinak" (spinach)
"ziemniaki smazone" (fried potatoes)
"ziemniaki tłuczone" (mashed potatoes)

"Salatki" (Salads)

"cwikla" (red beet salad with horseradish)
"mieszana sałatka" (mixed salad)
"sałatka jarzynowa" (vegetable salad)
"sałatka owocowa" (fruit salad)
"sałatka pomidorowa" (tomato salad)
"sałatka sledziowa" (herring salad)
"sałatka w galarecie" (jellied salad)
"sałatka z cebuli" (onion salad)
"sałatka z ziemniakow" (potato salad)

"<u>Deser</u>" (dessert)

"babka" (round cofee cake)
"budyń" (pudding)
"budyń czekoladowy" (chocolate pudding)
"chrust" (Polish fried cookies)
"galaretka porzeczkowa" (currant jelly)
"gruszki w rumie" (pears in rum)
"kompot" (compote)
"kompot morelowy" (apricote compote)
"kutia" (wheat grain and honey dessert)
"lody" (ice cream)
"lody waniliowe" (vanilla ice cream)
"lody czekoladowe" (chocolate ice cream)
"makownik" (poppy seed cake)
"mus jablkowy" (creamed apples)
"paczki" (cherry stuffed batter balls)

"suflet kawowy" (cofee souffle)

"Napoje Orzezwiajace" (Refreashments)

"Napoje gorace" (Hot drinks)

"biała kawa" (coffee with cream)
"czarna kawa" (black coffee)
"herbata" (tea)
"kakao" (cocoa)
"mleko" (milk)
"surówka owocowa" (fresh fruit salad)
"truskawki" (strawberries)

"<u>Napoje Alkocholowe</u>" (Alcoholic Drinks)

"ajerkoniak" (eggnog vodka)
"ajerowka" (sweet sedge vodka)
"ciemne piwo" (dark beer)
"cytrynowka" (lemon vodka)
"jarzębiak" (rowanberry vodka)
"jasne piwo" (light beer)
"kminkowka" (caraway seed vodka)
"krupnik" (peppercorns, vanilla, honey vodka)
"miód pitny" (mead, honey wine)
"morelowka" (apricot vodka)
"piwo" (beer)
"piwo słodowe" (malt liquor)
"pomaranczówka" (orange vodka)
"śliwowica" (plum brandy)
"winiak" (wine brandy)
"wiśniówka" (cherry cordial)
"wódka" (vodka)
"wódka wyborowa" (choice grain vodka)
"wyszynk" (retail of alcoholic drinks)
"złota woda" (golden vodka)
"zubrowka" (bison grass vodka)
"zytnia wódka" (rye vodka)

CARDINAL NUMBERS	-	LICZEBNIKI GŁÓWNE
0	nought, zero, cipher	- zero
1	one	- jeden, raz
2	two	- dwa
3	three	- trzy
4	four	- cztery
5	five	- pięć
6	six	- sześć
7	seven	- siedem
8	eight	- osiem
9	nine	- dziewięć
10	ten	- dziesięć
11	eleven	- jedenaście
12	twelve	- dwanaście
13	thirteen	- trzynaście
14	fourteen	- czternaście
15	fifteen	- piętnaście
16	sixteen	- szesnaście
17	seventeen	- siedemnaście
18	eighteen	- osiemnaście
19	nineteen	- dziewiętnaście
20	twenty	- dwadzieścia
21	twenty-one	- dwadzieścia jeden
22	twenty-two	- dwadzieścia dwa
23	twenty-three	- dwadzieścia trzy
24	twenty-four	- dwadzieścia cztery
30	thirty	- trzydzieści
40	forty	- czterdzieści
50	fifty	- pięćdziesiąt
60	sixty	- sześćdziesiąt
70	seventy	- siedemdziesiąt
80	eighty	- osiemdziesiąt
90	ninety	- dziewięćdziesiąt
100	one hundred	- sto
101	one hundred and one	- sto jeden
110	one hundred and ten	- sto dziesięć
200	two hundred	- dwieście
777	seven hundred seventy seven	- siedemset siedemdziesiąt siedem
1,000.	one thousand	- tysiąc
1,500.	fifteen hundred	- tysiąc pięćset
1978	nineteen hundred and seventy eight	- tysiąc dziewięćset siedemdzie-siąt osiem
500,000.	five hundred thousand	- pięćset tysięcy
1,000,000.	one million	- milion
3,000,000.	three million	- trzy miliony
1,000,000,000.	one billion	- miliard

XVII

ORDINAL NUMBERS	–	LICZEBNIKI PORZĄDKOWE

1st	first	– pierwszy
2nd	second	– drugi
3rd	third	– trzeci
4th	fourth	– czwarty
5th	fifth	– piąty
6th	sixth	– szósty
7th	seventh	– siódmy
8th	eighth	– ósmy
9th	ninth	– dziewiąty
10th	tenth	– dziesiąty
11th	eleventh	– jedenasty
12th	twelfth	– dwunasty
13th	thirteenth	– trzynasty
14th	fourteenth	– czternasty
15th	fifteenth	– piętnasty
16th	sixteenth	– szesnasty
17th	seventeenth	– siedemnasty
18th	eighteenth	– osiemnasty
19th	nineteenth	– dziewiętnasty
20th	twentieth	– dwudziesty
21st	twenty-first	– dwudziesty pierwszy
22nd	twenty-second	– dwudziesty drugi
23rd	twenty-third	– dwudziesty trzeci
24th	twenty-fourth	– dwudziesty czwarty
30th	thirtieth	– trzydziesty
40th	fortieth	– czterdziesty
50th	fiftieth	– pięćdziesiąty
60th	sixtieth	– sześćdziesiąty
70th	seventieth	– siedemdziesiąty
80th	eightieth	– osiemdziesiąty
90th	ninetieth	– dziewięćdziesiąty
100th	(one) hundredth	– setny
101st	(one) hundred and first	– sto pierwszy
102nd	(one) hundred and second	– sto drugi
103rd	(one) hundred and third	– sto trzeci
104th	(one) hundred and fourth	– sto czwarty
200th	two hundredth	– dwusetny
500th	five hundredth	– pięćsetny
1,000th	(one) thousandth	– tysięczny
3,000th	three thousandth	– trzytysięczny
1978th	nineteen hundred and seventy eighth	– tysiąc dziewięćset siedemdziesiąty ósmy
500,000th	five hundred thousandth	– pięćsettysięczny
1,000,000th	millionth	– milionowy
3,000,000th	three millionth	– trzy milionowy

ENGLISH – POLISH
APPENDIX OF BUSINESS TERMS

with

COMPLETE PHONETICS

A

a [ej] art. jeden; pewien;
pierwsza litera angielskiego
alfabetu; pierwszej kategorii
A-O'k [ej okej] zupełnie
gotów
aback [e'baek] adv. wstecz;
w tył; do tyłu; nazad
abandon [e'baendon] v.
opuszczać; porzucić;
zarzucić; (dobrowolnie)
zaniechać; oddać się
abandonment
[e'baendonment] s.
opuszczenie; brak
pohamowania;
zrezygnowanie z prawa do
własności, bez naznaczenia
następnego właściciela
abandonment clause
[e'baendonment 'klo'z]
exp.: prawo zrezygnowania
z asekurowanej własności z
zachowaniem prawa do
odszkodowania
abatement [e'batment] s.
zniżka; zmniejszenie
abatement of taxes
[e'batment of taxys] exp.:
zniżka podatku
ABC method [ej bi si 'meţod]
exp.: inwentaż według
wartości; "A" - najdroższe,
"B" mniej drogie i "C"
najmniej wartosciowe
towary
above par [e'boew] exp.:
ponad nominalna wartość
abrogate ['aebrogejt] v.
obalić; unicestwić;
odwoływać; zno-sić
(ustawę, zarządzenie etc.)
absence rate ['ab.sens 'rejt]

exp.: częstotliwość
opuszczania pracy przez
zatrudnionych
absenteeism [,ab.sen.'tizem]
s. częstotliwość
opuszczania pracy przez
zatrudnionych
absentee owner [,ab.sen.'ti]
s. olner] exp.: właściciel
nie zarządzający albo nie
mieszkający w posiadanej
własności
absorbed costs [eb.'sorbd
'kosts] exp.: pośrednie
koszty produkcji (podatki od
nieruchomości, premie
asekuracyjne, etc.)
absorption costing
[eb.'sorbszyn 'kostyn] exp.:
koszt na jednostkę
produkcji
absorption rate [eb.'sorbszyn
'rejt] exp.: prognoza rocznej
sprzedaży (procent od
maksimum)
abstract of record [ab.'strakt
of ry.'kord] exp.:
streszczenie sprawy
sądowej na użytek sądu
apelacyjnego
abstract of title [ab.'strakt of
'tajtl] exp.: wyciąg
hipoteczny z historią
poszczególnej własności
ziemskiej
abusive tax shelter [e.'bjuzyf
'taks 'shel.ter] exp.:
nielegalne zmniejszanie
podatku z powołaniem się
na niewłaściwe przepisy
acceleration clause
[aek'slerejszn 'klo'z] exp.:
klauzula natychmistowego
zwrotu pożyczki na
rządanie wierzyciela
access right ['ak.,ses 'rajt]
exp.: prawo dostępu
właściciela to jego
własności

access time ['ak.,ses 'tajm]
exp.: czas potrzebny
komputerowi lub
automatycznej drukarce do
znalezienia w pamięci
danych lub instrukcji i
przekazania ich oraz
zarejestrowania w miejscu
przeznaczenia
accident and health insurance
['ak.sed.ent 'end 'hel<u>s</u>
yn.'szur.ens] exp.: polisa
asekuracyjna od wypadku
w pracy i chorby
pokrywająca koszty
szpitala, leczenia, zabiegów
oraz zwrot straconych
zarobków
accommodate [e'komedejt] v.
przystosować; pogodzić;
zakwaterować; wygodzić;
wyświadczyć (przysługę);
załagodzić (spór, etc.)
accommodation
[e,kome'dejszyn] s.
wygoda; dostosowanie;
kwatera; pogodzenie się;
ugoda; kompromis; usługa
accord [e'ko:rd] s. zgoda; v.
uzgadniać; dać; licować
accord and satisfaction
[e'ko:rd end
,sat.ys.'fak.szyn] exp.:
uznanie spłacenia długu w
zamian za sumę mniejszą
niż należna
according [e'ko:rdyng] prep.
według; zależnie od
accordingly [e'ko:rdyngly]
adv. odpowiednio; więc;
zatem
account [e,kaunt] s.
rachunek; sprawozdanie; v.
wyliczać; wytłumaczyć;
uważać; oceniać; być
odpowiedzialnym
accountability
[e'kaunt.e'bylyty] s.
odpowiedzialność zarządu
za działaność

organizacyjną, finansową, i
zatrudnieniową;
odpowiedzialność
manadżera (niższej rangi)
wobec jego przełożonych
accountancy [e.'kauntensy]
s. teoria i praktyka
księgowości
account for [e'kaunt fo:r] v.
dać powód; wytłumaczyć
accountant [e'kauntent] s.
księgowy, księgowa
accounting [e'kauntyng] s.
księgowość
accounting software
[e'kauntyng 'soft.łaer] exp.:
program do prowadzenia
księgowości za pomocą
komputera
accrued interest [e.'krud
'yn.trest] exp.:
nagromadzone odsetki
(niezapłacone)
accumulate [e'kju:mju,lejt] v.
gromadzić; zbierać;
piętrzyć
accumulated depreciation
[e'kju:mju,lejtyd
di,pry:szy,ejszn] exp.: suma
amortyzacji zaksięgowanej
(do danej daty)
acid-test ratio [aesyd test
'rej,szo] exp.: suma
gotówki, papierów
wartościowych i
należności podzielona przez
zadłużenie
acknowledge [ek'nołlydż] v.
uznać; potwierdzić;
przyznać (się); nagrodzić
acknowledgement
[ek'nołlydżment] s.
przyznanie; potwierdzenie;
uznanie; dowód uznania
acquire [e'kłajer] v. nabywać
acquisition [,aekły'zyszyn] s.
nabytek; nabycie; zdobycz;
przejęcie kontroli jednej
firmy przez drugą
acquisition cost

[,aekły'zyszyn 'kost] exp.:
całkowity koszt zakupu
własności włącznie z
pośrednictwem, rejestracją,
etc.

acquit [e'kłyt] v. zwolnić;
wywiązać się; spławić;
uniewinnić (kogoś); uiścić

acquittal [e'kłytl] s.
zwolnienie; uiszczenie;
wywiązanie się

acre ['ej.kr] s. morga
amerykańska = 0.405
hektara

acronym ['ak.re.nym] s.
akronim

accross the board [e'kros dy
bo:d] exp.: wszystko w
pewnej grupie; na całym
froncie; powszechnie
(podnieść płace, etc.)

active market ['ak.tyv
'mar.ket] exp.: okres
wielkiej ilość tranzakcji na
giełdzie

act of God ['akt of god] exp.:
katastrofa spowodowana
siłą wyższą przyrody
(powódź etc.)

actuarial science
[,ak.cze.'ler.jel 'sy.ents]
exp.: asekuracyjne dokładne
obliczenia ryzyka i jego
prawdopodobieństwa w
celu wyznaczenia
wysokości premii
ubezpieczeniowych

ad [aed] s. ogłoszenie;
reklama (od advertisement)

adapt [e'daept] v.
dostosować; przerobić;
przystosować; dostrajać;
nadawać się (do)

adaptation ['aedaep'tejszyn]
s. przystosowanie;
dostrojenie

add [aed] v. dodać; doliczyć

addendum [e.'den.dem] s.
dodatek dołączony do
kontraktu (dotyczący spłat,

inspekcji, etc.)

addition [e'dyszyn] s.
dodawanie; dodatek; (in
addition = ponadto)

additional [e'dyszynl] adj.
dodatkowy; dalszy

add-on interest [aed on
'yn.trest] exp.: odsetki
dodane do pożyczki

address [e'dres] s. adres;
mowa; odezwa; v. zwracać
się; adresować (do);
skierować (prośbę);
przemawiać

addressee [,aedre'si:] s.
adresat; adresatka (listu
itp.)

ad infinitum [aed
yn.'fyn.etem] exp.: bez
końca; bezgraniczna suma;
bezgraniczny okres

administer [ed'mynyster] v.
dawać; sprawować;
administrować; zarządzać

administration
[ed,myny'strejszyn] s.
zarząd; rząd; administracja;
ministerstwo; wymiar (kary
itp.)

administrative law
[ed,myny'strejtyv 'lo] exp.:
prawo adminstracyjne

administrative
[ed'mynystrejtyw] adj.
administracyjny

administrator
[ed,myny'strejter] s.
administrator mianowany
przez sąd w celu
wykonania decyzji sądu
dotyczącej spadku
pozostawionego bez
testamentu

advanced reservation
[ed'waenst rezerwejszyn]
exp.: rezerwacja z góry
zamówiona (załatwiona)

adversary ['aedwersery] s.
strona w sprawie sądowej;
przeciwnik; przeciwniczka

advertise ['aedwertajz] v.
ogłaszać; reklamować
advertisement
['edwertysment] s.
ogłoszenie; reklama
advertising ['aedwertajzyng]
s. reklama; ogłoszenie
handlowe
advice [ed'wajs] s. rada;
informacje; porada;
pouczenie
advisable [ed'wajzebl] adj.
wskazany; rozsądny;
ostrożny
advise [ed'wajz] v. radzić;
powiadamiać; pouczać
adviser [ed'wajzer] s.
doradca; radca (prawny
etc.)
advocate ['aedwekejt] v.
zalecać; bronić; s.
rzecznik; orędownik;
adwokat; adwokatka
affidavit [,aefy'dejwyt] s.
oświadczenie złożone pod
przysięgą (w sądzie, u
notariusza, lub wobec
urzędnika uprawnionego do
oficjalnego poświadczania
dokumentów
affiliated chain [,aefy'ljetyd
chajn] exp.: stowarzyszenie
niekonkurujących sklepów
w celu uzyskiwania
optymalnych cen zakupów
na wielką skalę
agency ['ejdżensy] s. ajencja;
działanie; pośrednictwo
agenda [e'dżenda] s. agenda;
lista; porządek dzienny
agent ['ejdżent] s.
pośrednik; ajent; czynnik;
przedstawiciel
agglomeration
[e,glome'rejszn] s.
skupienie; nagromadzenie;
gromadzenie; skupisko;
zlepek; aglomeracja
aggregate income ['ag.ry.get
'yn,kem] exp.: suma

wszystkich dochodów w
gospodarce uwzględniająca
inflację, podatki i dodwójne
księgowanie
agreement [e'gri:ment] s.
zgoda; umowa;
porozumienie; układ między
dwoma lub więcej stronami
prowadzący do zawarcia
kontraktu
agribusiness ['ag.ry,byznys]
s. wielkie przedsiębiorstwo
rolne produkujące i
sprzedające artykuły
przemysłowe i rolnicze
air-conditioning [,eer-
ken'dyszynyn] s.
klimatyzacja
airline ['eerlajn] s. linia
lotnicza (system transportu
lotniczego)
airmail ['eermejl] s. poczta
lotnicza; przesyłka lotnicza
airplane ['eerplejn] s. samolot
airport ['eerpo:rt] s. lotnisko
air traffic ['eer-traefyk] ruch
lotniczy (samolotów,
poczty, pasażerów;
ładunków itp.)
airway ['eerłej] linia lotnicza
algorithm ['al.ge,ryt.em] s.
dokładna procedura
rozwiązania problemu lub
osiągnięcia celu; program
komputerowy napisany
językiem zrozumiałym dla
komputera
alienation [,a.lje.'naj.szn] s.
dobrowolne przekazanie
tytułu do nieruchomości od
jednej do drugiej osoby
prawnej
alimony ['aelimeny] s.
alimenty
ambassador [aem'baesede:r]
s. ambasador;
przedstawiciel
amendment [e.'men(d).ment]
s. prawomocne uzupełnienie
lub zmiana w dokumencie,

który w nowej formie jest
nadal prawomocnym
amount [e'maunt] v.
wynosić; s. suma; kwota;
wynik
amount to [e'maunt tu] v.
wynosić (w sumie);
przedstawiać sobą
analytical review
[,an.'l.yt.ulel ry.'vyu] exp.:
kontrola ksiąg i analiza
zależności kont od zmian
ekonomicznych
annual report ['an.yel ry.port]
exp.: roczne sprawozdanie
podsumujące bilans i
dochód firmy (prawnie
wymagane)
annuity [e'njuyty] s. renta
roczna; renta dożywotnia
annul [e'nal] v. unieważniać;
anulować; skasować;
pozbawić (czegoś);
kasować
apologize [e'poledżajz] v.
usprawiedliwiać;
przepraszać
apology [e'poledży] s.
usprawiedliwienie; obrona
(ideologii etc.); przeprosiny
appendix [e'pendyks] s.
dodatek; uzupełnienie;
ślepa kiszka
appliance [e'plajens] s.
przyrząd; urządzenie;
akcesoria
applicant ['aeplykent] s.
petent; zgłaszający się;
kandydat
application [,aeply'kejszyn] s.
podanie; użycie;
zastosowanie; przykładanie;
pilność; sposób używania
apply [e'plaj] v. używać;
stosować; odnosić się;
naciskać; być pilnym;
prosić o; mieć
zastosowanie
apply for [e'plaj fo:r] v.
starać się o ...; wnosić

podanie o
apply to [e'plaj tu] v.
zwracać się do ...;
zgłaszać się do (o coś);
stosować się (do)
appoint [e'point] v.
mianować; wyznaczać;
ustanawiać; ustalić (datę,
miejsce etc.)
appointment [e'pointment] s.
nominacja; oznaczenie
czasu i miejsca; umówione
spotkanie
apportion [e'po:rszyn] v.
wyznaczyć; wydzielać;
przydzielać; wydać udziały
appraise [e'prejz] v. oceniać;
szacować; ustalić cenę
appreciate [e'pri:szjejt] v.
cenić wysoko; zyskiwać
na war-tości; ocenić;
oszacować; docenić;
dobrze myśleć o
appreciation [e'pri:szjejszyn]
s. ocena; uznanie; wzrost
wartości; zrozumienie
czegoś; uznanie (jakości)
apprentice [e'prentys] s.
czeladnik; uczeń;
terminator
apprenticeship [e'prentsszyp]
s. termin; nauka rzemiosła
approval [e'pru:wel] s.
aprobata; uznanie;
zatwierdzenie
approximate [e'proksymyt]
adj. zbliżony; przybliżony;
mniej więcej; v. zbliżać
(się); być około; przybliżać
(coś)
archive storage ['a:rkajw
'sto.rydż] exp.: archiwum
(miejsce, zabezpieczenie i
zbiory starych
dokumentów)
archives ['a:rkajwz] pl.
archiwa; archiwum (miejsce
i zbiory)
area code ['e:rje koud] exp.:
trzy cyfrowy przedrostek

numeru telefonicznego
oznaczający region
geograficzny w celu
rozmów zamiejscowych
arithmetic [´aery_t´metyk] s.
rachunki; arytmetyka; adj.
arytmetyczny; rachunkowy
arrears [e´rierz] pl. zaległości
(w końcu okresu); długi;
zaległe płace (płatności)
article [´a:rtykl] s. rodzajnik;
artykuł; warunek; paragraf
(dokumentu); temat
articles of incorporation
[´a:rtykls of
yn.´kor.perejszn] exp.:
document założenia
prywatnej korporacji
zgodnie z prawem
państwowym
articulate [a:rtykjulejt] v.
wyrażać jasno;
artykułować; adj.
artykułowany; wyraźny;
łączony stawami;
wygadany
artificial intelligence
[‚a:ty´fyszel yn.´tel.y.dżens]
exp.: część nauk
komputerowych
poświęcona zastosowaniu
komputerów do
symulowania ludzkiego
myślenia twórczego
as is [ez yz] exp.: (termin
handlowy) przyjęcie zakupu
w stanie zgodnym z
przeglądem bezpośrednio
przed kupnem
assemblage [e´semblydż] s.
zebranie; zbiór;
zmontowanie; skupowanie
terenów przez jednego
nabywcę
assemble [e´sembl] v.
zbierać; montować;
nagromadzać; złożyć;
wpasować (w coś)
assembly [e´sembly] s.
zebranie; zbiórka; montaż;

legislatura
assembly language [e´sembly
´lan.głtdż] exp.: język
komputerowy w którym
każde wyrażenie odpowida
wyrażeniu w języku
maszyny zakodowanym
dwójkowo
assembly line [e´sembly,lajn]
taśma montażowa; linia
mon-tażowa (w fabryce
etc.)
assent [e´sent] s. zgoda;
pogodzenie się; v. zgadzać
się; uznawać; wyrażać
zgodę
assent to [e´sent tu] v.
zgadzać się na coś;
zatwierdzać coś
assert [e´se:rt] v. twierdzić;
upominać się; dowieść;
stawiać się; potwierdzić
assess [e´ses] v. szacować;
oceniać; wymierzać;
opodatkować; nałożyć
podatek na; określić
wysokość podatku; ustalić
wartość posesji w celach
opodatkowania
assets [´aesets] pl.
własności; aktywa
(ściągalne); wartościowi
pracownicy; cokolwiek
wartościowego
assign [e´sajn] v. przydzielać;
ustalać; odnosić;
przekazywać; przypisywać
(do pracy); podpisywać akt
kupna-sprzedaży
assignee [‚as.y.ni] s. osoba
prawna przejmująca
kontrakt (odpłatnie)
assignment [e´sajnment] s.
przydzielenie; przypisanie;
przekazanie; przydział;
podział; przekazanie
uprawnienia w ramach
polisy ubezpieczeniowej
innej osobie prawnej
assignment of income

[e'sajnment ow 'yn.,kem]
exp.: prawne przekazanie
dochodu i związanego z
nim opodatkowania
assignment of lease
[e'sajnment ow 'li:s] exp.:
prawne przekazanie
dzierżawy
assignor [a:s'y.no:r] s. osoba
prawna przekazująca
kontrakt i związane
uprawnienia drugiej osobie
prawnej
assimilate [e'symylejt] v.
upodabniać; wcielać;
wchłaniać; asymilować;
przyswajać sobie; strawić
assimilation [e'symylejszn] s.
wykupienie nowych akcji
giełdowych pozostałych po
sprzedaży przez agentów
gwarantujących
assist [e'syst] v. pomagać;
brać udział; być przy
assistance [e'systens] s.
pomoc (pieniężna); asysta;
wsparcie
assistant [e'systent] s.
asystent; pomocnik; adj.
pomocniczy
assizes [e'sajzyz] pl.
okresowe sesje sądu
(wyjazdowe) w Anglii (ich
czas i miejsce)
association [e,souszy'ejszyn]
s. łączenie; współpraca;
kojarzenie; przyłączenie się;
związek; organizacja; grupa
osób prawnych
stowarzyszona a jakimś
celu
assort [e'so:rt] v. sortować;
dobierać; obcować;
klasyfikować;
porządkować
assorted [e'so:rtyd] adj.
dobrany; posortowany;
mieszany
assumption of mortgage
[e.'sem.szn ow 'mo:r.gydż]

exp.: przejęcie spłat
hipotecznych i
odpowidzialności prawnej
za nie
assurance [e'szu:rens] s.
zapewnienie; pewność;
zaufanie; ubezpieczenie
assure [e'szu:r] v.
zapewniać; ubezpieczać;
zabezpieczać
assured [e'szu:rd] adj. pewny
(siebie); s. ubezpieczony
at par [aet 'pa:r] exp.: za
cenę równą wartości
nominalnej
at risk [aet rysk] exp.:
narażony na
niebezpieczeństwo lub
stratę
attach [e'taecz] v.
przywiązywać;
przyczepiać; przydzielać;
łączyć; przymocowywać;
nalepiać
attachment [e'taeczment] s.
załącznik; przymocowanie;
więź; przywiązanie;
dodatek do polisy
ubezpieczeniowej
wyjaśniający szegółowo
warunki ubezpieczenia
attention line [e.'ten.szn
'lajn] exp.: miejsce na
adresie gdzie wpisane jest
nazwisko osoby która ma
otrzymać przesyłkę
attest [e'test] v.
poświadczyć; stwierdzać;
zalegalizować; potwierdzić
jako prawdziwe
at the close [aet dy klouz]
exp.: zakup lub sprzedaż
akcji giełdowych w czsie
ostatnich 30 sekund
dziennych transakcji
at the market [aet dy
'ma:kyt] exp.: po najlepszej
cenie osiągalnej w danym
momencie
attractive nuisance

[e'traektyv 'nju:sns] exp.:
własność z natury
niebezpieczna dla dzieci
(prywatny basen pływacki
etc.)

attrition [e'tryszn] s.
normalny i nie nadający się
do kontrolowania proces
pensjonowania, wymierania,
chorowania i
przeprowadzek siły
roboczej. Metoda
zmniejszania siły roboczej
bez usuwania ludzi z pracy

auction ['o:kszyn] s.
licytacja; (publiczna) aukcja;
sprzedaż po najwyższej
zaoferowanej cenie na
licytacji

auction off ['o:kszyn of] v.
licytować; sprzedawać na
licytacji; wystawiać na
(publiczną) licytację

auction sale ['o:kszyn sejl]
exp.: licytacja; (publiczna)
aukcja; sprzedaż po
najwyższej zaoferowanej
cenie na licytacji

audience communications
['o:djens ke,mju:ny'kejszns]
exp.: ilość osób do których
można dotrzeć za pomocą
danego środka przekazu

audit ['o:dyt] s. sprawdzenie
rachunków; rozliczenie;
kontrola księgowości
(włącznie z procedurą); v.
kontrolować rachunki

auditor ['o:dyter] s. urzędnik
państwowy odpowiedzialny
za kontrolę wydatków ze
skarbu państwa; rewident
księgowy

audit program ['o:dyt
'pro.gram] exp.: lista
czynności wymaganych od
rewidenta księgowego

audit trail ['o:dyt trejl] exp.:
zapis czynności rewidenta
księgowego i wykazanie

pochodzenia zapisów
księgowych

authentication
[o:tenty'kejszn] s.
poświadczenie;
zalegalizowanie; legalizaja;
nadanie ważności przez
potwierdzenie i pieczątkę
urzędnika państwowego

authority ['o:teryty] s.
władza nad podwładnymi w
organizacji włącznie z
zatrudnianie i usuwaniem z
pracy

authorize ['o:terajz] v.
upoważniać; zatwierdzać;
dać prawo (urząd);
aprobować

autograph ['o:tegraef] s.
podpis; autograf; podpis
własny

automat ['o:temaet] n.
automat; automat na
monety do sprzedaży
(porcji) jedzenia

automatic [,o:te'maetyk] adj.
automatyczny; machinalny

automatic merchandising
[,o:te'maetyk
'mer.czen.,dajzyn] exp.:
sprzedaż za pomocą
automatów

automation [,o:te'mejszyn] s.
automatyzacja; robotyzacja

automobile ['o:temeby:l] s.
samochód; auto; slang: wóz

average ['aeverydż] s.
przeciętna; średnia
arytmetyczna

average cost ['aeverydż
'kost] exp.: przeciętny
koszt; suma kosztów
podzielona przez ilość
jednostek
wyprodukowanych lub
zakupionych

average fixed cost ['aeverydż
'fykst 'kost] exp.:
przeciętny koszt stały;
koszty stałe podzielone

przez dochód
average tax rate ['aeverydż
'taks rejt] exp.: przeciętny
podatek; suma podatków
podzielona przez dochód
avoidance of tax [e'wojdens
of 'taks] exp.: metoda
legalnego unikania
podatków

B

baby bond ['bejby bond]
exp.: bony wartości
poniżej 1000 dolarów
(zwykle 500 do 25
dolarów)
back dating ['baek 'dejtyn]
exp.: wpisywanie
wcześniejszej daty na
dokumencie niż data
tranzakcji
backlog ['baek,log] s.
zaległości
back pay ['baek 'pej] exp.:
nie wypłacone zarobki z
poprzedniego okresu
wypłaty
bad debt ['baed det] exp.:
nieściągalny dług
bezwartościowy dla
wierzyciela
bad title ['baed 'tajtl] exp.:
niewystarczający dowód
własności
baggage ['baegydż] s. bagaż
baggage check ['baegydż,
czek] exp.: kwit bagażowy
bail [bejl] s. kaucja; poręka
bail bond ['bejl bond] exp.:
kaucja pieniężna
gwarantująca stawienie się
oskarżonego na rozprawę
bailee ['bej,li] s. powiernik
mający chwilowo cudzą
własność w opiece

bail out [bejl'ałt] v. zwolnić
za kaucją; wywinąć się z
opresji
bailiff ['bejlyf] s. woźny
sądowy (powiatowy);
komornik; rządca majątku
bait and switch ['bejt end
'słycz] exp.: wabienie na
okazyjną cenę żeby
sprzedać inny towar za
wyższą cenę (z wysokim
zyskiem)
balance ['baelens] s. waga
(przyrząd); bilans;
równowaga; suma na
rachunku (czekowym etc.)
v. równoważyć;
bilansować; wahać się;
przeciwdziałać
balance sheet ['baelens 'shit]
exp.: datowane zestawienie
stanu posiadania i długów
firmy
bale [bejl] s. zwój płótna;
bela; snop (siana); v. zob.
bail
ballast ['baelest] s. balast; v.
obciążać balastem
ball-bearing ['bo:lbearyn] s.
łożysko kulkowe (też jedna
z kulek)
balloon payment [ba.'lon
'pey,ment] exp.: ostatnia
rata większa niż poprzednie
ballot ['baelet] s. (tajne)
głosowanie (na
reprezentantów związku
zawodowego w fabryce,
etc.) ; kartka do
głosowania; v. tajnie
głosować
ballot box ['baeletboks] s.
urna wyborcza
ball-point pen ['bo:l-point-
pen] s. kulkowy pisak;
długopis
bank [baenk] s. brzeg; łacha;
nasyp; skarpa; bank; stół
roboczy; rząd; nachylenie
toru; zasób; zbiór; wał

przeciw-powodziowy; v.
prowadzić bank; składać w
banku; piętrzyć; pochylać;
slang: polegać;
obwałować; pochylić
jezdnię

bank bill ['baenk,byl] s.
banknot

banker ['baenker] s. bankier

banking ['baenkyng] s.
bankowość; transakcje
banku

banknote ['baenknout] s.
banknot; papierowy
pieniądz

bank-rate ['baenkrejt] s.
stopa dyskontowa; stopa
procentowa (obciążająca
pożyczki)

bankrupt ['baenkrept] s.
bankrut

bankruptcy ['baenkreptsy] s.
bankrutctwo

bar ['bar] s. legalna sankcja
przeciw ponownemu
procesowi przeciw
oskarżonemu lub
pozwanemu; adwokatura

bar code ['bar koud] exp.:
drukowane linie równoległe
(o rozmaitej szerokości)
przedstawiające zapis cen
towaru odczytywanych
przez komputer kasjera

bargain basement ['bar.gejn
'bej.sment] exp.: część
dużego sklepu gdzie
sprzedaje się towary
przecenione

bargain hunter ['bar.gejn
'hant.er] exp.: kupujący po
najniższej cenie (towary,
akcje giełdowe, etc.)

barrister ['baeryster] s.
adwokat; adwokatka;
obrońca; obrończyni
(głównie w Anglii)

barter ['bart.er] s. handel
wymienny; wymiana
(bezgotówkowa)

base pay rate ['bejs 'pej 'rejt]
exp.: podstawowa stawka
no podstawie której oblicza
się zapłatę za nadgodziny,
etc.

bear ['baer] s. giełdziarz
spekulujący na zniżkę

bear hug ['baer hag] exp.:
przejęcie korporacji przez
wykup jej udziałów po
cenie wyższej niż rynkowa

bear market ['baer 'ma:kyt]
exp.: dlugi okres niżu na
giełdzie

below par [by'lou 'par] exp.:
cena poniżej wartości
nominalnej

benchmark ['bencz.'ma:k] s.
punkt odniesienia;
jednostka służąca jako
standart do porównań

benefits, fringe ['benifit
'fryndż] exp.: pośrednie
wynagrodzenie (asekuracja
życia i zdrowia oraz
emerytura, etc.)

bequest [by'kłest] s. zapis;
spadek; spuścizna; legat

bid bond [byd bond] exp.:
kaucja wymagana od
przedsiębiorcy, który
zaoferowal najniższą cenę
wykonania projektu (na
przetargy)

big board [byg 'bo:rd] exp.:
giełda nowojorska

bill [byl] s. rachunek; kwit;
afisz; plakat; v. ogłaszać;
afiszować; oblepiać
afiszami

billboard ['byl,bo:rd] s.
tablica ogłoszeniowa

billfold ['byl,fould] s. portfel
(na dokumenty i pieniądze)

billion ['byljen] s. tysiąc
milionów (USA); miliard

bill of exchange ['byl,ow
'eksczendż] weksel

blackmail ['blaekmejl] s.
szantaż; wymuszenie; v.

szantażować
black-market ['blaek ma:rkyt]
s. czarny rynek
blank [blaenk] adj. biały;
pusty; czysty; nie
wypełniony; s. puste
miejsce; nie wypełniony
formularz; ślepak
blockade [blo'kejd] s.
blokada; v. blokować;
robić zator
board [bo:rd] s. deska;
władza naczelna; tablica;
rada; pokład
bonus ['bounes] s. premia
book [buk] s. książka;
rejestr; v. księgować;
rezerwować; aresztować;
rejestrować
booked up ['bukt ap] adj.
wyprzedany; pełny
bookcase ['bukkejs] s. półka
na książki; biblioteczka
booking clerk ['bukyn,klerk]
s. kasjer kolejowy
booking office ['bukyn,ofys]
biuro biletowo-rezerwacyjne
bookkeeper ['buk,ki:per] s.
księgowy; księgowa
bookkeeping ['buk,ki:pyng] s.
księgowość
booklet ['buklyt] s.
książeczka
bookseller ['buk,seler] s.
księgarz
book shop ['bukszop] exp.:
księgarnia
bookstore ['buksto:r] s.
księgarnia
boom [bu:m] s. huk; nagła
zwyżka; bom; bariera; v.
zwyżkować; podbijać ceny
boss [bo:s] s. szef; v.
rządzić
box office ['boks,ofys] exp.:
kasa w teatrze; kasa
biletów wstępu
boycott ['bojkot] s. bojkot; v.
bojkotować
branch [bra:ncz] s. gałąź;

odnoga; filia; v. odgałęziać
się; zbaczać; rozwidlać się
brand [braend] s. głownia;
żagiew; wypalony znak na
skórze; piętno; żelazne
narzędzie do wypalania
znaku; znak własności;
znak firmowy; marka
towaru; pochodzenie
towaru; gatunek towaru; v.
naznaczać; piętnować;
wryć (w pamięć)
brand new [,braen'nju] adj.
nowiutki; nowiusieńki; jak
spod igły
bribe [brajb] v. dawać
łapówkę; przekupywać; s.
łapówka
bribery ['brajbery] s.
przekupstwo; łapownictwo;
korupcja
brief [bri:f] s. streszczenie;
zestawienie; odprawa;
krótkie majtki; v. zwięźle
streścić; pouczyć;
informować; zrobić
odprawę; mówić krótko;
adj. krótkotrwały; treściwy;
zwięzły; krótki
briefcase ['bri:f,kejs] s.
teczka
brochure ['broszjuer] s.
broszura
budget ['badżyt] s. budżet;
v. budżetować;
asygnować
bulletin ['buletyn] s.
komunikat; biuletyn
bulletin board ['buletyn,bo:rd]
exp.: tablica na ogłoszenia
bullion ['buljen] s. złoto i
srebro w sztabach
bureau ['bjurou] s. komoda;
biuro; sekretarzyk; urząd
bureaucracy [bju'rokresy] s.
biurokracja
business ['byznys] s. interes;
zajęcie; sprawa;
przedsiębiorstwo;
transakcja; handel; adj.

handlowy; urzędowy
business hours ['byznys,aurs]
exp.: godziny urzędowe
business letter ['byznys,leter]
exp.: oficjalny list
businesslike ['byznys,lajk]
adj. rzeczowy; solidny;
poważny; praktyczny;
dokładny
businessman ['byznysman] s.
przedsiębiorca; człowiek
interesów; handlowiec
business trip ['byznys,tryp]
exp.: podróż służbowa
businesswoman
['byznys'łumen] s. kobieta
interesu; właścicielka
przedsiębiorstwa
bylaw ['bajlo:] s. przepis;
zarządzenie (miejscowe
etc.)

C

cab [kaeb] s. taksówka;
dorożka; szoferka; budka
maszynisty
cable ['kejbl] s. przewód;
lina; depesza; v.
depeszować;
umocowywać liną;
przesyłać kablem
cabdriver ['kaeb,drajwer] s.
taksówkarz
cabstand ['kaeb staend] s.
postój taksówek
call [ko:l] v. wołać;
wzywać; telefonować;
odwiedzać; zawijać do
portu; wyzywać; s. krzyk;
wezwanie; apel; powołanie;
wizyta; nazwanie; żądanie;
sygnał
call back ['ko:l,baek] exp.:
odtelefonować; odwołać z
powrotem

call up ['ko:l,ap] exp.:
telefonować; wywoływać
(duchy etc.)
campaign [kaem'pejn] s.
kampania; akcja; v.
odbywać kampanię;
agitować
cancellation [,kan.se.'lejszyn]
s. skasowanie; skreślinie
(lotu, etc.); odwołanie
(rezerwacji, etc,)
cancellation clause
[,kan.se.'lejszyn 'kloz] exp.:
warunek wkontrakcie
upoważniający do
unieważnienia
zobowiązania wobec z góry
zastrzeżonej zaszłości
capacity [ke'paesyty] s.
zdolność; kompetencja;
pojemność; właściwość;
nośność; objętość
capital ['kaepytl] s. stolica;
kapitał; adj. główny;
zasadniczy; stołeczny;
fatalny
capitalism ['kaepytlyzem] s.
kapitalizm
car [ka:r] s. samochód; wóz
carbon paper
['ka:rben,pejper] exp.: kalka
card ['ka:rd] s. karta; bilet;
pocztówka; legitymacja;
atut
cardboard ['ka:rdbo:rd] s.
tektura; adj. tekturowy
cardboard box ['ka:rdbord
boks] exp.: karton
card index ['ka:rd yndeks]
exp.: kartoteka
car papers [ka:r pejpers]
exp.: dokumenty
samochodowe
car parking ['ka:r-pa:rkyŋg]
exp.: parking samochodowy
catalog ['kaetelog] s. katalog
category ['kaetygery] s.
kategoria
cater ['kejter] v. dostarczać
żywności; obsługiwać

certificate [se'rtyfykyt] s.
świadectwo;
poświadczenie; dyplom;
metryka; v. zaświadczać;
dyplomować
certify ['se'rtyfaj] v.
zaświadczać; zapewniać;
uznawać za
chairman ['czeermen] s.
przewodniczący; prezes
change [czejndż] s. zmiana;
wymiana; drobne; v.
zmienić; przebierać (się);
wymieniać; rozmieniać (na
drobne)
change one's mind ['czejndż
,łans'majnd] exp.: zmienić
czyjeś zdanie (przekonania
etc.)
charge account [cza:rdż
e'kaunt] exp.: otwarty
kredyt (w banku)
charge card [cza:rdż 'kard]
exp.: karta kredytowa do
zakupów
charter [cza:rter] s. statut;
przywilej; dyplom; akt
nadania prawa do ...; v.
nadawać; zakładać na
statutach; wynajmować
statek lub samolot
charter plane [cza:rter plejn]
exp.: s. samolot wynajęty
grupowo; samolot
czarterowy
check [czek] s. wstrzymanie;
przerwa; sprawdzenie;
czek; kwit; szach; adj.
szachownicowy; kontrolny;
podkreślony; v. hamować;
sprawdzać; zakreślać;
nadawać; zgadzać się;
szachować; ganić;
krytykować; opanowywać
check in [czek yn] v.
wmeldowywać się (w
pracy, w wojsku, w hotelu,
etc.)
check out [czek aut] v.
wymeldowywać się;

zapłacić za hotel
circular ['se:rkjuler] s.
okólnik; adj. okrągły; kolisty
circulate ['se:rkjulejt] v.
krążyć; cyrkulować;
puszczać w obieg; być w
obiegu
circulation ['se:rkjulejszyn] s.
krążenie; obrót; nakład
classification
[klaesyfy'kejszyn] s.
klasyfikacja; klasyfikowanie
classify ['klaesyfaj] s.
klasyfikować; sortować;
zaklasyfikować
clause [klo:z] s. klauzula;
zdanie; punkt umowy
cocktail ['koktejl] s. cocktail
coin [koyn] s. moneta; v. bić
monety; spieniężać; ukuć
(nowe pojęcie); tłoczyć
collect ['ke'lekt] v. zbierać;
odbierać; inkasować
collected ['ke'lektyd] adj.
skupiony; opanowany;
spokojny
collection ['ke'lekszyn] s.
zbiór; kolekcja; inkaso;
zainkasowane pieniądze
collective ['ke'lektyw] adj.
zbiorowy; wspólny; s.
kolektyw
collector ['ke'lektor] s.
inkasent; poborca; zbieracz
commerce ['kome:rs] s.
handel
commercial [ke'me:rszel] adj.
handlowy; s. ogłoszenie (w
radio ...)
common market ['komen
'ma:rkyt] exp.: wspólny
rynek (Zachodniej Europy)
company ['kampeny] s.
towarzystwo; załoga;
goście; partnerzy; spółka;
kompania; trupa teatralna
compensate ['kompen,sejt] v.
wyrównywać; nagradzać;
wypłacić odszkodowanie;
kompensować

compensation
[‚kompen'sejszyn]
s. rekompensata;
wynagrodzenie;
odszkodowanie;
wyrównanie
compete [kem'pi:t] v.
konkurować; rywalizować;
ubiegać się
compete for [kem'pi:t‚fo:r] v.
(o coś) współzawodniczyć;
współubiegać się;
prześcigać się
competence ['kompytens] s.
fachowość; kwalifikacja;
uzdolnienie; zasobność;
dobrobyt
competent ['kompytent] adj.
właściwy; kwalifikowany;
odpowiedni; kompetentny
competition [‚kompy'tyszyn]
s. konkurencja; konkurs;
zawody; turniej;
współzawodnictwo
competitor [kem'petyter] s.
rywal; konkurent;
współzawodnik;
współzawodniczka; rywalka
computation
[‚kompju'tejszyn] s.
obliczenie; kalkulacja
computer [kem'pju:ter] s.
kalkulator; komputer;
przelicznik
concern [ken'se:rn] s. interes
concession [ken'seszyn] s.
koncesja; ustępstwo;
przyzwolenie
confer [ken'fe:r] v. naradzać
się; nadawać; przyznawać
confiscate ['konfyskejt] v.
konfiskować;
skonfiskować
consideration
[ken‚syde'rejszyn] s.
wzgląd; rozważanie;
warunek; uprzejmość;
rekompensata
consign [ken'sajn] v.
przekazać; powierzać;

złożyć do (banku, grobu
etc.)
consignment [ken'sajnment]
s. przesyłka; powierzenie
consumer [ken'sju:mer] s.
konsumer; spożywca;
odbiorca; użytkownik
consumer research
[ken'sju:mer ry.'sercz] exp.:
badania (jakości, cen, etc.)
z punktu widzenia
konsumerów (spożywców,
odbiorców, użytkowników,
etc.); badania nastawienia
spożywców przez
przedsiębiorstwa
consumption [ken'sampszyn]
s. zużycie; suchoty; pylica
container [ken'tejner] s.
zasobnik; zbiornik; naczynie
contract ['kontraekt] s.
umowa; układ; kontrakt;
obietnica
contract [ken'traekt] v.
ściągać; kurczyć;
zobowiązywać
contractor [ken'traekter] s.
przedsiębiorca (budowlany
etc.); kontrahent
control [ken'troul] v.
sprawdzać; rządzić;
kontrolować; opanować; s.
kontrola; sterowanie;
regulowanie; ster; władza
controller [ken'trouler] s.
kontroler; regulator;
zarządca
co-op [kou'op] s. spółdzielnia
cooperate [kou'operejt] v.
współpracować;
współdziałać
cooperation [kou‚ope'rejszyn]
s. współpraca;
współdziałanie; kooperacja;
spółdzielczość
cooperative [kou‚ope'rejtyw]
adj. spółdzielczy;
uspołeczniowy; uczynny;
współpracujący
cooperator [kou'ope‚rejter] s.

współpracownik;
spółdzielca
copartner [kou'pa:rtner] s.
uczestnik; wspólnik;
udziałowiec (we wspólnym
interesie)
copybook ['kopy,buk] s.
zeszyt
copyright ['kopy,rajt] s.
prawo autorskie; v. chronić
prawem autorskim
corporation [,ko:rpe'rejszn] s.
korporacja; zrzeszenie;
osoba prawna zbiorowa
correspondence
[,korys'pondens] s.
zgodność; korespondencja
correspondent
[,korys'pondent] s.
korespondent; adj.
odpowiedni; zgodny z;
odpowiadający
corruption [ke'rapszyn] s.
zepsucie; korupcja; rozkład;
fałszowanie
cost [kost] v. kosztować; s.
koszt; strata; cena
costly ['kostly] adj.
kosztowny; wspaniały;
drogi; cenny
counsel ['kaunsel] s. rada;
zamysł; radca prawny; v.
radzić; doradzać;
przyjmować radę
count [kaunt] v. liczyć;
sądzić; liczyć się;
znaczyć; s. rachuba;
liczenie; suma; zarzut;
hrabia
countdown [kaunt-dałn] s.
liczenie do startu (rakiety)
count in [kaunt yn] v. brać
w rachubę; wliczać;
włączyć
count out [kaunt aut] v.
wyliczyć; nie brać w
rachubę
counter ['kaunter] s. kantor;
lada; licznik; żeton
counterfeit ['kaunterfyt] adj.

fałszywy; podrobiony; v.
udawać; fałszować
coupon ['ku:pon] s. odcinek;
kupon wymienny (w
sklepie, banku ...)
court of justice
['ko:rt,ow'dżastys] exp.:
sąd
courtroom ['ko:rt,ru:m] s.
sala sądowa (rozpraw)
coverage ['kawerydż] s.
pokrycie ubezpieczeniem;
zasięg radiowy; omówienie
w prasie
credit ['kredyt] s. kredyt;
wiara; autorytet; powaga;
uznanie; chluba; v. dawać
wiarę; zapisywać na
rachunek; zaliczać;
przypisywać (coś komuś)
creditable ['kreditebl] adj.
zaszczytny; godny
pochwały; chlubny
credit card ['kredyt ka:rd]
exp.: karta kredytowa do
zakupów
creditor ['kredyter] s.
wierzyciel (handlowy,
prywatny etc.)
crisis ['krajsys] s. przesilenie;
kryzys; krytyczna sytuacja
crises ['krajsi:z] pl.
przesilenia; kryzysy; opały
cross out ['kros,aut] v.
wykreślać; skreślać;
przekreślać
currency ['karensy] s.
waluta; obieg; potoczność;
popularność
curriculum vitae [ke'rykjulem
,wajti:] exp.: życiorys
customer ['kastemer] s.
klient
customhouse ['kastem-haus]
s. komora celna; urząd
celny
custom-made ['kastem-mejd]
adj. zrobiony na
zamówienie
customs ['kastemz] pl. cło

customs clearance ['kastemz klierenz] exp.: odprawa celna

customs declaration ['kastemz ,dekle'rejszyn] s. deklaracja celna (przy przekraczaniu granicy etc.)

customs examination ['kastemz ig,zamy'nejszyn] exp.: rewizja celna (bagażu, towarów etc.)

D

damage ['daemydż] s. szkoda; uszkodzenie; odszkodowanie; (slang) koszt; v. uszkodzić; ponieść szkody; uwłaczać

data ['dejte] pl. dane; podstawa odniesienia; dane liczbowe

data processing ['dejte 'prousesyng] exp.: przetwarzanie danych (na komputerze)

date [dejt] v. datować (list) nosić datę; chodzić z kimś; s. data; spotkanie; randka; umówienie się; termin; palma daktylowa; daktyl

date from ['dejt ,from] exp.: data z ... (dnia, miejsce, miasto etc.)

day [dej] s. dzień; doba

deadline ['dedlajn] s. nieprzekraczalny termin; ostateczna granica (czegoś)

deadlock ['dedlok] s. impas; martwy punkt; v. powodować impas (zastój)

deal [di:l] v. zajmować się; traktować o; załatwiać (coś); przestawać z (kimś); postępować;

handlować; rozdzielać (karty); s. ilość; sprawa; sporo; wiele

deal with ['di:l łyt] v. postępować z ...; mieć do czynienia (z kimś, czymś)

dealer ['di:ler] s. kupiec; handlarz; rozdający karty

dealing ['di:lyng] s. postępowanie z; stosunki; transakcje; konszachty

dear Sir ['dier,se:r] exp. Szanowny Panie; Drogi Panie

debit ['debyt] s. debet; obciążenie rachunku

debrief [dy'bri:f] s. przesłuchania po (akcji); v. przesłuchiwać po (akcji wojskowej etc.)

debt [det] s. dług

debtor ['deter] s. dłużnik (czyjś); dłużniczka (czyjaś)

decide [dy'sajd] v. rozstrzygać; postanawiać; decydować się (na coś); zadecydować; skłaniać się (ku czemuś)

decipher [dy'sajfer] v. odcyfrować (depeszę, etc.); rozszyfrować; rozwiązać

decision [dy'syżyn] s. rozstrzygnięcie (czegoś); postanowienie (o czymś); decyzja; zdecydowanie; stanowczość; wygrana na punkty; ustalenie; rezolutność

deduct [dy'dakt] v. potrącać; odciągać (kwotę etc.); odejmować; odtrącać (kogoś)

deduction [dy'dakszyn] s. potrącenie; odciągnięcie; wnioskowanie; wniosek; wydedukowanie; wywód

deed [di:d] s. czyn; wyczyn; akt; v. przekazywać aktem (własność); przekazywać

(komuś) pieniądze etc.
defendant [dy'fendent] s.
pozwany; oskarżony;
obrońca
defender [dy'fender] s.
obrońca (w prawie i
sporcie)
defer [dy'fe:r] v. odraczać;
ustępować; ulegać; mieć
wzgląd; skłaniać się
(przed)
deficiency [dy'fyszynsy] s.
brak; niedobór; należność
niezapłacona; niedostatek;
słabość (natury człowieka
etc.)
deficit ['defysyt] s. deficyt;
niedobór; nadwyżka
rozchodu
defunct ['dy'fankt] adj.
zmarły; zlikwidowany; już
nie istniejący; wymarły;
rozwiązany
delay [dy'lej] v. odraczać;
opóźniać; zwlekać; s.
odroczenie; zwłoka;
opóźnienie
delegate ['delegejt] s.
zastępca; wysłannik; v.
delegować; udzielać
delegacji; zlecać (władzę);
udzielać (władzy,
pełnomocnictwa komuś)
delegation [,dely'gejszyn] s.
delegacja; grupa delegatów
delinquent [dy'lynkłent] a.
winny; zaniedbany;
zalegający z zapłatą
(podatkiem); s. winowajca;
przestępca (nieletni); osoba
zalegająca etc.
delivery [dy'lywery] s.
doręczenie; dostawa;
roznoszenie; poród;
wydanie (jeńca); poddanie
(fortecy, etc.)
demise [dy'majz] s. zgon;
przekazanie spadku; v.
przekazywać (coś)
testamentem lub zgonem

demurrage [dy'me:rydż] s.
przestój; opłata za
postojowe
department [dy'pa:rtment] s.
wydział; ministerstwo; dział
department store
[dy'pa:rtment ,sto:r] exp.:
dom towarowy
deposit [dy'pozyt] s. osad;
warstwa; kaucja; depozyt;
v. składać do depopzytu;
osadzać; deponować;
nawarstwiać; złożyć (jaja
etc.)
depositor [dy'pozyter] s.
depozytor; deponent
depot [depou] s. stacja
kolejowa; skład; remiza;
kadra
depression [dy'preszyn] s.
przygnębienie; depresja
designer [dy'zajner] s.
projektant; konstruktor;
rysownik; intrygant;
projektodawca; autor;
autorka; kreślarz
desk [desk] s. biuro; referat;
pulpit; ambona; ławka
szkolna
desk set ['desk set] exp.:
zestaw przyborów do
pisania
detail ['di:tejl] s. szczegół;
wyszczególnienie; v.
wyłuszczać; przydzielać do
zadań
devaluation
[,dy:waelju'ejszyn] s.
dewaluacja; zdewaluowanie
diagram ['dajegraem] s.
wykres; schemat; diagram;
plan
dial ['dajel] s. tarcza
numerowa (zwłaszcza
zegarowa); v. mierzyć;
nakręcać (numer telefonu)
dial tone ['dajel,toun] exp.:
sygnał połączenia
(telefonicznego)
dictation [dyk'tejszyn] s.

dyktat; dyktowanie;
wyraźny nakaz
dictionary ['dykszeneeri] s.
słownik; mała encyklopedia
digest [dy'dżest] v. trawić;
przetrawiać; s.
streszczenie; skrót;
przegląd; zbiór praw
dinner jacket
['dyner,dżaekyt] exp.:
smoking (tuxedo)
dinner party ['dyner,pa:rty]
exp.: przyjęcie; obiad
proszony
diploma [dy'plouma] s.
dyplom
director [dy'rektor] s.
dyrektor; reżyser; celownik;
kierownik; zarządzający;
nadzorca
directory [dy'rektery] s.
książka adresowa,
telefoniczna (lub
przepisów); skorowidz
discount ['dyskaunt] s.
dyskonto; rabat; odjęcie; v.
potrącać; odliczać; nie
dawać wiary (komuś,
czemuś)
disembark ['dysym'ba:rk] v.
wyładować; wysiadać;
lądować (samolotem,
statkiem)
disengage ['dysen'gejdż] v.
odczepiać; wyłączać;
odwikłać; rozłączyć;
odhaczyć
disqualify [dys'kłolyfaj] v.
dyskwalifikować
distribute [dys'trybju:t] v.
udzielać; rozmieszczać;
rozdać; rozprowadzać
(ludzi)
distribution [dys'trybju:szyn]
s. rozdział; podział;
dystrybucja; roznoszenie; a.
rozdzielczy
district ['dystrykt] s. okręg;
powiat; dystrykt; dzielnica;
rejon (kraju, państwa)

divide [dy'wajd] v. dzielić;
rozdzielać; oddzielać;
różnić
divide by [dy'wajd,baj] v.
dzielić przez (liczbę,
mianownik)
division [dy'wyżyn] s.
podział; rozdział; dzielenie;
dział; wydział; oddział;
dywizja
document ['dokjument] s.
dokument; v. poprzeć
dokumentami;
udokumentować
documentary
[,dokju'mentery] s. & adj.
dokumentalny (film etc.)
draft [dra:ft] s. szkic; brulion;
zarys; przekaz; pobór;
rysunek; ciąg w kominie; v.
szkicować; projektować;
rysować;
odkomenderować
draftsman ['dra:ftsmen] s.
kreślarz (techniczny);
rysownik; projektodawca
drive-in ['drajw,yn] s. obsługa
w samochodzie, w banku,
jadłodajni etc.; kino; sklep;
poczta
due [dju:] adj. należny;
płatny; należyty; adv. w
kierunku na (wschód); s. to
co się należy; należności;
opłata; składka
due to ['dju:,tu] exp. z
powodu

E

earn [e:rn] v. zarabiać
(pracą, etc.); zasługiwać;
zapracować; zdobywać
(sławę)
earnest ['e:rnyst] adj.
poważny; gorliwy; nie

żartujący; s. zadatek
(dowód kupna domu)
earnings [′e:rny<u>nz</u>] pl. zarobki
ecology [i′koledży] s.
ekologia; związek między
środowiskiem a
organizmem (część biologii
i inżynierii)
economic [,i:ke′nomyk] adj.
ekonomiczny; gospodarczy
economical [,i:ke′nomykel]
adj. oszczędny;
ekonomiczny
economics [,i:ke′nomyks] pl.
nauka o ekonomii
(gospodarce)
economist [i′konemyst] s.
ekonomista; specjalista od
działania gospodarki
economize [i:kone,majz] v.
oszczędzać; zmniejszać
wydatki i marnotrawstwo;
gospodarowac oszczędnie;
używac (coś) wydajnie
economy [i′konemy] s.
ekonoomia; gospodarka;
gospodarowanie;
zapobiegliwość
economy class
[i′konemy,kla:s] exp.:
druga klasa (w pociągu,
samolocie); klasa
turystyczna
edition [i′dyszyn] s. wydanie;
nakład (książki, gazety
etc.)
editor [e′dyter] s. redaktor;
wydawca; pisarz "od
redakcji"
editorial [,edy′to:rjel] s.
artykuł od redakcji
(wydawcy); adj.
redakcyjny; redaktorski
efficacy [′efykesy] s.
skuteczność; dawanie
porządnych wyników
(skutków etc.)
efficiency [i′fyszency] s.
wydajność; skuteczność;
sprawność (przy minimum

nakładów, wysiłków i strat)
efficient [i′fyszent] adj.
skuteczny; wydajny;
sprawny adj. starszy (z
dwóch); należący do
starszyzny
electrical engineer [e′lektry
kel,endży′nier] exp.:
inżynier elektryk
(dyplomowany)
electron [i′lektron] s. elektron
embargo [em′ba:rgou] s.
zakaz handlowania, wjazdu,
wyjazdu
embark [im′ba:rk] v. ładować
(się); wsiadać (na statek);
załadować (wojsko, towar);
rozpoczynać;
przedsięwziąć
embark upon [im′ba:rk e′pon]
v. rozpoczynać;
przedsięwziąć
embassy [′embesy] s.
ambasada
embed [im′bed] v. osadzić;
sadzić; wmurować; wryć;
zalać; wkopać; wbijać w
coś
embedded [im′bedyd] adj.
osadzony; wsadzony;
wryty; wmurowany; wbity;
wkopany
embezzle [ym′bezl] v.
sprzeniewierzać (cudzą
własność); zdefraudować
(pieniądze)
emit [y′myt] v. wydawać;
wysyłać (światło, fale
radiowe, ciepło, opinie);
wypuszczać (banknoty);
nadawać przez radio
(audycję); emitować
employ [ym′ploj] v.
zatrudniać; używać;
zajmować się; poświęcać
(czas); posługiwać się;
zastosować coś
employee [,emploj′i:] s.
pracownik; siła (robocza)
employer [em′plojer] s. szef;

pracodawca;
pracodawczyni
employment [ym'plojment] s.
zatrudnienie; używanie;
zajęcie; praca (najemna)
employment agency [ym'ploj
ment'ejdżensy] exp.:
agencja pośrednictwa
pracy; biuro zatrudnienia
bezrobotnych
empower [ym'pałer] v.
upełnomocnić;
upoważniać; umożliwiać
(coś, komuś)
enact [y'naekt] v.
postanawiać; uchwalać;
grać (rolę); odgrywać
(sztukę); uprawomocnić;
wydawać zarządzenia;
zagrać role (na scenie)
enclosure [yn'kloużer] s.
ogrodzenie; załącznik; płot
encore [en'ko:r] s. bis
(zagrać, zaśpiewać na
bis); bisowanie
endorse [yn'do:rs] v.
potwierdzać; popierać;
żyrować; podżyrować;
notować na odwrocie;
indosować coś
endow [yn'dał] v. uposażyć;
wyposażyć; ufundować;
zapisywać; obdarzyć
kogoś
engagement [yn'gejdżment]
s. zobowiązanie; zaręczyny
enterprise ['enterprajz] s.
przedsięwzięcie;
przedsiębiorstwo;
przedsiębiorczość; zadanie;
inicjatywa
envelope ['enweloup] s.
koperta; otoczka; teczka
(papierowa)
equalize [i'kłelajz] v.
wyównywać; równać;
zrównywać (się);
(s)kompensować (coś)
equip [i'kłyp] v. wyposażać;
zaopatrywać; uzbrajać;

ekwipować (kogoś w coś)
equipment [i'kłypment] s.
wyposażenie; ekwipunek;
sprzęt
equitable ['ekłytebl] adj.
słuszny; sprawiedliwy;
godziwy
equivalent [i'kływeilent] adj.
równowartościowy;
równoznaczny; równej
wielkości; s. równoważnik;
równowartość;
równoważność
escalator ['eskelejter] s.
ruchome schody; ruchoma
skala płac (według kosztów
utrzymania etc.)
establish [ys'taeblysz] v.
zakładać; osądzać;
ustalać; wprowadzać;
udowodnić; ufundować;
ustanawiać
establishment
[ys'taeblyszment] s.
założenie; osadzenie;
ustalenie; ustanowienie;
zakład; gospodarstwo; koła
rządzące; organizacja
państwowa lub wojskowa;
firma; przedsiębiorstwo
estate [ys'tejt] s. majątek;
stan majątkowy; położenie
w życiu
estate tax [ys'tejt,taeks]
exp.: podatek spadkowy,
od nieruchomości
(majątkowy)
estimate ['estymejt] v.
oceniać; szacować; s.
szacunek; kosztorys; ocena;
opinia; oszacowanie;
obliczenie
estimation [,esty'mejszyn] s.
szacowanie; poważanie;
szacunek; zdanie;
mniemanie; sąd
evasion [y'wejżyn] s.
uniknięcie; wymknięcie się;
obejście; wykręt; oszustwo
(podatkowe)

event [y'went] s.
wydarzenie; możliwość;
wynik; rezultat; zawody
(sportowe); konkurencja
eventual [y'wenczuel] adj. w
końcu pewny
eventually [y'wenczuely] adv.
w końcu na pewno
exact [yg'zaekt] adj.
dokładny;
ścisły; v. wymagać;
ściągać; egzekwować;
wymuszać
example [yg'za:mpl] s.
przykład; wzór; precedens
excess luggage
[yk'ses,lagydż] exp.:
nadwyżka bagażu
exchange [yks'czendż] s.
wymiana; zamiana; giełda;
centrala telefoniczna; v.
wymienić; zamienić (się);
adj. wymienny; walutowy
exhibition [,eksy'byszyn] s.
wystawa; wystawianie;
pokazywanie; pokaz;
widowisko; popis
exhibitor [yg'zybyter] s.
wystawca; wystawczyni
exit visa ['eksyt,wyza] exp.:
wiza wyjazdowa
expense [yks'pens] s. koszt;
wydatek; rachunek; strata;
ofiara
expert ['ekspe:rt] s. biegły;
ekspert; znawca; adj.
biegły; światły;
mistrzowski; wykonany
przez eksperta
exponent [yks'pounent] adj.
interpretujący; s.
eksponent; wyraziciel;
interpretator; wykładnik
(potęgi); przedstawiciel
export [yks'po:rt] v.
wywozić; eksportować; s.
wywóz; eksport; towar
wywozowy; wywożenie
express [yks'pres] s. ekspres;
przesyłka pośpieszna; adj.

wyraźny; umyślny;
dokładny; adv. pośpiesznie;
ekspresem
extent [yks'tent] s. obszar;
rozmiar; zasięg; miara;
stopień; wysokość;
oszacowanie
extort [yks'tort] v.
wymuszać; zdzierać
(pieniądze); wydrzeć
extra ['ekstre] adj. specjalny;
dodatkowy; luksusowy;
nadzwyczajny; ponad
normę; adv. nadzwyczajnie;
dodatkowo; s. dodatek;
dopłata; rzecz szczególnie
dobra; statysta
extra charge ['ekstre,cza:rdż]
exp.: dopłata; nadpłata

F

facsimile [faek'simily] s.
dokładna reprodukcja;
kopia; FAX
falsehood ['fo:lshud] s. fałsz;
kłamstwo; nieprawda;
kłamliwość
falsify ['fo:lsyfaj] v.
fałszować przekręcać;
kłamać; zawodzić;
podrabiać; oszukać
family name ['faemyly ,nejm]
exp.: nazwisko
fashion ['faeszyn] s. moda;
fason; kształt; wzór;
sposób; v. kształtować;
fasonować; modelować;
urabiać
FAX ['faeks] s. elektroniczna
transmisja kopii
dokumentów; system
przesyłania kopii
dokumentów przez telefon
(zob. facsimile)
fee [fi:] s. opłata; wpisowe;

należność; honorarium; v.
płacić honorarium; płacić
wpisowe
feud [fju:d] s. lenno; waśń
rodowa; wojna między
klanami (rodami)
file [fajl] s. rejestr; archiwum;
seria; pilnik; v. archiwować
fill in ['fyl,yn] v. zapełniać;
wypełniać (formularze,
blankiety)
finance [faj'naens] s. finanse;
skarbowość; v.
finansować; udzielać
pożyczki
financial [faj'naenszel] adj.
pieniężny; finansowy
financier [,fynaen'sjer] s.
finansista; v. spekulować;
sprzeniewierzać pieniądze
fine [fajn] adj. piękny;
misterny; czysty; przedni;
wyszukany; dokładny; adv.
świetnie; wspaniale; s.
grzywna; kara; v. ukarać
grzywną
firm [fe:rm] s. firma; adv.
mocno; adj. pewny;
stanowczy; trwały; v.
ubijać; osadzać (mocno);
umacniać się
first class ['fe:rst'klas] exp.:
pierwsza klasa; a. najlepszej
jakości
first-rate ['fe:rst,rejt] adj.
pierwszorzędny; adv.
pierwszorzędnie; bardzo
dobrze
foot [fut] s. stopa; dół; spód;
miara (30.5 cm); piechota;
v. płacić
foot the bill ['fut,ty'byl] v.
zapłacić rachunek
foreign ['foryn] adj. obcy;
obcokrajowy; cudzoziemski
foreign currency
[,foryn'karensy] s. obca
waluta
form [fo:rm] v. formować
(się); kształtować (się);

utworzyć (się);
organizować (się);
wytworzyć; s. forma;
kształt; postać; formuła;
formułka; formularz;
blankiet; styl; układ
formulate ['fo:rmjulejt] v.
formułować; wyrażać;
redagować
fortune ['fo:rczen] s.
szczęście; los; majątek;
traf; ślepy los
fraction ['fraekszyn] s.
ułamek; część; odłam;
frakcja
franchise ['fraenczajz] s.
przywilej; prawo do
prowadzenia filii lub firmy,
do głosowania
free [fri:] adj. wolny;
bezpłatny; nie zajęty; v.
uwolnić; wyzwolić;
oswobodzić; adv. wolno;
swobodnie; bezpłatnie
freight [frejt] s. przewóz;
fracht; v. przewozić;
frachtować statek; adj.
towarowy (pociąg)
freighter ['frejter] s.
frachtowiec; statek
towarowy

G

gauge [gejdż] s. wskaźnik;
miara; skala; v. kalibrować;
oceniać; szacować;
oszacować
going rate ['gouyn,rejt] exp.:
bieżący kurs (dolara,
oprocentowania, etc.)
gold [gould] s. złoto; adj.
złoty
gold digger ['gould,dyger]
exp.: poszukiwacz złota;
naciągaczka

government ['gawernment] s.
rząd; ustrój; okręg; a.
rządowy

governor ['gawerner] s.
gubernator; zarządca;
naczelnik; szef

gown [gaun] s. suknia; toga;
v. układać togę; ubierać
suknię

groceries ['grouserys] pl.
towary spożywcze

grocery ['grousery] s. sklep
spożywczy; artykuł
spożywczy

gross estate [grous ,ys;tejt]
exp.: stan posiadania przed
odjęciem długów,
podatków etc.

gross profit ratio [grous
'pref.it rej.szo:] exp.:
stosunek między zyskiem i
zakontraktowaną ceną
kupna

gross weight [grous 'wejt]
exp.: waga zawartości i
opakowania (do transportu)

groundless ['graundlys] adj.
bezpodstawny; gołosłowny

groundwork ['graundłerk] s.
podstawa; podłoże; zasada;
fundament; tło; osnowa;
kanwa (utworu)

group [gru:p] s. grupa; v.
grupować;
rozsegregowywać na grupy

guarantee [,gaeren'ti:] v.
gwarantować; poręczać; s.
poręczyciel; poręka;
rękojmia

guarantor [,gaeren'to:r] s.
poręczyciel; poręczycielka

guardian ['ga:rdjen] s.
opiekun; kustosz; adj.
opiekuńczy

guardianship ['ga:rdjenszyp]
s. opieka; opiekuństwo;
kuratela

H

haberdasher ['haeberdaeszer]
s. kupiec galanteryjny;
szmuklerz

handbill ['haendbyl] s. ulotka

handbook ['haend-buk] s.
podręcznik; poradnik

hand luggage ['haend,lagydż]
exp.: bagaż ręczny

hard up ['ha:rd,ap] v. być w
kłopotach pieniężnych

head [hed] s. głowa; łeb;
szef; naczelnik; nagłówek;
szczyt; v. prowadzić;
kierować (się)

headquarters ['hed'kło:terz]
pl. kwatera główna; główne
biuro

heavy traffic ['hewy'traefyk]
ciężki ruch (np. kołowy)

heir [eer] s. spadkobierca;
dziedzic; następca

heiress ['eerys] s.
spadkobierczyni;
następczyni; dziedziczka
(majątku, tytułu)

heritage ['herytydż] s.
spuścizna; spadek;
dziedzictwo

hire [hajer] s. najem; opłata
za najem; v. najmować;
wynajmować; dzierżawić;
odnajmować

hire out ['hajer aut] v.
wynajmować (się do pracy,
na służbę ...)

hire purchase
['hajer'pe:rczys] exp.:
wynajem - zakup na raty

hock [hok] s. pęcina; v.
zastawić (się) w
lombardzie

holding ['houldyn] s.
posiadłość; portfel akcji;
dzierżawa; uchwyt; ujęcie;
trzymanie

home trade ['houm-trejd] s.

handel wewnętrzny
horsepower ['ho:rs,pałer] s.
koń mechaniczny = 746
watów
hotel [hou'tel] s. hotel
how much is it?
['hau,macz'yz ,yt] exp.: ile
to kosztuje?

I

identical [aj'dentykel] adj.
taki sam; identyczny;
tożsamościowy; zupełnie
podobny
identification
[ajdentyfy'kejszyn] s.
utożsamienie; identyfikacja;
stwierdzenie tożsamości
identification papers
[aj,dentyfy 'kejszyn'pejpers]
exp.: dowód tożsamości;
dowód osobisty
identify [aj'dentyfaj] v.
utożsamić; identyfikować
identity [aj'dentyty] s.
tożsamość; identyczność
identity card [aj'dentyty
ka:rd] exp.: dowód osobisty
ignition key [yg'nyszyn,ki:]
exp.: klucz do zapłonu (w
aucie)
import [ym'po:rt] s. import;
treść; v. oznaczać;
importować; przywozić z
zagranicy; adj. importowy
import ['ympo:rt] s. treść;
znaczenie; ważność;
doniosłość
importation [,ympo:r'tejszyn]
s. przywóz; importowanie
incalculable [yn'kaelkjulebl]
exp.: adj. nieobliczalny;
nieprzewidzialny
inch [yncz] s. cal (2.54 cm);
v. posuwać cal po calu
income ['ynkam] s. dochód

income tax ['ynkam,taeks]
exp.: podatek dochodowy
incoming ['yn,kamyng] adj.
nadchodzący; następujący;
przyrastający; s. przybycie;
dochód
incorporate [yn'korperejt] v.
jednoczyć; wcielać;
zrzeszać; [yn'ko:rperyt] adj.
zrzeszony
incorporated [yn'ko:rperejtyd]
adj. zarejestrowany;
zalegalizowany; wcielony;
złączony
indebted [yn'detyd] adj.
dłużny; zobowiązany;
wdzięczny; zawdzięczający
index ['yndeks] s. wskaźnik;
indeks; v. umieszczać w
spisie (indeksie); robić
indeks
indorse [yn'do:rs] v.
potwierdzić (podpisem)
inexpensive [,ynyks'pensyw]
adj. niedrogi; niekosztowny;
tani
inflation [yn'flejszyn] s.
inflacja; nadymanie;
nadmuchanie; zwyżka cen
information [,ynfer'mejszyn]
s. wiadomość; wiedza;
objaśnienie; informacja;
doniesienie
information desk
[,ynfer'mejszyn ,desk] exp.:
punkt informacyjny (w
banku, hotelu, na
wystawie)
information officer [,ynfer
'mejszyn 'ofyser] exp.:
oficer informacyjny (w
banku etc.)
injury ['yndżery] s. szkoda;
krzywda; rana; uszkodzenie
injustice [yn'dżastys] s.
niesprawiedliwość;
krzywda
ink [ynk] s. atrament; tusz
inquiry [yn'kłajry] s. badanie;
zasięganie informacji;

śledztwo; poszukiwanie;
ankieta; wywiad
insolvent [yn'solwent] adj.
niewypłacalny; s. bankrut;
bankrutka
inspect [yn'spekt] v.
oglądać; doglądać; mieć
nadzór; badać
inspection [yn'spekszyn] s.
przegląd; oglądanie;
inspekcja; doglądanie;
sprawdzanie; kontrola
inspector [yn'spekter] s.
inspektor; nadzorca;
kontroler
institute ['ynstytju:t] s.
instytut; v. zakładać;
ustanawiać; zarządzać
(śledztwo etc.)
institution [,ynsty'tju:szyn] s.
instytucja; ustanowienie
instrument ['ynstrument] s.
instrument; przyrząd;
dokument
insurance [yn'szuerens] s.
ubezpieczenie; adj.
ubezpieczeniowy
insurance policy [yn'szuerens
'polysy] exp.: polisa
ubezpieczeniowa; polisa
asekuracyjna
insure [yn'szuer] v.
ubezpieczać (się);
asekurować; zabezpieczać
intelligence [yn'telydżens] s.
inteligencja; informacja;
wywiad; wiadomości;
nowiny
intelligent [yn'telydżent] adj.
inteligentny; łatwo uczący
się
interchange [,ynte:r'czejndż]
s. wzajemna wymiana; v.
wymieniać się; zmieniać
się
interest ['yntryst] s.
zainteresowanie;
ciekawość; odsetki;
interes; procent; v.
zainteresować

invalid [yn'waelyd] adj.
nieważny; nieprawomocny
invalidate [yn'waelydejt] v.
unieważniać (prawnie etc.)
invest [yn'west] v.
inwestować; wyposażać;
oblegać; obdarzać
investigator [yn'westygejtor]
s. badacz; agent
(prokuratury)
investment [yn'westment] s.
inwestycja; lokata;
oblężenie; osaczenie;
obleczenie
invoice ['ynwois] s. faktura;
v. fakturować
I.O.U. = I owe you
['ajou'ju:] s. kwit; skrypt
dłużny
itemize ['ajte,majz] v.
wyszczególniać (rachunek,
spis)

J

janitor ['dżaenitor] s. portier;
dozorca; sprzątacz biurowy
jeep [dżi:p] s. łazik;
samochód terenowy (silnie
zbudowany)
job [dżob] s. robota; zajęcie;
zadanie; posada; v.
pracować; robić;
handlować; wynajmować
job [dżob] v. ukłuć;
dźgnąć; dziobnąć; s.
dźgnięcie; praca;
dziobnięcie; zadanie;
robota; fach
jobless ['dżoblys] adj.
bezrobotny; bez pracy
job work ['dżobłerk] exp.:
praca na akord (zob. piece-
work)
joint stock ['dżoynt,stok] adj.
akcyjny (bank); udziałowy

judge [dżadż] v. sądzić;
osądzać; rozsądzać; s.
sędzia; znawca; znawczyni;
człowiek biegły w ocenach
judgment ['dżadżment] s.
sąd; sądzenie; wyrok;
rozsądek; opinia; ocena;
decyzja
judicial [dżu'dyszel] adj.
sądowy; sędziowski;
bezstronny; krytyczny;
sądownie zrzeszony
jumble sale ['dżambl,sejl]
exp.: wyprzedaż
wysortowanych towarów
(często dobroczynna)
junk ['dżank] s. złom;
szmelc; slang: narkotyki; v.
wyrzucać
jurisdiction [,dżurys'dykszyn]
s. wymiar sprawiedliwości;
sądownictwo; zasięg
władzy
jurisprudence
[,dżurys'pru:dens] s.
prawoznawstwo
juror ['dżuerer] s. sędzia
przysięgły; ławnik;
zaprzysiężony; juror
jury ['dżuery] s. sąd
przysięgłych; sąd
konkursowy
justice ['dżastys] s.
sprawiedliwość;
słuszność; sędzia (pokoju,
sądu najwyższego)
justification
[,dżastyfy'kejszyn] s.
uzasadnienie;
usprawiedliwienie;
wykazanie
justify ['dżastyfaj] v.
usprawiedliwić;
wytłumaczyć;
umotywować; uzasadnić;
dać dowody

K

know-how ['nouhau] s.
umiejętność; znajomość
rzeczy

L

lab [laeb] s. (slang)
laboratorium; adj.
laboratoryjny
label ['lejbl] s. nalepka;
etykieta; naklejka;
przezwisko; v. przylepiać
etykiety (na coś, komuś);
przezywać
labor ['lejber] s. praca;
robota; trud; mozół;
wysiłek; klasa robotnicza;
poród; v. ciężko
pracować; mozolić się;
borykać się; łudzić się;
brnąć; opracować;
rozwodzić się; rodzić;
szczegółowo opracować
laboratory [lae'boretery] s.
laboratorium; pracownia
laborious [le'bo:rjes] adj.
pracowity; mozolny;
wypracowany; ciężko
pracujący
labor union ['lejber'ju:njen]
exp.: związek zawodowy
laborer ['lejberer] s. robotnik
płatny na godzinę (fizyczny)
lag behind ['laeg,by'hajnd] v.
pozostawać w tyle;
zalegać
lager ['la:ger] s. wystałe
piwo
landholder ['laend,houlder] s.
właściciel ziemski;
dzierżawca
landlady ['laend,lejdy] s.

właścicielka domu, hotelu etc.; gospodyni (pensjonatu)
landlord ['laend,lo:rd] s. właściciel domu czynszowego; gospodarz odnajmujący pokój
landowner ['laend,ołner] s. właściciel ziemski
last name ['laest,nejm] exp.: nazwisko
law [lo:] s. prawo; ustawa; reguła; sądy; posłuszeństwo prawu
lawsuit ['lo:sju:t] s. proces (sądowy); sprawa sądowa
lawyer ['lo:jer] s. prawnik; adwokat; radca prawny
leader ['li:der] s. przywódca; lider; przewodnik; prowadzący
leadership ['li:der,szyp] s. przywództwo; kierownictwo; przewodnictwo; umiejętność przewodzenia
leakage [li:kydż] s. przeciekanie (sekretów); wyciekanie (pieniędzy); rozproszenie
legislation [,ledżys'lejszyn] s. prawodawstwo; ustawodawstwo
legislative ['ledżysletyw] adj. prawodawczy; ustawodawczy
legislator ['ledżyslator] s. prawodawca; poseł do parlament (sejmu, senatu etc.)
legitimate [ly'dżytymyt] adj. ślubny; prawowity; słuszny; uzasadniony; logiczny; rozsądny
let go ['let,gou] v. wypuszczać; zwalniać; pozwolić odejść
let know ['let,nou] v. zawiadomić; donieść; powiadomić

letter ['leter] s. litera; list; czcionka; v. drukować; oznaczać literami; kaligrafować
liability [,laje'bylyty] s. odpowiedzialność; obowiązek; obciążenie; zadłużenie; ryzyko
liable ['lajebl] adj. odpowiedzialny; podlegający; podatny; skłonny; narażony; mający widoki
liable to ['lajebl,tu] adj. skłonny do ...; adv. łatwo (zgnije)
liaison [ly'ejzo:n] s. łączność; związek; romans (nielegalny)
life assurance ['lajfe'szuerens] exp.: ubezpieczenie na życie
life insurance ['lajn,yn'szuerens] exp.: ubezpieczenie na życie
limited liability ['lymytyd ,laje'bylyty] s. ograniczona odpowiedzialność
livelihood ['lajwly,hud] s. utrzymanie; środki do życia
loan [loun] s. pożyczka; v. pożyczać
lobby ['loby] s. przedpokój; kuluar; v. urabiać senatora lub posła na czyjąś korzyść (przekupywać)
lobbyist ['lobyst] s. interwencjonalista kuluarowy (często oficjalnie rejestrowany w USA); lobbyista
log [log] s. kłoda; kloc; log; dziennik operacyjny (statku, szybu); v. wycinać drzewa; ciąć na kłody; wciągać do dziennika okrętowego etc.
logbook ['logbuk] s. dziennik pokładowy; książka raportowa
long distance call

['lon'dystans ,kol] exp.:
telefon międzymiastowy;
rozmowa międzymiastowa
lottery ['lotery] s. loteria
luggage ['lagydż] s. bagaż;
walizki
luggage carrier
['lagydż'kaerjer] exp.:
bagażowy
luggage rack ['lagydż'raek]
exp.: półka na walizki
luggage slip ['lagydż'slyp]
exp.: kwit bagażowy
luggage van ['lagydż'waen]
exp.: wóz bagażowy
lunch hour ['lancz'auer] exp.:
przerwa obiadowa (w
południe)
lunch time ['lancz 'tajm]
exp.: pora obiadowa;
południe

M

magazine [maege'zi:n] s.
czasopismo; magazynek (na
kule); skład broni dla
wojska
mailbox ['mejl,boks] s.
skrzynka pocztowa
mailman [mejlmen] s.
listonosz
mail-order house ['mejl,order
,haus] s. firma sprzedająca
przez pocztę (z katalogu)
maintenance ['mejntenens] s.
utrzymanie; utrzymywanie;
poparcie; wyżywienie
manage ['maenydż] v.
kierować; zarządzać;
posługiwać się; obchodzić
się; opanowywać;
poskramiać; radzić sobie
management ['maenydżment]
s. zarząd; kierownictwo;
dyrekcja; posługiwanie się;

obchodzenie się; sprawne
zarządzanie
manager ['maenydżer] s.
kierownik; zarządzający;
gospodarz
manageress ['maenydżeres]
s. (Brit.) kierowniczka
woman manager ['łumen
'maenydżer] s.
kierowniczka
mandate ['maendejt] s.
mandat; pełnomocnictwo
do sprawowania funkcji
pochodzącej z wyboru;
pismo władzy wyższej;
grzywna; rozkaz; komenda;
wola wyborców przekazana
wybranemu
reprezentantowi
manifest ['maenyfest] adj.
jawny; oczywisty; v.
manifestować; ujawniać;
s. manifest okrętowy
(szczegółowa lista ładunku)
market ['ma:kyt] s. rynek;
zbyt; targ; v. robić zakupy;
sprzedawać na targu
marketing ['ma:rkytyng] s.
organizowanie rynku;
handlowanie
marketplace ['ma:rkytplejs] s.
rynek; plac targowy
matter-of-fact
['maeter,ow'faekt] adj.
rzeczowy; praktyczny
medium ['mi:djem] s. środek;
średnia; przewodnik;
środek obiegowy;
środowisko; rozpuszczalnik;
sposób; środkowa droga;
adj. średni; adv. średnio
meeting ['mi:tyng] s.
spotkanie; połączenie się;
posiedzenie; zgromadzenie;
wiec; zawody; konferencja;
pojedynek
merger ['me:rdżer] s.
połączenie; zlanie się; fuzja
middle class ['mydl,kla:s]
exp.: klasa średnia; klasa

średniozamożna; adj. ze
średniozamożnej klasy
middle name ['mydl,nejm] s.
drugie imię
mind your own business
['majnd ,jo: 'ołn 'byznys]
exp.: pilnuj swego nosa; nie
wtrącaj się
mint [mynt] s. mięta;
mennica; slang: majątek;
źródło; v. bić pieniądze;
slang: wymyślać; tworzyć;
kuć
mismanage [,mys'maenydż]
v. źle prowadzić; źle
pokierować
model ['modl] s. model;
wzór; modelka; manekin; v.
modelować
monetary ['manytry] adj.
monetarny; pieniężny;
walutowy
money ['many] s. pieniądze
money order ['many,o:rder]
exp.: przekaz pieniężny
monopolize [me'nopelajz] v.
monopolizować; skupiać
na sobie uwagę wszystkich
etc.
monopoly [me'nopely] s.
monopol
mortgage ['mo:rgydż] s.
hipoteka; v. hipotekować
multiple ['maltypl] s.
wielokrotna; adj.
wielokrotny; złożony
multiplication
[,maltyply'kejszyn] s.
mnożenie; rozmnażanie się
multiplication table
[,maltyply'kejszyn tejbl]
exp.: tabliczka mnożenia
multiply ['maltyplaj] s.
mnożyć (się); rozmnażać
się; pomnożyć
municipal [mju:'nysypel] adj.
miejski; samorządowy;
komunalny

N

name [nejm] s. imię; nazwa;
nazwisko; v. nazywać;
mianować; wymieniać;
naznaczyć (datę)
national ['naeszenl] adj.
narodowy; państwowy; s.
członek narodu; obywatel;
ziomek
nationality [,naesze'naelyty]
s. narodowość;
obywatelstwo
nationalize ['naesznelajz] v.
upaństwowić; nadawać
obywatelstwo (imigrantom)
necessity [ny'sesyty] s.
potrzeba; konieczność;
artykuł pierwszej potrzeby;
niedostatek; los; zrządzenie
losu
negotiate [ny'gousjejt] v.
pertraktować; omawiać;
załatwiać; przezwyciężać;
przebić się przez; uporać
się; przekazać lub
sprzedać
negotiation
[ny,gouszy'ejszyn] s.
pertraktacje; omawianie w
celu osiągnięcia
porozumienia
newsstand ['nju:staend] s.
kiosk z gazetami
nominal ['nomynl] adj.
nominalny; imienny;
symboliczny; tylko z nazwy
norm [no:rm] s. norma;
wzorzec; standard
normal ['no:rmel] adj.
normalny; prostopadły;
prawidłowy; s. stan
normalny; prostopadła
normalize ['no:rmelajz] v.
normalizować; unormować
notary public
['noutery'pablyk] exp.:

notariusz
notation [nou'tejszyn] s.
znakowanie; notacja;
symbol
note [nout] s. nuta; znak;
znamię; uwaga; notatka;
banknot; v. zapisywać;
zauważać
notepaper ['nout,pejper] s.
papier listowy; blok
nought [no:t] s. nic; zero
null and void ['nal,end'woid]
exp.: nieważny; bez
znaczenia; unieważniony;
nic nie znaczący
number ['namber] s. liczba;
numer; ilość; v. liczyć;
numerować; wyliczać;
zaliczać
numeral ['nju:merel] adj.
liczbowy; cyfrowy; s.
liczebnik; cyfra (pisana,
mówiona etc.)
nylon ['najlon] s. nylon;
pończochy nylonowe

O

oath [ou_s_] s. przysięga;
przekleństwo;
świętokradztwo etc.
obligation [obly'gejszyn] s.
zobowiązanie; obowiązek;
obligacja; dług
(wdzięczności)
occupant ['okjupent] s.
mieszkaniec; posiadacz
(faktyczny)
occupation [,okju'pejszyn] s.
okupacja; zawód; zajęcie;
zajmowanie;
zamieszkiwanie
occupy ['okjupaj] v.
okupować; zajmować (się
czymś); zatrudniać
official [e'fyszel] s. urzędnik;

adj. urzędowy; oficjalny
offset [o':fset] s. offsetowy
druk; gałąź; odgałęzienie
oil [ojl] s. oliwa; olej; ropa;
nafta; farba olejna; v.
oliwić smarować;
przetapiać; pochlebiać
operator ['operejter] s.
operator; pracownik;
obsługujący maszynę;
telefonista; kierownik;
przemysłowiec; finansista;
spekulant
order ['o:rder] s. rozkaz;
zlecenie; zarządzenie;
przekaz; porządek; szyk;
układ; stan; zakon; order;
obrzęd; zamówienie;
zadanie; v. rozkazywać;
zamawiać; komenderować;
zarządzać; wyświęcać;
porządkować
organization
[,o:rgenaj'zejszyn] s.
organizacja; organizowanie;
struktura; zrzeszenie
organize ['o:genajz] v.
organizować; zrzeszyć;
nadawać ustrój
organizer ['o:genajzer] s.
organizator
outbid [aut'byd] v.
przelicytować; dać więcej
(niż inny)
outfit ['autfyt] s.
wyposażenie; drużyna;
zespół; towarzystwo;
zestaw narzędzi; v.
wyposażyć; zaopatrywać
wyekwipować
outlet ['autlet] s. wylot;
rynek zbytu; wyjście;
ujście
outline ['autlajn] s. zarys;
szkic; v. konturować;
szkicować; przedstawiać
(plany etc.)
out-of-date [autew'dejt] adj.
przestarzały; niemodny
output ['autput] s.

wydajność; wydobycie;
moc; produkcja
overcharge [,ouwer'cza:rdż]
v. przeciążać; zdzierać
(pieniądze); stawiać za
wysokie ceny
overdraw [,ouwer'dro:] v.
wyczerpać (konto);
przesadzać; pisać czeki
bez pokrycia
overdue [,ouwer'dju:] adj.
zaległy; zapóźniony
(pociąg)
overestimate
[,ouwer'esty,mejt] v.
przeceniać; s. za wysoka
ocena; zbyt duże
oczekiwania
overrate ['ouwer'rejt] v.
przeceniać; spodziewać się
zbyt dużo
overtime ['ouwertajm] s.
godziny nadliczbowe; adv.
nadprogramowo; adj.
nadprogramowy; v.
prześwietlić;
przeeksponować
owner ['ołner] s. właściciel
ownership ['ołnerszyp] s.
własność; posiadanie

P

package ['paekydż] s.
pakunek; paczka
package deal ['paekydż'di:l]
exp.: przyjęcie złożonej
propozycji bez zmian
packer ['paeker] s. pakier;
przedsiębiorca od
pakowania artykułów
spożywczych; maszyna do
pakowania
packet ['paekyt] s. pakiet; v.
zawijać
packing ['paekyn] s.

pakowanie; opakowanie;
uszczelka; okładzina;
tampon
packthread ['paektred] s.
szpagat
pact [paekt] s. pakt; układ
paper ['pejper] s. papier;
gazeta; tapeta; rozprawa
naukowa; papierowe
pieniądze; adj. papierowy;
rzekomy; v. zawinąć w
papier; tapetować
paperback ['pejper,baekt] adj.
w paperowej okładce; s.
kieszonkowe wydanie
książki
paper money ['pejper'many]
exp.: papierowe pieniądze
parcel ['pa:rsl] s. paczka;
działka; v. dzielić;
pakować w paczki
part [pa:rt] s. część; ustęp;
udział; rola; strona;
przedział (włosów); v.
rozchodzić (się);
rozdzielać; dzielić; pękać;
robić (przedział);
wyjeżdżać; adj. mniejszy
niż całość
partake [pa:r'tejk] v. brać
udział; dzielić coś z kimś;
(zob. take)
particulars [per'tykjulers] s.
dane osobiste
partner ['pa:rtner] s.
wspólnik
partnership ['pa:rtnerszyp] s.
spółka
part-time ['pa:rt,tajm] adv. na
niepełnym etacie; na
niepełnym czasie; adj.
niepełnoetatowy
passport ['pa:s,po:rt] s.
paszport
password ['pa:s,ło:rd] s.
hasło
patent ['paetnt] s. patent; v.
opatentować; adj.
patentowany;
opatentowany; oczywisty

patent ['pejtnt] adj. jasny;
otwarty; oczywisty;
chroniony patentem
pawn [po:n] s. zastaw; fant;
pionek; v. zastawiać;
dawać w zastaw
pawnbroker ['po:n,brouker] s.
lichwiarz pożyczający pod
zastaw; właściciel
lombardu
pawnshop ['po:n-szop] s.
lombard; sklep zastawniczy
pay [pej] v. płacić; zapłacić;
wynagradzać; udzielać
(uwagi); dawać (dochód);
opłacać (się); s. płaca;
zapłata; pobory;
wynagrodzenie; adj. płatny
(np. automat telefoniczny);
opłacalny
pay back ['pej baek] v.
zwrócić dług; odpłacać
payday ['pej dej] s. dzień
wypłaty
pay down ['pej dałn] v.
dawać zadatek; płacić
pierwszą ratę gotówką
pay for ['pej,fo:r] v. płacić
(za coś)
pay in ['pej,yn] v. wpłacać
pay off ['pej,of] v. spłacać
pay out ['pej,aut] v.
wydatkować; wypuszczać
linę (na statku); wypłacać;
płacić
pay up ['pej,ap] v.
wyrównywać (dług);
zapłacić
payable ['pejebl] adj. płatny;
dochodowy; opłacający się
payee ['pej'i:] s. odbiorca
płatności
payer ['pejer] s. płatnik
payment ['pejment] s.
płatność; wypłata; zapłata
peak hour ['pi:k'auer] exp.:
godzina szczytu ruchu
peddle ['pedl] v. sprzedawać
po domach; być
domokrążcą; wydzielać po

trochu
peddler ['pedler] s.
domokrążcą
peddlar ['pedler] s.
przekupień; handlarz
pencil ['pensl] s. ołówek; v.
rysować; pisać
pencil sharpener
['pensl'sza:rpner] exp.:
strugaczka do ołówka
penholder ['pen,houlder] s.
piórnik; obsadka; stojak na
pióro
penniless ['penylys] adj. w
nędzy; bez grosza
penny ['peny] s. cent; grosz;
pl. pennies ['penyz]; Brit.:
pl. pence [pens]
pennyworth ['penyłe:rs̲] s.
wartość centa; exp.: za
centa
pension ['penszyn] s. renta;
emerytura; pensjonat; v.
wyznaczać pensję;
pensjonować
pension off ['penszyn,of] v.
przenosić na emeryturę
pensioner ['penszener] s.
emeryt; emerytka; rencista;
rencistka
percent [per'sent] s. odsetek;
od sta
percentage [per'sentydż] s.
odsetek; procent; od sta
permit [per'myt] s. pisemne
zezwolenie; pozwolenie; v.
pozwalać; zezwalać;
dopuszczać
personnel [,pe:rse'nel] s.
personel
personnel manager
[,pe:rse'nel 'maenydżer]
exp.: kierownik oddziału
personalnego; personalny
petition [py'tyszyn] s.
petycja; prośba; podanie;
v. prosić; wnosić podanie
petroleum [py'trouljem] s.
ropa naftowa; olej skalny
petty cash [,pety'kaesz] exp.:

gotówka podręczna
phone [foun] s. telefon
(slang)
placard ['plaeka:rd] s. afisz;
plakat; [ple'ka:rd] v.
rozlepiać plakaty
plainclothes man
['plejn,klozmen] exp.: tajny
policjant; detektyw
plaintiff ['plejntyf] s. powód
(zaskarżający); powódka
plank down ['plaenk,dałn] v.
slang: wybulić gotówkę
plant ['pla:nt] s. roślina;
fabryka; zakład; wtyczka;
(slang) oszustwo;
włamanie; kant; v.
zasadzać; zakładać;
umieszczać; pozorować;
ukrywać; wtykać; sadzić
(rośliny)
pledge [pledż] v.
zobowiązywać (się);
zastawiać; s. zastaw;
gwarancja; przyrzeczenie
plenipotentiary [,plenype
'tenszery] s. pełnomocnik;
adj. pełnomocny
pocketbook ['pokyt,buk] s.
portfel
pocket money ['pokyt,many]
exp.: kieszonkowe
poll [poul] s. głosowanie;
rejestrowanie głosów;
wyniki głosowania; lista;
wykaz; lokal wyborczy;
urny wyborcze; ankieta
possession [pe'zeszyn] s.
posiadanie; posiadłość;
własność; dobytek;
opanowanie
possessor [pe'zeser] s.
posiadacz; właściciel
post [poust] s. słup; posada;
posterunek; poczta; v.
ogłaszać; wywieszać;
zalepiać plakatami
postage ['poustydż] s. opłata
pocztowa
postage stamp ['poustydż

,staemp] exp.: znaczek
pocztowy
postal ['poustel] adj.
pocztowy
postal order ['poustel'o:rder]
exp.: przekaz pocztowy
postcard ['poust,ka:rd] s.
pocztówka
post code ['poust,koud] =
zip-code [,zyp'koud]
pocztowy numer
kierunkowy
poste restante
['poust'resta:nt] exp.: list
lub·przesyłka do odebrania
na poczcie
poster ['pouster] s. plakat
postman ['poustmen] s.
listonosz
postmark ['poust,ma:rk] s.
stempel pocztowy
postmaster ['poust,ma:ster]
s. naczelnik poczty
post office ['poust,ofys]
exp.: poczta
post office box ['poust,ofys
'boks] exp.: skrytka
pocztowa
postpaid ['poust,pejd] s.
opłata pocztowa z góry
uiszczona
prepay ['pry'pej] v. opłacać z
góry
price [prajs] s. cena; koszt;
v. wyceniać
principal ['prynsepel] adj.
główny; s. kierownik;
zleceniodawca; kapitał;
sprawca
prize [prajz] v. podważyć;
zajmować; cenić; s.
nagroda; premia; wygrana;
łup; a. kapitalny
produce ['produ:s] s. 1.
produkty; plony; wynik;
produkcja; wydajność;
wydobycie; produkty rolne
produce [pre'dju:s] v. 2.
wytarzać; produkować;
dostarczać; wydobywać;

wystawiać; okazywać
producer ['produ:ser] s.
wytwórca (filmowy);
producent
product ['predakt] s. produkt;
wynik; iloczyn; wytwór
(natury etc.)
production [pre'dakszyn] s.
wytwórczość; wydobycie;
produkcja; utwór; produkty;
adj. produkcyjny
productive [pre'daktyw] adj.
wydajny; produktywny;
produkcyjny; urodzajny;
żyzny
profitable ['profytebl] adj.
korzystny; intratny;
zyskowny
profiteer [,profy'tier] v.
paskować; spekulować; s.
paskarz; spekulant (na
czarnym rynku etc.)
proof [pru:f] s. dowód; próba
(np. złota); sprawdzian;
wypróbowanie; korekta;
próbna odbitka; adj.
odporny; wypróbowany;
sprawdzony;
nieprzemakalny
property ['property] s.
własność; właściwość;
cecha; nieruchomość
proprietary [pre'prajetery] adj.
należący; będący
własnością prywatną; s.
właściciel; własność
proprietor [pre'prajeter] s.
właściciel; posiadacz;
gospodarz
prospect ['prospekt] s.
widok; perspektywa;
ewentualny klient;
potencjalne złoża; v.
przeszukiwać (okolice);
próbnie eksploatować
kopalnię; szukać złota etc.;
badać (teren etc.)
prospective [pres'pektyw]
adj. dotyczący przyszłości;
przyszły; działający na

przyszłość; zapowiedziany;
spodziewany
prototype ['proute,tajp] s.
prototyp; model
publicity [pab'lysyty] s.
rozgłos; reklama; a.
reklamowy
publish ['pablysz] v.
publikować; wydawać;
ogłaszać; rozgłaszać;
wydawać drukiem
publisher ['pablyszer] s.
wydawca; nakładca
publishing house
['pablyszyng,haus] exp.:
firma wydawnicza
purchase ['pe:rczes] s.
zakup; kupno; dźwignia; v.
kupić; okupić; nabywać;
podnosić (np. kotwicę);
sprawiać sobie
purchaser [pe:rczeser] s.
nabywca; kupujący
purvey [pe:r'wej] v.
dostarczyć; zaopatrywać;
być dostawcą
purveyor [pe:rwejer] s.
dostawca
pyramid ['pyremyd] s.
piramida; ostrosłup; v.
zarabiać na spekulacji;
wznosić (się) piramidalnie;
budować jak piramidę

Q

qualification [,kłolyfy'kejszyn]
s. warunek; określenie;
kwalifikacja; uzdolnienie (do
pracy)
qualified ['kłolyfajd] adj.
wykwalifikowany;
uwarunkowany;
kwalifikujący się
quality ['kłolyty] s. jakość;
gatunek; właściwość;

zaleta
quantity ['kłontyty] s. ilość;
wielkość; hurt; obfitość
quart [kło:rt] s. jedna czwarta
galonu (0.946 l.); kwarta
piwa
quarter ['kło:ter] v.
ćwiartować; kwaterować;
rozpłatać; stacjonować; s.
ćwierć; ćwiartka;
kwadrans; kwartał;
kwatera; 25 centów
(moneta); kwadra
(księżyca); dzielnica;
mieszkanie; strona świata;
czynniki wpływowe; (pl.)
sfery (rządzące); kwartał
quarterly ['kło:terly] adj.
kwartalny; adv. kwartalnie;
s. kwartalnik; pismo
kwartalne
questionnaire [,kłejstje'neer]
s. kwestionariusz
queue [kju:] s. warkocz;
ogonek; kolejka; v. czekać
w kolejce; czekać w
ogonku
queue up ['kju:,ap] v.
ustawiać się w kolejce
quid pro quo [,kłyd.,prou.
'klou] exp.: coś dane w
zamian czegoś innego
quota ['kłouta] s. udział;
kontyngent; norma
quotation [kłou'tejszyn] s.
cytata; cytowanie;
notowanie; przytaczanie
(bieżącej ceny)
quotation marks
[kłou'tejszyn,ma:rks] pl.
cudzysłów
quote [kłout] v. cytować;
przytaczać; umieszczać w
cudzysłowie; notować;
podawać kurs; powoływać
się na kogoś
quotient ['kłouszent] s. iloraz

R

racket ['raekyt] s. rakieta;
rak; zabawa; hulanka;
awantura; hałas; afera;
granda; nieuczciwe
interesy; kant; v.
hałasować; hulać;
bumblować; zabawiać się;
awanturować się
racketeer [,raeky'tier] s.
szantażysta; opryszek; v.
szantażować; robić grandę
raise [rejz] v. podnosić;
wskrzeszać; wznosić;
wynosić; hodować;
wychowywać; wysuwać;
wytaczać; wzniecać;
zrywać; wywoływać;
budzić; zbierać (np.
fundusze); wydobywać;
przerywać (np. oblężenie);
znosić (zakaz); s.
podwyżka (płac);
podwyższenie
rake-off ['rejk,of] s.
nielegalna prowizja;
łapówka
rate [rejt] s. stopa; stosunek;
proporcja; wysokość;
poziom; szybkość; cena;
stawka; opłata; podatek;
stopień; klasa; v.
szacować; oceniać;
ustalać; zaliczać;
opodatkować; zasługiwać;
besztać; wymyślać
rate of exchange ['rejt of
yks'czejndż] exp.: kurs
wymiany
rate of interest [,rejt of
'yntryst] exp.: stopa
procentowa
readout ['ri:daut] s. odczyt
wyników komputera
real estate ['ryel,es'tejt] s.
nieruchomość; realność
realization [,ryelaj'zejszyn] s.

realizacja; spełnienie;
wykonanie; spieniężenie;
uświadomienie sobie
realize ['ry:e,lajz] v.
urzeczywistnić; realizować;
uprzytamniać; zdawać
sobie sprawę; uzyskiwać;
zdobywać (majątek)
realtor ['ryelter] s. pośrednik
sprzedaży nieruchomości
realty ['ryelty] s.
nieruchomość
rebate [ry'bejt] s. rabat;
zwrot (części kwoty); v.
udzielać rabatu; potrącać
(z rachunku);
zamortyzować; przytępiać
rebel ['rebel] s. buntownik; v.
buntować się; adj.
zbuntowany; buntowniczy
re-book ['ry:buk] v.
zamawiać na nowo
(program teatralny, bilety
lotnicze etc.)
receipt [ry'si:t] s.
pokwitowanie; odbiór;
recepta
receiver [ry'si:wer] s.
odbiornik (radiowy);
słuchawka (telefoniczna);
odbiorca; syndyk; zarządca
upadłości
reception [ry'sepszyn] s.
przyjęcie; odbiór; recepcja
reception desk
[ry'sepszyn,desk] exp.:
biuro do przyjmowania
interesantów; portiernia;
biuro przyjęć
receptionist [ry'sepszynyst]
s. recepcjonistka;
sekretarka przyjmująca
klientów; portier
recession [ry'seszyn] s.
cofnięcie; recesja
(gospodarcza); wgłębienie;
wnęka; kryzys; zastój
reciprocal [ry'syprekel] adj.
wzajemny; odwrotny; s.
odwrotność (w

matematyce)
reckoning ['rekenyng] s.
obliczanie (położenia);
rachuba; obrachunek;
kalkulacja; rozliczenie
record ['ryko:rd] v.
zapisywać; notować;
rejestrować; zaznaczać;
nagrywać; s. zapiska;
archiwum; rejestracja;
dokument; przeszłość
(czyjaś); pamięć o kimś;
nagranie; rekord
recorder [ry'ko:rder] s.
rejestrator; aparat
zapisujący; pisak; pisarz
archiwista
recruit [ry'kru:t] s. rekrut;
poborowy; v. werbować;
uzupełniać (stan
zatrudnienia)
reduction [ry'dakszyn] s.
zmniejszenie; redukcja;
obniżka; sprowadzenie;
dostosowanie; odtlenienie;
wytapianie
reference book
['referens,bu:k] exp.: tekst
podręczny; podręcznik
refund [ry'fand] s. zwrot;
spłata; v. zwracać
pieniądze
register ['redżyster] v.
rejestrować;
zapamiętywać; wysyłać
polecony list; prowadzić
rejestr; wstrzeliwać się;
wyrażać minami
registered letter
['redżysterd,leter] exp.: list
polecony
registration [,redżys'trejszyn]
s. rejestracja; meldunek;
ilość zarejestrowana
reliability [ry,laje'bylyty] s.
rzetelność; solidność;
pewność
remainder [ry'mejnder] s.
reszta; pozostałość;
remanent

remit [ry'myt] v.
przekazywać (pieniądze);
darować (dług);
odpuszczać (grzechy);
odsyłać; przywracać;
łagodzić; łagodnieć;
słabnąć
remittance [ry'mytens] s.
przesyłka pieniężna;
wypłata
remnant ['remnent] s.
resztka; pozostałość; ślad
czegoś
rend [rend] v. drzeć; targać;
wydzierać; urągać;
rozdzierać
render ['render] v. uczynić;
zrobić; oddawać;
okazywać; składać;
wydawać; płacić;
odpłacać; oczyszczać;
wytapiać; tynkować; s.
odpłata (np. w naturze);
pierwsza warstwa tynku
rent [rent] s. komorne;
czynsz; renta; najem;
rozdarcie; szczelina; rozłam;
parów; v. wynajmować;
dzierżawić; pobierać
czynsz; być
wynajmowanym
rental ['rentl] s. czynsz;
komorne; wypożyczanie;
adj. czynszowy
rental agency
['rentl'ejdżensy] exp.: biuro
wynajmu (narzędzi,
mieszkań etc.)
rent-free ['rent'fri:] adj.
wolny od opłaty
czynszowej
reparation [repa'rejszyn] s.
naprawa; remont;
odszkodowanie
repay [ry:'pej] v. spłacić;
zwrócić; wynagrodzić;
odwzajemnić się; oddać
reporter [ru'po:rter] s.
dziennikarz; sprawozdawca;
reporter

requisition [,rekły'zyszyn] s.
żądanie; nakaz;
zapotrzebowanie; v.
wydawać zapotrzebowanie;
zapotrzebowywać;
rekwirować; zażądać
dostaw
residence permit
['rezydens,per'myt] exp.:
prawo pobytu
retail ['ri:tejl] s. detal; adj.
detaliczny; v. sprzedawać
detalicznie; szczegółowo
opowiadać; adv. detalicznie
retailer [ri:'tejler] s.
sklepikarz; detalista;
plotkarz
retired [ry'tajerd] adj.
emerytowany; ustronny;
odosobniony
retirement [ry'tajerment] s.
przejście w stan
spoczynku; ustronie;
odosobnienie; wycofanie
(weksla); odwrót
return flight [ry'te:rn,flajt]
exp.: lot powrotny
return ticket [ry'te:rn,tykyt]
exp.: powrotny bilet
revaluation [ri:'wael'juejszyn]
s. ponowna ocena;
przewartościowanie (po
ponownej ocenie)
revaluate [ri:'waelju':ejt] v.
ponownie ocenić;
przewartościować (dom w
celach podatkowych)
revenue ['rewy,nu:] s.
dochód (z podatków)
revenue office
['rewy,nu:'ofys] exp.: urząd
podatkowy (finansowy)
rider ['rajder] s. jeździec;
dżokej; poprawka; dodatek;
klauzula; ciężarek
przesuwany; nasadka;
poprawka na dokumencie
ring [ryng] v. dzwonić;
dźwięczeć; brzmieć;
rozbrzmiewać;

wydzwaniać; telefonować;
wybijać czas na zegarze
kontrolnym; sprawdzać
monetę dźwiękiem; s.
dzwonek; dzwony; dźwięk;
brzęk; telefonowanie
ring off ['ryng,of] s.
skończyć rozmowę
telefoniczną
ring the bell ['ryng,dy'bel] v.
dzwonić (do drzwi etc.)
ring up ['ryng,ap] v. wybijać
kwotę (na kasie
rejestracyjnej);
zatelefonować (do kogoś)
robot ['roubot] s. robot
royalty ['rojelty] s.
królewskość; honorarium
autorskie

S

safe [sejf] adj. pewny;
bezpieczny; s. schowek
bankowy; kasa pancerna;
spiżarnia wietrzona; (slang):
kondon
safeguard ['sejfga:rd] v.
ochraniać; zabezpieczać;
gwarantować; s.
zabezpieczenie; gwarancja
safety ['sejfty] s.
bezpieczeństwo;
zabezpieczenie; bezpiecznik;
adj. dający bezpieczeństwo
safety belt ['sejfty,belt] s.
pas bezpieczeństwa (np. w
samochodzie)
safety lock ['sejfty,lok] s.
zamek bezpieczeństwa
sale [sejl] s. sprzedaż;
wyprzedaż
saleslady ['sejls'lejdy] s.
sprzedawczyni
salesman ['sejlsmen] s.
sprzedawca

sales manager
[,sejls'maenydżer] exp.:
kierownik działu sprzedaży
sample ['sa:mpl] s. próbka;
wzór; v. próbować; dawać
próbki
save [sejw] v. ratować;
oszczędzać; zachowywać
pozory; zbawiać; uniknąć;
zyskiwać (czas); prep.:
oprócz; wyjąwszy; poza;
pominąwszy; conj.: że;
poza tym; chyba że; z
wyjątkiem
save for a car
['sejw,fo:r'ej,ka:r] exp.:
oszczędzać na samochód
saver ['sejwer] s. osoba
oszczędzająca; przedmiot
oszczędzający (np. czas)
saving ['sejwyng] adj.
zbawienny; oszczędny;
(preposition:) wyjąwszy
savings bank
['sejwynz'baenk] exp.: kasa
oszczędności
scarce [skeers] adj. rzadki;
niewystarczający
scarcely ['skeersly] adv.
zaledwie; ledwo; z trudem;
z trudnością
scarcity ['skeersyty] s.
niedostatek; niedobór; brak
schedule ['skedżul] s. rozkład
jazdy; wykaz; zestawienie;
tabela; taryfa;
harmonogram; lista; plan; v.
planować; wciągać na
listę; naznaczać (według
planu)
scheme [ski:m] s. intryga;
podstęp; plan
scrap iron ['skraep,ajern]
exp.: złom żelazny
secure [sy'kjuer] v.
zabezpieczać (się);
umacniać; uzyskiwać;
zapewniać sobie; adj.
spokojny; bezpieczny;
pewny

security [sy'kjueryty] s.
bezpieczeństwo;
zabezpieczenie; pewność;
zastaw; papier
wartościowy; zbytnia
ufność
self-interest ['self'yntryst] s.
interesowność; własne
dobro
self-service ['self'se:rwys] s.
samo-obsługa
sell [sel] v. sprzedawać;
zaprzedawać;
sprzeniewierzyć; wykiwać;
mieć zbyt; być na
sprzedaż; wyprzedawać
sell out ['selaut] v.
wyprzedawać
seller ['seler] s. sprzedawca
semicolon ['semy'koulen] s.
średnik
sender ['sender] s. nadawca;
nadajnik (np. radiowy)
serial ['sierjel] adj. seryjny;
periodyczny; kolejny;
odcinkowy
series ['sieri:z] s. seria;
szereg; rząd
service ['se:rwys] s. służba;
obsługa; praca; urząd;
zaopatrzenie; instalacja;
uprzejmość; grzeczność;
przysługa; pomoc;
użyteczność;
nabożeństwo; serw; serwis
(stołowy); wręczenie; v.
doglądać; naprawić; kryć
(samice)
serviceable ['se:rwysebl] adj.
pożyteczny; użyteczny;
praktyczny; wygodny;
mocny; trwały
service-station ['se:rwys -
'stejszyn] exp.: stacja
obsługi i sprzedaży benzyny
settle [setl] v. osiedlić (się);
umieścić (się);
uregulować; osadzić (się);
ustalić; rozstrzygnąć;
zapłacić (dług);

zamieszkać; usadowić
(się); uspokoić (się);
zawierać (umowę);
układać (się)
settle down ['setl,daln] v.
ustatkować się; osiedlić
się; zabrać się do czegoś
settlement ['setlment] s.
osiedle; osada; kolonia;
osiadanie; sedymentacja;
załatwienie; rozstrzygnięcie;
ustalenie
share [szeer] s. udział;
należna część; lemiesz; v.
rozdzielić; dzielić (się);
podzielać; brać udział
shareholder ['szeer,houlder]
exp.: akcjonariusz
shipment ['szypment] s.
załadunek; przesyłka; fracht
shipowner ['szyp,olner] s.
armator
shipping ['szypyn] s. flota
handlowa; żegluga;
załadunek; usługi
żeglugowe; przesyłka; adj.
spedycyjny; okrętowy
shipping company ['szypyn
'kampeny] exp.: firma
okrętowa; armator
shop [szop] s. sklep;
pracownia; warsztat;
zakład; v. robić zakupy
shopkeeper ['szop,ki:per] s.
kupiec; sklepikarz
shoplifter ['szop,lyfter] s.
złodziej sklepowy
shopping center ['szopyn
,senter] s. skupisko
sklepów; ośrodek zakupów
shopping mall ['szopyn ,mol]
exp.: skupisko sklepów
wzdłuż krytej hali; pasaż
handlowy
shop window ['szop'lyndoł]
exp.: wystawa
shortage ['szo:rtydż] s. brak;
niedobór; deficyt
shorthand ['szo:rthaend] s.
stenografia

short-term ['szo:rt'term] adj.
krótkoterminowy;
krótkotrwały
show business ['szou'byznyz]
exp.: przemysł
widowiskowy
shyster ['szajster] s. chytry
(polityk) bez zasad;
adwokat-krętacz
sick benefits ['syk'benefyc]
exp.: zasiłek chorobowy
sick leave ['sykli:w] exp.:
zwolnienie lekarskie; urlop
chorobowy
sign [sajn] s. znak; omen;
godło; napis; wywieszka;
szyld; skinienie; oznaka;
objaw; ślad; znak drogowy;
hasło; odzew; v. znaczyć;
naznaczyć; podpisać;
skinąć
sign up ['sajn,ap] v.
zapisywać się
sign out ['sajn,aut] v.
wypisywać się
signal ['sygnl] s. sygnał;
znak; v. sygnalizować;
zapowiadać; dawać znak
signature ['sygnyczer] s.
podpis; sygnatura; klucz
signboard ['sajnbo:rd] s.
wywieszka; szyld; godło
single out ['syngl,aut] v.
wybierać
sketch ['skecz] s. szkic;
skecz; zarys; v. szkicować;
przedstawić w ogólnych
zarysach (w krótkich
słowach); robić wstępny
rysunek
sketch block ['skecz,blok]
exp.: szkicownik
sketchbook ['skecz,bu:k] s.
szkicownik
slide rule ['slajd,ru:l] exp.:
suwak logarytmiczny
small change ['smo:l,czejndż]
exp.: drobne (pieniądze)
snafu [snae'fu:] v.
zabałaganić; s. bałagan

(slang)
snow job ['snou,dżob] s.
naciąganie pochlebstwami
social security ['souszel
sy'kjueryty] exp.:
ubezpieczenia społeczne
social welfare
['souszel,łelfeer] exp.:
opieka społeczna
sold [sould] adj. sprzedany;
v. (zob. sell)
solicitor [se'lysyter] s. radca
prawny; akwizytor; agent
firmowy
solution [so'ljuszyn] s.
rozczyn; roztwór;
rozwiązanie (problemu)
spare [speer] v. oszczędzać;
zaoszczędzić; odstępować;
obywać się; zachować;
przeznaczać; szanować
(uczucia); szczędzić; adj.
zapasowy; oszczędny;
skromny; drobny; szczupły;
wolny (np. czas); s. część
zapasowa; koło zapasowe
spare time ['speer,tajm] exp.:
wolny czas
spare tire ['speer,tajer] exp.:
koło zapasowe
special ['speszel] adj.
specjalny; wyjątkowy;
osobliwy; dodatkowy;
nadzwyczajny; s.
dodatkowy autobus;
nadzwyczajne wydanie;
reklamowa dzienna zniżka
ceny w sklepie
specialist ['speszelyst] s.
specjalista; specjalistka
specialize ['speszelajz] v.
wyspecjalizować (się);
wyszczególniać;
ograniczać; precyzować;
różniczkować (się);
ograniczać (się)
specialty [,speszy'aelyty] s.
1. specjalność; specjalna
cecha
specialty ['speszelty] s. 2.

fach; specjalizacja; umowa
specimen ['spesymyn] s.
okaz; przykład; wzór; typ;
próba; numer okazowy
speculate ['spekjulejt] v.
spekulować; rozmyślać
nad ...; rozważać
speculation [,spekju'lejszyn]
s. spekulacja; domysł;
rozmyślanie
square [skłeer] s. kwadrat;
czworobok (budynków);
plac; kątownik; węgielnica;
adj. kwadratowy;
prostokątny; prostopadły;
uporządkowany; zupełny;
uczciwy; v. robić
kwadratowym, prostym;
podnosić do kwadratu;
płacić (dług); adv. w
sedno; rzetelnie; wprost
stagflation ['staegflejszyn] s.
stagnacja, rosnące
bezrobocie i inflacja
jednocześnie
stall [sto:l] v. działać
opóźniająco; zwlekać;
przewlekać; kręcić;
zwodzić; przetrzymywać;
dławić motor; utykać;
grzęznąć; trzymać bydło w
oborze; zaopatrywać w
przegrody; s. stajnia; obora;
stragan; kiosk; przegroda;
komora (w kopalni); (slang):
trik; kruczek
standard ['staenderd] s.
sztandar; norma; miernik;
wzorzec; wskaźnik; stopa
(życiowa); próba; słup;
podpórka; adj.
znormalizowany; normalny;
typowy; przeciętny;
wzorcowy; klasyczny;
literacki (język)
standardize ['staenderdajz] v.
normalizować;
dostosowywać do normy;
mierzyć wzorcem;
porównywać z wzorcem

standpoint ['staend,point] s.
punkt widzenia; punkt
obserwacyjny
standstill ['staendstyl] s.
zastój; przerwa; martwy
punkt; unieruchomienie
state [stejt] s. państwo;
stan; zajęcie; parada;
pompa; ceremoniał; stan
prac; adj. państwowy;
stanowy; uroczysty;
paradny; formalny; v.
stwierdzać; wyrażać (też
symbolami); określać
state department ['stejt
,dy'pa:rtment] exp.: (w
USA) ministerstwo spraw
zagranicznych
statement ['stejtment] s.
wyrażenie; twierdzenie;
sprawozdanie; wyciąg;
oświadczenie; deklaracja;
zeznanie
state room ['stejt,rum] s.
prywatny pokój; kabina;
przedział
stateside ['stejt,sajd] adj.
amerykański; w stanach
statesman ['stejtsmen] s.
mąż stanu
stay [stej] s. pobyt; zwłoka;
odroczenie; opóźnienie;
zawieszenie; podpora;
wanta; zatrzymanie;
przerwa; wytrzymałość; v.
zostać; przebywać;
wytrzymać; odraczać;
kłaść kres; zaspokajać
(głód)
steer [stier] v. sterować;
kierować; prowadzić; s.
wskazówka; młody wół na
mięso
steering wheel ['stieryng,hłi:l]
exp.: kierownica; koło
sterowe
stenographer [ste'negraefer]
s. stenograf; stenografistka
steward ['stu:erd] s.
zarządca; ekonom; kelner;

v. zarządzać; być
stewardem
stewardess ['stu:erdys] s.
stewardessa
stipulate ['stypjulejt] v.
zażądać; uwarunkować;
zastrzegać w umowie
stock [stok] s. zapas; zasób;
bydło; pień; trzon; kłoda;
łożysko; ród; rasa;
surowiec; kapitał
udziałowy; akcje giełdowe;
obligacje; wywar; v.
zaopatrywać;
zagospodarować; zarybiać;
mieć na składzie; adj.
typowy; seryjny; w stałym
zapasie; repertuarowy
stockade [sto'kejd] s.
palisada; częstokół; obóz
stockbroker ['stok,brouker] s.
makler giełdowy
stock exchange ['stok
,eks'czejndż] s. giełda
stockholder ['stok,houlder] s.
akcjonariusz; udziałowiec
stock market ['stok-'ma:rkyt]
exp.: giełda
storage ['sto:rydż] s. skład;
przechowywanie;
magazynowanie
store ['sto:r] s. zapas; sklep;
skład; mnóstwo; składnica;
v. magazynować; mieścić
w sobie; zaopatrywać;
wyposażać
store up ['sto:r,ap] v.
zamagazynować;
zachować
storehouse ['sto:rhaus] s.
skład; magazyn; skarbnica;
kopalnia
storekeeper ['sto:r,ki:per] s.
sklepikarz; kupiec
strongbox ['strong,boks] s.
sejf; kasa ogniotrwała
strongroom ['strong,rum] s.
skarbiec
studio ['stju:djou] s. studio;
pracownia

stumbling block ['stamblyng
,blok] s. przeszkoda;
zawada; szkopuł; trudność
subdivision [,sabdy'wyżyn] s.
dzielnica (miasta, osiedla);
podział
subscribe [seb'skrajb] v.
zaprenumerować;
podpisywać (np. obraz);
pisać się na coś; dawać
na cel
subscribe for [seb'skrajb,fo:r]
v. zapisywać się na (nową)
książkę
subscribe to [seb'skrajb,tu] v.
abonować gazetę
subscriber [seb'skrajber] s.
abonent; człowiek
popierający
subscription [seb'skrypszyn]
s. prenumerata; przedpłata;
podpisanie; zgoda pisemna;
podpis dołączony
subsidiary [seb'sydjery] adj.
pomocniczy; subsydiowany
(zależny); s. pomocnik
subsidiary company
[seb'sydjery 'kampeny] s.
firma zależna od innej firmy
substandard [sab'staenderd]
adj. poniżej poziomu;
ordynarny (język)
succession [sek'seszyn] s.
następstwo; kolej;
kolejność; sukcesja;
spadkobiercy; szereg
successive [sek'sesyw] adj.
kolejny
successor [sek'seser] s.
następca; dziedzic;
spadkobierca
sum [sam] s. suma; w sumie;
rachunek; v. dodawać;
zbierać; podsumowywać
sum up ['sam,ap] v.
dodawać; zbierać;
podsumowywać
summarize ['samerajz] v.
streszczać; zbierać;
podsumowywać

summary ['samery] s.
streszczenie; skrót; adj.
pobieżny; doraźny; krótki
summons ['samens] pl.
wezwanie urzędowe; v.
doręczać wezwanie
urzędowe
super-duper [,su:per-'du:per]
adj. (slang): b. dobry;
luksusowy; bardzo
elegancki
superintend [,su:peryn'tend]
v. nadzorować; doglądać;
kierować
superintendent
[,su:peryn'tendent] s.
nadzorca; dozorca;
nadinspektor
supermarket ['su:per'ma:rkyt]
s. supersam; duży sklep
samoobsługowy
(żywnościowy)
supplement ['saplyment] s.
dodatek; uzupełnienie; v.
uzupełniać
supplier [se'plajer] s.
dostawca
supply [se'plaj] s. zapas;
aprowizacja; zaopatrzenie;
dostarczenie; dostawy;
kredyty; podaż; dopływ;
zasilanie; v. dostarczać;
zaopatrywać; zaradzić;
zastępować
surcharge [se:r'cza:rdż] s.
nadpłata; nadmierny ciężar;
dodatkowy ciężar; opłata
(karna); przeładowanie; v.
ściągać opłatę podatkową;
nakładać grzywnę;
przeładować;
przedrukować (znaczek)
surname ['se:rnejm] s.
nazwisko; przydomek;
[se:r'nejm] v. przezywać;
nadawać przydomek
survey [se:r'wej] s. przegląd;
oględziny; inspekcja;
pomiary; plan
(topograficzny); opis;

ankieta; statystyka; v.
przeglądać; robić pomiary;
wymierzać; oglądać
surveying [se:r'wejyng] s.
miernictwo
surveyor [se:r'wejer] s.
mierniczy; inspektor celny
sweepstake ['sli:pstejk] s.
wyścigi; loteria; nagroda
(zbiorowa) w wyścigach
swindle ['słyndl] s. oszustwo;
v. oszukiwać
switch on ['słycz,on] v.
włączać
switchboard ['słyczbo:rd] s.
tablica rozdzielcza; łącznica
(telefoniczna etc.)
swivel chair ['sływl,cze:r]
exp.: krzesło ruchome (na
przygubie i na kółkach)
synopsis [sy'nopsys] s.
streszczenie
syntax ['syntaeks] s. składnia
system ['systym] s. system;
układ; metoda; sieć
(kolejowa); organizm
(człowieka); formacja; ustrój

T

tab [taeb] s. patka; wieszak
(przyszyty); język (buta);
naszywka; języczek; ucho;
przywieszka; rachunek;
kontrola; pilnowanie; v.
prowadzić ewidencję;
tabelować; zaopatrywać w
(języczek lub ucho etc.)
table ['tejbl] s. stół; stolik;
tablica; tabela; tabliczka
(np. mnożenia); płyta;
płaskowyż; blat; v. kłaść
na stole; odraczać (na
długo); wciągać na
agendę; adj. stołowy
tabloid ['taeb'loid] s. gazeta,

zwykle małego wymiaru,
zawierająca krótkie
ilustrowane, często
sensacyjne, wiadomości
bieżące (przeważnie w
skrócie); gazeta brukowa,
sensacyjna, często płacąca
wysokie wynagrodzenia za
rewelacje skandaliczne; adj.
ściśnięty; prasowany
tabloid journalism ['taeb'loid
'dźe:rne,lysem] s.
wiadomości dziennikarskie
podawane w skrócie;
polowanie na rewelacje
skandaliczne dotyczące
zwykle znanych osobistości
tag [taeg] s. skuwka;
etykieta; kartka; strzęp;
przywieszka; znaczek
tożsamości; marka;
mandat karny (pisany);
ucho; igliczka; wieszadło
(przyszyte); błyszczka;
dodatek; morał; frazes;
banał; cytat; refren; ogon;
zabawa w gonionego; v.
przyczepiać: skuwkę,
kartkę, znaczek, markę,
ucho, wieszadło, igliczkę,
ogon; dawać: mandat
karny, morał; bawić się w
gonionego; tańczyć
odbijanego; wymierzać
wyrok; przeznaczać;
włóczyć się za kimś;
dołączyć do czegoś
tailor-made ['tejlermejd] adj.
uszyty na zamówienie
take-in ['tejk'yn] s.
oszukanie; naciąganie
takeover ['tejkouwer] s.
opanowanie firmy przez
manipulacje giełdowe lub
finansowe
take over ['tejk,ouwer] v.
przejmować (firmę);
przyjmować (obowiązki);
dominować
tape recorder ['tejp

ry,ko:rder] exp.:
magnetofon
tape recording ['tejp
ry,ko:rdyng] exp.: nagranie
na taśmę
tariff ['taeryf] s. cło; taryfa;
cennik; v. clić wg taryfy;
układać taryfę celną
tax [taeks] s. podatek;
wysiłek; ciężar; obciążenie;
v. opodatkować; obarczać;
obciążać; nadwerężać;
sprawdzać; wymagać
wysiłku; zarzucać coś
taxation [taek'sejszyn] s.
opodatkowanie
tax collector ['taekske,lekter]
exp.: poborca podatkowy
taxi ['taeksy] s. taksówka; v.
jechać taksówką; wieźć
taksówką
taxi driver ['taeksydrajwer]
exp.: taksówkarz
taximeter ['taeksy,mi:ter] s.
licznik (w taksówce);
taksometr
taxpayer ['taeks,pejer] s.
podatnik
tax return ['taeks,ry'te:rn] s.
podatek (zapłata ze
sprawozdaniem)
technical ['teknykel] adj.
techniczny; formalny;
spekulacyjny
telegram ['telygraem] s.
telegram
telegraph ['telygra:f] s.
telegraf
telephone ['telyfoun] s.
telefon; v. telefonować
telephone booth
['telyfoun,bu:s] exp.: kabina
telefoniczna
telephone call ['telyfoun,ko:l]
exp.: rozmowa
telefoniczna
telephone directory
['telyfoundy,rektory] exp.:
książka telefoniczna
telephone exchange

['telyfoun eks,czejndż]
exp.: centrala telefoniczna
na zagranicę
telephone kiosk ['telyfoun-
kiosk] exp.: kiosk
telefoniczny
teleprinter ['tely,prynter] s.
dalekopis
telescope ['telyskoup] s.
teleskop
teletypewriter [,tely'tajprajter]
s. dalekopis
televise ['telywajz] v.
nadawać przez telewizję
television ['telywyżyn] s.
telewizja
television set
['telywyżyn,set] exp.:
telewizor; odbiornik
telewizyjny
televisor ['telywajzer] s.
telewizor
tenant ['tenent] s. lokator;
dzierżawca; v.
zamieszkiwać; dzierżawić
terms [te:rms] pl. warunki
(kontraktu, porozumienia);
stosunki wzajemne
terminal ['te:rmynel] adj.
końcowy; terminowy;
ostateczny; s. zakończenie;
końcówka; uchwyt;
końcowa stacja
terminate ['te:rmynejt] v.
skończyć; zakończyć;
kończyć (się); ograniczać;
upływać; rozwiązywać
(umowę); ustawać;
wygasać; wymawiać pracę
termination [,te:rmy'nejszyn]
s. koniec; wypowiedzenie
(pracy); wygaśnięcie;
zakończenie; końcówka
testament ['testement] s.
testament
text [tekst] s. tekst
textbook ['tekstbuk] s.
podręcznik
thief [ṭi:f] s. złodziej
  thieves [ṭi:ws] pl. złodzieje

ticker ['tyker] s. telegraf;
zegarek; serce (slang)
ticket ['tykyt] s. bilet; kwit;
znaczek; wywieszka; lista
kandydatów (USA); v.
zaopatrywać w bilet,
etykietkę; umieszczać na
liście kandydatów
ticket office ['tykyt'ofys]
exp.: kasa biletowa
timetable ['tajm,tejbl] s.
rozkład jazdy, zajęć etc.
toll [toul] s. opłata (np.
telefoniczna); myto:
mostowe, drogowe; miejski
podatek; trybut; danina;
dzwonienie; v. uiszczać
opłatę; wydzwaniać;
dzwonić jednostajnie;
wabić (zwierzynę)
toll bar ['toulba:r] s. szlaban
tollgate ['toulgejt] s. rogatka
wjazdowa na płatny most
lub autostradę
tonnage ['tanydż] s. tonaż;
opłata od tony ładunku
total ['toutel] adj. ogólny;
zupełny; całkowity; totalny;
kompletny; v. zliczać;
wynosić ogółem; (slang):
niszczyć całkowicie (np.
samochód w wypadku)
trace [trejs] s. ślad;
postronek; drążek
przekaźnikowy; v. iść
śladami; kopiować
rysunek; przypisywać
czemuś; wytyczać;
nakreślać; kreślić
trade [trejd] s. zawód;
zajęcie; rzemiosło; handel;
wymiana; klientela; branża;
kupiectwo; v. handlować;
wymieniać; frymarczyć;
przewozić towary;
kupczyć; przehandlować
trademark ['trejd,ma:rk] s.
znak ochronny; v. przybijać
znak ochronny; rejestrować
znak ochronny

trader ['trejder] s.
handlowiec; statek
handlowy; spekulator
giełdowy
trade union ['trejd 'ju:njen]
exp.: związek zawodowy
trade unionist
['trejd'ju:njenyst] exp.:
działacz związku
zawodowego
traffic ['traefyk] s. ruch
(kołowy, pasażerski,
towarowy, telegraficzny,
telefoniczny, drogowy etc.);
handel czymś; v.
frymarczyć; kupczyć
traffic jam ['traefyk-dżaem]
exp.: zator ruchu
transact [traen'saekt] v.
załatwiać; pertraktować;
przeprowadzać
transaction [traen'saekszyn]
s. transakcja;
przeprowadzenie sprawy;
pl. sprawozdania naukowe;
rozprawy
transcribe [traens'krajb] v.
nagrywać na taśmie;
przepisywać
transcript ['traenskrypt] s.
kopia; transkrypcja
transfer [traens'fe:r] v.
przemieścić; przenieść
(się); przewozić;
przekazać; s. ['traensfe:r]
przeniesienie; przewóz;
przedruk; przekaz; przelew;
odstąpienie
transferable [traens'fe:rebl]
adj. przenośny
transistor [traen'zyster] s.
tranzystor
transit ['traensyt] s. przejazd;
przelot; przewóz; tranzyt;
teodolit
transition [traen'syszyn] s.
przejście; zmiana
transitive ['traensytyw] adj.
przechodni
translate [traens'lejt] v.

przetłumaczyć; przełożyć
translation [traens'lejszyn] s.
tłumaczenie; przekład
translator [traens'lejter] s.
tłumacz
transport [traens'po:rt] v.
przewozić; zachwycać; s.
['traenspo:rt] przewóz;
zachwyt; uniesienie
transportation
[,traenspo:r'tejszyn] s.
przewóz; transport;
deportacja; zesłanie
travel agency
['traewl'ejdżensy] exp.:
biuro podróży
traveler ['traewler] s.
podróżnik; wodzik nitkowy;
komiwojażer
traveler's check
['traewlers,czek] exp.: z
góry wykupiony czek do
użytku w podróży
traveling bag
['traewlyng,baeg] exp.:
torba podróżna
treasure ['treżer] s. skarb; v.
zaskarbiać; cenić; strzec
skarbu
treasurer ['treżerer] s.
skarbnik
treasury ['treżery] s. urząd
skarbowy; skarbnica
Treasury Department
['treżery,dy'pa:rtment]
exp.: ministerstwo skarbu
(USA)
treaty ['tri:ty] s. traktat;
układ; umowa
trend [trend] s. dążność;
ogólna tendencja; ogólny
kierunek; v. dążyć; mieć
tendencję; kształtować się;
ciągnąć się
trespass ['trespas] v.
wdzierać się w cudze;
nadużywać; naruszać;
wykraczać; grzeszyć; v.
przekroczenie; wykroczenie;
grzech; szkoda wyrządzona

na cudzym terenie
trespasser ['trespaser] s.
człowiek naruszający
przepisy, prawo (czyjeś)
tribunal [traj'bju:nl] s.
trybunał; sąd
trunk road ['tra<u>n</u>k-roud] exp.:
szosa główna
trust [trast] s. pewność;
zaufanie; wiara; nadzieja;
kredyt; opieka;
powiernictwo; trust; v.
zaufać; mieć zaufanie;
ufać; wierzyć; polegać (na
pamięci swojej etc.);
powierzać; kredytować
tune up ['tu:n,ap] v.
nastrajać (np. motor)
typewriter ['tajp,rajter] s.
maszyna do pisania
typist ['tajpyst] s.
maszynistka

U

unauthorized ['an'o:<u>t</u>erajzd]
adj. nieupoważniony
undercharge ['ander'cza:rdż]
v. za mało policzyć; za
słabo naładować
underestimate
['ander'estymejt] v.
niedoceniać; za nisko
oszacować
underpay ['ander'pej] v. za
mało płacić
undertaking [,ander'tejky<u>n</u>g]
s. przedsięwzięcie;
zobowiązanie; obietnica;
przyrzeczenie;
przedsiębiorstwo
pogrzebowe
undervalue [,ander'waelju] v.
niedoceniać; za nisko
szacować
underwrite ['ander-rajt] v.

(zob. write);
zakontraktować
(ubezpieczenie); podpisać
(się); wydawać (polisę
ubezpieczeniową);
zobowiązywać się
underwriter ['ander-rajter] s.
ajent ubezpieczeniowy
unemployment
[an'emplojment] s.
bezrobocie
uninsured ['anyn'szurd] adj.
nieubezpieczony
union ['ju:njen] s. połączenie;
złącze; łączność; związek;
zjednoczenie; klub;
małżeństwo; zgoda;
łącznik; złączka; godło
unionist ['ju:njenyst] s.
związkowiec; zwolennik
związku
unofficial ['ane'fyszel] adj.
nie urzędowy; nieoficjalny
unpaid ['an'pejd] adj.
niezapłacony;
bezinteresowny
unproductive [,anpro'daktyw]
adj. niewydajny; nie
wytwórczy; niepłodny
unprofessional ['anpre'feszn1]
adj. laicki; niezawodowy;
dyletancki; amatorski
unprofitable [an'profytebl]
adj. niepopłatny;
niekorzystny; nierentowny;
jałowy
upkeep ['apki:p] s.
utrzymanie; koszty
utrzymania
usurer ['ju:żerer] s. lichwiarz
utility [ju'tylyty] s. pożytek;
użyteczność; firma
dostarczająca gaz,
elektryczność lub wodę
ludności w USA

V

vacancy ['wejkensy] s. wolne mieszkanie; wolne pokoje motelowe; wakans; próżnia; pustka; bezczynność
vacant ['wejkent] adj. pusty; próżny; wolny; wakujący; bezczynny; bezmyślny; obojętny
vacate [we'kejt] v. opróżniać; opuszczać; unieważniać
vacation [we'kejszyn] s. wakacje; ferie; opróżnienie; zwolnienie (mieszkania); ewakuacja
valuables ['waljuebls] pl. kosztowności
valuation [,walju'ejszyn] s. oszacowanie; cena
value ['waelju:] s. wartość; cena; stopień jasności barwy (w obrazie); v. szacować; cenić; oceniać
valueless ['waelju:lys] adj. bezwartościowy
valuer ['waelju:er] s. taksator
vend [wend] v. sprzedawać
vender ['wender] s. (uliczny) sprzedawca; automat do sprzedaży
vending machine ['wendyng,me'szi:n] exp.: automat do sprzedaży
venture ['wenczer] s. ryzyko; stawka; spekulacja; impreza; interes; próba; v. odważać się; ośmielać się; ryzykować; śmieć; narazić się
vice-president ['wajs'prezydent] s. wiceprzewodniczący; wiceprezydent
video ['wydjou] s. telewizja; adj. telewizyjny

videotape ['wydi:ou,tejp] s. taśma magnetowidowa; v. nagrać (obraz i dźwięk) na taśmie
vie [waj] v. współzawodniczyć; rywalizować; współubiegać się
violation [,waje'lejszyn] s. pogwałcenie; zgwałcenie; gwałt; zbezczeszczenie; naruszenie (też praw ruchu)
visa ['wi:za] s. wiza; v. wizować
volt [woult] s. wolt (elektr.); wolta; v. robić woltę (na koniu)
voltage ['woultydż] s. napięcie prądu; woltaż
vouch [waucz] v. ręczyć; gwarantować; potwierdzać; zapewnić
voucher ['wauczer] s. dowód kasowy
vouch for ['waucz,fo:r] v. ręczyć za kogoś

W

wage [łejdż] s. płaca; zarobek; zapłata; v. prowadzić (np. wojnę)
wage earner ['łejdż,e:rner] exp.: człowiek zarobkujący
wages ['łejdżyz] s. zapłata
walkout ['ło:kaut] s. strajk
wallet ['łolyt] s. portfel
Wall Street ['łolstri:t] exp.: ośrodek finansowy (USA)
warehouse ['łeerhaus] s. magazyn; składnica; dom składowy; v. magazynować; składować
warrant ['łorent] v. usprawiedliwiać; uzasadniać; gwarantować;

s. upoważnienie;
gwarancja; nakaz prawny
(aresztu, rewizji etc.);
pełnomocnictwo dla
adwokatów; patent
starszego podoficera (USA)
warranty ['łorenty] s.
gwarancja; poręka;
rękojmia; podstawa;
usprawiedliwienie;
upoważnienie; dokument
sądowy
warranty deed ['łorenty ,di:d]
exp.: kontrakt
gwarantujący ważność
tytułu własności
sprzedawcy
water rate ['ło:ter,rejt] s.
opłata za wodę; cena wody
watt [łot] s. (electr.) wat
wealth [łels] s. bogactwo;
dobrobyt
wealthy ['łelsy] adj. bogaty
weather bureau
['łedzer,bjuerou] exp.:
instytut meteorologiczny
weather chart ['łedzer,cza:rt]
exp.: wykres
meteorologiczny
weather forecast
['łedz,fo:rka:st] exp.:
komunikat meteorologiczny
welfare state ['łelfeer'stejt]
exp.: państwo o bardzo
wysokich świadczeniach
społecznych
wholesale ['houl,sejl] s. hurt;
handel hurtowy; adj.
hurtowy; masowy; adv.
hurtem; masowo
wholesaler ['houl,sejler] s.
hurtownik
wholesale trade
['houlsejl,trejd] exp.: handel
hurtowy
wholesome ['houlsem] adj.
zdrowy; zdrowotny
window dressing ['łyndou
,dressyng] exp.: dekoracja
wystawy sklepowej

window-shopping
['łyndouszopyng] v.
oglądać wystawy (ale nie
kupować)
workbook ['łe:rk,buk] s.
podręcznik ze
wskazówkami; dziennik
pracy
workday ['łe:rkdej] s. dzień
roboczy; dzień powszedni
worker ['łe:rker] s.
pracownik; robotnik
workhouse ['łe:rk,haus] s.
dom poprawczy; przytułek
working ['łe:rkyng] adj.
pracujący; pracowniczy;
roboczy; praktyczny;
działający; czynny;
ruchomy; powszedni; s.
praca; robota; działanie;
ruch; roboczodniówka;
obróbka
working capital
['łe:rkyng'kaepytl] exp.:
kapitał obrotowy
working knowledge
['łe:rkyng'nolydż] exp.:
wiedza praktyczna
working-class ['łe:rkyng'kla:s]
exp.: klasa robotnicza
working day ['łe:rkyngdej]
exp.: dzień pracy
working hours
['łe:rkyng,auers] exp.:
godziny pracy
working load ['łe:rkyng,loud]
exp.: ciężar użyteczny;
nośność
workingman ['łe:rkyng,men]
exp.: robotnik
working pressure ['łe:rkyng
,preszer] exp.: ciśnienie
robocze
workless ['łe:rklys] adj. & s.
bezrobotny
work-like ['łe:rklajk] adj.
dobrze wykonany; dobrze
nastawiony do pracy
workman ['łe:rkmen] s.
robotnik (fizyczny);

fachowiec
workmen ['łe:rkmen] pl.
robotnicy
workmanship ['łe:rkmanszyp]
s. wykonanie; jakość
wykonania; faktura; twór
workwoman ['łe:rkłumen] s.
robotnica; pracownica
fizyczna
workwomen ['łe:rkłymyn]
pl. robotnice
wrapping ['raepyng] s.
opakowanie
wrapping paper ['raepyng
pejper] exp.: papier do
pakowania
wrapped [raept] v.
zapakowany; opakwany;
(zob.: **wrap**)
writ [ryt] s. nakaz pisemny,
prawny
writing desk ['rajtyng,desk]
exp.: biurko; pulpit
writing ink ['rajtyng,ynk]
exp.: atrament
writing paper ['rajtyng,pejper]
exp.: papier listowy; papier
do pisania
writing table ['rajtyng,tejbl]
exp.: biurko

Y

yard [ja:rd] s. jard (91.44
cm); podwórze; dziedziniec;
v. umieszczać w
ogrodzeniu
yardage ['jarrdydż] s. metraż
yardstick ['jard,styk] s.
listewka do mierzenia,
kryterium
yearbook ['jer:,buk] s. rocznik
(statystyczny etc.)
year-end ['jer:,end] exp.:
koniec roku obrotów
finansowych; adj.
(zestawienie, etc.) zrobione
z końcem roku; (zdarzający
się, etc.) z końcem roku
yield [ji:ld] v. wydawać;
dawać; rodzić; przynosić;
oddawać (się); porzucać;
ustępować; s. plon; zysk;
wydajność
yielding [ji:ldyng] s.
wydajność; adj. ustępliwy;
wydajny; gnący się

X

x-ray ['eks'rej] adj.
rentgenowski; v.
prześwietlać; robić zdjęcie
rentgenowskie
x-ray diagnosis
['eks'rej,dajeg'nouzys] exp.:
rozpoznanie rentgenowskie
x-ray examination
['eks'rej,yg'zaemynejszyn]
exp.: badanie
rentgenowskie
x-ray picture
['eks'rej'pykczer] exp.:
zdjęcie rentgenowskie

Z

zero ['zierou] s. zero; v.
ustawiać na zero; brać na
cel; wstrzeliwać się
zero hour ['zierou 'awer]
exp.: moment rozpoczęcia
akcji (wojskowej, etc.)
zero-sum ['zierou ,sam] exp.:
wygarna jednej storny
równa się stracie drugiej
strony
zero-sum game ['zierou ,sam
'gejm] exp.: wygrana jednej

storny równa się stracie
drugiej strony
zero-zero ['zierou 'zierou]
adj. całkowicie
uniemożliwiony przez
pogodę; całkowity brak
widoczności
zillion ['zyl.yen] s.
nieokreślenie wielka ilość
zip code ['zyp,koud] exp.:
numeracja pocztowa
miejscowości
zloty ['zlouty] s. złoty
(pieniądz polski)
zone ['zoun] v. wyznaczć
okręgi; dzielić na okręgi;
dzielić na strefy
zoning ['zoun,in] s.
wyznaczanie okręgy
(przemysłowego,
mieszkalnego, etc.)
zoning map ['zoun,in maep]
exp.: mapa wyznaczonych
okręgów (przemysłowych,
mieszkalnych, etc.)
zoom [zu:m] v. buczeć;
wzlatywać; wzbijać się
szybko; śmigać; s.
poderwanie (samolotu);
soczewka zbliżająca w
kamerze filmowej oraz w
aparacie fotograficznym;
obiektyw o zmiennej
ogniskowej

Other Hippocrene Dictionaries and Language Books of Interest . . .

ALBANIAN-ENGLISH/ENGLISH-ALBANIAN PRACTICAL DICTIONARY
400 pages 4⅜ x 7 18,000 entries 0-7818-0419-1 $14.95pb (483)

ENGLISH-ALBANIAN COMPREHENSIVE DICTIONARY
1000 pages 60,000 entries 0-7818-0510-4 $60.00hc (615)

ALBANIAN-ENGLISH STANDARD DICTIONARY
510 pages 5¼ x 7½ 20,000 entries 0-87052-077-6 $14.95pb (293)

ENGLISH-ALBANIAN STANDARD DICTIONARY
441 PAGES 9½ X 6¾ 20,000 entries 0-7818-0021-8 $14.95pb (518)

ARMENIAN-ENGLISH/ ENGLISH-ARMENIAN CONCISE DICTIONARY
378 pages 4 x 6 10,000 entries 0-7818-0150-8 $11.95pb (490)

ELEMENTARY MODERN ARMENIAN GRAMMAR
196 pages 5½ x 8¼ 0-87052-811-4 $8.95pb (172)

ARMENIAN-ENGLISH/ ENGLISH-ARMENIAN COMPACT DICTIONARY
379 pages 3½ x 4¾ 9,000 entries 0-7818-0500-7 $8.95pb (608)

WESTERN ARMENIAN DICTIONARY IN TRANSLITERATION
139 pages 6 x 9 4,000 entries 0-7818-0207-5 $11.95pb (59)

ENGLISH-AZERBAIJANI/ AZERBAIJANI-ENGLISH CONCISE DICTIONARY
144 pages 5½ x 7 8,000 entries 0-7818-0244-X $14.95pb (96)

BOSNIAN-ENGLISH/ ENGLISH-BOSNIAN CONCISE DICTIONARY
331 pages 4 x 6 8,500 entries 0-7818-0276-8 $14.95pb (329)

BOSNIAN-ENGLISH/ ENGLISH-BOSNIAN COMPACT DICTIONARY
332 pages. 3½ x 4¾ 8,500 entries 0-7818-0499-X $8.95pb (204)

BEGINNER'S BULGARIAN
207 pages 5½ x 8½ 0-7818-0300-4 $9.95pb (76)

BULGARIAN-ENGLISH/ ENGLISH-BULGARIAN PRACTICAL DICTIONARY
323 pages 4⅜ x 7 6,500 entries 0-87052-145-4 $14.95pb (331)

BULGARIAN-ENGLISH/ ENGLISH-BULGARIAN COMPACT DICTIONARY
323 pages 3½ x 4¾ 6,500 entries 0-7818 0535-X $8.95pb 623)

BULGARIAN-ENGLISH COMPREHENSIVE DICTIONARY
1,050 pages 6¾ x 9¾ 47,000 entries 0-7818-0507-4 $90.00 2-volume set (613)

ENGLISH-BULGARIAN COMPREHENSIVE DICTIONARY
1,080 pages 6¾ x 9¾ 54,000 entries 0-7818-0508-2 $90.00 2-volume set (614)

BYELORUSSIAN-ENGLISH/ ENGLISH-BYELORUSSIAN CONCISE DICTIONARY
290 pages 4 x 6 6,500 entries 0-87052-114-4 $9.95pb (395)

CHECHEN-ENGLISH/ ENGLISH-CHECHEN DICTIONARY AND PHRASEBOOK
160 pages 3¾ x 7 1,400 entries 0-7818-0446-9 $11.95pb (183)

BEGINNER'S CZECH
200 pages 5½ x 8½ 0-7818-0231-8 $9.95pb (74)

CZECH-ENGLISH/ENGLISH-CZECH CONCISE DICTIONARY
594 pages 3½ x 5⅜ 7,500 entries 0-87052-981-1 $11.95pb (276)

CZECH-ENGLISH COMPREHENSIVE DICTIONARY
1,400 pages 6 x 9 60,000 entries 0-7818-0509-0 $49.50hc (616)

CZECH PHRASEBOOK
220 pages 5½ x 8½ 0-87052-967-6 $9.95pb (599)

CZECH HANDY EXTRA DICTIONARY
186 pages 5 x 7¾ 0-7818-0138-9 $8.95pb (63)

ENGLISH CONVERSATIONS FOR POLES
250 pages 5½ x 8 ½ 0-87052-873-4 $9.95pb (225)

ENGLISH FOR POLES SELF-TAUGHT
496 PAGES 6 x 8⅜ 455 lessons 3,600 entries
0-7818-0273-3 $19.95pb $19.95pb (317)

AMERICAN P HRASEBOOKS FOR POLES, 2ND EDITION
154 pages 5 ½ x 8 ½ 0-7818-0554-6 $8.95pb (644)

AMERICAN-ENGLISH FOR POLES IN FOUR PARTS
828 pages 5¾ x 8-32140-152-X $24/95pb (441)

ESTONIAN-ENGLISH/ENGLISH ESTONIAN CONCISE DICTIONARY
300 pages 3⅝ x 3⅜ 6,500 entries 0-87052-081-4 $11.95pb (379)

ESTONIAN-ENGLISH/ ENGLISH-ESTONIAN CONCISE DICTIONARY
300 pages 3⅝ x 5⅝ 6,500 entries 0-87052-081-4 $11.95pb (379)

FINNISH-ENGLISH/ ENGLISH-FINNISH CONCISE DICTIONARY
411 pages 3½ x 4¾ 12,000 entries 0-87052-813-0 $11.95pb (142)

FINNISH-ENGLISH COMPREHENSIVE DICTIONARY
793 pages 5½ x 8½ 80,000 entries 0-7818-0380-2 $24.95 (467)

MASTERING FINNISH
278 pages 5½ x 8½ 0-7818-0233-4 $14.95pb (184)
2 Cassettes: 0-7818-0265-2 $12.95 (231)

**GEORGIAN-ENGLISH/ ENGLISH-GEORGIAN CONCISE
DICTIONARY**
346 pages 4 x 6 8,000 entries 0-87052-121-7 $8.95pb (392)

**GEORGIAN-ENGLISH/ENGLISH-GEORGIAN DICTIONARY AND
PHRASEBOOK**
150 pages 3¾ x 7 1300 entries 0-7818-0542-2 $11.95pb (630)

**HUNGARIAN-ENGLISH/ ENGLISH-HUNGARIAN CONCISE
DICTIONARY**
282 pages 4 x 6 7,000 entries 0-7818-0317-9 $14.95pb (40)

HUNGARIAN-ENGLISH STANDARD DICTIONARY
650 pages 4½ x 8½ 40,000 entries 0-7818-0390-X $40.00pb (43)

ENGLISH-HUNGARIAN STANDARD DICTIONARY
541 pages 4½ x 8½ 40,000 entries 0-7818-0391-8 $40.00pb (48)

BEGINNER'S HUNGARIAN
200 pages 5½ x 7 0-7818-0209-1 $7.95pb (68)

HUNGARIAN BASIC COURSE
266 pages 5½ x 8½ 0-87052-817-3 $14.95pb (131)

HUNGARIAN HANDY EXTRA DICTIONARY
209 pages 5 x 7¾ 0-7818-0164-8 $8.95pb (2)

LITHUANIAN-ENGLISH/ ENGLISH LITHUANIAN CONCISE DICTIONARY
382 pages 4 x 6 10,000 entries 0-7818-0151-6 $14.95pb (489)

LITHUANIAN-ENGLISH/ ENGLISH LITHUANIAN COMPACT DICTIONARY
400 pages 3½ x 4¾ 10,000 entries 0-7818-0536-8 $8.95pb (624)

MACEDONIAN-ENGLISH/ ENGLISH-MACEDONIAN CONCISE DICTIONARY
400 pages 4 x 6 14,000 entries 0-7818-0516-3 $14.95pb (619)

POLISH-ENGLISH UNABRIDGED DICTIONARY
3,800 pages 250,000 entries 2-volume set 0-7818-0441-8 $150.00hc (526)

BEGINNER'S POLISH
200 pages 5½ x 8½ 0-7818-0299-7 $9.95pb (82)
BEGINNER'S POLISH CASSETTES
2 Cassettes: 0-7818-0330-6 $12.95 (56)

POLISH HANDY EXTRA DICTIONARY
125 pages 4 x 6 0-7818-0504-X $11.95pb (607)

HIGHLANDER POLISH-ENGLISH/ENGLISH-HIGHLANDER POLISH DICTIONARY
111 pages 4 x 6 2,000 entries 0-7818-0303-9 $9.95pb (297)

POLISH-ENGLISH/ENGLISH- POLISH CONCISE DICTIONARY
With Complete Phonetics
408 pages 3⅝ x 7 8,000 entries 0-7818-0133-8 $9.95pb (268)

POLISH-ENGLISH/ENGLISH- POLISH COMPACT DICTIONARY
240 pages 4 x 6 9,000 entries 0-7818-0496-6 $8.95pb (609)

POLISH-ENGLISH/ ENGLISH-POLISH PRACTICAL DICTIONARY
703 pages 5¼ x 8½ 31,000 entries 0-7818-0085-4 $14.95pb (450)

POLISH-ENGLISH/ENGLISH-POLISH STANDARD DICTIONARY,
Revised Edition With Business Terms
780 pages 5½ x 8½ 32,000 entries 0-7818-0282-2 $19.95pb (298)

POLISH PHRASEBOOK AND DICTIONARY
252 pages 5½ x 8½ 0-7818-0134-6 $9.95pb (192)

POLISH PHRASEBOOK AND DICTIONARY COMPANION
CASSETTES
Volume I 2 Cassettes: 0-7818-0340-3 $12.95 (492)
Volume II 2 Cassettes: 0-7818-0384-5 $12.95 (486)

MASTERING POLISH
288 pages 5½ x 8½ 0-7818-0015-3 $14.95pb (381)
2 Cassettes: 0-7818-0016-1 $12.95 (389)

DICTIONARY OF 1,000 POLISH PROVERBS
131 pages 5½ x 8½ 0-7818-0482-5 $11.95pb (628)

BEGINNER'S RUSSIAN
200 pages 5½ x 8½ 0-7818-0232-6 $9.95pb (61)

MASTERING RUSSIAN
278 pages 5½ x 8½ 0-7818-0270-9 $14.95pb (11)
2 Cassettes: 0-7818-0271-7 $12.95 (13)

ENGLISH-RUSSIAN COMPREHENSIVE DICTIONARY
800 pages 8½ x 11 50,000 entries 0-7818-0353-5 $60.00hc (312)
0-7818-0442-6 $35.00pb (50)
RUSSIAN-ENGLISH COMPREHENSIVE DICTIONARY
800 pages 6 x 9 40,000 entries 0-7818-0506-6 $60.00hc (612)

RUSSIAN-ENGLISH/ENGLISH-RUSSIAN STANDARD DICTIONARY,
Revised Edition With Business Terms
418 pages 5¼ x 8½ 32,000 entries 0-7818-0280-6 $16.95pb (322)

RUSSIAN-ENGLISH/ ENGLISH-RUSSIAN CONCISE DICTIONARY
400 pages 4½ x 6 10,000 entries 0-7818-0132-X $11.95pb (262)

DICTIONARY OF RUSSIAN VERBS
750 pages 5½ x 8½ 20,000 fully declined verbs 0-7818-0371-3 $45.00 (572)
0-88254-420-9 $35.00pb (10)

DICTIONARY OF RUSSIAN PROVERBS, Bilingual
477 pages 8½ x 11 5,335 entries index 0-7818-0424-8 $35.00pb (555)

RUSSIAN PHRASEBOOK AND DICTIONARY, Revised
256 pages 5½ x 8½ 3,000 entries, subway maps of Moscow and St. Petersburg
0-7818-0190-7 $9.95pb (597)

RUSSIAN PHRASEBOOK AND DICTIONARY CASSETTES
2 cassettes: 120 minutes 0-7818-0192-3 $12.95 (432)

**RUSSIAN-ENGLISH/ ENGLISH-RUSSIAN DICTIONARY OF
BUSINESS AND LEGAL TERMS**
800 pages 5½ x 8½ 40,000 entries 0-7818-0163-X $50.00 (66) $35.00pb
0-7818-0505-8 (480)

SERBIAN-ENGLISH/ENGLISH-SERBIAN CONCISE DICTIONARY
400 pages 4 x 6 14,000 entries 0-7818-0556-2 $14.95pb (326)

SERBO-CROATIAN HANDY DICTIONARY
120 pages 5 x 7¾ 0-87052-051-2 $8.95pb (328)

**SERBO-CROATIAN-ENGLISH/ENGLISH-SERBO-CROATIAN
PRACTICAL DICTIONARY**
400 pages 5⅝ x 7 24,000 entries 0-7818-0445-0 $16.95pb (130)

SLOVAK-ENGLISH/ ENGLISH-SLOVAK CONCISE DICTIONARY
360 pages 4 x 6 7,500 entries 0-87052-115-2 $11.95pb (390)

SLOVAK HANDY EXTRA DICTIONARY
200 pages 5 x 7¾ 0-7818-0101-X $12.95pb (359)

SLOVAK-ENGLISH/ ENGLISH-SLOVAK COMPACT DICTIONARY
360 pages 3½ x 4¾ 7,500 entries 0-7818-0501-5 $8.95pb (107)

SLOVENE-ENGLISH/ ENGLISH-SLOVENE MODERN DICTIONARY
935 pages 5½ x 3½ 36,000 entries 0-7818-0252-0 except Slovenia $24.95pb
(19)

**UKRAINIAN-ENGLISH/ ENGLISH-UKRAINIAN STANDARD
DICTIONARY**
590 pages 5½ x 8½ 32,000 entries 0-7818-0374-8 $24.95pb (193)

UKRAINIAN-ENGLISH STANDARD DICTIONARY
286 pages 5½ x 8½ 16,000 entries 0-7818-0189-3 $14.95pb (6)

UKRAINIAN-ENGLISH/ ENGLISH-UKRAINIAN PRACTICAL DICTIONARY, Revised Edition With Menu Terms
406 pages 4¼ x 7 16,000 entries 0-7818-0306-3 $14.95pb (343)

BEGINNER'S UKRAINIAN
130 pages 5½ 8½ 0-7818-0443-4 $11.95pb (88)

UKRAINIAN PHRASEBOOK AND DICTIONARY
205 pages 5½ x 8½ 3,000 entries 0-7818-0188-5 $11.95pb (28)

UKRAINIAN PHRASEBOOK COMPANION CASSETTES
2 cassettes: 120 minutes 0-7818-0191-5 $12.95 (42)

UKRAINIAN-ENGLISH/ENGLISH-UKRAINIAN COMPACT DICTIONARY
448 pages 3½ x 4¼ 8,000 entries 0-7818-0498-1 (151) $8.95pb

All prices subject to change. **TO PURCHASE HIPPOCRENE BOOKS** contact your local bookstore, call (718) 454-2366, or write to: HIPPOCRENE BOOKS, 171 Madison Avenue, New York, NY 10016. Please enclose check or money order, adding $5.00 shipping (UPS) for the first book and $.50 for each additional book.

Self-Taught Audio Language Courses

Hippocrene Books is pleased to recommend Audio-Forum self-taught language courses. They match up very closely with the languages offered in Hippocrene dictionaries and offer a flexible, economical and thorough program of language learning.

Audio-Forum audio-cassette/book courses, recorded by native speakers, offer the convenience of a private tutor, enabling the learner to progress at his or her own pace. They are also ideal for brushing up on language skills that may not have been used in years. In as little as 25 minutes a day — even while driving, exercising, or doing something else — it's possible to develop a spoken fluency.

Polish Self-Taught Language Courses

Conversational Polish (Beginning Course)
8 cassettes (7 hr.), 327-p. text, $185.
Order #HP500.

Readings And Conversation In Polish
(Intermediate Course) 1 cassette (1 hr.) and
booklet, $24.50. Order #HP600.

All Audio-Forum courses are fully guaranteed and may be returned within 30 days for a full refund if you're not completely satisfied.

You may order directly from Audio-Forum by calling toll-free 1-800-243-1234.

For a complete course description and catalog of 264 courses in 91 languages, contact Audio-Forum, Dept. SE5, 96 Broad St., Guilford, CT 06437.
Toll-free phone 1-800-243-1234. Fax 203-453-9774.